W9-ACS-677

World Resources 1987

Director J. Alan Brewster
World Resources **Staff**
Donald Hinrichsen, *Editor-in-Chief*
Mary E. Paden, *Managing Editor*
Robert M. Kwartin, *Research Director*
Czech Conroy, *Senior Research Associate (London)*
Ed Barbier, *Research Associate (London)*
Lauren Wenzel, *Research Associate*
Esther Runnalls, *Researcher*
John Dorries, *Intern*

Senior Advisors
Jessica Tuchman Mathews, *Vice President, WRI*
David Runnalls, *Vice President, IIED*
Richard Sandbrook, *Vice President, IIED*
Peter S. Thacher, *Distinguished Fellow, WRI*

Editorial Advisory Board
Dr. M.S. Swaminathan (India), *Chairman*
Mr. Anil Agarwal (India)
His Excellency Abdlatif Y. Al-Hamad (Kuwait)
The Honorable Serge Antoine (France)
Professor Bert Bolin (Sweden)
The Honorable Enrique Iglesias (Uruguay)
Ms. Yolanda Kakabadse (Ecuador)
Professor Victor Kovda (USSR)
Dr. Thomas A. Lambo (Nigeria)
Dr. Istvan Lang (Hungary)
Dr. Jingyi Liu (People's Republic of China)
Dr. Uri Marinov (Israel)
Mr. Robert S. McNamara (United States)
Dr. Liberty Mhlanga (Zimbabwe)
Mr. James Gustave Speth (United States)
Mr. Brian Walker (United Kingdom)

World Resources 1987

A Report by
The International Institute for
Environment and Development

and

The World Resources Institute

Basic Books, Inc., New York

The cover is a Landsat 4 Thematic Mapper image of the Mississippi River's Balize, or "bird foot" delta. The mouths of the delta have built to the edge of the continental shelf.

The sedimentation at the mouths of the delta is clearly illustrated by the Landsat color composite, which combines bands 1, 3 and 4 in the visible and near-infrared portions of the spectrum.

More than 210 million metric tons of sediments flow into the delta and the Gulf of Mexico per yer. Landsat images are used to monitor the flood-prone Mississippi River for management and control measures throughout the year.

Photo courtesy of Earth Observation Satellite Company, Lanham, Maryland.

The World Resources Institute and the International Institute for Environment and Development gratefully acknowledge permission to reprint from the following sources:

Part II: Tables 2.1 and 2.2, Population Reference Bureau; Tables 2.3, 2.4, and 2.6, The Population Council; Table 2.12, MacMillan Education, Ltd., Figures 2.1, 2.2, and 2.3, Population Reference Bureau; Table 3.3, J.M. Hobcraft; Table 3.9, Oxford University Press; Table 4.4, International Food Policy Research Institute; Table 4.10, American Agriculture Economics Association; Table 5.4, Elsevier Scientific Publishing Company; Table 5.5, International Council for Research in Agroforestry; Table 5.7, *Science;* Table 6.1, International Union for Conservation of Nature and Natural Resources; Table 6.3, South West African Department of Agriculture and Nature Conservation; Table 6.4, Heinemann Publishers, Ltd.; Table 6.5, World Wildlife Fund; Table 6.6, Van Nostrand Reinhold Co.; Figure 6.3, Elsevier Science Publishers;

Table 7.1, 7.2, 7.3, 7.4, 7.5, and 7.6, British Petroleum International Ltd.; Table 7.9, Geothermal Resources Council; Figures 7.1, 7.2, and 7.4, British Petroleum International Ltd.; Box 7.2, Figure 1, *The New York Times,* Table 8.4, W.R. Rangeley; Table 8.5, Worldwatch Institute; Table 8.9, Arthur D. Little, Inc.; Figure 8.1, *Scientific American;* Figure 8.2, *AMBIO;* Table 9.1, International Union for Conservation of Nature and Natural Resources; Table 9.6, Antenne Museum; Box 9.2, Figure 1, *AMBIO;* Tables 10.3, and 10.4, *AMBIO;* Table 10.5, Swedish Environmental Research Institute; Table 10.7, R.A. Rasmussen and M.A.K. Khalil; Figure 10.2, Robert I. Bruck; Figure 10.3, MacMillan Journals, Ltd.; Box 10.1, Table 1, American Chemical Society; Box 10.2, Figure 1, Robert I. Bruck; Table 11.4, American Institute of Biological Sciences; Figures 11.3 and 11.4, Joint Institute for the Study of the Atmosphere and Ocean.

Part III: Table 13.3, Island Press; Table 13.4, American Chemical Society.

Part IV: Tables 22.5 and 22.6, World Bureau of Metal Statistics.

World Map, Rand McNally & Co.

Copyright© 1987 by the International Institute for Environment and Development and the World Resources Institute
Library of Congress International Standard Serial Number:
0887-0403
ISBN 0-465-09238-1 Cloth
ISBN 0-465-09239-X Paper
Printed in the United States of America

Graphic design and production assistance provided by
The Forte Group, Alexandria, Virginia
86 87 88 89 MPC 9 8 7 6 5 4 3 2 1

Contents

Preface   ix

Acknowledgments   xi

Note to the Reader   xiii

Part I Perspectives

    1. Global Connections   1

Part II World Resources Reviews

    2. Population and Health   7

Population Trends; Factors That Influence Fertility Decisionmaking;
Regional Patterns of Fertility; **Focus On: Declining Fertility in
Western Europe and North America;** The State of Health; Trends
in Mortality; Factors Affecting Health; Health Priorities in the Third
World; *Recent Developments:* The Kenya Contraceptive Prevalence
Survey, Progress on the Global Strategy for Health for All by the Year
2000.

    3. Human Settlements   25

Global Trends in Human Settlements; **Focus On: Rural-Urban Disparities in Living Conditions;** Rural-Urban Dynamics; *Recent
Developments:* China Redefines Its Urban Population, The International Year of Shelter for the Homeless.

    4. Food and Agriculture   39

Agricultural Output: Trends and Prospects; Agricultural Commodities:
Production and Price Trends; **Focus On: Trends in Cash and Food
Crop Production;** Increasing Production and Its Environmental Costs:
The United States and the European Community; Innovations in Third
World Agriculture; *Recent Developments:* U.N. Special Session on
Africa, The Year of the Locusts.

    5. Forests and Rangelands   57

Forest Resources; Forest Management; Trends in Commercial Forests;
Focus On: Agroforestry; Rangeland Resources; Condition of Range-
lands; Desertification; Improving Rangeland; *Recent Developments:*
Progress on the Tropical Forestry Action Plan, U.S. Consumers
Demand Leaner Meat.

6. Wildlife and Habitat   77

The Economic Value of Wildlife; Regional Trends in Wildlife Manage-
ment; **Focus On: Freshwater Wetlands;** *Recent Developments:*
World Bank Adopts Wildlands Policy, Toxic Materials Threaten U.S.
Wildlife.

7. Energy   93

Energy Production and Consumption By Region; Major Energy
Sources; **Focus On: Energy Efficiency;** *Recent Developments:*
Clean-Coal Technologies, Biomass Users Network.

8. Freshwater   111

Freshwater: The Resource; Water Use; Water Pollution; **Focus On:
Groundwater;** *Recent Developments:* Desalination: The Industry
Matures, Great Lakes: Bilateral War on Toxics, Water Markets: The
Debate Grows.

9. Oceans and Coasts   125

Focus On: Marine Pollution; Coastal Wetlands and Estuaries; World
Fisheries; Fish Consumption and Trade; Regional Seas: The Baltic;
Recent Developments: The South Pacific Comes of Age, Wetlands
Receive Increased Attention.

10. Atmosphere and Climate   143

Emissions and Ambient Air Quality; Indoor Air Pollution; Trends in
Acid Deposition; Air Pollution and Acid Rain in the Third World: A
Case Study of China; Effects of Air Pollutants on Agricultural Crops;
Multiple Pollutants and Forest Decline; **Focus On: Decreasing Levels
of Stratospheric Ozone;** *Recent Developments:* Earth's Climate
Warming Faster Than Predicted, Depletion of the Ozone Layer, Hole
in Ozone Layer Studied, Czechoslovakia Works To Improve Its
Environment.

11. Global Systems and Cycles   163

The Carbon Cycle; Ocean-Atmosphere Interaction; **Focus On: The
Role of Tropical Oceans;** Geosphere-Biosphere Interactions: The
Case of Soils; New Tools; *Recent Developments.*

12. Policies and Institutions   181

International Environmental Law; Prospects for Success; Resource
Agreements Involving Two-Four Countries; Regional Agreements;
Global Agreements; Conclusions.

Part III World Resources Issues

13. Managing Hazardous Wastes: The Unmet Challenge   201

What is Hazardous Waste? Hazardous Wastes: How Much and Where?
The Multimedia Hazards of Toxic Wastes; Assessing Health Risks; Living With Past Mistakes: Hazardous Waste Dumps; Managing Hazardous Wastes; Conclusion.

14. Elements of Success: Sustainable Development in Sub-Saharan Africa   **221**

The Dimensions of Crisis; The Background to Crisis; The Response; Building Sustainable Agriculture; Reforesting Africa; Easing the Fuelwood Shortage; The Lessons.

Part IV   World Resources Data Tables

15. Basic Economic Indicators   **239**

15.1 Gross National Product, 1965-84.
15.2 External Debt Indicators, 1970-85.
15.3 World Commodity Indexes and Prices, 1960-86.
Figure 15.1: Price Index of 33 Nonfuel Commodities.

16. Population and Health   **247**

16.1 Estimated Size and Growth of Population, 1955-2000.
16.2 Births, Deaths, Fertility, and Age Dependency, 1960-90.
16.3 Health Indicators, 1964-90.
16.4 Malaria and Cholera Incidence, 1979-84.
16.5 Unmet Need for Contraception, 1980.

17. Human Settlements   **259**

17.1 Urban and Rural Populations, 1960-90.
17.2 Drinking Water and Sanitation in Developing Countries, Early 1980s.
17.3 World's 85 Largest Urban Agglomerations, 1985.
17.4 Waste Generation in Selected Countries, 1980.

18. Land Use and Cover   **267**

18.1 Land Area and Use, 1964-87.
18.2 Selected Internationally Important Wetlands, 1980s.
18.3 Land Use, 1850-1980.

19. Food and Agriculture   **275**

19.1 Food and Agricultural Production, 1964-85.
19.2 Agricultural Land Distribution, 1960-80.
19.3 Irrigation and Salinization, 1974-84.
19.4 Soil Erosion in Selected Countries, 1970-86.

20. Forests and Rangelands   **283**

20.1 Forest Resources, 1980s.
20.2 Wood Production, 1966-84.
20.3 Trade in Forest Products, 1966-84.
20.4 Extent of Desertification, Early 1980s.

21. Wildlife and Habitat   **291**

21.1 National and International Protection of Natural Areas, 1986.
21.2 Protected Areas Classified By Biogeographical Realm and Province, 1985.
21.3 Nationally Threatened Vertebrate Species, Early 1980s.
21.4 Globally Threatened Vertebrate Species, Early 1980s.

22. Energy and Minerals   **299**

    22.1 Production and Consumption of Commercial Energy, 1970-84.
    22.2 Production of Electricity, 1960-84.
    22.3 Reserves and Resources of Commercial Energy.
    22.4 Nuclear Power and Waste Generation, 1970-85.
    22.5 Producers and Consumers of Selected Metals, 1965-85.
    22.6 Recovery of Selected Materials, 1964-85.

23. Freshwater   **313**

    23.1 Freshwater Availability and Use, 1959-85.
    23.2 Large Dams.
    23.3 River Water Quality, 1979-86.
    23.4 Production Costs and Tariffs for Drinking Water, Early 1980s.

24. Oceans and Coasts   **325**

    24.1 Coastal Areas and Resources, 1974-86.
    24.2 Marine Mammals, 1920-85.
    24.3 Marine Fish Catch, 1979-84.
    24.4 Accidental Oil Spills, 1973-86.

25. Atmosphere and Climate   **333**

    25.1 Atmospheric Concentrations of Environmentally Important Trace Gases, 1959-86.
    Figure 25.1: Trends in Atmospheric Concentrations of Environmentally Important Trace Gases, 1975-85.
    25.2 Annual Emissions of Environmentally Important Trace Gases, 1925-85.
    Figure 25.2: Annual Emissions of Environmentally Important Trace Gases, 1925-85.
    Figure 25.3: Acidity of North American Precipitation, 1984.
    Figure 25.4: Acidity of European Precipitation, 1978-82.
    25.3 Indoor Air Pollution in Developing Countries, 1968-86.

26. Policies and Institutions   **341**

    26.1 Participation in Global Conventions Protecting the Environment, 1986.
    26.2 National and Regional Sources of Environmental Information, 1986.
    26.3 Official Development Assistance, 1964-84.
    26.4 Public Opinion on Environmental Issues, 1979-86.

World Map   **354**

Index   **356**

*The blue tabs along the sides of pages connect
Part II chapters with the corresponding data tables
in Part IV.*

Preface

At the launching of the *World Resources* series, former World Bank President Robert S. McNamara welcomed it into the "family of documents" that increase our understanding of the natural, economic, and political forces that shape our world. *World Resources* is designed to complement the established annual reports that survey the economic and political landscape by providing an objective, current, *global* assessment of the natural resource base that supports the world economy.

Events of the past year, such as growing evidence of global warming and the nuclear accident at Chernobyl, confirm our belief that protection of environmental quality and wise management of the world's natural resources are essential to the well-being of all nations. But as these issues come to the forefront of national and international attention, the critical need for up-to-date reliable information combined with objective analysis of conditions and trends of the world's natural resources becomes ever more apparent. *World Resources 1987* continues our commitment to meeting this critical need.

We have been encouraged in this course by the overwhelmingly positive response to *World Resources 1986*—from governmental and nongovernmental organizations concerned with the environment, from the international assistance community, from teachers and students, and most important, from individuals directly concerned with resource management and economic development around the world. This response is reflected in the many personal communications we have received and also in the wide interest in the book. The initial print run in English sold out. Publishers are proceeding with editions in Chinese, German, and Arabic. The book has been adopted as a course text or reference document at many universities in the United States, Europe, and elsewhere. Advance orders for *World Resources 1987* are already in hand.

With this strong start, we are confident that the ambitious undertaking begun by our two institutions more than three years ago is on its way to fulfilling the vital role we intended.

World Resources 1987 is a product of the good efforts of many people. The *World Resources* staff, once again, contributed its time and talents in greater measure than anyone could ask for. Its commitment and dedication made it all possible. The Editorial Advisory Board, chaired by Dr. M.S. Swaminathan, provided critical advice and support. The many others who contributed to this edition are noted in the Acknowledgments.

We deeply appreciate the financial support of those organizations that share our view of the importance of this series: The Ford Foundation; the United States Agency for International Development; the John D. and Catherine T. MacArthur Foundation; the J.N. Pew Jr. Charitable Trust; the United Nations Environment Programme; the German Marshall Fund of the United States; The United Nations Development Programme; and the World Bank. Such support is essential if *World Resources* is to continue to meet the many objectives we have set for the series.

World Resources 1987 updates and expands on issues and information covered in *World Resources 1986*. It also addresses new issues such as the management of hazardous wastes and the global systems and cycles that control the earth's climate and make life on earth possible. As the series develops, it will continue to address many of the most important issues of our time.

James Gustave Speth
President
World Resources Institute

Brian Walker
President
International Institute
    for Environment and
    Development

Acknowledgments

We are indebted to a long list of people who contributed to making *World Resources 1987* a reality. First and foremost are those who generously provided financial support. We thank: the Ford Foundation; the United States Agency for International Development; the John D. and Catherine T. MacArthur Foundation; the J.N. Pew Jr. Charitable Trust; the United Nations Environment Programme; the German Marshall Fund of the United States; the United Nations Development Programme; and the World Bank.

Our colleagues at the International Institute for Environment and Development and at the World Resources Institute provided invaluable assistance and advice throughout the planning and editing of this edition. Without their help it could not have been done. We thank them all.

A number of writers and technical experts assisted in drafting Part II and III chapters. They are: Gill Sheperd and Lesley Doyal (Population and Health); David Satterthwaite, Robert Fox and Herb Werlin (Human Settlements); John Madeley (Food and Agriculture); Jay Heinrichs, Thadis Box, Dean Treadwell, Steve Berwick, and Chris Elfring (Forests and Rangelands); James Teer and Steve Berwick (Wildlife and Habitat); Richard Munson (Energy); Larry Mosher and Lisa Jorgenson (Freshwater); Nora Berwick (Oceans and Coasts); Michael B. McElroy, Robert W. Stewart, Ruth S. DeFries, John Eddy, and Jerry M. Melillo (Global Systems and Cycles); Armin Rosencranz (Policies and Institutions); and Paul Harrison (Elements of Success: Sustainable Development in Sub-Saharan Africa).

Dozens of individuals in universities, governments, international organizations, research institutions, and elsewhere generously provided data (some of it not previously published), reviewed drafts, or wrote short sections. The length of the list does not diminish their individual contributions or our gratitude to each of them. They are: Richard Andrews, M.A. Acheson, Silvio Barabas, Roger Batstone, John Beddington, Nigel Bell, Miriam Bennett, Bob Berg, Chris Bernabo, Albert Binger, Deborah Bleviss, Bryan Boulier, Howard Braham, Mary Brandt, Marcia Brewster, Lester Brown, Robert Bruck, Lynton Keith Caldwell, David Carroll, Luis Castro, Henry Caufield, Ramesh Chander, Wan-Li Cheng, Dennis Childs, David Cies-likowski, Rod Coggin, Jim Craig, Ken Creighton, Pierre Crossen, Annick DeMarffy, E. Denti, Bengt Dieterich, Anne Dingwall, Betty Dow, Jean-Bernard Dubois, R.A. Duffield, Lloyd Duscha, Don Dwyer, Nicola Ellen, Paul Erlich, Malin Falkenmark, John Firor, Richard Ford, Peter Freeman, Robert Friedman, Bruce Fuller, Bjorn Ganning, Pietro Garau, Tom Geary, Jim Gibson, John Gladwell, Howard Goldberg, Edward Goldsmith, Galal Gorchev, Elizabeth Festa Gormley, Robert Greene, Martin Haigh, Nigel Haigh, Charles Hakkarinen, David Hall, Andrew Hamer, Lawrence Hamilton, N. Hample-Baker, Jeremy Harrison, Carl Haub, Gerry Hawkes, Harold Heady, Don Heisel, Richard Helmer, Howard W. Hjort, Bob Hofmann, Howard Hogg, R.A. Houghton, Norman Hudson, Hans Hurni, Fran Irwin, Charles Jelinek, Peter Johnson, Janis Jolly, Christopher Joyner, C.D. Keeling, Mick Kelly, M.A.K. Khalil, Charles Kimball, Lee Kimball, Albert Kohler, Christine Kronauer, Hans Landsberg, J.P. Lanly, Susan Lapham, Charles Larkin, Bill Long, Francisco Lopez, Margaret Lorenz, Gordon MacKerron, Sheila Macrae, Tom Magness, Jean Margat, Joan Martin-Brown, Larry Mason, Elaine Matthews, Marek Mayer, Arthur McKenzie, John Miller, Donald Mitchell, Robert Mitchell, L. Molineaux, Konrad von Moltke, Dave Moody, Sidney Moore, Jackie Myles, F. Najmabadi, Dan Navid, Martha Noble, Anthony Olsen, Bengt Owe-Jansson, R.K. Pachauri, Francesco Pariboni, Glenn Paulson, Henry M. Peskin, Rob Peters, Dale Pierce, David H. Pletscher, Cynthia Pollock, Sandra Postel, J.J. Rabier, R.A. Rasmussen, John Richards, Jane Robertson, Michael Robinson, Henning Rodhe, Peter Rogers, Dennis Rondinelli, Ralph Rotty, Peter Sandman, Stephen Sanford, David J. Sarokin, Jan Schaug, Doug Scheffler, Fred Schottman, Joseph Schuster, John Scott, James Shaw, T.C. Sheng, Kirk Smith, David M. Smith, Dick Soulen, Odyer Sperandio, Ronald St. John, Bevan Stein, Richard Tabor, Vivian Thompson, B.G. Thompson, Jane Thornback, Barbara Torrey, Jeffrey Tschirley, Dan Tunstall, Arthur Upton, Francis Urban, A. Vessereau, Horst Vogel, P.A. Wardle, Gregg Watters, Ann Way, Harold J. Weeks, Mary Beth Weinberger, Charles Westoff, Dean Wilkinson, Robert Williams, John Winter, Bob Winterbottom, Douglas Wolfe, Daniel Yergin, Jim Ypsilantis, William Zajac, and M.S. Zehni.

(continued on next page)

Producing this volume was a challenge to everyone involved. Our dedicated team of copy editors, fact checkers and proofreaders worked long and unpredictable hours: Leslie Bates (production assistant), Sheila Mulvihill and Richard Danca (copy editors), and Bart Brown (indexer). In addition we wish to acknowledge the fine work done by our secretarial team: Audrey Holley, Ahmey Katheryn Solee, and Novella Murray. Maurice Allen entered most of the data for Part IV with near perfect accuracy. We thank them all for their commitment, skill, and high professional standards.

Finally, we would like to acknowledge the excellent design and production work of The Forte Group of Alexandria, Virginia.

J. A. B.

Note to the Reader

World Resources 1987 is the second edition of an annual series. It is not an updated version of World Resources 1986, but rather a companion volume. Each new volume discusses different topics within the same broadly-defined framework. While each edition can stand on its own, readers will find optimal benefit in using it as part of a series.

Material discussed in World Resources 1986 is usually not repeated here. Rather a cross reference is given to last year's volume. As the series builds over the years, we hope readers will find it an increasingly valuable reference tool.

Like its predecessor, World Resources 1987 contains four main sections: Part I, Perspectives; Part II, World Resources Reviews; Part III, World Resources Issues; and Part IV, World Resources Data Tables. Any method of organization tends to separate issues into digestible pieces, but doing so raises the danger of losing sight of their interconnectedness. It is these interconnections that make natural resource issues so complex. In several areas of the book we attempt to cut across standard discussions such as atmosphere, freshwater, and wildlife to make these critical connections. Part I highlights these connections to stress some of the major themes that run through the entire book. In Part II, two chapters—Chapter 11, "Global Systems and Cycles" and Chapter 12, "Policies and Institutions"—are designed to provide a cross-cutting look at the issues covered by the other chapters.

There are three new chapters in World Resources 1987. As indicated, Chapter 11, "Global Systems and Cycles," looks across the narrower boundaries of other Part II chapters to examine the connections between, for example, the earth's atmosphere and its oceans. Each year, this chapter will also look at one of the major biogeochemical cycles essential to life—this year the carbon cycle. Human impacts on the carbon cycle are altering the conditions for life on earth. Carbon released by burning fossil fuels has increased the concentration of carbon dioxide in the atmosphere, which is the largest contributor to global warming. Understanding these systems and cycles is essential to understanding the ultimate consequences of our actions in altering our environment.

The other new chapters are in Part III, where we delve more deeply into issues of particular concern. This year one Part III chapter examines the persistent problem of hazardous wastes, one of the most serious environmental issues facing industrialized countries. Another looks at several successful projects in sub-Saharan Africa in a search for the keys to sustainable development of agriculture.

Other Part II chapters are retained from last year but focus on new topics. For example, Chapter 2, "Population and Health," examines the effects of a dramatic drop in fertility (below the level at which population replaces itself over time) in developed countries and reviews the state of human health in the world. Chapter 4, "Food and Agriculture," examines trends in cash crops and food crops in the developing world and the environmental impacts of increasing agricultural production in the developed world. Chapter 7, "Energy," analyzes major energy trends, assesses new and renewable sources of energy, and looks at nuclear power after Chernobyl. Chapter 12, "Policies and Institutions," examines the growing trend toward international agreements on transboundary pollution problems and shared natural resources.

As in last year's edition, Part IV contains data for 146 countries on the extent, condition, use, and value of many of the natural resources analyzed in Part II. In addition, this section includes two other chapters on "Basic Economic Indicators" and "Land Use and Cover." Overall, about half the data tables are new this year; the other half update last year's tables. Among the tables unique to this volume are "Unmet Need for Contraception" (Table 16.5), "Selected Internationally Important Wetlands" (Table 18.2), "Recovery of Selected Materials" (Table 22.6), "Large Dams" (Table 23.4), "Marine Mammals" (Table 24.2), and "Public Opinion on Environmental Issues" (Table 26.4).

The tables in Part IV continue to show many areas where data are incomplete or entirely missing. Throughout World Resources 1987 we have attempted to point out where serious gaps in data exist, in order to encourage organizations and agencies to fill these gaps. As the World Resources series grows, it will touch on other major issues and present more comprehensive data tables as these data become available.

1. Global Connections

One year ago, *World Resources 1986* was published as the first of an annual series devoted to providing objective, accurate, and up-to-date information on the world's environment and natural resources. This series was launched with the belief that wise management of natural resources and the protection of environmental quality are intimately linked to achieving sustainable economic growth, alleviating poverty, promoting public health, coping with the pressures of population expansion, and ensuring long-term political and economic stability.

By coincidence, during the week that *World Resources 1986* was released, world attention focused on the small town of Chernobyl in the Soviet Union. The nuclear reactor accident there released a cloud of radiation that passed over most of Europe and raised fears that it might encircle the globe. The governments of most European countries scrambled to assess the full extent of the radiation and to devise strategies for dealing with fallout and contamination while they wondered what could have been done to prevent or at least to respond better to such a crisis. That single event, more than any other in 1986, dramatized our dependence on the environment and our ability to affect it significantly.

Thirty-one people died as a result of the accident. The radiation cloud from the Ukraine recognized no political boundaries. The health and well-being of millions of people depended on the vagaries of wind and rain as the radiation spread over most of Europe. Traces were detected throughout the northern hemisphere. Contamination of crops, livestock, and soil was widespread, causing substantial economic losses. Long-term effects include an estimated additional 5,000–50,000 deaths over the next 30–60 years. Chernobyl dispelled any lingering notion that a nation can independently ensure the protection of its environment and the welfare of its citizens. (See Chapter 7, "Energy," Box 7.2, Chernobyl: An International Accident.)

In November, a large volume of toxic chemicals, including mercury, insecticides, and dyes, spilled into the Rhine River as a result of a fire at the Sandoz chemical plant in Basel, Switzerland. As at Chernobyl, the pollutants quickly moved across international boundaries. The spill caused massive fish kills in Germany and France, required substantial cleanup efforts, and threatened human health throughout the Rhine basin. In response to demands from downstream neighbors, both Sandoz and the Swiss Government promised to compensate victims for financial losses after the economic and health costs are fully assessed. (See Chapter 12, "Policies and Institutions," The Rhine River.)

These and other less dramatic events in 1986, such as continuing famine and food shortages in Africa and the confirmation of the seasonal thinning of the ozone layer over Antarctica, exemplify two related themes that run throughout *World Resources 1987*:

■ *The global environment is an interconnected web.* The links among the natural systems of air, water, land, and the living biota are often global. Disturbing any one of them can have unexpected results that are remote in both space and time.

■ *The human race relies on the environment and therefore must manage it wisely.* The prosperity of nations and individuals depends upon the quality of the environment and the availability of natural resources. Yet it is principally human activities that degrade the global environment and deplete the world's natural resource base. Our future health and well-being depend on our ability to manage the earth's environment successfully.

These two themes are exemplified by the following major environmental and natural resource issues, which are drawn from the many topics covered in *World Resources 1987*.

Depletion of Stratospheric Ozone

Stratospheric ozone depletion was a leading global environmental issue during 1986. The presence of ozone in the stratosphere is vital to human health because it substantially reduces the amount of ultraviolet (UV) radiation that reaches the earth's surface from the sun. Depletion or loss of this protective shield would substantially increase radiation, resulting in an increase in skin cancers among humans, possible damage to the human immune system, and a variety of impacts on other species. In the United States, it is estimated that a 1 percent increase in UV radiation would increase the number of nonmalignant skin cancers by up to 5 percent and the number of deaths from the rarer malignant melanomas by about 1 percent. Research also suggests that increased UV radiation would damage some crops and the sensitive planktonic organisms that support marine food chains, although the magnitude of these effects has not been estimated.

Unfortunately, humans are probably beginning to cause depletion of the ozone layer, primarily because of atmospheric emissions of a group of highly stable synthetic compounds called chlorofluorocarbons (CFCs) that destroy ozone. These chemical compounds, first manufactured in the early 1930s, found widespread use in a variety of commercial and industrial applications, including refrigeration, industrial solvents, and propellants for aerosols. Highly valued because they are nontoxic, nonreactive, and "safe" to use, production and use of CFCs grew substantially and atmospheric emissions rose. In 1985, an estimated 650,000 metric tons of the two most common forms, CFC-11 and CFC-12, were emitted. Concentrations of CFCs in the atmosphere have almost doubled in the past ten years, increasing from 320 to 607 parts per trillion for CFC-11 and CFC-12. (See Chapter 25, "Atmosphere and Climate," Table 25.1, Atmospheric Concentrations of Environmentally Important Trace Gases, 1959-86, and Table 25.2, Annual Emissions of Environmentally Important Trace Gases, 1925-86.)

Theoretical work first reported in 1974 by U.S. scientists suggests that CFCs, through a complex physical and chemical process, can migrate to the stratosphere, where they can chemically react with ozone and destroy it. Although the destructive impact of CFCs on the ozone layer has not been validated empirically, several nations restrict CFC use and production. In 1985, continuing concerns led to signing of the Vienna Convention for the Protection of the Ozone Layer, an initial agreement in principle to control CFC use. However, no agreement was reached on exactly how and when to achieve a reduction. Since 1985, the signatories to the Convention have met several times to discuss such an implementing protocol, but they have not yet reached an agreement.

In late 1985, British scientists reported evidence of a "hole" in the ozone shield over Antarctica during the late winter and early spring months (August-November).

Monitoring data, which go back more than 30 years, show that ozone concentrations over Antarctica are now 40 percent less during this season than they were in the mid-1970s and that the area of the hole is growing. No damage is apparent, but the head of Argentina's National Meteorological Service has warned that the hole may soon be large enough to expose southern Argentina to potentially dangerous amounts of ultraviolet radiation.

Although there remains some scientific debate over the causes and implications of the ozone hole and its possible relationship to a global depletion of the ozone layer, the entirely unexpected appearance of this Antarctic phenomenon has stimulated considerable public discussion and concern over the ozone shield. These growing concerns have helped fuel efforts to reach agreement on the protocol to the Vienna Convention. Even the U.S. chemical industry has modified its resistance to restrictions on CFCs. The Alliance for Responsible CFC Policy—a coalition of about 500 users and producers of CFCs—now publicly supports the need for limitations, and the world's largest producer (DuPont) favors a policy to encourage the development of environmentally acceptable substitutes that can be introduced over the next five years. (See Chapter 10, "Atmosphere and Climate," Focus On: Decreasing Levels of Stratospheric Ozone, and Recent Developments: Depletion of the Ozone Layer, and Chapter 12, "Policies and Institutions," Stratospheric Ozone.)

Agricultural Production in Sub-Saharan Africa

The population of sub-Saharan Africa is growing faster than that of any other region of the world. Although total agricultural output has risen, it has not kept pace with population growth. Per capita agricultural production and per capita food production have both fallen consistently over the past 20 years, resulting in increased poverty and malnutrition. Even before the 1983-84 drought, 99 million people were acutely malnourished. With 71 percent of the labor force in agriculture and 77 percent of the population living in rural areas, the health, nutrition, and income of the majority of Africans are inseparably linked to agriculture. In a continent where the use of fertilizers, irrigation, and new seeds is the lowest in the world, agriculture depends on the health of the environment and vice versa.

Africa's environment is not naturally favorable to agriculture. The soils are poor—55 percent have severe fertility constraints. In addition, many African soils have limited water-holding capacity and are highly susceptible to erosion. Sub-Saharan Africa shares with other tropical regions the problems of rain that falls predominately in erosive downpours, the stresses that dry seasons place on vegetation, the high temperatures that accelerate decomposition of organic matter, and the absence of a cold winter to kill pests and reduce disease. Outside the humid zones, rainfall is highly variable and prolonged drought is a constant threat.

Human activities have degraded the already fragile natural resource base. Traditional agricultural systems—shifting cultivation and nomadic pastoralism—used abundant land for only a limited time before abandoning it, a practice that allowed natural restoration of the land through relatively long periods of inactivity. With larger and rapidly growing populations, land is less abundant. Fallow periods have been reduced in many areas and are no longer sufficient to restore fertility or provide adequate grazing or fuelwood. In many countries, crop yields are stagnant or declining, fallow and farmland are overgrazed, and fuelwood needs are met by depleting the stock rather than by replanting. Vegetation cover is weakened, runoff increases, erosion accelerates, and topsoil is irrevocably lost, further reducing soil fertility and continuing the downward spiral.

In 1980, Africa's forests were being cleared at the rate of 3.7 million hectares per year—0.6 percent of the continent's total undisturbed forests. Annual rates of deforestation reached 4 percent in Nigeria and almost 6 percent in the Cote d'Ivoire during the early 1980s. Throughout sub-Saharan Africa, deforestation outpaced new tree planting 29:1. Desertification of dry lands—the loss of the biological productivity of land, which can lead to desert-like conditions—affects 80 percent of rangelands and rain-fed croplands and 30 percent of irrigated land.

Soil erosion is widespread, with annual topsoil losses of up to 296 metric tons per hectare on relatively steep slopes in Ethiopia. Even moderate slopes can erode rapidly when unprotected by vegetation. In West Africa, losses of 30–55 metric tons per hectare have been reported on slopes of only 1–2 percent. Wind erosion, significant in drier areas, erodes even flat land. (See Chapter 14, "Elements of Success: Sustainable Development in Sub-Saharan Africa," The Dimensions of Crisis; and Chapter 19, "Forests and Rangelands," Table 20.4, Extent of Desertification.)

Efforts to increase agricultural productivity are often limited by the lack of funds for fertilizer, improved seeds, and tools. Yet, even when funds have been available, many efforts at intensifying agricultural production fail to recognize Africa's environmental realities. By promoting monocropping instead of intercropping, increased cattle production on fragile lands, and tractor plowing or machine clearing methods on soils that demand minimal disturbance, these efforts often led to less rather than more productivity despite the expenditure of considerable sums.

Several projects in sub-Saharan Africa demonstrate the feasibility of reversing this process of degradation. They include various forms of agroforestry, which combines farming with tree growing, thus raising the total productivity of a given piece of land. In semi-arid areas, planting trees for windbreaks can reduce soil erosion and improve water infiltration, increasing agricultural production. In the Majia Valley of Niger, windbreaks of neem trees increased crop yields 18–23 percent while providing a new and easily accessible source of fuelwood.

Alley cropping with rows of nitrogen-fixing trees, such as *Leucaena leucocephala*, alternating with rows of crops such as maize is effective in humid and subhumid areas; yield increases averaged 39 percent. There are other benefits as well. Soils become richer in organic matter and moisture levels increase. The higher yields are achieved on a sustainable basis, permitting continuous cropping and requiring no artificial nitrogen fertilizers. (See Chapter 4, "Food and Agriculture," Innovations in

Third World Agriculture; Chapter 5, "Forests and Rangeland," Focus On: Agroforestry; and Chapter 14, "Elements of Success: Sustainable Development in Sub-Saharan Africa," Case Study: Alleycropping.)

Hazardous Wastes

In the industrialized world, few issues have brought home more clearly the ability of humans to affect the quality of their environment and the complex interconnections of land, water, and air than have hazardous wastes. Twenty years ago, industrial wastes (including hazardous wastes) were dumped into a river, carried to a landfill, or poured onto the ground. An out-of-sight, out-of-mind mentality prevailed. No one worried that these materials might come back to haunt us.

Today, after too many discoveries of toxic and hazardous wastes' finding their way into the water we drink, the air we breathe, and the land on which we live, governments are struggling to deal with this history of uncontrolled dumping and to manage the continuing output of these substances. No one knows how many old waste dump sites there are. In the United States, estimates of the number of sites requiring priority cleanup under the federal Superfund program vary among U.S. government agencies between 2,500 and 10,000. Cost estimates for the sites are $23–$100 billion. But these figures cover just the worst problem sites. An estimated 75,000 active industrial landfill sites and 180,000 surface impoundments (ponds) may also contain hazardous wastes. It is estimated that nearly 2 percent of U.S. groundwater aquifers may be contaminated.

Many European countries face a similar situation. For example, the Netherlands Government estimates that up to 8 million metric tons of hazardous chemical wastes may be buried in Dutch soil—most of it in leaking metal drums. About 5,000 hazardous waste sites have been identified, of which more than 1,000 require immediate or priority attention. Total costs for cleanup could reach $5.6 billion. Similarly, the Federal Republic of Germany anticipates cleaning up 2,000 of its 21,000 abandoned waste sites at a cost of about $4 billion.

Up to 95 percent of all hazardous wastes generated in Eastern Europe are disposed of in landfills, many lacking any environmental controls. Because authorities did not generally keep track of potentially hazardous wastes until recently, no estimate of the total number of potential problem sites is available. However, the discovery of individual problem sites, such as the contamination of town wells for drinking water in Vac, Hungary, by chemicals from improperly stored waste drums at an abandoned waste site, suggests that the problem will grow.

Even less information is available in the developing world on the disposal of hazardous wastes. Although much less hazardous waste has been produced in the Third World than in the industrialized countries, adequate treatment and disposal are almost totally lacking.

The extent of health risks associated with individual dump sites is generally unknown and is extremely difficult to determine. Assessing risks requires knowing not only what wastes were dumped but also how they interact and how they spread through land, water, and air. In

World Resources 1987

a study of U.S. Superfund sites, 230 hazardous chemicals or groups of chemicals had made their way outside the sites—173 were found in nearby groundwater reservoirs, 162 in surface water, and 65 in the air. Further, health effects depend not only on the type of toxic or hazardous substance but also on its concentration, the type of exposure (ingestion, contact with skin, etc.), and the level and duration of exposure.

Despite the extreme difficulty of assessing environmental contamination from toxic wastes and extrapolating health effects, what we know about the chemicals in these dumps is certainly cause for concern. In a study of 900 hazardous waste sites in the United States, 444 toxic pollutants were found. Among the ten most common substances, seven are believed to cause cancer; seven, birth defects; and five, genetic damage. Some cause immediate poisoning, and low-level, long-term exposure to virtually all of them, particularly through contaminated drinking water, can damage human health.

In light of the sad history of toxic waste disposal, most OECD countries in the past 15–20 years have instituted regulations governing the handling and disposal of hazardous wastes. The regulations fall far short of dealing successfully with a threat of the magnitude of hazardous wastes. For example, U.S. industry produces an estimated 265 million metric tons of hazardous wastes annually. Although the U.S. Government has established a federal manifest system for tracking the wastes to ensure proper disposal, it applies only to the 4 percent of hazardous wastes that are transported away from their sites of origin.

Eighty percent of hazardous wastes in OECD countries are still disposed of in landfills or other land-based storage sites. Only 5–10 percent are incinerated or thermally destroyed, and no more than 5 percent are recycled, reclaimed, or reused. Land disposal, even under carefully controlled conditions, does not eliminate the threat of hazardous wastes; land disposal merely contains it for the immediate future. Landfills designed to contain hazardous wastes must be lined, but most experts argue that the clay or other barriers built to contain the wastes are generally inadequate to prevent hazardous wastes from eventually seeping into the surrounding soil. Significant risks to human health will continue until ways are found to stop piling up these wastes: through extensive recycling and reuse of these materials, further development of technologies for waste destruction, and increased source reduction—avoiding the creation of hazardous wastes in the manufacturing process in the first place. (See Chapter 13, "Managing Hazardous Wastes: The Unmet Challenge.")

Pollution of River Systems

The Rhine chemical spill was a catastrophe whose effects on the river were immediate and visible. It made headlines around the world. Yet every day the world's rivers receive an enormous stream of industrial discharges, human sewage, and surface runoff from urban and agricultural uses of the land. Rivers and streams are of major importance historically, providing water for drinking, washing, agriculture, transportation, and disposal of human wastes. More recently, rivers are used increasingly for power generation, industrial processes (such as cooling), and disposal of industrial effluents. Intensifying use is burdening rivers with an increasing load of pollutants that threaten the future usefulness of the rivers.

Growing populations and economic development produce increasing amounts of wastes and sewage, which can overwhelm a river unless they are adequately treated. But in many parts of the world, especially in most developing countries, water treatment and pollution control are either grossly inadequate or totally lacking. For example, in China, where waste water severely pollutes 70 percent of the country's 78 monitored rivers, an estimated 98 percent of all waste water goes untreated. During summer months, untreated waste water has accounted for up to 25 percent of the waters of the Huang-p'u River, Shanghai's primary source of drinking water.

Other Asian countries face similar situations. More than two thirds of India's water resources are polluted. One indicator of untreated human (and animal) sewage is fecal coliform bacteria in water. Although World Health Organization guidelines for safe drinking water call for 98 percent of all samples to be free from coliform, recent measurements in India's Mali and Napada Rivers averaged 550,000 and 260,000 per 100 milliliters, respectively. By failing to install waste treatment facilities, many of India's growing new industries have also exacerbated water pollution. (See Chapter 8, "Freshwater," Water Pollution, and Chapter 23, "Freshwater," Table 23.3, River Water Quality.)

Untreated or inadequately treated sewage and industrial effluents have caused water quality to deteriorate in the Philippines. Incredibly, domestic sewage constitutes 60–70 percent of Manila's Pasig River. Its dissolved oxygen content is now 3.1 milligrams per liter, the level at which aquatic life begins to die. In Malaysia, palm and rubber effluents, other industrial wastes, and sewage have caused 42 rivers to be officially labeled "dead."

Although data are scarce, countries in Africa appear to be facing similar problems. Agro-industrial activities, in addition to raw sewage, are a significant source of pollution. In Nigeria, the brewing, slaughtering, and sugar refining industries make little attempt to control water pollution; in Kenya, the coffee and tanning industries are the major source of pollution.

In South America, with the world's most abundant water resources, most municipalities and industries discharge their effluents virtually untreated. The mining industry is the worst offender, particularly in the Andean countries.

Data on river pollution in the developed world are most readily available among the Organisation for Economic Co-operation and Development (OECD) nations. Including many of the world's most industrialized and urbanized countries, OECD nations were among the first to confront water pollution—by installing waste water treatment plants. By 1983, over 50 percent of the population in 21 of the 24 OECD countries surveyed were served by a waste water treatment facility.

As a result, rivers in some areas are becoming cleaner. Biological oxygen demand (BOD)—the amount of oxygen used by microorganisms in oxidizing organic matter—has generally decreased since 1970. The biggest improvement was in the Seine River in France, where BOD dropped 60 percent between 1975 and 1983.

Progress in reducing the levels of other pollutants is mixed. For example, lead levels in the Rhine River at Bimmen in the Federal Republic of Germany dropped from 24 micrograms per liter in 1975 to 8 micrograms per liter in 1983, but nitrate concentrations more than doubled between 1970 and 1983.

In Eastern Europe, where data are scarce, the problem appears more severe. Poland's Vistula River, which runs through some of the country's most heavily industrialized regions, was so badly polluted in 1978 that for 636 kilometers—60 percent of its length—the water was considered unsuitable even for industrial use. The stretch running through Krakow was reportedly devoid of biological life. In 1977, 75 percent of the effluents dumped into the Soviet Union's Volga River were untreated. In Volgograd, industrial wastes accounted for 10 percent of the Volga's total annual flow. (See Chapter 7, "Freshwater," Water Pollution.)

Inevitably, a large proportion of riverborne pollutants flow into seas and oceans, with major effects felt along the coasts and in enclosed seas. For example, the Chesapeake Bay in the United States is a highly productive estuary fed by 150 rivers and streams, harboring about 200 species of fish and shellfish and 2,700 species of other aquatic animals and plants. Primarily as a result of pollution, the annual catch of striped bass fell 90 percent between 1970 and 1983. Oyster harvests dropped about 50 percent over the past 20 years. The principal pollutants are nitrogen, phosphorus, and toxic chemicals. Most of the phosphorus is from municipal sewage and industrial wastes, and most nitrogen is from agricultural runoff. High concentrations of toxic organic compounds and heavy metals are found in sediments near industrial areas, primarily along the major rivers. (See Chapter 9, "Oceans and Coasts," Box 9.1, Turning the Tide in the Chesapeake Bay.)

Enclosed seas such as the Mediterranean and the Baltic are also severely affected. About 85 percent of all pollutants reaching the Mediterranean are from land-based sources, the great majority of them carried by rivers.

The Baltic Sea is fed by some 250 river systems. The surrounding region is highly industrialized with over 200 major industrial complexes—including steel and metal works, chemical industries, and pulp and paper mills. Major pollutants reaching the Baltic include heavy metals, such as mercury, cadmium, lead, zinc, and copper; PCBs; DDT; and nutrients such as nitrogen and phosphorus. An estimated 1.1 million metric tons of nitrogen enter the Baltic each year. Although some progress has been made in reducing mercury and DDT levels over the past ten years, the high overall pollution levels have resulted in severe oxygen depletion in nearly half of the Baltic's deep waters (approximately 100,000 square kilometers). This lack of oxygen makes it virtually impossible for any life form to survive. (See Chapter 9, "Oceans and Coasts," Land-Based Sources of Pollution, and Regional Seas: The Baltic.)

Conclusion

Human activities are changing the global environment in many ways, too often to its detriment and the detriment of people. The effects are sometimes direct and obvious, but more often they are subtle, indirect, delayed or entirely unexpected.

Pollutants are carried by the natural flows of water and wind far from their origin, frequently across international boundaries. The person who becomes ill from drinking polluted river water may be hundreds of kilometers from the source of the pollutants. Groundwater may become contaminated by hazardous wastes seeping from an abandoned dump many years after the dumping took place. The unanticipated risks of an increased incidence of cancers and other effects of depletion of the ozone layer are becoming known decades after CFCs began to be widely used.

Deforestation, overcropping, and other stresses—caused by pressures to feed a rapidly growing population—inevitably lead to declining soil fertility and water-holding capacity. These declines, in turn, lead to increased soil erosion and further degradation of the soil's capacity to support agriculture in a steep downward spiral.

The environmental impacts of human activities in these examples are largely negative. But they need not be. People can also affect the environment positively, and a number of signs indicate a growing commitment to sustaining and improving the global environment. Public support for environmental protection and for governmental spending to achieve it is high. Public opinion polls in the OECD countries over the last seven years consistently show these attitudes to be strong. (See Chapter 26, "Policies and Institutions," Table 26.4, Public Opinion on Environmental Issues, 1979–86.)

There is also a growing recognition that effective management of natural resources and protection of the environment require cooperative actions by many nations. The result is a growing number of international negotiations and formal agreements on issues of shared natural resources and transboundary pollution. Although many of these agreements have achieved little actual reduction in pollution so far, they often embody research, monitoring, assessment, and consultation activities designed to lead to further action. (See Chapter 12, "Policies and Institutions.")

1986 saw several small steps which hold significant promise for the future.

A flood of international discussions followed the Chernobyl and Rhine accidents. In the case of Chernobyl, they have already led to new agreements on reactor safety and the handling of international nuclear emergencies. The more recent Rhine chemical spill prompted initiatives in five international organizations—the OECD, the United Nations Environment Programme, the Economic Commission for Europe, the Council of Europe, and the European Economic Committee—with the intention of improving control over hazardous materials and the handling of accidents involving hazardous chemicals. (See Chapter 7, "Energy," Box 7.2, Chernobyl: An International Accident; and Chapter 12, "Policies and Institutions," The Rhine.)

Global Connections

In May, an unprecedented Special Session of the United Nations was held on the problems of Africa. There was remarkable agreement on the need for both African governments and the donors of international assistance to focus on agricultural development. The necessity of ensuring the sustainability of agricultural development was also widely recognized. Unfortunately, the financial resources needed to accomplish the session's lofty goals may not materialize. (See Chapter 4, "Food and Agriculture," U.N. Special Session on Africa.)

Progress was also made on other fronts, particularly a gathering commitment to carry out the Tropical Forestry Action Plan (see Chapter 5, "Forests and Rangelands," Progress on the Tropical Forestry Action Plan) and the slow but steady progress toward an enforceable agreement to control CFC emissions.

Note must finally be made of another important event of 1986, one that could have a profound impact on our understanding and therefore our ability to manage the global environment. At the 21st General Assembly of the International Council of Scientific Unions (ICSU) in September, an ambitious long-term (10–20 year) program of global scientific research was unanimously approved: the International Geosphere-Biosphere Programme (IGPB). Its goals are unprecedented in scope—to describe and understand the interactive physical, chemical, and biological processes that regulate the total earth system, the unique environment that it provides for life, the changes that are occurring in this system, and the manner in which they are influenced by human actions. The program amounts to the birth of a new scientific discipline—earth systems science—that may ultimately enable us to use the earth's resources ever more intensively, yet without damage to their integrity. (See Chapter 11, "Global Systems and Cycles," Recent Developments.)

2. Population and Health

As the world population passes the 5 billion mark in 1987 (1), the overall rate of increase obscures large differences in population trends between the developed and the developing world. The developing world is growing 2.4 percent per year (2 percent if China is included), but the annual growth rate in the developed world is only 0.6 percent. In the Third World, a woman bears an average of five children (4.2, including China), and, in the industrialized world, two children per woman is the norm—a number that is below replacement level (2). (See Table 2.1.)

Much useful work has been done in investigating the social, economic, political, and cultural factors that influence population growth and decline. In general, high birth rates are found where mortality rates are high, where household labor is the key to agricultural production, and where children are essential to the well-being of parents in their old age. Falling birth rates, on the other hand, are normally found when educational opportunities for women and children increase and when women move from unpaid family labor to paid employment.

Regional differences in birth rates have much to do with underlying cultural norms. A key variable is the status of women, which is a function of their economic dependence on, or independence from, fathers and husbands. A greater degree of economic independence among women in the Caribbean and Southeast Asia, for example, has contributed to notable declines in birth rates. Whereas in South and Southwest Asia, young wives are subordinate in the extended households of their parents-in-law, and birth rates remain high.

Political events and philosophies also affect the fertility decisions of many people, both through explicit government population policies and through the influence of events and policies on economic, cultural, and social forces.

Many governments in both the First and Third Worlds worry about their countries' population growth rates—in the Third World, high growth rates often create problems for their national economies and add pressure to their resource base, and, in the First World, declining birth rates and aging populations may lead to heavy economic burdens on a reduced work force.

Health status is one of the most sensitive indicators of wider social and economic conditions. In a poor country, the population frequently suffers excess ill health and premature mortality. In a rich country whose wealth is unevenly distributed, sickness and death are distributed unequally. Health is a vital resource both for individuals and for the society in which they live. Without good health, people cannot participate fully in normal social and economic activities. Poor health is a major disaster for those whose lives are diminished or prematurely ended. For countries whose economic growth is limited by it, it is a liability. A look at the state of world health today reveals the fact that good health is unevenly distributed both around the world and within particular countries. Major policy initiatives are needed if health conditions are to improve.

CONDITIONS AND TRENDS

POPULATION TRENDS

In 1750, there were approximately 760 million people in the world. By 1950, there were 2.5 billion (3), and most recent estimates calculate that the world's population will pass the 5 billion mark in 1987. Although the overall growth rate is declining, the world population is expected to increase another 3 billion between 1985 and 2025. In the 200 years between 1750 and 1950, the total population of the world increased by a factor of 3.3. Current estimates for the year 2025 suggest that in just 75 years it will have grown by another factor of 3.3 (4). (See Figure 2.1.)

Regional Growth

There have been two major periods of worldwide population expansion: 1750–1950 and 1950–1985. The first was triggered by the Industrial Revolution (5). The most rapid growth rates occurred in Europe and in the Americas and Oceania, where the Europeans settled. (In absolute numbers, Asia's population increase was the highest because its population was so large to begin with.)

The second major period began in the middle of this century, and growth has been concentrated in the Third World. Improved standards of living and improvements in public health have reduced death rates while birth rates have remained high. Growth rates in industrialized countries are now low: population in the developed world

Table 2.1 Global Population Statistics

	World	Developed	Developing	Developing (excluding China)
Population mid-1986 (millions)	4,942	1,180	3,762	2,712
Crude Birth Rate[a]	27	15	31	37
Crude Death Rate[b]	11	10	11	12
Natural Increase (annual, percent)	1.7	0.6	2	2.4
Population "Doubling Time" in Years (at current rates)	41	122	34	29
Population Projection to 2000 (millions)	6,157	1,264	4,893	3,703
Population Projection to 2100 (millions)	10,445	1,417	9,028	7,457
Infant Mortality Rate (number of deaths before the age of 1 year per 1,000 live births)	82	17	92	99
Total Fertility Rate (average number of births per woman)	3.7	1.9	4.2	5
Percent of Population Under 15/Over 65 Years of Age	35/6	23/12	39/40	41/4
Life Expectancy at Birth (years)	62	73	58	56
Urban Population (percent)	43	72	34	34
Population Growth 1950-85 (millions)	2,321	342	1,979	1,486
Population Growth 1985-2020 (millions)	2,986	203	2,783	2,415
Per Capita GNP, 1983 (U.S. dollars)	$2,760	$9,510	$ 700	$ 870

Notes:
a. Average annual number of births per 1,000 population.
b. Average annual number of deaths per 1,000 population.
Source: Adapted from Population Reference Bureau, Inc. (PRB), *World Population Data Sheet 1986* (PRB, Washington, D.C., 1986).

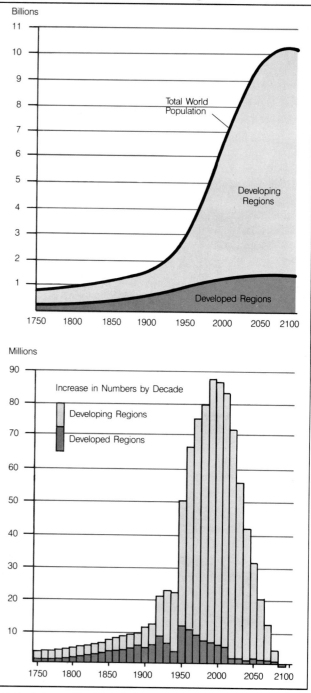

Figure 2.1 World Population Growth: Developing and Developed Regions, 1750–2100

Developing Regions = Africa, Asia (excluding Japan), and Latin America.
Developed Regions = Europe, the USSR, Japan, and Oceania (including Australia and New Zealand) and North America (Canada and the United States).
Source: Thomas W. Merrick, *et al.*, "World Population in Transition," *Population Bulletin*, Vol. 41, No. 2 (1986), Figure 1, p. 4.

increased 41 percent, compared to 117 percent in the Third World, between 1950 and 1985 (6). (See Figure 2.1.)

The highest growth rates currently are in Africa and Latin America. Between 1985 and 2025, Africa is expected to increase its share of the total world population from 11.5 percent to nearly 20 percent. The corresponding increase in Latin America is from 8.4 percent to 9.5 percent (7). (See Table 2.2.)

In sheer numbers, China and India dwarf all other nations with their populations of 1,050 million and 785 million, respectively. The third largest country, the Soviet Union, with a population of 280 million, is about one-quarter the size of China, while the next three largest countries—the United States, Indonesia, and Brazil—have a combined total of only 553 million (8).

Long-Range Projections

Long-range projections of world population size and distribution are based on assumptions about fertility rates, mortality rates, and international migration patterns. As such, they are educated extrapolations of trends, and they may be incorrect, but they are useful indicators of the implications of current trends. Long-range projections by the United Nations (U.N.) indicate that the world population will more than double by the year 2100. Ninety-five percent of the increase will be in the Third World; by then, the population of developing countries is estimated at 8.8 billion, compared to 1.4 billion in developed regions (9).

Africa's projected growth rate is the highest of all regions, increasing from 555 million in 1985 to almost 2.6 billion in 2100. Latin America and the Caribbean are expected to grow from 405 million in 1985 to 1.2 billion in 2100. Asia is projected to add the largest number of people, growing from 2.7 billion to 4.9 billion. Developed regions are expected to follow a low-growth pattern; by 2100, they are expected to account for only 14.1 percent of the total population, compared to 24.4 percent today (10).

Stabilization

The U.N. Medium Variant Projection, the U.N.'s best estimate of population trends, assumes that, worldwide, average fertility rates will drop to the replacement level of 2.1 births per woman by 2035. Although the United Nations foresees fertility rates remaining higher in some developing countries, these will be offset by the industrialized countries where fertility rates are already generally below two (11).

The U.N. Medium Variant projects stabilization of the world population by 2100 at 10.2 billion if the replacement fertility level is reached by 2035. However, the

World Bank estimates that the population will not stabilize until it reaches 11.2 billion. The differences between these projections illustrate the uncertainties of long-range projections. In fact, the U.N. has prepared five different projections based on differing sets of world population assumptions that result in estimates of world population in 2100 that vary from 7.2 billion to 14.9 billion (12). The Medium Variant Projection is used throughout this chapter.

These projections are sensitive to variations in assumed fertility rates. A 20 year delay beyond 2035 in reaching the replacement level fertility rate of 2.1 births per woman results in a projected stable population that is 2.8 billion larger. A 20-year advance in achieving this fertility rate implies 2.2 billion fewer people. The difference in the eventual size of total world population resulting from this 40-year shift equals the present world population (13).

FACTORS THAT INFLUENCE FERTILITY DECISIONMAKING

Fertility levels reflect complex social phenomena. Analyses of the World Fertility Survey (14), a survey conducted by the International Statistical Institute of the Netherlands of over 30,000 married women in 62 countries during 1974-82, and other studies have focused attention on the complex individual and family decision-making processes and on the effects of socioeconomic, political, and cultural factors on reproductive behavior in households (15).

Socioeconomic and Cultural Factors

Socioeconomic and cultural factors that appear to affect fertility most significantly include:
■ the importance of children as part of the family labor force,
■ the costs of raising and educating children,
■ the social status of women,
■ the educational attainment and employment patterns of women, and
■ urbanization (16).

Although these factors operate with each other in complex ways (and also interact with each other), correlations between them and average fertility rates in various countries and regions of the world are strong.

The Total Fertility Rate (TFR) is the number of children whom an average woman bears in a lifetime. TFRs tend

Table 2.2 Population Growth, 1750–2100
(millions)

Region	1750 Number	1750 Percent	1900 Number	1900 Percent	1950 Number	1950 Percent	1985 Number	1985 Percent	2000 Number	2000 Percent	2025 Number	2025 Percent	2100 Number	2100 Percent
Developing Regions	569	74.9	1,070	65.6	1,681	66.8	3,657	75.6	4,837	79.0	6,799	82.9	8,748	85.9
Africa	100	13.2	133	8.2	224	8.9	555	11.5	872	14.2	1,617	19.7	2,591	25.4
Asia (excluding Japan)	455	59.9	867	53.2	1,292	51.4	2,697	55.8	3,419	55.8	4,403	53.7	4,919	48.3
Latin America[a]	14	1.8	70	4.3	165	6.6	405	8.4	546	8.9	779	9.5	1,238	12.2
Developed Regions	191	25.1	560	34.4	835	33.2	1,181	24.4	1,284	21.0	1,407	17.1	1,437	14.1
Europe, USSR, Japan, Oceania[b]	189	24.9	478	29.3	669	26.6	917	19.0	987	16.1	1,062	12.9	1,055	10.4
North America[c]	2	0.3	82	5.0	166	6.6	264	5.5	297	4.9	345	4.2	382	3.8
World Total	**760**	**100.0**	**1,630**	**100.0**	**2,516**	**100.0**	**4,837**	**100.0**	**6,122**	**100.0**	**8,206**	**100.0**	**10,185**	**100.0**

Notes: Population estimates from this source vary slightly from those in the U.N. Department of International Economic and Social Affairs, *World Population Prospects, Estimates and Projections as Assessed in 1984,* the major source used in *World Resources 1987.*
a. Latin America includes Mexico and the Caribbean.
b. Oceania includes Australia and New Zealand.
c. North America includes Canada and the United States.
Source: Thomas W. Merrick, *et al.,* "World Population in Transition," *Population Bulletin,* Vol. 41, No. 2 (1986), Table 1, p. 12.

Population and Health

to be high where the costs of bearing and rearing children are low and the benefits high, for example, where children help with agricultural and domestic tasks from an early age and customarily look after their aged parents. Availability of mass education tends to alter these relationships. Education withdraws children from household production, imposes direct costs upon parents for fees and uniforms, and makes it more likely that children will live elsewhere as adults, contributing less to parents in their old age (17).

When women have limited access to paid employment and education and their primary task is unpaid family labor, the TFR is usually high. (See Table 2.3.) In such situations, women tend to marry young, they often marry men who are considerably older, and their social status is lower than men's. Improved education and health services contribute to a lower fertility rate. A recent study comparing 79 Third World countries in 1970 and 1980 shows strong correlations between falling TFRs and rising educational attainment, increased employment outside the family, and increased age at the time of marriage. (See Table 2.3.)

Very high average TFRs—seven or more children per woman—correlate closely with high infant mortality rates. Infant mortality rates vary with living conditions, available health services, and climate. In parts of the world that often experience famine, the high death rates that result from famines are often quickly compensated for. In Bangladesh, for example, the approximately 1.5 million additional deaths caused by the 1974 famine were offset by additional births in less than one year (18). Such short-term responses change mortality and fertility patterns, but not long-term patterns of population growth.

Although "modernization" (in the form of health services, women's education, and abandonment of polygyny in favor of the nuclear family) leads in the long term to lower fertility, in the short term it may cause a fertility rise. Women who have been to school know more about child health and hygiene, and they frequently abandon traditional child-spacing practices that limited the total number of children a woman might have (19). This phenomenon appears to have happened in the countries with the highest TFR levels shown in Table 2.3. (For a more extensive discussion of socioeconomic and cultural factors affecting fertility, see *World Resources 1986*, Chapter 2, "Population," Focus On: Fertility, pp. 15–22.)

Political Factors and Government Policies

Individual governments can affect fertility rates through specific policies for provision of family planning programs and health care and by their political positions on desired family size and population growth rates. The attitudes of many Third World governments have changed considerably since the early 1970s. At the 1974 World Population Conference in Bucharest, Third World governments were reluctant to support the call for government family planning programs. The general consensus was that "development is the best contraception." By 1984, at the Mexico City International Population Conference, greater recognition of the need for family planning and for reduction of fertility rates was apparent (20). Where official population-planning policies have been in effect for some time, gradual decreases in fertility rates can be observed. Table 2.4 shows birth rate decreases since the introduction of government policies in nine developing countries.

Table 2.4 Decreases in Birth Rates in Nine Developing Countries since Introduction of Government Population Planning Policies

	Year Government Adopted Official Positive Policy	Births per 1,000 Population in Year Policy Adopted	Births per 1,000 Population, 1980–85 Estimates
Indonesia	1968	45	34 (1982)
Thailand	1970	42	28 (1982)
India	1952	42	33.3 (1982)
Pakistan	1960	47	43
Bangladesh	1971	50	45
Vietnam	1977	40	31
Sudan	1970	44	34
Mexico	1974	42	34
Brazil	1974	36	31

Source: Adapted from D.L. Nortman, *Population Family Planning Programmes—A Compendium of Data through 1983* (Population Council, New York, 1985), Table 6, pp. 33–34.

REGIONAL PATTERNS OF FERTILITY

Table 2.5 shows key population indicators by regions of the world ranked by fertility rates. These indicators are useful in assessing progress toward the low-fertility low-growth patterns that are now the norm in Europe, North America, and the rest of the developed world. (For more information, see "Focus On: Declining Fertility in Western Europe and North America," below.)

East Asia

East Asian population statistics are dominated by China. The region's currently low TFR is due primarily to the stringent population policies imposed by China to reduce its population growth rate. In 1960, China's TFR was 5.9 (21); now it is 2.1 (22). This drop in fertility took place when there were massive changes in China in the social and economic factors that affect fertility. China's achieve-

Table 2.3 The Relationship between Women's Access to Paid Employment and Education and the Total Fertility Rate in 79 Third World Countries, 1980

Number of Countries	Total Fertility Rate[a]	Women's Share of Paid Employment	Percent of Women Working as Unpaid Family Workers	Women's Illiteracy Rate	Women's Elementary School Completion Rate	Women's Secondary School Enrollment Rate	Women's Average Age at Marriage
9	>7.0	10.6	46.9	65.7	17.3	24.4	20.3
35	6.1–7.0	16.5	31.7	76.9	9.7	14.4	18.6
10	5.1–6.0	24.5	27.1	46.0	25.5	26.5	21.0
25	≤5.0	30.3	18.1	22.6	54.3	49.3	21.8

Note: a. Data averaged from countries in each TFR category.
Source: Adapted from C. Safilios-Rothschild, *The Status of Women and Fertility in the Third World in the 1970-80 Decade* (Population Council, New York, 1985).

Table 2.5 Regional Demographic Indicators

Region	Ranking by Fertility Rates	Total Fertility[a] 1980–85	Infant Mortality[b] 1980–85	Annual Population Growth Rate[c] 1980–85 (percent)	Urban[d] Population as Percentage of Total Population 1985
North America[e]	1	1.83	11	0.90	74.1
Europe[f]	2	1.88	15	0.30	71.6
East Asia	3	2.34	36	1.22	28.6
Oceania	4	2.65	31	1.51	71.0
Caribbean[e]	5	3.34	65	1.53	56.5
Southeastern Asia	6	4.11	73	2.05	26.3
Latin America[e,g]	7	4.17	61	2.34	70.1
Southern Asia	8	4.72	115	2.14	25.2
Western Asia	9	5.22	81	2.79	55.0
Africa	10	6.34	112	2.92	29.7
World Average		**3.52**	**78**	**1.67**	**41.0**

Notes:
a. The number of children an average woman would have if current age-specific fertility patterns remained constant through her reproductive years.
b. The number of babies who die before their first birthday in a given year divided by the number of births in that year, multiplied by 1,000.
c. Includes the effects of international migration.
d. The definition of "urban" varies widely across countries.
e. Mexico and Central America are included under Latin America; the Caribbean is listed separately.
f. Does not include the USSR.
g. Data were derived by population-weighting of disaggregated statistics for Central America, Temperate South America, and Tropical South America.
Source: U.N. Department of International Economic and Social Affairs, *World Population Prospects, Estimates and Projections as Assessed in 1984*, ST/ESA/SER.A/98 (United Nations, New York, 1986).

ment is also the result of strong government policies and political pressures. Since 1982, one-child families have benefited from larger pensions, free health care, and priority housing, education, and employment. The rate of natural population increase is lower now than at any time since 1949 (23).

In the rest of East Asia, Japan exhibits the low birth rate and low population growth rate pattern typical of developed nations. In the Republic of Korea and in Hong Kong, relatively high incomes, high enrollment levels of women in school (more than 90 percent in primary school), a predominantly urban population, and effective family planning programs contribute to relatively low and declining fertility rates and population growth rates.

Oceania

The developed nations of Australia and New Zealand, with their low fertility rates (below replacement rates) and low population growth rates, are predominant in this region. Among the many (often small) islands that make up the rest of Oceania, variation is substantial, but high total fertility rates are common, reaching 7 in the Solomon Islands (24).

The Caribbean

The Caribbean has experienced some success in controlling fertility. Moderate rates of total fertility are found throughout the region. The highest rate is 5.5 in Haiti, which is the most impoverished country in the Caribbean. No other country's total fertility rate exceeds 4.2, and several nations are below replacement levels (25). Emigration also moderates population growth in the region (26). During the 1960s, the TFR was much higher (as high as 7), and infant mortality rates were also higher (27). Increasingly available family planning services have been a key factor in reducing TFRs.

Southeastern Asia

Fertility rates in Southeast Asia have dropped fairly consistently over the past 20 years. In Indonesia, the largest country in the region, the 1965–70 average TFR was 5.6 and by 1980–85, the average TFR had fallen to 4.1. Corresponding figures for the Philippines and Thailand show declines from 6.0 and 6.1 to 4.4 and 3.5, respectively (28). Taking into account the large rural population and the low per capita income, these decreases in TFR are considerable. The decline is due largely to a strong government commitment to raise levels of women's education, lower infant mortality rates, and effect family planning (29). The egalitarian relationship of men and women in many Southeast Asian societies would also seem to be an important factor (30).

Latin America

Fertility rates vary substantially in Latin America. The TFR is less than three in Chile and Uruguay but over six in Bolivia and Honduras (31). Fertility rates have been consistently lower in the Southern Cone countries (Argentina, Chile, and Uruguay) than in other parts of Latin America for the past 30 years. They have been declining, however, in the rest of the region. During 1960–65, only one country had a TFR less than six, but by 1980–85, the average TFR had fallen to just over 4.2.

Economic development and rising incomes have contributed to this decreased fertility, as have official population policies—notably in Colombia and Mexico, where rates declined one third between 1970 and 1980. Rural fertility rates remain higher than urban rates (32).

Southern Asia

In spite of low per capita income and high infant mortality rates, Southern Asia has made some progress in lowering fertility rates. Although the current TFR of 4.7 remains substantially above the world average, the rate has declined more than 20 percent since the 1960s. The most notable declines were in India and Sri Lanka. In 1984, the World Bank reported that: "No other country at India's level of socioeconomic development—measured by low literacy and per capita income and high infant mortality—has a lower level of fertility" (33). In other parts of Southern Asia, fertility rates remain high.

Bangladesh and Pakistan, the region's second and third most populous countries, still have TFRs of 6.2 and 6.7, respectively. Limited access to family planning services is a major constraint to their success. In Bangladesh in 1981, 19 percent of the women of child-bearing age practiced contraception, and only 5 percent did in Pakistan. By contrast, in India and Sri Lanka, these figures were 28 and 55 percent, respectively. Sterilization is a major form of contraception in this region, particularly in India (34).

Other socioeconomic factors contribute to the higher rates of fertility. In 1986, the average infant mortality rate (outside India and Sri Lanka) was over 120 per 1,000 live births. Family structures are patriarchial or extended in much of South Asia and male children are preferred. A young wife lives with her husband's family and has little control over her own child-bearing (35).

Western Asia

The largest country in Western Asia is Turkey, which accounts for 44 percent of the region's population. The rest of the region is predominately Middle-Eastern Arab countries, including some wealthy oil-exporting nations. Among the Arab nations, fertility rates are consistently high (many with a TFR above 6.5). The non-Arab nations (Turkey, Israel, and Cyprus) have TFRs below 4 (36).

Cultural factors are important in the Arab countries, particularly the status of women (37). Turkey, which initiated a family planning program in 1965, has achieved the most significant drop in fertility in the region—from 6.0 in 1960–65 to 4.0 in 1980–85 (38).

Africa

Africa has the world's highest fertility rates and population growth rates, and the sub-Saharan countries have the highest fertility rates in Africa. Except for several small island countries off the coast of Africa, there are only two African nations with a TFR below five. The TFR is six or higher in 38 countries, and Kenya continues to have the world's highest fertility rate, a TFR of 8.0 (39). (See *World Resources 1986*, p. 18.)

Sub-Saharan Africa (excluding South Africa) is the only area of the world where the average fertility rate in 1980–85 was higher than at any time during the previous 30 years (40). Fewer than 10 percent of women use modern methods of contraception (41). This region is also the poorest—with a predominately rural population, a low literacy level, and high mortality rates. Life expectancy is 49 years.

The demand for children is still high. A six-country survey found that six to nine children were desirable in each family, primarily because of their high value for labor (42). Fear of infertility discourages fertile women from using contraceptives. In the 1950s and 1960s, 12 percent of African women from 18 sub-Saharan countries had passed their child-bearing age and were childless because of infertility, compared to 2–3 percent in developed countries. Although childlessness in younger women is not as high (because of improved medical care), fear of the consequences of infertility—ostracization, abandonment, or divorce—still discourages their using contraceptives (43).

The lack of reliable demographic statistics and awareness of the size of the population problem has hindered development of planning policies in Africa. The Ghanaian and Senegalese Governments have now recognized the need for family planning policies and taken action, but only after increased population growth rates were documented in census data (44).

The countries of North Africa have an average TFR of 5.8, lower than the rest of Africa but still high relative to the average world rate. Individual country TFRs range from 4.9 in Tunisia to 6.9 in Libya. This region has a predominantly Islamic heritage and levels of female education remain low. Women still marry young. The legal age limits for marriage are low: in Morocco, the legal age is 15. In Tunisia, it was raised to 15 in 1956 and to 17 in 1964. Fewer women marry early as a result. Between

1956 and 1975, the percentage of women in Tunisia who married between ages 15 and 19 dropped from 42 to 6. Egypt, Morocco, and Tunisia have official family planning policies; they also have lower fertility rates than other North African countries. (45).

FOCUS ON: DECLINING FERTILITY IN WESTERN EUROPE AND NORTH AMERICA

Although much of the Third World struggles with rates of natural increase that will double their populations in 23–40 years, Western Europe and North America will grow slowly. (See Figure 2.2.) Their share of the world's population fell from 22.3 percent to 15.6 percent between 1950 and 1985, and it is likely to fall to well under 10 percent by 2025. (See Box 2.1.)

The Causes of Low Birth Rates

As previously noted, fertility decisions are complex socioeconomic phenomena. Changing perceptions of the costs and benefits of having children and the changing economic and social roles of women in North America and Western Europe are important factors in lower birth rates.

The Rising Costs of Raising Children

Birth rates tend to fall as the costs of raising children rise. With changes in the social structure of western soci-

Figure 2.2 Population Doubling Times by Region, at Current Rates of Growth

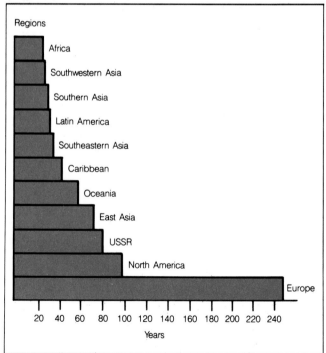

Source: Adapted from Population Reference Bureau, Inc. (PRB), *World Population Data Sheet 1986* (PRB, Washington, D.C., 1986).

Box 2.1 France: A Case of Declining Birth Rates

Because of its unique demographic history, France has long feared depopulation, though the views of government and people are not always aligned (1).

FRANCE FROM 1800 to 1900

Death rates in Western Europe first began to fall substantially in the second half of the 18th Century. In France alone, for poorly understood reasons, the birth rate also fell, long before that of other Western European nations.

In 1800, with a population of 28 million, France was the most populous and militarily the most successful country in Europe. But during the 19th Century, its population grew only 25 percent while that of other European countries tripled. By 1900, France had been overtaken in size by Germany, England, Italy, and Russia. French military and economic strength had also declined in relative terms. After losing the Franco-Prussian War in 1870, France began to associate population decline with political and economic weakness and with a loss of French vitality and culture (2).

FROM WORLD WAR I TO 1942

Pronatalist associations, founded largely by France's intellectual elite before the First World War, pointed with alarm at Germany's superior numbers. After the war, they successfully lobbied the government for strong antiabortion and anticontraception laws (enacted in 1920) and for family allowances (that became law in 1932). Throughout the 1930s, none of these efforts had much effect on population size, which remained at around 40 million from the late 19th Century to 1940 (3).

THE BABY BOOM

Like all other industrialized countries, France experienced a baby boom from after World War II until about 1964. The reunification of couples separated by the war and a common desire to replace those who had died were key factors, although birth rates remained high after replacement levels were reached. Suddenly, both government and people were united in their desire for population growth. The Government's Family Allowance Program took 22 percent of the country's gross national product by 1949, and a 1947 public opinion poll showed that 70 percent of the people wanted the population to increase. Active pronatalism gradually became unnecessary as high birth rates continued for most of the next 20 years (4).

1964 To 1974

After 1964, again in common with the rest of Europe, France experienced a steep decline in the birth rate. Demographers still debate its precise cause, but contributing to

it were the introduction of oral contraceptives and the liberalization of abortion laws from the mid-sixties onwards. In addition, those now choosing to defer childbirth were the postwar babies themselves—in an era that celebrated unmarried youth.

French birth rates actually fell less steeply than those of Germany, England, and Scandinavia. But the decline caused great alarm in France, especially when, in 1974, the total fertility rate fell below the replacement level of 2.1 for the first time (5).

AFTER 1974

Government Attitudes

When President Giscard d'Estaing came to power in 1974, he took a more active pronatalist line than any French Government had done since the 1940s. He introduced the most generous and comprehensive family policy in Europe, with the declared aim of restoring birth rates to a level just above replacement. During the 1970s, new allowances were introduced and intentions declared to make better housing available to large families and to make it easier for women to work and have children.

Attitudes of the French Population

In 1974, 1975, 1976, and 1978, the Institut National d'Etudes Demographiques (INED) conducted national opinion polls to gauge public understanding of fertility decline and reactions to it (6). INED's 1976 inquiries showed that the French were well aware of the demographic picture: over 90 percent answered all the demographic questions correctly (7). It was thus clear that fertility decline was due, not to the ignorance of the population, but to their reluctance or inability to conform to the pronatal aims of the political elite.

The surveys also attempted to investigate women's fertility decisionmaking by offering them choices among a variety of possible policy measures and asking them to suggest the circumstances in which they would be prepared to have another child (8).

The surveys reveal a gap between the two children whom parents felt they could afford and the three children they would ideally like. There was little hostility, as the decade wore on, to the government's interest in promoting births, but there was no tangible response to it either.

Measures most likely to produce a third child were discussed in the 1978 poll, and it became clear that women's decisionmaking about childbearing was constrained by the difficulties of combining motherhood with work (9). The majority indicated a desire for several years' maternity leave with the right to return to work, more part-time work, salaries for mothers who decided to stay at home to rear children, and pensions for

mothers with three or more children. Such opportunities were preferred to lump sums at the birth of a child and, to some extent, even to allowances and tax rebates (10).

DECISIONMAKING ABOUT FERTILITY

The poll responses make it clear how high the opportunity costs of having children have become in France, now that employment for women is the norm. Parents expect to forego many thousands of dollars in order to have the number of children they want. But to respond to the government's desire for more children, French parents know they would have to take on yet further costs, which could include a complete loss of career for women.

Although France spends a higher percentage of its GNP on family policy measures than any other European Community country, it clearly cannot begin to compensate women for the loss of income and job security that extended childbearing brings with it. The French would like to see a rise in the birth rate, which is currently only 1.8 children per family, and the general public is dismayed by the dwindling numbers of French people. However, as parents, most individuals feel that they cannot afford a third child, and the French Government cannot afford the truly enormous incentives that would be required to enable them to do so (11).

References and Notes

1. J.J. Spengler, *France Faces Depopulation* (Duke University Press, Durham, North Carolina, 1938).
2. A. Sauvy, *La Prevention des Naissances: "Birth Control"* (Presses Universitaires de France, 1962).
3. M.M. Huss, *Demography, Public Opinion and Politics in France*, QMC Occasional Papers in Geography No. 16 (University of London, United Kingdom, 1980).
4. A. Armengaud, *La Population Francaise au XXe Siecle* (Presses Universitaires de France, 1973).
5. Institute National d'Etudes Demographiques (INED), *Rapport sur la Situation Demographique de la France en 1974* (INED, Paris, 1976).
6. C.A. McIntosh, "Low Fertility and Liberal Democracy in Western Europe," *Population and Development Review*, Vol. 7, No. 2 (1981).
7. A. Girard and L. Roussel, "Fecondite et Conjuncture: Une Enquete d'Opinion sur la Politique Demographique," *Population*, Vol. 34, No. 3 (1979).
8. *Op. cit.* 6.
9. *Op. cit.* 7.
10. *Op. cit.* 2.
11. *Op. cit.* 2.

eties, both the monetary and time costs of raising children have increased. Conversely, the economic benefits of having children have been largely eliminated in the western industrial countries. Child labor is generally illegal (and school is mandatory), and public and private pension systems have replaced reliance on children for economic security in old age (46). As a result, the reasons for having children are almost entirely noneconomic (47).

The monetary costs of raising a child in industrialized countries can impose a serious burden on parents. In addition to the direct costs of food, clothing, shelter, etc., a child may prevent one spouse from working or reduce the amount of time available for employment outside the home, thereby reducing family income. A recent study of the costs of raising a first child in the United States estimated a life time cost of $175,000 (48).

The Changing Role of Women

As the costs of raising children have grown and families have become smaller, women are spending less of their adult lives rearing children. (See Table 2.6.) In this century, the change coincides with increased longevity and introduction of commercial products and labor-saving devices that speed and simplify domestic work (49). As a result, women are able to devote more time to paid employment, and they have entered the labor force in growing numbers.

Over 50 percent of U.S. wives are employed outside their homes, and the proportion continues to rise. In 1981, the fraction of employed wives in the European Community had reached 36 percent (50). The breadwinner model of society—with the married couple as a societal unit internally divided into a cash earner and a provider of domestic services—has been eroded. As employment opportunities for women increased and their salaries improved, the opportunity costs of staying at home to look after children rose dramatically, reinforcing the trend toward having fewer children (51).

Table 2.6 Years Spent Rearing Children Compared to Years Spent Free of Them

	Rural North India, 1956	United States 1880s	United States 1950s
Years from Birth of First Child to Age 18 of Last Child	36.8	27.9	24.9
Years From Age 18 of Last Child to Death of Mother	None	21.3	34.1

Source: Kingsley Davis and P. van den Oever, "Age Relations and Public Policy in Advanced Industrial Societies," *Population and Development Review*, Vol. 7, No. 1, 1981, p. 1–18.

The Consequences of Declining Fertility

Although fertility rates in the United States and Western Europe have fallen below replacement levels, their populations will increase in absolute terms for a few more decades. Europe's point of zero population growth is already on the horizon. Western Europe's baby boom was shorter lived than in the United States, and Europe's immigration level is lower. The U.S. population will stabilize later, beginning to decline in about 2050, assuming a projected annual average of 500,000 legal immigrants (52).

Aging Populations

As birth rates decline, populations age—that is, there are relatively fewer individuals in lower age categories and more in higher ones. In Western Europe and North America, about 13 percent of the population is now in the over-64 age category, and 22 percent is under 15 years of age. This profile contrasts sharply with the developing world, where 39 percent of the population is less than 15 years old and only 4 percent is over 64 (53).

The relative aging of the population is reinforced by continuing increases in longevity, which the industrialized countries are also experiencing. Life expectancy is aproaching 75 years in Western Europe and North America. As a result, the 65-and-older group is the fastest growing segment of the population in these regions.

With the elderly proportion of a country's population increasing, the age structure is disturbed, which can affect all institutions in society. To illustrate the impact, examining the progress of the U.S. baby boom cohort through the population structure is useful (54). (See Figure 2.3.) The baby boom cohort as defined here includes only children born between 1950 and 1959.

By 1980, this cohort of people was between 20 and 29 years old. (See Figure 2.3.) There are approximately 40 million in this age group—18 percent of the population. In 1960, there were only 22 million people in this age bracket, or 12 percent of the population. When this group reaches the peak years of employment, their numbers are likely to increase job competition and thus decrease promotion prospects (55).

In both Europe and North America in the past 30 years, the direct burden of support for the elderly has largely shifted from their own children to the government. Social and geographic mobility has separated parents and children so that parents tend to rely on themselves and on the government in their old age. In the process, their per capita incomes have risen almost to those of young workers in society. About 94 percent receive some kind of social security (56).

The elderly are not yet a great burden on society. Although the fact is not generally realized, children are more costly than the elderly on a per capita basis. As a result, shrinking numbers of youthful dependents and rising numbers of aged dependents are a lighter, not a heavier, burden (57). Further, dependency rates are actually declining in Europe because so many wives and mothers have joined the work force and are no longer dependent (58).

The real problem lies in the more distant future. In the United States, the baby boom generation will begin reaching age 65 after 2010. By 2030, there will be an estimated 59 million elderly (59). The demands on Social Security—the publicly funded retirement system in the United States—will increase considerably. In 1969, the elderly required 17 percent of the U.S. federal budget. This share could reach a peak of 40 percent by 2025 (60).

Figure 2.3 Progress of Depression Cohort, Baby Boom Cohort, and Baby Bust Cohort through U.S. Population Age–Sex Pyramid: 1960–2050[a]

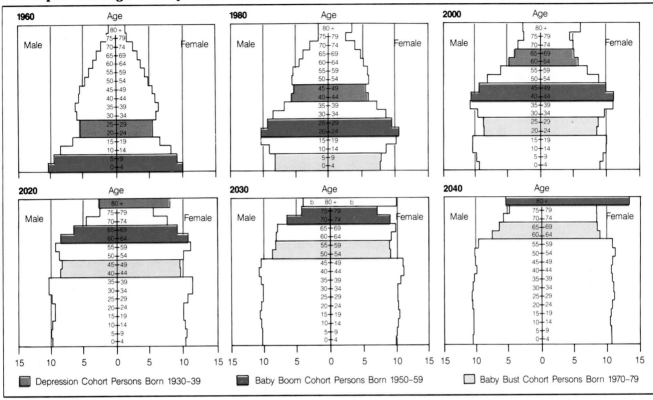

Notes:
a. 1980–2050 projections assume a total fertility rate rising to 2.0 births per woman by 1985 and constant thereafter; life expectancy at birth rising to 72.8 years for males and 82.9 years for females by 2050; and net immigration constant at 750,000 persons per year.
b. Includes survivors of Depression cohort.
Source: Leon F. Bouvier, "America's Baby Boom Generation: The Fateful Bulge," *Population Bulletin*, Vol. 35, No. 1 (1980), pp. 18–19.

Under the present system, it is unlikely that the high benefit levels enjoyed by today's elderly will be available to the elderly of the future.

Immigration in the Context of Stabilizing Populations

In the late 1950s and until the early 1970s, while the baby boom generation was being reared, labor shortages in many Western European countries were met by encouraging the immigration of foreign workers. The general recession of 1973 stopped the immigration of new male workers abruptly, but family members continued to arrive during the 1970s. For most European countries, immigrants came from Eastern and Southern Europe; in addition, North Africans came to France and members of the Commonwealth came to the United Kingdom (61).

Both natural increase and immigration contributed to growth of the U.S. population from 75 million in 1900 (62) to 241 million in 1986 (63). Immigration has been consistently high. By 2030, if the U.S. fertility rate continues to be below replacement level, immigration will account for all the U.S. population growth (64).

There has been a dramatic shift in the origin of immigrants to the United States. In the first half of the 20th Century, the majority came from Europe. By the 1970s, only 13 percent of legal immigrants were European, 42 percent were Latin American and 39 percent were Asian. The number of illegal U.S. immigrants ranges from 100,000 to 500,000 per year. The vast majority comes from Latin America, especially Mexico (65).

Immigration in Times of High Unemployment

With the baby boom generation entering the work force, the labor supply in Europe and the United States has been relatively abundant. Under such conditions, high immigration levels cause considerable controversy. Historically, immigration has been economically positive. At the beginning of the 20th Century, when the United States was relatively underpopulated, immigrant labor was valued (66). Although continuing high levels of immigration have been questioned given the high levels of unemployment, attributing unemployment mainly to high levels of immigration while ignoring the impact of national economic policies is inaccurate.

There is little evidence to support the view that immigrants take jobs away from more vulnerable sections of the indigenous population—such as minorities, youths, women, and the unskilled—and keep wages low. Immigrants contribute to economic growth in many ways (67). The labor market is more flexible because immigrants tend to be more mobile and respond to labor needs in particular parts of the country. Migrants create a demand for goods and services, which has a multiplier effect and increases the availability of various jobs (68). A report of the U.S. House of Representatives Select Commission on Immigration and Refugee Policy concluded that "immigration has been and continues to be a force for economic growth in the U.S." (69).

Birth rates of immigrants are frequently higher than those of the host country when the immigrants are from less developed nations (70). The impact of immigrant fertility rates is likely to be more significant than total immigration figures in determining the future size of the U.S. population (71). However, even when populations emigrate from high fertility countries, their birth rates tend to conform gradually to those of the host populations, controlling for income-level differences (72).

THE STATE OF HEALTH

The World Health Organization (WHO), in its most recent *Report on the World Health Situation*, divides nations into three major groups, each with a different pattern of health and illness (73). (See Table 2.7.)

The first group of countries has high levels of mortality accompanied by high rates of infectious and parasitic diseases and malnutrition, resulting in high infant mortality rates and low life expectancy at birth. This group includes the poorest countries in the world, most of them in Africa and Asia.

The intermediate group consists of those countries undergoing rapid demographic change accompanied by new patterns of health and illness. Fertility is beginning to decline and life expectancy to increase. Although infectious and parasitic diseases are still the major causes of death, the chronic diseases of an aging population and the social-environmental health problems associated with urbanization and industrialization are evident. In this group are developing countries that have taken off into

Table 2.7 Health and Related Socioeconomic Indicators

	Least Developed Countries	Other Developing Countries	Developed Countries
Number of countries	29	90	37
Total population (millions)	283	3,001	1,131
Infant mortality rate (per 1,000 live births)	160	94	19
Life expectancy (years)	45	60	72
Percentage of newborns with a birth weight of 2,500 grams or more	70%	83%	93%
Coverage by safe water supply	31%	41%	100%
Adult literacy rate	28%	55%	98%
GNP per capita	$170	$520	$6,230
Per capita public expenditure on health	$1.7	$6.5	$244
Public expenditure on health as percent of GNP	1.0%	1.2%	3.9%

Note: The figures are weighted averages, based on data for 1980 or the latest available year.
Source: World Health Organization (WHO), *Global Strategy for Health for All by the Year 2000* (WHO, Geneva, 1981), p. 24.

Table 2.8 Number of Countries with Life Expectancy at Birth of More Than 60 Years, by WHO Regions
(number of countries)

Life Expectancy At Birth[a]	Africa	Americas	South-east Asia	Europe	Eastern Mediter-ranean	Western Pacific	Total
Below 60 Years	38	5	6	0	10	4	63
60 Years and More	5	29	5	33	12	12	96
No Information	1	0	0	2	0	4	7
Total	**44**	**34**	**11**	**35**	**22**	**20**	**166**

Note: a. The average number of years lived given age-specific mortality rates at the year of birth.
Source: World Health Organization (WHO), *Evaluation of the Strategy for Health for All by the Year 2000: Seventh Report on the World Health Situation* (WHO, Geneva, 1986), Table 17, p. 62.

economic growth, almost all of them in Asia and Latin America.

The third group of countries has low fertility rates and high average life expectancy. They have relatively little infectious or parasitic disease but a high incidence of circulatory diseases, cancers, and mental disorders. The level of health problems associated with life style and behavior is high. Most of the industrialized countries and a few that are usually classified as developing are in this category.

TRENDS IN MORTALITY

In developing countries in particular, the mechanisms for collecting vital statistics are relatively inefficient, so that official mortality figures are likely to underestimate the true situation. Life expectancy and infant mortality rates are the most sensitive indicators available, however, and therefore are widely used to illustrate global differences in health status. WHO recently adopted as minimum health objectives for the year 2000 a life expectancy at birth of 60 years and an infant mortality rate of fewer than 50 deaths per thousand births (74).

The least developed countries have the shortest average life expectancy. In Africa, the average is still below 50 years in most countries; it is above 60 in only five. (See Table 2.8 and Chapter 16, "Population and Health," Table 16.3.) In Latin America, many countries have moved into the 60–75-year range, and all the industrialized countries now have a life expectancy exceeding 70. Overall, 96 countries representing 62 percent of the world population have now achieved a life expectancy of 60 years or more, mainly by reducing childhood deaths. Information is not available for seven countries representing 4 percent of the world population (75).

Infant mortality rates (IMRs) show a broadly similar pattern, with great variation between rich and poor countries. In the past decade, the IMR has decreased in nearly 120 countries, but inequalities still remain. (See Table 2.9 and Chapter 16, "Population and Health," Table 16.3.) The rates in most African and Asian countries are still in excess of 50 per 1,000 live births, and the rates in more than one quarter of all countries (representing 29 percent of the world population) are higher than 100 per 1,000 live births. In developed countries, on the other hand, rates are as low as 12 per 1,000 in the United States and seven per 1,000 in Sweden.

Table 2.9 Infant Mortality per 1,000 Live Births, by WHO Regions
(number of countries)

Infant Mortality Rate[a]	Africa	Americas	South-east Asia	Europe	Eastern Mediter-ranean	Western Pacific	Total
Below 50	2	24	4	27	7	12	76
50.0-99.9	9	7	3	3	8	3	33
100 and More	32	3	4	2	7	1	49
No Information	1	0	0	3	0	4	8
Total	**44**	**34**	**11**	**35**	**22**	**20**	**166**

Note: a. Infant mortality rate is the annual number of deaths of infants under one year of age per 1,000 live births.
Source: World Health Organization (WHO), *Evaluation of the Strategy for Health for All by the Year 2000: Seventh Report on the World Health Situation* (WHO, Geneva, 1986), Table 20, p. 65.

Although international differences in mortality rates are very important, so too are intracountry variations. In most countries, women have a longer life expectancy than men. In many developed countries, the gap is now as wide as six or seven years, a fact that can be explained primarily by the less hazardous life styles of most women (76). The pattern is reversed, however, in a few countries, including Pakistan and Bangladesh. It can be traced to the low status of women and to discriminatory practices that affect their health, often resulting in high rates of mortality during their child-bearing years (77). In developed countries, maternal mortality rates are now low—currently about 10 per 100,000 births in the United States—but, in most Third World countries, maternal mortality is still the largest single cause of death among women in their reproductive years. In parts of Asia, one woman dies for every 100 births. Although statistics on maternal deaths are particularly difficult to obtain, the World Health Organization estimates that worldwide some 500,000 women die from pregnancy-related causes each year and most of the deaths are preventable (78).

Mortality rates among different socioeconomic groups within countries vary markedly, a point that is especially important for health planners. The class differences are often substantial, even in developed countries. For example, in the United Kingdom, a male child of an unskilled or semiskilled laborer has a life expectancy about seven years less than a male child of wealthy parents (79). Differences between rich and poor are even greater in the Third World, although there are few data available to quantify the inequalities. One study of child mortality rates in Costa Rica showed a fivefold difference between higher and lower social groups in the likelihood of surviving to two years of age (80). (See Table 2.10.)

Table 2.10 Probability of Dying between Birth and Two Years of Age, by Social Class, Costa Rica, 1968-69

Social Class	Number of Deaths per 1,000 Births
High and Middle Bourgeoisie	20
Middle Class	39
Proletariat	80
Agricultural Workers	99
Average	**80**

Source: H. Behm, "Socioeconomic Determinants of Mortality In Latin America" in *Proceedings of the Meeting on Socioeconomic Determinants and the Consequences of Mortality* (United Nations/World Health Organization, Mexico City, 1979), p. 160.

FACTORS AFFECTING HEALTH

Health Problems of the Developed World

In developed countries, the main causes of death are diseases of the circulatory system (ischemic heart disease and cerebrovascular disease, in particular). They account for about one quarter of deaths worldwide, but, in the industrialized countries, about half of all deaths and considerable disability are caused by cardiovascular diseases alone. Although some countries—including Australia, Finland, Japan and the United States—have recently shown a decline in heart disease, rates in most other countries are stable or are even increasing. Many factors have been implicated in the high incidence of heart disease in industrialized countries. Diet, smoking, and lack of exercise are recognized as risk factors, but it is clear that stress also plays a significant part. Heart problems are not restricted to coronary-prone executives and, in fact, tend to be more common among the lowest socioeconomic groups (81) (82).

Cancer is the second most common cause of death in industrialized countries, accounting for around 20 percent of all deaths. Stomach, intestinal tract, and lung cancers are the most common among men, and breast cancer is most common for women in industrialized countries. Both stomach and lung cancers have been linked with environmental and occupational pollution, but cigarette smoking is the single most important cause of lung cancer (83). Men began smoking long before women, a fact that is reflected in their high rates of mortality from lung cancer. Women, who did not begin smoking in significant numbers until after World War II, began to show a rapid rise in deaths from lung cancer 30 years later. In some countries lung cancers are overtaking breast cancer as the most common cause of death from cancer (84). About 50 percent of all breast cancer deaths occur in North America and Europe (excluding the USSR)—which have only 18 percent of the world's population. There are no obvious reasons for this, but having the first pregnancy at a late age and diets high in fat have been implicated (85). Cervical cancer, on the other hand, is relatively uncommon in the developed world and is declining where effective screening policies have been implemented. Eleven of 26 European countries reported a decline in deaths from this cancer of women under the age of 65 (86).

In addition to these life-threatening, often fatal, and physically disabling conditions, the populations of industrialized countries also suffer mental and neurological disorders. They are particularly difficult to measure, but WHO has estimated that severe mental disorders affect about 2 percent of most populations, and an additional 3–8 percent are disabled by less serious problems, such as neurotic and psychosomatic disorders, alcohol, or drug dependency (87). The incidence of problems would be considerably higher if hidden distress, which is not treated clinically, were taken into account (88). In many developed countries, suicide is among the top ten causes of death, and most European countries report a steady increase. Alzheimer's Disease, which leads to senile dementia, is recognized increasingly as a medical problem. It affects an estimated 10–20 percent of people over age 70 in industrialized countries.

Health Problems of the Developing World

More than 11 million children under the age of five die every year in the Third World (89). Malnutrition and infectious diseases are responsible for 50–90 percent of these infant and child deaths (90). Although the two sometimes strike independently of each other, more often they act together, intensifying the effects of each. Both will need to be treated if the poor countries of the world are to achieve a health status anywhere nearly approaching that of industrialized countries (91).

Estimates of worldwide malnutrition vary according to how it is defined and measured. WHO estimates that at least 430 million—nearly 10 percent of the world population—are currently affected. An estimated 100 million children under the age of five suffer from protein energy malnutrition, over 10 percent from a severe form that is usually fatal if not treated, and 39 percent from chronic malnutrition (92). The proportion of underweight children in Third World countries appears to have remained at around 42 percent in the 1963–73 and 1973–78, although the numbers involved have risen from

126 million to 145 million because of population growth (93). Thus, despite advances in agriculture, there are nearly 20 million more malnourished children now than there were ten years ago.

Undernourishment can be a primary cause of death, especially among the very young, but more often it produces chronic ill health and debility. It also lowers resistance to infectious diseases and considerably increases their severity. A recent study of Latin American countries found that nutritional deficiencies were associated with more than 60 percent of deaths from measles and diarrheal disease. (See Table 2.11.)

Lack of adequate nourishment for mothers is one of the major causes of low birth weight in babies (94). In 1985, some 20 million of the 129 million children born weighed less than the 2.5 kilos thought necessary for optimum health, and 19 million of them were in developing countries. This figure represented about 17 percent of all infants born in those countries, whereas the comparable figure for developed countries is only 4–8 percent. Little improvement has been reported in the Third World over the past five years (95). Weight at birth is the single most important determinant of future well-being; babies weighing less than 2.5 kilos at birth are three times more likely to die in infancy.

Box 2.2 The AIDS Epidemic Spreads

Since it was first identified in 1981, AIDS—Acquired Immune Deficiency Syndrome—has spread rapidly throughout the world. In December 1986, 110 countries reported a total of 36,539 cases to the World Health Organization (WHO) (1), more than double the number of cases reported by 71 countries a year earlier (2). Health officials feel the disease is seriously underreported in many countries—especially in Latin America—which would make the total number of cases much greater (3). Accounting for unreliable reporting, up to 10 million people worldwide may be infected with HIV (human immunodeficiency virus) (4), which causes AIDS in many of those it infects.

Recognized a few years ago as a serious problem in homosexual communities in developed countries, AIDS is now considered an epidemic in both developed and developing nations. In Africa the HIV infection occurs equally among men and women and is spread by heterosexual intercourse. In central Africa, the area that seems to be the most seriously affected, the annual incidence of AIDS may be 550 to 1,000 cases per million adults (5). In some central African cities shockingly high percentages of certain populations are infected: 18 percent of the blood donors in Kigali carried the HIV virus, 33 percent of the men aged 30-35 in Lusaka, and 88 percent of the female prostitutes in Nairobi (6). At least 1 million people, mostly in central Africa, are expected to die within the next decade of AIDS (7).

Not all those with HIV develop AIDS, but studies in the United States suggest that at least 25 to 50 percent of those infected will

develop AIDS within 5 to 10 years of becoming infected (8). This long, often unrecognized period of asymptomatic infection, during which an infected person can infect others, complicates control of the spread of the virus (9). Because of the delay between HIV infection and the appearance of AIDS, most of the persons who will develop AIDS between now and 1991 already are infected (10).

AIDS destroys the body's defenses against disease, making the infected person susceptible to so-called "opportunistic infections" that rarely cause illness in those with normal immune systems. Throughout the world, HIV spreads primarily through sexual contact (both homosexual and heterosexual), and also through intravenous drug use, through transfusions of blood and blood products, and from an infected mother to her infant in the womb or at birth. There is no evidence that casual contact or insect vectors spread the virus.

Prevention is the only known way to stop the spread of AIDS, although research on a cure continues throughout the world. The World Health Organization (WHO) has sponsored two international conferences on AIDS and has initiated a global program to control the disease. The WHO program will coordinate the exchange of information; prepare and distribute guidelines for diagnosis, prevention, and control; provide advice on safe blood and blood products; coordinate research; and cooperate with member states' national programs to control HIV (11).

As yet there is no satisfactory treatment for HIV infection, and a vaccine probably will not be developed for at least five years. One drug has recently shown benefits in the treatment

of AIDS, but a safe and effective long-term treatment is also not likely be available for at least five years (12).

References and Notes

1. World Health Organization (WHO), "WHO AIDS Programme: Recent Developments," Note to the Press (WHO, Geneva, December 9, 1986).
2. World Health Organization (WHO), "WHO Activities for the Prevention and Control of Acquired Immunodeficiency Syndrome (AIDS)," Report by the Director General (WHO, Geneva, November 25, 1985), p. 1.
3. Op. cit. 1.
4. Institute of Medicine, Confronting AIDS: Directions for Public Health, Health Care, and Research (National Academy Press, Washington, D.C., 1986), pp. 28–29.
5. Fakhry Assaad, M.D., et al., "AIDS—An International Perspective," WHO Features, No. 103, World Health Organization (WHO), Geneva, November 1986, p. 1.
6. Jon Tinker, AIDS and the Third World, Panos Dossier No. 1 (Panos Institute, London, 1986), p. 20.
7. Ibid.
8. Op. cit. 4, p. 7.
9. Op. cit. 4, p. 7.
10. Op. cit. 4, p. 8.
11. Op. cit. 5, p. 3. WHO adopted its strategy at the 39th World Health Assembly in May 1986.
12. Op. cit. 4, p. 8. The IOM notes, however, that the drug, known as AZT (azidothymidine), is only used for AIDS patients with a specific opportunistic disease, Pneumocystis carinii pneumonia.

Table 2.11 Nutritional Deficiency as Associated Cause of Death of Children under Five Years of Age, by Underlying Cause of Death in 13 Latin American Projects[a]

Underlying Cause of Death	Nutritional Deficiency as Associated Cause (percent)
All Causes	47
Infective and Parasitic Diseases	61
Diarrheal Disease	61
Measles	62
Other	59
Diseases of Respiratory System	32
Other causes	33

Note: a. Excluding neonatal deaths.
Source: Ruth Puffer and Carlos W. Serrano, *Patterns of Mortality in Childhood* (Pan American Health Organization, Washington, D.C., 1973), reproduced in David Saunders, *The Struggle for Health: Medicine and the Politics of Underdevelopment* (Macmillan Publishing Co., Inc., New York, 1985), p. 22.

Specific dietary deficiencies can also lead to a range of chronic diseases. Nutritional anemia affects both sexes and all age groups but is especially prevalent among women. In developing countries, it affects an estimated two thirds of the women who are pregnant and about half those who are not. It causes fatigue and lowers resistance to disease, contributing significantly to maternal morbidity and mortality (96).

More than 500,000 children are blinded by xerophthalmia each year because their diet lacks Vitamin A. When young children are malnourished and contract an infectious disease such as measles, their Vitamin A requirements increase greatly. If these needs are not met, xerophthalmia all too often results (97). It is the single most common cause of blindness in developing countries, and it often strikes the most needy children in refugee camps and feeding centers.

The infectious and parasitic diseases of poverty are best classified according to the ways that they are spread, enabling possible preventive strategies to be planned. (See Table 2.12.) The most common are the water-related diseases that occur in the absence of potable water and adequate sanitation. Diarrheal disease in particular is a major problem in all developing countries, often exacerbating existing problems of malnutrition. In 1980, an estimated 5 million children under five years of age died from diarrhea—about ten every minute of every day. A recent study of young children in Bangladeshi villages revealed that each child suffered on average 6–8 episodes of diarrhea per year, lasting a total of 55 days, or 15 percent of the year (98). Often the hazards of diarrhea are compounded by infestation with parasites such as hookworm. Cholera is another water-related disease that continues to threaten life and health in the Third World. Although it has become less common in recent years, it is still endemic in many countries, particularly in Africa. (See Chapter 16, "Population and Health," Table 16.4.)

Some of the most common "tropical" diseases are also water related. About 200 million people are said to be infected with schistosomiasis (also known as bilharzia). This chronic and debilitating disease is acquired through infestation by a parasite living in snails that inhabit the canals, lakes, and slow-moving rivers where people bathe, wash clothes, fish and perform other daily tasks. In many areas, incidence of the disease increased after irrigation canals and hydroelectric projects were constructed without attention to their ecological implications. New drugs being developed to control schistosomiasis give some hope of combating the disease more successfully.

Onchocerciasis and malaria are transmitted by insects that live in water at some stage in their life cycles. In the 1970s, about 100,000 people in West Africa were blinded by onchocerciasis; the total population at risk was about 12.5 million. Recent control projects have interrupted the transmission cycle, allowing many new areas to be opened for development. Malaria is a major public health problem in many developing countries—over 50 percent of the world population lives in areas where it is endemic.

Table 2.12 Classification of Most Disease in Developing Countries

Nutritional	Airborne		Communicable Water-Related	
Malnutrition and Associated Vitamin Deficiencies	Viral	Influenza Pneumonia Measles Chicken-pox	Waterborne or water-washed:	Cholera Typhoid Diarrhoeas, dysenteries, amoebiasis, infectious hepatitis, poliomyelitis, intestinal worms
	Bacterial	Whooping-cough Diptheria Meningitis Tuberculosis	Water-washed: Skin and eye infection	Trachoma Skin infection Leprosy
			Skin infestation	Scabies Louseborne typhus
			Water-based: Penetrating skin	Schistosomiasis (bilharzia)
			Ingested	Guinea worm
			Water-related insect vectors: Biting near water	Sleeping sickness
			Breeding in water	Malaria Yellow fever Onchocerciasis (river blindness)

Airborne = Disease spread by breathing airborne respiratory secretions of infected persons.
Waterborne = Disease transmitted when water containing pathogen is ingested.
Water-washed = Disease whose prevalence will fall when increased quantities of water are used for drinking and hygienic purposes (the water should be clean but need not be pure).
Water-based = Disease in which pathogen spends part of its life cycle in an intermediate aquatic host or hosts.
Source: Adapted from David Sanders, *The Struggle for Health: Medicine and the Politics of Underdevelopment* (MacMillan Education Ltd., London and Basingstoke, 1985), p. 20.

Malaria is transmitted through the bite of infected mosquitoes (which breed in water). Despite considerable expenditures, progress in combating malaria has been slow, and some strains of mosquitoes are resistant to most of the common insecticides. Some parasites in humans have also developed resistance to chloroquine, making treatment of infected individuals more difficult. As a result, improvement in some countries is offset by worsening conditions in others. (See Chapter 16, "Population and Health," Table 16.4.) According to WHO, malaria still kills about 1 million Africans under the age of 14 each year.

The other major diseases prevalent in the developing world are airborne—they are spread by the victim breathing the respiratory secretions of an infected person. This situation is facilitated by the overcrowded housing common in the Third World, particularly in urban areas. WHO estimates that "between a quarter and a third of child mortality in the world can be attributed directly or indirectly to acute respiratory infections" (99). Throughout the world, they are the most common reason people use health services, and they cause 30–70 times more deaths in the Third World than in developed countries. Tuberculosis also continues to be a major public health problem in the poorest parts of the world; urban dwellers who are undernourished are particularly at risk.

The major diseases of childhood—diphtheria, whooping cough, neonatal tetanus, poliomyelitis, measles, and tuberculosis—are preventable by vaccination. They have been singled out by WHO and national governments for special immunization projects. In the developed countries, incidence of these diseases has been greatly reduced, or their effects have been attenuated by improved housing and nutrition and comprehensive public health programs. However, they continue to kill or disable several million children every year. (See Table 2.13.)

The traditional diseases of poverty exact an enormous toll in the Third World; yet some of the world's poorest people are also exposed to diseases more commonly associated with affluence. In developing countries, 16 percent of the deaths are caused by cardiovascular disease, a figure exceeded only by infectious diseases (21 percent) and parasitic diseases (18 percent). Cancer is also becoming a major public health problem in many parts of the Third World. The incidence of lung cancers, in particular, is rising markedly. This trend is certain to continue in line with the increased promotion of cigarettes in Third World countries (100). There is also evidence of growing occupational and environmental health problems as some parts of the Third World undergo rapid and relatively uncontrolled industrialization. They are particularly serious in the Latin American countries with severe water and air pollution in large urban centers, Sao Paulo, Rio de Janeiro, and Mexico City, for example.

HEALTH PRIORITIES IN THE THIRD WORLD

Much of the disease and death found in the poorest parts of the world results from the lack of basic medical care, potable water, and adequate sanitation.

Table 2.13 Number of Deaths from Selected Vaccine-Preventable Diseases

(thousands)

	Estimated Annual Deaths			
	Neonatal Tetanus[a]	Measles[b]	Whooping Cough[c]	Total
India	298	782	189	1,269
Pakistan	132	163	66	361
Bangladesh	119	173	69	361
Indonesia	71	218	63	352
Nigeria	64	171	68	303
Mexico	31	57	19	107
Ethiopia	16	60	25	101
Zaire	21	45	19	85
Philippines	12	59	12	83
Brazil	28	34	18	80
Burma	20	43	16	79
Thailand	10	57	11	78
Vietnam	12	46	19	77
Kenya	9	37	15	61
Egypt	16	32	13	61
South Africa	11	35	14	60
Sudan	8	36	15	59
Afghanistan	11	27	11	49
Iran	17	19	9	45
Algeria	10	25	8	43
Morocco	10	21	5	36
Turkey	8	16	5	29
Colombia	9	14	6	29
Tanzania	6	7	6	19
Republic of Korea	5	10	2	17
Total	**954**	**2,187**	**703**	**3,844**
All other developing countries	181	411	139	731
Grand Total	**1,135**	**2,598**	**842**	**4,575**

Notes:

a. Based on survey data or, in the absence of survey data, estimated using data from countries with similar socioeconomic conditions.

b. Based on immunization coverage data reported to Expanded Programme on Immunization (EPI)/World Health Organization (WHO), assuming that 95 percent of the vaccine is efficacious and that 90 percent of the children not immunized will acquire measles. Coverage is assumed to be zero in countries from which data are not available.

c. Based on immunization coverage data reported to EPI/WHO, assuming that 85 percent of the vaccine is efficacious and that 80 percent of children not immunized will acquire whooping cough. Coverage is assumed to be zero in countries from which data are not available.

Source: United Nation's Children Fund, *The State of the World's Children 1985* (Oxford University Press, United Kingdom, 1984), p. 36.

Medical Care: An Appropriate Technology?

The distribution of medical resources around the world is uneven, with those most in need having access to the least. Developing countries presently spend only a small fraction of their limited per-capita GNPs on health. In 1983 in low income countries, public expenditure on health averaged 2.7 percent of total government expenditures while in middle income countries it averaged 4.5 percent compared to 10.7 percent in the United States (101). In 1980, there was one qualified physician for every 490 relatively healthy people in Sweden and one for every 650 in the United Kingdom, compared with one for every 7,970 in the Philippines and every 69,390 in Ethiopia (102). Similarly, there was one nurse for every 5,460 people in India compared to 140 in the United States. The average for industrialized countries is now one nurse to every 180 people, but for the low-income countries (excluding India and China), it is one to every 8,697.

Medical services are unevenly distributed within individual countries as well. Doctors are concentrated in the towns—particularly in capital cities—and few practice in rural areas where most of the people live. In India, 80 percent of all doctors work in the cities, but 80 percent of the people live in rural areas (103). Similarly, a recent study in Ghana showed that between one-third and one-half the population lived outside the reach of basic health care units (104). This uneven distribution of health services reflects the emphasis on high-technology curative medicine found in most Third World countries (with the exception of China and a few other countries that emphasize preventive medicine). National health budgets are spent primarily on hospital-based urban medical services, even though money spent on preventive health care would yield a far greater return in improved health.

Limited access to trained health care providers is aggravated by the emigration of qualified doctors and nurses (105). Attractive professional opportunities and income in the developed world, often combined with limited professional opportunities at home, lead to this emigration. Trained doctors are a particularly valuable resource loss. Considerable public funds are spent on their education, so that their migration to another country is a financial loss as well as a loss of valuable skills. About 140,000 doctors (6 percent of the world total) now work permanently in countries other than where they were trained. About 119,000 (80 percent) work in only five countries: the United States (77,000), the United Kingdom (21,000), Canada (11,000), West Germany (6,000), and Australia (4,000). The majority were trained in developing countries, with those from India and the Philippines forming the largest single groups. Indeed, in the Philippines some years ago, a football stadium was hired to hold all the doctors taking the qualifying examination to go to the United States. Less is known about the migration of nurses, but they appear to follow a broadly similar pattern, with about 6 percent of nurses working outside their own countries, chiefly in the United States, the United Kingdom, and Canada.

This loss of medically trained personnel is only partially offset by medical aid to Third World countries. In 1960–70, the annual financial loss to Latin America caused by the flow of doctors to the United States equaled the total value of medical aid from the United States to Latin America over the entire decade (106). Although some developing countries are beginning to control emigration of medically trained people, and some of the developed countries are restricting entry, the overall situation has changed little during the 1980s.

The current provision of medical care in the Third World can best be described by the "three-quarters rule" developed by the pediatrician David Morley: "Although three quarters of the population in most countries in the tropics and subtropics live in rural areas, three quarters of the spending on medical care is in urban areas, and also three quarters of the doctors (and other health workers) live there. Three quarters of the deaths are due to conditions that can be prevented at low cost, but three quarters of the medical budget is spent on curative services, many of them provided at high cost" (107).

The World Health Organization Strategy for Health for All by the Year 2000

The International Conference on Primary Health Care held at Alma Ata in the Soviet Union in 1978 marked the beginning of a new approach to health policy for WHO. Participants at the conference called for a more equitable distribution of health resources to enable all the people in the world to become healthier and more productive. They stressed the point that the poor health of millions of people was morally unacceptable, and they formulated a strategy to close the gap between the "haves" and the "have nots." Their report was endorsed by both WHO and the U.N. General Assembly in 1979. In 1981, it was adopted by the Thirty-Fourth World Health Assembly as the Global Strategy for Health for All by the Year 2000, and all WHO member countries were urged to implement their own strategies according to local circumstances. The objectives of the Global Strategy may be summarized in terms of the 12 basic indicators used for monitoring the progress of individual nations in achieving Health for All (108):

■ *national endorsement of health for all as policy at the highest official level* accompanied by the establishment of a suitable organizational framework and the allocation of adequate resources;
■ *creation of mechanisms for effective community participation* in health-related decisions;
■ *at least 5 percent of GNP to be spent on health*;
■ *a reasonable percentage of national health expenditure to be spent on local health care*, with the exact amount to be determined according to particular circumstances;
■ *resources to be equally distributed* among different geographical areas and social groups;
■ *sustained support of developing country strategies by developed nations*;
■ *primary health care to be available to the whole population*, including at least:
  1. safe water in the home or within 15 minutes' walk and adequate sanitary arrangements,
  2. immunization against diphtheria, tetanus, whooping cough, measles, poliomyelitis, and tuberculosis,
  3. local health care, including availability of at least 20 essential drugs within one hour's walk or travel, and
  4. trained personnel to be available for attending pregnancy and childbirth and caring for children up to the age of one year;
■ *the nutritional status of children to be adequate*, in that:
  1. at least 90 percent of newborn infants to have a birth weight of at least 2,500 grams and
  2. at least 90 percent of children to have attained a reasonable weight for their age;
■ *the infant mortality rate for all identifiable subgroups to be below 50 per 1,000 live births*;
■ *life expectancy at birth to be over 60 years*;
■ *the adult literacy rate for both men and women to exceed 70 percent*; and
■ *the GNP per capita to exceed $500.*

The aims of the Global Strategy are wide ranging, and they recognize the link between health and socioeconomic development. The Strategy recognizes the fact that health goals are ultimately achieved not by medical care alone but by policies outside the immediate health sector, particularly those designed to ensure a reasonable income for all. The ultimate aim of the Strategy is to ensure that "as a minimum, all people in all countries should have at least such a level of health that they are capable of working productively and of participating actively in the social life of the community in which they live." (See "Recent Developments," below.)

Access to Safe Water and Adequate Sanitation

Without an adequate supply of clean water and effective sanitation, health is certain to suffer. Against this background, the International Drinking Water Supply and Sanitation Decade was inaugurated in 1981. At the end of 1983, WHO reviewed progress and found that about 75 percent of the urban population in the developing countries had access to piped water supplies, with 61 percent served through house connections (109). In rural areas, on the other hand, only 40 percent of the population had reasonable access to safe water. The coverage of sanitation services was less extensive, with just over 50 percent of the urban dwellers having facilities for disposal of excreta and about 36 percent having connections to public sewers. These figures represent some improvement on 1970 figures, but progress was too slow to achieve the target for the decade.

Better sanitation and water supplies alone can rarely improve health, but they are a necessary prerequisite for progress. Their impact on disease patterns is complex, depending on the number of people covered, the ways in which they use (or do not use) the services, the social and economic status of the population, and existing health problems.

Experience in many countries shows that well-planned projects can achieve a considerable reduction in diarrheal diseases, cholera, and typhoid (110) (111). In fact, the potential benefits can extend to improving the nutritional, educational, and ultimately the economic status of those involved (112). But the financial costs are high. A recent estimate suggests that the minimal cost of providing safe water for all those who need it in all the developing countries would be around $300 billion (113). In view of the fact that the total GNP of all developing countries was around $2,000 billion in 1980, the cost of providing safe water would amount to 15 percent of the total GNP, or about 1.5 percent per year spread over ten years. Millions of people are therefore likely to remain unhealthy without considerable aid from the industrialized countries, which have so far not provided it.

RECENT DEVELOPMENTS

THE KENYA CONTRACEPTIVE PREVALENCE SURVEY

World Resources 1986 noted that Kenya has the highest birth rate in the world, with a TFR of eight, an annual population growth rate of 4.2 percent, and a population doubling time of only 17 years. However, a recent study, the Kenya Contraceptive Prevalence Survey (KCPS), indi-

cates that some important changes may be taking place that could lead to declining fertility (114).

The Kenya Fertility Survey (KFS) was conducted in 1977–78. In 1984, the KCPS obtained updated information on fertility and attitudes toward contraception. A comparison of the findings of the two studies reveals several encouraging trends.

■ The level of education attained in Kenya has increased since 1977, especially among young women, and was found to be positively associated with small families (actual and desired), contraceptive knowledge, and use.

■ The average desired family size among women who have been married dropped from 7.2 to 6.2 children since 1977.

■ In 1984, 69 percent of currently married women wanted to stop bearing children or to pause before the next child, suggesting a considerable unmet need for family planning services. (See Figure 2.4.)

Awareness of family planning and contraception is high. About 80 percent of all women have heard of at least one contraceptive method. There was a notable increase in the number of married women currently using contraception—the proportion rose from 7 percent to 17 percent over the seven-year period. Current use of contraception has doubled in almost every age group, with the largest increase in the 25–29 age group. In urban areas, 21 percent of all women use contraception; the figure for rural women is 14 percent. Modern methods of contraception are more popular in the towns,

Figure 2.4 Percent of Married Kenyan Women Who Do Not Want More Children, 1977–78 and 1984

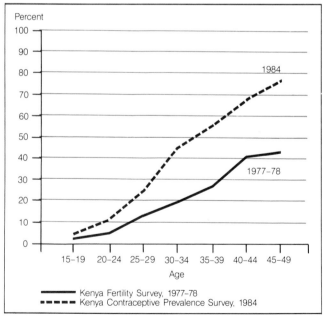

Percent

15–19 20–24 25–29 30–34 35–39 40–44 45–49

Age

——— Kenya Fertility Survey, 1977–78
- - - - Kenya Contraceptive Prevalence Survey, 1984

Note: Surveys included only currently married, fecund women.
Source: Ministry of Planning and National Development, Central Bureau of Statistics, *Kenya Contraceptive Prevalence Survey 1984: Summary Report* (Ministry of Planning, Central Bureau of Statistics, Nairobi, 1986), Table 6.1, p. 9.

in contrast to a higher proportion of rural women using traditional methods, such as rhythm and abstinence.

Among nonusers of contraception, attitudes are positive. Of women who have been married and who knew of a family planning method but were not users, 76 percent approved and only 11 percent disapproved of contraception.

Access to a source of contraceptive supplies in rural areas is a major barrier to use. About 60 percent of rural dwellers live more than an hour from the nearest outlet, and only 7 percent use modern methods. Users were asked why people interested in obtaining contraception might not go to family planning outlets. Thirty percent mentioned costs as a disincentive, 24 percent mentioned lengthy travel, 25 percent mentioned fear of nurses, and 13 percent mentioned the poor quality of service offered.

This increase of almost two-and-a-half times the contraceptive prevalence rate, from 7 percent to 17 percent in only seven years, is a major step forward for the Kenya Family Planning Programme, and it shows what can be done with a high level of government and donor commitment. Although the principal gains have been in towns and in rural areas near Nairobi, plans for the next phase include a much more concerted effort to bring modern contraceptives to rural areas using lay, community-based distributors.

The changes are not yet reflected in a significant reduction in fertility or population growth rates, but they are encouraging signs of an impending decline.

PROGRESS ON THE GLOBAL STRATEGY FOR HEALTH FOR ALL BY THE YEAR 2000

The World Health Organization's (WHO) Global Strategy for Health for All by the Year 2000 is an ambitious and attractive vision that has led to a change in the rhetoric if not always in the reality of health policy and planning since its adoption in 1981. The first evaluation of the Global Strategy, covering 1978–84, was completed in 1986, with the active participation of 146 of the 166 Member States of WHO. Because this was the first evaluation, a lack of historical baseline data and weaknesses in data collection methods and procedures made it difficult to assess the early effectiveness of the Strategy [115]. Early indications are that while the Global Strategy has been endorsed by most Member States at the highest political levels, economic constraints have limited the resources necessary to follow through on this commitment. There are some indications of progress on the availability of primary health care, particularly in rural areas, and efforts to increase immunization have increased in a few countries. However, access to medical care remains highly uneven in most Third World countries, and sustained community involvement is difficult to attain in the face of poverty, illiteracy, and traditional attitudes [116]. It is still too early to measure the impact of the Global Strategy on mortality and morbidity rates, but large disparities in infant mortality rates and life expectancy persist on both a national and an international scale [117].

References and Notes

1. U.N. Department of International Economic and Social Affairs, *World Population Prospects, Estimates and Projections as Assessed in 1984*, ST/ESA/SER.A/98 (United Nations, New York, 1986), p. 19. As discussed further in this chapter, all population estimates are based on projections of trends and census data that may be 10 or more years old. Therefore, the precise point in time when the world population reaches 5 billion is an estimate. While one estimate indicated that this occurred in 1986, most projections indicate that this milestone will be reached in mid-1987.
2. Population Reference Bureau, Inc. (PRB), *World Population Data Sheet 1986* (PRB, Inc., Washington, D.C., 1986).
3. Thomas W. Merrick, *et al.*, "World Population in Transition," *Population Bulletin*, Vol. 41, No. 2 (1986), p. 16.
4. *Ibid.*
5. *Op. cit.* 3, p. 18.
6. U.N. Department of International Economic and Social Affairs, *World Population Prospects, Estimates and Projections as Assessed in 1984*, ST/ESA/SER.A/98 (United Nations, New York, 1986), p. 20.
7. *Op. cit.* 3, p. 13.
8. *Op. cit.* 2.
9. United Nations (U.N.), "Long-Range Global Projections as Assessed in 1980," *Population Bulletin of the United Nations*, No. 14 (1983), pp. 17–22.
10. Thomas W. Merrick, *et al.*, "World Population in Transition," *Population Bulletin*, Vol. 41, No. 2 (1986), Table 1, p. 12.
11. *Op. cit.* 3, p. 15.
12. *Op. cit.* 9, pp. 17–20.
13. T. Frejka, "Long-Term Prospect for World Population Growth," *Population and Development Review*, Vol. 7, No. 3 (1981), pp. 489–511.
14. International Statistical Institute (ISI), World Fertility Survey, *Major Findings and Implications* (ISI, Voorburg, The Netherlands, 1984).
15. Centre for Population Studies, Population Council, *Research on the Determinants of Fertility: A Note on Priorities* (Population Council, New York, 1981).
16. U.N. Department of International Economic and Social Affairs, *Fertility and the Family* (United Nations, New York, 1984), pp. 45–47.
17. Benjamin White, "The Economic Importance of Children in a Javanese Village," *Population and Social Organization*, Moni Nag, ed. (Mouton Publishers, The Hague, 1975), pp. 127–147.
18. J. Bongaarts and M. Cain, *Demographic Responses to Famine* (Population Council, New York, 1981), p. 13.
19. Moni Nag, *Modernization and Its Impact on Fertility: The Indian Science* (Population Council, New York, 1982), pp. 1–22.
20. Thomas W. Merrick, *et al.*, "Population
Pressures in Latin America," *Population Bulletin*, Vol. 41, No. 3 (1986), p. 40.
21. *Op. cit.* 6, p. 159.
22. *Op. cit.* 2.
23. H. Yuan Tien, "China Demographic Billionaire," *Population Bulletin*, Vol. 38, No. 2 (1983), p. 10.
24. *Op. cit.* 2.
25. *Op. cit.* 2.
26. The World Bank, *World Development Report 1984* (Oxford University Press, New York, 1984), pp. 169–170.
27. *Op. cit.* 6, p. 102.
28. *Op. cit.* 6, Table A12, p. 104.
29. *Op. cit.* 26, pp. 173–174.
30. T. Dyson and M. Moore, "On Kinship Structure, Female Autonomy, and Demographic Behavior in India," *Population and Development Review*, Vol. 9, No. 1 (1983), pp. 35–60.
31. *Op. cit.* 2.
32. *Op. cit.* 26, pp. 170–171.
33. *Op. cit.* 26, p. 173.
34. *Op. cit.* 26, pp. 173–174.
35. *Op. cit.* 30.
36. *Op. cit.* 6, p. 104.
37. J. Minces, *The House of Obedience, Women in Arab Society* (Zed Press, London, 1982), pp. 29–49 and pp. 57–71.
38. *Op. cit.* 6, p. 104.
39. *Op. cit.* 2.
40. *Op. cit.* 6, p. 102.
41. *Op. cit.* 26, p. 162.
42. *Op. cit.* 26, p. 163.

43. *Op. cit.* 26, p. 166.
44. *Op. cit.* 26, p. 163.
45. *Op. cit.* 26, pp. 167–169.
46. Kingsley Davis and P. van den Oever, "Age Relations and Public Policy in Advanced Industrial Societies," *Population and Development Review*, Vol. 7, No. 1 (1981), pp. 1–18.
47. *Op. cit.* 26, pp. 122–123.
48. A. Carlson, "The Depopulation Bomb," *The Washington Post* (April 13, 1986).
49. Kingsley Davis, "Wives and Work: The Sex Role Revolution and Its Consequences," *Population and Development Review*, Vol. 10, No. 3 (1984), pp. 347–418.
50. European Community, *Labor Force Sample Survey: Results for 1981* (Eurostat, Luxembourg, 1983).
51. *Op. cit.* 46.
52. Population Reference Bureau, Inc., "U.S. Population: Where We Are; Where We're Going," *Population Bulletin*, Vol. 37, No. 2 (Washington, D.C., 1982), pp. 44–45.
53. *Op. cit.* 2.
54. Leon F. Bouvier, "America's Baby Boom Generation: The Fateful Bulge," *Population Bulletin*, Vol. 35, No. 1 (1980), p. 15.
55. Celia Evans Miller, "The Aging Children of the Baby Boom," *ZPG National Reporter*, Vol. 8, No. 5 (June 1976), p. 5, cited in Leon F. Bouvier, "America's Baby Boom Generation: The Fateful Bulge," *Population Bulletin*, Vol. 35, No. 1 (1980), p. 17.
56. U.S. Government, *Economic Report of the President* (Government Printing Office, Washington, D.C., 1985), pp. 159–186.
57. Hilde Wander, "Zero Population Growth Now: The Lessons from Europe" in *The Economic Consequences of Slowing Population Growth*, T.J. Espenshade and W.J. Serow, eds. (Academic Press, New York, 1978), pp. 55–59.
58. M. Kirk, *Demographic and Social Change in Europe 1975–2000* (Liverpool University Press, United Kingdom, 1981), pp. 54–55.
59. *Op. cit.* 54, p. 29.
60. *Op. cit.* 54, p. 30.
61. *Op. cit.* 58, pp. 60–64.
62. Leon F. Bouvier, *The Impact of Immigration on U.S. Population Size* (Population Reference Bureau, Inc., Washington, D.C., 1981), pp. 1–19.
63. *Op. cit.* 2.
64. Elaine M. Murphy and Patricia Cancellier, *Immigration Questions and Answers* (Population Reference Bureau, Inc., Washington, D.C., 1982), p. 2.
65. *Op. cit.* 52, pp. 21–22.
66. *Op. cit.* 64, p. 8.
67. Kathleen Newland, *International Migration: The Search for Work* (Worldwatch Institute, Washington, D.C., 1979), p. 16.
68. *Ibid.*, p. 19.
69. *Op. cit.* 64, p. 9.
70. *Op. cit.* 52, p. 9.
71. *Op. cit.* 52, pp. 5–6.
72. F.D. Bean and J.P. Marcum, "Differential Fertility and Minority Group Hypothesis: An Assessment and Review" in *The -Demography of Racial and Ethnic Groups*, F.D. Bean and W. Parker Frisbie, eds. (Academic Press, New York, 1978), pp. 189–211.
73. World Health Organization (WHO), *Evaluation of the Strategy for Health for All by the Year 2000: Seventh Report on the World Health Situation* (WHO, Geneva, 1986), pp. 60–61.
74. World Health Organization (WHO), *Development of Indicators for Monitoring Progress towards Health for All by the Year 2000* (WHO, Geneva, 1981), p. 10.
75. *Op. cit.* 73.
76. Alan D. Lopez, "Sex Differentials in Mortality," *WHO Chronicle*, Vol. 38, No. 5 (1984), pp. 212–224.
77. Stan D'Souza and Lincoln C. Chen, "Sex Differentials in Mortality in Rural Bangladesh," *Population and Development Review*, Vol. 6, No. 2 (1980), pp. 257–272.
78. *Op. cit.* 73, p. 65.
79. Peter Townsend and Nick Davidson, *Inequalities in Health: The Black Report* (Penguin, Harmondsworth, United Kingdom, 1982).
80. H. Behm, "Socioeconomic Determinants of Mortality in Latin America" in *Proceedings of the Meeting on Socioeconomic Determinants and the Consequences of Mortality* (United Nations/World Health Organization, Mexico City, 1979), p. 160.
81. Michael G. Marmot, "Socioeconomic and Cultural Factors in Ischaemic Heart Disease" in *Advances in Cardiology: Psychological Problems Before and After Myocardial Infection*, H. Denolin, ed., Vol. 39 (1982), pp. 68–76.
82. R.F. Heller, *et al.*, "How Well Can We Predict Coronary Heart Disease? Findings in the United Kingdom Heart Disease Prevention Project," *British Medical Journal*, Vol. 288, No. 6428 (1984), pp. 1409–1411.
83. Richard Doll and Richard Peto, *The Causes of Cancer* (Oxford University Press, United Kingdom, 1981), p. 1220.
84. Bobbie Jacobsen, *Beating the Ladykiller: Women and Smoking* (Pluto Press, London, 1986), p. 18.
85. *Op. cit.* 83, p. 1237.
86. *Op. cit.* 73.
87. *Op. cit.* 73, p. 73.
88. George W. Brown and Tirrell Harris, *Social Origins of Depression: A Study of Psychiatric Disorders in Women* (Tavistock, London, 1978).
89. Vicente Navarro, *Crisis, Health and Medicine: A Social Critique* (Tavistock, London, 1986), p. 212.
90. David Sanders, *The Struggle for Health: Medicine and the Politics of Underdevelopment* (MacMillan Education Ltd., London and Basingstoke, 1985), p. 20.
91. N.S. Scrimshaw, *et al.*, *Interactions of Nutrition and Infection* (World Health Organization, Geneva, 1968).
92. *Op. cit.* 73, pp. 79–80.
93. "Nutritional Surveillance: Global Trends in Protein-Energy Malnutrition Surveillance," *Weekly Epidemiological Record*, No. 25 (1984), pp. 189–191.
94. *Op. cit.* 90.
95. *Op. cit.* 73, p. 79.
96. E. Royston, "The Prevalence of Nutritional Anaemia among Women in Developing Countries: A Critical Review of Available Information," *World Health Statistics Quarterly*, Vol. 35, No. 2 (1982), pp. 52–91.
97. David Morley and M. Woodland, *See How They Grow* (Macmillan Publishing Co., Inc., New York, 1979), p. 97.
98. K.M. Elliott and W.A.M. Cutting, "Carry on Feeding," *Diarrhoea Dialogue*, No. 15 (1983), p. 5.
99. *Op. cit.* 73, p. 67.
100. Mike Muller, *Tobacco and the Third World: Tomorrow's Epidemic?* (War on Want, London, 1978).
101. World Bank, *World Development Report 1986* (Oxford University Press, New York, 1986), Table 22, pp. 222–223.
102. The World Bank, *World Development Report 1985* (Oxford University Press, United Kingdom, 1985), p. 220.
103. Claire Whittemore, *The Doctor Go Round* (Oxfam, London, 1976), p. 7.
104. Anne Mills, "Vertical versus Horizontal Health Programs in Africa: Idealism, Pragmatism, Resources and Efficiency," *Social Science and Medicine*, Vol. 17, No. 24 (1983), pp. 1971–1981.
105. A. Mejia, *et al.* *Physician and Nurse Migration: Analysis and Policy Implications* (World Health Organization, Geneva, 1979).
106. Vicente Navarro, "The Political and Economic Origins of the Underdevelopment of Health in Latin America," in Vicente Navarro, *Medicine under Capitalism* (Croom Helm, London, 1976), p. 14.
107. David Morley, *Paediatric Priorities in the Developing World* (Butterworths, London, 1973), p. 4.
108. World Health Organization (WHO), *Global Strategy for Health for All by the Year 2000* (WHO, Geneva, 1981), pp. 74–76.
109. Fredrik L.O. Deck, "Community Water Supply and Sanitation in Developing Countries, 1970–1990: An Evaluation of the Levels and Trends of Services," *World Health Statistics Quarterly*, Vol. 39, No. 1 (1986), p. 5.
110. J. Briscoe, "Intervention Studies and the Definition of Dominant Transmission Routes," *American Journal of Epidemiology*, Vol. 120, No. 3 (1984), pp. 449–455.
111. J. Briscoe, "The Role of Water Supply in Improving Health in Poor Countries (with Special Reference to Bangladesh)," *American Journal of Clinical Nutrition*, Vol. 31, No. 11 (1978), pp. 2100–2113.
112. Branko Cvjetanovic, "Health Effects and Impact of Water Supply and Sanitation," *World Health Statistics Quarterly*, Vol. 39, No. 1 (1986), pp. 105–117.
113. Mahesh Patel, "An Economic Evaluation of 'Health for All'," *Health Policy and Planning*, Vol. 1, No. 1 (1986), pp. 37–47.
114. Ministry of Planning and National Development, Central Bureau of Statistics, *Kenya Contraceptive Prevalence Survey, 1984: Summary Report* (Ministry of Planning, Central Bureau of Statistics, Nairobi, 1986).
115. *Op. cit.* 73, p. 97.
116. *Op. cit.* 73, pp. 97–101.
117. Brian Abel-Smith, "The World Economic Crisis. Part 1: Repercussions on Health," *Health Policy and Planning*, Vol. 1 (1986), pp. 202–213.

3. Human Settlements

Worldwide, roughly three people live in rural areas for every two urban dwellers, and agriculture is the main source of livelihood for more than half the world's population. Most Asian and African nations have predominantly rural populations, as do some Latin American nations. However, over the past century, there has been an unprecedented growth in the world's urban population and in the number and size of large cities. An increasingly integrated and city-based world economy has been the driving force. The "million city" is now commonplace throughout the world, even in relatively rural regions, and a growing number of cities now have populations of 5–15 million. Such urban growth challenges governments in providing adequate facilities and services for residents and businesses.

Most of the larger and more rapidly growing cities are in the Third World. Rates of natural increase are generally higher than in the developed world, and rapid economic, social, and political change has stimulated urbanization. In addition, under colonial rule, many Third World nations had small urban populations, with movement to cities often strongly controlled. Thus, urban rates of growth often appear particularly high in recent decades because they began with a small base.

Despite the rapid growth of some large cities, they house only a small part of the world's population. In 1980, only 6 percent of the world's population lived in cities with more than 4 million people. Even in many of the most urbanized regions such as Japan and Western Europe, less than half the population now lives in urban centers with 100,000 or more inhabitants.

The United Nations predicts that all the world's inhabited regions will become increasingly urban up to the year 2025 and that most of the largest cities will continue to grow rapidly. But recent censuses suggest that this prediction may not be realized. In North America and much of Europe, recent trends have been toward counterurbanization with less concentration in the largest older cities. In the Third World, many of the largest cities are growing more slowly than expected. Indeed, in some countries, the largest cities have some of the slowest urban growth rates, but certain relatively small urban centers, often near the largest cities, are growing more rapidly and becoming important concentrations of new industries and service enterprises. If these trends are sustained, there will be fewer and smaller megacities than projected by the United Nations.

Should a slowdown in Third World urbanization occur, it is likely to be the result of economic stagnation. Rapid population growth in any city presents problems, particularly in providing necessary services, because city governments typically lack the power to levy taxes for roads, water supplies, sewers, drains, and public transportation and to intervene in land markets to ensure that residents have access to legal and affordable land sites. However, a stagnant or declining economy that slows or stops people from moving to the cities may prove a more intractable problem for developing nations than rapid urban growth.

World Resources 1987

Worldwide, poverty is more a rural than an urban phenomenon: most of the world's poorest people live in the predominantly rural nations of Africa and Asia. Many have no land of their own or their holdings are too small to provide an adequate standard of living for their families. They cannot grow enough food, nor are they able to find other work that pays adequately. They are usually the worst served by health care, schools, safe and convenient water supplies, transportation, and other public services. In the past 30 years, the movement of rural poor to urban areas to seek a more secure basis for their own survival is one of the main factors behind urbanization in the Third World.

The distinction between rural and urban areas is made by all governments. But definitions vary widely, complicating international comparisons. Nevertheless, the differences between living conditions in rural and urban areas in most developing nations are generally consistent.

There have been major advances in understanding the dynamics of rural-to-urban migration in recent years. Most research findings show that migration flows are rational responses to changing economic circumstances and that recent city migrants often provide much of the cheap labor on which the urban economy is based.

All government policies and expenditures influence rural-urban dynamics. Some of the most powerful influences derive from policies with no explicit spatial aims or objectives. Thus, macroeconomic policies can encourage or discourage migration to cities. For example, import substitution policies often help concentrate businesses and factories in one or two large cities. The strength and competence of local government influence the spatial distribution of urban development; a highly centralized government with weak and ineffective local governments increases the dominance of national capitals. If governments wish to slow migration flows to large cities, they may have to do more than concentrate on agrarian reform and agricultural and rural development—they may have to change their economic and pricing policies and strengthen the power, resources, and representative nature of local governments.

CONDITIONS AND TRENDS

GLOBAL TRENDS IN HUMAN SETTLEMENTS

During 1987, the world population will pass the 5 billion mark, and United Nations (U.N.) projections suggest that it will exceed 6.1 billion by the turn of the century. In 1985, an estimated 59 percent of the global population lived in rural areas, most of them in developing countries. Asia and Africa were 71.9 and 70.3 percent rural, respectively. By contrast, the developed nations were 71.5 percent urban, and Latin America was 68.9 percent urban (1).

Urban Change

These international comparisons as to levels of urbanization are marred by major differences in the way governments define "urban." The dividing line between urban and rural varies considerably since there is no general agreement as to what constitutes an urban area. Occasionally, changes in the definition of urban areas can significantly affect statistics. (See Recent Developments, China Redefines its Urban Population, below. For a more complete discussion of the problems of defining urban and rural areas, see *World Resources 1986*, p. 32.)

In spite of this difficulty, it is clear that within the past century there has been an unprecedented increase in both the number and the proportion of people living in settlements defined as urban throughout the world. The form and scale of this urban growth and the time at which it began differ greatly from region to region. Until the 19th Century, predominantly rural and agricultural or pastoral societies were the norm throughout the world, and until the second half of the 19th Century, nations with more than one person in ten living in an urban area were unusual (2). Today more than one person in ten lives in an urban area in most nations, and in many countries more than seven in ten do. In 1800, some 50 million people—about 5 percent of the total population—lived in urban areas throughout the world. By 1985, more than 2 billion people—about 42 percent of the total population—lived in urban areas.

In recent decades, the nations with the most rapidly growing urban populations have been in the Third World. There are several reasons. First, the rates of natural increase in population are generally much higher in the Third World, so that even urban areas with little in-migration often grow 2–3.5 percent a year. In addition, for many Third World nations, relatively few people lived in urban centers in 1950; urban growth rates have been high relative to the developed countries because growth is measured against a small urban population base. For example, Tanzania's urban population growth of around 1 million people between 1967 and 1978 appears rapid because there were only 621,000 urban inhabitants in 1967. At the same time, Australia, which has a smaller national population than Tanzania, also experienced an urban population growth of about 1 million people, but because Australia was already a predominantly urban society by the 1960s, the growth rate appears slow.

Urban population growth has also been more rapid in many Third World nations in recent decades because of rapid economic, social, and political changes since 1950 (including, for many, the attainment of political independence). These changes have generally led to a concentration of new employment and educational opportunities in urban areas, especially in one or two of the largest cities. In turn, these opportunities have stimulated large-scale population movements from rural areas and frequently from smaller urban centers as well. Urban centers whose populations did not grow rapidly were almost always those whose economies remained stagnant or declined, and many of their inhabitants often moved to cities where new opportunities were concentrated.

During 1950–85, the level of urbanization (i.e., the proportion of the population living in urban areas) increased in all regions of the world. (See Table 3.1.) U.N. figures indicate that in Africa the urban population increased from 15 to 32 percent of the total population, with East

Table 3.1 Proportion of the Population Living in Urban Areas: World, More Developed and Less Developed Regions, and Major Regions, 1950–2000

(percent)

Area	1950	1960	1970	1975	1980	1985	1990	1995	2000
World	**29.2**	**34.2**	**37.1**	**38.4**	**39.6**	**41.0**	**42.6**	**44.5**	**46.6**
More Developed Regions	**53.8**	**60.5**	**66.6**	**68.8**	**70.2**	**71.5**	**72.5**	**73.5**	**74.4**
Less Developed Regions	**17.0**	**22.2**	**25.4**	**27.2**	**29.2**	**31.2**	**33.6**	**36.3**	**39.3**
Africa	15.7	18.8	22.5	24.5	27.0	29.7	32.7	35.8	39.1
Latin America	41.0	49.2	57.4	61.4	65.3	68.9	72.0	74.6	76.8
North America	63.9	69.9	73.8	73.8	73.9	74.1	74.3	74.6	74.9
Eastern Asia	16.8	25.0	26.9	27.6	28.1	28.6	29.5	30.9	32.8
South Asia	16.1	18.4	21.3	23.3	25.4	27.7	30.2	33.2	36.5
Europe	56.3	60.9	66.7	68.8	70.2	71.6	72.8	74.0	75.1
Oceania	61.3	66.3	70.8	71.7	71.4	71.0	70.9	71.0	71.3
USSR	39.3	48.8	56.7	60.0	63.1	65.6	67.5	69.4	70.7

Note: North America includes Bermuda, Greenland, and St. Pierre and Miquelon.
Source: U.N. Department of International Economic and Social Affairs, *World Population Prospects: Estimates and Projections as Assessed in 1984*, Population Studies No. 98 (United Nations, New York, 1986), pp. 140-143, p. 150, p. 156, p. 162, p. 173, and p. 180.

Africa the most rapidly urbanizing subregion, growing from 5 to 19 percent. Latin America became a predominantly urban continent, growing from 41 percent urban in 1950 to 69 percent urban in 1985. In Asia, the level of urbanization increased from 17 percent to 28 percent.

In spite of rapid urbanization in the developing world, prior to 1980 the absolute increase in the rural population continued to exceed the urban increase because of its much larger base. Based on U.N. projections, since 1980, for the first time, the absolute growth in urban population in developing countries is higher than the absolute growth in rural population. This change is important historically. (See Table 3.2.)

Table 3.2 Increases in Urban and Rural Population, 1950–80 and 1980–2000

(millions)

	1950–80		1980–2000	
	Urban	Rural	Urban	Rural
World	**1,030**	**904**	**1,089**	**583**
More Developed Regions	**351**	**−46**	**152**	**−12**
Less Developed Regions	**679**	**950**	**937**	**595**
Africa	94	161	211	181
Latin America	169	28	183	2
North America	80	6	36	9
East Asia	218	287	154	145
South Asia	244	459	400	267
Europe	119	−27	44	−17
Oceania	9	2	5	2
USSR	97	−11	55	−6

Note: North America includes Bermuda, Greenland, and St. Pierre and Miquelon.
Source: Adapted from U.N. Department of International Economic and Social Affairs, *World Population Prospects as Assessed in 1984*, Population Studies No. 98 (United Nations, New York, 1986), pp. 140-143, p. 150, p. 158, p. 162, p. 168, p. 173, and p. 180.

Rural Populations

Despite the attention given by policymakers and the media to rapid urban change and to urban and large-city problems, most of the world population continues to live in rural rather than urban areas. In 1985, 59 percent of the world population lived in rural areas, and agriculture provided the livelihood for more than half the world population.

Throughout the world, there is a strong correlation between the proportion of a nation's population living in rural areas and the proportion of its labor force working in agriculture. In addition, the larger the relative size of the rural population, the poorer the country is likely to be. These correlations can be seen by looking at groups of nations categorized by per capita Gross National Product. The World Bank divides the countries of the world with more than 1 million inhabitants (1983) into six major categories.

The poorest nations are classified as "low income economies." In most of these countries, 70–90 percent of the labor force works in agriculture. The 35 nations in this category include India and China and contain nearly half the world population. Although many farmers live in small urban centers—and a few in larger urban centers— the predominance of agriculture is reflected in the small proportion of national populations, typically 10–30 percent, living in urban centers.

In the 36 nations classified as "lower middle income economies," about 40 percent of the labor force works in agriculture and half the population lives in rural areas. This group of nations is diverse; it includes relatively urbanized nations like Cuba and Colombia, with less than 30 percent of their labor force in agriculture, as well as predominantly rural and agricultural countries like Senegal and Mauritania.

The 22 nations with "upper-middle income economies" have an average of just 30 percent of their labor force working in agriculture and one third of their population living in rural areas. This group includes Latin America's most urbanized and industrialized nations, such as Brazil, Chile, Mexico, and Venezuela, and the poorer European nations, such as Portugal and Greece.

Among the five high income oil exporter nations, the proportion of the labor force working in agriculture is low and the proportion living in urban centers relatively high, with the exception of Oman, where much of the population remains nomadic. In addition, roughly 40 percent of the population in Saudi Arabia still derives its livelihood from pastoralism.

In the industrial market economies, including Japan, North America, and most of Western Europe, less than a quarter of the population lives in rural areas and just 6 percent of the labor force works in agriculture. Here the link between agricultural employment and rural residence begins to break down. An increasing fraction of the rural population no longer works on farms.

There is considerable diversity among the East European nonmarket economy nations. In predominantly rural Albania, 61 percent of the labor force still worked in agriculture in 1981. At the other end of the spectrum, highly urbanized East Germany has only 10 percent of its work force in agriculture.

Trends in Urbanization

The United Nations projects that all regions will continue to urbanize up to 2025 and that more than 60 percent of the world population will live in urban areas by then. Recent census data from North America, Western Europe, and some Third World nations raise questions about these projections. Censuses undertaken in the last 10 years show that many nations are not urbanizing as rapidly as U.N. figures suggest. Further analysis of the factors that underpin urbanization in the Third World has brought into question the validity of some of the assumptions on which the U.N. projections are based (3). One key assumption is that urban trends in the past few decades provide a valid guide to the future.

The relatively slow population growth that Calcutta has experienced in recent years illustrates how inaccurate such population projections can be. During the 1970s, Calcutta was projected to have 40–50 million inhabitants by the year 2000 (4). The projection was based on extrapolating Calcutta's rapid population growth rate in the 1940s and 1950s far into the future. But the rapid population growth was largely due to the influx of refugees from what was formerly East Pakistan (now Bangladesh) after the partition of India in 1947. More than 2 million settled in Calcutta. But such rapid inflows of people have not taken place since 1960; indeed, between 1971 and 1981, more people moved out of Calcutta than into it. With a total population of some 9 million in 1981, Calcutta is unlikely to exceed even 15 million inhabitants by the year 2000, let alone the 40 or 50 million predicted during the 1970s.

In the richer Western nations, the fact that the proportion of people living in urban areas is hardly growing or in some instances is even decreasing is a result of a productive and sophisticated economic structure (including far less reliance on traditional heavy industry and far more on service enterprises) and of advances in transportation and communications. Some businesses are able to operate from cheaper rural greenfield sites. For others, it is attractive to decentralize operations. Many professionals and executives are attracted by jobs that offer what have traditionally been urban comforts and levels of services but in rural surroundings. If urbanization does continue in parts of North America and Western Europe, it is likely to be through rural populations moving to relatively small urban centers, not to large cities.

In contrast, a slowdown in urbanization (5) is far more likely to be associated with a slowdown in economic development in most of the Third World. In recent decades, cities like Mexico City, Lagos, and Dar es Salaam have been the main focus of rural-to-urban migration within their national boundaries because they were the places with the most new employment opportunities. They no longer appear to offer such great opportunities, relative to other urban centers and other regions. Recent economic stagnation and the current debt crisis in many developing nations are likely to be reflected in substantial slowdowns in urbanization rates, which will be apparent when new census results become available.

If this slowdown is occurring, the developing world may be far less urban by the year 2025 than the United Nations projects. If Africa and Asia are to change from predominantly rural regions to become nearly 60 percent urban in less than 40 years, their economies will have to be transformed during these years.

Small Urban Centers

Despite the attention given to the problems of cities like New York, Mexico City, Calcutta, Cairo, and Manila, only a small proportion of the world population lives in very large cities. In 1980, only 6 percent lived in cities with 4 million or more inhabitants while only 25 percent lived in urban centers with 100,000 or more people. Even in many of the most urbanized nations of the world such as Japan and the nations of Western Europe, less than half the population lives in urban centers with 100,000 or more inhabitants. In many Third World nations, at least half the urban population lives outside the national capital and the largest cities. They live in small or medium-size urban centers of great diversity in terms of economic base and potential for further development. For example, in India, the 1981 census showed that only a quarter of the urban population lived in the 12 largest cities (6).

In many nations, the urban areas with the highest rates of population growth are relatively small urban centers. In the United States, most of the cities (7) that grew more rapidly between 1970 and 1980 had fewer than 250,000 inhabitants (8). In Kenya, the two largest urban centers—Nairobi and Mombasa—had among the slowest rates of population growth for the nation's urban centers with 5,000 or more inhabitants between 1969 and 1979 (9). Lima, the largest city in Peru, had one of the slowest rates of population growth between 1972 and 1981 among that country's urban centers with more than 50,000 inhabitants (10). In Ecuador, several relatively small urban areas experienced much higher growth rates than the two largest cities, Guayaquil and Quito, in recent intercensal periods. A dramatic example is the town of Machala, which grew from 7,549 inhabitants in 1950 to 105,521 inhabitants in 1982, turning it from a small, unimportant town to the fourth largest urban center in Ecuador (11). In India, most of the more rapidly growing urban centers during the 1970s had fewer than 500,000 inhabitants (12).

A surprising aspect of rapid urban growth is the lack of new urban centers. The growth in urban population is primarily concentrated around long-established urban centers. The few new cities that have emerged are generally the result of explicit government policies rather than natural economic and social forces. In order to get these new cities going, governments have poured money into their creation. In Latin America, virtually all national capitals and most provincial capitals were founded as towns prior to independence; the continent's ten largest cities were all founded more than 400 years ago (13). In East Africa, virtually every urban area with more than 20,000 inhabitants in the mid-1970s was an established colonial administrative center by 1910 (14). A study of three districts in India with 34 urban centers in 1981 found that virtually all had been administrative centers under colonial rule in the 19th Century, and many were important towns within their areas for hundreds of years (15). A comparable study in Southwest Nigeria also found that most urban centers there had histories as important settlements stretching back hundreds of years (16).

Whether smaller urban centers will grow enough to moderate the dominance of the largest cities will vary from country to country. In some nations, they show signs of doing so already, but it is not clear whether this trend will be sustained into the next century. If the richer and more industrialized Third World nations develop high standards of interregional transportation and communications, an increasing number of new businesses may locate outside the largest cities, as they have done in North America and much of Europe.

FOCUS ON: RURAL-URBAN DISPARITIES IN LIVING CONDITIONS

The Difficulties of Pinpointing Disparities

It is clear that a high proportion of the world's most impoverished people live in rural areas. This poverty is frequently the result of landlessness or the inadequate size or poor quality of landholdings, combined with a lack of alternative employment opportunities either within or outside the agricultural sector. The poverty of hundreds of millions of rural dwellers is reflected, not surprisingly, in their one-room homes that are typically made of materials which are most immediately available and for which little or no payment is needed.

Rural dwellers in the developing world are also likely to be worse off than urban dwellers in terms of access to the kinds of services and infrastructure that are usually the responsibility of governments: roads, telephones, postal service, public transportation, safe water supplies and sanitation, education, and public health services.

Comparisons of living conditions in rural and urban areas are difficult to make and must be carefully interpreted. The most important reason is simply that the data base is extremely limited, both in the types of living conditions measured and in the number of nations covered. Beyond availability, there is also a problem of quality of the information. Data are frequently obtained through surveys of national government agencies, and they may be based on limited knowledge of actual conditions in remote rural areas or they may be exaggerated. A second major problem in interpreting these data is the diversity of conditions within both rural and urban areas in most nations. Statistical averages for all rural areas or urban centers frequently mask large differences among towns or rural areas. A third problem is that poor living conditions often correlate more closely with low incomes or with a particular ethnic group than with the location of dwellings. Particularly in cities, averages for an entire city tend to hide large individual differences that are relevant for policymaking. Even with these limitations, it is important to understand differences in living conditions in rural and urban areas, especially in many parts of the developing world where those differences are greatest.

Urban and Rural Mortality Rates

Mortality rates are one of the most useful and important indicators of the effects of differences in overall living conditions, including housing, access to potable water, sanitation, education, health care, nutrition, and income.

During the Industrial Revolution in Europe and North America, mortality rates were higher than birth rates in most urban areas; their populations would have declined without a constant influx of people from the countryside.

Rural-to-urban migration, not natural increase, was usually the main source of urban population growth.

Over the past century, urban mortality rates declined significantly. Although there is some debate about the most important causes, it is generally agreed that improved diet—made possible primarily through rising incomes and cheaper food—probably was the single most important factor. Direct government action was also important in improving water supplies, sanitation, the disposal of household refuse, and other services. So too, in some instances, was public action to restrict working hours and exploitation of labor.

More recently, rural-urban differences in terms of life expectancy and infant mortality have largely disappeared in North America and Europe. Although differences persist between rural and urban areas in some regions, a lower than average life expectancy is more commonly associated with low income or with specific locations in cities where high concentrations of low-income people are concentrated.

In the Third World, rural-urban disparities are more significant. Table 3.3 demonstrates the fact that for selected nations where data are available, infant and child mortality in urban areas is substantially below rural levels. The data, which are based on an extensive survey of Latin American, Asian, and African nations, show that in both the first year of life and in the first five years of life, metropolitan areas tend to have the lowest mortality rates, followed by other urban areas and then by rural areas (17).

Not all urban areas in the Third World have lower mortality rates than rural regions do. Conditions in some

Table 3.3 Mortality Rates during First Five Years of Life by Type of Residence for Selected Countries

(per thousand births)

Country	Mortality during First Year of Life				Mortality during First Five Years of Life			
	Metropolitan	Other Urban	Rural	Total	Metropolitan	Other Urban	Rural	Total
Senegal	82	81	146	127	167	187	332	287
Lesotho	(132)		145	144	(192)		190	190
Kenya	(94)	95	102	101	(145)	126	165	162
Sudan	81	66	83	81	120	121	148	140
Haiti	162	(90)	140	144	221	(137)	215	214
Peru	58	115	144	115	76	165	222	170
Mexico	72	76	92	82	88	103	135	114
Colombia	41	71	89	74	66	101	139	112
Costa Rica	55	80	87	78	63	94	108	95
Guyana	64	(62)	53	56	75	(77)	70	71
Panama	37	50	57	49	46	67	76	65
Jamaica	37	50	46	44	43	59	65	58
Trinidad and Tobago	47	39	40	43	52	48	49	49
Nepal	(119)		174	173	(145)		262	259
Bangladesh	(133)	127	148	146	(180)	188	218	215
Pakistan	97	130	150	141	143	174	216	202
Indonesia	77	82	118	111	143	137	188	180
Thailand	(47)	(69)	92	88	(57)	(83)	122	116
Jordan	69	71	88	75	85	96	123	100
Syria	56	60	88	73	72	78	115	95
Philippines	39	47	62	57	57	77	98	90
Sri Lanka	52	54	63	61	71	74	87	84
Korea	46	59	58	55	63	87	90	83
Malaysia	36	34	52	47	42	46	68	61

Note: Rates based on fewer than 500 births are shown in parentheses.
Source: Adapted from J.N. Hobcraft, *et al.*, "Socio-Economic Factors in Infant and Child Mortality: A Cross National Comparison," *Population Studies*, Vol. 38, No.2 (1984).

major cities seem to be worse than in rural areas. For example, infant mortality in Nairobi, Kenya's capital and largest city, is 30 percent higher than in the surrounding countryside. By contrast, the mortality rate in Mombasa, Kenya's second largest city and major port, is 40 percent lower than in nearby rural areas (18).

In addition, health surveys in squatter communities or other city districts with a high proportion of low-income residents often show higher infant mortality rates than surveys made in rural areas, even if the city average is lower than the rural average. An example is the slums of Haiti's capital, Port-au-Prince, where the infant mortality rate was 200 deaths per 1,000 live births, with another 100 deaths of children between the ages of 1 and 2 years—nearly three times the mortality rates in rural areas (19). Infant mortality rates in the "bustees" (slums) of New Delhi, India's capital, were 221 per 1,000, but they were double this figure for some castes (20). In Manila, the infant mortality rate in the squatter communities was three times that of the city.

Access to Potable Water and Sanitation Facilities

The United Nations launched the International Drinking Water Supply and Sanitation Decade in 1980 in an effort to improve access to potable water and sanitation in the Third World. As part of this intensive campaign to persuade governments to place a much higher priority on water and sanitation services, considerable effort has been devoted to collecting information on access to water and sanitation.

Most of the data come from U.N. questionnaires completed by individual governments. As such, the data may contain errors and overstatements that the United Nations has little capacity to correct. But the statistics strongly indicate that rural populations have poorer access than urban populations to safe water supplies and sanitation

facilities. U.N. data show that by 1983 only 39 percent of the rural population in 92 reporting countries had access to safe drinking water, compared to 74 percent of the urban population. Similarly, only 14 percent of people in rural areas had access to sanitation facilities, compared to 52 percent of urban dwellers in these countries (21). (See Table 3.4.)

Tables 3.5 and 3.6 show water and sanitation data for individual countries. The pattern of a higher proportion of urban than rural populations with access to piped water and sanitation is consistent across a wide spectrum of countries and regions. However, some care must be taken in interpreting these data—access to piped water includes people living within 100 meters of a piped supply, not just those who have running water. Carrying water from a public tap 100 meters away is hard work and it is time consuming, quite different from having a piped supply in the house. In addition, piped water is not guaranteed safe. The water supply in many cities is contaminated, often from sewage seeping into the pipes of the water distribution system when water pressure drops because of overloading or poor maintenance.

The statistics on access to toilets and latrines in Table 3.6 can also be misleading. Many poorly designed and maintained latrines are a major cause of infection, especially in high-density settlements and where they are shared by many. Even relatively sophisticated flush toilets can be centers of infection when, as is common in tenements or cheap boarding houses, 30 or more people share a facility.

Housing Conditions

One of the few standardized indicators of housing conditions is the number of persons per room in occupied housing. Yet the statistic is a limited measure of conditions because it does not include information on room size, quality of construction, cost to the inhabitants, and

Table 3.4 Total Population with Access to Clean Drinking Water and Sanitation Facilities, 1983
(population in thousands, percentages in parentheses)

WHO Region	Number of Reporting Countries/Territories	Population			Population With Access to Safe Drinking Water				Population With Access to Sanitation Facilities			
		Total	Urban	Rural	Urban[a]			Rural	Urban[a]			Rural
					Total	by HC[b]	by PS[c]		Total	by SC[d]	by Other	
Africa	26	270,965	65,481 (24)	205,484 (76)	37,914 (61)	21,152	17,424	52,372 (26)	15,755 (68)	4,877	18,535	27,782 (25)
Americas	24	367,525	246,098 (67)	121,427 (33)	182,088 (85)	170,397	25,680	44,358 (40)	109,089 (80)	96,671	43,183	14,815 (18)
Southeast Asia	9	1,076,049	253,160 (24)	822,889 (76)	166,521 (66)	4,525	2,610	356,721 (43)	77,963 (31)	854	4,509	57,834 (7)
Eastern Mediterranean	12	139,813	45,396 (32)	94,417 (68)	37,206 (86)	12,350	5,044	23,614 (26)	25,447 (64)	5,281	6,616	5,037 (7)
Western Pacific	21	180,804	72,127 (40)	108,677 (60)	23,947 (70)	18,503	5,422	48,871 (45)	23,355 (80)	3,968	19,457	53,318 (57)
Totals	92	2,035,156	682,262 (34)	1,352,894 (66)	447,676 (74)	226,927	56,180	525,936 (39)	251,609 (52)	111,651	92,300	158,786 (14)

Notes:
a. Coverage does not necessarily add up to the value for total coverage because all countries did not report the breakdown. The sample countries were not always the same.
b. HC = house connection.
c. PS = public standpost.
d. SC = sewer connection.
Source: Adapted from World Health Organization (WHO), *The International Drinking Water Supply and Sanitation Decade Review of Regional and Global Data*, WHO Offset Publication No. 92 (WHO, Geneva, 1986), p. 13.

Table 3.5 Percentage of Housing Units in Selected Countries with Access to Piped Water[a], 1975–84

	Total	Urban	Rural
Africa			
Cameroon	22.0	57.6	7.9
Egypt[b]	35.1	69.2	5.5
Malawi	12.4	62.1	8.6
Tunisia	26.4	54.7	3.0
North and Central America			
Canada	99.5	99.8	97.5
Cuba[c]	74.1	90.3	35.9
Panama	75.4	95.6	50.9
South America			
Bolivia	39.3	84.2	8.8
Brazil	53.2	75.8	3.2
Uruguay	80.6	87.8	41.7
Asia			
India[b]	90.4	94.0	78.3
Japan	92.7	95.0	84.5
Korea Rep	51.2	83.1	23.5
Pakistan	20.3	58.3	5.4
Sri Lanka	17.3	46.5	10.9
Thailand	13.9	79.4	2.6
Europe			
Bulgaria[d]	66.0	84.4	43.6
Czechoslovakia	91.6	97.0	80.1
Finland	90.6	95.2	82.7
Hungary[c]	81.2	94.4	65.8
Poland	69.7	90.1	37.1
Oceania			
French Polynesia	89.5	99.9	76.9

Notes:
a. Piped water refers to water provided within housing units by pipe from community-wide systems or from individual installations such as pressure tanks and pumps. Water source must be within 100 meters of dwelling.
b. U.N. Statistical Office, New York, unpublished data.
c. Distance from dwelling to piped water source not specified.
d. Indoor only.
Source: Adapted from United Nations (U.N.), *Compendium of Human Settlement Statistics, 1983* (U.N., New York, 1985), pp. 264-282.

Table 3.7 Average Number of Persons per Room in Urban and Rural Areas for Selected Countries, 1975–84

	Total	Rural	Urban
Cameroon	1.2	1.3	1.2
Tunisia	3.1	3.8	2.6
Canada	0.5	0.5	0.5
Cuba	1.0	1.0	1.0
El Savador	3.3	4.5	2.4
Greenland	1.5	2.2	1.4
Panama	1.8	2.1	1.6
Uruguay	2.1	2.1	2.1
Iran	2.0	2.2	1.8
Israel	1.2	1.4	1.2
Japan	0.8	0.7	0.8
Pakistan	3.6	3.8	3.2
Sri Lanka	2.1	2.1	2.3
Bulgaria	1.0	0.9	1.1
Czechoslovakia	0.9	0.9	0.9
Finland	0.8	0.8	0.8
France	0.8	0.8	0.4
Hungary	1.0	1.0	1.0
Poland	1.2	1.3	1.1
Sweden	0.6	0.6	0.6

Source: Adapted from United Nations (U.N.), *Compendium of Human Settlements Statistics 1983* (U.N., New York, 1985), pp. 251-263.

terms of persons per room, suggest that overcrowding is more of a problem in rural areas than in urban areas, although in some countries, notably Japan, Sri Lanka, and Bulgaria, the reverse appears to be true.

Access to electricity sharply distinguishes urban and rural households in the developing world. (See Table 3.8.) Although availability of electricity differs little between rural and urban areas in Europe and North America, in nearly all developing countries access in rural areas is much more limited (22). Although electricity is probably not a high priority for most rural households, compared to safe and convenient water supplies and health care services, for example, it is an indicator of differences in investments in infrastructures between rural and urban areas in the developing world.

the level of security provided: middle-class apartments are indistinguishable from temporary shacks. Even as an index of overcrowding, the number of occupants is inadequate because the definition of a room varies and differences in room size are not considered. The limited data available on overcrowding (see Table 3.7), as measured in

Table 3.6 Percentage of Housing Units in Selected Countries with Access to Toilets and Latrines[a], 1975—84

	Total	Urban	Rural
Africa			
Cameroon	72.4	92.8	64.2
North & Central America			
Canada	99.1	99.6	96.9
Cuba	91.1	95.8	79.7
El Salvador	62.4	92.2	37.2
Panama	87.0	96.6	75.5
US Virgin Islands	94.5	88.9	96.4
South America			
Bolivia	21.8	47.6	4.3
Brazil	76.1	92.6	41.9
Uruguay[b]	93.0	95.7	78.2
Asia			
Israel	90.0	98.5	90.9
Korea Rep	98.4	98.0	98.8
Sri Lanka	66.5	80.2	63.4
Thailand	50.3	95.4	42.5
Europe			
Finland	85.5	92.7	73.1
France	73.8	79.8	56.5
Oceania			
French Polynesia	97.3	99.2	94.9

Notes:
a. A toilet includes both flush and nonflush types (e.g., water closets, latrines, outhouses).
b. Data refer to households.
Source: United Nations (U.N.), *Compendium of Human Settlements Statistics 1983*, (U.N., New York, 1985), pp. 264-282.

Table 3.8 Percentage of Housing Units in Selected Countries with Access to Electricity, 1975–84

	Total	Urban	Rural
Africa			
Cameroon	5.9	19.2	0.5
Egypt[a]	45.7	77.0	18.6
Tunisia[a]	34.2	68.2	6.0
North & Central America			
Cuba	82.9	98.6	45.7
Panama	64.8	90.7	33.3
Trinidad and Tobago	83.6	91.6	75.5
US Virgin Islands	97.6	97.5	97.6
South America			
Bolivia	34.3	76.2	5.8
Peru	12.5	17.5	4.2
Uruguay	80.7	89.4	34.2
Asia			
Indonesia	13.9	46.7	5.5
Iran	48.3	X	14.2
Pakistan	30.6	71.0	14.7
Sri Lanka	14.9	45.9	8.0
Thailand	24.0	92.2	12.2
Oceania			
French Polynesia	74.7	93.0	50.9
Tonga	21.9	57.4	12.1

X = not available.
Note: a. U.N Statistical Office, New York, unpublished data.
Source: Adapted from United Nations (U.N.), *Compendium of Human Settlements Statistics, 1983* (U.N., New York, 1985), pp. 283-302.

Table 3.9 Availability of Complete Primary Schools in Urban and Rural Areas

	Countries	Complete Schools (percentage of total) Urban	Rural
Countries by Per Capita GNP (U.S. dollars)			
Up to $120 (excluding India)	9	53	36
India		57	49
$121-$250	7	72	32
$251-$750	16	77	62
$751-$1,500	2	89	56
Over $1,500	6	100	99
By Major Region			
Africa	16	79	54
Asia (excluding India)	9	94	66
India		57	49
South and Central America	10	88	34
Europe	5	98	99

Note: Table shows percentages of the total number of primary schools in each category (rural and urban) that offer the complete number of grades.
Source: Johannes F. Linn, *Cities in the Developing World: Policies for Their Equitable and Efficient Growth* (Oxford University Press, New York, 1983), p. 27.

Education

Urban dwellers generally have better access to schools than do rural dwellers. Table 3.9 shows the percentage of primary schools offering a complete number of grades in rural areas compared with urban areas. Rural areas are consistently behind urban areas in all developing regions. As a result of this differential access to schooling, the educational levels of urban populations tend to be higher than those of rural areas. (See Table 3.10.) Throughout the developing world, a higher proportion of rural people

Table 3.10 Distribution of Population Age 25 Years and Over without Schooling in Selected Countries, 1970–81

(percent)

	Year of Data	Percent Urban	Rural
Algeria	1971	73.5	89.9
Botswana[a]	1981	23.3	48.1
Cameroon	1976	57.0	78.4
Mali	1976	83.5	97.5
Morocco	1971	82.6	97.8
Canada	1981	1.9	2.3
Costa Rica	1973	7.2	23.6
Cuba	1981	2.0	8.1
Dominican Republic	1970	22.9	52.8
El Salvador[b]	1980	15.5	42.2
Guatemala	1973	85.2	98.7
Honduras	1974	29.5	64.5
Panama	1980	0.3	1.1
Puerto Rico	1980	40.9	63.1
Bolivia	1976	23.2	65.0
Brazil	1980	22.8	57.7
Chile	1970	8.3	29.8
Colombia	1973	14.2	38.4
Paraguay	1972	11.3	25.5
Afghanistan	1980	72.4	91.5
Indonesia	1980	24.4	45.3
Japan	1980	0.3	0.7
Malaysia	1970	32.5	47.5
Poland	1978	1.5	4.5
USSR[b]	1979	27.6	50.8

Notes:
a. 12 years and older.
b. 10 years and older.
Source: United Nations Educational, Scientific and Cultural Organization (UNESCO), *UNESCO Statistical Yearbook 1984 and 1985* (UNESCO, Paris, 1984, 1985).

lack schooling. In addition to availability of schools in urban areas, it is also the better educated young people who frequently migrate to urban areas (23).

Despite the availability of educational services in urban areas, an estimated 40 million urban children in the Third World do not attend school. Even where schooling is available, many cannot go because they must work. In Calcutta, for example, over 60 percent of all school-age children do not attend school because they work in tea-shops or in the homes of wealthy families or they must look after young siblings (24). Because these many children are forced to work, it is estimated that nearly half of all school-age children in the Third World (both urban and rural) drop out before they complete fourth grade (25).

RURAL-URBAN DYNAMICS

The dynamics of movement between rural and urban areas are often extremely complex. Although the world continues to become more urban, movement is not just one way—from rural areas to urban centers. The importance of urban-to-rural movement in some developed nations has already been noted. In many Third World nations, rural-to-rural movements are larger than rural-to-urban shifts, usually as a result of new land colonization programs. There are also substantial urban-to-urban and urban-to-rural movements in most nations.

Many people who move to an urban area do not expect to remain there permanently (26). Some rural-to-urban migrations are seasonal, for example, farmers and agricultural workers who go to cities when farm work is sparse. Others work mostly in the city in order to send money back to their families in the rural areas. This arrangement is common in many parts of sub-Saharan Africa, where husbands earn cash in the cities (or mines) and wives tend the farm and raise the children.

Changes in the economic and social structure of a society are the most important influences on population movements within a country. The rapid decline of the rural population in most developed countries during this century was due in large measure to two related factors: most new jobs were nonagricultural and were located in urban areas, and intensification of agriculture through mechanization, use of fertilizers and pesticides, and development of high-yielding varieties of grain and other food crops led to a greatly reduced demand for agricultural labor.

Such changes are also evident in some areas of the Third World. Increasing intensification of agriculture has reduced the number of rural jobs. Mechanized commercial agriculture tends to increase the concentration of land ownership, pushing small-scale largely subsistence farmers off their land.

But rural-urban migration in much of the Third World is more directly related to survival. Rural population growth is often rapid, in spite of increasing urbanization. Although there is no guarantee of an adequately paid job in urban centers, many people lose all possibility of making a livelihood in rural areas.

Links between Agricultural Development and Rural-Urban Migration (27)

Agricultural development can go hand in hand with rising prosperity for many local people and with rapidly increasing numbers employed in agriculture and agriculture-associated jobs. It can also go hand in hand with rapid impoverishment for most of the local population and the consequent migration to other regions. Box 3.1 illustrates the first point with the story of agricultural development in the Upper Valley of the Rio Negro in Argentina. Box 3.2, on the other hand, focuses on a small region in Brazil and illustrates what can happen when government policies designed to encourage agricultural development lead to more rapid rural-to-urban migration.

Several factors help determine the balance between these two extremes (28). One critical factor is concentration of land ownership. When land ownership is concentrated in a small group of people, decisions are likely to be based on maximizing their individual returns rather than on maximizing returns to the entire local population. If there is also a rural labor surplus (usually the case), landowners can keep wages low. Then agricultural production on plantations or large farms can be highly profitable—without raising the level of income among local people. Large landowners may also seek to expand their holdings, thereby driving small subsistence farmers off their land, as in Brazil. (See Box 3.2.) In the upper valley of the Rio Negro in Argentina, land ownership was distributed more widely, with most farmers able to obtain a good income on relatively small holdings. (See Box 3.1.)

In many cases, the impact of the Green Revolution in Asia and the development of commercial farming in Latin America have increased agricultural production and productivity at the price of impoverishment for many rural people in the area. Inequitable land ownership was a principal cause.

A second critical factor is the type of agricultural product being produced. The labor needed per hectare of land can vary by a factor of 100 or more for different crops and products. At one extreme, pastoralists may need 100–200 hectares or more per person. At the other extreme, an intensively cultivated farm of one or two hectares can provide a reasonable living for an entire family (29). One reason why Uruguay is among the world's most urbanized nations with so much of its urban population concentrated in Montevideo, the national capital, is because of the economic importance of cattle ranching. Cattle ranching requires large tracts of lands and relatively little labor. Concentration on this form of agriculture, combined with inequitable land ownership, means that only a relatively small rural population can earn a decent living. Further, cattle ranchers usually deal directly with banks, export houses, and industrial, transportation, and retail enterprises in the national capital, with little or no stimulus given to businesses in smaller urban centers near the ranches (30). Whereas, in the Upper Valley of the Rio Negro in Argentina, many small, relatively affluent farmers bought goods and services from local enterprises and stimulated local urban development (see Box 3.1), Uruguayan cattle ranchers stimulated business in Montevideo. This steering of profits from local business and employment to other locations is a third

---

Box 3.1 Balanced Agricultural and Urban Development (1)

Development of the Upper Valley of the Rio Negro in Argentina illustrates the possibility of positive links among agricultural, rural, and urban development. Within a 700-square-kilometer fertile river valley, the total population has grown from around 5,000 inhabitants in 1900 to more than 300,000 in 1981. Although growth and diversification of agricultural production have been the main engine of growth, more than 80 percent of the Upper Valley's population lives in urban centers with 5,000 or more inhabitants.

One hundred years ago, the first colonists had just begun to grow crops; establishment of a military fort there in 1879 provided the nucleus for the first town and provided much of the demand for food and fodder. But the Upper Valley's prosperity began to grow when a railway linked it to Buenos Aires in 1899 and thus gave local farmers access to both national and international markets and when government investment in a dam and flood control-irrigation system encouraged intensive agriculture.

For the first quarter of the 20th Century, in-migration to the region was rapid, including many foreign immigrants. Initially, alfalfa was the main crop, but it was gradually replaced by fruit trees—particularly apple and pear. The land-owning structure that developed was

relatively equitable: most of the land came to be farmed by farm owners who had sufficient capital to invest in intensive production. Relatively small farms producing a good income were the norm.

The growing number of prosperous farmers was a considerable stimulus to local urban development. Despite the region's small area of only 700 square kilometers, no single dominant urban center emerged. Rather, a chain of urban centers developed around railway stations along the river valley. Each had shops and businesses selling to farmers in their immediate vicinities, and they shared specialized businesses and government offices that served the whole valley.

Increasing agricultural production also stimulated many urban-based enterprises. First, cold storage plants were built. Because fruit crops usually ripen within a relatively short period, the transport system is strained during a small part of the year. Cold storage plants allowed the packaging and transportation of fruit to be spread over a longer time. In addition, industries developed to produce packing material and boxes and to produce cider, apple juice, jams, and dried and tinned fruits. Industries also grew to support the farmers; a large agricultural chemicals factory and a factory to produce machines for preparing the

land and picking fruit were built.

In 1957, the two national territories in which the Upper Valley was located became provinces. This change considerably increased power and resources available to the provincial government, and one of the Upper Valley's urban centers became the provincial capital. As the provincial administrative machinery grew to meet increased responsibilities, this also stimulated and supported urban development, although this stimulus was confined largely to the provincial capital.

Although the Upper Valley has not been without economic problems, it illustrates how growth in agricultural production can be linked to growth in employment related to agriculture and growth in urban centers.

References and Notes

1. This box is based on Mabel Manzanal and Cesar A. Vapnarsky, "The Development of the Upper Valley of Rio Negro and Its Periphery within the Comahue Region, Argentina," in *Small and Intermediate Urban Centres: Their Role in National and Regional Development in the Third World*, Jorge E. Hardoy and David Satterthwaite, eds. (Hodder and Stoughton, London, 1986).

Box 3.2 Growth in Agricultural Production, Rural Poverty, and Out-Migration (1)

Cruz das Almas is in the Reconcavo region of Northeast Brazil. Most farmers there cultivate cassava (the main subsistence food crop) and citrus fruits or tobacco as cash crops for sale. Small amounts of other food crops for family consumption are also grown.

Traditionally, farmers' choice of the mix of crops was based largely on availability of land and family labor. Farmers with small holdings tended to grow tobacco because it maximized farm income per hectare. When family size grew too large for the farm income to support, family members commonly migrated to

cities; the cash they sent back to the farm was important for many households. But as family members moved, the mix of crops was adjusted to the availability of fewer laborers.

The Brazilian Government has encouraged citrus production and supported it by favorable prices. As a result, citrus production has grown at the expense of cassava and tobacco. However, citrus production requires less labor and more capital than cassava and tobacco. As citrus cultivation has expanded, the demand for labor declined and small farms were absorbed by larger farms, resulting in a sharp rise in migration from the area.

Between 1960 and 1975, there was a sharp drop in the number of tenants and sharecroppers.

Government policies designed to encourage growth in agricultural production also encouraged concentration of landownership and migration from this rural area, most of which has been to cities.

References and Notes

1. This box is based on William S. Saint and William D. Goldsmith, "Cropping Systems, Structural Change and Rural-Urban Migration in Brazil," *World Development*, Vol. 8 (1980), pp. 259–272.

factor affecting agricultural and rural development, with a resulting impact on rural-to-urban migration. Such a removal of profits can also result from foreign or absentee ownership of large commercial agricultural enterprises.

Macroeconomic Policies, Sectoral Priorities, and Rural-Urban Dynamics (31)

Virtually every government policy, action, and expenditure has some impact on urban or rural distribution of development and the form that it takes. Many powerful influences on rural-urban migration arise from government policies with no explicit urban or rural purposes.

The extent to which government policies and actions help concentrate population in capital cities is illustrated in Lima, Peru. With 4.4 million metropolitan inhabitants in 1981, Lima was 10 times the size of the next largest city, Arequipa. A 1985 study concluded that "Lima has received a disproportionately high share of infrastructure and public investments, a response to the more vocal political pressures in the capital and greater awareness of the extent of public service lags in Lima than elsewhere. Utilities such as water and domestic electricity have been subsidized heavily in Lima. In an attempt to rationalize the invasion process, the government has supplied free lots in many peripheral areas to migrant households; mortgage finance has been heavily subsidized with most of the loans made in Lima. Until very recently, gasoline was priced far below the world price, again benefiting Lima because two thirds of the country's motor vehicles are concentrated there. Food prices have also been subsidized, shifting the internal terms of trade against the rural areas and resulting in heavy government support for the food import bills for urban consumers. The persistent over-valuation of the currency harmed the agricultural areas and natural resource regions (i.e., the periphery) by eroding their export potential and subsidizing the main focus of import demand, Lima itself (32)."

Many governments have tried to support industries producing import substitutes with policies that have significantly affected rural-urban migration. In most instances, subsidizing industrial investment has resulted in concentrating productive investment (and people) in the largest cities—often the national capitals. In Brazil, the states of Sao Paulo and Rio de Janeiro (containing Brazil's two

largest metropolitan centers) have benefited most from government incentives to promote import substitution while some of the poorest most rural states benefited least (33). In Nigeria, indirect subsidies from national trade policies have favored enterprises in Lagos (with more than 5 million people) and the region around it (34). In Thailand, enterprises in Bangkok, much the largest city, have benefited from import substitution policies. By the end of the 1960s, protected industries in Thailand were given full duty exemption for capital goods and raw materials (most of this protected industry is located in Bangkok) (35).

For countries that are traditionally major exporters of agricultural produce, the exchange rate of the national currency against those of major trading partners affects the return that export crop farmers receive. An overvalued national currency to cheapen imports reduces farmers' returns. One reason for rural-urban migration in Nigeria during the 1970s was the fact that oil exports kept the exchange rate of the Nigerian currency high against the currencies of nations that had previously been major markets for its agricultural exports. This policy led to extremely low prices for export crops and lowered the costs of imports, including basic foodstuffs. Rural incomes suffered and urban consumers benefited (36). Similarly, the fact that the Argentine peso became increasingly strong against the U.S. dollar and currencies of other nations to which Argentina exported during the second half of the 1970s seriously affected the income of farmers producing export crops (37).

The governments of many developing nations set prices for agricultural products. These price-setting policies can be designed to accomplish several goals. They can favor urban dwellers by keeping food costs low, or they can stimulate agricultural development by creating attractive price incentives for greater production. A study of agricultural pricing in Thailand, Egypt, Argentina, and Pakistan found that government intervention in setting crop prices had the effect of taxing the farm sector with large income transfers to urban areas (38). In Pakistan, low urban food prices have helped to keep wages low in industry, which, combined with the low prices of cotton and other raw materials, helped maintain export industries' competitive position in the world market (39).

Farmers in many sub-Saharan African nations received less than half the world market value for their crops from government crop-purchasing agencies. One main reason for the rapid decline in cocoa production in Ghana from 1967 to 1983 was the heavy tax imposed on farmers by the government through the Cocoa Marketing Board's pricing policies (40). Ghana subsequently revised its agricultural pricing policies in 1983, with a substantial positive effect on agricultural production and incomes.

A recent study of development in Mexico (41) illustrates how government policies helped ensure that the Mexico City Metropolitan Area remained the main focus for rural-urban migration throughout the 1950s and 1960s. The Federal District (the central part of the metropolitan area) received the highest share of public investment in transport, water, and power, a "disproportionately large share" (42) of total outlays on education and subsidized prices for water, corn, electric power, diesel fuel, and public transportation. Further, railroad freight rates "were structured to favor routes to and from Mexico City" while property in the Federal District "was relatively under-valued for tax purposes and other states were taxed at relatively high rates" (43). Mexico City and its wider metropolitan area also received many of the new industries encouraged by the federal import substitution policy.

Thus many government policies and expenditures whose objectives are social, economic, or political have major impacts on urban and rural development, effecting rural-to-urban migration. As one study stressed, "eliminating sectoral distortions may do more for decentralized development than all the myriad spatial efforts conventionally proposed by Third World policy makers" (44).

Government Structure and Rural-Urban Dynamics

In Third World nations, power and resources are frequently highly centralized in the national government, much more so than in developed nations. Local government employees in most developed countries usually outnumber their national counterparts. But in many developing nations, central government employees greatly outnumber local government employees. According to a recent survey of local government in the Third World, many local governments are "fragmented, confused about their functions and all too often either invisible or largely ceremonial" (45). This centralization of power and resources also helps ensure that government policies and expenditures tend to concentrate in national capitals, whereas investments made elsewhere often do not match local needs and resources.

RECENT DEVELOPMENTS

CHINA REDEFINES ITS URBAN POPULATION

According to official statistics, China's urban population grew from 212 million in 1982 to 382 million by 1985. At the same time, the rural population fell from 804 million to 663 million (46). This dramatic change, however, did not result from massive and sudden population shifts, but rather from the redefinition of what constitutes an urban area.

During 1978–82, China's urban population grew an average of 6.1 percent a year (47). This impressive growth rate was due to several factors that occurred in the post-Mao period. First, during 1978 and 1979, many of China's educated young people rebelled against the long-standing policy of sending new graduates to rural areas, and many who had been exiled from the cities during the Mao period practiced civil disobedience until they were allowed to return home. Studies of one city show that more than two thirds of the in-migration during the late 1970s was returnees sent to the countryside during the Cultural Revolution. Second, changes in economic policy during the post-Mao period made it possible for peasants to become entrepreneurs, selling agricultural produce and household products at village markets. Third, in 1979, a number of jurisdictions that had lost their city status in the 1950s and 1960s were reclassified as urban areas. In addition, some towns expanded to form new cities. Together, these measures account for most of the 12.5 million increase in urban population in 1979.

In 1983, however, China's urban population suddenly swelled by 30 million, an increase of 13.1 percent, when 44 cities were either newly created or reinstated as urban areas through redefinition of some rural areas and expansion of the boundaries of some cities, particularly those with populations between 500,000 and 2 million (48). An estimated 70 percent of the 1983 urban population growth was due to redefinition and boundary expansion; only 30 percent was due to migration (49).

Beginning in 1984, even more dramatic increases in the urban population resulted from adjustments in the criteria for designating incorporated towns. Previously, in order to be incorporated, communities were required to have populations of 3,000 or more, with at least 70 percent of the total categorized as nonagricultural workers eligible for grain rations (50). (Towns with populations of 2,500–3,000 qualified as urban areas if 85 percent of the inhabitants were engaged in nonagricultural activities.)

The new criteria for urban areas established in 1984 varied by province. In Sichuan Province, for example, communities were required to have at least 2,500 people, at least 50 percent of them categorized as nonagricultural. Gansu Province required that communities have at least 2,000 people, of whom 25 percent are nonagricultural, in order to be incorporated as an urban area. In other places, the criteria included measures of industrial output (51). These variations in requirements, an effort to take account of local reality, will probably continue to change as China's urbanization policy evolves.

China's redefinition of its urban population has had a significant impact on the population statistics of the nation. At the end of 1984, there were more than twice as many towns as the year before. China's urban population had increased 31 percent, or 89 million, with 70 million attributed to the new criteria for urban areas. In 1985, another 52 million urban dwellers were added to the list, bringing the total urban population up to 382 million (52).

Such a major change in the population statistics of a country that contains about 40 percent of Asia's total population—and nearly a quarter of the world population—significantly affects regional and world data on urbanization. The U.N. estimates of China's population in 1985, based on the old definition of urban places, showed China with 21 percent of its population in urban areas. (See Chapter 17, "Human Settlements," Table 17.1.) On the basis of the new definitions, China's urban population in 1985 was 36.6 percent of the total. This redefinition shifts the percentage of Asia's urban population from 28.2 to 34.1.

THE INTERNATIONAL YEAR OF SHELTER FOR THE HOMELESS

The United Nations has declared 1987 as the International Year of Shelter for the Homeless. Departing from a more traditional definition of homelessness, the United Nations has defined a much larger category of people who lack a "real home." This new definition relates not merely to the physical structure of the dwelling but also to the economic and social role that a home plays in everyday life. A "real home" must have basic services such as access to potable water and sanitation. It must also guarantee the inhabitants a measure of safety and security. Thus a squatter household living with the daily fear of being bulldozed cannot be said to have a real home. Further, a real home must be within easy reach of centers of employment, education, and health care. In most Third World cities, there are large concentrations of illegal developments on the periphery of cities from which the dwellers have to travel several hours a day to and from work. Similar travel times are necessary for any visit to health services. These too cannot be regarded as "real homes." (Also see Box 3.3.)

The United Nation intends the Year of Shelter for the Homeless to center world governments' attention on the need for increased efforts to provide adequate housing for the poor. Major efforts during 1987 will focus on collecting information on the extent and severity of the problem of "homelessness" and on publicizing the need for government action.

Box 3.3 The Pavement People of Bombay (1)

Homelessness has been a continuous problem in India for decades. During the 1961 Indian national census, nearly 1.5 million "house-less persons" were counted, with over 62,000 of them in Greater Bombay (constituting 1.5 percent of the city's population at that time). Nearly all these people live on the pavements or sidewalks of India's major cities.

In order to learn more about the most destitute group of people in India, a nongovernmental organization called the Society for Promotion of Area Resource Centres (SPARC) in Bombay instituted the first detailed survey of pavement people ever carried out in India. SPARC conducted the survey in 1985 and concentrated on one section of central Bombay, which included 6,000 pavement households comprising nearly 27,000 individuals.

The startling results of this unique census shed light not only on the basic demographics of this neglected group but also on a number of important trends in urban population dynamics, factors that India's city planners will have to reckon with if they are to cope with the swelling numbers of urban poor.

ECONOMIC PROFILE

The economic profile that emerged from the survey was revealing, if unanticipated. Rather than finding a high rate of joblessness, the researchers discovered that the proportion of wage earners to the total pavement population was 43 percent, somewhat higher than the national average of 38 percent. Like the national trend, however, 73 percent of the men were wage earners, while only 27 percent of the women earned an income.

However, unlike the national trends, 74 percent of the pavement people surveyed earned less than $1.80 a day, well below Bombay's minimum wage. Overall, 67.6 percent of the working men fell into this category, along with an overwhelming 90.9 percent of the women wage earners. Only one quarter—26 percent—earned more than 19 rupees a day.

Another finding of the survey was the diverse kinds of employment performed by this group of pavement dwellers. In all, over 90 different occupations were listed during the census, but were grouped for analysis into five major categories. Predictably, the largest group—33.4 percent—were unskilled workers toiling away at strenuous jobs as manual laborers on construction sites, as dock workers and as headloaders. Surprisingly, the second largest group (21.5 percent) consisted of traders or vendors of edible goods and other items, usually hawked from door to door in the middle-class neighborhoods of the city. Self-employed people accounted for 14 percent, while domestic servants comprised the fourth category (12 percent), followed by less than 12 percent engaged in skilled labor such as metal-working, machinery, tailoring, and plumbing.

MIGRATION HISTORY

Another unexpected finding was that almost 60 percent of all the pavement people surveyed had migrated to Bombay over a decade ago; only 20 percent had arrived within the last six years. This discovery dispels the widespread notion that pavement people are rootless transients and terminal derelicts. Living in the street has become a way of life for most of them.

When asked why they migrated to Bombay, 67 percent cited abject poverty, landlessness, and lack of employment opportunities in their native provinces. The majority of pavement dwellers (52.4 percent) claimed to own no assets whatsoever before coming to Bombay—certainly a powerful reason to move to the city in search of better opportunities.

CONCLUSIONS

If some 27,000 pavement people reside in only one small section of central Bombay, their total numbers must be staggering. This entire segment of the population—at the bottom of the economic ladder—has been almost totally neglected by city administrators and planners. And their ranks are growing as more destitute and landless people stream in from the countryside in search of a better life. This group of displaced people performs important and vital tasks for the economy of the city, such as collecting garbage and recycling discarded metals, plastic, and glass.

Very low wages eliminate them from the housing market, even from slum dwellings, so they are restricted to the streets, where they live in makeshift "houses" fashioned out of cardboard, canvas, and other scrap materials.

If city planners in India and other Third World countries are to begin to tackle the immense human problems posed by slums and squatter settlements, they must also recognize the plight of the pavement dwellers.

References and Notes

1. This box is based on Society for Promotion of Area Resource Centres (SPARC), *We the Invisible: A Census of Pavement Dwellers* (SPARC, Bombay, 1985).

References and Notes

1. U.N. Department of International Economic and Social Affairs, *World Population Prospects: Estimates and Projections as Assessed in 1984* (United Nations, New York, 1986), pp. 140–157.
2. Tertius Chandler and Gerald Fox, *3,000 Years of Urban Growth* (Academic Press, New York and London, 1974).
3. Jorge E. Hardoy and David Satterthwaite, "Urban Change in the Third World: Are Recent Trends a Useful Pointer to the Urban Future," *Habitat International*, Vol. 10, No. 3 (1986).
4. Lester Brown, *In the Human Interest* (W.W. Norton and Company, New York, 1974).
5. Care should be taken not to confuse increasing urbanization with urban growth. Increasing urbanization is an increase in the proportion of the national population living in urban centers. It is largely the result of net movement of rural population into urban areas. Natural population increase does not lead to increasing urbanization unless rates of natural increase are more rapid among urban populations than they are among rural populations. Urban population growth derives both from net movement of formerly rural inhabitants into urban centers and from a natural increase in urban centers. To some extent, both urban population growth and increasing urbanization can be increased by rural settlements' growing sufficiently that they become redefined as urban centers (i.e., a formerly rural population is suddenly 'urban'). Both can also increase through an extension of cities' boundaries, which then encompass people who were formerly designated as rural. Note that a nation can stop urbanizing (i.e., the proportion of the national population living in urban centers stabilizes) but still have quite rapid urban population growth from a natural increase.
6. Jorge E. Hardoy and David Satterthwaite, "Small and Intermediate Urban Centres: What Role for Governments?" forthcoming.
7. Cities here are standard metropolitan statistical areas with populations exceeding 100,000 in 1980.
8. Nigel Harris, "Some Trends in the Evolution of Big Cities: Studies of the U.S.A. and India," *Habitat International*, Vol. 8, No. 1 (1984), pp. 7–28.
9. Derived from statistics in Government of Kenya, *Economic Survey 1981* (Central Bureau of Statistics, Nairobi).
10. Calculated from census data cited in Harry W. Richardson, "Planning Strategies and Policies for Metropolitan Lima," *Third World Planning Review*, Vol. 6, No. 2 (1984) pp. 123–137.
11. Derived from census data cited in Carlos Larrea Maldonado, "Crecimiento Urbano y Dinamica de las Ciudades Intermedias en el Ecuador," in *Poder Local y Ciudades Intermedias en America Latina* (CLACSO-CIUDAD, Quito, Ecuador, 1985).
12. M.N. Buch, "Urbanization Trends in India: The Emerging Regional Patterns" (unpublished, 1985).
13. Jorge E. Hardoy and David Satterthwaite, "A Survey of Empirical Material on the Factors Affecting the Development of Small and Intermediate Urban Centers," in *Small and Intermediate Urban Centres: Their Role in Regional and National Development in the Third World*, Jorge E. Hardoy and David Satterthwaite, eds. (Hodder and Stoughton, London, 1986), pp. 279–334.
14. Edward W. Soja and C.E. Weaver, "Urbanization and Underdevelopment in East Africa," in *Patterns of Urbanization and Counter-Urbanization*, B.L.J. Berry, ed. (Sage Publications, Beverly Hills, California, 1976), pp. 232–266.
15. B.S. Bhooshan, "Bangalore, Mandya and Mysore Districts," in *Small and Intermediate Urban Centres: Their Role in Regional and National Development in the Third World*, Jorge E. Hardoy and David Satterthwaite, eds. (Hodder and Stoughton, London, 1986), pp. 131–184.
16. David Aradeon, *et al.* "Southwest Nigeria," in *Small and Intermediate Urban Centres: Their Role in Regional and National Development in the Third World*, Jorge E. Hardoy and David Satterthwaite, eds. (Hodder and Stoughton, London, 1986), pp. 228–278.
17. Walter Mertens, "Fertility and Mortality Trends and Policies and the Urban Future," presented at the International Conference on Population and the Urban Future, Barcelona, Spain, May 1986.
18. *Ibid.*
19. J.E. Rodhe, "Why The Other Half Dies: The Science and Politics of Child Mortality in the Third World," in *Assignment Children 61–62* (1983), cited in A. Rossi-Espagnet, *Primary Health Care in Urban Areas: Reaching the Urban Poor in Developing Countries: a State of the Art Report* (United Nations Children's Fund and World Health Organization, Geneva, 1984).
20. S.S. Basta, "Nutrition and Health in Low Income Urban Areas of the Third World," *Ecology of Food and Nutrition*, Vol. 6 (1977), pp. 113–124.
21. World Health Organization (WHO), *International Drinking Water Supply and Sanitation Decade Review of Regional and Global Data*, Publication No. 92 (WHO, Geneva, 1986), p. 13.
22. United Nations (U.N.), *Compendium of Human Settlements Statistics, 1983* (U.N., New York, 1985), pp. 283–302.
23. Johannes F. Linn, *Cities in the Developing World: Policies for Their Equitable and Efficient Growth* (Oxford University Press, New York, 1983), p. 27.
24. *Op. cit.* 17.
25. *Op. cit.* 17.
26. Joan M. Nelson, "Sojourners versus New Urbanites: Causes and Consequences of Temporary versus Permanent Cityward Migration in Developing Countries," *Economic Development and Cultural Change*, Vol. 24, No. 4 (1976), p. 721.
27. This section is based on Jorge E. Hardoy and David Satterthwaite, "A Survey of Empirical Material on the Factors Affecting the Development of Small and Intermediate Urban Centres," pp. 335–397, and "Government Policies and Small and Intermediate Urban Centres," pp. 279–334, in *Small and Intermediate Urban Centres: Their Role in Regional and National Development in the Third World*, Jorge E. Hardoy and David Satterthwaite, eds. (Hodder and Stoughton, London, 1986).
28. *Op. cit.* 27, p. 298.
29. In some areas with fertile soil and climates that permit double or triple cropping, an adequate living for a family of six or seven members can be made from less than 1 hectare. Chinese farmers are reported to have maintained their families on holdings of between one fifth and one tenth of a hectare during the 1930s; fertilizers were pig, buffalo, horse, and human excreta, often gathered from roads, inns, sties, and drains in the locality. H.T. Fei and C. Chang, *Earthbound China* (University of Chicago Press, 1945), cited in Gerald Leach, *Energy Food Production* (International Institute for Environment and Education, London, 1975).
30. Anne Collin Delavaud, *Uruguay: Medium and Small Cities* (Institut des Hautes Etudes de l'Amérique Latine, Laboratoire Associé du Centre National de la Recherche Scientifique, Paris, 1976).
31. This section is based on Jorge E. Hardoy and David Satterthwaite, "Government Policies and Small and Intermediate Urban Centres," in *Small and Intermediate Urban Centres: Their Role in Regional and National Development in the Third World*, Jorge E. Hardoy and David Satterthwaite, eds. (Hodder and Stoughton, London, 1986).
32. *Op. cit.* 10, pp. 123–124.
33. William G. Tyler, *The Brazilian Sectoral Incentive System and the Regional Incidence of Non Spatial Incentive Policies* (The World Bank, Washington, D.C., 1983).
34. M. Daly, *Development Planning in Nigeria* (University of Ibadan Planning Studies Programme, Nigeria, 1977), p. 2, cited in Michael O. Filani, "Nigeria: The Need to Modify Centre-Down Development Planning" in *Development from Above or Below*, Walter B. Stohr and D.R. Fraser Taylor, eds. (John Wiley and Sons, Chichester, United Kingdom, 1981), p. 297.
35. Mike Douglass, "Thailand: Territorial Dissolution and Alternative Regional Development for the Central Plains," in *Development from Above and Below*, Walter B. Stohr and D.R. Fraser Taylor, eds. (John Wiley and Sons, Chichester, United Kingdom, 1981), p. 194.
36. A.M. O'Connor, *Secondary Cities and Food Production in Nigeria* (International Institute for Environment and Development, London, 1984).
37. Mabel Manzanal and Cesar A. Vapnarsky, "The Development of the Upper Valley of Rio Negro and its Periphery Within the Comahue Region, Argentina," in *Small and Intermediate Urban Centres: Their Role in Regional and National Development in the Third World*, Jorge E. Hardoy and David Satterthwaite, eds. (Hodder and Stoughton, London, 1986).

38. Malcolm D. Bale and Ernst Lutz, *Price Distortions in Agriculture and Their Effects: An International Comparison* (The World Bank, Washington, D.C., 1979), p. 26.

39. Carl Gotsch and Gilbert Brown, *Prices, Taxes and Subsidies in Pakistan Agriculture 1960-76* (The World Bank, Washington, D.C., 1980).

40. The World Bank, *Accelerated Development in Sub-Saharan Africa* (The World Bank, Washington, D.C., 1981), p. 26.

41. Ian Scott, *Urban and Spatial Development in Mexico* (The Johns Hopkins University Press, Baltimore, Maryland, 1982).

42. *Ibid.*, page 111.

43. *Op. cit.* 41, p. 118.

44. Andrew M. Hamer, *Decentralized Urban Development and Industrial Location Behavior in Sao Paulo, Brazil: A Synthesis of Research Issues and Conclusions* (The World Bank, Washington, D.C., 1984), pp. 18–19.

45. Glynn Cochrane, *Policies for Strengthening Local Government in Developing Countries* (The World Bank, Washington, D.C., 1984) pp. 3–4.

46. Judith Banister, *Urban-Rural Population Projections for China* (U.S. Bureau of the Census, Washington, D.C., 1986).

47. *Ibid.*, Table 2, p. 4.

48. *Op. cit.* 46, p. 4 and pp. 11–12.

49. *Op. cit.* 46, p. 13.

50. *Op. cit.* 46, p. 2 and p. 14.

51. *Op. cit.* 46, p. 15.

52. *Op. cit.* 46.

4. Food and Agriculture

Record cereal harvests and continuing food shortages for millions continue to dominate global food and agriculture. Supported by government subsidies and protectionism, agriculture in industrialized market economies, particularly in North America and Europe, continues to produce large food surpluses. However, there is growing concern that such policies are becoming financially burdensome and that, in the long run, these high levels of production may be environmentally unsustainable.

Although the green revolution increased food production in some regions of the Third World (e.g., India and Indonesia), in other areas, such as sub-Saharan Africa, food production has not kept pace with population growth. About 14 percent of all cropland in developing countries grows export crops, most of which face gloomy prospects in world markets. Chronic food shortages call into question whether this land is being used to best advantage. The need for food security requires new patterns of agricultural production capable of making a positive and lasting impact on the income and nutritional requirements of the poor.

Substantial increases in the production of cash crops have led to lower prices for key export crops. Agricultural exports provide valuable foreign exchange for most developing countries; yet long-run price declines and the impact of mounting debt on global demand have undercut these earnings. These trends have important implications for agricultural development, allocation of resources, and management of the resource base.

A crucial concern is whether current trends in agricultural production and the allocation of resources between cash and food crops are leading to a sustainable system of global agriculture. The choice of crops is crucial to the sustainable use of land and other resources. There is no general rule that either cash crops or food crops are ecologically more sustainable; instead, the main concern is striking a balance between protecting resources and earning foreign exchange while improving conditions of the poor and malnourished.

The environmental costs of increasing production in the United States and the European Community (EC) suggest the need for reforms. Recent farm legislation in the United States attempts to combat both resource mismanagement, especially soil erosion, and surplus production. In the EC, there is concern that excessive use of fertilizers is causing environmental and health hazards.

Technological innovations in Third World agriculture may offer the best possibility of increasing production of the basic staple food crops. Investment in ecologically sound agricultural techniques for the Third World has occurred in three major categories: alternative agricultural systems, such as agroforestry and intercropping, that enhance productivity while conserving resources; new high-yielding, low-input varieties of staple crops; and biotechnology.

CONDITIONS AND TRENDS

AGRICULTURAL OUTPUT: TRENDS AND PROSPECTS

Underlying the recent expansion in global agricultural output are many important variations among regions and types of produce.

Food and Agriculture

Table 4.1 Total Cereal Production
(million metric tons)

	1971	1974	1977	1980	1981	1982	1983	1984	1985
Developed Market Economies	467.1	442.0	506.7	532.5	605.4	608.5	481.9	622.9	643.7
Eastern Europe and USSR	242.8	263.3	265.9	264.1	234.6	261.7	272.5	259.9	273.7
Total[a] Developed	**709.9**	**705.3**	**772.7**	**796.7**	**840.0**	**870.1**	**754.4**	**882.8**	**917.4**
Africa	43.4	44.1	43.3	50.7	48.7	51.8	44.6	45.8	59.7
Latin America	72.6	78.0	86.1	88.5	104.4	105.2	98.6	106.9	112.4
Near East	44.0	45.2	51.5	55.6	59.7	58.5	56.1	54.0	61.1
Far East	209.5	211.3	252.2	273.5	289.7	276.3	316.9	319.5	321.4
Asian Centrally Planned Economies	236.3	249.1	272.0	303.1	310.1	341.4	373.3	395.0	369.0
Total[a] Developing	**605.8**	**627.7**	**705.1**	**771.5**	**812.8**	**833.3**	**889.6**	**921.2**	**923.6**
World	**1,315.7**	**1,333.1**	**1,477.8**	**1,568.1**	**1,652.8**	**1,703.4**	**1,644.0**	**1,804.0**	**1,841.0**

Note: a. Totals may not add due to rounding.
Sources:
1. United Nations Food and Agriculture Organization (FAO), *Production Yearbook* 1972, 1976, 1980, and 1984 (FAO, Rome, 1973, 1977, 1981, and 1985).
2. United Nations Food and Agriculture Organization (FAO), *FAO Monthly Bulletin of Statistics*, Vol. 9, No. 4 (1986).

Supplies of the world's cereals—wheat, rice, and coarse grains—will likely reach record levels in 1986–87. The United Nations Food and Agriculture Organization (FAO) forecasts cereal supplies at 2.058 billion metric tons, some 3 percent higher than in 1985–86 (1). This increase reflects large opening stocks and favorable prospects for 1986 harvests. World cereal production, however, was expected to drop from 1.84 billion metric tons in 1985 to 1.82 billion metric tons in 1986. The drop is partly attributable to an expected 3.5 percent decline in coarse grains due mainly to reduced plantings in the United States (2). This drop could mark the start of an era when surplus production in the United States is less pronounced, particularly as the provisions of the 1985 Farm Act take effect. Generally, there has been an upward trend in world food production since the early 1970s. (See Table 4.1.)

Up to 1983, the developed world produced more cereals than the developing world, but recently the position has been reversed. Most of the rise in Third World output, however, has come from two countries: India and China. Until 1985, cereal production in Africa had been stagnant, reflecting the devastating drought conditions of the mid-1970s and 1983–84. (See Table 4.1.)

Noncereal food production also increased steadily since the early 1970s. Only Eastern Europe and the Soviet Union experienced little growth. In 1985, for the first time, developing nations outproduced developed nations in noncereals. (See Table 4.2.)

There is also an upward trend in principal nonfood export crop production. Only the developing countries of Africa and the Near East experienced no growth in this sector during the 1970s and early 1980s. By contrast, the most rapid growth has taken place in the Asian Centrally Planned Economies. (See Table 4.3.) In 1985 commodity prices and export earnings came under increased pressure from weaker demand associated with a slowdown in world economic growth while supplies of most primary commodities remained stable. Because of their heavy dependence on export crops, developing countries have generally felt the impact of depressed world market prices more than most developed countries (3). Faced with foreign exchange constraints and huge debt repayments, many developing countries have little alternative but to expand export crop production and curb imports, including agricultural imports.

Of all the developing regions, Africa suffers from the most severe agricultural problems, which are the culmina-

Table 4.2 Noncereal Food Production[a]
(million metric tons)

	1971	1974	1977	1980	1981	1982	1983	1984	1985
Developed Market Economies	561.3	577.0	586.6	615.1	613.9	636.8	626.3	637.7	642.4
Eastern Europe and USSR	379.1	402.3	398.2	361.6	385.9	392.7	408.0	428.1	395.8
Total[b] Developed	**940.4**	**979.3**	**984.8**	**976.7**	**999.8**	**1,029.5**	**1,034.3**	**1,065.8**	**1,038.2**
Africa	114.3	122.0	130.6	148.8	152.5	158.2	156.1	164.4	167.3
Latin America	173.4	180.0	192.4	200.9	206.6	211.9	204.7	210.8	214.4
Near East	59.1	64.8	74.6	85.0	89.0	93.5	95.2	95.1	100.0
Far East	168.8	184.9	216.3	237.9	252.0	258.5	266.2	274.6	280.7
Asian Centrally Planned Economies	261.0	273.2	240.8	288.7	278.6	285.1	305.3	312.4	316.5
Total[b] Developing	**776.6**	**824.9**	**854.7**	**961.3**	**978.7**	**1,007.2**	**1,027.6**	**1,057.3**	**1,078.9**
World	**1,717.0**	**1,804.2**	**1,839.5**	**1,938.0**	**1,978.5**	**2,036.7**	**2,061.9**	**2,123.1**	**2,117.1**

Notes:
a. Includes root crops, pulses, vegetables and melons, fruits, nuts, sugar, meat, milk, and eggs.
b. Totals may not add due to rounding.
Sources:
1. United Nations Food and Agriculture Organization (FAO), *Production Yearbook* 1972, 1976, 1980, and 1984 (FAO, Rome, 1973, 1977, 1981, and 1985).
2. United Nations Food and Agriculture Organization (FAO), *FAO Monthly Bulletin of Statistics*, Vol. 9, No. 4 (1986).

Table 4.3 Nonfood Production[a]
(million metric tons)

	1971	1974	1977	1980	1981	1982	1983	1984	1985
Developed Market Economies	5.8	6.0	6.7	6.0	7.1	6.3	5.1	6.5	6.8
Eastern Europe and USSR	4.3	4.6	4.7	4.6	4.6	4.7	4.7	4.4	4.7
Total[b] Developed	**10.1**	**10.6**	**11.4**	**10.6**	**11.7**	**11.0**	**9.8**	**10.9**	**11.5**
Africa	3.8	3.9	3.6	3.6	3.7	3.5	3.6	3.8	4.1
Latin America	6.4	7.1	6.6	6.9	8.0	7.3	7.3	7.4	8.2
Near East	2.1	2.2	2.1	2.0	1.9	2.0	2.1	2.1	2.1
Far East	10.2	10.4	10.8	11.4	11.6	11.4	11.3	12.2	13.4
Asian Centrally Planned Economies	4.2	5.5	4.8	5.9	7.0	8.1	8.4	10.9	10.9
Total[b] Developing	**26.7**	**29.1**	**27.9**	**29.8**	**32.2**	**32.3**	**32.7**	**36.4**	**38.7**
World	**36.7**	**39.7**	**39.3**	**40.4**	**43.9**	**43.3**	**42.5**	**47.3**	**50.2**

Notes:
a. Includes cocoa beans, green coffee, tea, vegetable fibers, tobacco, natural rubber, and greasy wool.
b. Totals may not add due to rounding.
Sources:
1. United Nations Food and Agriculture Organization (FAO), *Production Yearbook* 1972, 1976, 1980, and 1984 (FAO, Rome, 1973, 1977, 1981, and 1985).
2. United Nations Food and Agriculture Organization (FAO), *FAO Monthly Bulletin of Statistics*, Vol. 9, No. 4 (1986).

tion of rapid population growth, insufficient and inappropriate innovation, cultivation of marginal and sensitive lands, severe deforestation and erosion, and misguided agricultural policies (4). While per capita food production increased substantially everywhere else since the early 1970s, it declined in Africa. (See Figure 4.1.) In sub-Saharan Africa, per capita consumption of cereals has fallen with production, while dependence on imports—particularly wheat and rice—increased. (See Figure 4.2.) Although the worst impacts of the 1983–84 drought and

Figure 4.1 Per Capita Food Production in Asian and African Developing Countries, 1971–84

(1974–76 = 100)

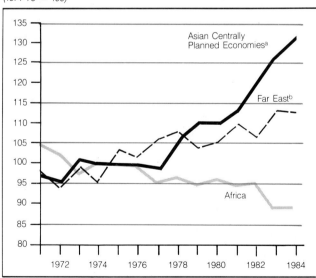

Notes:
a. Asian Centrally Planned Economies include China, Mongolia, Democratic Kampuchea, Viet Nam, and the Democratic People's Republic of Korea.
b. Far East includes Bangladesh, Bhutan, Brunei Darus-salam, Burma, East Timor, Hong Kong, India, Indonesia, Republic of Korea, Laos, Macau, Malaysia, Maldives, Nepal, Pakistan, Philippines, Singapore, Sri Lanka, and Thailand.
Sources:
1. United Nations Food and Agriculture Organization (FAO), *Production Yearbook 1982* (FAO, Rome, 1983), Table 10.
2. United Nations Food and Agriculture Organization (FAO), *Production Yearbook 1984* (FAO, Rome, 1985), Table 9.

famine seem to be over, in mid-1986 FAO declared that six African countries were still facing "exceptional food emergencies" (5).

Total consumption of basic food staples expanded at an average annual rate of 3.3 percent between 1966 and 1980 in all developing countries. (See Table 4.4.) The amount used directly for food rather than animal feed accounts for about 70 percent of the total.

Between 1980 and 2000, increased total food demand is projected to exceed the growth of food output in all developing regions except Asia, despite the fact that per capita food production in Latin America, North Africa, and the Middle East will continue to grow. Even though Latin America's increased production rate is projected to be the most rapid, the demand has been expanding rapidly as well, outstripping the growth in output. With its rapid population growth, sub-Saharan Africa's food consumption is expected to grow 3.6 percent a year, substantially outpacing the estimated growth in food output. Per capita food production is projected to decline in the region (6). (See Table 4.4.)

In summary, although total world production of food is expanding faster than demand, causing global prices to decline, the increase will not keep pace with growing populations in some regions, notably sub-Saharan Africa. Many developing countries are also increasing production of agricultural commodities for export, despite global surpluses and depressed prices for some commodities. The key question facing planners is how agricultural resources and production should be allocated to ensure sufficient food for the world's poor, stable income for Third World exporters, and a sustainable resource base for future production.

AGRICULTURAL COMMODITIES: PRODUCTION AND PRICE TRENDS

Many developing countries depend on agricultural exports for a sizable share of export earnings. Twelve of the most important export crops for the Third World are coffee, cocoa, sugar, rubber, cotton, tea, palm oil, tobacco, wheat, maize, rice, and soybeans (7). (See Box 4.1 for

Figure 4.2 Production, Consumption, and Imports of Cereals in Sub-Saharan Africa, 1965–84

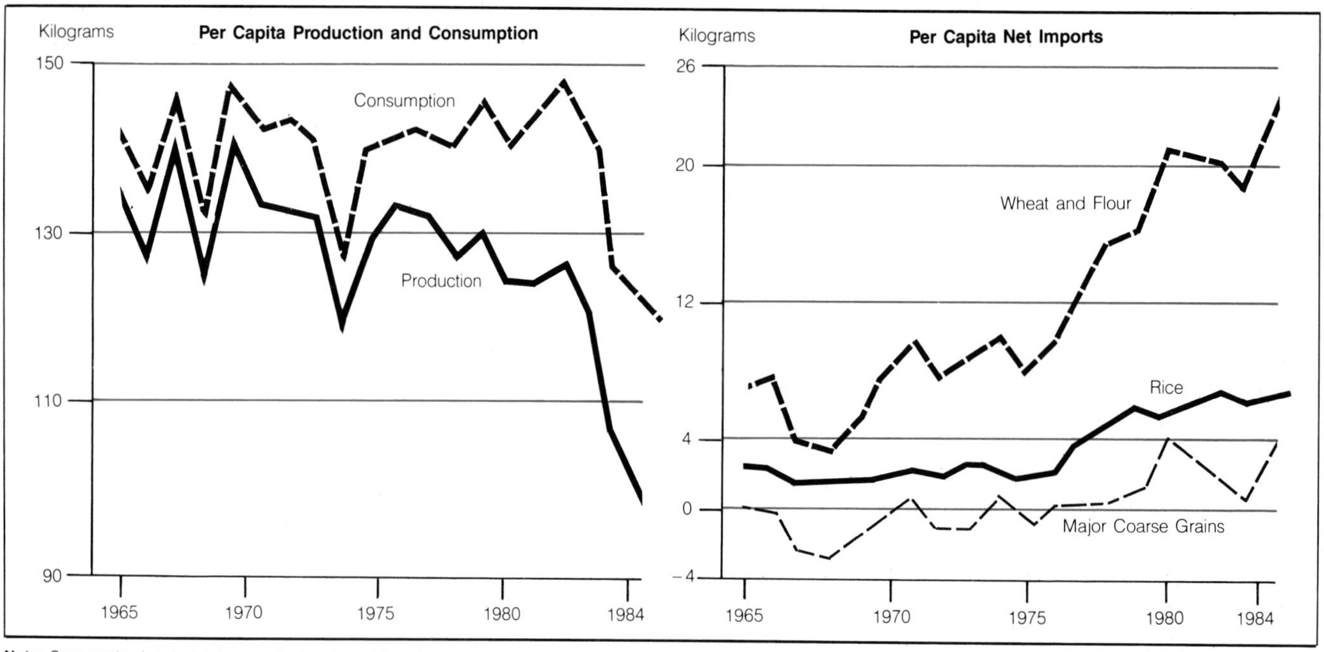

Note: Consumption is calculated as production plus net imports.
Source: United Nations Food and Agriculture Organization, cited in The World Bank, *World Development Report 1986* (Oxford University Press, New York, 1986), p. 77.

details of worldwide production and trade of these commodities.)

The real prices of most of these commodities have fallen since 1960 (see Table 4.5), and the downward trend shows little sign of easing in the 1980s. The price declines can be attributed mainly to steady increases in production and supply resulting from substantial improvements in crop yields. (See Table 4.6.) Export earnings of developing countries from 11 of these commodities (excluding tobacco) fell 17 percent from 1980 to 1985 (8). The International Monetary Fund believes that only large and unforeseen reductions in harvests could change the trend (9).

Although international agreements exist for coffee, cocoa, sugar, and rubber, none has effectively stabilized long-term prices in the face of the growing production of these commodities in the Third World. In fact, these agreements have not reduced short-term fluctuations in prices.

While the gloomy prospects for world commodity prices will benefit importers, developing countries that rely heavily on agricultural export earnings to service their debt burdens will continue to feel the squeeze. In the past, countries with balance of payment difficulties relied on the Compensatory Financing Facility of the International Monetary Fund to finance shortfalls in export earnings and excess costs of cereal imports. During 1984–85, five members made record total purchases of Special Drawing Rights worth the equivalent of roughly $473 million: $88 million for excess cereal import costs and $384 million for export shortfalls under the combined export shortfall/cereal import facility (10).

For five years beginning March 1, 1985, compensatory assistance is also being provided by the Third Lome Convention between the African, Caribbean, and Pacific (ACP) Group of developing countries and the European Community (11).

Table 4.4 Trends for Consumption of Basic Food Staples in Developing Countries, 1966–80 and Projections for 1980–2000
(percent)

| | Average Annual Growth Rate of Consumption 1966–80 | | | Projected Annual Growth Rate 1980–2000 | | | | Share of Food in Total Consumption | |
| | | | | Production Per Capita | Consumption[a] | | | | |
	Total	Food	Feed[b]		Total	Food	Feed[b]	1980	2000
Developing Countries	3.3	3.2	4.3	1.0	2.7	2.1	4.6	69.3	61.8
Asia	3.3	3.3	4.2	1.4	2.3	1.9	4.4	75.1	68.9
Northern Africa/ Middle East	3.9	3.7	4.8	0.2	3.8	2.5	6.1	55.3	42.6
Sub-Saharan Africa	2.2	2.5	3.1	-1.2	3.6	3.5	5.5	72.7	71.0
Latin America	3.1	2.4	4.4	0.9	3.2	2.3	4.0	45.7	38.5

Notes:
a. Based on 1966-80 income growth trend and 1980 trend estimates. Consumption refers to the total domestic use of the major food crops, including food, fuel, seeds, allowances for waste, and other nonfood uses.
b. Includes bran and cake.
Source: Leonardo A. Paulino, *Food in the Third World: Past Trends and Projections to 2000*, Research Report 52 (International Food Policy Research Institute, Washington, D.C., 1986), Tables 7, 11, and 22.

Table 4.5 Commodity Price Trends, 1960–85
(1980 constant prices)

	1960	1970	1975	1980	1985
Cocoa[a]	2.05	1.93	1.98	2.60	2.36
Coffee[a]	2.81	3.45	2.94	4.58	3.50
Cotton[a]	2.27	1.81	1.85	2.05	1.38
Maize[b]	150.90	167.30	190.50	125.30	117.50
Palm Oil[a]	795.10	745.30	691.40	583.50	524.20
Rice[b]	435.00	413.00	578.20	434.00	226.10
Rubber[a]	293.40	132.70	104.90	162.40	96.75
Soybeans[b]	321.00	335.00	350.00	296.00	235.00
Sugar[a]	.24	.23	.23	.72	.63	.09
Tea[a]	4.96	3.14	2.21	2.23	2.08
Tobacco[b]	2,812.00	2,831.00	2,416.00	2,300.00	2,101.00
Wheat[b]	219.20	179.90	288.70	190.80	181.50

Notes:
a. U.S. dollars per kilogram.
b. U.S. dollars per metric ton.
Source: The World Bank, *Commodity Trade and Price Trends* (The World Bank, Washington, D.C., 1986), pp. 49–52, pp. 54–56, pp. 64–65, p. 68, p. 73, and p. 77; and The World Bank, unpublished data.

Table 4.6 World Commodity Production Trends, 1960–84
(million metric tons)

	1960	1969–71	1974–76	1980	1984
Cocoa	1.2	1.5	1.5	1.6	1.7
Coffee	3.9	4.3	4.3	4.7	5.2
Cotton	11.1	11.7	13.0	14.0	17.8
Maize	215.9	283.0	333.7	395.9	452.9
Palm Oil	1.1	2.0	3.2	5.0	6.8
Rice	239.8	309.8	347.5	399.1	471.0
Rubber	2.0	2.9	3.4	3.7	4.2
Soybeans	27.3	43.5	58.1	80.9	90.3
Sugar (cane)	430.4	567.8	649.4	719.8	935.8
Sugar (beet)	185.2	223.3	261.0	262.9	293.5
Tea	0.9	1.3	1.5	1.9	2.2
Tobacco	3.6	4.6	5.4	5.2	6.2
Wheat	245.0	327.9	383.4	446.1	509.9

Source: United Nations Food and Agriculture Organization (FAO), *Production Yearbook* 1972, 1976, 1980, and 1984 (FAO, Rome, 1973, 1977, 1981, and 1985).

FOCUS ON: TRENDS IN CASH AND FOOD CROP PRODUCTION

Many of the poorest developing countries depend on certain export crops to generate the foreign exchange needed to meet development goals and to import food for their growing populations. Some nations are heavily dependent on a single crop. In 1979, for example, Burundi was 93 percent dependent on coffee, Mauritius relied on sugar for 68 percent of its exports, and the Sudan was tied to cotton for 65 percent of its exports (12). Given the long-term decline in real commodity prices and the current global oversupply of many export crops, these countries are trapped between low domestic productivity for essential food crops on one hand and weak markets for their export products on the other. At the end of 1984, some 65 low-income, food-deficit countries—most in sub-Saharan Africa—lacked both a surplus of basic foodstuffs as a hedge against drought and starvation and the income to buy sufficient supplies from abroad (13).

An interesting question is whether the land and resources devoted to export crops in developing countries could better be used for growing domestic food crops. There is also concern that cash crops are increasingly grown on the more fertile lands, forcing subsistence cultivators into marginal areas. Moreover, current cultivation practices for some cash crops may entail significant environmental and health risks. Critics of cash crop production argue that food consumption and the nutritional status of the poorest households have declined in areas where cash cropping has increased.

Nonetheless, distinctions between cash crops and food crops are not clear-cut. "Cash crops" and "export crops" are often used synonymously. Strictly speaking, however, a cash crop may be either a food or nonfood commodity sold at home or abroad, whereas an export crop is a cash crop that is ultimately exported from the country producing it. The major nonfood export crops are cocoa, coffee, fiber crops, rubber, tea, and tobacco. "Food crop" refers to domestic production of basic staples (cereals, pulses, roots, and tubers). Although they are the principal subsistence crops, food crops are also marketed (14). In

Asia, for example, a sizable proportion of rice and wheat, which are basic food staples, is sold for cash. Rice is a major export crop for Burma, China, Pakistan, and Thailand. (See Box 4.1.)

Because of these overlaps, distinguishing between food and export crops may not help in understanding the problems of agricultural development. Nor may the distinction be appropriate for assessing problems of resource conservation and environmental protection. Given the significant regional variations in agricultural development patterns in the Third World, there appears to be no general rule that either cash crops—even those that are predominantly exported—or food crops are more ecologically sustainable.

The choice of which crops to grow, and how, is heavily influenced by government agricultural policies and global trade and price trends. Many developing countries continue to promote industrialization at the expense of agricultural development by protecting domestic industries and by overvaluing their exchange rates. The result is that prices of domestic substitutes for industrial imports rise relative to the prices of domestic agricultural products, which effectively taxes agriculture and reduces its profitability (15). Government subsidies of irrigation water, agricultural chemicals, and farm machinery tend to promote large-scale industrial farming practices that can deplete natural resources and cause pollution from residues and wastes (16). In many developing countries, producers of export crops are being squeezed between taxes levied to encourage domestic food production, raise revenues, or promote processing by agro-industries (17) and the long-term decline in many commodity prices.

Although national and international policies clearly influence the overall allocation of agricultural resources, it is often at the village level where the final decision is made about the mix of crops to grow. A subsistence farming family decides what to grow based on how much land is needed to grow the food it requires, together with the mix of crops it can sell to yield the best possible return. If cash cropping leads to greater income fluctuations, requires longer fallow or gestation periods, and substantially reduces soil fertility, farmers may assess these risks in deciding the optimal crop mix.

Food and Agriculture

Further, the choice of crops may depend on whether men or women control household cash or food income.

The amount of land growing both export and food crops in developing market economies has increased in the past ten years mainly because of the new (mostly forest and marginal) land brought into production. As can be seen in Table 4.7, the land under export crops expanded 8.1 million hectares between 1976 and 1984, and land growing basic food crops increased 27.1 million hectares. In Africa, the region most critically affected by food shortages, the amount of land given over to food staples increased 3.9 million hectares, whereas land growing export crops hardly increased at all. About 12.8 percent of Africa's cropland is growing export crops, a slightly lower proportion than in the rest of the developing world.

A recent study compared changes in the production of cash crops on arable land with changes in the production of basic food staples in 78 developing countries [18]. Between 1968 and 1982, only six countries showed an increase in the share of land used for cash cropping while experiencing a decline in per capita food production. The majority of countries with positive growth in per capita production of basic staples simultaneously expanded the area devoted to cash crops. In sub-Saharan Africa, constant or declining per capita food production has been associated with constant or declining shares of land allocated to cash crops. In general, countries either manage sufficient growth in both cash crops and staple food production or they fail in both [19].

Modern agricultural development in the Third World often requires imported inputs, and policies that discriminate against export crops may actually inhibit overall agricultural development, including food production. In sub-Saharan Africa, the incentive to produce export crops is severely hampered by export taxes and overvalued exchange rates. Because of high taxes during the 1970s and early 1980s, the farm price of coffee in Togo was only a third of the international (border) price. Similarly, cotton and groundnut farmers in Mali received half the

Box 4.1 Trends in Agricultural Commodities

Trends in 12 agricultural commodities of significant economic importance to developing countries are detailed here. Food commodities include coffee, cocoa, sugar, tea, vegetable oil, wheat, maize, rice, and soybeans. Nonfood commodities include rubber, cotton, and tobacco.

Brazil normally accounts for 30 percent of world **coffee** production and 25 percent of world exports, sufficient to give it a dominant influence over prices [1]. Other major exporters include Colombia, the Côte d'Ivoire, Indonesia, Mexico, Guatemala, El Salvador, and Uganda [2]. As a result of severe drought in Brazil, global output in 1986 was expected to be around 85 million 60-kilogram bags, 8 million fewer than in 1985 [3]. Because coffee consumption is not rising significantly, the long-term price trend seems unlikely to improve.

Although the real price of **cocoa** rose from 1960 to 1984 (see Table 4.5), this is not a sign of a long-term upward trend; the price in 1960 was considerably below the average 1950s' real price of $3.10 per kilogram [4]. Most cocoa is produced in West Africa by the Côte d'Ivoire, Ghana, Nigeria, and Cameroon. The 1986 world output is estimated at about 1.89 billion metric tons and consumption at 1.82 billion metric tons [5]. With Ghana, once the world's largest producer, trying to revive output, cocoa production is likely to outpace demand in the near future.

Most **sugar**, either cane or beet, is consumed in the country where it is produced; only about one fourth the global production is exported. The main exporters include Cuba, the European Community, Brazil, Australia, Thailand, the Philippines, and the Dominican Republic [6]. The real free market price of sugar has fallen dramatically in the 1980s. (See Table 4.5.)

Global output of sugar cane has more than doubled since 1960. Cane-sugar exporting countries can usually make a profit from some of their crop because of their special trade arrangements with developed countries. Major sugar importers, like the United States, pay above the cost of production for a given quantity. This kind of arrangement accounts for about a third of the sugar traded each year. The main sugar routes are from Cuba to the Soviet Union; from the Philippines, Central America, and the Caribbean to the United States; and from African, Caribbean, and Pacific countries to the European Community. As of August 1986, FAO estimated the world output of sugar at 97.9 million metric tons, against a consumption of 100 million metric tons [7]. However, the increased availability of alternative sweeteners continues to reduce sugar prospects. Fructose sweeteners, made from maize, are estimated to be capturing 10 percent of the world sweetener market [8]. Third World producers are also concerned about competition from the European Community, the world's largest producer of beet sugar.

The long-term trend of world **tea** prices is downward. (See Table 4.5.) World output of tea rose over 4 percent in 1985, from 1.45 to 1.51 million metric tons. Demand was less buoyant, increasing from 1.43 to 1.45 million metric tons [9]. India, China, Indonesia, Sri Lanka, Kenya, Malawi, and Tanzania produce the bulk of global tea output, over a third of which is exported [10].

Palm oil competes with soybean, groundnut, coconut, rapeseed, cottonseed, and sunflower seed oil for industrial frying, margarine, and soap production. Subsidies given by some countries to produce soya, rape, and sunflower have encouraged increased output of vegetable oils and contributed to reduced prices of

palm oil. Worldwide production of vegetable oils in 1985–86 was 53.9 million metric tons, 7.6 million of which was palm oil [11]. The main world producers are Malaysia, Indonesia, and Nigeria [12]. Output has been increasing rapidly since 1960. (See Table 4.6.) Expansion of acreages under palm oil, allied to productivity gains, have allowed Malaysia and Indonesia to increase output substantially [13].

The main producers of **wheat** are China, the USSR, the European Community, the United States, India, Canada, Turkey, Australia, Argentina, and Pakistan [14]. Argentina is the major Third World exporter. Production by developing countries was forecast to rise from 205 million metric tons in 1984 to 214.6 million metric tons in 1986, reflecting record or near-record harvests for China, India, Pakistan, and Turkey and good prospects for Argentina and Brazil [15]. However, prices have been declining steadily since 1980, and have fallen more steeply since early 1985 [16].

The United States produces about 43 percent of the world's **maize** (corn) crop; other major producers include China, Brazil, the European Community, the Soviet Union, Romania, Yugoslavia, Argentina, and Mexico. The major Third World exporters are China, Argentina, and Thailand [17]. Although maize is an important staple food in many countries, approximately half the world maize production is used for animal feed, particularly for poultry. With global production continuing to rise and total utilization expected to fall, maize stocks are forecast to rise to 111 million metric tons in 1985–86, about double the level at the end of 1984–85. This buildup in stocks is expected to depress maize prices in 1986 and 1987 [18].

Most of the world's **rice** is consumed in the countries where it is grown, and only 4 percent of production is exported. Because 90 border prices, and in Cameroon and Ghana cocoa producers received less than half. The domestic price of export crops relative to their border prices declined 27 percent in real terms for all sub-Saharan countries between 1971 and 1983 (20).

Although sub-Saharan Africa's food problems are often ascribed to an overemphasis on cash crops, in 25 of 38 countries, the growth rate for both food and nonfood production fell in the period 1970–82, compared with the 1960s. Only in Kenya and Malawi, both self-sufficient in food, did food production slow while nonfood production accelerated (21). As agricultural export earnings stagnated or declined in most of sub-Saharan Africa between 1970 and 1982, countries in the region were unable to import necessities like spare parts or chemical fertilizers; consequently, per capita food production declined (22).

Despite evidence that cash cropping for export has not expanded at the expense of staple food production in most developing countries, in some cases where planned expansion has taken place, it has occurred on fertile land

that once grew food. When cocoa first came to the southern Volta region of Ghana, for example, it was planted on the best land, and food production was displaced to less fertile areas (23). In Kenya, the government has promoted sugar plantations for its own processing industries and fuel production. But it was the farmers in Kenya's traditional bread basket, the Western province, who responded to government incentives and switched from growing maize to growing sugar (24). In the Cauca Valley of Colombia, large export crop estates employ permanent and contract laborers who also work their own subsistence farms on marginal lands. It is on these lands that the worst soil erosion and flooding occur (25).

In Burkina Faso, cotton production increased 25-fold between 1960 and 1984, whereas food production remained the same. Cash crops are usually grown on irrigated land along the rivers in Senegal and Niger. Because cash crops require less labor per hectare than subsistence farming, food production is pushed northward into areas of lower rainfall and poorer soils that cannot

Box 4.1

percent of all rice is grown in Asia, the vagaries of the monsoons can cause considerable instability in availability and prices (19). The main producers are China, India, Indonesia, Bangladesh, Thailand, Burma, Japan, and Vietnam (20), but major exporting countries include Burma, China, Pakistan, Thailand, and the United States (21). World paddy production is expected to fall to around 464–466 million metric tons in 1985–86 from the 1984–85 record of 467 million metric tons. After collapsing in the second half of 1984, rice prices weakened again in 1985. Given the ample supplies of the world's major exporters, no early recovery in prices is expected (22).

The main world producers of **soybeans** are the United States, Brazil, Argentina, and China; all but China are major exporters as well. The world market is dominated by the United States, which accounts for 56 percent of production. World production for 1985–86 is forecast at a record 94.3 million metric tons, up 3.7 percent from the 1984–85 record of 91 million metric tons. With world prices declining, major producing countries are expected to reduce acreage as prices of competing crops become more favorable (23).

Malaysia, Indonesia, Thailand, China, India, and Sri Lanka produce about 90 percent of the world's natural **rubber**. Malaysia, Indonesia, and Thailand account for about 85 percent of world exports (24). Production is expected to rise to 4.735 million metric tons in 1987 from 4.34 million metric tons in 1985. Consumption is likely to grow at a slower rate, from 4.35 million metric tons in 1985 to 4.55 million metric tons in 1987 (25). Prospects appear to hinge as much on the strength of competition from synthetics as on growth in industrial economies.

China is the world's largest producer of **cotton**, followed by the United States and the

Soviet Union (26). Third World exporters include Pakistan, Egypt, and Mexico (27). Cotton production rose 30 percent in 1984–85, reaching 19.1 million metric tons, while consumption increased only marginally to 15.1 million metric tons (28). China's huge expansion of land under cotton cultivation accounted for much of the increase; output also rose in India, Pakistan, Australia, and Brazil. Prices are expected to remain depressed as worldwide stocks accumulate.

Three quarters of all harvested **tobacco** is used for cigarettes in the country where it is grown. China, India, the United States, and Brazil produce more than half the global output. Of the one quarter that enters world trade, 70 percent comes from nine countries: Brazil, Bulgaria, Greece, India, Italy, Malawi, Turkey, the United States, and Zimbabwe. Worldwide exports of tobacco in 1985 were 1.4 million metric tons, about 0.56 million metric tons of which came from the main Third World producers (29). There are now stocks of 7.19 million metric tons, more than a year's output and an amount that is far larger than for any other agricultural commodity (30). Thus tobacco prices are likely to stay low.

References and Notes

1. United Nations Food and Agriculture Organization (FAO), *Commodity Review and Outlook 1985–86* (FAO, Rome, 1986), Table 2.2, p. 33.
2. The Economist Intelligence Unit, *World Commodity Outlook 1986* (The Economist Publications Ltd., London, 1985), p. 83.
3. Based on information provided by the International Coffee Organization, London, July 1986.
4. The World Bank, *Commodity Trade and Price Trends*, 1986 edition (The World Bank, Washington, D.C., 1986), p. 49.
5. Based on information supplied by Gill and Duffus, commodity brokers, London, July 1986.
6. *Op. cit.* 2, p. 100.
7. United Nations Food and Agriculture Organization (FAO), *Food Outlook*, No. 9 (FAO, Rome, October 1986), p. 21.
8. David Dembo, *et al.*, "The Biorevolution and the Third World," in *Third World Affairs 1985* (Third World Foundation for Social and Economic Studies, London, 1985), p. 318.
9. *Op. cit.* 7, pp. 5–6.
10. *Op. cit.* 2, p. 15.
11. *Op. cit.* 2, pp. 26–39.
12. International Monetary Fund (IMF), *Primary Commodities: Market Developments and Outlook* (IMF, Washington, D.C., May 1986), pp. 17–19.
13. *Ibid.*, p. 19.
14. *Op. cit.* 2, p. 15.
15. *Op. cit.* 7, pp. 5–6.
16. *Op. cit.* 2, p. 15.
17. *Op. cit.* 2, pp. 26–29.
18. *Op. cit.* 12.
19. *Op. cit.* 12, p. 19.
20. *Op. cit.* 2, p. 44.
21. *Op. cit.* 1, p. 52.
22. *Op. cit.* 2, p. 44 and p. 49.
23. *Op. cit.* 2, pp. 55–59.
24. *Op. cit.* 1, Table 2.23, p. 85.
25. Malaysian Rubber Producers Association, unofficial estimates, London, July 1986.
26. *Op. cit.* 12, Table 30, p. 49.
27. *Op. cit.* 4, pp. 14–18.
28. *Op. cit.* 1, pp. 72–73.
29. *Op. cit.* 2, p. 44.
30. *Op. cit.* 1, p. 52.

tolerate cropping year after year (26). In southeast Mexico, there is concern that the introduction of agricultural techniques unsuitable to tropical lowlands to grow cash crops may be displacing traditional maize cropping, maize-bean-squash intercropping, and home garden systems that could be developed further as a more appropriate agricultural base (27).

The input requirements of cash crops may also have important distributional and ecological impacts. For example, in many developing countries, imported agricultural machinery and equipment receive favorable tariff and exchange rates, are accorded high priority when scarce foreign exchange is rationed, and are purchased through subsidized credit and run on subsidized diesel fuel. In Brazil, this benefits the larger farmers, who also get a tax shelter that allows them to claim up to six times the purchase price of farm machinery in depreciation allowances (28). In Sri Lanka, the replacement of water buffaloes by tractors in paddy cultivation has saved human labor and raised yields, but it has depressed the labor market in rural villages and penalized the landless peasants who are employed as agricultural labor. If fuel must be imported, the costs of operating tractors can reach four times the cost of plowing with buffaloes (29).

Currently, about 25 percent of pesticide use is in developing countries, mainly on cash crops (30), including rice—an important staple and cash food crop in Asia (31). Pesticides (almost entirely herbicides) are applied heavily to maize in the United States, but virtually none is used on maize in developing countries. Because nearly 70 percent of the world's cotton production is concentrated in the Third World, 70 percent of insecticide use on cotton also occurs in developing countries. Although some developing countries can achieve cotton yields of over 1,000 kilograms per hectare, this yield requires intensive cropping on large areas, with extensive irrigation and chemical pest control (32). Pesticide and fertilizer imports for cash crops are often heavily subsidized by governments in developing countries. Where these crops are

grown on large estates, the distribution of subsidies favors the larger farmers. Yet the side effects of pesticide use—contaminated water supplies and high levels of pesticide residues in food—adversely affect the entire population (33). In Honduras, for example, insecticide use averages about three kilograms per hectare, nearly an order of magnitude higher than the U.S. rate. Insecticides are mainly used on large plantations producing export crops such as coffee, cotton, sugar, and bananas (34).

Because many subsistence farmers lack cash incomes, basic food staples do not receive as many applications of pesticides and fertilizers as do cash crops. Even so, the inputs required for certain food crops cause environmental hazards. For example, the increasing severity of resistant pest populations in Southeast Asia is resulting in more intensive applications of pesticides. Rice is often sprayed or dusted at 10–14-day intervals, and because the new early-maturing, high-yielding rice varieties can now be grown continuously on irrigated land, pesticide applications 10–20 times a year may become common (35). Similarly, because of the high rainfall in the tropics and the rapid growth of new leaves, cabbage requires pesticide applications every three or four days (36). In Indonesia, Malaysia, and Thailand, fish stocks in irrigated rice paddies, irrigation channels, and ponds have been greatly reduced by pesticide poisoning (37).

Some undesirable environmental impacts from the production of both food and cash crops can be mitigated through intercropping. (See "Innovations in Third World Agriculture," below.) For example, a ground cover of legumes, vines, or grasses can reduce soil erosion and conserve organic matter in oil palm groves, as can intercropping with bananas, coffee, cocoa, and other tree crops (38). Between 1971 and 1981, Rwanda increased yields of both root crops (13 percent) and coffee (49 percent) by intensifying farming through traditional multicropping and soil conservation techniques, such as heavy use of mulches on coffee groves, terracing on ridges, digging crop residues into cultivated fields, and mixing bananas, coffee, and cassava with food crops to protect the soil against erosion (39).

In general, the risks of environmental damage are much greater in monocultures than in multicropping systems. In Rajasthan, India, the establishment of a multipurpose system involving tree crops, forage crops, and livestock produced higher net returns per hectare than the returns from cultivating annual crops alone. This approach also increases soil fertility, controls soil erosion, and improves wildlife habitats (40). (Also see Chapter 5, "Forests and Rangelands," Focus on: Agroforestry.)

Although the main advantage of cash cropping is that it allows farming households an increased source of cash income, it may have unforeseen consequences because of social and cultural traditions. In Sukumuland, Tanzania, the introduction of cotton in food crop systems successfully increased farmers' cash incomes. But because there was no outlet for this cash other than to purchase cattle, livestock numbers increased dramatically, placing greater strains on communal grazing areas. When the herds began to decline, farmers increased cultivation of cotton

Table 4.7 Harvested Areas Growing Basic Food and Export Crops
(million hectares)

	All Developing Countries		Africa	
	1974–76 (average)	1984	1974-76 (average)	1984
Food				
Cereals	301.9	322.2	69.7	70.9
Roots and Tubers	20.7	23.1	11.2	13.0
Pulses	46.9	51.3	11.7	12.6
Total	**369.4**	**396.5**	**92.6**	**96.5**
Export Crops				
Cotton	20.2	20.7	4.0	3.9
Coffee	8.6	10.1	3.3	3.3
Cocoa	4.4	4.9	3.2	3.3
Tea	1.0	1.3	0.1	0.2
Tobacco	2.3	2.2	0.3	0.3
Sugar	11.4	15.0	0.5	0.6
Palm Oil	3.9	4.8	0.7[a]	0.9[a]
Rubber	5.6	6.5	0.2[a]	0.2[a]
Total	**57.4**	**65.5**	**12.3**	**12.7**

Note: a. Estimated.
Sources: Compiled from United Nations Food and Agriculture Organization (FAO), *Production Yearbook 1984* (FAO, Rome, 1985); and FAO unpublished data.

in an attempt to recoup their losses, a ploy that further reduced communal grazing areas and exacerbated the problem (41).

Even if the real income of poor households increases as a result of cash cropping, the nutritional standard of the family may not improve. Studies in Tanzania, Nicaragua, Colombia, and Nigeria show that, even at fairly low income levels, families may devote only a small portion of an increased income to augmenting the caloric intake of the households (42). Moreover, cash payments in lump sums are more likely to be spent on consumer durables than on food (43). In many cultures, men control cash income and women control food income. Findings in Nigeria, India, and Nepal suggest that to the extent that women's income decreases as cash cropping increases, family consumption and nutrition, particularly the nutritional status of children, may decline. In general, the nutritional status of preschool children is better on farms with a mix of subsistence and cash crops as opposed to mainly cash crops (44).

The issue of whether Third World countries should concentrate on domestic food crops rather than export crops is complicated. The choice is influenced by such diverse factors as agricultural policies and prices, the relative impacts on land allocation, and the pattern of land ownership, environmental degradation, the availability of inputs, household income, the status of women, and family nutrition. A main concern is striking a balance between protecting resources while improving conditions of the poor and malnourished. In recent years, however, many Third World countries have had to take into account the additional pressures of rising debt repayments and scarce foreign exchange.

Debt and Export Crops

During the past ten years the external debt of most developing countries has grown by massive proportions. Africa's debt, for example, swelled more than sevenfold to $175 billion (nearly half the continent's annual income) between 1974 and 1985 (45). The need to service these debts is leading some governments to expand export crops, even though the long-term real prices for many of these crops are declining, partly because of the debt crisis itself. Agricultural exports have grown in Latin America—the continent with the highest overall debts— but not generally in sub-Saharan Africa, which has a higher debt burden relative to its income. Such trends could further depress world prices.

Countries saddled with huge debt obligations often attempt to increase their agricultural exports at the expense of food crops, altering income distribution and access to food for the poorer segments of society (46). If export crops, including food crops, are produced mainly on capital-intensive plantations and domestically consumed food crops are produced by semi-subsistence peasants, a shift of resources to the export crop sector can reduce the income of poor peasants.

Agricultural export earnings in the Third World have also been hobbled by protectionist agricultural policies in industrialized countries. Exporters of commodities that are in surplus in industrial countries, such as dairy products, beef, cereals, and sugar, are particularly affected. In order to reduce its surpluses of rice, the United States lowered its export price from $8 per hundredweight to $4.20 in mid-April 1986. This move severely cut into Thailand's foreign exchange income, which is heavily dependent on rice exports (47). The sugar policies of the European Community are estimated to cost Third World producers $2 billion a year in lost export earnings (48). A study based on 1975–77 data suggests that developing countries could have increased their real export revenues in 1977 by almost $6 billion, or 11 percent, if countries in the Organisation for Economic Cooperation and Development had cut their tariffs on 99 commodities by 50 percent (49). Eliminating both protectionism in industrial countries and distortionary pricing policies in the Third World for grains, meat, rice, dairy products, and sugar might increase the real national income of developing countries by $18 billion annually (50).

INCREASING PRODUCTION AND ITS ENVIRONMENTAL COSTS: THE UNITED STATES AND THE EUROPEAN COMMUNITY

Historically, the primary aim of agricultural policies in the United States and the European Community has been to stabilize and increase farmers' incomes by subsidizing domestic prices, storing surpluses, controlling international trade, and, in the United States, reducing cultivated acreage. Support of farm incomes, however, has also contributed to more rapid technological change and higher production. As a result, in an era of falling real prices for most agricultural commodities, U.S. and EC farm programs are paying more than ever before to prop up domestic prices and store surplus stocks.

Agricultural spending accounts for approximately 70 percent of the total EC budget, rising from $5.6 billion in 1974 to $23.5 billion in 1984 (51). In the United States, the cost of agricultural policies has increased from $3 billion in 1980–81 to $11.9 billion in 1984, and it could exceed $30 billion in fiscal year 1986 (52). The World Bank estimates that the loss of real national income to the European Community from its Common Agricultural Policy (CAP) through higher food prices that mislead producers into using too many resources and consumers into purchasing less reached $15.4 billion in 1980. The United States lost some $4 billion in 1984–85 because of its agricultural policies (53).

In view of the fact that it essentially subsidizes agricultural production and farmers' incomes, increased agricultural spending in the EC and the United States will continue to stimulate both growth in agricultural output and the accumulation of surplus stocks. Real expenditures on dairy market support in the EC and United States have continued to increase. Yet, despite attempts to dispose of surpluses at subsidized prices in domestic and international markets, stocks of butter and cheese totaled more than 1.5 million metric tons in the EC during 1984–85 (54). As direct payments to major crop producers in the United States increased in the 1980s, so did production and surplus stocks. (See Table 4.8.) Similarly, buildup of

Food and Agriculture

Table 4.8 U.S. Surplus of Major Crops[a] and Program Costs

Item	1950s Average	1960s Average	1970s Average	1980	1981	1982	1983	1984	1985
Production[b]	150.8	200.9	280.2	311.5	376.0	385.0	246.8	358.2	396.9
Ending Stocks[b]	67.9	82.9	59.3	70.0	106.7	147.9	74.4	97.4	173.6
Planted Area[c]	99.5	88.3	100.2	112.4	115.3	115.1	100.4	111.2	110.2
Diverted Area[c,d]	0.0	15.9	16.4	0.0	0.0	7.1	28.5	9.8	10.9
Direct Payments[e,f]	0.0	1,489.0	1,438.0	649.0	1,648.0	1,960.0	2,419.0	4,848.0	3,765.0

Notes:
a. Includes feed grains (corn, sorghum, barley, and oats), wheat, and soybeans.
b. Million metric tons.
c. Million hectares.
d. Area diverted from production.
e. Deficiency payments, diversion payments, disaster payments, and producer storage payments.
f. Million dollars.
Source: U.S. Department of Agriculture (USDA), Commodity Credit Corporation, "CCC Estimates: CCC President's Budget Estimates," Presentation No. 86-003 (USDA, Agricultural Stabilization and Conservation Service, Washington, D.C., 1986).

surplus cereals in the EC is expected to continue until 1990–91. (See Table 4.9.)

Increasing agricultural production using mechanization, irrigation, drainage, fertilizers, and pesticides has aggravated problems of soil erosion, depletion of water supplies, and pollution in the United States and the EC. By encouraging maximum yields per acre and intensive livestock rearing, U.S. and EC agricultural policies have contributed to these environmental problems. A crucial question is whether future policies for controlling agricultural production can also promote the long-term conservation of land and water resources.

United States

Since the 1930s, the main U.S. policy tools for ensuring adequate agricultural production at prices capable of supporting farm incomes have included short-term loans from the Commodity Credit Corporation (CCC), target price deficiency payments, voluntary acreage-reduction programs, and farmer-owned reserves of grains. The 1970s boom in world trade provided a further outlet for U.S. agricultural expansion. Recent estimates suggest, however, that annual growth in U.S. grain trade for the remainder of the century will be less than half the 7.5 percent realized annually from 1969 to 1982 (55). Controlling production and disposing of surplus reserves are expected to be serious problems in the near future as the CCC continues to accumulate surpluses.

By encouraging maximum yields per hectare and by failing to discourage "sodbusting" (conversion of reserve land to intensive use), past U.S. farm programs have provided incentives for farming highly erodible soils (56). Evidence suggests that although technical innovations have helped to increase agricultural production, they have worsened soil erosion problems, both onsite and offsite (57). Onsite damage has reduced soil quality; offsite damage includes accelerated fertilizer runoff, water pollution, and sedimentation. The 1982 National Resources Inventory revealed that 13 percent (55 million acres, or 22.3 million hectares) of U.S. cropland exhibits erosion rates exceeding soil-loss tolerance levels by up to twice its value. Another 20.6 million hectares exceed the tolerance level by more than two times. The loss tolerance level of soil is the maximum rate of annual soil loss that will still support crop productivity. It averages about 10.2 metric tons of soil lost per hectare per year (58). In the Corn Belt, soybean and corn yields on highly erodible cropland could be 15–30 percent lower within 50 years

(59). For the entire United States, crop yields could well decline an average of 8 percent over the next 50 years because of erosion if no corrective measures are taken (60).

The total offsite damages of erosion were estimated at $6.1 billion (in 1980 dollars) (61). The cost of agricultural chemicals and plant nutrients lost through erosion and runoff may range from $1–$4 billion annually (62). In addition, the potential ecological impacts of sediment and nutrient runoff could be serious, contributing to the eutrophication of water bodies and causing habitat destruction.

In general, because U.S. farm program benefits have been proportional to the acreage kept in erosion-prone crops (maize, wheat, and soybeans), these benefits essentially subsidized production on marginal land that could have been kept in hay, pasture, forest, or wildlife cover (63). This production occurred despite the fact that U.S. farm program benefits are partly conditional on participation in set-aside programs. Comparison of the 1977 and 1982 National Resource Inventories reveals that an estimated 4.4 million hectares of new croplands, mostly under maize, wheat, and soybeans, are eroding at a rate that is 1.4 times the national average. Highly erodible soils account for about 46 million metric tons (70 percent) of sheet and rill erosion on the new acreage (64).

Attempts to limit production through acreage reduction programs have had limited success in promoting soil con-

Table 4.9 European Community Surplus Buildup of Cereals, 1980–91
(million metric tons)

	Usable Production (1)	Internal Consumption (2)	Imports (3)	Exportable Surplus (4)[a]	Exports (5)	End of Season Stocks (cumulative) (6)[b]
1980–81	124.5	119.0	18.0	23.5	24.0	13.0
1981–82	122.5	115.5	15.0	22.0	24.0	11.0
1982–83	131.0	114.0	11.0	28.0	23.0	16.0
1983–84	124.0	113.5	10.0	20.5	20.5	16.0
1984–85[c]	143.0	114.0	7.5	41.5	25.0	32.5
1985–86	133.0	115.5	7.5	25.0	25.0	32.5
1986–87	137.0	115.5	7.5	29.0	25.0	36.5
1987–88	141.0	116.0	7.5	32.5	25.0	44.0
1988–89	145.5	116.5	7.5	36.5	25.0	55.5
1989–90	149.5	117.0	7.5	40.0	25.0	70.5
1990–91	153.5	117.5	7.5	43.5	25.0	89.0

Notes:
a. Column (4) = (1) − (2) + (3).
b. Net addition to column (6) = (4) − (5).
c. Data after 1984–85 are estimates. Cereals include wheat, corn, sorghum, barley, oats, rye, millet, and mixed grains.
Source: Home Grown Cereals Authority, evidence presented to the *Select Committee on the European Communities, 6th Report* (House of Lords, Session 1985–1986, London, 1986), Table 1.

servation; the least profitable land is usually retired, and it is not necessarily the most erodible. There is only limited overlap between excess crop acreage and erodible acres. For example, about 2.9 million hectares of wheat are highly erodible; yet three times this area must be idled to eliminate surpluses (65).

The 1985 Farm Act is rectifying some of these problems through controls on sodbusting and "slippage" (acreage reduction exceeded by increases in new cropland) and establishment of a "conservation reserve" to ensure retirement of up to 18.6 million hectares of land for conservation purposes over the next 10 years. Farm program benefits will be denied farmers who convert fragile grasslands or wetlands to agricultural production after January 1, 1986, or cultivate erosive lands after January 1, 1990. Conservation reserve costs are estimated at $5 billion for the first five years, and eligibility is limited to lands that are considered unsuitable for farming or that are eroding faster than three times the natural rate of soil formation (66). Anticipated ecological benefits include reducing soil erosion 680 million metric tons a year, reducing sedimentation of streams and other surface water more than 180 million metric tons each year, reducing pesticide use almost 30 million kilograms annually, and improving the quality of fish and wildlife habitat. Planting new trees will improve environmental quality, will provide future income for landowners, and will be of economic value to communities (67).

Many farmers cultivating highly erodible lands do not participate in U.S. farm programs and thus will not be affected by the new regulations. Moreover, because tax and market incentives to convert land are not included, the amount of nonprogram land farmed may grow if market prices rise enough for the benefits of cultivating fragile lands to outweigh those of conservation (68). Results of the first round of bids for the conservation reserve in the Palouse Valley of Washington state are disappointing. The low values of the accepted bids, the failure to link bids to soil erodibility, and confusion among farmers about the ramifications of the program have resulted in the most erodible land in the Palouse not being enrolled (69).

Conversion of wetlands is a major source of new farmland. From the 1950s to the 1970s, the United States lost an average of 185,000 hectares of wetlands each year, with agricultural development accounting for 87 percent of the recent loss (70). In North Carolina, mass agricultural conversion during the 1970s increased freshwater runoff and flooding, salinity, and nitrogen concentrations (71). Conversion of wetlands may be financially attractive to the individual farmer or developer, but the costs to society as a whole from the loss of ecological services may be large. (See Chapter 9, "Oceans and Coasts," and Chapter 6, "Wildlife and Habitat.") In the past, wetlands conversion has been subsidized essentially by farm program benefits that are proportional to the acreage cropped; however, a surprise provision in the 1985 U.S. Farm Act eliminates indirect federal incentives to convert wetlands by denying eligibility for farm program benefits to landowners who convert wetlands to crop production ("swampbusting"). These regulations will be an effective

deterrent to conversion only in areas where farm programs offer important subsidies and where participation in the program is high. In many areas, income tax deductions still offer significant counterincentives to convert wetlands to agriculture (72).

Increased agricultural production, spurred by U.S. farm supports, may have serious consequences for depletion of water supplies, particularly in the arid regions of the Great Plains and the Southwest. The majority of the 9.5 million hectares of irrigated agriculture in the Great Plains depends on the Ogallala Aquifer. At current use rates, 2 million hectares will have no remaining groundwater by the end of the century (73). For western states, protection of aquatic ecosystems requires that depletion not exceed 40 percent of a stream's average annual flow. But current use is 60–80 percent of streamflow in many river basins (74).

The impact of increased pesticide application in U.S. agriculture on human health and wildlife is also a major concern; the use of herbicides, for example, rose 280 percent between 1968 and 1981 (75). Sixty percent of the global herbicide market for maize and 90 percent of the pesticide market for soybeans are in the United States.

European Community

Established in 1957, the Common Agricultural Policy (CAP) sets the overall direction for agricultural policy and national farming legislation in the European Community. The CAP aims to support farmers' incomes and agricultural production by maintaining price levels. This is achieved through variable taxes on imports, the use of intervention boards to maintain floor prices, subsidies on exports for surplus produce to achieve world price levels, and, in rare cases, subsidies on imports when world market prices exceed domestic prices. In addition, land improvements and conversion and farm investments are sometimes funded through the CAP and by national government programs.

Over the past 20 years, the EC has experienced an average increase in agricultural productivity per laborer of 7 percent per year and has achieved relatively secure supplies and prices (76). As in the United States, the 1970s boom in world agricultural trade provided an outlet for excess EC production. In the 1980s, slackening world trade, bigger budget costs, and mounting surpluses have caused some revisions in the CAP, notably quotas on milk production and limits on price increases. Yet surplus production is expected to continue. (See Table 4.9.)

The higher agricultural prices resulting from EC policies have led to an intensification of production and increased land values, along with such adverse environmental consequences as fertilizer pollution, livestock waste runoff, field drainage, soil erosion, and habitat destruction. In some regions, higher prices, especially for cereals, have encouraged conversion of marginal and unexploited areas. An estimated 790,000 hectares of nonagricultural land in France was converted between 1969 and 1984 (77). With the real prices of cereals to farmers declining in the past three years, this trend may be abating.

Considerable funding to improve agricultural productivity through field drainage is available through national grants and CAP subsidies. In 1983–84, about 140,000 hectares were drained in France and 120,000 in the United Kingdom. Although most drainage in the EC is on existing agricultural land, in France much of it is for the conversion of wetlands (78). The impact on natural ecosystems and habitats is greatest when land is drained for the first time or where existing agricultural acreage is significantly upgraded (79).

Agricultural yields have been raised by the intensive application of nitrogenous fertilizers, which price supports make more economically attractive. In 1979–80, the average annual application of nitrogen fertilizer in the EC was 75 kilograms per hectare, but it ranged from a low of 33 kilograms (Greece) to 240 kilograms per hectare (the Netherlands) (80). Crops that require increased fertilizer applications are sometimes favored by higher crop and land prices. For example, because of favorable CAP prices, the area of oilseed rape cultivation in the United Kingdom grew about 30 percent annually between 1973 and 1981, from 6,000 to 100,000 hectares. Rape receives the heaviest application of nitrogen fertilizers—272 kilograms per hectare, compared with an average of 121 kilograms for all crops and grasses (81).

Although use of nitrogen fertilizers has increased yields substantially throughout the EC, the fertilizers are not always entirely absorbed by crops and they may leach into groundwater supplies and contaminate surface water. Under normal conditions in northwestern Europe, leaching from uncultivated land into groundwater amounts to less than three kilograms of nitrate per hectare annually. A yearly dosage of 180 kilograms of nitrogen fertilizer per hectare, corresponding to about 60 kilograms of nitrogen, will generally increase leaching to between 30 and 45 kilograms per hectare (82).

In several European countries, there are areas where nitrate levels in groundwater exceed the EC maximum admissible concentration for drinking water (83). Rising levels of nitrate in groundwater have been discovered in France, the Netherlands, the United Kingdom, and West Germany, although the major source may not be limited to chemical fertilizers; human wastes and excessive spreading of slurries of animal wastes also contribute.

Eutrophication is another problem. Nitrate and phosphate runoff, along with untreated sewage discharges, are thought to be major sources of eutrophication in the EC (84) (85). Another major source is detergents. The result is an excessive growth of water plants and algae, which leads to eutrophication and lowers water quality. In Belgium almost all nonwoodland water courses are eutrophic (86). (Also see Chapter 8, "Freshwater.")

Intensive livestock rearing and applications of slurries of animal wastes can also lead to problems of nitrate and phosphate runoff and leaching (87) (88). Excessive and inappropriate use of slurry can lead to soil contamination by numerous trace elements, such as copper, zinc, and manganese from the antibiotics, fungicides, and heavy metals contained in animal feed.

Subsidized crop prices mean that pesticides become more affordable. Pesticide applications, particularly herbicides, have increased in EC countries. These chemicals can also cause runoff and leaching problems. Nonpest

species and natural habitats may be the most seriously affected by pesticides. Chemical pesticides have caused a 60–80 percent reduction in the 800 groups or species of fauna in the Paris basin, of which only 5 percent are harmful to cereal crops (89).

EC subsidies have intensified production of more erosion-prone crops, such as maize and wheat, that need careful management on poor quality soils. This has led to soil erosion, particularly in areas with alluvial soils. Some parts of Belgium and France experience soil losses of between 12.8 and 15.6 metric tons per hectare per year. In France, loss of revenues from erosion of cropland is estimated at $32–$53 per hectare (90). Current practices of field drainage, intensive crop production, and destruction of natural barriers such as hedgerows can contribute to worsening erosion problems.

Although the CAP does not yet provide for a conservation reserve, such as the one that was recently proposed in the United States, a similar set-aside policy could be designed for EC conditions to promote soil conservation (91). Some member governments are proceeding with limited measures to promote conservation-oriented agriculture. For example, the United Kingdom recently designated five areas in England and one in Wales for the encouragement of environmentally sensitive farming and nature conservation (92).

INNOVATIONS IN THIRD WORLD AGRICULTURE

In the 1960s, the chief innovations in Third World agriculture were the development and dissemination of high-yielding seeds of rice and wheat in what came to be known as the "green revolution." Similar advances are now needed for the production of other staple foods in the Third World. In recent years, there has been a growing worldwide effort to research such basic foods. From 1972 to 1979, for example, national and international programs in 25 countries spent 21 percent of research funds on potatoes, 15 percent on cassava, and 11 percent on beans. (See Table 4.10.) Although increasing in absolute terms, investment in agricultural research and extension as a percentage of agricultural Gross Domestic Product in

Table 4.10 Research Spending by National and International Programs for 25 Developing Countries, Average 1972–79
(percent)

Commodity	National Research Expenditures as a Share of the Value of Output			Spending by National and International Programs as a Share of Total Research Expenditures
	Africa[a]	Asia[b]	Latin America[c]	
Wheat	1.30	0.32	1.04	4
Rice	0.44	0.21	0.41	7
Maize	0.44	0.21	0.18	11
Cassava	0.09	0.06	0.19	15
Beans	1.65	0.08	0.60	11
Potatoes	0.21	0.19	0.43	21
Groundnuts	0.57	0.12	0.60	2
Beef	1.82	0.65	0.67	2

Notes:
a. Egypt, Ghana, Kenya, Nigeria, Sudan, Tanzania, Tunisia, and Uganda.
b. India, Indonesia, Korea, Malaysia, Pakistan, Philippines, Sri Lanka, Taiwan, Thailand, and Turkey.
c. Argentina, Brazil, Chile, Colombia, Mexico, Peru, and Venezuela.
Source: Robert E. Evenson, et al., "The Influence of International Research on the Size of National Research Systems," American Journal of Agricultural Economics, Vol. 67 (1985), pp. 1074-1079.

low-income developing countries is still smaller than in middle-income developing, semi-industrialized, and industrialized countries.

Technological innovations in Third World agriculture may offer the best possibility for increasing output of the basic staple crops and products while maintaining the resource sustainability of agricultural systems. Improvements in ecologically sound agricultural techniques are occurring in three important categories: alternative agricultural systems, such as agroforestry and intercropping, that enhance productivity and conserve resources; new high-yield, low-input varieties of staple crops; and biotechnology.

Agroforestry combines agricultural and forestry methods for cultivating woody plants and agricultural crops or livestock on the same land in an attempt to increase the total productivity of the plot. Currently, at least 11 major international research programs help finance agroforestry and community forestry projects in more than 50 developing countries, with expenditures totaling $750 million between 1972 and 1984. (See Chapter 5, "Forests and Rangelands.") One of the potentially most significant agroforestry systems for Africa is alley-cropping, a form of intercropping in which food crops are grown between regularly pruned hedgerows of fast-growing, nitrogen-fixing trees and shrubs. Because alley-cropping increases the organic matter, usable nutrients, and moisture levels of soils, it allows continuous cropping with improved crop yields even without additional inputs. (See Chapter 14, "Elements of Success: Sustainable Development in Sub-Saharan Africa.")

Research done at a number of the Consultative Group on International Agricultural Research centers, and followed up in farmers' fields, has demonstrated that intercropping often increases yields of basic foods. Work at the International Potato Center at Lima, Peru, shows that farmers enjoy higher total yields per unit of land when they intercrop maize with potatoes. The growing maize shades the soil from the hot sun, protecting the potato tubers but allowing the sun to reach the potato plants after the maize is harvested (93).

Intercropping is proving to be a valuable technique with many applications around the world. In Rwanda, farmers successfully intercrop potatoes with maize, beans, wheat, sorghum, taro, peas, and tobacco. Potatoes and maize are planted simultaneously, and four months later the potatoes are harvested. Then a bean crop is planted, using the maize stalks as support; after the maize is harvested, the stalks remain for the beans. In trials in Bangladesh and Mauritius, sugarcane was intercropped with potatoes, again with significantly increased yields (94). In the Cauca Valley of Colombia, intercropping maize and beans provides better control of the fall army worm in maize and leafhoppers in beans than is possible when the same crops are grown separately (95).

In the past few years hybridization has significantly improved yields of cowpeas—a nutritious crop that can survive drought conditions—again with the aid of intercropping. The International Institute for Tropical Agriculture reports that new varieties planted in Burkina Faso, Mali, Niger, and Nigeria have the potential to treble cowpea yields (96). During trials in Niger, only 150 millimeters of rain fell; yet 33 new lines yielded between 600 and 1,500 kilograms per hectare when grown as a single crop. Twenty of these lines produced more than 200 kilograms per hectare when intercropped with millet (97). The new varieties matured earlier than local cowpeas, which produce about 185 kilograms per hectare. In 1983, six new varieties were tested in Burkino Faso. Cowpeas that were mulched on untilled land produced substantially higher yields than plants that were not mulched on ploughed land (98).

The India-based International Crops Research Institute for the Semi-Arid Tropics (ICRISAT) helped develop higher-yielding strains of millet in the last five years that could have important consequences for the world's rural poor. Millet is the staple for millions in Africa and Asia. It is the only major grain crop that can survive in areas with as little as 190 millimeters of rain a year. It is these low rainfall areas that are cultivated by the poorest farmers who cannot afford irrigation (99).

In India, a strain of pearl millet, ICMV 1, was released to farmers in 1982; it is now planted on about half a million hectares. ICMV 1 is both higher yielding and resistant to downy mildew, a fungus that can devastate millet. Other new millets are performing well in tests in West African countries. Two varieties bred in regional trials at the Institut du Sahel in Senegal are showing encouraging results. In Mali, new millet strains are expected to yield up to 3,000 kilograms per hectare; average millet yields are currently 800 kilograms per hectare (100).

There have also been advances in the Sudan in developing an improved variety of sorghum. Hageen-Durra-1 has been bred by scientists from ICRISAT and the Sudan Agricultural Research Corporation. In the dry conditions of 1984, the new hybrid yielded nearly 900 kilograms per hectare when planted on dryland farms. Local varieties, by contrast, yielded only 200–300 kilograms per hectare. Under irrigation, yields of the new sorghum soared to 5,189 kilograms per hectare, against 1,112 kilograms per hectare for local varieties. Hageen-Durra-1 performed well with both high and low levels of fertilization. ICRISAT says that the seed is relatively easy to produce (101).

In Asia, developing new varieties of hybrid rice is still essential as population pressures on arable land continue to increase. Especially in the current period of low and stagnant rice prices, farmers look to hybrid rice varieties to provide an opportunity to increase efficiency and lower production costs. The result may be a reduction in the amount of land given over to rice production, leading to diversification into other crops, livestock, and household industry and increasing the earning potential of rice-growing households. The major success of hybrid rice is in temperate China, where it is important to national food self-sufficiency. This success was achieved by the development of early-maturing (less than 115 days) hybrids suitable for cultivation in the first crop season in double-cropping areas. However, because the current varieties favor irrigated and temperate rain-fed areas, only similar regions outside China would benefit from use of these new varieties (102).

Food and Agriculture

Biotechnology refers to the integrated use of biochemistry, microbiology, and chemical engineering to exploit the technological applications and biological capacities of natural species. Conventional animal- and plant-breeding methods take time; biotechnology can accelerate the processes with techniques such as cell and tissue culture, protoplast fusion, and genetic engineering (103). It could mean that food output is stepped up more quickly, with crops being produced that yield more, are tolerant to drought, heat, and salinity, and are less dependent on chemical fertilizers and pesticides. New technologies in embryology could make possible tremendous advances in genetic selection among larger animals that are more adaptable to Third World conditions.

Biotechnology is considerably more advanced in livestock than in crop applications. In industrialized countries, advances are being made in reproductive technologies, growth hormones, and new vaccines for livestock (104). Their potential benefits to the Third World include:

■ *diagnosis, prevention, and control of animal diseases,* using monoclonal antibody technology to diagnose, monitor, and research animal disease, and genetic engineering to expand the range of vaccines and other animal health care products
■ *promotion of animal nutrition and growth,* through the use of such biotechnology products as growth hormones and food additives
■ *genetic improvement of animal breeds,* ultimately involving the transfer of genes among different animal breeds (105).

The initial impact of biotechnology in the Third World is likely to be in livestock vaccines. For example, vaccines developed at the International Laboratory for Research into Animal Diseases in Kenya and other research centers could lead to major improvements in animal health in Africa (106).

The application of biotechnology to crops in the Third World is still at the research and development stages. It has two major goals. One is to improve specific plant characteristics by introducing or manipulating genes conferring resistance to disease, heat, or cold. The second is to manipulate microorganisms genetically to enhance the natural process of nitrogen fixation, to control pests and plant diseases, or to promote plant growth (107).

It is already possible to improve root crops using tissue culture techniques in vegetative reproduction (108). Almost 4,000 *in vitro* (test tube) cassava clones are now in storage at the Centro Internacional de Agricultura Tropical in Cali, Colombia (109). The International Board for Plant Genetic Resources believes that development of the full potential of *in vitro* culture, storage, and associated biochemical techniques would revolutionize the handling of germplasm (110).

RECENT DEVELOPMENTS

U.N. SPECIAL SESSION ON AFRICA

In the aftermath of the severe famine that hit Africa in 1984 and 1985, the General Assembly of the United Nations held a special session on Africa in May 1986. The first session ever held on a regional issue ended with the launching of the U.N. Programme of Action for African Economic Recovery and Development: 1986–1990, the heart of which is agriculture and related services (111). The Programme has two elements: "the determination and commitment" of African countries to undertake national and regional programs of recovery and development and "the response and commitment of the international community" to support and supplement the African development effort.

The U.N. Programme is designed to complement the Organization of African Unity's "Priority Programme for Economic Recovery," initiated by African heads of state in July 1985. African leaders then indicated a willingness to devote 20–25 percent of public investment to agriculture. At the special U.N. session, African officials did not hide the lack of priority accorded to agriculture in the past. Although no specific commitments were made, the international community pledged to support the development process that African countries are struggling to accomplish.

The Programme stresses immediate measures to combat food emergencies that aim to create and sustain national emergency preparedness, to institute effective early-warning systems, and to establish national food security programs. Medium-term measures will aim at raising substantially the level of agricultural investment; developing arable land and rendering it more productive; and establishing appropriate agricultural pricing policies, incentives, and credit schemes. The Programme also emphasizes the need to give small farmers the necessary inputs to increase yields, including better management of water resources, the establishment of low-cost irrigation schemes, reforestation programs, and drought and desertification control programs. These efforts are likely to cost $57.4 billion, slightly less than half the Programme's total budget of $128.1 billion.

Success will depend "on the parallel development of agriculture support sectors," whose importance is emphasized by their cost—$60.1 billion (112). This amount includes development of industries for producing agricultural tools and equipment; rehabilitation and upgrading of existing factories; utilization of renewable sources of energy, especially biomass and solar energy; establishment of a network for the production of spare parts and components; and provision of local training for project design and preparation.

African nations are committed to funding $82.5 billion of the Programme costs, leaving a gap of $45.6 billion. Participants at the session expressed doubts about whether the continent will be able to find the $82.5 billion if world commodity prices remain low and if they have to repay debts at existing levels—expected to be between $15 billion and $24 billion a year over the next five years. Again, the U.N. Programme contains no commitment by the international community either to help stabilize commodity prices or to relieve debt burdens.

The session was successful in highlighting some of the problems faced by Africa, and it should encourage increased domestic spending and aid flows to the continent's agricultural sector. But there are also doubts about whether the people most vulnerable to famine will be accorded any more priority than in the past. Although women farmers are a primary focus of the U.N. Programme, the developed market economy nations want African countries to reform their economies and encourage private investments. But prospective investors are unlikely to be interested, or indeed wanted, in the small-scale food production systems characteristic of Africa, where women do most of the work.

THE YEAR OF THE LOCUSTS

After two years of drought, the rains finally came to sub-Saharan Africa in late 1985 and early 1986. But with the rains came another threat: locusts. By mid-1986, at least four species of locusts and millions of grasshoppers were swarming over the Sahel and eastern Africa (113). Plagues of locusts are a common blight in Africa, but the 1986 invasion was particularly severe. Not since 1942 have the populations of all four major locust species exploded at the same time (114). Coming so soon after two years of famine, the invasion caused many African leaders and aid agency officials to predict ruined harvests and widespread hunger. However, the locust invasion was blunted by the well-coordinated efforts of the most seriously affected countries and the aid agencies.

In October 1986, the FAO announced that the worst of the threat was past. At least 90 percent of the foodcrops threatened by the Senegalese grasshopper in western

Africa had been saved, and eastern Africa had been spared the widely feared plague of red and African migratory locusts. The only remaining infestation is in southern Africa, where harried farmers are bracing for a second season of assaults from brown locusts (115). "From Mauritania in the west to Somalia in the east, Africans and the international community can be proud of a job well done," said FAO Director-General Edouard Saouma. "In the Sahel and eastern Africa, major food losses have been averted. We waged war on the farmer's oldest enemy and we won" (116). In the Sahelian region, more than 200,000 metric tons of food were saved that would otherwise have been eaten by rampaging grasshoppers and locusts (117).

But the costs were high. The FAO's Emergency Centre for Locust Operations coordinated a massive spraying operation in 13 African countries, involving 36 aircraft and 500 tons of pesticides sprayed over 1.6 million hectares (118). According to FAO reports, another 660,000 hectares remain to be sprayed. The total costs for the 1986–88 eradication program, estimated at $24 million, were provided entirely by bilateral and multilateral donors, mainly the United States, the EC, Canada, the Federal Republic of Germany, Italy, Japan, the Netherlands, France, Norway, and Sweden (119).

In addition, environmental costs may be involved. No assessment of the effects on the environment of these large doses of pesticides has yet been made.

References and Notes

1. United Nations Food and Agriculture Organization (FAO), *Food Outlook*, No. 9 (FAO, Rome, 1986), p. 3.
2. *Ibid.* 1, p. 4.
3. United Nations Food and Agriculture Organization (FAO), *Commodity Review and Outlook 1985–86*, FAO Economic and Social Development Series No. 40 (FAO, Rome, 1986), p. 4.
4. See "Agriculture in Africa," in World Resources Institute and International Institute for Environment and Development *World Resources Report 1986* (Basic Books, New York, 1986), pp. 55–56.
5. United Nations Food and Agriculture Organization (FAO), *Food Outlook*, No. 6 (FAO, Rome, 1986). The difficulty of analyzing shortages and surpluses was noted as six countries, including Sudan, faced "exceptional food emergencies" and seven countries, again including Sudan, actually had "exportable surpluses." Transportation problems make it difficult for surpluses to reach areas of need, but the more fundamental reason is poverty. "Surpluses" can exist in areas where there is great need but where local people have limited purchasing power.
6. Leonardo A. Paulino, *Food in the Third World: Past Trends and Projections to 2000*, Research Report 52 (International Food Policy Research Institute, Washington, D.C., 1986), pp. 38–39.
7. The World Bank, *Commodity Trade and Price Trends* (The World Bank, Washing-

ton, D.C., 1986), pp. 49–52, 54–56, 64–65, p. 68, p. 73, and p. 77.
8. International Monetary Fund (IMF), *Primary Commodities Market Developments and Outlook* (IMF, Washington, D.C., 1986), sections II–IV.
9. *Ibid.*
10. *Op. cit.* 3, p. 22.
11. *Op. cit.* 3, p. 22.
12. Barbara Dinham and Colin Hines, *Agribusiness in Africa* (Earth Resources Research, Ltd., London, 1983), pp. 187–188.
13. United Nations Food and Agriculture Organization (FAO), *International Trade and World Food Security* (FAO, Rome, 1985), p. 14 and Appendix A.
14. Joachim von Braun and Eileen Kennedy, *Commercialization of Subsistence Agriculture: Income and Nutritional Effects in Developing Countries*, Working Papers on Commercialization of Agriculture and Nutrition No. 1, CCP 85/15 (International Food Policy Research Institute, Washington, D.C., 1986), p. 1 and Table 1.
15. The World Bank, *World Development Report 1986* (Oxford University Press, New York, 1986), pp. 62–63.
16. Robert Repetto, "Economic Policy Reform for Natural Resource Conservation" (World Resources Institute, Washington, D.C., draft, 1986), p. 59.
17. *Op. cit.* 15, pp. 64–66.
18. *Op. cit.* 14.
19. *Op. cit.* 14, p. 36.

20. *Op. cit.* 15, pp. 67–68.
21. *Op. cit.* 15, pp. 77–78.
22. U. Lele, "Terms of Trade, Agricultural Growth, and Rural Poverty in Africa," in *Agricultural Change and Rural Poverty*, J.W. Mellor and G.M. Desai, eds. (Johns Hopkins University Press, Baltimore, Maryland, 1985), pp. 167–169.
23. United Nations Food and Agriculture Organization (FAO), *Women in Developing Agriculture* (FAO, Rome, 1985), p. 36.
24. *Op. cit.* 12, pp. 86–87.
25. Piers Blaikie, *The Political Economy of Soil Erosion in Developing Countries* (Longman, London, 1985), pp. 123–124.
26. L. Timberlake, *Africa in Crisis* (Earthscan, London, 1985), p. 73.
27. Stephen R. Gliessman, "Resource Management in Traditional Tropical Agroecosystems in Southeast Mexico," in *Agricultural Sustainability in a Changing World Order*, Gordon Douglas, ed. (Westview Press, Boulder, Colorado, 1984), pp. 191–201.
28. *Op. cit.* 16, p. 51.
29. Ranil Senanayake, "The Ecological, Energetic, and Agronomic Systems of Ancient and Modern Sri Lanka," in *Agricultural Sustainability in a Changing World*, Gordon Douglas, ed. (Westview Press, Boulder, Colorado, 1984), pp. 229–230.
30. I.F. Balk and J.H. Koeman, *Future Hazards from Pesticide Use*, Commission on Ecology Papers No. 6 (International Union for Conservation of Nature and Natural

Resources, Gland, Switzerland, 1984), pp. 18–19.

31. For example, 80 percent of all subsidized insecticides sold in Indonesia are used primarily on rice crops. Herbicides are used increasingly in rice production there, especially in the outer islands where labor for weeding is scarce. Robert Repetto, *Paying the Price: Pesticide Subsidies in Developing Countries* (World Resources Institute, Washington, D.C., 1985), p. 20.

32. Robert Goodland, *et al.*, *Environmental Management in Tropical Agriculture* (Westview Press, Boulder, Colorado, 1984), p. 65.

33. Robert Repetto, *Paying the Price: Pesticide Subsidies in Developing Countries,* Research Report No. 2 (World Resources Institute, Washington, D.C., December 1985), p. 1.

34. *Ibid.*, p. 11 and p. 24.

35. Gordon R. Conway, "The Future," in *Pesticide Resistance and World Food Production*, G.R. Conway, ed. (Imperial College Centre for Environmental Technology, London, 1982), p. 83.

36. *Ibid.*, p. 81.

37. *Op. cit.* 16, p. 33.

38. *Op. cit.* 32, p. 72.

39. Paul Harrison, "Boosting Food Production" in *The Greening of Africa* (Penguin Books, New York, and Paladin, London, in press, 1987).

40. T. Gupta, "The Economics of Tree Crops on Marginal Agricultural Lands with Special Reference to the Hot Arid Region in Rajasthan, India," *The International Tree Crops Journal*, Vol. 2, Alan Grainger, ed. (1983), pp. 155–194.

41. *Op. cit.* 25, p. 126.

42. *Op. cit.* 14, p. 52.

43. Larry Lev, "The Effect of Cash Cropping Among the Meru of Northern Tanzania," Working Paper 21 (Michigan State University, East Lansing, 1981), cited in Joachim von Braun and Eileen Kennedy, *Commercialization of Subsistence Agriculture: Income and Nutritional Effects in Developing Countries*, Working Papers on Commercialization of Agriculture and Nutrition No. 1 (International Food Policy Research Institute, Washington, D.C., 1986), p. 55.

44. *Op. cit.* 14, pp. 56–58.

45. U.N. Division for Economic and Social Information, pack prepared for the U.N. Special Session of the General Assembly on Africa, New York, May 1986.

46. United Nations Food and Agriculture Organization (FAO), *World Food Security: Selected Themes and Issues*, FAO Economic and Social Development Paper No. 53 (FAO, Rome, 1985), p. 17.

47. *Op. cit.* 15, p. 125.

48. Stuart Auerbach, "Farm Subsidies Have Global Impact," *The Washington Post* (July 13, 1986, Washington, D.C.), p. G6.

49. *Op. cit.* 15, p. 128.

50. *Op. cit.* 15, pp. 130–131.

51. *Op. cit.* 15, p. 122.

52. K. Schneider, "Cost of Farm Law Might Be Double Original Estimate," *The New York Times* (July 22, 1986), p. A15.

53. *Op. cit.* 15, p. 120.

54. *Op. cit.* 3, p. 123.

55. D.G. Johnson, "World Commodity Market Situation and Outlook," in *U.S. Agricultural Policy: The 1985 Farm Legislation*, B.L. Gardner, ed. (American Enterprise Institute for Public Policy Research, Washington, D.C., 1985), p. 35.

56. E.W. Learn, *et al.*, "American Farm Subsidies: A Bumper Crop," *The Public Interest*, No. 84 (1986), p. 77.

57. P.R. Crosson and A.T. Stout, *Productivity Effects of Cropland Erosion in the United States* (John Hopkins University Press, Baltimore, Maryland, 1983).

58. National Research Council (NRC), *Soil Conservation: Assessing the National Resources Inventory*, Vol. I, (National Academy Press, Washington, D.C., 1986) p. 11.

59. U.S. Department of Agriculture (USDA), *Soil, Water and Related Resources in the United States: Status, Conditions and Trends*, Part II (USDA, Washington, D.C., 1981), cited in American Farmland Trust (AFT), *Future Policy Directions for American Agriculture* (AFT, Washington, D.C., 1984), p. 54.

60. American Farmland Trust (AFT), *Soil Conservation in America: What Do We Have to Lose?* (AFT, Washington, D.C., 1984), p. 9.

61. E.H. Clark II, *et al.*, *Eroding Soils: The Off-Farm Impacts* (The Conservation Foundation, Washington, D.C., 1985), p. 174.

62. U.S. Congress, Office of Technology Assessment (OTA), "Impacts of Technology on U.S. Cropland and Rangeland Productivity" (OTA, Washington, D.C., 1982), cited in American Farmland Trust (AFT), *Soil Conservation in America: What Do We Have to Lose?* (AFT, Washington, D.C., 1984), p. 12.

63. *Op. cit.* 60, p. xvi.

64. C.W. Ogg, "New Cropland in the 1982 NRI: Implications for Resource Policy," in *NRC Soil Conservation: Assessing the National Resources Inventory*, Vol. II (National Academy Press, Washington, D.C., 1986), pp. 255–259.

65. Clive Potter, "Environmental Protection and Agricultural Adjustment: Lessons from the American Experience," Working Paper No. 1 (Department of Environmental Studies and Countryside Planning, Wye College, University of London, 1986), p. 10.

66. T.T. Phipps, "The Farm Bill, Resources, and Environmental Quality," *Resources*, No. 82 (Winter 1986), p. 4.

67. John R. Block, "Conserving Soil for America's Future," *Journal of Soil and Water Conservation*, Vol. 41 (1986), p. 30.

68. *Op. cit.* 66.

69. F. Steiner, "The New Federal Conservation Initiatives: Reactions from the Palouse," *Journal of Soil and Water Conservation*, Vol. 41, No. 3 (1986), p. 171.

70. E. Maltby, *Waterlogged Wealth: Why Waste the World's Wet Places?* (Earthscan, London, 1986), p. 90.

71. *Ibid.*, p. 106.

72. R.E. Heimlich and L.L. Lanner, "Swampbusting in Perspective," *Journal of Soil and Water Conservation*, Vol. 41, No. 4 (1986), pp. 219–224.

73. High Plains Associates, "Six-State High Plains Ogallala Aquifer Regional Resources Study" (U.S. Department of Commerce and High Plains Study Council, 1982), cited in American Farmland Trust (AFT), Future Policy Directions for American Agriculture (AFT, Washington, D.C., 1984), p. 60.

74. Sandra Postel, *Conserving Water: The Untapped Alternative*, Worldwatch Paper No. 67 (Worldwatch Institute, Washington, D.C., 1985), p. 10.

75. The Organisation for Economic Co-operation and Development (OECD), *The State of the Environment 1985* (OECD, Paris, 1985), p. 197.

76. F.R. Du Vivier, "Report on Behalf of the Committee on the Environment, Public Health and Consumer Protection on Agriculture and the Environment" (European Parliament, Strasbourg, France, 1986), p. 161.

77. P. Kromarek, *European Aspects of Soil and Ground Protection Policy* (Institute for European Environmental Policy, Bonn, West Germany, 1984), p. 7.

78. David Baldock, *Wetland Drainage in Europe: The Effects of Agricultural Policy in Four EEC Countries* (International Institute for Environment and Development and Institute for European Environmental Policy, London, 1984), p. 161.

79. *Ibid.*, p. 159.

80. *Op. cit.* 76, p. 30.

81. David Baldock, *The CAP Price Policy and the Environment—An Exploratory Essay* (Institute for European Environmental Policy, Bonn, West Germany, December 1984), p. 39.

82. *Op. cit.* 75, p. 191.

83. *Op. cit.* 77, p. 11.

84. A. Dam Kofoed, "Pathways of Nitrate and Phosphate to Ground and Surface Water," in *Environment and Chemicals in Agriculture*, F.P.W. Winteringham, ed. (Elsevier Applied Science Publishers, London), pp. 27–69.

85. M. Vighi and G. Chiaudani, "The Impact of Agricultural Loads on Eutrophication in EEC Surface Waters," in *Environment and Chemicals in Agriculture*, F.P.W. Winteringham, ed. (Elsevier Applied Science Publishers, London, 1985), pp. 71–85.

86. *Op. cit.* 76, p. 32.

87. *Op. cit.* 84.

88. *Op. cit.* 85.

89. *Op. cit.* 76, p. 34.

90. *Op. cit.* 77, p. 8.

91. *Op. cit.* 65, p. 10.

92. Nature Conservancy Council (NCC), *Nature Conservation Press Release* (NCC, London, August 14, 1986).

93. "Intercropping Pays Off," *International Agricultural Development*, Vol. 6, No. 5 (1986), p. 17.

94. *Ibid.*

95. C. Francis and R. Harwood, *Enough Food: Achieving Food Security through Regenerative Agriculture* (Rodale Institute, Emmaus, Pennsylvania, 1985), p. 13.

96. International Institute for Tropical Agriculture (IITA), *Research Highlights for 1984* (IITA, Ibadan, Nigeria, 1985), pp. 18–19.

97. *Ibid.*, pp. 20–21.

98. *Ibid.*, pp. 24–25.

99. "The Green Advance of Millet," *International Agricultural Development*, Vol. 5,

No. 3 (1985), p. 7.

100. *Ibid.*

101. "High Yields in Drought Conditions," *International Agricultural Development*, Vol. 5, No. 3 (1985), p. 20.

102. Hunan Provincial Association for Science and Technology, Hunan Hybrid Rice Research Center, and International Rice Research Institute, International Symposium on Hybrid Rice, "Recommendations, Program and Participants" (Changsha, Hunan, China, October 6–10, 1986).

103. D. Dembo, *et al.*, "The Biorevolution and the Third World," *Third World Affairs 1985* (Third World Foundation for Social and Economic Studies, London, 1985) pp. 311–312.

104. R.J. Kalter, *et al.*, "Biotechnology and the Dairy Industry: Production Costs and Commercial Potential of Bovine Growth Hormone" (Cornell University, Department of Agricultural Economics, Ithaca, New York, 1984), cited in R. Barker, "Research in Biotechnology in the United States: Implications for Developing Countries and IARCS" (International Rice Research Institute, Laguna, Philippines, 1986), p. 14.

105. John Elkington, *Double Dividends? U.S. Biotechnology and Third World Development* (World Resources Institute, Washington, D.C., 1986), p. 13.

106. R. Barker, "Research in Biotechnology in the United States: Implications for Developing Countries and IARCS" (International Rice Research Institute, Laguna, Philippines, 1986), p. 14.

107. *Op. cit.* 105, p. 29.

108. *Op. cit.* 106.

109. "Biotechnology and the CGIAR," *CGIAR Newsletter*, Vol. 5, No. 3 (Consultative Group on International Agricultural Research, 1985), p. 3.

110. Lyndsey A. Withers and J.T. Williams, "In Vitro Conservation," *IBPGR Research Highlights 1984–1985* (International Board for Plant Genetic Resources, Rome, 1985), p. 1.

111. U.N. General Assembly, *U.N. Programme of Action for African Economic Recovery and Development: 1986–1990*, A/RES/S-13/2 (United Nations, New York, 1986).

112. *Ibid.*, p. 8.

113. Debora MacKenzie, "Locusts Rampage over the Famine Fields of Africa," *New Scientist*, Vol. III, No. 1522 (1986), p. 15.

114. *Ibid.*

115. United Nations Food and Agriculture Organization (FAO), "Threat of Locust and Grasshopper Plague Recedes in Western, Eastern Africa; FAO Director-General Says Major Food Losses Averted" (FAO, press release, Rome, October 1986), p. 1.

116. *Ibid.*

117. *Ibid.*

118. *Ibid.*, p. 2.

119. United Nations Food and Agriculture Organization (FAO), *The State of Food and Agriculture 1986* (FAO, Rome, October 1986), p. 13.

5. Forests and Rangelands

Although the distinction between forests and rangelands seems obvious, the two ecosystems actually overlap a great deal. In areas where rain is relatively sparse and the soils poor, trees are scattered in "open woodlands" with varying degrees of density, making it difficult to tell where the grassland begins and the forest ends (1). Both woodlands and grazing lands may support livestock. In fact, there are many areas that both forest and rangeland managers claim as their own—areas that are managed for wood and fodder simultaneously.

In their natural state, forests tend to change little from year to year. Nonetheless, humans can effect a rapid change on large areas of forested land—often for the worse. Parts of Europe and the southeastern United States have suffered a decade and a half of severe forest fires, most of them caused by careless people. In Europe and North America, data suggest that air pollution is severely hampering growth rates and survival of trees over vast areas.

Even more devastating is the continuing destruction of forests in the tropics. While forested area in most temperate regions is declining only slightly, tropical forests in Central America have been reduced by 38 percent and in Africa by 23 percent in little more than 30 years. Little of the forested area is managed by professional foresters, or is under management plans. Worldwide, managed forests represent only 3 percent of the total; most of these are in developed countries.

International development banks and aid organizations are being forced to become more innovative in their approach toward forests in the developing world. Where appropriate, they are encouraging commercial management of cut-over forests. Plantations of commercially valuable trees are being established on increasingly large areas where capital is available. Most importantly, banks are beginning to apply more sophisticated economic analysis to forest-management projects that include benefits other than timber—including protection of watersheds, production of so-called "minor" forest products, such as rattan, fruits and resins, and recreation and tourism. Frequently these values are more important to local economies than the most valuable timber.

Techniques that manipulate the genetic makeup of trees, until recently almost the exclusive province of developed nations, have begun producing impressive results in the tropics with fast-growing species such as *Leucaena leucocephala*. Brazilian researchers working for a private company have revolutionized the use of rooted *Leucaena* cuttings to produce timber and fuelwood at unprecedented rates. Meanwhile, scientists have begun talking about a future in which artificial seeds—packages of genetic material whose every trait has been determined by humans—will be available to forest managers. Unfortunately, achieving those genetic advances requires huge amounts of cash and scientific resources, two of the scarcest commodities in developing nations.

For much of the Third World, research has centered increasingly on forestry methods that allow farmers to incorporate trees with their crops, obtaining forest benefits without having to exploit the remaining uncut woodlands. Many of the techniques of this form of management, or agroforestry, are improvements of methods that have been used sustainably by local people for hundreds or even thousands of years.

Rangelands, areas that provide forage for free-ranging livestock and wild animals, cover more than half of the world's land surface. Most of these lands are too dry, steep, rocky, or cold for agriculture, but can be used efficiently to produce animal protein.

Most of the world's rangelands have suffered some degree of degradation from overgrazing or mismanagement. While some degraded rangeland in developed countries has been restored to productivity, vast areas in Third World countries, especially in Africa and the Middle East, are under increasing pressure from growing numbers of people and livestock.

Although the United Nations Conference on Desertification drew world attention to the plight of drylands in 1977, the situation had not improved six years later when efforts to stem desertification were evaluated. Both development assistance agencies and developing nations have been reluctant to invest in range improvement projects that affect relatively few people and take many years to show results.

On the other hand, there have been some striking successes in range reclamation. In the United States, the Bureau of Land Management successfully plowed and reseeded a severely degraded area of 2.6 million hectares in Oregon. The vast area of the United States that was devastated by the Dust Bowl of the 1930s now has a stable grass cover and is productively used for grazing. In Somalia, a project sponsored by the World Bank and the U.S. Agency for International Development is stabilizing sand dunes to provide fodder for livestock.

CONDITIONS AND TRENDS

FOREST RESOURCES

At one time the world's forests and woodlands probably covered 6 billion hectares. By 1954, the total had declined to approximately 4 billion hectares because of the increasing use of land for agriculture, pasture, and settlements for a rapidly growing population (2).

Evaluating long-term trends is difficult. But one recent assessment (3) indicates that, historically, the greatest relative changes in the vegetation cover have occurred in temperate regions. Since large-scale land clearing for agriculture began around 8,000 years ago cold-winter deciduous forests (seasonal broadleaved forests) have been reduced by 32–33 percent. In contrast, most natural climax tropical vegetation has been reduced by only 15–20 percent over the past several millennia. Some 24–25 percent of all wooded savannas and tropical/subtropical deciduous forests have been cleared, while until recently only slight losses (4–6 percent) of tropical evergreen rainforests and tropical/subtropical evergreen needle-leaved forests have occurred (4).

The balance is changing, however. Over the past three decades, reduction of forested areas has been far greater in the tropics than in temperate regions. Temperate forest areas in Europe, Asia, and Oceania have grown slightly as reforestation and reversion of cropland to forestland more than offset losses to urbanization, roads, and other uses. In North America, the total forested area increased steadily in the early 20th Century, after centuries of decline. More recently, however, the total has again dropped slightly.

In tropical regions, deforestation rates have been 10–20 times greater than reforestation in recent years. Average annual deforestation is greatest in Latin America, and it is also high in Africa's open forests. In Central America the area of forests and woodlands declined 38 percent, from 115 to 71 million hectares, and in Africa by 23 percent, from 901 to 690 million hectares, between 1950 and 1983 (5). In the commercially unproductive (6) closed forests of Africa and Asia, deforestation rates were relatively low. In the early 1980s, annual losses equalled about 0.6 percent of all remaining forests in all three tropical regions, though exact amounts and rates varied more than a hundredfold among countries. (See *World Resources 1986*, p. 73, Table 5.10 for the deforestation rates and areas deforested annually in selected tropical countries.)

Estimates of forest area reveal little about the condition of forest resources (e.g., changes in the density of the tree cover or in the productivity or composition of forests). In general, as long as tree cover appears to exceed 10–20 percent, an area is considered forested, even though the forest may have been significantly degraded and the number of trees per hectare reduced from several hundred to fewer than 50.

One cause of the loss of forestlands has been the conversion of forests to agricultural land. Since 1976, 6–8 million hectares of open forests and woodlands have been cleared each year for agriculture (7). Annually, 4–5 million hectares of commercially productive closed forests are logged, and over 90 percent of this area later becomes cropland. Another 14.5 million hectares of fallow land that is regenerating as forests are cleared each year; of that, 3.3 million hectares are converted to permanent agriculture and the remainder returned to forest fallow by shifting cultivators (8).

Extent of the World's Forests

Until recently, studies of forest resources worldwide have been poorly coordinated and hampered by expensive and inefficient technology. For those reasons, global data on forests are controversial. Some of the most comprehensive statistics on tropical forests, gathered by the United Nations Food and Agriculture Organization (FAO), are more than a decade old. More accurate information now emerging from country-by-country studies, particularly in Africa and Asia, is superseding the FAO data on a national basis. Until these data can be made consistent with global assessments, however, policymakers continue to use the FAO statistics (9).

Table 5.1, which gives 1980 FAO statistics plus an updated estimate for 1985, shows that in 1985 closed-canopy forests covered 2.8 billion hectares (or 69 percent of the forested areas worldwide) and the less densely

Table 5.1 Distribution of the World's Forest Lands, 1985

(millions of hectares)

Region	Total Land Area	Closed Forest Broadleaved[a]	Closed Forest Coniferous	Open Forest	Total Forest Area	Percent of Total Land Area Forested	Other Wooded Land Shrubland[b]	Other Wooded Land Forest Fallow[c]	Total Wooded Area[d]	Percent of Total Land Area Wooded
North America[e]	1,835	168	301	215	684	37	X	NA	684	37
Europe	472	65	88	21	174	37	X	NA	174	37
USSR	2,227	147	645	128	920	41	X	NA	920	41
Other Countries[f]	950	50	22	70	142	15	X	NA	142	15
Developed Countries Subtotal	**5,484**	**430**	**1,056**	**434**	**1,920**	**35**	**X**	**NA**	**1,920**	**35**
Africa	2,966	216	2	500	718	24	450	160	1,328	45
Latin America	2,054	666	26	250	942	46	150	170	1,262	61
Asia (except China and Oceania)	1,640	317	30	83	430	26	45	76	551	34
China	933	97	25	15	137	15	30	X	167	18
Developing Countries Subtotal	**7,593**	**1,296**	**83**	**848**	**2,227**	**29**	**675**	**406**	**3,308**	**44**
1985 World Totals	**13,077**	**1,726**	**1,139**	**1,282**	**4,147**	**32**	**675**	**406**	**5,228**	**40**
1980 World Totals	**13,077[g]**	**1,827**	**1,121**	**1,372**	**4,320**	**33**	**624**	**407**	**5,381**	**41**

X = not available
NA = not applicable
Notes:
a. Includes bamboo and mangrove formations.
b. Includes area with woody vegetation greater than 0.5 meters and less than 7 meters in height; counted by the United Nations Food and Agriculture Organization as "other land" (see Table 5.6).
c. Includes wooded areas with forest regrowth following clearing for shifting cultivation within the past 20 years.
d. Includes forest area and other wooded land.
e. Canada and the United States.
f. Australia, New Zealand, Japan, Israel, and South Africa.
g. "World Totals" exclude Antarctica.
Sources:
1. For 1980 world totals: United Nations Food and Agriculture Organization (FAO)/Economic Commisson for Europe (ECE), *Forest Resources 1980* (FAO/ECE, Rome, 1985).
2. For 1985 world totals: R. Persson, unpublished report to Swedish International Development Authority (1985), Tables 1, 2, and 4.
3. For total and regional land area: United Nations Food and Agriculture Organization (FAO), *1983 Production Yearbook*, Vol. 37 (FAO, Rome, 1984), Table 1, p. 56.

wooded open forests covered 1.3 billion hectares for a total forested area of 4.1 billion hectares. In addition, natural shrublands and degraded forests covered 675 million hectares and forest regrowth on fallowed cropland covered 406 million hectares. The total, nearly 5.2 billion hectares of woody vegetation, covered about 40 percent of the world's total land area.

Excluding forest fallow, shrubland, and trees outside the forest, closed forests and open woodlands still cover three times as much area as croplands and 75 percent more than grasslands (10). Today, forests and woodlands account for 60 percent of the net productivity of biomass in terrestrial ecosystems; of that productivity, tropical forests account for 63 percent (11).

There are several ways to compare forestry statistics including whether they have open or closed canopies, are coniferous or non-coniferous, are in temperate or tropical zones, or are in developed or developing countries.

■ Seventy-seven percent (1.6 billion hectares) of the forests in temperate regions are categorized as having closed canopies (12), while about 62 percent of the tropical forests have closed canopies (13).

■ The world's coniferous forests, the source of most industrial wood production, cover 1.1 billion hectares, or 27 percent of the world's total forest area. Some 83 percent of these forests are in North America and the USSR. Non-coniferous forests (14) cover 1.7 billion hectares, or 42 percent of the forest area. About 1.6 billion hectares of these forests are found in South America and Africa, with another 567 million hectares in Asia and Oceania (15).

■ Tropical forests—including closed forests, open forests, shrubland, and forest fallow—cover nearly 3 billion hec-tares worldwide. An area roughly equal to one fifth of closed and open tropical forests now lies fallow—the result of clearing by shifting cultivators within the past 20 years. Latin America includes the largest expanses of closed tropical forests and Africa contains two thirds of all open tropical forests.

■ Slightly more than half the world's forests are in developing countries, where they cover 2.3 billion hectares, or 30 percent of the land area (16). In developed countries, forested areas amount to approximately 1.8 billion hectares or about 33 percent of these countries' land area (17).

FOREST MANAGEMENT

Most of the world's forests are not consciously managed for the sustained production of timber or for any other purpose. Management plans covered only 527 million hectares (23 percent) of the world's 4.1 billion hectares of forests, according to a report made during the 1960s by the United Nations Food and Agriculture Organization (FAO) (18). Table 5.2 shows that between 1963 and 1983 the amount of land under management plans increased in the Soviet Union, the United States, and tropical Asia, and has decreased in Europe, tropical Africa, Central America and the Caribbean, and tropical South America, but increased overall to 1 billion hectares.

Developing countries manage less of their forests than developed countries do. Of 1.2 billion hectares of tropical closed forests in developing countries, only 42 million hectares (4.7 percent) are under "intensive management" (19). (See Figure 5.1.) India contains most of these

Table 5.2 Management of Closed Forests
(thousands of hectares)

Region/Country	Total Area of Closed Forest[a]	Area of Productive Closed Forest[b]	Area Under Management Plans, 1963	Area Under Management Plans, 1983
Europe	145,486	133,304	93,010	83,484
Soviet Union	791,600	534,500	299,965	791,600
United States	195,256	189,961	84,378	102,362
Tropical Asia	305,510	200,989	37,370	39,790
Tropical Africa	216,634	163,033	10,610	1,735
Tropical America	678,655	521,651	2,444	522
World Total	**2,333,141**	**1,743,438**	**527,777**	**1,019,493**

Notes:
a. Closed-canopy forest that is suitable for industrial wood production (i.e., not commercial timberland).
b. "Productive" forests are those that can be logged. Table does not include data on open forests in the regions listed; the forest areas of China, Canada, and other countries in temperate Asia, Africa, and Latin America are also excluded.

Sources:
1. Data for tropical regions are from United Nations Food and Agriculture Organization (FAO), *Forest Resources of Tropical Asia* (FAO, Rome, 1981), Tables 1c and 1d; and FAO, *Los Recursos Forestales de la America Tropical* (FAO, Rome, 1981), Tables 1c and 1d, pp. 42–43.
2. Data for Europe and the Soviet Union are from Economic Commission for Europe (ECE)/United Nations Food and Agriculture Organization, *The Forest Resources of the ECE Region* (ECE, Geneva, 1985), pp. 19–20.
3. Data for the United States are from U.S. Forest Service, *An Assessment of the Forest and Rangeland Situation in the U.S.* (U.S. Department of Agriculture, Washington, D.C., 1980), p. 366.
4. Data on area under management plans for 1963 are from United Nations Food and Agriculture Organization (FAO), "Wood: World Trends and Prospects," *Unasylva*, Vol. 20., No. 80–81 (1966), Table III-A, p. 66.
5. Data on area under management plans for 1983 are from United Nations Food and Agriculture Organization (FAO), *Forest Resources of Tropical Asia* (FAO, Rome, 1981), Tables 1c and 1d; and FAO, *Los Recursos Forestales de la America Tropical* (FAO, Rome, 1981); and Economic Commission for Europe (ECE)/United Nations Food and Agriculture Organization, *The Forest Resources of the ECE Region* (ECE, Geneva, 1985), Table 2.3.
6. Data for United States are estimated from commercial forestland in tree farms or owned by the U.S. Forest Service, Bureau of Land Management, state forest agencies, and forest industries. See U.S. Forest Service, Source 3, above.

managed forests (78 percent), along with three other countries in Asia, four in Africa, and one in tropical America (20).

Natural Forest Management

Most of the managed forest throughout the world is natural forest—composed primarily of the tree species that existed before any logging and therefore not composed of artificially planted trees. In the tropics, for example, artificially regenerated or planted forests totaled only 17 percent (7.07 million hectares) of the forests under intensive management by 1980—or only 0.5 percent of tropical closed forests as a whole. The remaining 35 million hectares that are managed intensively are natural forests (21). These natural forests present foresters with some of their most difficult challenges.

Many nations in West Africa practice "zero treatment," in which officials prevent further exploitation of cut-over forests and wait until market demands make the remaining trees more valuable (22). At the other end of the spectrum is 'intensive management," in which foresters not only control logging but also suppress plants and trees that compete with valuable timber species and protect the forest against fire and disease (23). In "multiple-use" management, managers have broader goals: they work with some form of the original forest in order to attain a variety of benefits, such as watershed protection, recreation, wildlife habitat, genetic diversity, and non-timber wood products.

Not all managed natural forests are logged. Tropical moist forests, for example, are also important for retention of soil and water; for their influence on climate; as a source of new agricultural and timber species, gene pool,

food and shelter for animals and humans; as subjects of research; and for their supply of so-called "minor" forest products, including rattan, latex, fruits, medicinal plants, and resins. According to a survey by the International Union for Conservation of Nature and Natural Resources (IUCN), approximately one of every six species in tropical moist forests has some direct economic non-timber use (24). Minor forest products, for example, earned Indonesia $32 million in 1982 (25). Forests also serve to control the yields and quality of water for agricultural and urban areas. Studies in the United States show that properly managed forested watersheds can reduce flooding by as much as 35 percent and increase water yields by 7 percent while retaining water quality (26). This finding has important implications for developing countries, where some 150 million hectares of watershed have been degraded by human and livestock pressures (27).

In financial terms, however, timber is by far the most important benefit of natural forests, particularly in cash-poor developing nations. Annual production of sawlogs and veneer logs from natural tropical forests averaged nearly 140 million cubic meters between 1976 and 1979 (28). (See Table 5.3.) The value of logs exported from developing nations during those years totaled more than $2.7 billion (29). Previously untouched tropical forests are being logged at a rate of 4.4 million hectares per year; another 7.5 million hectares are cleared for agriculture and other purposes (30). As easily accessible virgin forests

Figure 5.1 Management of Tropical Closed Forests
(million hectares)

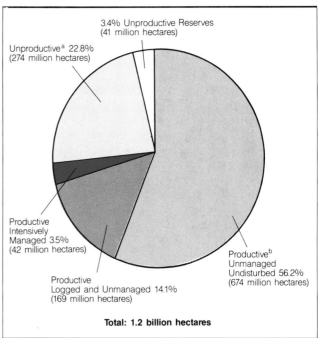

3.4% Unproductive Reserves (41 million hectares)

Unproductive[a] 22.8% (274 million hectares)

Productive Intensively Managed 3.5% (42 million hectares)

Productive Logged and Unmanaged 14.1% (169 million hectares)

Productive[b] Unmanaged Undisturbed 56.2% (674 million hectares)

Total: 1.2 billion hectares

Notes:
a. "Unproductive" forests are those that cannot be exploited commercially because of inaccessibility, topography, protected status, or other reasons. Such forests may be highly productive in an ecological sense.
b. "Productive" forests are those that can be logged.
Source: United Nations Food and Agriculture Organization (FAO), *Tropical Forest Resources,* Forestry Paper No. 30 (FAO, Rome 1982), Table 1d, p. 47.

Table 5.3 Annual Production of Logs in the Tropics[a], 1976-79

(thousand cubic meters)

Region	Total	From Natural Forests Only
Tropical America		
Broadleaved	22,140	21,400
Coniferous	20,250	12,000
Total	**42,390**	**33,400**
Tropical Africa		
Broadleaved	16,000	15,350
Coniferous	710	150
Total	**16,710**	**15,500**
Tropical Asia		
Broadleaved	77,250	73,550
Coniferous	2,770	2,750
Total	**80,020**	**76,300**
Total Tropics		
Broadleaved	115,390	110,300
Coniferous	23,730	14,900
Total	**139,120**	**125,200**

Note: a. Includes sawlogs and veneer logs.
Source: United Nations Food and Agriculture Organization (FAO), *Tropical Forest Resources*, Forestry Paper No. 30 (FAO, Rome, 1982), p. 59.

are diminished, commercial foresters are looking increasingly to secondary, or logged-over, forests to supply future timber needs. Unfortunately, many of the trees in such forests were deliberately left behind by loggers the first time around: less valuable species, trees of poor form, or trees with unworkable fiber or wood (31).

In developed nations, silviculture—the management of trees for economic uses—has been most successful with forests of a single species of trees that are all the same age, such as the Douglas fir forests in the northwestern United States (32). Tropical forests, on the other hand, contain an astonishing variety of trees. For example, an area of 126,000 square kilometers in the sultanate of Brunei and the neighboring state of Sarawak in Malaysia contains at least 2,500 native tree species. By contrast, in twice the area, Great Britain contains only 35 species (33).

Despite the diversity, silvicultural techniques to increase the volume and growth rate of valuable species in tropical moist forests have succeeded in relatively small areas in such countries as India, Ghana, Congo, Gabon, and Suriname (34). Techniques include shelterwood cuts that remove less valuable trees and allow desired species to reestablish themselves under their larger parents; selective logging that removes the larger trees and leaves smaller ones to grow; and "enrichment" planting, in which valued species are planted in gaps where trees have been logged. In general, however, natural forest management has produced disappointing results. In India, annual growth of natural forests is only 0.7 to 2.9 cubic meters of wood per hectare—compared to growth rates of 5 to 20 cubic meters of wood per hectare in plantations. Throughout the developing world, managed natural forests actually produce *less* wood than unmanaged forests mainly because managed forests are usually second-growth forests, while unmanaged forests are a mixture of virgin and second-growth stands. (See Table 5.4.) Because of selective culling of non-commercial species, however, the species present in managed forests tend to be more valuable (35).

Because trees grow so slowly in tropical natural forests, managing these forests for timber is usually less economically viable than using the same land for agriculture or pasture. In peninsular Malaysia, for example, the most commercially productive natural forest earns only one third the return from investment that would be gained if the same forest were converted to rubber or oil-palm plantations (36). One solution to this productivity problem is to rely increasingly on plantations for producing tropical timber, while protecting a large portion of natural forests to allow them to serve their important environmental and social purposes (37). However, plantation forestry still has a number of management problems, such as disease control, that limits its success in widely varying sites throughout the Third World. Monoculture plantation forests also reduce the biodiversity of plant and animal species and may alter the soil chemistry to prevent growth of other tree species. In the likely event that the massive planting necessary to meet future demands is not carried out, managers must rely instead on increasingly sophisticated management methods and on harvesting, planting, and processing technologies that make maximum use of both natural and planted forest land.

Table 5.4 Yields From Natural Tropical Moist Forests

(mean annual wood increment in metric tons per hectare)

Location	Unmanaged Forest	Managed Forest
Africa	2.3-5.8	0.6-1.3
America	0.9-1.9	0.6-2.0
Asia	3.7-4.5	1.3-2.6

Note: Data for unmanaged forest refer to stands that are essentially in balance; increment is only enough to offset losses caused by occasional natural catastrophes.
Source: Frank H. Wadsworth, "Production of Usable Wood from Tropical Forests," in *Tropical Rain Forest Ecosystems: Structure and Function*, F.B. Golley, ed. (Elsevier Scientific Publishing Company, New York, 1983), Table 14.4, p. 281.

TRENDS IN COMMERCIAL FORESTS

The most sophisticated research in forestry—applied genetics, or "tree improvement"—concentrates on the tree itself. For centuries, foresters have collected and cultivated seed from trees that exhibit favorable characteristics such as fast growth, good form, good wood quality, resistance to pests and disease, and tolerance to cold and drought. Historically, the process has been slow and inefficient; environmental factors often obscured the trees' genetic endowments, and improvement appeared in small increments over decades. Recent advances in genetic research and tree-propagation techniques make tree breeding a science that is yielding enormous benefits in forest management, particularly on plantations.

It is difficult to assess the rate of tree improvement around the world; all new plantations intentionally or unintentionally determine the resulting forest's gene pool simply by using a limited number of seeds or seedlings. Some of the most sophisticated tree-improvement methods, described below, are already in use in developed countries.

Seed Collection: Seed is gathered from trees that appear to be favorable for commercial use, including nearly all developed-world species used in plantations. Seed cooperatives and donor agencies, including the Central America and Mexico Coniferous Resources Cooperative (CAMCORE), the Danish International Development Agency (DANIDA), and the Commonwealth Forestry Institute (CFI), collect seed for tree breeding and conservation throughout the developing world (38). CFI cooperates with individual national research institutions to collect and test the genetic value of several tropical pine species. The network has conducted trials of Caribbean pine and *Pinus oocarpa* in 50 tropical countries (39).

Seed orchards: These genetic tree farms produce high-quality seed in quantity. The most common technique grafts branches from superior trees onto rootstock (hardy trees whose tops have been removed) and crossbreeds the graft with other superior trees. The offspring are subjected to "provenance" trials to select the best trees, and the process is repeated (40).

Rooted cuttings: This technique, which is much less expensive than grafting, is possible with only a limited number of species. Branches cut from superior trees are placed in a nutrient-rich medium and made to form roots; these rooted cuttings are clones of the original tree. Cuttings of several poplar species are grown widely in Europe, North America, and China. There are two major disadvantages of rooted cuttings: they are impossible to produce in most species, and the best cuttings are taken from immature trees whose eventual growth and form are uncertain.

Tissue culture: This newer method of cloning allows the replication of both old and young trees. Seed from a superior tree is allowed to germinate, and the tiny sprouts are removed and transferred to a series of solutions to grow buds, shoots, and roots. There are few programs in the field as yet. However, in the United States, the Weyerhaeuser Corporation—which pioneered the technique in the late 1970s—plans soon to begin producing 100,000 tissue-cultured clones of Douglas fir per year in the country's Northwest region (41).

Cell Culture and Bioengineering: In the future, geneticists hope to develop trees from individual cells—a technique that would allow the immediate propagation of an unlimited number of clones from a single tree. Successful experiments have already been conducted with crops such as tobacco, corn, and tomatoes. Recent advances in DNA research, in which individual genes have been identified and isolated, promise future breeding programs that allow favorable genetic traits to be inserted directly into tree cells and duplicated indefinitely. In addition, cells that have mutated naturally or have been artificially mutated might produce trees that survive high salt concentrations, cold, or drought (42). The ultimate goal, according to researchers, is to use cell culture to produce "embryoids," or microscopic infant trees, and manufacture them in capsule form as artificial seeds (43). These seeds would contain precisely the genetic structure that foresters desire.

Although the ability to grow trees from cell cultures is years away, current tree-improvement programs have already produced impressive results. (See Box 5.1.) The programs are generally most advanced in the developed countries, especially in Europe, Canada, the United States, and the Soviet Union (44). However, research on Caribbean pine and teak, two important species for the Third World, shows promise.

The new technology has raised concern that genetic selection might reduce the gene pool and limit the options for future breeding. Although many tree species have been considered for commercial purposes, they represent only a fraction of the possibilities. Unlike agriculture, the genetic base for forestry is still broad. In addition, by constantly "outbreeding" genetically manipulated trees with individuals from natural stands, most breeding programs attempt to increase, rather than restrict, the genetic base of individual plantations. In addition, increasing numbers of national parks and equivalent reserves are being established with genetic diversity as one of the criteria for management (45).

In the short term, more emphasis could be placed on using indigenous species for fuelwood, polewood, fencing and shelterbelts. Often, only fast-growing species are used, whereas the indigenous species are often better adapted to local conditions. Over the past 20 years, Malaysia has increased its number of commercial tropical forest tree species from 100 to more than 600 (46).

Box: 5.1 Aracruz: A Genetic Revolution in Brazil

Not all the successes in forestry genetics are restricted to the future, or to the temperate countries. In Brazil, forests of various *Eucalyptus* species grown from rooted cuttings by a private pulp company, Aracruz, have revolutionized plantation forestry in the region. The techniques have huge potential in other developing countries for raising fast-growing trees for pulp or fuelwood (1).

Established in 1967, Aracruz began planting *Eucalyptus* in Espirito Santo state on the coast of Brazil. In 1978, the company began operating the world's largest single plant for making bleached pulp. Aracruz now raises a total of 54 species, primarily *Eucalyptus*, and plants 14 million rooted cuttings per year. Workers fell selected trees and collect sprouts that form on the trunks. The cuttings are treated to stimulate root formation and grown in a nursery.

The average annual growth rate among Aracruz's 14 million trees is 70 cubic meters per hectare. The trees grow as fast as 2 centimeters per day, reaching 20 meters in height in less than three years (2).

References and Notes

1. John Spears, "Role of the Development Banks in Forestry Financing," *Proceedings, Society of American Foresters Annual Meeting* (Society of American Foresters, Bethesda, Maryland, 1985), p. 344.
2. Leopoldo Garcia Brandao, in *The New Eucalyptus Forest*, lectures given by the 1984 Marcus Wallenberg Prize winners, (Marcus Wallenberg Foundation, Falun, Sweden, 1984), pp. 3–15.

FOCUS ON: AGROFORESTRY

During the past decade, managers in developing nations have sought a comprehensive solution to the intertwined problems of deforestation and the need for increased production of food and fuelwood. One of the most promising "new" systems is agroforestry, a set of land-management techniques borrowed from both the latest science and from ancient practice. As the name implies, agroforestry combines agricultural and forestry methods to grow woody plants on the same land as agricultural crops or animals (47). By integrating different uses on a single tract, the manager attempts to increase the total productivity. When the technique is sustained, its benefits reach beyond the farm; increased harvests of fuelwood, food, meat, and other products lessen pressures on farmers to seek new agricultural lands at the expense of neighboring forests.

As early as 8,000 years ago, humans making the transition to agriculture from hunting and gathering developed a primitive agroforestry technique. They cut the forest, then dried and burned it to clear the land for planting, returning to the soil the nutrients trapped in the forest biomass. Cropping lasted for several years, and then the land was left for as long as a decade to allow the forest to rejuvenate—and to prepare it for another round of burning and cropping (48). Though it is the simplest of agroforestry methods, that technique—called shifting cultivation, or "swidden"—has by no means died out. Shifting cultivation is still practiced on 30 percent of the area where the technique is possible (49). However, over time swidden is not always beneficial, either to the people practicing it or to the land itself. Where populations are growing rapidly, farmers shorten the fallow periods and seek new forests to burn, often taking over tracts recently cut by the forest industry. In Africa, swidden is responsible for 70 percent of the continent's deforestation (50).

Within the past ten years, new forms of agroforestry have become recognized as an alternative to shifting cultivation, and international donor agencies have come to recognize that forestry and agriculture are inseparable in the developing world. Kenyans, for example, now meet 47 percent of their wood needs from agricultural lands, 25 percent from rangelands, and only 28 percent from forests. In both Pakistan and in Java, Indonesia, forest reserves produce only 40 percent of all timber and 10 percent of all fuelwood (51).

In recognition of farmland's increasing forestry burden, assistance organizations have shifted greater amounts of funding toward agroforestry and community forestry. Twenty years ago, funding for these projects was minimal. Today, at least 11 major international groups help finance agroforestry and community forestry projects in more than 50 countries. From 1972 to 1984, expenditures totaled $750 million (52). Forty percent of the U.S. Agency for International Development's forestry assistance to Asia now goes toward agroforestry and community forestry projects (53). Research and extension agencies have fol-

lowed suit. International groups researching or funding agroforestry projects include the International Council for Research in Agroforestry (ICRAF) in Kenya, the Tropical Agricultural Research and Training Center (CATIE) in Costa Rica, the Central Arid Zone Research Institute (CAZRI) in India, and the International Institute for Tropical Agriculture (IITA) in Nigeria. According to ICRAF, agroforestry projects are underway in approximately 100 developing nations.

The projects have demonstrated agroforestry's major benefits: maximum use of climate and site, increased productivity, and evenly distributed economic risk to the farmer (54). In addition, agroforestry's tree-cultivation techniques allow farmers to take advantage of woodland benefits even when they live far from natural forests (55). Trees grown among agricultural crops or on pasture land can provide fuelwood, timber, nuts, fruits, food for cattle, and fertilizer. Food crops can also benefit when the appropriate tree species are present to enrich the soil, prevent erosion, retain water, and shield crops and animals from damaging wind and excessive sunlight.

The range of products that can be grown on a single plot depends on the method used, but generally falls into one of three major categories: agro-silvicultural (trees and crops), silvo-pastoral (trees and livestock), and agro-silvo-pastoral (trees, crops, and livestock). (See Table 5.5.)

"Taungya," one system that combines crops and trees, is a controversial remnant of British colonial policies in Burma. Farmers are given the temporary right to grow crops in new forest plantations; in return, they help tend the young seedlings. In many cases the arrangement is only temporary; forestry takes precedence over farming, and when the trees begin to shade out the crops, the farmers must leave. Some critics thus consider taungya a system for afforestation rather than an agroforestry practice (56). Tanzania, regarding taungya as an "exploitive" practice, has abolished it (57).

Nevertheless, variations of taungya can be found elsewhere in Africa and in Asia and Latin America. Nigeria uses it to establish teak and *Gmelina arborea* plantations. Paid laborers intercrop plants among recently planted trees. In addition to providing a new source of rural income, the practice reportedly yields enough food for 1 percent of the nation's population (58). Similarly, Indonesia uses taungya to establish 40,000 hectares of teak plantations each year. To overcome taungya's temporary nature, the government of Thailand has established 26 forest villages with schools and medical clinics, in the hope that the farmers will settle permanently. The government offers garden plots, wages, and bonuses for successful tree care—as well as the traditional three-year right to grow crops between young teak, eucalyptus, and melia trees (59).

Other forms of agroforestry take better advantage of the mutual benefits of appropriate trees and crops. In Costa Rica, farmers use *Cordia alliodora*, a valuable timber tree, to shade coffee and cocoa plants. In the central highlands of Papua New Guinea, plots totalling approximately 25,000 hectares contain coffee, food crops such as

Forests and Rangelands

Table 5.5 Agroforestry Systems and Practices

Major Systems	Practices	Regions Where Present
Agro-Silvicultural	Improved ''fallow'' (in shifting cultivation areas)	Southeast Asia, East and Central Africa, American Tropics
	Taungya	South Pacific, Southeast Asia, South Asia, East and Central Africa, West Africa, American Tropics
	Tree gardens (primarily fruit and nut trees used also for firewood)	South Pacific, Southeast Asia, South Asia, Middle East and Mediterranean, American Tropics
	Hedgerow intercropping (alley cropping)	Southeast Asia, East and Central Africa, West Africa
	Multipurpose trees and shrubs on farmlands	Throughout developing world
	Crop combination with plantation crops	Throughout developing world
	Multipurpose fuelwood trees	South Pacific, Southeast Asia, South Asia, East and Central Africa, American Tropics
	Shelterbelts, windbreaks, soil conservation hedges	Throughout developing world
Silvo-Pastoral	Protein bank (cut and carry fodder production)	Southeast Asia, South Asia, East and Central Africa, West Africa, American Tropics
	Living fence of fodder trees and hedges	Southeast Asia, South Asia, East and Central Africa, American Tropics
	Trees and shrubs on pastures	Throughout developing world
Agro-Silvo-Pastoral	Woody hedges for browse, mulch, green manure, soil conservation, etc.	South Pacific, Southeast Asia, South Asia, East and Central Africa, West Africa, American Tropics
	Home gardens (with many herbaceous and woody plants)	Throughout developing world
Other	Aquaforestry (silviculture in mangrove swamps; trees in bunds of fish-breeding ponds)	Southeast Asia
	Shifting cultivation (e.g., swidden)	South Pacific, Southeast Asia, South Asia, East and Central Africa, West Africa, American Tropics
	Apiculture with trees (beekeeping)	South Pacific, Southeast Asia, South Asia, Middle East and Mediterranean, East and Central Africa, West Africa

Note: Table does not include data on Europe, where agroforestry is common on a small scale in foothills and middle reaches of mountain uplands. Along lowland regions, especially river valleys, poplars are often combined with grazing.
Source: P.K.R. Nair, "Some Examples of Prominent Agroforestry Systems and Practices in the Developing Countries," ICRAF Newsletter, No. 17 (May 1986), pp. 4–5.

bananas, and *Casuarina oligodon*, a tree that provides shade, timber, and fuelwood (60). In China, almost 1.3 million hectares of farmland have been intercropped with *Paulownia*, a fast-growing, broadleaved tree that loggers have long prized for its timber. In the wheat fields of the Yellow River Basin, masses of *Paulownia* protect the crops from hot, dry winds that can reduce harvest yields by as much as 40 percent (61).

Paulownia and *Acacia* are also important in silvo-pastoral schemes. *Paulownia*, which in five years can grow to 17 meters in height and 30 centimeters in diameter, produces good animal fodder as well as wood. A ten-year-old tree can yield 30 kilograms of dry leaves and 400 kilograms of young branches a year (62). Twenty mature *acacia* trees growing in just one hectare produce 1,500 to 2,500 kilograms of nutritious pods for cattle and other ruminants. The trees' pods and edible foliage are most bountiful during the hot, dry season.

Alley cropping uses hedgerows to substitute for fallow periods in restoring the soil. The system, which allows cropland to be used continuously, helps slow the destruction of forests by minimizing the amount of land needed by each farmer. Leguminous hedgerows of nitrogen-fixing *Leucaena leucocephala* and *Gliricidia sepium* flank crops and renew the soil with nutrient-rich leaf fall. Alley cropping thus duplicates the gains of shifting agriculture; yet it is a continuously productive farming system, yielding food at the same time that it restores the soil. One IITA alley-cropping project involving *Leucaena* and maize produced three to five tons of the grain per hectare—four times Africa's average yield (63).

Home gardens, the most common form of agro-silvopastoral systems, include livestock in the management mix. The Chagga home gardens on Tanzania's Mt. Kilimanjaro use limited space efficiently in "multi-storied" farm plots that raise a variety of products from root crops to soaring trees. Individual farm plots, averaging 0.68 hectares apiece, cover approximately 120,000 hectares on the south and east slopes of Africa's highest mountain. In addition to coffee, the major cash crop, farmers cultivate 53 tree species, many of which prevent or minimize soil erosion. Approximately 90 percent of the tree species produce fuelwood; 30 percent yield medicines for humans and livestock; 25 percent produce poles; 24 percent, shade; 23 percent, timber; 10 percent, fodder; and 19 percent provide other benefits such as mulch, fruit, and pesticides. The home gardens meet one quarter to one third of the farmers' fuelwood needs, and in most cases supply all the fodder for household livestock. The trees grow amid food crops such as bananas, beans, peas, potatoes, tomatoes, yams, maize, taro, and onions (64).

In Nyabisindu, Rwanda, farmers replaced shifting cultivation, overgrazing, and accompanying deforestation and soil erosion with a multi-storied agro-silvo-pastoral system. They planted trees and hedges in erosion-control strips that yield shade and increased humidity as well as fruit, wood, fodder, and green manure (plant material used as fertilizer). Results from test plots indicate that a typical family using the system could produce a fuelwood surplus of 25 to 50 percent beyond its own needs. A multi-storied plot yields 54 percent more calories, 31 percent more protein, and 62 percent more carbohydrates than a similar site that contains merely one crop (65).

Agroforestry is not restricted to the developing world. In hilly parts of Europe, small farmers traditionally graze livestock among cultivated trees, or grow trees among crops. Cattle can be seen among the 68,000 hectares of poplar plantations that have been established along river valleys in France and Germany (66). In Ontario, Canada, poplars grow between rows of corn and soybeans (67). In Australia and the southern United States, cattle graze amid pine plantations (68).

Agroforestry does not succeed everywhere, however. The successful mixture of trees with crops and pasture is more likely to occur (and often does so spontaneously) when three conditions are met. First, the environment must be favorable to the growth of trees, with sufficient rainfall and fertile soils. Second, populations must be dense enough to favor a more intensive use of land—and not so dense that short-term survival replaces sustained management. Finally, the social and economic climate must favor the growth and management of trees. Agroforestry has a chance of success when farmers hold tenure to their land, can protect their trees from browsing animals, and can successfully sell their products. When the right environmental and social conditions have been met, the benefits of agroforestry have been substantial.

RANGELAND RESOURCES

Rangelands are areas that provide forage for free-ranging livestock and wild animals. They typically have physical limitations that make them unsuitable for agriculture or intensive forestry. For instance, more than one third of the earth's surface is too dry for rainfed agriculture and is used as range instead. Other areas are too steep, too rocky, poorly drained, or too cold. About half the world's land surface is considered rangeland.

Rangelands provide forage for about 2.9 billion head of cattle, buffalo, sheep, and goats. These ruminants can turn cellulose, which is indigestible to humans, into protein-rich meat and milk. Globally, the total investment in domestic livestock is at least $400 billion (69). Worldwide, exports of fresh and frozen meat, milk, wool, and

live animals represented 12 percent of total agricultural exports in 1983. In many African and South American countries, livestock products account for a large portion of total agricultural exports (70).

The importance of rangelands varies considerably among different cultures. Countries with pastoral economies value rangelands because they provide forage for domestic livestock, wood for fuel, and other products necessary for daily living. As human populations increase and competition for land intensifies, there is increasing pressure to convert range into cropland. In developed countries such as those of North America, watershed conservation and recreation join livestock as important rangeland values. In a few countries, efforts are underway to preserve some range as wilderness or to use it for disposal of nuclear and hazardous wates.

Extent of the World's Rangelands

Despite their importance, knowledge of the extent of the world's rangelands is incomplete: no comprehensive global assessment exists. Part of the problem in conducting such an assessment is the overlapping definitions of range, pasture, grassland, and other types of land that produce forage.

The most complete rangeland data available were compiled by the FAO and are organized by type of vegetation. The total amount of range in the world is estimated to be about 6.7 billion hectares, or about 51 percent of the total land. (See Table 5.6.) This figure was derived by adding the area of permanent pasture, 3.16 billion hectares, plus the 1.37 billion hectares of open forest, plus about half of FAO's "other land" category, or 2.19 billion hectares of desert, tundra, and scrub. Other estimates may differ slightly, depending on how they count permanent pastures, deserts, open forests, and rangeland. (Also see Chapter 18, "Land Use and Cover," Table 18.1.)

About 75 percent of Oceania (Australia and New Zealand) and Africa is rangeland, mostly arid and semiarid lands. Fifty-eight percent of China is rangeland, mostly broad

Table 5.6 Distribution of the World's Pastures and Rangelands, 1955–83

	Area of Permanent Pasture[a] 1955 1975 1983 (million hectares)			Permanent Pasture as Percent of Land Area 1983	Open Forests[b] 1980 (million hectares)	Other Land[c] 1983 (million hectares)	Estimated Total Area Range and Pasture[d] (million hectares)	Rangeland As Percent of Total Land Area
North America (United States and Canada)	277	265	265	14	275	746	913	50
Europe	83	88	86	18	22	91	153	33
USSR	124	374	373	17	137	702	861	39
Central America (inclusive and Caribbean)	79	94	95	32	0.3	99	145	48
South America	330	446	456	26	248	230	819	47
Africa	615	785	778	26	508	1,317	1,945	65
Asia (except China)	279	372	359	21	61	602	721	41
China	194	286	286	31	45	415	538	58
Oceania	377	472	460	55	76	182	627	75
World Total[e]	**2,358**	**3,181**	**3,157**	**24**	**1,372**	**4,384**	**6,721**	**51**

Notes:
a. Includes permanent meadows and pastures and land that has been used for five years or more for the production of herbaceous forage crops, either cultivated or wild.
b. Includes wooded land with a grass understory beneath the open canopy. Livestock and wildlife browse on both the leaves and twigs of the trees and on the grasses.
c. "Other land" is a residual category defined by the United Nations Food and Agricultural Organization (FAO) in its *Production Yearbook*. About one third of this land is so dry it lacks plant cover. However, a significant percentage of this land may be grazed seasonally or in years of heavy rainfall. Half of this category is counted in the estimated total area of range and pasture.
d. Sum of areas of permanent pasture (1983), open forest (1980), and 50 percent of "other land" (1983).
e. Numbers may not add up to totals because of rounding.

Sources:
1. Data on "permanent pasture" and "other land" are from United Nations Food and Agriculture Organization (FAO), *1983 Production Yearbook* Vol. 38 (FAO, Rome, 1985), Table 1, pp. 47–48; and FAO, *1955 Production Yearbook* (FAO, Rome, 1955).
2. Data on open forests and other wooded land are from United Nations Food and Agriculture Organization (FAO)/Economic Commission for Europe (ECE), *Forest Resources 1980* (FAO/ECE, Rome, 1985).

steppes, mountains, and deserts. About half of North and South America is range. On these continents, rangelands include the true grasslands, such as the prairies of the United States and the pampas of Argentina, as well as deserts, open forests, and land that was cleared of forest.

Europe, the USSR, and Asia (excluding China) are less than 40 percent rangeland. In these areas, permanent pastures, open forests, and humid wastelands combine with grasslands to provide the major grazing lands. (See Table 5.6.)

Systems for Using Rangeland

Although there are many specific systems for using rangeland, they fall into two general categories: those that use the land to produce goods that are removed or exported from the land (ranches) and those that provide subsistence for the people who own the livestock (pastoral systems). Neither system is inherently a better method of managing the resource; problems in either are caused by a variety of factors such as type and intensity of use.

The ranch system is typified by the ranches of Australia, Europe, and the Americas. Such ranches use investments of capital and various management techniques on large acreages of land to increase cattle production. Labor inputs are relatively low. Fencing, water development, brush control, selective breeding, and grazing management can be used to varying degrees (71).

Ranch systems generally require more land per animal than pastoral systems, although this is not true in places such as Europe where ranching occurs on intensively managed "tame" pastureland. Ranch systems often rely on a sizable amount of privately-owned land, sometimes augmented with public rangeland as is common in the United States. While there is no aggregate figure for the amount of ranch land worldwide, there are figures for certain countries. Brazil has the greatest area in ranches, about 175 million hectares that produced 94.7 million head of cattle in 1985. Of this area, about 60.6 million hectares are improved range and 13.9 million hectares are in a natural state (72). Australia has 450,000 hectares of ranches. At least 300,000 hectares of this rangeland is extremely arid and it supports only 5 percent of the country's cattle even though it represents two thirds of the land. The average size of a ranch in this region is 76,268 hectares and the stocking rates are as low as one head of cattle per 40 hectares (73).

The pastoral system is common in Africa, the Middle East, and Asia. Pastoral systems rely on few mechanical or chemical inputs and are highly labor intensive. Pastoral systems involve moving livestock herds from one location to another, usually following seasonal patterns of forage or water sources. Individual land ownership is uncommon in traditional pastoral systems, and land management, particularly any activities that require capital inputs, is minimal (e.g., setting of range fires or broadcast seeding before moving on).

Because of the nature of this system, it is difficult to estimate the amount of range used by pastoralists. However, livestock supports an estimated 30–40 million nomadic people in developing countries besides being

essential to millions of farmers. The importance of cattle in a pastoral system is many-fold and livestock are more than sources of milk and meat.

Livestock is a common means of accumulating capital and the size of a herd is a mark of social standing. Livestock are assets that can reproduce and can be liquidated if cash is needed. Rangelands in pastoral systems also serve as important sources of fuelwood, fencing materials, roof thatch, medicinal plants, gums, incense, tannins, and other useful products. The wildlife that roams many rangelands is often a major food source for local people: in Ghana, for example, nearly 75 percent of the meat consumed is from wild animals (74) and in Botswana the figure is 40 percent. In addition, certain native groups depend entirely on wildlife for subsistence (75). Rangelands also provide nuts, fruits, berries, tubers, and other human foods.

Livestock products are extremely important to farmers as well. Without livestock, it is estimated that developing countries would have to spend an additional $40 billion on mechanical power for agriculture and $6 billion on fertilizer (76). Animal power supplies half the nonhuman energy used in agriculture in developing countries (77). Dung, the traditional method of maintaining soil fertility, is still an important nutrient source. In India, it is estimated that dung supplies the equivalent of one third the chemical fertilizer produced annually (78). When fuelwood is scarce, as is increasingly the case, dung also supplies household fuel (to the detriment of soil fertility).

Range Productivity

The type and degree of management used on rangelands can make significant differences in their productivity. The productivity of Europe's intensively managed pasturelands, for example, has increased beyond 500 animal production units (APU) (79) per hectare per year, compared to less than 20 APU per hectare per year in most developing countries (80).

Pastoral systems are not by definition less productive than ranch systems and their potential often has been underestimated. African pastoral systems can be as productive per hectare as market-oriented ranching systems in areas of comparable rainfall in terms of the amount of protein produced per unit of land. Conventional ranching is more efficient from a labor perspective because it produces much more protein per hour of labor. But conventional ranching requires vastly greater energy inputs, something that most pastoral economies would find difficult to supply (81). (See Table 5.7.)

Although the number of livestock continues to grow, the growth lags slightly behind human population increases. Worldwide the inventory of livestock that use rangeland (cattle, buffalo, sheep, and goats) has grown from 2.7 billion head in 1974–76 to 2.9 billion head in 1985. The number of animals slaughtered annually has increased from 723 million to 842 million. However, because of human population increases over the same period, the number of livestock per capita fell from 0.68 in 1974–76 to 0.61 in 1985, and the number of livestock slaughtered per capita remained steady at 0.17 (82).

Table 5.7 Labor and Energy Inputs to Livestock Production in Three Regions

Region[a]	Protein (kilograms/year)		Fossil Energy Input (thousand kilocalories per worker-hour)
	Per Hectare	Per Worker-hour	
United States	0.3 to 0.5	0.9 to 1.4	25 to 35
Australia	0.4	1.9	150
Sahel			
Nomadism	0.4	0.01	0
Transhumance	0.6 to 3.2	0.01 to 0.07	0
Sedentary	0.3	0.04	0

Note: a. All regions have less than 500 millimeters of rainfall per year.
Source: H. Breman and C.T. de Wit, "Rangeland Productivity and Exploitation in the Sahel," *Science,* Vol. 221, No. 4,618 (1983), p. 1344.

Range Degradation

Most rangeland ecosystems are relatively susceptible to degradation: for example, arid lands, tundra, and high mountain pasture communities are less resilient to disruption than humid ecosystems. In dry areas, natural plant growth is slow and plants are adapted to extremes of wind, rainfall, and temperature (83).

Arid rangelands are especially prone to the process of xerification, or drying out, that can be caused or accelerated by overgrazing. If a range is overstocked, or if livestock cluster in one area such as around a watering hole, overgrazing can nearly eliminate the most palatable plants. Specifically, when a plant loses its leaves to grazing it moves nutrients from its roots to grow new leaves, causing the root area to shrink. This reduced root system absorbs less water even during rains. As more palatable plants are weakened, less palatable species become dominant. As even these are overgrazed, the plant cover becomes scarce and the soil is exposed to trampling, compaction, and severe erosion. When the infrequent, but heavy, rains characteristic of arid zones occur, the water simply runs off rather than penetrating the soil and recharging the groundwater.

In the worst cases, rangeland can become so dry and degraded as to become unproductive. (See "Desertification" below.) While moderately degraded range can usually be restored over time through management, severely degraded land may require expensive techniques such as plowing and reseeding, and this can mean the land is beyond the point at which it can be economically restored.

CONDITION OF RANGELANDS (84)

Range condition is a complex and inexact estimate in which the present condition of the soils and vegetation is compared with what is thought to be the most productive community possible on that land given the climate, native vegetation, and original soil type (85). Generally, range is in good condition if 75 percent or more of the native species are present and poor if 25 percent or less of the native species remain (86).

In practice, however, range conditions are reported from many different sources and many different measurement techniques are used. That makes comparisons among different countries difficult. Reasonably good data based on sound, standard techniques exist for some countries, such as those of North America. However, the data available for many areas, such as the countries of sub-Saharan Africa, are limited. In some cases, only subjective estimates or remote sensing data from satellite imagery are available.

Most of the world's rangelands have been degraded to some degree. In certain areas, such as the western United States, some restoration has taken place. In other areas, such as much of Western Asia, degradation continues.

North and South America

The most complete data available on range condition and how it has changed over time are from North America. Grazing by domestic animals has been a factor for just over a hundred years in most of the western United States and early explorers described the region as a livestock grower's paradise (87). These reports spurred investors to establish large ranching empires using the virgin rangelands. Within two or three decades, the herds grew far beyond the land's carrying capacity. Pressed by a series of severe droughts and blizzards during the 1890s, the livestock industry crashed.

The dramatic degradation of the Dust Bowl era in the 1930s—the climax of an abortive attempt to farm the arid rangelands—spawned a general conservation movement in the United States, and range management concepts became incorporated into laws. Since then, both public and private rangelands have improved and are in better condition today than at any other time in this century (88). However, these lands are still degraded from their ecological potential (89). Of the 883 million acres of rangeland in the United States (including Alaska), 32 percent is considered in good condition, 28 percent in fair condition, 28 percent in poor condition, and 12 percent in very poor condition (90).

Although it is not as easily documented, the rangelands of Canada and Mexico have followed a similar pattern of use, misuse, and gradual improvement. All three countries have areas that still need improvement, but overall the deterioration has been stopped and conditions are gradually improving.

The rangelands of South America, particularly those of Argentina, Paraguay, Uruguay, and Brazil, have also seen a pattern of overstocking and degradation. Management in this region is particularly complex because South America's rangelands cover a variety of environments, from humid tropics and cold deserts to coastal plains and alpine meadows. No overall assessment of their conditions has been made. One particular concern is the cutting of tropical forests to create both range and cropland, which sets in motion a chain of events that can seriously degrade the land's productivity.

Australia

The history of settlement and range use in Australia is similar to that in the Americas, and most ranges were fully stocked and overgrazed by the turn of the century. About three fourths of Australia's rangelands are naturally arid, and they are particularly susceptible to drought. One unique problem faced by Australia was the huge

Table 5.8 Rangeland Conditions in Selected Western Asian Countries

Country/Locality Size of Rangeland	Range Condition	Range Trend	Causes	Remedial Activities	Source
Syria Country-wide 8,700,000 ha (grasslands)	• Overgrazed	• Not specified, but either generally downward, or stable at minimal productivity	• Too many animals; most productive rangelands destroyed by plowing; uprooting of shrubs for fuel, establishment of water points (wells) without any grazing controls		1
Kamishly Area				• FAO integrated agricultural development project: introduction of forage legumes into large parcels of fallow lands (one third of cropland is typically fallowed) • Establishment of range management cooperatives (44 in 1977 with approximately 9,000 people)	
Interior Steppes; Arid Deserts	• Original plant community virtually eradicated; replaced by species of little interest to humans or animals	• Long history of degradation	• Overgrazing, especially by goats; development of wells permitted over-use of plant resources	• Arab Centre for the Study of Arid Zones and Dry Lands (ACSAD), includes range management work • Law permits each family in the western mountain region only one goat • Creation of the "Steppe Department" within the Ministry of Agriculture and Agrarian Reform	
People's Democratic Republic of Yemen Country-wide 9,000,000 ha (grassland) 2,500,000 ha (scrub forest)	• Degraded stage of retrogression	• Declining, or stable at minimal productivity	• Grazing pressure; fuelwood collection		2
Yemen Arab Republic 7,000,000 ha (pasture) 1,600,000 ha (woodland)	• Majority of "woodland" better classified as rangeland • Depleted plant cover	• Long history of degradation • Severe sheet and gully erosion • Decline in livestock numbers • World Bank believes range can be restored to some extent	• Overgrazing; fuelwood cutting	• Pilot project; "village development association and range improvement center" (Most of livestock owned by villagers and communally grazed near village)	3
Iraq Country-wide 4,000,000 ha (grassland) 33,000,000 ha (other lands)				• Establishment of the Directorate of Rangelands (1976); included 10 regional facilities	4
Steppe Zone 6,200,000 ha	• Predominance of unpalatable shrubs • Disappearance of natural vegetation	• Unspecified, but condition indicates historical downward trend • Continuing loss of rangeland	• Overgrazing • Conversion to dryland farms	• Project development: "improvement of grazing lands in the Hammad Valley" (10,000,000 ha)	
Mountain Range (Forest and Sub-alpine)	• Palatable perennial grasses generally scarce; annuals predominate		• Long history of overgrazing		
Alpine Meadows	• Good seasonal grazing (four months)	• Apparently stable	• Limited seasonal usage		
Southwestern Desert 16,700,000 ha	• Apparently fair— "luxuriant growth of annuals in the spring; shrubs available during summer and winter"	• Downward—"steady deterioration"	• Overgrazing, in part due to transhuming flocks from neighboring countries		
Country-wide 36,040,000 ha (grazing land, i.e., uncultivated) 100,000 ha (forage)	• Low productivity	• Long-term progressively downward trends	• Uncontrolled grazing; conversion of some desert lands to dryland farming (Jazeera locality)	• Number of sheep had to be reduced • Establishment of combined crop and sheep cooperatives and government farms • National support for sheep breeding programs; sheep and steer finishing projects; feed processing facilities	

World Resources 1987

Table 5.8

Country/Locality Size of Rangeland	Range Condition	Range Trend	Causes	Remedial Activities	Source
Oman 1,000,000 ha (permanent pasture) 20,208,000 ha (other land)					5
Desert and Mountain	• Not specified, however 1975 surveys noted "little evidence of damage to plant communities"	• Stable, perhaps upward (improving)	• Herd sizes decreasing in nomadic regions	• Apparently none	
Sain Katat and Batinah	• Over-used	• Not specified	• Excessive woodcutting; heavy grazing and trampling by livestock		
"Settled Areas"	• Not specified, but perhaps fair condition at present	• Possibly improving	• Although animals are concentrated in these areas, there is heavy reliance on fodder crops		
Jordan 8,316,253 ha (grazing and/or uncultivated)	• Loss of vegetation • Lack of water more limiting than lack of feedstuffs	• Degradation for hundreds of years, but utilization has become increasingly destructive in the past few decades • Substantially increased erosion • Goats have even been an obstacle to reforestation	• Overstocking, especially of goats	• Measures to restrict grazing in certain areas not very successful • Establishment of permanent settlements for nomadic herdsmen including water developments and irrigated forage production	6
	• Serious erosion, pavement-like soil	• Long-term, continuing degradation • Low level of productivity from rangelands in the future	• Sedentarization has concentrated more animals in smaller areas for longer periods • Human population increased six-fold over 55 years (2.5 million in 1983) with increased demand for red meat	• Tasks proposed for a "National Rangeland and Rainfed Watershed Program" (July 1984)	
Saudi Arabia country-wide 85,000,000 ha (pastureland) Arabian Shield-South 20,400,000 ha (9.5% of total country area)	• Increase in overall plant biomass production since 1967 (which was a drought period) but a shift in species composition towards more unpalatable plants indicates a degraded forage resource • Condition ratings based on field surveys of percent perennial species and cover measurements: Poor 40%, Fair 20%, Good 20%, Excellent 20% (Most of the area in excellent condition is in flat desert zone where animal use is restricted by limited water availability)	• Human-caused destruction of rangeland has increased significantly • Rangelands are now less suitable for sheep (grazing), and better suited for camel and goat (woody browse) • Trend ratings for major range zones were calculated from measurements of indicators such as seedling establishment, plant vigor, plant residue amount and soil surface condition; all zones (flat desert; hilly plateau; mountains and foothills) can be rated at the lower end of "stable"	• Widespread availability of trucks allows transport of animals and water to remote areas previously used infrequently • Animal production units have increased 1.8 times since 1967 study		7
Iran Country-wide 1,100,000 ha (specified as pastureland)	• Severe depletion of range; disappearance of most preferred perennial species (e.g. *Artemisia* and *Aristida*)	• Severe and continuing deterioration • Serious soil erosion and flash run-offs • The need to reconcile stock reductions to restore biological equilibrium with the goal of increased meat production presents a major problem	• Heavy overstocking— estimated to exceed carrying capacity by 4 times; fuel gathering, including the uprooting of shrubs in cold winter areas; widespread encroachment of dryland cultivation into traditional grazing areas; climatic fluctuations	• Some very good vegetation studies, but no detailed survey for monitoring baseline or range management trials • Administrative structure in place	8

Sources:
1. A.W.A. El Moursi, *Ecological Management of Arid and Semi-Arid Rangelands* (EMASAR—Phase II), Vol. VII, Near East (United Nations Food and Agriculture Organization, Rome, 1978), pp. 38-39; United Nations Food and Agriculture Organization (FAO), *Regional Study on Rainfed Agriculture and Agro-Climatic Inventory of Eleven Countries in the Near East Region*, World Soil Resources Report (FAO, Rome, 1982), pp. 88-89; U.S. Man and the Biosphere (USMAB), Draft Environmental Profile on Syria (Library of Congress, Washington, D.C., 1981), pp. 30-31, 41-51, p. 55, 63, 67.
2. A.W.A. El Moursi, *Ecological Management of Arid and Semi-Arid Rangelands* (EMASAR—Phase II), Vol. VII, Near East (United Nations Food and Agriculture Organization, Rome, 1978), pp. 45-46.
3. United Nations Food and Agriculture Organization (FAO), *1983 FAO Production Yearbook*, Vol. 37, FAO Statistics Series No. 55 (FAO, Rome, 1984); U.S. Man and the Biosphere (USMAB), *Environmental Profile of Yemen (Yemen Arab Republic)* (Office of Arid Lands Studies, University of Arizona, revised draft, Tucson, 1982), pp. 68-70, p. 77.
4. A.W.A. El Moursi, *Ecological Management of Arid and Semi-Arid Rangelands* (EMASAR—Phase II), Vol. VII, Near East (United Nations Food and Agriculture Organization, Rome, 1978), pp. 12-15; United Nations Food and Agriculture Organization (FAO), *Regional Study on Rainfed Agriculture and Agro-Climatic Inventory of Eleven Countries in the Near East Region*, World Soil Resources Report (FAO, Rome, 1982).
5. United Nations Food and Agriculture Organization (FAO), *1983 FAO Yearbook*, Vol. 37, FAO Statistics Series No. 55 (FAO, Rome, 1984); U.S. Man and the Biosphere (USMAB), *Draft Environmental Profile of the Sultanate of Oman* (Office of Arid Lands Studies, University of Arizona, Tucson, 1981), pp. 64-66, 84-85.
6. United Nations Food and Agriculture Organization (FAO), *Regional Study on Rainfed Agriculture and Agro-Climatic Inventory of Eleven Countries in the Near East Region*, World Soil Resources Report (FAO, Rome, 1982); U.S. Man and the Biosphere (USMAB), *Draft Environmental Report on Jordan* (Library of Congress, Washington, D.C., 1979), p. 51, 54, pp. 76-79; R.D. Child, R. Saunier, A. Al-Rimawi, W.A. Rabboh and W. Furtick, *A National Rangeland and Rainfed Watershed Program for Jordan*, Joint Environmental Service/w Contract No. 37-E (International Institute for Environment and Development, Washington, D.C., 1984), pp. 3-8.
7. United Nations Food and Agriculture Organization (FAO), *1983 FAO Yearbook*, Vol. 37, FAO Statistics Series No. 55 (FAO, Rome, 1984); MacLaren International, Ltd., *Draft Rangeland Inventory and Management, Annex 13*, Water and Agriculture Development Studies, Arabian Shield-South (Government of Saudi Arabia, Ministry of Agriculture and Water, 1978), pp. 3-53.
8. J. Calembert and L.R.N. Strange, *Ecological Management of Arid and Semi-Arid Rangelands* (EMASAR—Phase II), Vol. VI, Middle East (United Nations Food and Agriculture Organization, Rome, 1978), pp. 17-20.

overpopulation of introduced European rabbits that denuded many rangelands. Uncontrolled grazing by feral populations of horses, camels, and water buffalo is also a problem in some areas. Overall, however, Australia's rangelands have gradually improved in recent decades. The government has formed a national range research organization to give more attention to rangelands management. Most states now operate some system of rangeland monitoring. These institutional improvements, coupled with a better marketing system, will focus more attention on the rangelands that are still deteriorating.

Africa

About 65 percent (1,945 million hectares) of Africa is rangeland. Since livestock are and will continue to be an important part of African agriculture, rangelands will be increasingly important resources in the future. As Africa's human population grows, pressures to increase the number of livestock will intensify, and this will create additional conflicts with native wildlife. In several African countries mixed game and livestock ranches have been established. Like a mixed herd of wild animals, these herds can take advantage of a wide variety of range forage and browse. (See Chapter 6, "Wildlife and Habitat.")

The rangelands of Africa are a critical source of fuelwood. In some areas, almost anything burnable, including fodder trees, is cut for fuel or charcoal—a short-term necessity creating long-term problems. Some of the charcoal produced is used locally, but it is increasingly being transported hundreds of kilometers to population centers. The removal of shrubs and fodder trees reduces the amount of dry season forage available for both livestock and wildlife and increases the land's susceptibility to erosion and degradation. (For a country-by-country assessment of African rangelands see *World Resources 1986*.)

Europe

Rangelands in Europe are usually categorized as permanent pasture. Although only about 18 percent of the continent is permanent pasture, these lands are highly productive. (Thirty-three percent of Europe is rangeland including open forest and other land.) Some rangelands, such as those on the Iberian peninsula, are managed like rangelands in the rest of the world. However, most of Europe's pastures are managed so intensively that they may be more akin to cropland than to rangelands. These improved pastures are many times more productive than the arid rangelands common elsewhere in the world. Only a decade ago, many experts hoped that the developing countries could become major exporters supplying livestock products to Europe. But livestock production in Europe has increased substantially and these countries now supply not only their own markets, but they also are exporting meat products.

Western Asia

Western Asia is a region with arid climates, rough terrain, and barren soils. The land has been grazed continuously for centuries. This area has been the focus of a growing concern about the desertification of rangeland. The difference between the fertile land of Biblical description and the present conditions may be partly due to climate change, but is largely due to overgrazing and lack of management (91).

Western Asia, also known as the Middle East, includes Syria, The People's Democratic Republic of Yemen, Yemen Arab Republic, Iran, Iraq, Oman, Kuwait, Turkey, Lebanon, Jordan, Saudi Arabia, and Israel. Table 5.8 summarizes range conditions in selected countries. Although these conditions are alarming, it is also significant that studies in Syria, Jordan, and Kuwait show that rangelands can be improved with proper technical input and grazing control.

Range accounts for a large percentage of the land area of these west Asian countries. In many of these countries, a significant percentage of the population are nomads who earn their living from herding livestock. For example, in Iran, 6.1 percent of the total population and nearly 15 percent of the rural population is classified as nomadic (92). (This does not include farmers who also keep animals.)

The rangelands of Syria, Oman, Jordan, and Saudia Arabia are some of the driest areas continuously grazed by domestic livestock. Since the area is naturally arid, bare soil and sparse plant cover is the normal condition. It was in these areas that sheep, goats, and dromedaries probably were first domesticated.

Most reports indicate that rangeland in Western Asia is declining in productivity. (See Table 5.8.) For example, the steppes of Iraq have lost a significant amount of native vegetation and now have a preponderance of unpalatable shrubs. Similarly, on the interior steppes of Syria the original plant community has been virtually eradicated and replaced by species of little interest to humans or animals. In the Democratic Republic of Yemen, rangelands are severely degraded, and in Jordan eroded, arid range has become as hard as pavement. Overgrazing is invariably cited as a cause for these conditions, and goats in particular are problems in Syria and Jordan.

There are, however, other factors that contribute to problems on the region's rangelands. Degradation occurs in Iraq and Syria when rangelands are converted to dryland farming. Excessive wood-cutting in Oman, the Yemen Republics, and Syria, combined with the establishment of new wells without concurrent grazing controls, degrades range. In Saudi Arabia, the widespread availability of trucks has opened once-remote areas to use and overuse. According to current information, the countries with the most seriously degraded rangelands are Syria, the Democratic Republic of Yemen, and the Yemen Arab Republic.

The desert mountains of Iraq and Iran face similar problems and are also thought to be stable or declining in productivity. Iran's rangelands are severely depleted and they have lost most of the preferred perennial species. The major areas of concern are around population centers where pastoralists move their herds and flocks to be near the cities. Areas around wells and new water sources are also critical.

Asia

No comprehensive assessment of condition has been made of Asia's rangelands. These include arctic tundra, temperate grasslands, annual desert grasslands, semi-arid shrublands, monsoonal forests, and swamplands. They occur in a multitude of developed and developing countries in widely different geographic settings. The economies and cultures of the people are likewise varied. The largest areas of rangelands occur in the People's Republic of China and the Soviet Union. According to the FAO, about 31 percent of the People's Republic of China (2.8 million square kilometers) is permanent pasture and 58 percent of the country can be considered rangeland. (See Table 5.6.) Mongolia has about 1.2 million square kilometers in permanent pasture. In 1984 and 1985 Chinese and U.S. scientists held a series of symposiums on arid lands in China which reported that the pace of dry land degradation has increased dramatically over the past 50 years due to population pressure and unsound land use. Of the 171,000 square kilometers of human-caused deserts in the country, 119,000 square kilometers became deserts during the past 2,500 years and 52,000 square kilometers became deserts over the past 50 years (93).

DESERTIFICATION

Desertification—the expansion of desert-like landscapes into arid and semi-arid environments under the impact of human influences—is a critical problem worldwide, especially for the world's rangelands. It is a land degradation process that involves a continuum of change, from slight to very severe. The United Nations Environment Programme estimates that desertification threatens about one third of the world's land surface (48 million square kilometers) and affects the livelihood of at least 850 million people (94). Many of the world's major rangelands are at risk. (See Figure 5.2.) This desertification hazards map, compiled by several United Nations agencies, shows areas that are at greatest risk of desertification because of a combination of factors such as low rainfall, terrain, soil and vegetation conditions and high human and animal pressure.

Desertification can occur in a variety of environments and be caused by a number of factors, but rangelands are particularly at risk because they are often naturally arid. Overgrazing is a primary cause of desertification, but deforestation (particularly the cutting of fuelwood), overcultivation of marginal lands, and salinization caused

Figure 5.2 Areas at Risk of Desertification

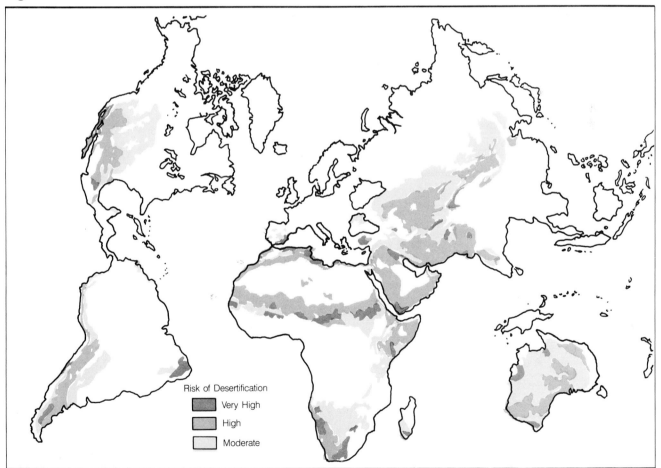

Risk of Desertification
- Very High
- High
- Moderate

Source: *United Nations Map of World Desertification,* United Nations Food and Agriculture Organization, United Nations Educational, Scientific and Cultural Organization, and the World Meteorological Organization for the United Nations Conference on Desertification, 1977, Nairobi, Kenya.

by poorly managed irrigation are also important influences (95) (96) (97).

Desertification first gained international attention in 1977 when the United Nations Conference on Desertification (UNCOD) was held in Nairobi following a serious drought in the Sahel. The conference confirmed that desertification was caused mainly by human activities, rather than by climate changes.

UNCOD issued a Plan of Action to Combat Desertification (PACD) consisting of 26 recommendations, with administration of the plan charged to the United Nations Environment Programme. UNEP set up three groups: the Desertification Branch within UNEP to carry out programs, an Interagency Working Group on Desertification to facilitate cooperation among U.N. agencies, and the Consultative Group of Desertification Control (DESCON) to secure funding for projects (98). From 1978 to 1983, bilateral and multilateral donor agencies spent an estimated $10 billion on desertification projects (99).

Despite this initial effort, by 1983 (six years after the conference) UNEP Executive Director Mostafa Tolba reported that he found "no signs that the war against the spread of desert-like conditions is being won" (100). He told the U.N. Governing Council that "the response by developed and developing countries alike has been totally inadequate" (101).

According to one estimate, it will take a total of $141 billion to fight desertification of rangelands and agricultural land, half of the amount going to rangelands. (See Table 5.9.) The number seems staggering, until it is considered that $141 billion is equal to the estimated losses of agricultural production to past desertification over about five and a half years (102). Not all desertified land is economically worth reclaiming because it would cost more to correct the problem than could ever be paid back, but there are social reasons for such investments, such as slowing the rural exodus to the cities (103).

According to an analysis by soils expert Harold E. Dregne, director of the International Center for Arid Land Studies at Texas Tech University, 90 percent of the $10 billion allocated for desertification-related assistance projects since the 1977 conference went to rural development projects such as improved water supplies, animal disease control, and road building. These do not directly combat desertification, and in some cases may even worsen it (104). Both donors and recipients prefer projects that offer immediate economic development over projects aimed at range management and other long-term soil conservation activities that show no immediate payoff. In fact, some countries have acutally rejected long-term planning against desertification as being in conflict with immediate development needs (105). Although

UNCOD issued a reasonable set of recommendations, it was not able to generate the political support necessary to put desertification on national agendas (106).

IMPROVING RANGELAND

Generally, improvement of overgrazed range calls for the use of some kind of grazing system that allows the vegetation to rest and recover periodically. A few of the important grazing elements to consider are intensity, timing, distribution of livestock, sequence of grazing, and type or combination of animals. Water management, brush control, reseeding, fertilization, and other techniques are sometimes also applied in conjunction with grazing management.

The approach taken varies with local environmental conditions and the severity of the degradation. For instance, fire, or prescribed burning, can be used widely in tropical savannas, but only sparingly in desert systems. Moderately degraded rangelands can usually be improved by management alone, such as by changing the grazing patterns. Severely degraded rangelands require additional efforts such as reseeding, control of noxious plants, terracing for soil stabilization, or some combination of approaches. The worse the degradation, the more dramatic the restoration efforts must be. Preventing range deterioration is typically cheaper than reclamation.

In Somalia, where 90 percent of the country's exports are derived from livestock and the rangeland is deteriorating from overuse, a comprehensive program, the Central Rangelands Development Project, has been instituted to try to reverse the trend of degradation and increase livestock production over the long term (107). This effort includes resource monitoring, field research, water development, training and education, and a variety of soil and water conservation projects to improve the range.

One approach being used in Somalia is sand dune stabilization. In 11 villages, areas of shifting sand have been enclosed by a living fence of *comiphera* cuttings to exclude livestock, and panels of natural bush have been erected to block the prevailing winds. Grass and shrubs are planted to permanently stabilize the area, and in time the villagers are able to harvest fodder crops to feed to cattle off site (108).

A classic example of successful restoration of severely degraded range is the U.S. Bureau of Land Management's (BLM) Vale District in the southeast corner of Oregon. Over 11 years, from 1963 to 1974, the United States spent $10 million rehabilitating the 2.6 million hectare Vale District (109). Under this intense effort, the abused range was transformed into a showplace of range management and restoration experiments: innovative seedings, water development, fencing, brush control, and grazing systems (110).

The project did not attempt to treat the entire vast acreage; rather, the managers intensively treated scattered tracts totaling about 10 percent of the land. Combined with sound management and some temporary herd reductions, this alleviated grazing pressures on the degraded native range and gave it time to recover. A special effort was made to accommodate wildlife and recreational users. Preliminary findings of a reassessment

Table 5.9 Cost of Combatting Desertification

Type of Land Use	Area Desertified (thousand hectares)	Cost of Improvement Per Hectare	Total (billion US $)
Irrigated cropland	27,100	$750	$ 20.3
Rainfed cropland	173,100	250	42.2
Rangeland	3,071,600	25	77.5
Total			**$141.0**

Source: Harold E. Dregne, *Desertification of Arid Lands* (Harwood Academic Publishers, New York, 1983), p. 24.

World Resources 1987

being conducted in 1986 indicate that the project has been a long-term success (111).

Australia, France, and the United States are the leaders in developing range reclamation techniques, and the United States—partly because of environmental laws requiring reclamation of land that has been surface mined—does more reclamation than any other country. Efforts to restore severely degraded range require large capital inputs, thus they are difficult to implement successfully in developing countries. In addition, they are becoming increasingly expensive, putting some techniques out of the reach of even developed countries. Twenty years ago, for instance, dragging chains across a range to remove brush cost about $7 an acre in the United States; in 1986, it cost about $45. Herbicide spraying cost around $4 an acre and has increased to $15–20 (112). Because the expense of range treatments is so great, the U.S. Forest Service is reducing its use of costly methods of reclamation such as plowing and chaining, and herbicide use is limited by law. Less costly controlled burning is now the primary tool for public rangelands managed by the U.S. Forest Service (113).

Integrated Range Management

Sound range management that incorporates elements of range science, ecology, economics, political science, and sociology is sometimes referred to as integrated range management. In recent years, range scientists and managers have given increasing emphasis to this holistic approach to management, although actual use in the field is just beginning.

Integrated range management considers the total ecosystem, not just maximum livestock production (114). It incorporates a mixture of techniques to take advantage of the strengths of each method while minimizing any inherent drawbacks. Grazing management, water development, brush control, and institution-building might be combined to restore a range. The approach is flexible and site-specific, and it attempts to consider multiple uses of the resource (e.g., forage production, wildlife, watershed, etc.) so that overall productivity, not just livestock production, is optimized.

An element that is increasingly recognized as essential to range management, especially in developing countries, is the complex web of social and economic factors that affect the people who use a range. Technologies developed in the United States, Europe, Australia, and other developed areas are not necessarily appropriate or feasible for developing countries because they were designed for different environments and socioeconomic situations (115). In particular, grazing management is difficult if a region's land tenure system does not provide a clear method to control the land and the animals grazing on it (116).

Two examples of integrated range management are the Systems Planning for the Use of Rangeland (SPUR) Systems Model developed by the U.S. Department of Agriculture for small watersheds and private ranches and the Integrated Planning Technology developed by the U.S. Agency for International Development and used in Botswana to plan range wildlife and socioeconomic activities. Both

require interdisciplinary workshops, the development of conceptual models, and the use of computer models to test the possible effects of alternate rangeland use policies.

RECENT DEVELOPMENTS

PROGRESS ON THE TROPICAL FORESTRY ACTION PLAN

The Tropical Forestry Action Plan, an ambitious attempt to conserve tropical forests while increasing their productivity, has gained considerable international support since it was announced in November 1985.

The Action Plan was designed to unite countries in their efforts to substantially reduce tropical deforestation. It stresses fuelwood and social forestry, watershed rehabilitation, industrial forestry, conservation of forest ecosystems, and institution-building. The Plan was developed jointly by the United Nations Food and Agriculture Organization (FAO), the United Nations Development Programme, the bilateral development agencies, the World Bank and other development banks, several nongovernmental organizations (including the World Resources Institute), and representatives of more than 60 tropical countries.

During 1986, under the guidance of the Action Plan, development assistance agencies began coordinating their development assistance in forestry, and the World Bank has revised its lending programs to reflect the Plan's recommendations. These commitments, along with others to increase aid and loan flows for forestry, are the earliest signs of progress following a series of organizational meetings by the Tropical Forestry Advisory Group, an ad hoc committee of forestry advisors from the development assistance community and from nongovernmental organizations (NGOs). The money committed so far, however, is only a fraction of the $8 billion that the Plan recommends is needed over the next five years (117). To monitor and coordinate implementation of the Action Plan, the FAO established a special secretariat in Rome.

Considering the long history of debate and inaction surrounding efforts to stop tropical deforestation, the Plan has sparked impressive commitments during its first year. Specifically:

■ The World Bank revised and expanded its entire Africa loan portfolio in forestry in line with the Action Plan recommendations.

■ For the first time, development assistance agencies such as FAO, the United Nations Development Programme, and bilateral assistance agencies, as well as the World Bank and other development banks, are coordinating their development assistance in forestry. This coordination should reduce waste and duplication in development assistance to make better use of available financial resources. An ad hoc Tropical Forestry Advisory Group has met three times in the past year to find ways to coordinate grants and loans in line with the Action Plan.

■ Three countries—France, the Federal Republic of Germany, and the Netherlands—agreed to double their aid to forestry as a direct result of the Action Plan.

■ The Tropical Forestry Advisory Group is coordinating reviews of forest conditions in 30 countries to help national governments assess the status of their forests, estimate industrial potential, and evaluate training needs. As of late 1986, reviews were underway in 14 countries, and one for Sudan had been completed. In addition, National Forestry Plans are being written or revised in over a dozen countries, with technical and financial help from international development agencies (118).

■ Efforts are also underway to increase NGO participation in the Action Plan. Although most of the original work on the Plan was done by assistance agencies and governments, both international and local NGOs need to play vital roles in implementing reafforestation activities. Three international NGOs—the World Resources Institute, the International Institute for Environment and Development, and the International Union for Conservation of Nature and Natural Resources—organized three meetings in 1986 for NGOs to discuss their ideas. The meetings were held in Nairobi, Kenya; Bangkok, Thailand; and Panama City, Panama.

Effort is also being focused on a high-level forestry conference scheduled for July 1987 in Bellagio, Italy. At the meeting, ministers from at least 20 temperate and tropical nations will gather to discuss how their countries can work to help solve the deforestation crisis. The conference is being organized by FAO, UNDP, the World Bank, the Rockefeller Foundation, and the World Resources Institute.

U.S. CONSUMERS DEMAND LEANER MEAT

Health-conscious consumers in developing countries are beginning to affect how livestock is managed and readied for market. Since medical evidence has shown that too much fatty red meat in the diet can lead to health problems, many affluent consumers have turned to leaner sources of protein such as chicken and fish. In the United States, red meat consumption has fallen 20 percent since 1975 because of people's awareness of these health issues (119). The United States is still a major consumer of red meat, accounting for 28 percent of world consumption in 1985 (120). While it is a major producer of cattle, the United States also imports 8 percent of its red meat (121). Thus U.S. consumer trends stand to have a major influence on the cattle industry. Consumers in

Canada and Europe are beginning to show similar health concerns over red meat consumption. In other regions where beef consumption is high, such as Australia and parts of South America, leaner red meat has always been the preference.

Most of the industry responses include attempts to produce leaner, more healthful meat:

■ Largely in response to economic factors, U.S. cattle are being raised longer on forage and less on grain. This has the side effect of producing leaner meat. In 1972, for instance, a cow typically was switched from forage to grain in a feedlot when it weighed 135 to 180 kilograms. In 1986, cattle may stay on grass until they reach 315 kilograms (122).

■ In addition to shortening the "finishing period," some cattle are being slaughtered at a younger age, when they are more tender and thus more palatable without fattening. Again, the result is leaner meat.

■ In Europe, several countries have passed laws banning the use of hormones in livestock because of health concerns.

The cattle industry, like all complex industries, responds slowly to changes in consumer preference and most of the adaptations so far have occurred on a limited scale. However, there are innovators who are willing to take risks to explore new advances. Inspired by the consumer's growing health awareness, some range managers are considering how other types of animals might fit into the U.S. livestock system. For instance, longhorn cattle—the mainstay of the early American West—are both hardier and leaner than their contemporary counterparts and there is some interest in returning to the breed or crossbreeding it with modern cattle. In Florida, scientists are experimenting with water buffaloes, the oxlike beasts that have pulled carts and plowed rice paddies in Asia for thousands of years, to see if they can be produced on American farms. Water buffalo meat is also significantly lower in fat and cholesterol than beef, and blind taste tests indicate that it tastes at least as good as beef (123).

It is too early to tell how this trend might affect U.S. rangelands, but one could speculate that it could decrease the use of feed corn (much of which is grown on irrigated western lands) and increase the use of rangelands.

References and Notes

1. *Closed forest* has a cover of trees sufficiently dense to prevent the growth of grass underneath. *Open forest* has at least 10 percent tree cover, but allows enough light to penetrate the tree canopy to permit grass to grow.
2. World Resources Institute, International Institute for Environment and Development, *World Resources 1986* (Basic Books, New York, 1986), p. 61.
3. E. Mathews, "Global Vegetation and Land Use," *Journal of Climate and Applied Meteorology*, Vol. 22 (1983), pp. 474–487.
4. *Op. cit.* 2, p. 62.
5. United Nations Food and Agriculture Organization (FAO), *Production Yearbooks*; 1950-82 (FAO, Rome, 1951–83),

Table 1.
6. The term "unproductive" refers to forests that cannot be exploited commercially because of accessibility, topography, or other reasons. Such forests may be highly productive in an ecological sense. In the United States, these forests are called "non-commercial."
7. United Nations Food and Agriculture Organization (FAO), *Tropical Forest Resources*, Forestry Paper No. 30 (FAO, Rome, 1982), p. 80 and p. 84.
8. J.M. Melillo, *et al.*, "A Comparison of Two Recent Estimates of Disturbance in Tropical Forests," *Environmental Conservation*, Vol. 12, No. 1 (1985), pp. 37–40.
9. Statistical reports on forest resources include United Nations Food and

Agriculture Organization (FAO), *Tropical Forest Resources*, Forestry Paper No. 30 (FAO, Rome, 1982); and United Nations Food and Agriculture Organization/Economic Commission for Europe (ECE), *Forest Resources 1980* (FAO/ECE, Geneva, 1985).
10. *The World Environment 1972–1982*, M.W. Holdgate, *et al.*, eds., (Tycooly International Publishing Ltd., Dublin, 1982), p. 253.
11. J.S. Olson, "Productivity of Forest Ecosystems," in *Productivity of World Ecosystems* (National Academy Press, Washington, D.C., 1975), p. 41.
12. "Forestry Beyond 2000," *Unasylva*, Vol. 37, No. 147 (1985), p. 12.
13. *Op. cit.* 7, Table 1f, p. 50.

14. Broadleaved forests are also known by the "hardwood" they produce, as opposed to the "softwood" produced in coniferous or needle-leaved forests.

15. United Nations Food and Agriculture Organization (FAO)/Economic Commission for Europe (ECE), *Forest Resources 1980* (FAO/ECE, Rome, 1985).

16. United Nations Food and Agriculture Organization (FAO), *1983 Production Yearbook*, Vol. 37 (FAO, Rome, 1984), Table 1, p. 56.

17. *Ibid.*

18. "Wood: World Trends and Prospects," *Unasylva*, Vol. 20, No. 80-81 (United Nations Food and Agriculture Organization, Rome, 1966), Table III-A, p. 66.

19. Intensive management involves the frequent manipulation of trees and sites to improve a forest's commercial value. While other forms of timber management usually involve an immediate economic payoff, intensive forestry often pursues commercial benefits that lie in the future.

20. *Op. cit.* 7, p. 43.

21. *Op. cit.* 7, p. vii.

22. John Spears and Edward S. Ayensu, "Resources, Development, and the New Century: Forestry," in *The Global Possible: Resources, Development, and the New Century*, Robert Repetto, ed. (Yale University Press, New Haven, Connecticut, 1985), p. 330.

23. *Op. cit.* 7, pp. 56–58.

24. J. Davidson, *Economic Use of Tropical Moist Forests*, International Union for Conservation of Nature and Natural Resources (IUCN), Commission on Ecology Paper No. 9 (IUCN, Gland, Switzerland, 1985), p. 9.

25. Norman Myers, *The Primary Source: Tropical Forests and Our Future* (W.W. Norton and Company, New York, 1984), p. 242.

26. U.S. Forest Service, *America's Renewable Resource: A Supplement to the 1979 Assessment of the Forest and Range Land Situation in the United States* (U.S. Forest Service, Department of Agriculture, Washington, D.C., 1984), pp. 69–70.

27. *Op. cit.* 22, p. 320.

28. *Op. cit.* 7, p. 59.

29. United Nations Food and Agriculture Organization (FAO), *Yearbook of Forest Products, 1984* (FAO, Rome, 1984), p. 119.

30. *Op. cit.* 7, p. vii.

31. U.S. Congress, Office of Technology Assessment (OTA), *Technologies to Sustain Tropical Forest Resources* (Government Printing Office, Washington, D.C., 1984), p. 196.

32. Chadwick Dearing Oliver, "Silviculture: The Past 30 Years and the Next 30 Years," in *Proceedings of the 1985 Society of American Foresters National Convention* (Society of American Foresters, Bethesda, Maryland, 1985), pp. 243–246.

33. *Op. cit.* 25, p. 26.

34. World Resources Institute (WRI), *Tropical Forests: a Call for Action*, Part I (WRI, Washington, D.C., 1985), p. 31.

35. World Resources Institute (WRI), *Tropical Forests: A Call for Action*, Part II: Case Studies (WRI, Washington, D.C., 1985), p. 25.

36. *Op. cit.* 25, p. 303.

37. Frank H. Wadsworth, "Production of Usable Wood from Tropical Forests," in *Tropical Rain Forest Ecosystems: Structure and Function*, F.B. Golley, ed. (Elsevier Scientific Publishing Company, Amsterdam, 1983), p. 287.

38. Gene Namkoong, "Issues in Forest Genetic Resource Conservation and Management," paper presented at the Ninth World Forestry Congress, Mexico City, July 1-10, 1985 (unpublished).

39. *Op. cit.* 34, pp. 40–41.

40. American Forest Institute, *Green America* (poster), Summer 1979.

41. Andrew H. Malcolm, "Scientists Try to Create Forest of Cloned Trees," *New York Times* (New York, February 4, 1986).

42. M. Thompson Conkle, "Decoding Tree DNA," *Journal of Forestry*, Vol. 84, No. 1 (1986), pp. 36–37.

43. W.J. Libby, "Clonal Propagation," *Journal of Forestry*, Vol. 84, No. 1 (1986), p. 38.

44. U.S. Congress, Office of Technology Assessment (OTA), *Wood Use: U.S. Competitiveness and Technology* (OTA, Washington, D.C., 1983), p. 114.

45. Stanley L. Krugman, "The Ethical Question," *Journal of Forestry*, Vol. 84, No. 1 (1986), p. 41.

46. F. William Burley, "Deforestation in the Tropics: Priorities for Research," unpublished (World Resources Institute, Washington, D.C., 1986).

47. Gerald Foley and Geoffrey Barnard, *Farm and Community Forestry*, Technical Report No. 3 (Earthscan, International Institute for Environment and Development, Energy Information Programme, London, August 1984), p. 160.

48. Napoleon T. Vergara, "Agroforestry Systems: A Primer," *Unasylva*, Vol. 37, No. 147 (United Nations Food and Agriculture Organization, Rome, 1985), p. 24.

49. David Spurgeon, "Agroforestry: A Promising System of Improved Land Management for Latin America," *Interciencia*, Vol. 5, No. 3 (1980), p. 37.

50. Hans Jurg Steinlin, "Monitoring the World's Tropical Forests," *Unasylva*, Vol. 34, No. 137 (1982), p. 7.

51. K.F. Wiersum, "Trees in Agricultural and Livestock Development," presented at the Ninth World Forestry Congress, Mexico City, July 1-10, 1985 (unpublished), p. 6.

52. *Op. cit.* 47, pp. 217–223.

53. Susan Braatz, "The Role of Development Assistance in Forestry: The Forestry Policies and Programs of the World Bank, the U.S. Agency for International Development, and the Canadian International Development Agency" (International Institute for Environment and Development, Washington, D.C., 1985), p. v.

54. *Op. cit.* 47, p. 161.

55. *Op. cit.* 51.

56. Michael D. Benge, Agroforester, U.S. Agency for International Development (U.S. AID), Washington, D.C., 1986 (personal communication).

57. Aron Myaeni, "The Complexities of Community Forestry," *CERES*, Vol. 18, No. 2 (United Nations Food and Agriculture Organization, Rome, 1985), p. 20.

58. *Op. cit.* 31, p. 224.

59. S.A. Boonkird et al., "Forest Villages: an Agroforestry Approach to Rehabilitating Forest Land Degraded by Shifting Cultivation in Thailand" in *Agroforestry Systems 2*, P.K. Nair, ed. (International Council for Research in Agroforestry, M. Nijhoff/Dr. W. Junk Publishers, Netherlands, 1984), pp. 87–102.

60. R.M. Bourke, "Food, Coffee, and Casuarina: an Agroforestry System From the Papua New Guinea Highlands," in *Agroforestry Systems 3*, P.K. Nair, ed. (International Council for Research in Agroforestry, M. Nijhoff/Dr. W. Junk Publishers, Netherlands, 1984), pp. 273–279.

61. Chin Saik Yoon and G. Toomey, "Paulownia: China's Wonder Tree," *Reports*, Vol. 15, No. 2 (International Development Research Centre, Ottawa, April 1986), pp. 11–13.

62. *Ibid.*, p. 12.

63. B.T. King, *et al.*, *Alley Cropping: A Stable Alternative to Shifting Cultivation* (International Institute of Tropical Agriculture, Ibadan, Nigeria, 1984), p. 18.

64. E.C.M. Fernandes et al., "The Chagga Homegardens: a Multistoried Agroforestry Cropping System on Mt. Kilimanjaro" in *Agroforestry Systems 2*, P.K. Nair, ed. (International Council for Research in Agroforestry, M. Nijhoff/Dr. W. Junk Publishers, Netherlands, 1984).

65. M.J. Dover, *Ecotechnology: New Direction for Agricultural Development* (World Resources Institute, Washington, D.C., in press).

66. European Community (EC), *Memorandum Forestry: Discussion Paper on the Community Action in the Forestry Sector* (EC, European Community Commission, Brussels, 1986), pp. 17–18.

67. International Society of Tropical Foresters (ISTF), ISTF News, Vol. 4, No. 1 (1983), p. 3.

68. *Op. cit.* 49, p. 177.

69. United Nations Food and Agriculture Organization (FAO), *State of Food and Agriculture 1982* (FAO, Rome, 1983), p. 79.

70. United Nations Food and Agriculture Organization (FAO), *FAO Trade Yearbook*, Vol. 37 (FAO, Rome, 1984).

71. T.L. Capps and J.P. Workman, *Management Productivity and Economic Profiles of Two Sizes of Utah Cattle Ranches*, Utah Agricultural Station Research Report No. 69 (Utah Agricultural Experiment Station, Logan, Utah, 1982).

72. Ed Allen, Brazil Country Specialist, U.S. Department of Agriculture (USDA), Economics Research Service, December 16, 1986 (personal communication). Data from USDA and "Anvario Estatistico do Brasil—1984" (Brazilian Institute of Geography and Statistics, Brasilia, 1974).

73. Sally Burn, Australia Country Specialist, U.S. Department of Agriculture, Economics Research Service, December 16, 1986 (personal communication). Data from Bureau of Agricultural Economics, "Australian Agriculture and Grazing Industries Survey: 1979-1980" (Australian Government Publishing Service, Canberra, 1983).

Forests and Rangelands

74. Al de Vos, "Game as Food," *Unasylva*, Vol. 29, No. 116 (United Nations Food and Agriculture Organization, Rome, 1977), pp. 2–12, cited in U.S. Congress, Office of Technology Assessment (OTA), *Technologies to Sustain Tropical Forests* (OTA, Washington, D.C., March 1984).

75. M.L. Murray, *Wildlife Utilization, Investigation and Planning in Western Botswana* (Government of Botswana Printing Office, Gaborone, 1978).

76. *Op. cit.* 69, Table 1-2, p. 79.

77. *Op. cit.* 69, p. 82.

78. Steve Berwick, "The Gir Forest: An Endangered Ecosystem," *American Scientist*, Vol. 64, No. 1 (1976), pp. 22-40.

79. An Animal Production Unit is the equivalent of one 453.6 kilogram (1,000 pound) cow.

80. R. Jizhon, *Range Production in the People's Republic of China* (New Mexico State University, Las Cruces, New Mexico, 1983).

81. H. Bremen and C.T. de Wit, "Rangeland Productivity and Exploitation in the Sahel," *Science* (September 30, 1983)

82. Livestock statistics taken from United Nations Food and Agriculture Organization (FAO), *Production Yearbooks*, 1984 and 1985 (FAO, Rome, 1985 and 1986). Population statistics taken from U. N. Population Division, *World Population Prospects as Assessed in 1984* (U. N. Population Division, New York, 1986).

83. U.S. Congress, Office of Technology Assessment (OTA), *Impacts of Technology on Land Productivity* (Government Printing Office, Washington, D.C., 1982), p. 68.

84. The assessments of rangeland condition in this section were taken from an unpublished manuscript prepared for *World Resources* by Dean Treadwell, currently the natural resources consultant to the U.S. Agency for International Development in Haiti.

85. U.S. Congress, Office of Technology Assessment (OTA), *Impacts of Technology on U.S. Cropland and Rangeland Productivity* (Government Printing Office, Washington, D.C., 1982).

86. L.A. Stoddart *et al.*, *Range Management* (McGraw Hill, 3rd Edition, New York, 1975), p. 181.

87. T.W. Box, *The Arid Lands Revisited*, faculty honor lecture (Utah State University Press, Logan, Utah, 1978).

88. Bureau of Land Management, *National Celebration of the Taylor Grazing Act* (U.S. Department of the Interior, Washington, D.C., 1985).

89. *Op. cit.* 85, p. 70.

90. U.S. Forest Service, *An Assessment of the Forest and Rangeland Situation in the United States* (U.S. Department of Agriculture, Washington, D.C., 1980), Table 5.2, p. 258.

91. W.C. Lowdermilk, "History of Civilization Without Soil and Water Management Planning," International Seminar on Soil and Water Utilization (South Dakota State College, Brookings, South Dakota, 1962), pp. 5–10.

92. J. Calembert and L.R.N. Strange, *Ecological Management of Arid and Semiarid Rangelands* (EMASAR-Phase II), Volume VI, Middle East (United Nations Food and Agriculture Organization, Rome, 1978).

93. Bill E. Dahl and Cyrus M. McKell, "Use and Abuse of China's Deserts and Rangelands," *Rangelands*, Vol. 8, No. 6 (1986), p. 267.

94. Mostafa Tolba, "Harvest of Dust," *Desertification Control Bulletin*, Number 10 (United Nations Environment Programme, Nairobi, May 1984), p. 2.

95. Alan Grainger, *Desertification* (Earthscan, International Institute for Environment and Development, London, 1982).

96. Salinization, a problem for dry land that has been converted to agriculture, affects a relatively small amount of land; but because that land is more productive, the economic loss per acre is three times a great as for similar areas of desertified rain-fed crop land and 100 times as great as for desertified rangeland. Harold E. Dregne, "Combating Desertification: Evaluation of Progress," *Environmental Conservation*, Vol. 11, Nos. 1 and 2 (The Foundation for Environmental Conservation, Geneva, 1984).

97. International Institute for Environment and Development (IIED), *Cropland or Wasteland*, Earthscan Press Briefing Document No. 38 (IIED, London, 1984).

98. Harold E. Dregne, "Combating Desertification: Evaluation of Progress," *Environmental Conservation*, Vol. II, No. 2 (The Foundation for Environmental Conservation, Geneva, 1984).

99. *Ibid.*, pp. 116–117.

100. James Walls, "Back to the War," *Desertification Control Bulletin*, Supplement to No. 10 (United Nations Environment Programme, Nairobi, October 1984), p. 6.

101. *Ibid.*, p. 6.

102. Harold E. Dregne, *Desertification of Arid Lands* (Harwood Academic Publishers, New York, 1983).

103. *Ibid.*

104. *Op. cit.* 98, p. 116.

105. *Op. cit.* 100, p. 8.

106. Peter T. Thacher, Former Assistant Secretary-General of the United Nations and Deputy Executive Director of the U.N. Environment Programme, November 1986 (personal communication).

107. *The Berger World*, Vol. xii, No. 3 (Summer 1982) p. 3.

108. The Louis Berger International Group, *Somalia Newsletter* (December 1985), p. 2.

109. Harold F. Heady and James Bartolome, *The Vale Rangeland Rehabilitation Program: The Desert Repaired in Southeastern Oregon* (Pacific Northwest Forest and Range Experiment Station, U.S. Department of Agriculture, Portland, Oregon, 1977).

110. *Op. cit.* 85, p. 200–205.

111. Harold F. Heady, Professor of Range Management, University of California, Berkeley, and author of the Vale District reevaluation, 1986 (personal communication).

112. Ed Schlutterer, Range Division, U.S. Forest Service, December 15, 1986 (personal communication).

113. *Ibid.*

114. R. Dennis Child, Program Officer, Winrock International, December 3, 1986 (personal communication).

115. U.S. Agency for International Development (U.S. AID)/National Parks Service (NPS), *Arid and Semiarid Lands: Sustainable Use and Management in Developing Countries* (U.S. AID/NPS Natural Resources Expanded Information Base Project, October 1984).

116. Winrock International (WI), *Arid and Semiarid Lands* (WI, Morrilton, Arkansas, 1984).

117. *Op. cit.* 34, p. 1.

118. F. William Burley, "The Tropical Forestry Action Plan: Recent Progress and New Initiatives," presented at the National Forum on Biodiversity, Washington, D.C., September 21–25, 1986.

119. Frank Baker, Winrock International, Diet and Health Section, December 15, 1986 (personal communication).

120. Foreign Agricultural Service, *Dairy, Livestock and Poultry: World Livestock and Poultry Situation* (Foreign Agricultural Service, U.S. Department of Agriculture, Washington, D.C., September 1986).

121. *Ibid.*

122. Ronald Gustafson, United States Department of Agriculture, Economic Research Service, National Economics Division-Animal Products Branch, December 15, 1986 (personal communication).

123. Boyce Rensberger, "Ancient Water Buffalo Groomed to Become Wonder Cow of the Future," *The Washington Post* (November 2, 1986, Washington, D.C.).

6. Wildlife and Habitat

The increasing pressures of population growth and development continue to threaten wildlife and its habitat throughout the world. In the industrialized countries much of the wildlife was destroyed by development and hunting over the past few centuries. Now some wildlife species are carefully husbanded for sport and recreation while many nongame species are threatened, mainly by loss of habitat. Many tropical, species-rich countries are just beginning their development process, which may lead to a far greater loss of species than in the relatively species-poor northern countries.

The first responses by wildlife agencies and organizations to threats to wildlife were to create habitat reserves (see *World Resources 1986*, pp. 94–99) and to form conventions to restrict trade in rare and endangered species. While many of these efforts have succeeded, others have run into the harsh reality of human poverty. In areas where preserving wildlife seems at odds with local residents' perceptions of their chances for a better life, wildlife often loses. Unfortunately there are many conditions in which wildlife simply cannot co-exist with intense human settlement. There are other conditions, however, in which wildlife can be an asset to human economic development.

Over the past few years, a number of wildlife projects have emphasized the economic value of wildife to local people. Of course, wildlife has always been harvested for food, furs, skins, medicines, and other purposes. But the current emphasis is on the sustainable economic management of wildlife through controlled hunting, cropping, or ranching.

How wildlife is managed and the priorities for management can depend as much on a region's cultural background as on the biological needs of its wildlife. For example, in Europe, where wildlife traditionally belonged to the crown, game is now intensely managed on private land and hunters are an elite and privileged group. By contrast, in the United States hunting has always been a right of the common person and game is managed on both public and private lands. Africa developed management laws to foster the safari hunting business but also pioneered the establishment of wildlife reserves. Currently rampant poaching has caused many countries to take drastic measures such as closing hunting seasons and patrolling with armed conservation officers.

While managing game has been the thrust of wildlife management in all three of these regions, trends are growing toward managing nongame animals—especially endangered species—and their habitat.

Wetland habitats have been especially vulnerable to damage from development. Some of the world's greatest wetland systems are threatened by development, to the misfortune of both the people who depend on them for their livelihoods and the species that inhabit them. On the other hand, the Everglades of Florida in the United States—an area greatly modified since the turn of the century—are now beginning to be restored by the state of Florida and the federal government.

Wildlife and Habitat

CONDITIONS AND TRENDS

Wildlife in most regions of the world has declined as the land has been settled and developed. Only about 1.6 million of an estimated 5–10 million plant and animal species are known to science (that is, have been classified and named). Because of degradation of the environment by humans, 20 percent of these are likely to become extinct by the end of the century, and in 50 years more than half will be gone if current rates of destruction continue (1). Some scientists estimate a much higher number for the total number of species. At a 1986 conference on biodiversity sponsored by the National Academy of Sciences and the Smithsonian Institution, Dr. E.O. Wilson, professor of science at Harvard University, estimated that the number of species not yet discovered could approach 30 million (2). Undoubtedly, many species with enormous potential to satisfy human needs will be destroyed before they are even known to science. Many of these could have economic value; but even species that would never be used by humans may play a critical role in ecosystem balance.

The number and size of wildlife parks and preserves has grown sharply since the 1950s, especially in developing countries (see Figure 6.1) (3). Unfortunately, some are little more than "paper parks," areas outlined on a map with no on-site administration or field force to protect them. They are encroached upon by humans seeking land for grazing and invaded by poachers looking for meat or animal products they can sell. Few parks or preserves are large enough to function as complete ecosystems, thus migratory wildlife is often vulnerable during its journeys out of the park. For example, the Serengeti National Park in Tanzania and the adjacent Masai Mara Game Reserve in Kenya encompass 25,000 square kilometers of tropical savannas, woodlands, and grasslands. Yet their population of more than 1.5 million wildebeest move seasonally beyond park boundaries (4). Many reserves are too small even to sustain all the non-migratory species found within them. For example, many of the large East African parks may lose large mammal species simply because the parks are too small to maintain viable long-term populations.

Even within protected areas, wildlife is threatened by the press of humans who poach for food or profit or kill animals that might harm their crops. A sociological study in Tanzania showed that local antagonism toward parks was universal, and that encroachment on park land and poaching increased as the human population grew in areas around the parks and reserves (5). Among the most seriously threatened reserves were those in the northern region of Tanzania, including the Serengeti National Park. But reserves are threatened in other regions as well. Table 6.1 describes 23 sites added to the list of threatened protected areas in 1986. The list, published by the International Union for Conservation of Nature and Natural Resources' Commission on National Parks and Protected Areas, now totals 74 areas in both developed and developing countries.

As many nations find that properly managed wildlife can bring considerable economic benefits, they are beginning to tailor strategies to protect wildlife that put eco-

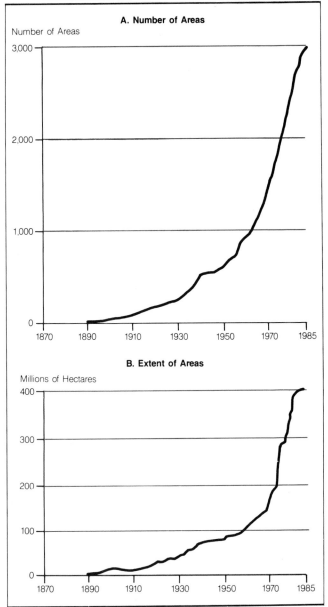

Figure 6.1 Growth of Global Network of Protected Areas, 1890–1985

Source: International Union for Conservation of Nature and Natural Resources (IUCN), *The United Nations List of National Parks and Protected Areas* (IUCN, Gland, Switzerland, 1985).

nomic forces to work in regional and national economies and seek to meet the needs of humans at local levels. Global conservation strategies as well are beginning to encourage sustainable use of wildlife by local people (6).

There are dangers involved in developing economic uses for wildlife. Once there is an economic incentive for their capture, some species may be overexploited, as has been the case with many fur-bearing animals in northern countries. Any successful plan for economic use of wildlife must foster a healthy base population and harvest animals only on a sustainable yield basis. In some cases, placing an economic value on wildlife has given private landowners an incentive to create and maintain habitat for valuable species.

Table 6.1 Threatened Protected Areas of the World, Additions for 1986[a]

Area	Country	Summary of Threats	Area	Country	Summary of Threats
South America			Dneprovsko-Teterevskoe Nature Hunting Reserve	USSR	Partly within zone A (total evacuation) of Chernobyl accident site
Iguazu National Park	Argentina	Transfer of lands within park to local government for development purposes	**Africa**		
			Selous Game Reserve	Tanzania	Drastic drop in rhinoceros and elephant population due to heavy poaching
Los Glaciares National Park	Argentina	Construction of new settlement Proposed excisions and hydro dam development	Ipassa-Makokou Nature Reserve	Gabon	Issue of logging permits, heavy poaching
Fernando de Noronda National Marine Park (proposed)	Brazil	Expansion of military facilities, siltation of reef due to land erosion	Mosi-Oa-Tunya National Park	Zambia	Rampant poaching, title deeds given for farming inside park
Paracas Nature Reserve	Peru	Proposed size reduction to exclude development zone	Kainji Lake National Park	Nigeria	Poaching, unauthorized fires, domestic livestock grazing, inadequate legislation and enforcement
North America			Gashaka-Gumti Game Reserve	Nigeria	Expansion of enclaves within reserve, rampant poaching, agriculture by park staff, inadequate management resources
Chincoteague National Wildlife Refuge	United States	Intensive recreational use by off-road vehicles, road redevelopment, serious impact on snow geese	Manovo-Gounda-St. Floris National Park	Central African Republic	Extirpation of rhinoceros and poaching of 75% of elephants Invasion by nomads from Chad and Sudan with large herds of livestock carrying bovine rinderpest
Lady Evelyn-Smooth Water Provincial Park	Canada	Wilderness values to be compromised by expansion of logging activities and road construction in buffer zone	Nickolo-Koba National Park	Senegal	Plan for construction of new road through park. Pressure from surrounding land uses and poaching
Forillon National Park	Canada	Air pollution, acid rain having severe effects on lakes and forests			
Europe			**Indonesia, China**		
Donana National Park	Spain	Diversion of water (wells) outside park for irrigation will result in serious dry-season droughts	Taman Negara National Park	Malaysia	Proposed construction of major road to interior of park
Rosca-Letea Biosphere Reserve	Romania	Hunting of pelicans by local fishermen, agricultural development plans for Danube Delta, water pollution	Kepulanan Seribu Marine Park	Indonesia	Proposed inappropriate tourism resort development
Stelvio National Park	Italy	Provincial authorities propose 50% reduction in size to allow additional forestry and hunting activities	Gunung Nyrut Nature Sanctuary	Indonesia	Expansion of shifting cultivation activities, overhunting and collecting of forest products, timber concessions
Hardangervidda National Park	Norway	Uncontrolled motorized traffic, road and cottage development, inadequate supervision, legal claims, acid rain	Datian Nature Reserve	China	Declassification of 25% of area for cattle ranch. Wood-cutting and poaching by reserve residents

Note: a. These 23 sites were added to the register of threatened protected areas in 1986. The current register now totals 74 sites worldwide.

Source: International Union of Conservation for Nature and Natural Resources (IUCN), *Commission on National Parks and Protected Areas Members Newsletter* (IUCN, Gland, Switzerland, October-November-December 1986).

It is clear that economic justification alone is not enough to conserve a diversity of species. Nonetheless, the development of economic uses for wildlife provides a powerful tool for its conservation.

THE ECONOMIC VALUE OF WILDLIFE

Some species have sustainable economic value in legal trade for their hides, horns, tusks, musk, and other products; as tourist attractions; in sport hunting; and in game cropping or ranching for their meat. Many such species are flourishing because their habitat is protected and their growth is fostered, but some are being decimated in illegal trade. Conversely, species deemed to have no value or species that compete with, prey upon, or carry diseases to economically valuable species are often controlled or eliminated.

Since countries do not usually keep records reflecting the contribution of wildlife-based industries or recreation to national economies it is difficult to assess the contribution on a global scale. One such assessment, however, indicates that wildlife does play a major economic role. A 1980 survey of fishing, hunting, and wildlife-associated recreation, conducted by the U.S. Fish and Wildlife Service, estimated that expenditures that year were $41 billion, "making fishing, hunting, and nonconsumptive wild-life activities a significant part of the American economy." (See Figure 6.2.)

Trade

Millions of people are dependent on or affected by wildlife trade. They range from those who literally live off the land and are dependent for their survival upon wildlife they can catch to those who are willing to pay a high price for something that serves as a status symbol (7). A recent estimate by TRAFFIC (USA), the trade monitoring program of the World Wildlife Fund, places the annual value of the legal, international trade in live animals and animal products at $5 billion (8).

While many animals have been hunted to extinction or near extinction, a more recent trend involves ranching or in some way husbanding wildlife to produce a sustainable harvest. Yet there is a risk for species that become valuable in trade. On one hand, their numbers may increase through careful management for harvest. On the other hand, a high price may encourage poachers to violate the boundaries of the management area and decimate the species in the wild. For example, crocodile ranchers (see below) commonly collect eggs from the wild and raise the young in captivity. Because the survival rate in a ranch is much higher than in the wild, the crocodile

Wildlife and Habitat

Figure 6.2 Expenditures on Wildlife-Based Recreation in the United States, 1980

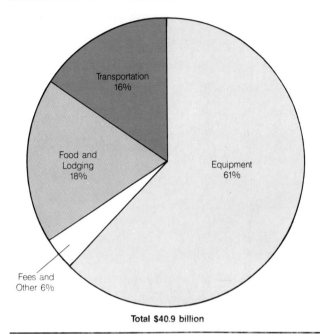

Total $40.9 billion

Source: U.S. Fish and Wildlife Service, *1980 National Survey of Fishing, Hunting, and Wildlife Associated Recreation* (U.S. Government Printing Office, Washington, D.C., 1982), p. 7.

population should increase, but if ranchers gather too many eggs from the wild, the natural population could be destroyed. Obviously, this risk is greatest where the potential profit from taking animals or eggs from the wild is high and where the enforcement of wildlife laws is lax.

Illegal trade in wildlife and wildlife products continues to be a major threat to many species. The World Wildlife Fund estimates that illegal trade in wildlife products totals $1 billion a year worldwide (9). Especially threatened are several species of rhinoceroses, crocodiles, and parrots. Rhinoceros horn is used to make coveted medicines in some countries. In 1986, an African rhino horn could bring $400–$600 a pound and a horn from a rare Asian rhinoceros could bring $2,000–$5,000 a pound, making rhinoceros especially tempting prey for poachers. Crocodilians are hunted mainly for their leather, and parrots for the pet market (10).

Ivory is another coveted trade item. About 900 metric tons of African elephant tusks, much of it taken illegally, are traded each year in a business worth $55 million (11). About 1.1 million elephants remained in Africa in 1982, but populations were declining in most countries mainly because of loss of habitat (12). To control the harvest of elephants in each country, an export quota system was developed by the 91 member nations of the Convention on International Trade in Endangered Species of Wild Flora and Fauna (CITES) at its Geneva convention in 1986. The quota calls for a total of 90,000 tusks, some of which are in storage, to be traded in 1986 (13).

Two of the growing number of enterprises that attempt to produce a sustainable harvest of wildlife for trade pur-

poses are the butterfly industry in Papua New Guinea and crocodile ranching in New Guinea, India, Africa, Australia, and Latin America.

The world trade in swallowtail butterflies, most of which are caught in the wild in Asia and Latin America, is worth about $100 million annually. Butterflies are sold to museums, students, hobbyists, and manufacturers of decorative objects and jewelry. In Papua New Guinea, villagers have developed butterfly ranches by cultivating the types of plants on which swallowtails lay their eggs. The chrysalises are collected and the metamorphosed butterflies are carefully handled and prepared for sale. Their quality and their prices are higher than wild-caught specimens. A butterfly rancher may earn up to $1,200 per year (14), a good wage in New Guinea. Far from depleting the species, this type of enterprise can promote its welfare. Because butterfly farmers want to maintain a steady income, they have an interest in seeing that the species does not die out. The trade is government controlled and monitored under CITES (15).

More than one million crocodiles, caimans, and alligators are marketed each year, most of them from wild populations (16). However, ranching of crocodiles is a new and growing venture in New Guinea, India, Africa, Australia, and Latin America. Eggs are collected from wild populations and hatched in pens, and the young are grown to two—four feet for the market. The caiman trade earns $120 million a year from markets largely in the United States and Europe.

The most traditional, and still the most extensively traded, animal product is fur. In the early 1980s the annual value of furs and hides from wildlife totaled $377 million in the United States, $44 million in Canada, $7.2 million in Australia, and $3 million in Finland (17). In the Soviet Union, hunting and trapping collectives harvest the Soviet Union's valuable fur-bearers, employing some 15,000 full-time professionals year-round and perhaps ten times that many at the peak of the harvest (18).

In Europe and North America, ranching of fur-bearing animals now accounts for a large portion of the industry. In the United States, virtually all mink and chinchilla and many fox are bred on farms. According to the American Fur Industry, mink accounts for an estimated 55 percent of retail fur sales (19).

Tourism

Wildlife is the chief attraction of the tourist trade in many regions where spectacular numbers or unique species occur. Estimates of expenditures on tourism in wildlife preserves and national parks are not available. However, it is known that some nations receive a large part of their foreign exchange from wildlife-associated tourism. Kenya, probably the chief beneficiary, netted $300 million from 500,000 visitors in 1985, making wildlife-based tourism Kenya's biggest foreign-exchange earner, ahead of its usual chief earners: exports of coffee and tea (20).

Since the 1960s, efforts at protecting wildlife have focused on preserving large tracts of habitat as the most reliable method of insuring the survival of species. More than 3,500 major protected areas, totaling over 4.25 million square kilometers, are listed in the *1985 United*

World Resources 1987

Nations List of National Parks and Protected Areas (21). (See Chapter 21, "Wildlife and Habitat," Table 21.1.) These protected areas not only aid wildlife, but they form the foundation of the wildlife tourist business.

Nowhere is wildlife-based tourism accomplished on such a grand scale as in Africa (22). Tourists come to see the great spectacles of plains game in natural habitats where some semblance of pristine nature still exists. A study of visitors to Amboseli National Park in Kenya determined that most came to see lions and other wildlife and had only passive interest in Mount Kilimanjaro (23). The great herds of plains game and other wildlife are responsible for the tourist circuit out of Nairobi through Kenya and Tanzania.

Using a model based on the amount of time visitors spend viewing lions and the amount of money they spend visiting Amboseli National Park in Kenya, Philip Thresher, an economist with the United Nations Food and Agriculture Investment Center in Rome, estimated that the average maned lion living to seven years of age would be worth $515,000 in foreign exchange receipts. As a hunting resource it would bring no more than $8,500, and if it were killed for its skin, its value would be between $960 and $1,325 (24). While the calculations make several tenuous assumptions and obviously do not consider many important factors (they ignore the number of lions needed to draw tourists and the other species of animals needed to sustain lions as wild creatures), Thresher's model clearly demonstrates the scale of the economic impact of animals in tourist industries.

Although air fares and other expenditures by overseas travelers may not reach the countries where the tourist industry is found, costs of housing, food, entry fees to parks and reserves, transportation, and other in-country services provide important sources of revenue, some of which may be put back into conservation.

Unfortunately, tourist expenditures do not always benefit local people adjacent to the parks. In Kenya, for example, foreign exchange earned from tourism stays largely in Nairobi where the service companies are headquartered. The bulk of the people who live near Amboseli's lions benefit little from tourism. Some may be employed by the park, and others may make curios for the tourist trade, but poaching still brings the most profit to local people. In fact, local farmers can suffer from their proximity to reserves, as migrating animals can damage their crops. Ten percent of the land area of Kenya is in protected reserves, but the outreach of migratory animals affects 80 percent of the country at some season of the year (25), and it is often the small farmer who takes the brunt of their numbers.

Sport Hunting

Sport hunting can range from an organized safari to a local villager shooting a predator. This section concerns only legal, organized sport hunting in which fees are paid for licenses, leases, travel, and equipment.

Canada and the United States are probably the most important countries in kills of animals for sport, with some countries of Europe and Africa not far behind. In the United States, 17.4 million persons hunted and 42.1

million fished in 1980 (26). Slightly more than 2 percent of the population of western Europe hunts (27). In the Soviet Union, only about 3 million, less than 1 percent of the population, hunt and fish (28). In Latin America, hunting has been limited to a small number of people who own land or are in the upper level of society (29), and much of the big game has been lost to overshooting and loss of habitat.

Although big game was once plentiful in Asia, today only a few areas support large animals of interest to sport hunters. Hunting is banned in most of Buddhist Asia because of religious beliefs and social mores. In Africa, big game hunting still attracts hunters from abroad, but many African countries—including Kenya, Tanzania, Mozambique, Angola, Uganda, and Zaire, formerly the most important African nations in the safari hunting business—have closed hunting, primarily because of political unrest, rampant poaching, and pressures of conservation organizations from abroad.

Worldwide figures on the economic value and kill of animals by sport hunting are fragmentary. In 1980, the 17.4 million U.S. hunters spent $8.5 billion on hunting fees, transportation, food and lodging, and equipment (30). Several African nations earn considerable income from sport hunting. Zimbabwe, for example, earned $6.2 million from marketing game through sport hunting in 1983, much of it coming from American and European trophy hunters (31). Hunters paid an average of $415 for hunting privileges, $767 for each buffalo, $2,987 for each elephant, and $1,125 for each lion they killed (32).

In Botswana, one of the few game-rich African nations that still permits hunting, hunting licenses bring in more money than national park entrance fees. (See Table 6.2.) Botswana, a desert country with little scenic grandeur but with a great diversity of large mammals and birdlife, finances its conservation agency largely from sales of licenses to hunters and concessions to safari companies.

European Community (EC) hunters (excluding those in Spain and Portugal) spent about $3.3 billion harvesting some 72,000 metric tons of wild game worth about $400 million—about 0.5 percent of the average EC consumer's annual intake of meat (33).

In some U.S. states, there is a trend toward the European style of hunting in which a hunter leases hunting rights on private land. In Texas, where commercial fee-hunting is highly developed, hunters annually pay landowners more than $100 million for access rights (34). According to a 1980 survey, 47 percent of those who hunted or fished in Texas did it on land they either leased or owned (35). In south and central Texas, income from hunting leases now exceeds that from livestock operations, and the economic value of wildlife has changed many patterns of ranching. The protection of game habitat in livestock ranching is now a common practice, whereas until recently, habitat such as woody brush was considered noxious because it reduced the carrying capacity for range livestock (36).

Around public lands, many businesses have developed to cater to hunters, fishermen, and other recreationists. In some U.S. states, like Alaska, guides are required by hunters entering primitive areas. A sizable industry has developed in the U.S. west for outfitting and guiding hunters,

Wildlife and Habitat

Table 6.2 Revenues from Wildlife and National Parks in Botswana, 1972–78
(thousands of $US)

Type of Revenue	1972	1973	1974	1975	1976	1977	1978
Hunting Licenses	355.4	298.9	358.2	397.4	386.1	444.6	309.7
National Parks Entrance Fees	10.7	13.5	22.6	29.9	51.8	28.4	25.6
Game Trophies and Sale of Ivory	26.0	39.5	0.5	21.7	0.3	41.1	0.5
Export Duty	52.9	47.3	19.3	26.1	41.4	54.7	46.9
Total Revenue	**445.1**	**399.2**	**400.6**	**475.1**	**479.6**	**572.8**	**382.7**

Source: Adapted from Botswana Department of Wildlife and National Parks, Central Statistics Office, *Statistical Abstracts 1979* (Gaborone, Botswana, 1980).

fishermen, and other recreationists. Charges of up to $1,000 per day for elk hunting are common in the better elk ranges. In 1983–84, there were 310 registered outfitters or guides in Alaska, 159 in Arizona, 172 in California, and 592 in Colorado (37).

Cropping

Cropping refers to culling animals from a wild herd in numbers that will not endanger the viability of the wild population. Cropping may be done either as a management technique to prevent the animals from overpopulating their habitat, with the animals' meat products as a secondary benefit, or it may be done primarily to produce meat and animal products under restrictions that prevent killing too many animals. Commercial harvests of animals from large herds have been a wildlife-based industry for the past 30 to 40 years.

In Africa, cropping is being done successfully in Namibia, Zimbabwe, Botswana, and the Republic of South Africa. Quotas are established by game departments on private and state lands, and the animals usually are shot at night and butchered in the field. Carcasses are transported either to local markets for sale or to cities, where they are frozen for export, primarily to Germany, France, and southern Europe. In 1979, a farmer in Namibia earned $21–$23 per head for springbok and $126–$152 per head for kudu (38). In 1980, some farmers earned between $31,000 and $47,000 from cropping game on their land. Gross income from export of meat rose from $1.3 million in 1978 to $2.4 million in 1979. Table 6.3 shows the number of animals cropped in the 1980 season.

"Nuisance" populations of larger species such as elephants and hippopotamuses have been reduced by cropping, but none have been harvested in a sustained yield program because annual recruitment for these large species is low. Elephants, buffalos, and hippos are cropped annually from herds in Kruger National Park in South Africa to prevent epizootic diseases among certain species and to protect the habitat from overuse by the large herbivores. Between 1967 and 1981, 9,456 elephants, 25,857 buffalos, and 828 hippos were removed from Kruger Park. The cropped animals are transported to a central *abattoir* where the meat is either canned or dried as biltong. Skins, ivory, horns and other products are saved for sale and the offal and bones are rendered into carcass meal for animal food. A net profit of $217,500 per year was attained during 1977–81 (39).

Cropping of kangaroos, mainly the red and gray species, has been a major activity in Australia since 1851, when 29,000 skins were traded. Ranchers regard kangaroos as serious competitors for forage with range livestock and have subjected them to control by shooting and poisoning. Kangaroos have been taken in large numbers since the mid-1950s for their hides, for pet food, and in some cases for human food. A total of 597,040 kilograms of kangaroo meat worth $823,779 and 1.8 million kangaroo skins worth almost $8.5 million was exported from Australia in 1982–83 (40).

In the Soviet Union, about 200,000 saiga antelope are cropped in an average year. Between 1957 and 1976, commercial exploitation of saiga by the Soviet state in Kazakhstan amounted to 600,000 metric tons of meat, 3 million hides, and 10 metric tons of horns worth approximately $100 million (41).

In some cases, however, cropping enterprises have failed. Organized schemes for cropping animals from free-ranging populations were attempted several times in East Africa, either to provide food for local peoples or to reduce numbers of large mammals, including elephants, that were damaging their habitats by overgrazing. Most were not continued beyond first trials (42). Some were not economically profitable because of long distances to markets and the lack of sanitation and refrigeration in remote areas. Others were stopped through pressures of world opinion and, in some cases, from opposition by the livestock industry because of competition in the market place. An ambitious project of the United Nations Food and Agriculture Organization (FAO) in the Kajiado District of Kenya failed because of difficulties in harvesting sufficiently large numbers (from 100 to 200 per day) of seven species of large herbivores by capture and shooting and because of poor marketing strategies (43).

Statistics on tonnage of game meat in international trade are coarse and sketchy. (See Table 6.4.) However, the amount of meat produced from wildlife is large and important as food and as a source of revenue. Most of the wild meat from New Zealand and the European nations is from red deer, roe deer, and chamois. From Argentina it is largely European hares and rabbits released there (44).

Although wildlife is unlikely to compete with livestock as a source of food on a large scale, it can be expected to provide meat for some time in the future in areas where domestic livestock cannot be raised profitably or efficiently. This is especially true in regions such as deserts and tundra that support wildlife more efficiently

Table 6.3 Results of the 1980 Game Cropping Season in Namibia for Export of Meat[a]

	Springbok	Kudu	Gemsbok
Number of Animals Offered	45,748	4,610	4,082
Number of Animals Cropped	40,232	3,491	3,297
Number of Carcasses Approved by Health Inspectors	39,035	3,437	3,220
Number of Carcasses Condemned	938	54	77

Note: a. The animals were cropped in 279 nights on 268 farms by four cropping teams.
Source: E. Joubert, et al., "An Appraisal of the Utilization of Game on Private Land in South West Africa," *South West Africa Journal of Nature Conservation and Desert Research*, Vol. 13, No. 3 (1983).

Table 6.4 Exports of Game Meat From Selected Countries, 1966–78
(metric tons)

	1966–70	1971–75	1976	1977	1978
Argentina	7,200	11,100	13,200	14,100	17,000
United Kingdom	X	X	6,200	8,200	8,100
New Zealand	3,100	4,200	2,800	4,100	4,000
France	500	370	2,700	2,800	3,000
Austria	2,300	2,800	4,000	4,400	2,900
Netherlands	900	1,700	2,200	1,800	1,500
Yugoslavia	600	600	1,100	900	1,100
Others	2,000	7,600	3,800	5,700	3,000
Total	**16,600**	**28,370**	**36,000**	**42,000**	**40,600**

X = not available.
Source: Graeme Caughley, *The Deer Wars: The Story of Deer in New Zealand* (Heineman Publishers, Auckland, New Zealand, 1983), Table 1, p. 103.

because the wild species have become adapted to extreme environmental conditions (45).

Game Ranching

In contrast to cropping, game ranching is the raising of game on ranches, often mixed with cattle or other livestock. In game ranching the landowner provides some inputs—food and water from the land—whereas the game cropper provides no inputs to raising the game.

In many countries in southern Africa, where game ranching is most popular, laws allow ranchers to claim all wildlife within the fenced borders of their property. By mixing wildife and livestock a rancher can make more efficient use of range vegetation, as different animals feed on different types of vegetation. For example, cattle eat grass and many wild ungulates browse on low branches.

In South Africa game ranching is practiced by about 8,200 landowners, according to estimates provided by provincial departments of nature conservation (46). From a survey of game ranchers in South Africa, Delwin E. Benson of Colorado State University in the United States determined that 52 percent of 2,207 landowners who responded sought income from wildlife. Thirty-two percent did not seek income but used wildlife, and 16 percent said they were not using game on their farms (47). The ranchers marketed wildlife through sport hunting, cropping of several species for meat, skins, and other products, and by capturing live animals for sale to other farmers for restocking. Benson estimated that wildlife on private land contributed between $28.6 and $33.6 million to South Africa's gross farm income in 1984 (48). Most ranches and farms had livestock—cattle, sheep, and goats—in the same pastures with their wildlife and 81 percent had fenced their property to keep wildlife inside (49).

Perhaps the best known game ranch in east Africa is the 8,100-hectare Hopcraft Ranch south of Nairobi, Kenya. The owner, David Hopcraft, is an ecologist and conservationist who hopes to demonstrate the viability of game ranching. Hartebeest, impala, Thompson's and Grant's gazelles, and wildebeest are killed on the ranch and the carcasses sold to restaurants in Nairobi catering to the tourist trade. This operation is particularly important because of studies being conducted on yields of various species of antelope and the economics of the game farming system. Hopcraft reports that his mixed cattle and

game ranch is more profitable than nearby cattle ranches. Whether his operation can be duplicated by other ranches is questionable, because the market may not support more than is now being sold (50).

In New Zealand, cropping of introduced deer evolved into deer ranching over a period of about 50 years (51). Because the deer had no natural enemies in New Zealand, they increased to levels that seriously damaged native forests and pine plantations (52). Initially, professional hunters were hired to shoot deer only for their skins. Carcasses were left to rot because there were insufficient markets at home or abroad to absorb all that were taken. However, in the early 1950s, markets for venison were developed in Europe, and between 1959 and 1983 more than 1.5 million carcasses were exported by the game-meats industry.

By the early 1980s, cropping had dramatically reduced deer in the wild and the industry turned to game ranching red, sika, and fallow deer to sustain the game-meat markets that had been developed, as well as the Asian demand for antler velvet, which is used for medicinal purposes. By 1976 an estimated 50,000 deer were on ranches and by 1986 the number grew to 350,000 on 3,000 ranches (53). The industry is now undergoing retrenchment because more venison is being produced than can be sold in New Zealand or in European markets.

REGIONAL TRENDS IN WILDLIFE MANAGEMENT

Wildlife management in various regions of the world has grown out of different cultures and different pressures facing wildlife. Three wildlife management systems—those of Europe, Africa, and the United States—are examined here.

Europe

In medieval Europe wildlife was the exclusive property of the king. In England, lands not parceled out to nobility were declared "royal forests" in which the king alone had the right to hunt (Robin Hood was a poacher in the king's forest). Franchises were granted to nobles to take game on their own land and in some cases to pursue game across the lands of others (54). In England and most other European countries, access to wildlife was and still is essentially controlled by the landowners.

Currently, in most European countries hunters can pay landowners for the privilege of hunting on their lands. Leases are made through a system of *reviers*, plots of land assigned for hunting. Leasing a *revier* can cost $5,000 or more per year, and carries the responsibility for the welfare of the game even to being liable for any damage done by it on the *revier* or to adjacent property (55). Although the government may administer wildlife resources through regulations, management is largely a landowner and hunter responsibility. Wildlife is carefully managed and harvested for sustained yields of trophy animals and meat.

Clearly, the system of hunting in Europe is restricted to those who can afford it. In most European countries hunters are highly regarded members of society who are required to master legal and traditional hunting skills.

They are organized into hunter associations or clubs that lease hunting rights (56).

Management of wildlife in Europe is concerned mainly with producing animals for sport hunting. Even though only a small percentage of the population hunts, harvests of big game and game birds are enormous. Hunting is an economic asset to both private and public purses (because of taxes on land leases), and nowhere in the world is management more intensive than in European *reviers*. Gamekeepers actively control predators, protect game from poachers, select specific trophy animals for the harvest, crop those of inferior quality, and protect the habitat (and croplands) from damage by the animals. Many are trained as foresters and use silvicultural techniques to favor multiple use of forest products including wildlife.

Attitudes toward management of nongame species vary considerably from country to country in Europe. In some countries, nonconsumptive uses of wildlife are vastly more popular than hunting. In England anti-hunting and animal-rights movements are popular. Nature study is extremely popular, as evidenced by the number of books and television programs about wildlife and by the number of people involved in birdwatching and nature study organizations. In other countries nonconsumptive activities have a low priority. In Italy, Spain, and Greece, for example, songbirds are regularly hunted for food.

A relatively high percentage of Europe's wildlife is considered "nationally threatened," that is, threatened within a country's borders though not threatened globally. For example, 57 percent of mammals are threatened in France, 53 percent in Spain, 51 percent in the United Kingdom, and 46 percent in Austria. This compares to 8 percent in the United States, 6 percent in Canada, and 2 percent in Japan. (See Chapter 21, "Wildlife and Habitat," Table 21.3.)

Germany, the Netherlands, Spain, and Turkey report many more species of birds have declining populations than have increasing populations. Of the European countries, only Finland and Norway report species with increasing populations (57).

Protection of nongame species is regulated by the Convention on the Conservation of European Wildlife and Natural Habitats, also known as the Bern Convention, which has been ratified by 13 European countries and the European Community. Another seven states have signed but not yet ratified the Convention, which came into force in 1982.

The Convention imposes a legal obligation on signing parties to protect all important breeding and resting sites of hundreds of species of animals, to prohibit killing of these species, and to prohibit the picking or uprooting of 119 species of plants. Unlike many conventions, the Bern Convention imposes mandatory provisions and has an administrative structure to oversee implementation (58). The Convention's Secretariat has taken an active role in urging countries to adopt specific measures to preserve the listed species. For example, the Secretary General wrote to French, Spanish, and Italian authorities to draw their attention to the danger of extinction of the brown bear in the Pyrenees and the Alps. He also urged Bel-

gium, Denmark, and the Netherlands to take necessary measures to prevent the disappearance of certain populations of black grouse that were threatened by changes in peatland habitat (59).

Africa

Management of wildlife in Africa was patterned after European systems and, until recently, most management programs were for game species. The first international agreement to conserve wildlife in Africa was signed in London in 1900 by the European colonial powers that then governed much of Africa—France, Germany, Great Britain, Italy, Portugal, and Spain—"to prevent the uncontrolled massacre and to insure the conservation of diverse wild animal species . . . which are useful . . . or inoffensive" (60). This Convention was the first treaty to encourage the establishment of nature reserves. It prohibited the killing of certain rare animals, but its primary purpose was to preserve a good supply of game for trophy hunters, ivory traders, and skin dealers. It also urged signatories to "reduce" certain other species of predators or nuisance animals including lions, leopards, and wild dogs (61). The 1900 Convention was supplanted by another Convention in 1933, which refined some of the provisions and ended the concept of nuisance animals.

As African nations gained independence, a new treaty was needed and in 1968 the African Convention on the Conservation of Nature and Natural Resources was endorsed by the Organization of African Unity and ratified by 28 nations (another 14 have signed but not yet ratified). This treaty has been called "the most comprehensive multilateral treaty for the conservation of nature yet negotiated" (62), because it addresses the conservation of soil and water as well as wildlife. Unlike Europe's Bern Convention, however, the African Convention failed to establish a secretariat to oversee its implementation; thus little has been done to encourage signatories to abide by its provisions (63).

Most African countries are signatory parties to the Convention on International Trade in Endangered Species of Flora and Fauna, which prohibits all trade in species that are believed threatened with extinction. Since the Convention came into force in 1975 the list of restricted species has grown to more than 200, including both plants and animals. Administered by the United Nations Environment Programme (UNEP), CITES has a secretariat, which works with designated management authorities in each country.

Africa's spectacular wildlife is currently under severe stress from loss of habitat to agricultural development and grazing and from poaching. In most countries of Africa, burgeoning numbers of people, most of whom live in rural areas, compete with wildlife for habitable land. The rate of population increase in sub-Saharan Africa is the highest in the world. Growing at 3.2 percent per year, the present population of 450 million will triple by 2100 to 2.5 billion people. (See Chapter 2, "Population and Health.") Figures are not available on precisely how much wildlife habitat is being lost. Currently Africa is underpopulated by the standards of the more densely set-

tled developed countries with large tracts of nonpark
land used by wildlife. It is this type of land that is most
likely to be developed, but there is some pressure on
reserves as well. For example, the Kenyan Government is
encouraging the development of huge wheat plantations
west of the Masai Mara Reserve in one of the country's
few areas suitable for agriculture. As land is converted to
agriculture, Masai cattle herders are being forced onto the
reserve where their cattle compete with wildlife and may
be in danger of overgrazing the range (64).

Widespread poverty and human misery exacerbated by
drought and political unrest have turned some regions of
Africa into killing fields for organized poaching for sale
of animal products in foreign trade. Some 65,000 black
rhinos have been reduced to a mere 4,500 in east, central, and southern Africa since 1970 (65), and pressures
continue on those remaining. At $400–$600 per pound,
up from $17 per pound in the early 1970s (66), a single
rhino horn may bring a price worth more than a year's
wages.

Eight thousand of the total population of 11,000
elephants in the Central African Republic have been
taken by poachers for their ivory. Ninety percent of
Zaire's elephant population has been eliminated by
poaching. One recent estimate is that 95 percent of
Africa's elephant population will be killed if poaching
continues unabated (67).

In East Africa, poaching of elephants, rhinoceroses,
leopards, zebras, and other animals of high value in commercial trade became so serious in the late 1960s and
1970s that in 1976 the Kenyan Government banned hunting. Other nations followed suit. Kenya and some of its
neighboring states are reluctant to reopen hunting seasons even though many areas support huntable populations of game, because hunting could encourage illegal
traffic in protected animals.

Some wildlife experts, on the other hand, contend that
hunting guides actually helped protect the wildlife from
poachers. Guides who held a permit for a certain tract of
land had a vested interest in maintaining a viable population of game animals and would sometimes apprehend
poachers in the vicinity (68). Since the ban, wildlife and
park agencies have suffered a loss of revenue from sale
of licenses and permits for concessions and other activities associated with the safari business. Lack of government funds as well as loss of support from external aid is
responsible for the closing of Kenya's once-active field
research stations in Tsavo West Park and the Masai Mara
Game Reserve, as well as the Serengeti Research Institute
and the research station in the Selou Game Reserve in
Tanzania. Operation of parks in most East African countries has been curtailed.

Despite efforts by African countries—including banning
hunting and patrolling with armed game rangers—poaching
continues unabated in many places. Countries in which
civil disturbances are taking place and where firearms
are readily available tend to have the most serious problem with poaching. These include Uganda, Central African Republic, Chad, and Sudan.

In Malawi, on the other hand, a combination of armed
anti-poaching patrols and police investigations to break

up local illegal trade rings has resulted in a sharp drop in
the poaching of elephants. (See Table 6.5.)

Zimbabwe actually has too many elephants. Conservation and management efforts have increased the number
of elephants from 200 at the turn of the century to
40,000 in 1987. The government is now trying to reduce
the number to 30,000, which it considers a sustainable
population (69).

United States

The United States has put considerable resources into
conservation and wildlife management. Fifty-nine percent
of its citizens fish, hunt, or engage in other wildlife-
related recreation (70). Over the past 10 years there was a
substantial trend toward nonconsumptive wildlife activities, such as photography, birdwatching, and nature walks,
while the number of hunters held steady and the number of fishermen increased slightly, according to the U.S.
Fish and Wildlife Service, which has published a survey
of fishing, hunting, and wildlife-associated behavior every
five years since 1955. Before 1970, nonconsumptive uses
of wildlife were not even included in the study, but they
are now growing faster than fishing or hunting. In 1980
the survey reported 83 million people engaged in nonconsumptive activities, up from 43 million in 1975, with
an even larger number expected in the next report to be
issued in late 1987 (71). The number of sportsmen
increased only slightly between 1975 and 1980, from 45.8
million to 46.9 million, mainly because of an increase in
fishermen (72), and it is expected to remain fairly steady
in the 1985 survey.

As in other places, wildlife laws were introduced in the
United States to manage and protect game animals. The
states were primarily responsible for game management,
particularly big game and fur-bearing mammals. But the
federal government—the U.S. Fish and Wildlife Service
and the National Marine Fisheries Service—has taken an
increasingly active role in managing migratory game and
nongame birds and marine mammals over which they
have jurisdiction, as well as the management and recov-

**Table 6.5 Effects of Anti–Poaching Programs
on the Number of Elephants Poached in Two
Areas of Malawi, 1977–84**

	Kasungu[a] National Park	Vwaza Marsh[b] Game Reserve
1977	16	X
1978	15	X
1979	26	X
1980	35	22
1981	55	21
1982	29[c]	23
1983	7	29
1984	7	13[d]
1985	X	5

X = not available.
Notes:
a. Kasungu National Park is in central Malawi near the Zambia border. The estimated total elephant population is 250.
b. Vwaza Marsh Game Reserve is in northern Malawi near the Zambia border. The estimated total elephant population is 800.
c. Anti-poaching programs began halfway through 1982.
d. Anti-poaching programs began in 1984.
Source: Thomas McShane, Africa Program, World Wildlife Fund (WWF), unpublished report to the Malawi Government (WWF, Washington, D.C., 1987).

World Resources 1987

85

ery of threatened and endangered plants and animals. As wildlife became less important as a food source and hunting and fishing became primarily recreational activities, laws began to reflect the idea that wildlife should be protected for its own sake (73). The Endangered Species Act of 1973 declares that endangered wildlife "are of esthetic, ecological, educational, historical, recreational, and scientific value to the Nation and its people" (74)—the most comprehensive official statement to date about the diverse value of wildlife.

However, most of the wildlife management funds are still directed toward game species. Of the approximately 3,700 vertebrate species in the United States, only 10 percent are classified as game animals. Yet about 90 percent of the more than $500 million spent annually on wildlife management by the state and federal governments goes to game animals (75). Although Congress passed the Fish and Wildlife Conservation Act (commonly called the "nongame act") in 1980 requiring each state to prepare conservation management plans for fish and wildlife, including nongame animals, no money has yet been appropriated. Game management is financed by hunting and fishing fees as well as by taxes on related equipment. Some states have passed legislation permitting funds for nongame programs to be obtained from special taxes or fees on automobile license plates. Thirty-one states allow citizens to check off a portion of their taxes for nongame wildlife conservation.

The amount of public land designated as state and federal parks and wildlife refuges grew continuously through the 1960s and 1970s, then took a huge jump in 1980 when large tracts of Alaskan lands were reclassified—more than doubling the amount of land in these categories and increasing by nearly fourfold the amount of land in the National Wilderness Preservation System (76). Since 1980 little land has been added to the public system, which now totals more than 109 million hectares.

Most game animals have steadily increased in numbers in most states, with the general exception of ducks, which have seen a downward trend in population since 1980, although individual species may be increasing (77).

Since 1880 more than 160 animals and plants are known to have become extinct in the United States (not including Hawaii, which had more than 140 extinctions since 1850) (78). The Endangered Species Act seems to have slowed the extinction rate: between 1982 and 1984 three fish, one mussel, and one bird were removed from the list because they were presumed extinct (79). A number of species have been reclassified as "threatened," meaning they are in less serious danger of extinction. Notable for their recovery have been the bald eagle, the osprey, the peregrine falcon, and the American alligator.

In its 1985 assessment of wildlife the National Audubon Society noted that animal species in severe danger of national extinction include the polar bear, wolf, sage grouse, and Kemp's Ridley sea turtle. Species in serious trouble include the woodland caribou, loon, black duck, spotted owl, loggerhead shrike, hooded warbler, and the Atlantic and Chinook salmon. The major threats to wildlife outlined in the report are excessive roadbuilding, overgrazing, oil and gas leasing, excessive timber cutting, and declining budgets for conservation (80).

FOCUS ON FRESHWATER WETLANDS

Wetlands are among the world's most important ecosystems. Avoided throughout most of human history as undesirable places to live, swamps and moors were thought to be evil and mysterious, the home of spirits and mystic animals. Once viewed as useless obstacles to agricultural and industrial interests, they are now recognized for their great values in chemical and biological materials and cycling, and especially for their rich diversity of life. Wetlands filter pollutants and act as reservoirs of nutrients in food chains, produce forage for domestic animals and fuel (peat) for humans, provide esthetic, recreational, and cultural benefits for society, and provide habitats for a host of plants and animals.

Size and Extent of Wetlands

Found on every continent except Antarctica (see Figure 6.3) and in every climatic zone, wetlands cover about 6.4 percent of the earth's land surface (see Table 6.6). They are patchy in distribution and generally small. Only those of the lowlands south of Hudson Bay in Canada and the Ob-Irtysh area in western Siberia are comparable in size to large deserts and coniferous forests (81). Most occur in the cooler regions of the world where precipitation exceeds evaporation. Two thirds of the total are probably in Canada and in the western and northern Soviet Union (82).

Wetlands have been mapped and quantified primarily in the developed regions of the world, including Europe, North America, Australia, New Zealand, the Soviet Union, China, and a few regions of Asia. Much of the wetlands in developing nations have yet to be delineated. Data compiled from several sources show that the alkaline mineral soil swamps and marshes make up 2–4 million square kilometers; and more acidic bogs, fens, and peatlands comprise 1.5–3.6 million square kilometers (83). Data in these and other estimates are usually sketchy and almost never comparable. One estimate places the total area of global wetlands at 8.5 million square kilometers (84).

The International Union for Conservation of Nature and Natural Resources (IUCN) has launched an extensive

Table 6.6 Estimated Area of Wetlands in the World by Climatic Zone

Zone	Climate	Wetland Area (thousand square kilometers)	Percent of Total Land Area
Polar	Humid; semihumid	200	2.5
Boreal	Humid; semihumid	2,558	11.0
Sub-Boreal	Humid	539	7.3
	Semiarid	342	4.2
	Arid	136	1.9
Subtropical	Humid	1,077	17.2
	Semiarid	629	7.6
	Arid	439	4.5
Tropical	Humid	2,317	8.7
	Semiarid	221	1.4
	Arid	100	0.8
World Total		**8,558**	**6.4**

Source: William J. Mitsch et al., Wetlands (Van Nostrand Reinhold Co., New York, 1986), p. 4.

Figure 6.3 Wetlands of the World

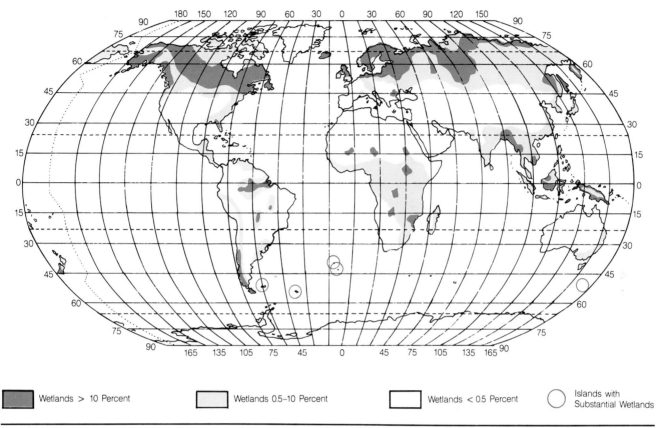

Wetlands > 10 Percent	Wetlands 0.5–10 Percent	Wetlands < 0.5 Percent	Islands with Substantial Wetlands

Source: A.J.P. Gore, *Ecosystems of the World*, Vol. 4A, *Mires: Swamp, Bog, Fen, and Moor: General Studies* (Elsevier Scientific Publishing Co., New York, 1983), inside cover.

worldwide effort to identify freshwater and salt water wetlands of international importance. IUCN coordinators work with specialists and organizations within each country to collect data for a series of *Directories* listing wetland sites, their ecology, flora and fauna, ownership, threats, and management plans. Two directories have been published: *A Directory of Neotropical Wetlands* and *Directory of Wetlands of International Importance in the Western Palearctic* (See Chapter 18, "Land Use and Cover," Table 18.2 and the Technical Notes for that table.) *Directories* for Africa and Asia are in preparation.

Value of Wetlands

Wetlands are among the most productive ecosystems in the world, producing greater net primary productivity (NPP) per unit area than any other natural system except perhaps tropical rain forests and coral reefs (85). (Net primary productivity is the amount of energy stored as organic matter less the cost of respiration required to produce it.) In an analysis of freshwater wetlands, Dr. Orie L. Loucks of the Holcomb Research Institute at Butler University, Indianapolis, Indiana, estimated that the NPP of wetlands is 7–14 percent of global terrestrial productivity (86). The most productive wetlands are shallow marshes and swamps on mineral soils with high nutrient and oxygen supplies. Bogs are the least productive; their

substrates are highly acidic and their nutrient supply is often stagnant. Although they are relatively unproductive in terms of NPP per unit area, bogs are important producers of organic materials, especially carbon, in the form of peat.

Most of the waterfowl harvested in North America is produced in wetland habitats of Canada; most is harvested in the United States. The Migratory Bird Treaty Act of 1916 between the United States and Great Britain regulates waterfowl harvest. A total of 9.2 million ducks and 1.7 million geese were shot and retrieved by hunters in the United States in 1985 (87). The harvest of beaver, mink, muskrat, nutria, and other wetland fur-bearers in 1975–76 in the United States amounted to about $35 million (88).

Loss of Wetlands

Loss of wetlands through natural events is insignificant compared to that caused by human action. Most losses are irreversible and even though some gains are made, especially in deep water habitats through damming of streams and other types of drainages, the gains do not offset losses. Between 25 and 50 percent of the world's swamps and marshes have been lost (89).

Wetlands are drained for a number of reasons, but primarily to create land for crops, forestry, and pasturage for domestic animals. Other activities that seriously affect wetlands include peat mining; pollution by toxic materials from agricultural and industrial chemicals; channelization and obstructions of waterways by dams, dikes, and levees; eutrophication caused by runoff water loaded with fertilizers and wastes; dredging and filling for navigation; flood protection; and housing developments.

Of the original 87 million hectares of wetlands in the United States, only 40 million hectares (46 percent) remained in mid-1970 (90). Of those, 37.9 million hectares were freshwater wetlands and 2.1 million were marine or estuarine wetlands. The annual loss between the mid-1950s and the mid-1970s was 185,000 hectares, with agricultural development accounting for 87 percent of the loss.

In Africa, two large wetland systems—the Okavango Swamps of Botswana and the Sudd Swamps of southern Sudan—face threats from development. The Okavango River flows out of the highlands of Angola to form the Okavango Swamps in Botswana, which range in size each year from 6,000–13,000 square kilometers, depending on the flow of water. Only 3 percent of the water that flows into the swamp exits at the swamp's outlet at Maun; the rest is lost to evaporation. The world's largest inland delta, the Okavango is one of the world's most untrammeled, pristine wetland ecosystems. It is surrounded by arid, heavily grazed lands.

Because only 4 percent of its land is arable, Botswana is interested in opening new irrigated farmland. Several experimental irrigated farms have been established on the delta's southern fringes. While traditional "molapo" farming, which involves plowing and planting as the swamp waters recede, seems successful, soil scientists warn that irrigation will seriously increase the natural salinity of the area's soil. On irrigated farms, flood waters would be kept out. Without flood waters to wash them away, salts brought to the surface by evaporating groundwater will accumulate, leaving the land unproductive (91).

Developers have looked at the Okavango Delta for years as a source of water for agricultural development and for use in mining diamonds and minerals. The Okavango may also face pressure from cattle grazing if a controversial World Bank project called Livestock III proceeds as planned. Tsetse flies have made cattle raising in the delta impossible, but the Botswana Government has recently begun spraying pesticides in the delta. Botswana is economically dependent on cattle, which have overgrazed much of the country's arid rangelands and could seriously damage the grasslands of the Okavango.

In southern Sudan, construction of the Jonglei Canal, which would divert a quarter of the flow of the White

Box 6.1 The Return of the Florida Everglades

Because wetland losses are usually irreversible, an experiment to restore the natural flow of water to a vast wetland in the southern United States—the Florida Everglades—has captured the attention of conservationists.

For more than 100 years, these wetlands were drained for agriculture and development. Now state and federal agencies are attempting to undo their channelization projects and restore the wetlands to their former productivity.

The Everglades, an immense freshwater wetland system of marshes, lakes, and natural drainage, stretches for 240 kilometers in the southern third of Florida (1). Hammocks (or tree islands), sawgrass prairies, mangrove swamps, pinelands and bayheads (mixtures of cypress and willows) occur in the matrix of several kinds of freshwater and marine communities. These afford unusual diversity in plants and animals not found in such numbers elsewhere in the United States. Among the native species of animals, some of which are endangered, are the Florida panther, round-tailed muskrat, Everglades mink, manatee, Everglade kite, bald eagle, peregrine falcon, osprey, American alligator, American crocodile, and green turtle.

Rains charge the system through the Kissimmee River watershed in central Florida (see Figure 1), which empties into Lake Okeechobee. During wet years, the lake would overflow its banks and feed the wetlands that now make up the Everglades National Park and adjacent marshes of southern Florida. The water ultimately reached Florida Bay in the Gulf of Mexico, where it provided nursery areas for a great wealth of finfish and shellfish resources.

In 1883, projects were begun to drain the wetlands for urban and agricultural purposes. A shallow canal was dredged to connect Lake Okeechobee with the Caloosahatchee River to the west, and five other canals were dredged from the lake to the Atlantic. Other projects followed, with the result that by the early 1930s the drainage between Lake Okeechobee and Florida Bay was completely severed. They are now separated by a wide band of agricultural land. South of Lake Okeechobee some 283,000 hectares were converted to agriculture, mostly sugar cane (2). Despite protests from the Florida Game and Freshwater Fish Commission, the U.S. Army Corps of Engineers completed channelization of the Kissimmee River in 1971 to prevent flooding of downstream cities and agricultural land. The 23,310 square-kilometer wetlands comprising the Kissimmee River-Lake Okeechobee-Everglades ecosystem was ultimately reduced by a third to 15,540 square kilometers. Meanwhile in that 100 years, the area's human population increased from 11,200 to about 4 million.

The drainage projects also resulted in eutrophication of Lake Okeechobee, lowering of the water table by two or more feet, and subsidence of peat lands at the rate of a foot per year. They also altered water quality in the Kissimmee basin and in Lake Okeechobee, increased salinities in the estuaries, allowed saltwater intrusion into some of the permeable limestone aquifers along the Atlantic Coast, and changed the composition of the vegetation communities through invasions of exotic plants.

Losses of fish and wildlife were enormous. About 2.5 million wading birds used the Everglades in the 1880s, but there are only about one tenth that number in south Florida today (3). Numbers of the once-abundant American alligator and catches of fin and shellfish by commercial and recreational fishermen were drastically reduced in freshwater and estuarine habitats. All species of wildlife were reduced in number as wetland habitats decreased.

Now the wetland losses are being reversed. The reversal was triggered by a plea from rangers in the Everglades National Park. In 1964 following several years of late rains and a total cut-off from the natural flow of water from the north, the park suffered a severe drought, which threatened long-term ecological damage. The National Park Service petitioned Congress for guaranteed deliveries of surface waters from the control structures. Six years of negotiations among various government agencies followed (4). Restoration of water flows finally began in 1970, when the U.S. Congress required the Corps of Engineers to deliver a monthly quota of 260,000 acre-feet of water to the drying Everglades. Further serious efforts were begun in 1983 with Florida's "Save Our Everglades" program, the goal of which is to restore the Everglades to its condition of 1900 by the year 2000 (5). The South Florida Water Management District began by attempting to mimic natural flows of water through a series of canals, gates, and pumps. While not entirely successful, it was a positive step. Dispersed "sheetflow" drainage was the original pattern of drainage through land that fell only an inch to the mile. A system of canals has

Nile's waters from the Sudd Swamps, has begun but is stalled because of civil strife in Sudan (92). The canal is designed to bring water from the Sudd Swamps to north Sudan and Egypt for irrigation projects and to improve river transportation between north and south Sudan. It will also change the water flow patterns that feed the swamps that stretch 360 kilometers along the Nile. The *toich*, or the rich grassland floodplain, will be greatly narrowed by the canal and its reduction, calculated at up to 50 percent, will threaten migratory tiangs (wild asses), Nile lechwes, shoebill storks, and the largest number of water birds anywhere in Africa. The migratory lifestyle of the pastoral people will be changed dramatically, schistosomiasis will probably take hold as snail larvae, which spread the disease, invade the canal, and the loss of pasturage will likely introduce new conflicts between various tribes already at odds over land and other resources (93). Due to be completed in 1985, the Jonglei Canal is now not expected to open until late in the decade. (See Chapter 12, "Policies and Institutions," The Nile River.)

Although drainage of large wetlands such as the Okavango and the Sudd Swamps may have drastic consequences for wildlife and local peoples, drainage of small marshes and swamps incrementally adds up over time to even greater losses. In the United States, for example, the prairie potholes of Iowa were destroyed in just that way, drained to provide farmland. Iowa's original natural wetlands comprised 930,000 hectares when settlement began, but only 10,715 hectares remain (94). This story is being repeated in a great many regions and nations throughout the world.

The United Nations Development Programme, multilateral lending agencies such as the World Bank, and the international assistance programs of several nations have adopted plans to protect natural resources and to reduce the environmental insults of projects they fund. For example, the United States Agency for International Development (U.S. AID) in 1985 adopted a policy of promoting biological diversity for all habitats, including wetlands, in its international programs (95). Legislation is pending in the U.S. Congress to require environmental considerations as a condition for approval of projects in the developing nations. Restoration and protection of wetlands are expensive. The U.S. Fish and Wildlife Service paid $701 million to purchase about 1 million hectares of wetlands in the United States from 1962 through 1985 (96). Ducks Unlimited, a private organization interested in waterfowl and wetlands habitat, has spent $227 million in Canada on restoration of wetlands since 1937, developing 747,457 hectares and reserving another 1.5 million hec-

Box 6.1

now been designed to allow water to flow southward in much the same fashion from shallow upstream reservoirs.

Current state and federal holdings and proposed acquisition of land for the Kissimmee-Lake Okeechobee-Everglades system total 1.4 million hectares (6). The National Park Service has taken steps to restore fisheries stocks and to preserve several endangered species, such as the Florida panther, and the Corps of Engineers has modified several of its water management structures and policies to accommodate increased flows. Much remains to be done, but there is now a commitment to restore the ailing Everglades to health.

References and Notes

1. J.M. Morehead, *Everglades National Park, U.S.A.: Attempts to Modify Significant Deterioration of a Park's Natural Resources*, pamphlet, 1986.
2. Jeffrey Kahn, "Restoring the Everglades," *Sierra* (September/October, 1986), pp. 40–43.
3. *Ibid.*
4. Gary Hendrix *et al.*, "Everglades National Park: An Imperiled Wetland," *AMBIO*, Vol. 12, No. 3-4 (1983), p. 155.
5. Office of the Governor of Florida, "Save Our Everglades, Report Card Number 6" (1986), p. 10.
6. Office of the Governor of Florida, "Land Acquisition Prior To and Since Save Our Everglades Program" (February 24, 1986), p. 8.

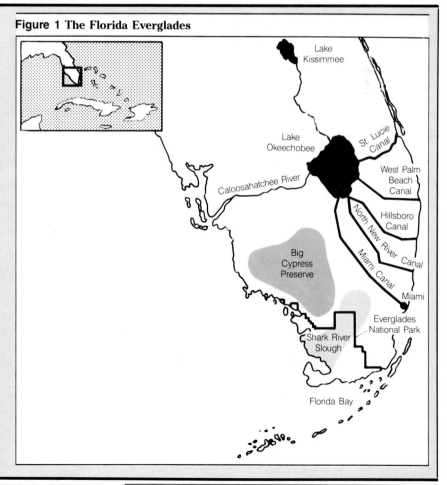

Figure 1 The Florida Everglades

Lake Kissimmee

Lake Okeechobee

Caloosahatchee River

St. Lucie Canal

West Palm Beach Canal

Hillsboro Canal

North New River Canal

Miami Canal

Miami

Big Cypress Preserve

Everglades National Park

Shark River Slough

Florida Bay

tares for waterfowl and other wildlife associated with wetland habitats (97).

A series of meetings, beginning with the Mouvement d'Action Rurale (MAR) conference in 1962, led to the signing of the Wetlands Convention at Ramsar, Iran, in 1972. Signatories to the Convention have imposed limitations upon themselves to protect and use wetlands wisely. This convention is a worldwide effort to control and administer these valuable resources. The number of contracting parties is 43, with the United States, Uruguay, Ireland, Suriname, and Belgium joining in the past year. The list of protected wetlands—called Wetlands of International Importance—now includes 353 sites covering more than 20 million hectares. Sites are listed by country in Chapter 21, "Wildlife and Habitat," Table 21.1.

While most efforts focus on preserving existing wetlands, an effort is underway in southern Florida to restore a wetland area—the Everglades—that has been systematically drained and developed since the 1880s. This is the first attempt to restore a wetland on this scale. (See Box 6.1.)

RECENT DEVELOPMENTS

WORLD BANK ADOPTS WILDLANDS POLICY

The World Bank, as part of a general shift toward more awareness of environmental concerns affecting its projects, adopted a wildlands management policy in June 1986. The policy specifies that the Bank "normally declines to finance (development) projects involving wildlands of special concern." It also states that conversion of less important wildlands must be justified and must be compensated by financing the preservation of an ecologically similar area in a national park or nature reserve, or by some other mitigatory measures (98).

The World Bank and other international lending agencies have been criticized by environmental groups for being insensitive to the environment in their development projects. One project highlighted as an example of unsustainable development was a plan to increase cattle ranching on arid lands in Botswana. Others involved encouraging agricultural development on fragile soils, such as the Polonoroeste project in Brazil, and constructing large dams that flooded tropical forest valleys.

In his address to the 1986 annual meeting of the Board of Governors of the Bank and the International Finance Corporation, newly appointed Bank President Barber Conable indicated that environmental considerations will play more of a role in Bank planning. Quoting Francis Bacon, he said: " 'Nature, to be commanded, must be obeyed.' To keep development in harmony with natural forces and resources, we must apply that lesson on the largest scale—from the planning stage through the execution of every significant project" (99).

An operational policy paper distributed to World Bank staff said that the following types of projects might affect wildlands: agriculture and livestock projects involving wildland clearing, wetland elimination, or wildland inundation for irrigation storage reservoirs; fishery projects involving elimination of important fish nursery or breeding sites, overfishing, or introduction of environmentally risky exotic species; forestry projects involving access roads, clearcutting, or other intensive logging operations; transportation projects involving construction of roads or canals that open wildlands to easy access; hydroelectric projects involving creation of reservoirs that flood wildlands or construction of power line transmission corridors; and industrial projects involving chemical and thermal pollution, mining, or wildland conversion for industrial fuels or feedstocks.

The paper also noted that the Bank had assisted with financing more than 40 wildland-protection projects over the past 15 years and would entertain other projects whose sole objective is wildland protection (100).

While critics of the Bank complain that changes in Bank policy are mostly talk so far, they acknowledge that the Bank is a huge organization that will take time to change. In late 1986 the Bank was undergoing a review of organizational changes designed to enable it to handle environmental and natural resource issues more effectively (101).

TOXIC MATERIALS THREATEN U.S. WILDLIFE

Setting aside protected habitat for wildlife may not be enough to ensure its survival in an industrialized country. A recent study in the United States found that pesticide runoff or hazardous wastes have contaminated wildlife refuges, in some cases causing breeding problems among wildlife.

A 1986 survey by the U.S. Department of the Interior found that 10 refuges were contaminated and another 74 were in danger of contamination. The survey, based on systematic sampling, was commissioned after a 1981 survey in which 121 refuge managers reported cases of serious water contamination. The 431 U.S. National Wildlife Refuges protect more than 36 million hectares harboring 459 species of birds, 147 species of mammals, 34 species of fish, plus various reptiles, amphibians, and insects (102).

The contamination comes from a variety of sources: agricultural or industrial runoff, oil and gas drilling activities, wastes from military activities, or even hazardous wastes previously buried on or near the refuge.

Perhaps the most seriously contaminated refuge is the Kesterson Refuge in California's central valley, where birds have produced grotesquely deformed offspring and many waterfowl have been killed. The marshes there were fed by agricultural drain water contaminated by heavy metals, including selenium, which causes mutations at high levels (103). Asbestos fibers have been found in the water of New Jersey's Great Swamp National Wildlife Refuge, and military wastes such as mustard gas, dioxin, and plutonium have been found at Johnston Atoll off Hawaii.

While the contamination has not often resulted in direct mortality of wildlife, scientists suspect that contaminants weaken animals, making them more susceptible to disease and reducing their ability to reproduce. Reports from Europe, Africa, and Japan indicate that avian diseases occurred after wastewater discharges into marshes (104).

Some wildlife refuges were actually created on land that had been used previously as a dumping ground for industrial or military wastes; as the refuge system expanded it often acquired cheap land that no one wanted, some of which was former industrial or dumping sites. For example, Crab Orchard National Wildlife Refuge in southern Illinois was the former site of a factory that made industrial and military explosives (105).

Funds have been requested for further study of the sit-

uation but so far no money has been earmarked for cleanup. Estimates for cleaning Kesterson Refuge alone range up to $150 million (106). The long-term solution is to keep toxic chemicals out of the environment by reducing them at their source or by proper disposal (see Chapter 13, "Managing Hazardous Wastes: The Unmet Challenge").

References and Notes

1. International Union for Conservation of Nature and Natural Resources (IUCN) and United Nations Environment Programme (UNEP), *An Introduction to the World Conservation Strategy* (IUCN/UNEP, Gland, Switzerland, 1984), p. 13.
2. Dr. E.O. Wilson, Harvard University, quoted in Philip Shabecoff, "Action is Urged to Save Species," *The New York Times* (September 28, 1986).
3. World Resources Institute (WRI), International Institute for Environment and Development (IIED), *World Resources 1986* (Basic Books, New York, 1986), Figure 6.2, p. 93.
4. A.R.E. Sinclair and M. Norton-Griffiths, *Serengeti* (The University of Chicago Press, Chicago and London, 1979).
5. F. Jurji, *Conservation Areas and Their Demographic Settings in Tanzania*, Research Report No. 18, Bureau of Land Use Practice, University of Dar es Salaam, Tanzania (1979).
6. *Op. cit.* 1, p. 29.
7. James G. Teer and Wendell G. Swank, "International Implications of Designating Species Endangered or Threatened," presented at the 43rd North American Wildlife and Natural Resources Conference, Phoenix, Arizona, 1978, pp. 33–41.
8. Ginette Hemley, director of TRAFFIC (USA), Trade Monitoring Program of the World Wildlife Fund, Washington, D.C., 1986 (personal communication).
9. TRAFFIC (USA), the trade monitoring program of the World Wildlife Fund, estimates that illegal trade is about 20 percent of legal trade worldwide. The figure is extrapolated from an estimate that illegal animal trade in the United States is equivalent to 25 percent of the legal trade. Since the United States has strict trade regulations, the illegal trade in other countries may be less, thus TRAFFIC (USA) uses an estimate of 20 percent worldwide. Ginette Hemley, director, TRAFFIC (USA), World Wildlife Fund, Washington, D.C., 1987 (personal communication).
10. *Ibid.*
11. "Of Butterfly Ranchers and Crocodile Catchers," *The Economist* (March 1, 1986), pp. 79–80.
12. Peter Jackson, "The Future of Elephants and Rhinos in Africa," *AMBIO*, Vol. 11, No. 4 (1982), pp. 202–203.
13. "Africa: The Last Safari?" *Newsweek* (August 18, 1986), pp. 40–42.
14. "Butterfly Trade: Net Profits," *South* (July 1986), p. 107.
15. *Ibid.*

16. *Op. cit.* 11.
17. Organisation for Economic Co-operation and Development (OECD), *The State of the Environment 1985* (OECD, Paris, 1985), p. 137.
18. A.M. Borodin, "The Hunting Economy of the USSR," *Transactions of the International Congress of Game Biologists* (1977), pp. 518–521; cited in Michael L. Wolfe and Douglas R. Weiner, *Wildlife Conservation in the Soviet Union*, Report No. 45 (Universities Field Staff International, Inc., Hanover, New Hampshire, 1982), p. 7.
19. American Fur Industry, *Fur Review* (May 1981), cited in TRAFFIC, World Wildlife Fund Wildlife Trade Monitoring Unit, *TRAFFIC Bulletin*, Vol. III, No. 5 (1981), p. 56.
20. *Op. cit.* 13.
21. International Union for Conservation of Nature and Natural Resources (IUCN), *The United Nations List of National Parks and Protected Areas* (IUCN, Gland, Switzerland, and Cambridge, United Kingdom, 1985).
22. S.K. Eltringham, *Wildlife Resources and Economic Development* (John Wiley and Sons, New York, 1984).
23. Philip Thresher, "The Economics Of A Lion," *UNASYLVA*, Vol. 33, No. 134, pp. 34–35.
24. *Ibid.*
25. Erik Eckholm, "New Tactics Transform Wildlife Conservation," *The New York Times* (November 18, 1986), p. C1.
26. U.S. Fish and Wildlife Service, *1980 National Survey of Fishing, Hunting, and Wildlife-Associated Recreation* (U.S. Government Printing Office, Washington, D.C., June 1982), p. 5.
27. "Fair Game?" *The Economist* (July 19, 1986), pp. 38–39.
28. *Op. cit.* 18.
29. M.J. Dourojeanni, *Renewable Natural Resources of Latin America and the Caribbean: Situation and Trends* (World Wildlife Fund-U.S., Washington, D.C., 1982), pp. 319–321.
30. *Op. cit.* 26, p. 4.
31. *Op. cit.* 11.
32. *Op. cit.* 11, p. 79.
33. *Op. cit.* 27.
34. C.A. Pope III, *et. al.*, "The Recreational and Aesthetic Value of Wildlife in Texas," *Journal of Leisure Research*, First Quarter (1984), p. 56.
35. *Op. cit.* 26.
36. *Op. cit.* 34, pp. 51–60.
37. Lewis E. Hawkes, "Trespass Fees for Hunting and Access to Public Land: The Over-Commercialization of Montana's Wildlife

Resources," *Western Wildlands*, Vol. 12, No. 2, Summer (1986), pp. 21–25.
38. E. Joubert, P.A.J. Brand, and G.P. Visagie, "An Appraisal of the Utilization of Game on Private Land in South West Africa," *Journal of Nature Conservation and Desert Research, South West Africa, MADOQUA*, Vol. 13, No. 3 (1983), p. 205.
39. V. de Vos, *et. al.*, "Population Control of Large Mammals in the Kruger National Park," in *Management of Large Mammals in African Conservation Areas*, R. Norman Owen-Smith, ed., proceedings of a symposium held in Pretoria, South Africa, April 20–30, 1982, pp. 213–231.
40. W.E. Poole, *Management of Kangaroo Harvesting in Australia (1984)*, Occasional Paper No. 9 (Australian National Parks and Wildlife Service, Canberra, 1984), p. 21.
41. *Op. cit.* 18.
42. James G. Teer, "Cropping Wildlife for Food and Profit," presented at the Symposium on Wildlife/Livestock Interfaces on Rangeland, Nairobi, Kenya, 1986, pp. 189–195.
43. Wendell G. Swank, *et. al.*, "Cropping, Processing and Marketing of Wildlife in Kajiado District, Kenya," Project Working Document No. 6 (The Government of Kenya and United Nations Food and Agriculture Organization, Nairobi, Kenya, 1974), pp. vi–vii.
44. Graeme Caughley, *The Deer Wars: The Story of Deer in New Zealand* (Heinemann Publishers, Auckland, New Zealand, 1983), p. 113.
45. *Op. cit.* 42.
46. Delwin E. Benson, "Sources of Income," Game Farming Survey No. 2, *Farmer's Weekly* (April 11, 1986), pp. 10–11.
47. *Ibid.*, p. 10.
48. *Op. cit.* 46.
49. Delwin E. Benson, "Management Techniques," Game Farming Survey No. 4, *Farmer's Weekly* (April 25, 1986), p. 21.
50. R.E. McDowell, *et. al.*, "Game or Cattle for Meat Production on Kenya Rangelands?" (Department of Animal Science, New York State College of Agriculture and Life Sciences, Cornell University, Ithaca, New York, 1983), p. 1–77.
51. *Op. cit.* 44.
52. C.N. Challies, "Commercial Hunting of Wild Red Deer in New Zealand," in *Game Harvest Management*, S.L. Beason and Sheila Roberson, eds. (Caesar Kleberg Wildlife Research Institute, Kingsville, Texas, 1983).
53. A.H. Leigh, forest officer, New Zealand Forest Service, 1986 (personal communication).

54. Michael J. Bean, *The Evolution of National Wildlife Law* (Praeger Publishers, New York, 1983), pp. 10–11.
55. John S. Gottschalk, "The German Hunting System, West Germany, 1968," *Journal of Wildlife Management*, Vol. 36, No. 1 (1972), p. 111.
56. George V. Burger and James G. Teer, "Economic and Socioeconomic Issues Influencing Wildlife Management on Private Land," proceedings of a symposium on Wildlife Management on Private Lands, Wisconsin Chapter of the Wildlife Society, Madison, Wisconsin, 1981, p. 253.
57. *Op. cit.* 17, p. 145.
58. Simon Lyster, *International Wildlife Law* (Grotius Publications Ltd., Cambridge, United Kingdom, 1985), p. 130.
59. Council of Europe, *Report of the Fourth Meeting of the Interim Committee of the Convention on the Conservation of European Wildlife and Natural Habitats* (January 21, 1982); cited in Simon Lyster, *International Wildlife Law* (Grotius Publications Ltd., Cambridge, United Kingdom, 1985), p. 152.
60. *Op. cit.* 58, p. 112.
61. *Op. cit.* 58, p. 113.
62. *Op. cit.* 58, p. 115.
63. *Op. cit.* 58.
64. Edward R. Ricciuti, "Paradise Lost?" *Animal Kingdom* (June-July 1984), pp. 31–32.
65. *Op. cit.* 13.
66. *Op. cit.* 13.
67. *Op. cit.* 13.
68. Steve Berwick, senior scientist, International Institute for Environment and Development, Washington, D.C., 1986 (personal communication).
69. Tomas McShane, Africa Program, World Wildlife Fund and the Conservation Foundation, Washington, D.C., 1987 (personal communication).
70. *Op. cit.* 26.
71. David Klinger, information office, U.S. Fish and Wildlife Service, Washington, D.C., 1983 (personal communication). Because the 1975 and 1980 surveys used different methods, these numbers may not be comparable, but there is an acknowledged trend toward nonconsumptive sports.
72. *Op. cit.* 26, p. 136.
73. *Op. cit.* 54, p. 411.
74. *Ibid.*
75. Philip Shabecoff, "U.S. Spending on Wildlife is Assailed," *The New York Times* (November 13, 1986), p. A27.
76. The Conservation Foundation, *State of the Environment: An Assessment at Mid-Decade* (The Conservation Foundation, Washington, D.C., 1985), p. 184.
77. Council on Environmental Quality (CEQ), *Environmental Quality 1982* (U.S. Government Printing Office, Washington, D.C., 1983), p. 260.
78. Paul A. Opler, "The Parade of Passing Species: A Survey of Extinctions in the U.S.," in *Environmental Problems* 2nd ed., Folkerte and Mason, eds. (William C. Brown and Co., Dubuque, Iowa, 1983); cited in The Conservation Foundation, *State of the Environment: An Assessment at Mid-Decade* (The Conservation Foundation, Washington, D.C., 1985), p. 181.
79. U.S. Fish and Wildlife Service, *Endangered and Threatened Wildlife and Plants* (U.S. Fish and Wildlife Service, Washington, D.C., January, 1986).
80. The National Audubon Society, *Audubon Wildlife Report 1985* (The National Audubon Society, New York, 1985).
81. J.A. Taylor, "The Peatlands of Great Britain and Ireland," in *Ecosystems of the World*, Vol. 4B, *Mires: Swamp, Bog, Fen, and Moor*, A.J.P. Gore, ed. (Elsevier Scientific Publishing Co., New York, 1983), p. 1–46.
82. D.W. Goodall, "The Future of Mires," in *Ecosystems of the World*, Vol. 4B, *Mires: Swamp, Bog, Fen, and Moor* A.J.P. Gore, ed. (Elsevier Scientific Publishing Co., New York, 1983), p. 395–396.
83. O.L. Loucks, "Biological Productivity" (Butler University, unpublished report, 1985), p. 3.
84. W.J. Mitsch and J.G. Gosselink, *Wetlands* (Van Nostrand Reinhold Co., New York, 1986).
85. G.E. Likens, "Primary Productivity of Inland Aquatic Ecosystems," in *Primary Productivity of the Biosphere*, H. Lieth and R.H. Whittaker, eds., Ecological Studies 14 (Springer-Verlag, New York, 1975), pp. 203–215.
86. *Op. cit.* 83, p. 12.
87. Office of Migratory Bird Management, "Waterfowl Harvest and Hunter Activity in the United States During the 1985 Hunting Season," Administrative Report (U.S. Fish and Wildlife Service, Washington, D.C., July 1986).
88. R.H. Chabreck, "Wildlife Harvest in Wetlands of the United States," in *Wetland Functions and Values: The State of Our Understanding*, P.E. Greeson, et. al., eds. (American Water Resources Association, Minneapolis, Minnesota, 1979), pp. 618–631.
89. *Op. cit.* 83.
90. H.B. Roe, and Q.C. Ayres, *Engineering for Agricultural Drainage* (McGraw Hill Book Co., New York, 1954); cited in R.W. Tiner, Jr., *Wetlands of the United States: Current Status and Recent Trends* (U.S. Government Printing Office, Washington, D.C., 1984), p. 29.
91. "Botswana Taps Okavango Delta," *World Water* (March 1986).
92. A.I. el Moghraby and M.O. el Sammani, "On the Environmental and Socioeconomic Impact of the Jonglei Canal Project, Southern Sudan," *Environmental Conservation*, Vol. 12, No. 1 (1985), pp. 41–48.
93. A. Charnock, "A New Course for the Nile," *New Scientist* (October 27, 1983), pp. 285–288.
94. R.W. Tiner, Jr., *Wetlands of the United States: Current Status and Recent Trends* (U.S. Government Printing Office, Washington, D.C., 1984), p. 35.
95. U.S. Agency for International Development (U.S. AID), *U.S. Strategy on the Conservation of Biological Diversity: An Interagency Task Force Report for Congress* (U.S. AID, Washington, D.C., 1985).
96. U.S. Fish and Wildlife Service, *Fish and Wildlife Service Land Acquisition Program Accomplishments, FY 1962-1985* (U.S. Fish and Wildlife Service, Division of Realty, Washington, D.C., 1986).
97. Ducks Unlimited, *Ducks Unlimited Progress Summary: 1985*, pamphlet (Ducks Unlimited, Lone Grove, Illinois, 1985).
98. The World Bank, "Wildlands: Their Protection and Management in Economic Development," operational policy paper (The World Bank, Washington, D.C., June 1986).
99. Barber B. Conable, "Address to the Board of Governors of The World Bank and International Finance Corporation" (The World Bank, Washington, D.C., September 30, 1986).
100. *Op. cit.* 98, p. 3.
101. John Walsh, "World Bank Pressed on Environmental Reforms," *Science*, Vol. 234 (November 14, 1986), pp. 813–815.
102. Maura Dolan, "Pollution Endangers U.S. Refuges," *Los Angeles Times* (July 6, 1986), p. 1.
103. *Ibid.*, p. 17.
104. *Op. cit.* 102, p. 18.
105. *Op. cit.* 102, p. 18.
106. *Op. cit.* 102, p. 18.

7. Energy

Rapidly changing developments in energy have significantly affected the short-term outlook for the mix of commercial energy use and the economic prospects of various types of energy production. The long-term implications of these events are not yet predictable, but continuing change in response to market forces, development needs, and environmental concerns seems likely. In 1986, two major energy developments startled most experts: a sudden drop in worldwide petroleum prices and the explosion and fire at the Soviet Union's Chernobyl nuclear power plant.

During the year, spot market prices for oil dipped below $10 per barrel (from a high of more than $30 in 1981) and the average U.S. price fell to $15 per barrel in early 1986, shaking predictions made as early as 1980 that costs would soar beyond $40 per barrel. Because of conservation efforts and an economic slowdown in the developed world, oil consumption settled at 2,809 million metric tons in 1985 (1), almost 40 percent below the estimates of many petroleum industry analysts only a few years before (2).

The Organization of Petroleum Exporting Countries (OPEC), once considered an invincible cartel, lost oil sales for the seventh year in a row. OPEC's share of world oil output dropped from 57 percent in 1975 to only 30 percent in 1985 (3) as non-OPEC countries expanded their production. Many Third World nations, strapped by heavy energy debts, were relieved to see prices falling. But oil exporting developing nations, such as Mexico, Venezuela,

and Nigeria, which had come to depend on oil revenues as an important source of income, were badly hurt.

As oil prices plunged, energy analysts watched the effect on renewable energy development and energy conservation efforts. Some nations have decreased their solar efforts, but others have advanced alternative energy technologies and dramatically expanded their use of renewable resources. Energy conservation in industrialized countries promises to continue, despite lower oil prices, because of investments made in efficient technologies during the 1970s and early 1980s. But energy use is rising in many sectors in response to lower prices.

In the Third World, energy conservation efforts are less established and analysts predict that as these countries grow their increasing energy demand could strain their economies if they spend more foreign exchange on oil imports. In countries that lack foreign exchange, energy demand could remain unmet, limiting development. Recent studies, however, suggest that developing countries could achieve Western living standards with only a 20 percent per capita increase in energy use if they adopt conservation measures as they switch to modern forms of energy.

The second major energy-related shock of 1986 occurred on April 26 when one of the Soviet Union's nuclear reactors at Chernobyl exploded and caught fire, spewing radioactive debris more than 2,000 meters into the air and over sizable portions of the Soviet Union and Europe (4). After the accident, more than 100,000 people

World Resources 1987

93

had to be evacuated to avoid the substantial amounts of radioactive fallout. Several months later, Soviet scientists announced that 31 people died and 203 remained hospitalized with radiation illness (5). The disaster's long-term effects on nuclear power development are not yet clear, but several countries have re-examined their nuclear programs and many others have placed a new emphasis on nuclear safety.

Another significant development over the past few years, one less reported by the international media, was the increase in the Soviet Union's natural gas production following its discovery in the early 1980s of three massive gas reserves in western Siberia, above the Arctic Circle, and near the Soviet border with Iran. Soviet gas production expanded some 45 percent from 1980 to 1985 (6), enabling the USSR to put more of its oil on the export market.

Overall, world energy markets have become increasingly competitive in the past few years. Once controlled by multinational oil companies and then by OPEC, oil production and prices are now shaped as much by market forces as by corporate or government decisions. The percentage of oil traded internationally under long-term contract dropped from 95 percent in the 1970s to about 60 percent in the 1980s (7). Electricity monopolies, particularly in the United States, are starting to feel competition from entrepreneurs employing small-scale generators. And suppliers of all energy resources are forced to compete for markets as oil prices drop, natural gas reserves expand, and energy conservation slows the growth of demand.

CONDITIONS AND TRENDS

ENERGY PRODUCTION AND CONSUMPTION BY REGION

Industrialized Countries

OECD nations, increasingly relying on efficient technologies, have weakened the link between economic expansion and the growth of energy use. From 1945 to 1973, when real energy prices remained relatively constant, the ratio of energy consumed per dollar of Gross Domestic Product (GDP) hardly changed. But the price hikes for oil during the 1970s spurred investments in energy-efficient machines and processes and encouraged a shift toward less energy-intensive industries and services. As energy efficiency has improved, the ratio of energy consumption to GDP has decreased in the United States, Japan, and Western Europe (8). (See Figure 7.1.)

The question now is whether lower oil prices will once again cause rapid growth in energy consumption. Few analysts expect oil demand to rise as fast as the 6 percent to 7 percent annual increases of the 1960s and early 1970s, particularly because of the efficiency improvements built into industrial equipment, buildings, and motor vehicles during that period (9). But U.S. petroleum demand in the first eight months of 1986 did rise 2.1 percent from the same period a year earlier (10). Even such relatively small increases represent a flood of oil. If demand were to expand by only 3 percent two years in

Figure 7.1 Ratio of Energy Consumption to Gross Domestic Product, 1965–85

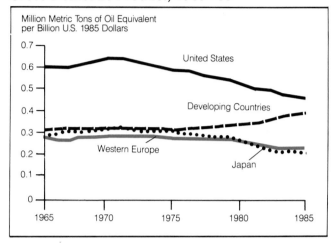

Source: British Petroleum (BP), *BP Statistical Review of World Energy, 1986* (BP, London, 1986).

a row, for instance, U.S. petroleum consumption would rise about 1 million barrels a day, or about one-fifth of U.S. oil imports in 1985. If lower prices spur oil consumption and also reduce efforts to explore for domestic resources, OECD officials fear that industrialized nations will again face tight petroleum supplies, sharp price swings, and increased reliance on the volatile Middle East (11). At a 3 percent growth rate, that situation could occur by the early 1990s.

As a group, industrialized nations reduced their oil use 19 percent between 1979 and 1985, but oil still accounted for almost 43 percent of their primary energy consumption at the end of this period (12). (See Figure 7.2.) Falling oil prices, therefore, promise major benefits for most of these nations. OECD calculates that a 30 percent price decline would boost economic output by almost 1 percent in the first year and by another 2 percent the following year (13).

Oil price declines have varied among the industrialized nations. Japan and the United States have enjoyed gradually falling prices since 1981 (see Figure 7.3), but exchange rates in most OECD countries led to price increases through 1985 and contributed to Europe's economic recession (14). Recently, the falling U.S. dollar has spread the benefits of lower oil prices to Western Europe, Australia, and New Zealand.

Production and consumption of nuclear energy expanded rapidly over the past decade, but the growth rate has slowed recently. France's accelerated atomic power program increased its output about 250 percent from 1980 to 1985, and nuclear energy now accounts for almost one-quarter of the country's primary energy. (See Figure 7.4.) Japan's nuclear consumption rose 67 percent during those five years (15). Although U.S. consumption rose 51 percent in the same period, U.S. utilities have placed no new reactor orders in more than eight years. In fact, all but two of the 41 U.S. nuclear plants ordered since 1974 have been subsequently canceled; no work

Figure 7.2 Regional Consumption Patterns of Primary Energy, 1985

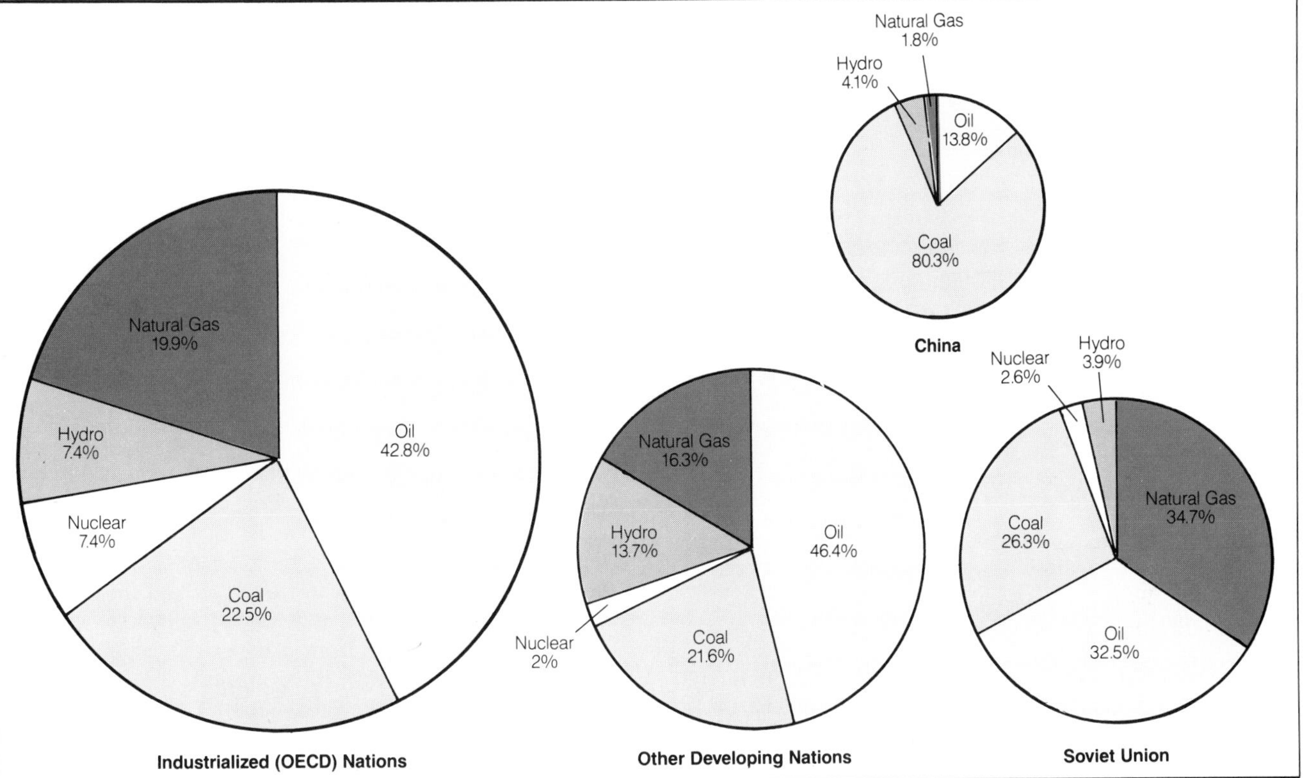

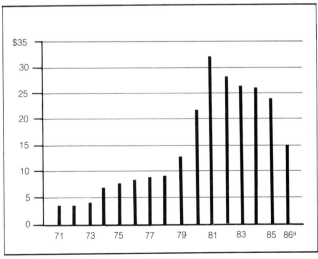

Note: The size of each circle represents the relative amount of energy consumed by that country or group of countries.
Source: Adapted from British Petroleum (BP), *BP Statistical Review of World Energy, 1986* (BP, London, 1986), p. 31 and p. 32.

has been done on even these two plants, and neither will probably ever be completed (16).

In the United States, overbudget nuclear plants and 1978 legislation requiring utilities to buy electricity from independent power producers have made the electricity market increasingly competitive. Entrepreneurs have invested in technologies that cogenerate steam and electricity, burn wastes, or harness the sun, wind, falling water, and geothermal steam. According to the U.S. Federal Energy Regulatory Commission, independent power producers will soon supply a quarter or more of the capacity in several regions of the country (17). California utilities report that since 1982 these independents increased their capacity from 100 to about 3,000 megawatts, approximately the equivalent of three nuclear reactors. Contracts for another 12,553 megawatts have been signed (18).

Table 7.1 shows changes in consumption patterns among industrialized nations during the first half of this decade: oil consumption fell by 12 percent, natural gas was down by 4 percent, coal consumption rose by 11 percent, hydropower jumped 46 percent, and nuclear rose by 90 percent. Table 7.2 shows production trends during the same period: oil up by 13.2 percent, natural gas down 9.8 percent, and coal up by 5 percent. For nuclear and hydropower, consumption and production are considered almost identical since there is little export of these

forms of power, except through international electrical grids, and virtually no storage.

Figure 7.3 Average U.S. Price per Barrel of Oil, 1971–86

Note: a. Estimate by industry sources.
Source: U.S. Department of Energy.

Figure 7.4 Nuclear Energy's Share of Total Energy Consumed, 1980–85

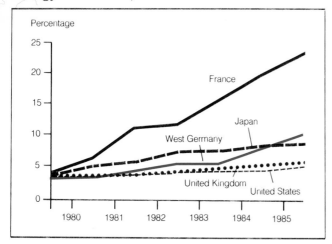

Source: British Petroleum (BP), *BP Statistical Review of World Energy, 1986* (BP, London, 1986), p. 29.

Soviet Union and Eastern Europe

The Soviet Union, which earns more than half its foreign earnings from oil, could be a major loser in an era of declining oil prices. Although it is still the world's largest oil producer—its 1985 output was more than triple that of Saudi Arabia (19)—the Soviet Union's production has been stagnating, and the cost of extracting new oil is rising as production moves to even less accessible parts of Siberia.

Soviet leaders have been trying to shift domestic energy consumption from oil to nuclear power and natural gas in order to free liquid petroleum for the export market. Between 1980 and 1985 nuclear production/consumption increased by 121 percent and the Soviets had planned to add 40,000 megawatts of nuclear capacity by 1990, more than doubling nuclear's share of total electrical output to 20 percent (20). But the effects of the Chernobyl accident may slow that rate.

In 1985, for the first time, the Soviet Union consumed more natural gas than oil. The Soviets have been extremely successful in expanding natural gas production: officials claim the Soviet Union has recently found enough gas "to last us through the 21st Century" (21). Russian geologists have determined that the huge Urengoi field in Western Siberia has reserves equaling almost 11 percent of the world's total known reserves in 1985.

Similar-sized fields exist at Yamburg, above the Arctic Circle, and at Sovetabad, near the Iranian border (22). By 1985, the USSR produced 37.7 percent of the world's gas at a rate more than 50 percent greater than its 1980 output. (See Table 7.3.) According to available evidence, the rate of increase of Soviet pipeline construction, field development, and gas reserves may moderate, but continued increases in production capability are likely (23).

Total energy consumption in the USSR and Eastern Europe increased 13 percent from 1980 to 1985, compared to a decrease of almost 1 percent in OECD countries. (See Table 7.1.) Coal consumption rose only 4 percent, while coal production rose 8.8 percent. Hydroelectricity use expanded 10.8 percent.

Developing Countries

Petroleum—even less-expensive petroleum—remains an unaffordable luxury for more than half the world's people who cook and heat with fuelwood, charcoal, animal wastes, and crop residues. Even in an era of falling petroleum prices, developing nations continue to obtain more than 40 percent of their energy from non-commercial sources such as fuelwood and other biomass.

On average, a person from a developing country consumes less than one-sixth the commercial energy used by a resident of an industrialized nation, and less than one-twelfth as much as the average U.S. citizen (24). Third World consumption, however, is rising. According to the International Monetary Fund, net oil-importing developing countries increased their oil use from 5.6 million barrels a day to 7.3 million barrels a day between 1973 and 1985 (25). The World Bank estimates that the Third World's share of global commercial energy consumption will increase from 20 percent in 1980 to slightly over 25 percent by 1995 (26). (See Figure 7.5.) The major commercial fuel in the Third World is oil, which accounts for 46.4 percent of consumption. (See Figure 7.2.)

The Bank also projects that Third World energy production, excluding the output from high-income oil exporters, will rise from 25 percent of the world's commercial energy in the 1970s to about 33 percent by 1995 (27). Several developing countries—including Brazil, Colombia, Egypt, Malaysia, and Pakistan—have significantly boosted their oil production in recent years, most of the fuel being burned for domestic consumption (28). China, for instance, increased its output 8.9 percent from 1984 to 1985, adding slightly more than 10 million metric tons (29).

Table 7.1 Commercial Energy[a] Consumption by Region and Fuels, 1985
(million metric tons of oil equivalent)
(numbers in parentheses reflect percent change from 1980 to 1985)

	Oil	Natural Gas	Coal	Hydro[b]	Nuclear[b]	Total
OECD Industrialized Countries	1,591 (−12%)	739 (−4%)	837 (+11%)	276 (+46%)	275 (+90%)	3,718 (−1%)
USSR and Eastern Europe	554 (+0.5%)	570 (+40%)	658 (+4%)	67 (+9.5%)	47 (+121%)	1,896 (+13%)
Developing Countries	664 (+6%)	183 (+39%)	783 (+27%)	155 (+37.5%)	15 (+348%)	1,800 (+22%)
World Total	**2,809 (−6%)**	**1,492 (+14%)**	**2,278 (+14%)**	**498 (+16%)**	**337 (+99%)**	**7,414 (+7%)**

Notes:
a. Commercial Energy excludes wood, peat, and animal wastes.
b. Consumption and production are approximately the same.
Source: British Petroleum (BP), *BP Statistical Review of World Energy, 1986* (BP, London, 1986).

Table 7.2 Commercial Energy[a] Production by Region and Fuels, 1985

(million metric tons of oil equivalent)
(numbers in parentheses reflect percent change from 1980 to 1985)

	Oil		Natural Gas		Coal	
OECD Industrialized Countries	800.3	(+13.2%)	663.0	(−9.8%)	820.1	(+5.0%)
USSR and Eastern Europe	616.8	(−1.5%)	639.3	(+48.2%)	669.7	(+8.8%)
Developing Countries	1,372.4	(−21.6%)	233.0	(+29.0%)	781.1	(+24.9%)
World Total	**2,789.5**	**(−9.5%)**	**1,535.3**	**(+14.0%)**	**2,270.9**	**(+12.3%)**

Note: a. Commercial Energy excludes wood, peat, and animal waste.
Source: Adapted from British Petroleum (BP), *BP Statistical Review of World Energy, 1986* (BP, London, 1986).

Many middle-income developing countries have rapidly increased their electrical capacity with domestic coal burning, hydroelectric dams, and nuclear reactors. South Korea and Taiwan, for instance, leapt to electrification over the past 30 years. China, India, and Indonesia are following their lead (30).

Because of cutbacks by OPEC nations, oil production in developing countries fell almost 22 percent over the past five years, while natural gas production rose 29 percent and coal production increased almost 25 percent. (See Table 7.2.)

Consumption of all commercial fuels by developing countries rose 22 percent from 1980 to 1985, reflecting continued economic development. Nuclear power use increased 348 percent from a small base, hydroelectricity rose 37.5 percent, natural gas 39 percent, coal 27 percent, and oil 6 percent. (See Table 7.1.)

MAJOR ENERGY SOURCES

Oil

Petroleum is one of the world's most unevenly distributed resources. Ninety-five percent of proven reserves are in only 20 countries, and Arab nations and Iran control 56.3 percent of the world's total (31). (See Table 7.4.) Most petroleum experts believe remaining petroleum reserves will become increasingly concentrated in the Middle East

Table 7.3 Production of Natural Gas, 1985

(million metric tons)

	1985	Percent Change 1980 to 1985	1985 Share of Total
North America	489.2	−13.3%	31.9%
Western Europe[a]	156.4	−0.8%	10.3%
Oceania[b]	15.4	+41.3%	1.8%
Japan	2.0	0	0.1%
USSR	578.6	+52.2%	37.7%
Eastern Europe[c]	60.7	+18.6%	3.0%
Middle East[d]	45.7	+8.8%	3.0%
Other Developing Countries[e]	175.8	+39.1%	11.4%
China	11.5	−5.7%	0.7%
World Total	**1,535.3**	**+14.0%**	**100.0%**

0 = zero or less than 0.05.
Notes:
a. Western Europe includes Austria, Belgium, Denmark, Federal Republic of Germany, Finland, France, Greece, Iceland, Republic of Ireland, Italy, Luxembourg, the Netherlands, Norway, Portugal, Spain, Sweden, Switzerland, Turkey, and United Kingdom.
b. Oceania includes Australia, New Zealand, Papua New Guinea, Southwest Pacific Islands.
c. Eastern Europe includes Bulgaria, Czechoslovakia, German Democratic Republic, Hungary, Poland, Rumania, and Yugoslavia.
d. Middle East includes Abu Dhabi, Dubai Iran, Iraq, Kuwait, Neutral Zone, Oman, Qatar, Saudi Arabia, and Syria.
e. Developing Countries includes all Latin American, African, South Asian and Southeast Asian countries.
Source: Adapted from British Petroleum (BP), *BP Statistical Review of World Energy, 1986* (BP, London, 1986).

Figure 7.5 Shares of Country Groups in World Commercial Energy Consumption, 1970–95

(Tons of oil equivalent [toe])

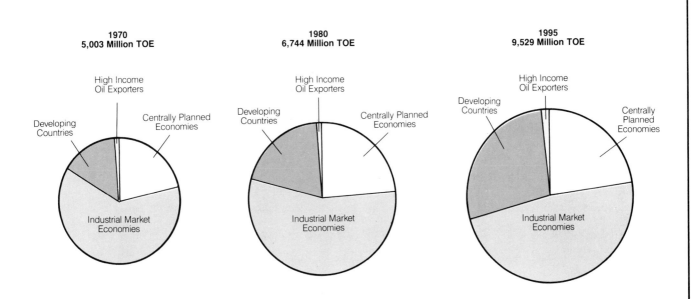

1970
5,003 Million TOE

1980
6,744 Million TOE

1995
9,529 Million TOE

Source: The World Bank, *The Energy Transition in Developing Countries* (The World Bank, Washington, D.C., 1983), p. 5.

Table 7.4 Gas, Oil, and Coal Reserves, 1985

	Billion Metric tons of Oil	Share of Total Oil	Trillion Cubic Meters of Natural Gas	Share of Total Natural Gas	Billion Metric tons of Coal	Share of Total Coal
North America	5.6	6.0%	8.4	8.6%	262.9	27.6%
Western Europe[a]	3.4	3.7%	6.1	6.5%	99.3	10.4%
Oceania[b]	0.2	0.2%	0.7	0.7%	67.2	7.0%
Japan	0	0	0	0	1.0	0.1%
USSR	8.3	8.6%	42.5	43.2%	241.0	25.2%
Other Centrally Planned Economies[c]	0.3	0.3%	0.5	0.5%	101.9	10.7%
Middle East[d]	54.0	56.3%	24.2	24.6%	0	0
Other Developing Countries[e]	21.6	22.3%	14.8	15.0%	82.2	8.6%
China	2.4	2.6%	0.8	0.9%	99.0	10.4%
World Total	**95.8**	**100.0%**	**98.0**	**100.0%**	**954.5**	**100.0%**

0 = zero or less than 0.05.

Notes:
a. Western Europe includes Austria, Belgium, Denmark, Federal Republic of Germany, Finland, France, Greece, Iceland, Republic of Ireland, Italy, Luxembourg, the Netherlands, Norway, Portugal, Spain, Sweden, Switzerland, Turkey, and United Kingdom.
b. Oceania includes Australia and New Zealand.
c. Other Centrally Planned Economies includes Albania, Bulgaria, Czechoslovakia, Cuba, German Democratic Republic, Hungary, Kampuchea, North Korea, Laos, Mongolia, Poland, Rumania, Vietnam, and Yugoslavia.
d. Middle East includes Abu Dhabi, Dubai, Iran, Iraq, Kuwait, Neutral Zone, Oman, Qatar, Saudi Arabia, Syria.
e. Developing Countries includes non-centrally planned countries in Latin America, Africa, South Asia, and Southeast Asia.
Source: Adapted from British Petroleum (BP), *BP Statistical Review of World Energy, 1986* (BP, London, 1986).

as Arab states and Iran cut their production and non-OPEC countries rapidly pump out their oil (32). Since 1980, the Middle East's output has declined 42.6 percent, while production in the North Sea, Australia, and China has continued to grow. In the same period, there has been little change in oil output in the United States, the USSR, and Eastern Europe. (See Table 7.5.)

How much oil is left to be found and economically pumped remains controversial among geologists and government officials. Optimists point to fields in Mexico that have delivered substantially more than expected; pessimists focus on the multi-million dollar exploration projects off the Atlantic coast of the United States that have turned up virtually nothing. The United States spent $250 billion on domestic petroleum exploration between 1980 and 1984 (33), but proven reserves of crude oil dropped almost 5 percent during that period and a total of 27 percent since 1970 (34).

Exxon Corporation, a major petroleum company, believes declining reserves will soon be a worldwide phenomenon. Oil production, the company calculates, "eventually will reach a plateau—probably sometime early in the next century—and then begin to drop" (35). As noted, lower oil prices result in less exploration and development. An industry survey suggests that if the price of oil settles at $15 a barrel U.S. outlays for exploration will drop from about $70 billion in 1985, to $38 billion in 1987, and to $32 billion in 1991 (36). Some North Sea fields already cost more than $20 per barrel to exploit and are uneconomical to operate at 1986 prices (37). If oil market signals are accurate, of course, reduced oil development will create scarcities, which will lead in turn to higher oil prices and subsequently stimulate exploration.

Natural Gas

Natural gas, long a neglected resource that was commonly flared—or burned off—at oil wells, is now coveted as a clean-burning, efficient fuel. Geologists now estimate that recoverable gas reserves are almost as large as those for oil.

World consumption of natural gas rose from 1,084 million metric tons of oil equivalent in 1975 to 1,492 million metric tons in 1985. Increases, however, were not evenly shared among nations. Consumption in the United States, for instance, fell during the early 1980s because of rising prices and temporary shortages caused by government actions. In the rest of the world, average gas use jumped 79 percent between 1975 and 1985; in the Soviet Union it soared 107 percent (38).

The Soviet Union has dramatically increased its natural gas output, becoming the world's leading producer. (See Table 7.3.) About 50 developing countries, including 30 that import oil, have natural gas reserves, but they have not organized systematic exploration or development, in large part because of the high cost of building a gas distribution system. The World Bank surveyed 15 Third World nations with sizable gas reserves and found that their average current production is only 16 percent of the level that proven reserves could support. Nonetheless, the Bank projects a fourfold increase in natural gas production in developing countries by 1995 (39).

Utility planners have tended to avoid burning relatively high-priced natural gas in inefficient electricity-generating turbines. But renewed interest in cogeneration—the production in a common facility of both electricity and heat for industrial process and other applications—has sparked dramatic improvements in the efficiency of gas turbines and may expand gas markets. Using technologies developed for aircraft engines, engineers have increased the turbine's efficiency by 50 percent. Utilities and entrepreneurs, as a result, may be able to build low-cost, short-lead-time facilities that provide gas-powered electricity priced competitively with coal- and nuclear-generated electricity (40). (See Box 7.1.)

A few scientists, notably Thomas Gold of Cornell University, believe massive quantities of natural gas, and possibly oil, are contained in deep reservoirs throughout the world. They argue that gas is not a fossil fuel—the product of decayed organic matter—but is derived from the cloud of material that formed the planet. Much of this fuel was trapped in the earth's molten core, they claim, and has since percolated upward, only to be

Table 7.5 Production of Oil, 1985
(million metric tons)

	1985	Percent Change 1980 to 1985	1985 Share of Total
North America	578.4	+2.2%	20.7%
Western Europe[a]	191.2	+57.5%	6.8%
Oceania[b]	30.2	+57.3%	1.1%
Japan	0.5	+25.0%	0
USSR	594.5	−1.4%	21.3%
Eastern Europe[c]	22.3	−3.3%	0.8%
Middle East[d]	532.5	−42.6%	19.2%
Other Developing Countries[e]	715.2	−0.1%	25.6%
China	124.7	+17.9%	4.5%
World Total	**2,789.5**	**−9.5%**	**100.0%**

0 = zero or less than 0.05.
Notes:
a. Western Europe includes Austria, Belgium, Denmark, Federal Republic of Germany, Finland, France, Greece, Iceland, Republic of Ireland, Italy, Luxembourg, the Netherlands, Norway, Portugal, Spain, Sweden, Switzerland, Turkey, and United Kingdom.
b. Oceania includes Australia and New Zealand.
c. Eastern Europe includes Bulgaria, Czechoslovakia, German Democratic Republic, Hungary, Poland, Rumania, and Yugoslavia.
d. Middle East includes Abu Dhabi, Dubai, Iran, Iraq, Kuwait, Neutral Zone, Oman, Qatar, Saudi Arabia, and Syria.
e. Developing Countries includes all Latin American, African, South Asian and Southeast Asian countries.
Source: Adapted from British Petroleum (BP), *BP Statistical Review of World Energy, 1986* (BP, London, 1986).

trapped by an impermeable layer of cap rock. Most geologists reject the claim, but the theory is being tested in Sweden's Siljan Ring where drilling of a 5,000-meter-deep well began in July 1986 with results expected by early 1987 [41].

Coal

The world's coal resources are enormous, and at current production levels reserves will last about 500 years [42]. Use of the resource, however, has been limited by the inefficiencies of the international coal industry's management, the inconvenience of storing and shipping the fuel, and the environmental consequences of large-scale coal burning. (See Chapter 10, "Atmosphere and Climate.")

World coal consumption rose 14 percent over the past five years. (See Table 7.1.) China logged the largest increase—26 percent—to become the world's premier user. World coal production rose 12.3 percent from 1981 to 1985 (see Table 7.6), with big advances in China, India, and Australia. The largest coal reserves are in the United States and the USSR [43]. (See Table 7.4.)

About 35 developing countries produce coal for domestic use. The World Bank maintains that "coal will only be a viable alternative to oil if the governments improve the management of all aspects of the coal chain, including exploration, production, transport, and use." The Bank projects that China and India will account for the largest production increases in the next decade [44].

Nuclear Power

Worldwide nuclear electricity consumption rose 99 percent between 1980 and 1985, with the largest increases in France and the Soviet Union. (See Table 7.1 and Figure 7.4.) But much of this increase is because plants begun several years ago are finally coming on line. The number of new plants being constucted has declined over the past few years because of construction cost overruns and safety concerns, and this trend seems likely to continue. (See Figure 7.6.)

West Germany obtains about 10 percent of its total energy from nuclear power, but has ordered only one nuclear plant since 1975, and construction has not begun

Box 7.1 Cogeneration Catches On

With electricity rates rising, one energy-efficient technology—cogeneration—is enjoying a dramatic renaissance among petroleum refiners, wood and food processors, steel and chemical producers, cement manufacturers and other companies that need both heat and electric power [1]. In a typical cogeneration system, fuel (usually natural gas, although wood, plant wastes, coal, and residual oil are used) is burned in a boiler to produce steam. The steam spins an electric generator, and, then rather than being lost as it is in typical power plants, is captured for heating, refrigerating or manufacturing processes. The hybrid machines can more than double the useful energy obtained for each dollar invested in fuel. A power plant producing only electricity is approximately 32 percent efficient; an industrial cogenerator using the same amount of fuel can be 80 percent efficient [2].

Large industrial businesses that need both heat and electricity usually purchase custom-designed cogenerators, using the steam for their own operations and selling excess electric power to the local utility. Commercial establishments—such as hospitals, restaurants and dairy farms—demand smaller, packaged units. Cogeneration systems usually cost between $500 and $1,000 per kilowatt of electrical capacity—less than half the price of new coal or nuclear plants [3].

In the United States, serious interest in cogeneration was spurred when Congress approved the Public Utilities Regulatory Policies Act (PURPA) of 1978. PURPA forces a utility to buy electrical power from cogenerators and small-power producers at the utility's "avoided cost," or what the utility would have spent to produce the same amount of power. By mid-1986, U.S. firms had installed or were building 23,500 megawatts of cogeneration facilities [4]. The picture is varied in other countries. Canadian capacity totalled about 1,200 megawatts in 1985 and is expected to rise to 3,500 megawatts within ten years [5]. Although Europeans and Russians have long used advanced district heating systems that heat buildings with the waste heat from coal and nuclear plants, their use of industrial cogeneration has not been extensive. The United Kingdom and West Germany, however, recently approved PURPA-type legislation to spur industrial development. Reliable statistics are not available on activities in developing countries, but the International Cogeneration Society reports that Third World nations have begun to express substantial interest in small-scale cogeneration applications [6].

Lower oil prices promise little impact on cogeneration. Few utilities burn oil, so electricity rates should not decline significantly. Falling natural gas prices, in contrast, will benefit many cogenerators. And some oil suppliers, trying to develop new markets for the currently abundant oil, have begun to promote oil-fired cogeneration.

References and Notes

1. Richard Munson, *The Power Makers*, (Rodale Press, Emmaus, Pennsylvania, 1985), pp. 149–150.
2. Marc Ross, "Energy Consumption by Industry," *Annual Review of Energy*, Vol. 6 (1981), pp. 379–416.
3. Glenn Lovin, International Cogeneration Society, Washington, D.C., 1986 (personal communication).
4. Glenn Lovin, International Cogeneration Society, "Cogeneration Installation by State," July 17, 1986.
5. Laurence F. Moore and Anthony P. Rockingham, "An Overview of Alternative Energy Development in Canada," *Alternative Sources of Energy*, Vol. 84 (October 1986), p. 45.
6. *Op. cit.* 3.

Table 7.6 Production of Coal, 1985
(million metric tons of oil equivalent)

	1985	Percent Change 1980 to 1985	1985 Share of Total
North America	534.2	+6.6%	23.5%
Western Europe[a]	192.1	−6.6%	8.5%
Oceania[b]	82.9	+31.6%	3.6%
Japan	10.9	−6.8%	0
USSR	363.2	+4.5%	16.0%
Eastern Europe[c]	306.5	+14.4%	13.5%
Middle East[d]	0.6	+20.0%	0
Other Developing Countries[e]	267.6	+18.2%	11.8%
China	512.9	+28.7%	22.6%
World Total	**2,270.9**	**+12.3%**	**100.0%**

0 = zero or less than 0.05.

Notes:
a. Western Europe includes Austria, Belgium, Denmark, Federal Republic of Germany, Finland, France, Greece, Iceland, Republic of Ireland, Italy, Luxembourg, the Netherlands, Norway, Portugal, Spain, Sweden, Switzerland, Turkey, and United Kingdom.
b. Oceania includes Australia and New Zealand.
c. Eastern Europe includes Bulgaria, Czechoslovakia, German Democratic Republic, Hungary, Poland, Rumania, and Yugoslavia.
d. Middle East includes Abu Dhabi, Dubai, Iran, Iraq, Kuwait, Neutral Zone, Oman, Qatar, Saudi Arabia, and Syria.
e. Developing Countries includes all Latin American, African, South Asian and Southeast Asian countries.
Source: Adapted from British Petroleum (BP), *BP Statistical Review of World Energy, 1986*, (BP, London, 1986).

on eight units ordered before then, largely because of political opposition. In the United States, utilities abandoned more than $18 billion of investment in 113 proposed nuclear reactors, largely because of cost overruns and lower-than-expected demand for electricity (45). Direct construction costs per kilowatt of installed capacity increased fourfold (in constant dollars) in the United States from the early 1970s to the early-1980s; expenses for some reactors soared above $5,000 per kilowatt (46). Moreover, construction times doubled, and plant reliability remained mediocre at best (47). By 1986, major contractors such as Westinghouse and General Electric were no longer even designing nuclear plants for the U.S. market (48).

Nuclear power has become an important energy source throughout the Eastern bloc, supplying 32 percent of Bulgaria's electricity, 12 percent of East Germany's, and 8 percent of the Soviet Union's in 1984 (49). But the USSR and Eastern Europe obtain only about half as much electricity from nuclear power as was projected a decade ago (50). Economic setbacks and the Chernobyl accident may further curtail Soviet plans to supply 20 percent of the region's electricity with nuclear power by 1990.

Six newly-industrialized countries—Argentina, Brazil, India, Pakistan, South Korea, and Taiwan—employed a total of 18 reactors in 1986 and supplied about 6 percent of the world's nuclear capacity. At least three other Third World nations are building plants, but high costs have reduced plans for expansive nuclear programs in developing countries strapped for foreign exchange (51).

The Chernobyl disaster (see Box 7.2) and the risk of similar accidents elsewhere caused several governments to rethink their commitment to nuclear power and other governments to put increased emphasis on safety, including the development of safer reactor designs.

Renewable Energy

More than half the world's people rely on renewable sources of energy for cooking, heating, and other needs. Although most official energy statistics ignore the impor-

tant role of woodfuels, biomass, and other traditional fuels, renewable sources supply the equivalent of 1,400 million metric tons of oil per year, about one-fifth the world's primary energy and four times the nuclear contribution (52).

Largely in response to the shock of oil price increases in 1973 and 1979, many countries began aggressive programs to harness renewable energy for commercial uses. Brazil, China, India, the Philippines, Sweden, and the United States achieved some impressive results, but efforts in other nations stalled because institutions failed to provide strong management for the programs and because some technologies proved too expensive (53). The major forms of renewable energy—hydropower, wind power, solar power, biomass, and geothermal—are discussed below.

Hydropower

Substantial potential exists to convert falling water into electricity and motor power. Worldwide hydroelectric consumption rose 16 percent from 1980 to 1985 (see Table 7.1), with the largest gains in China, the USSR, and South Asia. In 1985, dams accounted for 498.2 million metric tons of oil equivalent, about 6.7 percent of the world's primary energy (54). The World Energy Conference has projected that hydropower will supply almost 8 trillion kilowatt-hours of electricity by 2020, about six times the current output (55).

Two thirds of the unexploited hydropower potential lies in developing countries. OECD nations have exploited about 50 percent of their usable opportunities, and the USSR and Eastern Europe have tapped about 20 percent, but Third World nations have utillized only 7 percent of their available resources. Among them, Brazil, China, Colombia, India, Peru, and Zaire have the largest untapped potential (56). Table 7.7 shows hydropower potential and use by region.

Most hydropower projections include only large dams, but a great deal can be expected from decentralized, small-scale "mini-hydro" (less than 10 megawatts) and "micro-hydro" stations (less than 1 megawatt). Because these units use local energy sources to satisfy local needs, they can contribute to rural development out of proportion to the amount of energy they deliver. By 1982, China had built some 80,000 small dams, averaging about 70 kilowatts. Small-scale hydro stations in the United States, many of which have come on line since 1978, numbered 1,410, with a combined capacity of 7,019 megawatts in 1983. In 1980, 1,060 micro-hydro stations provided 1 percent of France's electricity (57).

Further hydro development will be restricted more by a lack of money and markets for the power than by a lack of possible sites for projects. Construction costs for dams have increased less sharply than for nuclear or thermal generating stations, but the World Bank projects that $10 billion will be needed for dam construction between 1982 and 1990 if hydropower is to meet the Bank's goal of 43 percent of Third World electricity production in 1995 (58).

Environmental and social problems also limit large-scale dam construction projects. Reservoirs often flood valuable farmland, displace people from their homes, and spread

Figure 7.6 Nuclear Reactor Construction Starts and Grid Connections, 1971–86

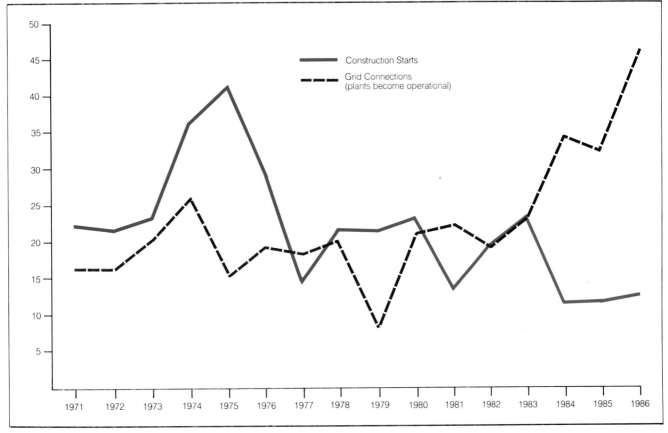

Note: Estimates, based on scheduled grid connections and construction starts available to the International Atomic Energy Agency.
Source: Adapted from *International Atomic Energy Agency Bulletin* Vol. 28, No. 2 (International Atomic Energy Agency, Vienna, Austria, 1986), p. 66.

water-borne diseases such as schistosomiasis. Dams can also restrict the flow of nutrient-rich silt to agricultural lands downstream. Moreover, that trapped sediment often fills reservoirs, eventually curtailing the dam's ability to store water and generate electricity. The Sanman Gorge Dam in Central China, for example, has lost three-quarters of its 1,000 megawatt power capacity because of sediment from the Yellow River.

Windpower

Wind energy machines contributed little to the global energy budget a decade ago, but more than 50,000 units have been installed since 1974, particularly in Denmark and California. By early 1986, entrepreneurs had placed more than 13,000 wind turbines throughout California, providing 1,100 megawatts of capacity (59). That is a significant increase from 1980 when the global capacity of wind generators was only 600 megawatts (60). Most machines are located at "wind farms" where clusters of small turbines line mountain passes and are connected to the electrical grid. The California Energy Commission expects wind energy machines to supply at least 8 percent of the state's electricity by the century's end (61).

Wind-turbine developers have reduced average per-kilowatt costs from $3,100 in 1981 to less than $1,200 (current dollars) in 1986. Some turbines cost only $1,000

per kilowatt, and wind industry officials predict average costs will fall to about $700 per kilowatt within three to five years (62). Wind farms have also been built in Denmark, India, and the Netherlands, and planning continues in Great Britain, Mexico, Spain, Sweden, and several islands in the Caribbean (65).

Wind availability, of course, varies by region. Relatively few sites possess the average wind speeds of at least 24 kilometers per hour necessary to produce electricity economically. Even in appropriate areas, winds are often intermittent, and turbines tend to operate only about 30

Table 7.7 Hydropower Potential and Use, by Region

	Technically Exploitable Potential (megawatts)	Share of Potential Exploited (percent)
Asia	610,100	9
South America	431,900	8
Africa	358,300	5
North America	356,400	36
USSR	250,000	12
Europe	163,000	59
Oceania	45,000	15
World Total	**2,214,700**	**17**

Source: World Energy Conference (WEC), *Survey of Energy Resources, 1980* (WEC, Munich, 1980).

Box 7.2 Chernobyl: An International Accident

In April 1986, the name of a small industrial town in the western Soviet Union became the code word for potential nuclear disaster when a reactor near Chernobyl exploded and caught fire, becoming nuclear power's first international accident. Because radiation released by the April 26 accident spread quickly to many European countries, government leaders and protesting citizens began to look across national borders at nuclear safety issues, challenging the assumption that each country had only to meet its own safety criteria.

By late summer, several countries were considering an unprecedented step: allowing safety inspections of their nuclear power plants by the United Nations International Atomic Energy Agency (IAEA). In addition, IAEA members had adopted an agreement pledging signatories to provide timely information to other countries during a transboundary nuclear accident. Another agreement pledging signatories to provide assistance to countries that suffered such an accident was gaining support.

Two other agreements proposed by IAEA seemed less likely to be ratified. One calls for the development of a revised—and perhaps binding—set of reactor safety standards, and the second would establish a case for compensation for international damage done by a nuclear accident (1).

Sweden, which claims to have suffered damage of "hundreds of millions of Swedish crowns" because of nuclear contamination of agricultural products, is pushing for a compensation agreement; so are the Netherlands, Norway, Austria, and West Germany. The Soviet Union insists it has no responsibility to compensate anyone beyond its borders, and is, not surprisingly, opposed to such an agreement (2).

The accident also shocked many countries into reexamining their own nuclear

programs—although it did not significantly change the course of any country. Pro-nuclear nations remained pro-nuclear, perhaps with a heightened sense of caution, while anti-nuclear countries saw the accident as further

Figure 1 Spread of the Radioactive Cloud from the Chernobyl Nuclear Accident

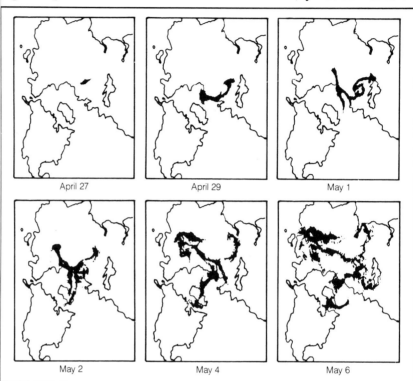

April 27   April 29   May 1

May 2   May 4   May 6

Note: a. The maps give a good qualitative picture of the cloud's dispersion, but are restricted to high altitudes and contain no information about terrain, particle size, or vertical distribution.
Source: a. Based on U.S. Air Force weather data and computer simulation by Lawrence Livermore National Laboratory in California. Copyright 1986 by the New York Times Company. Reprinted with permission.

proof that their position was correct. The accident also gave impetus to research programs aimed at developing safer nuclear reactors.

Another result was the immediate increase

---

percent of the time compared to about 60 percent for conventional power plants. Moreover, if not connected to an electrical grid, wind systems require expensive and cumbersome storage systems such as batteries, and back-up systems such as diesel engines. Simple mechanical wind machines can also be used for irrigating semi-arid regions where wind speeds average only eight miles per hour. Wind pumps provide particular opportunities for East Africa, northern Argentina, northeastern Brazil, Mexico, and Peru.

Solar Power

This section concentrates on one type of solar power: photovoltaics, palm-sized wafers that convert sunlight into electricity and that require little maintenance, have no moving parts, and produce no pollution in use. Future editions of *World Resources* will examine solar thermal technologies. Photovoltaics are not yet a significant

energy source, but they hold promise of providing electricity under a decentralized system and could have broad applications in the future.

One of the major barriers to photovoltaic use—a high price—has been steadily crumbling. The original solar or photovoltaic cells, first devised in 1954, cost almost $600 a peak watt, several hundred times more than conventional sources. Successors of these early designs proved to be the most efficient means of powering satellites. Rising electricity prices in the early 1970s brought interest in solar cells down to earth, where scientific advances quickly lowered costs to approximately $50 a peak watt. By mid-1986, the bulk price for terrestrial modules with a ten-year warranty had fallen to $5, much closer to the $1.50 now considered necessary to compete with conventionally generated electricity (63).

The lowest-cost system installed to date—a 300-kilowatt, grid-connected unit, complete with power-conditioning equipment—was purchased by the City of Austin (Texas) Power & Light Company in 1985 for $9.80 per watt.

in antinuclear protests in West Germany, Great Britain, and the United States. Like the radiation, the protests spilled over national borders. At a protest held at one of France's newest nuclear plants near the border of West Germany and Luxembourg, most of the 10,000 protesters chanting "Chernobyl is everywhere" were German (3). In Austria, a country that renounced nuclear power in a 1978 referendum, the antinuclear movement is now aimed at halting construction of a West German nuclear fuel reprocessing plant in neighboring Bavaria. The controversy has prompted high-level meetings, including one between West German Chancellor Helmut Kohl and Austrian Chancellor Franz Vranitzky (4).

In late August, more than 500 scientists from 50 countries gathered in Vienna at a symposium sponsored by IAEA. There, they heard a five-day presentation by Soviet scientists on the causes and extent of the Chernobyl disaster. Unlike their reticent behavior in the early days after the accident, the Soviets openly offered information and analysis.

The *IAEA Bulletin* published after the meeting reported that "International response... clearly has centered on a major immediate lesson: the need for stronger international cooperation to improve nuclear safety and to reduce the consequences of accidents when they do occur" (5). The agreement that binds states to promptly notify each other of a nuclear accident was quickly ratified by 51 countries and was scheduled to go into effect in late October (6). The need for timely information was a major concern of European countries, since the Soviet Union had denied for two days that there had been an accident, then offered only minimal information as shifting weather patterns brought nuclear rains down over Europe. (See Figure 1.) As the reactor core continued to burn and release radiation, information on the danger to any given country on any given day was sketchy. Without a reliable source of information, governments reacted with a range of responses from ignoring the whole affair

(France) to advising children and pregnant women to stay indoors (the Austrian state of Carinthia) (7).

A team of senior scientists assembled in Copenhagen shortly after the accident reported to the World Health Organization that some of the precautions had not been necessary and that the real trouble spots were areas in which "heavy rainfall coincided with the passage of the radioactive cloud" (8). Unfortunately, there was no monitoring system in place to identify such spots. The group stressed the need to establish an international system to collect and interpret information on any future large-scale nuclear accident so that the public could accurately and promptly be advised of the danger (9).

The worst effects of the accident, of course, were near the plant. Thirty-one people, mostly firefighters, died and several hundred were hospitalized. The town of Pripyat was evacuated and will remain uninhabitable for many years. The long-term health effects in the Soviet Union and Europe remain uncertain, with estimates of from 5,000 to 50,000 additional deaths from cancer over the next 30 to 60 years (10).

For several months following the disaster, many countries—both in Europe and as far away as Brazil—slowed their nuclear programs awaiting the results of studies of the accident. While the accident probably won't permanently slow nuclear development in pronuclear countries such as France and the Soviet Union itself, it may prove to be the key to nuclear power's demise in countries such as Sweden, the Netherlands, and Denmark—which were already considering terminating their nuclear programs. Many countries—including Great Britain, West Germany, and the United States—are continuing limited nuclear programs with opposition from antinuclear protesters, who can now argue that the accident that experts said could never happen has happened.

Another result of the accident was a new interest in developing safer nuclear plant tech-

nology. Some experts advocate a new generation of technically advanced and passively safe plants, such as the U.S.-designed Modular High Temperature Gas-Cooled Reactor (MHTGR) or the Swedish-designed Process Inherent Ultimately Safe Reactor (PIUS), that would shut themselves down in the event of a problem (11). The Soviets attributed the accident to an improbable series of operator actions combined with a plant design that was highly sensitive, leaving little room to correct errors. Operators had manually overridden safety shut-down systems to conduct a routine test when the disaster occurred.

References and Notes

1. Walter Pincus, "Chernobyl is Focus of IAEA Session," *The Washington Post* (September 30, 1986, Washington D.C.), p. A22.
2. *Ibid.*
3. Michael Dobbs, "Fission Splits France, W. Germany," *The Washington Post* (August 4, 1986, Washington D.C.), p. A15.
4. James M. Markham, "Europe is Bracing for Chernobyl's Grim Nightmare," *The New York Times* (August 31, 1986, New York), Section 4, p. 1.
5. International Atomic Energy Agency (IAEA), "Response to Chernobyl," *IAEA Bulletin* (IAEA, Vienna, Austria, Vol. 28, No. 2, Summer 1986), p. 61.
6. International Atomic Energy Agency (IAEA), *IAEA Newsbriefs*, Vol. 1, No. 1 (IAEA, Vienna, October 1, 1986), p. 1.
7. "Deadly Meltdown," *Time* (May 12, 1986), p. 44.
8. *Op cit.* 5, p. 64.
9. *Op cit.* 5, p. 64.
10. John Ahearne, "Nuclear Power After Chernobyl," speech (Resources for the Future, Washington D.C., September 24, 1986), p. 11.
11. Harold M. Agnew and Thomas A Johnson, "Chernobyl: The Future of Nuclear Power," *Issues in Science and Technology* (Fall 1986), p. 36.

Experts believe photovoltaic systems will be installed for $4.50-$6 per watt by 1992 or 1993; that price is competitive with small diesel generators used throughout developing countries and in rural areas of industrialized nations. When that goal is reached, photovoltaics could compete for the multi-gigawatt market in rural areas that now have no electrical service (64).

Even at today's price, installing solar cells is less expensive than extending the utility grid to many remote sites for uses such as lighthouses, buoys, mountaintop radio relays, and irrigation pumps. But solar is still far from becoming a major conventional energy source. In 1985, 25 megawatts of capacity were shipped, up from about 3 megawatts in 1980. (See Figure 7.7.) By 1990, the worldwide photovoltaic industry will have the capacity to produce 100–120 megawatts of solar cells (65). (By contrast, a single large nuclear plant has 1,200 megawatts of capacity.)

Over the past five years, research and production procedures have shifted from wafers of silicon crystals to

thin films of amorphous silicon. Amorphous silicon cells are less expensive to produce and more optically absorptive than crystalline forms. The films are less efficient, however, and tend to degrade after long exposure to sunlight, a problem researchers and manufacturers are trying to overcome. In 1985, amorphous silicon accounted for 32 percent of the world photovoltaics market, up from 3 percent in 1981 (66).

The relatively high cost of photovoltaics is largely a result of their relatively low efficiency in converting sunlight into electricity. Until recently, the best silicon-based solar cell had an efficiency of only 21 percent. In April 1986, however, researchers at Stanford University unveiled a new design that uses a parabolic mirror to concentrate sunlight to 500 times its normal intensity, increasing the cell's efficiency to 27.5 percent. With modifications, the new design's efficiency is expected to reach 30 percent (67). If laboratory tests continue to be successful, production of these more efficient cells could begin in two to three years.

Energy

Figure 7.7 World Photovoltaic Shipments, 1980–85

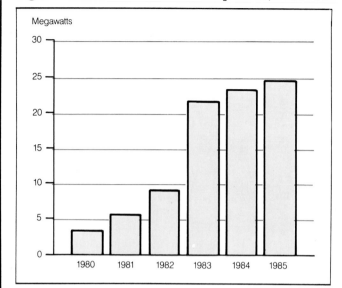

Source: Solar Energy Research Institute, "Amorphous Silicon Advances Significant in 1985", *In Review*, Vol. 8, No. 3 (1986), p. 1.

Scientists also have high hopes for cells employing multiple layers of semiconductors that respond to different segments of the solar spectrum. Multi-layer photovoltaics have the advantage over previous cells of being able to generate electricity from diffuse sunlight in cloudy or hazy regions. One major manufacturer now guarantees 20 percent efficiency for its multi-layered film cells (68).

Photovoltaics have been promoted as an ideal solution to energy problems in developing countries that lack centralized power grids but enjoy brilliant sunshine. Decentralized solar cells can be installed at the point of need without building expensive transmission lines, although improved electricity storage systems are generally needed.

Because high initial costs stand in the way of the widespread use of photovoltaics, Third World energy planners argue that production facilities must be constructed locally so that developing countries expend little foreign currency on this capital-intensive technology. In the past five years, Japanese and U.S. companies have responded to that request by delivering complete photovoltaic cell manufacturing plants to Algeria, Brazil, China, India, and Yugoslavia (69).

Biomass

Wood, organic wastes, and other biomass accounted for approximately 14 percent of total global energy use in 1980 (70). For Nepal, Ethiopia, and Tanzania, more than 90 percent of total energy comes from biomass. (See Table 7.8.) Fuelwood use increased 33 percent worldwide between 1970 and 1982 (71).

The use of wood for cooking—the largest use of biomass fuel—presents serious environmental and social problems because wood is being used faster than it is being replaced. As discussed in *World Resources 1986*, fuelwood scarcities now affect 1.3 billion people (72). The United Nations Food and Agriculture Organization predicts

that by the year 2000, unless immediate corrective actions are taken, almost 3 billion people either will be forced to consume wood faster than it is grown or will simply be unable to meet their minimum energy needs (73).

Unlike fossil fuels, biomass is a widely available resource that can be produced renewably with good management practices. Biomass can be converted to alcohol, an efficient, clean-burning fuel for cooking or transportation, or can be burned to generate electricity. Its low-sulfur, low-ash content makes biomass a cleaner feedstock than coal. Moreover, its production and conversion are inherently labor-intensive, an attractive feature for developing countries facing severe unemployment problems. But the low efficiency of photosynthesis requires huge land areas for energy crops if significant quantities of biomass fuels are to be produced (74).

Several countries have expanded their use of biomass for electricity generation since the 1973 oil embargo. U.S. industries, for instance, have added more than 2,000 large wood-fired boilers and many thousands more small facilities since 1973, accounting for 10 percent of all U.S. boiler sales (75).

The Philippine government wants to help build a 3-megawatt, base-load, wood-fired power plant for each of the country's 100 rural electric cooperatives. Beginning in 1977, it identified parcels of marginal and unused federal land for 100-hectare wood plantations that are rented to 10 to 15 farmers. The National Electrification Administration provides loans for the cooperatives to build the power plants and for the farmers to plant the trees. Program managers estimate that the wood-fired electricity will cost 5.6 cents per kilowatt-hour, about 34 percent less than the marginal cost of electricity in 1981 (76).

The Philippine plan originally called for 114 megawatts of capacity by 1985, but technical problems and budget constraints limited progress. Capacity reached only 12.7 megawatts in 1984, and about three-quarters of the original plantations failed because of poor site selection and belated planting caused by bureaucratic delays. Program managers now hope for 200 megawatts of capacity by 1990.

Table 7.8 Contribution of Biomass Energy in Developing Countries, 1978
(kW per capita)

Country	Commercial Energy	Biomass Energy	Total Energy	Percentage of Energy from Biomass
Bangladesh	0.038	0.095	0.13	71
Niger	0.035	0.25	0.29	86
The Gambia	0.098	0.22	0.32	69
Morocco	0.27	0.073	0.34	21
India	0.17	0.19	0.36	53
Ethiopia	0.019	0.37	0.39	95
Nepal	0.009	0.43	0.44	98
Somalia	0.092	0.48	0.57	84
Bolivia	0.34	0.26	0.60	44
Sudan	0.16	0.63	0.79	80
Thailand	0.30	0.52	0.83	63
Tanzania	0.06	0.81	0.87	93
China	0.78	0.32	1.10	29
Brazil	0.74	0.37	1.10	34
Mexico	1.30	0.13	1.40	9
Libya	1.80	0.095	1.90	5
Developing Countries (average)	**0.549**	**0.416**	**0.96**	**43**

Source: Adapted from D.O. Hall *et al.*, *Biomass for Energy in the Developing Countries* (Pergamon Press, New York, 1982), Table 2.3, p. 18.

Brazil has utilized its large sugar cane production to develop perhaps the world's most aggressive alcohol fuels program, cutting imported oil from 34 percent of its energy use in 1980 to 22 percent in 1984. Brazil's combination of subsidized loans, regulations, and price supports helped increase alcohol fuel output from about 500 million liters in 1975 to 3.7 billion liters in 1980. The future of alcohol fuel programs in Brazil and other countries is difficult to predict because of high production costs and uncertain demand. All-time-low sugar prices could encourage many developing countries to convert sugar to a valuable energy source, but lower oil costs may decrease efforts to displace imported petroleum (77). The Biomass Users Network, an organization of Third World countries, was recently formed to promote the development of biomass production and markets. (See Recent Developments, below.)

Geothermal

The earth's natural interior heat is enormous but difficult to harness with present technologies. Nonetheless, world geothermal capacity grew by 8.3 percent per year from 1920 to 1978, and by 16.5 percent per year from 1978 to 1985. In 1985, an estimated 4,763 megawatts were produced; by 1990, output is expected to increase to 6,398 megawatts. (See Table 7.9.)

The United States, which leads the world in geothermal capacity, increased that capacity more than threefold since 1975 to 2,022 megawatts in 1985 (78). Mexico has developed three major geothermal fields for 645 megawatts of capacity. Hungary, Iceland, Italy, and the Philippines have recently added significant geothermal output (79).

Tapping geothermal resources requires tools and procedures similar to those employed for oil exploration. Drilling costs are high. The lack of scientific surveys of potential thermal areas is also retarding rapid geothermal development. And although geothermal's environmental impacts are minor compared to those of other energy sources, they include possible pollution of surface waters and groundwater by non-toxic chlorides, sulfates, and carbonates or silica.

Conventional geothermal resources, which draw steam or hot water from natural underground reservoirs, can be economically exploited only where molten rock lies within 3,000 meters of the earth's surface, although engineers hope to develop technologies by the year 2000 that will enable drilling and heat extraction as deep as 5,000 meters (83). Scientists are also trying to find ways to use more abundant, lower-temperature water or steam for electricity generation.

In July 1986, scientists at the United States' Los Alamos National Laboratory announced success with an experimental hot dry rock system that does not depend on the availability of geysers or hot springs. Millions of liters of water were pumped about 4,000 meters deep into a region of fractured, naturally hot rock. The water, heated to more than 175 degrees Celsius and placed under high pressure, was pumped back up a second well to the surface, where it turned into steam that drove turbines to generate enough electricity for a town of 2,000

Table 7.9 Worldwide Geothermal Power Capacity, 1984–90
(megawatts electric)

Country	1984[a]	1985[b]	1990[c]
United States	1,454	2,022	2,516
Philippines	781	894	1,042
Italy	472	519	519
Mexico	425	645	965
Japan	215	215	215
New Zealand	167	167	283
El Salvador	95	95	95
Iceland	41	39	39
Nicaragua	35	35	70
Indonesia	32	32	362
Kenya	30	45	45
USSR	11	11	91
China	8	14	14
Portugal (Azores)	3	3	3
Turkey	0.5	21	21
France (Guadeloupe)	0	4	4
Greece	0	2	2
Costa Rica[d]	0	0	50
Saint Lucia[d]	0	0	30
Chile[d]	0	0	15
Guatemala[d]	0	0	15
India[d]	0	0	1
Rumania[d]	0	0	1
Australia[d]	0	0	0.5
Total	**3,769.5**	**4,763**	**6,398.5**

Notes:
a. Through June 1984.
b. Projected.
c. Estimated.
d. Facilities may come on line between 1986 and 1990.

Sources:
1. Ronald Di Pippo, "Geothermal Power Development: 1984 Overview and Update," *Geothermal Resources Council*, Vol. 13, No. 9 (October 1984), p. 3.
2. Deepak Kenkeremath (Meridian Corporation) and Dr. John E. Mock (U.S. Department of Energy), "International Geothermal Market Opportunities," 1985 International Symposium on Geothermal Energy, August 26–30, 1985.

people. Similar experiments are being conducted by Great Britain in Cornwall, by the European Community in Soultz, France, and by Japan in Hijiori (80).

The hot dry rock system requires scientists to use highly-refined listening and mapping tools in order to create a closed loop between the two wells. Despite the engineering challenges, advocates say the technology can be used almost everywhere, unlike traditional geothermal plants that must rely on unusual geological circumstances for natural underground water and steam. Moreover, the Los Alamos experiment was free of the pollution problems that often plague traditional geothermal facilities. Tests on the recirculated water in New Mexico showed it was sometimes clean enough to meet drinking water standards (81).

FOCUS ON: ENERGY EFFICIENCY

Efficient Technologies

Industrialized nations consumed about 1 percent less primary energy in 1985 than in 1980, a significant shift from the 26 percent increase in the five years before the 1973 oil embargo (82). Part of the decline was caused by an economic downturn, but higher energy prices certainly spurred consumers and businesses to adopt simple housekeeping measures, such as turning down thermostats and driving more slowly. Major conservation gains, however, also came from the growth of less energy-intensive service sectors of the economy and from the development of more efficient appliances, buildings, automobiles, and motors.

Energy

Since the 1973 oil embargo, energy conservation has become an established science. Architects in Sweden and the United States have designed thermally-tight new buildings that require 90 percent less heat than typical houses (83). Engineers in Western Europe developed socketed fluorescent lights that use 65–75 percent less energy than conventional incandescent bulbs. Designers in Japan created refrigerators that consume one-third the energy of the average current model (84). And automotive engineers in Japan, Western Europe, and the United States are building cars that travel three times further on a liter of gasoline than the present global-average vehicle; and their prototype automobiles are almost four times more efficient (85).

The potential for further efficiency is enormous. The United Nations Economic Commission for Europe predicts industrialized nations can cut their energy needs for the year 2000 by about 20 percent from current government forecasts if they adopt currently available conservation measures (86). Other researchers find that half the electricity used for lighting in the United States could be saved (87), as could half the total energy used in U.S. buildings (88). Japan expects to dramatically increase fuel efficiencies above current prototypes with lighter-weight, non-metallic automobiles based on ceramics and plastics (89). And engineers say new steel plants using virgin ore can reduce energy use 25 percent below that of the world's average mill; plants using recycled steel can achieve even larger savings (90).

Energy Conservation in the Third World

Concern about energy efficiency has historically focused on the rich, industrialized countries that consume most fossil fuel energy. Developing nations use fewer commercial energy resources to begin with and are often unable to devote scarce capital to improve efficiency. To enhance their standards of living, therefore, Third World regions have tended to focus more on promoting development—regardless of energy use—than on conserving energy.

Currently, developing nations use only one sixth as much commercial energy as developed nations. In 1980, per capita primary energy use averaged 6.3 kilowatts in industrialized countries but only about 1 kilowatt in developing nations, including 0.4 kilowatts of noncommercial energy use (91). But if developing countries were to follow the pattern of the developed countries, global energy use would need to double or quadruple over the next four to five decades in order for the world's impoverished majority to achieve a decent standard of living, according to most international energy analysts. Supplying that much additional energy would present enormous economic and environmental problems.

Throughout the 1970s, per capita commercial energy use in developing countries grew at a vigorous average annual rate of 3.6 percent. If that pace continues until 2020, and if population doubles by then as expected, the increment in energy use by developing countries would equal 1.3 times total world energy use in 1980 (92). Outside Middle Eastern and North African countries, such an increase in demand could not be met with domestically produced oil and gas. Oil-importing developing countries, already spending about half their export earnings to import oil, would confront further restrictions on their economic development and additional dependence on the Persian Gulf region. In 1982, oil-importing Third World nations also spent some $25 billion of foreign exchange to expand their domestic energy supplies (93).

If coal use were dramatically expanded, major global climatic changes could occur in a matter of decades as a result of the "greenhouse effect" associated with the build-up in the atmosphere of carbon dioxide released in fossil fuel combustion. To meet half the projected incremental energy requirements with nuclear energy would require building 100 large reactors a year until 2020. In addition to the huge capital costs for such projects, the increased amounts of plutonium produced as a byproduct of those plants could encourage the spread of nuclear weapons capability. Renewable energy sources, while promising, would not be able to make major contributions to these requirements without major technological breakthroughs (94).

These and other problems inherent in expanding the energy supply have led many analysts to gloomy forecasts of the energy outlook for many developing countries. Yet there is major potential for new energy "supply" through conservation. According to a recent study, if developing countries were to adopt a menu of energy-efficient technologies that are now available, they could provide services comparable to those of Western Europe today with only a 20 percent increase in per capita energy use. Third World nations, according to this analysis, could achieve much higher standards of living without significantly increasing the average energy use per capita if emphasis were given to modern energy sources and energy efficiency improvements as economic development proceeds (95). The study notes that conservation-conscious Western Europeans enjoy a per-capita Gross Domestic Product (GDP) 10 times higher than that of residents of developing countries, but they use only two-and-a-half times more energy per capita than their Third World neighbors for purposes other than space heating.

Third World nations, of course, face enormous obstacles in making the transition to energy-efficient technologies and modern energy sources. The potential for increased efficiency varies enormously between industrial and residential energy uses and between the relatively rich, who tend to rely on oil and electricity for their needs, and the poorest, who depend on traditional energy technologies that employ fuelwood, animal dung, and crop residues.

In the industrial and commercial sectors alone, developing countries could realize significant energy savings in factories and transportation. Third World factories, for instance, devote two to five times more power to a specific operation that do modern plants in OECD nations (96).

Several developing countries have adopted aggressive and successful energy conservation programs. China, for instance, achieved its goal of a 5 percent annual savings among its major energy-intensive industries from 1980 to 1985. In January 1986, China's State Council approved a series of ambitious additional energy regulations and requirements for energy conservation plans and targets (97).

In India, where oil imports consumed 80 percent of the country's foreign-exchange earnings in 1981, automobile manufacturers have shifted to producing more fuel-efficient cars. New, domestically-manufactured, five-passenger cars use about half the fuel of the typical automobile on the road in India (98).

Insufficient cash on hand and the inability to raise capital under favorable terms have prevented many firms from replacing antiquated and wasteful factory equipment (99). However, where new plants and equipment are being installed or where expansion and modernizing are being supported by industrial lending and aid, relatively small investments can yield significant long-term payoffs in reduced energy costs.

Will Cheap Oil Reduce Efficiency?

In an era of lower oil prices, projecting the future pace of energy conservation in developed and developing countries is difficult. No clear statistics are yet available on conservation trends related to oil price drops in 1986. On one hand, the International Energy Agency reports that many industrialized countries have already pared down their conservation programs (100); the rise in efficiency of new automobiles in Europe and North America has leveled off since the early 1980s, for example (101).

Yet even as oil prices decline, electricity costs remain high enough to encourage consumers to conserve. Moreover, the billions of dollars invested in efficient technologies over the past decade will continue to bear fruit in the years ahead. (For one example, see Box 7.1.)

RECENT DEVELOPMENTS

CLEAN-COAL TECHNOLOGIES

Recent data suggest that engineers may have developed technologies that significantly reduce emissions from coal-fired power plants. Three new techniques, coal gasification, fluidized bed combustion, and furnace limestone injection, offer dramatic environmental improvements by substantially reducing pollution from coal-burning plants. For countries with coal deposits, they offer one of the best hopes for meeting new energy demand while helping to resolve the problems of acid rain and other air pollution.

In the United States, the Cool Water Coal Gasification Program removed 97 percent of the sulfur from low-sulfur coal and reduced emissions to one tenth of existing federal standards. The test facility also cut sulfur output from high-sulfur coal to about one third of the mandated level (102). The 100-megawatt Cool Water unit in California's Mojave Desert mixes pulverized coal with water and oxygen and converts it into a gas. Combustion of the gas drives the main turbine, and water converted into

superheated steam during the gasification process spins another engine.

In atmospheric fluidized bed combustion, coal is mixed with inexpensive limestone and burned above an upwelling flow of air. The limestone reacts chemically with the coal to capture most of the sulfur. Because the unit operates at lower temperatures than conventional boilers, it also reduces the output of nitrogen oxides. A more advanced version is the pressurized fluidized bed combustor, in which hot, pressurized combustion gases power a turbine. While industries have used atmospheric fluidized beds for years, the pressurized combustor for large scale power generation is less well developed (103).

Attempts to capture sulfur dioxide by injecting limestone into a furnace date from the 1960s, but only recently have advancements made the procedure effective. In this process, dry pulverized limestone is fed into the furnace, where it is reduced to lime and reacts with sulfur dioxide to form dry, solid calcium sulfate, or gypsum. Because these reactions occur most effectively at reduced temperatures, the process also suppresses nitrogen oxides. Japanese researchers testing limestone injection at small pilot plants have achieved as much as 50 percent sulfur removal. West German engineers expect better than 60 percent removal from a 300-megawatt demonstration facility that burns low-sulfur coal (104).

BIOMASS USERS NETWORK

Faced with heavy oil debts and falling prices for their export commodities, a group of 20 Third World nations recently formed an organization that proposes, among other things, to convert unprofitable export crops such as sugar cane into biomass fuel for local consumption.

Inaugurated at a meeting in Bangkok, Thailand in October 1985, the Biomass Users Network (BUN) aims to stimulate rural development, create new markets for agricultural products, preserve foreign exchange, and conserve natural resources through effective biomass management (105).

BUN proposes to share information on biomass technologies by publishing case studies, sponsoring workshops, and maintaining a catalog of experts who can provide direct assistance. The first case studies focus on the Phillippines' wood-burning power program, Brazil's alcohol and industrial charcoal program, and Guatemala's biogas program (106).

BUN is supported by foundations and has offices in Washington, D.C. and San Jose, Costa Rica. It proposes five initial programs, each with a three-year lifespan: diversification of the sugar cane industry; using arid, semi-arid, and degraded lands for biomass production; producing biomass fuels for commercial and domestic uses; identifying biomass crops' germplasm; and offering special support for country and regional programs. During its first year, BUN's membership doubled to 40. Member countries are not required to make a financial contribution, but must appoint a representative who will devote a substantial amount of time to serving on BUN committees and projects.

Diversification of the sugar cane industry is especially important to BUN Executive Director Albert Binger, a

Energy

Jamaican who headed that country's Agricultural Development Agency, and who has watched the effects of falling sugar cane prices on the country's economy.

"Since the price of sugar cane has fallen, the lending agencies would like us to ditch cane and find alternative crops that we can sell to the North so we can import oil," he said. "But we have 300 years of experience growing sugar cane. Why not simply make alcohol fuel from the sugar cane? As the country develops, it will need more energy. The market would be much steadier than the international commodity market. Give the farmers a market and they will produce biomass fuel" (107).

About half of BUN's members are large-scale sugar cane producers, a few of which are already using sugar cane as a source of liquid fuel, electricity, and animal feed. Cane can also be used for paper pulp, construction materials, and chemical feedstocks. A BUN task force of industry and technical members is looking into markets for potential sugar cane products and evaluating technologies for various conversions.

References and Notes

1. Unless otherwise stated, statistics on global, regional, and national energy consumption and production are taken from British Petroleum (BP), *BP Statistical Review of World Energy, 1986* (BP, London, 1986). Note that the statistics on global, regional, and national energy consumption and production used in Chapter 22, "Energy and Minerals," are taken from United Nations (U.N.) Statistical Office, *1984 Energy Statistics Yearbook* (U.N., New York, 1986). The U.N. statistics are more comprehensive in terms of the number of countries and the classes of production and consumption they include.
2. Gulf Oil Corporation, "World Petroleum Outlook," unpublished, November 1978.
3. British Petroleum (BP), *BP Statistical Review of World Energy, 1986* (BP, London, 1986), p. 6.
4. Celestine Bohlen, "Chernobyl Blunders Spelled Out," *The Washington Post* (August 22, 1986, Washington, D.C.), p. 1.
5. *Ibid.*
6. PennWell Publishing, *International Petroleum Encyclopedia* (PennWell Publishing, Tulsa, Oklahoma, 1985), pp. 222–239.
7. Cheryl Trench, Director of Research, Petroleum Industry Research Foundation, New York, 1986 (personal communication).
8. *Op. cit.* 3, p. 35.
9. James Tanner, "Many Oil Men See U.S. Again Relying Heavily on Uncertain Imports," *Wall Street Journal* (New York, May 23, 1986), p. 1 and p. 10.
10. Energy Information Administration (EIA), *Monthly Energy Review, June 1986* (EIA, Washington, D.C., September 1986), p. 40.
11. *Op. cit.* 9, p. 1 and p. 11.
12. *Op. cit.* 3, p. 10.
13. Melvyn Westlake, "Impact of the Third Oil Shock," *South* (April 1986), pp. 79–80.
14. *Ibid.*
15. *Op. cit.* 3, p. 28.
16. U.S. Department of Energy (DOE), "Commercial Nuclear Power: Prospects for the United States and the World" (DOE, Washington, D.C., 1985), p. 114.
17. James Liles, Special Assistant, Regulatory Analysis Program, Federal Energy Regulatory Commission, Washington, D.C., 1986 (personal communication).
18. Southern California Edison Company (SCE), *Cogeneration/Small Power Projects: Quarterly Report to the California Public Utilities Commission* (SCE, Rosemead, California, 1986); and similar reports from

Pacific Gas and Electric Company and San Diego Gas and Electric Company.
19. *Op. cit.* 3, p. 5.
20. "The Harm of Nuclear Power," *The Economist* (May 3, 1986), p. 57.
21. *Op. cit.* 6, p. 222.
22. *Op. cit.* 6, p. 223.
23. American Gas Association (AGA), *World Natural Gas Consumption Trends* (AGA, Arlington, Virginia, 1986), p. 4.
24. *Op. cit.* 3.
25. International Monetary Fund (IMF), *World Economic Outlook* (IMF, Washington, D.C., 1985), p. 143.
26. The World Bank, *The Energy Transition in Developing Countries* (The World Bank, Washington, D.C., 1983), p. 5.
27. *Op. cit.* 7.
28. Christoper Flavin, *World Oil: Coping with the Dangers of Success* (Worldwatch Institute, Washington, D.C., 1985), p. 143.
29. *Op. cit.* 3, p. 4.
30. David J. Rose, *et al.*, "Reducing the Problem of Global Warming," *Technology Review*, Vol. 87, No. 4 (May/June 1984), p. 54.
31. *Op. cit.* 3, p. 2.
32. *Op. cit.* 9, p. 10.
33. U.S. Congress, Office of Technology Assessment (OTA), *Oil and Gas Technologies for the Arctic and Deepwater* (OTA, Washington, D.C., 1985), pp. 1–15.
34. Energy Information Administration (EIA), *Annual Energy Review 1985* (U.S. Department of Energy, EIA, Washington, D.C., 1986), p. 91.
35. Exxon Corporation, *How Much Oil and Gas?* (Exxon Corporation, New York, 1982), p. 14.
36. *Op. cit.* 9, p. 1 and p. 11.
37. Roger Vielvoye, "Oil Production Up, Activity Levels High Off Northern Europe," *Oil and Gas Journal* (June 10, 1985), p. 92.
38. *Op. cit.* 3, p. 24.
39. *Op. cit.* 26, p. 36.
40. Robert H. Williams and Eric D. Larson, "Steam-Injected Gas Turbines and Electric Utility Planning," *IEEE Technology and Society Magazine* (March 1986), pp. 29–31.
41. David Osborne, "The Origin of Petroleum," *The Atlantic*, Vol. 257, No. 2 (1986), pp. 39–54.
42. Michael Chadwick, *et al.*, "Developing Coal in Developing Countries," *AMBIO*, Vol. 14, No. 4-5 (1985), p. 249.
43. *Op. cit.* 3, p. 25.

44. *Op. cit.* 26, p. 36.
45. Richard Munson, *The Power Makers* (Rodale Press, Emmaus, Pennsylvania, 1985), p. 5.
46. Charles Komanoff, *Power Plant Cost Escalation: Nuclear and Coal Capital Costs, Regulation, and Economics* (Komanoff Energy Associates, New York, 1981).
47. U.S. Congress, Office of Technology Assessment (OTA), *Nuclear Power in the Age of Uncertainty* (OTA, Washington, D.C., 1984), pp. 58–59.
48. John Aherne, "Nuclear Power After Chernobyl," speech (Resources for the Future, Washington, D.C., October 1, 1986), p. 20.
49. World Resources Institute and International Institute for Environment and Development, *World Resources 1986* (Basic Books, New York, 1986), p. 294.
50. Christopher Flavin, *Nuclear Power: The Market Test* (Worldwatch Institute, Washington, D.C., 1983), p. 49.
51. *Ibid.*, p. 51.
52. *Op. cit.* 28, p. 41.
53. *Op. cit.* 26, p. 5.
54. *Op. cit.* 3, p. 30.
55. World Energy Conference (WEC), *Survey of Energy Resources, 1980* (WEC, Munich, 1980).
56. Ellis L. Armstrong, "Hydraulic Resources," in *Renewable Energy Resources: The Full Report to the Conservation Commission of the World Energy Conference* (IPC Science and Technology Press, Munich, 1981).
57. Renewable Energy Institute (REI), *Annual Renewable Energy Technology Review* (Renewable Energy Institute, Washington, D.C., 1986), p. 125 and p. 127.
58. World Bank, *A Survey of the Future Role of Hydroelectric Power in 100 Developing Countries* (The World Bank, Washington, D.C., 1984), p. i.
59. Thomas Gray, Executive Director, American Wind Energy Association, Alexandria, Virginia, 1986 (personal communication).
60. "The U.N. Conference on New and Renewable Sources of Energy: UNERG," *AMBIO*, Vol. 10, No. 5 (1981), p. 232.
61. Kathleen Gray, former Director of Wind Energy Programs, California Energy Commission, Sacramento, California, 1986 (personal communication).
62. *Op. cit.* 59.
63. Paul D. Maycock, President, Photovoltaic Energy Systems, Inc., Casanova, Virginia, 1986 (personal communication).

64. *Ibid.*
65. *Ibid.*
66. Solar Energy Research Institute, "Amorphous Silicon Advances Significant in 1985," *In Review,* Vol. 8, No. 3 (1986), p. 1.
67. Walter Sullivan, "Solar Energy Gets a Boost from Flurry of Designs," *New York Times* (April 29, 1986), p. C1.
68. *Op. cit.* 64.
69. Paul D. Maycock, "Boomer's Corner," *PV News* (March 1986), p. 1.
70. Alan S. Miller, Irving M. Mintzer, *et al., Growing Power: Bioenergy for Development and Industry* (World Resources Institute, Washington, D.C. 1986), p. 6.
71. United Nations (U.N.), *United Nations Energy Statistics Yearbook* (U.N., New York, 1984), p. 254.
72. *Op. cit.* 49, p. 111.
73. U.N. Food and Agriculture Organization (FAO), *Fuelwood Supplies in Developing Countries* (FAO, Rome, 1983), p. 117 and p. 118.
74. Robert H. Williams, "Potential Roles for Bioenergy In An Energy-Efficient World," *AMBIO,* Vol. 14, No. 4-5 (1985), pp. 201–209.
75. *Op. cit.* 45, p. 159.
76. Al Binger, Executive Director, Biomass Users Network, Washington, D.C., 1986 (personal communication).
77. *Ibid.*
78. Ronald DiPippo, "Geothermal Power Development: 1984 Overview and Update," *Geothermal Resources Council,* Vol. 13, No. 9 (1984), p. 3.
79. Ronald DiPippo, "Development of Geothermal Electric Power Production Overseas," presented at the 11th Energy Technology Conference, Washington, D.C., March 1984.
80. James Gleick, "New Mexico Project Mines Earth's Interior Heat," *New York Times* (July 7, 1986), p. A1.
81. *Ibid.,* p. 1.
82. *Op. cit.* 3, pp. 31–33. "Primary energy" is an estimate of the amount of fossil fuel required to produce secondary sources of energy such as electricity. Estimates for hydropower and nuclear power are based on the amount of oil required to fuel an oil-fired plant to produce the same amount of electricity. Biomass fuels are excluded.
83. Thomas B. Johansson and Robert H. Williams, "Energy Conservation in the Global Context," presented at the Soviet-American Symposium on Energy Conservation, Moscow, June 1985.
84. Howard S. Geller, Associate Director, American Council for an Energy-Efficient Economy, Washington, D.C., 1986 (personal communication).
85. *Ibid.*
86. United Nations Economic Commission for Europe (ECE), *An Efficient Energy Future: Prospects for Europe and North America* (Butterworths, London, 1983), pp. 3–4.
87. Nadine Lihach and Stephen Partusiello, "Evolution in Lighting," *EPRI Journal* (June 1984).
88. Arthur H. Rosenfeld, "Residential Energy Efficiency: Progress Since 1973 and Future Potential," in *Energy Sources: Conservation and Renewables* (American Institute of Physics, New York, 1985), p. 92.
89. Philip Burget, "Japan Aims for Non-Metallic Auto in '90s," *American Metal Market/Metalworking News* (April 25, 1983).
90. *Op. cit.* 85.
91. Jose Goldemberg, *et al.,* "Basic Needs and Much More with One Kilowatt per Capita," *AMBIO,* Vol. 14, No. 4–5 (1985), p. 190.
92. *Ibid.*
93. The World Bank, *The Energy Transition in Developing Countries* (The World Bank, Washington, D.C., 1983), p. XIX.
94. *Op. cit.* 91, pp. 190–200.
95. World Resources Institute (WRI), *Journal '86* (WRI, Washington, D.C., 1986), p. 47.
96. Jose Goldemberg and Robert H. Williams, "The Economics of Energy Conservation in Developing Countries: A Case Study for the Electrical Sector in Brazil," in *Energy Sources: Conservation and Renewables,* David Hafemeister, *et. al.,* eds. (American Institute of Physics, New York, 1985), p. 34.
97. U.S. Embassy in Beijing, "China's New Energy Conservation Measures" (unclassified cable to Secretary of State, January 1986).
98. *Op. cit.,* p. 197.
99. Michael Fisher, "Innovative Approach to Financing Energy Conservation Investments in Developing Countries," *Natural Resources Forum,* Vol. 9, No. 2 (1985), p. 105.
100. International Energy Agency, *Energy Policies and Programmes of IEA Countries: 1984 Review* (Organisation for Economic Co-operation and Development, Paris, 1985), p. 74.
101. International Energy Agency, *Fuel Efficiency of Passenger Cars* (Organisation for Economic Co-operation and Development, Paris, 1984), p. 113.
102. Thomas O'Shea, Technology Transfer Manager, Electric Power Research Institute, Palo Alto, California, 1986 (personal communication).
103. Leslie Braunstein, "Clean Coal Technology: Just in Time," *Electric Perspectives* (Fall 1985), p. 8.
104. Ralph Whitaker, "Developing the Options for Emissions Control," *EPRI Journal* (November 1983), p. 48.
105. Biomass Users Network (BUN), *Biomass Users Network: Workplan 1986–1988* (BUN, Washington, D.C. 1986), p. 4.
106. *Op. cit.* 76.
107. Albert Binger, Executive Director, Biomass Users Network, Washington, D.C., July 11, 1986.

8. Freshwater

Worldwide, the total supply of freshwater is more than adequate to meet current and forseeable human needs. But a growing challenge is to accommodate the increasing water demands of households, agriculture, and industry with a global supply that is often not abundant locally—and is increasingly polluted. Population growth and increasing urbanization may strain the availability of drinking water supplies, particularly in parts of Africa and East Asia. Increased agricultural irrigation, which already accounts for over 70 percent of worldwide water use, could help meet the food needs of the world's growing population. But many of today's irrigation systems use far more water than necessary and contribute to the degradation of high-quality land through extensive salinization and waterlogging. The expansion of sophisticated micro-irrigation techniques such as drip or trickle systems have the potential to conserve vast amounts of water. But more important, inexpensive improvements to the common gravity flow systems used throughout the world could make an enormous impact on water use.

Potable water supplies are fouled by untreated municipal and industrial wastes in many areas of the Third World. The developed countries of Europe and North America face increasing contamination of groundwater reserves. Up to 2 percent of the aquifers in the United States may be unfit for drinking water. Nonpoint sources of pollution, such as fertilizer and pesticide residues in farm runoff, are partly to blame. But inadequate disposal of chemical and other hazardous wastes is also an important factor in localized groundwater contamination.

By and large, the industrialized countries have managed, albeit at great costs, to prevent the pollution of their surface waters from growing worse and, in some cases, to improve over the last decade, mainly by upgrading sewage and industrial waste water treatment plants. In the developing countries, however, water quality is worsening as industrialization takes place without the benefits (or costs) of pollution control. Although half the Third World population has access to safe drinking water, only a fifth has adequate sanitation facilities. Goals set by the United Nations International Drinking Water Supply and Sanitation Decade in 1980 are being adjusted downwards, particularly in Africa, where rapid urbanization is taxing municipal water services.

Participants at the United Nations World Water Conference, held in Argentina in 1977, developed an instructive anecdote that illustrates the finite nature of global freshwater resources. If a half-gallon bottle held all the planet's water, the amount of usable freshwater would fill only half a teaspoon; of that amount, a single drop would represent the amount of water in rivers and streams. The remaining half teaspoon would be groundwater. The earth's freshwater is a precious resource. Its uses touch every human need: drinking water and food, cleanliness, electricity, industry, transportation, and recreation. But water is often wasted and mismanaged in many parts of the world.

CONDITIONS AND TRENDS

FRESHWATER: THE RESOURCE

Most of the earth's 1.4 billion cubic kilometers (km^3) of water is saline; 97 percent forms the oceans. About 30 million km^3 of the remaining freshwater is locked in icecaps and glaciers, and a large portion of the 4–60 million km^3 of groundwater remains essentially inaccessible (1). Thus the supply of freshwater available for human use depends on the global hydrological cycle.

Each year evaporation from the oceans yields about 453,000 km^3 of water to the atmosphere (1 cubic kilometer equals 1 trillion liters). Over 90 percent returns to the oceans as precipitation. The approximate 41,000 km^3 remaining is carried by winds to land, where it combines with slightly more than 72,000 km^3 of water evaporated from land masses and falls as precipitation (2) (3). This gross continental precipitation—about 113,000 km^3—creates enough water to cover the earth's land surface to a depth of 83 centimeters. The rainfall recharges soil moisture and groundwater, which form the 41,000 km^3 of river water that returns to the seas to complete the hydrological cycle (4). (See *World Resources 1986*, Figure 8.2, p. 122.)

But of this 41,000 km^3, only about 14,000 km^3 is available as stable runoff (5), while the rest flows back to the sea as flood runoff. (See Figure 8.1.) Of this 14,000 km^3, about 5,000 km^3 flows through unpopulated or sparsely populated areas like the Amazon River Basin, leaving only 9,000 km^3 readily available for human use (6).

Population variations, of course, also affect the adequacy of water availability. Per capita water availability varies from about 122,000 cubic meters per year in Canada to 70 cubic meters per year in Malta (7). (See *World Resources 1986*, Table 8.3, p. 124.) Most sub-Saharan African and Middle Eastern countries suffer chronic water shortages, but so do parts of the United States, Australia, and the Soviet Union. Some countries, such as Haiti, Poland, and Belgium, may have substantial water resources but are still considered water poor because of their high population densities. Belgium, for example, receives an average 12.5 km^3 of freshwater annually compared to Oman's 0.66 km^3. But Belgium's per capita share is only slightly more than twice Oman's: 1,270 cubic meters per year, compared to Oman's 540 cubic meters per year (8).

Some experts contend that where the number of persons dependent on one flow unit (1 million cubic meters of water per year) exceeds 2,000, there is an inherent vulnerability to water deficits. About 350 people compete for that amount of water in the United Kingdom, Italy, France, India, and China, compared to 2,000 persons in Tunisia and 4,000 in Israel and Saudi Arabia. Fewer than 100 people compete for one flow unit of freshwater in Nepal, Bangladesh, Indonesia, and Sweden. Just over 100 compete for one flow unit in the United States; slightly more than 200 do in Japan (9). (See *World Resources 1986*, p. 124, Figure 8.4; p. 123, Table 8.3; and pp. 301–307.)

Another determinant of water availability is the interannual variability of rainfall. The areas of highest variability, where rainfall varies more than 40 percent over the long-term average, are sub-Saharan Africa, southwestern Africa, Saudi Arabia, southern Iran, Pakistan, western India, southwestern United States and northwestern Mexico, northern Chile, and Brazil's eastern tip (10). Sahelian Africa also experienced a significant decline in average annual rainfall recently, although such drought cycles are common to the region. A Mali measuring station, for example, registered a mean annual rainfall of 715 millimeters (mm) during the 50-year period ending in 1983, compared to 577 mm during the last 15 years of that period (11). Figure 8.2 shows the earth's areas of water surplus and deficiency, defined as the difference between annual precipitation and the loss of water by evaporation from soil and plants.

The scarcity of water caused by rainfall variability should not be confused with how human activity affects water availability. Figure 8.2 does not take into account the use of underground aquifers and interbasin water transfer systems that provide water in some arid regions, such as the southwestern United States and the central Asian republics of the Soviet Union.

WATER USE

The amount of freshwater actually used (as opposed to the amount available) is estimated at between 2,600 and 3,500 km^3 (12) (13). People need less than one cubic meter (m^3) of drinking water a year to survive. However, to sustain a quality of life as defined by most developed countries, at least 30 m^3 of water is required per year per person for domestic use (14). Domestic and recreational needs account for only 6 percent of the world's freshwater use. Irrigated agriculture accounts for 73 percent of the water used and industry accounts for the remaining

Figure 8.1 Global Water Supply and Demand

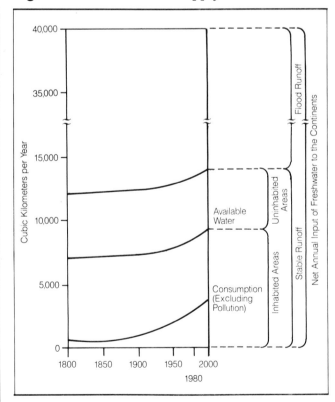

Source: Adapted from R.P. Ambroggi, "Water," *Scientific American*, Vol. 243, No. 3 (1980).

Figure 8.2 **Global Water Surplus and Deficiency**[a]
(millimeters per year)

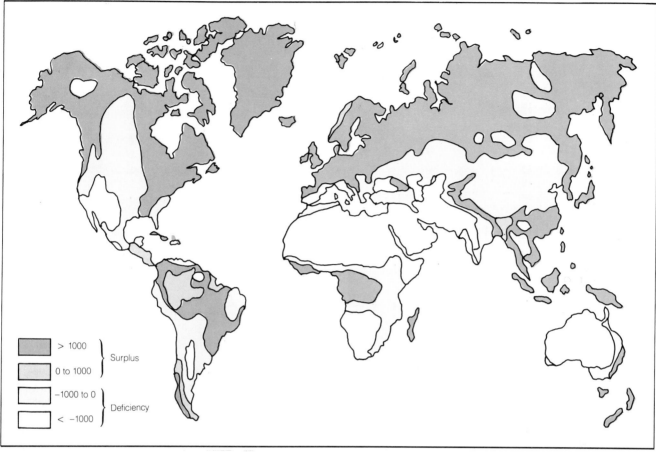

> 1000 ⎫
0 to 1000 ⎬ Surplus

−1000 to 0 ⎫
< −1000 ⎬ Deficiency

Note: a. Defined as difference between annual precipitation and evapotranspiration. Evapotranspiration corresponds to the water demand from a potential crop not suffering from water deficiency.
Source: M. Falkenmark, "Water and Mankind — A Complex System of Mutual Interaction," *AMBIO*, Vol. 6, No. 1 (1977), p. 3.

21 percent [15]. But this pattern varies from region to region. Industries in Eastern Europe use up to 80 percent of that region's available freshwater, compared to less than 10 percent in such countries as Turkey (9 percent), Mexico (7 percent), and Ghana (3 percent) [16] [17]. But even in countries with otherwise good statistical data, water data are not always available.

This analysis ignores a harsh reality: the distribution of the earth's freshwater supply often does not coincide with where people live. Some countries are relatively water rich because their per capita water use is small compared to per capita water availability. For example, in 1980 Canada had 122,000 cubic meters of water available per year for each person but used only about 1,500 cubic meters per person per year. On the other hand, Egypt's per capita water withdrawal of 1,180 cubic meters in 1976 was already pushing the per capita limit of about 1,470 cubic meters available per person per year [18].

At the global level, according to the Organisation for Economic Co-operation and Development (OECD), North America leads the world in per capita water use at 2,230 cubic meters per person per year (in 1980). (See Figure 8.3.) European OECD countries, on the other hand, used 656 cubic meters per person per year; Japan, Australia, and New Zealand averaged 945 cubic meters per person per year [19].

Despite the abundance of water globally, the rapid increase in the world's water usage since 1950 is cause for concern, especially for those areas that are water poor. Total water use increased from just over 1,000 cubic meters in 1950 to nearly 3,600 cubic meters in 1980; over the same period per capita use rose from almost 300 cubic meters to about 800 cubic meters [20].

Drinking Water and Sanitation in the Third World

In the developing countries, the availability of freshwater for domestic use varies widely; it also provides a measure of public health. Domestic uses include water for drinking, washing, and removing and treating sewage. In Africa, 13 percent of Lesotho's population had access to safe drinking water and 14 percent had access to sanitation services in 1980; in Libya, the percentages were 96 and 90, respectively. In India, 55 percent had access to drinking water but only 8 percent had sanitation services.

Freshwater

Figure 8.3 Water Withdrawal per Capita, 1980

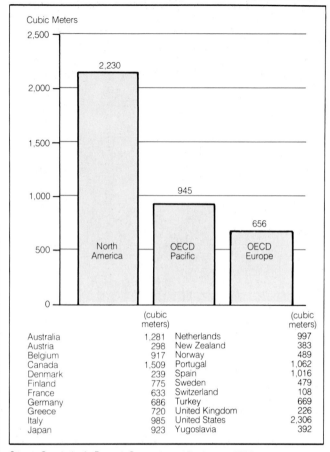

	(cubic meters)		(cubic meters)
Australia	1,281	Netherlands	997
Austria	298	New Zealand	383
Belgium	917	Norway	489
Canada	1,509	Portugal	1,062
Denmark	239	Spain	1,016
Finland	775	Sweden	479
France	633	Switzerland	108
Germany	686	Turkey	669
Greece	720	United Kingdom	226
Italy	985	United States	2,306
Japan	923	Yugoslavia	392

Source: Organisation for Economic Co-operation and Development (OECD). *The State of the Environment 1985* (OECD, Paris, 1985), p. 50.

Conversely, in Paraguay, only 25 percent of the population had potable drinking water available, but 87 percent had sanitation services of some kind (21).

Some 1.2 billion people, or 24 percent of the world's population, lack safe drinking water (22). About 1.4 billion people have no sanitary waste disposal facilities. About 5 million people die every year from such waterborne diseases as cholera, typhoid, diarrhea, dysentery, malaria, and intestinal worm infections (23). At the end of 1983, three years into the International Drinking Water Supply and Sanitation Decade, 49 percent of the populations of Third World countries reporting to the World Health Organization had access to safe drinking water, but only 20 percent had access to adequate sanitation facilities (24). Considering population growth, these figures represent a 4 percent improvement in access to safe drinking water but a 4 percent loss of access to adequate sanitation since 1980. (For more information on the U.N. International Drinking Water Supply and Sanitation Decade, see Chapter 3, "Human Settlements.")

Industrial Water Use and Reuse

Industrial water use is categorized by whether it is used for electric power generation or for process industries.

Cooling water for electric power generation accounts for over 60 percent of total industrial demand (25). Of the remaining 40 percent, two thirds is used by five process industries: primary metals, chemical products, petroleum refining, pulp and paper, and foods.

Developing countries use little water—about 20–40 cubic meters per person per year compared to such industrialized nations as the United States, which uses about 2,300 cubic meters per person per year (26). Only 2 percent of this water, however, is consumed or is not returned to the water cycle (27). Table 8.1 shows how water withdrawals varied among 22 countries reporting to OECD in 1980. The amount used by industries ranged from 2.1 percent in Greece to 74.4 percent in Sweden. Further, while industrial withdrawals increased in Canada, Portugal, and Turkey, they decreased in Finland, the Netherlands, and the United Kingdom (28). These differences are due to variations in economic development, changes in industrial mix, and the application of recycling technologies required to comply with more stringent water quality laws.

In order to meet stricter pollution standards, process industries—the big polluters—are recirculating more water, thus reducing their water use. In Japan, for example, industrial water withdrawals more than doubled from 1965 to 1974, but at the end of that period Japanese plants were recycling two thirds of their water, compared to one third in 1965 (29). In the United States, industries recently began using less water, mostly because of more stringent pretreatment pollution control regulations enacted in 1977. Between 1978 and 1983, U.S. industry's water intake had fallen 23 percent from 49.2 billion cubic meters to 38 billion cubic meters, despite a 6 percent increase in the number of industrial installations using more than 75.7 thousand cubic meters a year included in a U.S. Department of Commerce census (30). (See Table 8.2.)

The amount of water reused varies considerably within the five industrial groups that use most of the freshwater withdrawn for industrial purposes. Table 8.3 shows the breakdown in the United States, where the manufacture of chemicals, pulp and paper, petroleum and coal, primary metals, and food take nearly 90 percent of all the water used by industries, not including water used for cooling. The petroleum and coal industries recirculated 87 percent of the water they used in 1983, compared to 54 percent recirculated by the food industry (31).

In Sweden, the pulp and paper industry uses 80 percent of the country's industrial water withdrawals. From 1930 to the mid-1960s, Sweden's industrial water demand increased fivefold. Prodded by tough pollution control

Table 8.2 U.S. Industrial Water Use 1964–83
(billions of cubic meters)

Year	Total	Intake	Volume Reused	Percent Reused	Volume Discharged	Percent Treated	Number of Users[a]
1983	128.1	38.0	90.1	70	33.7	45	10,262
1978	168.5	49.2	129.5	72	44.2	40	9,605
1973	178.7	56.9	X	X	53.6	43	10,668
1968	135.2	58.6	X	X	54.0	30	9,402
1964	113.0	53.0	X	X	49.6	29	8,925

X = not available.
Note: a. Installations reporting intakes of 75,720 cubic meters or more per year.
Source: Adapted from U.S. Department of Commerce, Bureau of Census, *Water Use Manufacturing* (U.S. Government Printing Office, Washington, D.C., 1986), p. 6.

Table 8.1 Total Water Withdrawal by Major Uses, Selected Countries, 1980

	Total[a] (millions of cubic meters)	Cubic Meters per Capita	Percent Public Use	Percent Irrigation	Industry		
					Percent Process Industries	Percent Electrical Cooling	Percent Total Industrial
Canada[b]	36,153	1,509.0	12.6	7.8	11.6	36.8	48.4
USA	525,053	2,306.3	8.9	39.5	10.3	39.8	50.1
Japan[c]	107,772	922.8	12.5	X	0.0	0.8	0.8
Australia[d]	17,800	1,211.5	12.1	57.1	4.6	X	4.6
New Zealand	1,200	383.3	41.7	X	X	X	X
Austria[e]	2,240	298.3	26.8	1.8	24.6	46.9	71.5
Belgium	9,030	917.0	7.3	X	10.0	50.9	60.9
Denmark[f]	1,210	236.2	X	X	X	X	X
Finland[g]	3,702	774.5	10.5	1.4	38.3	2.6	40.9
France[c,h,i]	27,000	502.7	15.9	19.3	20.4	44.4	64.8
Germany[j]	42,204	685.5	11.8	0.4	6.8	60.4	67.2
Greece[k]	6,945	720.2	10.8	82.7	1.3	0.8	2.1
Italy[e]	56,200	984.8	14.2	57.3	14.2	12.5	26.7
Netherlands	14,209	997.4	7.4	X	1.2	70.9	72.1
Norway	1,999	489.1	19.5	2.0	70.0	X	70.0
Portugal[c]	10,500	1,062.3	15.0	46.9	37.5	X	37.5
Spain[f]	36,170	967.5	X	X	X	X	X
Sweden[c,l]	3,979	478.8	24.0	1.6	74.4	X	74.4
Switzerland[f]	690	108.3	X	X	X	X	X
Turkey[c,m]	29,928	669.0	12.5	77.8	9.7	X	9.7
United Kingdom[c,n]	12,639	225.7	46.6	0.3	14.4	37.9	52.3
Yugoslavia[o]	8,767	392.4	17.2	7.9	2.9	31.9	34.8

X = not available.

Notes:
a. Withdrawal from the four major sectors presented in the table do not necessarily add up to 100 percent because agricultural uses other than irrigation, industrial cooling, and other uses are not included.
b. Public use data are based on residential and commercial withdrawal only; industrial (municipal) withdrawal is included in industry water use.
c. Industry: cooling water included.
d. Industry: industrial and electrical cooling included.
e. Public use: data are estimates.
f. Total and per capita data refer to 1975 for withdrawal and to 1980 for population.
g. Irrigation: data represent mean withdrawal during dry years, which occur two to three times per decade.
h. Public use: nonirrigation agriculture uses included.
i. Data refer to 1975; per capita figure refers to 1975 for withdrawal and to 1980 for population.
j. Public use, irrigation, electrical cooling, and industry: 1979 data (percentage of 1980 total).
k. Irrigation: data refer to total agriculture water withdrawal.
l. Industry: 1975 data (percentage of 1980 total).
m. Irrigation: small-scale removal excluded.
n. England and Wales only.
o. Industry: water consumption only.
Source: Organisation for Economic Co-operation and Development (OECD), *OECD Environmental Data Compendium 1985* (OECD, Paris, 1985), p. 51.

laws, the industry cut its water use in half while more than doubling production by applying recirculation processes. By the late 1970s, the industry had increased its water efficiency fourfold (32).

Scarcity also is driving industries to use water more efficiently. In Israel, the government has established water use standards per unit of production for each industry. These standards are used to set quotas for each plant based on anticipated production, and these quotas motivate plant managers to use less water. Over the past two decades, Israel has cut its average water use per unit value of industrial production 70 percent (33). The discipline created by water scarcity, however, is lacking in most developing countries, where industrialization is beginning to gather momentum.

Whether these countries will adopt water-efficient technologies to make more freshwater available for other uses remains to be seen. India's developing industries, for example, use only about 4 percent of the country's available water, but that share is expected to increase fourfold by the year 2025, when India's water demands are predicted to exceed its maximum usable water supply (34).

In many Third World countries, industries have yet to treat their effluents. In India, for example, plants manufacturing chemicals in Goa, rayon in Kerala, pulp in Amlai, and leather products in Tamil Nadu have resisted pressures to install pollution control systems (35).

Irrigation: Emphasis on Efficiency

During the first half of this century, world water use doubled; it will double again by 1990. The use of irrigated agriculture and global population growth are the main causes (36). From 1950 to 1970, the gross irrigated area of the world doubled (37). Agriculture now accounts for about 73 percent of total freshwater usage (38); Table 8.4

Table 8.3 Major U.S. Industrial Water Users, 1983
(billions of cubic meters)

Industrial Group	Total	Volume Reused	Percent Reused	Volume Discharged	Percent Treated	Number of Sources[a]
Chemical Products	36.5	23.6	65	11.3	33	1,315
Paper and Pulp	28.1	21.0	74	6.7	73	600
Petroleum and Coal	23.4	20.3	87	2.6	54	260
Primary Metals	22.3	13.3	60	8.0	42	776
Food Processing	5.3	2.9	54	2.1	36	2,656
Total[b]	115.6	81.1		30.7		5,607

Notes:
a. Installations reporting water intake of 75,720 cubic meters or more per year.
b. Accounts for 90 percent of all industrial use, excluding water for cooling.
Source: Adapted from U.S. Department of Commerce, Bureau of Census, *Water Use in Manufacturing* (U.S. Government Printing Office, Washington, D.C., 1986), p. 7.

Freshwater

Table 8.4 Growth in Irrigated Area by Continent, 1950–85

Region	Total Irrigated Area (millions of hectares) 1985	Growth in Irrigated Area[a] (percent) 1950–60	1960–70	1970–80
Africa	13	25	80	33
Asia[b]	184	52	32	34
Europe[c]	29	50	67	40
North America	34	42	71	17
South America	9	67	20	33
Oceania	2	0	100	0
World	271	49	41	32

Notes:
a. Percentage increase between 1970 and 1982 prorated in 1970–80 to maintain comparison by decade.
b. Includes the Asian portion of the USSR.
c. Includes the European portion of the USSR.
Source: Adapted from W.R. Rangeley, "Irrigation and Drainage in the World," presented at the International Conference on Food and Water, College Station, Texas, May 26–30, 1985, p. 9.

shows the growth by continent. Most of the recent growth has occurred in the European part of the Soviet Union, Africa, Asia, and South America (39). About 18 percent of the world's cropland is now irrigated, producing about 30 percent of the world's food (40), but the environmental costs are high. The relatively sudden increase in water withdrawals has depleted aquifers, particularly in arid areas, and reduced or eliminated crop production in some fertile regions through salinization, alkalization, and waterlogging.

Salinity now seriously affects productivity on about 20 to 30 million hectares—or about 7 percent—of the world's irrigated land (41). The salinization of fertile croplands is running between 1 and 1.5 million hectares a year. The world's affected areas include Egypt, Iraq, Syria, Iran, the Soviet Republics of Uzbekistan and Tadzhikistan, Western China, Pakistan, India, Australia, and the Southwestern United States (42). In the U.S. Colorado River Basin, annual loadings of up to 10 million metric tons of salt cause crop yield losses valued at about $113 million a year (1982 dollars). These losses are expected to reach $267 million a year by 2010 if the salinization is not controlled, but progress in that region's salinity control has been disappointing (43).

A major cause of salinization is excessive irrigation ditch flows that deposit salts in the soil. One of the many ways to reduce salinization and waterlogging is to improve the efficiency of irrigation water use. Again, the irrigated world has much room for improvement. Water efficiencies vary widely. The more technologically advanced countries use about half the amount of water per hectare that the less advanced countries use. About 75 percent of today's 271 million hectares of irrigated land are in developing countries (44). But crop yields in many developing countries are only about a third of those obtained in the more developed countries (45).

Irrigated agriculture often loses half the water that it uses through evaporation and transpiration (46). Improving irrigation efficiency is necessary to provide additional water for irrigating more land. If the Indus region of Pakistan increased its water efficiency by 10 percent, for example, the water saved could irrigate another 2 million hectares (47).

Gravity irrigation down parallel furrows still typifies the method used by most of the world's farmers. This 5,000-year-old practice contrasts sharply with such technological improvements as center-pivot sprinklers, now used on one third of all irrigated land in the United States. These devices, which water a circular area of about 50 hectares from a rotating central arm, can increase water efficiency about 70 percent. Saudi Arabia has installed some 12,000 sprinklers in its drive to become self-sufficient in grain (48).

During the past decade, Israel, South Africa, France, Mexico, New Zealand, Australia, and the United States began using micro-irrigation techniques such as drip or trickle systems that deliver water directly to crop roots though perforated tubes. Table 8.5 shows how use of this method has grown eightfold since 1974, improving water efficiency an additional 20–25 percent over center-pivot sprinklers. Israel now uses sprinklers and the drip method on about half its irrigated land. Nevertheless, micro-irrigation still accounts for only 1 percent of the world's total irrigated area (49).

Less costly improvements to the gravity flow system, such as leveling the land and recycling the excess water with the aid of ponds and pumps, remain the most practical alternative for most of the developing world. Simply reducing the difference in levels between the top and bottom of irrigation furrows by only three centimeters can reduce a farmer's water use up to 40 percent. A surge technique developed in the United States (Texas) also can cut water and energy use 10–40 percent. Instead of running the irrigation water continuously, a timed valve releases the water at intervals to permit initial wettings to seal the soil. This method allows a more even distribution of water (50).

In 1979, the International Food Policy Research Institute in Washington, D.C., projected food deficits in 36 selected developing countries. It predicted that if these countries were to avoid a 70-million-metric-ton food deficit by 1990, they would almost have to double their past 2 percent-a-year growth rate for irrigated agriculture. Instead of adding another 27 million hectares under irrigation by 1990, they would need to add another 40 million hectares. The major food deficit areas are Bangladesh, India,

Table 8.5 Use of Micro-Irrigation Techniques[a]
(hectares)

Country	1974	1981–82
United States	29,060	185,300
Israel	6,070	81,700
South Africa	3,480	44,000
France	X	22,000
Australia	10,120	20,050
Soviet Union	X	11,200
Italy	X	10,300
China	X	8,040
Cyprus	160	6,600
Mexico	6,470	5,500
All Other	1,010	21,970
Total	56,370	416,660

X = not available.
Note: a. Includes primarily surface and subsurface drip methods and micro-sprinklers.
Sources: Sandra Postel, Conserving Water: The Untapped Alternative (Worldwatch Institute, Washington, D.C., 1985), p. 15; 1974 estimates from Don Gustafson, "Drip Irrigation in the World—State of the Art," in Israqua '78: Proceedings of the International Conference on Water Systems and Applications (Israel Centre of Waterworks Appliances, Tel Aviv, 1978); and 1981-82 estimates adapted from J.S. Abbott, "Micro-Irrigation—World Wide Usage," Bulletin of the International Commission on Irrigation and Drainage, January 1984.

Nigeria, Egypt, and the Sahel region of Africa. But the average rate of expansion in irrigation is not meeting even the lower figure (51). India is ahead of its growth prediction and should be self-sufficient in cereals by 2000. But sub-Saharan Africa, where the potential for irrigation development is limited, lacks both the investment capital and a tradition in irrigated agriculture; it is apparent that irrigated croplands will not make a significant contribution to that region's food needs by the end of the century (52). Factors other than irrigation can help, such as growing crops that need less water.

WATER POLLUTION

Controlling the world's growing municipal and industrial water pollution appears to be a never ending struggle. In 24 OECD countries, progress toward cleaner rivers and lakes has been spotty although measurable. Biological oxygen demand (BOD) has generally decreased since 1970. BOD—a primary indicator of water quality—reveals the presence of bacteria from untreated household sewage and industrial organic wastes that consume the oxygen in water, destroying the water's ability to support aquatic life. The lower the BOD, the cleaner the water. Figure 8.4 shows how water quality has improved in some of the rivers monitored from 1970 to 1983. France's Seine River, for example, registered the most dramatic improvement, with a BOD value of 4 milligrams per liter in 1983, down from 10 milligrams per liter in 1975. On the other hand, Japan's Yodo River and the Delaware River in the United States showed slight increases (53).

The levels of other pollutants—nitrates, phosphorus, lead, cadmium, chromium, and copper—showed mixed trends. Lead levels in the Rhine River at Bimmen, Federal Republic of Germany, for example, dropped from 24 micrograms per liter in 1975 to 8 micrograms per liter in 1983, but nitrates rose from 1.8 micrograms per liter in 1970 to 3.9 micrograms per liter in 1983. Phosphorus levels remained about the same, and values for cadmium, chromium, and copper decreased substantially (54).

Installation of primary (mechanical), secondary (biological), and tertiary (biological and chemical) treatment plants by municipalities and industries accounts for most of the progress. Waste water treatment plants served slightly more than half the populations of 21 OECD countries surveyed in 1983 (55). Table 8.6 shows the progress since 1970: Sweden, the only country that has shifted almost entirely to tertiary treatment, had 100 percent service; Denmark, 90 percent; Norway, 51 percent; Japan, 33 percent; Ireland, 11.2 per cent (1980); and Greece, 0.5 percent (1980).

United States

These national percentages provide only a rough estimate of progress. For example, in the United States, 70 percent of the population was served by waste water treatment plants in 1983. But in 1984, the U.S. Environmental Protection Agency (EPA) reported that out of a national total of 1.8 million stream-miles, water quality improvements for only 47,000 stream-miles were reported by the states for 1972–82, compared to 11,000 that were degraded

Figure 8.4 Water Quality: Biological Oxygen Demand (BOD) at Mouth of Selected Rivers[a]

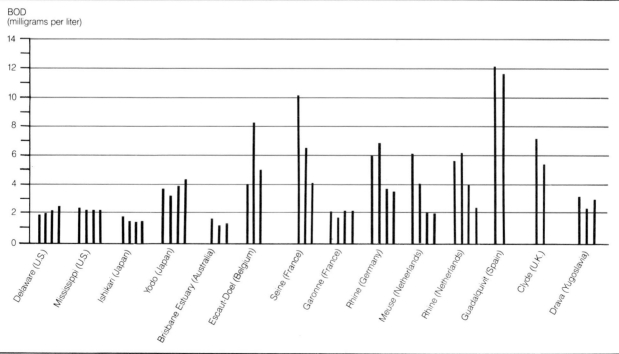

Notes: a. Data refer to 1970, 1975, 1980, and 1983. "Mouth" refers to either the mouth or the downstream frontier of the river.
Source: Organisation for Economic Co-operation and Development, *The State of the Environment 1985* (OECD, Paris, 1985), p. 53.

Table 8.6 Population Served by Waste Water Treatment Plants, Selected OECD Countries, 1970–83
(percentage)

	Primary Only				Primary and Secondary and/or Tertiary				Total Served			
	1970	1975	1980	1983	1970	1975	1980	1983	1970	1975	1980	1983
Canada[a]	X	X	13.0	13.0	X	X	43.0	43.0	X	49.0	56.0	56.0
United States[b,c]	X	23.0	17.0	14.6	X	44.0	53.0	55.5	X	67.0	70.0	70.1
Japan[d,e]	X	X	X	X	16.0	23.0	30.0	33.0	16.0	23.0	30.0	33.0
New Zealand[f]	X	9.0	10.0	X	X	47.0	49.0	X	52.0	56.0	59.0	X
Austria[g]	11.0	X	10.0	X	5.0	X	30.0	X	16.0	X	40.0	X
Belgium[h]	0.0	0.0	0.0	X	3.8	5.5	22.9	X	3.8	5.5	22.9	X
Denmark[i]	31.9	29.0	X	20.0	22.4	41.6	X	70.0	54.3	70.6	X	90.0
Finland[j]	5.0	3.0	0.0	0.0	22.0	47.0	65.0	69.0	27.0	50.0	65.0	69.0
France[k]	X	X	2.5	X	X	X	59.0	X	X	40.0	61.5	63.7
Germany[l]	20.5	18.4	10.2	X	41.3	56.4	71.6	X	61.8	74.8	81.8	84.0
Greece	X	X	0.0	X	X	X	0.5	X	X	X	0.5	X
Ireland	X	X	0.2	X	X	X	11.0	X	X	X	11.2	X
Italy[m]	8.0	X	X	X	6.0	X	X	X	14.0	X	30.0	X
Luxembourg	X	X	0.0	X	X	X	76.0	X	X	X	76.0	83.0
Netherlands[d]	X	8.0	7.0	7.0	X	37.0	61.0	65.0	X	45.0	68.0	72.0
Norway	1.0	2.0	2.0	3.0	20.0	25.0	35.0	48.0	21.0	27.0	37.0	51.0
Portugal[k]	1.0	2.0	3.0	3.5	2.1	4.0	7.0	8.5	20.1	24.0	30.0	33.5
Spain	X	7.0	8.8	X	X	7.3	9.1	X	X	14.3	17.9	X
Sweden[n]	12.0	4.0	1.0	2.0	66.0	94.0	98.0	98.0	78.0	98.0	99.0	100.0
Switzerland	X	X	X	X	35.0	55.0	70.0	81.0	35.0	55.0	70.0	81.0
United Kingdom[o]	X	X	X	7.0	X	X	X	76.0	X	X	X	83.0

X = not available.
Notes:
a. Secondary treatment usually includes primary treatment and refers to waste stabilization ponds. Tertiary treatment refers to secondary treatment with phosphorus removal. 1975 data refer to 1976.
b. 1975 data refer to 1976.
c. 1983 data refer to 1982. 1983 data for the second category include 1.8 percent of nondischarge treatment.
d. 1983 data refer to 1981.
e. Data for the second category may include data for primary treatment only.
f. 1970 data are Secretariat estimates.
g. Estimated data.
h. 1980 data refer to 1979.
i. 1975 data refer to 1977.
j. Networks serving fewer than 200 inhabitants are excluded. Primary treatment is defined as mechanical, secondary as biological, and tertiary as combined chemical-biological treatment.
k. 1983 data are Secretariat estimates.
l. 1970 data refer to 1969. 1983 data are estimates.
m. 1970 data refer to 1971.
n. Urban population only (84 percent of total population). Definitions: Primary treatment: removal of sediments. Secondary: chemical or biological treatment. Tertiary: chemical and biological and complementary treatment.
o. England and Wales only. Definitions: Primary treatment: removal of gross solids. Secondary: removal of organic material or bacteria under aerobic conditions. Tertiary: removal of suspended solids following secondary treatment.
Source: Organisation for Economic Co-operation and Development (OECD), *OECD Environmental Data Compendium 1985* (OECD, Paris, 1985), p. 53.

over the same period. Water quality for another 296,000 stream-miles monitored by the states remained about the same (56). About 42 percent of U.S. streams are checked at least quarterly to monitor possible changes in pollution levels. The remaining 58 percent are considered generally free from water quality problems (57). EPA nonetheless called this record "a major accomplishment" in view of the "substantial increases in population, industry, and development pressures" that took place during the ten-year period. The nation's population, for example, grew by 11 percent.

Eastern Europe

Eastern European nations and the Soviet Union are only now beginning to deal with severe municipal and industrial pollution of their rivers and lakes. Water pollution data from the Soviet Union are still hard to obtain. According to a 1977 source, however, three quarters of the effluents dumped into the Volga River were untreated. At Volgograd, industrial wastes accounted for 10 percent of the river's average flow (58). Although an effort was launched to install treatment facilities along the Volga, poor enforcement has reportedly undercut implementation. Thus, as industrial water demand continues to grow, the river's quality is expected to worsen by the turn of the century (59).

The quality of the water in Poland's Vistula River, on the other hand, may significantly improve by the year 2005, if the ambitious Vistula Program is carried out as planned. The Vistula, which winds through some of Poland's most heavily industrialized regions, was so badly polluted in 1978 that only 432 kilometers of its total length of 1,068 kilometers was suitable even for industrial use. The rest was "so polluted as to be utterly useless." The stretch that runs through the historic city of Krakow was reportedly "devoid of biological life." Of the 3.3 billion cubic meters of sewage flowing into the river then, only half received any form of treatment (60) (61). In 1980, the Polish Government initiated a plan to build 188 new purification plants to treat a total of 5.7 billion cubic meters of domestic and industrial waste. Another 200 facilities with combined capacities of 1 billion m^3 will treat only toxic industrial waste water. According to Poland's Institute for Shaping the Natural Environment in Katowice, 16 percent of the Vistula and its tributaries will attain first class quality and 45 percent second class status by 2005. Only 3 percent is expected to remain as polluted as before (62).

Hungary faces a different water pollution problem: 95 percent of its water supply originates outside its borders. Although Hungary's water demands from the Danube River are increasing, the worst pollution sources have been eliminated, and the river is now of higher water quality when it leaves Hungary than when it enters (63). Hungary is also moving to control eutrophication of Lake Balaton, one of the largest bodies of freshwater in Europe. The lake, which has an average depth of only 3.1 meters, is a tourist magnet because of its sandy beaches and warm water. But during the past 25 years, the amount of nutrients—mainly phosphorus and nitrogen from agricultural runoff—has increased by a factor of 10–20. The government is now trying to control farmland runoff into the lake and its tributaries and plans to build tertiary treatment plants to reduce the phosphorus intake (64).

Third World
Asia

Water pollution control is still either totally lacking or grossly inadequate in most Third World countries. Some data are available, but they tend to be anecdotal rather than comprehensive. China, for example, installed its first major waste water treatment plant in Beijing in 1980, but the facility's capacity is already insufficient (65). Waste water severely pollutes 70 percent of the country's 78 monitored rivers, but China is treating only an estimated 2 percent of its total waste water (66). Data from 1980 show that 41 of the 44 major cities relying on groundwater draw on "contaminated supplies and nine of these are seriously polluted" (67). During the summer, untreated waste accounted for up to 25 percent of the Huangpujiang River, Shanghai's primary drinking water source (68).

Throughout East Asia, the wastes from rapid industrialization, the runoff from increased use of pesticides and fertilizers, and excessive water withdrawals are destabilizing the hydrological cycle. Destruction of East Asia's water resources is regarded as the region's most critical ecological threat, according to N.D. Jayal, regional councilor for the International Union for Conservation of Nature and Natural Resources (69). More than two thirds of India's water resources are polluted, a condition exacerbated by the growth of new industries that have not installed waste treatment facilities. Over the past decade, for example, India's pulp and paper industry—one of the country's major users and polluters of water—quadrupled in size (70).

In Malaysia, palm oil and rubber effluents, in addition to other industrial wastes and sewage, have caused 42 rivers to be officially labeled "dead" (71). Philippines surface water quality continues to deteriorate from untreated or inadequately treated sewage and industrial effluents. Domestic sewage constitutes 60–70 percent of Manila's Pasig River. The river's dissolved oxygen content is now 3.1 milligrams per liter, the threshold at which aquatic life begins to die (72). In Bangladesh rivers, fecal coliform bacteria levels vary erratically from the wet summer season to the drier winter months: in 1981, the coliform count on the Sitalakhya River shifted from 225 per 100 milliliters of water in July to 3,000 per 100 milliliters of water in December (73). Untreated sewage in Pakistan—which in some cases exceeds industrial wastes fourfold—is polluting both its urban and rural areas. From half to two thirds of all illnesses in Pakistan are related to such waterborne diseases as typhoid, diarrhea, dysentery, and infectious hepatitis (74).

Africa

Africa is no better off. In addition to raw sewage, agro-industrial activities are a significant source of pollution. In Nigeria, the brewing, slaughtering, and sugar refining industries make little attempt to control either air or water pollutants. Coffee wastes are the worst offenders in Kenya, although the tanning industry's organic wastes—hair and fats—and inorganic residues of chromium and sulfide are also serious pollutants (75). The rapid urbanizing trend in sub-Saharan Africa will only increase its current pollution problems. While Mombasa's human population is expected to double by 1996 to 665,000 (from 324,000 in 1974), city wastes will more than triple (76). Likewise, in Dar es Salaam, where three quarters of all Tanzanian industry is located, many sewage pumping stations have broken down from overloading. By one account, 127 factories are discharging untreated wastes into the city's sewers and rivers (77).

Latin America and the Caribbean

Latin America's water resources are the world's richest; its surface runoff accounts for 31 percent of the world's total. Yet here, too, most municipalities and industries are discharging their effluents virtually untreated (78). Mining—lead, zinc, and silver—is Latin America's leading water pollution source, particularly in the Andean countries. Oil deposits in the central Amazon Basin and in the Andean foothills of Bolivia, Peru, and Ecuador constitute another major source of pollution. Three of Bolivia's rivers are badly polluted, as are 21 in Chile, 13 in Peru, including the Mantaro, and the La Plata River between Argentina and Uruguay (79).

Latin American cities, however, still have relatively healthy drinking water despite the growth of petrochemical, chemical, and cellulose industries. More than 400 urban waste water treatment plants have been installed, but some operate inefficiently or not at all (80). Agricultural pollution from pesticides, fertilizers, and soil erosion is expected to increase over the next two decades, particularly as deforestation accelerates.

In the Caribbean Basin, water pollution is growing from insufficient sewage treatment that has not kept up with gains made in the supply of domestic water. The percentage of urban populations served by sewage systems varies from virtually none in Haiti to 31 percent in Guatemala and to 69 percent in Trinidad (81). The region's critical pollution sources include discharges from sugar refineries and distilleries, which have a high BOD, oil refineries in Trinidad and Tobago, and the bauxite industries in Jamaica and Guyana. Jamaica's red mud, a toxic residue from bauxite mining, is polluting groundwater by increasing its sodium level (82). A slow-starting Regional Seas strategy initiated by the United Nations Environment Programme is now focusing Caribbean Basin attention on correcting these problems (83).

FOCUS ON: GROUNDWATER

Not much is known about the availability and quality of the earth's groundwater except in Europe, parts of Africa and North America, and small parts of Asia. Recent estimates of freshwater stored in geologic formations to a depth of 4,000 meters vary from 8.1 million km^3 to 10.5

million km^3. Although only about 0.1 percent of these reserves takes part in the average year's hydrological cycle (84), the planet's groundwater is an immense resource. In the United States, for example, the "volume of groundwater within a half mile of the surface is estimated to be four times that of the Great Lakes" (85). It equals the amount of water discharged by the Mississippi River into the Gulf of Mexico over the past 200 years (86).

In the past 25 years, the world began to use more of its groundwater. The Chinese dug more than 2 million tube wells in their North Plain between 1960 and 1980. In India, the number of tube wells proliferated from fewer than 5,000 in the 1950s to more than 2 million by the late 1970s (87). In the United States, groundwater withdrawals have increased 190 percent since 1955 (88); half the nation's drinking water comes from the ground, as does 40 percent of the water used in irrigation (89). Groundwater is the principal supplier of freshwater for Denmark, Cyprus, and Malta and is the sole provider of drinking water for more than 60 percent of the towns in the Soviet Union (90). In general, however, Europe's aquifers provide less usable water than the continent's surface waters. The percentage of groundwater to surface flows originating in a country's borders varies from 2 in Finland to 68 in Hungary. The figures are 7.6 percent in the United Kingdom, 10 percent in Belgium and Czechoslovakia, and 15 percent in Poland (91). Because of this limitation, Europe's groundwater resources cannot satisfy additional demands, and nearly all U.N. Economic Commission for Europe countries will have to limit withdrawals to 1982 levels (92). Indeed, the proportion of groundwater used for drinking water is expected to decrease 30 percent by the year 2000 in Belgium, Czechoslovakia, Poland, and Canada.

Groundwater data for Latin America are sparse. Havana, Cuba, relies almost exclusively on groundwater, as do the arid regions of Argentina, Brazil, Chile, Peru, and Mexico (93). However, thousands of Andean communities in Bolivia, Colombia, Chile, Ecuador, Peru, and Venezuela have always relied on springs for drinking water and for irrigating small farms. Estimates of annual withdrawals range from 62 million cubic meters in Trinidad and Tobago to 16.5 billion cubic meters in Mexico (94). (See Table 8.7.)

Over the past decade, droughts have plagued more than 20 African countries, causing famine and population migrations. At the same time, African populations have expanded faster than any other parts of the world. By the end of the century, Kenya's per capita water supply is expected to shrink by half. Nigeria faces a 42 percent reduction, Egypt a 33 percent decrease (95). On the other hand, the African continent is estimated to hold 24 percent of the planet's groundwater reserves (96). Nevertheless, most sub-Saharan African countries do not have enough information about their groundwater locations, recharge areas, and available volumes to develop plans. Mali is currently producing a groundwater survey with a $15 million loan from the United Nations Environment Programme. The United Nations, which has published groundwater compendiums on other regions of the world,

Table 8.7 Volume of Groundwater Extracted Annually and Number of Wells in Selected Countries of Latin America and the Caribbean

Country	Volume of Groundwater (millions of cubic meters)	Number of Wells Drilled
Argentina	4,700	300,000
Cuba	5,200	X
Chile[a]	1,690	2,507
El Salvador	149	1,685
Mexico	16,565	X
Peru	1,289	11,290
Trinidad and Tobago	62	X

X = not available.
Note: a. Deep wells only.
Source: U.N. Economic Commission for Latin America (ECLA), *The Water Resources of Latin America and Their Utilization* (ECLA, Lima, Peru, 1984), p. 9.

is only now in the process of reporting on Africa and Asia. In addition, the World Bank is financing a program to develop an efficient hand pump suitable for Third World production and use that could allow better access to groundwater in Africa's drought-stricken areas (97).

A major threat to groundwater is the practice of water mining, the long-term drawing down of an aquifer at a rate that exceeds its replenishment. Beijing's groundwater is being withdrawn four times faster than it is being replaced. Agricultural pumping in India's Tamil Nadu region has caused its water table to drop 25–30 meters in a decade. The Ogallala Aquifer, which underlies eight of the U.S. high plains states, is already partially depleted from wells dug for irrigation (98).

When the groundwater adjacent to coastal river systems is overdrawn, salt water may intrude, creating an additional problem of pollution. Salt water intrusion has already occurred in the Federal Republic of Germany, the Netherlands, the United Kingdom, the United States, Malta, India, Pakistan, and Thailand. Ten percent of Thailand is now underlain by saline water. Bangkok's water table has dropped 25 meters since 1958 and is now declining at a rate of nearly 4 meters per year. Salt water is encroaching inland at a rate of 500 meters per year, contaminating shallow wells. As a result, the Thai Government has imposed restrictions on new wells less than 300 meters deep (99).

Groundwater exhaustion can also lead to land subsidence—the sinking of land surfaces caused by depletion of the groundwater below. Subsidence is a major problem in at least 42 areas around the world according to the United Nations Educational Scientific and Cultural Organization's *Guidebook to Studies of Land Subsidence*. For example, in the San Joachim Valley in California a 6,200 square kilometer area experienced subsidence of up to 9 meters from 1930 to 1975. In Mexico City an area of 225 square kilometers dropped up to 9 meters from 1891 to 1978 and in Tokyo an area of 3,420 square kilometers dropped up to 4.6 meters from 1918 to 1978. To combat this problem, more than 20 countries have initiated artificial groundwater recharge programs (100).

Pollution, especially from synthetic organic chemicals, also threatens the world's vast supplies of groundwater. Groundwater quality varies naturally, depending on surrounding geology. It may contain dissolved calcium, salts, trace metals such as arsenic and selenium, and even radionuclides (101). Recently developed techniques that permit measurement of minuscule amounts of toxics (to parts per billion) are now confronting governments with a new dilemma: setting water quality standards when the health effects of trace amounts of most chemicals remain unknown. The science of quantitative risk assessment—still in its infancy—continues to be controversial (102).

Sources of groundwater pollution include hazardous waste sites, septic tanks, leaking underground sewer lines, underground petroleum storage tanks, agricultural runoff containing pesticides and fertilizers, runoff from city streets and highways that includes de-icing salts, underground and surface mines, and the municipal and industrial pollutants affecting surface waters that connect to aquifers (103).

Nitrates, primarily from fertilizers, are becoming a serious drinking water pollutant, and as the use of fertilizers spreads throughout the Third World, this developed country affliction may become a worldwide problem, although nitrate leaching is less serious in tropical climates (104). In the United States, 6 percent of more than 124,000 wells sampled in 1984 exceeded the EPA drinking water limit of 10 milligrams per liter of water for nitrates. Some 20 percent of the wells surveyed had maximum nitrate-nitrogen concentrations greater than 3 milligrams per liter, warranting continued monitoring (105). Nitrate pollution is also a growing problem in some Latin American cities like Buenos Aires and Sao Paulo, primarily because of nitrate leaching from surrounding farmland into wells supplying these cities.

Volatile organic compounds, such as trichloroethylene (TCE), a common substance used in household cleaners and industrial degreasants, have been contaminating aquifers in North America and parts of Europe for years. TCE is now the primary organic contaminant of Florida's Key Biscayne Aquifer because of its common use for cleaning septic tanks in southern Florida (106) (107).

In June 1986, the U.S. Environmental Protection Agency announced that a third of the nation's 796,000 mostly steel underground fuel tanks probably leak because of structural defects or corrosion. Although the U.S. Congress required fiberglass construction in 1984, EPA sampled 433 tanks and concluded that fiberglass was no safer than steel (108). Major oil companies had previously estimated that no more than 5 percent of the underground tanks leaked.

In the United States, 58 percent of all hazardous wastes are disposed of by injection into deep wells, and 40 percent are disposed of in landfills and surface impoundments (109). Hazardous waste is now infiltrating the groundwater at half the 2,000 abandoned waste sites that require cleanup under the EPA's Superfund Program (110). A congressional committee investigating the sites discovered that many were not being monitored as required (111).

An EPA survey of 466 randomly sampled utilities supplying drinking water found that water from 22 percent of them contained detectable levels of volatile organic chemicals (112). Although efforts continue to find cost-

effective methods for removing these contaminants and meeting new drinking water standards, the most desirable way of controlling groundwater contamination is to prevent pollution at the source. (See Chapter 13, "Controlling Hazardous Wastes: The Unmet Challenge.")

RECENT DEVELOPMENTS

DESALINATION: THE INDUSTRY MATURES

New desalination technologies are emerging that promise to revolutionize the industry. As arid and semiarid regions face increasing water shortages, desalination will become an increasingly important option. Further, as more freshwater is affected by poorly drained irrigation projects, new and cheaper desalination technologies hold promise for restoring freshwater quality. Attention is focused on the recently developed reverse osmosis (RO) systems, which use a membrane that allows water molecules to pass through under pressure but block most dissolved organics and inorganics. These systems can reduce the salt concentration of brackish water 90-95 percent and that of sea water more than 99 percent. By early 1985, about 500 million gallons (1.8 billion liters) per day of RO capacity had been built, of which only 567 million liters per day of capacity was in the arid Middle East (113). The most common desalinization process currently in use—multistage flash distillation (MSF)—can deliver higher quality freshwater with a salt concentration of only 10 parts per million. However, MSF plants require about twice the energy of RO plants.

By 1985, the world's total desalting capacity had reached 2.6 billion gallons a day (9.8 billion liters) (114). Despite the drop in world oil prices, which has depressed the market for desalination equipment, the "confidence level to deliver increasingly economical desalination plants continues to grow" (115). Table 8.8 shows that the Middle East and North Africa account for 69 percent, and the United States 12 percent, or 300 million gallons a day (1.1 billion liters).

The U.S. figure will increase significantly when the Yuma Desalting Plant in Arizona begins to operate at full capacity in 1989, adding another 72 million gallons (272 million liters) a day (116). The plant is designed to help fulfill the U.S. treaty obligations to deliver to Mexico 1.3 million acre-feet of Colorado River water annually with an average salinity content no higher than 115 milligrams per liter of water over the annual average salinity of water arriving at Imperial Dam near Yuma. The Yuma plant, which was 60 percent completed by mid-1986, will use reverse osmosis. The investment cost will be $3 per

Table 8.8 World Desalinating Capacity, 1985

Region	Millions of Liters per Day	Percentage of Total
Middle East and North Africa	3,785	69
United States	1,135	12
Balance of World	1,892	19
Total	**6,812**	**100**

Source: Arthur D. Little, Inc., Cambridge, Massachusetts, cited in J.D. Birkett, "Alternative Water Resources in the Middle East," *U.S.-Arab Commerce* (November-December 1985), p. 14.

World Resources 1987

gallon per day or $792 per cubic meter per day of installed capacity (117).

This cost compares favorably with successful 1985 installation bids around the world. Two Japanese companies (Susakura and Mitsui) contracted to build eight multistage flash distillation units in Kuwait to generate 208,000 cubic meters a day at an investment cost of $1,000 per cubic meter per day. Water Services of America, a U.S. company, is building a 10,000-cubic-meter-per-day reverse osmosis plant in Curaçao to desalinate at $1,020 per cubic meter a day. Hydranautics, another U.S. company, was low bidder ($300 per cubic meter per day) to construct a reverse osmosis system using brackish water in Englewood, Florida. In Tamil Nadu, India, however, a smaller 50-cubic-meter-per-day, brackish-water reverse osmosis plant will be built by Bharat Heavy Electricals at a cost of $1,570 per cubic meter per day of installed capacity (118).

Still, source alternatives such as treating and reusing water and transporting it by pipe or aqueduct are more cost effective than desalination in many instances.

Regardless of how efficient water treatment becomes, its application for drinking water will be limited by public attitudes and, in the Islamic world, by religious restrictions. Long water pipelines continue to be laid, even in the Middle East and North Africa. Libya is currently building its $3.3 billion "Great Manmade River," which will transfer groundwater from the country's barren southern interior to its Mediterranean coastal populations (119).

Desalination, however, will continue to be a practical source of freshwater when the alternatives are more costly. Evaporative and membrane technologies are available at predictable costs. International competition among suppliers is increasing, a situation that will act to keep capital costs down. Membrane design improvements and hardware refinements have significantly cut energy needs, and they are expected to continue to do so. But capital and operating costs are still beyond the reach of most oil-importing Third World countries, and many developing countries lack the skilled operators needed to run the sophisticated equipment (120).

GREAT LAKES: BILATERAL WAR ON TOXICS

The Toxic Substances Control Agreement, approved by eight U.S. states and two Canadian provinces in 1986, pledges "to continue reducing toxics in the Great Lakes Basin to the maximum extent possible." It is the third recent international agreement affecting Great Lakes water quality, following a 1985 Great Lakes charter, which deals with new water diversions, and a 1986 ban on oil drilling (121). The toxic substance agreement bans the reduction of pollution control standards to encourage economic development, establishes a coordinated control plan for toxic discharges, asks for an overall plan to reduce, recycle, and treat hazardous waste safely by January 31, 1987, requires the notification of other states or provinces of accidental toxic discharges, and standardizes procedures for describing fish contamination and identifying toxic effects on human health and wildlife.

As part of the Toxic Substances Control Agreement, Canadian Environmental Minister Thomas McMillan and U.S. Environmental Protection Agency Administrator Lee M. Thomas signed an agreement in May 1986 for the reduction of toxic loadings into the Niagara River and Lake Ontario. A goal was set to lower loadings of toxic chemicals 50 percent by 1995. In February 1985, the eight U.S. states and two Canadian provinces bordering the Great Lakes signed the Great Lakes Charter. They agreed to consult each other concerning any major proposal involving intrabasin diversion or consumption. The charter was two years in the making (122). Treaties involving U.S. and Canadian boundary waters fall under the purview of the permanent International Joint Commission, founded in 1909. (See Chapter 12, "Policies and Institutions.")

WATER MARKETS: THE DEBATE GROWS

In the United States, water marketing—using economic forces to affect the available water supply—is being discussed in the arid west with increasing urgency. "We talk scarcity," the governor of Colorado wryly observes, "yet we have set our largest cities in the deserts, and then have insisted on surrounding ourselves with Kentucky bluegrass. Our words are those of the Sahara Desert; our policies are those of the Amazon River" (123). How the United States experiments with water pricing and market structures will offer other countries facing similar problems a test tube view of employing market forces to allocate scarce water.

Environmental economists have recognized the need to value water more in order to conserve it. They contend that big users of water would rapidly install water-saving devices, more water would be reused, and fewer costly dams would be needed to impound water if there were an open market for water (124). Earlier U.S. studies showed that water is price elastic and that the use of water meters can cut domestic water consumption as much as 45 percent (125). Studies of an electric power plant's demand for cooling water showed that as the price increased from about one cent per 1,000 gallons (3,700 liters) to five cents per 1,000 gallons, water use dropped from 50 gallons per kilowatt hour (kWh) of energy generated in once-through cooling to 0.8 gallons per kWh in a cooling tower. Thus a fivefold price increase led to a fiftyfold reduction in water use (126).

Changing conditions in the United States—population shifts, declining groundwater supplies and quality, and less government willingness to finance major interbasin water transfers—are forcing changes in the way water is being allocated and used. "American laws, institutions, and culture continue to reflect the naive belief that water supplies can be expanded indefinitely—while the challenge of the future will be learning to live with less," the Freshwater Foundation of Minneapolis, Minnesota, stated in a special report on water values and markets (127).

Those economists who advocate water markets prefer to compare water to oil and minerals. "Until some pattern is agreed upon that permits economic and market forces to be the prime element in the allocation and use of water," contends Thomas C. Campbell, professor of economics at Virginia Commonwealth University, "waste and other inefficient uses are inevitable" (128). On the other hand, Williamson B. C. Chang, associate professor of law at the University of Hawaii, argues against treating water as a commodity. "Freshwater is simply too important to be given over to free market forces," he says (129). Chang notes that on the island of Oahu, with a population of 800,000, the two biggest groundwater users are the municipal water system and the sugar industry. He fears that the sugar industry would exploit the market approach to the further detriment of food production, citing the demise of Hawaii's rice industry as a case in point.

Idaho administers one of the first water market experiments in the United States. The Idaho Snake River Water Bank was initiated after a severe drought in 1977 to rent excess water impounded by four U.S. Bureau of Reclamation projects. The Idaho Power Company rents most of the water from such suppliers as canal companies, irrigation districts, and individual farmers who purchased excess storage from the federal government as insurance against another drought (130). The rental arrangement allows agricultural water use to be shifted to generate power without the owners losing their water rights under the prior appropriation doctrine of "use it or lose it" that governs water rights in the western United States.

In May 1986, Congressman George Miller of California introduced a bill to establish a "water exchange" in northern California to allow San Joaquin Valley farmers beset with selenium-tainted agricultural drainage to sell their water rights to the state's thirsty cities in the south. The bill would set aside 75 percent of the "profits" to deal with the polluted drainage problem, thus resolving another water-market issue—preventing owners of subsidized water from reaping windfall profits by selling cheap government-provided water (131).

References and Notes

1. United Nations Economic and Social Commission for Asia and the Pacific (UNESCAP), *State of the Environment in Asia and the Pacific*, Vol. 2 (UNESCAP, Bangkok, 1984), p. 122.
2. M.T. L'vovitch, "World Water Resources Present and Future," *AMBIO*, Vol. 6, No. 1 (1977), p. 20.
3. M. Falkenmark, "Do We Need Hydrologic Research?" (in Swedish), *Forskning och Framsteg*, No. 5 (Stockholm, 1974).
4. *Ibid.*
5. Stable runoff is runoff that flows from groundwater into rivers. It is a conservative estimate of water availability that ignores seasonal runoff stored in reservoirs, lakes, or groundwater.
6. Peter P. Rogers, "Fresh Water," in *The Global Possible: Resources, Development, and the New Century*, Robert Repetto, ed. (Yale University Press, New Haven, Connecticut, 1985), pp. 261–262.
7. J. Forkasiewicz and J. Margat, *Tableau Mondial de Donnees Nationales D'Economie de L'Eau, Ressources et Utilisations*, 79 SGN 784 HYD (Department Hydrogeologie, Orleans, France, 1980).
8. *Ibid.*
9. *Ibid.*
10. Asit K. Biswas, "Climate and Water Resources," in *Climate and Development*, Vol. 13, Asit K. Biswas, ed. (Tycooly International Publishing Ltd., Dublin, 1984).
11. A.V. Todorov, "Sahel: The Changing Rainfall Regime and the 'Normals' Used for Its Assessment," *Journal of Climate and Applied Meteorology*, Vol. 24, No. 2 (1985), p. 102.
12. United Nations Environment Programme (UNEP), *The State of the World Environment: 1972–82* (UNEP, Nairobi, 1982), p. 22.
13. Sandra Postel, *Water: Rethinking Management in an Age of Scarcity* (Worldwatch Institute, Washington, D.C., 1984), p. 12.
14. R.P. Ambroggi, "Water," *Scientific American*, Vol. 243, No. 3 (1980), p. 101.
15. *Ibid.*
16. E. Fano and M.R. Brewster, "Industrial Water Pollution Control in Developing Countries," in *Water Resources Management in Industrial Areas* (1982), p. 219.
17. World Resources Institute and International Institute for Environment and Development, *World Resources 1986* (Basic Books, New York, 1986), pp. 302–303.
18. *Op. cit.*
19. Organisation for Economic Co-operation and Development (OECD), *The State of the Environment 1985* (OECD, Paris, 1985), p. 50.
20. *Op. cit.* 13.
21. World Resources Institute and International Institute for Environment and Development, *World Resources 1987* (Basic Books, New York, 1987), Table 17.2.
22. Asit K. Biswas, ed., *Water Development Supply and Management, United Nations Water Conference: Summary and Main Documents*, Vol. 2 (Pergamon Press, New York, 1978), p. xiv.
23. *Ibid.*, p. xv.
24. World Health Organization (WHO), *The International Drinking Water Supply and Sanitation Decade Review of Regional and Global Data*, Offset Publication No. 92 (WHO, Geneva, 1986), p. 13.
25. *Op. cit.* 14, p. 111.
26. *Op. cit.* 14, p. 106.
27. W.B. Solley, *et al.*, *Estimated Use of Water in the United States in 1980* (U.S. Geological Survey, Alexandria, Virginia, 1983).
28. *Op. cit.* 19, p. 51.
29. *Op. cit.* 12.
30. U.S. Department of Commerce, *1982 Census of Manufacturers: Water Use in Manufacturing*, MC82-S-6 (U.S. Government Printing Office, Washington, D.C., March 1986), pp. 6–7.
31. *Ibid.*
32. *Op. cit.* 13, p. 43.
33. *Op. cit.* 13, p. 43.
34. Centre for Science and Environment, *The State of India's Environment: 1984-85, The Second Citizen's Report* (Centre for Science and Environment, New Delhi, 1985), p. 29.
35. *Ibid.*, pp. 26–27.
36. Council of Ministers of the USSR and Committee for the International Hydrological Decade, *World Water Balance and Water Resources of the Earth* (United Nations Educational, Scientific and Cultural Organization, Paris, 1974).
37. W.R. Rangeley, "Irrigation and Drainage in the World," presented at the International Conference on Food and Water, College Station, Texas, May 26–30, 1985, p. 8. Note: "gross irrigated area" refers to the total land area brought under some form of irrigation and does not include the land taken out of irrigation for environmental or economic reasons.
38. M.I. L'vovich, *World Water Resources and Their Future* (translated by the American Geophysical Union) (LithoCrafters Inc., Chelsea, Michigan, 1979), p. 250.
39. *Op. cit.* 37, p. 9.
40. *Op. cit.* 37, p. 10.
41. V.A. Kovda, "Loss of Productive Land due to Salinization," *AMBIO*, Vol. 12, No. 2 (1983), p. 92.
42. *Ibid.*
43. M.T. El-Ashry, *et al.*, "Salinity Pollution from Irrigated Agriculture," *Journal of Soil and Water Conservation*, Vol. 40, No. 1 (1985), p. 50.
44. *Op. cit.* 37, pp. 17–18.
45. *Op. cit.* 37, p. 27.
46. *Op. cit.* 13, p. 11.
47. *Op. cit.* 37, pp. 17–20.
48. "Saudis Convert Oil to Water and Food," *The Groundwater Newsletter* (February 28, 1985).
49. *Op. cit.* 13, pp. 14–16.
50. *Op. cit.* 13, pp. 12–13.
51. *Op. cit.* 37, pp. 23–24.

52. *Op. cit.* 37, p. 25.
53. Organisation for Economic Co-operation and Development (OECD), *OECD Environmental Data Compendium 1985* (OECD, Paris, 1985), p. 55.
54. *Ibid.*, pp. 56–59.
55. *Ibid.*, p. 53.
56. U.S. Environmental Protection Agency (EPA), *National Water Quality Inventory, 1984 Report to Congress,* EPA-440/4-85-029 (EPA, Washington, D.C., 1985), p. 10.
57. Association of State and Interstate Water Pollution Control Administrators (ASIWPCA), *America's Clean Water: The States' Evaluation of Progress 1972–1982* (ASIWPCA, Washington D.C., 1984), p. 2.
58. *Op. cit.* 20, pp. 19–20.
59. T. Gustafson, "Transforming Soviet Agriculture: Brezhnev's Gamble on Land Improvement," *Public Policy* (Summer 1977).
60. Don Hinrichsen, "Poland: Coming to Grips with Pollution," *AMBIO*, Vol. 10, No. 1 (1981), p. 40.
61. E. Pudlis, "Poland Launches Major Program to Restore and Regulate Country's Largest River System," *AMBIO*, Vol. 10, No. 1 (1981), pp. 41–42.
62. *Ibid.*, p. 42.
63. G. Kovacs, "Water Quality Control," *AMBIO*, Vol. 13, No. 2 (1984), pp. 101–102.
64. *Ibid.*, pp. 102–103.
65. V. Smil, *The Bad Earth: Environmental Degradation in China* (M.E. Sharpe, Inc., New York, 1984), pp. 100–101.
66. V. Smil, "Ecological Mismanagement in China," *Bulletin of the Atomic Scientists*, Vol. 38, No. 8 (1982), p. 22.
67. *Op. cit.* 65, p. 95.
68. *Op. cit.* 65.
69. N.D. Jayal, "Destruction of Water Resources—The Most Critical Ecological Crisis of East Asia," presented at the 16th Technical Meeting, International Union for Conservation of Nature and Natural Resources, Madrid, November 1984, p. 1.
70. *Ibid.*, p. 5.
71. *Op. cit.* 69, p. 96.
72. National Environmental Protection Council, *Report on the State of the Philippine Environment 1982* (Ministry of Human Settlements, Manila, 1982), pp. 34–35.
73. *Op. cit.* 1, p. 162.
74. *Op. cit.* 1, p. 175.
75. *Op. cit.* 16. p. 221.
76. *Renewable Resource Trends in East Africa* (Program for International Development, Clark University, Worcester, Massachusetts, 1984), pp. 79–80.
77. *Ibid.*
78. U.N. Economic Commission for Latin America (ECLA), *The Water Resources of Latin America and Their Utilization,* E/CEPAL/SES.20/G.6 (ECLA, Lima, 1984), p. 44.
79. M.J. Dourojeanni, *Renewable Natural Resources of Latin America and the Caribbean: Situation and Trends* (World Wildlife Fund-U.S., Washington, D.C., 1982), p. 250.
80. *Ibid.*, p. 251.
81. R. Reid, "Environment and Public Health in the Caribbean," *AMBIO*, Vol. 10, No. 6 (1981), p. 315.

82. *Ibid.*, p. 317.
83. Lawrence Mosher, "At Sea in the Caribbean," in *Bordering on Trouble: Resources and Politics in Latin America,* J.W. Brown and A. Macguire, eds. (Adler & Adler, Bethesda, Maryland, 1986), pp. 233–267.
84. *Op. cit.* 22, p. 40.
85. T. Moore, "Groundwater: Examining a Resource at Risk," *EPRI Journal* (October 1985), p. 7.
86. L. Schroeder, "Out of Sight, Out of Mind: Understanding Groundwater," *The Journal of Freshwater*, Vol. 9 (1985), p. 4.
87. *Op. cit.* 34, p. 51.
88. U.S. Geological Survey, *National Water Survey 1984* (U.S. Government Printing Office, Washington, D.C., 1985).
89. *Op. cit.* 85, p. 10.
90. U.N. Economic Commission for Europe (ECE), *Long-Term Perspectives for Water Use and Supply in the ECE Region* (ECE, New York, 1981), p. 9.
91. *Ibid.*
92. U.N. Economic Commission for Europe (ECE), *Policies and Strategies for Rational Use of Water in the ECE Region* (ECE, New York, 1982), p. 2.
93. *Op. cit.* 78, p. 7.
94. *Op. cit.* 78, p. 9.
95. *Op. cit.* 13, p. 11.
96. United Nations Educational, Scientific and Cultural Organization (UNESCO), *World Water Balance and Water Resources* (UNESCO, Paris, 1978), p. 2.
97. R. Dijon, "International Cooperation and Coordination of Groundwater Development in Rural Water Supply," presented at the Workshop on Groundwater in Rural Water Supply, Paris, 1984, p. 28.
98. *Op. cit.* 13, p. 24.
99. U.N. Department of Technical Cooperation for Development, *Groundwater in Continental Asia,* Natural Resources/Water Series No. 15 (U.N., New York, 1985), pp. 303–306.
100. J. Lehr, "Recharge, a Solution to Many U.S. Water Supply Problems," *Groundwater*, Vol. 20, No. 3 (1982), pp. 262–266.
101. *Op. cit.* 85, p. 10.
102. Lawrence Mosher, "The Revisionist: William D. Ruckelshaus," *The Amicus Journal* (Spring 1984), pp. 33–34.
103. Veronica I. Pye, *et al., Groundwater Contamination in the United States* (University of Pennsylvania Press, Philadelphia, 1983), pp. 15–28.
104. G.N. Golubev, "Economic Activity, Water Resources, and the Environment: A Challenge for Hydrology," *Hydrological Sciences Journal*, Vol. 28, No. 1 (1984), p. 57.
105. *Op. cit.* 88, p. 3.
106. U.S. Environmental Protection Agency (EPA), *Remedies: An Update of Hazardous Waste Issues,* Issue No. 3, Biscayne Aquifer Project (EPA, Atlanta, 1984).
107. U.S. Environmental Protection Agency (EPA), *South Florida Drinking Water Investigation of Broward, Dade, and Palm Beach Counties* (EPA, Denver, 1984).
108. U.S. Environmental Protection Agency (EPA), *Underground Motor Fuel Storage Tanks: A National Survey* (EPA, Washington, D.C., 1986).

109. U.S. Environmental Protection Agency (EPA), *National Survey of Hazardous Waste, Generators, Treatment, Storage, and Disposal Facilities Regulated under RCRA in 1981* (EPA, Washington, D.C., April 20, 1984), p. 205.
110. Superfund, authorized by the Comprehensive Environmental Response, Compensation and Liability Act of 1980 (CERCLA), assesses an excise tax on the sale or use of petroleum and 42 chemicals used commercially to produce hazardous substances plus a tax on all industries with annual incomes exceeding $2 million. The fund is used to pay for liability, compensation, cleanup, and emergency response for hazardous substances released into the environment and the cleanup of inactive hazardous waste disposal sites. The program, administered by the U.S. Environmental Protection Agency, is authorized to spend $9 billion over the next five years.
111. "Ground Water Ills: Many Diagnoses, Few Remedies," *Science*, Vol. 232 (June 20, 1986), p. 1491.
112. F.T. Mayo, *et al.*, "Removal of Organic Contaminants from Groundwater: Status of EPA Drinking Water Research Program," presented at the National Water Supply Improvement Association's First Biennial Conference, Washington, D.C., June 8–12, 1986.
113. J.D. Birkett, "Alternative Water Resources in the Middle East," *U.S.-Arab Commerce* (November-December 1985), p. 14.
114. *Ibid.*
115. J.D. Birkett, Senior Research Associate, Arthur D. Little, Inc., Cambridge, Massachusetts, 1986 (personal communication).
116. K.M. Trompeter, "The Yuma Desalting Plant—A Status Report," presented at the National Water Supply Improvement Association's First Biennial Conference, Washington, D.C., June 8–12, 1986, p. 2.
117. *Ibid.*, p. 5.
118. J.D. Birkett, "Economic Factors in Desalination" (The World Bank, unpublished, Washington, D.C., 1986).
119. *Op. cit.* 113, p. 16.
120. *Op. cit.* 118.
121. International Joint Commission (IJC), *Focus*, Vol. 11, No. 2 (IJC, Ontario, Canada, 1986), pp. 10–11.
122. Lawrence Mosher, *Water Information News Service* (February 15, 1985, Washington, D.C.), p. 4.
123. Freshwater Foundation, *Water Values and Markets: Emerging Management Tools* (Freshwater Foundation, Navarre, Minnesota, 1986), p. 8.
124. Institute of Government Studies, *Economic Development and Environmental Quality in California's Water System,* Zack Willey, ed. (University of California, Berkeley, 1986).
125. *Op. cit.* 6, p. 264.
126. *Op. cit.* 6, p. 269.
127. *Op. cit.* 123, p. 52.
128. *Op. cit.* 123, p. 11.
129. *Op. cit.* 123, p. 18.
130. *Op. cit.* 123, p. 37.
131. Lawrence Mosher, *The Water Reporter,* Vol. 10, No. 22 (Washington, D.C., 1986), p. 162.

9. Oceans and Coasts

The United Nations Environment Programme (UNEP) proclaimed that the world's oceans were in relatively good health in 1982, but it still raised some warning flags. Although the oceans' capacity to absorb humanity's castoffs seems limitless—more than two thirds of the earth's surface is salt water—a number of coastal regions are suffering from serious pollution problems. Due in large measure to the tremendous amount of research that has taken place since the Stockholm Conference on the Human Environment 14 years ago, scientists know much more about the environmental effects of a whole range of pollutants on marine life. Many coastal states also have a better idea of where their own pollution "hot spots" are and what measures they can take to reduce the risks to marine life and human health.

The world community, however, still has a considerable burden to bear in reducing marine pollution. Oil pollution of the world's seas seems to be on the increase, particularly along tanker routes, despite concerted control efforts. Persistent toxic substances, like PCBs and DDT—although banned throughout much of the industrialized North by the late 1970s—continue to show up in fish, shellfish, and marine mammals in measurable quantities. Further, a new generation of poisons, like the organohalogens, pose daunting challenges for marine scientists, resource managers, and decisionmakers.

There are more disturbing trends. Whereas the oceans continue to yield up their bounties for human consumption—total fish catches are still on the increase, although per capita consumption is decreasing—estuaries and other coastal wetlands, which provide nurseries for roughly two thirds of all fish caught, are under increasing development pressures throughout much of the world. And, of course, coastal waters are the ocean areas most affected by land-based sources of pollution.

With the declaration of 200-mile Exclusive Economic Zones (EEZs) by virtually all coastal countries, the "high seas" have been reduced by around 30 percent (see *World Resources 1986*, pp. 143–145). Coastal developing countries, which now control some of the richest fishing grounds, are embroiled in disputes between artisanal (traditional) fishermen and their more mechanized counterparts. Meanwhile, national fleets are often outcompeted for fish, even within their own EEZs, by more efficient international fleets. Resource conflicts, in turn, put increasing pressures on existing stocks of economically valuable fish and shellfish.

One promising development is the increase in the amount of both freshwater and marine organisms cultivated and farmed for the table. Aquaculture is becoming a multimillion-dollar industry, accounting for nearly 11 percent of the total take of fish, shellfish, and plants (principally kelp and seaweed) in 1984. If this momentum can be maintained, cultured species may provide a margin of safety, making up the shortfall in captured fisheries that is being predicted for the turn of the century.

Since 1970, international conventions and agreements—like those inaugurated in the Baltic and Mediterranean Seas—have been established to control or limit the amount of pollution, regulate shipping, provide for a sustainable harvest of marine life, and generally husband marine resources. Such arrangements can provide the best means of protecting the oceans, if they are given regulatory teeth and effective enforcement.

CONDITIONS AND TRENDS

FOCUS ON: MARINE POLLUTION

Like the atmosphere, oceans mix and transport pollutants over great distances. This point was recently underscored by the detection of cesium-137 in the Arctic Ocean and of lead in open-ocean surface layers (1). The patterns of ocean pollution, however, are not easy to study, let alone model or map.

The seas are on the receiving end of billions of tons of society's castoffs: pollutants mainly from the discharge of municipal sewage and industrial waste from point sources and runoff from pesticides and fertilizers from nonpoint sources; pollutants from shipping and offshore drilling operations (mainly oil); toxic or hazardous waste dumped at sea, including radioactive waste; and diverse atmospheric and terrestrial inputs from both anthropogenic and natural sources. Although a sizable portion of the total pollution load reaching the seas is from natural sources—for example, the high mercury content of the western Mediterranean is thought to be due, in part, to natural weathering processes acting on local rocks and soils—human activities have had serious and perhaps long-term effects on vulnerable marine ecosystems in certain regions.

So far little is known about the amounts of pollutants in the open ocean or their effects on marine organisms. Knowledge of marine pollution and its effects comes mainly from laboratory studies or site-specific work carried out in nearshore waters. Of necessity, pollution loads are based on estimates of discharges from known and quantifiable sources. But because many sources of pollution are neither known nor quantifiable, total estimates of pollutants entering the marine environment tend to be rather crude. Even for seas bordering on countries with highly developed statistical reporting systems, the data are relatively poor; for seas situated largely in the developing world, pollution data are practically nonexistent, with the exception of a few regions including China, India, East Africa, and parts of the Caribbean.

Despite the fact that the United Nations Environment Programme (UNEP) pronounced the "water planet" to be in relatively good health in 1982 (2), there is concern that the world's oceans continue to be used, indiscriminately, as waste bins. And since the worst effects of pollution are concentrated along coastlines—where a substantial portion of the global population resides—monitoring the health of coastal ecosystems is an ongoing endeavor throughout much of the developed world, particularly within the nations of the Organisation for Economic Co-operation and Development (OECD).

Though the overall picture of ocean pollution is sketchy, it appears that oil pollution is on the increase, with the worst affected areas in the Caribbean, Mediterra-

nean, and Red Seas, the west coast of Africa, the Arabian Gulf, much of the coastline of the Indian Ocean, and a substantial portion of the "Asian Mediterranean," which stretches from the East Asian seas surrounding Indonesia north into the South China Sea and east to the Philippines. Levels of DDT and PCBs, on the other hand, appear to be decreasing, at least for some OECD countries. This improvement is offset, however, by a general increase in toxic pollutants, especially heavy metals, in the sediments and biomass of certain heavily polluted regional seas (e.g., the Baltic, North, and Mediterranean Seas).

Land-Based Sources of Pollution

Land-based pollutants often have severe effects on coastal marine resources. Roughly 41,000 cubic kilometers of freshwater flow from rivers and streams into the oceans each year, carrying with them some 20 billion metric tons of suspended matter and dissolved salts, including less well-determined amounts of metal and organic contaminants (3). Even at low levels, these pollutants are often toxic to the larval stages of fish, crustaceans, and mollusks found in salt marsh nurseries. In addition to being damaged by pollution, salt marshes are directly destroyed by draining and filling to permit expansion of agricultural and industrial activities and construction of subdivisions and resorts. The increased amount of suspended sediments in nearshore waters caused by harbor dredging and construction can kill valuable seagrass beds and smother coral reefs. Further, dredge spoils from polluted harbors often contain high levels of heavy metals and other toxic substances that have settled out of the water. When dumped near coasts, dredge spoils can release these toxic contaminants, causing the formation of "dead sea" areas. In addition, the discharge of municipal sewage along with industrial wastes can result in serious hazards to marine life as well as to human populations.

Municipal Effluents

Municipal effluents are one of the principal sources of chronic pollution of the marine environment, and there is evidence that the discharge of these pollutants is increasing, particularly in the Third World. But even in relatively developed regions, sewage and industrial effluents are often pumped into the ocean untreated. The amount of organic matter discharged into the Mediterranean every year has a biological oxygen demand (BOD) of roughly 3.3 million metric tons (4). (BOD is a water quality measure that indicates the amount of oxygen consumed by bacteria in the process of breaking down organic matter. Thus bacteria used 3.3 million metric tons of oxygen to break down the amount of organic matter discharged into the Mediterranean.) Only an estimated 30 percent of the discharge is treated in some way before being pumped into coastal waters (5).

A large proportion of sewage is organic matter and nutrients, in addition to numerous microorganisms (bacteria and viruses) and parasitic worms. Large amounts of untreated sewage in coastal waters greatly increase the nutrient content of the water, overstimulating plant growth and creating algal blooms that, in turn, deplete the water of oxygen, especially when the plants begin to decay. This process is called "eutrophication." In relatively enclosed waters where water renewal is slow (e.g., lagoons, mangrove swamps, creeks, bays, estuaries), the loss of oxygen can impoverish the marine environment. Sewage from urban and industrial areas can contain petroleum hydrocarbons and heavy metals plus a host of other chemicals.

In extreme cases, such as the central Baltic Sea, deposited organic material along with toxic substances can lead to anoxic conditions (total lack of oxygen) on the bottom and in the immediate overlying water layers. Then the bottom-dwelling organisms may be reduced to a few types of worms capable of tolerating such conditions (see "Regional Seas: The Baltic," below).

Near large urban centers where masses of raw sewage and other municipal effluents are dumped, local "hot spots" of pollution are created. For OECD countries, these areas include: Athens, Barcelona, Venice, Marseilles, New York, San Francisco, Sydney, and Tokyo (6). Despite some cleanup attempts, the harbors and nearshore waters of virtually every major port city in the Third World are polluted with untreated sewage and industrial discharges of some kind.

Municipal effluents generally have local effects on marine fauna and flora. Large amounts of untreated sewage and other urban wastes dumped into coastal estuaries and salt marshes can contaminate shellfish beds, particularly those of filter feeders like clams, mussels, and oysters. These shellfish concentrate bacteria and viruses, as well as toxic metals and organochlorines, from sewage while feeding. Human consumption of contaminated shellfish exposed to untreated sewage can lead to hepatitis and other viral diseases, respiratory infections, and, more commonly, gastroenteritis (7).

PCBs and DDT: Persistent Toxic Pollutants

The most toxic chemicals are often the least biodegradable. They consist mainly of persistent hydrocarbons and halogenated organic compounds like polychlorinated biphenyls (PCBs), DDT, chlorinated hydrocarbons, aldrin, and dieldrin, and heavy metals like mercury, cadmium, and lead. These compounds are discharged into the sea by industries or leached from farm fields along coasts or are drained into oceans from river basins like the Mississippi in North America and the Rhone and Rhine Rivers in Europe. (See Chapter 8, "Freshwater.")

Two chemicals in particular—PCBs and DDT, both organochlorines—are known to have serious and long-term effects on ocean biomass.

PCBs were used extensively in electrical transformers and condensers, among other applications, until the late 1970s, and, as a result of improper disposal, their residues are widespread in surface waters and in the bottom sediments of regional seas located in the industrial-ized regions of the world. (PCBs are still used extensively in the Third World.) Generally speaking, the highest levels of PCB residues in marine organisms occur near large urban, industrialized areas. In relatively unpolluted waters, PCB values of less than 0.1 micrograms per kilogram wet weight are observed. However, where there are large inputs of PCBs, residues well above 1 microgram per kilogram wet weight (about 1 part per billion, or ppb) have been found in fish, and levels as high as 300 milligrams per kilogram (300 parts per million, or ppm) have been found in extractable fat in fish (8). This figure is well above 5 ppm, the level considered dangerous for human consumption by the U.S. Food and Drug Administration (9).

Two aspects of PCB pollution are disturbing: PCBs tend to bioaccumulate in the food chain, and they are long lived. Monitoring studies carried out in North America and Europe suggest that, even in areas like Scandinavia—where PCBs are now banned—the rate of disappearance is extremely slow (10). One exception is the U.S. east coast, where scientists have observed a general decrease in PCB concentrations in mussels (11).

PCBs have a cumulative toxic effect: organisms exposed to PCB concentrations over a long period are more likely to die than are organisms exposed to the same concentrations for shorter periods. UNEP reports that the lethal dose (LD50) for different cohorts of rainbow trout vary from 38 micrograms per liter up to 326 micrograms per liter for a ten-day exposure, but when the exposure is extended to 20 days, the LD50 ranges from only 6.4 to 49 micrograms per liter (the LD50 is the lethal dose that kills half the test animals) (12). The longer marine organisms are exposed to PCBs, even in small quantities, the greater the risks.

Marine organisms, including fish, take up PCBs from water and food. Several effects have been observed in the laboratory. High concentrations of PCBs are fatal; lower levels retard growth, interfere with reproduction, and render the organism more susceptible to stress and disease. Low-level PCB contamination in the Baltic and North Seas has reportedly resulted in poor reproductive successes and even spontaneous abortions in harbor, gray, and ringed seals (13). PCBs are also found in Baltic herrings, in Antarctic penguins, and even in Pacific whales, evidence of their widespread presence in the marine environment.

DDT is one of the best known of the toxic synthetic organic chemicals. DDT and its main metabolites (DDD and DDE) are relatively stable under ambient conditions, are highly lipophilic (nonsoluble in water), and are resistant to breakdown. On a global scale, DDT has been the most extensively used pesticide; in 1974 world production reached roughly 60,000 metric tons (14). Like PCBs, residues of DDT are found in rain water in pristine environments, in Antarctic snow, and in soils and lakes far from where it is used.

Under laboratory conditions, the lethal concentration of DDT for zooplankton begins at 0.01 micrograms per liter of water; for fish (including fry) at 0.1 micrograms per

Oceans and Coasts

liter; and for phytoplankton, crustaceans, and mollusks at concentrations above 1 microgram per liter (15).

Residues of DDT in fish muscle from coastal areas range from 0.01 to 10 milligrams per kilogram wet weight (or 0.01–10 ppm), considerably higher than residues found in the same species of fish taken from the open ocean (16). Some coastal areas in the developing world regularly haul in fish with DDT levels above the safe limit, which, according to the U.S. Food and Drug Administration, should not exceed 5 milligrams per kilogram (5 ppm) (17). However, no global estimate of the extent and severity of DDT contamination of edible fish and shellfish is available.

The widespread use of both PCBs and DDT was curtailed by the late 1970s in most of the industrialized North. As a result, concentrations of both substances in estuaries and coastal waters along the North Atlantic and Pacific have shown a slow downward trend (with the exception of the California coast of the United States, where levels in mussels are still high, and throughout the Baltic Sea, where little if any reduction is evident). But throughout much of the developing world, particularly in Latin America, industrial and agricultural applications of these two organochlorines is increasing (18).

Plastics

The seas are becoming increasingly littered with persistent solids, especially plastics. In general, most plastics come to the marine environment from sea-based garbage disposal and dumping. Estimates of the oceans' total load of plastics have yet to be made, but it is known that approximately 6.4 million metric tons of shipboard litter are tossed into the world's seas every year from normal maritime operations and more than 5 million plastic containers are thrown overboard each day (19). According to the U.S. National Academy of Sciences, commercial fishermen dump more than 22,000 metric tons of plastic packaging into the sea and lose or discard about 136,000 metric tons of plastic nets, lines, and buoys every year (20) (21). Further, polyethylene and polypropylene packing pellets have been found in densities as high as 1,000—4,000 per square kilometer on the surface of the North Atlantic, South Atlantic, and Pacific Oceans (22).

Because plastic is not readily broken down by natural processes, it tends to accumulate in the oceans. There is mounting concern that plastic debris is becoming a menace to marine life and in some cases to marine transportation. Marine mammals and birds often ingest plastic, mistaking it for food, or they become tangled in plastic netting or other debris and die. In some areas, ships' propellers run afoul of plastic fishing lines and nets. A recent study of Laysan albatross chicks and wedge-tailed shearwaters on Midway Island in the Pacific found plastic debris in the digestive systems of 90 percent of the chicks observed (23). It is estimated that up to 1 million seabirds and approximately 100,000 cetaceans and seals die each year because of plastic pollution (24). With plastic production doubling every 12 years or so, the amount of litter in the oceans can be expected to increase.

Heavy Metals

Following a widely publicized incident in Minamata Bay, Japan, in the 1950s and 1960s, in which 1,385 villagers suffered mercury poisoning and 649 died from eating fish and shellfish contaminated by industrial discharges of mercury (25) (26), increased attention has been given to monitoring the concentrations of certain toxic metals in edible fish and shellfish. Today, scientists are concerned about a range of toxic metals and other chemical contaminants, but routine monitoring is usually carried out only for mercury, lead, copper, and cadmium. Generally, when mercury levels in edible fish exceed 1 milligram per kilogram (1 ppm) in Europe and North America, a ban on human consumption is imposed. Mercury levels have frequently exceeded 1 ppm in North Sea herring over the past several decades, prompting Danish and British authorities to impose bans from time to time.

Little is known about the concentrations of lead in fish, but average levels in the range of 0.1–0.4 milligrams per kilogram (0.1–0.4 ppm) have been reported (27). In 1972 a joint United Nations Food and Agriculture Organization/World Health Organization expert committee made a provisional recommendation that adults ingest no more than 3 milligrams (3 ppm) of lead per week (28). However, no national government has set health standards for lead in fish.

Mining operations are another source of toxic metal contamination of the marine environment. The Fal Estuary in England, for example, has long been the repository of large amounts of copper and zinc from nearby mine tailings; elevated levels of copper have turned up in the Rio Tinto Estuary in Spain (as high as 165 milligrams per kilogram wet weight in oysters, or 165 ppm); and mercury concentrations of up to 47 ppm have been noted in the sediments along the southern coast of Tuscany, Italy, and in the northern part of the Gulf of Trieste (29).

In the United States, high levels of heavy metals have been recorded in New York and New Haven harbors (30). Along the French Mediterranean coast, mercury concentrations as high as 300 micrograms per kilogram (300 ppb) and cadmium levels reaching upwards of 1,000 micrograms per kilogram (1,000 ppb, or 1 ppm) have been found in mussels (31).

Oil Pollution of the World's Oceans

UNEP reports that every year somewhere between 2 and 20 million metric tons of oil are discharged into the world's oceans from both land- and sea-based operations (32). OECD, on the other hand, estimates the total at roughly 3.5 million metric tons a year from all sources (33). Scientific consensus narrows the figure to between 3 and 6 million metric tons per year (34). Even with the lower OECD estimate, at least 1 metric ton is spilled or dumped for every 1,000 metric tons extracted (35).

According to OECD, oil pollution of the seas is nearly evenly divided between land- and sea-based sources. (See Table 9.1.) Many experts disagree, however, claiming that

Table 9.1 Sources of Oil Pollution of the Sea

Source	Million Metric Tons per Year
Sea-based (52%)	
Maritime transport	1.49
Nonaccidental	1.08
Accidental	0.41
Production platforms	0.05
Natural seeps, erosion	0.30
Land-based (48%)	
Municipal, industrial wastes, runoff	1.40
Atmospheric	0.30
Total	**3.54**

Source: J. MacNeil, "Sources of Oil Pollution of the Sea: Problems and Solutions," *AMBIO*, Vol. 13, No. 4 (1984), p. 230; and J.M. Baker, "Impact of Oil Pollution on Living Resources" *The Environmentalist* Supplement 4 (International Union for Conservation of Nature and Natural Resources, Geneva, 1983), p. 6.

up to 90 percent of the oil may come from land-based sources (36).

The main source of marine-based oil pollution is shipping, as shown in Table 9.1. Of the roughly 1.5 million metric tons of oil discharged into the sea from shipping operations every year, the bulk of it (1.1 million metric tons) is not accidental; only about 400,000 metric tons results from tanker accidents (37). The major sources of oil pollution are virtually unnoticed by the public; it is the tanker accidents and platform spills that make the headlines and focus regulatory attention on oil pollution. (See *World Resources 1986*, p. 315.)

As the amount of oil entering the marine environment increases, so too does the price tag. The total cost of damages from accidental spills and deliberate discharges from tankers worldwide is around $500 million a year (38). This figure includes damages paid by shipping companies as well as quantifiable losses of nearshore fisheries, particularly maricultured species like clams, oysters, and kelp.

MAPMOPP Surveys Ocean Pollution

With the blessings of the U.N. General Assembly, the International Oceanographic Commission and the United Nations World Meteorological Organization joined forces to form the Integrated Global Ocean Station System, which put together the Marine Pollution Monitoring Pilot Project (MAPMOPP). That comprehensive global survey of the world's oceans, carried out from 1975 to 1978, included nearly 100,000 visual observations of the sea surface to detect floating pollutants (39).

The results confirmed the fact that surface contamination in the form of slicks and floating tar was most prevalent along and near major tanker routes (see Figure 9.1) and that concentrations of dissolved/dispersed petroleum residues in the microgram-per-liter range were present almost everywhere at a depth of one meter in the water column (40).

As a result of the prodigious amount of data generated by MAPMOPP, it is now possible to map oil pollution of the world's oceans and seas in a general way. Surprisingly, the Baltic and North Seas—both highly polluted regions—do not have as much chronic oil pollution as do the Mediterranean and Red Seas, where oil slicks were

noted in more than 10 percent of the observations made during the three-year survey. Taken as an aggregate, virtually the entire surface of both seas had visible oil slicks at some point during the study.

Other areas with a high percentage of surface slicks include: a large part of the Caribbean, most of the coast of Brazil, almost the entire west coast of Africa, the east coast of Africa from Tanzania north through the Arabian Gulf to the Indian subcontinent, and a substantial section of the "Asian Mediterranean" from Malaysia through the Indonesian archipelago to the South China Sea and west to the Philippines. In many cases, oil pollution coincided with the major tanker lanes running from the Arabian Gulf to Europe and Japan. (See Figure 9.1.)

Two interesting results emerge from the MAPMOPP surveys when examining total oil pollution, rather than just surface oil slicks. First, the North Atlantic is not nearly so polluted with oil as was previously believed (41). MAPMOPP researchers calculated the concentration of tar in the North Atlantic at 4.4 milligrams per square meter, mostly along the tanker lanes. Using these data, they estimated the "standing crop" of particulate oil residues on the surface of the North Atlantic at 15,000–20,000 metric tons. A second discovery was the fact that the Indian Ocean is perhaps the most oil-fouled body of salt water in the world. For the Indian Ocean as a whole, the MAPMOPP data contained few values below 10 micrograms per liter, and some values exceeded 300 micrograms per liter (42). In the southwestern part of the Indian Ocean, a section of sea stretching along the East African coast from Somalia to South Africa is known to be badly polluted with oil slicks and petroleum residues. In one sense, this is the fast lane of the world's oil highway. On any given day, an estimated 224 tankers pass through these waters, carrying 475 million metric tons of oil a year from the Middle East to Europe and North and South America. The amount of oil discharged by tankers and other ships sailing through the region, just from normal operations, has been estimated at 33,440 metric tons a year, excluding oil spills from tanker accidents and other sources (43).

Environmental Effects

There is no doubt that marine organisms absorb oil or that it can be lethal, but there is little convincing evidence for its bioaccumulation. Toxicity is largely associated with the aromatic hydrocarbon fraction of oil, although for some organisms the nonhydrocarbon components are most toxic.

Oil slicks at sea can kill or adversely affect zooplankton, including planktonic species of copepods, as well as the planktonic eggs and larvae of fish and benthic invertebrates (44). Shellfish are particularly susceptible to oil pollution because they spend much of their life cycles in nearshore waters and estuaries where spilled oil often accumulates, and they cannot digest or degrade petrochemical hydrocarbons. When a Swedish coastal tanker sank 11 nautical miles off the Baltic island of Oland, spilling a modest 300 metric tons of oil, some 60

Figure 9.1 **Location of Visible Oil Slicks, Early 1980s**

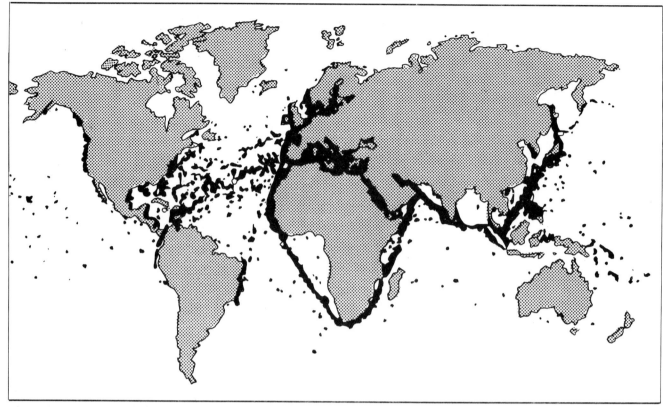

Source: Organisation for Economic Co-operation and Development (OECD), *The State of the Environment 1985* (OECD, Paris, 1985), p. 84.

tons of coastal marine organisms, mostly mollusks and crustaceans, were killed immediately (45).

Likewise, oil—even in small doses—can be fatal to marine mammals and seabirds. In February 1969, when a tanker discharged 100–200 metric tons of bunker oil into the Dutch Wadden Sea, 40,000 seabirds were killed, mostly eider ducks and common scoters (46).

It is known that water-soluble aromatic hydrocarbons can be lethal to adult animals in relatively low concentrations (1–100 parts of oil per million parts of water) as well as to the more sensitive larval stages at even lower concentrations (0.1–1 ppm) (47). Apparently crustaceans and certain bottom-dwelling organisms, especially the burrowers, are the most sensitive to oil pollution, usually succumbing to concentrations as low as 1–10 ppm. Fish and bivalves are moderately sensitive, dying at levels of 10–100 ppm, although their larval and juvenile forms can succumb to concentrations as low as 0.1–1 ppm (48). Chronic oil pollution is a menace to most marine life—it can interfere with reproduction and, in severe cases, wipe out entire larval and juvenile classes of fish and shellfish.

Dumping and Incineration of Wastes at Sea

Several developed countries—Canada, the United States, New Zealand, Belgium, Denmark, France, the Federal Republic of Germany, the Netherlands, and the United

Kingdom—routinely dump thousands of tons of wastes at sea every year. (See Figure 9.2.) Although there is no international agreement on dumping nontoxic wastes, the London Dumping Convention of 1972 (now ratified by 58 countries) was formed to regulate the dumping of hazardous and toxic wastes at sea.

Four main types of waste are currently dumped at sea: dredge spoils, industrial waste, sludge from sewage treatment plants, and radioactive waste. All of them can contain hazardous substances.

Dumping of Dredge Spoils

Dredge spoils are usually dumped at sea fairly near the coast. This one source accounts for the lion's share of waste dumped at sea. (See Figure 9.2.) In 1979, for example, the United States dumped 67.4 million metric tons of dredge spoils into the sea, as opposed to 8.7 million metric tons of other wastes (49). The reason for this massive amount of dredging and dumping is that harbors and channels must be kept clear for ocean-going traffic. The problem is that dredge spoils often contain high levels of toxic contaminants, particularly PCBs, DDT, hydrocarbons, and heavy metals that have settled out of the water. In 1979, when U.S. officials discovered high concentrations of PCBs in dredge spoils from New York harbor, they suspended dumping permits until the disposal problem could be solved (50). However, no long-term option has been identified, and in 1985, authorities simply prohibited the dumping of dredge spoils within 12 nautical miles of the coast (51). A similar problem paralyzed Hamburg, West Germany, when high levels of dioxin were discovered in a waste dump situated near the harbor. Researchers suspected that dioxin had been carried into the harbor by the Elbe River, which flows through heavily industrialized areas (52).

Liquid Wastes and Industrial Sludge

There is some evidence that the discharge of industrial waste into the ocean is growing, particularly as managers of land-based disposal sites become increasingly reluctant to be responsible for treating and disposing of highly toxic industrial waste products (53). Figure 9.2 indicates that the United States, France, the Federal Republic of Germany, Ireland, and the United Kingdom dump substantial quantities of industrial waste at sea.

Industrial waste includes chemical residues covering a wide range of organic and inorganic substances, residues from milk processing plants, sludge and debris from mining operations, waste from plants producing phosphogypsum, and in some cases residues from titanium dioxide production (54).

Figure 9.2 Industrial Waste, Sewage Sludge, and Dredge Spoils Dumped at Sea, 1981

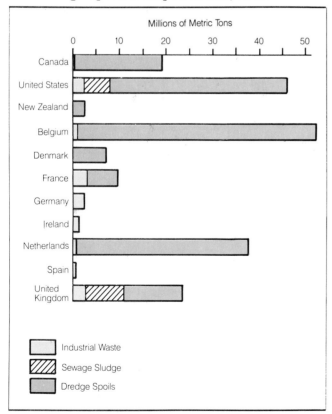

Source: Organisation for Economic Co-operation and Development (OECD), *The State of the Environment 1985* (OECD, Paris, 1985), p. 79

This kind of dumping can severely affect the marine environment, but damage is usually confined to particular areas. In the New York and New Jersey bights, for example, mutant and crippled fish are common. Fishermen routinely report catching fish lacking fins and tails (55).

Sewage Sludge

Only two countries currently dump significant quantities of sewage sludge at sea, the United States and the United Kingdom. (See Figure 9.2.) Sludge from urban industrial areas often contains heavy metals like mercury, cadmium, and lead as well as an abundance of organic and inorganic matter. The environmental effects of the sludge are well known; in enclosed areas it generally results in eutrophication of the waters used as a dump site—creating a dead sea area where virtually no marine life can survive (e.g., parts of the New Jersey bight).

Incineration of Toxic Waste at Sea

As costs increase for proper land-based disposal of toxic waste, incinerating toxic chemicals at sea is being considered as an alternative for industries and municipalities. Sea-based incinerators are used to dispose of organohalogen compounds and other chemicals that can be destroyed by high temperature combustion.

At present, only the Netherlands, France, the Federal Republic of Germany, and the United Kingdom regularly incinerate hazardous chemical wastes at sea; nearly all of it is handled by two incineration vessels operating in the North Sea. Incineration began in 1969 and the amount of waste now disposed of in this manner totals around 90,000–100,000 metric tons a year (56).

So far, little information is available on the environmental effects of this type of disposal. However, mounting concern has led the signatory nations to the Oslo Convention (which regulates dumping in the North Sea) to consider a total ban on incinerating toxic chemicals in the North Sea. (For more information on incinerating highly toxic wastes at sea, see Chapter 13, "Controlling Hazardous Wastes: The Unmet Challenge.")

Radioactive Waste

During the past two decades, four European countries—the United Kingdom, Belgium, the Netherlands, and Switzerland—have dumped low-level radioactive waste in an area of the Atlantic Ocean off the coast of Spain at a depth of 4,000 meters (57). The amount dumped between 1967 and 1982 remained roughly the same every year, but the radioactivity level of the waste increased as the waste at the site accumulated. The radioactivity levels for the alpha and beta-gamma emitters (58)—which totaled, respectively, 250 curies and 7,600 curies in 1967—reached 1,428 curies and 49,539 curies (59), respectively, by 1982 (60). The more dangerous types of radiation (beta and gamma) comprise the bulk of the radioactive emissions at this site.

As Figure 9.3 illustrates, the accumulated amount of radioactive waste dumped in the ocean by all OECD

Figure 9.3 Accumulation of Nuclear Waste Dumped at Sea, 1967–83

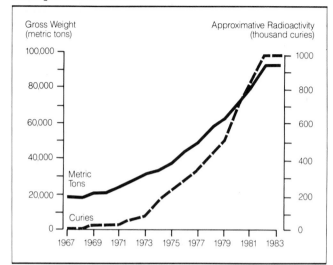

Note: Includes all types of radiation.
Source: Organisation for Economic Co-operation and Development (OECD), *The State of the Environment 1985* (OECD, Paris, 1985), p. 79.

countries grew from about 20,000 metric tons in 1967 to more than 90,000 metric tons in 1983, and the accumulated radioactivity now amounts to more than 1 million curies.

Dumping radioactive waste in the sea is an emotional issue in the OECD countries. Because of public concern, signatories to the London Dumping Convention temporarily halted ocean disposal of low-level radioactive wastes in 1983, pending scientific review of the risks. The moratorium will probably remain in effect until completion of important risk-related environmental studies. (For further information, see *World Resources 1986*, pp. 152–153.)

COASTAL WETLANDS AND ESTUARIES

Estuarine wetlands, which represent the ecological coupling of land and sea water, are often associated with deltas, marshes, and mangrove forests. The dominant feature of estuarine ecosystems is their salinity, which is governed by the tides and the amount of freshwater runoff from the land. The mixing of fresh and salt water, coupled with the type of substrate or bottom composition (i.e., mud, peat, or sand), influences the various types of estuarine wetland communities.

Freshwater, brackish water, and saline wetlands occupy an estimated 6 percent of the world's land surface from the tundra to the tropics (61). However, no reliable estimates of the total extent of coastal wetlands and estuaries are available on a global basis (62). (For more information on freshwater wetlands, see Chapter 6, "Wildlife and Habitat" and Chapter 18, "Land Use and Cover," Table 18.2.)

Coastal wetlands are among the most productive ecosystems on earth. (See Box 9.1.) Mangrove forests, salt marshes, and estuaries produce a vast amount of organic material that equals or exceeds the productivity of most terrestrial communities of comparable size, including cultivated land. (See Table 9.2.) The fecundity of tidal marshes is a result of the interface between land and sea. As dissolved organic and inorganic nutrients and detrital material enter the marsh estuary from inflowing rivers and streams, they are met by a wedge of salt water pushed along the bottom by the incoming tide. The mixing of these nutrient-rich waters is the basis for a diverse food chain capable of supporting a host of nearshore marine life, including the larval and juvenile stages of commercially important fish and shellfish.

Swamplands include not only the cypress swamps of the southern United States, the Melaleuca swamps of Papua New Guinea, and the mangrove forests of the tropics but also the reed swamps of North and South America, Europe, and Australia and the papyrus swamps characteristic of many African wetlands (63). Coastal swamps dominate more than 25 percent of Indonesia: 30 percent of Sumatra is coastal swampland, and Kalimantan has an estimated 20 million hectares of swamp, more than half of it peat soils (64).

Mangrove swamplands are particularly important because they are the primary source of inorganic and organic compounds for tropical estuarine fisheries and they support commercially valuable species of nearshore fin- and shellfish as well. These swamplands dominate at least 75 percent of low-lying tropical coastlines with freshwater drainage. An estimated 24 million hectares of mangrove forests cover intertidal, lagoonal, and riverine flatlands globally, reaching their greatest extent along the coasts of South and Southeast Asia, Africa, and South America (65). Approximately 20 percent of the world's total mangrove area borders the Sunda Shelf region enclosed by Vietnam, Thailand, Malaysia, Sumatra, Java, and Borneo (66). Indonesia alone has an estimated 2.2

Table 9.2 Comparative Productivity of Selected Ocean, Coastal, and Terrestrial Ecosystems
(grams of carbon per square meter per year)

Ecotype	Average Gross Primary Production	Average Net Primary Production
Mangrove Forest[a]	2,300-5,110	X
Marine Grass Beds	4,650	2,500
Coral Reef	4,200	2,500
Tropical Rain Forest	X	2,500
Salt marsh (U.S.)	X	2,000
Estuaries	X	1,500
Open Ocean	X	125
Upwelling Zones (e.g., Peruvian Current)	3,650	X
Sugar Cane Fields	3,450	X
Cultivated Land	X	650
Field Grass, Minnesota	500	X

X = not available.
Note:
a. Receives wet season terrestrial nutrient runoff.
Sources:
1. J.B. Lewis, "Processes of Organic Production on Coral Reefs," *Biological Review*, Vol. 52 (1977), pp. 305–347.
2. A.E. Lugo and S.C. Snedaker, "The Ecology of Mangroves," *Annual Review of Ecological Systems*, Vol. 5 (1974), pp. 39–64.
3. S.C. Snedaker and M.S. Brown, *Water Quality and Mangrove Ecosystem Dynamics* (U.S. Environmental Protection Agency, Environmental Research Laboratory, Gulf Breeze, Florida, 1981).
4. R.H. Whittaker and G.E. Likens, eds., "The Primary Production of the Biosphere," *Human Ecology*, Vol. 1, No. 4 (1973), pp. 299–369.

Box 9.1 Turning the Tide in the Chesapeake Bay

The Chesapeake Bay on the U.S. east coast, one of the richest estuaries in the world, has long been a marvel of productivity. The 314-kilometer-long estuary is fed by 150 rivers, creeks, and streams that drain a vast watershed of 165,760 square kilometers [1]. It harbors about 200 species of fish and shellfish and 2,700 species of other aquatic animals and plants [2]. It is edged by 201,540 hectares of wetlands [3] that attract tens of thousands of waterfowl during fall migrations.

The Chesapeake supports a nationally important commercial fishery. It is the largest blue crab producer in the world and the largest single source of oysters in the United States [4]. The bay is important for recreation (especially boating and sport fishing), industry, and shipping for the 14 million people who live nearby. It has two major ports, Baltimore on the north and Norfolk/Portsmouth on the south. Other cities in its drainage basin include Washington D.C., Annapolis, Maryland, and Richmond, Virginia.

As one might expect, increasing development and population pressures have taken a severe toll. In the late 1970s, watermen noticed declines in the catches of rockfish (striped bass) and oysters. Rockfish commercial catches fell from 2,608 metric tons in 1970 to 272 metric tons in 1983. Oyster harvests fluctuated, but they dropped by 50 percent in the past 20 years [5].

In 1983, a major study by the U.S. Environmental Protection Agency (EPA)—seven years in the making, at a cost of $27 million—concluded that the bay was in a decline caused by pollution and that immediate action should be taken to reverse the trend. The study found an overabundance of both nutrients (mainly nitrogen and phosphorus) and toxic chemicals. Most of the nitrogen came from runoff from farms and urban and suburban development; most of the phosphorus came from municipal effluents (sewage) and industrial wastes [6]. High concentrations of toxic organic compounds and heavy metals were found in the sediments near industrial areas, mainly along the bay's major rivers. Extensive beds of submerged aquatic vegetation that once served as food for waterfowl and nursery grounds for fish and shellfish larvae had virtually disappeared in many areas due to pollution and sedimentation.

The study recommended that the federal government and the states in the Chesapeake watershed form a basin-wide plan to control the flow of pollutants into the bay. In December 1983—just three months after the study was published—the governors of Virginia, Maryland, and Pennsylvania, the mayor of the District of Columbia, the EPA administrator, and the Chesapeake Bay Commission sponsored a two-day conference attended by 700 people to discuss the study. By the end of the meetings, the sponsors had signed an agreement to create a Chesapeake Executive Council of high-ranking officials to "assess and oversee the implementation of coordinated plans to improve and protect the water quality and living resources of the Chesapeake Bay"[7].

The various government units displayed an extraordinary degree of cooperation in establishing and funding cleanup programs. One of the states involved—Pennsylvania—does not even border on the bay, but it earmarked $2 million to control erosion of soil carrying pesticide and fertilizer residues from its rolling farmlands down the Susquehanna River and into the bay [8]. Over the next three years, numerous committees were appointed, assessments made, and programs initiated. About $100 million was spent toward improving water quality in the bay [9].

Several programs—especially those aimed at controlling runoff or "nonpoint source pollution"—were truly innovative. The Chesapeake Bay Foundation, a nonprofit citizen's group with 40,000 members, set up a model farm on donated property to experiment with minimum tillage practices that reduce erosion. The experimental plots are worked by foundation staff and farmers who make themselves available to explain the techniques to other local farmers, government officials, and students [10]. To control runoff from rapidly expanding suburban development along the waterfront, Maryland boldly put strict controls on valuable waterfront property limiting the density of new development within 1,000 feet of the shoreline. About $7.5 million of the annual $10 million contributed by the federal government for a four-year period for bay cleanup was allocated to programs to control runoff [11].

Meanwhile, however, industries and municipal sewage plants continued to discharge thousands of tons of sewage and toxic wastes into the bay, often in violation of their discharge permits under the 14-year-old Clean Water Act. A *Washington Post* investigation of 124 of these "point sources" of pollution revealed that every one of them had exceeded its legal levels of discharge for one or more pollutants. During the study period—July 1983 through June 1985—Maryland and Virginia officials had rarely punished the violators [12].

More than 2,641 facilities hold permits to discharge into the bay or the tidal portion of its major tributaries [13]. The total discharge from Maryland and Virginia sources amounts to 15 trillion liters of wastewater per year—about one fifth the amount of water in the bay at any given time [14].

The permit program does check some major polluters. During 1985, for example, 13 facilities had such significant violations that they were dealt with by EPA rather than by the states, but by the end of the year all had "returned to compliance" [15].

Both EPA and citizen watchdog groups agree, however, that many of the permits allow the discharge of too much waste; some were based on historical discharge rates or were written before identification of toxic chemicals was required. Discharge of toxins by sewage treatment plants may be reduced by a new requirement that makes cities and towns responsible for ensuring that all hazardous waste is pretreated—either at the source or by the municipality—before it is discharged

from a municipal treatment plant. And some discharge permits are being rewritten. According to EPA Administrator Lee M. Thomas, tighter permit requirements should force Bethlehem Steel Corporation, one of the bay's biggest polluters, to reduce its discharge 95 percent by June 1987. He said the company has spent some $25 million in recent years to meet increasingly strict permit requirements [16].

After three years of effort, the states and the federal government have created an infrastructure for bay clean-up, but they have not yet effected any improvement in water quality. Nevertheless, people involved in bay cleanup remain optimistic. In the 1985 annual report, Chesapeake Bay Foundation Chairman Godfrey Rockefeller wrote: "On one hand we have a Bay with serious problems to be solved. On the other hand, we have an aroused citizenry that is determined to save the Bay. We are proud to be a major force in the process" [17].

References and Notes

1. U.S. Environmental Protection Agency (EPA), *Chesapeake Bay Program: Findings and Recommendations* (EPA, Washington, D.C., 1983), p. 5.
2. U.S. Environmental Protection Agency (EPA), Chesapeake Bay Program, *Chesapeake: An Environmental Fact Sheet* (EPA, Annapolis, Maryland, April 1985).
3. *Op. cit.* 1, p. 16.
4. Lee M. Thomas, "Can We Save the Chesapeake Bay?" *Sunday News Journal* (July 13, 1986, Wilmington, Delaware), p. H1.
5. Maryland Department of Natural Resources, Fisheries Division, *Chesapeake Bay Landings and Dockside Value 1962–1984* (Maryland Department of Natural Resources, Annapolis, Maryland, 1985).
6. *Op. cit.* 1, p. 29.
7. Chesapeake Executive Council, *First Annual Progress Report under the Chesapeake Bay Agreement* (Washington, D.C., 1985), p. 1
8. *Ibid.*, p. 8.
9. Rodney A. Coggin, Public Affairs Director, Chesapeake Bay Foundation, Annapolis, Maryland, 1986 (personal communication).
10. *Ibid.*
11. *Op. cit.* 4.
12. Victoria Churchville, "The Poisoning of the Chesapeake Bay," *The Washington Post* (June 1, 1986, Washington, D.C.), p. 1.
13. Joseph Galda, Chief Water Permits Branch, Water Management Division, U.S. Environmental Protection Agency, Region III, Baltimore, Maryland, 1986 (personal communication).
14. *Op. cit.* 14, p. 1.
15. *Op. cit.* 13.
16. *Op. cit.* 4.
17. Chesapeake Bay Foundation, 1985 Annual Report (Chesapeake Bay Foundation, Annapolis, Maryland, 1985), p. 2.

million hectares of mangroves. Other countries with vast mangrove areas include Brazil (2.5 million hectares), Australia (1.2 million hectares), and Nigeria (973,000 hectares) (67).

Peat bogs—including freshwater bogs—cover an estimated 500 million hectares worldwide, occurring in all continents from the high latitudes of the Northern Hemisphere to marsh and swamplands associated with tropical coastal floodplains. Although it is not possible to say what percentage of this immense figure is found along coasts, some 75 percent of all tropical peat soils border the western, southern, and eastern extremities of the South China Sea (68). Peat bogs are also typical of coastal areas in Western Europe, the Kamchatka Peninsula in the USSR, southern Chile, southwest New Zealand, and the Antarctic islands (69).

Delta floodplains are formed when large fingers of river sediment mix with sediments from the ocean. One of the greatest coastal deltas in the world is the area of the Sundarbans, bordering India and Bangladesh, which drains both the Ganges and Brahmaputra Rivers. Here more than 90,000 square kilometers of land are subjected to seasonal flooding. Other coastal deltas of significance include the Huanghe (Yellow River) of China, the Senegal River in West Africa, the 31,000-square-kilometer delta of the Irrawaddy River in Burma, the Nile delta, and the increasingly modified regime of the Mekong delta where an estimated 30 percent of its 74,000 square kilometers is no longer flooded because of channel construction (70).

Resource Value

Coastal wetlands are a sustainable source of staple food and nonfood plants that benefit human populations directly. In addition, they provide food chain support for estuarine and nearshore fisheries, grazing land for domestic animals, habitat for waterfowl and other wildlife, fuel from peat bogs, and flood control protection. They also act as natural filters for pollutants and they stabilize the shoreline.

Coastal marshes, floodplains, and estuaries provide highly productive spawning, nursery, and feeding areas for fish and shellfish. Globally, an estimated two thirds of all fish caught are hatched in tidal areas (71). In 1976, the yield of fish and shellfish dependent on wetlands was worth more than $700 million (72). Roughly two thirds of the major U.S. commercial fisheries—and 98 percent of all fish caught in the Gulf of Mexico—depend upon estuaries and salt marshes as nursery and spawning grounds (73). Further, an estimated 80 percent of the Indian fish catch from the lower delta region of the Ganges-Brahmaputra comes from the Sundarbans (74).

Nutrients and particulate organic matter originating in offshore waters concentrate in coastal wetlands and estuaries. This phenomenon is important to increasing the fertility of areas like the Wadden Sea, which borders on parts of the Netherlands, the Federal Republic of Germany, and Denmark. According to Edward Maltby, a lecturer in geography at the University of Exeter, United Kingdom, the Wadden Sea supports an estimated "60 percent of the North Sea's brown shrimp, more than 50

percent of the sole, 80 percent of the plaice, and nearly all the herring population during some part of their life cycle" (75). In 1983, the dockside value of the Wadden Sea-based fishery was estimated at $110 million (76).

Although coastal wetlands in developed nations produce large amounts of commercially valuable products, economic and nutritional dependence on wetlands is greatest among smaller Third World countries. Half the current 500,000-metric-ton annual catch in the Lower Mekong Basin, for example, is of wetland origin. Consequently, in 1981, the fisheries value of the Mekong delta directly contributed $90 million to the economies of Kampuchea, Thailand, and Vietnam while supplying 50–70 percent of the protein needs of the delta's 20 million people (77).

Coastal Wetland Loss

Despite the fact that it is not possible to estimate the loss of coastal wetlands on a global scale, their destruction is accelerating in the United States, France, the United Kingdom, parts of the Caribbean, and the Indo-Pacific region (78).

By the mid-1970s, the United States had lost roughly half its original coastal wetlands. In 1983, the National Marine Fisheries Service calculated the U.S. fisheries loss at $208 million per year from 1954 to 1978 due to the loss of vital estuaries (79). To date, estuarine wetland losses have been greatest in five states: California, Florida, Louisiana, New Jersey, and Texas. In fact, Louisiana's loss rate is 10,000 hectares per year due to coastal subsidence and other causes.

The outlook for Europe's few remaining areas of undisturbed coastal wetlands is grim. Some 40 percent of the coastal wetlands of Brittany, France, disappeared in the last 20 years, and two thirds of the remainder is being seriously affected by drainage and other development activities (80). Most of the United Kingdom's coastal estuaries disappeared years ago, with 20,000 hectares of salt marsh and mudflats in The Wash (on the east coast of England in East Anglia) reclaimed for agriculture since the 1950s.

Large-scale wetland losses are a more recent phenomenon in the Third World, but the pace of destruction is staggering. Only one quarter of Puerto Rico's original mangrove area of 24,000 hectares remains; between 1967 and 1975, the Philippines lost 24,000 hectares of mangroves a year; at least 5,000 hectares a year are lost in Malaysia for the production of wood chips; and Thailand has lost a full 20 percent of its mangrove forests in the past decade (81).

The causes of wetland destruction are underlined by the following problems: the tendency to view wetlands as wastelands, the association of wetlands with disease, the flooding hazards that accompany the use of wetlands, the lack of government interest, and the lack of financial support for wetland protection and management (82).

Despite this negative assessment, some critical estuaries are coming under regulatory protection. (See Box 9.1.) As governments begin to recognize the value of estuaries as fish and shellfish nurseries, the upward trend in fish catches may be sustained into the 1990s.

WORLD FISHERIES

Marine Fisheries Harvest

Of the 20,000 known species of fish, around 9,000 are currently exploited (83). However, only 22 species are routinely harvested in quantities exceeding 100,000 metric tons a year, with just five groups—herrings, cods, jacks, redfishes, and mackerels—accounting for roughly half the annual catch (84). Since 1950, world fish yields have risen almost fourfold, from about 20 million metric tons to more than 82 million metric tons in 1984; 73 million metric tons consisted of marine fish, mollusks, crustaceans, and algae. (See Table 9.3.) However, the spectacular growth rate of catches has slowed dramatically since the 1970s. The United Nations Development Programme (UNDP) attributes this fact to overfishing of certain species and areas, increasing amounts of pollutants entering the ocean, degradation of coastal estuaries and wetlands, high fuel costs for fishing boats in the Third World, and old, outdated equipment and process facilities, particularly in the Third World (85).

The United Nations Food and Agriculture Organization (FAO) believes that the world's seas cannot sustain a maximum commercial catch rate of more than 100 million metric tons per year from *conventional resources* without critically depleting certain valuable species, like herring and cod (86). (See Chapter 24, "Oceans and Coasts," Table 24.3.) If projections of fish consumption by the year 2000 are correct, then the sustainable catch from world fisheries could be exceeded by some 19–30 million metric tons (87). This figure totally disregards the estimated 24 million metric tons of fish harvested every year by small-scale fishermen operating outside the official sector. Considering the fact that some stocks have already been overfished and mismanaged, the prognosis is not encouraging. For example, overexploitation has led to a sharp decline in catches of Northeast Atlantic cod and herring since the early 1970s. Both these species were subject to catch quotas in the mid-1970s, and in some areas (i.e., the North Sea) fishing was banned until the stocks recovered (88). The same factors contributed to the dwindling stocks of California sardines in the 1950s. The dramatic collapse of the Peruvian anchovy fishery in 1971–72 resulted not only from overfishing in response to demands for fishmeal and oil but also from the weather patterns collectively known as El Niño. (See Chapter 11, "Global Systems and Cycles.") The catch of Peruvian anchovy is beginning to increase once again, but at a slow rate.

The growth in aquaculture and mariculture activities over the past decade holds promise for narrowing the gap between the sustainable supply from capture fisheries and projected consumption by the turn of the century. In 1985, world aquaculture production exceeded 10 million metric tons, amounting to over 11 percent of the total world harvest of fish and shellfish (89). Between 1975 and 1980, aquaculture production grew at an annual rate of over 7 percent, compared to about a 2 percent aggregate growth rate for all other food-producing sectors (90). Although aquaculture production tapered off from 1980–85, given current production and potential growth rates, the International Aquaculture Foundation predicts an increase in world aquaculture production of around 5.5 percent a year between now and the year 2010, resulting in a total aquaculture harvest of more than 18 million metric tons a year by the turn of the century (91).

Two of the most heavily fished regions in the world are the Northeast Atlantic and the Northwest Pacific. FAO estimates the Northeast Atlantic catch at around 12 million metric tons a year, taken mostly by fleets operating out of Norway, the USSR, Denmark, Iceland, the United Kingdom, Spain, France, the Netherlands, and the Federal Republic of Germany. The Northwest Pacific, on the other hand, is fished mainly by Japan, which has the highest catch of any country in the world. In 1983, Japan hauled in 11 million metric tons of fish and shellfish from the Northwest Pacific, out of a total of 21 million metric tons for the region (92).

Artisanal Fisheries

Artisanal (traditional) fisheries—although often excluded from official catch totals because there is no routine registration of landings from village fishermen or small, independent operations—nevertheless provide a substantial amount of the protein consumed in coastal developing countries.

It has been estimated that somewhere between 8 and 10 million artisanal fishermen worldwide harvest roughly 24 million metric tons of fish and shellfish a year for local consumption (93). Further, FAO recently calculated

Table 9.3 Annual Fisheries Catches, 1950–84

	1950–54[a]	1955–59	1960–64	1965–69	1970–74	1975–79	1980	1981	1982	1983	1984
North Atlantic	9.2	10.2	11.2	14.3	15.3	15.5	14.7	14.5	13.6	13.9	13.9
Central Atlantic	2.0	2.3	3.1	3.9	5.9	6.4	6.9	6.8	7.2	7.2	7.2
South Atlantic	0.9	1.2	1.9	3.5	3.7	3.9	3.9	4.0	4.3	4.3	4.0
North Pacific	2.8	3.5	4.7	13.2	17.9	20.0	20.7	21.9	22.6	23.6	26.4
Central Pacific[b]	5.1	7.7	10.2	4.0	6.1	7.1	7.9	8.5	8.2	7.8	8.5
South Pacific	0.3	1.2	7.2	13.3	8.2	5.7	6.6	7.2	8.3	6.7	8.7
Indian Ocean	1.2	1.4	1.7	2.6	2.8	3.3	3.6	3.6	3.7	4.0	4.3
Antarctic	X	X	X	X	0.1	0.3	0.6	0.6	0.7	0.4	X
Total Marine	**21.6**	**27.7**	**40.0**	**51.6**	**60.0**	**63.7**	**64.4**	**66.7**	**68.1**	**67.7**	**73.1**
Inland	**3.1**	**4.5**	**6.2**	**7.9**	**7.9**	**7.4**	**7.6**	**8.1**	**8.5**	**9.1**	**9.7**
World Total	**24.7**	**32.2**	**46.2**	**59.5**	**67.9**	**72.1**	**72.0**	**74.9**	**76.6**	**76.8**	**82.8**

X = not available.
Notes:
a. Data for 1950–79 are five-year averages.
b. The division between Central Pacific and North Pacific was shifted northward after 1965.
Source: United Nations Food and Agriculture Organization (FAO), *Yearbook of Fishery Statistics: Catches and Landings* (FAO, Rome, relevant years).

Oceans and Coasts

that one seagoing fisherman provides work for two to three workers onshore, thus raising the number of people involved in small-scale fisheries to 25 million. These additional workers, in turn, are thought to support families numbering upwards of 100 million people (94). Uncertain as the numbers may be, there is little doubt that a significant portion of the coastal population of the world subsists on artisanal fisheries.

Artisanal fisheries are the largest single supplier of animal protein for several hundred million people in developing countries. In the majority of tropical Asian countries, for example, artisanal fisheries contribute more than 50 percent of the animal protein intake. (See Table 9.4.) Further, the production from artisanal fisheries as a percentage of total fisheries production per nation ranges from 20 percent in Hong Kong to 100 percent in Tanzania, Guyana, Trinidad, and St. Vincent and the Grenadines. (See Table 9.5.)

Coral Reef Fisheries

Because of their incredible diversity of fauna and flora, coral reefs are the marine counterparts of tropical rain forests. There is much disagreement over the commercial potential of coral reef fisheries, but if harvests are not limited to a few species like jacks, groupers, and snappers, which feed at the upper trophic levels, then the productive potential is immense. Table 9.6 provides data on fish and invertebrate harvests from selected reef systems. Unfortunately, catch statistics are fragmentary because overall data from reef fisheries do not exist (95). Relatively good data exist for the United States (i.e., Hawaii, Florida, Guam, and Puerto Rico), but the reefs are so lightly fished that it is difficult to draw reliable conclusions about the limits of coral reef productivity.

The most heavily exploited reefs are in the Eastern Caribbean, in the Philippines, and near major urban centers throughout the tropics. In St. Vincent and the Grenadines, for example, artisanal fishermen report a 50 percent drop in finfish landings and a 30 percent decrease in the size of groupers, snappers, and jacks in

Table 9.4 Importance of Fish as a Source of Protein Supply for Selected Countries, mid-1970s

Country	Fish as Percentage of Total Animal Protein Supply 1974–76	Fish as Percentage of Total Protein Supply 1974–76	Per Capita Fish Consumption (kilograms per year)
Bangladesh	58.9	7.9	10.8
Burma	55.3	7.5	13.6
Hong Kong	31.2	18.1	50.5
India	22.4	2.3	3.4
Indonesia	63.6	8.3	10.4
Kampuchea	47.8	8.4	9.9
Malaysia	47.3	17.0	34.7
Pakistan	1.9	0.5	1.4
Philippines	58.2	22.6	33.1
Singapore	31.6	15.2	42.4
Sri Lanka	54.7	8.4	10.9
Thailand	52.8	13.2	22.6
Viet Nam	56.3	14.0	21.8

Source: B. Darus, "The Management of South East Asian Small-Scale Fisheries and the Example of the Bubun Coastal Village Development Project, North Sumatra Province, Indonesia," in *The Traditional Knowledge and Management of Coastal Systems in Asia and the Pacific*, K. Ruddle and R.E. Johannes, eds. (United Nations Educational, Scientific and Cultural Organization, Jakarta Pusat, Indonesia, 1983), p. 211.

Table 9.5 Production from Artisanal (Traditional) Fisheries as a Percentage of the Total Fisheries Production

Country	Year	Percentage of Production from Artisanal Fisheries
Hong Kong	1978	20
India	1977	62
Indonesia	1978	96
Malaysia	1976	80
Pakistan	1987	40
Philippines	1976	61
Sri Lanka	1979	98
Bangladesh	1975	95
Burma	1972	83
Thailand	1970	30
Burundi	1975	58
Cape Verde	1976	75
The Gambia	1976	79
Ghana	1976	73
Nigeria	1970	99
Senegal	1975	79
Sierra Leone	1976	93
Tanzania	1975	100
Togo	1976	83
Brazil	1976	50
Guyana	1970	100
Trinidad	1971	100
Uruguay	1974	31
St. Vincent	1986	100
Turkey	1977	50
Yemen, AR	1974	95
Yemen, PDR	1975	90

Sources:
1. B. Darus, "The Management of South East Asian Small-Scale Fisheries and the Example of the Bubun Coastal Village Development Project, North Sumatra Province, Indonesia," in *The Traditional Knowledge and Management of Coastal Systems in Asia and the Pacific*, K. Ruddle and R.E. Johannes, eds. (United Nations Educational, Scientific and Cultural Organization, Jakarta Pusat, Indonesia, 1983), p. 211.
2. Nora L. Berwick, "Artisanal Fisheries of St. Vincent and the Grenadines" (unpublished, 1986).
3. A. Sfeir-Younis, The World Bank, Washington, D.C. (unpublished paper, 1981).

addition to an estimated 35 percent drop in lobster and conch catches since 1980 (96). Both lobster and conch, usually shallow water inhabitants, are now found only at depths of 24–52 meters and 18–24 meters, respectively. In some cases, the reef systems have been completely degraded as a result of blast fishing and the use of tangle nets. These areas are now producing very low harvests despite intensive fishing.

The larger harvests shown in Table 9.6 were taken in reef areas where all species of edible fish and invertebrates are consumed locally. On the basis of present evidence, a sustainable harvest of all edible fish, crustaceans, and mollusks averaging 15 metric tons per square kilometer per year could be derived from coralline areas at depths of less than 30 meters (97). This potential global harvest of some 9 million metric tons a year is the equivalent of 11 percent of the world's current total fish production. But reef systems do not lend themselves to industrial-scale fishing because of their rugged topography. Further, the diversity of species, the remoteness of many areas from major markets, and the presence of ciguatoxic (poisonous) fishes are all factors likely to limit the catch of fish and shellfish from coral reefs for the near future (98).

FISH CONSUMPTION AND TRADE

The trade in fish and fish products is an increasingly important source of foreign exchange earnings. World exports of the major fishery commodities now exceed $15 billion annually (99). Prices for fish and fish products

World Resources 1987

Table 9.6 Harvests per Unit Area for Selected Coral Reef Areas

Country	Area Type of Fishery	Habitat	Area fished (square kilometers)	Groups Included	Total Catch (metric tons)	Average (metric tons per square kilometer per year)
Puerto Rico (1978)	A	Coralline shelf	5,300	Neritic[a] fish and crustaceans	2,140	0.5
Ontong Java	S	Coral atoll	122	All	79	0.6
Kaapingamarangi Atoll	S	Coral atoll	400	X	280	0.7
Jamaica (1980)	A	Coralline shelf	3,305	Neritic fish and crustaceans	4,496	1.4
Jamaica (1968)	A	Coralline shelf	3,422	Neritic fish and crustaceans	5,983	1.7
Tanzania coast	A,S	Coralline shelf	12,160	All	21,980	1.8
Tarawa, Kiribati	A,S	Coral atoll	500	Reef and lagoon fish	220	4.4
Mauritius	A	Coralline shelf	350	All	1,645	4.7
Kora and Lakeba, Fiji	A,S	Fringing reefs	8.40	All	42	5.0
Ifaluk Atoll	S	Reef and lagoon	6	All	30.6	5.1
Philippines (1976–77)	A	Coralline shelf	27,000	All	130,000	4.9
Philippines	A	Reef	1.56	Demersal[b] fish and octopus	9	5.8
Apo Island				Demersal and pelagic fish	17.7	11.3
Philippines	A	Reef	0.50	Demersal fish	10.1	20.2
Sumilon Island			0.65	Demersal and pelagic fish	11.0	18.3
American Samoa	S	Reef and reef flat	X	Fish and invertebrates	X	12
American Samoa	S	Reef and reef flat	3	Fish only	63	21.2
			X	All fish and invertebrates	94	26.6

X = not available. A = artisanal. S = subsistence.
Notes:
a. Neritic fish are those found along the coast to a depth of 200 meters.
b. Demersal fish are those found on or near the bottom of the sea.
Source: J.L. Munro and D.M. Williams, "Assessment and Management of Coral Reef Fisheries: Biological, Environmental and Socio-Economic Aspects," in *Proceedings of the Fifth International Coral Reef Congress* (Papeete, Tahiti, 1985), p. 26.

range from $100 per metric ton to more than $5,000 per metric ton. Although the data are limited, it appears that in most countries fish prices have risen more rapidly than the prices of other foods, probably because of increased demand and a constricted supply (100).

An analysis of catches by economic group reveals the fact that although developed countries still harvest more than half the world catch, there has been a steady upward trend in the harvests of developing countries, especially those in Asia. Developing countries collectively increased their annual fish harvests 3.5 percent from 1977 to 1981; developed countries' harvests grew by a modest 0.7 percent. Today, six of the top 11 fish-producing nations are developing countries: China, Chile, Peru, India, the Republic of Korea, and Indonesia. However, Japan heads the list, which includes four other developed countries: the Soviet Union, the United States, Norway, and Denmark. (See *World Resources 1986*, Table 9.3, page 143, and Table 10.1, pp. 310–311.)

Developing nations are also increasing their share of the international trade in fish and fish products. Between 1974 and 1982, the volume of exports of fish and fish products from the Third World doubled and their value tripled. The Republic of Korea, Mexico, Thailand, India, Chile, Peru, Indonesia, Senegal, and Argentina are among the countries with the most significant increases in fish exports (101).

REGIONAL SEAS: THE BALTIC

The concept of a regional sea first evolved in the mid-1970s as a result of initiatives taken by the United Nations Environment Programme to deal with the increasing pollution of the world's seas. UNEP's first regional seas program concentrated on the Mediterranean, followed by nine other programs around the world. (See Chapter 12, "Policies and Institutions.") However, it was the seven nations bordering on the Baltic Sea that first recognized the importance of controlling the amount of pollutants discharged into their common sea. These states took independent action (not under the umbrella of UNEP) in 1973 and 1974 to salvage their common heritage. Since then, the concept of a regional sea has entered the lexicon, signifying attempts by groups of countries bordering on the same sea (whether enclosed like the Mediterranean, Red, and Baltic Seas or relatively open like the Caribbean or the East African and South Pacific regions) to deal rationally and collectively with

Oceans and Coasts

their environmental problems. This is the first in an annual series of "regional seas" profiles in *World Resources*.

In order to tackle the environmental deterioration evident in the late 1960s and early 1970s in the Baltic Sea, the seven states met in Helsinki in May-June 1973 to create an international legal framework. Sweden and Finland spearheaded the initial efforts. In March 1974, all the Baltic states—Sweden, Finland, the Soviet Union, Poland, the German Democratic Republic, the Federal Republic of Germany, and Denmark—signed a comprehensive agreement. Six years later, the Helsinki Convention on the Protection of the Marine Environment of the Baltic Sea was ratified by the Federal Republic of Germany (the last signatory to do so), permitting the Convention to enter into force on May 3, 1980 (102). (See Box 9.2 for background information on the Baltic Sea.)

The Helsinki Convention

As one of the first comprehensive agreements of its kind on the marine environment, the Helsinki Convention is a model of international environmental cooperation. When UNEP launched the Regional Seas Program in the mid-1970s, it studied the Helsinki process carefully.

The Convention's 29 articles and six annexes call on all contracting parties to implement "individually or jointly all appropriate legislative, administrative, or other necessary measures to prevent and/or reduce pollution to the Baltic." It specifically covers: discharges from land-based sources, including airborne pollution; discharges from ships, including oil, chemicals, sewage, and garbage; dumping of hazardous wastes; international cooperation to combat oil spills; and formation of the Baltic Marine Environment Protection Commission (the Helsinki Commission, or HELCOM), charged with carrying out the spirit and terms of the Convention (103). Like most commissions, HELCOM has no power to enforce its decisions on the contracting parties. Decisions are reached unanimously by the members of HELCOM and are regarded as recommendations to the signatory governments. However, recommendations are expected to be incorporated into national legislation as soon as practicable, and the Commission monitors progress toward that end (104).

The Helsinki Commission has five main duties: "to keep the implementation of the Convention under continuous review; to recommend measures relating to the purposes of the Convention; to recommend amendments to the

---

Box 9.2 The Baltic Sea's Vital Statistics

Geography: Bordered by Sweden, Finland, the Soviet Union, Poland, the German Democratic Republic, the Federal Republic of Germany, and Denmark, the Baltic Sea has a surface area of 366,000 square kilometers—only 0.1 percent of the surface area of the world's oceans—and contains some 22,000 cubic kilometers of brackish water (1)(2). The Baltic is divided into seven distinct zones: Bothnian Bay at its northern-most end, the Bothnian Sea, the Gulf of Finland, the Gulf of Riga, the Baltic Proper, the Belt Sea (including The Sound) around Denmark, and the Kattegat, which leads out to the North Sea (see Figure 1).

Water Inputs: The Baltic receives 500 cubic kilometers of freshwater every year (3) from some 250 river systems (4). This large input of freshwater gives the sea a rather low salinity compared to open ocean water. The Baltic is a relatively enclosed sea, and its brackish waters have a residence time of 25 years, with a mean depth of only 60 meters.

Human Population: The drainage area of the Baltic comprises the entire area of Sweden, Finland, and Poland, a large part of the western Soviet Union, most of Denmark, and the northern parts of the Federal Republic of Germany and the German Democratic Republic. The population in the drainage area of the Baltic was nearly 80 million in the early 1980s, with a combined Gross National Product (GNP) of $3.7 billion, about 6 percent of the world's total GNP (5). A total of 16 million people live along the coast of the Baltic. The region is highly industrialized, and agriculture plays a relative-

ly minor role except in Poland and parts of the Soviet Union. There are at least 200 major industrial complexes within the Baltic's drainage area—mostly steel and metal works, chemical industries, and pulp and paper mills. Nearly all of them are in the category of polluting industries (6).

Shipping: On an average day, around 700 ships plus an equal number of fishing vessels operate on the Baltic, making it a heavily trafficked body of water. As of the mid-1970s, 50 million metric tons of goods were transported in and out of the Baltic via the Kiel Canal, and another 125–150 million metric tons were shipped by way of the straits (through the Kattegat) (7).

Fishing: Fish and fish products are still big business in the Baltic. The catch increased tenfold from 1930 to 1980, largely because of improved fishing gear, and amounted to 900,000 metric tons in 1980 (8). Between 80 and 90 percent of this total consists of sprat, herring, and cod. The Soviet Union continues to take more than one third of the catch (one third of the herring and two thirds of the sprat). Denmark and Poland take the largest shares of the cod fishery, which has been running at about 200,000 metric tons a year since the late 1960s (9).

The actual condition of the Baltic's fish stocks is uncertain. Some scientists claim that the fish biomass of the Baltic is increasing because of the elevated nutrient content in the water, a direct result of eutrophication. But most marine scientists agree that the primary commercial species are being fished near their maximum yields (10).

Fauna and Flora: The Baltic is characterized

by a rather poor assortment of fauna and flora, at least in terms of species numbers. Of the 1,500 macroscopic animals found off the Norwegian coast in the North Sea, only around 70 species survive in the central Baltic. Likewise, while 150 species of macroscopic algae are found on the west coast of Norway only 24 species are found on the Finnish coast (11). The soft bottom communities of the central Baltic support a mere 4–7 species, with the biomass being dominated by the blue mussel (*Mytilus edulis*) (12).

Pollution: Over the past 30 years, the Baltic has been severely affected by anthropogenic sources of pollution. Nearly half the Baltic's deep waters, covering 100,000 square kilometers, have become virtual "dead seas" of oxygen-starved water, where no marine life—except microscopic organisms—can survive (13). These anoxic conditions are thought to be caused, in large measure, by the tremendous input of pollutants from land-based sources, with atmospheric deposition playing an important role in some areas. The current annual nutrient load to the Baltic from all sources, particularly from municipal and industrial effluents, amounts to nearly 1.7 million metric tons of BOD (Biological Oxygen Demand), including 1.1 million metric tons of nitrogen and 77,000 metric tons of phosphorus (14). For phosphorus and nitrogen, these figures are 3 and 1.5 times higher, respectively, than earlier calculations.

Toxic substances such as mercury, DDT, and PCBs accumulate in marine plants and animals, increasing human health risks. Populations of gray and ringed seals have plummeted as a result of contamination from

Convention and its Annexes; to define pollution control criteria and objectives for the reduction of pollution; and to promote scientific and technological research" (105).

Some progress in reducing the amount of toxic pollutants entering the Baltic has been made. In the past 10 years, concentrations of mercury in fish from certain coastal areas have decreased two thirds. Concentrations of DDT (but not PCBs) have also begun to fall. Since 1974, when the Convention was signed, the use of DDT has been banned in all seven countries, and the use of PCBs has been severely limited (only the Soviet Union and Poland continue to use them). A new group of hazardous chemicals known as PCTs (polychlorinated terphenyls) has been added to the list of toxic substances that may not be discharged into the Baltic (the list includes heavy metals like lead, cadmium, and mercury; persistent pesticides; lignin; oil; and radioactive materials) (106).

Oil remains a persistent problem. In the early 1980s, oil spilled or discharged from routine shipping operations in addition to that from land runoff amounted to around 40,000 metric tons a year (107). The figure may be lower today as a result of a concerted effort to reduce oil pollution from both land- and sea-based sources. Several provi-

sions in the Convention address oil pollution: the discharge of oil from ships is strictly limited; reception facilities for ships' wastes, including petroleum residues, have been established in many Baltic ports; and rules and guidelines for cooperation in combatting oil spills have been established. In addition, a reporting system for ships transporting hazardous or toxic cargoes has been set up (108).

When the Helsinki Commission met in February 1986, it emphasized further reducing pollution from land-based sources. The Commission adopted several resolutions designed to limit discharges of pollutants from urban areas and agriculture, pertaining mostly to development of adequate sewage treatment facilities, pre-treatment of industrial waste waters, and treatment of storm water in the Baltic's catchment area (109). The Commission is particularly concerned about further limiting discharges of mercury, cadmium, lead, zinc, copper, and oil. Another important item before HELCOM is working out recommendations designed to combat the accidental discharge of hazardous chemicals into the Baltic.

Although the Helsinki Convention is certainly not perfect, it has provided the Baltic countries with a practical framework for addressing common environmental con-

PCBs, DDT, and heavy metals. Until recently, the white-tailed eagle (*Haliaetus albicilla*) was nearly extinct over much of the Baltic because of environmental contaminants.

References and Notes

1. H. Cederwall and R. Elmgren, "Biomass Increase of Benthic Macrofauna Demonstrates Eutrophication of the Baltic Sea," *Ophelia*, Supplement 1 (August 1980), p. 287.
2. Bengt-Owe Jansson, "Natural Systems of the Baltic," *AMBIO*, Vol. 9, No. 3-4 (1980), p. 129.
3. *Ibid.*
4. E. Leppäkoski, "Man's Impact on the Baltic Ecosystem," *AMBIO*, Vol. 9, No. 3–4 (1980), p. 174.
5. "The Political Geography of the Baltic," *AMBIO*, Vol. 9, No. 3-4 (1980), p. 137.
6. Leif Bruneau, "Pollution from Industries in the Drainage Area of the Baltic," *AMBIO*, Vol. 9, No. 3-4 (1980), pp. 145–152.
7. Gunnar Alexandersson, "Shipping in the Baltic," *AMBIO*, Vol. 9, No. 3-4 (1980), p. 160.
8. R. Rosenberg, ed., *A Review—Eutrophication in Marine Waters Surrounding Sweden*, Report No. 3054 (National Swedish Environmental Protection Board, Stockholm, 1986), p. 67.
9. Fritz Thurow, "The State of Fish Stocks in the Baltic," *AMBIO*, Vol. 9, No. 3–4 (1980), pp. 153–154.
10. *Ibid.*
11. *Op. cit.* 2, p. 130.
12. *Op. cit.* 8, p. 52.
13. *Op. cit.* 8, p. 7 and p. 51.
14. Ulf Larsson, *et al.*, "Eutrophication and the Baltic Sea: Causes and Consequences," *AMBIO*, Vol. 14, No. 1 (1985), pp. 11–13.

Figure 1 Drainage Basins and Subregions of the Baltic Sea

Note: Blue lines show Baltic Sea subregions and their corresponding drainage basins. Names of major rivers are given.
Source: M. Falkenmark and Z. Mikulski, *Hydrology of the Baltic Sea — General Background to the International Project* (International Hydrological Decade, Stockholm and Warsaw, 1974), cited in Lief Bruneau, "Pollution from Industries in the Drainage Area of the Baltic," *AMBIO*, Vol. 9, No. 3 – 4, p. 145 (1980).

cerns. Indeed, the Baltic is now one of the most intensively studied seas in the world.

RECENT DEVELOPMENTS

THE SOUTH PACIFIC COMES OF AGE

As a result of the 1982 U.N. Convention on the Law of the Sea, the area of "open ocean" was reduced by roughly 30 percent. The high seas have been apportioned rapidly by the declaration and general acceptance of 200-mile Exclusive Economic Zones (EEZs) by more than 159 countries (as of June 1986) [110]. The legal concept of the treaty is significant, particularly because it recognizes the coastal states' sovereign rights over all fishing within 200 miles of their coasts. (See *World Resources 1986*, pp. 143–145.) Although the treaty has not been ratified by the requisite number of countries for it to have the full force of international law, nearly all coastal developing countries endorse it. So far, only 26 countries, plus the U.N. Council for Namibia, have ratified the Convention; another 34 ratifications are needed before it comes into force.

As a result of the Convention, the South Pacific island countries' EEZs have virtually made the South Pacific into a closed sea [111]. This situation infuriated some long-distance fishing fleets, especially those of the U.S. tuna industry. The United States recognizes the validity of the 200-mile zones, but not some countries' claims over migratory fish, like tuna, within the zones. Because the United States is the only country that does not recognize exclusive fishing rights within declared EEZs, U.S. tuna fleets fish with impunity in the exclusive waters of a number of South Pacific countries, which have no navies to enforce their claims. This practice is angering some island nations. Kiribati (formerly the Gilbert Islands) recently concluded an agreement with the Soviet Union, allowing Soviet fleets to fish within its EEZ for $1 million a year—a costly but welcome fishing license for the Soviets [112]. Vanuatu is also contemplating a similar arrangement with the USSR.

A Soviet fishing presence is making the U.S. Navy nervous because the Pacific has been firmly under western influence since World War II. Meanwhile, the South Pacific Forum's Fisheries Agency is trying to persuade its members to grant the United States and other countries licenses to fish within the 200-mile zones [113].

In response to the Soviet overtures, the United States made an offer of $5.5 million a year to a collection of South Pacific nations—including Kiribati, the Solomons, and Vanuatu—for the right to continue fishing in their EEZs [114]. So far no agreement has been reached.

WETLANDS RECEIVE INCREASED ATTENTION

In 1985, the World Wildlife Fund (WWF) and the International Union for Conservation of Nature and Natural Resources (IUCN) launched a major campaign to increase public awareness of wetlands and their values. A major aim of the WWF/IUCN Wetlands Conservation Program is to establish a wetlands data base at the IUCN Conservation Monitoring Centre in Cambridge, England.

The Centre for Environmental Studies at the University of Leiden, the Netherlands, is involved in Project EDWIN. The goals of this project are threefold: the establishment of an information base on the impacts of various development schemes on wetlands; the evaluation of sound wetlands development that maintains ecological processes; and the development of recommendations to improve the design of drainage works, polders, and dams. EDWIN's main focus is on the problems of tropical developing countries, where the loss of wetlands is greatest and gaps in scientific data are also the greatest.

The Ramsar Convention of 1971 is the main mechanism for international cooperation in wetland conservation. Signatories to the Convention are required to include wetland conservation issues in their national planning initiatives, to establish protected areas of wetlands, and to designate wetlands for inclusion on the List of Wetlands of International Importance, maintained at IUCN's Conservation Monitoring Centre. As of the end of June 1986, the list included 335 sites covering an estimated 20 million hectares. In 1985, Uruguay, Ireland, Belgium, and Suriname joined the Ramsar Convention, and Mali, Egypt, and Mexico were in the process of signing. In September 1985, the United States ratified the Convention, as did France, bringing the total membership of the Convention to 42 contracting parties [115]. For a list of internationally important wetlands, see Chapter 18, "Land Use and Cover," Table 18.2.

References and Notes

1. United Nations Environment Programme (UNEP), *The Health of the Oceans*, UNEP Regional Seas Reports and Studies No. 16 (UNEP, Geneva, 1982), p. 1.
2. *Ibid.*, pp. 1–7.
3. *Ibid.*, p. 12.
4. United Nations Environment Programme (UNEP), *Pollutants from Land-Based Sources in the Mediterranean*, UNEP Regional Seas Reports and Studies No. 32 (UNEP, Geneva, 1984), p. 20.
5. P. Ress, "The Mediterranean—Surely but Slowly Cleaner" (United Nations Environment Programme, press release, July 1986), p. 1.

6. Organisation for Economic Co-operation and Development (OECD), *The State of the Environment 1985* (OECD, Paris, 1985), p. 70.
7. United Nations Environment Programme (UNEP), *Marine Pollution*, UNEP Regional Seas Reports and Studies No. 25 (UNEP, Geneva, 1983), p. 6.
8. *Op. cit.* 1, p. 41.
9. U.S. Food and Drug Administration (FDA), *Action Levels for Poisonous and Deleterious Substances in Human Food and Animal Feed* (FDA, Washington, D.C., 1985), p. 13.
10. *Op. cit.* 1, p. 41.

11. *Op. cit.* 6, p. 81.
12. *Op. cit.* 1, p. 42.
13. "The Case of Baltic Seals," *AMBIO*, Vol. 9, No. 3–4 (1980) p. 182.
14. *Op. cit.* 1, p. 43.
15. *Op. cit.* 1, p. 44.
16. *Op. cit.* 1, p. 43.
17. *Op. cit.* 9, p. 4.
18. *Op. cit.* 7, p. 3.
19. Ruth Norris, "A Tide of Plastic," *Audubon*, Vol. 88, No. 5 (1986), p. 20.
20. National Research Council, *Assessing Potential Ocean Pollutants* (National Academy Press, Washington, D.C., 1985).
21. M.W. Cawthorn, "Entanglement in, and

Ingestion of, Plastic Litter by Marine Mammals, Sharks, and Turtles in New Zealand Waters," in *Proceedings of the Workshop on the Fate and Impact of Marine Debris*, R. Shomura and H. Yoshida, eds. (U.S. Department of Commerce, National Oceanic and Atmospheric Administration, National Marine Fisheries Service, November 27–29, 1984, Honolulu, Hawaii), pp. 336–337.

22. V. Alexander, "Arctic Ocean Pollution," *Oceanus*, Vol. 29, No. 1 (1986), p. 34.

23. D.M. Fry, *et al.*, "Ingestion of Plastic Debris by Laysan Albatross and Wedge-Tailed Shearwaters in the Hawaiian Islands," *Marine Pollution Bulletin* (Pergamon Press, New York, in press).

24. "Ocean Plastic Debris Killing Marine Mammals; International Shipping Laws Seen Lacking," *World Environment Report*, Vol. 12, No. 17 (1986), p. 133.

25. J. Ui, ed., *Polluted Japan* (Jishu-Koza, Tokyo, 1972).

26. A. Abrams, "The Problem at Minamata," *The Asia Magazine*, June 29, 1975, pp. 3–11.

27. United Nations Environment Programme (UNEP), *GESAMP: Cadmium, Lead and Tin in the Marine Environment*, UNEP Regional Seas Reports and Studies No. 56 (UNEP, Geneva, 1985), p. 53.

28. *Ibid.*, p. 52.

29. *Op. cit.* 1, p. 49.

30. *Op. cit.* 6, p. 81.

31. *Op. cit.* 6, p. 86.

32. *Op. cit.* 1, p. 44.

33. *Op. cit.* 6, p. 73.

34. *Op. cit.* 1, p. 44.

35. *Op. cit.* 6, p. 73.

36. United Nations Environment Programme, *The World Environment 1972–1982*, Martin Holdgate, *et al.*, eds. (Tycooly International Publishing, Ltd., Dublin, 1982), p. 90.

37. *Op. cit.* 6, p. 74.

38. Jim MacNeill, "Sources of Oil Pollution of the Sea: Problems and Solutions," *AMBIO*, Vol. 13, No. 4 (1984), p. 230.

39. E. Levy, "Oil Pollution in the World's Oceans," *AMBIO*, Vol. 13, No. 4 (1984), p. 226.

40. *Ibid.*

41. *Op. cit.* 39, p. 232.

42. *Op. cit.* 39, p. 234.

43. J. Ferrari, "Oil on Troubled Waters," *AMBIO*, Vol. 12, No. 6 (1983), pp. 354–355.

44. International Council for the Exploration of the Sea (ICES), *Biological Effects on Marine Pollution and the Problems of Monitoring* (ICES, Copenhagen, 1980), p. 179.

45. Don Hinrichsen, "Oil Makes Troubled Waters," *Scanorama Magazine* (July-August 1983), p. 103.

46. J.M. Baker, *Impact of Oil Pollution on Living Resources* (International Union for Conservation of Nature and Natural Resources, Geneva, 1983), p. 14.

47. P. Nounou, "The Oil Spill Age," *AMBIO*, Vol. 9, No. 6 (1980), p. 299.

48. *Ibid.*, pp. 299–300.

49. *Op. cit.* 6, p. 78.

50. *Op. cit.* 6, p. 78.

51. Lee A. Kimball, Executive Director, Council on Ocean Law, Washington, D.C., 1986 (personal communication).

52. R. Spilker, "Poisonous Waste Threatens Hamburg," *AMBIO*, Vol. 13, No. 2 (1984), pp. 124–125.

53. M. Wald, "Experts See Value in Oceans as Sites for Wastes," *The New York Times* (July 7, 1986).

54. *Op. cit.* 6, p. 78.

55. J. Sullivan, "Much Ocean Pollution Gets its Start on Shore," *The New York Times* (August 3, 1986).

56. Graham Bennett, "Ocean Incineration: The Solution to the Toxic Waste Disposal Problem?" *The Environment in Europe*, No. 36 (Institute for European Environmental Policy, Brussels, 1986), p. 1.

57. *Op. cit.* 6, p. 80.

58. *Alpha* radiation consists of positively charged particles with two protons and two neutrons. Alpha radiation can be stopped completely with a sheet of paper, and the outer layer of human skin will repel the rays. However, if alpha particles enter the body through inhalation or ingestion, they can cause cancer. *Beta* radiation is more potent than alpha, and beta particles are similar to electrons. Beta is more penetrating than alpha radiation and can pass through 0.5–1 centimeter of human flesh or water. When inhaled, beta radiation can also be a dangerous carcinogen. *Gamma* radiation consists of photons (wave energy) that can penetrate deep, passing entirely through the human body, causing massive damage in high enough doses. Dense materials such as thick concrete and lead are used as shielding against gamma radiation.

59. A curie is a measure of radiation named after Marie Curie, the discoverer of radium. A curie represents a decay rate among fission products of 37 billion radiation emissions a second. Because of the extremely small amounts of radioactive material in the environment, it is often more convenient to use fractions of a curie (e.g., millicurie or one thousandth of a curie; microcurie or one millionth of a curie; and picocurie, one trillionth of a curie).

60. *Op. cit.* 6, p. 80.

61. Edward Maltby, *Waterlogged Wealth* (International Institute for Environment and Development, Earthscan, London, 1986), p. 10.

62. Edward Maltby, Lecturer in Geography, University of Exeter, United Kingdom, 1986 (personal communication).

63. *Op. cit.* 61, pp. 39–42.

64. *Op. cit.* 61, p. 41.

65. S.C. Snedaker and C.D. Getter, *Coasts: Coastal Resources Management Guidelines*, Renewable Resources Information Series: Coastal Publications No. 2 (Research Planning Institute, Columbia, South Carolina, 1985), p. 27.

66. *Op. cit.* 61, p. 42.

67. *Handbook for Mangrove Area Management*, L.S. Hamilton and S.C. Snedaker, eds. (Environment and Policy Institute, East-West Center; International Union for Conservation of Nature and Natural Resources; United Nations Educational, Scientific and Cultural Organization; and United Nations Environment Programme, 1984), p. 11.

68. Edward Maltby, "Issues and Trends in Global Wetlands," in D.D. Hook, *et al.*, *Proceedings of the International Symposium on the Ecology and Management of Wetlands*, Charleston, South Carolina, June 16-20, 1986 (Croom Helm, Ltd., Beckenham, United Kingdom, in press.)

69. *Op. cit.* 61, pp. 50–51.

70. *Op. cit.* 61, pp. 60–61.

71. *Op. cit.* 61, p. 19.

72. *Op. cit.* 61, p. 19.

73. W.N. Lindall and C.H. Saloman, "Alteration and Destruction of Estuaries Affecting Fishery Resources of the Gulf of Mexico," *Marine Fisheries Review Paper*, Vol. 39, No. 9 (1977), p. 1262.

74. B. Christensen, "Mangroves—What Are They Worth?" *Unasylva*, Vol. 35, No. 139 (1983), pp. 7–8.

75. *Op. cit.* 61, p. 19.

76. C. Macartney, "These Wastelands Are Vast Storehouses," in *World Wildlife Fund Wetlands Pack 2* (World Wildlife Fund/International Union for Conservation of Nature and Natural Resources, Gland, Switzerland, 1985).

77. V.V. Pantulu, *Effects of Water Resource Development on Wetlands in the Mekong Basin* (Mekong Secretariat, Environmental Unit, Bangkok, 1981).

78. The areas of greatest wetland loss were identified by the World Resources Institute and the International Institute for Environment and Development from a variety of sources, most of which are cited elsewhere in this chapter.

79. R. Tiner, Jr., *Wetlands of the United States: Current Status and Recent Trends* (U.S. Department of the Interior, Fish and Wildlife Service, Washington, D.C., 1984), p. 36.

80. *Op. cit.* 68.

81. D.J. Macintosh, "Riches Lie in Tropical Swamps," *Geographical Magazine*, Vol. 55, No. 4 (1983), pp. 184–188.

82. *Op. cit.* 68.

83. United Nations Development Programme (UNDP), *World Fisheries* (UNDP, New York, 1986), p. 2.

84. Lester Brown, "Maintaining World Fisheries," *State of the World—1985* (Norton Publishing Co., New York, 1985), pp. 74–75.

85. *Op. cit.* 83, p. 3.

86. J.A. Gulland, *The Fish Resources of the Ocean* (Fishing News Books, Ltd., West Byfleet, United Kingdom, 1971), p. 251.

87. Francis T. Christy, Jr., Senior Fishery Planning Officer, United Nations Food and Agriculture Organization, Rome, "Global Perspectives on Fisheries Management: Disparities in Situations, Concepts and Approaches" (draft, 1985), p. 3.

88. *Op. cit.* 6, p. 86.

89. R. Rhodes, "Status of World Aquaculture: 1985," *Aquaculture Magazine Buyers Guide '86*, p. 6.

90. *Ibid.*

91. *Op. cit.* 89.

92. *Op. cit.* 6, p. 88.

93. D. Thomson, "Conflict within the Fishing Industry," *ICLARM Newsletter*, Vol. 3, No. 3 (1980), p. 4.

94. *Ibid.*
95. J.L. Munro and D.M. Williams, "Assessment and Management of Coral Reef Fisheries: Biological, Environmental, and Socio-Economic Aspects," in *Proceedings of the Fifth International Coral Reef Congress* (Papeete, Tahiti, 1985), p. 2.
96. Nora L. Berwick, "Tourism and the Near-shore Marine Environment in St. Vincent and the Grenadines" (unpublished, 1986).
97. *Op. cit.* 95.
98. *Op. cit.* 95, pp. 2–3.
99. United Nations Food and Agriculture Organization (FAO), *Utilization of Fish and its Role in Human Nutrition* (FAO, Rome, 1981), p. 11.
100. *Op. cit.* 87, p. 3.
101. United Nations Food and Agriculture Organization (FAO), *State of Food and Agriculture, 1984* (FAO, Rome, 1985), p. 63.
102. Bertil Hägerhäll, "International Cooperation to Protect the Baltic," *AMBIO,* Vol. 9, No. 3-4 (1980), p. 183.
103. *Ibid.*, pp. 183–184.
104. Helsinki Commission (HELCOM), *Ten Years of Environment Protection of the Baltic Sea* (HELCOM, Helsinki, 1984), p. 8.
105. *Op. cit.* 102, p. 184.
106. *Op. cit.* 104, p. 10.
107. Erkki Leppäkoski, "Man's Impact on the Baltic Ecosystem," *AMBIO,* Vol. 9, No. 3-4 (1980), p. 180.
108. *Op. cit.* 104, p. 9.
109. "Measures to Reduce Pollution," *Environmental Policy and Law,* Vol. 16, No. 2 (1986), pp. 75–76.
110. U.S. Department of State, *GIST* (U.S. Department of State, Washington, D.C., June 1986), p. 1.
111. "Fishy Business in the Pacific," *Economist* (November 16, 1985), p. 37.
112. *Ibid.*
113. *Op. cit.* 111, p. 38.
114. "Fishing for a Foothold," *Time Magazine* (August 4, 1986), p. 29.
115. Daniel Navid, "Developments under the Ramsar Convention," in D.D. Hook, *et al., Proceedings of the International Symposium on the Ecology and Management of Wetlands,* Charleston, South Carolina, June 16-20, 1986 (Croom Helm, Ltd., Beckenham, United Kingdom, in press).

10. Atmosphere and Climate

Despite the progress made during the past decade to reduce atmospheric concentrations of chemical pollutants, the global air pollution picture is still not a pleasant one. The 24 member nations of the Organisation for Economic Co-operation and Development (OECD) (and Yugoslavia) have managed—at great cost—to reduce emissions of sulfur oxides from power plants and industrial sources. Yet the same countries have had mixed results in reducing nitrogen oxide pollution. Until 1985, only the United States and Japan had been able to implement comprehensive legislation reducing vehicle emissions of nitrogen oxides, hydrocarbons, and carbon monoxide and eliminating (or greatly reducing) the lead content of petrol (gasoline). European OECD countries were able to reduce pollution loads from stationary sources, but until recently vehicles eluded them. Vehicle emissions of carbon monoxide, hydrocarbons, and nitrogen oxides will begin to level off over the next few years in Europe as the European Community (EC) implements new emission control legislation for all new vehicles.

One group of pollutants that is clearly increasing throughout the developed world is photochemical oxidants, particularly ozone. The average ambient ozone concentration for industrialized cities in Europe and North America is around 300 micrograms per cubic meter, well above the damage levels for crops and vegetation which begin at between 100 and 200 micrograms per cubic meter. This potent pollutant also corrodes building materials and is a health threat for people and animals.

Yet there has been real progress in improving air quality in many of the world's big cities. According to data generated by the urban air monitoring program of the Global Environmental Monitoring System (GEMS)—operated by the United Nations Environment Programme and the World Health Organization—between 1973 and 1980, sulfur dioxide concentrations were reduced over much of the network, which includes some Third World cities. Concentrations of suspended particulate matter (SPM), on the other hand, have shown mixed trends, with generally higher levels reported for cities in Eastern Europe and the Third World compared to urban areas in OECD countries.

The highly industrialized countries of Europe, Asia, and North America are facing a relatively new group of pollutants: toxic organic chemicals. Until a few decades ago, these potentially dangerous pollutants were little known, but scientists have now identified a number of them as powerful carcinogenic and mutagenic agents, causing cancer and birth abnormalities in human beings and test animals. Levels of toxic organic compounds in ambient city air may be up to 1,000 times higher than in relatively remote regions.

Another health risk is the lurking problem of indoor air pollution. A major radon scare made headlines in the United States in mid-1986, when the U.S. Environmental Protection Agency announced that as many as 8 million homes in 30 states could have radon levels exceeding the new recommended maximum of 4 picocuries per liter of indoor air.

As acid rain research becomes more sophisticated, policymakers are discovering that this issue too is more complex than they had thought. Not only has the acid rain issue broadened to incorporate a multitude of pollutants that may be involved in forest declines in Europe and North America, but there is also mounting evidence that acid rain is an emerging problem in parts of the industrializing Third World. Large urban areas in Africa, Asia and Latin America are beginning to document damage from acid deposition.

One of the most surprising events of the past few years was the announcement in 1985 that British scientists had detected a decade-long decline in the springtime stratospheric ozone concentrations over one Antarctic monitoring station. When this finding was checked against several years of archived satellite data, a "hole" in the earth's ozone layer over the Antarctic continent was confirmed for each October observation. The hole—about as big as the continental United States—had not been predicted by atmospheric-chemical models, and it had grown larger each year.

Recent atmospheric models suggest that the continued production and release of chlorofluorocarbons (CFCs) could lead to substantial global depletion of the stratospheric ozone layer by the middle of the next century. However, in anticipation of continued assaults on the earth's ozone shield, 28 nations signed the Vienna Convention for the Protection of the Ozone Layer in March 1985. The Convention established a framework for international cooperation in research but left the means to achieve reductions in CFC use to subsequent negotiations (which resumed in December 1986).

CONDITIONS AND TRENDS

EMISSIONS AND AMBIENT AIR QUALITY

The industrialized countries of OECD are by far the largest emitters of the four regularly monitored groups of pollutants: carbon monoxide, nitrogen oxides, sulfur oxides, and particulate matter. In 1980, OECD countries spewed out a total of 149 million metric tons of carbon monoxide, 37 million metric tons of nitrogen oxides, 54 million metric tons of sulfur oxides, and 16 million metric tons of particulate matter, representing, respectively, about 77, 54, 50, and 27 percent of the world's total emissions of these pollutants. (See Figure 10.1.) The United States and Canada account for 51–66 percent of the total OECD emissions of these four categories of pollutants, while Europe emits 29–44 percent of the total [1].

As can be seen from Box 10.1, "Trends in Traditional Pollutants," levels of sulfur dioxide, carbon monoxide, and particulate matter have generally decreased in urban areas throughout much of the industrialized world (and in some Third World cities). However, levels of nitrogen oxides show mixed trends, with decreases registered for most OECD countries (except for those in southern Europe and for France and the Federal Republic of Germany) and increases noted for most large cities in the Third World. Concentrations of ozone, on the other hand, demonstrated a consistently upward trend over the past decade, particularly in urban areas.

Atmospheric Trace Pollutants

Highly industrialized societies are increasingly affected by a growing number of substances that occur in the atmosphere in much smaller concentrations (trace amounts) than the "traditional" pollutants described in Box 10.1. Many of these trace pollutants are suspected or known carcinogens, mutagens, or teratogens (substances that cause birth defects); they are often referred to as toxic or hazardous air pollutants as a way of distinguishing them from the traditional air pollutants of concern. In the United States, for example, the U.S. Environmental Protection Agency (U.S. EPA) listed the following air pollutants as hazardous under the Clean Air Act: inorganic arsenic, asbestos, benzene, beryllium, coke oven emissions, mercury, radionuclides, and vinyl chloride. In 1985–86, the U.S. EPA published notices for ten more compounds—including cadmium and halogenated organic compounds—signifying the Agency's intention to list these substances as hazardous, should emission standards prove warranted [2]. Another 30 substances are under consideration [3].

The majority of the other OECD countries are also expressing concern about the same substances listed by the U.S. EPA, but with the broad addition of polycyclic organic compounds (a wide group of substances suspected of posing threats to human health) [4].

Toxic Metals

Global anthropogenic emissions to the air of lead, arsenic, mercury, and cadmium currently reach about 2 million metric tons, 78,000 metric tons, 11,000 metric tons, and 5,500 metric tons per year, respectively. According to OECD, these figures are 20–300 times higher than natural (background) levels [5].

As a rule, data on ambient concentrations and deposition patterns of lead, arsenic, mercury, and cadmium exist only for the OECD countries, and even these data are incomplete. Predictably, the data indicate that urban areas are much more polluted with heavy metals than rural regions (except for those rural areas that have ore smelting operations). However, emerging evidence points to high concentrations of heavy metals—particularly lead, zinc, and copper—in the soils of higher elevation wilderness areas throughout the eastern United States and Central Europe [6]. (See "Multiple Pollutants and Forest Decline," below.)

Lead has been a priority concern in nearly all OECD countries since the late 1970s [7]. As of 1986, the United States phased out *all* lead in petrol, and the 12 members of the European Community (EC) are moving in the same direction, although more slowly. The majority of European countries (including Scandinavia) will still have leaded petrol—with a lead content of around 0.15 grams per liter—until the early 1990s. The Federal Republic of Germany introduced unleaded petrol in 1984 and is offering tax rebates to German motorists who retrofit their older model cars with catalytic converters in order to accelerate the conversion to nonleaded petrol.

According to OECD, on the basis of available data and analyses of atmospheric metal deposition preserved in

Figure 10.1 Emissions of Air Pollutants in OECD Countries, 1980

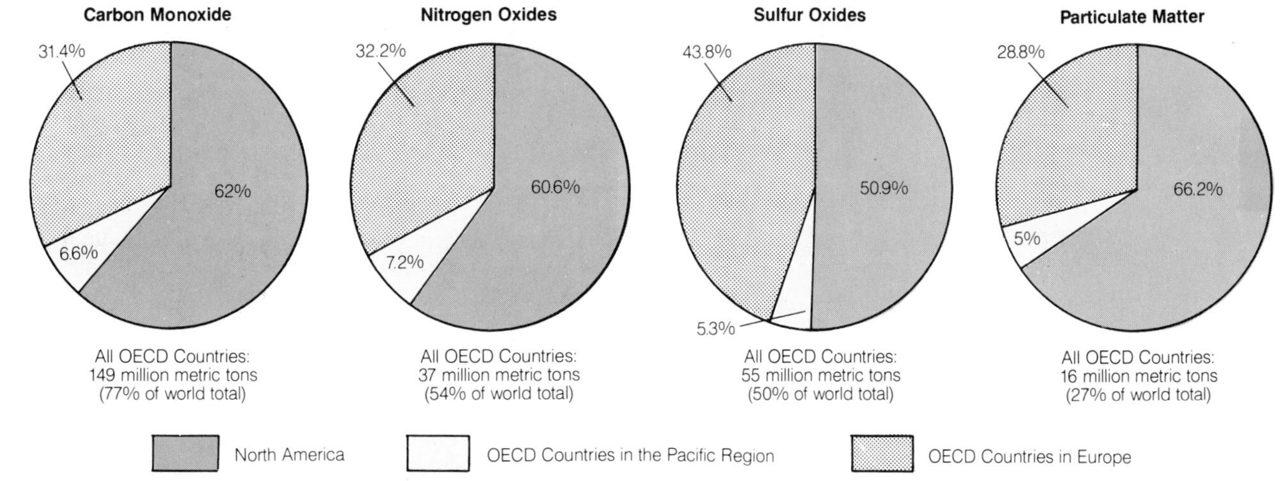

Carbon Monoxide

31.4%

62%

6.6%

All OECD Countries:
149 million metric tons
(77% of world total)

Nitrogen Oxides

32.2%

60.6%

7.2%

All OECD Countries:
37 million metric tons
(54% of world total)

Sulfur Oxides

43.8%

50.9%

5.3%

All OECD Countries:
55 million metric tons
(50% of world total)

Particulate Matter

28.8%

66.2%

5%

All OECD Countries:
16 million metric tons
(27% of world total)

North America   OECD Countries in the Pacific Region   OECD Countries in Europe

Source: Adapted from Organisation for Economic Co-operation and Development (OECD), *The State of the Environment 1985* (OECD, Paris, 1985), p. 19.

glaciers, peat bogs, soils, and ocean sediments, it appears that of all the heavy metals, lead and cadmium have shown the greatest increase in emissions and concentrations due to human activity (8).

Toxic Organic Compounds

Organic compounds, including most hydrocarbons, are known to be injurious to human health and vegetation in relatively low concentrations. Studies show that organic compounds such as some aldehydes, polycyclic aromatic compounds, benzene, and some organic acids, for instance, adversely affect human health; others, like ethylene, damage vegetation. Laboratory tests underscore the potential of many of these organic compounds to cause mutations and/or cancers (9).

Table 10.1 lists a number of such potentially toxic organic compounds, their main emission sources, and their environmental life spans. Roughly three quarters of all the substances listed in Table 10.1 proved to be carcinogenic in animal tests (10). Of these compounds, benzene, benzidine, bis (chloro-methyl) ether, 2-naphthylamine, and vinyl chloride are also classified by the International Agency for Research on Cancer as known human carcinogens. Others, like carbon tetrachloride, chloroprene, epichlorohydrin, and polychlorinated biphenyls are potentially powerful teratogens, causing reproductive abnormalities. In higher concentrations or when exposure is chronic, some organochlorine solvents (e.g., perchloroethylene) have caused central nervous disorders and liver dysfunction in humans. Exposure to phenols resulted in serious poisonings, and the aldehydes, particularly formaldehyde, cause respiratory, eye, and skin irritations (11).

Major sources of organic compounds include the chemical industry, municipal and industrial incineration, solvent use, and incomplete fuel combustion, particularly from vehicle exhausts.

Unfortunately, data on atmospheric concentrations are available only for selected organic pollutants. In the case of benzene, for example, people in large metropolitan areas may be exposed to 1,000 times the levels found in remote regions (12). A 1983 U.S. EPA study showed that average concentrations of selected synthetic organic chemicals in urban areas of the United States were 1–2 orders of magnitude (10–100 times) higher than in remote environments (13).

The vast number of trace organic compounds, plus the analytical difficulty and costs to obtain accurate measurements of ambient concentrations of these compounds, makes it very difficult to pin down human exposure rates, even in large cities. It is clear that in urban areas throughout the world, the ambient air is contaminated by a veritable alphabet soup of organic and inorganic chemicals. Many of these chemicals are found only locally, near their anthropogenic sources; others—like carbon tetrachloride, a suspected carcinogen—are persistent and are widely dispersed in the atmosphere (14).

There is still considerable uncertainty regarding the actual health risks associated with ambient air pollution in urban areas. OECD states that "epidemeological studies seem to point to a cancer risk contribution from air pollutants, but are not capable of proving its existence" (15). In Sweden, however, an expert group recently reported that the number of additional cancer cases the country could expect every year from air pollution ranged between 100 and 1,000 (out of a total population of slightly over 8 million) (16). The U.S. EPA, on the other hand, studied 16 groups of organic compounds and concluded that ambient levels would cause an additional 1,530 cancers per year, or 6.7 cases per 1 million inhabitants per year, not as high a rate as the Swedish study indicated (17).

Box 10.1 Trends in Traditional Pollutants

SULFUR DIOXIDE (SO₂) AND SUSPENDED PARTICULATE MATTER (SPM)

Sources. In North America and Europe, as well as many other industrialized areas, more than 90 percent of all sulfur in ambient air comes from anthropogenic sources. The energy sector is the principal contributor, particularly from burning coal and oil in power plants. Industrial processes also constitute major sources of SO_2 pollution.

Although natural sources of particulate matter are important, especially in arid regions with high levels of soil and dust, anthropogenic sources are of greater concern because they can carry toxic (including carcinogenic) trace substances and the particulates themselves may be toxic. Fine particulates (aerosols) can be formed in the atmosphere as secondary pollutants from gaseous emissions.

The principal anthropogenic contributors to particulate matter include industrial processes and fuel combustion from stationary and mobile sources. Diesel engines, in particular, emit significantly higher levels of fine and toxic particulates than petrol (gasoline) engines.

Emission and air quality trends. At 52 sites in the Global Environmental Monitoring System (GEMS) network where SO_2 and SPM concentrations were measured simultaneously for at least five years, 30 percent showed decreasing annual average concentrations of both pollutants; 20 percent of the sites showed stationary trends for both pollutants; and none of the sites demonstrated firm upward trends for both pollutants (the remaining sites showed mixed trends).

These trends do not mean, however, that cities in the GEMS network are free from sulfur dioxide and SPM pollution. As Tables 1 and 2 indicate, the ranges are rather broad: for sulfur dioxide, the median value is 45 micrograms per cubic meter ($\mu g/m^3$) per year, with a range of 3–242 $\mu g/m^3$ per year; for SPM, the median value is 89 $\mu g/m^3$ per year, with a range of 24–547 $\mu g/m^3$ per year [1]. (For comparison with National Ambient Air Quality Standards for the United States see *World Resources 1986*, Table 10.3, p. 162.)

Some cities are still plagued by rather high concentrations of suspended particulate matter and sulfur dioxide. Both Sao Paulo and Milan have composite annual averages of SO_2 that exceed 100 $\mu g/m^3$. Tokyo, Manila, Madrid, Tehran, Glasgow, Brussels, London, and Zagreb all have composite annual averages exceeding 50 $\mu g/m^3$ [2]. (For more information, see *World Resources 1986*, pp. 162–168).

With SPM concentrations, however, the ranges among individual sites in each city are smaller. The composite averages extend in a rather regular fashion from 59 $\mu g/m^3$ per year in Tokyo to 142 $\mu g/m^3$ in Zagreb. Both Tehran and Calcutta have extremely high average levels—more than 300 $\mu g/m^3$ per

year—but they are not caused entirely by industrial pollution; naturally high dust levels also contribute [3]. (See *World Resources 1986*, pp. 162–168).

Sulfur oxide and SPM concentrations in the United States show a consistently downward trend for the past decade. Sulfur oxide emissions decreased 16 percent from 1975 to 1984; at the same time, SPM levels decreased 33 percent [4]. (See Table 3.)

By and large, 1980 data from the GEMS network indicate that cities in Eastern Europe and the Third World are consistently more polluted with SO_2 and SPM than most cities in OECD countries [5].

NITROGEN OXIDES (NOₓ)

Sources. The major anthropogenic sources of NO_x are the transportation sector and stationary fuel combustion in the industrial and energy sectors. In urban areas, NO_x gives the atmosphere a yellow-brown cast. Nitrogen oxides are also critical to formation of photochemical smog and oxidants (particularly ozone).

Emission trends. From 1970 to 1979, NO_x emissions from stationary sources remained relatively stable in the OECD countries, but in the transportation sector they increased significantly. However, for 1979–84, there was an overall decrease or stabilization of NO_x emissions in Japan, North America, and most of OECD Europe, with the notable exceptions of southern Europe, France, and the Federal Republic of Germany, where emissions are still increasing. Between 1970

and 1983, NO_x emissions increased 4 percent in France and 15 percent in West Germany [6].

Overall, emission trends reflect the increased volume of road traffic since the 1960s as well as the number of diesel cars. In the United States, however, the rate of increase in emissions has been dropping because of the controls placed on vehicle emissions since the mid-1970s: NO_x increased 9 percent from 1970 to 1984, with only a 3 percent increase noted from 1975 to 1984. (See Table 3.)

Only in Japan has there been a significant decrease in total NO_x: emission levels dropped more than 90 percent despite a dramatic increase over the past 20 years in the number of passenger vehicles. This improvement results from the fact that in the mid-1960s, Japan began to impose strong NO_x emission controls on both mobile and stationary sources [7].

Air quality trends. Generally, trends in NO_2 air quality are similar to estimated NO_x emissions. For selected cities in the OECD network, ambient NO_2 levels remained relatively stable from 1975 to 1979, except in London, where they decreased.

In 1980, the annual average concentration of NO_2 in OECD cities was below 80 $\mu g/m^3$ with some notable exceptions in southern Europe—Milan, Rome, and Athens—where much higher levels were recorded [8].

By contrast, annual average NO_2 concentrations increased in the United States from 1975 to 1979, decreased through 1983, and then increased slightly in 1984. However, because

Table 1 Measurements of Sulfur Dioxide in the GEMSᵃ Network, 1973–80

Year	Number of Cities	Number of Representative Annual Data Sets	Annual Average Concentrations (micrograms per cubic meter)	
			Median	Range
1973	12	31	73	20-195
1974	10	28	71	14-178
1975	17	45	63	15-149
1976	40	78	46	3-149
1977	36	81	48	3-215
1978	40	94	40	4-240
1979	40	101	41	3-153
1980	35	83	40	7-242
1973-80	NA	541	45	3-242

NA = not applicable.
Note: a. Global Environmental Monitoring System.
Source: Burton G. Bennett, et al., "Urban Air Pollution Worldwide," *Environmental Science and Technology*, Vol. 19, No. 4 (1985), p. 301.

Table 2 Measurements of Suspended Particulate Matter in the GEMSᵃ Network, 1973–80ᵇ

Year	Number of Cities	Number of Representative Annual Data Sets	Annual Average Concentrations (micrograms per cubic meter)	
			Median	Range
1973	6	15	127	64-365
1974	6	16	126	48-519
1975	10	27	86	28-547
1976	23	45	84	26-380
1977	25	53	90	24-419
1978	28	64	93	30-450
1979	24	59	89	32-498
1980	24	55	84	30-535
1973-80	NA	334	89	24-547

NA = not applicable.
Notes:
a. Global Environmental Monitoring System.
b. Includes high-volume gravimetric sampling, nephelometry, membrane filter sampling, and beta absorption methods.
Source: Burton G. Bennett, et al., "Urban Air Pollution Worldwide," *Environmental Science and Technology*, Vol. 19, No. 4 (1985), p. 301.

the 1984 "composite average NO_2 level is 10 percent lower than the 1975 level," the long-term trend in the United States is downward [9].

CARBON MONOXIDE (CO)

Sources. In most industrialized countries, local sources in urban areas are responsible for the relatively high ambient concentrations of carbon monoxide. The transportation sector contributes about 90 percent of all anthropogenic CO emissions.

Emission trends. According to OECD data [10], total emissions decreased significantly from 1970 to 1979 in North America and Japan, with mixed trends in Western Europe. An overall decline—or at least a stabilization—of CO emissions has continued since 1979 in the OECD countries. (See Figure 10.1.)

Despite a continuing increase in vehicular traffic, CO emissions have decreased since 1975, mainly as a result of auto emissions control programs, especially in Japan and the United States. In Japan, for example, emission levels decreased more than 50 percent between 1971 and 1981. In the United States, CO emissions decreased 14 percent between 1975 and 1984 [11]. (See Table 3.)

Air quality trends. For OECD countries, there has been a general decline or stabilization in the ambient level of carbon monoxide from 1975 to 1979. The annual average concentrations in Japan peaked around 1960 and have been declining steadily since then. The trend in the United States indicates a decrease of 34 percent between 1975 and 1984, with only a 1 percent improvement from 1983 to 1984 [12].

OZONE (O_3) AND OTHER PHOTOCHEMICAL OXIDANTS

Sources. Ozone is not emitted in significant quantities directly; rather, it is the atmospheric byproduct of other primary pollutants, namely volatile organic hydrocarbons (sometimes called volatile organic compounds, or VOCs) and nitrogen oxides. Ozone is formed when these two precursors react with oxygen in the presence of sunlight, particularly when ultraviolet radiation is high. The primary anthropogenic sources of VOC and NO_x include fossil fuel-fired power stations, industrial processes, refineries, vehicle exhausts, and volatilization of organic solvents and fuels. Once in the atmosphere, this chemical "brew" is highly reactive.

Meteorological conditions and photochemistry have a major influence on the formation of ozone. Although many complex oxidants are formed from VOC and NO_x emissions (i.e., hydrogen peroxide, peroxyacetyl nitrate, and peroxyproprionyl nitrate), ozone is an indicator of the degree of photochemical pollution.

Emission trends. OECD data indicate a consistent, although slight, increase in the emissions of volatile organic compounds in most OECD countries since 1970, with the exception of the United States, where VOC

emissions increased 47 percent from 1940 to 1970, then decreased 21 percent from 1970 to 1984. (See Table 3.)

Nitrogen oxide levels, on the other hand, have stabilized or even decreased slightly in North America, Japan, and northern Europe, except for France and the Federal Republic of Germany. In southern Europe—Spain, Italy, Yugoslavia, and Greece—NO_x emissions are expected to continue increasing unless additional pollution controls are implemented [13].

Air quality trends. Available data indicate that during the latter half of the 1970s and early 1980s, maximum hourly ozone concentrations ranged up to 340 $\mu g/m^3$ in large metropolitan areas of Japan and Europe, with a maximum half-hour value of 664 $\mu g/m^3$ measured at Mannheim-Mitte, West Germany—the highest recorded half-hour concentration ever measured in Central Europe. Cities in North America and Australia, on the other hand, reported maximum hourly values between 340 and 860 $\mu g/m^3$ [14]. The *average* ozone concentration for industrialized cities in Europe and North America was around 300 $\mu g/m^3$. Ozone concentrations in rural areas were roughly 200 $\mu g/m^3$ with highs of 340 $\mu g/m^3$ in Canada and lows of around 100 $\mu g/m^3$ in Japan [15].

These data demonstrate the fact that tropospheric ozone levels are generally high throughout much of the industrialized world and that the World Health Organization (WHO) recommended maximum hourly levels of 100-200 $\mu g/m^3$ of ambient air are exceeded regularly, even in relatively remote clean air regions [16].

References and Notes

1. Burton G. Bennett, *et al.*, "Urban Air Pollution Worldwide," *Environmental Science and Technology*, Vol. 19, No. 4 (1985), p. 301.
2. *Ibid.*, p. 302.
3. *Op. cit.* 1.
4. U.S. Environmental Protection Agency (EPA), *National Air Pollutant Emission Estimates, 1940–1984* EPA-450/4–85–014 (Washington, D.C., 1986), pp. 3–7 and pp. 3–12.
5. United Nations Environment Programme and World Health Organization (WHO), *Urban Air Pollution, 1973–1980* (WHO, Geneva, 1984), Annex 4, pp. 71–96.
6. H. Rodhe and M.J. Rood, "Temporal Evolution of Nitrogen Compounds in Swedish Precipitation since 1955," *Nature*, Vol. 321, No. 6072 (1986), p. 764.
7. Japan Environmental Agency, *Quality of the Environment in Japan—1982* (Environment Agency, Tokyo, 1983), pp. 184–185.
8. Organisation for Economic Co-operation and Development (OECD), *The State of the Environment 1985* (OECD, Paris, 1985), p. 24.
9. U.S. Environmental Protection Agency (EPA), *National Air Quality and Emissions Trends Report, 1984*, EPA-450/4–86–001 (EPA, Washington, D.C., 1986), pp. 3–27.
10. *Op. cit.* 8, p. 21.
11. *Op. cit.* 4, p. 2.
12. *Op. cit.* 9, pp. 3–21. Because CO monitoring sites are often located in traffic saturated areas, they reflect local air quality conditions. If the air quality levels at these locations improve, it is generally at a faster rate than the rate for nationwide reductions in emissions.
13. *Op. cit.* 8, p. 34.
14. David T. Tingey, "The Effects of Ozone on Plants in the United States," in *The Evaluation and Assessment of the Effects of Photochemical Oxidants on Human Health, Agricultural Crops, Forestry, Materials and Visibility*, Peringe Grennfelt, ed. (Swedish Environmental Research Institute, Gothenburg, 1984), p. 81.
15. *Op. cit.* 8, p. 34.
16. *Op. cit.* 8, p. 34.

Table 3 National Emission Estimates in the United States, 1940–84

Year	Suspended Particulate Matter (SPM)[a]	Sulfur Oxides (SOx)[a]	Nitrogen Oxides (NOx)[a]	Volatile Organics (VOC)[a]	Carbon Monoxide (CO)[a]	Lead (Pb)[b]
1940	22.8	18.0	6.8	18.5	81.6	NA
1950	24.5	20.3	9.3	20.8	86.3	NA
1960	21.1	20.0	12.8	23.6	88.4	NA
1970	18.1	28.2	18.1	27.1	98.8	203.8
1971	16.7	26.8	18.6	26.5	96.8	220.8
1972	15.2	27.4	19.7	26.5	94.4	231.7
1973	14.1	28.7	20.2	25.8	90.0	202.7
1974	12.4	27.0	19.7	24.2	85.1	162.1
1975	10.4	25.6	19.2	22.8	81.2	147.0
1976	9.7	26.2	20.3	24.0	85.9	153.1
1977	9.1	26.3	21.0	23.9	81.9	141.2
1978	9.2	24.5	21.0	24.5	81.5	127.9
1979	9.0	24.5	21.1	23.9	78.4	108.7
1980	8.5	23.2	20.4	22.7	76.2	70.6
1981	7.9	22.3	20.5	21.4	73.5	55.9
1982	7.0	21.3	19.7	19.9	67.4	54.4
1983	6.7	20.6	19.1	20.5	70.4	46.3
1984	7.0	21.4	19.7	21.5	69.9	40.1
Change 1940–84	−69%	+19%	+190%	+16%	−14%	NA
Change 1970–84	−61%	−24%	+ 9%	−21%	−29%	−80%
Change 1975–84	−33%	−16%	+ 3%	− 6%	−14%	−73%

NA = not applicable.
Notes:
a. Unit of measurement is teragrams/year (10^6 metric tons/year).
b. Unit of measurement is gigagrams/year (10^3 metric tons/year).
Source: U.S. Environmental Protection Agency (EPA), "National Air Pollutant Emission Estimates, 1980–1984," EPA-450/4-85-014 (EPA, Research Triangle Park, North Carolina, 1986), p. 2.

INDOOR AIR POLLUTION

Little is known about the quality of indoor air despite the fact that many people spend most of their lives inside homes, apartments, offices, factories, hospitals, restaurants, schools, recreational facilities, and vehicles. Attempts to characterize indoor air are fraught with pitfalls; the pollutants vary from place to place, between neighboring structures, and even between rooms in the same house. Concentrations of indoor pollutants, in turn, are influenced to a large extent by lifestyles, whether the occupants smoke, whether they own pets, what heat source they use for cooking, and how well ventilated the building is, to name but a few factors. To date, only a few pilot studies have been completed on indoor air pollution and its hazards to health (18). However, the available data, mostly from residences in the developed countries of Europe and North America, strongly indicate that indoor levels of many compounds—particularly organic chemical compounds emitted from consumer products—routinely exceed outdoor levels.

Table 10.2 shows the sources, possible concentrations, and locations of selected indoor air pollutants.

Radon

The data base on sources and concentrations of indoor radon has been established only since the early 1980s. Radon is a chemically inert radioactive gas formed from the disintegration of radium, primarily from natural sources. Radon scares in Sweden, the Federal Republic of Germany, and, most recently, the United States prompted authorities to launch extensive surveys and monitoring projects. Initial attention focused on building materials and groundwater. But more recent evidence from regional studies, principally in Sweden and the United States, suggests that the soils under buildings may be more important sources of radon (19).

Once released, radon undergoes radioactive decay. As a result, indoor air contains both radon gas and alpha-emitting decay nuclides (often referred to as radon progeny or daughters). The latter become attached to

Table 10.1 Toxic Organic Compounds: Sources and Environmental Presence, 1985

Toxic Organic Compound[a]	Major Emission Sources	Remarks on Environmental Presence
Acetaldehyde (Ethanal)	Coffee roasting; manufacture of acrylic acid, acetic acid, and vinyl acetate; car exhaust	Atmospheric half-life: 1–2 days
Acrylonitrile (2-Propenenitrile)	Intermediate in the production of polymers and other chemicals	
Allyl chloride (3-Chloro-1-propene)	Synthetic intermediate chemical	
Benzene (C_6H_6)	Petrol-fueled internal combustion engines, raw material in production of other chemicals, petroleum refineries, gasoline storage and handling, coke ovens	
Benzidine ($C_{12}H_{12}N_2$) [(1,1-Biphenyl)-4,4-diamine]	Manufacture of dye, paper, textiles, leather	Atmospheric half-life: 1–4 days
Benzo(a)pyrene (Indicator pollutant for polycyclic organic matter)	Byproduct of incomplete combustion of coal (coke ovens), wood, charcoal, diesel fuel	
Benzyl chloride (Chloromethylbenzene)	Manufacture of polychlorinated biphenyls, n-butylbenzyl phthalate, benzyl alcohol, quaternary ammonium compounds, benzyl acetate	
Bis (Chloro-methyl) ether	Manufacture of polymethylene and polyphenyl isocyanate	
Carbon tetrachloride (CCl_4)	Dichlorodifluoromethane and trichlorofluoromethane production, fire extinguishers, dry cleaning agents, cleaning agents for machinery and electrical parts	Atmospheric half-life: 10 years; half-life in water: 70,000 years
Chlorofluorocarbons	Aerosol propellant, refrigerant, foaming agents in plastics industry	Potential effect on stratospheric ozone layer allowing possible increase of UV radiation and possible climatic changes
Chloroform ($CHCl_3$)	Production of chlorodifluoromethane, miscellaneous (industrial solvent, fumigant, pharmaceuticals, solvent, rubber industry)	Atmospheric half-life: 1–2 years
Chloroprene (2-Chloro-1,3-butadiene)	Production of neoprene	Atmospheric half-life: 10 hours
Dioxins such as TCDD (Polychlorinated dibenzo-p-dioxins)	Waste incinerators, herbicides	Half-life in soil: 10–12 years
Epichlorohydrin (1-Chloro-2,3-epoxypropane)	Production of synthetic glycerinepoxy resins and elastomers	
Ethylene dibromide ($C_2H_2Br_2$) (1,2-Dibromoethene)	Scavenger in leaded gasoline, soil and seed fumigant, dye production, pharmaceuticals, solvent	Atmospheric half-life: 20 hours
Ethylene dichloride ($C_2H_4Cl_2$) (1,2-Dichloroethane)	Production of vinyl chloride	Atmospheric half-life: 1,000 days
Ethylene oxide (C_2H_4O) (Oxirane)	Intermediate in production of ethylene glycol, production of polyester fiber and film and non-ionic surface active agents	Atmospheric half-life: 3 hours–1.6 days

Note: a. Includes known and potentially toxic organic compounds.
Source: Organisation for Economic Co-operation and Development (OECD), *The State of the Environment 1985* (OECD, Paris, 1985), pp. 42-43.

particulate matter, such as tobacco smoke and house dust, and can be inhaled and retained in the lungs. Indoor concentrations of radon and its daughters are also affected by ventilation and other factors.

Chronic exposure to elevated levels of radon and its daughters is known to result in lung cancers, but scientists cannot agree on a threshold for radon exposure. The U.S. EPA estimates that exposure to indoor radon results in 1,000-20,000 cases of cancer per year just in the United States [20], although the number of people at risk from high radon levels is not known.

Data from several studies in the United States and Sweden indicate that concentrations of indoor radon-222 (a common isotope of radon) vary by at least two orders of magnitude, with mean values in the United States of around 1.5 picocuries per liter (or 55 Becquerels per cubic meter) [21] and mean values in Sweden of 2.7 picocuries per liter (101 Becquerels per cubic meter) [22]. The U.S. National Research Council reports that this large range of values is not surprising "inasmuch as the studies included various types of buildings, building materials,

underlying materials, and ventilation rates and used many different measurement techniques" [23].

In August 1986, the U.S. EPA reported that as many as 8 million homes in some 30 states could have radon levels exceeding the new recommended guideline of 4 picocuries per liter of indoor air [24]. In some homes tested along the east coast from Georgia north to New York state, radon levels were as high as 300-1,000 picocuries per liter of air—enough radiation to expose the occupants to the equivalent health risk of smoking more than four packs of cigarettes a day [25] [26].

Sweden's relatively high action level (maximum health standard) of nearly 11 picocuries per liter, or 400 Becquerels per cubic meter of air, means that some 35,000 homes with up to 90,000 people are at risk from elevated radon levels [27].

Aldehydes

Concentrations of aldehydes—formaldehyde is the most important—are always higher indoors than outdoors. Sources of aldehydes include urea-formaldehyde (UF) insu-

Toxic Organic Compound[a]	Major Emission Sources	Remarks on Environmental Presence
Formaldehyde (CH_2O) (Methanal)	Charcoal manufacturing, catalytic cracking in petroleum refining, internal combustion engine exhausts, resin production, formaldehyde production, storage	
Hexachlorobenzene (C_6Cl_6)	Origin partly unknown	Atmospheric half-life: 2 days
Methyl chloroform (1,1,1-Trichloroethane)	Metal cleaning and cleaning plastic molds	
Methylene chloride (CH_2Cl_2)	Major component in paint strippers	Atmospheric half-life 1–2 years
2-Naphtylamines ($C_{10}H_9N$)	Research purposes	
Nitrobenzene ($C_6H_5NO_2$)	Production of aniline	
Nitrosamines	Limited commercial production but formed in air, water, and food from precursors, amines, nitrogen oxides, and nitrates	
Perchloroethylene (C_2Cl_4) (1,1,2,2-Tetrachloroethene)	Chlorination of acetylene, dry cleaning solvent, decreasing metals	
Phenol (C_6H_5OH)	Manufacture of explosives, fertilizer, coke, illuminating gas, lampblack, paints, paint removers, rubber, asbestos goods, wood preservatives, synthetic resins, textiles, drugs, pharmaceutical preparations, perfumes, bakelite and other plastics (phenoloformaldehyde resins); disinfectant in petroleum, leather, paper, soap, toy, tanning, dye, and agricultural industries	
Phosgene (CCl_2O) (Carbonyl chloride)	Manufacture of dyestuffs based on triphenylmethane, coal tar, and urea used in organic synthesis of isocyanates and their derivatives, in carbonic acid esters (polycarbonates) and in manufacture of some insecticides and pharmaceuticals	
Polychlorinated biphenyls ($C_{12}Cl_xH_{10-X}$) (PCBs)	Production, storage, and transport of PCBs, incineration of waste PCBs (electrical transformers and capacitors), solid waste disposal, evaporative losses of plasticisers, volatilization of PCB-containing paints and coatings	Atmospheric half-life: 26 days; a widespread pollutant of fish and wildlife
Propylene oxide (C_3H_6O) (Methyl oxirane)		Atmospheric half-life: 23 hours
Trichloroethylene (C_2HCl_3) (1,1,2,Trichloroethene)	Solvent in degreasing operations, PVC production, inks, surface coatings, adhesives, dry cleaning, pharmaceuticals	
Vinyl chloride (C_2H_3Cl) (1-chloroethene)	Production of polyvinyl chloride	Atmospheric half-life: 12 hours
Vinylidene chloride ($C_2H_2Cl_2$) (1,1-dichloroethene)	Monomer and polymer synthesis (latex coatings, extrusion resins), fabrication, polymer processing	

Table 10.2 Sources and Possible Concentrations of Selected Indoor Air Pollutants

Pollutant	Source	Possible Indoor Concentration[a]	Indoor/Outdoor Concentration Ratio[b]	Location
Carbon monoxide	Combustion equipment, engines, faulty heating systems	100 ppm	>>1	Homes, offices, cars, shops, skating rinks
Respirable particles	Stoves, fireplaces, cigarettes, condensation of volatiles, aerosol sprays, cooking	100-500 $\mu g/m^3$	>>1	Homes, offices, cars, public facilities, bars, restaurants
Organic vapors	Combustion, solvents, resin products, pesticides, aerosol sprays	NA	>1	Homes, restaurants, public facilities, offices, hospitals
Nitrogen dioxide	Combustion, gas stoves, water heaters, dryers, cigarettes, engines	200-1,000 $\mu g/m^3$	>>1	Homes, skating rinks
Sulfur dioxide	Heating systems	20 $\mu g/m^3$	<1	Homes, offices, public buildings
Total suspended particles (excluding cigarette smoke)	Combustion, heating systems	100 $\mu g/m^3$	1	Homes, offices, transportation, restaurants
Sulfate	Matches, gas stoves	5 $\mu g/m^3$	<1	Homes, offices
Formaldehyde	Insulation, product binders, particleboard	0.05-1.0 ppm	>1	Homes, offices
Radon and progeny	Building materials, groundwater, soil	0.1-30 nCi/m^3	>>1	Homes, buildings
Asbestos	Fireproofing	<1 fiber/cc	1	Homes, schools, offices
Mineral and synthetic fibers	Products, cloth, rugs, wallboard	NA	–	Homes, schools, offices
Carbon dioxide	Combustion, humans, pets	3,000 ppm	>>1	Homes, schools, offices
Visible organisms	Humans, pets, rodents, insects, plants, fungi, humidifiers, air conditioners	NA	>1	Homes, hospitals, schools, offices, public facilities
Ozone	Electric arcing, ultraviolet light sources	20 ppb 200 ppb	<1 >1	Airplanes Offices

ppm = parts per million; ppb = parts per billion; $\mu g/m^3$ = micrograms per cubic meter; nCi/m^3 = picocuries per cubic meter; NA = not applicable.
Notes:
a. Concentrations listed are only illustrative of those reported indoors. Both higher and lower concentrations have been measured. No averaging times are given.
b. >1 means that the concentrations are generally greater indoors than outside; (>> 1 means much greater); <1 means that ambient outdoor concentrations are higher than typical indoor concentrations.
Source: U.S. National Research Council, *Indoor Pollutants* (National Academy Press, Washington, D.C., 1981), pp. 23-24.

lation, building materials (especially particleboard and plywood), and, to a lesser extent, combustion appliances (e.g., stoves, water heaters, incinerators), other consumer products, and tobacco smoke.

Two of the most common sources of aldehyde indoors are urea-formaldehyde foam used as thermal insulation throughout much of Europe and particleboard and plywood formaldehyde-based resins (used extensively in the United States).

Urea-formaldehyde resin is the most common adhesive used in the manufacture of indoor plywood and particleboard. Plywood is composed of several sheets of wood glued together with UF resin, while particleboard is made by saturating small wood shavings with UF resin, then pressing the mass together under high temperatures. In most cases, indoor concentrations of formaldehyde result from the extensive use of pressboard or particleboard in building construction. Roughly 80 million homes in the United States were constructed using particleboard, which can emit high levels of formaldehyde for several months and even years (28).

Elevated levels of formaldehyde can cause eye and upper respiratory irritations, and chronic exposure may result in higher incidences of cancer. In the United States, for example, exposure to formaldehyde and five other organic substances—carbon tetrachloride, benzene, chloroform, tetrachloroethylene, and trichloroethylene—is estimated to cause up to 1,600 cancer cases a year (29).

Normal indoor concentrations of formaldehyde generally range between 0.05 and 0.3 parts per million (ppm), but in some unusual instances, concentrations of several parts per million have been measured in houses with extensive UF foam insulation. In residences and offices with high formaldehyde emission rates, concentrations can range from 0.01 ppm to over 1 ppm (30).

Asbestos and Other Fibers

Because of its fire-resistance and high tensile strength, asbestos now has more than 3,000 industrial and commercial applications. As of 1980, global production of asbestos was nearing 5 million metric tons per year and is now well above that level (31). Asbestos consumption in the United States, at 600,000 metric tons in 1979, is expected to reach perhaps 900,000 metric tons by the turn of the century (32).

Over 90 percent of the asbestos used in the United States is imported from Canada; 70 percent of the total is consumed by the construction industry. Asbestos fibers are widely used in roofing and flooring products, cement, panels, pipes, sheets, coating materials, textiles, papers and felts, friction materials, filters and gaskets, and thermal and acoustic insulation (33).

Inhalation of asbestos fibers can result—many years later—in pulmonary fibrosis, lung cancers, and mesothelioma of the pleura and peritoneum, all of which have high mortality rates (34).

According to the U.S. National Research Council, "most contamination [of the indoor environment with asbestos] is episodic, activity-related, and local" (35). Yet, indoor fiber counts have been found to exceed those outdoors, and sometimes they have reached the occupational safety limit of two fibers per cubic centimeter of air (36). This situation is a real problem in public buildings like hospitals and schools, where elevated fiber counts in the air prompted local health authorities to recommend replacing the asbestos with other insulating or sound-proofing material.

Smoking

Tobacco smoke is a major source of both gaseous and particulate pollution in the indoor environment, affecting both smokers and nonsmokers. Studies show that nonsmokers can absorb measurable amounts of carbon monoxide and nicotine (but not nearly as much as heavy smokers do). Involuntary or passive smoking can result in lung cancers, especially if exposure is chronic. In the United States, the estimated cancer incidence associated with indoor passive smoking ranges from 500 to 5,000 cases per year (37).

Residences occupied by smokers often have higher indoor concentrations of suspended particulate matter (SPM). The average smoker adds approximately 20 micrograms per cubic meter of SPM to home air (38). The annual ambient air quality standard in the United States is 75 micrograms per cubic meter (39). Because the typical range of indoor residential 24-hour SPM values is 30–100 micrograms per cubic meter, with an observed maximum of 600 micrograms per cubic meter (40), indoor concentrations often exceed outdoor values.

Indoor Air Pollution in the Third World

Organic fuels like firewood, dried dung, and agricultural wastes provide much of the domestic energy consumed in the developing countries of Asia, Africa, and Latin America. When these fuels are consistently burned inside dwellings—for cooking, space heating, or boiling water—high levels of toxic pollutants can accumulate. The combustion of organic fuels, particularly indoors, results in the release of measurable amounts of carbon monoxide, sulfur dioxide, nitrogen oxides (including nitrogen dioxide), ammonia, hydrochloric acid, hydrocarbons, and particulate matter. Of these pollutants, three are produced in relatively large amounts: suspended particulate matter, hydrocarbons, and carbon monoxide. (See Chapter 25, "Atmosphere and Climate," Table 25.4.)

If these pollutants are not vented properly (and most huts have no chimneys), they can pose serious health risks. The World Health Organization (WHO) reviewed the effects of indoor air pollutants on Third World populations and found that an increasing number of people were suffering from a variety of debilitating and fatal diseases, all linked to prolonged exposure to the combustion products of biomass. Five major categories of illness were identified: chronic obstructive lung disease (Nepal and Papua New Guinea); heart disease, particularly *cor pulmonale* caused by pulmonary damage (Nepal and India); cancers, especially lung and nasopharynx cancers (Indonesia, Kenya, and Malaysia); acute respiratory infections, particularly in children, due to destruction of the respiratory defense mechanisms (Africa and Papua New Guinea); and low birth weights caused, in part, by the chronic exposure of mothers to high levels of indoor pollutants (41). According to WHO, acute respiratory infections in children are a major cause of infant mortality in developing countries (42).

As a result, WHO estimates that somewhere between 300 and 400 million people, mostly in rural areas of developing countries, are adversely affected by high concentrations of indoor air pollutants formed from biomass combustion (43). In the central highlands of Papua New Guinea, for example, researchers found that native huts contained up to 5,000 micrograms per cubic meter of smoke, aldehyde levels of up to 3.80 parts per million, and carbon monoxide concentrations reaching 150 milligrams per cubic meter of indoor air (44). Similarly, in rural Guatemala, carbon monoxide concentrations averaged 35–45 milligrams per cubic meter of air in poorly ventilated homes, and a number of women tested had carboxyhemoglobin levels above 2 percent—levels thought to be damaging to fetal growth (45).

TRENDS IN ACID DEPOSITION

Acid deposition is a major air quality issue in Europe and North America, and it is emerging as a significant problem in parts of Asia, Africa, and Latin America. Many adverse environmental effects have been attributed to acid rain, including damage to lakes, streams, groundwater, forests, agriculture, buildings, statues, and human health.

Acid rain is a popular label for the complex scientific phenomena associated with atmospheric deposition. But acidic substances are not only deposited in rain, snow, fog, and dew; they also fall from the atmosphere as dry particles and gases.

The acid rain issue has changed significantly in the past few years:

■ Scientific and policy concerns now extend beyond the threat of acidification of aquatic ecosystems and materials damage. Observed changes in forest growth and condition are receiving increased attention.

■ Although acid deposition is still seen as the primary atmospheric agent damaging aquatic ecosystems, many other air pollutants are probably also important in the widespread forest declines of Europe and North America observed over the past five years.

■ The geographic area now perceived as threatened by acid rain and the other airborne chemical pollutants associated with atmospheric deposition has expanded far beyond Scandinavia, Central Europe, and eastern North America. It now encompasses nearly the whole of Europe (including the European part of the Soviet Union), parts of the western United States and Canada, and some industrialized areas of the Third World.

Transport and Deposition

It is now widely accepted that the dry deposition of gaseous pollutants and their derivatives is more important near the source (within 300 kilometers) and wet deposition is important farther from the source (upwards of 500–2,000 kilometers). (For more complete information on transport, see *World Resources 1986*, pp. 167–169).

A long-term perspective on atmospheric deposition of acidic compounds in the Northern Hemisphere is provided by ice cores taken from the Greenland ice shelf. An analysis of the cores, which span more than a century (from 1869 to 1984), indicates that sulfates have dominated deposition since the early 20th Century, and nitrates have been prominent since about 1960 (46). These trends roughly parallel anthropogenic emissions over the same period.

The recent patterns of acid precipitation for North America and Europe are shown in Chapter 25, "Atmosphere and Climate," Figures 25.3 and 25.4.

The pH scale, used to determine the extent of acidity or alkalinity of a solution, ranges from 0 to 14; 7 is neutral. The more acidic a solution is, the higher is its hydrogen ion concentration and the *lower* is its pH value (battery acid, for example, has a pH of 1). High pH values indicate alkaline solutions (lye has a pH of 13). Normal rainfall has a pH between 5.6 and 6.8. Because the pH scale is logarithmic, a change of one unit represents a tenfold change in the hydrogen ion concentration. Hence, a solution at pH 4 is ten times as acidic as a solution at pH 5 and 100 times as acidic as a solution at pH 6.

Large areas downwind from major emission sources routinely experience precipitation with pH averages of 4.1–4.5. Individual weather events can have rainfall as acidic as pH 2.2 or below (47). This analysis is supported by data from the European Monitoring and Evaluation Program (EMEP), which now consists of 82 monitoring stations in 23 countries. Long-term mean values show that a large section of central Europe has pH levels of

4.2 or below (48). According to OECD, in polluted areas in Scandinavia, Japan, Central Europe, and eastern North America, annual pH values ranged from 3.5 to 5.5, the sulfate content of rainfall (SO_4) varied from 1 to 12 milligrams per liter, and nitrate concentrations (NO_3) averaged 0.5–6 milligrams per liter (49).

More spatially and temporally detailed analyses of trends over recent decades are possible using monitoring data available for the northern European sites of the European Air Chemistry Network (EACN). The EACN was inaugurated in Sweden in the early 1950s and was the first to detect increasing acidity and sulfate concentrations in precipitation (50). Over the years, the number of participating stations varied from 50 to slightly over 100, but all the non-Swedish stations have been gradually absorbed by national institutions, and European monitoring is now coordinated by the EMEP network (51). Sulfate concentrations in precipitation increased an average of about 2.5 percent per year from 1955 to 1975 at 12 sites in Scandinavia (52). Throughout much of the network, anthropogenic emissions of sulfur increased 50 percent between 1955 and 1970, but 1972–82 emissions in the United Kingdom, the Federal Republic of Germany, the Netherlands, Sweden, Norway, and Denmark decreased substantially (in Sweden nearly 50 percent) (53). Since 1975, sulfate concentrations have either decreased—an average of 20 percent in Norway and Sweden—or remained constant over most of the network (54). These observations are consistent with the estimated decrease in emissions over the past decade.

Nitrate concentrations have generally increased since the 1950s. A recent analysis of EACN data revealed that nitrate concentrations doubled at most stations between the late 1950s and the early 1970s, with a less pronounced increase in ammonium (55). For the 12 sites in Scandinavia, increases in nitrate averaged about 6 percent per year from 1960 to 1980 (56). However, for 12 stations in Sweden, no further increases of nitrate or ammonium were detected between 1972 and 1984 (57). These overall deposition trends roughly follow the pattern of nitrogen emissions for Western Europe during the monitoring period.

North America's monitoring efforts, which began much later, can provide less historical data. Only one site in the United States—Hubbard Brook, New Hampshire—has a record extending over 20 years (58). The data from this northeastern site show no marked trend in acidity, but they do show a general decrease in sulfate accompanied by a roughly compensating increase in nitrate concentrations from about 1964 to 1977. The trends in sulfate and nitrate deposition correspond to sulfur and nitrogen emissions. (For more information on deposition, see *World Resources 1986*, pp. 168–169).

The Costs of Damage Control

The European Community calculated that reducing SO_2 emissions 55–65 percent (between 1980 and 2000) would cost its member nations $4.6–$6.7 billion per year (59). Reducing nitrogen oxide levels a modest 10 percent by the year 2000 would cost members $100–$400 million a year (60).

Although the damage costs from material and fish losses are estimated to run up to $3 billion a year for OECD countries, air pollution damage to crops, forests, and human health have yet to be assessed adequately (61).

AIR POLLUTION AND ACID RAIN IN THE THIRD WORLD: A CASE STUDY OF CHINA

Although acid rain is unlikely to be a major concern in most developing countries, it is already threatening some heavily industrialized areas, particularly in China, Brazil, Nigeria, and South Africa (62).

China suffers from elevated levels of both sulfur dioxide and suspended particulate matter. This situation is caused principally by the large amount of coal burned in the country—in 1982, 459 million metric tons of coal were consumed which is 74 percent of the total amount of energy used (63).

Concentrations of SPM have been relatively high throughout China. The highest levels are recorded in the northern cities, with Shenyang reporting an annual average value of 470 micrograms per cubic meter of ambient air. (See Table 10.3.) These high levels are thought to be caused by the larger volumes of coal consumed in the North coupled with natural soil dust contributions. SPM also contains large amounts of heavy metals and hydrocarbons. Measurements carried out in the northern cities of Beijing and Tianjin revealed that hydrocarbons (benzene-soluble matter) composed approximately 8 percent of the particulates, and concentrations of lead, cadmium, and arsenic were 0.27, 0.003, and 0.13 micrograms per cubic meter, respectively (64).

In 1982, SO_2 emissions from coal combustion amounted to between 15 and 18 million metric tons, accounting for more than 90 percent of the total sulfur dioxide emitted in China (65).

Sulfur dioxide concentrations tend to be high throughout much of China, but the highest annual averages are reported for the southern cities, with Chongqing and Guiyang recording values of 430 and 413 micrograms per cubic meter, respectively. (See Table 10.3.) The main sources for most of this sulfur and particulate pollution are the large number of small and medium-size coal-burning stoves and furnaces used throughout the country (66).

Nitrogen oxide concentrations in Chinese cities still appear to be relatively low, reflecting the small number of motor vehicles. In 1981, the daily average NO_x concentration in 28 northern cities was 60 micrograms per cubic meter, and for 26 southern cities, it was only 40 micrograms per cubic meter (67).

Acid rain surveys conducted in cities throughout China since 1982 demonstrate a clear pattern of acidity in some parts of the country. More than half of all "rain events" in large areas south of the Yangtze River have a pH of less than 5.6 (68). The lowest annual average pH of rainwater is found in the cities of Chongqing (pH 4.14), Guiyang (pH 4.02), and neighboring areas in southwestern China (see Table 10.4)—values comparable to those in the eastern United States and Central Europe.

Some southern cities where acid rain seems rather common have relatively low SO_2 concentrations, but some northern cities heavily polluted by sulfur dioxide (i.e., Beijing and Tianjin) have no acid rain at all. Researchers have discovered that in northern China large amounts of ammonia combined with airborne alkaline particles buffer the acids before they reach the ground (69).

In contrast, paddy rice in the Chongqing area has been observed to turn yellow after a rainfall with a pH below 4.5, and the soil in some parts of the city has lower pH values than two decades ago (70). Further, acid rain has seriously corroded metal structures and concrete works in both Chongqing and Guiyang (71).

In order to determine more precisely the areas affected by acid deposition in China and its effects on crops, forests, soils, and cities, officials have launched an ambitious multidisciplinary research project, with results expected in the early 1990s.

EFFECTS OF AIR POLLUTANTS ON AGRICULTURAL CROPS

The harmful effects of ozone and sulfur dioxide on crops and vegetation have been known for more than 35 years (72). In 1980, the U.S. EPA launched the National Crop Loss Assessment Network (NCLAN) in an effort to ascertain the economic consequences of crop losses caused by air pollution. Among its original goals, the program was to determine the relationships between crop yields and

Table 10.4 Rainwater pH in Selected Cities in China, 1981–83

Location	City	Year	pH
North	Beijing	1981	6.80
North	Tianjin	1981	6.26
North	Lanzhou	Jan. 1981–Aug. 1982	6.85
South	Nanjing	June–Nov. 1981	6.38
South	Hangzhou	Sept.–Dec. 1981	5.10
South	Wuhan	Jan.–July 1983	6.44
South	Fuzhou	May 1982	4.49
South	Nanning	June–Nov. 1981	5.74
South	Yibin	1982	4.87
South	Chongqing	1982	4.14
South	Guiyang	1982	4.02

Source: Dianwu Zhao and Bozen Sun, "Air Pollution and Acid Rain in China," *AMBIO*, Vol. 15, No. 1 (1986), p. 4.

Table 10.3 Air Pollution in Residential Areas of Selected Cities in China, 1982

(micrograms per cubic meter)

Location	City	July Average	December Average	Annual Average
Total Suspended Particulates				
North	Shenyang	324	769	470
North	Beijing	165	585	403
South	Shanghai	161	322	244
South	Guangzhou	133	194	174
Sulfur Dioxide				
North	Shenyang	9	691	132
North	Beijing	53	388	158
South	Shanghai	53	121	65
South	Guangzhou	48	53	52
South	Chongqing[a]	280	610	430
South	Guiyang[a]	347	409	413

Note: a. Chinese Academy of Sciences, unpublished data.
Source: Dianwu Zhao and Bozen Sun, "Air Pollution and Acid Rain in China," *AMBIO*, Vol. 15, No. 1 (1986), p. 2.

three phytotoxic air pollutants and their mixtures: ozone, sulfur dioxide, and nitrogen dioxide (73). European scientists began to show renewed interest in the effects of photochemical oxidants and other pollutants on crops and forests about the same time. In the past few years, researchers have also begun to study the synergistic or additive interactions among ozone, sulfur dioxide, and nitrogen dioxide. All this work has given rise to a formidable literature, particularly on the effects of ozone on cash crops in Europe and North America.

Effects of Ozone on Crops

Visible injury to plants is one of the most obvious signs of ozone damage, but most plants initially suffer from unseen physiological effects of exposure to ozone. In addition to affecting leafy surfaces of plants, ozone also limits growth, decreases yields, lowers crop quality, and increases plant susceptibility to abiotic and biotic stresses (74).

Ozone enters a plant through its leaf openings (stomata). If enough ozone penetrates the sensitive cells of a leaf, photosynthesis, which is necessary for plant growth and development, is disrupted. Injury to the leaf (e.g., necrosis) is visible, and the secondary effects are manifested in reduced root growth and/or reduced yield of seeds or fruits (75).

Analyses of more than 100 studies of agricultural crops and 18 studies of tree species performed in the United States show that foliar injury on sensitive agricultural crops can be caused by ozone concentrations as low as 0.04–0.09 parts per million and on trees and shrubs with concentrations of 0.06–0.17 parts per million for a four-hour exposure (76). In general, the data indicate that ozone concentrations of 0.10 parts per million (frequently the lowest concentration used in the studies) for a few

hours a day for several days to several weeks caused significant yield reductions of 10–50 percent (77).

As can be seen from Table 10.5, a wide variety of plant cultivars and trees is susceptible to ozone damage at ambient levels. (See Box 10.1.) Research has documented the fact that ambient levels of ozone and other oxidants significantly reduce both yield and quality of citrus fruits, grapes, tobacco plants, cotton, potatoes (78), tomatoes, beans (79), soybeans (80), two sweet corn cultivars (81), and even native plants like forbes, grasses, and sedges (82). Bean yields, for example, decreased up to 22 percent in response to ozone concentrations in excess of 0.06 parts per million (83). In some cases, ozone damage to both beans and tobacco plants was more severe over a short period than the same dose spread over a longer time. On the other hand, low concentrations of ozone probably predispose the plants to damage from subsequent episodic ozone exposures (84).

Experiments in the United Kingdom also revealed that a number of crop species are sensitive to ozone exposure at ambient levels. Significant reductions in plant growth and yield were evident in white clover, red clover, French beans, peas, spinach, radish, and barley (85). Similar experiments in Denmark revealed the fact that ambient ozone levels damaged rape, pea, and bean plants (86).

Photochemical oxidants impair plant reproductive capacity, interfering with fertilization in soybeans, corn, wheat, and ornamental plants (87). Further, chronic ozone exposure predisposes both crops and trees to root rot and damage from insects, fungi, nematodes, and other disease organisms (88).

The Costs of Ozone Damage

Economists working with the U.S. National Crop Loss Assessment Network believe that ozone damage to U.S.

Table 10.5 Ozone Concentrations at Which Certain Plants Suffer Yield Losses

Plant Species	Duration of Exposure	Percent of Yield Reduction	Ozone Concentration (parts per million)
Alfalfa	7 h/d, 70 d	51, top dry wt[a]	0.10
Alfalfa	2 h/d, 21 d	16, top dry wt	0.10
Pasture grass	4 h/d, 5 d/wk, 5 wk	20, top dry wt	0.09
Ladino clover	6 h/d, 5 d	20, shoot dry wt	0.10
Soybean	6 h/d, 133 d	55, seed wt/plant	0.10
Sweet corn	6 h/d, 64 d	45, seed wt/plant	0.10
Sweet corn	3 h/d, 3 d/wk, 8 wk	13, ear fresh wt	0.20
Wheat	4 h/d, 7 d	30, seed yield	0.20
Radish	3 h	33, root dry wt	0.25
Beet	2 h/d, 38 d	40, storage root dry wt	0.20
Potato	3 h/d, every 2 wk, 120 d	25, tuber wt	0.20
Pepper	3 h/d, 3 d/wk, 11 wk	19, fruit dry wt	0.12
Cotton	6 h/d, 2 d/wk, 13 wk	62, fiber dry wt	0.25
Carnation	24 h/d, 12 d	74, flower bud no	0.05-0.09
Coleus	2 h	20, flower no	0.20
Begonia	4 h/d, once every 6 d for a total of 4 times	55, flower wt	0.25
Ponderosa pine	6 hr/d, 126 d	21, stem dry wt	0.10
Western white pine	6 h/d, 126 d	9, stem dry wt	0.10
Loblolly pine	6 h/d, 28 d	18, height growth	0.05
Pitch pine	6 h/d, 28 d	13, height growth	0.10
Hybrid poplar	12 h/d, 102 d	58, height growth	0.15
Hybrid poplar	8 h/d, 5 d/wk, 6 wk	50, shoot dry wt	0.15
Red maple	8 h/d, 6 wk	37, height growth	0.25
American sycamore	6 h/d, 28 d	9, height growth	0.05
Sweetgum	6 h/d, 28 d	29, height growth	0.10
White ash	6 h/d, 28 d	17, total dry wt	0.15
Green ash	6 h/d, 28 d	24, height growth	0.10
Willow oak	6 h/d, 28 d	19, height growth	0.15
Sugar maple	6 h/d, 28 d	12, height growth	0.15

h = hours; d = days; wk = weeks; h/d = hours per day; d/wk = days per week; wt = weight; no = number.
Note a. Alfalfa yields were reduced 51 percent as measured by dry weight.
Source: David T. Tingey, "The Effects of Ozone on Plants in the United States," in *Proceedings of an International Workshop on the Evaluation and Assessment of the Effects of Photochemical Oxidants on Human Health, Agricultural Crops, Forestry, Materials and Visibility,* Peringe Grennfelt, ed. (Swedish Environmental Research Institute, Gothenburg, 1984), p. 69.

crops amounts to $1–$5 billion a year. NCLAN researchers have determined that a 25 percent reduction in current ozone levels throughout North America would result in a benefit to society of from $1.6 to $1.9 billion a year, depending on the underlying assumptions. Conversely, a 25 percent increase in ambient ozone concentrations would cost society $1.9–$2.3 billion a year in lost production (in 1980 dollars) (89).

MULTIPLE POLLUTANTS AND FOREST DECLINE

Forest Declines in Europe

As of the end of 1985, at least 7 million hectares of forest lands in 15 European countries had been affected by *Waldsterben* (forest death). The massive forest decline observed in the Federal Republic of Germany over the past six years appears to be leveling off—at least in terms of its geographical distribution—but *Waldsterben* is increasing in extent and severity in Switzerland, Austria, Czechoslovakia, Poland, the German Democratic Republic, France, Italy, Yugoslavia, and Sweden. *Waldsterben*-like symptoms are seen in the United Kingdom, but government officials have yet to acknowledge them formally (90). (For more information on forest declines in Europe and North America, see *World Resources 1986*, pp. 203–224).

Swiss forests, which cover a full quarter of the country, were particularly hard hit in 1985–86. Overall, at least 36 percent of the country's forests are affected by *Waldsterben* (91). The most severely affected regions are mainly in the Swiss Alps, where trees are vital barriers against avalanches. Switzerland's Federal Office of Forestry reported that the disease syndrome has attacked or killed some 43 percent of the trees in the central alpine region situated between the French and Italian borders to the west and the Austrian border to the east. In addition, at least 56 percent of the trees in the mountainous canton of Grisons (in the southeast) have been stricken (92).

The Federal Republic of Germany is still the most seriously affected country, with 3.8 million hectares, or 52 percent of its forests, in various stages of decline and death (93).

There is some optimism, however, that some of the declines in West Germany can be reversed. Trees suffering from deficiencies of calcium, magnesium, potassium, zinc, and manganese in the Black and Bavarian Forests recently recovered when they were carefully fertilized with the appropiate combination of soil nutrients (94). Scientists cautioned that this measure is not a cure for *Waldsterben*, only a stopgap until overall pollution loads are reduced. This method of treatment, of course, does not apply to all afflicted forest stands, only those where nutrient deficiencies dominate other symptoms. Nonetheless, it holds promise as an immediate way to reduce damage from *Waldsterben*.

The forest declines observed in Poland, the German Democratic Republic, and Czechoslovakia are thought to be far more severe than official figures indicate. Unofficial estimates place the amount of damage at up to 1.5 million hectares for Poland, 2.5 million hectares for the German Democratic Republic, and more than 1 million hectares for Czechoslovakia (95).

Forest Declines in North America

North America's higher elevation eastern coniferous forests have experienced a rapid and severe deterioration since 1983–84. The most severely affected areas are in the Appalachian Mountains from Georgia to New England. (For a more extensive discussion of forest declines in Europe and North America, see *World Resources 1986*, pp. 203–224.)

A six-state study in the southern Appalachian region recently revealed that Eastern white pine (*Pinus strobus*) is suffering from pollution-related declines in 23 percent of the stands surveyed. The area with the highest incidence of decline was in Kentucky, where 77 percent of all the white pine surveyed showed air pollution damage (96). Even more alarming is the finding that trees with air pollution damage "were growing 49 percent less volume on the average than healthy trees, resulting in an annual loss of $708,000" (97). The main pollutant known to damage white pine is ozone, along with other photochemical oxidants.

An extensive research program is underway on Mount Mitchell, North Carolina, to study the widespread decline of both Fraser fir and red spruce noted over the past three years. (See Box 10.2.)

Recent studies indicate that Canadian forests are also threatened by acid deposition, heavy metals, and ozone. Of Canada's 161 million hectares of productive and accessible forests, 46 million hectares, or 28 percent of the total, receive wet acid sulfate depositions greater than 20 kilograms per hectare per year (the threshold at which sensitive lakes are known to become acidified) (98). Even higher levels have been recorded. Wet acid sulfate deposition exceeding 40 kilograms per hectare per year falls regularly on southwest Ontario and southeastern Quebec (99), and acid nitrate ranging from 10 to 30 kilograms per hectare per year is found over smaller areas in western and eastern Canada (100). Clearly, some Canadian forests receive excessive amounts of acidic deposition, but so far no massive *Waldsterben*-like declines have been reported.

A Comparison of Declining and Healthy Forests

Dr. Robert I. Bruck of North Carolina State University in Raleigh has compiled the results of a three-year study comparing the relative health and growth of higher-elevation stands of conifers in the Black Forest area of the Federal Republic of Germany; the southern Appalachian Mountains, the Mount Hood area of Oregon's Cascade range, the Gothic Mountain-Gunnison area of the Colorado Rocky Mountains, and the Alaska Range surrounding Mt. McKinley in the United States; and the Mount Everest Solu-Khumbu region of the Himalayas. The results, depicted in Figure 10.2, show significant decreases in annual radial growth rates only in Central Europe and eastern North America, areas known to be

Atmosphere and Climate

Box 10.2 Disaster on Mount Mitchell

Mount Mitchell, North Carolina, is the highest peak in eastern North America. But if its high elevation spruce-fir forests continue to decline as rapidly as they are at present, the entire crown of the mountain will either be bald or its once lush coniferous ecosystem will be replaced with something entirely different.

According to Robert I. Bruck, the project director on Mount Mitchell, whatever replaces the spruce-fir ecosystem must be able to withstand the alphabet soup of pollutants that spills over the mountain almost daily. During the summer of 1986, Dr. Bruck and his colleagues discovered unusually high levels of pollution at two monitoring stations high on the mountain. On a number of occasions, ozone concentrations were observed above 120 parts per billion—the standard set by the U.S. Environmental Protection Agency (EPA) that should not be exceeded for more than one hour a year. In one 35-day period, that concentration was exceeded 11 times, generally for several hours (1). Similarly, the acidity of the clouds that swaddle the mountain in mist and fog for seven days out of ten is extremely high: pH levels range from 2.4 to 4.7, with many cloud events showing a pH of 2.6 or below—1,000 times more acidic than normal rainfall at pH 5.6 (2). In addition, elevated levels of heavy metals have also been found, with lead concentrations reaching two grams per square meter of forest floor (up to ten times the normal concentration) (3).

The result is a dramatic and sustained decline in both radial growth and needle retention for Fraser fir and red spruce.

Although some biological factors affected the decline of Fraser fir, no significant biotic or nonpollution-related abiotic factors were associated with the red spruce declines. Figure 1 illustrates the rapidity of the decline syndrome. In 1984, nearly 80 percent of the red spruce on Mount Mitchell showed the normal range of defoliation (0–10 percent). By 1986, over 60 percent of the spruce was suffering foliage losses of 11–50 percent, with a total stand mortality of nearly 10 percent.

Although Dr. Bruck cautions that scientists may never find any smoking pistols in this decline syndrome—definitely linking specific air pollutants to the decline symptoms—strong correlative evidence suggests that airborne chemical pollutants are important to this process of destruction.

References and Notes

1. Associated Press, "Ozone Blamed for Ailing Appalachian Trees," *The Charlotte Observer* (August 11, 1986, Charlotte, North Carolina).
2. Robert I. Bruck, Professor, North Carolina State University, Raleigh, 1986 (personal communication).
3. Robert Bruck, "Boreal Montane Ecosystem Decline in the Southern Appalachian Mountains: Potential Role of Anthropogenic Pollution," in *Air Pollutants Effects on Forest Ecosystems* (Acid Rain Foundation, St. Paul, Minnesota, 1985), p. 150.

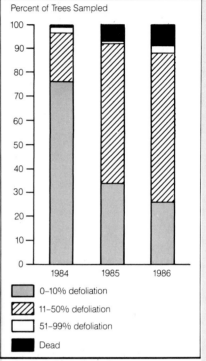

Figure 1 Decline of Red Spruce, Mount Mitchell, North Carolina, 1984–86

Percent of Trees Sampled

- ▨ 0–10% defoliation
- ▨ 11–50% defoliation
- ☐ 51–99% defoliation
- ■ Dead

Source: Jaime Cavalier, Robert Bruck, *et al.*, *Summary of Initial Observations at Mount Mitchell* (North Carolina State University, Raleigh, 1986).

---

affected by high levels of atmospheric contaminants. Further, the growth rates of the afflicted trees had been decreasing for 20–30 years before any visible symptoms of damage appeared.

Elevated levels of heavy metals were also detected in the soils of declining forests in Central Europe and the southern Appalachians, levels not found in healthy forests. High concentrations of lead, usually over 400 milligrams per kilogram of soil, were found in the West German (Bavarian) Alps, and, in the southern Appalachian Mountains, levels were consistently over 200 milligrams per kilogram of soil sampled (101).

FOCUS ON: DECREASING LEVELS OF STRATOSPHERIC OZONE

Ozone (O_3) is a variant of oxygen, present throughout the atmosphere but concentrated in a belt between 10 and 50 kilometers above the earth's surface. Although ozone in the troposphere (nearest the earth's surface) is a potent pollutant adversely affecting human health and plant life, it is a valuable component of the upper atmosphere, where it acts as a filter, absorbing harmful wavelengths of ultraviolet radiation (UV). Without this radiation shield, more UV radiation would reach the surface of the earth, damaging plant and animal life and greatly increasing the risk of skin cancers (102).

In 1974, two scientists, Mario Molina and F.S. Rowland of the University of California, postulated that the widespread use of chlorofluorocarbons (CFCs)—highly stable compounds used in aerosol propellants, refrigeration, foam-blowing, and industrial solvents—could have adverse effects on the world's ozone shield (103). They hypothesized that CFC gases could add chlorine to the stratosphere and, through complex chemical reactions, reduce the amount of stratospheric ozone, allowing more harmful UV radiation to reach the earth's surface.

This hypothesis had a profound effect on both the CFC industry and national governments. The United States, Canada, and Sweden first banned the nonessential uses of CFC propellants in spray products, and several other Nordic countries followed suit. According to OECD, this action resulted in an initial decrease in the world production of the two major chlorofluorocarbons—CFC-11 and CFC-12—from 850,000 metric tons in 1974 to around 740,000 metric tons by 1979 (104). However, total CFC production data have not been available since 1975,

Figure 10.2 Tree Growth in Six Boreal Forests, 1920 – 85[a]

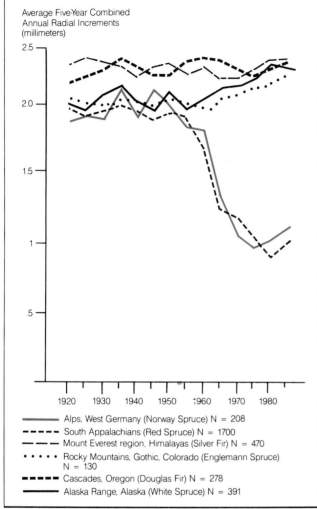

Average Five-Year Combined Annual Radial Increments (millimeters)

——— Alps, West Germany (Norway Spruce) N = 208

- - - - South Appalachians (Red Spruce) N = 1700

— – — Mount Everest region, Himalayas (Silver Fir) N = 470

• • • • Rocky Mountains, Gothic, Colorado (Englemann Spruce) N = 130

▬ ▬ ▬ Cascades, Oregon (Douglas Fir) N = 278

——— Alaska Range, Alaska (White Spruce) N = 391

Note: a. Average of five-year combined annual radial increments taken from six boreal montane ecosystems on three continents. All trees were dominant or co-dominant from well-stocked undisturbed stands. Trends show significant decreases in annual radial growth rates only in Central Europe and eastern North America.
Source: Robert I. Bruck, "Studies Concerning the Incidence of Forest Decline on Three Continents" (unpublished, North Carolina State University, Raleigh, 1986), p. 61.

when the Soviet Union, Eastern Europe, and China stopped reporting production levels (105).

Current estimates are based mainly on data provided by manufacturers in the OECD plus a few developing countries (e.g., Brazil and India) to the Chemical Manufacturers Association (CMA). According to CMA data, the production of CFC-11 and CFC-12 increased from 694,500 metric tons in 1984 to 703,200 metric tons in 1985 (106). Recent estimates provided by the Rand Corporation and the U.S. EPA indicate that the world use of CFC-11 and CFC-12 in 1985 (including estimates for the centrally planned economies) amounted to more than 785,000 metric tons, with the United States accounting for about one quarter to one half the world use of CFCs and other fully halogenated halocarbons (107). (See Table 10.6.) The

numbers are uncertain because of the absence of any centralized reporting for halogenated chemicals—other than CFC-11 and CFC-12—and on releases of some other halogenated halocarbons thought to be increasing rapidly. If these figures are accurate, the initial decrease in production registered in 1974 has been offset by increases in CFC use, particularly within OECD countries, most likely as blowing agents in closed-cell foam and as solvents. It is thought that non-OECD countries also increased production and use of CFCs between 1984 and 1985, although no comprehensive figures are available (108).

According to the CMA, the cumulative amount of CFC-11 and CFC-12 produced through 1985 is estimated at 6.3 million metric tons and 8.5 million metric tons, respectively (109).

Emissions of CFC-11 and CFC-12 from 1925 to 1985 are shown in Chapter 25, "Atmosphere and Climate," Table 25.2 and Figure 25.2. Emissions grew steadily and peaked in the early 1970s. Although they declined during the late 1970s, they began climbing again in the early 1980s.

Trace Gases and Ozone Concentrations

Stratospheric ozone is particularly affected by changes in the concentrations of the CFCs, carbon dioxide, methane, and nitrous oxide, the same gases that affect global temperatures and drive climate change (110). (See Chapter 25, "Atmosphere and Climate," Figure 25.1.) As of the end of 1985, average global atmospheric concentrations of CFC-11 and CFC-12 amounted to 230 parts per trillion volume and 400 parts per trillion volume, respectively. Concentrations of these chlorofluorocarbons are increasing annually at rates of about 5 percent for CFC-11 and CFC-12 (111) and 10 percent for CFC-113. Concentrations of methane and nitrous oxide were also increasing: methane concentrations were 1.65 parts per million volume at the end of 1985, increasing at an average annual rate of about 1 percent (112); average global nitrous oxide concentrations were about 304 parts per billion volume (as of late 1985), increasing at an annual rate of 0.2 percent (113). Carbon dioxide concentrations have been increasing at a rate of 0.4 percent per year. (See Table 10.7.)

Table 10.6 Estimated World Use of Potential Ozone-Depleting Substances, 1985

(thousands of metric tons)

Chemical	World	United States	Other Reporting Countries	Centrally Planned Economies[a]
CFC-11	341.5	75.0	225.0	42.5
CFC-12	443.7	135.0	230.0	78.7
CFC-113	163.2	73.2	85.0	5.0
Methyl chloroform	544.6	270.0	187.6	87.0
Carbon tetrachloride	1,029.0	280.0	590.0	159.0
Halon 1301	10.8	5.4	5.4	0.0
Halon 1211	10.8	2.7	8.1	0.0

Note: a. Estimated data. The centrally planned economies, including the USSR, China, and Eastern Europe, have not reported total production and use figures since 1975. The USSR, however, reported some figures in September 1986.
Source: James K. Hammitt, et al., Product Uses and Market Trends for Potential Ozone-Depleting Substances, 1985-2000, R-3386-EPA (Rand Corporation, Santa Monica, California, 1986), p. 2.

Table 10.7 Increasing Concentrations of Trace Gases, 1985

Gas	Rate of Increase (percent per year)	Effects	Sources	Lifetime (years)
Carbon dioxide	0.4 0.2–0.7	Added greenhouse effect	Natural, combustion (i.e., fossil fuels)	10–15
Methane	1.3 1–2	Added greenhouse effect	Natural, food production	7–10
Nitrous oxide	0.2–0.3	Added greenhouse effect, ozone depletion (stratosphere)	Natural, combustion, agriculture	100
CFC–11 and CFC–12	>5	Added greenhouse effect, ozone depletion (stratosphere)	Anthropogenic	50–100
Others CFC–113 CFC–22 Methyl chloroform Carbon tetrachloride	10 11 5–7 1–3	Ozone depletion (stratosphere), added greenhouse effect	Anthropogenic	Long 15 6 >50

Source: Adapted from R.A. Rasmussen and M.A.K. Khalil, "The Behavior of Trace Gases in the Troposphere," *The Science of the Total Environment*, Vol. 48 (1986), p. 177.

Concentrations of two other gases that have less impact on stratospheric ozone depletion have also been increasing. They are methyl chloroform (130 parts per trillion volume, increasing at a rate of 7 percent per year) and carbon tetrachloride (125 parts per trillion volume, increasing at a rate of 1 percent per year) (114).

Early estimates, based on limited data and the use of one-dimensional models, indicate that the continued use of CFCs at mid-1970s levels would result in an ozone reduction of 7–13 percent by the middle of the next century (115). However, newer one-dimensional models based on the long-term release of CFCs at 1980 rates suggest that the vertical ozone column would be reduced about 5–8 percent by 2050 (116). This figure assumes no increase in the other key trace gases (mentioned above). Using the same base year (1980) and assumptions as the earlier estimates, two-dimensional models predicted a global decrease in the ozone column of about 9 percent by 2050, involving a reduction of around 4 percent in the tropics, 9 percent in the temperate zones, and up to 14 percent in the polar regions (117).

In 1985, when British scientists monitoring the ozone layer over Antarctica reported a thinning of the ozone shield (commonly called a "hole"), the debate switched into high gear (118). The hole is now roughly the size of the continental United States, and it appears to be growing larger every year. In this hole, springtime ozone levels have decreased more than 40 percent since the mid-1970s (119). (See Figure 10.3.) According to Dr. Rowland, the hole is "unprecedented anywhere else in the atmosphere. It was not predicted. The questions now are will it spread and how rapidly will it spread"(120).

The hole in the ozone layer has prompted another debate about its probable causes. Chlorofluorocarbons are suspect, of course, but so too are solar radiation, polar

winds, and some complex chemical processes that may result from the unique meteorological conditions in the polar regions. According to the National Air and Space Administration, however, "it is not yet evident whether the behavior in Antarctic ozone is an early warning of future changes in global ozone or whether it will always be confined to the Antarctic due to the special geophysical conditions that exist there" (121). Preliminary results of studies carried out in late 1986 indicate that the hole reappeared and that chlorine (caused by CFCs) remains one of several plausible explanations of the phenomenon. (See Figure 10.3 and "Recent Developments," below.)

Figure 10.3 Monthly Means of Total Ozone at Halley Bay, Antarctica, October 1957–85

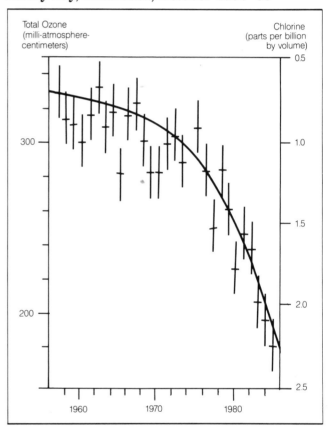

Source: F. Sherwood Rowland, University of California at Irvine (unpublished, October 1986).

RECENT DEVELOPMENTS

EARTH'S CLIMATE WARMING FASTER THAN PREDICTED

Nineteen eighty-six may well be remembered in science circles as the year when a consensus, of sorts, was reached on global climate change. New, more sophisticated computer models (called GCM-mixed layer ocean models), using better data, indicate that the earth's climate is not only growing warmer but it is doing so faster than scientists had previously predicted. As a result of increasing levels of carbon dioxide, combined with rising concentrations of other important trace gases like CFCs, methane, and nitrous oxide (see Table 10.7), global temperatures may increase 3.5–4.2°C by the middle of the next century (122). In support of this prognosis, the World Meteorological Organization (WMO) reported that the increased growth of climate-impacting greenhouse gases is now 3–10 times greater than the mean rate for the period 1850–1960, mainly because of increases in the production rates of carbon dioxide and of other important trace gases (123). (For further discussion of climate change, see *World Resources 1986*, pp. 173–177.)

Although there is now a general consensus within the scientific community that the world's climate is likely to grow warmer, how soon and what policy responses should be implemented to deal with the change are still disputed. An Advisory Group on Greenhouse Gases (AGGG) was established in 1986 as a result of the 1985 Villach Conference. (See *World Resources 1986*, p. 175.) Meeting in Geneva in June-July 1986, AGGG agreed that limiting emissions of the greenhouse gases—carbon dioxide, methane, CFCs, ozone, and nitrous oxide, among others—should be achieved primarily through energy conservation (124).

Other meetings, in Vienna and Washington, D.C., echoed the concern expressed by the AGGG. Scientists and policymakers alike are concerned about the impending rise in sea levels predicted by the newer climate change models. According to the latest assessments, global sea levels are expected to rise 20–140 centimeters by the year 2050 as a result of melting polar ice, shrinking continental glaciers, and the oceans' natural tendency to expand when heated (125) (126) (127). As a result, both the Geneva and Vienna groups recommended regional studies on the impacts and policy responses to such climatic side effects as drier grain belts and rising sea levels. Climatologists are urging that the first areas to be evaluated for potentially harmful impacts from climate change should be North America's Great Lakes region, Southeast Asia, and Europe's boreal forests (128).

Climate change is a much more complicated issue than it was a few years ago, when controlling carbon dioxide emissions (from burning fossil fuels) was thought to be the main solution. The scientific community now maintains that ozone depletion and climate modification can no longer be considered unrelated issues because the same trace gases affect both ozone levels and global climate.

DEPLETION OF THE OZONE LAYER

International negotiations began in December 1986 on implementation of the Vienna Convention for Protection of the Ozone Layer, signed by 28 countries in 1985. The United States proposed an immediate freeze on production of chlorofluorocarbons and a gradual phase-out. In 1985 The European Community proposed a freeze on production *capacity*, which would allow a growth of about 30 percent in production, under current capacity. Several nongovernmental organizations, including the World Resources Institute, proposed an immediate reduc-

tion in production of CFCs followed by a gradual phase-out.

In the fall of 1986 U.S. and European CFC manufacturers reversed their previous positions and supported a limit on production. The DuPont Company, the largest CFC manufacturer, went a step further and said that if production of CFCs is totally or almost totally banned, it could economically produce safe and effective substitutes within five years. It already has a product, F-22, which has less effect on stratospheric ozone. F-22 is already in widespread use in refrigeration and air conditioning applications. DuPont, which has been looking for substitutes for CFC-11 and CFC-12 since 1979, is also experimenting with CFC-134a, which deteriorates before reaching the upper atmosphere. Because retooling for and producing substitutes for the current chlorofluorocarbons would be costly, no single manufacturer is likely to take action in the absence of direct incentives or an international agreement to limit or ban CFC-11 and CFC-12.

A study by the World Resources Institute concludes that global CFC emissions could be quickly and affordably reduced one third by using CFC substitutes, banning aerosols, and recycling CFCs (129).

HOLE IN OZONE LAYER STUDIED

In August-October 1986, 15 scientists from a variety of institutions flew to Antarctica to study the hole in the earth's ozone shield that appears over the frozen continent in the Antarctic spring. The scientific team launched 33 balloons with upper atmospheric measuring instruments and took spectrometric ground readings in an effort to understand interactions of the gases involved in ozone depletion.

The U.S. National Science Foundation reported that the expedition confirmed a large hole or depression in the ozone layer, but so far there are not enough data to establish its cause(s). Team Leader Susan Solomon, a chemist with the National Oceanic and Atmospheric Administration in Boulder, Colorado, stated that "we suspect a chemical process is fundamentally responsible," thus dampening theories that polar winds or high solar activity causes the hole to appear each spring (130). However, scientists hope that when all the data from the expedition are finally analyzed, a clearer picture of the cause(s) of the hole will emerge.

CZECHOSLOVAKIA WORKS TO IMPROVE ITS ENVIRONMENT

Czechoslovakia, one of the most polluted countries in Europe, is beginning to take action to reduce air pollution. In mid-1986, the government announced that it was taking steps to clean the air by spending a rather modest $200 million over the next few years to combat air and water pollution (131).

Part of the money will go toward developing new techniques for cleaning the dirty brown coal burned throughout much of the country, eventually eliminating up to 90 percent of the sulfur oxide emissions.

Meanwhile, thousands of hectares of damaged forest lands in the northern part of the country are being

Atmosphere and Climate

pelted with "lime bombs" dropped from aircraft. In July 1986, 1,350 hectares of the Besklds Mountains forest, south of the city of Ostrava, were sprayed with dolomite lime in an effort to promote its recovery from heavy assaults of acid rain and other pollutants. In August 1986, another 1,450 hectares of degraded forest land in

Jeseniky, near the Polish border, were dosed with lime (132). Yet it is doubtful that liming damaged forest soils will help reverse forest decline; only reductions of pollutants at their source will bring long-term relief to the country's threatened forest lands.

References and Notes

1. Organisation for Economic Co-operation and Development (OECD), *The State of the Environment 1985* (OECD, Paris, 1985), p. 18.
2. Vivian E. Thomson, Environmental Protection Specialist, Office of Air and Radiation, U.S. Environmental Protection Agency, 1986 (personal communication).
3. Elaine Haemisegger, *et al.*, *The Air Toxics Problem in the United States: An Analysis of Cancer Risks for Selected Pollutants*, EPA-450/1-85-011 (U.S. Environmental Protection Agency, Washington, D.C., 1985), p. 16.
4. Organisation for Economic Co-operation and Development (OECD), *Polycyclic Aromatic Compounds in the Air—Report of an Expert Meeting* (OECD, Paris, 1983).
5. *Op. cit.* 1, p. 38.
6. World Resources Institute and International Institute for Environment and Development, *World Resources 1986* (Basic Books, New York, 1986), pp. 217–219.
7. *Op. cit.* 1, p. 38.
8. *Op. cit.* 1, p. 38.
9. *Op. cit.* 1, p. 41.
10. *Op. cit.* 1, p. 41.
11. *Op. cit.* 1, p. 41.
12. *Op. cit.* 1, p. 43.
13. H.B. Singh, *et al.*, *Measurements of Hazardous Organic Chemicals in the Ambient Atmosphere* (U.S. Environmental Protection Agency, Environmental Sciences Research Laboratory, Research Triangle Park, North Carolina, 1983), p. 80.
14. *Op. cit.* 3, pp. 30–42.
15. *Op. cit.* 1, p. 43.
16. *Op. cit.* 1, p. 43.
17. *Op. cit.* 3, pp. 38–42.
18. National Research Council, *Indoor Pollutants* (National Academy Press, Washington, D.C., 1981), p. 30.
19. *Ibid.*
20. *Op. cit.* 3, p. 74.
21. A.V. Nero, *et al.*, "Distribution of Airborne Radon 222 Concentrations in U.S. Homes" (submitted to *Science*, June 1986).
22. Gun Swedjemark and Lars Mjones, *Exposure of the Swedish Population to Radon Daughters* (National Institute of Radiation Protection, Stockholm, 1986), p. 39.
23. *Op. cit.* 18.
24. Mark Uehling *et al.*, "Radon Gas: A Deadly Threat," *Newsweek* (August 18, 1986), pp. 60–61.
25. Michael Weisskopf, "Cancer-Causing Gas Radon in 1 of 8 Homes, EPA Says," *The Washington Post* (August 15, 1986), pp. A7–A8.
26. Robert Pear, "Safety Standard Is Set on

Radon in U.S. Homes," *The New York Times* (August 15, 1986).
27. *Op. cit.* 22.
28. *Op. cit.* 18, p. 84.
29. *Op. cit.* 3, p. 74.
30. *Op. cit.* 3, p. 31.
31. U.S. Department of Interior, Bureau of Mines, *Mineral Industry Surveys—Asbestos* (U.S. Department of Interior, Washington, D.C., 1979).
32. *Op. cit.* 18, p. 112.
33. S. Speil and J.P. Leineweber, "Asbestos Minerals in Modern Technology," *Environmental Resources*, No. 2 (1969), pp. 166–208.
34. *Op. cit.* 18, p. 39.
35. *Op. cit.* 18, p. 32.
36. *Op. cit.* 18, p. 32.
37. *Op. cit.* 3, p. 74.
38. *Op. cit.* 2.
39. *Op. cit.* 2.
40. *Op. cit.* 18, p. 33.
41. H.W. de Koning, *et al.*, "Biomass Fuel Combustion and Health," *Bulletin of the World Health Organization*, Vol. 63, No. 1 (1985), pp. 20–21.
42. *Ibid.*, p. 21.
43. *Ibid.*, p. 11.
44. G.J. Cleary and C.R.B. Blackburn, "Air Pollution in Native Huts in the Highlands of New Guinea," *Archives of Environmental Health*, Vol. 17 (1968), pp. 785–794, cited in H.W. de Koning, *et al.*, "Biomass Fuel Combustion and Health," *Bulletin of the World Health Organization*, Vol. 63, No. 1 (1985), p. 17.
45. *Op. cit.* 44, p. 18.
46. P.A. Mayewski, *et al.*, *A Detailed Record (1869–1984) of Sulfate and Nitrate Concentrations from South Greenland* (in press, 1985).
47. Environmental Resources Ltd., *Acid Rain, A Review of the Phenomenon in the EEC and Europe* (Environmental Resources Ltd., London, 1983).
48. Economic Commission for Europe (ECE), *Report of the Second Phase of EMEP* (ECE, Geneva, 1985), pp. 2–4.
49. *Op. cit.* 1, p. 32.
50. L. Granat, "Sulphate in Precipitation as Observed by the European Atmospheric Chemistry Network," *Atmospheric Environment*, Vol. 12 (1978), pp. 413–424.
51. H. Rodhe and L. Granat, "An Evaluation of Sulfate in European Precipitation 1955–1982," *Atmospheric Environment*, Vol. 18, No. 12 (1984), p. 2627.
52. A.S. Kallend, *et al.*, "Acidity of Rain in Europe," *Atmospheric Environment*, Vol. 17, No. 1 (1983), pp. 127–137.
53. *Op. cit.* 51, p. 2636.
54. *Op. cit.* 51, p. 2627 and p. 2637.

55. H. Rodhe and M.J. Rood, "Temporal Evolution of Nitrogen Compounds in Swedish Precipitation since 1955," *Nature*, Vol. 321, No. 6072 (1986), pp. 762–764.
56. *Ibid.*
57. *Op. cit.* 55.
58. G. Likens, *et al.*, "Variations in Precipitation and Streamwater Chemistry at the Hubbard Brook Experimental Forest during 1964 to 1977," in *Proceedings of the NATO Conference on Effects of Acid Precipitation on Vegetation and Soils* (Toronto, Canada, 1978).
59. *Op. cit.* 1, pp. 32–33.
60. *Op. cit.* 1, p. 33.
61. *Op. cit.* 1, p. 33.
62. Robert Lamb, "Acidification Threatens Southern Hemisphere," *AMBIO*, Vol. 13, No. 4 (1984), pp. 284–285.
63. Dianwu Zhao and Bozen Sun, "Air Pollution and Acid Rain in China," *AMBIO*, Vol. 15, No. 1 (1986), p. 2.
64. Wang Mingxing, *Environmental Sciences in China* (in Chinese), Vol. 4 (1984), p. 36, cited in Dianwu Zhao and Bozen Sun, "Air Pollution and Acid Rain in China," *AMBIO*, Vol. 15, No. 1 (1986), pp. 2–3.
65. *Op. cit.* 63, p. 3.
66. *Op. cit.* 63, pp. 3–4.
67. *Op. cit.* 63, p. 4.
68. *Op. cit.* 63, p. 4.
69. *Op. cit.* 63, p. 4.
70. *Op. cit.* 63, p. 13.
71. *Op. cit.* 63, p. 13.
72. Richard M. Adams, *et al.*, *The Economic Effects of Ozone on Agriculture*, EPA-600/3-84-090 (U.S. Environmental Protection Agency, Corvallis, Oregon, 1984), p. ix.
73. "Statement of Dr. Leonard H. Weinstein and Dr. Jay S. Jacobson," in U.S. House of Representatives, Committee on Agriculture, Subcommittee on Forests, Family Farms, and Energy, *Review of Effects of Acid Deposition on Other Air Pollutants on Forest Productivity; Forest Ecosystems and Atmospheric Pollution Act of 1985; and the Endangered Forest Research Act of 1985*, Hearings, May 13, 1986, House Serial No. 99–27, p. 4.
74. David T. Tingey, *The Impact of Ozone on Vegetation*, EPA-600/D-34-291 (U.S. Environmental Protection Agency, Corvallis, Oregon, 1984), p. 1.
75. *Ibid.*
76. David T. Tingey, "The Effects of Ozone on Plants in the United States," in *The Evaluation and Assessment of the Effects of Photochemical Oxidants on Human Health, Agricultural Crops, Forestry, Materials and Visibility*, Peringe Grennfelt, ed. (Swedish Environmental Research Insti-

tute, Gothenburg, 1984), pp. 61–62.

77. *Op. cit.* 74, p. 13.

78. U.S. Environmental Protection Agency (EPA), *Air Quality Criteria for Ozone and Other Photochemical Oxidants,* EPA-600/8–78–004 (EPA, Research Triangle Park, North Carolina, 1978), cited in David T. Tingey, *The Impact of Ozone on Vegetation,* EPA-600/D–34–291 (EPA, Corvallis, Oregon, 1984), p. 15.

79. D.C. MacLean and R.E. Schneider, "Photochemical Oxidants in Yonkers, New York," *Journal of Environmental Quality,* Vol. 5 (1976), pp. 75–78, cited in David T. Tingey, *The Impact of Ozone on Vegetation,* EPA-600/D–34–291 (U.S. Environmental Protection Agency, Corvallis, Oregon, 1984), p. 15.

80. *Op. cit.* 74, p. 15.

81. C.R. Thompson, *et al.,* "Effects of Ambient Photochemical Oxidants on Growth, Yield, and Ear Characteristics of Two Sweet Corn Hybrids," *Journal of Environmental Quality,* Vol. 5 (1976), pp. 410–412.

82. S.F. Duchelle, *et al.,* "Effects of Ozone on the Productivity of Natural Vegetation in a High Meadow of the Shenandoah National Park of Virginia," *Journal of Environmental Management,* Vol. 17 (1983), pp. 299–308.

83. H.E. Heggestad and J.H. Bennett, "Photochemical Oxidants Potentiate Yield Losses in Snap Beans Attributable to Sulfur Dioxide," *Science,* Vol. 213 (1981), pp. 1008–1010, cited in David T. Tingey, *The Impact of Ozone on Vegetation,* EPA-600/D–34–291 (U.S. Environmental Protection Agency, Corvallis, Oregon, 1984), p. 16.

84. J. Johnston and A.S. Heagle, "Response of Chronically Ozonated Soybean Plants to Acute Ozone Exposure," *Phytopathology,* Vol. 73 (1982), pp. 387–389.

85. M.R. Ashmore, "Effects of Ozone on Vegetation in the United Kingdom," in *The Evaluation and Assessment of the Effects of Photochemical Oxidants on Human Health, Agricultural Crops, Forestry, Materials and Visibility,* Peringe Grennfelt, ed. (Swedish Environmental Research Institute, Gothenburg, 1984) pp. 92–102.

86. Helge Ro-Poulsen, *et al.,* "Effects of Ozone on Some Danish Agronomic Crops," in *The Evaluation and Assessment of the Effects of Photochemical Oxidants on Human Health, Agricultural Crops, Forestry, Materials and Visibility,* Peringe Grennfelt, ed. (Swedish Environmental Research Institute, Gothenburg, 1984), pp. 105–112.

87. *Op. cit.* 80, p. 20.

88. *Op. cit.* 80, p. 22.

89. *Op. cit.* 72, p. 71.

90. John Ardill, "Acid Rain Damage to Trees Worse than Thought, Scientist Claims," *The Guardian* (August 10, 1985), p. 2.

91. "Swiss Forests Are Depleted Further by Pollution," *The New York Times* (December 9, 1985).

92. *Ibid.*

93. Federal Ministry of Food, Agriculture and Forestry, *1985 Forest Damage Survey* (Federal Ministry of Food, Agriculture and Forestry, Bonn, West Germany, October 1985), Table 1.

94. Reinhard Huettl and Joe Wisniewski, "Fertilization as a Tool to Mitigate Forest Decline" (unpublished, Freiburg, West Germany, 1985), p. 9.

95. These figures were compiled by the author, based on estimates provided by researchers in Eastern Europe.

96. Robert Anderson, *et al.,* "Occurrence of Air Pollution Symptoms on Eastern White Pine in the Southern Appalachian Mountains" (U.S. Department of Agriculture, Forest Service, Asheville, North Carolina, draft, 1986), p. 1.

97. *Ibid.*

98. "Statement of Allen Torrenueva," in U.S. House of Representatives Committee on Agriculture Subcommittee on Forests, Family Farms, and Energy, *Review of Effects of Acid Deposition and Other Air Pollutants on Forest Productivity; Forest Ecosystems and Atmospheric Pollution Act of 1985; and the Endangered Forest Research Act of 1985,* Hearings, May 13, 1986, House Serial No. 99–27, p. 3.

99. *Ibid.*

100. Peter Rennie, "Air Pollution, Knowledge-Transfer and Abatement," *Workshop on Forests in Danger* (Royal Swedish Academy of Engineering Sciences, Ottawa, Canada, April 8, 1986), pp. 1–13.

101. Robert I. Bruck, "Studies Concerning the Incidence of Forest Decline on Three Continents" (unpublished, North Carolina State University, Raleigh, 1986), pp. 57–62.

102. National Research Council, *Causes and Effects of Changes in Stratospheric Ozone: Update 1983* (National Academy Press, Washington, D.C., 1984), pp. 164–167.

103. M.J. Molina and F.S. Rowland, "Stratospheric Sink for Chlorofluoromethanes: Chlorine Atom-Catalysed Destruction of Ozone," *Nature,* Vol. 249, No. 5460 (1974), pp. 810–812.

104. *Op. cit.* 1, p. 36.

105. The Soviet Union released data on CFC use in September 1986 for the first time since 1975.

106. Chemical Manufacturers Association (CMA), *Production, Sales, and Calculated Releases of CFC-11 and CFC-12 through 1985* (CMA, Washington, D.C., 1986), pp. 7–8.

107. James K. Hammitt, *et al., Product Uses and Market Trends for Potential Ozone-Depleting Substances, 1985–2000,* R-3386-EPA (Rand Corporation, Washington, D.C., May 1986), pp. 2–3.

108. *Op. cit.* 1, p. 36.

109. *Op. cit.* 106, p. 9.

110. R.T. Watson, *et al., Present State of Knowledge of the Upper Atmosphere: An Assessment Report,* Reference Publication 1162 (National Aeronautics and Space Administration, Washington, D.C., 1986), pp. 14–15.

111. *Ibid.,* p. 30.

112. *Ibid.,* p. 35.

113. *Ibid.,* p. 37.

114. *Ibid.,* p. 30.

115. A. Miller and I. Mintzer, *The Sky Is the Limit: Strategies for Protecting the Ozone Layer* (World Resources Institute, Washington, D.C., 1986).

116. World Meteorological Organization (WMO), *Atmospheric Ozone 1985: Assessment of our Understanding of the Processes Controlling its Present Distribution and Change,* Volume III, Global Ozone Research and Monitoring Project Report No. 16 (WHO, Geneva, 1986), p. 786.

117. *Ibid.*

118. *Op. cit.* 110, pp. 14–15.

119. *Op. cit.* 110, pp. 14–15.

120. Cass Peterson, "Decrease in Antarctic's Ozone Alarms Experts," *The Washington Post* (April 24, 1986).

121. *Op. cit.* 110, p. 15.

122. Richard A. Kerr, "Greenhouse Warming Still Coming," *Science,* Vol. 232 (May 2, 1986), p. 573.

123. *Op. cit.* 116, p. 875.

124. United Nations Environment Programme (UNEP), "A Warmer World" (UNEP, press release, Geneva, July 1986), pp. 1–3.

125. *Ibid.*

126. R.A. Rasmussen and M.A.K. Khalil, "The Behavior of Trace Gases in the Troposphere," *The Science of the Total Environment,* Vol. 48 (1986), p. 183.

127. United Nations Environment Programme, World Meteorological Organization (WMO), and International Council of Scientific Unions, *An Assessment of the Role of Carbon Dioxide and of Other Greenhouse Gases in Climate Variations and Associated Impacts* (WMO, Geneva, 1985).

128. *Op. cit.* 124, p. 2.

129. *Op. cit.* 115.

130. National Science Foundation (NSF), "Scientists Closer to Identifying Cause of Antarctic Ozone Depletion," (NSF, press release, Washington, D.C., October 20, 1986), pp. 1–2.

131. William Mahoney, "Czechoslovakia to Double Spending for Air, Water Improvements in Prague, Bohemia Region," *World Environment Report,* Vol. 12, No. 15 (1986), p. 118.

132. "Lime Bombs," *New Scientist,* Vol. 111, No. 1518 (1986), p. 19.

11. Global Systems and Cycles

We are witnessing the birth of a sweeping new science. From it will come a powerful new understanding of the planet's structure and metabolism that could vastly improve the chances of sustaining billions more people.

This new science, which is an integration of the traditional disciplines of geology, oceanography, ecology, meteorology, chemistry, and other sciences, has a variety of names—earth systems science, global change, and biogeochemistry. Its subject is nothing less than the composition, behavior, and interactions of the planet's nonliving realms or phases—the atmosphere, geosphere, and hydrosphere—and its living realm, the biosphere, which encompasses parts of each of the others.

This science also concerns the planetary distribution and the cycles of the chemical elements essential to life, especially carbon (C), nitrogen (N), phosphorus (P), and sulfur (S). These four are of greatest importance because they are required in large amounts by every living organism: carbon because it is the basis of life as we know it, nitrogen because of its structural role in all proteins, phosphorus because it links nucleic acids (the genetic material) and because high-energy phosphate bonds are the energy currency of all cells, and sulfur because of the sulfhydryl bonds that give proteins their three-dimensional structure and hence their specific activities. The cycles of each of these elements, like the planet's phases, interact with each of the others in both living and nonliving systems. For example, the local carbon-nitrogen balance regulates the rate of decomposition of organic matter, and the amount of phosphorus that is available strongly controls the rate of biological nitrogen fixation. On the other hand, abiotic nitrogen-sulfur interactions are pervasive in both soils and the atmosphere.

This new science is emerging now for three principal reasons. First, research over the past 30 years has produced a dramatically new understanding of the planet, revealing it to be in a state of constant motion and change rather than fully formed and stable. Manifestations of this planetary activity, such as earthquakes, volcanic activity, mountain building, and continental drift, can now be consistently explained. In addition, advancing understanding of the atmosphere, geosphere, hydrosphere, and biosphere has revealed a degree of interaction among them that was previously unrecognized. In turn, this understanding leads to the realization that, as complex as each phase is, none can be studied or understood in isolation from its interactions with the others. For example, the exchange of heat, water, and momentum between the atmosphere and the hydrosphere largely creates the global climate. On a more local scale, a mutually reinforcing interaction between vegetation loss (in the biosphere) and surface albedo, the reflective power of the earth's surface (in the geosphere), may create or prolong droughts.

A second reason for the emergence of this new science at the present time is that recent advances in technology have only now made it possible to measure and monitor the globe on a vast scale and to analyze and store the mass of data that are required. Remote sensing devices on satellites and other airborne platforms and developments in computer capabilities are the key advances but by no means the only ones. Extremely sophisticated sensors of various kinds on land and at sea are also providing unprecedented insights. For example, a new long-range sidescan sonar developed in Great Britain, called GLORIA, can be towed behind a ship to produce detailed scans of the seabed. On its first trip, GLORIA revealed 28 new volcanoes on the ocean floor. In a 1984 program, GLORIA scanned 850,000 square kilometers in 96 days, providing nearly complete coverage of the U.S. Exclusive Economic Zone on the west coast from Canada to Mexico at a cost of about 40 cents per hectare (1).

The forging of this new science, which requires scientists to move beyond the familiar disciplinary niches in which they are trained, is the result of a growing sense of urgency. It is clear that human activities have reached a scale great enough to affect planetary biogeochemical cycles. Carbon released from fossil fuel burning (and perhaps as a result of deforestation) has altered the carbon cycle, just as industrial nitrogen fixation and the release of nitrogen from chemical fertilizers have changed the natural nitrogen cycle. Synthetic choloroflourocarbons are depleting the stratospheric ozone layer—with ramifications throughout the atmosphere. Erosion and deforestation caused by humans have accelerated the flow of sediments and nutrients to the ocean, while irrigation systems have interrupted the flow. Deforestation in the Amazon drainage basin could multiply its discharge manyfold in the near future. Conversely, the Colorado and the Nile, which once discharged more than a million tons of suspended matter per year, now discharge essentially none (2).

These examples are a few of the dozens that could be cited. The characteristic they all share is that the consequences of these human interventions are largely unknown. The driving sense of urgency behind the emergence of the science of global change is the recognition that it is essential to understand these natural systems if humanity is to live successfully with its new ability to alter them.

Because of this intimate connection to humanity's long-term survivability on the planet, this chapter of *World Resources* will be devoted to the earth's systems and cycles. Each year the chapter will describe one of the key biochemical cycles: this year, the carbon cycle. Each chapter will also cover aspects of the emerging understanding of the role and composition of the planet's phases and the large-scale interactions among them. Ocean-atmosphere interactions and the geosphere-biosphere interactions that occur in their important interface, the soils, are discussed this year. Further, each chapter will treat developments and issues relating to the new techniques and technologies that make earth systems science possible. This year's chapter explores some of the capabilities, limitations and present applications of remote sensing technologies, and related analytical developments to human needs.

CONDITIONS AND TRENDS

THE CARBON CYCLE

The amounts of the essential chemical elements in the earth-atmosphere system are fixed. They do not change over time. However, the distribution of these elements—the amounts lodged in the atmosphere, oceans, soils, biota, etc.—can vary dramatically as can their chemical state and hence their availability to living organisms. The cycles of these elements, and their characteristic sources and sinks, are thus in large part responsible for establishing the conditions of life. If the cycles are perturbed, fundamental planetary characteristics, from the weather to the chemical composition of sediments, can change. Similarly, shifts in concentrations affect living organisms. More nitrogen present as ammonia, for example, is good for plant growth but is toxic to humans. Thus, understanding the essential biogeochemical cycles is a prerequisite to managing human impacts on the earth's systems in such a way as to avoid destructive change or eventually, perhaps, to improve conditions for plant growth or other human needs.

The carbon cycle is the obvious place to begin. The carbon atom is the backbone of biological matter. Atmospheric carbon—principally as carbon dioxide, methane, and carbon monoxide—accounts for the greenhouse effect and thereby the global climate. Solar energy becomes available for human use as chemical energy

Table 11.1 Major Carbon Reservoirs
(petagrams[a])

Atmosphere	Amount	Source
Carbon dioxide	729	1
Methane	3.4	2
Carbon monoxide	0.2	3
Total Atmosphere[b]	**733**	
Ocean		
Dissolved inorganic carbon	37,400	4
Dissolved organic carbon	1,000	5
Particulate organic carbon	30	5
Biota	3	6
Total Ocean	**38,400**	
Terrestrial Biota and Soils		
Biota	560	4
Litter	60	7
Soils	1,500	8
Peat	160	7
Total Terrestrial	**2,280**	
Lithosphere		
Sediments	56,000,000	9, 10
Rock	9,600,000	9, 10
Total Lithosphere	**66,000,000**	

Notes:
a. 1 petagram = 1 quadrillion grams (10^{15} grams).
b. Mid-1980s.

Sources:
1. T.J. Conway, et al., "Recent Results from the NOAA/GMCC CO_2 Flask Sampling Network," in Atmospheric Carbon Dioxide—Its Sources, Sinks, and Global Transport (International Association of Meteorology and Atmospheric Physics, Commission on Atmospheric Chemistry and Global Pollution, Kandersteg, Switzerland, 1985), pp. 2-9.
2. D.R. Blake, et al., "Methane Concentrations and Source Strengths in Urban Locations," Geophysical Research Letters, Vol. 11, pp. 1211-1214.
3. H. Niki, et al., "Carbon Cycle," in Global Tropospheric Chemistry—A Plan for Action, T. Malone, ed. (National Academy Press, Washington, D.C., 1984), pp. 122-127.
4. B. Bolin, et al., "The Global Biogeochemical Carbon Cycle" in The Global Carbon Cycle, SCOPE, Report No. 13, B. Bolin, et al., eds. (John Wiley and Sons, Chichester, United Kingdom, 1979), pp. 1-56.
5. K. Mopper and E.T. Degens, "Organic Carbon in the Ocean: Nature and Cycling," in The Global Carbon Cycle, SCOPE Report No. 13, B. Bolin, et al., eds. (John Wiley and Sons, Chichester, United Kingdom, 1979), pp. 293-316.
6. C.G.N. DeVooys, "Primary Production in Aquatic Environments," in The Global Carbon Cycle, SCOPE Report No. 31, B. Bolin, et al., eds. (John Wiley and Sons, Chichester, United Kingdom, 1979), pp. 259-292.
7. G.L. Atjay, et al., "Terrestrial Primary Production and Phytomass," in The Global Carbon Cycle, SCOPE Report No. 13, B. Bolin, et al., eds., (John Wiley and Sons, Chichester, United Kingdom, 1979), pp. 129-182.
8. W.H. Schlessinger, "The World Carbon Pool in Soil Organic Matter," in The Role of Terrestrial Vegetation in the Global Carbon Cycle, Measurement by Remote Sensing, SCOPE Report No. 23, G.M. Woodwell, ed. (John Wiley and Sons, Chichester, United Kingdom, 1984) pp. 111-127.
9. S. Kempe, "Carbon in the Freshwater Cycle," in The Global Carbon Cycle, SCOPE Report No. 13, B. Bolin et al., eds. (John Wiley and Sons, Chichester, United Kingdom, 1979), pp. 317-342.
10. S. Kempe, "Carbon in the Rock Cycle," in The Global Carbon Cycle, SCOPE Report No. 13, B. Bolin et al., eds. (John Wiley and Sons, Chichester, United Kingdom, 1979), pp. 343-378.

Table 11.2 Average Residence Time for a Representative Carbon Atom during One Cycle

(years)

Atmosphere	2,000
Land Biomass	800
Soil Humus	3,000
Ocean above Thermocline	
Inorganic Matter	3,000
Organic Matter	8,000
Biota	30
Deep Ocean	83,000
Sediments	100,000,000

Source: Michael McElroy, "Chemical Processes of the Solar System: A Kinetic Perspective," *The Industrial Review of Science*, Physical Chemistry Series Two, Vol. 9 (1976), pp. 127-211.

through photosynthesis, by which plants convert atmospheric carbon dioxide to sugar. Changes in the natural carbon cycle are likely to affect every aspect of life on the planet.

Carbon Reservoirs

The lithosphere—approximately the first 50 miles of the earth's crust—contains the vast majority of the earth's store of carbon. Most lithospheric carbon is in the form of carbonate and noncarbonate sediments, with a smaller amount found in sedimentary rock. The ocean is the second most abundant reservoir for carbon. The atmosphere, biosphere, and soils play a minor role by comparison. (See Table 11.1.)

Carbon atoms are in a state of continuous motion, flitting back and forth among these reservoirs. The carbon atom that we ingest as food we exhale as carbon dioxide. During its time in the atmosphere-geosphere-biosphere-upper ocean, a representative carbon atom may linger awhile as structural material of a tropical tree. It will be ingested many times by bacteria. It can move from pole to pole, from troposphere to stratosphere and from atmosphere to the upper ocean. The deep ocean is more stagnant. Once there, the atom is stranded for about 1,000 years until the water returns to the surface. Altogether, the atom may wander the face of the fluid earth for as long as 100,000 years before finally escaping to sediments at the bottom of the sea. (See Table 11.2.)

Most of this 100,000 years will be spent in the deep sea, below the thermocline. Only 2,000 years will be spent in the atmosphere. About 800 years will be spent as part of the land biomass, most probably incorporated in the wood tissue of trees. The atom will spend an average of about 3,000 years as a component of humus in the soil, 3,000 years as inorganic carbon above the thermocline in the sea, 8,000 years as marine organic carbon, and a total of less than 30 years in the ocean's thinly populated biosphere.

Once captured in the deep ocean sediments, the stay is much longer, about 100 million years, though still temporary. The sediments are transported on giant plates that keep the continents in perpetual motion. Eventually the carbon atom will be withdrawn to the lithosphere, raised to high temperatures, and ejected explosively in a volcano or a hot spring. The cycle then begins anew. It is a story that has been repeated at least 20 times over the history of the planet. It will continue for as long as there is life, and as long as there is energy from the sun

and the earth's interior to maintain the exquisite state of thermodynamic disequilibrium that distinguishes earth from its neighbors in space.

Carbon Fluxes

Large amounts of carbon are exchanged between the terrestrial biota and soils and the atmosphere and between the oceans and the atmosphere each year. (See Table 11.3.) It should be noted that the magnitude of many of these individual annual fluxes is poorly understood, and some—such as the contribution from fossil fuel combustion—are changing rapidly.

The exchange between the terrestrial biota and soils and the atmosphere is primarily associated with the biological processes of photosynthesis and respiration. Green plants annually convert a net total of about 55 petagrams (1 petagram equals 1 quadrillion [10^{15}] grams) of carbon from carbon dioxide to organic carbon, which they use to sustain themselves. Eventually this organic carbon is

Table 11.3 Major Carbon Fluxes

(petagrams per year[a])

	Amount	Source
Atmosphere to Land		
Atmosphere to green plants (net flux)	55	1
Land to Atmosphere		
Soil respiration	55	1
Fossil fuel combustion (1979-1982)	5.1–5.4	2
Deforestation (net)	0.9–2.5	3
Land to Ocean		
River transport (inorganic)	0.7	4
River transport (organic)	0.5	5
Atmosphere to Ocean		
Atmosphere to surface water	92.5	6
Ocean to Atmosphere		
Surface water to atmosphere	90.0	6
Within Ocean Fluxes		
Biotic turnover	40	7
Detritus fallout of surface water	4	7
Circulation of surface water into deeper water	38	6
Circulation of deep water into surface water	40	6
Ocean to Lithosphere		
Sedimentation (inorganic)	0.15	4, 8
Sedimentation (organic)	0.04	4, 8

Note:
a. 1 petagram = 1 quadrillion grams (10^{15} grams).

Sources:
1. R.H. Whittaker and G.E. Likens, "The Biosphere and Man," cited in "Primary Productivity of the Biosphere," *Ecological Studies*, H. Lieth, *et al.*, eds., Vol. 14 (Springer-Verlag, Berlin, 1975), pp. 305-328.
2. G. Marland and R.M. Rotty, "Carbon Dioxide Emissions from Fossil Fuels: A Procedure for Estimation and Results for 1950-1982," *Tellus*, Vol. 36B (1984), pp. 232-261.
3. R.A. Houghton, *et al.*, "Net Flux of Carbon Dioxide from Tropical Forests in 1980," *Nature*, Vol. 316 (1985), pp. 617-620.
4. S. Kempe, "Carbon in the Freshwater Cycle," in *The Global Carbon Cycle*, SCOPE Report No. 13, B. Bolin, *et al.*, eds. (John Wiley and Sons, Chichester, United Kingdom, 1979), pp. 317-342.
5. M. Meybeck, "Carbon, Nitrogen and Phosphorus Transport by World Rivers," *American Journal of Science*, Vol. 282 (1982), pp. 401-450.
6. B. Bolin, "On the Role of the Atmosphere in Biogeochemical Cycles," *Quarterly Journal of the Royal Meteorological Society*, Vol. 105 (1979), pp. 25-42.
7. C.G.N. DeVooys, "Primary Production in Aquatic Environments" in *The Global Carbon Cycle*, SCOPE Report No. 13, B. Bolin, *et al.*, eds. (John Wiley and Sons, Chichester, United Kingdom, 1979), pp. 259-292.
8. S. Kempe, "Carbon in the Freshwater Cycle," in *The Global Carbon Cycle*, SCOPE Report No. 13, B. Bolin *et al.*, eds. (John Wiley and Sons, Chichester, United Kingdom, 1979), pp. 317-342.
9. S. Kempe, "Carbon in the Rock Cycle," in *The Global Carbon Cycle*, SCOPE Report No. 13, B. Bolin, *et al.*, eds. (John Wiley and Sons, Chichester, United Kingdom, 1979), pp. 243-378.

transferred to the soil where it is broken down by microbes and returned to the atmosphere primarily as carbon dioxide.

The combustion of fossil fuels currently results in a transfer of about 5 petagrams of carbon each year from the land to the atmosphere. (See Figure 11.1.)

The exchange of carbon between the oceans and the atmosphere involves about 90 petagrams of carbon annually. The magnitude of this exchange is controlled by the concentrations of carbon dioxide in the atmosphere and dissolved inorganic carbon in the surface waters of the oceans, with the ocean carbon concentration controlled partly by physiochemical factors and partly by biological processes. In response to the increasing concentration of carbon dioxide in the atmosphere, the oceans are accumulating a small additional amount—about 2.5 petagrams—of carbon each year. (See Figure 11.1.)

The annual exchanges of carbon between the lithosphere and the other carbon reservoirs are small. (See Table 11.3 and Figure 11.1.) For example, sedimentation accounts for a transfer of about 0.2 petagrams of carbon per year from the oceans to the lithosphere.

Carbon in the Oceans and Atmosphere

On time scales of a few hundred years or longer, the abundance of carbon dioxide (CO_2) in the atmosphere is determined by the dynamics, chemistry, and biology of the ocean. Most ocean carbon is present in cold, relatively stagnant water at great depths. Carbon moves from the surface to the deep as part of the overall circulation

of the ocean and as a component of the organic waste formed in the upper layers of the sea. It returns to the atmosphere in association with a slow upwelling motion at low latitudes. As surface waters cool and sink at high latitudes, they draw carbon from the atmosphere in roughly equal amounts. Water sinks to great depths in only a few regions of the world's oceans, in the North Atlantic, where waters are relatively saline and consequently dense enough to sink as they cool, and in the regions around Antarctica, notably in the Weddell Sea, where the formation of sea ice contributes to locally high concentrations of salinity. In general, carbon enters the ocean mainly at high polar latitudes and is released at low tropical latitudes.

The concentration of CO_2 in the earth's atmosphere has risen steadily over the past 100 years, from about 280 parts per million (ppm) in 1850 to almost 350 parts per million today. The change is due largely to combustion of fossil fuel. Since the Industrial Revolution, we have mined and consumed almost 150 billion metric tons of organic carbon as coal, oil, and natural gas. In fact, carbon dioxide is the largest single waste product of modern society. The average individual on the planet is responsible for the release of almost four metric tons of CO_2 per year, more than that in the developed world. The global emission in 1985 was nearly 5.4 billion metric tons.

Approximately half the carbon emitted since the Industrial Revolution persists in the atmosphere today. The balance is presumed to have made its way into the ocean or to have been incorporated in organic matter on land.

The most abundant carbon component of the ocean is the bicarbonate ion (HCO_3). Bicarbonate is in equilibrium with carbonate (CO_3) and neutral CO_2. The apportionment of inorganic carbon among these three species is controlled by pH (the ocean is alkaline, with a pH of about 8). Addition of CO_2 to the ocean tends to lower pH, switching carbon from CO_3 to HCO_3 and dissolved neutral CO_2. However, there is a limit to this switching, fixed by the alkalinity of the ocean. Alkalinity can be altered only by addition of salts supplied, for example, by the dissolution of calcite ($CaCO_3$) in sediments. The balance among these various processes and equilibria has very important implications for the size of the eventual greenhouse warming caused by the rising concentration of atmospheric CO_2.

The Changing Carbon Cycle

A continuing rise in atmospheric CO_2 seems inevitable. Current estimates of fossil fuel reserves are about 4 trillion metric tons, and assuming that half of this reserve is used up over the next 100 years, the level of CO_2 could rise above 1,000 parts per million. Supposing, more conservatively, that annual consumption of fossil fuel will double over the next 100 years, CO_2 may be expected to grow to about 500 parts per million, approximately twice the 1980 level. Such a doubling is expected to raise the average global surface temperature beyond that experienced in recorded human history. (For a discussion of the greenhouse effect, the warming that results from rising CO_2 concentrations, see *World Resources 1986*, pp. 173–177.) These estimates assume that the ability of the

Figure 11.1 The Global Carbon Cycle

(petagrams)

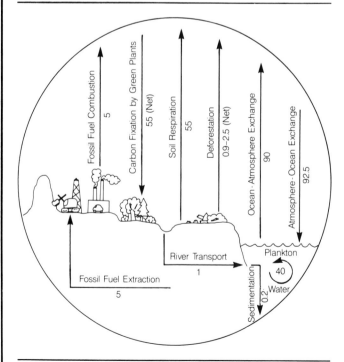

Source: Table 11.3

ocean to take up CO_2 is limited solely by the concentration of dissolved CO_3 at the surface. The sediments are taken to be passive. On a longer time scale, the release of calcite from sediments would add to the alkalinity of the oceans and the oceans would be a more efficient sink for CO_2. This state would not occur, however, for a thousand years or more.

Clearance of land for agriculture and the associated burning of vegetation can also add to the atmospheric concentration of CO_2. Over the past 100 years, this source appears to be comparable to that from fossil fuel. The weight of the evidence suggests, however, that the *current* net biospheric contribution is small, although the subject is a matter of great controversy (3) (4). The argument is as follows. If the magnitude of the source from fossil fuel burning is known and the rate at which CO_2 is absorbed by the ocean can be calculated with adequate accuracy, measurements of atmospheric CO_2 should reveal the approximate contribution from all other sources. This analysis suggests that the "missing" source is small, certainly less than 25 percent of the contribution from fossil fuel. Indeed, some scientists believe that we may need to identify an additional carbon *sink* rather than a source.

It is difficult to reconcile this view that the current net biospheric contribution is small with the evidence for rapid and growing rates of deforestation in the tropics (5). Production of CO_2 from freshly cleared areas may be offset in part by enhanced uptake in other regions, particularly those that have been abandoned recently by shifting cultivators. In addition, a significant fraction of carbon in areas cleared by the slash-and-burn technique may be converted to charcoal rather than to CO_2. The dilemma attests to the extent of our ignorance. There is an urgent need for data to define the current stock of carbon in major ecosystems, not only in plants but also in soils (6). There is a similarly great need for accurate records of change over time and for studies to define the effects of documented disturbances on specific ecosystems.

Further investigation is also needed on the effects of changing climate. There is increasing evidence that the average temperature of the earth is rising. What are the consequences for the capacity of ecosystems to acquire and retain carbon? Rates of bacterially mediated decomposition may accelerate. In this case, the carbon stock of soils could decline. On the other hand, plant growth could accelerate, aided by enhanced temperature and moisture and by the fertilization effect of a higher level of CO_2. Boundaries of major ecosystems could shift. Even a small change in the distribution of ecosystems could have a significant impact on CO_2. There is a range of possible feedbacks, both positive and negative. We can only guess at the magnitude and signs of the resulting effects on carbon and, hence, on the basic conditions for life.

Methane and Carbon Monoxide

The steadily rising atmospheric concentrations of methane (CH_4) and carbon monoxide (CO) provide further evidence of the changing carbon cycle.

Methane is a potent greenhouse gas, so that changes in its atmospheric concentration are important in the global warming trend. Methane in the atmosphere has more than doubled since the 16th Century. This unusual 400-year record is provided by measurements of air bubbles trapped in glacial ice. Since 1950, for still mysterious reasons, the rate of increase has risen sharply. The abundance of CH_4 was about 1.14 parts per million in 1951. It had risen to 1.58 parts per million by 1981, representing a mean annual increase of 1.1 percent over this 30-year period. Methane is believed to be produced by bacteria in anaerobic environments. Their activity represents part of the global cycle governing decay of organic material. Natural swamps and rice fields are therefore important environments for methane production. So also are termites and the intestines of ruminants, such as cattle. A portion of the increase in CH_4 can be attributed to expansion in rice cultivation facilitated by the "green revolution." Some can be charged to the growing population of sheep and cattle. However, the methane cycle is not yet well enough understood to assign causes with any degree of confidence. Measurements of the isotopic composition of methane in the atmosphere, combined with isotopic measurements of the gas produced in specific environments, could provide major clues. Rapid progress is expected. It is especially important to define the magnitude of the source due to burning vegetation in the tropics and to investigate the role of biological activity in seasonally flooded areas of the Arctic tundra.

Carbon monoxide is produced by combustion. The abundance of CO in the northern hemisphere is approximately twice that in the southern hemisphere. The concentration is currently increasing at about 2 percent per year. Carbon monoxide, which has a lifetime in the atmosphere of only about one month, is removed mainly by reaction with the hydroxyl radical (OH), which in turn is formed in the atmosphere by photochemical processes involving ozone and water. Reaction with carbon monoxide and a similar reaction with methane are the dominant paths for OH removal (7). This leads to an interesting dilemma. An increase in the release of carbon monoxide, a dangerous pollutant, will depress the concentration of OH, choking back the potential of the atmosphere to oxidize other substances. As a result, gases that would normally be removed by OH are more persistent. The result is an increase in carbon monoxide greater than would be expected simply from an enhancement of the source. Other gases, notably methane, are affected similarly. Perhaps as much as half the observed increase in methane can be attributed to depression of OH.

Interactions with Other Cycles

None of the biogeochemical cycles functions apart from the others, and this point is especially true of the carbon cycle. The importance of the carbon-nitrogen balance in regulating nitrogen release from decomposing crop residues, for example, has been recognized for more than 50 years (8). The ratios of carbon, nitrogen, and phosphorus required by marine phytoplanton interact with the sulfur and oxygen cycles to regulate the primary productivity of the oceans (9)(10). Dozens of similar examples could be cited.

But not only is the carbon cycle being altered by human activities, so are the other cycles, further complicating delineation of their interactions. For example, biological nitrogen fixation was once the only significant pathway for transferring the biologically unavailable form of atmospheric nitrogen (N_2), which constitutes more than 99 percent of the nitrogen in the atmosphere, to biologically available forms. Industrial nitrogen fixation, through the production of nitrogen fertilizer, now equals about half the nitrogen fixed through biological processes (11). The extra source could be as large as 100 million metric tons per year. If this nitrogen were employed to stimulate new growth of plants, the associated sink for carbon could be significant. If all the extra nitrogen were bound up in trees, whose carbon-nitrogen ratio could be as large as 100:1, the additional carbon sink—10 billion metric tons per year—could be comparable to the source from fossil fuel burning. Plants with less stature, and correspondingly lower requirements for carbon, could consume as much as 1 billion metric tons of carbon per year. It is therefore highly important to discover the ultimate disposal of anthropogenically fixed nitrogen. Studies of ecosystems in the industrialized nations where anthropogenic nitrogen is relatively abundant merit special attention. To date, these ecosystems have received little emphasis in attempts to balance the budget of either carbon or nitrogen.

OCEAN-ATMOSPHERE INTERACTION

It is useful at times to take a somewhat distant view of the earth and describe it in the way one would describe another planet. From this point of view, the surface of the earth is dominated by the existence of two fluid envelopes: a gaseous one, the atmosphere, that covers the entire earth and a liquid one, the ocean, lying below the atmosphere and covering nearly three quarters of the surface. From this distant viewpoint, the oceans are a striking anomaly: none of the other planets has oceans (or large reserves of liquid water in any form) (12).

Fundamental Characteristics of Oceans and the Atmosphere

A most important characteristic of the atmosphere is its transparency. A large fraction—about half—of the incoming radiation from the sun passes through the atmosphere and reaches the earth's surface, most of which is ocean. All the heat received by the earth from the sun must again be radiated away to space. However, the atmosphere is not transparent to the infrared radiation produced by the earth. (The relative transparency to incoming radiation and relative opacity to outgoing radiation create the natural greenhouse effect without which the planet would be icebound.) Heat must somehow work its way up through the atmosphere to higher levels before it is effectively radiated into space. The atmosphere therefore receives heat at a comparatively high temperature and pressure at the surface and releases it at a comparatively low temperature and pressure at altitude.

Receiving heat at a high temperature and pressure and releasing it at a low temperature and pressure are characteristic of a heat engine—which the atmosphere indeed is. The motions produced by this engine are the great atmospheric circulations and their fluctuations that determine weather and climate.

Weather and climate would both exist in the absence of the ocean. However, the ocean dramatically modifies the situation. The most important way it does so is through evaporation at the ocean surface. When water evaporates, it absorbs the latent heat of vaporization (about one megajoule, or one third of a kilowatt hour per kilogram). This heat is released again when the vapor condenses into clouds. The clouds may evaporate and recondense several times, but eventually they precipitate. When they do, the water returns to the surface and the heat remains aloft. This evaporation-precipitation process thus transports heat both vertically and geographically.

The second central characteristic of the ocean is its ability to store heat. The top three meters of the ocean have as much thermal capacity (i.e., can store as much heat energy) as the entire atmosphere (13). Thus the ocean is able to absorb and to give up great quantities of heat with little change in temperature. This capability has dramatic effects upon climate. For example, in areas where the air is dry, the day-night temperature difference can be 40°. Over the ocean, the difference is generally only a few degrees or less at the surface (14). At middle latitudes in midcontinent, the temperature difference between the summer maximum and winter minimum can reach 80°. Over the ocean, the spread rarely exceeds 10°.

The third important characteristic of the ocean is its ability to transport heat. The best-known and one of the most important examples is the North Atlantic circulation. Water heated by the sun in the tropical and subtropical Atlantic is transported northward in the Gulf Stream and then distributed over the entire North Atlantic, some proportion spreading as far north as the Norwegian Sea. The return-flowing water, much of it at great depths, is much colder. The resulting heat transfer, quantitatively about one petawatt (1 quadrillion watts), is a significant fraction of the north-south heat transfer effected by the atmosphere itself (15). The prevailing westerly winds at the latitude of the North Atlantic transport this heat across all of Europe, producing a significantly warmer climate there than would be anticipated from its latitude.

The reverse phenomenon can be seen off the coast of California. In this region, the ocean circulation moves warm surface water away from the coastline. It is replaced by much cooler water brought by subsurface circulation from higher latitudes. Thus, in this region, both the water and the adjacent land are much cooler than might be expected considering the latitude.

Ocean-Atmosphere Coupling

Although the ocean strongly influences the atmosphere, it is the atmosphere that largely drives ocean movements.

The ocean is also a heat engine, but a relatively inefficient one; the temperature range over which it works is much smaller than that of the atmosphere. The deep circulation of the ocean, below about 100 meters, is largely caused by heating and cooling and by changes in salinity produced by evaporation and precipitation. However, the more vigorous surface motions, which are responsible for much of the heat transport, are wind driven.

The way in which the ocean responds to surface wind is greatly complicated by the fact that the earth is a rotating spherical body. Although the details are beyond the scope of this discussion, what is most important to note is that the ocean-atmosphere system is closely coupled. The distribution of sea surface temperature has important effects on activity in the atmosphere, and wind driving is a dominant factor in setting up ocean currents, which in turn determine the distribution of sea surface temperature. Ideally, this system would be described and studied through a coupled ocean-atmosphere model, but today that remains a long-term scientific goal.

Atmospheric motions are now quite well described by advanced numerical models. Weather forecasts in all developed countries are generated by such models that are now capable of reproducing today's climate with considerable accuracy. The same is not true of ocean models. Motions corresponding to the large-scale cyclone-anticyclone systems in the atmosphere are also important in the ocean, but the physical scale of these oceanic motions is only a few percent of that of the corresponding atmospheric motions. Thus a full-scale oceanographic model comparable to an atmospheric model must have much finer resolution. Such models can be conceived, but running them is beyond the capability of even the most powerful of modern computers. Indeed, it will be near the end of this century before computers can handle the demands of ocean modeling.

Coupled analysis of the two systems is further complicated by the fact that they operate on different time scales. Atmospheric fluctuations are typically on the order of a few days, which is much too fast a time scale to be followed by the ocean. Oceanic fluctuations generally take place over several months (16).

Although the basic physics of ocean movements are believed to be reasonably well understood, the lack of data severely limits the possibilities of refining this general understanding. A major international experiment, the World Ocean Circulation Experiment (WOCE), is being planned under the auspices of the international Committee on Climatic Change and the Ocean (CCCO). WOCE is expected to become operational in the 1990s, when special satellites required for its success will be in orbit. WOCE goals include determining the three-dimensional oceanic circulation, the oceanic fluxes of heat and freshwater, and the exchanges of heat and water between the ocean and the atmosphere as well as delineating the annual cycle and long-term variability of these patterns (17). In the meantime, understanding the oceans remains more conceptual than detailed, and the capability to predict is extremely limited.

FOCUS ON: THE ROLE OF TROPICAL OCEANS

Despite the absence of a detailed understanding of ocean circulation, it is clear that tropical oceans are central to the large-scale ocean-atmosphere interaction and to global climate. In simplest terms, tropical oceans represent the input portion of the atmospheric heat engine.

Some reasons for the importance of tropical oceans relate to the basic physical properties of water. The relation between temperature and the vapor pressure of water is strongly nonlinear. Vapor pressure increases by a factor of approximately two for every 10° rise in temperature. Although the evaporation rate also depends on wind speed and the humidity of the overlying air, the most important factor is the vapor pressure of the water. Thus the rate of evaporation is highly dependent on temperature, and, except at quite low temperatures, the majority of the heat transfer from the ocean to the atmosphere occurs through evaporation. The fact that this transfer increases rapidly with temperature, plus the fact that nearly half the world's oceans are in the tropics, underscores the importance of tropical oceans in the supply of both moisture and energy to the atmosphere.

Although the influence of the tropical oceans can be traced throughout the global atmosphere, the most important influences are in tropical and subtropical regions. Because these regions contain most of the earth's population, changes in the ocean-atmosphere regime in the tropical areas have correspondingly large impacts on human affairs. Such well-known phenomena as El Niño, variations in the timing and strength of the South Asian monsoons, and the rainfall regimes in Brazil, the Sahel, and eastern tropical and subtropical Africa are examples that have come to world attention in recent years.

The importance of these phenomena is such that a large international ten-year experiment, the study of the interannual variation of the Tropical Ocean and the Global Atmosphere, has been inaugurated by the Joint Scientific Committee for the World Climate Research Program, the CCCO, and a variety of intergovernmental and nongovernmental bodies (18). To date, the tropical Pacific has received the most study and may be the most important area. Thus it is well suited to illustrate the phenomena involved.

Ocean Circulation in the Tropical Pacific

In global atmospheric circulation, winds typically blow from the east in tropical regions and from the west at midlatitudes. This behavior is the rule over the Pacific Ocean. Because of the earth's rotation and other factors, the response of the ocean to wind forcing is extremely complex, and wind in a particular direction does not necessarily drive the underlying water in the same direction. However, in this case, an easterly wind does generate a westward flow of surface water. Warm water, heated by the tropical sun, therefore tends to pile up against the archipelago that marks the western borders of the Pacific. (See Figure 11.2A.)

Figure 11.2 Sea Surface Temperatures in the Pacific During a Normal Year (1984) and an El Niño Event (1983)

Figure 11.2A Normal Distribution of Sea Surface Temperature, January 20, 1984

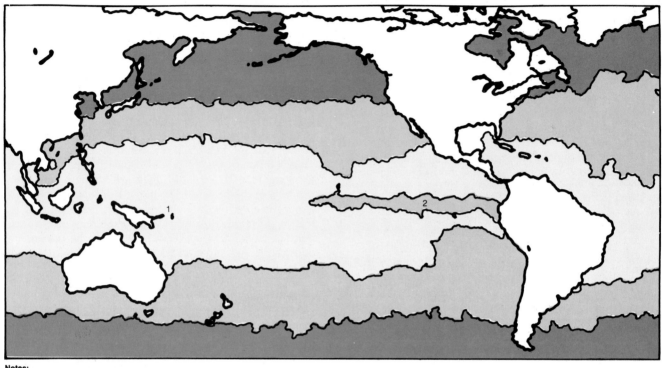

Notes:
1. Warm water is pushed by easterly winds to the western Pacific.
2. A tongue of relatively cold water is created when easterly winds push warm surface waters away from the equator.

Figure 11.2B Distribution of Sea Surface Temperatures during the El Niño Event of 1982–83, January 20, 1983

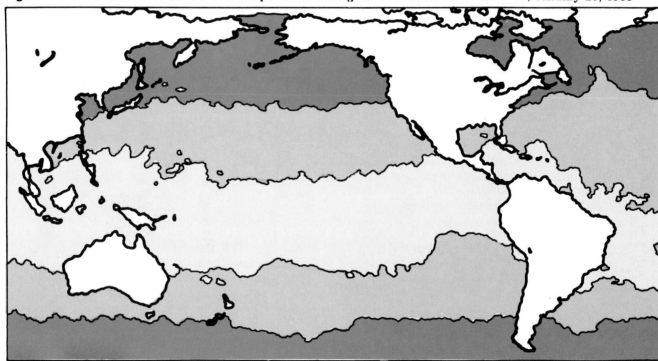

Note: A slackening of easterly winds allows warm surface water to slosh back to the east. No upwellings of nutrient-rich cold water were visible during the 1982–83 El Niño.

Source: Adapted from National Aeronautics and Space Administration (NASA), *Oceanography from Space*, information packet (NASA, Washington, D.C., 1986). The maps were produced by Richard Legeckis of NASA's Environmental Satellite Data and Information Service using data collected by the Advanced Very High Resolution Radiometer carried aboard NOAA-7, a polar-orbiting meterological satellite. They were prepared with a spatial resolution of 100 kilometers.

25–30°C   13–24°C   0–12°C

But the situation is much more complex. The first effect of a wind stress is the movement of surface water to the right of the wind in the northern hemisphere and to the left of the wind in the southern hemisphere. Thus an easterly wind along the tropics tends to cause water to move away from the equator in both hemispheres. In addition, complex ocean dynamics create a strong sub-surface current of cool water flowing eastward along the equator. The combination of these two phenomena usually causes the equatorial surface water to be appreciably cooler than that lying adjacent to the north and south. (See Figure 11.2A.)

Normally, the surface layer of warm water in this part of the world is quite thin, and, as it is blown away, much cooler water replaces it from below. This upwelling phenomenon has important biological consequences. Typically, the surface waters of the ocean are depleted in nutrients because the nutrients are incorporated into the tissues of microscopic plants growing near the surface. The plants are grazed by small animals that are in turn eaten by larger animals all the way up the food chain. Fecal matter excreted by these animals and the uneaten remnants of their bodies fall through the water column. This matter is decomposed by bacteria as it settles, and the nutrients are returned to the water, but at greater depths, beyond the reach of sunlight and so incapable of sustaining plant life. Thus, in upwelling areas, nutrient-rich water is brought into the euphotic zone, where there is sufficient light for plant growth. Vigorous growth takes place, nourishing the entire food chain. The richest fisheries in the world are found in these regions. In the tropical Pacific, wind tends to drive surface water away from the coast, creating the upwelling regions conveniently near the shore.

The Southern Oscillation and El Niño

The atmosphere, which is largely responsible for the distribution of sea surface temperature, also responds to it. Where surface water is warm, moist warm air rises to levels where condensation and clouds occur and precipitation is frequent. Where it is relatively cool, compared with surrounding regions, air sinks, clouds evaporate, and precipitation is rare. Thus western equatorial South America, where the water is relatively much cooler, is so dry as to be effectively a desert, and islands near the equator in the central and eastern Pacific receive little rainfall. On the other hand, islands of the western Pacific, the Malaysian peninsula, northern Australia, and tropical islands not near the equator receive plentiful rainfall.

Every few years a climatological event dramatically changes this situation. The event is best documented on the coasts of equatorial South America and the adjacent waters. Its most usual occurrence is toward the end of the calendar year, and the local Spanish-speaking population named it "El Niño," the child, referring to Christmas. The expression has been universally adopted. During the El Niño event, the surface water off the coasts of tropical South America becomes much warmer than usual. There is substantial rainfall. Nutrient-rich water no longer rises

into the euphotic zone, and there is a great reduction in phytoplankton growth. The result is a sharp reduction of fish populations in the area, with serious consequences to those whose lives depend on these fish—both fishermen and marine birds.

Until fairly recently, El Niño was considered a local phenomenon. However, research in the past decade revealed that it is a local manifestation of an oceanwide, perhaps worldwide, phenomenon.

It is now understood that the phenomenon begins with a relaxation of the wind stress that normally drives warm water toward the west. The deep pool of warm water in the western Pacific floods back. Once more the influence of the earth's rotation is dominant. Instead of spreading over the whole ocean, the water moves eastward in an equatorially trapped wave. After several months, this wave reaches the coast of South America, where it is in part reflected and in part transmitted north and south along the coast.

Details of the wind and wave action are scant and fragmented. The ocean is vast and oceanographic research vessels few—and not many of them are stationed in the Pacific. Thus the World Meteorological Organization arranged for regular commercial ships to obtain data on sea surface temperature and winds. These ship observations have been importantly augmented by careful installation and use of tide gauges on tropical islands in the Pacific.

From these scanty observations was constructed a theory for the development of El Niño that seemed to fit the data concerning El Niños occurring before 1980. According to this theory, the "preparation" for an El Niño is a period of anomalously strong east winds over the tropical Pacific. The resulting strong westward wind stress leads to an increased piling up of the warm surface water in the western Pacific. This warm water is substantially lighter than the cooler deep water. It floats higher, and the resulting higher sea level can be detected on tide gauges. When the winds return to normal, the warm water pool also has to return to normal and, in doing so, sheds a wave that surges eastward across the Pacific.

On the basis of this theory, it was confidently predicted in 1982 that no El Niño would occur that year. There had been no anomalous winds and no anomalous buildup of warm water in the western Pacific. Ironically, these predictions corresponded with the largest recorded El Niño and a series of events that have been referred to as the climatic disturbance of the century.

The basic phenomenon was the same as described in the theory. The difference was that instead of anomalously strong easterly winds followed by a return to normal, a rather ordinary situation was followed by a period of much reduced westward driving of the water.

The eastward surge of warm water exceeded anything previously recorded. (See Figure 11.2B.) Torrential rains occurred in normally arid areas as far apart as California and Ecuador. On the other side of the Pacific, great forest fires raged in parts of New Guinea normally drenched with rain. Australia, South Africa, India, and Indonesia all suffered serious droughts. On tropical islands famous for

Figure 11.3 Sea Surface Temperature and Fish Catch, During the 1982–83 El Niño

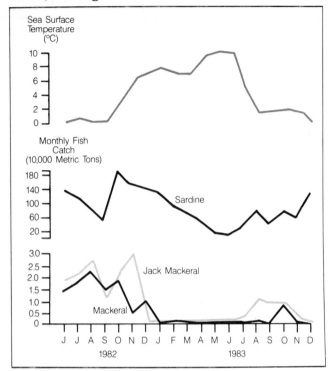

Source: H. Santander *et al.* "Impact of the 1982–83 El Niño on the Pelagic Resources Off Peru," *Tropical Ocean-Atmosphere Newsletter*, No. 28 (November 1984), pp. 9–10.

the nesting sites of multitudes of sea birds, bird populations were virtually wiped out—partly because of lack of food in the nutrient-poor water and partly because the nesting sites, parent birds, and fledglings were soaked with rain. Though no reliable study of the damages has been done, hundreds of millions of people are known to have been severely affected, and estimates of the costs run around $10 billion (19).

Ocean surface temperatures shifted, bringing extreme biological changes in their wake. Figure 11.3 shows the surface temperature anomaly (the departure from the usual average) measured off the coast of Peru, beginning with the onset of El Niño in this region in the fall of 1982. This large warming (up to 10°C) was accompanied by severe declines in many fish catches (Figure 11.3). Most severely damaged was the anchovy (20). The decline was also reflected in a steep drop in marine primary productivity (photosynthesis by phytoplankton), as shown in Figure 11.4. This decline represents a drop calculated at 1.1 petagrams in the amount of carbon fixed in the coastal and equatorial Pacific regions during the El Niño (21). Using food chain theory to convert primary productivity to fish production, scientists calculated a theoretical 1983 fish production deficit of 94 million metric tons (22). By comparison, this loss exceeds the total world fish catch for 1981 (23). Although the actual loss was almost certainly less than this figure, the calculations suggest that the actual loss was indeed very significant even in global terms (24).

On the other hand, species well adapted to the warmer temperatures, or that profited from the decline in competition for food or the disappearance of predators, flourished. The Peruvian shrimp catch in 1983—at the height of El Niño—was seven to eight times larger than in 1982; the scallop harvest leapt from an annual average of about 500 metric tons to an estimated 18,000–20,000 metric tons (25) (26).

At the same time, anomalous weather occurred widely throughout the world. It is still not known whether these other weather anomalies were caused by the redistribution of ocean water associated with the 1982–83 El Niño or were part of the large-scale atmospheric anomaly that was responsible for El Niño. Certainly the evidence is that the whole atmosphere moved more strongly than usual toward the east (that is, increased westerly winds and decreased easterly winds) around the end of December 1982. The effect was even evident in measurements of the length of day, which was longer than had been recorded since accurate measurements commenced a few years earlier (27).

Figure 11.4 Effect of the 1982–83 El Niño on Primary Marine Productivity

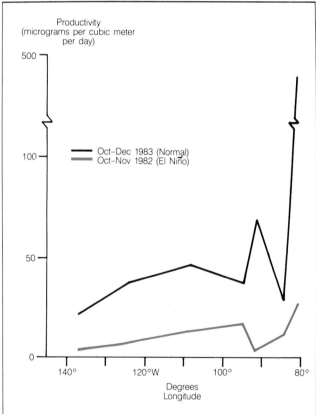

Note: Primary productivity measured during onset (October–November 1982, blue line) and after recovery (October–November 1983, black line) of the 1982–83 El Niño. The observations extend from 0°, 92°W, to 2°S, 85°W, and then to 5°S and 82°W.
Source: Francisco P. Chavez *et al.*, "El Niño and Primary Productivity: Potential Effects on Atmospheric Carbon Dioxide and Fish Production," *Tropical Ocean-Atmosphere Newsletter*, No. 28 (November 1984), p. 1.

Summary

The atmosphere and oceans are globally connected, and one of the difficult problems associated with understanding climatic fluctuations is separating cause from effect in their interactions.

Predicting climatic fluctuations would provide substantial advantages to populations afflicted by such variations and to agencies attempting to alleviate these afflictions. Substantial progress has been made in understanding the ways in which the ocean responds to changes in atmospheric driving—and to the ways in which the atmosphere responds to changes in sea surface temperature distribution. However, the ability to predict is frustrated by a present inability to forecast the behavior of the atmosphere with any reasonable success more than approximately a week in advance. Thus the future driving of the ocean by the atmosphere remains hidden.

These problems are being attacked within the World Climate Research Program and, in particular, within the Tropical Ocean and Global Atmosphere Study. However, at the present time even the extent to which it will be theoretically possible to make predictions remains unclear. It may well be some decades before the predictions reach a useful level of reliability.

GEOSPHERE–BIOSPHERE INTERACTIONS: THE CASE OF SOILS

The world's soils—the foundation for plant and, consequently, animal life on land—are at the interface of the geosphere and the biosphere. In the lower horizons of the soil, minerals in the geologic substrate weather, determining the chemical composition of the soil. On the soil surface, dead organic matter from the overlying vegetation decomposes and forms the humic material so essential for many soil processes.

The significance of the soils in the biosphere is widely unappreciated. In fact, the below-ground biomass of plant roots, animals, and microorganisms is at least 10 percent —and perhaps as much as 50 percent—of the estimated above-ground biomass (28).

Soil Functions

Several soil functions are necessary for maintaining plant life. First, soils retain water so that it is available to plants between precipitation events. Without this water-holding capacity, not only would plant growth generally be impossible, but rapid runoff would cause flooding of streams and rivers, altering the ways people use the biosphere for agriculture and other purposes. Soils also provide the physical substrate to which plant roots attach. Perhaps soils' most important roles lie in their ability to store plant nutrients and provide a habitat for microorganisms that convert nutrients to forms usable by plants. It bears repeating that without the world's soil resources, neither plant life nor animal life, which depends on plants for food, would be possible.

Soils and their microbial communities play a significant role in the biogeochemical cycling of many elements required for plant growth. A major portion of the annual flux of global nitrogen occurs either within the soil or between vegetation and the soil. Nitrogen fixation, one of the most important processes taking place in soils, occurs when microorganisms mineralize the biologically unavailable form of nitrogen, N_2—which accounts for more than 99 percent of the nitrogen in the atmosphere—and convert it to an inorganic form that can be taken up by plants.

Human interventions in the natural nitrogen cycle are substantial, many of them affecting soil function. For example, industrial production of nitrogen fertilizer is now about half as large as the total amount of nitrogen fixed biologically. In the other direction, combustion of fossil fuels and biomass produces a large net flux of nitrogen into the atmosphere, some of which returns to the biosphere and soils through acid deposition. High inputs of nitrogen from acid deposition on forests may be responsible for some of the forest decline seen in industrialized areas of the world (29). (See *World Resources 1986*, Chapter 12, "Multiple Pollutants and Forest Decline.") Heavy use of fertilizers also pollutes the rivers and lakes that drain agricultural areas. Using microorganisms or genetically engineered plants to fix nitrogen could reduce dependence on chemical fertilizers, a situation that would also reduce these and other disruptions of the natural cycle (30).

The phosphorus cycle is simple, but equally important. Because phosphorus is fairly abundant in insoluble forms, it is frequently the limiting nutrient for plant growth. Phosphorus must be liberated through weathering of apatite and other mineral complexes in the soil. However, soluble phosphorus is quickly immobilized by iron, by aluminum, and sometimes by calcium in the soil. Thus its overall availability for plant growth depends on soil type (31).

Soil processes are also essential to the global carbon cycle, providing the basis for food and fiber production and organic waste through mineralization. The activity of small animals in aerating the soil and the mineralization of dead organic matter by soil microorganisms are vital links in the decomposition processes of the cycle (32).

Soil Characteristics

The availability of plant nutrients in the soil, the amount of organic matter, overall soil depth, the depths of soil layers, and other soil characteristics vary, depending on the interplay of the major soil-forming factors: climate, parent material, biota, slope, and amount of time for soil development. Maps of the world's soils are at such a coarse scale that much local and even regional detail is not included. The maps are generally based on prevailing environmental conditions, so that they strongly reflect vegetation and climate patterns. The maps thus illustrate probable rather than actual soil types. The most authoritative map of the world's soils is the United Nations Food and Agriculture Organization/United Nations Educational, Scientific and Cultural Organization World Soils Map, which has a scale of 1:5 million (33).

The interaction of the various soil-forming factors is evident in the characteristic soils of different parts of the earth. For example, in tropical regions the warmer temperatures increase the effectiveness of weathering ten times that in the arctic regions and three times that in the temperate regions (34). Thus tropical soils are characterized by extensive weathering, and they can be layered as deep as 30 meters. Because of rapid decomposition of dead organic matter in warm climates, nutrients are generally stored in the biomass above ground rather than in the soil humus, as is characteristic of temperate soils. In the humid tropics, intensive weathering and leaching deplete the reserves of weatherable minerals and consequently lead to the formation of soils with low fertility and little agricultural value.

Soil Degradation

Human activities affect the world's soil resources and their long-term capacity to support the biosphere. Soil degradation, a general term referring to partial or total loss of the productive capacity of the soil, can be caused by water and wind erosion, salinization, waterlogging, desertification, soil pollution, conversion to urban land use, and other processes. Estimates of the rate of soil depletion, degradation, and destruction range from 5 million to 15 million hectares per year (35) (36).

Saline soils occur naturally in arid climates as moisture evaporates and the salts in solution are deposited on the surface. However, irrigation systems with inadequate drainage have caused salinization to a much greater extent than under natural conditions. Decline in productivity of agricultural land, 1–1.5 million hectares per year, is attributable to salinization in such diverse areas as the Indian subcontinent, the plains of China, the central valley of California, and the Middle East (37). Four million hectares of irrigated land in the United States (38), almost 2 million hectares in Australia, and more than 1 million hectares in Canada (39) are affected. Reclaiming salinized soils is extremely costly.

Soil erosion too is a natural process that human activities have accelerated. Recent research using the radioactive trace element Beryllium-10 measures the balance between the amount of the tracer carried by a river and the calculated amount deposited each year in rainfall. In the rivers studied, the output in the river sediment exceeded the rainfall input by factors ranging as high as 14 for China's Huanghe (Yellow River) and 24 for India's Narbara River, suggesting strongly that in large areas of the world, soils are being eroded far more rapidly than they are being formed (40). Moreover, the high erosion areas are often those with high population density, least able to afford the loss. Overall, erosion is believed to be responsible for approximately 30 percent of the loss of arable land caused by soil degradation (41). However, erosion rates are extremely variable and are dependent on local conditions, so that national or even regional estimates are difficult to calculate and are generally unreliable.

Major factors controlling soil erosion are vegetative cover, slope, and rainfall intensity. How much soil erosion can occur without decreasing soil production capacity is known as soil loss tolerance, basically, the rate of soil for-

mation. (See Chapter 4, "Food and Agriculture," Increasing Production and its Environmental Costs: The United States and the European Community.) This rate is estimated at 0.5–2.0 metric tons per hectare per year, but it also varies in ways that have not been quantified under different climatic regimes and soil conditions. The most severe erosion occurs in mountainous areas where steep slopes are cleared for logging, agriculture, grazing, and other purposes, as in the frequently cited case of Nepal. Experiments have been carried out to quantify the effects of varying these factors on local rates of erosion. (See *World Resources 1986*, pp. 52–55, for a description of some experiments and for further discussion of soil erosion.)

Natural deserts caused by climatic and geologic conditions cover approximately 48 million square kilometers, or 37 percent, of the earth's land surface. Stresses such as intensive agriculture and overgrazing in arid and semiarid regions with naturally extreme fluctuations in climate have caused desertification of an additional 9 million square kilometers (42). This process, which does not always result in the appearance of actual deserts, always leads to a decline in soil productivity and in the ability of the land to support plant and animal populations. (See Chapter 5, "Forests and Rangelands," Desertification.)

Soil pollution is a type of soil degradation that is only recently recognized for its serious consequences. Toxic and other hazardous substances released by mining and industrial activities and the application of pesticides directly affects human health by their contamination of soil and of the food products grown in the soil. Chemicals leached from the soil into groundwater contaminate wells used for drinking water and irrigation. Thousands of sites where the soil is contaminated have been identified in the United States, Japan, and some European countries. The extent of the problem is not fully known, but the potential is great.

The most extreme mode of soil degradation is conversion of land from its natural state or from agricultural production to use for settlements and other purposes such as mining and hydropower development. The worldwide significance of this problem is debatable, but rapid urban growth on fertile agricultural land can be consequential locally or regionally. From 1970 to 1980, between 1 and 3 percent of agricultural land in Organisation for Economic Co-operation and Development countries was converted to urban use—2.8 percent in the United States, 1 percent in France, 2.5 percent in Italy, and 1.2 percent in the United Kingdom (43).

Soil degradation occurs slowly and quietly, and it is difficult to monitor, so the hazard easily escapes the attention of policymakers. Because many aspects of soil degradation and its effects are not fully understood, precise predictions of losses in agricultural production are difficult to make. That the consequences can be catastrophic for human populations, however, cannot be denied. Investigations and global monitoring of soil cover, soil type, and soil moisture and studies of the geochemistry of various ecosystems are therefore all high priorities for research in the coming decades (44).

NEW TOOLS

Advances in technology have just recently made global science possible. Satellite-based remote sensing, paired with digitized geographical information systems and global-scale computer models, are giving scientists the means to gather global information, store and handle it, and use it to simulate and predict the workings of global systems and cycles.

Although ground- and sea-based measurements and sensors mounted on aircraft and balloons remain essential, the deployment of remote sensors on satellites has made synoptic worldwide data collection possible for the first time. Satellite-mounted sensors ensure compatibility of data measurements across both time and space.

Because satellites can transmit remote sensing data in digital form (rather than on photographic film), powerful new analytic techniques have been developed that take advantage of the high-speed data processing the digital form allows. Especially important is the fixing of data from a variety of sources to a common geographical base, a technique known as Geographical Information Systems (GIS).

Remote Sensing

Satellite-mounted sensors differ in three general dimensions. They measure energy of different frequencies, have either fine- or coarse-resolution sensors, and may be placed in a variety of orbits. Each remote sensing device is designed to accomplish specific tasks requiring different spectral, spatial, and temporal resolutions.

Spectral bands currently used for data collection range from several visible portions of the electromagnetic spectrum to nonvisible infrared, thermal, and ultraviolet frequencies and include "active" radar-like frequencies. The lapsed time of their bounceback to the satellite can be used to determine the precise altitude of the land or water beneath, even the height of ocean waves.

Spatial resolution obtained by remote sensors in satellites can be fine, such as the 10-meter ground resolution of the French SPOT panchromatic devices or the 30-meter resolution of the Thematic Mapper and the 80-meter resolution of the Multispectral Scanner System (MSS) devices, both on the U.S. Landsat satellites. Coarser spatial resolutions are suitable for several remote sensing objectives, such as meteorological monitoring.

Temporal resolution is determined by the satellite's orbit. Whereas Landsat satellites may overfly any given point on the surface within a matter of weeks, the low-orbiting weather satellites routinely visit each area daily, and geostationary satellites (which orbit at the same rate as the earth's rotation, effectively remaining stationary in relation to the ground below) provide continuous coverage of much larger areas.

Characteristics of several leading sensors are summarized in Table 11.4. Some monitoring methods offer spatially detailed data; others sacrifice spatial resolution for better temporal detail (i.e., the same area or process is monitored daily, rather than monthly or annually). Trade-offs are necessary, depending upon the type of information desired. For example, whereas geological features that indicate underground mineral deposits hardly change at all and therefore do not need frequent imagery, high spectral resolution is desirable for useful analysis, even if only from a single image. On the other hand, crop yield estimates require repeated coverage at precise times during the growing cycle, with high spatial detail needed for discriminating among crops and among various forms of stress affecting total production.

Measuring seasonal or annual changes in vegetative cover requires, at a minimum, an annual inventory. However, no single satellite sensor can do the job alone. U.S. National Oceanic and Atmospheric Administration (NOAA) polar orbiting meteorological satellites carry a sensing device, the Advanced Very High Resolution Radiometers (AVHRR), that can be used to estimate green leaf density on the surface below. The AVHRR has a fairly coarse resolution. A satellite picture can be visualized as a mosaic of many sections or "tiles." An AVHRR tile is about one kilometer by one kilometer square as the satellite looks down over the equator (45). Tiles are much larger at the edge of a swath and in high latitudes. For economy and ease of handling, the data from 4 of every 15 tiles are averaged and the 15 tiles assigned the average value. This method yields an effective tile of about 3 by 5 kilometers over the equator (46). This level of resolution may be adequate for global carbon modeling, for example, but only broad characteristics of vegetation can be determined: closed or open forest, grassland, desert, etc. The data cannot be used to classify specific vegetation characteristics (species, morphology, condition) or to measure any but the grossest disturbances.

Table 11.4 Characteristics of Various U.S. Satellite Sensors

	CZCS[a]	AVHRR[b]		MSS[c]	
	Nimbus-7	NOAA-6,8	NOAA-7,9	Landsat 1-3	Landsat 4,5
Visible and near-infrared bands	5	2	2	4	4
Orbit altitude	955 km	850 km	850 km	920 km	705 km
Equator crossing	12:00	7:30	14:30	9:30	9:30
Nadir ground resolution	825 m^2	1100 m^2	1100 m^2	79 m^2	83 m^2
Swath width	1566 km	2700 km	2700 km	185 km	185 km
Field of view	±39°	±56°	±56°	±5.5°	±7°
Effective repeat coverage	6 days	2 days	2 days	18 days	16 days

Notes:
a. Coastal zone color scanner.
b. Advanced very high resolution radiometer.
c. Multispectral Scanner System.

Source: N.E. Roller and J.E. Colwell, "Coarse-Resolution Satellite Data for Ecological Surveys," *BioScience*, Vol. 36, No. 7 (1986), pp. 468-475. ©1986 American Institute of Biological Sciences.

Other sensors offer much finer spatial resolution. Landsat's MSS, whose resolution is about 80 square meters, approximately 100 times finer than the most detailed AVHRR imaging, and the Thematic Mapper and French SPOT systems are much finer. Two sacrifices must be made for this fine spatial resolution, however. First, a single Landsat (there have been five) overflies a swath only once every 18 days instead of the daily coverage by NOAA orbiters. Clouds can obscure the ground for either scanner, but the loss of a Landsat overflight means losing a month's information about vegetation change. In tropical areas with frequent rainfall, the probability of a clear view is 1 in 5. A second difficulty with fine-resolution data is their volume. For example, Landsat MSS data are handled in square "frames" 185 by 185 kilometers; each frame has more than 7.5 million tiles, and each tile is scanned in four spectral bands. Each frame, therefore, is defined by more than 30 million measurements (47). About 12,000 of these scenes would be required for a complete picture of the earth (48). At least 1,200 of the scenes are required to cover the area where 90 percent of all tropical deforestation is occurring. Acquisition costs alone are prohibitive, and the task of storing and processing such a mass of information would be astronomical. Fine resolution data, therefore, are most useful for intensive monitoring of specific sites (such as regions of rapid deforestation) and for refining vegetation surveys based on AVHRR or data from other sources.

Satellite sensors monitoring vegetation were used in 1986 to monitor the potentially catastrophic locust swarms that followed the return of rain to the Sahel. The warning afforded by such monitoring allowed eradication teams to be deployed in advance to the targeted areas (49).

Remote scanners are also being used, for example, to detect, identify, and quantify the advancing symptoms of forest decline over broad areas. Although the causes of the decline are not yet known, reliable indicators of damage that can be remotely sensed are being developed (50).

Geographical Information System

A digitized Geographical Information System is a series of computerized "maps" that can be manipulated in the same ways as other computer data. The maps are actually arrays of measurements of specific parameters such as altitude, population, and vegetation. Each data point in the array has two elements: its geographic location and the value of the specified parameter.

Paper maps also show more than one kind of information; the most common show latitude and longitude, political boundaries, and altitude on the same sheet. Digitized GISs differ from paper maps in one critical respect; because they are housed on computers, GISs can integrate many kinds of information and derive numerical values from them.

One might want, for example, to know the relationship between population density and average altitude in each country of the world on a subnational or "district" level. Showing two kinds of district-level information for the whole world would be an arduous map-making job, and

after creating such a map, one would be hard pressed to discern the resulting mathematical relationships. Collecting worldwide district-level information and locating all the districts for a digitized GIS would also be a formidable task, but once accomplished, various kinds of information could easily be compared mathematically on any desired level. The results can then be shown in a number of ways: in computer-generated map form, with data shown at the district level or integrated over countries; in tabular form, by district or country; and with descriptive statistical graphics, such as a histogram showing the number of districts corresponding to specific altitude-population density relationships.

As a tool for studying global systems and cycles, GIS methods can be used in three ways. First, they can serve simply as a potent data storage and management tool. This capability is no small consideration given the volume of remote sensing data. Second, GISs add flexibility to displaying global data: data can be processed to highlight particular features or variables, and they can be displayed in a variety of map projections and aggregated or disaggregated to represent various scales and degrees of resolution. The third and most powerful use is integrating or "overlaying" many kinds of data sharing a common geographical framework. This end is generally accomplished with computer models, which easily handle digitized data. Used in this way, GISs become strong analytical tools, allowing resource managers to pinpoint specific areas requiring priority action. (See Box 11.1.)

Institutional Concerns

At a time when human interventions have impacts far beyond the local area and on generations yet unborn, these technologies are vital tools for understanding global systems and improving local planning and decisionmaking. Yet today there are only two operational remote sensing satellite systems deployed for civilian sensing of the land portion of the planet, the aging U.S. Landsat and the new French SPOT system. All others either are for military and intelligence purposes or are meteorological systems that, with related ground observations, permit timely analysis and prediction of weather.

Virtually all the many satellite systems with remote sensing capabilities of enormous potential for natural resource management have been deployed only experimentally and are not funded on a continuing basis. Delays caused by their commercialization, and other factors, have reduced confidence in the continuity of their coverage and have led to hesitancy on the part of investors, whose support for earth stations and analytical capabilities is vital if the practical benefits of satellites are ever to be realized.

The reasons for this lag in the continuous operational use of this tool are less a matter of technical than of institutional and policy obstacles.

At the international level, the gap between nations with technical know-how and those with the greatest need to know builds suspicion and distrust and hampers cooperation. In mid-1986, broad agreement was reached on a set of draft principles governing remote sensing of the earth by satellites. The 15 principles, which are await-

Box 11.1 Putting It All Together: Desertification Hazards Assessment

The combined power of remote sensing, Geographical Information Systems (GIS), and global models is well illustrated by the Desertification Hazards Assessment undertaken by the United Nations Food and Agriculture Organization (FAO) and the United Nations Environment Programme (UNEP) (1).

Desertification is the degradation of the productive capacity of land, specifically land in the arid and semiarid regions of the world. (See Chapter 5, "Forests and Rangelands.") The visible manifestations of desertification include impoverishment of the vegetative cover, soil erosion, nutrient loss from soils, structural breakdown of the soil, etc. The causes of desertification are complex, but they appear to hinge on the delicate balance between land productivity and human demands on that productivity. Agricultural use of marginal land, overstocking of livestock beyond the carrying capacity of the range, and poorly managed irrigation systems all contribute to desertification.

Desertification affects hundreds of millions of people, often among the poorest in the world. It is difficult to assess the current *extent* of desertification, and directly monitoring its spread is almost impossible. (See Chapter 20, "Forests and Rangelands," Table 20.4.) However, an index of desertification *hazards*

has been developed using remote sensing data, GIS, and a global model; it can be used to locate the areas most likely to experience desertification.

Producing the final FAO/UNEP map of desertification hazards required the use of several intermediate analyses that integrated even more fundamental GISs in various combinations. The basic data at this fundamental level included maps of world soils at 1:5 million scale, world climate (including mean annual rainfall, wind velocity, wet days, and precipitation/evaporation ratios) at 1:5 million, animal density at 1:1 million, human population density, potential population-supporting capacity, and agricultural areas. Note that some of these maps are impossible to create from satellite remote sensing data and others can best be created by satellite remote sensing. All these data were digitized for GIS use and then modeled using various treatments to produce seven subindicators of desertification hazards:

1. Soil constraints: world soils were evaluated for their ability to support rainfed crops.
2. Water hazard: the impact of precipitation on soils was modeled by integrating GISs of soils, topography, precipitation, and natural vegetation.
3. Wind hazard: this factor was modeled by integrating GISs of wind speed and variabil-

ity, sand movements, soil moisture, soil texture, surface roughness, and land use.
4. Salinization hazard: the salinization hazard model incorporated information on soil salt content, precipitation-evaporation indicators, soil texture, and topography.
5. Livestock carrying capacity: this factor was estimated from climate and vegetation growing-period data combined with soil condition, vegetation, and land use data.
6. Livestock pressure: current animal density was compared with livestock carrying capacity.
7. Population pressure: human population was evaluated in relation to the potential population-supporting capacity of the land.

Integration of these seven subindexes produced the World Map of Desertification Hazards at 1:25 million scale (more detailed data were used for Africa, allowing a map at 1:5 million scale).

Notes and References

1. Todor G. Boyadgiev, "Report on the Modelling for Compilation of the Maps of Desertification Hazards in Africa and Soil Elements Used in Assessing Desertification and Degradation in the World" (United Nations Food and Agriculture Organization, Rome, 1984).

ing adoption by the U.N. General Assembly, delineate agreed obligations and rights for sensed and sensing states and call for technical assistance and other measures to build mutual trust and the sharing of benefits between rich and poor.

For example, the principles call for nondiscriminatory access by a sensed state to data regarding its territory on a reasonable cost basis and for access to analyzed information. To protect the earth's natural environment, sensing states are called upon to disclose information capable of averting harmful phenomena as well as information about pending natural disasters. These plans are not merely theoretical possibilities. In 1985, the U.S. Office of Foreign Disaster Assistance provided advance notice of a cyclone, saving thousands of lives in Bangladesh. The office relied on remote sensing data combined with computer models of tidal predictions and historical storm-surge records for the Bay of Bengal (51).

However, the U.S. need (and that of other major space powers) to transfer the costs of satellite systems from national treasuries to the private sector has led to the systems' commercialization (accompanied by heavy government subsidies). The effect thus far is that information about critical renewable resources has been priced beyond the reach of those in greatest need. On the other hand, profit margins for energy and nonrenewable resource extraction information are generally sufficient to absorb the costs of obtaining the data.

International cooperation between space and nonspace powers will be vital to the success of the International Geosphere-Biosphere Programme (IGBP), the main

research effort of the science of global change. This global research program for the 1990s will rely on space-borne sensors and large computer models. However, as the planning document notes, "the program cannot be based on space techniques alone. It will demand an even larger observational effort from the ground, on land and sea and ice, as well as from supporting aircraft. A part of this ground-based effort will be needed to validate and calibrate spaceborne measurements, but a larger part will be devoted to local studies of biomass and climatic zones in selected land or water regions, to understand the interdependence of changes on regional and global scales" (52).

RECENT DEVELOPMENTS

A kind of ecumenical movement has swept through the biological and earth sciences communities in recent years, driven by forces that call, in effect, for a reorganization of science and a bold new attack on understanding the earth as a planet. Research plans highlight two gnawing inadequacies of modern global science—the lack of an adequate understanding of how the global environmental system operates (especially the interactive coupling between living and nonliving parts) and an inability to identify the impacts of humans against the natural background of environmental change. An oft-cited example is that of predicting the ultimate effects of rising levels of carbon dioxide and other greenhouse gases. Here causes and effects are tangled problems that transcend the bounds of scientific disciplines and the political boundaries of nations. Similar problems are met in issues of tropical deforestation, regional desertification, acid deposition, the changing chemistry of soils and ground-waters, and the rapid decline in the numbers of plant and animal species.

This trend toward global science has spawned a sequence of proposed programs of multidisciplinary research with goals and names that are much alike. In 1982, at the U.N. Conference on the Peaceful Uses of Outer Space (UNISPACE) in Vienna, the Administrator of the U.S. National Aeronautics and Space Administration (NASA) proposed a radical Global Habitability program to strengthen understanding of the earth as the support system for life—a new international endeavor, based chiefly on data taken from downlooking spacecraft—to monitor global changes in fundamental chemistry, land cover, water, and other resources and to build understanding of the near future of the earth [53]. At about the same time, a panel of atmospheric chemists and meteorologists in the United States proposed a comprehensive plan for a coordinated study of tropospheric chemistry on a global scale—a program of pure science prompted by increasing concerns about the influence of human activity on the life-giving chemistry of the planet [54]. In 1983, the U.S. National Research Council took steps to define a new international program of research, modeled after the International Geophysical Year (IGY) of 1957–58, that would address problems of global change on a multidisciplinary basis—to be organized, as was the IGY, under the aegis of the International Council of Scientific Unions (ICSU) [55]. Also in 1983, NASA organized its own prestigious multidisciplinary committee on Earth Systems Science (ESSC) to define the needs of a research program in whole-earth science and to design, in effect, a new science of the earth [56]. Soon after, the U.S. National Science Foundation initiated a new high-priority thrust, Global Geosciences, aimed at the same issue [57]. The member nations and scientific unions of ICSU began considering these programs as international endeavors in 1984, following a resolution of the 20th General Assembly of that body in Ottawa [58].

These disparate efforts reached fruition in Bern, Switzerland, in September 1986, when the 21st General Assembly of ICSU, made up of the scientific academies and research councils of 71 nations and the representatives of 20 international scientific unions, voted unanimously to launch the International Geosphere-Biosphere Programme, to begin immediately and reach full force in about 1992 [59]. The IGBP endorsed at Bern will solicit the cooperation of all nations of the earth in a 10- to 20-year scientific endeavor focused on selected pressing global problems. Its goal is to describe and understand the interactive physical, chemical, and biological processes that regulate the total earth system, the unique environment that it provides for life, the changes that are occurring in this system, and the manner in which they are influenced by human actions [60]. The program will try to build a new base of knowledge and understanding that will serve as a basis for assessing likely changes on the earth in the next 100 years through programs of observation, process studies, numerical modeling, and the recovery of records of natural changes in the past. Remarkable at Bern was the unanimity of opinion of all nations, from China to the United States to the USSR, on the need for and urgency of the program and on the basic elements of its scientific focus and definition.

IGBP will enlist an international army of space and ground-based scientists from the fields of biology, oceanography, geology, atmospheric science, hydrology, glaciology, soils science, and solar-terrestrial physics [61] [62]. It will be the biggest effort that science has ever organized, the first in which physical, chemical, and biological scientists will actively collaborate, and the most practical in terms of its ultimate goals. Principal funding will come through national programs of research that are dedicated to the aims of IGBP, for example, NASA (Earth System Science) and the National Science Foundation (Global Geosciences) in the United States. Headquarters for IGBP have been established in Stockholm through a pledge of about $150,000 per year from the Swedish Government.

The cost to each nation depends a great deal on how the accounting is done, because much of the program rests on research in individual scientific diciplines that are already planned or underway. IGBP is certain to require a new generation of downlooking spacecraft; major efforts in field studies on the ground, on ice, and on the seas; establishment of a worldwide computer-based communications and data-handling system; and the evolution of comprehensive numerical models of the global environment, adequate to predict the effects of natural and human perturbations of the earth's interdependent systems. How fast plans for these needs will evolve depends most of all upon national priorities for science funding in the next 10 years. In the United States at present, the program seems in good stead to receive favored treatment even in these times of severe budgetary constraints [63].

References and Notes

1. Herbert Friedman, "The Science of Global Change—An Overview," keynote address presented at the Symposium of Global Change on the 20th General Assembly of the International Council of Scientific Unions, Ottawa, Canada, September 24, 1984, pp. 21–22. A related version of this paper is reproduced in *Global Change*, T.H. Malone and J.G. Roederer, eds. (Cambridge University Press, Cambridge, United Kingdom, 1985).
2. *Ibid.*, p. 19.
3. Ariel E. Lugo and Sandra Brown, "Brazil's Amazon Forest and the Global Carbon Problem," *Interciencia*, Vol. 11, No. 2 (1986), pp. 57–58.
4. Philip M. Fearnside, "Brazil's Amazon Forest and the Global Climate Problem: Reply to Lugo and Brown," *Interciencia*, Vol. 11, No. 2 (1986), pp. 58–64.
5. George M. Woodwell, "Importance of Tropical Forests in Global Cycles, Especially the Carbon Cycle," presented at the Workshop on Biogeochemistry of Tropical Rain Forests: Problems for Research, Piracicaba, Sao Paulo, September 30-October 4, 1985.

6. George M. Woodwell, ed., *The Role of Terrestrial Vegetation in the Global Carbon Cycle: Measurement by Remote Sensing*, SCOPE Report No. 23 (John Wiley and Sons, Chichester, United Kingdom, 1984).
7. Paul J. Crutzen and Louis T. Gidel, "A Two-Dimensional Photochemical Model of the Atmosphere: The Tropospheric Budgets of the Anthropogenic Chlorocarbons CO, CH_4, CH_3Cl and The Effect of Various NO_X Sources on Tropospheric Ozone," *Journal of Geophysical Research*, Vol. 88 (August 1983), pp. 6641–6661.
8. A.G. Norman, "The Biological Decomposition of Plant Materials, VIII: The Availability of the Nitrogen of Fungal Tissue," *Annuals of Applied Biology*, Vol. 20, pp. 146–164.
9. W.S. Broecker, *Chemical Oceanography* (Harcourt, Brace, Jovanovich, New York, 1974).
10. B. Bolin and R.B. Cook, eds., *The Major Biogeochemical Cycles and Their Interactions*, SCOPE Report No. 21 (John Wiley and Sons, Chichester, United Kingdom, 1983).
11. United Nations (U.N.), *Statistical Yearbook 1979/80* (U.N., New York, 1981).
12. Devendra Lal and Wolfgang Berger, "Global Environmental Change and the Ocean," in *Global Change*, T.F. Malone and J.G. Roederer, eds. (Cambridge University Press, Cambridge, United Kingdom, 1985), p. 157.
13. *Op. cit.* 1, p. 5.
14. R.W. Stewart and F.P. Bretherton, "Atmosphere-Ocean Interaction," in *Global Change*, T.F. Malone and J.G. Roederer, eds. (Cambridge University Press, Cambridge, United Kingdom, 1985), p. 148.
15. World Climate Research Programme (WCRP), "'CAGE' Experiment: A Feasibility Study" (WCRP, c/o World Meteorological Organization, Geneva, 1982).
16. *Op. cit.* 14, p. 150.
17. *Op. cit.* 12, p. 170.
18. P. Morel, "The World Climate Research Programme," in *Global Change*, T.F. Malone and J.G. Roederer, eds. (Cambridge University Press, United Kingdom, 1985), pp. 171–181.
19. *Op. cit.* 1, p. 8.
20. Haydee Santander and Jorge Zuzunaga, "Impact of the 1982–83 El Niño on the Pelagic Resources off Peru," *Tropical Ocean-Atmosphere Newsletter*, No. 28 (University of Washington, Seattle, November 1984), pp. 9–10.
21. Francisco P. Chavez, *et al.*, "El Niño and Primary Productivity: Potential Effects on Atmospheric Carbon Dioxide and Fish Production," *Tropical Ocean-Atmosphere Newsletter*, No. 28 (University of Washington, Seattle, November 1984), pp. 1–2.
22. *Ibid.*, p. 2.
23. United Nations Food and Agriculture Organization (FAO), *Yearbook of Fishery Statistics* (FAO, Rome, 1983), p. 75.
24. *Op. cit.* 21, p. 2.
25. Juan Velez, *et al.*, "Effects of the 1982–83 El Niño on Fishes and Crustaceans off Peru," *Tropical Ocean-Atmosphere Newsletter*, No. 28 (University of Washington, Seattle, November 1984), p. 12.
26. Matthias Wolff, "Impact of the 1982–83 El Nino on the Peruvian Scallop *Argropecten purpuratus*," *Tropical Ocean-Atmosphere Newsletter*, No. 28 (University of Washington, Seattle, November 1984), p. 8.
27. *Op. cit.* 1, p. 8.
28. V.A. Kovda, *The Role and Functions of the Soil Cover in the Earth's Biosphere* (preprint, Academy of Sciences of the USSR, Scientific Center of Biological Research, Puschino, 1985), to be published in *Proceedings of the Institute of Soil Science and Photosynthesis* (International Congress of Soil Science, Hamburg, Germany, 1986), p. 4.
29. Bengt Nihlgard, "The Ammonium Hypothesis—An Additional Explanation to the Forest Dieback in Europe," *AMBIO*, Vol. 14, No. 1 (1985), pp. 2–8.
30. T. Rosswall, "The Biogeochemical Nitrogen Cycle," in *Some Perspectives of the Major Biogeochemical Cycles*, SCOPE Report No. 17, G.E. Likens, ed. (John Wiley and Sons, Chichester, United Kingdom, 1981), p. 34.
31. U. Pierrou, "The Global Phosphorus Cycle," in *Nitrogen, Phosphorus and Sulphur: Global Cycles*, SCOPE Report No. 7, B.H. Svensson and R. Soderlund, eds. (Ecological Bulletin No. 22, Stockholm, 1976), pp. 75–88.
32. B. Bolin, *et al.*, "The Global Biogeochemical Carbon Cycle," in *The Global Carbon Cycle*, SCOPE Report No. 13, B. Bolin, *et al.*, eds. (John Wiley and Sons, Chichester, United Kingdom, 1979), p. 1 and p. 22.
33. United Nations Food and Agriculture Organization (FAO) and United Nations Educational, Scientific and Cultural Organization (UNESCO), *Soil Map of the World*, Vol. 1, *Legend* (UNESCO, Paris, 1974).
34. E.M. Bridges, *World Soils* (Cambridge University Press, New York, 1978), p. 25.
35. *Op. cit.* 28, p. 11.
36. U.S. National Research Council, *Chemistry and World Food Supplies: Research Priorities for Development: Report of a Workshop Held at Los Banos, Philippines, December 11–14, 1982* (National Academy Press, Washington, D.C., 1983), p. 19.
37. V.A. Kovda, "Loss of Productive Land due to Salinization," *AMBIO*, Vol. 12, No. 2 (1983), p. 92.
38. World Resources Institute and International Institute for Environment and Development, *World Resources 1986* (Basic Books, New York, 1986), p. 132.
39. Organisation for Economic Co-operation and Development (OECD), *The State of the Environment* (OECD, Paris, 1985), p. 101.
40. *Op. cit.* 1, p. 19.
41. *Op. cit.* 36, p. 19.
42. *Op. cit.* 39, p. 94.
43. *Op. cit.* 39, p. 98.
44. *Op. cit.* 28, p. 11.
45. Compton J. Tucker, *et al.*, "Continental and Global Scale Remote Sensing of Land Cover," in *The Changing Carbon Cycle: A Global Analysis*, John R. Trabalka and David E. Reichle, eds. (Springer-Verlag, New York, 1986), p. 221 and p. 230.
46. *Ibid.*, p. 230.
47. R.M. Hoffer, "Remote Sensing to Measure the Distribution and Structure of Vegetation," in *The Role of Terrestrial Vegetation in the Global Carbon Cycle: Measurement by Remote Sensing*, SCOPE Report No. 23, George M. Woodwell, ed. (John Wiley and Sons, Chichester, United Kingdom, 1984), p. 143.
48. George M. Woodwell, *et al.*, "Measurement of Changes in the Vegetation of the Earth by Satellite Imagery," in *The Role of Terrestrial Vegetation in the Global Carbon Cycle: Measurement by Remote Sensing*, SCOPE Report No. 23, George M. Woodwell, ed. (John Wiley and Sons, Chichester, United Kingdom, 1984), p. 232.
49. Donald L. Rheem, "'Spy Satellites' Take on New Roles," *The Christian Science Monitor* (August 8, 1986), p. 3.
50. B.N. Rock, *et al.*, "Remote Detection of Forest Damage," *BioScience*, Vol. 36, No. 7 (1986), pp. 439–445.
51. *Op. cit.* 49, p. 4.
52. International Council of Scientific Unions (ICSU), *The International Geosphere-Biosphere Programme: A Study of Global Change* (ICSU, Paris, 1986), p. 4.
53. M. McElroy, *Global Change: A Biogeochemical Perspective* (Jet Propulsion Laboratory, Pasadena, California, 1983), p. iii and p. 1.
54. U.S. National Research Council, *Global Tropospheric Chemistry: A Plan for Action* (National Academy Press, Washington, D.C., 1984), p. ix.
55. U.S. Committee for an International Geosphere-Biosphere Program, Commission on Physical Science, Mathematics, and Resources, National Research Council, *Global Change in the Geosphere-Biosphere: Initial Priorities for an IGBP* (National Academy Press, Washington, D.C., 1986), p. vii and p. 5.
56. U.S. National Aeronautics and Space Administration (NASA), *Earth System Science Overview: A Program for Global Change* (NASA, Washington, D.C., 1986).
57. Mitchell Waldrop, "Washington Embraces Global Earth Sciences," *Science*, Vol. 233 (September 5, 1986), pp. 1040–1042.
58. T.F. Malone and J.G. Roederer, eds., *Global Change* (Cambridge University Press, Cambridge, United Kingdom, 1985), p. xviii.
59. Walter Sullivan, "Global Study of Changes in Earth's Livability Set," *The New York Times* (September 22, 1986), p. 14.
60. International Council of Scientific Unions (ICSU), "The International Geosphere-Biosphere Programme: A Study of Global Change," final report of the Ad Hoc Planning Group (ICSU, Paris, August 4, 1986), p. 3.
61. Thomas F. Malone, "Mission to Planet Earth," *Environment*, Vol. 28, No. 8 (1986), p. 6.
62. Philip H. Abelson, "The International Geosphere-Biosphere Program," *Science*, Vol. 234 (November 7, 1986), p. 657.
63. *Op. cit.* 57, p. 1042.

12. Policies and Institutions

Natural resources such as rivers and seas have helped shape the political boundaries of nations, dividing them in one sense, but also linking their future well-being inextricably to wise management of these resources. Because they are essential to all those whose boundaries they touch or cross, shared resources are frequently the focus of competition and conflict. As populations grew and technological capacities (and wastes) increased, water, air, and other resources have been used more intensely.

In 1986, two events served as stark reminders of the dramatic impacts that the quality of the air and water in one country can have on other countries: the nuclear accident at Chernobyl in the Soviet Union and the toxic chemical spill into the Rhine at Basel, Switzerland. In these cases—as in many other, less publicized abuses of shared resources—pollution had no respect for political boundaries.

In recent years, nations have increasingly recognized how the actions of other nations can significantly affect both the quality and quantity of the resources available to them. National leaders have begun to perceive mutual interests in protecting shared resources. As a result, they have attempted to reach a variety of formal and informal agreements concerning transboundary pollution and the management of shared resources.

This year's "Policies and Institutions" chapter examines some of these agreements and the cooperative arrangements that have been devised to manage rivers, seas, and the atmosphere. It looks separately at agreements involving two-to-four states, regional agreements involving a larger number of states, and global agreements involving most of the world's nations. This categorization, though not precise, is helpful for purposes of analysis.

Although it might be assumed that institutional arrangements involving the smallest number of participating countries can be conducted most quickly, enforced

most effectively, and have the best prospects for success, the examples below show that this assumption is not always correct. Nevertheless, when the interests of the countries involved are nearly equal and when cooperation focuses on specific limited objectives, the chances for successful cooperation seem to be enhanced.

INTERNATIONAL ENVIRONMENTAL LAW

In recent years, a body of international law, practice, and standards has evolved whose effect is to encourage equitable apportionment of resources, to discourage the externalization of pollution, and to promote cooperation among countries. Without these guidelines, individual nations would presumably export as much of their pollution, and take as much from shared resources, as they wished. But because of them, a growing number of attempts are being made to prevent and resolve environmental disputes in cooperative and mutually beneficial ways.

The foremost principle of international environmental law is that one's property should not be used in ways that endanger the property of one's neighbor. This principle, rooted in Roman legal tradition, was upheld 50 years ago in a landmark case between Canada and the United States, in which Canada was required to pay damages to Washington state for fumes from a British Columbia smelter [1]. In 1947, the principle was placed firmly in the body of international law by the *Corfu Channel* case, in which the International Court of Justice declared: "Every state is under an obligation not to allow its territory to be used for acts contrary to the rights of other states" [2].

The 1972 United Nations Conference on the Human Environment, held in Stockholm, adopted Principle 21, which recognizes a nation's right to exploit its own natural resources, providing that such exploitation does not

Policies and Institutions

damage the environment of other nations. The language of Principle 21 has since been incorporated into numerous regional and global conventions (3) (4).

This principle received further validation in the international community in 1979, when the U.N. General Assembly adopted a set of principles, based on the Stockholm Conference, for the "Conservation and Harmonious Utilization of Natural Resources Shared by Two or More States," to be used in the formulation of bilateral and multilateral conventions on environmental subjects (5).

PROSPECTS FOR SUCCESS

In the areas of pollution abatement and resource sharing, even modest successes are significant. An agreement to prevent air or water pollution may not result in cleaner air or water initially, but it may slow the rate of deterioration.

Even with a strong commitment on all sides, an agreement can take years to become established or effective. For example, the convention on "Long Range Transboundary Air Pollution," whose purpose is to address the critical problem of acid rain in Europe, was signed in 1979, came into force in 1983, and had an implementing protocol added to it in 1985 (6); the results will not be ascertained until 1993. Compared with other international environmental agreements, however, this convention has produced rather speedy and concerted international action.

International environmental problems are most successfully managed when all the participating countries recognize that their long-term national self-interests lie in mutual collaboration. Countries cooperate on resource sharing and pollution control because they believe it is in their interests to do so—either in the short term (e.g., cessation of a neighbor's misuse of the resource) or in the long term (proper management of a valued resource or improved relations among countries). Successful international agreements do not necessarily require giving up national sovereignty (such a requirement would most likely retard progress), but they do require a recognition of, and respect for, the rights and needs of the partner countries.

A number of conditions—including a history of amicable relations, compatible economies and cultures, and shared environmental values—contribute to a high degree of cooperation among countries. But there are no "givens"—no conditions that guarantee success.

Nonetheless, one can identify various factors that often influence the likelihood of achieving workable intergovernmental arrangements. These include:
■ the severity of the problem—once a problem is widely acknowledged as critical, it may be easier to make progress;
■ science—how much technical agreement there is about what actions are needed;
■ geography—the extent to which countries are similarly or differently affected;
■ law—whether countries have laws protecting the environment and whether foreigners have equal access to court and administrative proceedings to enforce those laws;
■ domestic interests and pressures—who favors and who opposes action on the issue in each country;
■ formal institutions and policies—whether there is a mechanism in place for cooperative action among the countries;
■ history—whether there is a tradition of cooperation or conflict among the countries;
■ relative economic strength, military power, and population—large disparities in size or strength may hinder agreement unless the stronger country depends on the weaker for the resource;
■ outside influences—whether there are third parties such as U.N. agencies or other nations that influence the process without being signatories to the agreement;
■ timing—it may be easier to reach agreement before various interests are entrenched.

Each of the cases discussed in this chapter entails unique circumstances—a particular problem involving particular groups of advantaged and disadvantaged countries dealing with their own domestic economic and political pressures. Collectively, however, the cases represent a broad array of institutional structures and mechanisms available for dealing with resource and pollution issues, they illustrate the factors that affect prospects for reaching and implementing agreements, and they provide insight into the behaviors of countries balancing narrow self-interests with long-term mutual interests in the protection of scarce, and ultimately finite, resources.

RESOURCE AGREEMENTS INVOLVING TWO—FOUR COUNTRIES

Issues of shared resource management and cross-boundary pollution that affect relatively few nations tend to be more immediate than those that affect a large number of countries. The direct benefits as well as the specific costs of the actions of individual nations are easier to define with precision, as is the question of who is doing what to whom. These characteristics may make agreement among a small number of nations easier in terms of defining specific actions or remedies required. On the other hand, a clearer understanding of the costs of specific actions may make it more difficult to reach agreement.

The Great Lakes Basin

The Great Lakes are one of the most important natural resources shared by Canada and the United States. (See Figure 12.1.) One seventh of the U.S. population resides in the Great Lakes basin, including four of the 12 largest cities in the United States, and one sixth of U.S. national income is generated in the basin. Sixty percent of Canada's total population lives in the basin, and nearly one third of Canada's national income is generated there. The U.S. population in the basin is almost five times that of the Canadian population (7). Use of the Great Lakes reflects this population difference—the United States accounts for 87 percent of the water consumed from the lakes and discharges 80 percent of conventional pollutants from sewage treatment plants. The two countries' discharges of toxic chemicals are likely to be similarly disproportionate (8).

The major legal instrument governing the Great Lakes is the Boundary Waters Treaty of 1909 (9), which extends to all U.S.-Canadian boundary waters. It established the International Joint Commission (IJC) as a permanent body to implement portions of the Treaty. The IJC is often portrayed as a successful model institution for dealing with transboundary disputes, especially disputes over water quantity issues (levels and flows of water) (10).

Part of the IJC's effectiveness in resolving disputes results from its relatively limited use. Canada and the United States originally created the IJC to deal exclusively with problems such as water diversion, flood control, and hydroelectric power generation, the solution of which could benefit both nations (11). Under Articles III and IV of the Treaty, the IJC can make binding, unreviewable decisions about applications regarding such issues (12). But in general, Canada and the United States do not refer problems to the IJC unless their national interests coincide (13). Under Article X of the Boundary Waters Treaty, if the two countries consent, the IJC can sit as arbitrator and render a binding decision on almost any issue arising under the Treaty. To date, the two countries have not exercised this option (14).

The IJC's effectiveness in water use issues arises primarily from its role as neutral adviser and factfinder. The IJC's advisory boards are staffed by impartial professionals. Throughout its existence, the IJC's commissioners, particularly the two chairs (one from the United States and one from Canada), have respected and maintained the Commission's role as neutral problem solver. The two governments view IJC recommendations as both technically competent and uncompromised by national biases. Over its 75-year history, about 80 percent of the IJC recommendations have been accepted by both governments. The IJC has generally not tried to stretch its power by setting policy or devising regulations. Implementation of IJC recommendations is left to each country (15).

Controlling pollution within the Great Lakes basin has proven to be a more difficult issue than controlling water use, and it is challenging the IJC's effectiveness. The Great Lakes Water Quality Agreements of 1972 and 1978 assigned the IJC a significant role in the joint U.S.-Canadian efforts to clean up the lakes. The 1972 Agreement focused on pollution from traditional sources, such as municipal sewers, that were causing severe eutrophication (16) of the lower Great Lakes (17). The 1978 Agreement relates mainly to toxic pollutants. The responsibility of the IJC was to oversee implementation of the agreements, to report on the adequacy of progress being made to meet the objective of the agreements, and to coordinate data collection, research, monitoring, and surveillance in both countries intended to meet the goals of the agreements (18). Binational boards and advisory groups were also established to advise the IJC on water pollution problems (19).

Primarily through unilateral domestic efforts, progress has been made in controlling pollution from conventional sources. Eutrophication of the lakes has been slowed and

Figure 12.1 The Great Lakes Basin

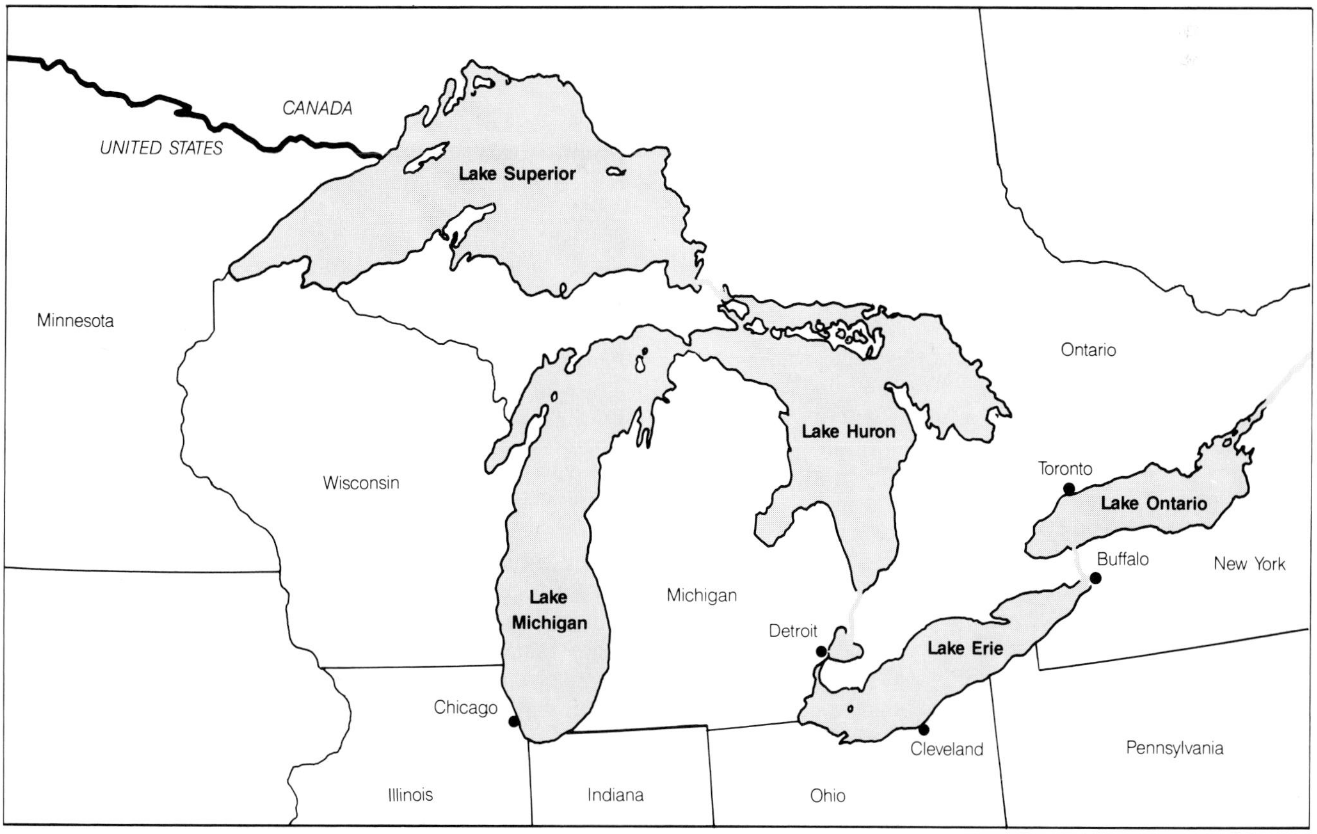

Policies and Institutions

in some places stopped (20). The IJC supports this effort through research and monitoring. On the other hand, an effective toxic substances control strategy has not been developed. Allocation of permitted discharges into the lakes is controversial. Canada would base the discharge allocation on land area instead of population. The United States favors allocation based on population, which would greatly favor the United States. This controversy also reflects divergences in the ways Canada and the United States control domestic water pollution. In the United States, regulations require the control of water pollution at the source, with a goal of zero discharge. Canadian regulations assume that water receiving pollutants has a given assimilative capacity. Regulation is on a case-by-case basis with the overall objective of staying within the assimilative capacity (21). In addition, a significant source of toxic pollutants in the lakes is air pollution, over which the IJC has not attempted to exercise any control.

Progress in dealing with Great Lakes water quality, however, does not depend solely on a binational administrative framework such as the IJC. Numerous conditions in the Great Lakes basin favor bilateral dispute resolution (22). For example, there is neither an upstream polluting country nor a downstream victim country. Industries and municipalities on both sides contribute to the pollution load. Although the United States produces the much larger share of the lakes' pollution, overall pollution affects both countries.

International cooperation is also fostered by subnational cooperation among the basin's states and provinces. Basin governance is diffused among the two federal governments, eight U.S. states, and the Canadian province of Ontario (23). The states and, to a greater extent, the province of Ontario have authority within their federal systems to regulate activities affecting the lakes' water quality. In May 1986, the governors of states bordering the Great Lakes approved a Toxic Substances Control Agreement as a first step toward developing a more comprehensive plan to reduce the dumping of chemicals into the lakes (24). Ontario and Quebec officials voiced support for the agreement, and they plan to develop a similar accord. Many provisions of the Toxic Substances Control Agreement echo those of the 1978 Great Lakes Water Quality Agreement.

Earlier in 1986, the governors of the eight Great Lakes states signed a joint resolution banning oil drilling in the Great Lakes. Ontario endorsed a draft "statement of purpose" on the subject. The IJC had not considered the drilling issue because lake beds are state lands and thus are outside federal jurisdiction (25). Michigan and Ontario also signed a pact in 1985 that commits both parties to virtually eliminate toxic chemicals from boundary waters by the year 2000 (26). These subnational cooperative efforts augment cooperative national efforts to clean up the lakes.

Nongovernmental organizations (NGOs) in both countries also strongly encourage international cooperative efforts to control toxic pollution. The Canadian Government has even taken the unusual step of funding Canadian environmental groups participating in U.S. lawsuits aimed at forcing cleanup of toxic waste dumps (27).

Environment Canada, Canada's environmental agency, is putting its informational and technical resources at the disposal of environmental groups. The Canadian Environment Minister has said: "Direct legal involvement [by the Canadian Government] might be self-defeating. If we lost in the courts, we might be encumbered in going through the political route. We don't want to hamstring ourselves" (28). U.S. environmental groups have not yet attempted to intervene in cases before Canadian courts; thus it remains to be seen whether U.S. environmental groups can gain equal access to Canadian courts (29).

The Great Lakes Water Quality Agreement of 1978 is slated to come under joint governmental review. The U.S. National Research Council and the Royal Society of Canada have reviewed progress under the Agreement and made recommendations. Their joint report suggests that the IJC should consider assuming a higher profile by exercising its authority to initiate reviews of water pollution issues (30) (31). This recommendation would strengthen the IJC role in protecting and managing the lakes.

In summary, Canada and the United States have developed fairly effective mechanisms for handling Great Lakes water issues. Success is most evident in issues of controlling water flow and diversion, with the IJC serving an important administrative function. Water quality is a newer issue, and progress on cleaning up the lakes is more limited, especially for toxic pollutants. When called upon, the IJC is effective in investigating and recommending solutions to Great Lakes' water quality problems, but the IJC is called upon only when Canada and the United States agree on the nature of a problem. The IJC may be a model for other situations—but only if the nations involved have strong incentives to cooperate.

The Nile River

Egypt and Sudan share the waters of the Nile, the world's second longest river. (See Figure 12.2.) The vast majority of Egypt's population lives within the Nile River Valley. Egypt's homogeneous population of about 50 million lives in a cultivable land area of some 30,000 square kilometers, with an average density of 1,000 people per square kilometer (32). Since the beginning of recorded history, "life in Egypt has . . . been based totally on agriculture irrigated by the waters of the River Nile" (33). Sudan, by contrast, has a heterogeneous population of about 20 million, but a population density of only seven people per square kilometer; 60 percent of Sudan's vast land surface is arable and habitable (34).

The Nile is so important to both countries that their presidents apparently negotiate any major problems or development schemes in bilateral discussions. Because of Egypt's total dependence on Nile water flowing from Sudan, it seems to be a cornerstone of Egyptian foreign policy that there be a friendly government in Khartoum. Egypt presumably would respond militarily if a hostile Sudan Government attempted to disrupt the flow of the Nile into Egypt.

The first Nile Water Agreement between Egypt and Sudan was signed in 1929 (35). Their current sharing arrangement was formalized in 1959. The 1959 "Agree-

World Resources 1987

184

Figure 12.2 The Nile River

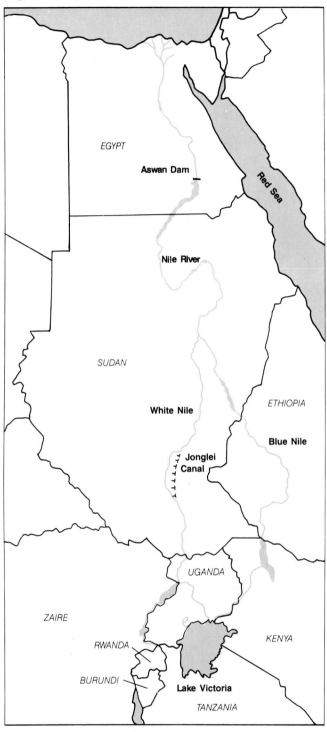

ment for the Complete Utilization of the Nile Waters" set up a Permanent Joint Technical Commission, which has been operating since then (36) (37). The Commission performs a limited research, data gathering, planning, and coordinating function. It is staffed by engineers and technical personnel from both countries.

The Permanent Joint Commission has no independent authority. It has facilitated the two countries' cooperative efforts to finance and build the Jonglei Canal project—

begun in 1978 to reclaim most of the Nile flow through the southern Sudan's *Sudd* swamp (50 percent of the Nile's total flow) that is currently lost by evaporation and seepage (38).

Egypt and Sudan now share equally in the costs, and they expect eventually to share in the water benefits of the Jonglei project (39). Underway since 1978 but nowhere near completion, the project has been completely stopped by political unrest in southern Sudan (40). Many believe that the project's adverse environmental consequences will be massive (41) (42). It will certainly displace large groups of native people and obliterate the fishing stock on which their livelihood and diet depend. (See Chapter 6, "Wildlife and Habitat," Focus On: Freshwater Wetlands.)

Sudanese Government leaders seem to have identified strongly with the Jonglei Canal project, just as Egypt's leaders had identified with the Aswan High Dam. Both projects fed on nationalism, and now each nation's self-image and self-esteem seem to be involved in the project's success.

The Joint Commission also helped to work out the formula for dividing the water from the Aswan Dam. These bilateral arrangements involve no loss of sovereignty and seem likely to work so long as they are mutually beneficial.

The 1959 Agreement formalized the acquired or historic rights of both countries to Nile waters in a proportion of 12 to 1 in favor of Egypt (43). Egypt has a larger population and is much stronger economically and militarily. The long-term problem for Egypt and Sudan is that both depend on their upstream riparians. Egypt, the most downstream riparian of the nine nations on the Nile, depends entirely on upstream nations, including Sudan, for its vital supply of Nile water.

At least 86 percent of Nile waters flow out of Ethiopia (44). If Ethiopia were unilaterally to divert any substantial percentage of its own Blue Nile waters for domestic use, a critical water shortage would undoubtedly result in both Egypt and the Sudan. Ethiopia and Egypt are vastly different culturally, economically, and politically. In the absence of problems, Egypt and Sudan seem to be reluctant to initiate discussions with Ethiopia (45). Accordingly, Ethiopia has been completely outside Nile planning and development. Although no major Ethiopian diversions of Blue Nile waters are foreseen, even a small diversion could cause serious problems for Sudan and Egypt. Sudanese needs for water may soon exceed its supply—after Egypt receives its guaranteed allocation—and Egypt too is hard pressed for water to support the rising agricultural needs of its burgeoning population.

The White Nile, which supplies about 14 percent of the water flowing annually through the Aswan Dam, originates in Lakes Victoria, Kioga, Edward, Albert, and George, whose six riparian states—Uganda, Kenya, Tanzania, Rwanda, Burundi, and Zaire—are essential to any future development of the Nile Basin (46). Because the nine nations of the Nile Basin had not met to discuss cooperative action, the United Nations Development Programme invited the water ministers of the nine Nile countries to a meeting in Bangkok in 1985 (47). No agreement was reached at the meeting, and Ethiopia appeared to be most reluctant to commit to any cooperative agreement that would limit its rights to control the Nile waters in its territory (48).

In the Nile basin, the greatest challenges would seem to lie ahead. Upstream riparians are likely eventually to claim Nile waters for their own hydropower and irrigation schemes. Thus a cooperative arrangement is especially important to Egypt and Sudan for the protection of their water needs.

The Ganges-Brahmaputra River Basin

The Ganges River rises in the Himalayas of India and Nepal and flows 2,700 kilometers through north India, joining the Bay of Bengal through deltaic Bangladesh. Its role as the sacred river of 600 million Hindus obscures for the outside world its economic, and specifically agricultural, importance. Like the Nile, the highly seasonal Ganges over millennia has created an alluvial basin with a distinct civilization whose cultivation now is the support of a third of a billion Indians, Nepalis, and Bangladeshis. The Brahmaputra, a slightly larger in volume and less seasonally varying river, after a long eastward course in Tibet, turns west to drain the Indian state of Assam and joins the Ganges in Bangladesh about 200 kilometers above the Bay of Bengal. (See Figure 12.3.)

Unlike the situation in the Nile basin, Bangladesh, the most downstream riparian, is militarily and economically much weaker than its upstream neighbor, India, which also dwarfs the highest riparian, Nepal. The latter impoverished Himalayan kingdom has by a good deal the smallest population and has virtually no major export resources except the large hydroelectric potential of its rivers that flow into the Ganges, effectively usable only by India. The Himalayas, primarily in Nepal, are the source of the silt the system carries. Because the Himalayas are geologically young and steep mountains, siltation is inevitably heavy, but speed of run-off and the sediment load have grown due to extensive deforestation of the slopes, increasing to an undetermined degree the wet season-dry season contrast, flood danger, problems of navigation, and the cost of dams.

In the 1950s, when Bangladesh was East Pakistan, India decided to build a barrage (dam) across the Ganges at Farakka just above the border. Its purpose was to divert a portion of the scarce low season water into the Hooghly channel which remains within India, ostensibly to flush silt from the economically stagnating port of Calcutta. The barrage (with movable gates) was constructed through the 1960s notwithstanding Pakistani protests. At the same time a deeper water Hooghly port was built closer to the sea at Haldia largely as a substitute for Calcutta (49). As the Farakka Barrage approached completion, and in the wake of Bangladesh's 1971 achievement of independence with the assistance of the Indian forces, the Indo-Bangladesh Joint Rivers Commission (JRC) was established in 1972 "to make Joint Recommendations to the two governments as to how (their common) waters might be optimally developed and appropriated by either country for their mutual benefit (50)." Each country's representation to the JRC is led by a minister, and meet-

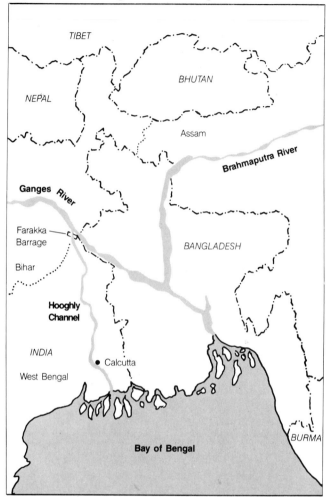

Figure 12.3 Ganges—Brahmaputra River Basin

TIBET

BHUTAN

NEPAL

Assam

Brahmaputra River

Ganges River

Farakka Barrage

BANGLADESH

Bihar

Hooghly Channel

INDIA

• Calcutta

West Bengal

Bay of Bengal

BURMA

ings were intended to be held four times a year. During the monsoon season, when excess water is the problem, the JRC has served to transmit information about Ganges flows, enabling Bangladesh to take protective measures against flooding (51), but concerning the critical low-water season (April and May), the JRC has not yet become an instrument of active cooperation.

Especially since the 1975 fall of Bangladeshi independence leader Mujibur Rahman, India has shown caution and reserve in several spheres of its relations with the Bangladesh government. In 1976, India unilaterally used Farakka to shift part of the Ganges low flow to the Hooghly (52). Bangladesh asserted that the reduced flow for Bangladesh not only diminished water available for food production but also caused Bangladeshi wells in the southwestern part of the country to dry up or to be invaded by salt water from the Bay of Bengal. In the absence of any resolution of the problem through the JRC, Bangladesh appealed to the General Assembly of the United Nations in 1976, leading to a consensus statement that helped persuade India to negotiate with Bangladesh over its use of the Barrage at Farakka (53).

After such exchanges, in 1977 India and Bangladesh agreed to a five-year sharing of dry-season Ganges waters at Farakka that gave 966 cubic meters per second (54) (55), or roughly 60 percent, to Bangladesh. It was also agreed that the two countries would jointly seek ways to augment the availability of low-season Ganges water. The 1977 "sharing" agreement has since been extended twice, but for shorter periods, and with less firm guarantees than the original ones to Bangladesh (56) (57).

There has been effectively no progress toward cooperative plans to "augment" the dry season flow of the river. A perennial proposal of Indian engineers has been to construct a canal through Bangladesh to divert Brahmaputra water upstream at the Assam-Bangladesh border into the Ganges in eastern Bihar state. This canal would cover the water needs of West Bengal and Calcutta permitting greater withdrawals by upstream farmers in Uttar Pradesh and western Bihar to irrigate the dry season "green revolution" crops that a growing population makes more imperative each year. The Bangladesh Government is deeply opposed to such a canal. It believes that Bangladesh needs all the dry-season water that historically both rivers have brought it, in order to resist salt invasion from the Bay of Bengal and to combat an asserted increased sedimentation said to lead to faster elevation of channel beds and a greater risk of flooding in the delta (58). Perhaps even more important, Bangladeshi nationalist feeling strongly rejects a canal as an intrusion of Indian interests and power into Bangladesh territory. Because Bangladesh had agreed to discuss augmentation of the waters, and because the Farakka Barrage gives India the powerful leverage of being able to control virtually completely the dry season flow of the Ganges into Bangladesh, Bangladesh countered the link canal suggestion with a proposal to construct storage dams in Nepal to hold the monsoon water of Ganges tributaries for use in the dry season. Until recently India has strongly resisted bringing Nepal to the table when it discusses water with Bangladesh. More important, it has been clear from the outset that Nepal has no reason to sacrifice its populated valleys as storage sites to solve the Indo-Bangladeshi problem (59).

As less water reaches Farakka each year due to increasing upstream irrigation use in the politically potent "Hindi belt" of North India, the "augmentation" efforts under the 1977 agreement remain deadlocked. It is not clear whether India will use its control of the Ganges flow at Farakka to increase pressure on Bangladesh to accede to interbasin transfer of water from the Brahmaputra. "Instead of making attempts to resolve differences through accommodations and a pooling of resources," observed one Bangladeshi scholar, "each country is determined to get more than its fair share (60)."

The Rhine River

The four major Rhine riparians—Switzerland, West Germany, France, and the Netherlands (61)—have similar cultures, standards of living, political values, and environmental controls. (See Figure 12.4.) These four countries have a long history of cooperation on issues concerning their shared river resource. In 1885, for example, they joined in a treaty on salmon fishing, and since then there have been several treaties on Rhine navigation.

The Rhine basin has a population of approximately 40 million people, including the majority of the residents of Switzerland and the Netherlands and about one third of West Germany's population (62). This concentrated population in the Rhine basin has resulted in the use of the Rhine to discharge much of the area's waste products. The highly publicized chemical spill in November 1986 that occurred in Basel, Switzerland, was merely the worst and most recent example of the tons of toxic chemicals, mineral wastes containing heavy metals, and organic compounds that have been dumped in the Rhine over the years, seriously degrading its water quality. Chlorides (common salt) have been the Rhine's most pervasive pollutant. (In 1975, at the place where the Rhine flows into the Netherlands, the river carried an annual average of 12.2 million metric tons of chlorides (63).)

In response to increasing pollution, the four states agreed in 1963 to their first environmental compact, establishing the International Commission for the Protection of the Rhine against Pollution (64). The International Commission imposes no specific obligation on the contracting states apart from their agreement to cooperate with the Commission. It conducts pollution research and proposes various abatement measures to the riparian states. Essentially, it has a monitoring and advisory function and no decisionmaking power (65). Three of the four main Rhine riparians—West Germany, France, and the

Figure 12.4 The Rhine River

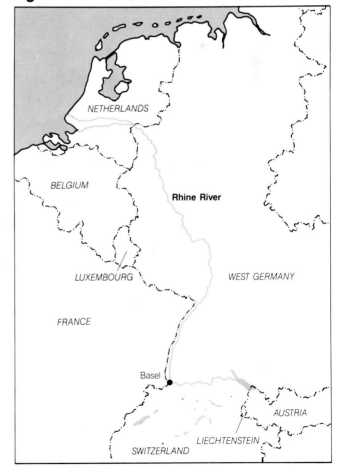

Policies and Institutions

Netherlands—are also members of the European Economic Community (EC), which has adopted a variety of directives concerning water pollution. (A directive of the EC is binding on each member nation.) The fourth riparian, Switzerland, is not a member of the EC.

In 1976, the four Rhine states signed two additional conventions: the Convention for the Protection of the Rhine against Chemical Pollution (66) and the Convention on the Protection of the Rhine against Pollution by Chlorides (the Rhine Salt Convention) (67). The Rhine Chemical Convention, modeled after a similar EC directive, established a "black list" of dangerous chemicals that should be gradually eliminated and a "grey list" of substances whose discharge into the Rhine needs to be strictly regulated by national authorities (68).

Until the spill of more than 1,000 metric tons of chemicals from a chemical storage warehouse in Basel, Switzerland, the effects of the Chemical Convention had been mixed. Levels of some pollutants, particularly heavy metals, had decreased since the mid-1970s, but levels of nitrates had risen. (See *World Resources 1986*, Part IV, Table 9.2, pp. 304–305.) Action on adding new chemicals to the list is slow because the three EC member countries look to the EC for new directives on specific chemicals (69).

Chloride pollution is not directly covered by any EC directive, and no real progress has yet been made in cleaning it up. The massive salinization of the Rhine has resulted from growing industrial and mining activities in the Rhine basin. About one third of the salt is discharged by potash mines in the Alsatian region of France (70). Under the terms of an annex to the Rhine Salt Convention, the French Government was to install a salt injection system in the subsoil of Alsace (71). The other three riparians were to (and did) pay France for this storage and disposal in disproportionate amounts. The Netherlands, the most victimized of the riparian states, paid the largest share, thus directly contradicting the widely subscribed "polluter pays" principle of the Organisation for Economic Co-operation and Development (OECD). The Netherlands paid 34 percent of the estimated cost of the salt injection system, Germany and France each paid 30 percent, and Switzerland paid 6 percent (72).

Because Alsatian farmers resisted the salt injection process, their delegates to the French National Assembly resisted ratification of the agreement for almost nine years. The Rhine Salt Convention was not ratified until September 1985 (73), and implementation action has not yet been taken. At a meeting of the International Rhine Commission in June 1986, the French Government announced that it had abandoned plans to inject salt effluents into the Alsatian subsoil (74). It pledged to come up with an alternative solution early in 1987 (75). France now appears to be ready to implement an alternative solution that will involve storing salts above ground. The cost is likely to be significantly higher than subsoil injection, and France will pay the added cost (76). Although action may now be forthcoming, French inaction to this point has prevented significant progress on reducing salt pollution.

Meanwhile, a Dutch district court held in 1983 that the French discharger of the salts, *Mines Dominiales des Potasses d'Alsace* (MDPA), was obliged both by international law and the Rhine Salt Convention to compensate Dutch farmers for damage from the salt discharge (77). The polluter was eventually found liable under both international and Dutch tort law. A Dutch appeals court upheld the lower court's finding in September 1986 (78). In an earlier related case (1983), a French administrative tribunal in Strasbourg, responding to a petition from 10 Dutch plaintiffs, declared illegal the discharge permit issued by the local prefect to MDPA. The court declared that French authorities were obliged to prohibit activities with harmful consequences outside the limits of national jurisdiction (79) (80) (81). Although the appeals courts in both cases did not rest their decisions on international law, the lower court decisions may be seen as small steps forward in the development of international environmental law. They also show how equal access to all the courts in a region (in this case, Western Europe) can help in the international resolution of transboundary environmental disputes. (See Box 12.1.)

Box 12.1 Equal Access to the Courts

Several western European countries afford citizens of neighboring states access to their courts and administrative proceedings on the same footing as citizens of the forum state (1). Under the Nordic Convention of 1974 on the Protection of the Environment (2), Norway, Sweden, Denmark, and Finland handle national pollution discharges causing damage *beyond* national borders in the same way that they handle discharges causing local damage (3). In environmental suits for compensation or injunctive relief, the Nordic Convention guarantees citizens of the four countries equal access to their countries' courts (4).

This principle is not yet well established in North America. U.S. citizens generally do not have the right in Canadian courts to seek legal remedies in cases involving transboundary pollution. Although U.S. courts are somewhat more flexible, no international agreement exists between Canada and the United States guaranteeing equal access (5). However, recent efforts by the Uniform Law Conference of Canada and the U.S. National Conference of Commissioners on Uniform State Laws have resulted in adoption of the Transboundary Pollution Reciprocal Access Act by at least five U.S. states and two Canadian provinces. The act guarantees equal access to the courts where the pollution originated (6).

References and Notes

1. Since 1974, the Organisation for Economic Co-operation and Development (OECD) has been advocating equal rights of access and nondiscrimination for foreigners seeking transboundary pollution remedies in domestic courts and administrative proceedings. OECD, Recommendation for Equal Right of Access in Relation to Transfrontier Pollution, Document C(74)224 (1974).
2. "Nordic Convention on the Protection of the Environment," February 19, 1974, reprinted in *International Legal Materials*, Vol. 13 (1974), p. 591.
3. *Ibid*, Article 2.
4. *Ibid*, Article 3 and Article 4.
5. Armin Rosencranz, "The Uniform Transboundary Pollution Reciprocal Access Act," *Environmental Policy and Law*, Vol. 15, No. 3/4 (1985), p. 105.
6. *Ibid*.

On November 1, 1986, a massive spill of dyes, insecticides, and mercury in the Rhine resulted from a fire (and attempts to extinguish it) at a Sandoz chemical company warehouse in Basel, Switzerland. The spill is reported to have destroyed most of the fish and many other life forms in the river (82). Although both Sandoz and the Swiss Government have made pledges of compensation, the spill continues to cause a major public outcry and is leading to increased multinational efforts to deal with accidental pollution. In a meeting of the Environmental Committee of the OECD on December 10, three top priorities were identified for research, reporting, and policy recommendations: hazardous waste, hazardous chemicals, and accidental pollution. According to Dr. Henri Smets of the OECD Environment Directorate, this is a striking change in priorities. Within two months of the spill, five international organizations had begun to focus major attention on accidental pollution—OECD, the United Nations Environment Programme (UNEP), the U.N. Economic Commission for Europe (ECE), the Council of Europe, and the EC (83). As a result, one long-term effect of the spill may be to create the political will to act aggressively against pollution of the Rhine and other rivers in Europe.

The preceding four cases involved formal international agreements. For a very different type of arrangement, see Box 12.2.

REGIONAL AGREEMENTS

The Mediterranean Sea

The Mediterranean Sea is one of the most vital and heavily trafficked waterways of the world. It is bordered by 18 nations with widely varying economic, political, and social systems, all of which contribute to and are affected by the pollution of this enclosed sea. (See Figure 12.5.) In spite of growing signs of coastal pollution during the 1960s, no agreement was reached on the severity, or even a diagnosis, of the problem. In the absence of a good understanding of the relationships among sources, pathways, and risks of key pollutants, there was little incentive for local action by individual countries—and even less incentive given no assurance of parallel action by other countries on the Mediterranean.

The process by which 17 of these 18 nations reached agreement on an overall Action Plan leading to the Barcelona Convention for the Protection of the Mediterranean Sea against Pollution in 1976 illustrates the importance of independent third parties in facilitating groups of nations' diagnosis and corrective action on common environmental problems. In this case, UNEP and associated U.N. agencies played strategic roles. The process also highlights the problems confronted by any effort to integrate environmental concerns into day-to-day decisionmaking.

During preparations for the 1972 Stockholm Environment Conference, marine pollution was identified as a priority item. Although the importance of reducing maritime sources of ocean pollution had led to action in the 1960s, it was not until the early 1970s that land-based activities were recognized as the most significant source of marine pollution. At the Stockholm Conference, agreement was reached on basic principles for developing a comprehensive approach to environmental issues. The principles embraced both assessment and management actions, emphasizing problems of enclosed and semienclosed seas, such as the Mediterranean.

These principles were confirmed at the first meeting of UNEP's Governing Council in 1973 (84) (85), and work on pollution of the Mediterranean began in 1974 (86). Positive action by the governments concerned was also encouraged by a number of meetings under NGO sponsorship. In 1973, for example, the United Tourist Organization, representing 132 municipalities in 16 Mediterranean countries, held a conference in Beirut that issued a "charter" calling for an international antipollution code for Mediterranean cities (87). In addition, the International Commission for Scientific Exploration of the Mediterranean Sea initiated scientific studies of pollution, further stimulating concerns in the region (88).

Building on activities begun by other U.N. agencies (notably the Food and Agriculture Organization), UNEP convened a series of meetings of scientific and legal experts from the region who drafted a comprehensive Action Plan for government approval. The plan suggested coordinated research and monitoring activities to improve assessments. It also suggested that governments enter into formal treaty obligations on a continuing basis and that they consider the assessment results in their domestic economic planning.

Broad agreement was reached at an intergovernmental conference convened by UNEP and FAO in Barcelona in 1975, when 16 Mediterranean countries and the EC approved the Action Plan for the Protection of the Mediterranean (MAP) (89). This plan began a process that led, only one year later, to signing the Barcelona Convention and to the first of a number of associated protocols relating to several categories of pollution sources, such as dumping, oil spills, and—ultimately—land-based activities (90). A further result is a series of coordinated research and monitoring programs that involve more than 80 national institutions.

Initially, MAP led to immediate action at the international level—specifically, the signing and entry into force of protocols and initiation of scientific work. The most significant progress under the Action Plan was assessment. A group of monitoring and research programs has already produced significant new insights into relevant conditions and trends. But as the effort focused on steps necessary to curb critical land-based activities, negotiations became more difficult. Although 85 percent of Mediterranean pollution is land based (91), several years of study were needed to support negotiations on a protocol relative to these sources; it was not adopted until 1980 and entered into force in 1983 (92). The economic implications of cleaning up these sources, as well as scientific uncertainties, have prevented action at the national level from keeping pace with the international agreements in principle.

Under the Action Plan, for example, there was agreement on the need for common environmental criteria for establishing minimum standards to safeguard the public from mercury in seafood and microbial contamination of

Box 12.2 The Jordan River Basin (1)

Not all shared resources require formal agreements. The Jordan River Basin is a rare case in which an implicit and informal arrangement seems to work. Jordan and Israel share the Jordan River, which forms the boundary between the two countries for much of its length. (See Figure 1.) A major northern tributary of the Jordan is the Yarmuk River, whose riparian areas are Syria, Jordan, and the territory occupied by Israel, including the Golan Heights. Syria has long had a tense relationship with Jordan, and both Jordan and Syria are nominally at war with Israel. Nonetheless, a tacit arrangement has evolved; Israel derives most of its water and irrigation needs from the Jordan River, whose headwaters lie mainly within Israel's boundaries. Lake Tiberias stores these Jordan River waters; a major pumping station and a conduit system running down the entire west side of Israel to the Egyptian border is located at the north end of Lake Tiberias.

Jordanian agriculture is supported almost exclusively by the Yarmuk, which flows into the Jordan River below Lake Tiberias. Some ten miles before the two rivers merge, a weir diverts much of the Yarmuk's flow into the East Ghor Main Canal, which, with additional water from the lower Jordan tributaries and groundwater wells, supplies virtually all Jordan's irrigation needs. A portion of the Yarmuk waters is also taken by canal to Lake Tiberias for use in Israel. There are no adequate storage facilities on the Yarmuk, and, during the rainy season, most of the Yarmuk's flood waters flow into the Jordan River. A portion of these Yarmuk flood waters is stored by Israel in its Naharayim reservoir beside the Jordan River. From there it is pumped and piped back to Lake Tiberias.

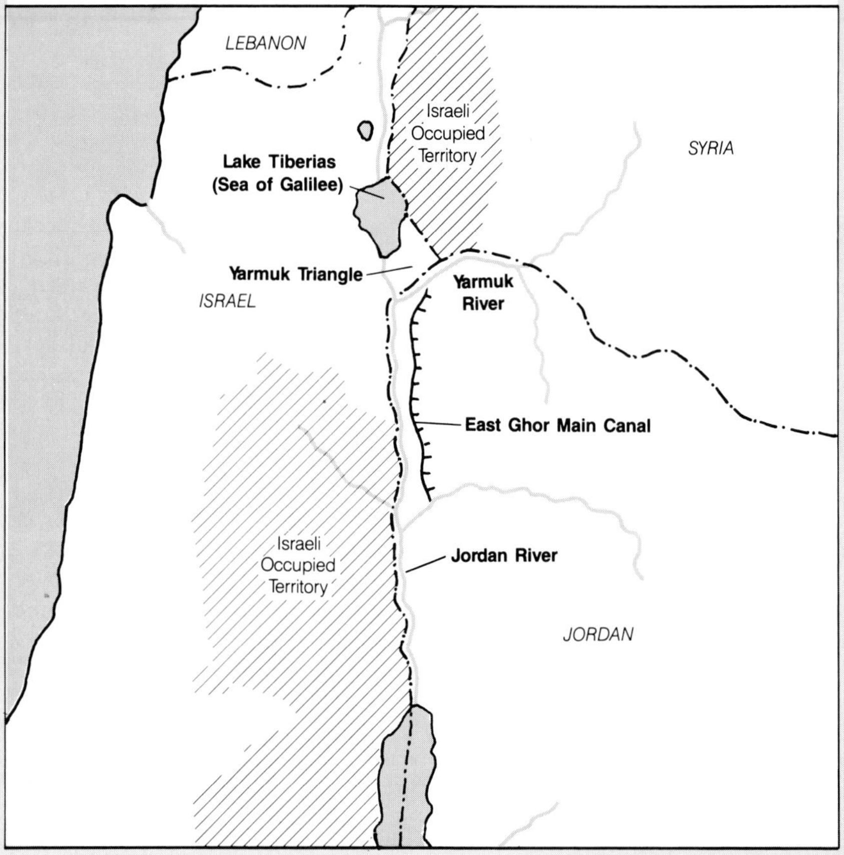

Under the Johnston Plan for sharing Jordan basin waters drawn up by U.S. special envoy Eric Johnston in the early 1950s and implicitly accepted since then by both Jordan and Israel, Jordan is entitled to all that it can take of the Yarmuk's flow, except for 25 million cubic meters that is allocated annually to irrigate the "Yarmuk Triangle"—a section of Israeli territory lying south of Lake Tiberias and flanked by the Jordan and Yarmuk Rivers. Neither country is allowed to do anything that would change the natural flow of the river without the agreement of the other.

For several years during the early 1980s, Israel and Jordan negotiated over a large sandbar in Israeli waters of the Yarmuk just at the point where the weir diverts the waters into the East Ghor Main Canal. The sandbar had appreciably diminished the flow of Jordan's vital irrigation waters into the canal. Years of negotiations between Jordan and Israel were facilitated by several parties includ-

Figure 1 The Jordan River

ing the United Nations Truce Commission, the International Red Cross, and U.S. diplomats in the area. Israel refused to allow destruction of the sandbar, apparently using it as a bargaining chip in a bid to construct a permanent water diversion at the Naharayim reservoir. Jordan opposed the diversion fearing Israel would use more than its share of water to irrigate the West Bank. Just following the 1984 change of government in Israel from the hardline Likud to the more conciliatory Labor-led coalition, Israel agreed to dig out the sandbar cooperatively with Jordan.

Of the three countries, Jordan is the weakest economically and militarily. Nonetheless, there has been no major recent dispute between Israel and Jordan over the uses or apportionment of the Jordan-Yarmuk River Basin. Both sides cultivate right up to the river bank, and technical cooperation between the two countries is achieved through informal discussions held under U.N. or U.S. auspices.

Why does the *de facto* water-sharing arrangement work? Every Israeli official understands the importance of a *modus vivendi* with Jordan. The Israelis understand how vital the Yarmuk waters are for Jordan, and they undoubtedly recognize that any unilateral Israeli action decreasing the Yarmuk's flow into the East Ghor Main Canal would be both provocative and destabilizing. Any such action could also give Jordan and Syria common cause against Israel. Accordingly—and so long as its economic self-sufficiency is maintainable—Israel is likely to handle water shortages in ways that do not disrupt its tacit arrangement with Jordan.

References and Notes

1. This discussion is based on personal communications in 1986 with U.S. State Department and Agency for International Development personnel, especially Samuel W. Lewis, former U.S. Ambassador to Israel, and Richard Viets, former U.S. Ambassador to Jordan.

bathing and shellfish-growing waters. The first proposed criteria took the form of recommended "Provisional Tolerable Weekly Intake of Mercury in Seafood," but in September 1985, the Contracting Parties chose to "take note" rather than adopt them for national enforcement.

An assessment of microbial pollution in recreational waters, shellfish-growing waters, and seafood was the basis for areawide actions. But in 1985, governments were not prepared to agree on these steps, and, although interim criteria for bathing waters were accepted for guidance, common action was postponed until the next meeting of Contracting Parties in late 1987.

Progress has also been slow on the most ambitious element of the Action Plan—the "integrated planning" component—whereby pollution concerns are to be converted into region-wide planning so as to ensure continued socioeconomic growth throughout the region on a sustainable basis.

A main activity of this component, a three-phase approach, known as the "Blue Plan," was initiated in 1975. Because of budgetary and methodological problems, the first phase—taking stock of development in relation to the environment in the Mediterranean Basin countries—was not completed until mid-1983 and was not forwarded to the governments until 1984 (93). The resulting reports made it clear that expected population increases as well as industrial, agricultural, and other growth will pose severe risks to the natural resources and productivity of the basin unless more thoughtful strategies are adopted.

The second phase of the Blue Plan will formulate possible development scenarios in order to highlight policy choices for governments of the region to consider. The third phase will include the presentation and discussion of results and recommendations among the Contracting Parties. These phases are not expected to be completed until the end of 1987 (94). However, measurable progress on reducing pollution flows into the Mediterranean has not been achieved. In fact, although effluent and environmental quality standards have been developed as part of the ongoing research, they have yet to be adopted and enforced by participating states.

In summary, the *process* set up by the Mediterranean Action Plan and the Barcelona Convention continues to move the participating countries in the direction of cleaning up the Mediterranean, but significant progress in reducing pollution levels has not been achieved. Building consensus for action is a slow process, particularly when there is uncertainty about the scientific facts, there are substantial economic costs of action, and there is a large number of diverse nations, all of whom must participate if real progress is to be made.

UNEP has initiated similar agreements for 10 regional seas (95). More than 120 countries, 14 U.N. agencies, and 12 other international organizations take part in the program (96). Like the Mediterranean, other Regional Seas Programs begin by producing regional sea Action Plans that provide for pollution monitoring, the exchange of information, and scientific investigation of pollution problems. The plans also anticipate agreement on formal conventions and implementation of protocols for reducing specific pollutants and on suggestions for control. Like the Mediterranean, these programs depend on voluntary actions by participating countries (97).

With MAP, the Regional Seas Program developed the framework for action that UNEP officials have transferred to other regions (98). As in the Mediterranean, the urgency of pollution problems and UNEP's pollution control negotiations have succeeded in bringing hostile participants into the regional programs. For example, Iran and Iraq participate in the Kuwait Program.

It is clearly in the interest of all coastal countries to abate marine pollution. Joint research, monitoring, and exchanges of information can lead only to heightened consciousness of marine pollution problems and to the adoption of national measures designed to ameliorate those problems gradually. The Regional Seas Programs share a major positive feature. They all establish a legal

Figure 12.5 The Mediterranean, A Regional Sea

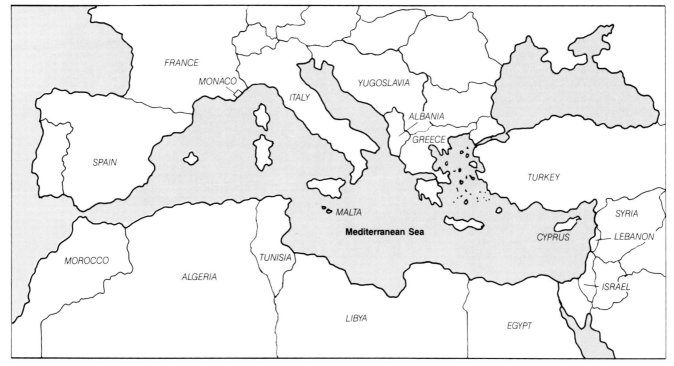

framework and provide a vehicle for data collection and dissemination that can be used when nations reach a consensus on international action to control marine pollution.

Transboundary Air Pollution in Europe and North America

In November 1979, the first broad international agreement covering air pollution, the Convention on Long Range Transboundary Air Pollution (99) (100), was signed in Geneva by 34 countries under the framework of ECE. The Convention was the first multilateral agreement on air pollution and the first environmental accord involving all the nations of Eastern and Western Europe and North America. The more recent Thirty Percent Protocol to the Convention—in which signatories pledged to reduce sulfur emissions 30 percent—is a rare instance of multilateral acceptance of a specific numerical environmental goal.

Concern over the effects of transboundary air pollution grew first in Sweden and Norway, where scientists began to detect rising levels of acidity in lakes and streams in the late 1950s and the 1960s (101). They postulated that this phenomenon was linked to the long range transport of air pollutants. Recognizing the transboundary dimension of the problem, Sweden and Norway chose to pursue a European-wide solution. Sweden brought the acidification problem to international attention at the 1972 Stockholm Conference. Throughout the 1970s, additional research conducted by the World Meteorological Organization, OECD, and others continued to increase awareness of the problems of acid deposition and its transboundary origins (102).

A new opportunity for an international agreement on transboundary air pollution grew out of a statement by President Leonid Brezhnev of the Soviet Union at the 1975 East-West meeting of the Conference on Security and Cooperation in Europe. Brezhnev challenged his fellow conferees to reach multilateral solutions to three pressing problems affecting all of Europe: energy, transportation, and the environment. Swedish and Norwegian environmental officials saw in Brezhnev's Helsinki speech an opportunity for international discussion, negotiation, and perhaps resolution of the acidification problem.

The most suitable, if not ideal, forum for an agreement on transboundary air pollution was the ECE. Thirty-two nations of Eastern and Western Europe are members of ECE, as are the United States and Canada. The Scandinavians realized that no multilateral accord with 34 signatories would be likely to have any teeth. But Swedish scientists had determined that up to one third of the sulfur compounds in Sweden's atmosphere originates in Eastern Europe, primarily in East Germany, Poland, and Czechoslovakia. Thus any hope for substantial control of acid deposition in Scandinavia would depend on Eastern European cooperation.

West Germany originally opposed the ECE Convention and was brought to the signing table in Geneva only by a combination of domestic pressures and appeals from Sweden, Norway, the United States, and other members of the European Community (103).

The terms of the Convention were hammered out as a compromise between the insistence of Norway and Sweden on "standstill" and "rollback" clauses (104) and the reluctance of Western Europe's two largest polluters, West Germany and the United Kingdom, to bind themselves to *any* formal agreement. The West Germans successfully resisted the standstill and rollback positions, required the words "economically feasible" to be added to the Norway-Sweden provision that air pollution reduction in the ECE region be achieved with the "the best available technology" (105), and receded from their opposition to an "executive body" to administer the Convention under the aegis of the ECE Secretariat. Several signatory nations remained unconvinced that the costs of preventing acid rain by controlling pollution at the source would be justified by the benefits.

Since 1979, Norway and Sweden have tried to persuade the other signatories that the benefits of control do indeed outweigh the costs. Canada and West Germany have joined their Scandinavian colleagues as strenuous advocates of acidification abatement. By the time of the 1982 multilateral conference in Stockholm on Acidification of the Environment, West German officials had been convinced by their scientists and foresters that massive forest death (*Waldsterben*) in Germany and elsewhere in Central Europe was resulting from air pollutants, including the sulfur and nitrogen pollutants that are the principal components of acid rain. (See Chapter 10, "Atmosphere and Climate," Multiple Pollutants and Forest Decline.) Canadian officials were concerned over the increasing acidification of eastern Canada's lakes. West Germany and Canada were important allies. In contrast to Sweden and Norway, a significant portion of the acid rain falling on Germany and Canada originates in those countries. Germany and Canada are both polluters *and* victims. They export and import acidifying air pollutants to and from their neighbors. Having balanced the costs and benefits of abatement and chosen to favor abatement, their views carried considerable weight.

Those countries committed to abating the acidification problem have kept up the pressure for international abatement by convening four well-publicized ministerial conferences—Stockholm in 1982, Ottawa and Munich in 1984, and Amsterdam in 1986—to which all parties to the ECE Convention were invited. These meetings, dominated by the already converted, built an international consensus for concerted international action. The first three conferences led directly to the Thirty Percent Protocol.

An increasing number of the ECE Convention's other signatories also gradually became convinced that the benefits of abatement outweigh the costs. By July 1985, when the Convention's Executive Body held its third meeting in Helsinki, 21 of the Convention's signatories had undertaken to sign the Thirty Percent Protocol, pledging to reduce their sulfur emissions *at the source* at least 30 percent over their 1980 levels as soon as possible, at the latest by 1993 (106). The 30 percent commitment provides some teeth to the Convention in the form of numerical goals. It is a major step forward in international environmental law and policy. Outside ECE, the acceptance of explicit numerical targets is almost unheard of in multilateral environmental agreements.

The three most polluting holdout nations, which have refused to join the Thirty Percent Club, are the United Kingdom, the United States, and Poland (107). Political leaders, economic planners, and scientists in these three countries have not yet reached a consensus that the benefits of a 30 percent sulfur reduction justify the costs.

Several countries, including France, Canada, Norway, Sweden, Denmark, and West Germany, have gone beyond the requirements of the Thirty Percent Protocol and have pledged sulfur reductions of 40 to 50 percent by the mid-1990s.

Negotiations over nitrogen oxide reductions are expected to be much more difficult. Large differences in industrial structures, vehicular traffic, and perceptions regarding nitrogen oxide effects exist throughout the ECE region. As yet, there are no uniform, broadly accepted international air quality or emissions standards for nitrogen oxides. Complicating the matter further, the Eastern European countries oppose nitrogen oxide controls, citing scientific uncertainty about nitrogen oxide damage (108).

In all areas of the world, most nitrogen oxide pollution comes from motor vehicles. Catalytic converters to reduce vehicle emissions are costly to install and monitor. Eastern European resistance to nitrogen oxide controls is undoubtedly also linked to the countries' currently weak economies and their dependence on smokestack industries burning heavily polluting brown coal, which emit nitrogen oxides as well as sulfur dioxide.

At the May 1986 International Conference on Acidification and Its Policy Implications, held in Amsterdam, delegates urged that nitrogen oxides be given research priority along with sulfur dioxides (109). The Executive Body of the ECE Convention had already decided, at its third meeting in 1985, to add nitrogen oxides to the European Monitoring and Evaluation Program, a UNEP program coordinated by the ECE.

In summary, the tangible accomplishment of the Thirty Percent Protocol confirms the notion that a limited objective, coupled with converging economic and environmental concerns of several nations, can lead to successful cooperation. Here, the issue sought the institution: Norway and Sweden—the two states initially most interested in abating the acidification problem—brought the issue before the U.N. Economic Commission for Europe, whose members included all the states from which acidifying pollutants emanate. During the negotiations leading to the ECE Convention of 1979 on Long Range Transboundary Air Pollution, Norway and Sweden proposed a percentage reduction in sulfur emissions that preceded the Thirty Percent Protocol. Other ECE member countries were not ready to agree to percentage reductions in 1979. But in just seven years, 19 additional northern industrial countries saw it in their own national interests to join Norway and Sweden in trying to reduce their own sulfur emissions by at least 30 percent. The existence of the ECE framework and the 1979 Convention obviously facilitated the subsequent adoption of the Thirty Percent Protocol.

GLOBAL AGREEMENTS

The World's Oceans

The Third United Nations Conference on the Law of the Sea (UNCLOS III) ended in 1982 after nine years of negotiations. It produced a comprehensive Convention that addressed almost every issue concerning jurisdiction over ocean waters and use of ocean resources. As of December 1986, 32 nations had ratified the 1982 Convention on the Law of the Sea, which needs 60 ratifications to enter into force. The Convention reflects two different approaches to international agreement. In coastal zones (up to 200 miles from land), it allocates rights and obligations between the coastal countries and international shipping countries. Beyond the coastal zones, it protects freedom of navigation and assigns management authority for development of seabed resources to international institutions.

The provisions of the 1982 Convention have been widely accepted as customary international law, and they are the basis for further development of international, regional, and bilateral agreements, such as the UNEP Regional Seas agreements and various treaties developed by the International Maritime Organization governing maritime safety and pollution control. However, once the difficult task of balancing coastal state claims and freedom of navigation was accomplished, negotiations on deep seabed mining assumed center stage. The primary resource involved is manganese (110). With current mineral market conditions, commercial prospects for development of this resource is limited until well into the 21st Century.

Many nations, including the United States and the United Kingdom, West Germany, Canada, France, Japan, and Italy, are withholding signature or ratification of the 1982 Convention until details of the international seabed mining regime are clear. The conflict pits nations advocating some principles of the New International Economic Order against the major industrialized nations. The former group of nations seeks to give effect to the view that seabed resources are the common heritage of mankind and that all nations should benefit from their development. It would establish an International Seabed Authority (ISA) to regulate mining; create an international mining operation—the Enterprise—to carry it out in cooperation with private companies; develop mechanisms to protect and compensate land-based producers of the same minerals from adverse economic effects; and, during an interim period, require the transfer of technology to the Enterprise from private operators (111). The U.S. Government subscribes to the concept that deep seabed resources are common to all, but it objects to the system established in the convention to give effect to the concept. It contends that the ISA limits the powers of the major industrialized nations and that the resources should be available for exploitation with a minimum of regulation on a first-come, first-served basis (112).

As a result of this conflict, two international regimes for deep seabed mining are developing. The Preparatory Commission for UNCLOS III is working out the details of a mining regime to implement the 1982 Convention. Four countries—France, India, Japan, and the Soviet Union—

have applied for registration as "pioneer investors" under UNCLOS III to secure rights to mine sites in which they have already made substantial investments. If the pioneers fulfill certain obligations and meet application requirements under the convention, they will be guaranteed mining rights from the ISA. Before the pioneers may be registered, they must resolve their overlapping claims. The Preparatory Commission is facilitating these efforts (113).

The United States has refused to sign the Convention or to attend Preparatory Commission meetings even as an observer (114). Instead, under the 1980 Deep Seabed Hard Mineral Resources Act, the U.S. Secretary of State is authorized to negotiate multilateral treaties with other mining nations that recognize mine sites on a reciprocal basis (115). In 1982, the United States concluded an interim agreement with France, West Germany, and the United Kingdom in which the parties agreed to consult on overlapping sites (116). They do not believe that interim recognition of sites among themselves is contrary to UNCLOS III provisions. In 1984, representatives from West Germany, Belgium, France, Italy, Japan, the Netherlands, the United Kingdom, and the United States signed a "Provisional Understanding Regarding Deep Seabed Matters." The agreement incorporates overlapping claims settlements among companies from these countries and provides a vehicle for mutual recognition of the claims, clearing the way for national authorization of mining operations (117).

Also in 1984, the United States issued licenses to explore for seabed minerals to four consortia of private companies (118). The Preparatory Commission for the ISA has adopted declarations in response to these mini-treaty and unilateral activities, stating that any claim or action regarding the international seabed and its resources undertaken outside the Commission and incompatible with UNCLOS III would be regarded as wholly illegal. The United Kingdom and West Germany recently issued interim licenses to explore the deep seabed. In April 1986, the Preparatory Commission issued a declaration deploring these "illegal" activities (119).

In summary, there is an internationally negotiated regime for mining the deep seabed, but important countries, including the United States, do not recognize it, and controversy over the mining regime has delayed entry into force of the 1982 Convention. There is some concern that if the 1982 Convention does not enter into force for some time, the delicate balances struck between coastal and maritime nations may erode.

Most potential mining countries are hedging their bets, participating in the Preparatory Commission as well as protecting their claims through separate multilateral agreements. The greatest risk of this dual treaty situation is that the climate for seabed resources development will be unstable when it becomes economically attractive. Thus the verdict on the international seabed mining regime is not yet in. It is up to the Preparatory Commission to demonstrate that it can adequately address the controversial issues that remain.

Antarctica

The Antarctic Treaty (120), in force since 1961, has successfully reserved the Antarctic for peaceful scientific research and banned all military activities in the region. Seven of the Treaty's 12 original signatories—Argentina, Australia, Chile, France, New Zealand, Norway, and the United Kingdom—have territorial claims to Antarctica and those of the United Kingdom, Argentina, and Chile overlap. Neither the other original signatories—Belgium, Japan, South Africa, the Soviet Union, and the United States—nor any other nation in the world recognizes these claims.

The Treaty is a concerted international effort to avoid military activities in the region. At the time of its adoption in 1959, little was known about Antarctic resources. Competing sovereign claims gave rise to the possibility of conflicts, complicating and inhibiting attempts to explore the continent. National interests in claims were tempered by ignorance about the location and extent of potential resources. By preserving the positions of both claimant and nonclaimant nations, Article IV of the Treaty allows nations to explore and carry out scientific research in Antarctica peacefully and cooperatively. Controversy over claims is frozen until after 1991, when the Treaty may be reviewed (121).

Consultative meetings to discuss and exchange information about Antarctica further the principles and objectives of the Treaty. Full participation in the meetings is limited to Consultative Parties—the original signatories and other nations that have subsequently demonstrated their interest in the Antarctic by conducting substantial scientific research there. So far, Brazil, China, West Germany, India, Poland, and Uruguay have achieved consultative status. The system emphasizes consensus; therefore most highly controversial issues are deferred (122).

Although little is known about the availability of mineral resources in the Antarctic, parties to the Antarctic Treaty are now negotiating among themselves to elaborate a regime for administering possible exploitation of Antarctica's mineral wealth. This action raises the same questions that arose over exploitation of deep seabed minerals, and it has led to intense debate in the United Nations. Nations that have not joined the Antarctic Treaty, most of which do not have the technical resources to conduct substantial Antarctic research, now argue that Antarctic minerals are part of the "common heritage" as presented in UNCLOS III and that all nations should have a share in their management and exploitation. The Consultative Parties assert that any nation that accedes to the treaty may take part in negotiating the international legal regime for mineral exploitation, but many countries are wary of restrictions on their rights should they not qualify for full participation in meetings on the basis of activities conducted in Antarctica (123).

In December 1985, the U.N. First Committee (Political and Security) adopted draft resolutions expanding a 1984 U.N. study on Antarctica, inviting the Consultative Parties to inform the U.N. Secretary-General of their negotiations to set up a minerals regime and to exclude South Africa from participating in Consultative Parties' meetings. Sixteen of the 18 Consultative Parties refused to vote on the resolutions. They generally contended that issues concerning the Antarctic are adequately covered by the existing treaty. Australia argued that parties to treaties conducted outside U.N. auspices are not usually held accountable to the United Nations (124). In November 1986, a similar debate took place in the General Assembly. This controversy threatens to add a political dimension to the Antarctic Treaty, which, until now, has been an exemplary agreement for resolving and defusing conflicts over the continent. Its success rests on its limited focus on scientific and technical problems, postponing other more difficult issues.

Stratospheric Ozone

The atmosphere surrounding the earth is clearly a shared resource of global dimension. In the stratosphere (the layer of the atmosphere that extends from about 10–50 kilometers above the earth's surface), ozone plays a critical role in the amount of radiation that reaches the earth from the sun. Ozone—a gas whose molecules consist of three oxygen atoms—absorbs much of the sun's ultraviolet rays and prevents harmful doses of ultraviolet light from reaching the earth's surface. From laboratory and epidemiological studies, scientists predict that increased ultraviolet radiation will increase human skin cancers, reduce crop growth, and damage the delicate planktonic organisms that support marine food systems (125). (See Chapter 10, "Atmosphere and Climate.")

In 1974, two University of California chemists theorized that when manufactured chlorofluorocarbons (CFCs) are released into the atmosphere, they may reduce stratospheric ozone. CFCs are used in refrigerators and air conditioners, in the production of polyurethanes, and as aerosol propellants. Protracted debate about the effects of CFCs on the ozone layer ensued among scientists, environmentalists, chemical manufacturers, and government officials in the industrial countries. In the United States, Canada, and Sweden, the debate quickly resulted in the banning of CFC-propelled aerosol sprays (126).

The possibility of CFC depletion of the protective ozone layer can be addressed only internationally. Many nations contribute to the global CFC load; any unilateral reductions by one country can be offset by another's increase (127). Even if CFC emissions were stopped today, the damage to the ozone layer from CFCs already in the atmosphere could remain for years.

In 1977, the United States hosted a UNEP conference that agreed upon an action plan of research and analysis for protecting the ozone layer (128). The conference led to the establishment in 1981 of a working group of technical and legal experts to develop a framework for a global convention for the protection of the ozone layer. This sequence followed the pattern established by UNEP's Regional Seas Program of technical and legal meetings leading to adoption of a formal convention. The 1985 Vienna Convention established basic goals and a continuing process of research and consultation to achieve them. The Convention declared that nations must prevent environmental harm caused by human interference with the ozone layer; specified that nations have the duty to monitor effects, exchange information, and harmonize national measures, and created new international institutions to develop rules and produce specific protocols (129). An important and unique feature of the Vienna Conven-

tion is the fact that it attempted to avert an environmental problem *before* adverse effects were apparent.

However, Conference delegates failed to agree on a CFC reduction protocol. Polarization on the CFC issue occurred among three major groups. The Toronto Group, including the United States, Canada, Finland, Norway, and Sweden, had already banned or restricted the use of CFCs as aerosol propellants (130). The group advocated international regulations paralleling their own national regulations (131). The European Community countries (EC Group) also advocated decreased use of CFCs, but it was to be achieved by capping production of certain types of CFCs and by a 30 percent rollback in nonessential uses of CFC aerosols. This approach paralleled the one taken in the EC countries; it would have only a minor impact on EC production of CFCs (132). At the time of the Vienna Conference, the Toronto Group and the EC Group were not prepared to compromise on a regulatory scheme that might restrict their own industries. The third position, taken by Japan and the Soviet Union, advocated waiting for further scientific evidence before initiating any CFC regulatory program (133).

During the 1970s, the ozone depletion debate had focused on theoretical predictions of severe ozone depletion. In 1985, however, British scientists reported a seasonal "hole" in the ozone layer over the Antarctic. Observations by U.S. satellites confirmed the British report. The hole, a 40 percent thinning of the ozone layer in an area approximately the size of the United States, appears between August and November (134). Recent reexamination of data collected in Switzerland since the 1930s revealed a less severe shrinking of the ozone layer over the heavily populated northern temperate zone, mostly in winter (135). Although the holes have caused no apparent damages, the head of Argentina's National Meteorological Service has warned that the Antarctic hole could soon be large enough to expose southern Argentina to potentially dangerous amounts of ultraviolet radiation (136). The cause of these holes is unknown, but their appearance coincides with a threefold increase in concentrations of atmospheric CFCs during the 1970s (137).

With this new information providing an extra stimulus, a UNEP working group of representatives from the 22 signatories of the Vienna Convention and Japan has met twice since the 1985 Vienna Conference—in Rome in May 1986 and in Leesburg, Virginia, in September 1986—to discuss CFC control strategies (138). A Canadian proposal, made at Leesburg, to reduce global use of fluorocarbons (from the current 1,200 million kilograms to 812 million kilograms) generated much interest. The proposal included an allocation formula based on both a nation's Gross National Product and its population (139). Japan and the USSR took a more flexible position on CFC control during the Leesburg meeting (140).

The chemical industry has recently modified its resistance to CFC restrictions. Both the E.I. du Pont de Nemours Company, the leading American CFC manufacturer, and the Alliance for Responsible CFC Policy, a coalition of some 500 users and producers of CFCs, publicly supported the need for some limits (141). Du Pont stated that it can produce environmentally acceptable substitutes for CFCs in five years, although existing market and

World Resources 1987

regulatory incentives do not yet justify the cost of developing substitutes (142).

A formal diplomatic meeting of governments took place under UNEP auspices in December 1986 in Geneva. The participating countries displayed some added flexibility in their positions, and progress appears to have been made in narrowing the differences between the Toronto and the EC Groups. No agreement was reached, however, and another meeting is planned for early 1987.

CONCLUSIONS

The cases discussed above represent a variety of shared resource and transboundary pollution issues. The effectiveness of the parties in achieving formal agreements and in subsequently implementing the agreements varies substantially. The general conclusions that can be reached on the basis of these examples—about how nations can best achieve successful bilateral and multilateral agreements on issues of pollution and shared resources—are driven by some basic perceptions about why individual countries participate in any agreement. In order to participate in an international agreement, each country must perceive:

■ the existence of a problem or potential problem, which requires joint action for resolution;
■ a scientific, technical, and/or political solution to the problem;
■ the economic and/or political benefits of the agreement as outweighing the costs.

These basic conditions for agreement may appear obvious, but they affect every case and they define both the possibilities for agreement and the necessary steps required to reach agreement.

Shared Problems

Individual nations are unlikely to participate in an agreement with other nations concerning shared resources or transboundary pollution that does not resolve a current or potential problem. International agreements take a substantial amount of time and effort to negotiate. They usually involve economic or political costs such as those required to monitor a pollution source or abate pollution or to forego unrestricted use of a shared resource.

Some problems are easy to see and understand—such as the sharing of a finite resource. The classic case here is the agreement between Canada and the United States on the use, diversion, and flow of the Great Lakes. The signing of the Boundary Waters Treaty and the successful role of the IJC in dealing with issues of water use and diversion exemplify resolution of a well-defined problem when the parties agree on the nature and importance of a problem. The resource is finite (although not in scarce supply), and each nation is capable of taking unilateral actions that could affect availability and use of the water by the other party. Both nations, which have a historic friendship, also wanted to avoid disputes over use of the Great Lakes.

For a problem to be solved, all parties do not necessarily have to perceive it in the same way. In the case of the Nile River, Egypt's potential problem is that a diversion of water by Sudan would reduce the vital flow of

water to Egypt. The reverse situation does not apply. For Sudan, the potential problem is possible disruption of friendly relations with a powerful neighbor. Although the two issues are not identical, a shared set of problems can be successfully resolved by an agreement on water use.

When perception of a problem is not shared, agreement is hard to reach. Sweden and Norway strongly perceived the problem of acid rain before 1972, but other European countries did not share their level of concern. Although West Germany signed the Convention on Long-Range Transboundary Air Pollution in 1979, its effectiveness was limited until the West German Government became convinced that acid rain at least contributed to the death of its forests.

The need for a shared problem or problems requiring joint action for its/their solution suggests mechanisms that can help bring about international agreements. Research to develop scientific understanding is one mechanism. Particularly on matters of transboundary pollution, the scientific community is often a long way from defining cause and effect relationships clearly. Continuing research efforts in the Mediterranean helped focus attention on land-based sources of pollution, which led to the 1980 protocol on land-based sources. Although the link between the emission of CFCs and depletion of the ozone layer is far from being fully understood (or even fully agreed upon), the clear potential risk shown by discovery of the ozone hole over Antarctica has stimulated efforts to reach a global agreement on reducing the use of CFCs.

Another mechanism for compelling nations to recognize a problem is political and diplomatic pressure. Domestic political pressure, such as through NGOs, heightens awareness of environmental problems. Diplomatic pressure is effective if the nation toward which the pressure is being directed places a high value on amicable relations with the pressuring countries. This strategy has limits. West Germany agreed to the ECE Convention in part because of diplomatic pressures, but real support for action required a greater commitment. India modified its behavior regarding diversion of the Ganges River under pressure from the United Nations, but in the absence of a strong desire to have good relations with Bangladesh, India has resumed some diversion.

It is important to note that there appears to be a growing recognition that issues of shared resources and transboundary pollution are important problems requiring concerted international action. Since the 1972 Stockholm Conference on the Human Environment, the number of international agreements dealing with these issues has been increasing, and the number of nations involved has also been growing.

Scientific and Technological Solutions

Even when countries clearly agree that a problem exists, effective action requires a common view of the technical or scientific nature of the problem and the means necessary to deal with it. Pollution of the Mediterranean Sea was a fact that all the Mediterranean coastal countries clearly recognized 15 years ago. Because the extent and sources of the pollution were much less well understood, agreement on the steps necessary to combat the pollution was much harder to achieve.

In such circumstances, one obvious mechanism for reaching agreement is to initiate research and monitoring projects relating to the problem and then to disseminate the results. This activity cannot be a one-time event. An important component of most arrangements for dealing with shared resources and transboundary pollution discussed in this chapter is a continuing research and monitoring function. Prior to a formal agreement, such a function may best be established through an existing institution such as UNEP or ECE. After initial agreement, this function may reside in a new institution set up by the formal agreement, for example, the IJC or the Permanent Joint Commission for the Nile.

Research results must be effectively disseminated, particularly before the concerned nations reach a general consensus on the nature of a solution. The agreements are fundamentally political, and the political consensus must be based on a scientific consensus. Thus not only must the scientific results be known but also they must be perceived as unbiased. Here independent agencies such as UNEP can be crucial, particularly when individual countries may be distrustful of other participating countries.

Mutual Benefits

Any nation that decides to participate in an agreement on shared resources or transboundary pollution must believe that the benefits of participation outweigh the costs. This judgment is not merely one of economic benefits and costs, although they are a part of the decision. Political benefits and costs are important, and they can be both domestic and international. Domestic pressure can discourage or aid agreement, depending upon perceived costs and benefits of different groups within a country. Lack of a domestic consensus can be a major impediment to action, as is the case with acid rain abatement between the United States and Canada. The benefits of maintaining good international relations with the other parties to an agreement can be an important factor.

The lower the costs, the more likely there is to be an agreement. In the case of the Antarctic Treaty, the costs were low because all the parties agreed to defer the most difficult political disagreements.

In the case of mining the deep seabed, a number of major industrial countries, including the United States, the United Kingdom, and West Germany, perceive the cost of losing independent, unilateral access to strategic mineral deposits as outweighing all other benefits of the 1982 Convention on the Law of the Sea.

But perceptions of benefits and costs change. They can change with new information and technologies, evolving political views and domestic opinion, and external events. The recent chemical spill in the Rhine seems likely to stimulate new arrangements to reduce the likelihood of accidents and to improve emergency responses when accidents occur.

Achieving effective international agreements on shared resources and transboundary pollution issues is a difficult, time-consuming, and unending process. Many formal agreements have taken many years to achieve. Often the formal agreement was initially an agreement in principle without a specific solution to the problems at hand, which then required further research, discussion, and eventual adoption of implementing protocols.

Even when specific procedures, actions, or targets have been agreed upon, individual countries must take the necessary steps to implement these agreements. Implementing actions (especially regarding pollution) may still take years to achieve the desired result. This discussion suggests the importance of establishing ongoing processes, whether through special purpose entities such as the IJC or through existing international organizations such as U.N. agencies or other multilateral groups. Ongoing monitoring of performance remains an essential element of all successful agreements.

There is a growing momentum toward international agreements and action on shared resources and transboundary pollution issues. Stimulated by such disasters as the Rhine chemical spill and the Chernobyl nuclear accident, individual nations are increasingly aware of their dependence on other nations for the protection and management of shared resources. As the problem of ozone depletion in the stratosphere has shown, shared resources can be global in scale, requiring global action. Only if this momentum can be maintained will significant progress be made in dealing with these issues.

References and Notes

1. Henry C. Black, *Black's Law Dictionary*, 5th edition, Joseph R. Nolan *et al.*, eds. (West Publishing Co., St. Paul, Minnesota, 1979), p. 1238.
2. The International Court of Justice (ICJ), *Reports of Judgments, Advisory Opinions, and Orders* (ICJ, The Hague, 1949), p. 18.
3. Report of the United Nations Conference on the Human Environment, 21st plenary meeting (Stockholm, June 5–16, 1972), p. 5, reprinted in *Legal Materials*, Vol. 11 (1972), p. 1416 and p. 1420.
4. For general discussion of other principles of the Stockholm Declaration dealing more specifically with transboundary pol-

lution, see James A. Burros and Douglas M. Johnston, *The International Law of Pollution* (Free Press, New York, 1974).
5. Approved by Governing Council decision 6/14 of May 19, 1978, endorsed by U.N. General Assembly Resolution 34/186 ("Co-operation in the field of the environment concerning natural resources shared by two or more states"), December 18, 1979.
6. "A Firm Commitment," *Acid Magazine*, Vol. 3 (Swedish National Environment Protection Board, Autumn 1985), p. 29.
7. Leonard Dworsky, "The Great Lakes: 1955–1985," *Natural Resources Journal*, Vol. 26, No. 2 (1986), p. 294.

8. David LeMarquand, "Preconditions to Cooperation in Canada-United States Boundary Waters," *Natural Resources Journal*, Vol. 26, No. 2 (1986), pp. 226–227.
9. Boundary Waters Treaty, January 11, 1909, United States-Great Britain (Canada), *Statutes-at-Large*, Vol. 36, p. 2448; and *Treaty Series*, No. 548 (U.S. Department of State, Washington, D.C.).
10. John Carroll, *Environmental Diplomacy* (University of Michigan Press, Ann Arbor, 1983), p. 39.
11. John Carroll, "Water Resources Management as an Issue in Environmental Diplomacy," *Natural Resources Journal*,

Vol. 26, No. 2 (1986), pp. 207–208.

12. *Op. cit* 10, p. 47.

13. Barry Sadler, "The Management of Canada-U.S. Boundary Waters: Retrospect and Prospect," *Natural Resources Journal*, Vol. 26 (1986), p. 372.

14. *Op. cit.* 10, p. 47.

15. *Op. cit.* 10, pp. 52–53.

16. Eutrophication is an excessive growth of plankton or algae that results from an increased concentration of nutrients, particularly phosphorus and nitrogen, in bodies of water. Eutrophication results in increased turbidity and periodic oxygen depletion that can kill fish.

17. *Op. cit.* 10, pp. 131–132.

18. Frank Bevacqua, Information Specialist, International Joint Commission, 1986 (personal communication).

19. *Op. cit.* 10, pp. 44–45.

20. *Op. cit.* 13.

21. *Op. cit.* 11, pp. 216–217.

22. For a comprehensive review of factors favoring bilateral agreement in the Great Lakes Basin, see David LeMarquand, "Preconditions to Cooperation in Canada-United States Boundary Waters," *Natural Resources Journal*, Vol. 26, No. 2 (1986), pp. 220–242.

23. *Op. cit.* 7, p. 296.

24. Sally Cole-Misch, "Governors Sign Agreement to Control Toxics in the Great Lakes," *Focus on International Joint Commission Activities*, Vol. 11, No. 2 (1986), p. 10.

25. "Signature by All Eight Governors Expected on Resolution to Ban Oil Drilling in Lakes," *International Environment Reporter*, Vol. 9, No. 2 (1986), pp. 46–47.

26. "Pact Pledges End to Boundary Water Toxics by 2000," *International Environment Reporter*, Vol. 9, No. 1 (1986), p. 24.

27. "Canada Says It Will Support Intervention by Environmentalists in U.S. Court Actions," *International Environment Reporter*, Vol. 8, No. 2 (1985), p. 365.

28. *Ibid.*

29. Under Article II of the Boundary Waters Treaty, nationals of one country may obtain access to the courts of the other country when the issue is water diversion.

30. U.S. National Research Council and the Royal Society of Canada, *The Great Lakes Water Quality Agreement: An Evolving Instrument for Ecosystem Management* (National Academy Press, Washington, D.C., 1985).

31. For a concise review of the report, see Robert Stein and Jennifer Woods, "The Great Lakes Water Quality Agreement: An Evolving Instrument for Ecosystem Management," *Environment*, Vol. 28, No. 6 (1986), pp. 25–27.

32. John Waterbury, *Hydropolitics of the Nile Valley* (Syracuse University Press, Syracuse, New York, 1979), p. 8.

33. U.N. Department of Technical Cooperation for Development, *Experiences in the Development and Management of International River and Lake Basins*, Proceedings of the United Nations Interregional Meeting of International River Organizations, Dakar, Senegal, May 5–14,

1981, Natural Resources Water Series No. 10 (1983), p. 293.

34. *Op. cit.* 32, p. 9.

35. *Op. cit.* 33.

36. *Op. cit.* 33, p. 295.

37. C.O. Okidi, "Review of Treaties on Consumptive Utilization of Waters of Lake Victoria and Nile Drainage System," *Natural Resources Journal*, Vol. 22, No. 1 (1982), p. 161.

38. *Op. cit.* 33, p. 298.

39. *Op. cit.* 33, pp. 298–299.

40. Blaine Harden, "Rebellion in Sudan: We Are Not Fighting to Be Invited to Dinner," *The Washington Post* (national weekly edition, October 6, 1986), p. 17.

41. *Op. cit.* 37, p. 183 and p. 191.

42. R. Eshman, "The Jonglei Canal: A Ditch Too Big?" *Environment*, Vol. 25, No. 5 (1983), p. 15.

43. *Op. cit.* 33, p. 294.

44. *Op. cit.* 32, p. 23.

45. Ethiopia, however, shows signs of awakening. In 1978, the Ethiopian Ministry of Foreign Affairs declared that: "Ethiopia has all the rights to exploit her natural resources." The statements point out that Egypt built the Aswan Dam, which was to depend largely on the Blue Nile waters, "without even consulting Ethiopia." *The Ethiopian Herald* (May 14, May 21, and June 2, 1978, Addis Ababa), quoted in C.O. Okidi, "Review of Treaties on Consumptive Utilization of Waters of Lake Victoria and Nile Drainage System," *Natural Resources Journal*, Vol. 22, No. 1 (1982), p. 193.

46. *Op. cit.* 37, p. 198.

47. Jean Gauvin, Senior Project Management Officer, United Nations Development Programme, New York, 1986 (personal communication).

48. *Op. cit.* 37, p. 193.

49. M.F.A. Siddiqui, "Management of River Systems in the Ganges and Brahmaputra Basin for Development of Water Resources," in *River Basin Development*, Munir Zamen, ed. (1981), p. 146.

50. *Op. cit.* 33, p. 273.

51. *Op. cit.* 33, p. 276.

52. *Op. cit.* 33, p. 272–273.

53. *Op. cit.* 33, p. 276.

54. Dante Caponera, "Patterns of Cooperation in International Water Law: Principles and Institutions," *Natural Resources Journal*, Vol. 25, No. 3 (1985), p. 583.

55. B. Crow, "The Making and the Breaking of Agreement on the Ganges," in *Strategies for River Basin Management*, J. Lundquist *et al.*, eds. (D. Reidel Publishing Co., Dordrecht, The Netherlands, 1985), p. 257.

56. Several U.N. and U.S. officials contributed to this assessment of the situation, 1986 (personal communications).

57. *Op. cit.* 49, p. 148.

58. *Op. cit.* 49, pp. 147–148.

59. *Op. cit.* 56.

60. *Op. cit.* 49, p. 148.

61. Austria and Liechtenstein also border the Rhine for several miles each, and Luxembourg is part of the Rhine drainage basin. However, none of these three countries participates in the Rhine Com-

mission.

62. A. Kiss, "The Protection of the Rhine against Pollution," *Natural Resources Journal*, Vol. 25, No. 3 (1985), p. 613.

63. *Ibid.*, p. 614.

64. Agreement Concerning the International Commission for the Protection of the Rhine against Pollution, April 29, 1963, 994 U.N.T.S. 3.

65. *Op. cit.* 62, p. 621.

66. Convention for the Protection of the Rhine against Chemical Pollution, December 3, 1976, *Official Journal of the European Communities*, Vol. 20 (1977), p. 76.

67. Convention for the Protection of the Rhine against Pollution by Chlorides, Dec. 3, 1976, *International Legal Materials* (1977), p. 265.

68. *Op. cit.* 62, p. 626.

69. Henri Smets, Environment Directorate, Organisation for Economic Co-operation and Development, Paris, 1986 (personal communication).

70. *Op. cit.* 62, p. 629.

71. *Op. cit.* 62, p. 630.

72. *Op. cit.* 62, p. 632.

73. "French Court Decision Does Not Change Situation on Salt Discharge into Rhine," *International Environment Reporter*, Vol. 9, No. 5 (1986), p. 146.

74. "France Abandons Plan for Salt Injection, Pledges Alternate Solution by Next January," *International Environment Reporter*, Vol. 9, No. 6 (1986), p. 174.

75. *Ibid.*

76. *Op. cit.* 69.

77. *Op. cit.* 62, pp. 634–635.

78. "Dutch Appeals Court Rules in Favor of Greenhouses in Salt Pollution Case," *International Environment Reporter*, Vol. 9, No. 8 (1986), p. 344. The Appeals Court, however, declared that only Dutch law applied in the case; it held that international law regulates relationships only between nations.

79. *Op. cit.* 62, p. 636.

80. The Strasbourg court decision was partly overruled and partly affirmed by the French Council of State (*Conseil d'Etat*) on April 18, 1986.

81. "Dutch Appellants Call Court Decision on Permits Both Disappointing, Promising," *International Environment Reporter*, Vol. 9 (1986), pp. 146–147. The Council of State made no mention of any French obligations under public international law and based its decision entirely on French administrative law.

82. John Tagliabue, "Rhine Poisoning Stretching 185 Miles," *New York Times* (November 11, 1986), p. A1.

83. *Op. cit.* 69.

84. Peter Thacher, *Stanford Journal of International Studies*, Vol. 8 (Spring 1978), p. 79, cited in Peter Thacher, "The Mediterranean Action Plan," *AMBIO*, Vol. 6, No. 6 (1977), p. 308.

85. Peter Thacher, "The Mediterranean Action Plan," *AMBIO*, Vol. 6, No. 6 (1977), p. 308.

86. United Nations Environment Programme Governing Council, Decision 8, March 1974, cited in Peter Thacher, "The Mediterranean Action Plan," *AMBIO*, Vol. 6,

No. 6 (1977), p. 308.

87. Baruch Boxer, "Mediterranean Pollution: Problems and Response," *Ocean Development and International Law Journal*, Vol. 10 (1982), p. 331.

88. *Ibid.*, pp. 332–334.

89. The participating states were Algeria, Egypt, France, Greece, Israel, Italy, Lebanon, Libya, Malta, Monaco, Morocco, Spain, Syria, Tunisia, Turkey, and Yugoslavia. Cyprus subsequently joined the group, leaving Albania as the only non-participating Mediterranean coastal country.

90. United Nations Environment Programme (UNEP), "The First Ten Years of the Mediterranean Action Plan: A Critical Review" (UNEP, Nairobi, 1985), pp. 7–8.

91. "International Regional Conference Urges Achieving Genoa Goals as a Matter of Priority," *International Environment Reporter*, Vol. 8, No. 11 (1985), pp. 372–373.

92. *Op. cit.* 90.

93. *Overview of the Mediterranean Basin (Development and Environment)*, brochure (Medi-Media, Marseilles, 1985), derived from the Mediterranean Blue Plan (United Nations Environment Programme, Geneva).

94. "Report of the Fourth Ordinary Meeting of the Contracting Parties to the Convention for the Protection of the Mediterranean Sea Against Pollution and its Related Protocols," Document IG.56.5 (United Nations Environment Programme, Geneva, 1985).

95. Areas covered by the United Nations Environment Programme (UNEP) Regional Seas Program include the Mediterranean Sea, the Arabian Gulf, West and Central Africa, the Southeast Pacific, the Red Sea-Gulf of Aden, the Caribbean Sea, the Southeast Asia Region, the Southwest Pacific, and the Southwest Atlantic. Protection plans for these regions are in various stages of development. In addition, all Baltic nations have ratified the Convention on the Protection of the Marine Environment of the Baltic Sea Area. The Baltic Convention is not part of the UNEP Regional Seas Program. Henry Degenhardt, *Maritime Affairs—A World Handbook* (Longman Group Ltd., Harlow, United Kingdom, 1985), pp. 158–165.

96. Peter Hulm, "The Regional Seas Program: What Fate for UNEP's Crown Jewels?" *AMBIO*, Vol. 12, No. 1 (1983), p. 2.

97. United Nations Food and Agriculture Organization/United Nations Educational, Scientific and Cultural Organization/International Oceanographic Commission/World Health Organization/World Meteorological Organization/International Atomic Energy Agency/United Nations Environment Programme (UNEP), *Coordinated Mediterranean Pollution Monitoring and Research Programme (MEDPOL)—Phase I: Programme Description, UNEP Regional Seas Reports and Studies No. 23* (UNEP, Geneva, 1983), p. i and pp. 1–3.

98. *Op. cit.* 96, p. 4.

99. Reprinted in *International Legal Materials*, Vol. 18 (1979), p. 1442.

100. For a general analysis of the ECE Convention's background, provisions, and significance, see Armin Rosencranz, "The ECE Convention of 1979 on Long Range Transboundary Air Pollution," *American Journal of International Law*, Vol. 75 (1981), p. 975, and *Zeitschrift fur Umwelt Politik* (1981), p. 511.

101. United Nations Environment Programme, *The World Environment 1972–1982* (Tycooly International Publishing Ltd., Dublin, 1982), p. 38.

102. *Ibid.*, p. 38.

103. See Gregory Wetstone and Armin Rosencranz, *Acid Rain in Europe and North America* (Environmental Law Institute, Washington, D.C., 1983), pp. 141–144.

104. Norway and Sweden pressed for a "tough" agreement that, even if not enforceable, would at least call on signatories to hold the line against further increases in sulfur emissions (the "standstill" clause) and begin to abate sulfur pollution levels by fixed across-the-board percentages (the "rollback" clause).

105. Armin Rosencranz, "The ECE Convention of 1979 on Long Range Transboundary Air Pollution," *American Journal of International Law*, Vol. 75 (1981), p. 975.

106. Swedish Environment Protection Board, *Acid Magazine* (Autumn 1985), p. 29.

107. Armin Rosencranz, "The Acid Rain Controversy in Europe and North America: A Political Analysis," *AMBIO*, Vol. 15, No. 1 (1986), p. 47.

108. *Op. cit.* 106, p. 30.

109. "Conference Says Abatement Programs Have Not Reduced Acidification Enough," *International Environment Reporter*, Vol. 9, No. 6 (1986), pp. 183–184.

110. Robert Knecht, "Deep Ocean Mining," *Oceanus*, Vol. 25, No. 3 (1983), pp. 3–4.

111. Alexandra M. Post, *Deepsea Mining and the Law of the Sea* (Kluwer Academic, Hingham, Massachusetts, 1983), pp. 141–143.

112. James Malone, "Freedom and Opportunity: Foundation for a Dynamic Oceans Policy," *Department of State Bulletin* (December 1984), pp. 78–79.

113. "France, India, Japan, USSR Meet to Resolve Seabed Mining Claims," *International Environment Reporter*, Vol. 8, No. 1 (1985), p. 25.

114. Lee Kimball, "The Law of the Sea—On the Shoals," *Environment*, Vol. 25, No. 9 (1983), p. 15.

115. United States Code, Vol. 30, section 1401 *et seq.* (Supplement V, 1981).

116. *Op. cit.* 114, p. 42.

117. "Provisional Understanding Regarding Deep Seabed Matters," *Environmental Policy and Law*, Vol. 13, No. 3/4 (1984), pp. 125–126.

118. Corporations from the following countries are involved in private consortia: Canada, Japan, Belgium, Italy, the Netherlands, the United Kingdom, the United States, and West Germany. France, Japan, India, and the USSR have established public enterprises. J.K. Amsbaugh and Jan L. Van der Voort, "The Ocean Mining Industry: A Benefit for Every Risk?" *Oceanus*, Vol. 25, No. 3 (1982), p. 25.

119. "Sea-Bed Commission Condemns Issuing Of Licenses for Exploration of International Area," *UN Chronicle*, Vol. 23, No. 4 (1986), pp. 107–108.

120. Antarctic Treaty, 12 U.S.T. 794, T.I.A.S. No. 4780.

121. Henry Degenhardt, *Maritime Affairs—a World Handbook* (Longman Group Ltd., Harlow, U.K., 1985), pp. 216-217.

122. "First Committee Reviews the Question of Antarctica for Third Time, Three Texts Adopted," *UN Chronicle*, Vol. 23, No. 2 (1986), p. 69.

123. *Ibid.*, pp. 70–71.

124. *Op. cit.* 122, p. 68 and p. 72.

125. World Resources Institute and International Institute for Environment and Development, *World Resources 1986* (Basic Books, New York, 1986), pp. 171–173.

126. Paul Brodeur, "Annals of Chemistry: In the Face of Doubt," *The New Yorker* (June 9, 1986), pp. 70–75.

127. The United States produces 20 percent of the global CFC load, with Japan and Western Europe producing most of the remaining 80 percent. "U.S. Should Ratify Vienna Ozone Agreement 'Expeditiously,' Officials Tell Senate Panel," *International Environment Reporter*, Vol. 9, No. 4 (1986), pp. 117–118.

128. Peter Thacher, Senior Researcher, World Resources Institute, Washington, D.C., 1986 (personal communication).

129. Malcolm Forster, "Ozone Convention Signed," *Environmental Policy and Law*, Vol. 14, No. 2/3 (1985), p. 38.

130. A definition of essential use of CFCs depends on notions of cost-benefit and the perception of environmental harm caused by CFCs. CFCs are generally considered essential as refrigerants, at least until relatively safe substitutes can be developed.

131. Peter Sand, "Protecting the Ozone Layer: The Vienna Convention Is Adopted," *Environment*, Vol. 27, No. 5 (1985), p. 41.

132. *Ibid.*

133. *Op. cit.* 131, p. 40.

134. James Gleick, "Hole in Ozone over South Pole Worries Scientists," *New York Times* (July 29, 1986), p. C1.

135. Philip Shabecoff, "Chemical Process Seen in Ozone Hole," *The New York Times* (October 21, 1986), p. C3.

136. Boyce Rensberger, "Southern Exposure," *The Washington Post* (national weekly edition, October 20, 1986), p. 38.

137. *Op. cit.* 126, p. 78.

138. "Some UNEP Workshop Delegates Say Protocol on Ozone Protection Possible by Spring 1987," *International Environment Reporter*, Vol. 9, No. 10 (1986), pp. 346–347.

139. *Ibid.*, p. 347.

140. *Op. cit.* 138.

141. "CFC Alliance Issues New Policy Statement about U.S. Policy on Chlorofluorcarbons," *International Environment Reporter*, Vol. 9, No. 10 (1986), p. 354.

142. Alan Miller, Visiting Professor, Washington College of Law, The American University, Washington, D.C., 1986 (personal communication).

13. Managing Hazardous Wastes: The Unmet Challenge

Minamata Bay, Japan, was one of the first widely reported incidents in a long list of horror stories involving improper discharge, transport, storage, or disposal of hazardous wastes. Today, names like Love Canal, New York, and Times Beach, Missouri, in the United States; Lekkerkerk in the Netherlands; Reyersdorf-Schonkirchen in Austria; BT Kemi in Sweden; and Vac, Hungary, are synonymous with toxic wastes and the problems associated with their release into the environment.

Increasingly, governments and international agencies are attempting to control the growing problem of hazardous wastes, but it is a long and frustrating process. Regulation is complicated by the multimedia nature of hazardous wastes—they affect air, water, and soil; further, definitions of hazardous and toxic wastes differ among countries, as do the concentrations of those wastes considered hazardous to human health. In short, the problem is a regulatory nightmare. Undeniably, much progress has been made over the past decade to control the manufacture, distribution, and disposal of hazardous substances, particularly chemical wastes, but governments everywhere still struggle with the complexities and magnitude of the problem.

The chemical industry produces not only large profits—$450 billion for the Organisation for Economic Co-operation and Development (OECD) countries in 1980—but also large quantities of hazardous wastes. In the industrialized countries of Europe and North America, chemical and petrochemical industries are responsible for nearly 70 percent of all hazardous wastes; in developing countries, the figure is 50–66 percent (1). Most toxic and hazardous wastes come from the chemical and related industries that produce plastics, soap, synthetic rubber, fertilizers, synthetic fibers, medicines, detergents, cosmetics, paints, pigments, adhesives, explosives, pesticides, herbicides, and numerous organic and inorganic intermediate chemicals.

WHAT IS HAZARDOUS WASTE?

There are probably as many definitions of hazardous wastes as there are government agencies responsible for them. However, some general guidelines have emerged for classifying wastes as hazardous. Perhaps one of the most widely used definitions is contained in the U.S. Resource Conservation and Recovery Act of 1976 (RCRA). This landmark Act considers wastes toxic and/or hazardous if they "cause or significantly contribute to an increase in mortality or an increase in serious irreversible, or incapacitating reversible, illness; or pose a substantial present or potential hazard to human health or the environment when improperly treated, stored, transported, disposed of, or otherwise managed" (2).

The meaning of "toxic" and "hazardous" wastes is confusing. They are often used interchangeably. "Toxic" here refers to a narrow group of substances that causes death or serious injury to humans and animals. "Hazardous," the broader term, refers to all wastes, including those that are toxic, that present an immediate or long-term human health risk or that pose a risk to the environment, as defined under RCRA and other legislation.

The World Health Organization (WHO) suggests that countries attempting to grapple with a legal definition of hazardous wastes consider whether the wastes present "short-term acute hazards, such as acute toxicity by ingestion, inhalation, or skin absorption, corrosivity or other skin or eye contact hazards or the risk of fire or explosion; or long-term environmental hazards, including chronic toxicity upon repeated exposure, carcinogenicity . . . resistance to detoxification processes such as biodegradation, the potential to pollute underground or surface waters, or aesthetically objectionable properties such as offensive odors" (3). Table 13.1 lists broad categories of wastes that WHO would include on priority lists for regulation.

In practice, most countries attempting to regulate toxic and hazardous wastes simply draw up a list of specific substances for which there is sufficient scientific evidence linking them to adverse human health or environmental effects. Unfortunately, many potentially dangerous chemical compounds have yet to be tested adequately, so most lists include only the worst offenders. Countries contemplating regulation of chemical wastes must consider—for each chemical—not only how toxic it is but also how corrosive, how explosive, and how flammable it is and whether it will oxidize, produce mutations, or cause cancer. Regulators must look not only at the effects of one massive dose of a substance (acute toxicity), but also at the effects of exposure to small doses over longer periods (chronic toxicity). The latter may be lethal even though a single massive dose is not.

Most developed countries use one or more of the following identification criteria for listing hazardous substances: the type of hazard involved (flammability, corrosiveness, toxicity), the generic category of the products involved (pesticides, solvents, medicines), technological origins (oil refining, electroplating), and the presence of specific substances like PCBs, dioxin, and lead compounds (4). Most OECD countries exclude radioactive waste from their traditional lists of hazardous and toxic substances because the waste products of fission (except some low-level wastes from hospitals, laboratories, and military installations) are so toxic or long-lived as to warrant their being placed in a separate category. (For this reason, radioactive waste is not discussed in this chapter.)

Despite the evolution of comprehensive criteria to aid governments in defining and regulating toxic wastes, European and North American environmental agencies are becoming aware that too many hazardous industrial wastes are not covered by current regulations because of flaws in definitions. The result is that national lists of toxic wastes are being refined and expanded as new toxicological data become available (5). The U.S. Environmental Protection Agency (EPA), for example, listed about 300 chemicals and 80 waste streams as hazardous in 1980 (6), but, by January 1987, the list of hazardous chemicals, as defined by RCRA, had grown to 450 (7).

Another significant problem for regulators everywhere is defining the quantities or concentrations at which wastes become hazardous. Nearly all substances are toxic in sufficiently high doses. Some chemicals are deadly in microgram doses; others induce a toxic response only at doses measured in grams. However, most chemical wastes fall somewhere between, making it difficult to draw the line between "safe" and "toxic." Because of this dilemma, many countries set only hazardous rather than safe levels. Even when concentrations are set, as in Belgium, the Netherlands, or the United Kingdom, they vary. In the Netherlands, for example, 50 milligrams of cyanide per kilogram (mg/kg) is considered hazardous; in Belgium, next door, the toxicity standard is fixed at 250 mg/kg (8).

Further, the creation of new substances as a result of spontaneous reactions among chemicals placed together in dump sites is another problem. Most toxicological tests focus on a single compound despite the fact that in waste dumps they are usually found in mixtures.

Although the wastes may be relatively harmless as separate compounds, once mixed, they may become highly toxic. Often the toxic end products escape adequate regulation because they do not fit into the definitional framework of hazardous wastes (9).

HAZARDOUS WASTES: HOW MUCH AND WHERE?

The total amount of hazardous wastes generated each year throughout the world is nearly impossible to estimate with any degree of accuracy. Definitions and legislation vary radically among countries. In the Third World, because many nations have no laws whatsoever governing the production and disposal of toxic wastes, they have no idea how much of their industrial waste is hazardous.

While some attempts have been made to estimate the annual amounts of hazardous wastes generated globally, there is no general acceptance of any of these estimates. It is clear that the United States leads the world in the generation of hazardous wastes, with an annual total of about 264 million metric tons (10). But estimates for the rest of the world are largely speculative. One estimate of the global total was 330 million metric tons (11), while another estimate for only 19 countries was more than 100 million metric tons higher (12).

The broad discrepancies in the estimates of hazardous wastes generated throughout the world highlight the nature of the problem: in fact, little is known about how much hazardous wastes are generated, where they are generated, and what happens to them.

THE MULTIMEDIA HAZARDS OF TOXIC WASTES

Hazardous wastes contaminate the environment by many pathways. But even before hazardous wastes are disposed of, they pollute air, water, and soil simply by virtue of how they are stored or contained prior to final disposal. For example, surface impoundments (settling ponds), for which most countries in Europe and North America have set operating standards, remain a source of air pollutants because volatile organic compounds (VOC) often evaporate from the ponds (13). Yet because the wastes have not been formally disposed of, they are not covered by most hazardous waste legislation. Further, the ponds also threaten surface- and groundwater unless they are properly lined.

Another example of how potentially toxic wastes escape adequate regulation—and are transferred from one medium to another in the process—is the sludge generated by both wastewater treatment plants and air pollution control devices (14). These wastes often contain heavy metals, and they are potential hazards to human health and the environment. But they may not be regulated nationally or regionally. As a result, many end up in uncontrolled industrial or municipal landfills, where toxic substances in the wastes can migrate into surface- and groundwater and can pollute the soil.

Multimedia pollution also results from permissible discharges in accordance with permits granted by federal, state, or local governments. In the United States, for example, hazardous wastes classified under RCRA are not regulated in the same way as traditional water or air pollutants. According to the U.S. Office of Technology Assessment (OTA), a research arm of the U.S. Congress, "RCRA does not limit releases; it sets standards for the management (treatment, storage, and disposal) of whatever is produced. RCRA regulations apply to all industrial categories but unequally depending on the amount generated. The body of substances defined as RCRA hazardous wastes has always been much larger than those regulated either as air or water pollutants. Many RCRA hazardous wastes are not regulated under the Clean Air or Clean Water Acts as air or water pollutants although they can be the same chemical. Therefore, if it is technically possible and economically beneficial, a regulated RCRA hazardous waste can be legally emitted into the air or water"(15). Such provisions create legal opportunities for wastes to be shifted from one medium to another—from land to water to air and back again. Similar loopholes exist in the laws governing the handling and disposal of hazardous wastes in most other OECD countries.

Once toxic or hazardous wastes are treated and disposed of, they can still pose a persistent threat to human health and the environment through contamination of air, water, and soil. Uncontrolled incineration, whether on land or at sea, can contaminate the atmosphere and the surrounding environment. The discharge of hazardous substances into the sea or into lakes and rivers often kills fish. Further, disposal on land in abandoned dumps or improperly controlled landfills can pollute both the soil and the groundwater.

In 1983, an EPA study reported 230 hazardous chemicals or groups of chemicals present in the immediate vicinity of waste sites requiring Superfund action. (The

Table 13.1 Toxic and Dangerous Substances and Materials that Require Priority Consideration

■ Arsenic and compounds
■ Mercury and compounds
■ Cadmium and compounds
■ Thallium and compounds
■ Beryllium and compounds
■ Chromium (VI) compounds
■ Lead and compounds
■ Antimony and compounds
■ Phenolic compounds
■ Cyanide compounds
■ Isocyanates
■ Organohalogenated compounds, excluding inert polymeric materials and other substances referred to in this list or covered by other directives concerning the disposal of toxic or dangerous wastes
■ Chlorinated solvents
■ Organic solvents
■ Biocides and phytopharmaceutical substances
■ Tarry materials from refining and tar residues from distilling
■ Pharmaceutical compounds
■ Peroxides, chlorates, perchlorates, and azides
■ Ethers
■ Chemical laboratory materials, not identifiable and/or new, with unknown effects on the environment
■ Asbestos
■ Selenium and compounds
■ Tellurium and compounds
■ Polycyclic aromatic hydrocarbons
■ Metal carbonyls
■ Soluble copper compounds
■ Acids and/or basic substances used in the surface treatment and finishing of metals
■ PCBs

Source: Adapted from World Health Organization (WHO), *Management of Hazardous Waste* (WHO, Regional Office for Europe, Copenhagen, 1983), p. 14.

Superfund legislation, enacted in 1980, authorized EPA to identify and clean up abandoned toxic waste dumps that are a clear threat to human health and the environment.) Of the 230 chemical compounds, 173 were found in nearby groundwater reservoirs, 162 in surface waters, and 65 in the air (16).

Fortunately, there have been few incidents like Minamata, where hundreds died of mercury poisoning as a result of the deliberate discharge of toxic wastes. But these dramatic incidents are just the tip of the iceberg. The real danger lies in the long-term effects on human health and the environment from the millions of tons of hazardous wastes scattered about the earth—dumped in ditches, poured down drains, abandoned in fields, discarded in warehouses, sunk in the sea, injected into the ground, or incinerated with inadequate safeguards. Too much hazardous waste ends up seeping into drinking water, contaminating the food chain, or polluting the air.

Groundwater at Risk

Because most hazardous wastes are disposed of by dumping or burial on land, the most serious environmental effect is contaminated groundwater. The threat is alarming. In the United States alone, an estimated 75,000 active industrial landfill sites may be possible sources of groundwater contamination, along with 200 special facilities for disposal of both liquid and solid hazardous wastes, and some 180,000 surface impoundments (ponds) for all types of waste (17). All told, nearly 2 percent of North America's underground aquifers could be contaminated (18), but there are no global estimates at all.

The diversity of chemicals found in drinking water aquifers, situated near toxic waste dumps, is astounding. Some of the most common contaminants include chlorinated solvents, aromatic hydrocarbons, pesticides, trace metals, and PCBs (19). One salient feature of all these toxic substances once they migrate into groundwater is their long-term contamination (20).

Although the typical contaminated area is less than 1,600 meters long and 760 meters wide, once groundwater is fouled with hazardous wastes, the cost of reversing the damage is prohibitive. In fact, if an aquifer is contaminated with organic chemicals, restoring the water to its original state is seldom physically or economically feasible (21).

ASSESSING HEALTH RISKS

Because most hazardous wastes are chemical wastes, controlling chemicals and their waste products is a paramount issue in most developed countries. Every year roughly 1,000 new chemicals join the nearly 70,000 in daily use (22). By 1986, more than 5 million chemical compounds had been isolated from natural products or synthesized, although the majority never leave the laboratory (23). Of the chemicals marketed commercially in 1979, about 1,500 were active ingredients of pesticides, 4,000 were used in drugs, and 5,500 were food additives. The remainder consisted of industrial and agricultural chemicals (other than pesticides), fuels, and chemical-based consumer products (24).

Figure 13.1 Available Data for Health Hazard Assessment of Categories of Substances

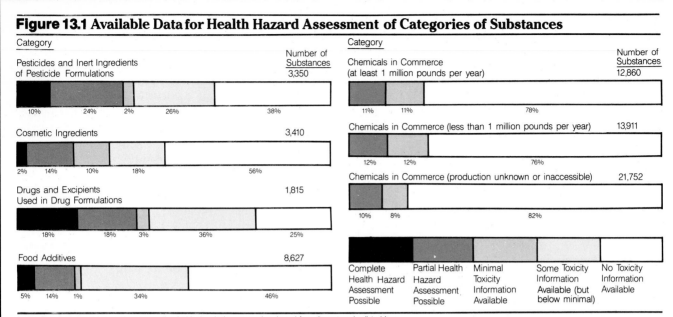

Category — Number of Substances

Pesticides and Inert Ingredients of Pesticide Formulations — 3,350
10% | 24% | 2% | 26% | 38%

Cosmetic Ingredients — 3,410
2% | 14% | 10% | 18% | 56%

Drugs and Excipients Used in Drug Formulations — 1,815
18% | 18% | 3% | 36% | 25%

Food Additives — 8,627
5% | 14% | 1% | 34% | 46%

Chemicals in Commerce (at least 1 million pounds per year) — 12,860
11% | 11% | 78%

Chemicals in Commerce (less than 1 million pounds per year) — 13,911
12% | 12% | 76%

Chemicals in Commerce (production unknown or inaccessible) — 21,752
10% | 8% | 82%

Legend: Complete Health Hazard Assessment Possible | Partial Health Hazard Assessment Possible | Minimal Toxicity Information Available | Some Toxicity Information Available (but below minimal) | No Toxicity Information Available

Note: This assessment is based on a sample of 100 chemical compounds selected from the categories listed here.
Source: U.S. National Academy of Sciences, National Research Council, *Toxicity Testing: Strategies to Determine Needs and Priorities* (National Academy Press, Washington, D.C. 1984), cited by Arthur C. Upton, *Availability of Toxicological Data on Existing Chemicals* (presented at the Seminar on Chemicals Testing and Animal Welfare, Stockholm, May 20-22, 1986), p. 11.

Many of these chemicals are toxic, but they are little threat to human health unless they are improperly treated and disposed of. Unfortunately, at the nub of the hazardous waste problem is the fact that the toxic byproducts of industry are all too often handled and disposed of in a cavalier manner. According to Bob Munro, an environmental consultant to several European governments and international agencies, "all this inadequately controlled toxic waste represents an incredible health risk for us and future generations. We must come to grips with it" (25).

Coming to grips with the medical consequences of exposure to toxic wastes is extremely complicated. Little is known because of the great diversity of wastes present in the environment, particularly chemical wastes. It is difficult enough, cautions Swedish toxicologist Dr. Erik Arrhenius, to identify with any degree of certainty potentially toxic chemicals, not to mention analyzing and controlling their production wastes. Further, some toxic chemicals, like PCBs and DDT, are so long lived and pervasive that trace amounts are found in nearly everyone on earth (26).

The problem of linking a particular chemical or other hazardous waste to specific injuries or diseases is compounded by the lack of toxicity data on most hazardous substances. "Although it is possible to perform risk assessments on individual chemicals for which adequate toxicity and exposure data exist," states U.S. toxicologist Dr. Peter Voytek, "such reliable data will be available for only a small percentage of the identifiable chemicals at most dump sites" (27). Of the millions of chemicals in existence, relatively few have been evaluated for toxicity. Further, as Dr. Voytek points out, "our inability to anticipate synergistic and antagonistic actions among chemicals makes it impossible to perform total risk assessments."

This bleak assessment of the situation was reinforced by a 1980–84 U.S. National Academy of Sciences study of

toxic chemicals carried out under the sponsorship of the National Toxicology Program (28). The Academy sampled 100 chemicals at random. For each chemical selected, researchers carried out extensive computer and literature surveys to obtain all pertinent toxicological information. The results, depicted in Figure 13.1, demonstrated the acute lack of toxicity data. "The quality and completeness of the data, evaluated on the basis of national and international guidelines, were sufficient to enable complete assessment of health hazards for only a small percentage of chemicals," states Dr. Arthur Upton of the Institute of Environmental Medicine at New York University's Medical Center. "For the vast majority of chemicals," concludes Dr. Upton, "the data were insufficient to enable even a partial health assessment" (29).

Toxicologists normally attempt to assess the effects of exposure to hazardous chemicals (or suspected toxins) by studying reproductive dysfunctions like impotence, sterility, fetal loss, stillbirth, low birth weight, birth defects, and infant illness and mortality (30). However, when it comes to tracking chemical wastes in a dump site to, for example, specific birth abnormalities, the trail goes cold.

Several studies confirm the presence of significant quantities of DDT, PCBs, and pesticide-related compounds in human blood (31). However, there is little evidence linking these levels to hazardous wastes or to various methods of disposal, except in extreme cases like Love Canal, where children suffered chemical burns (particularly on their arms and legs) and a disproportionate number of women gave birth to babies with birth defects (32).

By and large, only acute injuries have been linked to toxic wastes and in only a few incidents. In Toone, Tennessee, for example, chemical pollution of family water wells by endrin, dieldrin, and aldrin caused liver and urinary tract ailments, dizziness, nausea, and skin rashes to the local population—and one death (33). Similarly, in Legler, a small community in the Pine Barrens region of

New Jersey, residents reported skin rashes and sores, kidney ailments, cancers, and miscarriages when benzene, chloroform, trichlorethylene, and other toxic chemicals leached into the local drinking water aquifer. Latent medical problems included possible kidney, nervous system, blood, bone marrow, respiratory, and digestive tract damage (34).

Although assessing environmental contamination from toxic wastes and extrapolating health effects is extremely difficult, what little is known is certainly cause for concern. Most hazardous waste dumps, for example, contain dangerous and toxic chemicals along with heavy metal residues and other hazardous substances. In 1984, the Washington, D.C.-based Conservation Foundation reported that a total of 444 toxic pollutants had been identified at some 900 sites under investigation by the U.S. EPA for possible inclusion on the National Priorities List requiring Superfund cleanup (35). The 10 most common substances found at these sites were lead, trichloroethylene, toluene, benzene, PCBs, chloroform, phenol, arsenic, cadmium, and chromium (36). According to the Conservation Foundation, "some of these substances can cause immediate poisoning (e.g., arsenic and mercury). Virtually all of them can damage health as the result of low-level, long-term exposure, particularly through drinking water" (37). Seven of the ten are thought to cause cancer; seven, birth defects; and five, genetic damage. "The risk resulting from being exposed to more than one of these substances at the same time is not known," concludes the Conservation Foundation (38).

Of the 70,000 chemicals in trade, as many as 35,000 are classified by the U.S. EPA (39) and OECD as either definitely or potentially harmful to human health. A number of them, including some heavy metals (arsenic, cadmium) and certain organic compounds (toluene, carbon tetrachloride), are carcinogenic (cancer-causing). Others, like mercury, are mutagenic (causing mutations and genetic damage), and many tend to induce brain and bone damage (mercury, copper, lead), kidney diseases (cadmium), neurological damage, and a host of other debilitating and disfiguring diseases (40). (See Tables 13.2 and 13.3 for a review of acute and chronic health effects from exposure to selected hazardous wastes.)

LIVING WITH PAST MISTAKES: HAZARDOUS WASTE DUMPS

The industrial world is living with a deadly legacy: decades of uncontrolled and unregulated disposal of industry's toxic byproducts and other hazardous wastes. After nearly a century of uncontrolled dumping, ignorant of the environmental and human consequences of discarding toxic industrial wastes wherever it was convenient, industrialized countries (and increasing numbers of developing countries) are discovering that the cost of ignorance is high. In both Europe and North America, toxic waste dumps have displaced entire communities, fouled the air, poisoned surface- and groundwater, and adversely affected human health.

The problem of old dump sites is perhaps the most serious. The diversity of chemicals found in abandoned waste dumps, coupled with the paucity of documentation of what was dumped, underlines the enormity of the cleanup tasks involved in detoxifying these dumps and the futility of trying to characterize a typical site (41).

Nearly all industrialized countries are faced with costly cleanup bills, some of them massive. Despite progress, like the work being done in the European Community to regulate hazardous wastes (42), the situation still seems out of control. (See Box 13.1 for examples from Europe.)

Table 13.2 Acute Effects of Selected Hazardous Wastes

Type of Waste	Nervous System Damage	Gastrointestinal System Damage	Neurological System Damage	Respiratory System Damage	Skin Damage	Death
Pesticide wastes						
Halogenated organic pesticides	H		H	H		H
Methyl bromide			H			
Halogenated organic phenoxy herbicides					H	
2,4-D	H					
Organophosphorous pesticides	H		H	H		H
Organonitrogen herbicides (Paraquat® and Diquat®)		H				H
Carbamate insecticides	H		H	H		H
Dimethyldithiocarbamate fungicide compounds				H		
Aluminum phosphide		H				
Rotenone		H		H		
Polychlorinated biphenyls		A			H	
Cyanide wastes	H		H	H		H
Toxic metals						
Zinc, copper, selenium, chromium, nickel		H		H	H	
Arsenic		H			H	H
Organic lead compounds	H	H	H			
Mercury	H	H	H			H
Cadmium		H		H		H
Halogenated organics	H		H		H	
Nonhalogenated volatile organics			H	H		

H = statistically verifiable effects on human beings; A = statistically verifiable effects on laboratory animals.
Source: Governor's Office of Appropriate Technology, Toxic Waste Assessment Group, *Alternatives to the Land Disposal of Hazardous Wastes, An Assessment for California* (1981), cited in Benjamin A. Goldman, *et al.*, *Hazardous Waste Management: Reducing the Risk* (Island Press, Washington, D.C., 1986), p. 23.

Hazardous Waste

Not only is cleanup costly, but most government regulatory agencies do not know how to proceed. One expert testifying before the House of Lords Select Committee on Science and Technology (in the United Kingdom) told a stunned audience that "we do not know how much hazardous waste is produced in the UK, who produces it, what it is, and what happens to it" (43) (44). He could just as well have been addressing any other parliamentary or legislative body in Europe or North America.

Although OECD reports that abandoning hazardous wastes is prohibited in nearly all OECD countries (45), legislation regulating the handling, transport, and disposal of hazardous wastes did not take effect until the mid- to late 1970s. Sweden, one of the few countries in Europe to require "cradle-to-grave" manifests on hazardous wastes, did not bring its Ordinance on Environmentally Hazardous Waste into force until January 1, 1976. France's controlling legislation dates from 1975 and 1979. Likewise, the Netherlands passed the Chemical Waste Act in 1976 but failed to implement it until 1979. The Federal Republic of Germany's Federal Waste Disposal Act did not take effect until January 1, 1977. And the United Kingdom's key legislation dates from 1974, with important amendments in 1976 and 1981 (46). In effect, hazardous wastes were ignored until the mid-1970s. Says one West German official, "a decade ago, most of Western Europe's toxic garbage just disappeared down a black hole somewhere." Companies kept spotty records, if any, concerning the amount of hazardous wastes generated, what form they were in, or where they went. Decades of unregulated disposal have resulted in a profusion of toxic wastes in Europe and North America.

As to be expected from the amount of toxic wastes generated each year, the United States is near the top of the toxic heap, in terms of both the number of hazardous waste dumps needing immediate attention and the severity of their health threats (see below). Europeans are also paying a heavy price for their negligence. Every country in Europe (except Norway and Sweden) is plagued by an abundance of toxic waste sites—both old and new—needing urgent attention. Tiny, overcrowded Holland is a prime example. Authorities estimate that up to 8 million metric tons of hazardous chemical wastes may be buried in Dutch soil—most of it in leaking metal drums—with estimates of the cleanup bill ranging from $3.2 to $5.6 billion (47). (See Box 13.1.)

The United Kingdom faces the same situation. Of the estimated 5.5 million metric tons of notifiable hazardous wastes disposed of in 1980, three quarters were disposed of in municipal or industrial landfills with inadequate safeguards to prevent contamination of the environment (48). Further, there is no central authority in the United Kingdom charged with supervising the transport and disposal of hazardous wastes. Instead, there are 165 local waste disposal authorities, which are expected to cope with all manner of wastes in their jurisdictions. Although decentralization is often a good idea, it does not always work, particularly when standards vary from county to county. When the House of Lords Select Committee on Science and Technology circulated a questionnaire to these waste disposal authorities in 1981, of the 140 that replied, only 12 had hazardous waste disposal plans available, even though they had seven years to design them (49).

The United Kingdom is the only European country to encourage and endorse widespread codisposal of liquid industrial wastes and domestic solid wastes at the same site (50). The British approach is to mix the wastes, then allow soil chemistry processes to break down hazardous components. Little is done, however, to protect the soil or groundwater from contamination. Because of the uncontrolled nature of this technique, codisposal is seldom used in other OECD countries (51).

Because of the scarcity of data on hazardous waste in the Third World, little is known about how much is generated, what form it is in, or how it is handled or disposed of. Box 13.2 discusses the situation in two developing countries: India and Egypt.

Superfund: A U.S. Answer to Abandoned Waste Sites

The 1980 Comprehensive Environmental Response, Compensation, and Liability Act (CERCLA) established a federal fund, commonly called the Superfund, to support the identification and cleanup of abandoned hazardous waste sites. Funded from 1981 through September 1985 at the level of $1.6 billion, Superfund was supplemented by 10 percent matching grants from the states. Nearly 86 percent of the federal money was raised from a special tax imposed on feedstocks used by petroleum refining and chemical manufacturing industries, with the balance coming from federal appropriations (52). Though some 600

Table 13.3 Chronic Effects of Selected Hazardous Wastes

Type of Waste	Carcinogenic Effects	Mutagenic Effects	Teratogenic Effects	Reproductive System Damage
Pesticide wastes				
Halogenated organic pesticides	A	A	A	H
Methyl bromide				
Halogenated organic phenoxy herbicides 2,4-D	A	A	A	A
Organophosphorous pesticides	A	A	A	
Organonitrogen herbicides (Paraquat® and Diquat®)	A	A	A	
Carbamate insecticides				
Dimethyldithiocarbonate fungicide compounds				
Aluminum phosphide				
Rotenone				
Polychlorinated biphenyls	A		A	
Cyanide wastes				
Toxic metals				
Zinc, copper, selenium, chromium, nickel	H			
Arsenic				
Organic lead compounds				
Mercury		H	H	
Cadmium	H			
Halogenated organics	H	H		
Nonhalogenated volatile organics	A	A		

H = statistically verifiable effects on human beings. A = statistically verifiable effects on laboratory animals.
Source: Adapted from Benjamin Goldman, *et al., Hazardous Waste Management: Reducing the Risk* (Island Press, Washington, D.C., 1986), p. 24.

companies pay Superfund taxes—amounting to about 0.1 percent of their annual sales—10 major chemical and petroleum companies account for nearly 50 percent of the annual total of about $350 million (53).

The estimated number of hazardous waste dump sites throughout the country requiring urgent remedial action varies, depending on the government agency making the assessment. OTA estimates that 10,000 sites may eventually be placed on the National Priority List requiring Superfund cleanup. But, OTA points out, cleaning up these many hazardous dumps may well take 50 years and cost up to $100 billion (54). The Government Accounting Office believes that the National Priority List could reach more than 4,000 sites with maximum cleanup costs of around $40 billion. EPA, on the other hand, estimates that no more than 2,500 sites out of the 20,000 dumps identified will need to be placed on the National Priority List—costing around $23 billion to detoxify and taking 8–10 years to complete the work (55). As of August 1986, EPA had designated only 888 sites on the National Priority List (56).

Because of the long history of inadequate disposal practices, Superfund sites contain a bewildering variety of dangerous wastes. Table 13.4 shows the most common contaminants identified at Superfund sites. Heavy metals and volatile organics are the most prevalent pollutants. Many of the concentrations are extremely high (57).

After more than two years of Congressional and administration argument, the Superfund program was reauthorized and signed into law in October 1986. The new bill greatly increases the money available for hazardous waste cleanup: $9 billion for the next five years for the worst hazardous waste sites (58). The new money will be generated by a broader-based tax on corporate income, in addition to taxes on chemical and petroleum feedstocks and federal appropriations.

The new Superfund legislation requires EPA to resume work on 375 priority sites, work that was delayed because of the impasse in Congress, and to formulate standards for cleanup. It also provides funds for research and development of new hazardous waste disposal technologies (59). The new Superfund legislation promises to improve EPA's record. After the first five years, only 13 sites had been cleaned up and removed from the National Priority List, and there has been controversy over the effectiveness of some of these cleanups (60).

Box 13.1 Uncontrolled Dumping: The European Experience

Until the mid- to late 1970s, hazardous wastes were discarded indiscriminately throughout much of the world. Legislation governing the generation, transport, and final disposal of toxic wastes was virtually nonexistent or was in its infancy. Further, the environmental effects of hazardous wastes were not well understood, even by government agencies charged with protecting public health and welfare. The legacy of half a century of uncontrolled disposal of harmful industrial wastes began to surface in the 1970s and has continued to do so in virtually every industrialized country, including newly industrializing nations of the Third World.

The hazards of uncontrolled disposal and dumping are dramatically underlined by the following examples from Europe.

WESTERN EUROPE AND SCANDINAVIA

The Netherlands has been plagued with abandoned toxic waste dumps. About 5,000 hazardous waste sites have been identified, with at least 350 of them requiring immediate remedial action because they are clear threats to public health. Another 750 sites are located near residential areas or in watersheds and will need to be cleaned up in the near future (1). Commented one Dutch expert on toxic wastes, "It's a problem that has been swept under the rug too long. And now we have to pay" (2).

As a result, Holland is committed to spending $80 million per year for the next 15–20 years in an effort to clean up dangerous wastes (3). The eventual price tag, however, could be as high as $5.6 billion (4).

The dump sites being uncovered, most dating from the 1950s and 1960s, rival Love

Canal in the United States. The toxic waste issue broke the surface in 1980 with the discovery that over 270 homes in Lekkerkerk, a residential suburb of Rotterdam, had to be vacated because the soil and groundwater beneath the housing estate had been contaminated with chemical wastes containing toluene, xylene, and heavy metals. In all, some 900 people had to be relocated, 150,000 metric tons of polluted soil carted away and burned (5), and the entire area filled in with clean sand. The total cost of the operation ran upwards of $80 million (6).

When it was discovered that toxic wastes were buried under a new housing estate at Gouderak, health authorities had to evacuate 333 residents and pull down 99 houses. The ground was contaminated with 135,000 kilograms of polycyclic aromatics, 110 kilograms of benzenes, and more than 14,000 kilograms of PCBs (7).

Similarly, at Dordrecht, 106 houses had to be leveled and the residents moved elsewhere because they were sitting vulnerably atop a dumpsite containing hazardous chemical compounds like xylene, ethylbenzene, and dichlorobenzene. In all, around 35,00 square meters of soil were removed and burned (8).

The Federal Republic of Germany is faced with cleanup bills for about 2,000 of the country's 21,000 abandoned waste sites (9) (10). The total cost could exceed $4 billion and take decades to complete (11). Despite the fact that between 1972 and 1982 authorities managed to close down 50,000 unregulated dumps and open 5,000 new ones with some environmental safeguards, West Germany is haunted by its past industrial excesses (12).

The city of Hamburg has perhaps the worst record in the country. Two sites have made Hamburg synonymous with toxic wastes—an

abandoned factory that had been a chemical weapons complex and the Georgswerder waste dump near the suburb of Wilhelmsburg.

The Federal Republic's worst environmental disaster made headlines in 1979, when an eight-year-old boy was killed and two playmates critically injured by exploding chemicals found in an abandoned factory lot in a residential neighborhood of Hamburg. Horror-stricken investigators soon discovered that the abandoned factory was a waste dump containing an extremely lethal collection of chemical weapons left over from World War II (13). Some 61 chemical substances were discovered, including 30 liters of Tabun, an extremely potent nerve gas (one liter of it, when evaporating, reportedly could kill 200,000 people) (14). The surrounding neighborhood was evacuated as special cleanup crews from the police and army, wearing protective clothing, sifted through the abandoned factory grounds. Removal was complicated when quantities of three other deadly chemical weapons—phosgene, sarin, and soman (nerve gases)—were also uncovered (15). The delicate cleanup operations, which lasted from April 1980 until the end of 1981, cost an estimated $6.1 million. Federal authorities fear that an estimated 70 more such derelict waste dumps, containing potent chemical substances, including discarded nerve gases, remain to be found throughout West Germany (16).

A second dump, this one in the Hamburg suburb of Wilhelmsburg, also made headlines in the past few years. For more than two decades—until the dump was closed in 1979—Georgswerder received both municipal and hazardous industrial wastes from all over Europe. Known locally as "Monte Mortalis" because of its load of toxic garbage, Georg-

continued on next page

MANAGING HAZARDOUS WASTES

Managing hazardous wastes remains an unmet challenge in much of the world. "As report after report has recently shown, the field of toxic waste disposal has been characterized by mismanagement, rather than management," says Bob Munro. "Our management practices consist not of waste disposal in any real sense, but rather waste relocation. We don't deal with the problem, we are only postponing it" (61). But industrialized countries are beginning to introduce tougher legislation and enforcement procedures and are starting to employ innovative strategies to entice industries into reducing their production of hazardous wastes and using better treatment and disposal techniques.

How Most Wastes Are Managed

Despite the attention given to hazardous wastes over the past decade, most of industry's toxic wastes still end up in landfills; comparatively little is destroyed or recycled. OECD estimates that in its member states as much as 80 percent of all industrial hazardous wastes are disposed of in land-based sites, including deep wells and underground storage facilities. For the centrally planned economies of Eastern Europe and the Soviet Union, 90–95 percent of hazardous wastes are disposed of in or on the land (62). According to the limited amount of site data available, few of these dumps, particularly the old ones, have adequate safeguards to protect the environment from contamination.

In general, the United States, Canada, and Europe still rely principally on seven forms of hazardous waste management:
- deep-well injection into porous geological formations or salt caverns,
- discharge of treated and untreated liquids into municipal sewers, rivers, and streams,
- placement of liquid wastes or sludges in surface pits, ponds, or lagoons,
- storage of solid wastes in specially lined dumps covered by soil,
- storage of liquid and solid wastes in underground caverns and abandoned salt mines,
- dumping of wastes in sanitary landfills not specifically designed for toxic or hazardous wastes, and

---

Box 13.1 Uncontrolled Dumping: The European Experience (continued)

swerder exploded into a scandal in 1984, when health authorities found traces of dioxin in the dump (17). Further investigations revealed that because of the volatile and reactive nature of the chemical wastes discarded at Georgswerder, the abandoned dump is releasing about 100 million cubic meters of gas into the atmosphere each year. Municipal authorities fear that these "gas clouds" contain dangerously high levels of chlorinated hydrocarbons along with other toxic substances (18).

Denmark has its share of toxic troubles as well, despite the creation of an efficient nationwide central collection and disposal facility for hazardous wastes in 1976. (See discussion of Kommunekemi in main text.) Government authorities are in the process of cleaning up 380 abandoned chemical waste dumps (19), but there are widespread fears that many more dumps remain to be found.

In 1981, several hundred metric tons of toxic organic solvents, including toluene and benzene additives, were discovered buried beneath a busy city square in the middle of Copenhagen. The wastes had been discarded by a paint and varnish factory that had closed ten years earlier (20). Shocked by the discovery, the head of the Danish Environmental Board, Emmerik Moltke, admitted that "as contamination incidents become known it will show that much larger quantities of chemical waste are lying about than we in the Environmental Board were aware of" (21).

A short time later, health authorities in Harboore, western Jutland, discovered an abandoned dump on the coast that contained chemical wastes from the production of 2,4-D, parathion, and other pesticides, along with mercury wastes from the production of phenoxy-mercury acetate and ethylmercury

chloride left there by the Cheminova Chemical Company (22). Mercury levels in North Sea fish, including flounder, exceeded one part per million (the maximum level permitted by health standards), prompting the United Kingdom to ban the importation of Danish herring and flounder until the sources of contamination were found and remedied. Danish authorities quickly removed about 3,000 cubic meters of chemical wastes from the site at a cost of about $4 million (23).

In France, about 66 abandoned chemical waste sites, called *points noirs*—where hazardous wastes present grave risks to the environment—have received some form of remedial action, but the actual number of toxic dumps needing cleanup is not known (24). One of France's worst dump sites turned out to be a salt lagoon at Marais de Ponteau, where 30,000 cubic meters of oil wastes contaminated nearby surface waters. The lagoon had to be pumped out and the oily wastes shipped away for incineration and solidification at a total cost of about $1 million (25).

There are no official estimates available on the number of hazardous waste dumps in need of attention in the United Kingdom. But the country abounds in headline-grabbing abandoned toxic waste dumps. In 1981, a scandal wracked the county of Derbyshire when it was disclosed that a former chemical company had buried dangerous dioxin wastes somewhere near the tiny villages of Morton, Stretton, Shirland, and Higham (26). The situation was made worse because county authorities did not know exactly where the dioxin was buried, how much was there, or the extent of the health threat to the local residents.

There are other examples:
- In 1981, the Yorkshire County Council was forced to pay $178,000 to evacuate residents

in a housing estate in Ravenfield, excavate an abandoned landfill, and neutralize the sulfuric acid that it still contained six years after a local oil reclamation firm had stopped dumping its acid tars there. Children playing on the site had burns on their hands and feet (27).
- In the 1960s and early 1970s, a now defunct textile factory indiscriminately dumped asbestos wastes around the village of Hebden Bridge in West Yorkshire without bothering to record their locations. The result: more than 70 villagers have died from asbestos-related diseases (28).

No estimates of the number of abandoned toxic waste dumps are available for Austria, but the country is dotted with about 1,000 largely unregulated dumps for the disposal of both municipal and industrial garbage (29). Some of the worst dumps are government managed. An abandoned gravel pit in Reyersdorf-Schonkirchen in lower Austria has been used for years as a repository for dangerous petrochemical wastes. Despite the fact that the site is under the authority of the Austrian Mineral Oil Administration—the state oil company—it lacks any environmental safeguards to prevent the mix of toxic materials in the pit from seeping into the water table. According to reports, the acrid stench from the site brings tears to the eyes of visitors (30).

In a notorious case, a local privately operated disposal company in Vienna claimed to be handling and detoxifying 60,000 metric tons of hazardous wastes every year. Investigations by the Viennese Working Group of Concerned Scientists discovered that instead of disposing of the wastes as agreed, the delinquent firm was simply collecting huge fees for doing nothing more than stacking the toxic chemical wastes behind its plant in badly cor-

Table 13.4 Common Contaminants Found at Superfund Sites

Chemical	Average Occurrence (percent)	Average Concentration (parts per billion)
Lead	51.4	309,000
Cadmium	44.7	2,185
Toluene	44.1	1,120,000
Mercury	29.6	1,379
Benzene	28.5	16,582
Trichloroethylene	27.9	103,000
Ethylbenzene	26.9	540,000
Benzo[a]anthracene	12.3	148,000
Bromodichloromethane	7.0	20
Polychlorinated biphenyls	3.9	128,000
Toxaphene	0.6	12,360

Source: William Eckel, et al., presented at the National Conference on Hazardous Wastes and Environmental Emergencies, cited in Julian Josephson, "Implementing Superfund," *Environmental Science and Technology*, Vol. 20, No. 1 (1985), p. 28.

■ recovery of solvent liquids from other waste contaminants through fractional distillation (63).

In addition, a small but increasingly significant proportion of hazardous wastes is burned in industrial and commercial boilers as fuel supplements, incinerated or thermally destroyed, treated chemically through oxidation processes, or degraded biologically by soil microbes under aerobic conditions in carefully controlled and monitored landfills (64). (See Table 13.5 for an overview of treatment technologies.)

OECD countries were able to recycle, reclaim, or reuse only 12–16 million metric tons of hazardous wastes, roughly 4–5 percent of the total amounted generated in 1984 (65). At the same time, they incinerated or thermally destroyed 5–10 percent (66).

As mentioned above, the bulk of OECD's hazardous waste—as much as 85 percent—is pumped into deep wells, taken to landfills, stored in underground caverns, or treated and dumped into lagoons, rivers, and streams.

Tracking Systems for Monitoring Hazardous Wastes

By 1983, most OECD countries had instituted systems for tracking the movement of hazardous wastes from the site of origin to final disposal or were in the process of doing so (67).

In the United States, the Resource Conservation and Recovery Act of 1976 (RCRA) required that all generators of waste, as well as transporters and disposal firms, comply with a federal manifest system. All shipments of hazardous wastes from the site of their origin fall under this

Box 13.1

roded drums and broken plastic containers (31).

Switzerland produced 380,000 metric tons of hazardous wastes in 1985, including liquid industrial wastes that are handled by wastewater treatment plants. Other wastes are incinerated or deposited in controlled landfills. Switzerland's main problem is not abandoned toxic waste dumps but, rather, emissions from the country's 38 incineration plants that burn a variety of wastes, including hazardous chemicals (32). Prior to enforcement of the new air pollution ordinance (March 1986), the incinerators were annually discharging into the atmosphere some 5,000 metric tons of hydrochloric acids, 200 metric tons of hydrocarbons, and 140 metric tons of heavy metals, ranging from cadmium to mercury (33). The situation is slowly improving because all incineration plants are now required to meet stricter standards on air pollution and therefore must reduce harmful emissions.

Because about 75 percent of Sweden's hazardous wastes, which total about 520,000 metric tons a year, are generated by a few industries, toxic wastes are relatively easy to track (34). Still, good legislation and responsible industries have not spared Sweden from unscrupulous disposal practices. One famous case stands out. From 1965 to 1977, a chemical plant owned by BT Kemi manufactured pesticides at Teckomatorp in southern Sweden. During this period, the company was continuously at odds with the environmental protection authorities for discharging toxic wastes—mostly chlorinated phenols and phenoxy acids—into a small stream near the plant (35). Subsequent investigations revealed that, from 1975 to 1977, the company had also illegally buried more than 600 drums filled with toxic wastes containing high levels of pesticide residues, including chlorinated

phenols, phenoxy acids and their esters (Dinoseb and Lindane), as well as quantities of PCBs, chlorinated dioxins, and dibenzofurans (36). When this was discovered, the central government forcibly closed the plant in October 1977, after 12 years of litigation. But cleaning up the mess cost in excess of $7 million and took several years to complete (37).

EASTERN EUROPE

As mentioned earlier, up to 95 percent of all hazardous wastes generated in Eastern Europe are disposed of in landfills, many without any environmental controls whatsoever (38). Only in the past few years have countries like Hungary and Poland attempted to come to grips with their growing burden of toxic wastes.

Hungary had no legislation regulating the handling and disposal of hazardous wastes until 1984 (39). Most of the country's estimated 600,000 metric tons of hazardous wastes generated every year are disposed of in landfills; little is incinerated or shipped out of the country (40). The 1984 legislation was enacted largely in reaction to an incident at the small village of Vac, 40 kilometers north of Budapest on the Danube. In 1981, inspectors found high concentrations of chemical solvents in the drinking water from several of the town's wells (41). Investigators traced the chemicals to an abandoned waste site in the town, owned by Chinoin, the largest pharmaceutical company in Hungary. The chemicals had leaked out of improperly stored waste drums and seeped into the soil, contaminating the groundwater (42). In the aftermath of the revelations, 45,000 cubic meters of soil had to be transported elsewhere for burial, and Chinoin was forced to ship 2,000 metric tons of distillation residues to Austria

for incineration. The company was subsequently fined $6 million for negligence (43).

Poland's history of toxic waste legislation is also short. Until recently, authorities did not keep track of potentially hazardous wastes; much of industry's toxic waste was dumped in municipal landfills or industrial dumps with little or no environmental safeguards. Poland generates a lot of hazardous wastes. The chemical industry alone generated an estimated 125 million metric tons of wastes between World War II and 1980, much of it toxic (44). In 1976, according to one estimate, Poland produced nearly 23 million metric tons of hazardous wastes, of which nearly 20 million metric tons were from copper, zinc, and lead ore flotation; slurries and dust particulates from electrostatic precipitators; and industrial sludges generated in tanning, electroplating, and related process industries (45).

A study of toxic wastes in one region of the country—Lublin—revealed that most of the area's 61,000 metric tons of industrial toxic wastes were disposed of in landfills. According to Polish journalist Gene Pudlis, "the waste material is dumped around the towns of Lubartow and Kloda. However, none of these dump sites fulfills technological or sanitary requirements, creating a potential threat to the local water reservoirs and the soil. The same lack of basic regulations holds for municipal dumps outside the towns of Lublin and Krasnik, where wastes from the machine industry containing nickel, cadmium, lead, copper, zinc, molybdenum, iron and manganese are dumped" (46).

Responding, in part, to increasingly vocal demands from the Polish Ecological Club, a nationwide grassroots environmental organization, Polish authorities have recently devel-

continued on next page

regulation. The manifest, a form that contains information about the hazardous waste, accompanies the shipment from its point of origin to its ultimate destination (68). However, only about 4 percent of all hazardous wastes generated in the United States are transported off-site for treatment and disposal (69). Therefore, although the manifest system tracks a significant quantity of toxic wastes, most hazardous wastes are never recorded by the manifest system.

Europeans have instituted similar systems. The Federal Republic of Germany's "trip ticket" is an efficient national tracking system. Because most hazardous wastes generated in the Federal Republic are sent to central treatment and storage facilities, the trip ticket provides authorities with an elaborate tracking system. Each waste transfer is documented by a six-part form. One part is sent to federal authorities, one is kept by the facility, and four accompany the waste shipment. When the shipment arrives at its destination, the carrier sends one copy of the form to the federal authorities and one to the originating facility; both generators and disposers are responsible for the fate of the waste. In 1984, about 100,000 trip tickets were issued each month in the Federal Republic of Germany (70).

Europe's Centrally Managed Systems for Treating and Disposing of Hazardous Wastes

Europeans are beginning to monitor and manage their hazardous trash much more thoroughly than does the United States or Canada. In the Federal Republic of Germany, for example, nearly 85 percent of all hazardous wastes are sent to 15 large centrally managed treatment plants for destruction, reuse and recycling, or burial in controlled landfills and underground storage caverns (71).

Because of widespread public mistrust of landfills and storage, West Germany is not the only country to adopt regional or national integrated management systems. To varying degrees, France, Denmark, Sweden, Finland, Austria, the Netherlands, and Switzerland also rely on centrally managed collection and treatment systems, including both regional large-scale treatment and disposal centers and local smaller-scale plants.

Box 13.1 Uncontrolled Dumping: The European Experience (continued)

oped regional plans for reducing waste at the source, improving onsite disposal practices, and establishing centralized treatment facilities for especially hazardous industrial wastes (47).

References and Notes

1. Hans Erasmus, "Industrial Hazardous Waste Management in the Netherlands," *Industry and Environment* (United Nations Environment Programme special issue on industrial hazardous waste management), No. 4 (1983), p. 25.
2. Don Hinrichsen, "Europe's Plague of Poisons," *International Wildlife*, Vol. 13, No. 3 (1983), pp. 33–34.
3. Organisation for Economic Co-operation and Development (OECD), "Update on Activities—The OECD and Waste Management Policy" (OECD, unpublished, March 1986), p. 3.
4. Maurits Groen, "Holland's Toxic Troubles," *AMBIO*, Vol. 13, No. 4 (1984), p. 270.
5. Gary Yerkey, "Dutch Plan Major Cleanup of 3,000 Chemical Dumps," *International Herald Tribune* (January 15, 1981).
6. *Op. cit.* 4.
7. *Op. cit.* 4.
8. *Op. cit.* 4.
9. *Op. cit.* 3.
10. Michael Paparian, *et al.*, *Integrated Hazardous Waste Systems in the Federal Republic of Germany and Denmark* (California Foundation on the Environment and the Economy, Environmental Defense Fund, and Sierra Club, San Francisco, 1984), p. 20.
11. *Op. cit.* 3.
12. Reinhard Spilker, "Germany: A Black Hole in the North Sea for Toxic Wastes," *AMBIO*, Vol. 11, No. 1 (1982), p. 57.
13. *Op. cit.* 2, p. 34.
14. Reinhard Spilker, "The Stoltzenberg Syndrome: West Germany's Biggest Environmental Scandal Continues," *AMBIO*, Vol. 9, No. 5 (1980), p. 256.
15. *Ibid.*
16. *Op. cit.* 14, p. 257.
17. Reinhard Spilker, "Poisonous Waste Threatens Hamburg," *AMBIO*, Vol. 13, No. 2 (1984), p. 124.
18. *Ibid.*
19. Organisation for Economic Co-operation and Development (OECD), *Transfrontier Movements of Hazardous Wastes*, based on a conference held in Basel, Switzerland, March 26–27, 1985 (OECD, Paris, 1985), p. 5.
20. Judith M. Corcoran, ed., "Denmark Confronts the Effects of Toxic Dumping," *International Water Report* (summer 1981), p. 1.
21. *Ibid.*
22. Elaine Grandjean, "Denmark: Chemical Dumpsite Focuses Attention on Toxic Waste," *AMBIO*, Vol. 11, No. 1 (1982), p. 65.
23. *Ibid.*
24. *Op. cit.* 19.
25. Organisation for Economic Co-operation and Development (OECD), *Hazardous Waste "Problem" Sites—Report of an Expert Seminar*, ENV/WMP/81.10 (OECD, Paris, 1981), p. 46.
26. Catherine Caufield and Fred Pearce, "An Overburden of Toxic Waste," *New Scientist*, Vol. 90, No. 1252 (1981), p. 344.
27. Wendy Barnaby, "Great Britain: Relying on Luck to Avert Disaster," *AMBIO*, Vol. 11, No. 1 (1982), p. 55.
28. *Ibid.*
29. Hanswerner Mackwitz, "Austria: Unregulated Dumping and Government-Managed Polluters," *AMBIO*, Vol. 11, No. 1 (1982), p. 59.
30. *Ibid.*
31. *Op. cit.* 29.
32. D.B. Dubois, Federal Office of Environmental Protection, Basel, Switzerland, 1986 (personal communication).
33. Peter Hulm and Christoph Schweizer, "Switzerland: The Other Side of the Postcard Image," *AMBIO*, Vol. 11, No.1 (1982), p. 58.
34. Olov von Heidenstam, "Sweden: Managing Hazardous Waste," *AMBIO*, Vol. 11, No. 1 (1982), p. 66.
35. Ronny Ferm and Lars Renberg, "An Industrial Cover-Up: The Case of BT Kemi," *AMBIO*, Vol. 7, No. 5–6 (1978), p. 211.
36. *Ibid.*
37. *Op. cit.* 34.
38. H. Yakowitz, "Some Background Information Concerning Hazardous Waste Management in Non-OECD Countries" (Organisation for Economic Co-operation and Development, submitted, Paris, 1985), p. 5.
39. *Ibid.*, p. 30.
40. *Op. cit.* 38, p. 31.
41. Erika Laszlo, "Hungary: Beginning to Control Toxic Wastes," *AMBIO*, Vol. 11, No. 1 (1982), p. 60.
42. *Ibid.*
43. *Op. cit.* 41.
44. Eugeniusz Pudlis, "Poland: Heavy Metals Pose Serious Health Problems," *AMBIO*, Vol. 11, No. 1 (1982), p. 61.
45. Edward S. Kempa, "The Role of Low-Waste Technologies in the Management of Hazardous Waste in Poland," *Industry and Environment*, No. 4 (1983), p. 41.
46. *Op. cit.* 44, p. 62.
47. *Op. cit.* 38.

Box 13.2 Hazardous Waste Management in Selected Third World Countries

Most Third World countries have no legislation governing the production, handling, and disposal of toxic wastes. Industrial wastes are generally treated like municipal wastes and dumped indiscriminately in landfills or are discharged into rivers and streams or into the sea. There is also little information on hazardous wastes in the Third World.

In India, no study has been done on the nature and extent of toxic waste pollution (1). Although nearly all rivers in the country are polluted, most pollution is from domestic sewage and municipal effluents. However, rivers in the provinces of Gujarat, Rajasthan, Bihar, Maharashtra, Kerala, and Andhra Pradesh often contain high levels of heavy metal wastes, including mercury, cadmium, nickel, manganese, lead, chromium, copper, and antimony (2). Perhaps the most dramatic incident of hazardous waste release in India occurred in 1968, when the Ganges River near Monghyr (in Bihar Province) caught fire because of petrochemical wastes discharged from a refinery (3).

The production of hazardous wastes in India has grown significantly since the 1960s. Reports of fish kills in estuaries and rivers and the death of cattle from exposure to heavy metals and acids are a regular occurrence.

Further, as nonbiodegradable organic chemicals continue to enter the aquatic food chain, the threats to public health and welfare increase (4).

In other areas toxic wastes are simply dumped on land without regard for the environment or human health. In the highly industrialized area of Vapi in the province of Gujarat, chemical wastes are piled in the open with no protection. The problem of mismanaged toxic wastes is aggravated by India's weather systems. During the rainy season, the stockpiled chemical wastes leach into groundwater reservoirs, contaminating drinking water. During the eight months' dry season, wastes accumulating in small rivers and streams can become highly concentrated (5).

Egypt, like India, has no central agency responsible for managing hazardous wastes. The industries that generate toxic wastes are supposed to treat them before discharging them into public sewers, pumping them into rivers, or dumping them in landfills (6). The reality is often quite different. According to Ahmed Hamza, Director of the Industrial Waste Research Center in Alexandria, "since more than 75 percent of industrial establishments in Egypt are state-owned, it is virtually impossible to enforce the emission laws owing to economic, technological, and political con-

straints. The Prime Minister has stated recently that if the existing standards fixed by the Egyptian wastewater laws were to be met, nearly all factories would have no choice but to violate the law" (7).

The situation in most developing countries was succinctly summarized by Mateo Magarinos de Mello, an environmental lawyer from Uruguay: "Anybody can throw anything anywhere, at any time and in any quantity" (8).

References and Notes

1. David Davidar, "India: Every River Polluted, and Few Effective Controls," AMBIO, Vol. 11, No. 1 (1982), p. 63.
2. Ibid.
3. B.B. Sundaresan, et.al., "An Overview of Toxic and Hazardous Waste in India," Industry and Environment, No. 4 (1983), p. 70.
4. Ibid.
5. Op. cit. 1.
6. Ahmed Hamza, "Management of Industrial Hazardous Wastes in Egypt," Industry and Environment, No. 4 (1983), p. 31.
7. Ibid.
8. Mateo J. Magarinos de Mello, "General Guidelines for an Environmental Policy and a Preliminary Case Study in a Developing Country," Industry and Environment, No. 4 (1983), p. 53.

The West German and Danish Systems of Hazardous Waste Management

Although both West Germany and Denmark have tackled the problem of hazardous wastes by introducing centrally managed systems, their approaches are different.

Federal legislation in West Germany places hazardous waste management under the 11 German Länder, or states, allowing each one to develop its own implementation system. Nearly all have centralized treatment and storage facilities of some kind. However, the Bavarian system is particularly noteworthy. Three major integrated treatment-incinerator facilities, both private and state run, operate under the Company for Disposal of Special Wastes in Bavaria, abbreviated GSB (72). The facilities, located at Schweinfurt, Schwaback, and Ebenhausen/Gallenbach, receive hazardous wastes from more than 10,000 firms in Bavaria (73). In 1980, approximately 206,000 metric tons of hazardous wastes were delivered to GSB, an amount equal to nearly 90 percent of all such wastes generated in the state of Bavaria. Of this amount, 30 percent was incinerated, 30 percent required oil-water separation before it was discharged into municipal sewers, 24 percent was sent to Gallenbach for controlled landfill, 9 percent was treated by other methods, 2 percent consisted of solvents for recycling, and 5 percent was handled by unspecified methods (74).

The entire system originally cost $50 million, of which Bavaria subsidized $33 million through land grants and low-interest loans. Today, GSB's annual operating costs of about $10.5 million are fully covered by the disposal fees

paid by Bavaria's waste generators (75). GSB has also initiated a program to collect and dispose of hazardous household wastes such as: pesticides, oil-based paints, batteries, and waste oil.

Denmark has Europe's most centralized national treatment and disposal system. All wastes considered hazardous under Danish law are sent to one central facility—Kommunekemi—located in the city of Nyborg, about 30 kilometers east of Odense in central Denmark. Authorities set up 21 central collection stations throughout the country, in addition to 250 stations for handling toxic household wastes, thus ensuring that no source of hazardous wastes is far from a collection station (76). The collection stations do not pretreat the wastes but, rather, separate and store them until they can be transferred to Kommunekemi.

The Kommunekemi facility incorporates three separate treatment processes. First, waste oil is recovered, then upgraded and used to fuel the plant's incinerator. Second, organic wastes are treated through conventional detoxification processes, from pH adjustment and precipitation of heavy metals to dewatering the wastes. Detoxified waste water is then sent to a municipal sewage facility, and the filter cake (leftover toxic residue) is disposed of in landfills. Third, highly toxic organic wastes are incinerated in one of three large incinerators. Fly ash from the incinerators is subsequently sent to a nearby controlled landfill (77).

Despite this carefully controlled centralized system, industrial compliance is clearly below expectations; in the chemical industry alone, some 25 percent of all hazardous wastes are still not disposed of properly (78). The

Table 13.5 Common Treatment Technologies Used in North America and Europe

Advantages	Disadvantages	Limitations
Destruction/Detoxification Processes		
Biological Treatment		
Conventional:		
• Applicable to many organic waste streams • High total organic removal • Inexpensive • Well understood and widely used in other applications	• May produce a hazardous sludge that must be managed • May require pretreatment prior to discharge	• Microorganisms sensitive to oxygen levels, temperature, toxic loading, inlet flow • Some organic contaminants are difficult to treat • Flow and composition variations can reduce efficiency • Aeration difficult to depths of 2 feet • Many common organic species not easily biodegraded • Needs proper combination of wastes and hydrogeological characteristics • Must obtain proper mix of contaminants, organisms, and nutrients • Organisms may plug pores
In situ biodegradation		
• Destroys waste in place	• Limited experience • Extensive testing may be required • Containment also required	
Chemical Treatment		
Wet Air Oxidation		
• Good for wastes too dilute for incineration or too concentrated or toxic for biological treatment	• Oxidation not as complete as thermal oxidation or incineration • May produce new hazardous species • Extensive testing is required • High capital investment • High level of operator skills required • May require posttreatment	• Poor destruction of chlorinated organics • Moderate efficiencies of destruction (40–90%)
Chlorination for Cyanide		
• Essentially complete destruction • Well understood and widely used in other applications	• Specialized for cyanide	• Interfering waste constituents may limit applicability or effectiveness
Ozonation		
• Can destroy refractory organics • Liquids, solids, mixes can be treated	• Oxidation not as complete as thermal oxidation or incineration • May produce new hazardous species • Extensive testing required • High capital investment, high operation and maintenance	• Not well understood
Reduction for Chromium		
• High destruction • Well understood and widely used in other applications	• Specialized for chromium	• Interfering waste constituents may limit applicability or effectiveness
Permeable Treatment Beds		
• Limited excavation required • Inexpensive	• Developmental • Periodic replacement of treatment media required • Spent treatment medium must be disposed of	• Best for shallow plumes • Many reactants treat a limited family of wastes • Effectiveness influenced by groundwater flow variations
Chemical Injection		
• Excavation not required • No pumping required	• Developmental • Extensive testing required	• Best for shallow plumes • Need fairly homogeneous waste composition

Danish Parliament is attempting to impose more stringent penalties on violators in an effort to fashion a bigger enforcement stick.

Current Management Practices: Problems and Prospects

The Containment Dilemma

All the major containment technologies—surface impoundments, hazardous waste landfills, and sanitary landfills—seem to have inherent serious flaws.

In the United States, a study by the U.S. EPA found that over 70 percent of the estimated 80,000 surface impoundments accepting hazardous wastes in the country were unlined, and 90 percent of these were possible sources of groundwater contamination (79).

Even dumps designed to accept hazardous wastes often lack needed environmental controls. Throughout the OECD countries, regulations stipulate that these landfills must be lined, but most experts agree that the clay or soil barriers built to contain the wastes are often inadequate to prevent toxic mixtures from reacting and eventually seeping into the soil and contaminating groundwater. According to the U.S. EPA, less than 5 percent of all hazardous wastes disposed of in managed landfills are chemically or physically stabilized to reduce the chances of the wastes' migrating into the groundwater or leaching to the surface (80).

Sanitary landfills (municipal dumps) are not lined and therefore are not designed to accommodate hazardous wastes. But many such facilities in North America and Europe are riddled with toxic and hazardous wastes discarded before legislation governing the handling and disposal of such wastes was promulgated. Even where stringent laws exist, as in most OECD countries, loopholes in the definitions of hazardous wastes allow potentially toxic and harmful substances to escape regulation. In the United

Table 13.5

Advantages	Disadvantages	Limitations
Incineration		
Conventional Incineration		
• Destroys organic wastes (+99.99%)	• Disposal of residue required • Test burn may be required • Skilled operators required • Costly	
Onsite		
• Destroys organic wastes (+99.99%) • Transportation of wastes not required	• Disposal of residue required • Onsite feedstock preparation required • Test burn may be required • Skilled operators required • Costly	• Mobile units have low feed rate
Thermal Oxidation for Gases		
• Proven technology • High destruction efficiencies • Applicable to most organic streams	• May require auxiliary fuel • Operating and maintenence may be high	
Separation-Transfer Processes		
Chemical		
Neutralization-Precipitation		
• Wide range of applications • Well understood and widely used in other applications • Inexpensive	• Hazardous sludge produced	• Complexing agents reduce effectiveness
Ion Exchange		
• Can recover metals at high efficiency	• Generates sludge for disposal • Pretreatment to remove suspended solids may be required • Costly	• Resin fouling • Removes some constituents but not others
Physical Treatment		
Carbon Absorption for Aqueous Streams		
• Well understood and demonstrated • Applicable to many organics that do not respond to biological treatment • High degree of flexibility in operation and design • High degree of effectiveness	• Regeneration or disposal of spent carbon required • Pretreatment may be required for suspended solids, oil, grease • High operating and maintenance costs	• Many inorganics, some organics are poorly absorbed
Carbon Absorption for Gases		
• Widely used, well understood • High removal efficiencies	• High capital and operating and maintenance costs	• More effective for low molecular weight, polar species • Disposal or regeneration of spent carbon required
Flocculation, Sedimentation, and Filtration		
• Low cost • Well understood	• Generates sludge for disposal	
Stripping		
• Well understood and demonstrated	• Air controls may be required	• Applicable only to relatively volatile organic contaminants
Flotation		
• Well understood and demonstrated. • Inexpensive	• Generates sludge for disposal	
Reverse Osmosis		
• High removal potential	• Generates sludge for disposal • Pretreatment to remove suspended solids or adjust pH may be required • Costly	• Variability in waste flow and composition affects performance

Source: U.S. Office of Technology Assessment (OTA), *Superfund Strategy*, (U.S. Government Printing Office, Washington, D.C., 1985), pp. 188-189.

States, for example, roughly 23 million metric tons of inorganic wastes, chiefly metallic and nonmetallic dusts from the primary metals, steel, and iron foundry industries, were dumped in sanitary landfills in 1983—exempt from the regulations enacted under the umbrella of RCRA [81]. According to the U.S. Congressional Budget Office, because "some of these waste types have demonstrated significant hazards when deposited in unlined landfills, the use of this disposal method might threaten groundwater" [82]. In both Europe and North America, small-scale industries generating less than about 1 metric ton of hazardous wastes a month have also been generally excluded or made exempt from hazardous waste disposal regulations.

Incineration: A Necessary Option

When performed under controlled conditions, incineration can destroy 99.999 percent of organic wastes. (See Table 13.5.) Common incineration technologies include liquid injection, rotary kiln, hearth, and fluidized bed [83]. At the present time, incineration accounts for less than 2 percent of the disposal of hazardous wastes in the United States [84], where relatively high costs, compared with landfills, and concerns for the safety of surrounding areas in case of accident or improper operation have kept incineration from becoming a major form of hazardous waste disposal. In Europe, incineration is used more frequently but in most countries still accounts for well below half the wastes disposed of (85). The Federal Republic of Germany, for example, incinerates about 15 percent of its hazardous waste. However, as land-based sites for disposal become harder to find and as regulations become more stringent, especially for highly toxic organic wastes, incineration in specially built land-based facilities and at sea is becoming an increasingly important alternative to landfills and storage.

One promising new method for incinerating toxic and other hazardous wastes is the use of existing cement and lime kilns. In fact, this technique is emerging as an efficient and cost-effective alternative to costly centrally managed incinerators like those used throughout Europe. Tests at the Norcem cement plant outside Oslo proved successful. Not only were various kinds of wastes, including PCBs, incinerated, but the plant substituted selected toxic wastes for up to 30 percent of the fuel used to fire their cement kilns (86).

In the Swedish town of Stora Vika, a cement kiln successfully incinerated chlorinated aliphatics, PCBs, chlorophenols, phenoxy acids, and trichlorotrifluoroethane. During both short- and long-term tests, no major waste components were detected in the plant's stack gases (87). Similar tests were repeated successfully in Canada (involving waste oils contaminated with lead and zinc, PCBs, toluene, and a variety of chlorinated wastes) and in the United States (involving PCBs, chlorinated aliphatics, methyl ethyl ketone, toluene, methylene, chloride, trichloroethane, trimethylbenzene, xylene, chloroform, and carbon tetrachloride) (88).

Most cement and lime kilns are already fitted with advanced pollution control equipment, including high efficiency electrostatic precipitators that clean stack gases. In addition, the kiln materials—high in alkalinity—neutralize any acidic gases that may form (89). "The elegance of this solution," claims Roger Batstone, Industrial Pollution and Safety Engineer for the World Bank, "is that the cement companies are paid to incinerate the wastes and, in addition, are able to cut down on their own fuel consumption in the process. Moreover, capital investments are minimal, compared to full-scale incineration plants" (90).

Ocean incineration has also received publicity over the past few years, much of it unfavorable. Before it is accepted as an alternative to the other forms of incineration, not to mention disposal, several environmental stumbling blocks must be overcome. Incineration technologies used aboard the three ships currently operating are controversial. Critics of ocean incineration, like Greenpeace, claim that the toxic constituents of the wastes are insufficiently burned and, instead, are spread far and wide by the emissions plume (91). Opponents argue that tighter environmental controls, like mandatory scrubbers, need to be required for incineration vessels before they are licensed.

Even more worrisome is the possibility of a catastrophic accident or spill in discharging tons of highly toxic wastes into the ocean. The U.S. OTA, a proponent of ocean incineration, states that "for most hazardous materials, a significant spill in almost any location would result in considerable immediate destruction of biomass and loss of most organisms in and around the spill" (92).

Although no annual data are available for all hazardous wastes incinerated at sea on a global basis, in 1984, about 100,000 metric tons of highly toxic industrial wastes—about 80 percent were toxic organochlorines (93)—were incinerated by three specially equipped vessels operating out of Antwerp, Le Havre, and Rotterdam (94). Most of these wastes are incinerated in the North Sea off the coast of Belgium.

Six European countries produce nearly all the toxic wastes incinerated in the North Sea: the Federal Republic of Germany, the Netherlands, France, Belgium, Switzerland, and the United Kingdom (95). With the exception of Belgium, most toxic waste incineration by these countries is on land. (See Table 13.6.)

Promising New Technologies

Some new technologies show promise for improving treatment of hazardous wastes. As legislative restrictions on landfills grow and the costs and risks of traditional methods of disposal rise, new technologies become more attractive economically as well as technically.

Biotechnology

Genetically engineered microorganisms have been developed to biodegrade toxic wastes *in situ* and in closed reactors (96). Toxic chemicals like benzene, toluene, and xylenes along with other hydrocarbons can be oxidized *in situ* to carbon dioxide and water by microorganisms, provided that oxygen and such inorganic nutrients as phosphate and ammonium nitrogen are present (97). At one site where a large amount of oil had been spilled, 200 microorganisms per gram of soil were placed in the polluted earth; within 165 days the microorganisms had multiplied to more than 1 million per gram of soil and had digested 65 percent of the hydrocarbons (98). Occidental Chemical, one of the pioneers in this field, has filed patent applications covering nearly 100 strains of recombinant microorganisms for use in biodegradation (99).

Plasma Arc Destruction

This novel form of incineration obliterates all traces of organic toxic wastes. Developed by a Canadian engineer,

Table 13.6 Average Amounts of Hazardous Wastes Incinerated in Selected OECD Countries, Early 1980s

Country	Amount Incinerated (metric tons)	
	On Land	At Sea
Denmark	circa 32,000	0
Belgium	X	10,000
France	400,000	10,000
Federal Republic of Germany	675,000	41,000
Netherlands	66,000a	20,000
Switzerland	120,000	5,000
United Kingdom	80,000	3,500
United States	2,700,000b	0
Norway	X	8,000

X = Not available.
Notes:
a. The Netherlands incinerates about 86,000 metric tons of hazardous wastes each year on land and at sea.
b. This large figure is only 1 percent of the total amount of hazardous wastes generated in the United States. In contrast, West Germany incinerates 15 percent of its total amount of hazardous wastes. The U.S. Congress, Office of Technology Assessment, estimates that 10-20 percent of all U.S. hazardous wastes could, in theory, be incinerated.
Source: Adapted from U.S. Congress, Office of Technology Assessment (OTA), *Ocean Incineration: Its Role in Managing Hazardous Waste* (OTA, Washington, D.C., August 1986), pp. 198-201.

the plasma arc sends a powerful bolt of electricity between two electrodes, heating the air in a chamber to 45,000° F and creating an intense surge of energy known as the plasma state (100). Among a host of other applications, this technology is useful for destroying outmoded electrical transformers insulated with PCBs. When PCB-contaminated substances in concentrations of 22,000 parts per million have been fed into a plasma arc, there is no trace of PCBs after incineration (101).

Molten Salt Incineration

Soaking hazardous chemicals in a hot bath of molten salt is effective in destroying DDT powder, chemical warfare agents like mustard gas, corrosive solvents, and acids (102). The molten pool containing sodium carbonate is heated to about 1,650° F, well below levels necessary for some kinds of incineration. Less than 1 percent of the original waste volume remains after passing through the salt pool (103).

Source Reduction: Turning Off the Toxic Tap

Some companies that generate toxic wastes are beginning to cut off the flow of toxic wastes at the source—they are generating less hazardous materials in their manufacturing processes.

In the United States, Minnesota Mining & Manufacturing Corporation (3M) pioneered the concept of reducing pollution at the source instead of at the end of a pipe. In 1975, the company initiated a Pollution Prevention Pays program that by 1984 had eliminated 10,000 metric tons of water pollutants, 140,000 metric tons of sludge, and 90,000 metric tons of air pollutants. Further, the company cut its effluent discharge by 3.7 billion liters and saved 254,000 barrels of oil per year. This program used 1,200 employee suggestions and saved $192 million in less than ten years (104).

Laws and regulations dealing with solid and hazardous waste disposal are beginning to drive industrial behavior toward pollution prevention. It is no longer cheaper to pollute. In the United States and Europe, where strong waste disposal laws have been enacted over the past 15 years, the administrative machinery is reversing the economic incentives to pollute. These laws highlight the problem of cross-media pollution and the need for an integrated approach to waste management. "In the long run," concludes a U.S. Environmental Protection Agency researcher, "only the reduction in the generation of wastes and an increase in recovery and byproduct production will permit the achievement and maintenance of desired levels of environmental quality" (105).

Unfortunately, source reduction is still largely untried. The chemical and allied products industries account for roughly half the hazardous wastes generated in the United States (106). Yet in a recent study of 29 chemical plants, source reduction was being tried for only a small fraction of the toxic wastes being generated (107). The study by INFORM, a New York-based research organization, reported that "the largest reported waste reduction figures of two to three million pounds per year are dwarfed by the largest reported waste streams: 51.9 mil-

lion pounds of carbon tetrachloride wastes at Du Pont's Deepwater, New Jersey, plant; 17.5 million pounds of chromium wastes at International Flavors and Fragrances' plant in Union Beach, New Jersey; and 15.7 million pounds of phenol wastes at USS Chemicals' Haverhill, Ohio, plant" (108).

The INFORM study concluded that "waste reduction alternatives were seldom considered until circumstances virtually forced plants to review their waste management practices. Recycling, treatment, and disposal options prevailed" (109). Fewer than one quarter of the plants examined (12 of the 79) had made any reductions in wastes generated. At the Borden Chemical Company's Fremont, California, plant, managers first resorted to use of the traditional evaporation pond to meet a more stringent phenol limit in its wastewater discharge. Only when that technique failed did they seriously look at their waste reduction potential. By revising their equipment-rinsing procedures in resin operations, they cut the organic discharge by 93 percent. Eliminating the evaporation pond also reduced the generation of phenolic resin sludge from 350 to 25 cubic yards, saving the company $48,750 per year in disposal costs (110).

In the United States, pioneering pollution prevention research began at the University of North Carolina School of Engineering in 1972. The state of North Carolina now has a $600,000-per-year program to publicize successful pollution prevention efforts. The Institute for Local Self-Reliance in Washington, D.C., also provides technical information to promote waste elimination in urban areas (111). In Europe, a similar effort is conducted by *La Mission Technologies Propres de la Direction de la Prevention des Pollutions du Ministere de l'Environnement* in Paris. The French Government documented examples of industrial waste reductions in *"Les Techniques Propres dans l'Industrie Francaise,"* which has also been translated and published in the United States (112).

The biggest hurdle facing efforts to promote pollution prevention is company reluctance to share information. "Companies are hesitant to (accept) any outreach, whether it's from government or a nonprofit organization," says Roger Schecter, North Carolina's program director, "because they don't know whether the information is going to (result in) increased costs or increased regulations. Uncertainty about the use of the information has made a lot of industries gun-shy" (113). Many companies also argue that the information is proprietary. Yet, as Schecter points out, the 40 companies that participated in the North Carolina Pollution Prevention Pays program in 1985 saved a total of $12 million. Other major constraints to waste reduction are the relatively low costs of raw materials and water (114). What will sell pollution prevention at the source will be the rising costs of waste management and mismanagement. Until now, the costs of pollution control in the United States have amounted to only 1 or 2 percent of total business costs (115). But the 1984 amendments to the U.S. Resource Conservation and Recovery Act are expected to add an estimated 46 percent to industry's compliance costs by 1990.

As mentioned earlier, most Western European nations have made more progress in waste reduction and reuse than North America has. The first waste exchange was established in the Netherlands in 1969 (116), and it now lists 100–150 wastes annually. A waste exchange acts as an information clearinghouse and operates on the principle that one factory's waste can be another's feedstock. The leaders in pollution prevention now are the Federal Republic of Germany, France, the Netherlands, and Sweden (117).

The shift in emphasis from pollution control to pollution prevention, however, will remain uncertain and subtle. Most environmentalists and government officials believe that economic incentives alone will not motivate industries to look for waste reduction opportunities in their operations, at least in the short term. In a survey of how Japan, Canada, Sweden, Denmark, the Federal Republic of Germany, and the Netherlands approach waste reduction, Tufts University researcher Kenneth Geiser found that these governments are aggressive in promoting low- and nonwaste technologies. Sweden, for example, recently established a franchise board that considers waste reduction in issuing operating permits to industries. Denmark and the Netherlands have established competent technical assistance laboratories to work with companies. The Federal Republic of Germany and Norway motivate firms with large cash grants (118).

Yet it is recognized that government interference can stifle the kind of innovation that companies like the 3M Corporation have pioneered (119). As Professor Michael R. Overcash at North Carolina State University notes, "waste elimination is much more a thought process or problem-solving sequence that attempts to go further back into the source of waste" (120). How that process can be hastened remains one of pollution prevention's primary challenges.

Escalating Costs

Because the costs of safe hazardous waste disposal are mounting, waste handling firms—both private and public—are looking for better, cheaper ways to treat and dispose of highly toxic wastes. Without doubt the costs of dealing with industry's hazardous byproducts are rising. In 1983, European countries spent roughly $1.3 billion to dispose of their hazardous wastes (121), and 70 major U.S. industries spent an estimated $4.2–$5.8 billion on hazardous waste management (122).

The environmental costs of not managing hazardous wastes, as witnessed in virtually every industrialized country, are astronomical. And as major generators of hazardous wastes remain liable for past mistakes, economic and regulatory incentives for complying with hazardous waste regulations continue to encourage responsible management.

Transboundary Shipment of Hazardous Wastes

Although in the United States about 96 percent of all hazardous wastes generated each year are treated or disposed of onsite, that is, within factory grounds (123), the transboundary transport of hazardous wastes throughout Europe is a growing, troublesome phenomenon.

It is nearly impossible for countries to keep track of transboundary shipments. "Trip ticket" systems of follow-ing wastes from cradle to grave—like the highly efficient West German system—end at the border (124). Thus it is difficult, if not impossible, for officials to follow the wastes to their final destination, to ensure that the wastes are properly handled and disposed of. Once wastes cross borders, they are also subject to conflicting regulations: what is considered toxic in a given quantity in one country may not be regarded as toxic in another. Although both the European Community (EC) and OECD try to regulate transboundary shipments of hazardous wastes, only the EC has managed to introduce uniform guidelines in its member countries.

But the sheer magnitude of the problem makes management extremely difficult. In 1983, approximately 2.2 million metric tons of hazardous wastes made 100,000 border crossings in Europe (125). That same year (and, on average, every year), about 5,000 international shipments of toxic wastes took place in North America (mostly between the United States and Canada) (126). In OECD countries, a cargo of hazardous wastes crosses a national frontier once every 5 minutes, 24 hours a day, 365 days a year. "Many of these cargoes move across frontiers for reasons which are both sensible and legal," says an OECD official, "but certain crossings occur because controls are inadequate" (127).

The amount of hazardous wastes being shipped internationally is increasing. Between 1982 and 1983, the amount of wastes shipped abroad for final treatment or disposal in another country virtually doubled in OECD Europe (128). Part of the explanation for the increase in transnational shipments is the fact that as legislation tightens in one country, increasing disposal costs, some firms find it cheaper and more convenient to ship their toxic wastes to neighbors whose disposal regulations may be less stringent. For this reason, the market economies of Europe are shipping more wastes to Eastern Europe for final treatment and disposal. In 1983, 200,000–300,000 metric tons of toxic wastes were shipped from West to East for this purpose (129). Nearly all were eventually disposed of on or in land-based sites. By one estimate, the number of such West-East waste transfers is 10,000–20,000 each year (130).

Although most OECD nations regulate imports and exports of hazardous wastes, relatively few regulate hazardous wastes that are merely in transit. Hence, almost anything can pass through most countries, so long as its destination is elsewhere. Even if a country regulates importation of hazardous wastes, its provisions may fail to specify the types of toxic imports that waste firms may accept. In 1986, the OECD Waste Management Policy Group recommended that all OECD members adopt the following principles: 1) competent authorities should be empowered to prohibit waste exports in given cases; 2) wastes should not be exported unless explicit consent of the importing country and the tacit consent of the transit country are available and unless the wastes are directed to an adequate disposal facility; 3) the exporter is sure that the proposed disposal operation can be performed in an environmentally sound manner; and 4) either official contacts with the competent authorities of the importing country should be initiated by the exporter or such contacts should be initiated by the authorities of the exporting countries on the basis of information provided by the exporter (131).

The frequency of transboundary shipments is likely to grow, especially from North to South, as developing countries accept hazardous wastes in return for hard currency or needed industrial hardware. China, for example, reportedly proposed to accept toxic wastes from the Federal Republic of Germany in exchange for heavy machine tools and related equipment (132). The problem, of course, is that the hazardous wastes most likely to be sent to developing countries are those that are considered most toxic and therefore the most costly to handle in their country of origin. Nedlog Technology Group, a U.S. firm, reportedly offered the President of Sierra Leone $25 million for the right to send toxic wastes to his country for disposal, an offer that outraged many African leaders (133). A common fear is that developing countries will import environmental nightmares (134). (A report to be published in late 1987, sponsored by the World Bank, the United Nations Environment Programme, and WHO, reviews hazardous waste management in the Third World; it includes case studies of Mexico, Brazil, Malaysia, Thailand, and South Korea (135).)

CONCLUSION

Public recognition of the dangers of hazardous wastes is relatively recent. The industrialized countries of Europe and North America only began significant regulation of hazardous and toxic wastes during the past 15 years, and most developing countries require little or no controls of such substances. As a result, many countries are living with serious problems from prior uncontrolled dumping practices, while current systems for management of hazardous and toxic waste remain incomplete and incapable of even identifying all hazardous waste.

As discussed, there are a number of fundamental problems involved in hazardous waste management in both developed and developing countries. First, there is no agreement as to what constitutes a hazardous waste: definitions vary greatly from country to country. Moreover, little is known about the amounts of hazardous wastes generated throughout the world. The picture is further complicated by our limited understanding of the health effects of most hazardous wastes and the fact that large numbers of potentially hazardous chemicals are being developed faster than their health risks can be determined.

Management is also hampered by a set of technical and operational problems:
■ a long history of uncontrolled and undocumented dumping;
■ failure of the primary historical disposal method—landfilling—to protect the environment, even when performed under controlled conditions;
■ high costs of and limited facilities for complete destruction of hazardous wastes, and
■ limited technologies (with many still under development) for improved handling, storage, and destruction of such wastes.

In the face of these largely unresolved problems, many European countries have responded with tightly con-

trolled, centralized systems of management and disposal that minimize the amounts of wastes dumped in landfills. But despite safeguards and watchdogs, abuses have not been eliminated. The United States and Canada, on the other hand, have instituted decentralized systems that may encourage more innovative technological solutions but that have not yet contributed to an effective overall management structure. Too much toxic waste is not managed properly and ends up in hazardous waste dumps with inadequate safeguards.

Clearly, national policies regarding hazardous waste management must be improved. With some notable exceptions like the Federal Republic of Germany, Sweden, and Switzerland, most national governments need to devote more resources to identifying and tracking hazardous wastes, developing new technologies and building new facilities for the destruction or recycling of hazardous wastes, and researching the health and environmental effects of exposure to hazardous wastes.

There is also a need for concerted international action to control the transport and final disposal of hazardous wastes. A number of institutional frameworks could be used to initiate an international agreement, but two organizations working together—the U.N. Economic Commission for Europe (ECE) and the United Nations Environment Programme (UNEP)—might spearhead a new offensive against toxic wastes. These two international organizations could begin to initiate comprehensive negotiations aimed at controlling the transboundary transport of hazardous wastes, and to establish international guidelines on types and quantities of wastes regarded as hazardous or toxic. Such guidelines could serve as a model for national legislation, which must become more comparable among countries for real progress to be made towards solving the toxic waste puzzle. So far, efforts have been limited to Western Europe and North America. The umbrella of international negotiations in this field should be extended to cover Eastern Europe and the Soviet Union, the developed countries of Asia and the Pacific, and eventually, the major generators of hazardous wastes in the Third World.

The ECE-UNEP framework has two major advantages: first, the ECE administers the Long-Range Transboundary Air Pollution Convention, which includes provisions to encourage the dissemination and use of low and non-waste technologies that are crucial to reducing the generation of toxic wastes; and second, UNEP is already involved in programs aimed at managing hazardous wastes in the developing world.

As mentioned earlier, another pressing need is for comprehensive data on the health effects of potentially toxic substances. Increased support should be given to the International Register of Potentially Toxic Chemicals (IRPTC), administered by UNEP in Geneva, Switzerland. After nearly a decade of hard work, IRPTC has compiled information on more than 600 hazardous chemical compounds, including known health effects. Much more remains to be done, particularly in encouraging chemical industries to cooperate.

Finally, hazardous waste management must move beyond dumping. Industries everywhere need to be encouraged to generate less hazardous wastes in their manufacturing processes. Although the toxic spigot cannot be turned off entirely, hazardous wastes can be recycled and reused or destroyed. Dumping should not be a policy, but a last resort. Such steps are necessary if the world is to continue to enjoy the benefits of modern technology, while avoiding the consequences of a poisoned environment.

References and Notes

1. H. Jeffrey Leonard, "Hazardous Wastes: The Crisis Spreads," *Asian National Development* (April 1986), p. 36.
2. U.S. National Research Council, *Reducing Hazardous Waste Generation: An Evaluation and a Call for Action* (National Academy Press, Washington, D.C., 1985), p. 8.
3. Michael Suess and Jan Huismans, eds., *Management of Hazardous Waste*, World Health Organization (WHO), Regional Publications, European Series No. 14 (WHO, Copenhagen, 1983), p. 9.
4. Organisation for Economic Co-operation and Development (OECD), *Identification of Responsibilities in Hazardous Waste Management* (OECD, Paris, 1985), p. 15.
5. Selim M. Senkan and Nancy W. Stauffer, "What To Do With Hazardous Waste," *Technology Review*, Vol. 84, No. 2 (1981), pp. 40–41.
6. *Ibid.*, p. 40.
7. U.S. Environmental Protection Agency, Public Affairs Office, 1987 (personal communication).
8. *Op. cit.* 4.
9. *Op. cit.* 5.
10. U.S. Environmental Protection Agency (EPA), *National Survey of Hazardous Waste Generators and Treatment, Storage and Disposal Facilities Regulated Under RCRA in 1981* (EPA, Office of Solid Waste, Washington, D.C., 1984), p. 123.
11. H. Yakowitz, "Some Background Information Concerning Hazardous Waste Management in Non-OECD Countries" (Organisation for Economic Co-operation and Development, unpublished draft, Paris, 1985), pp. 2–3.
12. *Op. cit.* 1, pp. 36–37.
13. U.S. Congress, Office of Technology Assessment, *Serious Reduction of Hazardous Waste* (U.S. Government Printing Office, Washington, D.C., 1986), p. 147.
14. *Ibid.*
15. *Op. cit.* 13, p. 148.
16. Universities Associated for Research and Education in Pathology, Inc., *Health Aspects of the Disposal of Waste Chemicals* (Universities Associated for Research and Education in Pathology, Inc., Bethesda, Maryland, 1985), p. 2.4.
17. "Groundwater: Examining a Resource at Risk," *EPRI Journal*, Vol. 10, No. 8 (1985), p. 10.
18. *Ibid.*, p. 7.
19. *Op. cit.* 16, p. 3.1.
20. *Op. cit.* 16, p. 3.1.
21. Thomas Maugh II, "Just How Hazardous are Dumps?" *Science*, Vol. 215, No. 4532 (1982), p. 491.
22. United Nations Environment Programme (UNEP), *Chemicals: The Toxic Iceberg* (UNEP, press release, Geneva, 1982), pp. 1–5.

23. Arthur C. Upton, "Availability of Toxicological Data on Existing Chemicals," presented at the Seminar on Chemicals Testing and Animal Welfare, Stockholm, May 20–22, 1986, p. 1.
24. Paul Evan Ress, *Chemicals and the Environment* (United Nations Environment Programme, Geneva, 1979), p. 1.
25. Don Hinrichsen, "Europe's Plague of Poisons," *International Wildlife*, Vol. 13, No. 3 (1983), p. 34.
26. Ed Magnuson, "The Poisoning of America," *Time Magazine* (September 22, 1980), p. 58.
27. Peter E. Voytek, "Aspects of Risk Assessment," in *Assessment of Health Effects at Chemical Disaster Sites: Proceedings of a Symposium Held in New York City on June 1–2, 1981 by the Life and Sciences Public Program of the Rockefeller University*, William W. Lowrance, ed., cited in U.S. Congress, *Injuries and Dangers from Hazardous Wastes—Analysis and Improvement of Legal Remedies*, Part 2, Appendices, Serial No. 97-12 (U.S. Government Printing Office, Washington, D.C., 1982), pp. 217–233.
28. National Academy of Sciences/National Research Council, *Toxicity Testing: Strategies to Determine Needs and Priorities* (National Academy Press, Washington, D.C., 1984).
29. *Op. cit.* 23, p. 9.
30. Thomas Maugh II, "Biological Markers for Chemical Exposure," *Science*, Vol. 215, No. 4533 (1982), p. 644.
31. *Op. cit.* 21, p. 492.
32. U.S. Congress, *Injuries and Damages from Hazardous Wastes—Analysis and Improvement of Legal Remedies* (U.S. Government Printing Office, Washington, D.C., 1982), p. J-8.
33. *Ibid.*, p. J-14.
34. *Op. cit.* 32, p. J-7.
35. The Conservation Foundation, *State of the Environment: An Assessment at Mid-Decade* (The Conservation Foundation, Washington, D.C., 1984), p. 80.
36. *Ibid.*
37. *Op. cit.* 35.
38. "Text of EPA Draft 'Son of Superfund' Report," *Inside EPA Weekly Report*, Special Supplement (February 3, 1984), p. 3, cited in The Conservation Foundation, *State of the Environment: An Assessment at Mid-Decade* (The Conservation Foundation, Washington, D.C., 1984), p. 80.
39. *Op. cit.* 26.
40. Benjamin A. Goldman, *et al.*, *Hazardous Waste Management: Reducing the Risk* (Island Press, Washington, D.C., 1986), pp. 23–24.
41. *Op. cit.* 16, p. 3.1.
42. Nigel Haigh, *EEC Environmental Policy*

and Britain: An Essay and a Handbook (Environmental Data Services, Ltd., London, 1984), pp. 129–131.
43. Wendy Barnaby, "Great Britain: Relying on Luck to Avert Disaster," *AMBIO*, Vol. 11, No. 1 (1982), p. 53.
44. For a full account of hazardous wastes in Great Britain, see *Hazardous Waste Disposal* (House of Lords Select Committee on Science and Technology, London, July 28, 1981).
45. Organisation for Economic Co-operation and Development (OECD), *National Legislation and International Rules Applicable to Hazardous Waste Management in OECD Member Countries* 2nd revision (OECD, Paris, 1982), p. 25.
46. *Ibid.*, pp. 5–17.
47. Maurits Groen, "Holland's Toxic Troubles," *AMBIO*, Vol. 13, No. 4 (1984), p. 270.
48. *Op. cit* 43, p. 53.
49. *Op. cit.* 43, p. 54.
50. Robert A. Arnott, *Non-Regulatory Aspects of European Waste Management* (German Marshall Fund of the United States, Washington, D.C., 1984), pp. 5–6.
51. *Ibid.*
52. Julian Josephson, "Implementing Superfund," *Environmental Science and Technology*, Vol. 20, No. 1 (1986), p. 23.
53. U.S. Congress, Congressional Budget Office, Hazardous Waste Management: Recent Changes and Policy Alternatives (U.S. Government Printing Office, Washington, D.C., 1985), p. 32.
54. U.S. Congress, Office of Technology Assessment, *Superfund Strategy* (U.S. Government Printing Office, Washington, D.C., 1985), p. 3.
55. Jane Casler and Stephen Ramsey, *Super fund Handbook* (Environmental Research and Technology, Inc., Chicago, and Sidley & Austin, Concord, Massachusetts, 1985), p. iii.
56. U.S. Environmental Protection Agency, *Federal Register*, Vol. 51, No. 111 (U.S. Government Printing Office, Washington, D.C., June 10, 1986), p. 21099.
57. *Op. cit.* 52, p. 28.
58. Donald L. Rheem, "Superfund Clears Way for Cleanup of Worst Hazardous Waste Sites," *Christian Science Monitor* (October 20, 1986), p. 7.
59. *Ibid.*
60. Michael Weisskopf, "New Standards Set for Superfund Work," *The Washington Post* (August 1, 1986).
61. R.D. Munro, Environmental Consultant, 1983 (personal communication).
62. *Op. cit.* 11, p. 5.
63. *Op. cit.* 53, pp. 21–26.
64. Economic Commission for Europe (ECE), *Current Land Disposal Technologies and Practices for Hazardous Wastes* (ECE,

Geneva, December 1985, draft document), pp. 17–20.

65. Organisation for Economic Co-operation and Development (OECD), *Transfrontier Movements of Hazardous Wastes*, based on a conference held in Basel, Switzerland, March 26–27, 1985 (OECD, Paris, 1985), p. 5.

66. Estimated by Don Hinrichsen, Editor, *World Resources 1987*, from diverse sources.

67. *Op. cit.* 45, pp. 30–32.

68. U.S. Congress, Office of Technology Assessment, *Transportation of Hazardous Materials* (U.S. Government Printing Office, Washington, D.C., July 1986), p. 244.

69. *Ibid.*, p. 241.

70. Michael Paparian, *et al., Integrated Hazardous Waste Systems in the Federal Republic of Germany and Denmark* (California Foundation on the Environment and the Economy, Environmental Defense Fund, and Sierra Club, San Francisco, 1984), p. 13.

71. Bruce Piasecki, "Europe's Detoxification Arsenals: Lessons in Waste Recovery and Exchange," in *Beyond Dumping: New Strategies for Controlling Toxic Contamination*, Bruce Piasecki, ed. (Quorum Books, Westport, Connecticut, 1984), p. 103.

72. *Op. cit.* 50, pp. 10–11.

73. *Op. cit.* 70, p. 15.

74. *Op. cit.* 70, p. 15.

75. *Op. cit.* 70, p. 16.

76. *Op. cit.* 70, p. 23–26.

77. *Op. cit.* 70, p. 26.

78. *Op. cit.* 70, p. 29.

79. U.S. Environmental Protection Agency, *Surface Impoundment Assessment National Report* (Washington, D.C., 1983), cited in U.S. Congress, Congressional Budget Office, *Hazardous Waste Management: Recent Changes and Policy Alternatives* (U.S. Government Printing Office, Washington, D.C., 1985), p. 25.

80. *Ibid.*

81. *Op. cit.* 53, p. 26.

82. *Op. cit.* 53, p. 26.

83. For a complete description of common incineration technologies, see U.S. Congress, Office of Technology Assessment, *Ocean Incineration: Its Role in Managing* (U.S. Government Printing Office, Washington D.C., 1986), pp. 93–98.

84. *Op. cit.* 40, p. 43.

85. *Op. cit.* 83, pp. 198–201.

86. *Op. cit.* 71, p. 105.

87. Marvin Branscome, *Summary Report on Hazardous Waste Combustion in Calcining Kilns* (U.S. Environmental Protection Agency, Cincinnati, Ohio, draft, 1985), p. 23.

88. *Ibid.*, pp. 15–51.

89. Knut Trovaag, *Hazardous Waste Incineration in a Cement Kiln* (Norcem, Slemmestad, Norway, 1986), p. 3.

90. Roger Batstone, Industrial Pollution and Safety Engineer, The World Bank, Office of Environmental and Scientific Affairs, Washington, D.C., 1986 (personal communication).

91. Greenpeace International, "Ocean Incineration" (Greenpeace International, submitted to the London Dumping Convention, October 1986), p. 2.

92. *Op. cit.* 83, p. 163.

93. *Op. cit.* 83, p. 197.

94. *Op. cit.* 83, pp. 195–197.

95. U.S. Congress, Office of Technology Assessment (OTA), *Ocean Incineration: Its Role in Managing Hazardous Waste* (OTA, Washington D.C., 1986), pp. 198–201.

96. John Elkington, *Double Dividends? U.S. Biotechnology and Third World Development* (World Resources Institute, Washington, D.C., 1986), p. 21.

97. Philip H. Abelson, "Treatment of Hazardous Wastes," *Science*, Vol. 233, No. 4763 (1986), p. 509.

98. *Ibid.*

99. *Op. cit.* 96, p. 21.

100. Bruce Piasecki, "Unfouling the Nest: New Detoxification Strategies," in *Beyond Dumping: New Strategies for Controlling Toxic Contamination*, Bruce Piasecki, ed. (Quorum Books, Westport, Connecticut, 1984), p. 148.

101. *Ibid.*

102. *Op. cit.* 100, pp. 145–146.

103. *Op. cit.* 100, p. 146.

104. D. Huisingh, *et al., Proven Profits from Pollution Prevention: Case Studies in Resource Conservation and Waste Reduction* (Institute for Local Self-Reliance, Washington, D.C., 1986), p. 3.

105. T.E. Waddell, "Integrated Waste Management in Europe: A Tentative Assessment" (presented to the German Marshall Fund of the United States, Washington D.C., December 1981), p. 4.

106. *Op. cit.* 53, p. 20.

107. D.J. Sarokin, *et al., Cutting Chemical Wastes* (INFORM, New York, 1985), p. 31.

108. *Ibid.*, p. 146.

109. *Op. cit.* 107, p. 143.

110. *Op. cit.* 107, p. 187.

111. *Op. cit.* 104.

112. M.R. Overcash, *Techniques for Industrial Pollution Prevention* (Lewis Publishers, Chelsea, Michigan, 1986).

113. Rochelle L. Stanfield, "Drowning in Waste," *National Journal*, Vol. 18, No. 19 (1986), p. 1108.

114. *Ibid.*, p. 1109.

115. *Op. cit.* 113, p. 1109.

116. W. Gulevich, "Hazardous Waste Management Programs in Germany, Austria, and Switzerland" (presented to the German Marshall Fund of the United States, Washington, D.C., 1984), p. 3.

117. *Op. cit.* 105, p. 13.

118. K. Geiser, Center for Environmental Management, Tufts University, Medford, Massachusetts, 1986 (personal communication).

119. *Op. cit.* 113, p. 1110.

120. *Op. cit.* 112, p. 11.

121. *Op. cit.* 65, p. 7.

122. *Op. cit.* 53, p. 26.

123. *Op. cit.* 53, p. 26.

124. *Op. cit.* 70, p. 13.

125. *Op. cit.* 65, p. 6.

126. Organisation for Economic Co-operation and Development (OECD), "Update on Activities—The OECD and Waste Management Policy" (OECD, unpublished, Paris, March 1986), p. 3.

127. *Ibid.*

128. *Op. cit.* 65, p. 6.

129. *Op. cit.* 11, p. 3.

130. *Op. cit.* 11, p. 3.

131. Organisation for Economic Co-operation and Development (OECD), *Draft Council Decision and Recommendation on Exports of Hazardous Wastes from the OECD Area* (OECD, Paris, March 28, 1986), p. 2.

132. *Op. cit.* 11, p. 4.

133. Statement of Faith Campbell, in U.S. House of Representatives Committee on Foreign Affairs, Subcommittee on International Economic Policy and Trade, *Export of Hazardous Products*, Hearings, Ninety-sixth Congress, Second Session (U.S. Government Printing Office, Washington, D.C., 1980), p. 23.

134. *Op. cit.* 11, p. 4.

135. The World Bank, United Nations Environment Programme (UNEP), and World Health Organization (WHO), *Hazardous Waste Management in the Third World* (The World Bank/UNEP/WHO, in press, 1987).

14. Elements of Success: Sustainable Development in Sub-Saharan Africa

Sub-Saharan Africa poses the greatest challenge to world development efforts to the end of the century and beyond. Recurrent famine there is only the symptom of much deeper ills. Africa is the only major region where per capita income, food production, and industrial production have declined over an extended period: the only developing region where development appears to be moving in reverse (1).

The environment and agriculture are at the heart of Africa's problems. Some 71 percent of the labor force works in agriculture, and 77 percent of the population lives in rural areas (2). The health, nutrition, and income of the majority, overwhelmingly smallholders, are inseparably linked to the progress of agriculture. In a continent where inputs of fertilizers, irrigation, and new seeds are the lowest in the world, agriculture depends on the health of the environment, and vice versa.

In recent years, Africa's farmers and herders, its soils and forests, have been chasing each other down a vicious spiral of environmental degradation and deepening poverty. Conventional development efforts by donors and governments have largely failed to halt the spiral, indeed in some cases have aggravated it. The need to find solutions is urgent. Africa not only must increase its energy and food output in line with rapidly expanding populations, but must do so in a way that preserves the resource base and enhances the welfare and income of the majority.

Despite the general landscape of failure, a growing number of projects and programs—governmental, intergovernmental, and nongovernmental—have succeeded.

This chapter examines some of those "success stories" and attempts to draw some more general lessons that can point to a "recipe for success" in sub-Saharan Africa.

The focus for selecting case studies of successful projects has been on projects and programs that have long-term potential for restoring and sustaining the natural resources base, have an immediate positive impact on the well-being of individuals and families, and lead to economic growth. These case studies are not the only examples of success in Africa, nor is the concentration on resource management and agricultural development intended to suggest that long-term development of the countries of sub-Saharan Africa won't also require the development of industry, the improvement of governmental services, the reduction of civil strife, and progress on other fronts.

African governments and institutions have been making progress in dealing with these other concerns, reshaping policies and loans, adjusting programs, and developing staff competence. For example, in the face of the food crisis brought on by the most recent drought in 1983–84, some countries, notably Kenya, were successful in anticipating the need for food and implementing the necessary relief programs to avoid starvation (3). However, successful relief programs, while vitally important, do not lead to sustainable development. Similarly, many research efforts are underway in Africa to develop improved staple crops, increased resistance to disease among cattle, etc. The International Centre of Insect Physiology and Ecology in Nairobi has been making good progress in developing various approaches to combatting the tsetse fly, which is so destructive to people and livestock in many parts of Africa. But research programs take a long time to bear fruit and require the widespread transfer of their results to the field before complete success can be achieved.

This chapter focuses directly upon projects and programs that have been implemented successfully in the field.

THE DIMENSIONS OF CRISIS

The population of sub-Saharan Africa is growing faster than ever before, and faster than any other region in history. The current growth rate of 3.2 percent a year is expected to persist until around 2005 before it begins to decline. (See Chapter 2, "Population and Health.")

Total agricultural production has increased, but not fast enough to keep pace with this population growth. The result has been a steady decline in agricultural production per person over almost two decades. In the low-income countries, for example, per capita agricultural production fell by an average of 0.1 percent a year between 1965 and 1973, and by 1.5 percent a year from 1973 to 1984 [4]. Per capita food production in 1982, before the drought, was 11 percent lower than in 1969. In 1983 and 1984 it was 16 percent lower [5]. The result has been a steadily increasing dependence on food imports: cereal imports in sub-Saharan Africa rose by 155 percent in the decade from 1974, food aid by 185 percent [6]. (See Chapter 4, "Food and Agriculture," Figure 4.2.)

An emphasis on growing cash crops for export is often blamed for the decline in food production per person in Africa, but in fact, per capita cash crop production as a whole has dropped by more than per capita food production. Between 1971 and 1984, while food production grew by 2 percent a year, production of cash crops (coffee, cocoa, tea, fibers, tobacco, rubber, and wool) remained stable. (For an extensive discussion of cash and food crops, see Chapter 4, "Food and Agriculture.")

Since the overwhelming majority of Africans are small farmers, these trends have meant a steady decline in family incomes and a rise in the number of people in poverty. Between 1973 and 1984, per capita Gross Domestic Product fell by an average of 0.9 percent a year in the low-income countries, and by 1.4 percent a year in the middle-income countries [7]. The International Labour Organisation estimates that the number of people in absolute poverty in Africa rose from 205 million in 1974 to 258 million in 1982 [8]. The number of acutely malnourished people showed a steady rise, from 81 million in 1969-71 to 99 million in 1979-81, before the latest famine brought about by the drought of 1983-84 [9].

The Debt Crisis

Now that the immediate threat of major famine has receded from most of Africa, the financial crisis is a more serious short-term hazard, jeopardizing development efforts. The crisis has grown out of the structural weakness of the African economy and its dependence on primary commodities with fluctuating prices, most of which

have declined in real value over the last two decades. (See Chapter 4, "Food and Agriculture.") Between 1973 and 1984, of 25 commodities exported by African countries, only 8 saw even a nominal price increase, and the volume of exports increased for only 5 [10]. The terms of trade worsened over the 1970–84 period for no fewer than 17 of 22 non-oil exporters [11]. Total debt more than doubled from $38.5 billion in 1978 to nearly $80 billion in 1984. The cost of servicing the debt took a mounting share of foreign exchange earnings from exports, rising from a mere 8 percent in 1979 to 22 percent in 1984, and an estimated 33 percent in 1985 [12].

Total net flows of resources slumped, at the time of Africa's greatest need, from $8.2 billion in 1982, to only $2.75 billion two years later. Aid stagnated at $6.9–$7.3 billion while net private flows, which had brought in $4.2 billion in 1982, turned negative and took out $480 million in 1984 [13].

The financial crunch hit government budgets hard—37 of 42 African governments cut their per capita expenditures between 1980 and 1983 [14]. As jobs were politically hard to prune, cuts were often made in the hardware: school supplies, medicines, and spare parts for vehicles and water installations. The effectiveness of government services, from agriculture to education and health, has been drastically curtailed [15].

The Environmental Crisis

Most ominous of all is the environmental crisis, which threatens to perpetuate and deepen Africa's other problems.

Assessments of its extent can only be approximate. The United Nations Food and Agriculture Organization (FAO) reports that Africa's 703 million hectares of undisturbed forests in 1980 were being cleared at the rate of 3.7 million hectares a year—or 0.6 percent. Local rates ranged from 0.2 percent for the vast Cameroon-Congolese forest up to 4 percent a year in West Africa. Deforestation outstripped the rate of new tree planting, which was only 126,000 hectares per year, by 29 to 1 [16]. At the same time, 55 million Africans faced acute scarcity of fuelwood [17]. (See *World Resources 1986*, "Energy," pp. 111-113.)

Desertification affects primarily Africa's drylands. An assessment for 1983 suggests that in these areas 80–90 percent of the rangelands, 80 percent of the rainfed croplands and 30 percent of the irrigated land may be affected at least moderately. Of the dryland population of 118.5 million, 92 million lived in areas affected by desertification, 52.5 million of them in severely affected areas [18].

Soil erosion is widespread in all areas of sub-Saharan Africa. It is perhaps most serious in Ethiopia, where topsoil losses of up to 296 metric tons per hectare have been reported on 16-percent slopes, but even moderate slopes can erode rapidly when unprotected by vegetation. In West Africa per hectare losses of 10–21 metric tons have been reported on slopes as gentle as 0.4–0.8 percent, and of 30–55 metric tons on 1–2 percent slopes [19]. Wind erosion, significant in drier areas, can of course affect even flat land. Even more serious in the medium term is the gradual decline in fertility of all types of land.

Whatever the precise extent of these developments, it is clear that in almost all sub-Saharan countries the long-term capacity of the land to support population is being reduced at the same time the continent faces three decades of its most rapid population growth ever.

THE BACKGROUND TO CRISIS

Africa's environment has never been an easy one for agriculture. It shares with other tropical regions the problems of rain that falls predominantly in erosive downpours, the stress of dry seasons on vegetation, the high temperatures that accelerate the decomposition of organic matter, and the absence of a cold winter to kill off pests and diseases. But Africa has additional obstacles of particular severity. The continent's soil resources are poor. Outside the fertile soils of mountainous East Africa, most African soils are derived from ancient weathered rocks, highly leached, low in nutrients, and with a lower clay content than in most other major regions [20]. As a result, fertility and water-holding capacity are both lower. Only 19 percent of Africa's soils have no inherent fertility limitations [21] while 55 percent have severe or very severe soil constraints [22]. (See Figure 14.1.) The low clay and organic matter content makes many soils highly susceptible to erosion or to crusting once their cover of vegetation is removed.

The climate is problematic. Outside the humid zones, rainfall is highly variable from year to year—by 20 percent to 40 percent up or down from the mean each year. (See Figure 14.2.) The risk of more prolonged droughts is also high. Two thirds of the land area faces high or very high risk of drought, with the probability of two or more successive dry years occurring more than four times in a 50-year period [23]. The Sahel faces the additional problem of unusually wet or dry periods persisting for one or two decades. Even within years of "normal" rainfall the rains are spotty, and dry spells lasting weeks can come along unpredictably at key times in crop growth cycles [24]. (See *World Resources 1986*, pp. 124–127.)

Africa's farmers developed traditional crop-growing methods adapted to the continent's difficult circumstances. The primary adaptation was the system of shifting cultivation. After a year or two of cropping, the plot was left to revert to bush and forest. In the fallow period, nitrogen and organic matter were restored. Trees and shrubs lifted other leached nutrients from lower soil depths and deposited them on the surface with leaf fall, while vegetation cover protected against wind and rain erosion. Fallow areas also provided grazing and fuelwood and many other forest products [25].

On the cropped area, the simplicity of traditional hand tools ensured that tree roots were left in and that soil was not deeply disturbed. Intercropping was almost universal, often involving complex patterns of association, providing more protection against erosion and moisture stress than monocropping [26].

Shifting cultivation depends for its stability on abundant land. As Africa's population has grown, making increasing demands on available land, fallow periods have gradually been reduced in many areas to the point

Figure 14.1 Soil and Climate Constraints

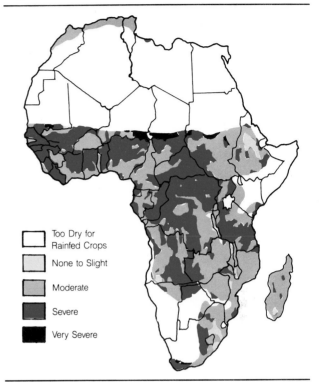

☐	Too Dry for Rainfed Crops
☐	None to Slight
▨	Moderate
▨	Severe
■	Very Severe

Source: Paul Harrison, *The Greening of Africa* (Penguin Books, New York and Paladin Books, London, in press). Data taken from United Nations Environment Programme (UNEP) *Map of Desertification Hazards* (UNEP, Nairobe, 1984) and United Nations Food and Agriculture Organization (FAO), "Report on the Agro-Ecological Zones Project," Vol. 1 of the *World Soil Resources Report*, No. 48 (FAO, Rome, 1978), p. 107.

where they are no longer sufficient to restore fertility or to provide adequate grazing or fuelwood. In other regions where shifting cultivation used to be practiced, a gradual change in technology and an increase in inputs have compensated for declining fallow periods [27]. In some parts of Africa—Nigeria's humid Southeast, the East African highlands—considerable intensification of agriculture has occurred under the pressure of high population density. Elsewhere there has been some intensification, such as the gradual adoption of improved traditional varieties, and the increasing use of valley bottom lands with hand-dug wells, and so on [28]. But over most of Africa the increases in inputs and conservation measures have not kept pace with rising population densities.

In many countries, crop yields are stagnant or declining, fallow and farmland are overgrazed, and fuelwood needs are met by depleting the stock rather than by replanting. Vegetation cover is weakened, erosion accelerates. topsoil is irrevocably lost. Why has Africa not intensified fast enough to avoid the makings of ecological catastrophe?

Other environmental factors are partly responsible for blocking the routes to intensification followed by Europe and Asia. For example, trypanosomiasis, the parasitic livestock disease carried by the tsetse fly, has blocked the development of mixed arable and livestock farming over the 10 million square kilometers affected. (See Figure 14.3.) It has virtually banned large draft livestock from

Figure 14.2 Interannual Variability of Rainfall

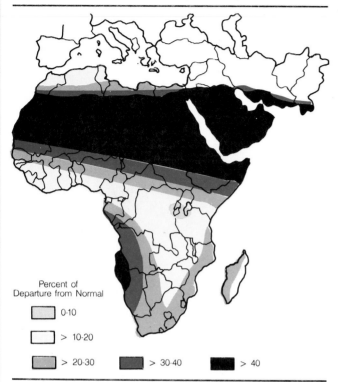

Percent of
Departure from Normal

- 0-10
- > 10-20
- > 20-30
- > 30-40
- > 40

Source: A. K. Biswas, "Climate and Water Resources," in *Climate and Development*, Vol. 13,
A. K. Biswas, ed., (Tycooly International Publishing Ltd. 1984).

the humid areas, and enforced the separation of cattle and agriculture during the rainy season in the subhumid and much of the semi-arid zones (29).

This separation has also contributed to Africa's peculiar labor shortage: human labor accounts for 84 percent of power inputs to agriculture in Africa, against only 66 percent in the Far East and 56 percent in Latin America (30). The labor shortage is intensified by male migration for work and the sexual division of labor—women produce an estimated 70 percent of subsistence foods in sub-Saharan Africa, as well as performing the onerous tasks of water- and wood-fetching along with child care, cooking, and so on (31). This labor shortage leads to late planting, late weeding and lost yields—and poses obstacles to labor-intensive conservation methods.

The unavailability of water resources probably hindered the emergence of extensive pre-modern irrigation schemes. Because of its generally flat topography, Africa has less surface water than other regions, and groundwater is often deep and difficult to obtain (32).

But human factors are equally to blame for the lag in intensification. One of these has been general uncertainty over ownership of land, forests, and rangelands in Africa. Communal control was traditionally the norm, but this is phasing gradually into *de facto* individual control, often inheritable and in some places saleable. However, since colonial times *legal* ownership of land, forests, and pastures in most countries has been vested in the government.

Equally significant have been the governmental policies of most African countries. Investment in agriculture has been low. State procurement agencies have paid generally low prices for food crops to provide cheap food for the cities, or they have siphoned off a high percentage of cash crop receipts as disguised taxation. Exchange rates have been kept artificially high. This has depressed the earnings in local currencies for export crops and made food imports artificially cheap, depressing the market price for home-grown food crops, like millet and sorghum, and shifting urban tastes to wheat and rice, which are costly or impossible to grow in most of Africa.

African farmers thus have had no incentive to increase their output of either cash crops or food crops. They have been starved of the cash earnings with which to make investments in purchased inputs, from fertilizer to better seeds or tools. At the same time, low prices have not made it worthwhile to invest in extra labor in home-produced inputs, from compost to conservation works. Low producer prices have perpetuated low-input farming and discouraged investment in protection of the natural resource base (33).

A Catalog of Failures

Government and aid interventions have been less successful in Africa than anywhere else. Africa has the highest failure rate in World Bank projects. A review of 994 World Bank projects evaluated at completion between 1974 and 1984 found that a global average of 14 percent

Figure 14.3 Zones Affected by Trypanosomiasis

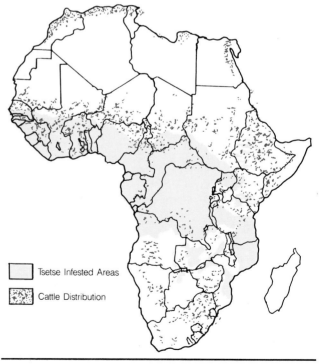

- Tsetse Infested Areas
- Cattle Distribution

Source: United Nations Food and Agriculture Organization (FAO), *Crisis of Sustainability: Africa's Land Resource Base* (FAO, Rome, 1985), p 57.

failed to achieve their objectives; in West Africa the failure rate was 18 percent, and in East Africa 24 percent. Agriculture had the worst performance of any sector, with failure rates of 30 percent in West Africa and no less than 51 percent in East Africa, against only 5 percent in South Asia (34).

The long-term performance of African projects may be even worse. The World Bank followed up 17 African agricultural projects five to ten years after completion. Thirteen of these projects had not sustained their benefits, and their average rate of return was only 2.7 percent (35). The record of decline in per capita agricultural and industrial output and incomes is clear evidence that government and donor projects and programs of all kinds have failed on a grand scale.

The policy environment—low producer prices and insecure tenure—was a major source of failure. But project design was often faulty in three major respects. First, projects frequently ignored Africa's environmental realities, e.g., pushing monocropping instead of intercropping, and fostering tractor plowing or machine clearing methods on soils that should have been disturbed as little as possible.

Second, failed projects often ignored the realities of life of African farmers, who work under a number of constraints. The most decisive of these, in addition to the traditional culture, society, economy, and technology, are shortages of cash and labor, and reluctance to take on any avoidable risk. Yet projects have regularly been launched that demand high labor inputs or high cash outlays, that involve radical changes in many spheres of life simultaneously, or that risk lower returns, in bad years, than the farmers' own practices.

The third major failing has been a tendency to ignore the economic and managerial realities of African governments, and to design projects that involved high recurrent costs, high imports, or high levels of expert or government input. As soon as the donor financing ceased and the national government had to take over, such projects became vulnerable to the import and public spending cuts that inevitably accompany Africa's endemic foreign exchange and budget crises, the breakdown of vehicles and equipment, or the shortage of skilled manpower (36).

THE RESPONSE

The task facing Africa now is threefold. Africa must increase its food output and possibly its output of cash crops as well; it must improve the incomes of the rural majority, so as to reduce poverty and malnutrition; and must do both in a way that is sustainable, conserves or enhances the resource base, and halts or reverses the processes of degradation. Production, distribution, and conservation must be pursued simultaneously. Africa's unique agrarian situation makes this possible, for in most of Africa land is more equally distributed than in most developing regions: smallholders make up the vast majority of farmers, and also control most of the land. Small African farmers and herders are the chief producers of food, mainly for their own consumption, as well as the chief custodians of the environment for good or ill. Thus only a strategy that includes a major focus

on the small producer can hope to solve the production, distribution, and conservation problems.

Despite the general background of failure, some agricultural and environmental projects have succeeded—in some cases spectacularly—and a number of promising technologies have emerged that could solve these three central problems simultaneously.

BUILDING SUSTAINABLE AGRICULTURE

An increasing number of countries have begun to implement policies to raise producer prices—often resulting in a swift response in increased output. They include Tanzania, Mauritania, Zaire, and Guinea. Ghana tripled the price of maize in 1983 and effected large devaluations in 1984–85. As a result, maize production in 1984 tripled over that of 1983, and was two thirds above pre-drought levels. In 1984 Zambia raised the official price of maize by 12 percent in real terms after substantial devaluations. The amount of maize marketed rose by an estimated 55 percent during 1984–85 and came close to meeting Zambia's needs for the first time since 1976 (37).

Case Study: Zimbabwe's Maize Miracle

Perhaps the most dramatic transformation in African agriculture has occurred among Zimbabwe's black farmers since the country achieved independence in 1980 (38). (See Photo 14.1.)

Under the former regime, white farmers got preferential prices for their maize, and preferential access to credit and extension advice. In 1979 they were getting maize yields of 5–6 metric tons a hectare—on a par with Canada or France. By contrast, the neglected communal farmers were getting a meager 0.6–0.7 metric tons per hectare—well below the African average of 0.9 metric tons.

The turnaround after independence in 1980 was dramatic. By 1985 average maize yields among black farmers had doubled, and yields of 2.5–4 metric tons per hectare were not unusual in the more favored regions. The black farmers harvested nearly 1.8 million metric tons of maize in 1985—more than three times the 1978 total. Zimbabwe's maize depots were overflowing, and the country had a surplus of around 1 million metric tons for export.

Zimbabwe's success was based on a comprehensive national government program aimed at small farmers. A package of inputs was formulated for the major zones; for maize in the higher potential zones, this included a massive dose of 500 kilograms of fertilizer per hectare, seed-dressing, and high-yielding seed varieties. The total cost for the higher potential areas was relatively high—Zimbabwe $226 (US$150) per hectare in 1985—but it was covered by credit, repayable from the crop proceeds (since the farmers had no land titles as collateral). The Agricultural Finance Corporation increased loans to black small farmers from a mere 4,400 in 1979–80 to 96,000 in 1985–86.

The credit repayment arrangements reduced the risk element for farmers, as did the use of a mixture of early- and medium-maturing maize varieties that would yield

Elements of Success

Photo 14.1. *Zimbabwe's maize miracle: Farmer Gerry Guyo (left) with his record maize harvest of 10 metric tons per hectare, 1985.*

<small>Photo by Paul Harrison</small>

something even in drier years. The high returns made the risk worthwhile. The package brought yield increases of 2–3 metric tons per hectare, worth Zimbabwe $360–$540 (U.S.$239–$358) at the 1985 price—a return of 60–140 percent on the investment. Maize prices were increased steeply after 1980; by 1981 they were up 57 percent in real terms compared to 1979. An extensive system of grain depots and collecting points made sure that farmers could get their produce to market.

The rural labor shortage is acute in Zimbabwe, due to male labor migration to mines and cities. The problem is being overcome by the creation of farmers' groups that work collectively, pooling their tools and their draft animals, reducing time wasted in individual visits to distant towns, in meal preparation, or in livestock herding.

Zimbabwe's high-input approach is economically sustainable, since the country produces its own high-yielding seeds and fertilizers. The program does not yet place sufficient emphasis on conservation, and has not yet developed a suitable package for dryland farmers. But it demonstrates dramatically the speed with which African farmers can adapt, and their capacity to feed themselves and their countries given adequate incentives.

A Green Revolution for Africa

Asia's Green Revolution, like Zimbabwe's success with maize, was based on a combination of high-yielding vari-

eties and increased inputs of fertilizer, pesticides, and management. All of Africa needs a Green Revolution just as urgently as Asia did, but the obstacles are higher. Africa's special environmental constraints mean that new varieties and practices must be developed to meet much more demanding and locally varied conditions. However, most African research programs have bred varieties at agricultural stations with superior soil and water conditions, good management, high fertilizer input, and monocropping. Most high-yielding varieties so far developed, therefore, are ill-adapted to the more common conditions of poor soils, labor shortage, low inputs, and intercropping. As an economist from the International Crops Research Institute for the Semi-Arid Tropics (ICRISAT) has remarked, on-farm test results average 40–60 percent worse than on-station results for the same input levels, and many "high-yielding" varieties perform worse than the farmers' own varieties under the farmers' actual conditions (39).

A new agenda is emerging for crop breeding programs. The aim is to develop new varieties that do at least as well as existing varieties under the worst conditions of drought, normal dry spells, disease incidence, soil constraints, and poor management and that are more capable than local varieties of responding to increasing inputs. Finally, the new varieties must be in keeping with farmers' priorities. In the semi-arid areas, for example, grain yield is not the sole consideration for cereal crops and cowpeas; stalk yield is also valued as fodder, roofing material, or fuel. In most areas new varieties must also be suitable for the main intercropping patterns.

In countries without adequate infrastructure or market networks, emphasis should at first be placed on open-pollinated varieties, which can be re-used for four years before showing much yield loss (40). Hybrid varieties, which offer higher yields than open-pollinated varieties but must be replaced each year, can be introduced at a later stage when the necessary supply networks are in place.

Case Study: High-Yielding Cassava

Perhaps the most promising low-input plant breeding program in Africa to date has been the root and tuber program at the International Institute of Tropical Agriculture (IITA), in Ibadan, Nigeria, which works with cassava, yams, and sweet potatoes.

The key to the program's success is that it selects its varieties under no-input conditions, without fertilizers, pesticides, or fungicides, and tests them on farms in areas with serious soil or disease problems.

This approach guarantees that new varieties are adapted to local conditions, and has paid handsome results. IITA has developed cassava varieties that are resistant to the major diseases, including cassava bacterial blight and mosaic virus. Five or more of these varieties are now in wide use in Nigeria, covering an estimated 200,000 hectares by 1983 (41). By 1985 they were estimated to cover 20 percent of the cassava area in Oyo state, tripling their area each year (42). The spread has been spontaneous, with farmers passing planting material on to neighbors.

The reasons for the rapid spread are clear. The new IITA varieties yield 50–300 percent more than local varieties, yet require no purchased inputs. Their yield is more reliable from year to year, since they are less susceptible to disease outbreaks. In addition, because they are bushier and thus shade the soil more, the new varieties reduce weeding labor (30 percent of total labor input) by two-thirds (43). They mature in 8 months instead of 12, yet can be left in the ground as a famine reserve.

Sweet potatoes may offer the next big breakthrough. Varieties developed at IITA are capable of massive yields of 14–18 metric tons per hectare in only four months, two or three times better than local varieties, (44) and up to 45–54 metric tons with good soil and management.

New varieties of other crops are beginning to spread widely enough to make an impact. Improved varieties of cowpea have been widely adopted in northern Nigeria (45). Improved maize varieties have been spreading in highland East Africa since the 1960s (46), while lowland varieties were released in Nigeria in 1975 and by 1983 covered 200,000 hectares (47). Improved sorghum is spreading rapidly in Sudan. For millet, the crop of the driest farming areas, however, no new varieties have yet been identified that perform better than local varieties under farm conditions (48).

Solving the Soil Fertility Problem

Improved varieties can offer yield increases with no extra inputs, especially in root crops and legumes, thanks to

improved disease resistance, plant architecture, and so on. But in the longer run, higher yields, particularly of cereals, can be sustained only with higher inputs of plant nutrients. This requirement must reckon with the inherently low fertility of Africa's agricultural soils.

The conventional path to increased inputs is fraught with difficulties in Africa. Farmers' cash reserves to buy inputs are low, and supply networks, whether public or private, are often underdeveloped. In many areas, especially in semi-arid zones, application of nitrogenous fertilizers is economically risky and may have damaging long-term effects, such as soil acidification, potassium deficiency, and aluminum toxicity (49).

Moderate use of phosphate—frequently deficient in African soils—is more promising. It can have a dramatic effect on yields, especially in the semi-arid regions. Research at ICRISAT's Sahelian Centre at Niamey, Niger, has found that as little as 15 kilograms of triple super-phosphate per hectare can boost millet yields by 100 percent, while the cheaper partly acidulated rock phosphate can give yield increases of 60 percent (50). In drier years the effects are greater. ICRISAT's test farmers were so impressed with the results after trying out phosphates on 5 percent of their land that they expanded their use to 60 percent, arranging their own supplies through a trader (51).

But for the near future, most increased inputs into African farming will have to be organic—from manure, crop residues, and nitrogen fixed by legumes. Organic inputs offer not only valuable yield improvements, but also reduce erosion and vulnerability to drought. They offer a simultaneous answer to the problems of production, conservation, and risk minimization. They continue to offer these advantages even when chemical fertilizers are later added, and must remain the foundation of agriculture in Africa.

Crop residues left in the field after harvest or applied as mulch can improve yields by 50–60 percent in humid areas (52) and by 80 percent in semi-arid areas (53). They also reduce soil erosion and runoff, and improve soil water-holding capacity and structure. On a 10-percent slope at Ibadan, for example, 6 metric tons of mulch per hectare cut soil loss from 27 to 0.03 metric tons per hectare (54). Because it improves water infiltration and soil moisture levels, mulching also offers better stability of yield through drought and dry spells. Mulch availability is high in humid areas, but in semi-arid areas crop residues are in high demand as fodder, fuel, and roofing materials; agroforestry (see below) will have to supply some of these needs before crop residues can be freed for mulching.

Use of legumes in intercrops and rotations is a source of additional nitrogen for associated or following crops. Intercropping generally offers significant advantages over monocropping in sub-Saharan Africa: higher total yield, more stable yield in drier years, reduced erosion, reduced runoff, more even labor distribution (55).

Conserving the Soil

Soil degradation is the most serious ongoing threat to improving productivity on a sustained basis. The loss of topsoil removes, preferentially, the layers richest in organic matter and nutrients. Soil depth and, therefore, often plant rooting depth are reduced. For example, in Nigeria, it has been estimated that a loss of 3 centimeters of topsoil cuts crop yields by 40-50 percent (56). Soil degradation also increases vulnerability to drought, since the reduction in organic matter cuts the soil's water-holding capacity, and plants with shallower roots resist dry spells less well. The more extreme forms of degradation, crusting, gullies, and sand dune encroachment, completely remove land from production even for pasture.

Yet efforts at soil conservation in Africa have been scattered and generally weak. Techniques and structures have often been designed by outside experts and executed by machinery, resulting in high cost and poor maintenance. They have focused on physical structures, and have ignored costs in lost food production or excess labor (57).

Case Study: Kenya's National Soil Program

Kenya's national soil conservation program, partly funded by the Swedish International Development Agency (SIDA), is generally regarded as one of the most successful in Africa. The program began in 1974 and by 1984 had terraced no fewer than 365,000 farms—two out of every five—regularly over-fulfilling its annual targets. In 1983–84 alone, 65,000 farms were terraced—46 percent more than the target (58).

A powerful factor in this success was that the techniques used were developed after extensive research into farmers' problems, felt needs, and existing techniques, which identified several effective traditional methods and perfected them with farmers.

The resulting methods could be executed with simple hand tools, at little or no cash cost to the farmer, and with labor costs kept low. Three main methods were spread: in *fanya juu*, or "work-up" terraces, a narrow trench is dug out and the soil thrown uphill to form a ridge. With trash lines, farm refuse is piled into lines along the contour. In both these systems, nature does the bulk of the work: as soil is washed downhill, it collects against the ridge or trash line, and level terraces form automatically. Grassed strips are also used (59).

Participation by farmers keeps the cost to government low, around $30 per farm terraced in 1983–84 (60), and increases farmers' commitment to maintenance. Terrace and drain layouts are planned by local agricultural extension workers. Local farmers do the work without payment, except for certain communal works like cutoff drains. In many areas the bulk of the work is done by women's groups; as in Zimbabwe, group work greatly increases labor productivity.

Tenure laws in Kenya help: most land is individually owned, so farmers know that they and their children will reap the long-term benefits of soil conservation. But the main attraction to farmers is the short-term economic benefit—investments are recouped within one year on moderate slopes in drier areas. A SIDA evaluation indicates that labor requirements are lower on flatter, terraced land than on slopes. Conservation works may boost crop yields by 30–65 percent, improve farm gross margins by 66–104 percent, and increase returns to labor by 39 percent (61) (62).

These gains point to a factor that should become the foundation of all soil conservation efforts in Africa. All conservation works and conserving cultivation practices slow runoff and increase infiltration. Therefore soil conservation also conserves water, reduces the loss of nutrients, and boosts crop yields even without purchased inputs; it is one of the most promising lines for low-cost intensification open to Africa.

Water Conservation

Water conservation and control are crucial to ensuring maximum output in all tropical zones with alternating wet and dry seasons—all the more so in sub-Saharan Africa where variable rainfall can bring weeks and sometimes years of low rainfall everywhere except the humid zone.

Africa therefore has a pressing need for controlled water supplies that can be used to even out climatic fluctuations. Yet irrigation is not well developed in Africa. Even when traditional systems are included, only 3 percent of the cultivated area of sub-Saharan Africa is irrigated, and more than half the irrigated area is in just two countries, Sudan and Madagascar (63). Africa's generally flat terrain, the shortage of surface or shallow groundwaters, the high seasonal variation of rivers, and the lack of infrastructure have all conspired to push the price of irrigation in Africa to around double its level in other continents. Yields often fall below the high levels needed to justify the investment costs of $5,000 to $25,000 per hectare (64). Large-scale schemes with centralized management have removed the autonomy of the individual farmer and sought to impose totally unfamiliar crops and cultivation methods (65).

The failure rate has been so high that by 1985 the World Bank had ceased to lend for new large-scale networks, and concentrated instead on rehabilitation of existing projects and small-scale projects. The emphasis is shifting onto low-cost ventures developing localized sources of water—small dams, cheap wells, and valley bottoms where water tables are close to the surface—in other words, sources that can be controlled by the individual farmer or small group and used to complement existing agricultural methods. Projects of this kind include Lutheran World Relief's dry-season gardens in Niger, with cheap wells irrigating plots surrounded by living fences of leguminous shrubs like *Prosopis juliflora*—which are useful for fodder and fuelwood (66). Other projects include the irrigation component of the World Bank's massive Kano Agricultural Development Project in northern Nigeria, which is using cheap tube wells, petrol pumps costing $500-$700 each, and washbores, metal screens inserted in a sandy river bed in the dry season to filter and extract subsurface water. These investments allow farmers to increase the area they irrigate by 15 times compared with traditional hand-operated *shadoofs*. Costs are recouped in a single season, with returns of 400 percent and more. Labor requirements per hectare are considerably reduced, and traditional cultivation methods are improved rather than supplanted (67).

Improving the water economy of rainfed agriculture is even more important than irrigation in Africa. This means increasing the share of rainfall that filters into the soil rather than running off. Methods to do that include water harvesting, water spreading, stone lines, soil conservation works, and increased vegetation cover. It means reducing moisture loss by using windbreaks and mulches. It also means encouraging deeper rooting by breeding and the use of phosphate fertilizers.

Case Study: Stone Lines in the Yatenga

One of the most impressive projects in Africa is Oxfam's water conservation project in the Yatenga plateau of Burkina Faso. The project began in 1979, aiming to introduce water harvesting techniques for tree planting. But local people were reluctant to divert land and labor from food production, or risk dry-season water needed for drinking (68).

Oxfam project director Peter Wright bowed to local priorities of improving food production. He focused on a traditional local technique: placing lines of stones across slopes to slow down runoff. He found that if the lines were exactly aligned with contours, they dammed water uphill and gave it time to infiltrate. However, as slopes were gentle—1 or 2 percent—local farmers had no way to determine the contour lines. Wright developed a $6 device: a transparent hose, 10–20 meters long, fixed at each end to stakes marked at half-centimeter intervals, and filled with water. When the bottoms of the two stakes are level, the water comes up to the same mark on each one. Farmers can be trained in one or two days to lay out contours on their own or neighbors' land. Once trained and supplied with the inexpensive level, they can make the lines with no further outside assistance.

The stone lines can be made during the dry season, so no labor is lost from food production. They take up only 1–2 percent of the cropland, yet boost crop yields by an average of 50 percent (69). The yield advantage is greater in drier years, so the lines reduce vulnerability to drought. They help to replenish sinking water tables. Perhaps the most remarkable feature is that they can regenerate the barren, crusted wasteland that now covers an estimated 15 percent of the Yatenga, as soil, organic matter, and seeds collect uphill and plants begin to grow again.

Not surprisingly, the lines have spread rapidly, both through Oxfam's training program and through the Naam movement, a network of self-help village cooperatives. As farmers still demand the evidence of their own eyes before adopting them, the time taken by the demonstration effect appears to be the only limit to the speed of their spread.

REFORESTING AFRICA

Trees play a crucial role in Africa's ecology. Along with most other types of vegetation, trees protect the soil against the erosive power of tropical rains, and of winds in the semi-arid areas; they aid infiltration and increase soil organic matter; and they may even stimulate cloud formation and rainfall.

Africa's low-fertility soils give trees a further essential role: through leaf fall they restore to the surface nutrients that have been leached down. This recycling is essential for the stability of African ecosystems, and is exploited in traditional shifting cultivation. Trees that regenerate in the fallow period restore nutrients depleted in the cropping period. In addition, areas of natural forest and tree fallow are the principal sources of wood and fodder, as well as of berries, leaves, fruits and nuts for food; of fibers and medicines; and of famine foods in time of drought.

Natural forest is under threat, primarily because of the expansion of farmed land and degradation on the fringes of the farmed area, due mainly to overgrazing. Tree fallows are also dwindling as fallow periods are whittled down and trees have insufficient time to re-establish themselves.

The conventional means of dealing with the problem of deforestation—professional forest management and plantations—have met with little success. Under-staffing, introduction of ill-suited exotics, and exclusion or even expropriation of local populations have all played their part. Even if every conventional forestry project could be made a success, the size of the task ahead makes this approach unrealistic. In 1985, according to FAO estimates, there were only 1.7 million hectares of managed natural forest and 2.4 million hectares of plantations—against a massive 683 million hectares of unmanaged natural forest plus another 178 million hectares of tree fallows (70). Unmanaged tree resources outnumber managed by more than 200 to 1.

This challenge can be met only by recognizing the inescapable fact that Africa's farmers are its de facto foresters, for ill perhaps at present, but potentially for good.

Two main strategies offer hope of reversing deforestation and forest degradation speedily, cheaply, and to the benefit of the rural majority: one is the management of natural forest with local participation, the other is the establishment of trees on cropland.

The Management of Natural Forest

The forestry laws of colonial powers—so often preserved by independent governments—nationalized most of the natural forest and sought to exclude people from their traditional rights. The people, in turn, reasserted their rights by uncontrolled grazing, tree felling, and encroachment. Most forestry efforts, by excluding local people, turned them into enemies.

Yet these same people can be transformed into an army of allies if traditional rights to manage the forest and enjoy its benefits are restored—this time under professional guidance and supervision to ensure enhanced productivity (71).

Case Study: The Guesselbodi Forest, Niger

The Forestry and Land Use Planning project (FLUP) in Niger, financed by the U.S. Agency for International Development (U.S. AID), is pioneering the rehabilitation of a degraded natural forest at Guesselbodi, 25 kilometers east of Niamey (72).

Guesselbodi has been a national forest reserve since 1948, but state protection has been powerless to prevent degradation. Colonial armies, encroaching farmers, years of low rainfall, two severe droughts, and overgrazing by local and nomadic livestock reduced the forest cover by 40 to 60 percent between 1950 and 1979. Most of the topsoil had been washed away, and many patches were crusted and barren.

The FLUP project aims to develop a complete inventory of Niger's forest resources, products and markets, along with a package of techniques for sustainable management of the natural forest. These are being developed at several pilot sites, of which Guesselbodi is the most advanced. After a detailed survey of soils, topography, vegetation and local use of the forest, a research and management plan was devised in 1983.

The idea was to test simple, small-scale, low-cost rehabilitation measures that could be carried out by villagers. The first plots were covered with water harvesting and water spreading structures: microbasins, earth banks, stone lines, rock dams to divert flash floods from gullies onto slopes. The earth banks and lines are already collecting soil, leaves, and seeds and local tree species are regenerating spontaneously. Perhaps the simplest and most spectacular regeneration technique on crusted areas is a mulch of twigs and small branches—of the kind that would be left over after extraction of saleable branches for firewood. The brushwood accumulates soil, sand, organic materials, and seeds, but also lowers soil temperature, protects against raindrop impact, and attracts termites, which aerate the soil. In the first year, 1983, when control plots of untreated crusted land produced no vegetation, the mulched plots yielded 210 kilograms per hectare dry weight. Plowed plots yielded 440 kilograms. But in 1984—a drought year—the plowed plots had re-crusted and produced only 30 kilograms of vegetation; the twig-mulched plots yielded five times as much.

The ultimate aim at Guesselbodi is to devise and institute a management plan for sustained yield of multiple products: fuelwood, poles, forage, honey, medicines and food. The first tests of cutting live *Combretum* trees—the dominant local species—showed regrowth of up to three meters a year. Cooperatives of local villagers will be created to take over the management and exploitation of the forest under the occasional supervision of forestry personnel. The first cooperative was launched in 1986, covering nine villages.

The economics of the project look extremely promising. Project economist Juan Sève calculated the costs and benefits of making 400 micro-catchments on one hectare, planting 100 with *Acacia* and cowpea, and 300 with millet and sorghum. The first year cost would be $400-$500 per hectare. Benefits would climb from $142 in the second year to $195 in the fifteenth, giving an annual return of 48 percent, six to eight times better than most Sahelian plantations. The cost estimate is based on hired labor paid at $2.50 per day. In practice villagers may well be induced to build the earthworks in the dry season in exchange for the crops that could be grown on them. For non-degraded forest the cost of local management would involve little more than firebreaks and guards, at an estimated $20 per hectare (73).

Perhaps the greatest benefits of this approach derive not from any concrete technology or physical works, but

from a shift in public attitudes: the forest is no longer an alienated resource to be poached from, but community property to be managed for the common good.

Turning Farms into Forests: Agroforestry

This shift in attitudes, however, will not be enough to prevent the clearing of forest for cropland. Cropland will continue to eat into forest as long as populations continue to grow rapidly, or until agricultural intensification allows yields per hectare to expand in line with population growth.

As forests and tree fallows shrink, it becomes more and more essential to establish or retain trees in the cropped area through agroforestry. Wherever attempts to establish agroforestry involve sacrificing of crop production to wood production, they are likely to fail. Yet techniques have now been developed to do it not only without loss, but in many cases with gains for production of food and fodder.

Case Study: Windbreaks in the Majjia Valley, Niger

In semi-arid areas, windbreaks provide an opportunity to introduce trees into cropland in a way that increases crop yields.

Perhaps the best known windbreak success story in Africa is the CARE project in the Majjia Valley, Niger. Here wind speeds reach up to 60 kilometers per hour, with soil losses averaging 20 metric tons per hectare. In the growing season, winds can bury seedlings in sand. They can also cause moisture loss, wilting and toppling of crops (74).

Planting of the windbreaks began in 1974. Each windbreak line is a double row of neem trees (*Azadirachta indica*), spaced four meters apart, with 100 meters between one line and the next. By 1985 there were 330 kilometers of windbreaks, with 80 kilometers added in 1985 alone.

Popular participation has been an element in the project's success. The whole project originated when villagers asked the forestry service for help with wind erosion. Windbreaks answered an urgent felt need. Farmers also participate in the work, digging holes, planting trees, weeding and protecting them in the wet season. Although farmers have not participated in the planning and management of the project so far, the favorable cost-benefit ratio has won their cooperation. Two separate studies have shown total crop yields up by 18–23 percent compared with unprotected areas—even after allowing for the 12–15 percent of cropland taken by trees and deep shade. The benefits in wood production come as a welcome bonus, as fuelwood has become a marketed commodity in this heavily deforested area. The project, plus the rising price of fuelwood, has fostered private tree planting: 60 farmers in the valley now have private tree nurseries and sell to neighbors.

In the traditional fallow system, the benefits of trees for the soil accrue to crops only after the trees have been cleared. They represent a limited capital that can be drawn on for only one to three years. Agroforestry, the growing of trees on and around farms, aims to preserve the capital and draw on the interest. It is exemplified by living fences around compounds or irrigated plots to produce wood or fodder, instead of dead fences that consume wood. Trees or hedges can be planted to stabilize terrace risers. Tree and shrub crops can be grown as windbreaks or in 10 meter-wide bands on slopes to promote infiltration of water that will benefit a food crop growing below them. In the millet growing zone, the *Acacia albida* is a traditional agroforestry species whose soil-enriching effects can double millet yields under its canopy (75). (Also see Chapter 5, "Forests and Rangelands," Focus on: Agroforestry.)

Multistory farming is particularly suitable for humid areas. It involves using complex mixtures of crops and trees of varying sizes, root depths, and growth periods that make complementary use of the available light, water and nutrients. Multistory farming has developed in southeastern Nigeria and around Mount Kilimanjaro; it mimics the layered effect of the rain forest, evens the demand for labor throughout the season, and spreads the food supply throughout the year (76).

Case Study: Alley Cropping

Perhaps the most sophisticated agroforestry system so far developed is alley cropping, where food crops are grown between regularly pruned hedgerows of fast-growing nitrogen-fixing trees.

Alley cropping was developed in 1976 at the International Institute of Tropical Agriculture by Dr. B. T. Kang and his colleagues. It began as a response to the failure of earth bunds (embankments) and chemical fertilizers to solve the erosion and fertility problems of soils at the Institute's headquarters at Ibadan. (See Photo 14.2.)

The basic system is simple. Leguminous trees like *Leucaena leucocephala*, *Cassia siamea* or *Sesbania sesban* are planted in rows, at four to ten to the meter. Crops are grown in 4–8 meter alleys between the rows. The seedling trees are weeded and protected along with the crop. During the dry season the trees continue to grow on residual moisture, putting on up to 4 meters. At the beginning of the next rainy season, the trees are pollarded to a height of 1–2 meters, and pruned up to five times to avoid shading the growing crop. The wood can be used for fuel or stakes. The twigs and leaves are dug in, applied as a surface mulch, or used as livestock fodder. When the next dry season arrives, the trees are allowed to shoot up again (77).

The benefits are multiple. Alley cropped soils are higher in organic matter and usable nutrients and have higher soil moisture levels. *Leucaena* produces as much as 6 metric tons of stakes per hectare each year, along with 15-20 metric tons of leaves and twigs containing

Photo by Paul Harrison

Photo 14.2. *Alley cropping: a Nigerian farmer builds a ridge for planting yams between rows of* leucaena *(right) and* gliricidium *(left).*

World Resources 1987

over 160 kilograms of nitrogen, 150 kilograms of potash and 15 kilograms of phosphorus (78). When these are applied to the soil, crop yields increase considerably and sustainably. In a six-year trial on a sandy soil at Ibadan, an alley-cropped plot cropped continuously without fertilizer maintained maize yields of around 2 metric tons a hectare—more than double the Nigerian average—where yields on a non-alley-cropped plot tailed off from about 1 metric ton in the first year to a quarter of a metric ton in the fourth year (79). In another Ibadan trial, the yield impact of 10 metric tons of dug-in *Leucaena* prunings was equal to applying 100 kilograms of chemical nitrogenous fertilizer (80).

Farm trials so far have been encouraging. Farmers have achieved yield increases averaging 39 percent (81). The largest farm trial so far began in 1984 at two villages near Oyo, run by the International Livestock Centre for Africa. By 1986 the number of volunteer participants had doubled to over 100, a clear sign of acceptability. Most of the plots were well run; some, indeed, looked better than the on-station plots.

The cash costs (excluding labor) of establishing and maintaining alley cropping are negligible. Labor input in farming is higher, mainly because of the pruning—but pruning yields fodder and fuelwood, which would have cost extra labor to gather. Total returns to labor are higher (82).

The benefits in soil conservation are considerable. The increased organic content makes the soil less vulnerable to erosion, while the hedgerows—if aligned with the contours, with weeding trash piled against the stems—collect washed soil on their upper sides, gradually creating level terraces with no other labor input.

Perhaps the greatest value of alley cropping is that it allows continuous cropping and improved crop yields, yet with no outside inputs. It is the most promising technique for sustainable, affordable intensification of agriculture in the humid and subhumid regions. It is highly flexible and compatible with traditional cultivation methods, yet can incorporate mechanization and chemical fertilization easily.

Two urgent priorities apply. One is research in semi-arid areas to see if alley cropping can be adapted using different species, spacings, and management methods. The other, now overdue, is application of alley cropping in large-scale development projects and government programs. If it is offered on a voluntary basis, as part of a menu of new approaches, there is nothing to lose, and a great deal to gain.

EASING THE FUELWOOD SHORTAGE

Africa's fuelwood shortages are—so far—a major cause of deforestation in only a few areas, near urban settlements, especially in the semi-arid zones, and in some semi-arid areas, for example in Ethiopia, Kenya, and Sudan, in which the sale of wood or charcoal to large cities has become a significant source of cash.

But fuel shortages do have serious human and environmental consequences elsewhere. In areas that are already heavily deforested—such as the Ethiopian highlands or the northern limits of rainfed agriculture in Niger—dung and crop residues are burned instead of being returned to the soil. Wherever fuelwood is growing scarcer, collection takes a mounting share of women's time, diverts labor from timely planting or weeding, and therefore depresses yields. Where a fuelwood market has developed, the rising price of fuel takes an increasing share of family budgets, affecting other basic needs such as food, clothing, and housing. Spreading fuel-efficient stoves, therefore, may have only a marginal impact on national rates of deforestation, but could have a significant beneficial effect on crop yields, soil structure, labor availability, and family welfare. Most stove programs in Africa have had limited success, distributing at best 5,000–8,000 stoves. Many of the designs were too expensive, ill-adapted to traditional cooking or heating requirements, and required cement and skilled masons to construct.

Case Study: Improved Charcoal Stoves, Kenya

The first large-scale breakthrough in fuel-efficient stoves came with the U.S. AID-funded Kenya Renewable Energy Development Project, launched in 1982 (83). The project's initial goal was modest but realistic: to sell or give away 5,000 fuel-efficient stoves by the end of 1986. Yet by the end of 1985 the project had given birth to a new industry whose main producers alone had sold 110,000 improved charcoal stoves at a profit. From the start, stove project director Max Kinyanjui aimed to capture a large slice of the one-unit-a-year market for cheap "jikos," scrap metal stoves costing around 60 Nairobe shillings (including replacement grates), with fuel efficiency of 19 percent. The new stove was designed to compete directly. The final design is a casing of scrap metal, waisted for stability, with an insulating ceramic liner, a built-in grate in the top half, and an ash chamber in the bottom. (See Photo 14.3.)

There was a high level of local participation in the design. Scrap metal artisans were consulted to make manufacturing easy. Prototypes were test marketed in 600 households to make sure they were acceptable.

The other main reason for the new stove's success is its overwhelmingly favorable cost benefit ratio. It costs 65–100 Nairobi shillings, but lasts longer than the old ones, resulting in an actual cost savings over two years.

The new stove's measured fuel efficiency is 29–30 percent, theoretically offering fuel savings of 34–37 percent, but many users report savings of 50 percent (probably due to more careful fuel use). For the average Nairobi family spending 170 shillings a month on charcoal, the stove pays for itself within eight weeks, and provides a handsome annual return of up to 1,000 percent on the investment.

The Kenya approach can be successfully adopted in countries with widespread cash availability, where fuelwood has become a marketed commodity. For poor and scattered rural populations, a different approach is called for. The path ahead may be indicated by Africa's second major stove breakthrough in Burkina Faso. Here the chosen design, developed at the Burkina Energy Institute, is basically a shielded traditional three-stone stove, with a circular shield built of clay, dung, millet chaff, and water

Photo 14.3. *An improved charcoal stove with white ceramic liner (left) and a traditional jiko (right).*

Photo by Paul Harrison

around three stones that act as pot rests. The stove can be built in half a day by a housewife to fit any desired pot size, and the simple design requires only half a day's training. The cash cost is nil. Fuel savings in use range between 35 and 70 percent. Most women recoup the investment of a day's labor within one or two weeks. The low-cost, high-benefit, and rapid-dissemination method ensured that by April 1986, some 85,000 improved three-stone stoves were in use (84).

THE LESSONS

The projects and programs outlined above show that success is possible for Africa in agriculture and environment, where success is most needed. Their common features also indicate how projects should be designed to stand the best chance of success in Africa, and suggest a set of tactics and a strategy that could bring it about.

The tactics concern the way projects and programs are designed and implemented, the "secrets of success" in Africa. It is sometimes suggested that only small-scale (i.e., localized) projects run by nongovernmental organizations can succeed. Zimbabwe's agricultural program and Kenya's soil conservation efforts show that this is not the case: government-run, nationwide programs can also succeed and must succeed if a wide and rapid enough impact is to be made. Both these projects are, however, small scale in the important sense that their ultimate goal is to bring about small-scale change on a widespread basis. Both also involve nongovernmental organizations

and depend on the cooperation of grass roots self-help groups.

The Secrets of Success

Many of the secrets of success are simply the reverse of the key reasons for failure. *Failures usually occur in Africa because of failure to understand the African context*, the realities of Africa's ecology, and the constraints under which African farmers and governments operate.

Successful projects take full account of these constraints, sometimes by chance or by intuition, but more often through careful preliminary research. The most reliable way of ensuring that projects harmonize with Africa's diverse ecological, economic, and cultural conditions is by involving local people directly in the design of technologies and programs. That occurred as consumer research in Kenya's stoves program, as action research in Kenya's soil conservation program and Oxfam's stone lines in Burkina Faso, and as on-farm research in IITA's alley cropping and cassava development. In all these cases the research ensured that the measures proposed fitted people's priorities, economic circumstances, labor availability, and cultural needs. In countries with varied cultures and environments, the adaptive research may need to be done in a representative range of locations.

The key elements as far as the farmer is concerned are *to minimize costs and risks, and to maximize benefits.*

As the African farmer is typically short of cash, low cash cost up front is a prime requirement. Many successful projects, such as the stone lines and the self-made stoves, involve no cash cost. Where medium to high cash investments are expected—as in Zimbabwe's maize program—a credit package, repayable from crop proceeds, is essential to ensure wide acceptance.

Low labor cost is also important, especially at key times in the crop calendar. This means that in conservation, techniques such as trash lines, grassed strips, or closely planted contour hedges are preferable (where they are adapted) to labor-intensive techniques like terracing. Increased labor input may be acceptable where the returns to labor are high; for example, the extra labor that may be involved in alley cropping is rewarded not only by much higher crop yields, but by fuelwood, stakes, and fodder.

One type of cost often overlooked is the cost in foregone benefits, for example the food that would have been produced from the land taken up by terracing or village wood lots, or the grazing that was provided by an area that has to be protected against animals. *Foregone benefits should be kept to an absolute minimum.* Stone terracing, for example, should never be used where an earth bund planted with fodder grasses, an alley hedge, or an infiltration strip of tree crops or thatch grass is possible. Where direct grazing is prohibited, people should be allowed to cut and carry fodder for their livestock.

Subsistence farmers exposed to severe climatic hazards are always reluctant to take on additional risks. *Most successful projects and programs are virtually risk free;* indeed many of them help to reduce the risk content of life—for example by reducing vulnerability to drought. It is a virtual precondition of success, especially in the semi-arid areas, that projects should not expose participants to additional hazards; any agricultural package offered should perform at least as well as indigenous methods and varieties in a year of bad rainfall.

Projects should provide maximum benefits. This means, for example, that no opportunity for increased useful output should be overlooked. *Fanya juu* ditches should be planted with bananas or papaya, terrace edges with trees. In a farm context, multipurpose trees should be preferred to purely fuelwood species; when fruit, timber, or fodder trees are planted, there will usually be enough surplus wood available from prunings or unwanted branches to meet fuelwood needs.

Subsistence farmers need *very attractive personal economic rates of return* before they will make an individual investment of cash or labor. Projects and programs should aim to provide returns for beneficiaries of 35 percent upward; many of the projects described here offered returns of 100 percent or more and recouped their full costs within a year, sometimes (as with the stoves) much less.

Development initiatives designed to last must also bear the realities of African government in mind. They should be built as far as possible to withstand periodic foreign exchange and budget crises.

They should be low in import content. Even where aid-financed projects pay for all associated imports, there are recurrent import requirements, for spare parts, for example. Most of the projects discussed involve virtually no imports except for essential vehicles. Zimbabwe's main

agricultural inputs, high-yielding seeds and fertilizer, are locally produced.

They should be low cost to government as well as to farmers. This means *maximum involvement of local people in providing labor, land, and other resources.* It may often mean local cash contributions in payment for tree seedlings or the costs of training village level workers—though these cash contributions should never be large. In some cases full payment can be expected from beneficiaries, for example, for the cost of wells for gardening, or improved stoves, so that the initial investment can be recycled in rolling funds that multiply the benefits. Contributions and payments, provided they are reasonable, generally result in higher commitment, higher effort, and better maintenance than subsidies and free provision. Local people should also be trained and equipped to maintain conservation works, such as wells and pumps. They should be empowered, and organized where necessary, to manage projects and to make any adjustments needed to adapt them to local circumstances.

Local participation, local labor, local resources, local contributions, local maintenance, local management: all these add up to *a strategy of fostering local self-reliance as far as feasible.* Self-reliance is desirable not only from a human point of view; in Africa it is the key to making village development less vulnerable to national economic problems, to ensuring that village development can carry on to some extent in spite of import restrictions, budget cuts, transport and supply problems, and shortages of skilled manpower.

The state then becomes less a direct provider and more an enabler, focusing on the dissemination of information and technologies for self-development, and the creation of a policy context favorable to self-development. If a technology fulfills the preconditions outlined above—low costs, low risks and high returns to labor, land, and capital—it will spread spontaneously, but unevenly, through formal and informal markets, and by the demonstration effect. With government backing, technologies—especially more complex ways of managing soils, crops, livestock or trees—will spread much more rapidly. The spread will be most rapid when every channel of communication is mobilized, including all media, primary and secondary schools, political parties, and community groups.

Lessons for African Governments

The strategy of success involves government and donor policies and institutions. Government policies must be framed so that they create the most favorable possible context for the spread of better technologies. Above all this means favorable prices, not just for cash and food crops, but also for wood and livestock. The experience of Zimbabwe, Zambia, and Ghana shows that favorable prices can translate very rapidly into increased output. More realistic exchange rates that make food imports more expensive and cash crop exports more profitable are also imperative, along with a reduction in the government rake-off from the proceeds of cash crop exports. Higher prices for producers will make intensification and conservation more worthwhile.

The second major policy area where government action is required is in laws and regulations on ownership and control of cropland, trees, forests, and rangeland. Heritable security of tenure is undoubtedly the most favorable context for conservation work to assure farmers (including women) that they will enjoy the long-term benefits of their efforts. For common resources like forests and rangeland, control and use rights are more important than formal ownership. Local populations must be given rights to manage and profit from common resources if the degradation of forests and grazing land is to be halted.

Incentives alone can boost production and sometimes productivity by making it worthwhile to invest extra labor and other available resources in food production. But other measures, including research and extension services, are needed to increase the effectiveness of incentives.

Research, including plant breeding, must relate much more closely to the real constraints, requirements, and priorities of smallholders. This means a much greater emphasis on on-farm and farming systems research, with priority to food crop production, agroforestry, and soil and water conservation, and emphasis on low cost, low risk, low labor technologies.

A high priority should go to creating or strengthening nationwide networks of multipurpose agricultural extension workers; there should be one extension worker for every 500–1,000 small farmers. Lack of skilled labor or funds is no real excuse for delaying the creation of a network. A pyramid training system developed in Burkina Faso allows a small number of national experts to train regional trainers, who train district trainers, and so on down to village level, where the farming equivalent of barefoot doctors can be elected and paid by their neighbors. Creating initial confidence is crucial, so the extension systems should begin by disseminating those low- or no-cost techniques that provide the highest returns with the lowest risk (85). (See Table 14.1.)

Because of Africa's unique cultural and ecological diversity these techniques will have to be adapted not only nationally but locally. The only people capable of ensuring this adaptation are smallholders themselves. They should be enlisted in adaptive research from the

Table 14.1 A Green Revolution for Africa

The Foundations

■ Improvement of producer prices for food and cash crops plus devaluation or currency de-regulation
■ Security of tenure and use of land, trees, pasture including full title for women
■ Functional integration of agriculture, livestock, forestry and conservation
    Research focused on farming systems
    Rapid creation of network of multipurpose agricultural
       extension agents using pyramid training
    Formation of farmer's groups
    Focus on food crops and women
    Production emphasis in conservation, and vice-versa

STAGE ONE: Dissemination of no cash cost and minimal cost techniques with high returns to labor, capital, land

Conservation of Soil, Water and Nutrients
    Stone lines
    Trash lines
    Planted bunds
    Grassed strips
    Infiltration zones
    Contour ridges
    Plus, for Semi-arid Areas:
    Waterharvesting
    Waterspreading
    Windbreaks
    Dune fixation
Improvement of Soil Fertility and Structure
    Nitrogen fixation by legumes in intercrops and rotations
    Mulching with crop residues
    Planted fallow of leguminous fodder or mulch crops
    Agroforestry with local varieties
        alley cropping (humid and subhumid)
        acacias etc. (semi-arid)
        multistory farming
Forestry
    Local management of natural forest
    Living fences
    Close hedges for terrace formation
    Tree crops
    Shade trees
    Emphasis on multi-purpose species
        Fuelwood
        Timber
        Fruit and nuts
        Fodder
        Nitrogen fixation
Small Scale Irrigation
    Valley bottoms
    Flood plains
    Earth dams
Improved Timing and Spacing of Planting

Livestock Measures
    Fodder banks of legumes and browse trees
    Increased use of camels and goats (semi-arid)
    Alley cropping for goats and sheep (humid)
    Hand dug wells, dispersed water points
    Controlled grazing in farming areas
Improved Labor Availability and Productivity
    Through reduced women's burdens
    Fuelwood from agroforestry
    Improved 3-stone stoves
    Farmer's groups to pool oxen and tools
    Improved health via charcoal water filters, latrines, homemade oral
       rehydration salts
    Childspacing, breast feeding

STAGE TWO: Low-cost techniques that require some nationwide distribution service, minimal imports and small cash investments

Improved Crop Varieties (open-pollinated) Bred For Performance Under Local Conditions
    Disease resistance
    Tolerance of poor soil
    Tolerance of dry spells
    Drought resistance:
        Early emergence
        Early maturity
        Deep rooting
    Equal to/better than local varieties in bad years
Improved Fertilizers as Booster for Legumes
Introduced Tree Species (*Leucaena* etc.)
Crossbreeding of Livestock
Low Cost Tsetse Traps
Multiplication of Trypano-tolerant Livestock
Cheap Wells
Hand-operated Pumps
Scooped Ponds
Improved Devices to Reduce Women's Burdens
    Hand grinders
    Shellers
Plus, For Semi-arid Areas
    Plowing—one-ox, chisel plough
    Tied ridging

STAGE THREE: Moderate cost techniques involving some imports, higher cash investment by farmers, and competent nationwide supply and maintenance systems

Hybrid Seeds
Moderate Levels of Carefully Chosen Nitrogenous and Potash Fertilizers
Selective Mechanization of Labor Bottlenecks
Washbores
Motorized Pumps
Biogas Using Bargain Technology e.g. Polythene Sausage
Plus For Humid and Subhumid Areas, Minimum Tillage With Herbicides

Notes: Each stage builds on and incorporates the previous stages, which create the surplus and capital needed for the later stages. The above list is suggestive, not exhaustive. All techniques and packages must be tried and adapted nationally and locally.
Source: Paul Harrison, *The Greening of Africa* (Penguin Books, New York and Paladin Books, London, in press).

beginning to overcome the research labor shortage. Extension workers should become an arm of research, not merely recommending new techniques to farmers, but gathering farmers' experiences, problems, adaptations, and requests for research back-up.

In many areas carefully chosen soil and water conservation measures may be the best starting point for dissemination and implementation. Because they reduce the loss of nutrients and water in runoff, they produce significant yield increases, especially in subhumid and semi-arid zones. It is important to integrate conservation and production much more closely than before. Wherever possible conservation methods should be chosen that increase production (e.g., alley cropping, or infiltration strips with tree or grass crops) and production methods that conserve soil and water (e.g. intercropping, use of organic residues).

Later agricultural innovations requiring higher incomes and a better infrastructure will not supersede but build on these foundations. (See Table 14.1.) Because of the fragile soils and erratic climate, even chemicals and mechanized farming in Africa must always have a firm base of organic inputs, soil and water conservation, and agroforestry.

This general approach will ease another area that is usually thought of as a government responsibility: inputs. In the poorer countries without adequate road and supply networks, the initial inputs will be local; labor for soil and water conservation, legumes and leguminous trees for nitrogen and other nutrients. Infrastructure can be improved in modest ways at first: feeder roads built and maintained with local labor and materials, small oil-driven agroprocessing plants, donkey carts to bring produce to collecting points. As infrastructure and farmers' incomes improve, more purchased inputs can be fostered, including improved seed varieties (open-pollinated at first), and chemical fertilizers formulated to suit specific African conditions. Rural credit schemes will be needed. Where land titles are absent, the crop itself can be used as collateral.

The most important input of all is the participation of local people. It is essential that neither African governments nor donors regard themselves as the sole source of services, priorities, or new technologies. Local people must be involved at every stage in every development activity, from research and design, to establishing local priorities and plans of action, through contributions of land, labor, materials and often cash, to ongoing maintenance and management. This participation is best organized on a group basis, establishing formal links between grass roots government workers and existing community organizations, or newly created ones where necessary. Self-help will be the emphasis but it will be self-help assisted by the technical support and advice of government.

These measures, especially if they are taken in combination, will result in a rapid gain in food and wood production and in yields on the order of 20 percent or more, with greater stability of yield. But a simultaneous effort must be launched to reduce the growth in demand for food, primarily by programs to bring down the birth rate.

Moderate reductions in population growth rates can bring massive reductions in the production required from agriculture over the long term. If Africa could, for example, achieve a population growth rate consistent with the U.N.'s low projection of population growth (birth rates falling from 44.4 per thousand in 1985–90 to 21.0 in 2020–25) instead of the medium projection (birth rates falling from 45.6 to 26.7 over the same period), the intensification effort required of agriculture by 2025 would be halved (86).

Lessons for the North

Focusing on low-cost, high-return ventures, African governments could make considerable progress with little external help. However, they will make more progress with the cooperation of northern industrialized countries.

For many decades to come, Africa will be the major challenge in world development and should command a higher proportion of aid funds. Even with no increase in aid flows, the effectiveness of aid could be massively increased if the lessons of the success stories were fully learned. Donors should avoid the temptation to push projects that involve high imports, high unit costs, and high skill requirements for initiation and maintenance. They should give far greater weight to the long-term sustainability of their activities, paying a greater proportion of local and recurrent costs. Their prime goal should no longer be to get specific things done but to strengthen the capacities of African governments and nongovernment organizations (NGOs) to do things for themselves. This means concentrating on nationwide programs rather than localized ventures (except for pilot and NGO projects) and accepting the African's prerogative to coordinate and standardize aid approaches within a given sector. It means accepting a normal funding horizon of at least ten years, two or three times longer than at present.

In the long term, the international economic environment, dominated by the north, will be crucial to Africa's success. Here the greatest priority should be a reduction in northern protectionism, particularly in agriculture. Farm subsidies, if they are judged particularly necessary, should take the form of income support for farmers rather than overpricing. Overpricing encourages overproduction, which depresses world prices for cereals and many cash crops. The resulting surpluses are dumped on African countries as food aid, depressing national prices. Both factors lead to lower incomes and incentives for African farmers. As FAO's recent report on African agriculture points out, aid in the form of fertilizer, pesticides, and appropriate tools would make a great deal more sense (87). Food aid (wherever possible given as food for conservation work in the home area) will of course be necessary in emergencies, though even here, cash-for-work programs may often be preferable for maintaining national food networks.

With this judicious combination of African and northern reforms and redirected development efforts, Africa's prospects could be transformed. Substantial progress on the triple goal of increasing self sufficiency in food, conserving the environment, and reducing absolute poverty could be realistically achieved within a decade.

References and Notes

1. This chapter is derived from *The Greening of Africa* by Paul Harrison, a book sponsored by the International Institute for Environment and Development and scheduled for publication in 1987 by Penguin Books, New York, and Paladin Books, London.
2. The World Bank, *Financing Adjustment With Growth in Sub-Saharan Africa 1986-90* (The World Bank, Washington D.C., 1986), pp. 94–95.
3. John M. Cohen and David B. Lewis, "Role of Government in Combatting Food Shortages: Lessons from Kenya 1984–85," in *Drought and Hunger in Africa: Denying Famine a Future*, Michael H. Glantz, ed. (Cambridge University Press, Cambridge, U.K., 1987), pp. 269–296.
4. The World Bank, *World Development Report 1986* (The World Bank, Washington, D.C., 1986), p. 182 and p. 228.
5. Calculated from United Nations Food and Agriculture Organization (FAO), *1979 FAO Production Yearbook* (FAO, Rome, 1980), p. 80; and *1984 FAO Production Yearbook* (FAO, Rome, 1985), p. 88.
6. *Op. cit.* 4, p. 190.
7. *Op. cit.* 4, p. 182 and p. 228.
8. Michael Hopkins, "Employment Trends in Developing Countries, 1960–80 and Beyond," *International Labour Review*, Vol. 122, No. 4, p. 474, Table 8.
9. United Nations Food and Agriculture Organization (FAO), *Fifth World Food Survey* (FAO, Rome, 1985), p. 26.
10. *Op. cit.* 2, p. 78.
11. *Op. cit.* 2, p. 77.
12. *Op. cit.* 4, p. 52.
13. *Op. cit.* 4, p. 52.
14. U.N. Secretary General, *The Critical Economic Situation in Africa*, AS/13/2 (United Nations, New York, 1986), p. 27.
15. United Nations Children's Fund (UNICEF), *Within Human Reach* (UNICEF, New York, 1985), pp. 10–16.
16. Jean-Paul Lanly, *Tropical Forest Resources*, Forestry Paper 30 (United Nations Food and Agriculture Organization, Rome, 1982), pp. 81–82 and p. 97.
17. United Nations Food and Agriculture Organization (FAO), *Fuelwood Supplies in Developing Countries* (FAO, Rome, 1983), pp. 16–17.
18. Jack A. Mabbutt, "A New Global Assessment of the Status and Trends of Desertification," *Environmental Conservation*, Vol. 11, No. 2 (1984), p. 106 and p. 108.
19. Chris Reij and Stephen Turner, *Soil and Water Conservation in Sub-Saharan Africa* (International Fund for Agricultural Development, Rome, 1985).
20. B.N. Okigbo, "Improved Permanent Production Systems as an Alternative to Shifting Intermittent Cultivation," in *Improved Production Systems as an Alternative to Shifting Cultivation*, Soils Bulletin No. 53 (United Nations Food and Agriculture Organization, Rome, 1984), pp. 54–56.
21. G.M. Higgins, *et. al.*, *Potential Population Supporting Capacities of Lands in the Developing World* (United Nations Food and Agriculture Organization, Rome, 1982), p. 16.
22. *Map of Desertification Hazards*, Explanatory Note (United Nations Environment Programme, Nairobi, 1978), Table 1.
23. United Nations Food and Agriculture Organization (FAO), *Crisis of Sustainability, Africa's Land Resource Base*, AGD/801/1 (FAO, Rome, 1985), p. 13.
24. Sharon Nicholson, *The Sahel: a Climatic Perspective* (Club du Sahel, Organisation for Economic Co-Operation and Development, Paris, 1982).
25. United Nations Food and Agriculture Organization (FAO), *Improved Production Systems as an Alternative to Shifting Cultivation*, FAO Soils Bulletin, No. 53 (FAO, Rome, 1984).
26. Les Fussell and Phil Serafini "Crop Associations in the Semi-Arid Tropics of West Africa" (International Crops Research Institute for the Semi-Arid Tropics, Sahelian Centre, unpublished draft, Niamey, Niger, 1985).
27. Ester Boserup, *The Conditions of Agricultural Growth* (Aldine Publishing Co., London, 1965).
28. Paul Richards, *Indigenous Agricultural Revolution* (Hutchinson and Co. Ltd., London, 1985).
29. Hans Jahnke, *Livestock Production Systems and Livestock Development in Tropical Africa* (Kieler Wissenschaftsverlag Vauk, West Germany, 1982), p. 19.
30. United Nations Food and Agriculture Organization (FAO), *Agriculture: Toward 2000* (FAO, Rome, 1981), p. 71.
31. Economic Commission for Africa (ECA), *The Role of Women in African Development*, E/CONF/BP/8 (ECA, Addis Ababa, Ethiopia, 1975).
32. United Nations Food and Agriculture Organization (FAO), *Consultation on Irrigation in Africa* (FAO, Lome, Togo, 1986), pp. 6–8.
33. *Op. cit.* 4, Chapters 4 and 5.
34. The World Bank, *Tenth Annual Review of Project Performance Audit Results* (The World Bank, Washington, D.C., 1985), pp. 19–24.
35. *Ibid.*, pp. 33–34.
36. This section is based on summary and analysis of evaluation documents, including The World Bank, *Tenth Annual Review of Project Performance Audit Results* (The World Bank, Washington, D.C., 1985), pp. 19–29; Robert Berg, *Foreign Aid in Africa* (Committee on African Development Strategies, Washington, D.C., 1984); Stephen Sandford, *Review of World Bank Livestock Activities in Dry Tropical Africa* (The World Bank, Washington, D.C., 1981); and Fred Weber, *Review of CILSS Forestry Sector* (U.S. Agency for International Development, Forestry Support Program, Washington, D.C., 1982).
37. *Op. cit.* 2, pp. 19–20.
38. This section is based on personal interviews and field visits in Zimbabwe, and on Paula Park and Tony Jackson, *Lands of Plenty, Lands of Scarcity* (Oxfam, Oxford, 1985); U.S. Agency for International Development (U.S. AID), *Zimbabwe, Country Development Strategy Statement, Financial Year 1987* (U.S. AID, Harare, Zimbabwe, 1985); G.L. Chavunduka, *Report of the Commission of Inquiry into the Agricultural Industry* (Government of Zimbabwe, Harare, 1982); The World Bank, *Zimbabwe Agriculture Sector Study* (The World Bank, Washington, D.C., 1983); Grain Marketing Board, *Annual Report 1985* (Harare, Zimbabwe, 1985); and Kate Truscott, *The Wedza Project* (Agritex, Ministry of Lands, Agriculture and Resettlement, Harare, Zimbabwe, 1985).
39. Peter Matlon, *A Critical Review of Objectives, Methods and Progress to Date in Sorghum and Millet Improvement*, Village Studies Report No. 15 (International Crops Research Institute For the Semi-Arid Tropics, Sahelian Centre, Niamey, Niger, 1985), p. 7.
40. International Institute of Tropical Agriculture (IITA), *Maize and Cowpea Improvement in Semi-Arid Africa* (IITA, Ibadan, Nigeria, undated), p. 18.
41. Dr. Sang Ki Hahn, Director of Root Crop Program, International Institute of Tropical Agriculture, Ibadan, Nigeria, 1986 (personal communication).
42. Sang Ki Hahn, *Tropical Root Crops: Their Improvement and Utilization* (International Institute of Tropical Agriculture, Ibadan, Nigeria, 1984), p. 6.
43. M.O. Akoroda, *et al.*, "Impact of IITA Cassava Varieties in Oyo State of Nigeria" (International Institute of Tropical Agriculture, Ibadan, Nigeria, unpublished, 1985).
44. International Institute of Tropical Agriculture (IITA), *Annual Report 1982* (IITA, Ibadan, Nigeria, 1983), p. 23.
45. S.R. Singh, *Impact of IITA's Grain Legume Improvement Programme* (International Institute of Tropical Agriculture, Ibadan, Nigeria, 1983), pp. 21–22.
46. Charles Johnson *et al.*, *Kitale Maize*, Project Impact Evaluation No. 2 (U.S. Agency for International Development, 1979), pp. 1–5.
47. *Op. cit.* 44, p. 14.
48. *Op. cit.* 39, p. 6.
49. Peter Matlon, "The West African Semi-Arid Tropics," in *Accelerating Food Production in Sub-Saharan Africa*, J.W. Mellor, *et al.*, eds. (Johns Hopkins University Press, Baltimore, Maryland, in press).
50. International Crops Research Institute for the Semi-Arid Tropics (ICRISAT), Sahelian Centre, *Annual Report 1983* (ICRISAT, Niamey, Niger, 1985), p. 61.
51. Les Fussell, Millet Agronomist, International Crops Research Institute for the Semi-Arid Tropics, Niamey, Niger, 1986 (personal communication).
52. Rattan Lal, *Role of Mulching Techniques in Tropical Soil and Water Management* (International Institute of Tropical Agriculture, Ibadan, Nigeria, 1975), p. 15.
53. Michael Klaij, Principal Soil and Water Engineer, International Crops Research

Institute for the Semi-Arid Tropics, 1986 (personal communication).

54. *Op. cit.* 52, p. 11.

55. *Op. cit.* 26.

56. *Op. cit.* 52, p. 6, Fig. 7.

57. *Op. cit.* 19, pp. 21–33.

58. *SIDA Sponsored Soil Conservation Projects,* Annual Report 1983/4 (Ministry of Agriculture and Livestock Development, Nairobi), pp. 10–11.

59. "Soil Conservation in Kenya," *AMBIO,* Vol. 12, No. 6 (1983), pp. 305–307.

60. *SIDA Sponsored Soil Conservation Projects,* Annual Report 1983/4, Ministry of Agriculture and Livestock Development, Nairobi, p. 4. Figure given is divided by number of farms terraced. US$1 = 15 Kenyan shillings.

61. Lars Hedfors, *Evaluation and Economic Appraisal of Soil Conservation in a Pilot Area* (Swedish International Development Agency, Stockholm, 1981), p. 8.

62. Eric Holmberg, *Evaluation and Economic Appraisal of Soil Conservation in Kalia Sub-Location* (Swedish International Development Agency, Stockholm, undated) p. 49.

63. Irrigated area from United Nations Food and Agricultural Organization (FAO), *Consultation on Irrigation in Africa,* AGL IA/86 Doc. I-A (FAO, Rome, 1986), pp. 15–16. Cultivated area from *FAO 1984 Production Yearbook* (FAO Rome, 1985), pp. 47–49.

64. H.W. Underhill, *Small-Scale Irrigation in Africa* (United Nations Food and Agriculture Organization, Rome, 1984), pp. 19–22.

65. Peter Benedict, *Sudan: The Rahad Irrigation Project,* Project Impact Evaluation Report No. 31 (U.S. Agency for International Development, Washington, D.C., 1982).

66. For a fuller description see Paul Harrison, *The Greening of Africa* (Penguin Books, New York and Paladin Books, London, in press), Chapter 9.

67. Personal interviews, Kano State Agricultural Research and Development Authority, Nigeria, November 1986.

68. Peter Wright, *La Gestion des Eaux de Ruissellement* (Oxfam, Ouagadougou, Burkina Faso, undated); and personal interviews and site visits in Burkina Faso.

69. *Ibid.*

70. *Op. cit.* 16, p. 57 and pp. 94–95.

71. J.K. Jackson, *et al., Management of Natural Forest in the Sahel Region* (Club du Sahel, Organisation for Economic Co-Operation and Development, Paris, 1983).

72. The Guesselbodi section is based on personal interviews and site visits in Niger and on John G. Heermans, "The Guesselbodi Experiment," 1985; rehabilitation results summarized in E. Boudouresque, and R. Chase, "Vegetative Regeneration Trials on Bare Soils in the Region of Niamey," 1984; costs and benefits from Juan Sève and J.A. Tabor, "Land Degradation and Simple Conservation Practices," 1985 (all unpublished documents of the Forestry and Land Use Planning Project, U.S. Embassy, Niamey, Niger). Costs for undegraded forest from J.K. Jackson, *et al., Management of Natural Forest in the Sahel Region* (Club du Sahel, Organisation for Economic Co-Operation and Development, Paris, 1983), pp. 51–52.

73. *Op. cit.* 71.

74. The Majjia section is based on personal interviews and site visits in Niger and on Steve Dennison, *et al.,* "Majjia Evaluation Study," interim reports and sociological reports (CARE, New York, unpublished, 1984 and 1985); and Amadou N'Tirgny Maiga, *Evaluation des Projets CARE a Bouza* (CARE, Niamey, Niger, 1983). Yield impact results from Else Bognetteau-Verlinden, "Study on Impact of Windbreaks in Majjia Valley" (Agricultural University Wageningen, The Netherlands, thesis, 1980), p. 68; and Michael Ahearn, Forestry Advisor, CARE, Niamey, Niger (personal communication).

75. C. Charreau and P. Vidal, "Influence de *Acacia albida* sur le Sol, Nutrition Minerale et Rendements du Mil," *L'agronomie Tropicale,* Vol. 6, No. 7 (1965), pp. 600–626.

76. For a detailed study of multistory farming in southeast Nigeria, see Johannes Lagemann, *Traditional Farming Systems in Eastern Nigeria* (Weltforum Verlag, Munich, 1977).

77. B.T. Kang, *et al., Alley Cropping* (International Institute of Tropical Agriculture, Ibadan, Nigeria, 1984).

78. *Ibid.,* p. 18.

79. *Ibid.,* p. 16.

80. *Ibid.,* p. 18.

81. International Institute of Tropical Agriculture (IITA), *IITA Annual Report 1983* (IITA, Ibadan, Nigeria, 1984), p. 184, Table 64.

82. J.E. Sumberg, *Alley Farming in the Humid Zone,* Bulletin No. 18 (International Livestock Center for Africa, 1984), pp. 2–6; and personal interviews and site visits at Ibadan and Oyo, Nigeria.

83. The charcoal stoves section is based on personal interviews and site visits in Kenya, and on Max Kinyanjui, *The Kenya Charcoal Stoves Programme, Interim Report* (Energy Development International, Nairobi, 1984); Henry Kerman, *et al., Kenya Renewable Energy Development Project, Mid-Term Evaluation* (U.S. Agency for International Development, Washington, D.C., 1984); Eric L. Hyman, *The Strategy of Decentralized Production and Distribution of Improved Charcoal Stoves in Kenya* (Appropriate Technology International (ATI), Washington, D.C., 1985); and Eric L. Hyman, *The Economics of Fuel-Efficient Charcoal Stoves in Kenya* (ATI, Washington, D.C., 1985).

84. Max Kinyanjui, Kenya Renewable Energy Development Project, Nairobi, 1986 (personal communication).

85. Paul Harrison, *The Greening of Africa* (Penguin Books, New York and Paladin Books, London, in press), p. 269 and p. 310.

86. Paul Harrison, *Land, Food and People* (United Nations Food and Agriculture Organization, Rome, 1974), p. 20.

87. United Nations Food and Agriculture Organization (FAO), *African Agriculture: The Next 25 Years,* Main Report (FAO, Rome, 1986).

15. Basic Economic Indicators

Employment, production, debt, and price statistics are basic economic indicators that are used to monitor levels of and predict changes in economic activity.

Gross National Product (GNP), perhaps the most important indicator of economic activity, measures the total market value of goods and services produced in a country in a year, including transactions with other countries. However, there are a number of problems with using GNP as a broader measure of development. Some economic activities are difficult to measure; others may be detrimental to a country's long-term development prospects. GNP data do not reflect the distribution of income and wealth within a country. In addition, comparability of GNP data among countries is limited.

GNP figures are more accurate for countries in which most economic transactions (trade in goods, services, and labor) go through a market place and can be accurately recorded. Data for many developing countries, where markets are not as well developed or where data collection systems are rudimentary, require extensive imputations. In all countries a fraction of economic activity occurs in black markets, and its value is not adequately represented in official statistics. Countries at war or suffering civil strife either do not report GNP data or provide incomplete data. For nonmarket economies, GNP data are difficult to calculate and interpret and, except for Hungary, are omitted from Table 15.1.

Comparing the GNP of one country to another requires use of a common currency (most often, U.S. dollars) and a common base year. However, currency exchange rates do not reflect the relative purchasing powers of currencies. For example, the price of labor services (such as carpentry) relative to those of commodities that enter international trade (such as wheat) differs systematically between high- and low-income countries. The GNP estimates in Table 15.1 were converted from local currencies to dollars using currency exchange rates that substantially overstate international differences in real living standards.

Official Development Assistance (ODA) flows can be an important component of GNP. These grants and loans on concessional terms are made by member countries of the Organisation for Economic Co-operation and Development, the Council for Mutual Economic Assistance and the Organization of Petroleum Exporting Countries, and by multilateral development banks. Fifteen African countries receive net flows of ODA (net of repayment of concessional loans) that are equal to 10 percent or more of their GNPs. (See Chapter 26, "Policies and Institutions," Table 26.3.) However, increasing payments of interest and principal on nonconcessional loans are now exceeding inflows of ODA for several developing countries.

The size and growth of GNP may prove to be poor indicators of long-term economic health. GNP data tell us little about a nation's wealth in human and natural resources, and they do not adequately account for changes in a nation's natural resource assets. Rapid depletion of natural resources could reduce a country's future income. Although the current economic gain from resource depletion is treated as a positive contribution to GNP, the value of the natural resources consumed is not subtracted.

External debt indicators, presented in Table 15.2, must be interpreted with caution. The ratios of debt to GNP and of debt service to exports indicate, respectively, a country's long- and short-term ability to finance its debt. These ratios are also influenced by the maturity of a country's loan portfolio; rescheduling agreements can convert current obligations into longer-term financing. The impact of debt upon a country's growth potential, employment opportunities, social welfare, and environmental quality is difficult to quantify and is not reflected in Table 15.2.

Although debt and debt ratios have generally risen throughout the developing world, growth has been uneven. From 1970 to 1984, the ratio of debt to GNP in Latin America and the Caribbean rose from the lowest of all regions to the highest. This change reflects the fact that Latin American and Caribbean countries accumulated almost 60 percent of all the new debt created between 1980 and 1984.

The commodity indexes and prices presented in Table 15.3 reflect transactions in world markets. These commodities are also traded within countries at prices that may vary widely from those of global markets because of transportation costs, tariffs, trade restrictions, subsidies, and other factors.

The constant price index for 33 nonfuel commodities, illustrated in Figure 15.1, has been declining since the early 1960s. For 1960–85, the 33-commodity price index has averaged a decline of slightly less than one point per year. For 1974–85, it declined at an average rate of 5.4 points per year.

Table 15.1 Gross National Product, 1965–84

	Gross National Product 1984		Average Annual Change in Real GNP (percent)		Distribution of Gross Domestic Product 1984 (percent)		
	Total (million $US)	Per Capita ($US)	1965–73	1973–84	Agriculture	Industry	Services
WORLD							
AFRICA							
Algeria	50,680	2,380	8.6	5.8	6	53	41
Angola	X	X	X	X	X	X	X
Benin	1,060	270	2.3	4.7	43	14	43
Botswana	940	910	13.0	10.8	6	45	48
Burkina Faso	1,040	160	2.7	3.0	43	20	38
Burundi	1,010	220	5.0	3.6	58	16	26
Cameroon	8,000	810	4.3	7.1	22	35	43
Cape Verde	100	320	X	7.1	X	X	X
Central African Rep	680	270	3.1	0.5	39	20	40
Chad	X	X	0.9	X	X	X	X
Comoros	X	X	5.2	4.0	X	X	X
Congo	2,060	1,120	6.4	7.9	7	60	33
Cote d'Ivoire	6,030	610	8.5	3.6	28	26	46
Djibouti	X	X	X	X	X	X	X
Egypt	33,340	720	3.5	8.7	20	33	48
Equatorial Guinea	X	X	X	X	X	X	X
Ethiopia	4,780	110	4.1	2.6	48	16	36
Gabon	2,830	3,480	6.9	1.0	X	X	X
Gambia	180	260	4.6	1.5	X	X	X
Ghana	4,730	350	3.3	-0.9	52	9	40
Guinea	1,810	300	3.0	2.0	41	21	38
Guinea-Bissau	160	180	X	2.0	X	X	X
Kenya	5,950	300	8.4	4.5	31	21	48
Lesotho	790	530	7.9	7.5	X	X	X
Liberia	990	470	7.2	1.6	36	26	38
Libya	29,790	8,230	7.2	2.7	2	64	34
Madagascar	2,600	270	3.7	-0.7	42	16	42
Malawi	1,430	210	6.1	2.7	37	18	45
Mali	1,060	140	3.0	3.9	46	11	43
Mauritania	750	450	3.5	2.4	30	27	42
Mauritius	1,100	1,100	2.5	3.3	14	25	61
Morocco	14,340	670	6.0	4.3	17	32	51
Mozambique	X	X	X	X	X	X	X
Niger	1,190	190	-1.1	4.1	33	31	37
Nigeria	74,120	770	9.1	0.6	27	30	43
Rwanda	1,610	270	6.3	5.6	X	X	X
Senegal	2,440	380	1.5	2.1	17	28	55
Sierra Leone	1,120	300	4.3	1.8	35	25	40
Somalia	1,360	260	3.5	2.5	X	X	X
South Africa	73,970	2,260	5.3	2.6	5	47	48
Sudan	7,360	340	0.8	4.9	33	16	51
Swaziland	590	800	8.8	4.5	X	X	X
Tanzania, United Rep	4,460	210	5.8	1.8	X	X	X
Togo	730	250	5.7	1.7	22	28	50
Tunisia	8,840	1,250	7.5	5.8	15	35	50
Uganda	3,290	230	4.1	-1.3	X	X	X
Zaire	4,220	140	3.6	-1.0	X	X	X
Zambia	3,020	470	2.7	0.6	15	39	46
Zimbabwe	6,040	740	7.1	3.0	14	40	46
NORTH & CENTRAL AMERICA							
Barbados	1,100	4,340	5.9	2.0	X	X	X
Canada	330,870	13,140	5.3	2.3	3	24	72
Costa Rica	2,930	1,210	7.1	1.9	21	30	49
Cuba	X	X	X	X	X	X	X
Dominican Rep	6,040	990	8.4	3.2	15	31	53
El Salvador	3,820	710	4.3	-0.5	21	21	58
Guatemala	9,110	1,120	6.0	2.2	X	X	X
Haiti	1,710	320	1.7	2.7	X	X	X
Honduras	2,980	700	4.5	3.6	27	26	47
Jamaica	2,480	1,080	5.8	-2.3	6	39	56
Mexico	158,310	2,060	7.7	4.5	9	40	52
Nicaragua	2,700	870	3.6	-1.1	24	30	45
Panama	4,210	2,100	7.4	4.4	9	19	72
Trinidad and Tobago	8,350	7,140	3.6	4.7	X	X	X
United States	3,670,490	15,490	3.2	2.4	2	32	66
SOUTH AMERICA							
Argentina	67,150	2,230	4.3	-0.2	12	39	50
Bolivia	2,560	410	4.2	-0.1	25	33	40
Brazil	227,280	1,710	9.6	4.0	13	35	52
Chile	20,340	1,710	3.6	2.0	6	39	56
Colombia	38,410	1,370	6.3	4.0	20	30	50
Ecuador	10,340	1,220	6.9	4.4	14	41	46
Guyana	470	580	4.2	-1.1	X	X	X
Paraguay	4,120	1,250	5.0	7.8	26	26	48
Peru	17,960	980	3.6	1.0	8	40	51
Suriname	1,350	3,520	4.9	2.4	X	X	X
Uruguay	5,900	1,970	2.5	1.5	14	29	57
Venezuela	57,360	3,220	5.9	1.8	7	43	50

World Resources 1987

Table 15.1

	Gross National Product 1984		Average Annual Change in Real GNP (percent)		Distribution of Gross Domestic Product 1984 (percent)		
	Total (million $US)	Per Capita ($US)	1965–73	1973–84	Agriculture	Industry	Services
ASIA							
Afghanistan	X	X	1.1	X	X	X	X
Bahrain	4,260	10,480	X	X	X	X	X
Bangladesh	12,360	130	0.1	4.6	48	12	39
Bhutan	X	X	X	X	X	X	X
Burma	6,620	180	2.8	5.9	48	13	39
China	318,310	310	7.8	6.6	36	44	20
Cyprus	2,390	3,590	14.9	5.1	X	X	X
India	197,210	260	4.0	4.3	35	27	38
Indonesia	85,400	540	8.0	6.6	26	40	34
Iran	X	X	12.2	X	X	X	X
Iraq	X	X	5.4	X	X	X	X
Israel	21,290	5,100	9.4	2.9	5	27	68
Japan	1,248,090	10,390	9.9	4.3	3	41	56
Jordan	4,340	1,710	X	9.6	8	30	62
Kampuchea, Dem	X	X	-2.7	X	X	X	X
Korea, Dem People's Rep	X	X	X	X	X	X	X
Korea, Rep	84,860	2,090	9.8	7.2	14	40	47
Kuwait	27,570	15,410	4.7	7.4	1	58	41
Lao People's Dem Rep	X	X	X	X	X	X	X
Lebanon	X	X	X	X	X	X	X
Malaysia	30,280	1,990	6.6	7.1	21	35	44
Mongolia	X	X	X	X	X	X	X
Nepal	2,630	160	1.7	3.1	56	12	32
Oman	7,380	6,230	18.6	8.6	X	X	X
Pakistan	35,420	380	5.7	6.2	24	29	47
Philippines	35,040	660	5.4	4.6	25	34	41
Qatar	6,020	20,600	X	-3.7	X	X	X
Saudi Arabia	116,380	10,740	10.8	8.0	3	60	38
Singapore	18,390	7,260	12.4	8.1	1	39	60
Sri Lanka	5,660	360	4.4	5.2	28	26	46
Syrian Arab Rep	18,540	1,870	6.3	7.1	20	24	57
Thailand	42,760	850	7.7	6.2	20	28	52
Turkey	57,810	1,200	6.9	3.5	19	33	47
United Arab Emirates	28,480	22,300	X	10.3	1	67	32
Viet Nam	X	X	X	X	X	X	X
Yemen	3,940	510	X	7.6	24	21	56
Yemen, Dem	1,130	560	X	X	X	X	X
EUROPE							
Albania	X	X	X	X	X	X	X
Austria	68,800	9,140	5.5	2.6	4	38	58
Belgium	83,070	8,430	5.2	1.5	3	34	64
Bulgaria	X	X	X	X	X	X	X
Czechoslovakia	X	X	X	X	X	X	X
Denmark	57,700	11,290	3.8	1.3	5	25	70
Finland	53,090	10,830	5.2	2.8	7	34	59
France	542,960	9,860	5.5	2.3	4	34	62
German Dem Rep	X	X	X	X	X	X	X
Germany, Fed Rep	678,880	11,090	4.7	2.0	2	46	52
Greece	36,940	3,740	7.7	2.7	18	29	53
Hungary	21,950	2,050	6.1	4.6	20	42	38
Iceland	2,250	9,380	4.3	2.3	X	X	X
Ireland	17,500	4,950	4.8	2.8	11	25	64
Italy	367,040	6,440	5.2	2.0	5	40	55
Luxembourg	4,980	13,650	5.8	2.5	X	X	X
Malta	1,210	3,370	7.7	8.7	X	X	X
Netherlands	135,830	9,430	5.3	1.4	4	32	64
Norway	57,080	13,750	4.0	3.5	4	43	54
Poland	X	X	X	X	15	52	33
Portugal	20,050	1,970	7.0	2.3	9	40	50
Romania	X	X	X	X	X	X	X
Spain	172,360	4,470	6.4	1.4	X	X	X
Sweden	99,060	11,880	3.6	1.1	3	31	66
Switzerland	105,060	15,990	4.4	0.9	X	X	X
United Kingdom	480,680	8,530	2.8	1.0	2	36	62
Yugoslavia	48,690	2,120	6.1	3.9	15	46	40
USSR	X	X	X	X	X	X	X
OCEANIA							
Australia	184,980	11,890	5.6	2.7	X	X	X
Fiji	1,250	1,840	8.0	3.1	X	X	X
New Zealand	23,530	7,240	3.8	1.2	9	32	60
Papua New Guinea	2,480	760	5.9	1.2	34	9	58
Solomon Islands	X	X	X	X	X	X	X

Source: The World Bank.
X = not available.
For additional information, see Sources and Technical Notes.

Basic Economic Indicators

Table 15.2 External Debt Indicators, 1970–85

	Disbursed Long-Term Public Debt (million $US)					Debt as Percentage of Gross National Product					Debt Service as Percentage of Exports of Goods and Services				
	1970	1975	1980	1984	1985	1970	1975	1980	1984	1985	1970	1975	1980	1984	1985
TOTAL 107 COUNTRIES	49,486	125,718	351,758	552,962	X	13	15	20	33	X	10	9	13	16a	X
SUB-SAHARAN AFRICA	5,433	13,992	41,018	57,306	X	15	16	23	38	X	5	6	7	17a	X
Benin	41	79	332	585	677	16	15	29	60	X	2	4	3	9a	X
Botswana	15	147	152	277	334	18	58	18	31	X	1	3	2	4	X
Burkina Faso	21	63	301	407	X	6	10	21	43	X	6	6	8	9a	X
Burundi	7	18	141	334	X	3	4	15	36	X	2	6	8	8a	X
Cameroon	132	372	2,049	1,738	1,975	12	15	31	23	25	3	5	9	9	8
Cape Verde	X	1	20	68	X	X	1	19	70	X	X	X	X	X	X
Central African Rep	24	71	160	224	X	14	19	20	37	X	5	7	1	12a	X
Chad	32	67	202	109	X	12	14	40	X	X	4	6	3	2	X
Comoros	1	5	43	101	129	5	8	36	X	X	X	X	2	25	X
Congo	144	423	1,132	1,396	X	54	57	71	76	X	11	13	10	21a	X
Cote d'Ivoire	256	943	4,347	4,835	X	18	25	43	84	X	7	9	24	21	X
Djibouti	X	X	26	62	98	X	X	8	X	X	X	X	X	X	X
Equatorial Guinea	5	25	58	103	X	8	24	X	X	X	X	X	X	X	X
Ethiopia	169	344	701	1,384	X	10	13	17	30	X	11	7	6	14	X
Gabon	91	797	1,356	725	X	29	40	36	24	X	6	5	17	9a	X
Gambia	5	13	106	161	X	10	11	46	101	X	1	1	1	8a	X
Ghana	495	689	1,100	1,122	X	26	25	25	23	X	5	6	8	13	X
Guinea	313	759	1,030	1,168	1,361	47	68	63	59	X	X	X	X	X	X
Guinea-Bissau	X	7	104	149	X	X	6	99	112	X	X	X	X	12a	X
Kenya	319	604	2,216	2,633	X	21	19	32	46	X	5	4	12	22	X
Lesotho	8	14	63	134	X	8	5	10	24	X	4	0	1	5	X
Liberia	158	179	567	781	874	50	31	58	80	X	8	8	6	4	X
Madagascar	93	174	1,021	1,636	X	11	10	32	73	X	4	3	11	24a	X
Malawi	122	257	647	731	X	43	42	76	45	X	7	8	22	23a	X
Mali	241	343	697	1,153	1,327	89	55	52	115	X	1	3	4	9	X
Mauritania	27	188	731	1,171	X	14	42	109	171	X	3	21	11	10a	X
Mauritius	32	46	296	354	X	14	7	26	35	X	3	2	6	15	X
Niger	32	112	399	678	X	9	17	22	62	X	4	5	6	18a	X
Nigeria	458	1,053	4,238	11,641	13,016	5	3	5	16	15	4	3	2	25	31
Rwanda	2	24	163	254	324	1	4	14	16	X	1	1	2	5	X
Senegal	100	304	926	1,555	X	12	17	32	69	X	3	6	20	7a	X
Seychelles	X	X	25	43	X	X	X	18	28a	X	X	X	0	4	X
Sierra Leone	61	149	350	330	391	15	24	33	34	52	11	10	14	10	X
Somalia	77	230	714	1,233	X	24	33	61	90	X	2	3	4	29	X
Sudan	307	1,235	3,802	5,659	X	15	29	55	77a	X	11	22	10	14	X
Swaziland	37	34	166	178	X	33	12	29	35	X	X	1	3	5	X
Tanzania, United Rep	250	803	2,011	2,594	X	20	31	41	68	X	5	6	11	14a	X
Togo	40	120	915	687	787	16	20	83	104	X	3	10	8	29	X
Uganda	138	212	603	675	X	7	9	20	14	X	3	5	7	21a	X
Zaire	311	1,718	4,288	4,240	4,825	18	49	74	137	X	4	15	17	8a	X
Zambia	623	1,147	2,185	2,779	X	36	49	61	114	X	6	11	18	11	X
Zimbabwe	239	190	697	1,413	1,526	16	6	13	28	X	2	1	3	20	X
EAST ASIA & PACIFIC	5,729	17,795	47,803	81,603	X	14	17	18	26	X	5	4	5	7a	X
Fiji	10	56	180	290	X	5	8	15	25	X	2	2	3	10	X
Hong Kong	2	21	485	270	X	0	0	2	1	X	0	0	0	0a	X
Indonesia	2,443	7,994	14,971	22,883	X	27	27	22	30	X	7	8	8	15	X
Korea, Rep	1,797	5,545	15,780	24,642	X	20	27	26	30	X	19	11	12	14	X
Malaysia	390	1,338	3,865	11,846	X	10	15	17	39	X	4	3	3	8	X
Papua New Guinea	39	275	510	949	1,010	6	21	21	41	X	X	X	6	13	X
Philippines	574	1,384	6,526	11,176	X	8	9	19	35	X	7	7	7	14	X
Singapore	154	550	1,320	1,905	1,791	8	10	12	11	X	1	1	1	1	X
Solomon Islands	X	X	8	26	X	X	X	6	15a	X	X	X	0	0	X
Thailand	326	616	4,100	7,538	9,800	5	4	13	18	25	3	2	5	12	15
Vanuatu	X	X	4	5	7	X	X	4	X	X	X	X	X	1	X
Western Samoa	X	16	55	64	65	X	X	X	X	X	X	7	16	14	X
LATIN AMERICA & CARIBBEAN	15,751	45,081	128,951	246,083	X	11	13	19	40	X	13	14	21	24a	X
Argentina	1,878	3,121	10,186	28,671	X	9	9	18	41	X	22	22	18	29	X
Bahamas	44	95	90	209	X	12	23	12	22	X	X	2	2	4	X
Barbados	13	27	98	302	352	7	7	12	27	X	1	2	3	3	X
Belize	4	5	47	76	94	9	5	28	44	X	X	X	X	X	X
Bolivia	481	824	2,227	3,204	X	35	34	53	98	X	11	15	27	38	X
Brazil	3,234	13,923	39,894	66,502	X	8	11	17	34	X	13	18	35	27	X
Chile	2,067	3,733	4,740	10,839	X	26	54	18	63	X	19	27	22	26	X
Colombia	1,299	2,377	4,084	7,980	X	19	19	12	23	X	12	11	9	21	X
Costa Rica	134	421	1,701	3,380	X	14	22	37	110	X	10	11	17	26	X
Dominican Rep	226	449	1,229	2,388	X	16	13	21	50	X	5	5	12	18a	X
Ecuador	193	434	3,300	6,630	X	12	10	29	76	X	9	4	19	33	X
El Salvador	88	196	527	1,388	X	9	11	15	35	X	4	9	3	17a	X
Grenada	6	9	22	40	X	30	28	35	49	X	X	X	4	10a	X
Guatemala	106	143	549	1,991	2,148	6	4	7	22	X	7	2	2	15	X
Guyana	85	296	566	681	721	34	60	103	161	X	4	5	17	20a	X
Haiti	40	57	267	494	534	10	8	18	27	X	8	7	7	6	X
Honduras	95	268	991	1,841	X	14	25	42	61	X	3	5	10	15a	X
Jamaica	160	695	1,396	2,175	X	12	32	58	105	X	3	7	14	21	X
Mexico	3,196	11,394	33,679	69,007	X	9	13	19	42	X	24	25	32	34	X
Nicaragua	147	593	1,687	3,835	X	15	36	81	142	X	11	12	16	18a	X
Panama	194	771	2,266	3,091	X	20	42	68	73	X	8	6	6	8	X
Paraguay	112	189	633	1,287	1,525	13	11	16	33	X	12	9	12	13	X

World Resources 1987

Table 15.2

	Disbursed Long-Term Public Debt (million $US)					Debt as Percentage of Gross National Product					Debt Service as Percentage of Exports of Goods and Services				
	1970	1975	1980	1984	1985	1970	1975	1980	1984	1985	1970	1975	1980	1984	1985
Peru	856	3,021	6,169	9,825	X	13	20	33	59	X	12	26	31	15	X
St. Vincent	1	3	10	21	23	3	10	18	22	X	X	X	1	2a	X
Trinidad and Tobago	102	159	623	915	1,087	12	7	10	10	X	5	2	6	5	X
Uruguay	269	618	1,127	2,545	2,686	11	18	11	52	X	22	41	12	30	X
Venezuela	728	1,262	10,873	17,247	X	7	5	18	38	X	3	5	13	13	X
NORTH AFRICA & MIDDLE EAST	**4,356**	**13,798**	**44,430**	**50,876**	**X**	**19**	**27**	**38**	**38**	**X**	**14**	**11**	**21**	**25a**	**X**
Algeria	937	4,477	16,298	12,052	X	19	31	41	24	X	4	9	27	32	X
Egypt	1,750	4,842	12,378	15,808	X	23	42	50	50	X	36	28	22	34	X
Jordan	119	340	1,265	2,336	X	24	33	39	56	X	4	5	8	15	X
Lebanon	64	46	197	179	X	4	X	X	X	X	X	X	X	X	X
Morocco	711	1,757	7,109	10,169	X	18	19	39	83	X	8	7	37	38	X
Oman	X	287	440	1,346	1,945	X	17	8	19	X	X	2	5	5	X
Syrian Arab Rep	232	685	2,107	2,453	X	11	10	16	15	X	11	8	12	11a	X
Tunisia	541	1,021	3,227	3,707	X	39	24	37	46	X	19	8	14	24	X
Yemen	X	244	900	1,688	1,868	X	26	30	44	X	X	9	6	27	X
Yemen, Dem	1	99	499	1,252	X	X	32	62	107	X	0	0	5	22	X
SOUTH ASIA	**11,419**	**19,819**	**32,898**	**42,627**	**X**	**15**	**17**	**16**	**17**	**X**	**18**	**15**	**10**	**13**	**X**
Bangladesh	X	1,605	3,549	5,155	5,966	X	11	28	37	39	X	18	7	14	17
Burma	101	281	1,453	2,219	X	5	8	25	35	X	16	17	23	37	X
India	7,940	12,244	17,574	22,403	X	15	14	11	12	X	22	13	9	10	X
Maldives	X	X	25	51	52	X	X	51	X	X	X	X	1	18	X
Nepal	3	34	174	427	527	0	2	9	17	X	X	X	2	3	X
Pakistan	3,081	5,099	8,785	9,990	10,681	31	45	34	30	32	24	19	18	27	32
Sri Lanka	321	597	1,344	2,422	2,815	16	20	34	41	X	11	22	6	11	X
EUROPE & MEDITERRANEAN	**6,798**	**15,234**	**56,658**	**74,467**	**X**	**14**	**10**	**20**	**33**	**X**	**8**	**7**	**11**	**18**	**X**
Cyprus	57	76	398	769	923	10	11	18	37	X	2	3	5	9	X
Greece	905	2,633	4,788	9,456	X	9	12	12	28	X	9	13	11	18	X
Hungary	X	X	6,376	7,380	X	X	X	29	38	X	X	X	14	24	X
Israel	2,274	5,915	11,495	15,415	X	41	46	62	77	X	3	19	12	18	X
Malta	26	32	101	104	106	10	7	8	10	X	2	1	0	1	X
Portugal	485	1,088	6,576	10,583	X	8	7	27	59	X	X	4	15	36	X
Romania	X	X	7,131	6,296	X	X	X	13	16	X	X	X	10	12	X
Turkey	1,854	3,165	15,195	15,774	X	14	9	26	32	X	22	13	28	23	X
Yugoslavia	1,199	2,325	4,598	8,690	X	9	8	7	22	X	10	7	5	7	X

Source: The World Bank.
Note: a. 1983 data.
0 = zero or less than half the unit of measure; X = not available.
For additional information, see Sources and Technical Notes.

Figure 15.1 Price Index of 33 Nonfuel Commodities

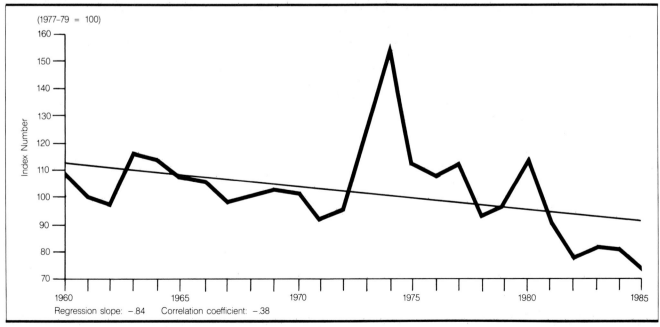

(1977–79 = 100)

Regression slope: −.84   Correlation coefficient: −.38

Source: Table 15.3

World Resources 1987

Table 15.3 World Commodity Indexes and Prices, 1960–86

COMMODITY INDEXES (index numbers based on constant prices with 1977-79 = 100)												
	1960	1961	1962	1963	1964	1965	1966	1967	1968	1969	1970	1971
33 Nonfuel Commodities	107	100	98	117	115	107	106	98	100	103	102	92
Total Agriculture	104	95	94	121	111	92	89	87	88	91	91	86
Total Food	92	87	85	121	109	86	83	82	82	86	89	83
Beverages	71	66	62	62	70	66	62	60	60	59	64	53
Cereals	114	120	130	132	129	125	136	143	140	132	113	103
Fats and Oils	104	106	98	105	106	117	110	103	100	94	104	99
Other Foods	111	96	97	223	167	84	76	79	80	105	109	116
Nonfood Agricultural Products	155	131	128	121	120	117	114	107	112	114	100	96
Timber	72	73	79	78	65	75	76	80	83	76	76	73
Metals and Minerals	125	120	115	115	138	158	164	136	140	146	143	117

COMMODITY PRICES (in constant 1980 $US per unit measure)															
	1972	1973	1974	1975	1976	1977	1978	1979	1980	1981	1982	1983	1984	1985	1986[a]
Cocoa (kg)	1.61	2.44	2.76	1.98	3.21	5.41	4.23	3.61	2.60	2.07	1.78	2.20	2.53	2.36	2.17
Coffee (kg)	2.81	3.29	2.86	2.94	5.17	9.70	3.97	4.26	4.58	3.85	3.25	3.27	3.48	3.50	6.09
Tea (kg)	2.63	2.28	2.48	2.21	2.41	3.84	2.72	2.36	2.23	2.01	1.98	2.42	3.65	2.08	1.96
Rice (metric ton)	367.5	754.3	959.3	578.2	399.5	388.9	456.5	363.3	433.9	480.4	300.1	287.2	265.9	226.1	225.0
Grain Sorghum (metric ton)	140.0	200.4	214.2	178.2	165.2	126.3	116.5	118.8	128.9	125.8	111.2	133.6	125.5	107.9	97.5
Maize (metric ton)	140.0	211.2	233.6	190.5	176.5	136.1	125.1	126.6	125.3	130.2	112.0	141.1	143.4	117.5	105.5
Wheat (metric ton)	178.3	317.2	369.4	288.7	234.1	165.4	167.5	189.0	190.8	195.4	170.6	175.8	174.5	181.5	189.2
Sugar (kg)	0.40	0.45	1.16	0.72	0.40	0.26	0.21	0.23	0.63	0.37	0.19	0.19	0.12	0.09	0.15
Beef (kg)	3.70	4.33	2.80	2.11	2.48	2.15	2.66	3.16	2.76	2.46	2.45	2.53	2.40	2.26	2.19
Lamb (kg)	2.46	2.98	2.32	2.27	2.42	2.36	2.70	2.60	2.89	2.73	2.44	2.00	2.03	1.93	2.35
Bananas (kg)	0.41	0.36	0.33	0.39	0.40	0.39	0.36	0.36	0.38	0.40	0.38	0.45	0.39	0.41	X
Black Pepper (kg)	2.55	2.76	3.31	3.19	3.08	3.59	2.91	2.32	1.99	1.58	1.59	1.75	2.41	X	X
Copra (metric ton)	352.3	761.0	1,171.7	408.1	431.7	574.7	584.4	737.6	453.8	377.0	321.9	514.5	749.1	404.2	196.4
Coconut Oil (metric ton)	585.5	1,105.6	1,766.4	626.6	656.2	826.0	848.7	1,079.5	673.8	567.1	475.8	757.2	1,217.9	618.0	295.2
Groundnut Meal (metric ton)	305.0	573.3	308.0	222.9	276.3	311.4	254.7	231.4	240.3	236.7	193.8	207.5	197.4	150.1	172.5
Groundnut Oil (metric ton)	1,064.8	1,177.2	1,905.8	1,364.7	1,163.3	1,217.6	1,340.6	974.5	858.8	1,037.8	599.3	737.5	1,072.5	947.5	611.2
Linseed (metric ton)	362.5	689.4	923.4	538.2	478.8	388.4	310.1	366.0	350.9	352.5	305.3	287.7	314.7	X	X
Linseed Oil (metric ton)	516.0	1,212.1	1,998.6	1,116.2	857.1	659.9	539.4	700.7	697.1	656.7	531.9	502.7	604.0	X	X
Palm Kernels (metric ton)	290.3	557.3	822.7	329.3	361.1	466.1	451.9	548.3	345.1	315.7	271.5	378.9	557.6	X	X
Palm Oil (metric ton)	543.3	813.6	1,184.1	691.4	638.2	757.1	745.6	716.9	583.5	567.9	456.1	520.1	768.8	524.2	271.1
Soybeans (metric ton)	350	625	490	350	363	400	333	327	296	287	251	293	298	235	225
Soybean Oil (metric ton)	675	1,002	1,407	986	688	823	754	726	597	504	458	547	764	599	389
Soybean Meal (metric ton)	323	651	326	247	311	329	265	267	262	251	224	247	208	165	194
Fish Meal (metric ton)	598	1,168	658	390	590	649	509	433	504	466	362	470	394	293	328
Cotton (kg)	1.98	2.92	2.50	1.85	2.66	2.22	1.95	1.85	2.05	1.84	1.64	1.92	1.88	1.38	1.09
Burlap (meter)	0.56	0.46	0.46	0.52	0.35	0.30	0.31	0.27	0.33	0.40	0.27	0.27	0.30	X	X
Jute (metric ton)	747.5	622.8	624.8	590.8	464.1	458.4	540.0	424.8	310.0	274.6	292.8	313.5	559.9	610.4	288.0
Sisal (metric ton)	600	1,136	1,869	924	736	733	609	775	765	642	608	584	616	550	537

World Resources 1987

COMMODITY INDEXES (Index numbers based on constant prices with 1977–79 = 100)

1972	1973	1974	1975	1976	1977	1978	1979	1980	1981	1982	1983	1984	1985
94	122	157	112	109	112	93	97	113	91	77	82	81	73
92	120	164	113	110	116	94	93	113	89	73	78	78	67
92	119	175	119	110	119	93	91	115	89	70	74	75	64
54	59	56	48	90	138	89	81	66	54	58	59	70	62
101	178	212	149	119	100	104	96	105	112	84	91	88	80
89	157	150	89	94	106	97	98	82	79	66	79	96	73
155	170	374	241	149	105	93	103	219	141	86	89	65	54
91	124	114	89	111	102	97	102	106	92	83	95	90	81
67	100	99	67	89	91	80	124	137	102	106	99	113	109
107	135	149	116	111	104	92	104	106	93	85	88	85	84

COMMODITY PRICES (in constant 1980 $US per unit measure)

	1972	1973	1974	1975	1976	1977	1978	1979	1980	1981	1982	1983	1984	1985	1986[a]
Wool (kg)	6.00	11.07	6.50	4.37	5.35	5.11	4.66	4.86	4.60	4.25	4.02	3.77	3.86	3.73	3.45
Natural Rubber (kg)	1.00	1.69	1.54	1.05	1.37	1.31	1.38	1.56	1.62	1.25	1.03	1.28	1.16	0.97	0.95
Logs (cubic meter)	94.0	141.4	139.1	94.4	125.0	128.3	114.0	175.7	192.9	143.9	148.8	140.3	159.3	138.2	153.5
Plywood (sheet)	2.39	4.07	2.70	1.94	2.32	2.36	2.35	2.88	2.74	2.44	2.38	2.38	2.39	2.21	2.75
Sawnwood (cubic meter)	265.0	336.4	253.3	265.0	263.9	220.1	255.2	371.8	365.1	312.6	309.4	315.7	323.6	289.3	278.3
Tobacco (metric ton)	2,405	2,073	2,266	2,416	2,215	2,386	2,099	2,336	2,300	2,338	2,469	2,329	2,101	X	X
Coal (metric ton)	47.90	45.04	78.80	86.42	84.08	77.51	69.24	61.95	55.70	57.76	57.79	59.62	61.00	X	X
Petroleum (barrel)	4.8	5.8	19.8	17.4	18.4	18.3	16.0	20.4	30.5	34.2	34.0	30.2	30.1	29.1	28.3
Gasoline (metric ton)	76.0	189.2	232.0	191.6	216.5	188.0	198.8	367.3	358.0	352.3	331.6	293.8	271.8	267.2	185.9
Jet Fuel (metric ton)	78.3	195.5	188.9	180.3	187.8	185.0	181.6	384.1	349.3	333.7	330.3	288.0	276.2	277.3	195.3
Gas Oil (metric ton)	67.0	180.2	182.8	159.2	168.6	168.3	159.8	340.9	307.1	297.2	296.8	257.5	251.6	251.1	174.4
Fuel Oil (metric ton)	35.3	61.9	123.0	98.9	107.5	108.9	94.0	146.5	170.2	182.6	168.0	169.5	188.2	158.8	84.8
Aluminum (metric ton)	1,080	1,429	1,671	1,099	1,353	1,416	1,298	1,667	1,730	1,331	1,087	1,551	1,446	1,163	1,331
Bauxite (metric ton)	30.00	26.94	41.06	40.29	42.70	44.00	42.61	40.13	41.20	39.80	36.89	36.00	35.06	X	X
Copper (metric ton)	2,678	3,849	3,644	1,970	2,199	1,870	1,696	2,177	2,183	1,733	1,516	1,652	1,453	1,484	1,478
Lead (metric ton)	755	927	1,050	664	699	883	822	1,325	906	723	559	441	467	409	396
Tin (metric ton)	9,425	10,405	14,515	10,940	11,903	15,374	16,035	16,950	16,775	14,089	13,141	13,473	12,904	12,507	X
Zinc (metric ton)	978	981	1,404	1,368	1,292	1,083	849	901	825	977	869	946	1,130	932	779
Iron Ore (metric ton)	32.0	36.9	33.6	36.0	34.4	30.9	24.1	25.6	26.7	24.2	26.5	24.9	24.5	23.8	22.9
Manganese Ore (10 kg Mn)	1.59	1.61	1.99	2.19	2.28	2.11	1.78	1.51	1.57	1.67	1.68	1.58	1.51	X	X
Nickel (metric ton)	7,700	7,270	6,770	7,277	7,808	7,433	5,729	6,563	6,519	5,924	4,957	4,847	5,013	5,130	4,216
Steel (metric ton)	449.3	403.5	452.2	461.9	464.2	460.9	452.1	444.4	452.8	505.4	547.8	566.5	570.3	X	X
Phosphate Rock (metric ton)	28.8	29.7	96.5	106.7	56.5	43.6	36.0	36.2	46.7	49.3	43.4	38.3	40.4	35.5	35.6
Diammonium Phosphate (DAP) (metric ton)	227.5	256.0	588.7	386.9	188.4	190.0	173.7	212.0	222.2	194.0	187.3	190.4	199.5	177.0	175.3
Potassium Chloride (metric ton)	83.8	91.6	107.1	129.5	86.3	72.9	70.1	84.1	115.7	111.8	83.6	78.1	88.3	88.0	76.8
Triple Superphosphate (metric ton)	170	216	538	322	143	139	122	161	180	160	141	140	139	127	136
Urea (metric ton)	148.3	204.3	558.9	315.3	175.8	182.0	179.9	189.6	222.1	214.9	162.7	140.5	180.7	142.7	114.5

Source: The World Bank.
Note: a. 1986 data refer to January through July.
X = not available.
For additional information, see Sources and Technical Notes.

Basic Economic Indicators

Sources and Technical Notes

Table 15.1 Gross National Product, 1965–84

Sources: GNP: The World Bank, *The World Bank Atlas 1986* (The World Bank, Washington, D.C., 1986). Change in GNP: unpublished World Bank data (October 1986). Distribution of Gross Domestic Product: The World Bank, *World Development Report 1986* (Oxford University Press, New York, 1986).

Gross National Product is the sum of two components: the Gross Domestic Product (the final output of goods and services produced by the domestic economy, including net exports of goods and nonfactor services) and net factor income from abroad. Net factor income from abroad is income residents receive on a net basis from abroad for factor services (labor, investment, and loans). Most countries estimate Gross Domestic Product by the production method. This method sums the final outputs of the various sectors of the economy (agriculture, manufacturing, government services, etc.) from which the value of the inputs to production have been subtracted.

Gross National Product in domestic currency was converted to U.S. dollars using a three-year average exchange rate, adjusted for domestic and U.S. inflation. 1984 GNP data are provisional.

The average annual percentage change of GNP was calculated by fitting a least-square regression line to the logarithmic values for GNP.

The agricultural sector includes farming, forestry, hunting, and fishing; the industrial sector includes mining, manufacturing, construction, and the provision of electricity, water, and gas; and the service sector summarizes all other economic activity. Because a sizable fraction of agricultural, forestry, hunting, and fishing output does not enter the money economy (especially in developing countries with large subsistence populations), the output of this sector and of GDP are often difficult to estimate.

Gross National Product data are produced by countries that use a market-oriented system of national accounts. World Bank economists periodically review the national income accounting practices of developing countries and adjust national GNP figures to fit common definitions. The Economic Analysis and Projection Department of the Bank reviews country data annually and further adjusts them as needed.

For additional information on procedures used to estimate GNP, see the Technical Notes to the World Development Indicators Annex, *World Development Report*.

Table 15.2 External Debt Indicators, 1970–85

Source: The World Bank, *World Debt Tables* and *First* and *Second Supplements* (The World Bank, Washington, D.C., March, July, and August 1986).

The World Bank operates the Debtor Reporting System (DRS), which compiles reports supplied by 107 of the Bank's member countries. Countries submit detailed reports on the annual status, transactions, and terms of the long-term external debt of public agencies and of publicly guaranteed private debt. Additional data are drawn from the World Bank, the International Monetary Fund (IMF), regional development banks, government lending agencies, and the Creditor Reporting System (CRS). The CRS is operated by the Organisation for Economic Co-operation and Development to compile reports from the members of its Development Assistance Committee.

A country's external liabilities include long-term debt, use of IMF credit, and short-term debt.

Long-term debt is an obligation with a maturity of at least one year that is owed to nonresidents and is repayable in foreign currency, goods, or services. Long-term debt is divided into long-term public and publicly guaranteed debt and long-term private debt. Public debt is an obligation of a national or subnational government or of their agencies and autonomous bodies. Publicly guaranteed debt is an external obligation of a private debtor that is guaranteed for repayment by a public entity.

The data described as "disbursed long-term public debt" are outstanding public and publicly guaranteed long-term debt. IMF credit, private nonguaranteed debt, and all short-term debt are excluded.

Private nonguaranteed debt is an external obligation of a private debtor that is not guaranteed by a public entity. Data for this class of debt are less extensive than those for public debt; many countries do not report these data through the DRS. Reporting has improved recently, however, with complete or partial data currently available from 36 countries and World Bank estimates available for 14 others. These 50 countries account for the majority of the private nonguaranteed debt of developing countries. In 1984, the private nonguaranteed debt of the 107 members of the DRS was estimated at one-fifth their "disbursed long-term public debt."

Short-term debt is public or private debt that has a maturity of one year or less. This class of debt is especially difficult for countries to monitor. Only a few countries supply these data through the DRS; the Bank supplements these data with creditor-country reports and information from international clearinghouse banks and other sources to derive rough estimates of short-term debt. In 1984, the short-term debt of the 107 members of the DRS was estimated at one quarter of their "disbursed long-term public debt."

Debt as a percentage of GNP is calculated using the "disbursed long-term public debt" described above. Gross National Product is defined in the Technical Note for Table 15.1. Total debt service comprises actual interest payments and repayments of principal made on the "disbursed long-term public debt" in foreign currencies, goods and services in the year specified. Exports of goods and services are the total value of goods and all services sold to the rest of the world. These data are from IMF files.

Debt data are reported to the Bank in the units of currency in which they are payable. The Bank converts these data to U.S. dollar figures using the IMF par values or central rates or, where appropriate, the current market rates. Debt service data are converted to U.S. dollar figures at the average exchange rate for the given year. Comparability of data among countries and years is limited by variations in methods, definitions, and comprehensiveness of data collection and reporting. Refer to the source for details.

Table 15.3 World Commodity Indexes and Prices, 1960–86

Sources: The World Bank, *Commodity Trade and Price Trends* (Johns Hopkins University Press, Baltimore, Maryland, 1986); and unpublished World Bank data (August 1986).

Price data are compiled from major international market places for standard grades of each commodity. For example, the gasoline series refers to 91/92 octane regular gasoline, in barges, f.o.b. (free on board) Rotterdam. Recent data are provisional.

The 1980 U.S. constant dollar figures were derived by converting current average monthly prices in local currencies to U.S. dollars using the monthly average exchange rate. These monthly average U.S. dollar figures were then averaged to produce an annual average dollar figure, which was adjusted to 1980 constant dollars using the Manufacturing Unit Value (MUV) index. The MUV index is a composite price index of all manufactured goods traded internationally. Current price data for January-July 1986 were adjusted to 1980 constant dollar values using the 1985 MUV index number.

The aggregate price indexes have the following components:
1. 33 Nonfuel commodities: individual items listed under 4–10 below;
2. Total agriculture: total food and nonfood agricultural products;
3. Total foods: beverages, cereals, fats and oils, other foods;
4. Beverages: coffee, cocoa, tea;
5. Cereals: maize, rice, wheat, grain sorghum;
6. Fats and oils: palm oil, coconut oil, groundnut oil, soybeans, copra, groundnut meal, soybean meal;
7. Other foods: sugar, beef, bananas, oranges;
8. Nonfood agricultural products: cotton, jute, rubber, tobacco;
9. Timber: logs;
10. Metals and Minerals: copper, tin, nickel, bauxite, aluminum, iron ore, manganese ore, lead, zinc, phosphate rock.

16. Population and Health

Population and health data are gathered in three ways: by enumeration, by survey, and by registration. *Enumerated* data, such as the size of population and its age structure, are collected directly through censuses. (See Tables 16.1 and 16.2.) *Surveys* are used to monitor a sample believed to be typical of the whole, e.g., women who responded to the contraception surveys should represent conditions throughout their countries. (See Table 16.5.) Because the burden of reporting falls on individuals, *registration* data are often incomplete. (See the Technical Note for Table 16.4.) Registration may be inconvenient, time-consuming, or impossible, given local conditions.

Another type of data shown in this chapter is modeled from measured information. Total fertility and life expectancy at birth (Tables 16.2 and 16.3) are two indicators that integrate current information into predictive tools. Life expectancy at birth, for example, assumes that the children born in a given year will experience, on average, the age-specific mortality rates current in that year. However, age-specific mortality rates will probably change as these children mature.

Demographic data from censuses and surveys are generally reliable, although developing-country data are less reliable than are developed-country data. Many countries are improving their data-gathering capabilities, often in cooperation with development assistance agencies such as the United Nations Fund for Population Activities (UNFPA), bilateral aid agencies, and private assistance organizations. In 1985, UNFPA alone allocated 8.2 percent of its total assistance budget ($11.5 million out of $141.4 million) to data collection programs; in sub-Saharan Africa the figure was 26 percent. Of the 146 countries shown in Tables 16.1–16.4, 129 conducted a national population census or major population survey between 1975 and 1985; 14 conducted their most recent census before 1975; and three have not conducted a modern census.

Data on legal international migration are weak, and those for illegal migration and refugee movements are even worse. Illegal migrants, fearing expulsion, avoid government census workers. Refugees, fleeing social, economic, environmental, or political turmoil, are difficult to count; they often return to their country of origin or move to a third country before they can be counted. Governments (of both the refugees' home and host countries) often have an interest in over- or understating the number of refugees. Also, the upheavals that turn thousands of people into refugees are usually so severe that host governments or international agencies give first priority to providing basic services and do not always take an accurate census.

Malaria and cholera data shown in Table 16.4 give a global picture of the spread and severity of these water-related diseases. However, because many countries either do not report or report only clinically diagnosed cases, the data do not reflect the real situation. Just in Africa, for example, about 98 million people suffer from malaria, according to the World Health Organization (WHO), whose estimates are based on the infections expected according to the degree of endemicity. In 1981, however, only 7.9 million cases of malaria were reported for the entire world.

Although reliable estimates of cholera incidence are unavailable, 5–10 percent of all diarrheal disease diagnoses are thought to be cholera, placing the annual incidence at 25–50 million in children under five years. Mortality due to malaria and cholera is unknown for many countries; it is not shown in Table 16.4.

Reported data for other water-related diseases are even less reliable than are those for malaria and cholera. WHO estimates that 20 million people suffer from oncheocerciasis, and more than 125 million are infected with schistosomiasis. (Country data for these diseases are not included here.)

Estimates of unmet need for contraception vary, depending on how "unmet," "need," and "contraception" are defined. (See Table 16.5.) Several factors are involved: first, because unmet need estimates are based on surveys of women, they do not reflect men's attitudes toward family size and contraceptive use. Second, many estimates exclude pregnant women and those who are breastfeeding, thereby not accounting for women who may need contraception in the near future. Third, many surveys polled only married women, omitting the contraceptive needs of the unmarried. Further, none of the surveys used accounts for contraceptive requirements for spacing births. For this reason especially, all estimates should be considered conservative.

Table 16.1 Estimated Size and Growth of Population, 1955–2000

	Estimated Population (thousands)			Estimated Average Annual Population Change (percent)				
	1960	1987	2000	1955-60	1965-70	1975-80	1985-90	1995-2000
WORLD	**3,018,878**	**4,997,609**	**6,121,813**	**1.86**	**2.04**	**1.75**	**1.63**	**1.51**
AFRICA	**280,051**	**589,208**	**871,817**	**2.31**	**2.62**	**2.97**	**3.02**	**2.99**
Algeria	10,800	23,157	33,444	2.12	2.85	3.06	3.21	2.48
Angola	4,816	9,220	13,234	1.64	1.52	3.39	2.67	2.82
Benin	2,251	4,307	6,532	1.20	2.06	2.77	3.12	3.24
Botswana	481	1,193	1,917	2.10	2.54	3.84	3.70	3.63
Burkina Faso	4,279	7,310	10,538	1.75	1.76	2.02	2.65	2.90
Burundi	2,927	4,999	7,226	1.76	1.45	1.80	2.84	2.80
Cameroon	5,483	10,438	15,168	1.94	2.13	2.57	2.80	2.91
Cape Verde	200	341	470	2.98	3.04	0.87	2.36	2.44
Central African Rep	1,605	2,701	3,750	1.33	1.63	2.22	2.42	2.57
Chad	3,064	5,265	7,308	1.53	1.82	2.10	2.44	2.56
Comoros	215	472	695	2.04	2.43	3.40	3.08	2.84
Congo	972	1,836	2,643	1.90	2.18	2.46	2.73	2.83
Cote d'Ivoire	3,731	10,529	16,006	1.58	4.15	3.77	3.45	3.17
Djibouti	126	388	604	2.19	2.42	7.41	3.32	3.39
Egypt	25,922	49,143	63,941	2.40	2.35	2.69	2.27	1.89
Equatorial Guinea	252	410	559	1.18	1.56	1.99	2.31	2.41
Ethiopia	24,191	45,997	66,509	2.19	2.41	2.32	2.79	2.82
Gabon	867	1,195	1,603	0.75	0.97	1.19	2.01	2.25
Gambia	374	670	898	1.36	2.24	2.15	2.13	2.30
Ghana	6,772	14,523	22,607	4.51	2.02	3.30	3.36	3.43
Guinea	3,660	6,380	8,879	1.38	1.95	2.17	2.48	2.57
Guinea-Bissau	540	925	1,229	0.73	0.06	5.04	2.08	2.21
Kenya	7,903	22,397	38,534	3.21	3.66	4.03	4.20	4.11
Lesotho	870	1,600	2,255	1.84	2.01	2.41	2.61	2.65
Liberia	1,047	2,336	3,615	2.11	2.73	3.36	3.25	3.43
Libya	1,349	3,883	6,082	3.61	4.04	4.03	3.67	3.28
Madagascar	5,362	10,605	15,550	2.02	2.32	2.70	2.90	2.95
Malawi	3,529	7,415	11,387	2.15	2.56	2.82	3.32	3.25
Mali	4,636	8,569	12,658	1.99	2.15	2.19	2.94	3.03
Mauritania	981	2,007	2,998	2.17	2.45	2.75	3.08	3.07
Mauritius	660	1,087	1,298	3.17	1.82	1.91	1.65	1.19
Morocco	11,626	23,014	29,512	2.75	2.78	2.27	2.30	1.66
Mozambique	6,545	14,724	21,104	1.54	2.28	4.42	2.69	2.79
Niger	3,234	6,489	9,750	1.36	2.08	2.59	3.01	3.19
Nigeria	42,305	101,992	161,930	2.63	3.23	3.49	3.49	3.57
Rwanda	2,753	6,488	10,123	2.84	3.05	3.31	3.36	3.43
Senegal	3,041	6,793	9,765	2.03	2.89	3.46	2.71	2.82
Sierra Leone	2,475	3,741	4,867	1.25	1.38	1.59	1.93	2.07
Somalia	2,143	4,862	6,671	1.83	2.14	4.23	2.11	2.80
South Africa	18,281	34,071	46,918	1.94	2.27	2.30	2.53	2.39
Sudan	11,165	22,828	32,926	1.91	2.29	3.08	2.89	2.75
Swaziland	333	691	1,048	2.35	2.39	2.90	3.14	3.23
Tanzania, United Rep	10,026	24,186	39,129	2.60	3.08	3.42	3.65	3.71
Togo	1,514	3,146	4,709	1.37	4.33	2.52	3.06	3.11
Tunisia	4,221	7,395	9,429	1.79	2.04	2.61	2.17	1.65
Uganda	6,562	16,584	26,262	3.33	3.95	3.19	3.49	3.55
Zaire	15,908	31,796	47,581	2.44	2.11	2.86	3.04	3.12
Zambia	3,141	7,135	11,237	2.63	2.96	3.08	3.43	3.52
Zimbabwe	3,605	9,430	15,130	3.97	3.61	3.39	3.61	3.64
NORTH & CENTRAL AMERICA	**268,579**	**411,933**	**487,379**	**2.03**	**1.60**	**1.53**	**1.38**	**1.21**
Barbados	231	256	284	0.29	0.30	0.28	0.60	0.94
Canada	17,909	25,963	28,927	2.59	1.72	1.16	1.01	0.71
Costa Rica	1,236	2,733	3,596	3.77	3.11	2.96	2.44	1.89
Cuba	7,029	10,214	11,718	1.79	1.87	0.84	0.98	0.99
Dominican Rep	3,224	6,531	8,407	3.10	2.80	2.34	2.21	1.75
El Salvador	2,574	5,906	8,708	2.98	3.52	2.93	3.10	2.90
Guatemala	3,964	8,434	12,222	2.89	2.77	2.77	2.88	2.81
Haiti	3,723	6,936	9,860	1.95	2.14	2.38	2.62	2.75
Honduras	1,943	4,657	6,978	3.34	2.72	3.53	3.10	3.18
Jamaica	1,629	2,409	2,880	1.10	1.20	1.24	1.52	1.26
Mexico	37,073	82,964	109,180	3.15	3.25	2.86	2.39	1.92
Nicaragua	1,493	3,502	5,261	3.12	3.18	2.81	3.36	2.95
Panama	1,148	2,274	2,893	2.54	2.88	2.26	2.07	1.69
Trinidad and Tobago	843	1,224	1,473	3.13	1.27	1.64	1.59	1.31
United States	180,671	242,159	268,239	1.70	1.08	1.06	0.86	0.73
SOUTH AMERICA	**146,839**	**279,384**	**356,351**	**2.73**	**2.45**	**2.27**	**2.08**	**1.73**
Argentina	20,616	31,500	37,197	1.71	1.45	1.61	1.46	1.18
Bolivia	3,428	6,730	9,724	2.19	2.37	2.59	2.76	2.88
Brazil	72,594	141,459	179,487	2.97	2.57	2.31	2.07	1.67
Chile	7,609	12,416	14,792	2.38	1.97	1.47	1.52	1.21
Colombia	15,538	29,943	37,999	2.98	2.77	2.14	2.05	1.68
Ecuador	4,413	9,923	13,939	2.96	3.17	2.88	2.79	2.48
Guyana	569	989	1,196	3.14	1.90	2.07	1.74	1.34
Paraguay	1,778	3,897	5,405	2.53	2.52	3.30	2.78	2.34
Peru	9,931	20,727	27,952	2.71	2.80	2.63	2.51	2.13
Suriname	290	386	469	2.97	2.28	-0.54	1.46	1.49
Uruguay	2,538	3,058	3,364	1.35	0.84	0.56	0.76	0.71
Venezuela	7,502	18,269	24,715	3.98	3.35	3.42	2.61	2.14

World Resources 1987

Table 16.1

	Estimated Population (thousands)			Estimated Average Annual Population Change (percent)				
	1960	1987	2000	1955-60	1965-70	1975-80	1985-90	1995-2000
ASIA	**1,668,165**	**2,913,191**	**3,548,994**	**1.95**	**2.43**	**1.86**	**1.63**	**1.43**
Afghanistan	10,775	18,110	26,035	2.03	2.42	0.87	4.83	2.06
Bahrain	156	467	693	3.10	2.79	4.87	3.72	2.61
Bangladesh	51,585	106,651	145,800	2.38	2.66	2.83	2.61	2.24
Bhutan	868	1,476	1,893	1.73	1.90	2.02	2.03	1.82
Burma	21,746	38,603	48,499	2.12	2.29	2.04	1.89	1.65
China	657,492	1,085,008	1,255,895	1.53	2.61	1.43	1.18	1.09
Cyprus	573	684	762	1.56	1.09	0.65	1.01	0.75
India	442,344	786,300	964,072	2.26	2.28	2.08	1.72	1.45
Indonesia	96,194	172,494	211,367	2.11	2.33	2.14	1.74	1.42
Iran	20,301	47,221	65,161	3.48	3.30	2.95	2.77	2.26
Iraq	6,847	17,010	25,377	2.94	3.19	3.75	3.31	2.92
Israel	2,114	4,399	5,302	3.80	2.98	2.31	1.65	1.31
Japan	94,096	122,053	129,725	0.93	1.07	0.93	0.51	0.46
Jordan	1,695	3,804	6,437	3.16	3.17	2.34	3.99	4.00
Kampuchea, Dem	5,433	7,688	9,772	2.31	2.44	-2.07	2.48	1.40
Korea, Dem People's Rep	10,526	21,390	28,166	2.91	2.76	2.57	2.36	1.95
Korea, Rep	25,003	42,672	50,981	3.04	2.40	1.87	1.89	1.45
Kuwait	278	1,982	3,007	6.67	9.17	6.24	4.15	2.68
Lao People's Dem Rep	2,355	4,322	5,789	2.25	2.60	1.44	2.43	2.10
Lebanon	1,857	2,762	3,617	2.82	2.75	-0.72	2.13	1.89
Malaysia	8,205	16,264	20,497	2.89	2.62	2.24	2.12	1.53
Mongolia	931	2,015	2,837	2.43	3.09	2.82	2.74	2.50
Nepal	9,404	17,253	23,048	1.61	2.10	2.41	2.28	2.16
Oman	505	1,331	1,973	2.09	2.71	5.01	3.18	2.99
Pakistan	50,093	105,195	140,961	2.38	2.77	2.84	2.23	2.13
Philippines	27,904	57,060	74,057	3.13	2.89	2.53	2.25	1.83
Qatar	45	355	569	5.03	9.28	5.42	5.44	2.84
Saudi Arabia	4,075	12,483	19,824	2.52	3.62	5.13	3.84	3.38
Singapore	1,634	2,616	2,947	4.48	1.97	1.30	1.09	0.78
Sri Lanka	9,889	16,725	19,620	2.51	2.28	1.71	1.48	1.11
Syrian Arab Rep	4,561	11,307	17,809	2.79	3.23	3.36	3.69	3.28
Thailand	26,867	53,150	65,503	2.85	3.04	2.34	1.61	1.59
Turkey	27,509	51,390	65,351	2.85	2.51	2.11	2.06	1.69
United Arab Emirates	90	1,437	1,939	2.69	8.70	13.27	3.46	1.84
Viet Nam	34,743	62,177	79,870	1.64	2.17	2.41	2.05	1.78
Yemen	4,039	7,251	10,881	2.05	1.47	2.49	2.92	3.22
Yemen, Dem	1,208	2,267	3,379	2.09	2.05	2.36	3.01	3.00
EUROPE	**425,129**	**494,529**	**512,474**	**0.83**	**0.64**	**0.42**	**0.27**	**0.27**
Albania	1,611	3,181	4,102	2.96	2.68	2.39	2.10	1.75
Austria	7,048	7,503	7,517	0.29	0.52	-0.04	0.01	0.00
Belgium	9,153	9,924	10,011	0.63	0.36	0.11	0.09	0.08
Bulgaria	7,867	9,147	9,535	0.96	0.75	0.32	0.38	0.30
Czechoslovakia	13,654	15,673	16,581	0.84	0.28	0.68	0.32	0.52
Denmark	4,581	5,121	5,082	0.63	0.71	0.25	-0.01	-0.10
Finland	4,430	4,926	5,055	0.90	0.18	0.29	0.30	0.14
France	45,684	54,965	57,162	1.01	0.77	0.38	0.31	0.29
German Dem Rep	17,240	16,810	17,149	-0.80	0.06	-0.13	0.15	0.18
Germany, Fed Rep	55,433	60,628	59,484	1.13	0.56	-0.09	-0.18	-0.17
Greece	8,327	9,959	10,437	0.89	0.56	1.28	0.41	0.32
Hungary	9,984	10,679	10,714	0.32	0.40	0.32	-0.07	0.10
Iceland	176	248	273	2.16	1.22	0.91	0.95	0.65
Ireland	2,834	3,700	4,320	-0.60	0.53	1.18	1.26	1.13
Italy	50,223	57,373	58,642	0.82	0.61	0.44	0.09	0.19
Luxembourg	314	363	358	0.58	0.43	0.09	-0.10	-0.10
Malta	329	388	418	0.93	0.35	1.32	0.66	0.52
Netherlands	11,480	14,610	15,082	1.31	1.17	0.51	0.34	0.16
Norway	3,581	4,158	4,215	0.88	0.81	0.39	0.17	0.06
Poland	29,561	37,753	40,816	1.61	0.72	0.89	0.70	0.58
Portugal	8,826	10,341	11,211	0.50	-1.36	0.95	0.64	0.58
Romania	18,407	23,331	25,571	1.03	1.35	0.88	0.68	0.70
Spain	30,303	39,004	42,237	0.84	1.14	1.00	0.62	0.59
Sweden	7,480	8,340	8,166	0.59	0.78	0.29	-0.11	-0.18
Switzerland	5,362	6,385	6,341	1.48	1.35	-0.25	0.04	-0.13
United Kingdom	52,559	56,160	56,354	0.52	0.35	-0.03	0.02	0.02
Yugoslavia	18,402	23,461	25,206	0.98	0.94	0.87	0.63	0.50
USSR	**214,335**	**283,993**	**314,736**	**1.77**	**0.91**	**0.93**	**0.93**	**0.73**
OCEANIA	**15,782**	**25,372**	**30,062**	**2.18**	**1.97**	**1.56**	**1.43**	**1.22**
Australia	10,315	16,102	18,628	2.20	1.95	1.51	1.25	1.03
Fiji	394	715	834	3.18	2.29	1.77	1.59	1.00
New Zealand	2,372	3,378	3,749	2.10	1.41	0.52	0.86	0.75
Papua New Guinea	1,920	3,686	4,933	1.92	2.40	2.70	2.38	2.15
Solomon Islands	124	292	447	1.72	2.79	3.01	3.96	2.84

Source: U.N. Population Division.
0 = zero or less than five one-thousandths of 1 percent.
For additional information, see Sources and Technical Notes.

World Resources 1987

Table 16.2 Births, Deaths, Fertility, and Age Dependency, 1960–90

	Estimated Crude Birth Rate (births per thousand population)		Estimated Crude Death Rate (deaths per thousand population)		Estimated Total Fertility Rate		Age Dependency Ratio (ratio of people age 0–14 and 65 + to those 15–64)		
	1965–70	1985–90	1965–70	1985–90	1965–70	1985–90	1960	1970	1985
WORLD	33.9	26.0	13.3	9.9	4.86	3.28	74.1	75.9	65.1
AFRICA	47.7	45.2	21.5	15.1	6.60	6.22	87.2	92.1	94.0
Algeria	49.8	41.1	17.4	9.1	7.48	6.15	90.9	110.5	97.7
Angola	49.1	47.2	28.1	20.6	6.38	6.39	80.4	84.2	90.9
Benin	49.5	50.5	28.9	19.4	6.86	7.00	92.3	93.0	97.3
Botswana	53.7	48.8	18.1	11.3	6.48	6.50	103.6	117.5	107.0
Burkina Faso	49.9	47.7	28.1	18.6	6.51	6.50	82.3	85.5	89.4
Burundi	46.5	45.7	25.0	17.4	5.83	6.31	76.7	80.8	90.8
Cameroon	41.9	42.5	20.6	14.5	5.68	5.79	76.8	81.6	87.9
Cape Verde	39.5	33.4	11.1	9.9	5.99	4.41	93.9	87.2	54.6
Central African Rep	43.2	44.3	27.0	20.1	5.69	5.89	74.5	78.9	86.2
Chad	45.2	44.2	27.0	19.9	6.05	5.89	76.2	81.6	84.8
Comoros	47.2	45.2	19.8	14.5	6.29	6.13	89.3	91.6	96.1
Congo	45.1	44.4	23.4	17.2	5.93	5.99	79.1	83.2	88.7
Cote d'Ivoire	43.9	45.2	22.7	14.3	6.63	6.60	83.7	86.7	92.5
Djibouti	X	X	X	X	X	X	X	X	X
Egypt	41.8	32.8	18.3	9.8	6.56	4.30	81.5	85.6	77.9
Equatorial Guinea	41.9	42.4	26.4	19.4	5.66	5.66	73.7	77.8	83.8
Ethiopia	48.7	49.3	24.6	22.3	6.70	6.70	87.0	90.0	93.6
Gabon	31.3	37.3	21.6	17.2	4.07	5.12	62.1	63.6	71.1
Gambia	47.2	48.2	32.5	26.9	6.40	6.39	76.3	81.7	83.6
Ghana	49.3	46.9	19.3	13.4	6.57	6.50	88.8	93.9	97.5
Guinea	48.5	46.6	29.1	21.9	6.41	6.19	84.4	83.0	85.2
Guinea-Bissau	41.2	40.8	26.2	20.0	5.19	5.38	69.3	73.4	81.8
Kenya	56.7	54.2	20.3	12.4	8.10	8.00	109.6	113.2	119.0
Lesotho	42.4	41.2	20.9	15.2	5.71	5.79	80.0	81.6	84.9
Liberia	45.6	48.1	21.2	15.6	6.27	6.90	83.8	87.1	99.3
Libya	49.5	43.9	16.8	9.4	7.48	6.87	89.7	91.1	95.2
Madagascar	43.6	44.1	20.4	15.2	5.83	6.09	78.9	82.5	90.8
Malawi	53.6	53.1	25.5	20.0	6.92	7.00	93.4	96.0	101.7
Mali	51.6	50.1	27.3	20.8	6.58	6.70	85.2	89.4	95.3
Mauritania	49.6	50.0	25.1	19.2	6.87	6.90	86.1	91.2	96.8
Mauritius	32.2	22.8	7.8	5.8	4.25	2.45	96.4	86.4	54.0
Morocco	48.2	32.5	17.4	9.5	7.09	4.31	90.1	107.2	94.6
Mozambique	45.1	45.2	24.1	18.4	5.87	6.09	77.8	83.9	92.9
Niger	49.4	50.9	28.6	20.9	7.10	7.10	89.3	93.1	99.9
Nigeria	52.3	50.5	22.0	15.7	7.10	7.10	91.3	97.4	102.8
Rwanda	50.6	50.7	20.2	17.2	7.00	7.31	88.8	99.3	105.0
Senegal	46.7	46.4	24.6	19.4	6.66	6.50	83.8	86.4	92.1
Sierra Leone	48.0	46.9	34.2	27.6	6.12	6.13	76.7	77.4	79.7
Somalia	46.0	47.7	24.7	22.6	6.60	6.60	80.4	83.4	91.2
South Africa	41.2	37.9	18.6	12.7	5.61	4.94	81.7	85.3	82.0
Sudan	47.0	44.2	23.0	15.4	6.68	6.38	89.6	89.0	92.0
Swaziland	47.4	47.1	20.9	15.8	6.33	6.50	85.4	90.0	95.9
Tanzania, United Rep	51.4	50.3	20.7	13.9	6.87	7.10	95.4	98.0	104.6
Togo	44.2	44.9	20.8	14.4	6.17	6.09	85.2	87.9	91.1
Tunisia	41.8	30.4	15.5	8.7	6.83	4.10	90.6	100.0	78.3
Uganda	49.1	50.1	18.7	15.4	6.91	6.90	96.8	98.4	104.2
Zaire	47.0	44.8	20.5	14.5	5.98	6.09	89.2	89.0	92.5
Zambia	48.9	47.9	19.3	13.7	6.65	6.76	90.8	94.4	100.0
Zimbabwe	47.1	47.0	16.5	11.0	6.61	6.60	93.0	96.9	101.4
NORTH & CENTRAL AMERICA	24.8	21.1	9.8	8.2	3.53	2.62	73.8	71.5	60.3
Barbados	23.8	18.6	8.5	8.6	3.44	2.00	81.2	83.8	58.6
Canada	18.8	14.9	7.5	7.6	2.51	1.75	69.6	61.4	47.3
Costa Rica	38.3	28.5	7.2	4.2	5.80	3.26	101.9	97.2	68.1
Cuba	32.0	18.2	7.4	6.7	4.30	1.97	64.4	75.7	52.1
Dominican Rep	45.5	30.9	13.1	7.1	7.01	3.63	104.6	106.4	77.7
El Salvador	44.9	37.9	12.8	7.0	6.62	5.10	92.2	97.2	92.2
Guatemala	45.6	40.8	15.9	8.9	6.60	5.77	95.7	94.0	85.4
Haiti	43.7	40.8	19.3	12.8	6.15	5.56	81.3	87.5	88.7
Honduras	50.0	39.4	15.9	8.4	7.42	5.59	91.4	99.7	99.2
Jamaica	37.3	26.0	8.0	5.5	5.43	2.86	85.1	110.7	74.4
Mexico	44.2	31.2	10.3	6.5	6.70	3.98	96.1	100.6	84.3
Nicaragua	48.4	41.8	14.7	8.0	7.09	5.50	101.3	102.9	97.1
Panama	39.3	26.7	8.4	5.2	5.62	3.14	90.5	93.3	72.5
Trinidad and Tobago	30.3	24.0	7.5	6.5	3.89	2.68	88.7	81.7	59.8
United States	18.3	15.7	9.5	9.0	2.55	1.91	67.4	61.4	50.0
SOUTH AMERICA	35.6	28.8	10.9	8.0	5.17	3.60	83.5	82.5	70.5
Argentina	22.6	23.2	9.1	8.6	3.04	3.26	57.0	57.0	65.4
Bolivia	45.6	42.8	20.2	14.1	6.56	6.06	85.3	86.2	88.5
Brazil	36.4	28.6	10.8	7.9	5.31	3.46	86.9	84.1	68.7
Chile	30.4	22.0	10.0	6.6	4.12	2.50	76.9	75.0	58.5
Colombia	39.6	29.2	10.4	7.4	5.94	3.58	97.5	93.6	69.3
Ecuador	44.5	35.4	12.8	7.6	6.70	4.65	92.3	96.7	90.7
Guyana	35.4	24.8	7.7	5.4	5.30	2.75	107.4	104.6	69.1
Paraguay	40.4	34.3	10.1	6.8	6.40	4.48	97.3	96.0	82.6
Peru	43.6	34.3	15.6	9.2	6.56	4.49	87.8	90.4	78.8
Suriname	40.0	25.9	8.8	6.1	5.94	2.97	107.1	109.3	88.8
Uruguay	20.5	18.9	9.6	10.2	2.81	2.61	56.2	58.2	60.3
Venezuela	40.6	30.7	7.7	5.4	5.90	3.77	94.8	94.5	78.5

World Resources 1987

Table 16.2

	Estimated Crude Birth Rate (births per thousand population)		Estimated Crude Death Rate (deaths per thousand population)		Estimated Total Fertility Rate		Age Dependency Ratio (ratio of people age 0–14 and 65+ to those 15–64)		
	1965–70	1985–90	1965–70	1985–90	1965–70	1985–90	1960	1970	1985
ASIA	**38.4**	**25.4**	**14.1**	**9.1**	**5.69**	**3.14**	**79.1**	**81.0**	**65.1**
Afghanistan	53.2	47.5	29.1	23.9	7.13	6.65	83.2	86.5	84.4
Bahrain	43.4	29.0	10.1	4.0	6.97	4.14	84.5	93.9	54.5
Bangladesh	47.5	41.7	21.0	15.6	6.91	5.53	81.4	95.7	95.4
Bhutan	41.8	37.0	22.7	16.7	5.89	5.33	76.7	76.8	76.5
Burma	39.1	28.8	16.2	9.9	5.74	3.69	73.8	83.2	81.8
China	36.9	18.4	10.9	6.6	5.97	2.11	76.8	80.3	55.9
Cyprus	21.0	18.3	9.9	8.2	2.78	2.31	74.3	69.9	53.9
India	40.2	28.1	17.5	10.9	5.69	3.69	83.1	82.7	69.0
Indonesia	42.6	28.6	19.3	11.3	5.57	3.48	77.0	83.0	72.1
Iran	48.5	38.5	15.6	10.8	7.55	5.21	96.7	97.3	86.9
Iraq	48.8	40.8	16.9	7.7	7.17	6.05	94.5	96.3	96.3
Israel	25.5	21.3	6.7	7.1	3.79	2.84	69.3	66.1	69.4
Japan	17.8	12.3	6.9	7.2	2.02	1.83	56.1	45.1	45.8
Jordan	48.0	46.4	16.3	6.6	7.17	7.28	94.2	96.0	102.4
Kampuchea, Dem	43.9	41.4	19.4	16.6	6.22	4.71	82.5	85.3	54.5
Korea, Dem People's Rep	38.8	28.9	11.2	5.4	5.64	3.60	88.8	90.0	72.1
Korea, Rep	31.9	23.2	10.4	5.9	4.49	2.50	82.7	83.0	51.7
Kuwait	49.6	34.6	6.3	3.1	7.48	5.74	58.9	82.3	74.2
Lao People's Dem Rep	44.8	38.1	18.9	13.9	6.13	5.41	77.2	81.2	84.7
Lebanon	38.8	28.9	11.8	7.7	6.05	3.38	87.2	95.3	74.2
Malaysia	38.5	27.1	10.4	5.9	5.91	3.30	96.4	93.6	68.2
Mongolia	41.9	34.7	11.2	7.4	5.89	4.82	84.1	88.5	79.7
Nepal	45.5	39.4	23.5	16.7	6.17	5.84	73.3	79.7	85.7
Oman	50.0	44.3	22.7	12.5	7.17	6.87	85.3	88.0	87.3
Pakistan	47.8	40.4	20.2	13.8	7.21	5.33	92.9	97.8	88.5
Philippines	40.2	30.8	10.7	7.6	6.01	3.91	102.1	92.9	71.5
Qatar	37.0	33.6	14.1	4.3	6.97	6.56	71.4	62.2	57.3
Saudi Arabia	48.1	40.6	19.2	7.4	7.26	6.87	87.4	91.1	84.7
Singapore	24.9	16.5	5.6	5.6	3.42	1.65	82.8	72.8	42.7
Sri Lanka	31.5	24.2	8.3	6.1	4.65	2.87	84.1	83.6	62.8
Syrian Arab Rep	47.6	45.4	15.3	7.0	7.79	6.83	93.0	114.1	104.1
Thailand	41.8	23.5	11.4	7.4	6.14	2.73	96.0	91.6	66.6
Turkey	39.6	29.2	13.6	8.4	5.80	3.65	81.1	83.6	70.5
United Arab Emirates	38.6	24.9	12.3	4.2	6.76	5.43	88.8	59.5	49.6
Viet Nam	38.3	29.6	16.6	9.2	6.70	3.69	77.2	80.5	78.9
Yemen	48.8	47.4	26.6	16.4	6.97	6.76	83.8	85.7	94.6
Yemen, Dem	49.0	46.6	25.3	15.7	6.97	6.56	91.0	92.6	92.0
EUROPE	**17.7**	**13.5**	**10.3**	**10.8**	**2.47**	**1.83**	**55.1**	**57.0**	**50.0**
Albania	34.8	26.5	8.0	5.4	5.09	3.32	86.3	88.0	67.6
Austria	17.3	12.4	13.0	12.3	2.53	1.61	51.9	62.9	48.1
Belgium	15.5	12.2	12.4	11.7	2.34	1.60	55.0	58.7	47.0
Bulgaria	15.8	14.9	8.7	11.0	2.16	2.21	50.5	47.9	50.8
Czechoslovakia	15.5	14.6	10.4	11.4	2.09	2.09	56.4	52.3	55.2
Denmark	16.6	10.9	10.0	11.5	2.24	1.47	55.8	55.2	50.7
Finland	16.3	12.6	9.7	10.2	2.06	1.64	60.3	51.0	45.6
France	17.1	13.7	11.1	10.6	2.61	1.83	61.3	60.5	49.9
German Dem Rep	15.1	14.2	13.7	12.8	2.30	1.90	53.3	63.8	48.1
Germany, Fed Rep	16.6	10.6	11.8	12.4	2.34	1.40	47.5	57.1	42.3
Greece	18.0	14.4	8.1	10.3	2.37	2.06	53.2	56.3	54.4
Hungary	14.3	12.1	10.8	12.8	1.99	1.84	52.4	47.8	51.9
Iceland	22.5	16.7	7.0	7.2	3.16	2.04	74.3	70.1	53.5
Ireland	21.5	21.4	11.5	8.8	3.85	2.93	73.2	73.5	70.7
Italy	18.3	11.6	9.7	10.7	2.49	1.60	52.1	53.9	49.8
Luxembourg	14.7	11.0	11.2	12.6	2.22	1.44	47.4	52.7	44.8
Malta	16.6	16.1	9.2	9.4	2.18	1.97	78.8	58.0	49.1
Netherlands	19.2	11.7	8.1	8.8	2.75	1.43	63.9	59.9	44.8
Norway	17.7	11.7	9.7	11.0	2.72	1.57	58.7	59.7	55.2
Poland	16.6	16.4	7.6	9.4	2.28	2.20	64.6	54.4	52.5
Portugal	21.4	16.6	8.1	9.4	2.84	2.09	59.1	61.5	54.5
Romania	21.3	16.9	9.2	10.1	3.06	2.37	53.6	52.6	53.0
Spain	20.5	15.1	8.7	8.9	2.91	2.05	55.4	60.6	55.6
Sweden	15.0	10.1	10.2	11.9	2.12	1.47	51.4	52.7	53.4
Switzerland	17.7	10.8	9.3	10.4	2.28	1.45	50.8	53.1	45.8
United Kingdom	17.6	13.1	11.7	12.3	2.53	1.78	53.7	59.2	51.6
Yugoslavia	19.8	15.2	8.8	8.9	2.49	1.99	58.3	54.4	46.8
USSR	**17.6**	**18.3**	**7.6**	**9.1**	**2.42**	**2.37**	**59.8**	**57.4**	**51.8**
OCEANIA	**24.5**	**20.0**	**10.3**	**8.2**	**3.49**	**2.56**	**67.7**	**65.2**	**57.8**
Australia	19.8	15.6	8.9	7.7	2.88	1.93	62.8	59.2	51.3
Fiji	32.0	27.3	7.6	5.0	4.57	3.19	102.0	85.0	64.2
New Zealand	22.6	15.6	8.7	8.4	3.22	1.86	71.0	67.3	52.2
Papua New Guinea	42.4	35.9	19.1	12.1	6.18	5.25	76.6	82.0	84.9
Solomon Islands	X	X	X	X	X	X	X	X	X

Source: U.N. Population Division.
X = not available.
For additional information, see Sources and Technical Notes.

Table 16.3 Health Indicators, 1964-90

	Estimated Infant Mortality (infant deaths per thousand live births)		Minimum Daily Calorie Requirement	Daily Calorie Supply as Percentage of Requirement			Estimated Life Expectancy at Birth (years)	
	1965-70	1985-90		1964-66	1974-76	1982-84	1965-70	1985-90
WORLD	**103**	**71**					**54.8**	**61.1**
AFRICA	**158**	**101**					**43.9**	**51.3**
Algeria	150	74	2,400	72	90	114	51.4	62.5
Angola	186	137	2,350	81	84	84	36.0	44.0
Benin	160	110	2,300	88	88	89	38.0	46.0
Botswana	110	67	2,320	88	91	90	48.5	56.5
Burkina Faso	183	139	2,370	91	91	88	38.9	47.2
Burundi	140	114	2,330	103	98	100	44.1	48.5
Cameroon	136	94	2,320	89	100	89	43.4	52.9
Cape Verde	120	63	2,350	75	93	108	50.1	61.5
Central African Rep	160	132	2,260	91	99	93	40.0	45.0
Chad	179	132	2,380	99	73	60	37.0	45.0
Comoros	115	80	2,340	94	89	95	45.0	52.0
Congo	110	73	2,220	101	102	113	40.5	48.5
Cote d'Ivoire	164	100	2,310	102	101	112	43.0	52.5
Djibouti	X	X	X	X	X	X	X	X
Egypt	170	85	2,510	97	107	128	49.7	60.6
Equatorial Guinea	173	127	X	X	X	X	38.0	46.0
Ethiopia	162	149	2,330	77	68	72	38.9	41.9
Gabon	147	103	2,340	81	86	103	43.0	51.0
Gambia	199	164	2,380	90	90	94	31.6	37.0
Ghana	118	90	2,300	87	96	72	48.0	54.0
Guinea	192	147	2,310	81	84	80	35.2	42.2
Guinea-Bissau	173	132	2,310	80	77	87	38.0	45.0
Kenya	108	72	2,320	98	97	86	45.4	55.3
Lesotho	140	100	2,280	89	91	103	43.3	51.3
Liberia	167	122	2,310	94	99	101	43.0	51.0
Libya	130	82	2,360	83	147	156	50.4	60.8
Madagascar	94	59	2,270	108	112	110	43.7	51.5
Malawi	197	150	2,320	91	107	104	39.5	47.0
Mali	206	169	2,350	83	79	81	37.0	44.0
Mauritania	166	127	2,310	88	78	95	39.0	46.0
Mauritius	67	23	2,270	103	113	121	61.6	68.2
Morocco	138	82	2,420	92	106	111	50.4	60.8
Mozambique	170	141	2,340	86	83	72	43.1	47.3
Niger	176	135	2,350	85	83	94	37.5	44.5
Nigeria	172	105	2,360	95	91	90	42.5	50.5
Rwanda	140	122	2,320	73	83	93	44.1	48.5
Senegal	168	131	2,380	104	96	101	38.7	45.3
Sierra Leone	218	169	2,300	79	84	85	30.2	36.0
Somalia	162	149	2,310	92	85	91	38.9	41.9
South Africa	120	72	2,450	107	119	120	47.5	55.5
Sudan	156	106	2,350	79	91	86	40.9	50.3
Swaziland	147	118	2,320	89	106	110	43.5	50.5
Tanzania, United Rep	135	106	2,320	85	97	99	44.1	53.0
Togo	141	93	2,300	101	91	98	43.0	52.5
Tunisia	138	71	2,390	94	109	120	52.1	63.1
Uganda	118	103	2,330	96	100	102	46.0	51.0
Zaire	137	98	2,220	98	103	97	44.0	52.0
Zambia	115	80	2,310	91	100	85	45.3	53.3
Zimbabwe	101	72	2,390	87	89	79	49.0	57.8
NORTH & CENTRAL AMERICA	**39**	**24**					**67.5**	**72.0**
Barbados	46	11	2,420	108	122	133	67.6	73.5
Canada	21	8	2,660	122	128	131	72.0	76.3
Costa Rica	66	18	2,240	104	114	114	65.6	73.7
Cuba	49	15	2,310	102	115	126	68.5	74.0
Dominican Rep	105	65	2,260	85	99	105	55.4	64.6
El Salvador	112	59	2,290	80	90	92	55.9	67.1
Guatemala	108	59	2,190	93	98	100	50.1	62.0
Haiti	172	117	2,260	88	86	84	46.2	54.7
Honduras	123	69	2,260	87	93	94	50.9	62.6
Jamaica	45	18	2,240	100	119	114	66.3	73.8
Mexico	79	47	2,330	111	116	127	60.3	67.2
Nicaragua	115	62	2,250	107	105	102	51.6	63.3
Panama	52	23	2,310	98	103	100	64.3	72.1
Trinidad and Tobago	41	20	2,420	103	110	121	65.7	70.2
United States	22	10	2,640	126	133	139	70.4	75.0
SOUTH AMERICA	**91**	**57**					**58.7**	**65.5**
Argentina	56	32	2,650	119	124	120	66.0	70.6
Bolivia	157	110	2,390	77	84	86	45.1	53.1
Brazil	100	63	2,390	100	104	106	57.9	64.9
Chile	95	20	2,440	108	107	107	60.6	70.7
Colombia	74	46	2,320	94	100	109	58.4	64.8
Ecuador	107	63	2,290	83	89	90	56.8	65.4
Guyana	56	30	2,270	101	103	103	62.5	69.8
Paraguay	67	42	2,310	112	118	122	59.5	66.1
Peru	126	88	2,350	98	97	91	51.5	61.4
Suriname	55	30	2,260	99	101	106	63.5	69.6
Uruguay	48	27	2,670	106	110	101	68.6	71.0
Venezuela	60	36	2,470	94	99	106	63.7	69.7

World Resources 1987

Table 16.3

	Estimated Infant Mortality (infant deaths per thousand live births)		Minimum Daily Calorie Requirement	Daily Calorie Supply as Percentage of Requirement			Estimated Life Expectancy at Birth (years)	
	1965-70	1985-90		1964-66	1974-76	1982-84	1965-70	1985-90
ASIA	**110**	**74**					**53.3**	**61.1**
Afghanistan	203	183	2,440	90	90	91	35.4	39.0
Bahrain	78	27	X	X	X	X	60.0	70.6
Bangladesh	140	119	2,210	91	83	85	43.3	49.6
Bhutan	164	128	2,310	X	X	X	40.6	47.9
Burma	110	63	2,160	89	99	116	49.5	60.0
China	81	32	2,360	86	94	115	59.6	69.4
Cyprus	29	15	2,480	108	122	137	70.3	74.6
India	145	99	2,210	89	87	96	48.0	57.9
Indonesia	120	74	2,160	81	95	113	45.1	56.0
Iran	150	107	2,410	87	115	128	53.2	59.0
Iraq	111	69	2,410	89	98	118	53.0	63.9
Israel	25	14	2,570	109	119	121	70.8	75.1
Japan	16	6	2,340	112	119	122	71.1	77.2
Jordan	102	44	2,460	93	96	120	51.7	66.0
Kampuchea, Dem	130	130	2,220	98	85	93	45.4	48.4
Korea, Dem People's Rep	58	24	2,340	99	118	133	57.6	69.4
Korea, Rep	58	24	2,350	96	117	120	57.6	69.4
Kuwait	55	20	X	X	X	X	64.4	72.7
Lao People's Dem Rep	147	110	2,220	86	82	94	45.4	52.0
Lebanon	52	39	2,480	99	103	119	62.9	67.2
Malaysia	50	26	2,240	101	111	114	59.4	68.6
Mongolia	82	45	2,430	106	103	114	58.0	64.5
Nepal	164	128	2,200	87	86	91	40.6	47.9
Oman	186	100	X	X	X	X	43.8	55.4
Pakistan	145	109	2,310	76	91	95	45.5	52.1
Philippines	70	45	2,260	82	94	106	56.2	63.5
Qatar	85	32	X	X	X	X	59.0	69.2
Saudi Arabia	140	71	2,420	79	83	132	49.9	63.7
Singapore	24	9	2,300	97	114	117	67.9	72.8
Sri Lanka	61	33	2,220	100	93	102	64.2	70.0
Syrian Arab Rep	107	48	2,480	89	101	126	54.0	65.0
Thailand	84	39	2,220	95	102	105	56.7	64.2
Turkey	153	76	2,520	105	118	126	54.4	64.1
United Arab Emirates	85	32	X	X	X	X	59.0	69.2
Viet Nam	133	67	2,160	97	94	101	47.9	60.8
Yemen	186	120	2,420	80	84	91	40.9	50.9
Yemen, Dem	186	120	2,410	84	79	95	40.9	50.9
EUROPE	**30**	**13**					**70.6**	**74.0**
Albania	77	40	2,410	102	107	114	66.2	72.1
Austria	27	10	2,630	126	126	133	69.9	73.9
Belgium	23	10	2,640	128	134	140	70.9	74.3
Bulgaria	31	15	2,500	137	141	146	70.8	72.6
Czechoslovakia	23	14	2,470	139	139	144	70.1	72.0
Denmark	16	7	2,690	127	125	132	72.9	75.1
Finland	15	6	2,710	116	116	114	69.6	74.6
France	21	8	2,520	135	137	140	71.5	75.2
German Dem Rep	21	10	2,620	122	133	143	71.3	73.1
Germany, Fed Rep	23	9	2,670	118	123	129	70.3	74.5
Greece	42	15	2,500	124	139	147	71.0	74.8
Hungary	37	17	2,630	122	130	135	69.2	71.3
Iceland	13	6	2,660	118	112	117	73.4	77.1
Ireland	23	9	2,510	138	139	145	71.1	73.8
Italy	33	11	2,520	124	137	140	71.0	75.2
Luxembourg	21	8	X	X	X	X	69.9	71.9
Malta	28	11	2,480	118	116	107	69.4	72.7
Netherlands	14	7	2,690	123	128	132	73.6	76.5
Norway	14	7	2,680	115	116	121	73.8	76.4
Poland	36	17	2,620	123	132	126	69.9	72.4
Portugal	61	17	2,450	107	123	125	66.1	73.0
Romania	52	23	2,650	114	125	128	68.4	71.1
Spain	33	9	2,460	117	133	136	71.6	75.0
Sweden	13	6	2,690	117	117	118	74.1	76.8
Switzerland	17	7	2,690	127	124	129	72.2	76.5
United Kingdom	19	9	2,520	133	129	126	71.4	74.5
Yugoslavia	61	25	2,540	128	138	142	66.6	71.7
USSR	**26**	**22**	**2,560**	**126**	**132**	**135**	**69.6**	**72.1**
OCEANIA	**48**	**26**					**64.2**	**69.1**
Australia	18	8	2,660	120	124	127	70.9	75.7
Fiji	55	26	2,660	93	99	109	62.7	70.4
New Zealand	18	11	2,640	127	131	134	71.3	74.5
Papua New Guinea	130	62	2,660	72	78	82	45.1	54.0
Solomon Islands	X	X	2,660	84	77	80	X	X

Source: U.N. Population Division.
X = not available.
For additional information, see Sources and Technical Notes.

Table 16.4 Malaria and Cholera Incidence, 1979–84

	Reported Malaria Cases						Reported Cholera Cases					
	1979	1980	1981	1982	1983	1984	1979	1980	1981	1982	1983	1984
WORLD												
AFRICA												
Algeria	73	36	67	71	41	32	2,513	1,075	X	X	218	45
Angola	522,385	797,688	X	X	X	X	X	X	X	X	X	X
Benin	122,405	131,909	142,872	X	X	X	X	3	2	3	X	1
Botswana	5,954	2,773	X	X	X	X	X	X	X	X	X	X
Burkina Faso	317,533	211,661	326,183	X	X	X	X	X	X	X	X	2,191
Burundi	94,049	79,181	X	X	X	X	915	2,039	582	351	477	180
Cameroon	X	X	X	X	X	X	16	229	243	5	55	392
Cape Verde	621	213	X	X	X	X	X	X	X	X	X	X
Central African Rep	167,346	X	X	X	X	X	X	X	X	X	X	X
Chad	X	X	X	X	X	X	X	X	X	X	X	X
Comoros	X	X	X	X	X	X	X	X	X	X	X	X
Congo	147,521	X	X	X	X	X	X	X	X	X	X	X
Cote d'Ivoire	349,046	X	X	X	X	X	3	X	X	34	X	X
Djibouti	123	69	640	X	X	X	X	X	X	X	X	X
Egypt	474	X	X	423	198	194	X	X	X	X	X	X
Equatorial Guinea	X	X	X	X	X	X	X	X	X	X	X	125
Ethiopia	31,658	X	X	X	X	X	X	X	X	X	X	X
Gabon	16,776	X	X	X	X	X	5	X	7	X	X	Y
Gambia	51,993	70,119	X	X	X	X	X	X	X	X	X	X
Ghana	X	X	X	X	X	X	1,783	260	581	1,784	14,160	1,015
Guinea	23,086	X	X	X	X	X	X	X	X	X	X	X
Guinea-Bissau	160,931	148,142	161,496	X	X	X	X	X	X	X	X	X
Kenya	437,660	X	X	X	X	X	1,070	2,808	2,424	3,498	1,049	14
Lesotho	X	X	X	X	X	X	X	X	X	X	X	X
Liberia	X	201,946	X	X	X	X	438	2,690	1,582	670	183	17
Libya	134	106	1,473	X	129	117	X	X	X	X	X	X
Madagascar	302,336	X	X	X	X	X	X	X	X	X	X	X
Malawi	23,237	X	30,234	X	X	X	X	X	261	X	513	X
Mali	180,176	149,308	X	X	X	X	X	X	X	X	X	1,795
Mauritania	X	X	X	X	X	X	X	X	X	X	X	492
Mauritius	128	470	607	X	X	X	X	X	X	X	X	X
Morocco	397	360	98	62	75	318	X	X	X	X	X	X
Mozambique	X	X	X	X	X	X	4,564	1,212	1,753	2,301	10,334	521
Niger	384,029	X	X	X	X	X	X	X	7	X	X	3,788
Nigeria	1,021,331	1,171,071	X	X	X	X	293	139	305	186	171	1,667
Rwanda	137,047	123,882	X	X	X	X	5	30	24	97	54	161
Senegal	508,010	X	498,895	X	X	X	103	X	428	X	X	712
Sierra Leone	79,991	X	X	X	X	X	X	X	X	X	X	X
Somalia	11,343	X	X	X	X	X	X	X	X	X	X	X
South Africa	2,007	1,059	X	X	X	X	2	859	4,180	11,968	4,715	1,182
Sudan	X	2,925,407	X	X	X	X	845	17	X	X	X	X
Swaziland	X	X	X	X	X	X	X	X	238	538	X	X
Tanzania, United Rep	X	X	X	X	X	X	2,559	5,196	4,241	4,071	1,816	2,600
Togo	294,562	X	X	X	X	X	X	X	X	X	X	X
Tunisia	6	7	1	X	X	X	X	X	X	X	X	X
Uganda	20,305	X	70,520	X	X	X	X	1,539	X	190	X	X
Zaire	317,533	X	X	X	X	X	5,515	1,051	2,379	10,328	2,977	162
Zambia	10,580	X	X	X	X	X	165	57	14	1,403	X	X
Zimbabwe	3,807	14,587	X	X	X	X	X	X	X	X	X	X
NORTH & CENTRAL AMERICA												
Barbados	2	1	1	X	X	X	0	0	0	0	0	0
Canada	X	631	538	X	X	X	0	3	0	0	2	0
Costa Rica	307	376	168	110	245	569	0	0	0	0	0	0
Cuba	295	307	573	X	X	X	0	0	0	0	0	0
Dominican Rep	3,080	4,780	3,596	4,654	3,801	2,370	0	0	0	0	0	0
El Salvador	77,976	95,835	93,187	86,202	65,377	66,874	0	0	0	0	0	0
Guatemala	69,039	62,657	67,994	77,375	64,024	74,132	0	0	0	0	0	0
Haiti	41,252	53,478	46,703	65,354	53,954	54,896	0	0	0	0	0	0
Honduras	25,297	43,009	49,377	57,482	37,536	27,332	0	0	0	0	0	0
Jamaica	5	X	1	X	X	X	0	0	0	0	0	0
Mexico	20,983	25,734	42,104	49,993	74,172	85,501	0	0	0	0	0	0
Nicaragua	18,418	25,465	17,434	15,601	12,907	15,702	0	0	0	0	0	0
Panama	316	310	340	334	341	125	0	0	0	0	0	0
Trinidad and Tobago	8	3	3	X	X	X	0	0	0	0	0	0
United States	894	2,062	1,388	X	X	X	1	10	21	0	1	0
SOUTH AMERICA												
Argentina	936	341	323	567	535	437	0	0	0	0	0	0
Bolivia	14,712	16,619	9,774	6,699	14,441	16,338	0	0	0	0	0	0
Brazil	147,630	176,237	205,544	221,939	297,687	378,257	0	0	0	0	0	0
Chile	X	X	X	X	X	X	0	0	0	0	0	0
Colombia	60,957	57,346	60,972	78,601	105,360	55,268	0	0	0	0	0	0
Ecuador	8,207	8,748	12,745	14,633	51,606	78,599	0	0	0	0	0	0
Guyana	2,294	3,202	2,065	1,700	2,102	3,017	0	0	0	0	0	0
Paraguay	116	140	73	66	49	544	0	0	0	0	0	0
Peru	17,127	14,982	14,812	14,613	28,563	36,621	0	0	0	0	0	0
Suriname	903	4,445	2,479	2,805	1,943	3,849	0	0	0	0	0	0
Uruguay	X	X	X	X	X	X	0	0	0	0	0	0
Venezuela	4,705	3,884	3,354	4,127	8,388	11,127	0	0	0	0	0	0

Table 16.4

	Reported Malaria Cases						Reported Cholera Cases					
	1979	1980	1981	1982	1983	1984	1979	1980	1981	1982	1983	1984
ASIA												
Afghanistan	34,444	47,285	67,668	110,309	118,684	155,720	X	X	X	X	X	X
Bahrain	273	256	274	X	X	X	39	X	X	X	X	X
Bangladesh	49,776	67,727	45,902	38,204	40,303	31,787	2,154	X	X	X	X	X
Bhutan	5,375	X	X	X	5,213	18,356	X	X	X	X	X	X
Burma	14,515	16,469	42,019	42,021	36,647	60,488	874	1,018	54	X	989	X
China	2,384,543	3,300,349	3,059,653	2,041,359	1,377,647	903,802	85	88	X	X	X	X
Cyprus	1	2	6	X	X	X	X	X	X	X	X	X
India	3,064,697	2,844,815	2,622,639	2,160,447	1,911,149	2,023,462	5,073	9,522	5,237	4,656	8,542	2,519
Indonesia	165,911	175,239	149,576	220,129	147,887	92,527	28,738	5,541	18,354	8,183	12,964	7,921
Iran	22,175	32,635	29,655	42,808	45,916	30,835	1,856	1,599	6,034	427	270	531
Iraq	4,012	2,815	X	3,326	2,422	3,340	X	X	X	1	X	X
Israel	16	43	44	X	X	X	X	X	X	X	X	X
Japan	53	55	41	X	X	X	11	22	16	16	35	55
Jordan	320	202	274	X	X	X	141	X	908	X	X	X
Kampuchea, Dem	X	X	X	10,114	X	X	X	X	X	X	X	X
Korea, Dem People's Rep	X	X	X	X	X	X	X	170	X	X	X	X
Korea, Rep	X	X	X	X	X	X	X	145	X	X	X	X
Kuwait	98	98	142	X	X	X	3	X	9	X	X	X
Lao People's Dem Rep	X	12,603	X	X	5,564	7,210	X	X	X	X	X	X
Lebanon	9	4	9	X	X	X	X	X	X	X	X	X
Malaysia	44,912	44,552	59,422	43,915	22,218	32,094	502	106	479	516	2,195	67
Mongolia	X	X	X	X	X	X	X	X	X	X	X	X
Nepal	12,131	12,265	15,978	16,907	16,719	28,208	22	1	24	X	X	X
Oman	2,247	1,340	2,218	30,566	34,885	16,590	X	X	X	X	X	X
Pakistan	12,304	17,707	37,923	56,708	49,160	73,996	X	X	4	X	X	X
Philippines	87,668	105,750	97,557	97,531	90,319	107,301	933	836	864	345	X	X
Qatar	124	62	116	X	X	X	X	X	X	X	X	X
Saudi Arabia	3,192	6,496	5,543	15,167	17,956	11,091	23	2	13	X	X	X
Singapore	208	200	261	X	X	X	10	18	34	31	14	40
Sri Lanka	48,004	47,949	47,383	38,566	127,264	149,470	46	104	574	309	86	X
Syrian Arab Rep	2,550	1,481	1,828	2,183	1,260	840	689	X	X	X	X	X
Thailand	302,568	396,705	427,792	419,763	243,906	306,569	1,788	4,331	39	638	1,495	645
Turkey	29,323	34,154	55,551	X	66,681	55,382	X	X	X	X	X	X
United Arab Emirates	11,599	8,560	7,653	6,224	4,815	3,516	X	X	X	X	X	X
Viet Nam	40,782	31,763	42,714	50,920	63,649	58,806	365	978	374	50	390	22
Yemen	3,838	5,824	10,029	20,641	2,168	1,262	X	X	X	X	X	X
Yemen, Dem	4,083	2,153	4,079	7,609	9,294	3,615	1,953	720	X	X	X	X
EUROPE												
Albania	X	X	X	X	X	X	X	X	X	X	X	X
Austria	35	44	54	X	X	X	X	X	2	X	X	X
Belgium	56	59	30	X	X	X	X	1	X	X	X	1
Bulgaria	102	128	420	X	X	X	X	X	X	X	X	X
Czechoslovakia	6	15	2	X	X	X	X	X	X	X	X	X
Denmark	110	70	104	X	X	X	X	X	X	X	X	X
Finland	13	13	14	X	X	X	X	X	1	X	X	X
France	99	111	77	X	X	X	X	3	20	18	3	1
German Dem Rep	22	16	35	X	X	X	X	X	X	X	X	X
Germany, Fed Rep	486	570	319	X	X	X	X	5	4	1	X	X
Greece	44	53	64	X	X	X	X	X	X	X	X	X
Hungary	13	6	34	X	X	X	X	X	X	X	X	X
Iceland	X	X	X	X	X	X	X	X	X	X	X	X
Ireland	32	22	25	X	X	X	X	X	X	X	X	X
Italy	164	176	143	X	X	X	8	X	X	X	X	X
Luxembourg	X	X	7	X	X	X	X	X	X	X	X	X
Malta	X	X	1	X	X	X	X	X	X	X	X	X
Netherlands	113	101	128	X	X	X	5	X	2	X	2	X
Norway	32	25	35	X	X	X	X	X	X	X	X	X
Poland	23	X	29	X	X	X	X	X	1	X	X	X
Portugal	45	26	27	X	X	X	X	X	X	X	X	X
Romania	19	14	22	X	X	X	X	X	X	X	X	X
Spain	52	90	129	X	X	X	267	4	2	1	2	4
Sweden	104	98	123	X	X	X	1	X	X	X	X	X
Switzerland	93	95	138	X	X	X	X	X	X	X	X	X
United Kingdom	2,053	1,670	1,576	X	X	X	X	6	12	1	5	5
Yugoslavia	55	83	58	X	X	X	X	X	2	X	X	X
USSR	**399**	**386**	**304**	**X**	**X**	**X**	**X**	**X**	**X**	**X**	**X**	**X**
OCEANIA												
Australia	473	629	497	X	X	X	1	2	2	1	4	1
Fiji	X	X	X	X	X	X	X	X	X	X	X	X
New Zealand	X	65	39	X	X	X	X	1	X	X	X	X
Papua New Guinea	117,670	118,390	122,743	109,306	126,930	150,328	X	X	X	X	X	X
Solomon Islands	26,357	35,028	61,108	69,829	84,526	72,108	X	X	X	X	X	X

Source: World Health Organization.
0 = zero; X = not available.
For additional information, see Sources and Technical Notes.

Table 16.5 Unmet Need for Contraception, 1980

	Year of Survey	Percentage of Women Wanting No More Children and in Need of Contraception		Desired Number of Children		Year of Survey	Percentage of Women Wanting No More Children and in Need of Contraception		Desired Number of Children
		Low Estimate	High Estimate				Low Estimate	High Estimate	
AFRICA					**SOUTH AMERICA**				
Benin	1981–82	3	X	X	Colombia	1980	7	24	4.1
Botswana	1984	5	X	X	Ecuador	1979	13	26	X
Cameroon	1978	1	1	X	Guyana	1975	23	29	4.6
Cote d'Ivoire	1980–81	2	3	X	Paraguay	1979	9	17	5.1
Egypt	1984	X	21	4.1	Peru	1981	13	41	3.8
Ghana	1979	5	8	6.1	Venezuela	1977	10	22	4.2
Kenya	1977–78	6	10	7.2	**ASIA**				
Lesotho	1977	5	9	5.9	Bangladesh	1983–84	25	28	4.1
Mauritania	1981	6	X	9.2	Indonesia	1976	10	15	4.1
Mauritius	1985	3	X	X	Jordan	1983	20	X	6.3
Morocco	1980	11	X	X	Korea, Rep	1979	X	23	3.2
Nigeria	1981–82	2	X	X	Malaysia	1974	15	23	4.4
Sudan	1979	6	9	6.3	Nepal	1981	22	27	3.9
Tunisia	1983	10	19	X	Pakistan	1975	17	27	4.2
CENTRAL AMERICA & CARIBBEAN					Philippines	1978	11	29	4.4
Barbados	1981	X	19	2.4	Sri Lanka	1982	18	31	3.8
Costa Rica	1981	6	11	4.7	Syrian Arab Rep	1978	7	15	6.1
Dominican Rep	1975	12	21	4.6	Thailand	1981	13	17	3.7
Guatemala	1983	21	X	X	Turkey	1978	13	X	3.0
Haiti	1977	13	30	3.5	Yemen	1979	8	12	X
Honduras	1981	9	21	X	**EUROPE**				
Jamaica	1983	18	X	4.0	Portugal	1979–80	6	X	X
Mexico	1979	14	22	4.5	**OCEANIA**				
Panama	1984	13	X	4.2	Fiji	1974	10	15	4.2
Trinidad and Tobago	1977	14	19	3.8					

Sources: The World Bank; World Fertility Survey; Contraceptive Prevalence Surveys; Population Reference Bureau; and U.S. Centers for Disease Control.
X = not available.
For additional information, see Sources and Technical Notes.

Sources and Technical Notes

Table 16.1 Estimated Size and Growth of Population, 1955–2000

Source: U.N. Population Division, *World Population Prospects: Estimates and Projections as Assessed in 1984* (U.N., New York, 1986).

Population refers to the midyear population. Most data are estimates based on population censuses and surveys. All projections are for the medium-case scenario (see below). The average annual growth rate of population takes into account the effects of international migration.

Many of the pre-1980 data in Tables 16.1–16.3 are estimated using models. Several kinds of demographic information are required to estimate the growth and composition of a country's population: the size of the population, age and sex distribution, fertility and mortality rates by age and sex groups, the growth rates of both the urban and rural population, and the levels of internal and international migration.

Recent population censuses and surveys have collected information needed to calculate or estimate the above indicators, although the degree of accuracy varies. The Population Division of the U.N. Department of International Economic and Social Affairs compiles and evaluates national census and survey reports from all countries. When necessary, the data are adjusted for over- and under-enumeration of certain age and sex groups (infants, female children, young males), misreporting of age and sex distributions, changes in definitions, etc. These adjustments incorporate data from civil

registrations, population surveys, earlier censuses, and, when necessary, population models based on information from socioeconomically similar countries. (Because the figures have been adjusted, they are not strictly comparable to the official statistics compiled by the U.N. Statistical Office and published in the *Demographic Yearbook*.)

After the figures for size and age/sex composition of the population have been adjusted, the data are scaled to 1980. Because most countries conducted a population census or large-scale population survey in the 1970s or early 1980s, the scaling is usually minor. Similar estimates are made for each five-year period between 1950 and 1980. Historical data are used when deemed accurate, with adjustments and scaling similar to those described above. For many developing countries, however, accurate historical data do not exist. The Population Division estimates the main demographic parameters for these countries using available information and demographic models.

Projections are based on estimates of the 1980 base year population. Age- and sex-specific mortality rates are applied to the base year population to determine the number of survivors at the end of each five-year period. Births are projected by applying age-specific fertility rates to the projected female population. The births are distributed by an assumed sex ratio, and the appropriate age- and sex-specific survival rates are applied. Future migration rates are also estimated on an age- and

sex-specific basis. Combining future fertility, mortality, and migration rates yields the projected size and composition of the population.

Assumptions about future mortality, fertility, and migration rates—the three components of population growth—are made on a country-by-country basis and, when possible, are based on historical trends. Four scenarios of population growth (high, medium, low, and constant) are created using different assumptions about these rates. The medium-case scenario, for example, assumes medium levels of fertility, mortality, and migration, assumptions that may vary widely among the countries. The medium mortality assumption includes a five-year gain of 2.5 years in life expectancy at birth until it reaches 62.5 years. Life expectancy is assumed to increase more slowly thereafter. For countries that have had little or no reduction in mortality recently (some sub-Saharan African and South Asian countries), the five-year gain in life expectancy was assumed to be two years or less. Refer to the source for further details.

Table 16.2 Births, Deaths, Fertility, and Age Dependency, 1960–90

Source: U.N. Population Division, *World Population Prospects: Estimates and Projections as Assessed in 1984* (U.N., New York, 1986).

The crude birth rate is derived by dividing the number of live births in a given year by the midyear population. This ratio is then multiplied by 1,000.

The crude death rate is derived by dividing the number of deaths in a given year by the midyear population. This ratio is then multiplied by 1,000.

The total fertility rate is an estimate of the number of children that an average woman would have if current age-specific fertility rates remain constant during her reproductive years.

The age dependency ratio is a fraction whose numerator is the sum of the populations in the 0–14 and over–65 age groups and whose denominator is the population in the 15–64 age group.

For details on data collection, estimation, and projection methods, refer to the source or to the Technical Note for Table 16.1.

Table 16.3 Health Indicators, 1964–90

Sources: Infant mortality and life expectancy data: U.N. Population Division, *World Population Prospects: Estimates and Projections as Assessed in 1984* (U.N., New York, 1986). Minimum daily requirement of calories and calorie supply as percentage of requirements: United Nations Food and Agriculture Organization (FAO), unpublished data (FAO, Rome, September 1986).

The infant mortality rate is derived by dividing the number of babies who die before their first birthday in a given year by the number of live births in that year. This ratio is then multiplied by 1,000.

Life expectancy at birth is the average number of years that a newborn baby is expected to live if the age-specific mortality rates effective at the year of birth are applied.

The minimum daily calorie requirement is the energy intake necessary to meet the energy needs of an average healthy person. It is calculated for each country by the World Health Organization, which takes into account body size, age and sex distribution, physical activity level of the population, climate, and other factors.

The calorie supply as a percentage of requirements includes calories from all food sources: domestic production, international trade, stock drawdowns, and foreign aid. The quantity of food available for human consumption, as estimated by FAO, is the food that reaches the consumer. The number of calories actually consumed may be lower than the figures shown, depending on how much food is lost in home storage, preparation, and cooking plus what is fed to pets and domestic animals or is discarded.

Table 16.4 Malaria and Cholera Incidence, 1979–84

Sources: World Health Organization (WHO), *World Health Statistics 1984* (WHO, Geneva, 1984). WHO, *Weekly Epidemiological Record* (WHO, Geneva), Vol. 59, 1984, pp. 141–148; and Vol. 60, 1985, pp. 149–156. WHO, *World Health Statistics Quarterly* (WHO, Geneva), Vol. 37, No. 2, 1984; Vol. 38, No. 2, 1985; and Vol. 39, No. 2, 1986.

Malaria is a parasitic infectious disease carried by the *Anopheles* mosquito, which transmits the *Plasmodium* parasite from the blood of an infected person to that of an uninfected person. WHO estimates that over half the

world's population lives in areas where malaria is a serious public health problem.

Cholera, an acute diarrheal disease, is caused by bacteria found in feces-contaminated water. Though primarily a waterborne disease, it can be transmitted by food, particularly fish and shellfish from contaminated waters. Cholera is quickly spread in areas lacking safe drinking water or adequate sanitation. Estimates of drinking water supply and sanitation services are presented in Table 17.2.

The malaria and cholera cases shown here are those reported by countries to WHO and WHO regional offices. These data are limited, however, because many countries do not report and others provide incomplete reports. The diversity of reporting systems, as well as changes in these systems, allow only limited cross-country comparison. For example, most countries report only laboratory-confirmed cases of malaria and cholera, and data from sub-Saharan Africa generally refer to clinically diagnosed cases. Because WHO relies on reports of laboratory and clinically confirmed cases, the total number of cases is underreported. This problem is particularly true for cholera because cholera cases are often difficult to distinguish from other diarrheal diseases and frequently are not referred for laboratory analysis.

Although Africa now reports the largest number of cholera cases, the disease did not exist there until 1970, when a global pandemic, originating in Indonesia in 1961, reached the continent. Outbreaks occurred in southern Europe in the early 1970s, and the disease was reported in the South Pacific for the first time in 1977. In the Western Hemisphere, only the United States has reported cases of indigenous cholera. Most cases of malaria and cholera reported in Europe are not indigenous but are brought by people carrying the disease from infected areas. WHO estimates that about 4,000 cases of malaria are imported annually into Europe.

Table 16.5 Unmet Need for Contraception, 1980

Sources: Unmet need for contraception: The World Bank, *World Development Report 1984* (The World Bank, Washington, D.C., 1984); International Statistical Institute, World Fertility Survey (WFS), *The World Fertility Survey, Major Findings and Implications* (International Statistical Institute, Beatrixlaan, the Netherlands, 1984); Westinghouse Public Applied Systems (WPAS), *Botswana Family Health Survey 1984* (WPAS, Columbia, Maryland, December 1985); WPAS, *Fertility and Family Planning in Egypt 1984* (WPAS, Columbia, Maryland, July 1985); U.S. Centers for Disease Control (CDC), *1983 Jordan Fertility and Family Health Survey* (CDC, Atlanta, Georgia, 1983); CDC, *1983 Guatemala Family Planning/Maternal-Child Health Survey* (CDC, Atlanta, Georgia, 1983); CDC, *1984 Panama Maternal-Child Health/Family Planning Survey* (CDC, Atlanta, Georgia, 1984); CDC, *1985 Mauritius Contraceptive Prevalence Survey* (CDC, Atlanta, Georgia, 1985). Desired number of children: The World Bank, *World Development Report 1984* (The World Bank, Washington, D.C., 1984); and Mary M. Kent and Ann Larson, *Family Size Preferences: Evidence from the World Fertility Survey* (Population Reference

Bureau, Washington, D.C., April 1982).

Estimates of unmet need are based on surveys of women between the ages of 15 and 49 conducted between 1972 and 1985 by the WFS, contraceptive prevalence surveys (CPS), and maternal-child health surveys.

Both the WFS and CPSs provide information on fertility, contraceptive use, and attitudes toward fertility, but their purposes and methods differ. First, the WFS conducted surveys in both developing and developed countries, and CPSs were limited to developing countries. (Because developed countries conducted their own surveys for the WFS and modified the standard WFS survey, results are not strictly comparable to developing-country data. No estimates of unmet need have been compiled for developed countries.) Second, in assessing unmet need, the WFS addressed only married women's demand for contraception—and only for the purpose of limiting births. Several CPSs surveyed unmarried and married women, and they included questions on the use of contraception for spacing births, thus permitting identification of categories of unmet need that the WFS does not.

In Table 16.5, unmet need is defined as the percentage of married women of childbearing age who are fecund, do not want more children, and are not pregnant or protected from the risk of pregnancy. A range of estimates of unmet need is given for some countries. Low estimates treat women who are breastfeeding during the first year after a birth as protected from pregnancy, and include in the unmet need category only those women who are not using *any* form of contraception. High estimates do not treat breastfeeding as protection from pregnancy; they also consider women using inefficient methods of family planning as having an unmet need for contraception. Efficient methods of contraception include male and female sterilization, oral contraceptives, IUDs, injectables, diaphragms, and condoms. Inefficient methods include withdrawal, rhythm, and traditional methods. Because neither estimate includes the need for contraception to space births, all figures presented here should be considered conservative.

Surveys in four countries did not achieve national coverage: Sudan (northern population only), Mauritania (sedentary population only), Malaysia (Peninsular Malaysia only), and Indonesia (Java and Bali only).

Data for Benin, Nigeria, Mauritania, Morocco, Turkey, and Portugal were taken from the WFS. Estimates for Mauritius, Jordan, Panama, and Guatemala were provided by CDC. Only low estimates of unmet need are available for these 10 countries.

Desired family size is based on ever-married women's answers to the question, "If you could choose exactly the number of children to have in your whole life, how many would that be?" The data shown are the mean for respondents who gave numerical answers. However, these data can provide only a general indication of desired family size. Many women did not give numerical answers. Of those who did, the answers of a significant percentage were inconsistent with their answers to the same question in follow-up surveys. Further, the question is hypothetical for women with large families, because many would not wish for fewer children than they already have.

17. Human Settlements

This chapter presents data on a few indicators of human living conditions: national urbanization characteristics, rural and urban growth rates, access to safe drinking water and sanitation, the populations of the world's largest cities, and the amount of waste generated by developed countries.

The level of urbanization in a country and the rates of urban and rural growth can signal the onset of numerous environmental problems: air, water, and noise pollution in urban areas; overstressed land resources in rural areas; and shortages of necessary public services in high growth areas. Urban and rural growth rate data are more comparable across countries than are urbanization data. (See Table 17.1.) The U.N. Population Division does not use a standard definition of urban and rural to estimate the urban fraction of a country's population. Data are collected according to national definitions, which vary widely. For example, in Mauritius, urban areas are localities with 20,000 or more inhabitants. Peru, however, defines urban areas as populated centers with 100 or more occupied dwellings. Data on urban and rural *growth rates* are more useful for cross-country comparisons because national definitions are usually applied consistently over time. Although some countries have changed their urban area definitions, the U.N. Population Division revises all previous national data to fit the current national definition.

Provision of safe drinking water and sanitation services can help prevent the spread of water-related diseases (e.g., cholera and schistosomiasis). However, accurate data on access to safe drinking water and sanitation in developing countries are difficult to obtain. (See Table 17.2.) (Service levels in developed countries are usually around 100 percent.) Although most countries report data on access to safe services to the World Health Organization, the various interpretations of "access" and "safe" make the existence of facilities an inadequate indicator of protection from water-related diseases. Poor design, maintenance, and operation of supposedly "safe" water supply systems, for example, can permit or enhance the transmission of disease. A system's actual effectiveness must be evaluated to determine its health benefits.

Table 17.3 presents data on the population, area, and population density of the world's 85 largest urban agglomerations. The U.S. Bureau of the Census adjusted national data

to fit a common definition of "city," allowing comparison among cities in many countries for 1985. Historical population data are difficult to standardize for many cities because earlier data are often inadequate.

There are striking contrasts in the data for developed- and developing-world cities. Of the 85 cities, the ten with the lowest population density are in the developed world, nine in the United States. The ten cities with the highest population density are in developing countries, nine in Asia.

Most countries do not collect data on waste generation and disposal. Those that do usually collect data within a regulatory framework that requires waste generators to report their waste output. However, many countries lack legal and regulatory frameworks for managing wastes (especially hazardous and toxic wastes). Effective waste management requires supervised disposal sites, trained scientific and administrative personnel, laboratories, and adequate enforcement mechanisms, which many countries cannot afford. Even in countries with regulatory systems in place, data may not reflect the actual amount of waste generated. In Thailand, for example, although all factories generating hazardous waste are required to register with the Department of the Environment, only half have complied. In the United States, the U.S. Environmental Protection Agency's hazardous waste program excludes an estimated 600,000 small quantity generators (producing less than 1,000 kg of wastes per month) from its reporting requirements.

Even when reliable waste generation data exist, they are not easily translated into management data. Some wastes are disposed of improperly or illegally, and other wastes are shipped across international boundaries for disposal (sometimes illegally). Wastes that are improperly disposed of can contaminate air or groundwater: they can vaporize, leach through the soil, or travel on wind- and waterborne particles of dust and soil.

Ultimately the greatest concern is the impact of wastes on human health and wildlife. Numerous contaminants from leaking landfills, dumped wastes, spills, and agricultural runoff have been detected in surface and groundwater. (See Table 23.3.) Wildlife and human tissue studies have also detected the presence of contaminants.

Table 17.1 Urban and Rural Populations, 1960-90

| | Urban Population as Percentage of Total | | | Average Annual Change in Population (percent) | | | | | |
| | | | | Urban | | | Rural | | |
	1960	1970	1985	1965-70	1975-80	1985-90	1965-70	1975-80	1985-90
WORLD	**33.6**	**36.9**	**41.6**	**2.8**	**2.6**	**2.5**	**1.7**	**1.3**	**0.9**
AFRICA	**18.4**	**22.9**	**32.1**	**4.6**	**5.3**	**5.1**	**2.0**	**2.1**	**2.1**
Algeria	30.4	45.6	66.6	6.7	5.5	4.6	0.1	-0.3	0.5
Angola	10.4	15.0	24.5	5.1	6.7	5.5	0.9	2.6	1.6
Benin	9.5	16.0	38.5	8.9	8.5	6.3	1.0	0.5	0.7
Botswana	1.8	8.4	19.2	18.0	8.5	7.7	1.6	3.0	2.5
Burkina Faso	4.7	5.7	7.9	3.8	4.0	5.4	1.6	1.9	2.5
Burundi	2.2	2.2	2.5	1.5	2.4	5.3	1.5	1.5	2.6
Cameroon	13.9	20.3	42.4	6.3	7.5	5.7	1.1	0.2	0.0
Cape Verde	7.0	6.2	6.1	1.1	1.5	3.2	2.5	1.5	1.2
Central African Rep	22.7	31.1	45.7	4.7	4.7	4.3	0.4	0.5	0.7
Chad	7.0	11.4	21.6	6.7	6.4	5.8	1.3	1.3	1.4
Comoros	5.1	7.7	14.0	6.6	7.9	6.6	2.1	3.5	2.4
Congo	33.0	34.8	39.5	2.7	3.3	4.1	1.9	2.0	1.8
Cote d'Ivoire	19.3	27.4	42.0	7.6	6.8	5.4	3.0	2.5	1.6
Djibouti	X	X	X	X	X	X	X	X	X
Egypt	37.9	42.2	46.5	3.0	3.1	3.3	1.7	2.1	1.5
Equatorial Guinea	25.5	39.0	59.7	5.6	4.8	3.9	-0.7	-0.8	-0.3
Ethiopia	6.4	9.3	17.6	5.6	6.2	6.7	2.1	1.3	2.3
Gabon	17.4	25.6	40.9	4.7	4.5	4.1	-0.2	-0.2	0.2
Gambia	12.4	15.0	20.9	4.3	4.4	4.6	1.9	1.7	1.4
Ghana	23.3	29.1	39.6	4.2	5.2	5.2	1.2	2.1	2.0
Guinea	9.9	13.8	22.2	5.3	5.3	5.4	1.5	1.5	1.6
Guinea-Bissau	13.6	18.1	27.1	2.9	7.7	4.6	-0.5	4.3	1.1
Kenya	7.4	10.2	16.7	7.0	7.3	7.4	3.3	3.5	3.5
Lesotho	1.5	2.6	5.8	7.5	7.6	7.1	1.9	2.2	2.3
Liberia	18.6	26.0	39.5	6.0	6.2	5.4	1.7	2.0	1.7
Libya	22.7	35.8	64.5	10.3	7.8	5.3	1.2	0.0	0.2
Madagascar	10.6	14.1	21.8	5.1	5.6	5.7	1.9	2.1	2.0
Malawi	4.4	6.0	12.0	6.8	7.6	7.4	2.3	2.4	2.7
Mali	11.1	14.3	20.8	4.7	4.6	5.4	1.8	1.6	2.1
Mauritania	6.7	13.9	34.6	9.7	9.1	7.0	1.5	0.9	0.7
Mauritius	33.2	42.0	56.8	4.4	3.9	3.0	0.2	-0.1	-0.3
Morocco	29.3	34.6	43.9	4.4	4.5	4.7	2.0	1.9	1.8
Mozambique	3.7	5.7	19.4	6.6	12.8	9.2	2.0	3.4	0.9
Niger	5.8	8.5	16.2	6.5	6.9	6.7	1.7	2.0	2.2
Nigeria	13.1	16.4	23.0	5.4	5.8	6.0	2.8	2.9	2.7
Rwanda	2.4	3.2	5.1	5.9	6.4	7.1	3.0	3.2	3.4
Senegal	22.4	29.6	42.4	5.6	6.0	4.8	1.8	2.2	1.2
Sierra Leone	13.0	18.1	28.3	4.6	4.6	4.5	0.7	0.7	0.8
Somalia	17.3	23.1	34.1	5.0	10.4	3.4	1.3	6.8	-0.1
South Africa	46.7	47.9	55.9	2.5	3.3	3.5	2.0	1.2	1.2
Sudan	10.3	16.4	29.4	6.9	7.0	5.8	1.5	1.9	1.5
Swaziland	3.9	9.7	26.3	10.3	9.8	7.7	1.6	1.5	1.2
Tanzania, United Rep	4.8	6.9	14.8	7.5	8.5	7.7	2.8	2.8	2.9
Togo	9.8	13.1	20.1	7.2	5.2	5.8	3.9	1.8	2.2
Tunisia	36.0	43.5	56.8	4.0	4.5	3.7	0.7	0.7	0.3
Uganda	5.2	8.0	14.4	8.1	7.2	7.1	3.6	2.8	2.9
Zaire	22.3	30.3	44.2	5.0	5.4	4.9	0.9	1.4	1.4
Zambia	17.2	30.4	49.5	8.2	6.3	5.8	1.0	1.0	0.8
Zimbabwe	12.6	16.9	24.6	6.8	5.7	5.9	3.0	2.8	2.8
NORTH & CENTRAL AMERICA	**63.3**	**67.2**	**70.0**	**2.3**	**1.9**	**1.8**	**0.2**	**1.1**	**0.4**
Barbados	35.4	37.1	42.2	0.8	1.6	2.1	0.1	0.3	0.1
Canada	68.9	75.7	75.0	2.5	1.0	1.2	-0.4	1.7	0.7
Costa Rica	36.6	39.7	45.9	3.9	3.9	3.7	2.6	2.2	1.3
Cuba	54.9	60.2	71.8	2.8	2.0	1.8	0.6	-1.5	-1.4
Dominican Rep	30.2	40.3	55.7	5.6	4.5	3.8	1.1	0.4	-0.0
El Salvador	38.3	39.4	43.0	3.8	3.5	4.3	3.4	2.5	2.2
Guatemala	33.0	35.7	41.4	3.7	4.0	4.2	2.6	2.4	1.8
Haiti	15.6	19.8	28.0	4.5	4.7	5.0	1.6	1.7	1.6
Honduras	22.7	28.9	39.9	5.1	5.7	5.0	1.8	2.4	1.7
Jamaica	33.8	41.6	53.8	3.2	2.9	2.8	-0.1	-0.4	-0.2
Mexico	50.8	59.0	70.0	4.7	4.0	3.2	1.3	0.8	0.4
Nicaragua	39.6	47.0	59.4	5.1	4.4	4.5	1.6	1.0	1.5
Panama	41.2	47.6	51.9	4.3	2.8	2.9	1.7	1.8	1.1
Trinidad and Tobago	22.2	21.5	22.6	0.7	0.1	2.8	1.1	-0.4	0.7
United States	70.0	73.6	74.2	1.6	1.1	1.1	-0.2	1.0	0.1
SOUTH AMERICA	**51.7**	**60.3**	**72.4**	**4.0**	**3.6**	**3.0**	**0.4**	**-0.2**	**-0.3**
Argentina	73.6	78.4	84.6	2.0	2.1	1.8	-0.6	-0.6	-0.8
Bolivia	39.3	40.8	43.7	2.7	2.9	3.7	2.1	2.3	2.0
Brazil	44.9	55.8	72.7	4.6	4.1	3.2	0.2	-0.9	-1.3
Chile	67.8	75.2	83.4	2.9	2.4	2.0	-0.7	-1.0	-0.7
Colombia	48.2	57.2	67.4	4.1	3.2	2.9	1.1	0.3	0.2
Ecuador	34.4	39.5	47.7	4.2	4.3	4.4	2.2	2.1	1.8
Guyana	29.0	29.4	32.2	2.0	2.7	3.2	1.8	1.8	1.0
Paraguay	35.6	37.1	41.5	3.0	4.1	4.1	2.3	2.8	1.8
Peru	46.3	57.4	67.4	4.8	3.6	3.3	0.4	1.0	0.7
Suriname	47.3	45.9	45.7	1.8	-0.8	1.5	2.7	-0.8	0.0
Uruguay	80.1	82.1	85.0	1.1	0.8	1.0	-0.2	-0.6	-0.7
Venezuela	66.6	76.2	85.7	4.8	4.3	3.3	0.1	0.1	0.3

World Resources 1987

Table 17.1

	Urban Population as Percentage of Total			Average Annual Change in Population (percent)					
				Urban			Rural		
	1960	1970	1985	1965–70	1975–80	1985–90	1965–70	1975–80	1985–90
ASIA	**20.6**	**23.6**	**28.2**	**3.3**	**3.1**	**3.0**	**2.2**	**1.5**	**1.0**
Afghanistan	8.0	11.0	18.5	5.6	4.3	8.8	1.9	0.2	4.8
Bahrain	78.6	78.2	81.7	2.7	5.2	4.0	3.1	3.6	2.3
Bangladesh	5.1	7.6	11.9	6.7	5.5	5.4	2.4	2.5	2.2
Bhutan	2.5	3.1	4.5	4.1	4.6	5.3	1.8	1.9	1.9
Burma	19.3	22.8	30.0	4.0	4.3	4.5	1.8	1.8	1.5
China	16.8	19.3	21.0	2.7	2.2	2.2	2.6	1.3	0.7
Cyprus	35.6	40.8	49.5	2.4	2.0	2.3	0.2	–0.4	–0.4
India	18.0	19.8	25.5	3.4	3.9	3.6	2.2	1.6	1.1
Indonesia	14.6	17.1	25.3	3.9	4.9	4.1	2.0	1.4	0.6
Iran	33.6	41.0	55.0	5.5	5.0	4.2	1.9	1.2	0.8
Iraq	42.9	56.2	70.6	5.3	5.2	4.2	0.8	0.9	0.7
Israel	77.0	84.2	90.7	3.8	2.8	2.0	–0.8	–1.2	–1.0
Japan	62.5	71.2	76.5	2.2	1.0	0.6	–1.5	0.5	–0.1
Jordan	42.7	50.6	64.4	4.9	4.0	5.1	1.5	0.1	1.7
Kampuchea, Dem	10.3	11.7	15.6	4.0	–0.2	5.0	2.2	–2.4	2.0
Korea, Dem People's Rep	40.2	50.1	63.8	4.9	4.0	3.3	0.9	0.3	0.1
Korea, Rep	27.7	40.7	65.3	6.8	4.9	3.3	–0.4	–2.2	–2.9
Kuwait	72.3	77.8	93.7	9.2	7.7	4.5	9.1	–3.8	–3.1
Lao People's Dem Rep	7.9	9.6	15.9	5.5	5.9	5.6	2.3	2.1	1.7
Lebanon	39.6	59.4	80.4	6.4	1.2	2.9	–1.6	–5.7	–1.6
Malaysia	25.2	27.0	31.5	3.3	3.4	3.8	2.4	2.0	1.4
Mongolia	35.7	45.1	55.9	4.4	4.3	3.8	2.0	1.4	0.9
Nepal	3.1	3.9	5.8	4.3	5.0	5.5	2.0	2.3	2.1
Oman	3.5	5.1	8.8	6.4	8.6	6.7	2.5	4.6	2.7
Pakistan	22.1	24.9	29.8	3.9	4.2	3.6	2.4	2.5	1.5
Philippines	30.3	33.0	39.6	3.7	3.5	3.6	2.5	2.0	1.4
Qatar	72.4	80.3	88.0	10.2	7.9	3.6	5.8	3.9	0.6
Saudi Arabia	29.7	48.7	73.0	8.2	7.4	4.8	0.1	0.4	0.2
Singapore	77.6	75.3	74.2	1.7	1.3	1.4	2.9	1.3	0.5
Sri Lanka	17.9	21.9	21.1	4.2	1.3	2.1	1.8	1.8	1.8
Syrian Arab Rep	36.8	43.3	47.4	4.8	4.2	4.7	2.1	2.6	2.8
Thailand	12.5	13.2	15.6	3.6	3.4	3.9	3.0	2.1	1.3
Turkey	29.7	38.4	48.1	4.9	3.6	3.7	1.2	1.0	0.9
United Arab Emirates	40.0	71.5	77.8	13.4	12.8	3.4	0.2	15.3	3.4
Viet Nam	14.7	18.3	20.3	4.4	2.9	3.4	1.8	2.3	1.5
Yemen	3.4	7.5	20.0	9.3	8.5	7.0	0.9	1.0	1.4
Yemen, Dem	28.0	32.1	39.9	3.4	3.8	4.5	1.4	1.5	1.8
EUROPE	**60.5**	**66.1**	**73.3**	**1.5**	**1.1**	**0.9**	**–0.9**	**–1.2**	**–1.3**
Albania	30.6	33.5	39.3	3.5	3.5	3.6	2.3	1.8	1.1
Austria	49.9	51.7	56.1	0.9	0.5	0.7	0.1	–0.7	–0.9
Belgium	84.6	88.2	89.2	0.8	0.2	0.1	–2.6	–0.3	–0.9
Bulgaria	38.6	52.3	68.6	3.4	2.4	1.4	–1.8	–2.2	–2.1
Czechoslovakia	46.9	55.2	66.3	1.8	1.9	1.3	–1.4	–1.2	–1.5
Denmark	73.7	79.7	85.9	1.4	0.7	0.4	–1.8	–2.2	–2.1
Finland	38.1	50.3	66.9	2.9	2.2	1.3	–2.2	–2.4	–2.2
France	62.4	71.0	77.2	1.9	1.0	0.8	–1.7	–1.2	–1.4
German Dem Rep	72.3	73.7	78.2	0.3	0.3	0.3	–0.5	–1.4	–1.5
Germany, Fed Rep	77.4	81.3	86.1	1.0	0.3	0.1	–1.4	–2.0	–2.0
Greece	42.9	52.5	65.9	2.5	2.8	1.6	–1.4	–1.0	–1.6
Hungary	40.0	45.6	57.0	1.7	1.6	1.2	–0.7	–1.1	–1.6
Iceland	80.3	84.9	89.6	1.7	1.4	1.1	–1.5	–1.4	–1.3
Ireland	45.8	51.7	57.0	1.7	1.8	1.8	–0.7	0.4	0.1
Italy	59.4	64.4	71.7	1.4	0.8	0.8	–0.8	–1.4	–1.5
Luxembourg	62.1	67.8	81.8	1.9	1.4	0.5	–2.4	–3.7	–3.1
Malta	70.0	77.5	85.4	1.3	2.0	1.0	–2.6	–1.6	–1.7
Netherlands	76.8	78.3	92.5	1.4	2.3	0.8	0.5	–9.2	–6.8
Norway	32.1	42.0	80.3	3.5	4.8	1.8	–0.9	–6.9	–8.0
Poland	47.9	52.1	59.2	1.6	1.9	1.7	–0.1	–0.0	–0.6
Portugal	22.5	26.2	31.2	0.1	1.8	2.0	–1.9	0.2	0.0
Romania	34.2	41.8	54.8	3.4	2.7	2.1	–0.0	–0.8	–1.1
Spain	56.6	66.0	77.4	2.6	2.1	1.4	–1.5	–1.7	–1.6
Sweden	72.6	81.1	85.5	1.8	0.5	0.1	–3.1	–1.5	–1.9
Switzerland	51.0	54.5	60.4	2.0	0.6	0.4	0.6	–1.0	–1.7
United Kingdom	85.7	88.5	91.7	0.7	0.1	0.2	–1.9	–2.4	–1.9
Yugoslavia	27.9	34.8	46.3	3.1	2.8	2.3	–0.1	–0.4	–0.9
USSR	**48.8**	**56.7**	**66.3**	**2.5**	**2.0**	**1.8**	**–1.0**	**–0.7**	**–0.9**
OCEANIA	**66.3**	**70.8**	**71.7**	**2.6**	**1.6**	**1.5**	**0.5**	**1.7**	**1.3**
Australia	80.6	85.2	86.8	2.5	1.6	1.4	–0.8	1.0	0.2
Fiji	29.7	34.8	41.2	3.6	2.9	2.8	1.6	1.1	0.5
New Zealand	76.0	81.1	83.7	2.0	0.7	1.0	–0.8	–0.1	0.1
Papua New Guinea	2.7	9.8	14.3	15.1	5.0	4.7	1.4	2.9	2.2
Solomon Islands	X	X	X	X	X	X	X	X	X

Source: U.N. Population Division.
0 = zero or less than five one-hundredths of 1 percent; X = not available.
For additional information, see Sources and Technical Notes.

Table 17.2 Drinking Water and Sanitation in Developing Countries,

	Percentage of Population with Access to Safe Drinking Water			Percentage of Population with Access to Sanitation Services		
	Total	Urban	Rural	Total	Urban	Rural
AFRICA						
Algeria	X	X	X	X	X	X
Angola	31	90	12	18	29	15
Benin	19	26	15	21	48	4
Botswana	57	98	47	36	90	23
Burkina Faso	31	27	31	8	38	5
Burundi	24	90	22	52	50	52
Cameroon	X	X	X	X	X	X
Cape Verde	31	99	27	11	49	8
Central African Rep	X	X	X	X	X	X
Chad	X	X	X	X	X	X
Comoros	X	X	X	X	X	X
Congo	21	42	7	X	X	X
Cote d'Ivoire	X	X	X	X	X	X
Djibouti	X	80	40	X	75	18
Egypt	75	88	64	26	45	10
Equatorial Guinea	X	47	X	X	99	X
Ethiopia	X	X	X	X	X	X
Gabon	X	X	X	X	X	X
Gambia	49	100	36	X	X	X
Ghana	52	72	39	28	47	16
Guinea	17	69	2	13	54	1
Guinea-Bissau	33	21	37	19	22	18
Kenya	28	61	21	45	75	39
Lesotho	13	37	11	14	13	14
Liberia	40	71	20	X	24a	20
Libya	96	100	90	90	100	72
Madagascar	23	73	9	X	3a	X
Malawi	51	66	49	X	75	X
Mali	16	46	8	21	91	3
Malta	100	100	100	98	100	84
Mauritania	X	80	X	X	4a	0
Mauritius	99	100	98	96	100	90
Morocco	X	100	X	X	X	X
Mozambique	X	X	X	X	X	X
Niger	34	41	33	8	36	3
Nigeria	37	60	30	X	30b	X
Rwanda	60	55	60	60	60	60
Senegal	45	69	27	X	87	X
Sierra Leone	22	61	6	22	52	10
Somalia	36	65	21	20	48	5
Sudan	51	100	31	X	73	X
Swaziland	X	X	X	X	X	X
Tanzania, United Rep	46	88	39	52	83	47
Togo	34	68	26	11	24	8
Tunisia	X	100	X	X	X	X
Uganda	X	45c	12	X	34a	10
Zaire	22	43	5	X	X	10
Zambia	49	65	33	74	100	48
Zimbabwe	X	X	X	X	X	X
LATIN AMERICA						
Argentina	64	72	17	84	94	32
Barbados	53	100	18	X	1	X
Bolivia	41	78	12	23	40	9
Brazil	77	86	53	X	33a	X
Chile	86	100	18	84	100	4
Colombia	X	77c	X	69	96	13
Costa Rica	90	100	82	93	100	87
Cuba	X	X	X	X	X	X
Dominican Rep	62	85	32	27	41	9
Ecuador	58	98	21	44	64	26
El Salvador	52	67	40	49	80	26
Guatemala	52	90	26	36	48	28
Guyana	73	100	60	86	100	80
Haiti	34	58	25	20	41	12
Honduras	69	91	55	44	50	40
Jamaica	X	X	X	X	X	X
Mexico	76	91	40	58	78	12
Nicaragua	58	91	10	X	35a	X
Panama	63	97	26	X	61	X
Paraguay	25	46	10	87	92	84
Peru	55	73	18	39	57	1
Suriname	98	100	96	98	100	96
Trinidad and Tobago	97	100	96	97	100	96
Uruguay	81	95	3	X	5a	X
Venezuela	X	X	65	X	X	X

Early 1980s

Table 17.2

	Percentage of Population with Access to Safe Drinking Water			Percentage of Population with Access to Sanitation Services		
	Total	**Urban**	**Rural**	**Total**	**Urban**	**Rural**
ASIA						
Afghanistan	22	39	18	X	3b	X
Bahrain	100	100	100	100	100	100
Bangladesh	41	29	43	4	21	2
Bhutan	X	40c	14	X	X	X
Brunei	X	100	95	X	75	98
Burma	26	36	21	21	34	15
China	X	X	X	X	X	X
Cyprus	100	100	100	100	100	100
Hong Kong	99	100	93	X	X	X
India	55	80	47	8	30	1
Indonesia	32	40	29	30	31	30
Iran	68	82	50	72	96	43
Iraq	84	100	46	75	100	15
Israel	X	X	X	X	X	X
Jordan	88	100	65	73	94	34
Kampuchea, Dem	X	X	X	X	X	X
Korea, Dem People's Rep	X	X	X	X	X	X
Korea, Rep	77	86	60	100	100	100
Kuwait	87	86	100	100	100	100
Lao People's Dem Rep	21	28	20	5	13	4
Lebanon	X	X	X	X	X	X
Malaysia	79	97	71	72	100	59
Maldives	X	54	7	X	71	1
Mongolia	X	X	X	X	X	X
Nepal	14	71	11	2	16	1
Oman	23	100	16	21	100	13
Pakistan	40	78	24	20	53	6
Philippines	54	53	55	58	75	47
Qatar	72	76	43	X	X	X
Saudi Arabia	91	100	68	82	100	33
Singapore	X	100	NA	X	100	NA
Sri Lanka	37	76	26	67	80	63
Syrian Arab Rep	80	100	61	X	66a	29
Thailand	67	50	70	45	50	44
Turkey	78	95	62	X	56	X
United Arab Emirates	92	95	81	77	93	22
Viet Nam	X	X	31	X	X	70
Yemen	37	100	21	X	75	X
Yemen, Dem	53	73	39	47	69	33
OCEANIA						
American Samoa	X	100	64	100	100	100
Cook Islands	X	100	85	100	100	100
Fiji	69	100	48	70	85	60
Guam	100	100	100	100	100	100
Niue	X	100	NA	X	100	NA
Pacific Island Trust Terr	X	68	24	X	79	7
Papua New Guinea	16	55	10	16	91	3
Solomon Islands	X	96	45	X	80	21
Tokelau	X	NA	100	X	NA	50
Tonga	X	91	90	X	100	97
Tuvalu	X	X	X	X	X	X
Vanuatu	X	100	50	X	86	64
Western Samoa	X	95	94	X	82	86

Sources: World Health Organization; and U.N. Population Division.
Notes:
a. Data refer to sewerage only; b. data refer to sanitation by non-sewerage
means only; c. data refer to drinking water by house connection only.
0 = zero or less than half of 1 percent; X = not available; NA = not applicable.
For additional information, see Sources and Technical Notes.

Table 17.3 World's 85 Largest Urban Agglomerations, 1985

Population Rank	City	Country	1985 Population (thousands)	Residential Area (square kilometers)	Area Rank	Residential Density (population per square kilometer)	Density Rank	City Population as a Percentage of National Population
1	Tokyo/Yokohama	Japan	25,434	2,821	3	9,018	59	21
2	Mexico City	Mexico	16,901	1,352	8	12,501	54	21
3	Sao Paulo	Brazil	14,911	1,168	12	12,765	50	11
4	New York	United States	14,598	3,300	1	4,424	68	6
5	Seoul	Korea, Rep	13,665	886	21	15,427	41	22
6	Osaka/Kobe/Kyoto	Japan	13,562	1,282	9	10,578	57	11
7	Buenos Aires	Argentina	10,750	1,386	7	7,758	60	35
8	Calcutta	India	10,462	541	31	19,327	26	1
9	Bombay	India	10,137	246	50	41,199	4	1
10	Rio de Janeiro	Brazil	10,116	673	28	15,022	42	7
11	Moscow	USSR	9,873	982	17	10,058	58	4
12	Los Angeles	United States	9,638	2,875	2	3,352	77	4
13	London	United Kingdom	9,442	2,264	4	4,171	71	17
14	Paris	France	8,633	1,119	14	7,716	61	16
15	Cairo	Egypt	8,595	269	47	31,909	13	18
16	Manila	Philippines	8,485	487	33	17,426	32	16
17	Jakarta	Indonesia	8,122	197	60	41,262	3	5
18	Essen	Germany, Fed Rep	7,604	1,823	6	4,170	72	12
19	Tehran	Iran	7,354	290	46	25,352	19	16
20	Delhi	India	6,993	357	41	19,565	25	1
21	Shanghai	China	6,698	202	56	33,155	11	1
22	Chicago	United States	6,511	1,974	5	3,299	79	3
23	Karachi	Pakistan	6,351	492	32	12,906	49	6
24	Lagos	Nigeria	6,054	145	68	41,740	2	6
25	Beijing	China	5,608	391	37	14,339	44	1
26	Taipei	Taiwan	5,550	357	40	15,528	39	30
27	Lima	Peru	5,447	311	43	17,526	31	28
28	Hong Kong	Hong Kong	5,415	52	85	104,537	1	98
29	Istanbul	Turkey	5,389	427	34	12,610	53	11
30	Bangkok	Thailand	4,998	264	48	18,919	28	10
31	Madras	India	4,983	298	45	16,730	34	1
32	Bogota	Colombia	4,711	205	53	23,024	22	16
33	Santiago	Chile	4,700	332	42	14,177	45	39
34	Milan	Italy	4,635	891	20	5,202	66	8
35	Tianjin	China	4,622	127	74	36,420	9	0
36	Leningrad	USSR	4,569	360	38	12,691	51	2
37	Nagoya	Japan	4,452	795	25	5,599	65	4
38	Manchester	United Kingdom	4,151	925	18	4,489	67	7
39	Madrid	Spain	4,137	171	62	24,201	21	11
40	Shenyang	China	4,086	101	77	40,451	6	0
41	Philadelphia	United States	4,025	1,220	10	3,299	78	2
42	Pusan	Korea, Rep	3,996	140	70	28,571	15	10
43	Barcelona	Spain	3,842	225	52	17,051	33	10
44	San Francisco	United States	3,790	1,109	15	3,419	75	2
45	Bangalore	India	3,685	130	73	28,456	16	0
46	Lahore	Pakistan	3,603	148	67	24,406	20	4
47	Sydney	Australia	3,396	875	22	3,879	73	22
48	Baghdad	Iraq	3,371	251	49	13,418	47	21
49	Dhaka	Bangladesh	3,283	83	81	39,611	7	3
50	Athens	Greece	3,252	300	44	10,824	56	33
51	Ho Chi Minh City	Viet Nam	3,250	80	82	40,478	5	5
52	Guangzhou	China	3,248	205	54	15,874	37	0
53	Detroit	United States	3,133	1,212	11	2,585	84	NA
54	Miami	United States	3,123	1,160	13	2,691	81	1
55	Belo Horizonte	Brazil	3,059	205	55	14,950	43	2
56	Wuhan	China	3,048	168	63	18,105	29	0
57	Ahmadabad	India	3,037	83	80	36,643	8	0
58	Greater Berlin	Germany, Fed Rep / German Dem Rep	3,033	710	27	4,274	69	NA / NA
59	Hyderabad	India	3,022	228	51	13,259	48	0
60	Caracas	Venezuela	2,993	140	71	21,400	23	17
61	Toronto	Canada	2,972	399	36	7,451	62	12
62	Surabaja	Indonesia	2,962	111	76	26,596	18	2
63	Rome	Italy	2,944	179	61	16,474	35	5
64	Naples	Italy	2,862	161	64	17,823	30	5
65	Melbourne	Australia	2,852	847	23	3,367	76	18
66	Montreal	Canada	2,827	425	35	6,656	63	11
67	Kinshasa	Zaire	2,794	148	66	18,926	27	9
68	Guadalajara	Mexico	2,746	202	57	13,593	46	3
69	Alexandria	Egypt	2,660	91	78	29,344	14	6
70	Rangoon	Burma	2,558	122	75	21,014	24	7
71	Singapore	Singapore	2,556	202	58	12,652	52	100
72	Porto Allegre	Brazil	2,536	598	29	4,239	70	2
73	Harbin	China	2,518	78	83	32,407	12	0
74	Casablanca	Morocco	2,495	91	79	27,523	17	11
75	Kiev	USSR	2,489	161	65	15,500	40	1
76	Dallas	United States	2,486	1,085	16	2,291	85	1
77	Boston	United States	2,470	785	26	3,147	80	1
78	Washington	United States	2,456	925	19	2,656	82	1
79	Monterrey	Mexico	2,351	199	59	11,789	55	3
80	Ankara	Turkey	2,338	142	69	16,413	36	5
81	Budapest	Hungary	2,297	357	39	6,427	64	21
82	Cheng-tu	China	2,260	65	84	34,903	10	0
83	Birmingham	United Kingdom	2,211	578	30	3,828	74	4
84	Houston	United States	2,104	803	24	2,621	83	1
85	Bucharest	Romania	2,095	135	72	15,555	38	9

Source: U.S. Bureau of the Census.
0 = zero or less than half of 1 percent; NA = not applicable.
For additional information, see Sources and Technical Notes.

World Resources 1987

Table 17.4 Waste Generation in Selected Countries, 1980

	Average Annual Municipal Waste Generation			Industrial Waste Generation			Hazardous and Special Wastes	
	Total	Per Capita	Per Unit Area	Total	Per Industrial Gross Domestic Product[a]	Per Unit Area	Total	Per Unit Area
	(thousand metric tons per year)	(kilograms)	(metric tons per square kilometer per year)	(thousand metric tons per year)	(metric tons per million $US of Industrial GDP)	(metric tons per square kilometer per year)	(thousand metric tons per year)	(metric tons per square kilometer per year)
Australia	10,000	681	1.3	20,000	X	2.6	X	X
Austria	1,560	208	18.8	300	10	3.6	100	1.2
Belgium	3,082	313	93.4	8,000	186	242.4	915	27.7
Canada	12,600	526	1.4	61,000	730	6.6	3,290	0.4
Denmark	2,046	399	48.7	814	X	19.4	63	1.5
Finland	1,200	290	3.9	X	X	X	87	0.3
France	15,500	289	28.4	38,205	163	70.0	2,000	3.7
Germany, Fed Rep	20,780	338	85.2	52,469	X	215.0	4,892	20.0
Greece	2,500	259	19.1	X	X	X	X	X
Ireland	640	188	6.4	1,200	X	12.0	X	X
Israel	X	X	X	X	X	X	22.5	1.1
Italy	14,041	246	47.8	35,000	207	119.0	X	X
Japan	40,225	344	108.4	161,677	379	435.8	768	2.1
Netherlands	5,400	382	158.8	4,869	79	143.2	280	8.2
New Zealand	1,528	488	5.7	498	67	1.9	X	X
Norway	1,700	415	5.5	2,186	93	7.1	120	0.4
Portugal	1,500	152	16.3	11,200	1,110	121.7	X	X
Spain	8,028	215	16.1	X	X	X	X	X
Sweden	2,500	301	6.1	4,000	102	9.7	550	1.3
Switzerland	2,146	337	53.7	X	X	X	382	9.6
United Kingdom	15,816	282	65.4	89,749	490	370.9	1,500	6.2
United States	160,000	703	17.5	400,000	455	43.8	264,000	28.9

Sources: Organisation for Economic Co-operation and Development; and national sources.
Note: a. The portion of Gross Domestic Product contributed by industry.
For additional information, see Sources and Technical Notes.
X = not available.

Sources and Technical Notes

Table 17.1 Urban and Rural Populations, 1960–90

Source: U.N. Population Division, *World Population Prospects: Estimates and Projections as Assessed in 1982* (United Nations, New York, 1985).

Urban population is defined as the portion of the total population residing in urban areas. The remainder of the population is defined as rural. Definitions of urban area vary widely from country to country. For a list of individual country definitions, see U.N. Population Division, *Estimates and Projections of Urban, Rural, and City Populations, 1950–2025: The 1982 Assessment* (United Nations, New York, 1985). For additional information on methods of data collection and estimation, refer to the Technical Note for Table 16.1.

Table 17.2 Drinking Water and Sanitation in Developing Countries, Early 1980s

Sources: Drinking water and sanitation: World Health Organization (WHO), *The International Drinking Water Supply and Sanitation Decade: Review of National Baseline Data: December 1980* (WHO, Geneva, 1984); and unpublished WHO data (WHO, Geneva, September 1986). Urban and rural fractions of total population: U.N. Population Division, *World Population Prospects: Estimates and Projections as Assessed in 1982* (United Nations, New York, 1985).

Data were collected from national governments by WHO in 1980 and 1983 by means of questionnaires. The questionnaires were com-

pleted by public health officials, WHO experts, and Resident Representatives of the United Nations Development Programme. The data collected were used to develop a baseline of information from which to assess progress toward meeting global goals set for the International Drinking Water Supply and Sanitation Decade. One hundred and six developing countries responded to one or both of the questionnaires. These countries represent about 65 percent of the population of the developing world, including China. The total includes 38 African countries, covering 78 percent of the developing country population (South Africa is excluded); 23 North and South American countries, covering 97 percent of the developing country population; 33 Asian countries, covering 59 percent of the developing country population (including China); and 12 Oceanian countries, covering over 99 percent of the developing country population. Developed countries routinely report comprehensive provision of drinking water and sanitation services.

The definitions of urban and rural population were supplied by national governments. Urban and rural service levels were weighted by the 1985 urban and rural populations for the national total service levels. Refer to the Technical Note for Table 17.1 for details.

WHO defines reasonable access to safe drinking water in an urban area as water piped to a housing unit or to a public standpipe within 200 meters of a dwelling. In rural areas, reasonable access implies that a family member need not spend a disproportionate part of the day fetching water. "Safe" drinking water includes treated surface water and untreated water from protected springs, boreholes, and sanitary wells.

Other sources are considered unsafe.

Urban areas with access to sanitation services are defined as urban populations served by connections to public sewers or household systems such as pit privies, pour-flush latrines, septic tanks, communal toilets, etc. Rural populations with access were defined as those with adequate disposal such as pit privies, pour-flush latrines, etc.

Application of these definitions is clearly open to subjective judgment. Comparisons among countries may therefore be misleading because of varied interpretations of definitions as well as incomplete responses.

Table 17.3 World's 85 Largest Urban Agglomerations, 1985

Source: U.S. Bureau of the Census, *World Population Profile 1985* (U.S. Bureau of the Census, Washington, D.C., in press, September 1986).

Urban agglomerations are defined as areas with a population of at least 5,000 people per square mile (1,930 people per square kilometer). All agglomerations that had populations of 2 million or more in 1985 are included.

The geographical area of each agglomeration was determined by examining detailed maps. Population data were drawn from official estimates. An urbanized area having a population density of at least 5,000 per square mile was included in the population and area estimates of a nearby agglomeration if the two are separated by a distance of less than one mile (1.6 kilometers). When possible, parks, airports, industrial complexes, and bodies of water were excluded from the area measured for each agglomeration so that population density figures would refer to the residential portions only.

City population data are analyzed in conjunction with national population data. The U.S. Census Bureau obtains national data from a country's two most recent censuses, adjusting these data for over- and underenumeration of certain age and sex groups. Data are then projected from the most recent census year to 1985 using past and assumed future trends in fertility, mortality, and migration. The population of a particular city is scaled to 1985 using similar methods, together with information about national urban growth rates. These city growth rates reflect rural to urban migration, but they cannot incorporate recent changes in the rates or patterns of migration.

Administrative and political boundaries were disregarded in determining the populations and areas of the agglomerations. Berlin includes both East and West Berlin as well as the surrounding urbanized area in the German Democratic Republic. Detroit includes Windsor, Canada.

Table 17.4 Waste Generation in Selected Countries, 1980

Sources: Waste data: Organisation for Economic Co-operation and Development (OECD), *Environmental Data Compendium 1985*

(OECD, Paris, 1985); hazardous waste data for Israel: Uri Marinov, State of Israel Environmental Protection Service, Jerusalem, Israel, 1986 (personal communication); hazardous waste data for Switzerland: Jean-Bernard Dubois, Bundesamt für Umweltschutz, Bern, Switzerland, 1986 (personal communication). Gross Domestic Product: The World Bank, *World Development Report 1982* (Oxford University Press, New York, 1982). Geographical area: United Nations Food and Agriculture Organization (FAO), *FAO Production Yearbook 1984* (FAO, Rome, 1985).

Waste data were collected by OECD by means of a questionnaire completed by government representatives. Refer to the Technical Note for Table 15.1 for details concerning Gross Domestic Product. Area data refer to land area only; inland water bodies are excluded.

Municipal waste is the trash collected from households, commercial establishments, and small industries. It includes refuse from markets and gardens if collected and disposed of by the municipality. Depending on local consumption and production patterns, 25–50 percent of municipal waste is paper, cardboard, and plastic packaging. Other municipal waste includes organic matter, metals, leather, textiles, wood, and rubber.

Industrial waste contains both chemical and nonchemical materials. Amounts depend on the definition of waste used in a country, the

levels of industrial production, and the types of technology used.

Hazardous waste is that waste known to contain potentially harmful substances. Nuclear wastes are not included in this table. Refer to Chapter 22, "Energy and Minerals," Table 22.4 for data on spent fuel from nuclear reactors.

Country-specific information:

1. New Zealand—municipal waste includes demolition waste; industrial waste is non-chemical waste only.
2. Australia—special and hazardous wastes are included under industrial waste.
3. Netherlands—industrial waste includes wastes generated only by enterprises employing ten or more people and includes office and canteen wastes; hazardous waste refers to "notifiable" wastes only.
4. Norway—industrial waste includes chemical waste only.
5. United Kingdom—industrial waste includes some agricultural waste.
6. Canada—hazardous waste is measured in wet weight.
7. Denmark—includes only hazardous waste that has been legally disposed of.
8. France—hazardous waste is toxic or hazardous waste.

For a more detailed discussion of hazardous waste measurement see Chapter 13, "Controlling Hazardous Waste: The Unmet Challenge."

18. Land Use and Cover

The extent and condition of several land-based resources (cropland and soils, forests and rangelands, wildlife and habitat) are examined in individual chapters of *World Resources 1987*. This chapter presents data on *patterns* of land cover and land use, and on the impacts of human land use on natural land cover. These indicators can be used to examine cross-cutting topics, such as the relationship between land use and the global carbon cycle.

Ideally, land use and cover data would be available in fine vegetational, geographic, and temporal detail. Regular monitoring of land cover and the processes causing rapid land use changes (e.g., growth of urban areas, deforestation, desertification, cropland expansion) would enable policymakers to focus on those areas where attention is most needed. However, changes in the categories shown in Table 18.1—cropland, pasture, forest and woodland, and other land—indicate only gross changes in national land use. For example, between the mid-1960s and the early 1980s, the Philippines lost 29 percent of its forest and woodland area and cropland increased 22 percent. If mangroves, one type of "forest and woodland," were the source of the entire 29 percent decline, local fisheries and shoreline stability would suffer. But if the source of new cropland were upland forests, accelerated soil erosion and reduced groundwater recharge would be likely.

In the future, satellite remote sensing may permit continuous global monitoring of land cover and land use changes at somewhat finer levels of detail than the four categories used by the United Nations Food and Agriculture Organization (the source for Table 18.1). Remote sensing data with even higher resolution are currently available from aircraft and the LANDSAT and Spot Image satellites, but the vast quantities of information inherent in high-resolution monitoring are difficult and costly to process on a global basis.

Data on one land-cover type, wetlands, are presented in Table 18.2. "Wetlands" encompass a wide variety of ecosystems, such as coastal marshes, mangroves, riverine wetlands, swamps, and peat bogs. Formerly considered wasteland, wetlands are now recognized for their biological, hydrological and economic value. Wetlands provide habitat and breeding areas for many kinds of wildlife, including birds, amphibians, aquatic mammals, shellfish, and finfish. Coastal wetlands help stabilize shorelines against waves and storm erosion, and they buffer littoral ecosystems against salinity changes. Freshwater wetlands are important filters of industrial and agricultural pollu-

tants (until overloaded), and they help to moderate the flow of surface waters. The biological productivity of tropical and warm temperate wetlands is equaled only by that of tropical forests.

The wetlands data summarized in Table 18.2 represent only a small fraction of the world's wetlands; globally, wetlands occupy 5–10 million square kilometers. However, because the area and condition of wetlands in many countries have not been thoroughly investigated, even the "internationally important" wetlands shown are almost certainly undercounted. A few developed countries have estimated their rates of wetland destruction and the current condition of wetlands. For example, 56 percent of the original U.S. wetland area has been converted (mostly to agricultural uses), and losses continue at 190,000 hectares per year. Only qualitative assessments of wetlands conditions have been made for most developing countries. For further information, refer to Chapter 6, "Wildlife and Habitat," Focus On: Freshwater Wetlands, and Chapter 9, "Oceans and Coasts."

Data on long-term land use and land cover changes are presented in Table 18.3. This data base was developed to support studies of the impact of land use changes on the global carbon cycle. (See Chapter 25, "Atmosphere and Climate," Table 25.2.) Globally, the world's forest and woodland areas have been reduced 15 percent since 1850, and cropland has expanded over 170 percent. On a regional level, cropland has expanded in all ten regions defined by the study and forests have declined in nine of the ten. European land use has changed little since 1850, but the tropical regions have seen cropland expansion of several hundred percent.

The data and model supporting this table rely on several assumptions and simplifications, reducing the usefulness of the data for analyzing long-term land use changes. In many instances, only a few historical assessments of land use are available in the literature, and the authors had to interpolate much of the data. For developing regions, cropland expansion is assumed to be directly proportional to population growth, ignoring the impact of rising incomes on crop demand and cropland expansion caused by increasing international demand for agricultural commodities. Many forms of land use change, such as urban growth and desertification, were not included in the model. For these reasons, the data in Table 18.3 should be considered indicative of broad trends rather than exact measurements of the status of land use at a particular time.

Table 18.1 Land Area and Use, 1964–87

| | Land Area | | Land Use (thousand hectares) | | | | | | | |
| | Total (thousand hectares) | Per Capita 1987 (people per thousand hectares) | Cropland | | Permanent Pasture | | Forests and Woodland | | Other Land | |
			1982–84	Percentage Change Over 1964–66	1982–84	Percentage Change Over 1964–66	1982–84	Percentage Change Over 1964–66	1982–84	Percentage Change Over 1964–66
WORLD	**13,081,014**	**382**	**1,472,401**	**8.9**	**3,153,352**	**−0.3**	**4,091,350**	**−2.6**	**4,363,925**	**0.0**
AFRICA	**2,966,447**	**199**	**183,214**	**13.5**	**779,134**	**−0.8**	**703,251**	**−7.6**	**1,300,850**	**3.3**
Algeria	238,174	97	7,393	9.1	31,916	−14.6	4,384	37.0	194,480	1.9
Angola	124,670	74	3,500	5.6	29,000	0.0	53,490	−2.9	38,680	3.8
Benin	11,062	389	1,809	25.7	442	0.0	3,820	−22.4	4,991	17.1
Botswana	58,537	20	1,360	32.4	44,000	5.3	962	0.4	12,214	−18.7
Burkina Faso	27,380	267	2,633	20.8	10,000	0.0	7,020	−13.3	7,727	8.8
Burundi	2,565	1,949	1,307	32.3	910	44.7	63	31.3	286	−68.2
Cameroon	46,944	222	6,958	21.2	8,300	−6.4	25,310	−7.2	6,376	26.1
Cape Verde	403	846	40	0.0	25	0.0	1	0.0	337	0.0
Central African Rep	62,298	43	1,971	10.7	3,000	0.0	35,870	−0.5	21,457	−0.1
Chad	125,920	42	3,150	8.6	45,000	0.0	13,290	−10.8	64,480	1.2
Comoros	217	2,175	93	9.4	15	0.0	35	0.0	74	−9.8
Congo	34,150	54	674	8.0	10,000	0.0	21,300	−1.8	2,176	18.5
Cote d'Ivoire	31,800	331	3,993	49.6	3,000	0.0	8,380	−56.3	16,427	136.7
Djibouti	2,198	177	0	0.0	200	0.0	6	−14.3	1,992	0.1
Egypt	99,545	494	2,471	−6.9	0	0.0	2	0.0	97,072	0.2
Equatorial Guinea	2,805	146	230	3.6	104	0.0	1,295	0.0	1,176	−0.7
Ethiopia	110,100	418	13,930	12.0	45,250	−2.0	27,800	−6.1	23,120	5.5
Gabon	25,767	46	452	120.5	4,700	−6.9	20,000	0.0	615	20.1
Gambia	1,000	670	162	29.6	90	0.0	198	−34.9	550	14.3
Ghana	23,002	631	2,787	6.1	3,440	−5.0	8,560	−12.8	8,215	18.5
Guinea	24,586	259	1,575	0.3	3,000	0.0	10,360	−13.2	9,651	19.5
Guinea-Bissau	2,800	330	288	9.5	1,280	0.0	1,070	−2.7	162	3.2
Kenya	56,925	393	2,318	22.6	3,753	−3.6	3,770	−12.5	47,083	0.5
Lesotho	3,035	527	298	−16.5	2,000	−9.9	0	0.0	737	60.9
Liberia	9,632	243	371	−0.3	240	0.0	3,760	−2.6	5,261	2.0
Libya	175,954	22	2,104	5.4	13,267	32.7	632	26.1	159,952	−2.1
Madagascar	58,154	182	3,010	34.1	34,000	0.0	15,380	−14.4	5,764	46.6
Malawi	9,408	788	2,341	17.8	1,840	0.0	4,742	−6.7	486	−3.0
Mali	122,000	70	2,053	21.6	30,000	0.0	8,680	−7.7	81,267	0.4
Mauritania	103,040	19	195	−28.6	39,250	0.0	15,000	−0.9	48,595	0.4
Mauritius	185	5,876	107	15.1	7	0.0	58	−4.9	13	−45.8
Morocco	44,630	516	8,307	15.0	12,500	0.0	5,200	−0.4	18,623	−5.4
Mozambique	78,409	188	3,080	14.6	44,000	0.0	15,330	−11.7	15,999	11.4
Niger	126,670	51	3,727	64.9	9,220	−12.0	2,720	−28.4	111,003	0.8
Nigeria	91,077	1,120	30,635	4.9	20,940	8.5	15,500	−25.8	24,002	10.7
Rwanda	2,495	2,600	1,010	54.2	440	−48.8	511	−9.6	534	28.7
Senegal	19,200	354	5,225	16.1	5,700	0.0	5,942	−12.0	2,333	3.7
Sierra Leone	7,162	522	1,771	23.4	2,204	0.0	2,097	−2.0	1,090	−21.2
Somalia	62,734	78	1,066	8.7	28,850	0.0	9,000	−9.1	23,818	3.5
South Africa	122,104	279	13,623	4.4	79,850	−5.5	4,150	0.4	24,481	20.1
Sudan	237,600	96	12,448	11.1	56,000	0.0	48,010	−17.0	121,142	7.6
Swaziland	1,720	402	142	−0.7	1,147	−14.5	101	−21.7	330	211.3
Tanzania, United Rep	88,604	273	5,190	36.7	35,000	0.0	42,903	−4.7	5,511	15.3
Togo	5,439	578	1,427	27.1	200	0.0	1,550	−36.7	2,262	35.8
Tunisia	15,536	476	4,684	8.1	3,057	22.3	556	27.8	7,239	−12.4
Uganda	19,971	830	6,213	27.4	5,000	0.0	5,910	−6.6	2,848	−24.3
Zaire	226,760	140	6,458	13.9	9,221	0.0	176,620	−3.2	34,461	17.0
Zambia	74,072	96	5,158	6.1	35,000	0.0	29,590	−5.4	4,324	48.0
Zimbabwe	38,667	244	2,715	28.2	4,856	0.0	23,810	0.0	7,286	−7.6
NORTH & CENTRAL AMERICA	**2,139,185**	**193**	**274,122**	**7.8**	**359,590**	**−3.1**	**660,364**	**−5.8**	**845,110**	**1.8**
Barbados	43	5,953	33	0.0	4	0.0	0	0.0	6	0.0
Canada	922,097	28	46,347	11.5	23,900	16.3	326,129	1.2	525,721	−5.8
Costa Rica	5,066	539	636	31.1	2,167	102.0	1,599	−45.6	665	17.1
Cuba	11,086	921	3,222	74.5	2,490	−9.7	1,930	26.1	3,444	−30.5
Dominican Rep	4,838	1,350	1,460	39.0	2,092	0.0	629	−5.4	657	−36.3
El Salvador	2,072	2,850	725	10.2	610	0.3	122	−38.1	615	−1.1
Guatemala	10,843	778	1,805	16.9	1,334	5.9	4,310	−17.9	3,394	21.7
Haiti	2,756	2,517	900	23.3	502	−17.4	55	−24.7	1,299	−3.4
Honduras	11,189	416	1,772	17.6	3,400	0.0	3,810	−28.0	2,207	122.5
Jamaica	1,083	2,224	268	−6.6	202	−19.2	192	−8.6	421	9.6
Mexico	192,304	431	24,692	5.2	74,499	0.0	46,237	−18.1	46,876	23.8
Nicaragua	11,875	295	1,263	6.0	5,051	23.2	4,150	−32.9	1,411	257.2
Panama	7,599	299	562	0.7	1,161	12.7	4,080	−11.7	1,796	29.1
Trinidad and Tobago	513	2,386	159	14.4	11	57.1	227	−7.3	116	−4.9
United States	916,660	264	189,915	6.2	241,467	−6.4	265,188	−9.7	220,090	20.1
SOUTH AMERICA	**1,753,454**	**159**	**138,878**	**34.6**	**456,431**	**9.2**	**926,787**	**−6.9**	**231,358**	**−2.4**
Argentina	273,669	115	35,700	21.9	142,900	−2.1	59,883	−1.7	35,186	−6.0
Bolivia	108,439	62	3,378	106.0	26,950	−4.1	56,010	−5.8	22,101	14.8
Brazil	845,651	167	74,873	45.7	164,000	27.9	567,710	−5.5	39,068	−40.3
Chile	74,880	166	5,528	24.9	11,900	17.2	15,480	−0.1	41,972	−6.3
Colombia	103,870	288	5,688	12.6	30,000	0.0	50,750	−21.9	17,432	352.8
Ecuador	27,684	358	2,491	−1.4	4,573	107.9	14,250	−17.5	6,369	11.9
Guyana	19,685	50	495	36.7	1,227	22.8	16,369	−10.0	1,594	1228.3
Paraguay	39,730	98	1,940	114.8	15,550	11.1	20,450	−4.2	1,790	−48.5
Peru	128,000	162	3,516	32.8	27,120	−1.3	70,150	−6.0	27,214	17.2
Suriname	16,147	24	58	52.6	23	187.5	15,599	−0.2	467	0.2
Uruguay	17,362	176	1,447	2.9	13,632	−0.6	630	5.5	1,653	0.5
Venezuela	88,205	207	3,757	7.8	17,350	8.2	32,205	−13.9	34,893	11.6

World Resources 1987

	Land Area		Land Use (thousand hectares)							
			Cropland		Permanent Pasture		Forests and Woodland		Other Land	
	Total (thousand hectares)	Per Capita 1987 (people per thousand hectares)	1982–84	Percentage Change Over 1964–66	1982–84	Percentage Change Over 1964–66	1982–84	Percentage Change Over 1964–66	1982–84	Percentage Change Over 1964–66
ASIA	**2,679,071**	**1,087**	**455,220**	**4.1**	**644,349**	**−3.0**	**558,440**	**0.9**	**1,021,065**	**−0.3**
Afghanistan	64,750	280	8,054	2.1	30,000	0.0	1,900	−5.0	24,796	−0.3
Bahrain	62	7,532	2	0.0	4	0.0	0	0.0	56	0.0
Bangladesh	13,391	7,964	9,124	1.4	600	0.0	2,131	−4.2	1,536	−1.9
Bhutan	4,700	314	98	42.0	217	4.8	3,280	5.8	1,105	−16.5
Burma	65,774	587	10,072	−2.2	361	2.3	32,145	−0.1	23,196	−0.1
China	932,641	1,163	100,892	−3.4	285,690	0.0	131,318	21.7	414,740	−4.6
Cyprus	924	740	432	0.0	93	0.0	171	0.0	228	0.0
India	297,319	2,645	168,333	3.6	11,950	−19.1	67,420	10.9	49,616	−16.3
Indonesia	181,157	952	20,253	16.5	11,900	−4.8	121,800	−1.5	27,204	−1.0
Iran	163,600	289	14,840	−4.0	44,000	0.0	18,020	0.1	86,740	0.7
Iraq	43,397	392	5,450	11.2	4,000	0.0	1,907	−2.2	32,040	−1.5
Israel	2,033	2,164	437	7.4	818	−0.5	116	17.2	662	−6.1
Japan	37,103	3,290	4,805	−18.1	606	326.8	25,198	−1.2	6,494	16.2
Jordan	9,718	391	415	18.9	100	0.0	41	36.7	9,162	−0.8
Kampuchea, Dem	17,652	436	3,046	5.0	580	0.0	13,372	0.0	654	−18.3
Korea, Dem People's Rep	12,041	1,776	2,291	18.6	50	0.0	8,970	0.0	730	−33.0
Korea, Rep	9,819	4,346	2,171	−3.1	69	228.6	6,535	−1.4	1,043	12.3
Kuwait	1,782	1,112	2	100.0	134	0.0	2	0.0	1,644	−0.1
Lao People's Dem Rep	23,080	187	890	6.8	800	0.0	13,400	−11.8	7,990	27.9
Lebanon	1,023	2,700	298	2.4	10	11.1	83	−12.6	635	1.1
Malaysia	32,855	495	4,342	17.4	27	12.5	20,540	−17.4	7,946	86.1
Mongolia	156,500	13	1,300	55.9	123,403	−11.7	15,178	1.2	16,619	1756.9
Nepal	13,680	1,261	2,317	26.5	1,786	5.1	2,308	−3.8	7,269	−6.2
Oman	21,246	63	42	61.5	1,000	0.0	0	0.0	20,204	−0.1
Pakistan	77,872	1,351	20,280	5.4	5,000	0.0	3,050	48.9	49,542	−4.0
Philippines	29,817	1,914	11,250	22.1	1,120	36.9	12,050	−28.9	5,397	89.5
Qatar	1,100	323	3	200.0	50	0.0	0	0.0	1,047	−0.2
Saudi Arabia	214,969	58	1,142	48.9	85,000	0.0	1,200	−28.6	127,627	0.1
Singapore	57	45,895	6	−53.8	0	0.0	3	−25.0	48	20.0
Sri Lanka	6,474	2,583	2,187	16.6	439	56.8	2,383	−28.3	1,465	15.0
Syrian Arab Rep	18,405	614	5,687	−12.0	8,338	6.9	496	4.6	3,884	4.4
Thailand	51,177	1,039	19,380	53.7	308	0.0	15,493	−40.5	15,997	31.0
Turkey	77,076	667	27,040	3.2	9,200	−17.5	20,199	0.1	20,637	5.6
United Arab Emirates	8,360	172	15	66.7	200	0.0	3	NM	8,142	−0.1
Viet Nam	32,536	1,911	6,692	11.8	272	0.0	13,150	−6.4	12,422	1.6
Yemen	19,500	372	1,351	5.5	7,000	0.0	1,600	0.0	9,549	−0.7
Yemen, Dem	33,297	68	167	36.9	9,065	0.0	1,570	−10.3	22,495	0.6
EUROPE	**472,735**	**1,046**	**140,495**	**10.5**	**85,558**	**−4.3**	**155,082**	**7.0**	**91,611**	**3.2**
Albania	2,740	1,161	711	36.5	402	−43.8	1,032	−17.6	596	135.6
Austria	8,273	907	1,558	−9.0	2,004	−11.1	3,241	1.8	1,470	31.3
Belgium	3,282	3,024	828	−17.2	672	−16.0	702	2.2	1,080	35.7
Bulgaria	11,055	827	4,142	−9.3	2,035	66.5	3,861	6.9	1,017	−38.5
Czechoslovakia	12,547	1,249	5,169	−1.8	1,665	−6.3	4,582	3.1	1,132	4.9
Denmark	4,237	1,209	2,627	−3.3	236	−27.6	493	9.8	881	18.3
Finland	30,547	161	2,350	−7.0	141	17.5	23,321	6.7	4,735	−21.8
France	54,563	1,007	18,752	−8.7	12,514	−7.0	14,599	18.2	8,698	5.5
German Dem Rep	10,604	1,585	4,998	−0.2	1,252	−12.9	2,962	0.4	1,384	13.2
Germany, Fed Rep	24,428	2,482	7,449	−2.5	4,637	−14.5	7,328	0.7	5,013	22.4
Greece	13,080	761	3,966	3.0	5,255	3.7	2,620	0.6	1,239	−20.3
Hungary	9,234	1,156	5,295	−6.2	1,269	−3.1	1,636	15.0	1,034	20.4
Iceland	10,025	25	8	33.3	2,274	−0.2	120	0.0	7,623	0.0
Ireland	6,889	537	972	−22.4	4,858	10.4	335	67.5	724	−30.2
Italy	29,402	1,951	12,303	−19.6	5,014	−2.1	6,389	4.9	5,695	97.7
Luxembourg	X	X	X	X	X	X	X	X	X	X
Malta	32	12,125	13	−7.1	X	X	X	X	19	5.6
Netherlands	3,394	4,305	868	−10.0	1,142	−11.6	297	2.4	1,087	35.9
Norway	30,786	135	850	0.1	96	−41.1	8,330	16.3	21,511	−4.8
Poland	30,452	1,240	14,807	−6.1	4,075	−3.9	8,712	8.2	2,857	18.6
Portugal	9,164	1,128	3,548	−14.9	530	0.0	3,641	10.3	1,445	24.1
Romania	23,034	1,013	10,551	0.6	4,428	3.0	6,337	−0.7	1,718	−7.9
Spain	49,941	781	20,502	X	10,672	−11.8	15,607	16.2	3,151	−21.4
Sweden	41,162	203	3,004	−5.5	665	−2.8	26,424	0.4	11,069	0.9
Switzerland	3,977	1,605	412	2.2	1,609	−9.4	1,052	7.2	904	8.4
United Kingdom	24,160	2,325	6,993	28.3	11,703	−3.8	2,180	20.7	3,283	19.3
Yugoslavia	25,540	919	7,803	−6.0	6,378	−1.0	9,269	5.7	2,089	3.4
USSR	**2,227,200**	**128**	**232,290**	**1.3**	**373,133**	**0.1**	**928,000**	**8.3**	**693,776**	**−9.7**
OCEANIA	**842,919**	**30**	**48,182**	**23.5**	**455,157**	**−1.2**	**159,427**	**−15.4**	**180,154**	**16.5**
Australia	761,793	21	46,547	24.1	440,497	−1.5	106,000	−23.0	168,750	21.2
Fiji	1,827	391	237	15.0	60	−14.3	1,185	0.4	345	−7.0
New Zealand	26,867	126	469	−3.7	14,113	9.7	10,300	40.4	1,985	−67.9
Papua New Guinea	45,171	82	373	20.3	100	42.9	38,330	−0.9	6,368	4.4
Solomon Islands	2,754	106	53	6.0	39	0.0	2,560	0.0	102	−2.9

Sources: U.N. Food and Agriculture Organization; and U.N. Population Division.
0 = zero or less than five one hundredths of 1 percent; X = not available; NM = not meaningful.
For additional information, see Sources and Technical Notes.

Table 18.2 Selected Internationally Important Wetlands, 1980s

| | Wetland Sites of Measured Area | | Other Wetlands | | | | Additional Sites with Unreported Area |
| | | | Riverine Wetlands | | Coastal Wetlands | | |
	Number of Sites	Total Area (hectares)	Number of Sites	Total River Length (kilometers)	Number of Sites	Total Coastal Length (kilometers)	Number of Sites
NEOTROPICAL REALM							
Anguilla	10	326	—	—	—	—	0
Antigua and Barbuda	6	4,901	—	—	—	—	0
Argentina	57	5,797,930	1	100	1	160	1
Bahamas	21	428,606	—	—	—	—	0
Barbados	3	52	—	—	—	—	0
Belize	15	58,707	4	160	—	—	0
Bermuda	10	78	—	—	—	—	0
Bolivia	18	4,017,920	7	2,320	—	—	6
Brazil	38	59,789,773	1	170	—	—	2
British Virgin Islands	4	614	—	—	—	—	7
Cayman Islands	15	7,310	—	—	—	—	0
Chile	49	9,188,713	—	—	1	50	0
Colombia	36	1,928,389	1	100	—	—	3
Costa Rica	12	82,055	—	—	—	—	0
Cuba	17	1,746,500	—	—	—	—	0
Dominica	3	93	—	—	—	—	1
Dominican Rep	14	40,121	—	—	—	—	1
Ecuador	12	722,830	1	250	—	—	9
El Salvador	8	76,800	—	—	—	—	0
Falkland Islands	9	43,500	—	—	—	—	0
French Antilles	14	11,300	—	—	—	—	0
French Guiana	4	337,700	—	—	—	—	0
Grenada	7	476	—	—	—	—	0
Guatemala	24	220,187	—	—	—	—	0
Guyana	X	X	X	X	X	X	X
Haiti	11	112,900	—	—	—	—	0
Honduras	6	649,000	—	—	—	—	0
Jamaica	14	13,775	—	—	—	—	1
Mexico	40	3,377,900	—	—	—	—	0
Montserrat	2	20	—	—	—	—	0
Netherlands Antilles	11	5,329	—	—	—	—	0
Nicaragua	17	2,111,349	—	—	—	—	0
Panama	21	646,012	—	—	—	—	0
Paraguay	5	5,723,528	2	1,415	—	—	0
Peru	43	1,318,697	2	240	1	16	2
Puerto Rico	14	12,995	—	—	—	—	1
Saint Kitts—Nevis	4	352	—	—	—	—	0
Saint Lucia	3	314	—	—	—	—	0
Saint Vincent	3	1,003	—	—	—	—	0
Suriname	14	1,625,000	—	—	—	—	0
Trinidad and Tobago	9	21,280	—	—	—	—	0
Turks and Caicos Islands	111	64,669	—	—	—	—	0
U. S. Virgin Islands	15	979	—	—	—	—	0
Uruguay	12	773,500	—	—	—	—	0
Venezuela	29	14,447,155	1	250	—	—	0

Table 18.2

| | Wetland Sites of Measured Area | | Other Wetlands | | | | Additional Sites with Unreported Area |
| | | | Riverine Wetlands | | Coastal Wetlands | | |
	Number of Sites	Total Area (hectares)	Number of Sites	Total River Length (kilometers)	Number of Sites	Total Coastal Length (kilometers)	Number of Sites
WESTERN PALEARCTIC REALM							
Afghanistan	2	40,000	—	—	—	—	0
Albania	5	32,990	—	—	—	—	0
Algeria	7	630,637	—	—	—	—	0
Austria	17	29,427	—	—	—	—	2
Belgium	6	9,642	—	—	—	—	3
Bulgaria	5	14,500	—	—	—	—	1
Cyprus	3	10,101	—	—	—	—	0
Czechoslovakia	26	69,466	—	—	—	—	0
Denmark	39	591,730	—	—	—	—	0
Egypt	6	808,500	—	—	—	—	0
Finland	45	301,310	—	—	—	—	0
France	25	1,321,215	1	4.5	1	10	1
German Dem Rep	25	353,127	—	—	—	—	0
Germany, Fed Rep	49	720,525	—	—	—	—	5
Greece	10	86,580	—	—	—	—	3
Hungary	14	98,698	—	—	—	—	2
Iceland	28	442,550	—	—	—	—	0
Iran	33	1,416,810	—	—	1	650	0
Iraq	18	1,992,500	—	—	—	—	1
Ireland	28	115,104	—	—	—	—	0
Israel	6	169,762	—	—	—	—	0
Italy	32	194,551	1	8	—	—	1
Jordan	1	10,000	—	—	—	—	0
Lebanon	2	1,515	—	—	—	—	0
Libya	X	X	—	—	—	—	5
Liechtenstein	X	X	1	30	—	—	1
Luxembourg	X	X	1	30	—	—	1
Malta	1	112	—	—	—	—	2
Morocco	10	22,985	1	15	—	—	2
Netherlands	22	394,019	—	—	1	55	4
Norway	39	151,298	—	—	1	1.5	23
Pakistan	16	37,158	—	—	—	—	11
Poland	15	193,507	—	—	—	—	0
Portugal	8	84,743	—	—	—	—	1
Romania	11	482,527	—	—	—	—	1
Spain	10	445,000	—	—	—	—	3
Sweden	84	1,727,623	1	500	—	—	3
Switzerland	24	175,402	—	—	—	—	0
Syrian Arab Rep	1	37,500	1	500	—	—	0
Tunisia	15	868,303	—	—	—	—	0
Turkey	30	1,238,150	—	—	—	—	4
USSR	12	2,837,200	—	—	—	—	0
United Kingdom	87	449,184	—	—	—	—	0
Yugoslavia	15	110,088	1	14	—	—	0

Sources: International Union for Conservation of Nature and Natural Resources; and International Waterfowl Research Bureau.
0 = zero; X = not available; — = not reported.
For additional information, see Sources and Technical Notes.

Table 18.3 Land Use, 1850–1980

	Area (million hectares)														Percentage Change 1850 to 1980
	1850	1860	1870	1880	1890	1900	1910	1920	1930	1940	1950	1960	1970	1980	
TEN REGIONS															
Forests and Woodlands	5,919	5,898	5,869	5,833	5,793	5,749	5,696	5,634	5,553	5,455	5,345	5,219	5,103	5,007	-15
Grassland and Pasture	6,350	6,340	6,329	6,315	6,301	6,284	6,269	6,260	6,255	6,266	6,293	6,310	6,308	6,299	-1
Croplands	538	569	608	659	712	773	842	913	999	1,085	1,169	1,278	1,396	1,501	179
Tropical Africa															
Forests and Woodlands	1,336	1,333	1,329	1,323	1,315	1,306	1,293	1,275	1,251	1,222	1,188	1,146	1,106	1,074	-20
Grassland and Pasture	1,061	1,062	1,064	1,067	1,070	1,075	1,081	1,091	1,101	1,114	1,130	1,147	1,157	1,158	9
Croplands	57	58	61	64	68	73	80	88	101	118	136	161	190	222	288
North Africa and Middle East															
Forests and Woodlands	34	34	33	32	31	30	28	27	24	21	18	17	15	14	-60
Grassland and Pasture	1,119	1,119	1,118	1,117	1,116	1,115	1,113	1,112	1,108	1,103	1,097	1,085	1,073	1,060	-5
Croplands	27	28	30	32	35	37	40	43	49	57	66	79	93	107	294
North America															
Forests and Woodlands	971	968	965	962	959	954	949	944	941	940	939	939	941	942	-3
Grassland and Pasture	571	559	547	535	522	504	486	468	454	450	446	446	447	447	-22
Croplands	50	65	80	95	110	133	156	179	196	201	206	205	204	203	309
Latin America															
Forests and Woodlands	1,420	1,417	1,414	1,408	1,401	1,394	1,383	1,369	1,348	1,316	1,273	1,225	1,186	1,151	-19
Grassland and Pasture	621	623	625	627	630	634	638	646	655	673	700	730	751	767	23
Croplands	18	19	21	24	28	33	39	45	57	72	87	104	123	142	677
China															
Forests and Woodlands	96	93	91	89	86	84	82	79	76	73	69	64	59	58	-39
Grassland and Pasture	799	799	798	798	797	797	797	796	796	794	793	789	784	778	-3
Croplands	75	78	81	84	86	89	91	95	98	103	108	117	127	134	79
South Asia															
Forests and Woodlands	317	315	311	307	303	299	294	289	279	265	251	235	210	180	-43
Grassland and Pasture	189	189	189	189	189	189	190	190	190	190	190	190	189	187	-1
Croplands	71	73	77	81	85	89	93	98	108	122	136	153	178	210	196
Southeast Asia															
Forests and Woodlands	252	252	251	251	250	249	248	247	246	244	242	240	238	235	-7
Grassland and Pasture	123	123	122	121	119	118	116	114	111	108	105	102	97	92	-25
Croplands	7	7	8	10	12	15	18	21	25	30	35	40	47	55	670
Europe															
Forests and Woodlands	160	158	157	157	156	156	155	155	155	154	154	156	161	167	4
Grassland and Pasture	150	147	145	144	143	142	141	139	138	137	136	136	137	138	-8
Croplands	132	136	140	142	143	145	146	147	149	150	152	151	145	137	4
USSR															
Forests and Woodlands	1,067	1,060	1,052	1,040	1,027	1,014	1,001	987	973	961	952	945	940	941	-12
Grassland and Pasture	1,078	1,081	1,083	1,081	1,079	1,078	1,076	1,074	1,072	1,070	1,070	1,069	1,065	1,065	-1
Croplands	94	98	103	118	132	147	162	178	194	208	216	225	233	233	147
Pacific Developed Countries															
Forests and Woodlands	267	267	266	265	264	263	262	261	260	259	258	252	247	246	-8
Grassland and Pasture	638	638	638	637	635	634	632	630	629	627	625	617	609	608	-5
Croplands	6	6	7	9	12	14	17	19	22	24	28	42	56	58	841

Source: *Ecological Monographs.*
For additional information, see Sources and Technical Notes.

Sources and Technical Notes

Table 18.1 Land Area and Use, 1964–87

Sources: Land area and use: United Nations Food and Agriculture Organization (FAO), *FAO Production Yearbook* 1985 (FAO, Rome, 1986); and unpublished FAO data (FAO, Rome, September 1986). Population data: U.N. Population Division, *World Population Prospects: Estimates and Projections as Assessed in 1984* (United Nations, New York, 1986).

Data for land area and land use are provided to FAO by national governments in response to annual FAO questionnaires. FAO also compiles data from national agricultural censuses; for further details of these censuses, refer to the Technical Note for Table 19.2 in Chapter 19, "Food and Agriculture." When official information is lacking, FAO prepares its own estimates or relies on unofficial data.

Land area data are for 1984; they exclude major inland water bodies, national claims to the continental shelf, and Exclusive Economic Zones. (See Chapter 24, "Oceans and Coasts," Table 24.1.) Antarctica is excluded from the world total. The population density and land distribution figures for the world refer to the six inhabited continents.

Cropland includes land under temporary and permanent crops, temporary meadows, land used for market and kitchen gardens, and temporarily fallow land. Permanent cropland is land under crops that do not need to be replanted after each harvest: cocoa, coffee, rubber, fruit trees, vines, etc. (It excludes land used to grow trees for wood or timber.)

Permanent pasture is land used five or more years for forage, including natural crops and cultivated crops. Grassland not used for forage is included under "other land."

Forests and woodland includes land under natural or planted stands of trees as well as logged over areas that will be reforested in the near future.

Other land includes uncultivated land, grassland not used for pasture, built-on areas, wasteland, roads, etc.

Several countries use definitions of total area and land use that differ from those used above. Refer to the sources for details.

Table 18.2 Selected Internationally Important Wetlands, 1980s

Sources: Derek A. Scott and Montserrat Carbonell, *A Directory of Neotropical Wetlands* (International Union for Conservation of Nature and Natural Resources [IUCN], Cambridge, United Kingdom, and International Waterfowl Research Bureau [IWRB], Slimbridge, United Kingdom, 1986); and Eric Carp, *Directory of Wetlands of International Importance in the Western Palearctic* (IUCN, Gland, Switzerland, and United Nations Environment Programme, Nairobi, Kenya, 1980).

The term "wetland" subsumes a variety of more specifically defined ecosystems. The sources use the definition of wetland contained in the Convention on Wetlands of International Importance Especially as Waterfowl Habitat (Ramsar, Iran, 1971): "areas of marsh, fen, peatland or water, whether natural or artificial, permanent or temporary, with water that is static or flowing, fresh, brackish or salt, including areas of marine water the depth of which at low tide does not exceed six meters." Coral reefs are generally excluded. (For details concerning the Ramsar Convention, refer to Chapter 21, "Wildlife and Habitat," Table 21.1; Chapter 26, "Policies and Institutions," Table 26.1, and the Technical Notes to these tables.)

Both *Directories* categorize wetlands using the following framework:

■ *Coastal Ecosystems*: shallow sea bays and straits; estuaries and deltas; small offshore islands and islets; rocky sea coasts, sea cliffs, and sea beaches; intertidal mud- and sand-flats; coastal brackish and saline lagoons and marshes; and mangrove swamps and forests.

■ *River Valleys*: slow-flowing rivers and streams, fast-flowing rivers and streams, riverine lakes (including oxbows) and marshes, freshwater lakes and associated marshes, freshwater ponds and associated marshes and swamps, flood plains, and interior or dry deltas.

■ *Other Areas*: salt lakes, reservoirs, and dams; seasonally flooded grassland and savanna; rice paddies, flooded arable land, and irrigated land; swamp forest and temporarily flooded forest; fens and mires; artificial ponds; and peat bogs, wet montane meadows, and snow-melt bogs.

The criteria used to select sites for inclusion in the two *Directories* differ. For the Neotropical *Directory*, sites met the criteria (developed by an expert group convened by IUCN and IWRB) used to evaluate nationally nominated sites for inclusion in the global system of Wetlands of International Importance. To be considered a Wetland of International Importance, a site must:

1. support a significant population of waterfowl, threatened species, or peculiar fauna or flora; or
2. be a regionally representative example of a type of wetland or an exemplar of a biological or hydrogeomorphic process; or
3. afford outstanding opportunities for research, education, or recreation; and,
4. be physically and administratively capable of benefiting from protection and management measures.

In practice, the use of these criteria in selecting sites to be included in the Neotropical *Directory* was often impossible because information was lacking. As a result, many wetlands were included in the *Directory* based on the informed judgment of experts; the *Directory* notes these sites as deserving further study.

Most of the data for the Neotropical *Directory* were gathered from national sources. A national coordinator assembled data from specialists and organizations within each country and attempted to make the country report as comprehensive as possible. It was impossible to establish a national coordinator for several countries, and the *Directory* compilers used information submitted directly from national sources. In a few small Caribbean countries, no local contacts could be established, and the compilers relied on expatriate experts and on recent literature.

Reports were collected for all 45 countries in the Neotropical Realm. Comprehensiveness varies among the countries; in general, the smaller countries were able to provide the most complete inventories of wetlands. Data for the large countries of South America are

considered preliminary; most of the largest sites are known but unexplored; many smaller sites have yet to be identified and studied.

Mexico extends beyond the Neotropical Realm. Only the sites located within the Neotropical Realm are included in the table.

The Western Palearctic *Directory* lists sites included in, or eligible for, three wetlands networks. Project MAR, an initiative of IUCN in 1961, was an early attempt to catalog Palearctic Wetlands of International Importance. Approximately 200 sites were identified on the MAR list. A second program, Project AQUA, was undertaken to catalog lakes and rivers of significant limnological interest. The third list is based on the criteria adopted for the Ramsar Convention (see above). The Western Palearctic *Directory* attempts to include all wetland sites from these three networks that meet the criteria for Wetlands of International Importance.

The Western Palearctic *Directory* covers all of Europe, Central and South Asia (bounded by the Yenisey River in the east and the USSR-China and Pakistan-India borders in the south), Turkey, Syria, Lebanon, Israel, Jordan, Iraq, and the five African countries bordering the Mediterranean. Questionnaires were circulated by IUCN and IWRB to national contacts. Responses to these questionnaires were supplemented by published information when it was available.

Several simplifications have been made in the preparation of this table. If a site's area was recorded in a *Directory* as over or under a given size, the limiting number was used. For example, when a site's area was reported as "over 500 hectares," the site was assigned an area of 500 hectares. If a site was reported to be "several hundred" or "several thousand" hectares, the site was assigned an area of 300 or 3,000 hectares. If the area was reported as a range (e.g., 200–500 hectares), the average of the extremes was used. Many wetland sites extend over international borders; only the area of the site within a country was counted. Some sites have been divided into two or more separate units; because the *Directories* do not always list all the subunits of a site, only the main site was counted in the number and area of sites.

The *Directories* contain additional information about each wetland site: location, altitude, and water depth; descriptions of their ecology, fauna, and flora; analysis of threats to the site; status of management, protection, and ownership; current scientific research on the site; and a bibliography of reference material.

Two other *Directories* are in preparation: Africa (to be published in 1987) and Asia.

Table 18.3 Land Use, 1850–1980

Source: R.A. Houghton *et al.*, "Changes in the Carbon Content of Terrestrial Biota and Soils between 1860 and 1980: A Net Release of CO_2 to the Atmosphere," *Ecological Monographs*, Vol. 53, No. 3 (1983), pp. 235–262; and unpublished data supporting this study (R.A. Houghton and D. Skole, October 1986).

The data in Table 18.3 are largely modeled, using four sets of information: maps of natural vegetation, population size and growth data between 1700 and 1980, literature on historical land use and cover, and recent (post-1950)

land use data collected by the United Nations Food and Agriculture Organization (FAO).

Eleven categories of natural land cover were assumed to exist: seven types of forest and woodland (tropical moist forest, boreal forest, temperate woodland and shrubland, etc.) and four types of grassland (temperate grassland, tropical grassland, tundra, and desert scrub). The forest data in the table refer to the aggregate area of the seven forest types. The grassland and pasture area refers to the four natural nonforest types plus pasture. Area covered by snow, ice, rock, or desert is not included.

Three main types of land use change were assumed to have occurred from 1850 to 1980:

■ *Agricultural Expansion*. For 1850–1950, historical land use literature provided data for seven of the ten regions (Latin America, North Africa–Middle East, and Tropical Africa are the exceptions). The literature did not provide area measurements for all natural ecosystems and cropland for all years for all regions. In many cases, the authors interpolated many of the data points based on only a few literature values. Rates of change were assumed to be linear.

For the other three regions, literature estimates of historical land cover for 1850–1950 were insufficient, necessitating the use of a population-based model. The extent of cultivated land was assumed to be proportional to population, and, unless other information was available, growth in cropland area was assumed to be drawn from all kinds of natural ecosystems. Cropland expansion was drawn from natural ecosystems in direct proportion to their areas. The pre-agricultural areas of the natural ecosystems were estimated from maps of the likely extent of natural vegetation.

For 1950–80, land cover data for five regions (North America, Europe, USSR, China, and Pacific Developed Countries) were taken from the FAO *Production Yearbooks*. (For a discussion of FAO's land use statistics, refer to the Technical Note for Table 18.1.) A population-based model was used to estimate cropland growth for the other five regions; this model differs slightly from the model discussed above. It was assumed that after 1950, 40 percent of the increased crop output required by expanding populations was achieved by increasing agricultural output on existing cropland (through irrigation, use of fertilizers, etc.). The remainder of the increased crop requirement was assumed to have been satisfied through cropland expansion.

■ *Change in Pasture Area*. It was assumed that almost all expansion or contraction of pasture was drawn from, or added to, the area of natural grassland ecosystems. Because pasture is part of the grassland and pasture aggregate, these changes are not shown in Table 18.3. The exception is Latin America, where pasture has expanded at the expense of forest ecosystems since 1950.

■ *Afforestation*. Afforestation has been proceeding since 1850 in Europe, 1925 in the USSR, and 1970 in China. Data on the area afforested were taken from FAO sources. Afforestation was assumed to have taken place only on natural nonforest land, not on abandoned cropland.

Land Use and Cover

The regions are composed of countries and are not biogeographical groupings.

■ *North America*: Canada and the United States.

■ *Europe*: All countries of Europe, excluding the European portion of the USSR.

■ *USSR*: The European and Asian regions of the USSR.

■ *Latin America*: All countries of Central and South America and the Caribbean.

■ *South Asia*: Afghanistan, Bangladesh, Bhutan, Burma, India, Nepal, Pakistan, and Sri Lanka.

■ *Southeast Asia*: Brunei, Democratic Kampuchea, East Timor, Indonesia, Lao People's Democratic Republic, Malaysia, Philippines, Thailand, and Vietnam.

■ *Tropical Africa*: All countries of Africa except Algeria, Egypt, Libya, Morocco, and Tunisia.

■ *China*: China and Mongolia.

■ *Pacific Developed Countries*: Australia, Japan, New Zealand, Democratic People's Republic of Korea, Republic of Korea, Papua New Guinea, Taiwan, and the Pacific Islands.

■ *North Africa and Middle East*: Algeria, Egypt, Libya, Morocco, Tunisia, Israel, Jordan, Syria, Lebanon, the countries of the Arabian Peninsula, Turkey, Iraq, and Iran.

The model discussed above was designed for analyzing the history of carbon dioxide emissions from biotic sources. (See Chapter 25, "Atmosphere and Climate," Table 25.2.) The model makes use of several simplifications and assumptions in estimating land use trends, reducing the usefulness of the land use data and the carbon emission data. For example, for several regions, per-capita crop requirements were assumed to be constant over several decades. But crop requirements (and thus cropland requirements) probably vary through time; rising incomes could increase demand for food and nonfood crops, and the substitution of imported or synthetic products would reduce the demand for locally grown crops. There is also evidence that cropland expanded substantially in several regions to satisfy growing world demand for food and nonfood agricultural commodities. The model also makes no allowance for human impacts on land cover other than clearing of natural ecosystems for agriculture and pasture. The expansion of cities, roads, and industry has been extensive in the past 130 years, and desertification has removed crop and pasture land from productive use. (See Chapter 20, "Forests and Rangelands," Table 20.4.)

19. Food and Agriculture

The data in this chapter focus on issues of particular importance to developing countries—the productivity and sustainability of agriculture.

Globally, agricultural output has increased about 55 percent since 1964–66, but per capita output has increased only 7 percent. (See Table 19.1.) Cereal yields have increased in all regions over the past 20 years, but developing country yields remain lower than developed country yields. Africa's yields, which are one quarter those of Europe, have declined 5 percent in the past decade. The largest grain importer, the USSR, has achieved only modest yield increases since the mid-1960s. Roots and tubers (potatoes, cassava, yams, etc.) are an important food source in many tropical and subtropical countries where cereals are difficult to grow. Fourteen African countries (whose total population is 225 million) rely on these crops as their primary staple, but in the past decade, yields in 12 of the 14 countries have declined or failed to match population growth rates.

The World Censuses of Agriculture, coordinated by the United Nations Food and Agriculture Organization (FAO), are an important source of agricultural and land use data, including data on land distribution. Some regional characteristics are apparent in land distribution data. (See Table 19.2.) For example, in most African and Asian countries, almost all the agricultural area is farmed in small (less than 5 hectares) or medium-size (5–50 hectares) holdings. In Latin America, most holdings are small, but the majority of the agricultural area (57–96 percent in 1970) is farmed in holdings of more than 50 hectares. In Canada, Australia, and the United States, almost all of the agricultural area is in holdings larger than 50 hectares.

Many small holdings occupy marginal lands, and, in some countries, the size of these holdings is shrinking because of land scarcity and population pressures. In other countries, such as Brazil, the average size of small holdings has increased because new agricultural land has been created, most often by clearing forests.

When arable land becomes scarce, increasing agricultural production requires improving yields on existing croplands. Irrigation, along with improved crop varieties, mechanization, fertilizers, pesticides, and other inputs, is largely responsible for increased crop yields in many countries. (See Table 19.3.) Over 40 percent of the world's crops are produced on irrigated lands, which represent 15 percent of the world's croplands. However, relating changes in crop production to the use of agricultural inputs requires trend data on *all* inputs. Detailed data for one of the most important inputs—pesticides—are unavailable for most countries. (For data on fertilizer use and tractors, refer to *World Resources 1986*, Table 5.2, pp. 264–265.)

Irrigation data are provided to FAO by national governments. These data may differ from those reported in national or other sources because of varying definitions of irrigation and irrigated area. The definitions are often not supplied, so that differences in irrigation estimates are difficult to evaluate.

Although irrigation increases crop yields, poorly managed irrigation systems may reduce yields over the long term by salinizing and waterlogging the soil. Waterlogging, which prevents the aeration of soil and reduces fertility, occurs when irrigated soils are inadequately drained. Waterlogged soils become salinized when the water evaporates and minerals from the subsoil or irrigation water accumulate in the topsoil.

Salinization has been documented in many countries, but only rough estimates of the total area affected are available. In South America, for example, one half to one third of irrigated lands are thought to be affected by salinization, but data on the extent and severity of the problem do not exist for most countries.

In addition to salinization, soil fertility is also threatened by wind and water erosion. (See Table 19.4.) Although soil erosion is a natural process, erosion has been greatly accelerated in many parts of the world by poor agricultural practices and degradation of vegetation caused by overgrazing and deforestation. For various soil types in the United States, the U.S. Department of Agriculture estimates that erosion rates exceeding 2–12 metric tons per hectare per year cannot be sustained without damaging the productivity of the soil. Estimates of tolerable rates of soil loss for other regions differ according to soil type and other factors.

Erosion data are not strictly comparable across countries because different methods of estimation are used. Estimates vary depending on the causes of erosion and on measurement techniques. Most field measurements of erosion rates are carried out in areas where sheet and rill erosion is most serious.

Table 19.1 Food and Agricultural Production, 1964–85

	Index of Agricultural Production (1979-81 = 100)				Index of Food Production (1979-81 = 100)				Crop Yields					
									Cereals			Roots and Tubers		
	Total		Per Capita		Total		Per Capita		Kilograms per Hectare	Percentage Change Over		Kilograms per Hectare	Percentage Change Over	
	1964-66	1983-85	1964-66	1983-85	1964-66	1983-85	1964-66	1983-85	1983-85	1964-66	1974-76	1983-85	1964-66	1974-76
WORLD	**71**	**110**	**95**	**102**	**70**	**110**	**94**	**102**	**2,441**	**58**	**25**	**12,476**	**21**	**9**
AFRICA	**72**	**109**	**109**	**96**	**71**	**109**	**108**	**96**	**951**	**13**	**−5**	**7,478**	**22**	**13**
Algeria	67	113	104	99	67	112	105	98	732	39	7	7,373	1	0
Angola	118	101	176	92	85	102	127	92	480	−45	−37	14,045	21	7
Benin	66	123	94	109	66	120	94	107	744	38	3	7,586	23	−1
Botswana	82	98	135	86	81	98	134	86	230	−38	−62	5,641	41	22
Burkina Faso	83	111	110	101	85	111	113	101	622	20	17	4,440	32	−5
Burundi	75	108	94	98	79	108	100	97	1,166	19	3	7,406	−5	6
Cameroon	63	106	88	96	63	107	89	97	1,006	27	5	2,428	9	2
Cape Verde	121	95	162	90	122	96	163	90	477	−23	6	3,035	−26	−28
Central African Rep	72	106	95	97	71	105	94	96	559	−25	8	3,223	−9	0
Chad	94	105	126	96	92	103	124	94	565	−8	−1	4,981	9	23
Comoros	70	110	114	97	70	109	114	97	1,122	−14	1	3,306	−3	−4
Congo	77	104	110	94	78	104	110	94	578	−47	−13	6,396	29	13
Cote d'Ivoire	47	107	85	93	40	114	73	99	894	12	10	6,006	63	32
Djibouti	X	X	X	X	X	X	X	X	X	X	X	X	X	X
Egypt	73	113	102	102	70	116	98	105	4,238	19	8	18,993	9	7
Equatorial Guinea	X	X	X	X	X	X	X	X	X	X	X	2,408	−32	−12
Ethiopia	78	100	111	90	78	98	111	88	1,128	45	17	2,988	−2	−8
Gabon	93	106	110	100	93	106	110	100	1,489	−5	2	6,453	1	10
Gambia	107	119	150	110	109	119	152	110	1,093	4	17	3,000	−32	−8
Ghana	81	114	119	100	82	114	120	100	735	−19	−16	7,631	−8	24
Guinea	78	108	105	98	78	108	106	98	721	−11	−13	6,146	−18	−14
Guinea-Bissau	91	131	140	121	91	131	140	121	753	6	3	6,154	8	26
Kenya	60	112	108	95	67	109	119	92	1,462	19	−6	7,787	6	0
Lesotho	91	96	127	86	86	94	120	85	685	−12	−11	15,103	3	17
Liberia	61	110	96	97	60	113	95	99	1,235	96	1	4,005	−4	3
Libya	43	136	78	117	43	137	78	117	648	118	44	6,990	53	38
Madagascar	73	111	106	99	72	112	105	100	1,741	2	−4	5,887	−7	−4
Malawi	55	110	83	97	58	108	87	95	1,203	28	11	4,568	−6	1
Mali	70	108	97	97	73	107	100	96	751	−4	−4	9,568	16	6
Mauritania	97	96	143	85	97	96	143	85	416	15	0	1,899	−24	70
Mauritius	86	106	106	98	90	104	111	96	4,011	99	55	23,363	87	49
Morocco	73	110	110	96	73	110	110	96	910	26	−13	13,418	28	17
Mozambique	83	97	138	85	80	97	132	86	648	−30	−10	5,887	22	20
Niger	74	97	105	87	74	97	105	87	367	−30	−7	6,937	−14	5
Nigeria	76	108	126	95	76	109	125	95	719	7	9	10,573	34	5
Rwanda	47	108	76	94	48	107	78	93	1,271	1	23	8,376	53	1
Senegal	94	104	155	93	95	103	156	92	691	21	−4	4,095	−1	34
Sierra Leone	78	106	97	98	79	107	99	100	1,383	5	−3	3,381	−7	−21
Somalia	78	103	144	87	78	103	144	87	596	21	−6	10,815	8	0
South Africa	61	91	85	82	58	90	82	82	1,174	24	−16	11,870	43	−1
Sudan	62	109	93	97	59	105	89	94	469	−33	−28	3,484	1	−3
Swaziland	44	117	65	104	46	117	68	104	1,682	258	13	2,501	−36	−34
Tanzania, United Rep	59	106	96	92	54	108	87	94	1,062	35	8	11,016	108	57
Togo	77	102	119	91	77	101	118	90	1,072	127	14	14,686	23	13
Tunisia	69	113	96	102	70	113	96	102	820	18	−1	12,429	51	31
Uganda	73	127	119	110	67	125	110	109	1,196	33	−2	6,852	75	56
Zaire	76	114	110	101	75	113	110	101	870	27	17	6,990	4	1
Zambia	64	105	100	92	63	104	98	91	1,551	83	27	3,672	13	9
Zimbabwe	63	107	105	93	58	101	96	88	1,088	21	−23	4,749	18	19
NORTH & CENTRAL AMERICA	**73**	**102**	**92**	**96**	**71**	**103**	**90**	**97**	**3,532**	**44**	**22**	**19,196**	**23**	**6**
Barbados	98	89	106	86	98	89	106	86	2,500	30	−4	9,696	10	−9
Canada	82	109	100	104	82	109	100	104	2,153	23	6	23,595	27	10
Costa Rica	52	105	80	95	50	100	77	90	2,445	78	41	7,426	1	−11
Cuba	58	110	72	108	56	110	70	108	2,737	131	35	6,189	14	14
Dominican Rep	65	114	97	104	63	115	94	105	3,434	65	27	6,613	5	9
El Salvador	65	93	104	83	55	101	88	90	1,855	57	20	14,018	81	20
Guatemala	56	99	88	88	53	107	84	95	1,674	81	15	4,638	21	20
Haiti	80	104	112	94	77	103	108	93	1,035	−3	−12	4,049	−4	−6
Honduras	57	107	91	93	59	106	94	93	1,426	22	31	7,022	31	102
Jamaica	75	109	92	103	74	109	91	103	1,874	60	6	10,419	−3	2
Mexico	60	109	96	98	56	110	90	99	2,163	65	27	12,520	46	4
Nicaragua	70	93	111	82	63	93	99	81	1,962	91	88	4,041	−2	−1
Panama	63	105	93	96	63	103	93	94	1,482	54	24	8,070	−2	−2
Trinidad and Tobago	90	93	99	90	89	94	97	91	3,102	28	8	12,097	36	2
United States	74	100	86	96	72	101	84	97	4,279	48	28	30,334	41	11
SOUTH AMERICA	**66**	**107**	**94**	**98**	**64**	**107**	**91**	**98**	**2,015**	**42**	**23**	**11,043**	**−1**	**1**
Argentina	71	104	90	98	70	104	89	98	2,409	54	22	15,859	57	19
Bolivia	59	97	86	87	60	98	87	88	1,218	29	6	4,547	−17	−35
Brazil	61	111	88	102	56	111	81	101	1,708	28	20	11,489	−12	−4
Chile	77	106	100	99	76	106	100	99	2,666	52	59	12,357	34	26
Colombia	57	102	82	94	56	103	79	95	2,639	98	12	11,422	50	24
Ecuador	73	103	113	91	73	103	114	91	1,838	102	36	10,078	22	−6
Guyana	81	94	109	87	81	94	109	87	3,237	59	51	6,755	12	2
Paraguay	54	114	85	101	59	114	92	101	1,536	21	10	14,416	7	2
Peru	89	108	135	98	89	110	134	99	2,418	56	32	7,850	18	12
Suriname	83	105	88	105	81	105	86	105	3,947	29	9	6,156	−14	5
Uruguay	91	107	99	104	87	106	94	103	1,857	91	45	5,729	19	9
Venezuela	56	107	95	94	54	107	92	94	2,078	65	34	8,485	−2	11

Table 19.1

	Index of Agricultural Production (1979-81 = 100)				Index of Food Production (1979-81 = 100)				Crop Yields					
	Total		Per Capita		Total		Per Capita		Cereals			Roots and Tubers		
									Kilograms per Hectare	Percentage Change Over		Kilograms per Hectare	Percentage Change Over	
	1964-66	1983-85	1964-66	1983-85	1964-66	1983-85	1964-66	1983-85	1983-85	1964-66	1974-76	1983-85	1964-66	1974-76
ASIA	**66**	**118**	**92**	**110**	**66**	**117**	**92**	**109**	**2,477**	**77**	**36**	**14,021**	**58**	**16**
Afghanistan	80	104	105	105	79	104	104	105	1,339	26	1	14,403	44	5
Bahrain	X	X	X	X	X	X	X	X	X	X	X	21,905	10	1
Bangladesh	80	109	121	98	79	110	119	98	2,125	29	20	10,672	30	7
Bhutan	70	110	94	102	70	110	94	102	1,408	−1	−1	6,825	5	3
Burma	66	126	95	114	66	127	95	115	2,912	91	68	9,279	173	65
China	59	127	81	121	59	124	80	118	3,825	119	55	15,468	79	20
Cyprus	67	110	72	105	66	111	71	106	1,611	51	15	22,276	44	12
India	67	118	94	109	66	119	93	110	1,566	73	33	14,250	61	20
Indonesia	57	119	81	111	57	120	80	112	3,413	123	46	9,934	42	19
Iran	54	111	87	99	52	111	83	99	1,072	23	1	14,437	−20	−16
Iraq	64	116	106	101	63	115	104	100	795	2	−7	17,462	75	94
Israel	53	112	80	104	57	112	87	104	2,256	34	7	39,255	70	28
Japan	96	105	113	102	94	106	111	103	5,705	29	2	24,007	30	13
Jordan	128	129	191	112	129	129	193	112	814	−20	27	19,054	115	62
Kampuchea, Dem	191	150	201	135	182	149	191	134	1,097	−2	−14	8,006	−21	−5
Korea, Dem People's Rep	49	116	73	106	49	116	72	106	4,288	50	19	12,734	21	4
Korea, Rep	60	113	80	106	60	113	80	107	5,498	82	33	20,642	22	22
Kuwait	X	X	X	X	X	X	X	X	3,279	X	64	15,000	X	17
Lao People's Dem Rep	63	128	93	116	63	128	93	116	1,880	130	43	11,587	55	17
Lebanon	74	104	93	104	73	104	90	105	1,162	23	−5	14,967	27	114
Malaysia	47	114	68	104	43	118	63	107	2,689	29	−1	9,715	3	−7
Mongolia	88	110	136	99	88	112	136	101	1,249	60	38	11,405	44	49
Nepal	82	115	116	105	82	116	116	106	1,695	−7	−3	6,089	6	8
Oman	X	X	X	X	X	X	X	X	1,763	58	39	3,804	X	X
Pakistan	60	115	91	101	59	114	90	101	1,605	84	16	10,376	12	−4
Philippines	53	102	78	92	53	103	79	93	1,782	70	34	6,269	12	18
Qatar	X	X	X	X	X	X	X	X	3,464	X	−3	10,000	X	1
Saudi Arabia	41	226	80	192	41	226	80	192	2,604	94	254	14,049	60	178
Singapore	43	96	55	91	42	96	54	91	X	X	X	11,139	10	−5
Sri Lanka	63	97	84	89	51	96	68	88	2,871	61	57	11,953	94	170
Syrian Arab Rep	47	112	78	97	41	110	69	95	917	15	−3	16,771	67	29
Thailand	56	120	83	110	55	120	82	110	2,085	14	11	16,233	24	14
Turkey	65	108	92	98	64	108	91	98	1,910	62	21	16,692	43	20
United Arab Emirates	X	X	X	X	X	X	X	X	3,306	X	X	10,267	X	−35
Viet Nam	66	120	93	111	66	120	93	110	2,604	37	22	5,453	−6	−16
Yemen	78	103	102	94	78	103	101	94	572	−23	−30	13,910	125	27
Yemen, Dem	74	103	101	93	71	102	98	92	1,662	36	1	11,135	123	−2
EUROPE	**75**	**106**	**82**	**104**	**75**	**106**	**82**	**104**	**4,102**	**76**	**29**	**20,018**	**19**	**9**
Albania	61	109	88	99	59	109	85	100	3,011	168	43	8,971	9	28
Austria	79	108	82	108	79	108	82	108	5,035	91	26	26,678	30	13
Belgium	78	105	82	105	78	105	81	105	5,633	57	34	38,716	26	16
Bulgaria	75	103	81	102	72	104	77	103	4,038	65	17	10,176	−6	−9
Czechoslovakia	69	112	74	111	69	112	74	110	4,624	110	29	18,597	25	16
Denmark	89	109	95	109	89	109	95	109	4,754	23	28	33,296	45	48
Finland	87	110	91	108	87	110	91	108	3,045	70	18	17,911	19	24
France	76	106	85	104	76	106	84	104	5,550	88	47	32,973	78	58
German Dem Rep	75	104	73	104	75	104	73	104	4,353	59	22	20,997	18	36
Germany, Fed Rep	80	106	84	107	80	106	84	107	5,052	66	27	31,336	29	15
Greece	64	103	72	100	63	102	71	99	3,186	87	28	17,618	87	17
Hungary	64	109	68	109	64	109	67	110	5,098	124	34	18,487	104	49
Iceland	80	99	96	95	79	99	95	95	X	X	X	12,633	−6	19
Ireland	69	107	81	102	69	107	81	102	5,378	74	37	22,074	−4	−15
Italy	78	103	84	102	78	103	85	102	3,735	59	16	17,394	62	7
Luxembourg	X	X	X	X	X	X	X	X	X	X	X	X	X	X
Malta	68	106	79	103	68	106	79	103	3,616	137	73	7,065	12	−20
Netherlands	58	111	67	109	58	111	67	109	6,560	70	38	39,096	30	11
Norway	84	107	92	106	84	107	92	105	3,793	55	24	24,388	14	6
Poland	85	103	96	99	85	103	96	99	2,871	60	7	16,785	2	−10
Portugal	92	98	98	95	92	98	97	95	1,255	52	12	8,805	−6	0
Romania	55	111	64	109	55	111	64	109	3,593	94	37	20,272	135	60
Spain	63	108	74	104	63	108	73	104	2,472	97	35	16,715	45	19
Sweden	89	107	96	106	89	107	96	106	4,008	35	9	28,233	20	20
Switzerland	77	106	83	104	77	106	83	104	5,644	67	25	35,618	39	0
United Kingdom	79	109	81	108	79	109	81	108	5,856	59	49	34,303	43	34
Yugoslavia	70	105	80	102	69	105	79	102	3,968	73	21	9,064	10	2
USSR	**75**	**108**	**86**	**104**	**75**	**108**	**86**	**105**	**1,563**	**35**	**7**	**11,985**	**13**	**8**
OCEANIA	**74**	**109**	**98**	**103**	**70**	**109**	**92**	**103**	**1,611**	**25**	**13**	**10,772**	**13**	**8**
Australia	75	110	97	104	70	109	90	104	1,568	25	13	25,143	68	27
Fiji	69	92	94	86	70	92	95	86	2,168	25	−1	9,269	4	−2
New Zealand	76	110	91	107	73	111	87	108	4,915	46	41	27,459	33	8
Papua New Guinea	64	109	96	98	71	110	106	99	1,598	−28	−15	6,977	3	1
Solomon Islands	55	122	89	105	55	123	89	105	3,157	51	58	15,591	22	19

Source: U.N. Food and Agriculture Organization.
0 = zero or less than half of 1 percent; X = not available.
For additional information, see Sources and Technical Notes.

Table 19.2 Agricultural Land Distribution, 1960–80

	Distribution of Agricultural Holdings by Size of Holdings (percent)									Distribution of Agricultural Area by Size of Holdings (percent)								
	1960			1970			1980			1960			1970			1980		
	Less than 5 ha	5-50 ha	More than 50 ha	Less than 5 ha	5-50 ha	More than 50 ha	Less than 5 ha	5-50 ha	More than 50 ha	Less than 5 ha	5-50 ha	More than 50 ha	Less than 5 ha	5-50 ha	More than 50 ha	Less than 5 ha	5-50 ha	More than 50 ha
WORLD																		
AFRICA																		
Algeria	X	X	X	69	30	1	X	X	X	X	X	X	14	63	23	X	X	X
Angola	X	X	X	X	X	X	X	X	X	X	X	X	X	X	X	X	X	X
Benin	X	X	X	X	X	X	X	X	X	X	X	X	X	X	X	X	X	X
Botswana	X	X	X	74	26	0	X	X	X	X	X	X	26	74	0	X	X	X
Burkina Faso	X	X	X	X	X	X	X	X	X	X	X	X	X	X	X	X	X	X
Burundi	X	X	X	X	X	X	X	X	X	X	X	X	X	X	X	X	X	X
Cameroon	X	X	X	97	4	0	X	X	X	X	X	X	84	16	0	X	X	X
Cape Verde	X	X	X	X	X	X	X	X	X	X	X	X	X	X	X	X	X	X
Central African Rep	X	X	X	98	3	0	X	X	X	X	X	X	90	10	0	X	X	X
Chad	X	X	X	89	11	0	X	X	X	X	X	X	72	28	0	X	X	X
Comoros	X	X	X	X	X	X	X	X	X	X	X	X	X	X	X	X	X	X
Congo	X	X	X	99	1	0	X	X	X	X	X	X	98	2	0	X	X	X
Cote d'Ivoire	X	X	X	64	36	0	X	X	X	X	X	X	32	68	1	X	X	X
Djibouti	X	X	X	X	X	X	X	X	X	X	X	X	X	X	X	X	X	X
Egypt	90	10	0	X	X	X	X	X	X	51	34	16	X	X	X	X	X	X
Equatorial Guinea	X	X	X	X	X	X	X	X	X	X	X	X	X	X	X	X	X	X
Ethiopia	X	X	X	X	X	X	96	4	0	X	X	X	X	X	X	82	18	0
Gabon	X	X	X	100	0	0	X	X	X	X	X	X	100	0	0	X	X	X
Gambia	X	X	X	X	X	X	X	X	X	X	X	X	X	X	X	X	X	X
Ghana	X	X	X	86	14	0	X	X	X	X	X	X	47	54	0	X	X	X
Guinea	X	X	X	X	X	X	X	X	X	X	X	X	X	X	X	X	X	X
Guinea-Bissau	85	16	0	X	X	X	X	X	X	61	39	0	X	X	X	X	X	X
Kenya	74	25	1	90	10	0	X	X	X	14	21	65	38	18	43	X	X	X
Lesotho	94	6	0	96	4	0	X	X	X	77	23	0	84	16	0	X	X	X
Liberia	X	X	X	93	7	0	X	X	X	X	X	X	36	35	29	X	X	X
Libya	24	62	14	X	X	X	X	X	X	2	35	63	X	X	X	X	X	X
Madagascar	97	3	0	X	X	X	X	X	X	89	11	0	X	X	X	X	X	X
Malawi	X	X	X	100	0	0	X	X	X	X	X	X	100	0	0	X	X	X
Mali	68	32	0	X	X	X	X	X	X	37	63	0	X	X	X	X	X	X
Mauritania	X	X	X	X	X	X	X	X	X	X	X	X	X	X	X	X	X	X
Mauritius	X	X	X	X	X	X	X	X	X	X	X	X	X	X	X	X	X	X
Morocco	75	25	0	X	X	X	X	X	X	38	62	0	X	X	X	X	X	X
Mozambique	X	X	X	X	X	X	X	X	X	X	X	X	X	X	X	X	X	X
Niger	X	X	X	X	X	X	58	42	0	X	X	X	X	X	X	33	67	0
Nigeria	X	X	X	X	X	X	X	X	X	X	X	X	X	X	X	X	X	X
Rwanda	X	X	X	X	X	X	X	X	X	X	X	X	X	X	X	X	X	X
Senegal	72	28	0	X	X	X	X	X	X	41	59	0	X	X	X	X	X	X
Sierra Leone	X	X	X	94	6	0	X	X	X	X	X	X	80	20	0	X	X	X
Somalia	X	X	X	X	X	X	X	X	X	X	X	X	X	X	X	X	X	X
South Africa	5	19	76	X	X	X	X	X	X	0	0	100	X	X	X	X	X	X
Sudan	X	X	X	X	X	X	X	X	X	X	X	X	X	X	X	X	X	X
Swaziland	X	X	X	87	13	0	X	X	X	X	X	X	8	6	85	X	X	X
Tanzania, United Rep	X	X	X	95	5	0	X	X	X	X	X	X	79	21	0	X	X	X
Togo	87	13	0	97	3	0	100	0	0	57	43	0	74	27	0	100	0	0
Tunisia	41	55	4	X	X	X	X	X	X	6	54	40	X	X	X	X	X	X
Uganda	75	25	0	X	X	X	X	X	X	43	57	0	X	X	X	X	X	X
Zaire	X	X	X	99	1	0	X	X	X	X	X	X	60	5	35	X	X	X
Zambia	0	14	86	94	6	0	X	X	X	0	0	100	34	19	47	X	X	X
Zimbabwe	0	9	91	X	X	X	X	X	X	0	0	100	X	X	X	X	X	X
NORTH & CENTRAL AMERICA																		
Barbados	81	7	13	X	X	X	X	X	X	6	5	89	X	X	X	X	X	X
Canada	4	30	66	5	24	72	5	13	82	0	7	93	0	3	97	0	1	99
Costa Rica	39	48	15	49	37	15	X	X	X	2	22	76	2	18	80	X	X	X
Cuba	X	X	X	X	X	X	X	X	X	X	X	X	X	X	X	X	X	X
Dominican Rep	86	13	1	77	21	2	X	X	X	21	31	48	13	30	57	X	X	X
El Salvador	85	13	2	89	10	1	X	X	X	15	28	57	20	31	49	X	X	X
Guatemala	74	24	3	X	X	X	78	19	3	13	24	63	X	X	X	11	25	64
Haiti	X	X	X	96	4	0	X	X	X	X	X	X	78	23	0	X	X	X
Honduras	X	X	X	64	32	4	X	X	X	X	X	X	9	35	56	X	X	X
Jamaica	90	10	1	94	6	0	93	6	1	23	23	54	29	19	52	26	17	57
Mexico	66	22	12	60	26	14	X	X	X	1	3	96	1	4	96	X	X	X
Nicaragua	40	43	16	X	X	X	X	X	X	2	18	79	X	X	X	X	X	X
Panama	46	47	6	56	37	8	66	27	7	5	37	58	4	33	64	4	30	66
Trinidad and Tobago	72	27	2	X	X	X	X	X	X	20	34	46	X	X	X	X	X	X
United States	8	45	47	7	39	54	9	35	56	0	9	91	0	6	94	0	4	96
SOUTH AMERICA																		
Argentina	15	39	47	X	X	X	X	X	X	0	2	98	X	X	X	X	X	X
Bolivia	X	X	X	X	X	X	X	X	X	X	X	X	X	X	X	X	X	X
Brazil	31	51	19	37	47	16	37	45	16	1	13	86	1	14	85	1	12	87
Chile	38	44	18	X	X	X	X	X	X	1	5	94	X	X	X	X	X	X
Colombia	63	31	7	60	32	8	X	X	X	5	20	76	4	19	78	X	X	X
Ecuador	X	X	X	67	27	7	X	X	X	X	X	X	7	28	65	X	X	X
Guyana	X	X	X	X	X	X	X	X	X	X	X	X	X	X	X	X	X	X
Paraguay	44	51	6	X	X	X	X	X	X	1	7	92	X	X	X	X	X	X
Peru	84	14	2	78	20	2	X	X	X	6	8	86	7	14	79	X	X	X
Suriname	81	19	0	81	19	0	X	X	X	24	27	49	28	28	45	X	X	X
Uruguay	15	50	36	14	48	38	12	46	42	0	5	95	0	4	96	0	4	96
Venezuela	50	40	10	44	43	14	X	X	X	1	7	92	1	7	93	X	X	X

	Distribution of Agricultural Holdings by Size of Holdings (percent)									Distribution of Agricultural Area by Size of Holdings (percent)								
	1960			1970			1980			1960			1970			1980		
	Less than 5 ha	5-50 ha	More than 50 ha	Less than 5 ha	5-50 ha	More than 50 ha	Less than 5 ha	5-50 ha	More than 50 ha	Less than 5 ha	5-50 ha	More than 50 ha	Less than 5 ha	5-50 ha	More than 50 ha	Less than 5 ha	5-50 ha	More than 50 ha
ASIA																		
Afghanistan	X	X	X	X	X	X	X	X	X	X	X	X	X	X	X	X	X	X
Bahrain	X	X	X	100	0	0	72	28	0	X	X	X	35	63	3	33	65	1
Bangladesh	X	X	X	X	X	X	100	0	0	X	X	X	X	X	X	100	0	0
Bhutan	X	X	X	X	X	X	X	X	X	X	X	X	X	X	X	X	X	X
Burma	X	X	X	X	X	X	X	X	X	X	X	X	X	X	X	X	X	X
China	X	X	X	X	X	X	X	X	X	X	X	X	X	X	X	X	X	X
Cyprus	X	X	X	X	X	X	76	23	0	X	X	X	X	X	X	31	55	14
India	87	13	0	89	11	0	91	9	0	47	51	3	47	50	4	51	46	3
Indonesia	98	3	0	98	2	0	X	X	X	67	21	12	69	18	14	X	X	X
Iran	53	46	1	X	X	X	X	X	X	17	69	14	X	X	X	X	X	X
Iraq	57	36	7	49	49	2	X	X	X	2	19	79	8	66	26	X	X	X
Israel	X	X	X	68	30	3	X	X	X	X	X	X	12	30	58	X	X	X
Japan	98	2	0	99	2	0	98	2	0	84	16	0	83	17	0	79	21	0
Jordan	X	X	X	X	X	X	X	X	X	X	X	X	X	X	X	X	X	X
Kampuchea, Dem	X	X	X	X	X	X	X	X	X	X	X	X	X	X	X	X	X	X
Korea, Dem People's Rep	X	X	X	X	X	X	X	X	X	X	X	X	X	X	X	X	X	X
Korea, Rep	100	0	0	100	0	0	100	0	0	100	0	0	100	0	0	100	0	0
Kuwait	X	X	X	74	23	3	X	X	X	X	X	X	14	48	38	X	X	X
Lao People's Dem Rep	X	X	X	X	X	X	X	X	X	X	X	X	X	X	X	X	X	X
Lebanon	80	20	1	82	17	1	X	X	X	39	45	17	22	43	35	X	X	X
Malaysia	89	10	1	X	X	X	X	X	X	30	14	56	X	X	X	X	X	X
Mongolia	X	X	X	X	X	X	X	X	X	X	X	X	X	X	X	X	X	X
Nepal	X	X	X	97	3	0	97	3	0	X	X	X	72	27	1	71	29	0
Oman	X	X	X	X	X	X	X	X	X	X	X	X	X	X	X	X	X	X
Pakistan	80	20	0	68	31	1	73	26	0	32	68	0	30	58	11	34	57	9
Philippines	81	19	0	85	15	0	86	14	0	43	45	12	48	38	14	51	37	12
Qatar	X	X	X	X	X	X	X	X	X	X	X	X	X	X	X	X	X	X
Saudi Arabia	X	X	X	77	20	2	72	25	3	X	X	X	15	39	46	10	32	58
Singapore	X	X	X	100	0	0	X	X	X	X	X	X	98	0	0	X	X	X
Sri Lanka	97	3	0	98	2	0	99	1	0	53	20	28	58	42	0	73	6	21
Syrian Arab Rep	X	X	X	62	36	3	X	X	X	X	X	X	11	57	32	X	X	X
Thailand	72	28	0	X	X	X	72	28	0	43	57	0	X	X	X	39	61	0
Turkey	58	41	1	X	X	X	62	37	1	22	65	13	X	X	X	20	68	11
United Arab Emirates	X	X	X	X	X	X	X	X	X	X	X	X	X	X	X	X	X	X
Viet Nam	89	11	0	X	X	X	X	X	X	61	29	11	X	X	X	X	X	X
Yemen	X	X	X	X	X	X	89	11	0	X	X	X	X	X	X	44	52	5
Yemen, Dem	X	X	X	X	X	X	X	X	X	X	X	X	X	X	X	X	X	X
EUROPE																		
Albania	X	X	X	X	X	X	X	X	X	X	X	X	X	X	X	X	X	X
Austria	42	53	5	41	54	5	34	60	6	5	45	51	5	47	49	4	46	50
Belgium	62	37	1	53	46	1	44	53	3	16	73	11	10	77	13	6	74	20
Bulgaria	X	X	X	X	X	X	X	X	X	X	X	X	X	X	X	X	X	X
Czechoslovakia	X	X	X	98	2	1	90	10	0	X	X	X	7	5	88	7	6	87
Denmark	19	78	3	10	84	7	14	77	9	4	78	18	1	73	26	2	63	35
Finland	53	47	0	36	63	1	31	68	1	28	68	4	53	46	1	16	79	5
France	29	65	6	31	61	8	28	60	12	5	67	29	5	62	34	4	54	42
German Dem Rep	X	X	X	X	X	X	X	X	X	X	X	X	X	X	X	X	X	X
Germany, Fed Rep	55	44	1	39	59	2	35	61	4	17	71	12	9	77	14	6	74	20
Greece	X	X	X	80	21	0	X	X	X	X	X	X	45	53	3	X	X	X
Hungary	X	X	X	99	0	0	100	0	0	X	X	X	5	0	95	4	0	96
Iceland	X	X	X	X	X	X	X	X	X	X	X	X	X	X	X	X	X	X
Ireland	17	76	7	20	73	7	X	X	X	3	65	32	3	65	32	X	X	X
Italy	76	23	1	76	23	1	76	23	2	20	43	36	18	40	42	16	39	45
Luxembourg	X	X	X	25	63	13	27	58	15	X	X	X	3	83	14	2	58	40
Malta	75	25	0	91	9	0	97	3	0	77	23	0	77	23	0	83	17	0
Netherlands	54	46	1	35	64	1	33	65	2	12	79	9	6	85	9	4	81	15
Norway	69	31	0	57	43	1	49	50	1	42	56	2	34	64	2	16	55	29
Poland	63	37	0	62	38	0	X	X	X	24	61	15	26	74	0	X	X	X
Portugal	X	X	X	82	17	1	86	12	2	X	X	X	18	31	51	20	24	56
Romania	X	X	X	X	X	X	X	X	X	X	X	X	X	X	X	X	X	X
Spain	50	45	5	X	X	X	63	31	5	6	29	65	X	X	X	6	24	70
Sweden	37	60	3	26	67	7	16	72	12	10	68	22	16	64	21	9	62	29
Switzerland	X	X	X	45	54	1	42	57	1	X	X	X	9	86	5	6	88	6
United Kingdom	32	49	19	22	52	26	17	52	30	2	24	74	1	20	79	1	18	81
Yugoslavia	71	29	0	74	26	0	X	X	X	33	57	11	33	48	19	X	X	X
USSR	X	X	X	X	X	X	X	X	X	X	X	X	X	X	X	X	X	X
OCEANIA																		
Australia	7	25	69	8	24	69	X	X	X	0	0	100	0	0	100	X	X	X
Fiji	X	X	X	58	42	0	85	14	1	X	X	X	13	87	0	17	41	42
New Zealand	3	36	61	5	29	67	X	X	X	0	4	96	0	3	98	X	X	X
Papua New Guinea	X	X	X	X	X	X	X	X	X	X	X	X	X	X	X	X	X	X
Solomon Islands	X	X	X	X	X	X	X	X	X	X	X	X	X	X	X	X	X	X

Source: U.N. Food and Agriculture Organization.
0 = zero or less than half of 1 percent; X = not available.
For additional information, see Sources and Technical Notes.

Table 19.3 Irrigation and Salinization, 1974–84

	Area Irrigated 1984 (thousand hectares)	Percentage Change Over 1974-76	Percentage of Irrigated Lands Affected by Salinization		Area Irrigated 1984 (thousand hectares)	Percentage Change Over 1974-76	Percentage of Irrigated Lands Affected by Salinization
WORLD	**219,715**	**17**		**ASIA**	**136,962**	**13**	
AFRICA	**10,390**	**25**		Afghanistan	2,660	7	
				Bahrain	1	0	
Algeria	298	22	10–15	Bangladesh	1,920	42	
Angola	X	X		Bhutan	X	X	
Benin	22	47		Burma	1,064	9	
Botswana	16	60		China	45,420	6	15
Burkina Faso	8	33		Cyprus	94	0	25
Burundi	5	0		India	39,700	18	27
Cameroon	10	25		Indonesia	5,420	12	
Cape Verde	2	0		Iran	5,730	– 3	⟨30
Central African Rep	X	X		Iraq	1,750	11	50
Chad	7	0		Israel	220	21	13
Comoros	X	X		Japan	3,250	– 1	
Congo	4	100		Jordan	38	6	16
Cote d'Ivoire	62	63		Kampuchea, Dem	89	0	
Djibouti	X	X		Korea, Dem People's Rep	1,060	18	
Egypt	2,474	– 12	30–40	Korea, Rep	1,200	13	
Equatorial Guinea	X	X		Kuwait	1	0	
Ethiopia	94	2		Lao People's Dem Rep	118	181	
Gabon	X	X		Lebanon	86	0	
Gambia	33	32		Malaysia	336	9	
Ghana	7	– 53		Mongolia	40	74	
Guinea	70	9		Nepal	640	176	
Guinea-Bissau	X	X		Oman	42	24	
Kenya	40	– 2		Pakistan	15,320	13	⟨40
Lesotho	X	X		Philippines	1,430	30	
Liberia	5	150		Qatar	X	X	
Libya	232	16		Saudi Arabia	410	9	
Madagascar	1,000	103		Singapore	X	X	
Malawi	22	69		Sri Lanka	550	15	13
Mali	340	102		Syrian Arab Rep	617	13	30–35
Mauritania	8	14		Thailand	3,550	47	
Mauritius	17	13		Turkey	2,140	8	
Morocco	520	22		United Arab Emirates	5	0	
Mozambique	78	105		Viet Nam	1,750	65	
Niger	14	100		Yemen	245	7	
Nigeria	1,200	650		Yemen, Dem	62	9	
Rwanda	15	15		**EUROPE**	**15,616**	**21**	
Senegal	175	11	10–15	Albania	390	18	
Sierra Leone	16	23		Austria	4	0	
Somalia	130	8		Belgium	1	0	
South Africa	1,128	10		Bulgaria	1,210	8	
Sudan	1,700	– 2	⟨20	Czechoslovakia	193	42	
Swaziland	60	7		Denmark	400	122	
Tanzania, United Rep	140	150		Finland	60	54	
Togo	2	– 67		France	1,160	44	
Tunisia	210	71		German Dem Rep	165	4	
Uganda	16	0		Germany, Fed Rep	320	5	
Zaire	7	600		Greece	1,030	16	7
Zambia	20	11		Hungary	234	– 10	
Zimbabwe	170	136		Iceland	X	X	
NORTH & CENTRAL AMERICA	**27,414**	**20**		Ireland	X	X	
				Italy	2,970	9	
Barbados	X	X		Luxembourg	X	X	
Canada	630	26		Malta	1	0	
Costa Rica	84	133		Netherlands	520	21	
Cuba	1,030	74		Norway	80	95	
Dominican Rep	180	29		Poland	100	– 53	
El Salvador	110	244		Portugal	632	1	10–15
Guatemala	75	23		Romania	2,612	70	
Haiti	70	0		Spain	3,145	12	10–15
Honduras	85	9		Sweden	53	10	
Jamaica	34	10		Switzerland	25	0	
Mexico	5,100	13		United Kingdom	150	74	
Nicaragua	83	26		Yugoslavia	161	24	
Panama	30	30		**USSR**	**19,485**	**34**	
Trinidad and Tobago	21	11		**OCEANIA**	**1,869**	**15**	
United States	19,831	19	20–25	Australia	1,628	11	15–20
SOUTH AMERICA	**7,979**	**21**		Fiji	1	0	
				New Zealand	240	60	
Argentina	1,660	15		Papua New Guinea	X	X	
Bolivia	155	32		Solomon Islands	X	X	
Brazil	2,200	69					
Chile	1,257	1					
Colombia	322	16	20				
Ecuador	537	6					
Guyana	127	5					
Paraguay	62	17					
Peru	1,200	6	12				
Suriname	45	36					
Uruguay	92	61					
Venezuela	322	8					

Sources: U.N. Food and Agriculture Organization; and other sources.
0 = zero or less than half of 1 percent; X = not available; blank = no data available or salinization not a significant problem.
For additional information, see Sources and Technical Notes.

World Resources 1987

Table 19.4 Soil Erosion in Selected Countries, 1970–86

Extent and Location	Affected Area as Percentage of National Area	Amount of Erosion (metric tons per year)	Rate of Erosion (metric tons per hectare per year)	Year of Estimate
AFRICA				
Burkina Faso — Central plateau	X	X	5-35	1970s
Ethiopia — Total cropland (12 million ha)	10	500 million	42	1986
Central highland plateau (47 million ha)	43	1.6 billion	X	1970s
Lesotho — Grazing and croplands (2.7 million ha)	88	18.5 million	7	X
Madagascar — Mostly cropland (45.9 million ha)	79	X	25-250	1970s
High central plateau	X	12-40 million	25-250	1980s
Niger — Small watershed (11,700 ha)	0.01	468,000	40	X
Nigeria — State of Imo (900,000 ha)	1	13 million	14.4	1974
Jos Plateau	X	6 million	X	1975
Anambra	X	10-15 million	X	1975
Zimbabwe — Area with moderate to severe erosion (304,000 ha)	0.8	15 million	50	1979
NORTH & CENTRAL AMERICA				
Canada — Cultivated land New Brunswick	X	X	40	1980s
Cultivated land Nova Scotia	X	X	2-26	1980s
Fraser River valley British Columbia	X	X	up to 30	1985
Dominican Republic — Boa watershed (9,330 ha)	0.2	X	346	1970s
El Salvador — Cultivated land Acelhuate basin (46,300 ha)	2	X	19-190	1970s
Guatemala — Western highlands	X	X	5-35	1979
Jamaica — Total cropland (208,595 ha)	19	7.45 million	36	1980s
Upper Yalluhs Valley	X	X	90	X
United States — Total cropland (169 million ha)	19	1.66 billion	9.6	1982
SOUTH AMERICA				
Argentina, Brazil, and Paraguay — La Plata River basin	X	95 million	18.8	X
Peru — Entire country	100	1.9 billion	15	X
ASIA				
Burma — Irrawaddy River basin (43,000 ha)	.07	X	139	1980s
China — Loess Plateau region (60 million ha)	6.4	X	11-251	1980
India — Seriously affected cropland (80 million ha)	27	6 billion	75	1975
Cultivated land Deccan Black Soil region	X	X	40-100	1980s
Indonesia — Brantas River basin, Java	X	X	43	1970s
Nepal — Entire country	100	240 million	35-70	X
Turkey — Entire country	100	5 million	X	1980s
Yemen — Abandoned terraces Serat Mountains (4,900 ha)	0.03	X	150-400	1984
EUROPE				
Belgium — Central Belgium	X	X	10-25	1970s
USSR — Total cropland (232 million ha)	10	2.5 billion	11	1970s

Source: World Resources Institute and International Institute for Environment and Development. X = not available. For additional information, see Sources and Technical Notes.

Sources and Technical Notes

Table 19.1 Food and Agricultural Production, 1964–85

Source: Unpublished data (United Nations Food and Agriculture Organization [FAO], Rome, September 1986).

Indexes of agricultural and food production represent the disposable output (after deduction for feed and seed) of a country's agriculture sector relative to the base period 1979–81. The index for a given year is calculated as follows: the disposable output of a commodity in terms of weight or volume is multiplied by the 1979–81 unit value of the commodity according to average national producer prices. The product of this equation is the total value of the crop for that year in terms of 1979–81 prices. The values of all crop and livestock products are totaled to derive the value of all agricultural production in 1979–81 prices. The aggregate output for other years is then divided by the aggregate output for 1979–81 and multiplied by 100 to obtain the index number.

Indexes for continents and the world are computed by converting national production figures in local currencies to U.S. dollar equiva-

lents using International Monetary Fund exchange rates. Country outputs are then totaled to derive regional and global aggregates.

The agricultural production index includes all crop and livestock products. The food production index covers all edible agricultural crops that contain nutrients.

Yields are calculated from production and area data. Production data include cereal production for feed and seed. Area data refer to the area harvested. Cereals refer to all cereals harvested for dry grain, exclusive of crops cut for hay or harvested green. Roots and tubers refer to all root crops grown principally for human consumption; root crops grown principally for feed are excluded.

The data in Table 19.1 are supplied to FAO by national agriculture ministries or are derived from agricultural censuses. (See the Technical Note for Table 19.2.)

Table 19.2 Agricultural Land Distribution, 1960–80

Sources: 1960: United Nations Food and Agriculture Organization (FAO), *Report on the*

1960 World Census of Agriculture: Analysis and International Comparison of Results (FAO, Rome, 1971). 1970: FAO, *1970 World Census of Agriculture: Analysis and International Comparison of Results* (FAO, Rome, 1981). 1980: FAO, *Report on the 1980 World Census of Agriculture*, Census Bulletins 2–23 (FAO, Rome, October 1983–August 1986).

The years 1960, 1970, and 1980 refer to those rounds of the World Census of Agriculture organized by FAO. Data for 1960 were compiled from national censuses conducted between 1958 and 1964. The 1970 round of censuses covered 1966–1974. The 1980 census round includes national censuses conducted between 1977 and 1985. For specific dates of country censuses, refer to the sources.

Agricultural Holdings, as defined in the *World Census of Agriculture*, are agricultural production units comprising all livestock kept and all land used wholly or partly for agricultural holding may consist of one or more parcels of land, or of livestock without agricultural land. Common grazing land and lands producing only forest products are not

Food and Agriculture

considered holdings. Rented land is considered within the holding of the operator rather than that of the owner.

Agricultural Areas include all land under temporary or permanent crops and land used as permanent pasture. (See the Technical Note for Table 18.1 in Chapter 18, "Land Use and Cover.")

Countries sometimes deviate from the standard FAO definitions and survey techniques, making comparisons across countries (or across years for the same country) difficult. For example, the censuses of many countries exclude holdings below a given size or level of economic importance. In the 1980 census, several countries classified holdings by sizes different from those in the table. These countries' holdings were classified by applying the categories most closely approximating a holding's actual size.

Refer to FAO's census publications for additional information.

Table 19.3 Irrigation and Salinization, 1974–84

Sources: Irrigation: United Nations Food and Agriculture Organization (FAO), *Production Yearbook 1985* (FAO, Rome, 1986). Salinization: Argentina and Syria: Victor A. Kovda, *Land Aridization and Drought Control* (Westview Press, Boulder, Colorado, 1980); Algeria, Egypt, Senegal, Sudan, Iran, Pakistan, Portugal, Spain, Australia: Victor A. Kovda, Academy of Sciences of the USSR, Moscow, 1986 (personal communication); United States: Mohamed El-Ashry, *et al.*, "Salinity Pollution from Irrigated Agriculture," *Journal of Soil and Water Conservation*, Vol. 40, No. 1 (1985); India: Dan Yaron, ed., *Salinity in Irrigation and Water Resources* (Marcel Dekker, Inc., New York, 1981); Cyprus, Iraq, Jordan, and Lebanon: M.M. El Gabaly, "Effects of Irrigation in the Near East Region," in *Arid Land Irrigation in Developing Countries* (Pergamon Press, Oxford, 1977); China: E.B. Vermeer, "Agriculture in China—A Deteriorating Situation," *The Ecologist,* Vol. 14, No. 1 (1984); Sri Lanka: William R. Gasser, *Survey of Irrigation in Eight Asian Nations* (U.S. Department of Agriculture, Washington, D.C., 1981); Israel, Colombia, Peru, and Greece: K.K. Framji, ed., *Irrigation and Salinity, A Worldwide Survey* (International Commission on Irrigation and Drainage, New Delhi, 1976).

Irrigated Lands are areas purposely provided with water, including land flooded by river water for crop production or pasture improvement, whether this area is irrigated several times or only once during the year.

Salinization refers to the accumulation of salts and minerals in topsoil as a result of poor irrigation practices. It primarily affects arid and semiarid lands, which are often naturally saline to some degree and have poor drainage. When these lands are irrigated, the water table rises, bringing dissolved salts from the subsoil into the crop root zone. As the water evaporates, salts accumulate in the upper soil layers, reducing soil fertility and crop yields. This process is accelerated when saline water is used for irriga-

tion. Data shown are estimates, and do not indicate the severity of salinization.

Table 19.4 Soil Erosion in Selected Countries, 1970–86

Sources: Compiled by World Resources Institute and International Institute for Environment and Development from the following sources: **Burkina Faso:** International Science and Technology Institute, Inc. (ISTI), *Environmental Sector Assessment: Upper Volta* (ISTI, Washington, D.C., 1982). **Ethiopia** (cropland): Hans Hurni, unpublished data (Soil Conservation Research Project Ethiopia, Addis Ababa, August 1986); Central Highland Plateau, Ethiopia: United Nations Food and Agriculture Organization (FAO), *Protect and Produce: Soil Conservation for Development* (FAO, Rome, 1984). **Lesotho:** University of Arizona, Arid Lands Information Center, *Draft Environmental Profile of the Kingdom of Lesotho* (University of Arizona, Tucson, 1982). **Madagascar** (cropland): P. Randrianarijaona, "The Erosion of Madagascar," *AMBIO,* Vol. 12, No. 6 (1983); High Central Plateau, Madagascar: U.S. Agency for International Development (U.S. AID), *Draft Environmental Profile of Madagascar* (U.S. AID, Washington, D.C., 1981). **Niger:** S.A. El-Swaify, *et al.*, "Soil Erosion by Water," in *Natural Systems for Development: What Planners Need to Know* (MacMillan Publishing Company, New York, 1983). Jos Plateau, Anambra, **Nigeria:** D.O. Aneke, "Coping with Accelerated Soil Erosion in Nigeria," *Journal of Soil and Water Conservation,* Vol. 41, No. 3 (1986); Imo, Nigeria: G.E. Osuji, "The Gullies of Imo," *Journal of Soil and Water Conservation,* Vol. 39, No. 4 (1984). **Zimbabwe:** University of Arizona, Arid Lands Information Center, *Draft Environmental Profile of Zimbabwe* (University of Arizona, Tucson, 1982). British Columbia, **Canada:** Agriculture Canada, *Agricultural Soil and Water Resources in Canada: Situation and Outlook* (Agriculture Canada, Ottawa, 1985); New Brunswick and Nova Scotia, Canada: Agricultural Institute of Canada (AIC), *A Strategy for Soil and Water Conservation in Canada* (AIC, Ottawa, 1984). **Dominican Republic:** U.S. AID, *Country Environmental Profile* (U.S. AID, Washington, D.C., 1981). **El Salvador:** S.L. Wiggins, "The Economics of Soil Conservation in the Acelhuate River Basin, El Salvador," in *Soil Conservation: Problems and Prospects,* R.P.C. Morgan, ed. (John Wiley and Sons, Chichester, 1981). **Guatemala:** University of Georgia, Institute of Ecology, *An Environmental Profile of Guatemala* (University of Georgia, Athens, 1981). **Jamaica** (cropland): T.C. Sheng, *A National Soil Conservation Programme for Jamaica* (United Nations Development Programme/FAO, New York, 1984); Upper Yalluhs Valley, Jamaica: FAO, *Strengthening the National Soil Conservation Programme for Integrated Watershed Development, Jamaica, Terminal Report* (FAO, Rome, 1982). **United States:** Paul Rosenberry and Burton English, "Erosion Control Practices: Impact of Actual Versus Most Effective Use," in *Conservation Needs and Opportunities* (National

Research Council, Board of Agriculture, 1984) (data were taken from the 1982 Natural Resources Inventory, U.S. Department of Agriculture, Soil Conservation Service). **Argentina:** Organization of American States (OAS), *Cuenca del Rio de la Plata: Estudio para su Plantificacion y Desarollo* (OAS, Washington, D.C., 1974). **Peru:** Interview with Lorenzo Chang Novarro, Director of Peru's Department of Watershed, Soil, and Water Conservation, in Abraham Lama, "Peru: Rapid Soil Erosion Threatens Peruvian Agriculture," *Latin America Links* (1984). **China** (erosion data): Lee Hsiaotseng, "Soil Conservation in China's Loess Plateau," *Journal of Soil and Water Conservation,* Vol. 39, No. 4 (1984); China (area data): Zhu Ling, "Study Aims to Lift Flood Threat of Yellow River," *China Daily,* Vol. 4, No. 1069 (1984). **India** (seriously affected cropland): Das, "Soil Conservation Practices and Erosion Control in India—A Case Study," *Soils Bulletin* No. 33 (FAO, Rome, 1977); Deccan Black Soil region, India: Centre for Science and the Environment (CSE), *State of India's Environment, 1982* (CSE, New Delhi, 1982). **Indonesia:** T.E. Brabben, "Use of Turbidity Monitors to Assess Sediment Yield in East Java, Indonesia," in *Erosion and Sediment Transport Measurement* (International Association of Hydrological Science, Wallingford, 1981). **Nepal:** Library of Congress, Science and Technology Division, *Draft Environmental Report on Nepal* (Library of Congress, Washington, D.C., 1979). **Turkey:** Environmental Problems Foundation of Turkey (EPFT), *Environmental Profile of Turkey 1981* (EPFT, Ankara, 1981). **Yemen:** Horst Vogel, "Deterioration of a Mountainous Agro-Ecosystem in the Third World due to Emigration of Rural Labor," presented at the Workshop on African Mountains and Highlands: Ecodevelopment, Resource Management, and Food Security, Addis Ababa, October 18–27, 1986. **Belgium:** G. Richter, "Aspects and Problems of Erosion Hazards in the EEC Countries," in *Soil Erosion,* A.G. Prendergast, ed., (Commission of the European Communities, Luxembourg, 1982). **USSR:** Lester Brown, *et al., State of the World 1985* (Norton, New York, 1985).

Soil erosion is the removal of soil from the land by the erosive processes of moving wind and water. The natural rate of erosion is determined by climate, topography, soil type, and vegetative cover. It can be exacerbated by poor agricultural practices and by vegetation degradation caused by livestock overgrazing and deforestation.

Erosion rates can be estimated at three locations within a watershed. "Upstream methods" calculate the amount of erosion based on field observations, "midstream methods" are based on the sediment loads carried by rivers, and "downstream methods" are based on the volume of sediment deposited in lakes, in reservoirs, or at the drainage point of a water basin. Some data in the table are point estimates, based on a few measurements made at one time and extrapolated to reflect an annual average. Estimates of erosion take into account rainfall and runoff, soil type, slope, land use and cover, and management practices.

20. Forests and Rangelands

Forests and rangelands together occupy roughly three quarters of the world's land surface. Yet the statistics available for evaluating changes in these lands are weak, particularly compared to information on cultivated lands.

Data on the extent and condition of forests are greatly influenced by the definitions and techniques used. (See Table 20.1.) For example, the United Nations Food and Agricultural Organization's (FAO) taxonomy of forest types distinguishes between "closed" and "open" forests. The trees of a closed forest fully shade the ground, preventing the growth of grasses. Open forests may have as little as 10 percent tree cover, permitting a nearly continuous grass layer on the forest floor. However, some countries classify open forests as rangelands.

Forest fallow and shrublands, covering 1 billion hectares, are excluded from Table 20.1. Forest fallow is forest land that is cut, burned, and cultivated for a year or two and then allowed to regrow until the next slash-and-burn cycle. Shrublands are important sources of fuelwood, forage, and other products in densely settled rural areas where forests may have been largely degraded or even eliminated.

"Deforestation" has several definitions. In Table 20.1, deforestation refers to the clearing of closed forested land and its subsequent use for permanent agriculture or settlement. It does not include other alterations, such as selective logging of closed forests or active management of productive stands that can have substantial impacts on wildlife and its habitat, watershed stability, and the global carbon cycle.

There is considerable controversy over the estimated rate and extent of tropical deforestation. Global reviews of deforestation conducted in the early 1970s found smaller areas of tropical forest and higher rates of deforestation than are shown here. A new global assessment of tropical forests, to be conducted by FAO and the United Nations Environment Programme, is planned for the late 1980s. In the future, satellite remote sensing may permit continuous monitoring of forests and rangelands, but with poor resolution of vegetational and geographic detail.

Fuelwood and industrial wood production data are compiled by different methods and therefore should be interpreted separately. (See Table 20.2.) Fuelwood and charcoal production estimates for many countries are derived by multiplying the population by national per capita consumption factors. These factors were estimated by FAO in the early 1980s after an extensive literature review and limited field visits. Industrial wood data, how-

ever, are largely drawn from questionnaires completed by government agencies. FAO supplements these responses with information drawn from national yearbooks, reports, and unofficial sources.

Industrial wood production is concentrated in a few developed countries: 52 percent is produced by the United States, the USSR, and Canada. Brazil, China, Indonesia, and Malaysia are the largest industrial wood producers in the developing world, accounting for 14 percent of global production. Industrial wood production is increasing more rapidly in developing countries. Since the mid-1970s, U.S. production has increased only 4 percent and USSR production has declined, but Brazil's production has increased 93 percent and China's has increased 53 percent.

Because fixed per capita consumption factors are used to estimate fuelwood and charcoal output for many developing countries, output trends for these countries reflect only population growth. The data cannot be used to analyze the impacts of increasing fuelwood scarcity, rapidly changing settlement patterns, and fluctuating commercial fuel prices on fuelwood and charcoal consumption.

The global trade in forest products, shown in Table 20.3, is dominated by a few major importers and exporters. Japan accounts for 40 percent of all roundwood imports; the United States, Malaysia, and the USSR provide 53 percent of all exports. Canada is the source of 41 percent of sawnwood exports, and the United States imports 41 percent of the global sawnwood total.

Many other data series that would be useful to policymakers are missing from these tables: the volume and growth rate of economically valuable trees for timber production, the value of nonwood forest products, changes in forest conditions and in the composition of flora and fauna, the amount of carbon dioxide released from forests and soils as a result of deforestation, and information on reforestation and forest management.

Table 20.4 presents statistics on desertification. The "percent desertified" figures (which should be regarded as informed estimates) indicate the amount of land believed to have lost some of its original productive capacity. This productivity loss can range from 1 to 100 percent. Qualitative information on rangeland conditions in Middle Eastern countries is presented in Chapter 5, "Forests and Rangelands." Similar information for African countries may be found in *World Resources 1986*, pp. 76–79.

Table 20.1 Forest Resources, 1980s

	Extent of Forest and Woodland, 1980 (thousand hectares)		Deforestation of Closed Forests, 1981–85		Reforestation 1980s (thousand hectares per year)	Managed Closed Forest 1980 (thousand hectares)	Protected Closed Forest 1980 (thousand hectares)
			Average Annual Extent (thousand hectares per year)	Percent per Year			
	Open	Closed					
WORLD	1,338,242	2,845,178					
AFRICA	498,479	221,079	1,268	0.6	212	2,317	9,140
Algeria	746	1,021	0	0.0	52	0	8
Angola	50,700	2,900	34	1.2	3	0	0
Benin	3,820	47	1	2.6	0	0	0
Botswana	32,560	0	0	0.0	0	0	0
Burkina Faso	4,464	271	5	1.8	2	0	0
Burundi	14	27	0	1.5	3	0	9
Cameroon	7,700	17,920	80	0.4	1	0	0
Cape Verde	0	1	X	X	X	X	X
Central African Rep	32,300	3,590	5	0.1	0	0	0
Chad	13,000	500	0	0.0	0	0	0
Comoros	X	X	X	X	X	X	X
Congo	0	21,340	22	0.1	0	0	130
Cote d'Ivoire	5,376	4,458	290	6.5	6	1	648
Djibouti	100	6	X	X	X	0	0
Egypt	0	0	0	0.0	2	0	0
Equatorial Guinea	0	1,295	3	0.2	0	0	0
Ethiopia	22,800	4,350	6	0.1	10	0	0
Gabon	75	20,500	15	0.1	1	0	0
Gambia	150	65	2	3.4	0	0	0
Ghana	6,975	1,718	22	1.3	2	1,167	397
Guinea	8,600	2,050	36	1.8	0	0	0
Guinea-Bissau	1,445	660	17	2.6	0	0	0
Kenya	1,255	1,105	11	1.0	0	70	405
Lesotho	0	0	0	X	X	0	0
Liberia	40	2,000	42	2.1	2	0	0
Libya	112	78	0	0.0	32	0	0
Madagascar	2,900	10,300	128	1.2	12	0	930
Malawi	4,085	186	0	0.0	1	0	146
Mali	6,750	500	10	2.0	1	0	0
Mauritania	15,000	0	0	X	X	0	0
Mauritius	29	2	X	X	X	X	X
Morocco	2,549	687	0	0.0	13	421	3
Mozambique	14,500	935	10	1.1	4	0	25
Niger	2,900	0	0	0.0	2	0	0
Nigeria	8,800	5,950	300	5.0	26	0	0
Rwanda	110	120	3	2.3	3	0	11
Senegal	10,825	220	0	0.0	3	0	63
Sierra Leone	1,315	740	6	0.8	0	0	0
Somalia	7,510	1,540	3	0.2	2	0	0
South Africa	2,800	1,350	X	X	X	X	X
Sudan	47,000	650	4	0.6	13	50	0
Swaziland	50	100	X	X	X	X	X
Tanzania, United Rep	40,600	1,440	10	0.7	9	0	410
Togo	1,380	304	2	0.7	0	0	0
Tunisia	134	163	0	0.0	3	163	0
Uganda	5,250	765	10	1.3	2	440	45
Zaire	71,840	105,750	160	0.2	0	0	5,690
Zambia	26,500	3,010	30	1.0	2	5	220
Zimbabwe	15,000	465	X	X	X	X	X
NORTH & CENTRAL AMERICA	275,320	528,046	X	X	2,539	102,884	36,812
Barbados	X	X	X	X	X	X	X
Canada	172,300	264,100	X	X	720	X	4,870
Costa Rica	X	1,638	65	4.0	0	0	320
Cuba	0	1,455	2	0.1	12	200	0
Dominican Rep	0	629	2	0.4	0	0	0
El Salvador	0	141	4	2.8	0	0	0
Guatemala	X	4,442	72	1.6	8	0	62
Haiti	0	48	1	1.2	0	0	0
Honduras	200	3,797	48	1.3	0	58	0
Jamaica	0	67	2	3.0	1	0	2
Mexico	X	46,250	470	1.0	22	0	360
Nicaragua	0	4,496	105	2.3	1	250	0
Panama	0	4,165	36	0.9	0	0	0
Trinidad and Tobago	0	208	1	0.4	0	14	0
United States	102,820	195,256	X	X	1,775	102,362	31,198
SOUTH AMERICA	239,320	624,465	3,186	0.5	580	4,660	8,662
Argentina	32,300	7,670	X	X	38	X	X
Bolivia	22,750	44,010	87	0.2	1	0	0
Brazil	157,000	357,480	1,360	0.4	449	4,660	X
Chile	2,430	6,250	X	X	50	X	X
Colombia	5,300	46,400	820	1.8	8	0	2,280
Ecuador	480	14,250	340	2.4	4	0	350
Guyana	220	18,475	2	0.0	0	0	12
Paraguay	15,640	4,070	190	4.7	1	0	90
Peru	960	69,680	260	0.4	6	0	850
Suriname	170	14,830	2	0.0	0	0	580
Uruguay	0	580	X	X	5	X	X
Venezuela	2,000	31,870	125	0.4	18	0	4,500

World Resources 1987

Table 20.1

	Extent of Forest and Woodland, 1980 (thousand hectares)		Deforestation of Closed Forests, 1981–85		Reforestation 1980s (thousand hectares per year)	Managed Closed Forest 1980 (thousand hectares)	Protected Closed Forest 1980 (thousand hectares)
	Open	Closed	Average Annual Extent (thousand hectares per year)	Percent per Year			
ASIA	**94,540**	**456,605**	**1,762**	**0.4**	**5,679**	**48,705**	**17,786**
Afghanistan	500	710	0	0.0	0	100	0
Bahrain	0	0	0	0.0	0	0	0
Bangladesh	0	927	8	0.9	17	795	52
Bhutan	40	2,100	1	0.0	1	0	X
Burma	0	31,941	102	0.3	0	3,419	299
China	45,000	125,000	X	X	4,552	X	X
Cyprus	24	153	X	X	X	153	25
India	5,393	51,841	132	0.3	138	31,917	6,743
Indonesia	3,000	113,895	600	0.5	131	40	5,430
Iran	2,520	1,230	X	X	X	400	120
Iraq	1,160	70	0	0.0	2	0	0
Israel	20	80	X	X	2	56	7
Japan	1,390	23,890	X	X	240	X	X
Jordan	50	X	X	X	3	X	X
Kampuchea, Dem	5,100	7,548	25	0.3	0	0	0
Korea, Dem People's Rep	X	8,970	X	X	200	X	X
Korea, Rep	240	6,275	X	X	152	X	X
Kuwait	X	X	X	X	X	X	X
Lao People's Dem Rep	5,215	8,410	100	1.2	2	0	0
Lebanon	20	X	X	X	X	X	0
Malaysia	0	20,996	255	1.2	20	2,499	959
Mongolia	5,000	10,000	X	X	X	X	X
Nepal	180	1,941	80	4.1	4	0	330
Oman	X	X	X	X	X	X	X
Pakistan	295	2,185	1	0.0	7	410	15
Philippines	0	9,510	91	1.0	50	0	690
Qatar	X	X	X	X	X	X	X
Saudi Arabia	170	30	0	0.0	0	0	0
Singapore	X	X	X	X	X	X	X
Sri Lanka	X	1,659	58	3.5	13	0	193
Syrian Arab Rep	90	60	X	X	10	60	X
Thailand	6,440	9,235	244	2.6	24	0	2,220
Turkey	11,343	8,856	X	X	82	8,856	139
United Arab Emirates	0	0	0	0.0	0	0	0
Viet Nam	1,340	8,770	60	0.7	29	0	560
Yemen	10	X	X	X	X	X	X
Yemen, Dem	X	X	X	X	X	X	X
EUROPE	**21,887**	**137,005**	**X**	**X**	**1,031**	**74,628**	**1,732**
Albania	0	1,280	X	X	X	X	X
Austria	0	3,754	X	X	21	1,489	0
Belgium	80	682	X	X	19	272	0
Bulgaria	400	3,328	X	X	50	3,600	100
Czechoslovakia	145	4,435	X	X	37	4,435	X
Denmark	18	466	X	X	X	330	56
Finland	3,340	19,885	X	X	158	10,578	294
France	1,200	13,875	X	X	51	2,957	92
German Dem Rep	285	2,700	X	X	X	2,697	85
Germany, Fed Rep	218	6,989	X	X	62	3,886	X
Greece	3,242	2,512	X	X	X	1,603	55
Hungary	25	1,612	X	X	19	1,612	41
Iceland	100	X	X	X	X	X	X
Ireland	33	347	X	X	9	298	0
Italy	1,700	6,363	X	X	15	699	162
Luxembourg	X	X	X	X	X	38	0
Malta	X	X	X	X	X	X	X
Netherlands	61	294	X	X	2	225	0
Norway	1,066	7,635	X	X	79	1,130	60
Poland	138	8,588	X	X	106	8,099	103
Portugal	349	2,627	X	X	4	X	7
Romania	410	6,265	X	X	X	5,940	X
Spain	3,905	6,906	X	X	92	2,007	40
Sweden	3,442	24,400	X	X	207	14,301	230
Switzerland	189	935	X	X	7	627	7
United Kingdom	151	2,027	X	X	40	1,505	0
Yugoslavia	1,390	9,100	X	X	53	6,300	400
USSR	**137,000**	**791,600**	**X**	**X**	**4,540**	**791,600**	**20,000**
OCEANIA	**71,696**	**86,378**	**X**	**X**	**113**		
Australia	65,085	41,658	X	0.0	62	X	X
Fiji	350	850	X	0.0	4	X	X
New Zealand	2,300	7,200	X	0.0	43	X	X
Papua New Guinea	3,945	34,230	22	0.1	2	55	X
Solomon Islands	16	2,440	X	0.0	2	X	X

Sources: U.N. Food and Agriculture Organization; U.N. Economic Commission for Europe; U.N. Environment Programme; and country data sources.
0 = zero or less than half the unit of measure; X = not available.
For additional information, see Sources and Technical Notes.

Table 20.2 Wood Production, 1966–84

	Average Annual Production (thousand cubic meters)								
	Roundwood			Fuelwood and Charcoal			Industrial Wood		
		Percentage Change Since			Percentage Change Since			Percentage Change Since	
	1982–84	1974–76	1966–68	1982–84	1974–76	1966–68	1982–84	1974–76	1966–68
WORLD	**2,989,861**	**14**	**29**	**1,570,317**	**22**	**37**	**1,426,147**	**7**	**21**
AFRICA	**413,631**	**26**	**55**	**360,888**	**27**	**55**	**52,467**	**21**	**53**
Algeria	1,681	21	51	1,461	20	51	217	23	51
Angola	9,061	15	40	7,663	16	39	1,398	12	46
Benin	4,115	24	49	3,902	24	49	215	24	47
Botswana	796	7	27	729	5	24	68	37	80
Burkina Faso	6,432	19	37	6,137	19	37	294	20	38
Burundi	3,368	17	32	3,330	17	32	41	26	35
Cameroon	10,369	20	47	7,994	14	33	2,432	54	136
Cape Verde	X	X	X	X	X	X	X	X	X
Central African Rep	3,139	15	52	2,658	20	54	482	−4	43
Chad	3,405	19	39	2,923	19	39	482	19	39
Comoros	X	X	X	X	X	X	X	X	X
Congo	2,262	26	21	1,510	23	48	753	32	−12
Cote d'Ivoire	12,055	15	68	7,447	35	87	4,606	−8	44
Djibouti	X	X	X	X	X	X	X	X	X
Egypt	1,910	23	45	1,821	23	45	89	23	45
Equatorial Guinea	551	27	−34	444	15	29	102	106	−79
Ethiopia	30,359	20	23	28,562	19	21	1,797	37	72
Gabon	2,571	−6	−2	1,222	6	16	1,349	−15	−13
Gambia	743	−4	21	723	−5	20	20	99	106
Ghana	8,075	0	24	7,284	21	49	764	−62	−53
Guinea	3,626	16	37	3,085	16	39	585	21	39
Guinea-Bissau	557	11	23	422	7	16	135	24	55
Kenya	29,820	39	89	28,413	38	87	1,407	44	125
Lesotho	293	13	35	293	13	35	X	X	X
Liberia	4,199	26	53	3,723	36	42	476	−19	246
Libya	631	18	57	536	10	51	95	103	97
Madagascar	6,262	18	39	5,455	10	53	807	139	−13
Malawi	6,240	27	59	5,869	27	57	369	32	94
Mali	4,618	22	43	4,325	22	44	293	20	34
Mauritania	11	26	48	6	27	58	5	25	36
Mauritius	31	−23	−1	23	3	45	8	−54	−48
Morocco	1,685	30	103	1,120	44	130	519	1	51
Mozambique	14,763	45	73	13,817	50	80	938	1	11
Niger	3,701	24	48	3,473	24	48	229	24	48
Nigeria	89,303	35	76	81,943	32	71	7,360	96	153
Rwanda	5,295	6	39	5,050	2	34	244	307	339
Senegal	3,948	30	68	3,422	30	69	520	31	66
Sierra Leone	7,500	14	27	7,360	14	28	140	2	−2
Somalia	5,013	65	113	4,941	66	113	65	26	61
South Africa	19,614	14	33	7,000	1	3	12,614	24	59
Sudan	18,452	27	57	16,711	27	57	1,741	24	58
Swaziland	2,223	−4	110	560	20	47	1,663	−10	145
Tanzania, United Rep	21,348	31	67	20,121	32	70	1,227	28	27
Togo	715	22	58	561	22	55	155	20	68
Tunisia	2,695	22	43	2,593	22	43	101	11	38
Uganda	11,813	30	66	10,266	30	68	1,532	23	51
Zaire	31,661	26	68	29,114	26	70	2,344	12	34
Zambia	9,685	26	60	9,192	26	61	451	14	37
Zimbabwe	7,002	39	27	5,653	35	18	1,328	57	88
NORTH & CENTRAL AMERICA	**628,210**	**24**	**33**	**152,357**	**164**	**159**	**475,852**	**6**	**15**
Barbados	X	X	X	X	X	X	X	X	X
Canada	149,214	14	33	6,022	62	−17	143,192	12	37
Costa Rica	3,287	2	55	2,426	26	56	861	−33	51
Cuba	3,166	33	78	2,781	39	98	385	0	2
Dominican Rep	957	109	133	951	116	171	6	−64	−90
El Salvador	4,503	26	61	4,403	26	62	100	29	28
Guatemala	6,819	20	51	6,650	27	64	169	−62	−63
Haiti	5,624	20	42	5,385	21	45	239	0	0
Honduras	4,933	19	46	4,250	32	68	683	−28	−20
Jamaica	87	45	22	27	286	286	60	13	−6
Mexico	19,930	16	60	13,161	25	62	6,768	3	56
Nicaragua	3,405	20	83	2,525	27	64	880	3	172
Panama	2,047	28	58	1,708	17	46	339	141	169
Trinidad and Tobago	65	−30	−41	16	−6	−21	50	−35	−45
United States	423,886	29	30	101,922	434	318	321,964	4	7
SOUTH AMERICA	**290,375**	**31**	**65**	**209,838**	**21**	**47**	**80,484**	**67**	**141**
Argentina	12,628	24	51	7,732	22	37	4,896	27	79
Bolivia	1,278	5	41	1,103	23	50	174	−46	4
Brazil	218,494	33	69	160,933	20	46	57,561	93	195
Chile	13,854	31	66	5,896	15	31	7,958	47	108
Colombia	16,616	13	30	13,943	19	44	2,673	−10	−12
Ecuador	7,923	39	84	5,792	45	83	2,131	24	84
Guyana	200	−9	−17	11	17	42	181	−14	−22
Paraguay	6,822	41	69	4,410	17	37	2,412	130	191
Peru	7,773	10	73	6,517	21	81	1,256	−24	37
Suriname	260	−3	−5	13	−43	−51	202	−18	−19
Uruguay	2,974	71	98	2,758	88	105	216	−22	36
Venezuela	1,300	12	49	664	32	80	636	−2	26

Table 20.2

	Average Annual Production (thousand cubic meters)								
	Roundwood			Fuelwood and Charcoal			Industrial Wood		
		Percentage Change Since			Percentage Change Since			Percentage Change Since	
	1982–84	1974–76	1966–68	1982–84	1974–76	1966–68	1982–84	1974–76	1966–68
ASIA	**929,364**	**13**	**35**	**703,033**	**12**	**32**	**231,248**	**19**	**47**
Afghanistan	5,697	2	16	4,252	2	13	1,529	7	36
Bahrain	X	X	X	X	X	X	X	X	X
Bangladesh	25,787	23	52	24,919	25	56	868	−14	−13
Bhutan	3,224	15	34	2,946	14	35	278	17	17
Burma	19,062	25	44	16,026	22	48	2,981	39	21
China	230,296	19	47	154,636	10	29	82,100	53	122
Cyprus	78	−18	2	21	2	−28	57	−23	20
India	234,556	19	45	214,619	18	41	18,679	13	82
Indonesia	144,735	18	63	117,044	18	42	27,681	19	313
Iran	6,727	2	−3	2,351	3	37	4,376	1	−17
Iraq	133	16	46	83	28	32	50	0	76
Israel	118	20	177	11	−3	6	107	23	231
Japan	32,815	−11	−43	582	−37	−92	32,233	−11	−36
Jordan	9	−10	59	5	25	67	4	−33	50
Kampuchea, Dem	5,050	−1	2	4,483	−2	7	567	10	−24
Korea, Dem People's Rep	4,414	13	36	3,814	16	44	600	0	0
Korea, Rep	6,692	−18	−34	4,394	−22	−45	2,253	−11	5
Kuwait	X	X	X	X	X	X	X	X	X
Lao People's Dem Rep	4,140	22	52	3,889	23	51	244	9	61
Lebanon	468	−3	18	444	−4	16	24	20	60
Malaysia	40,079	35	104	7,244	21	48	32,833	39	122
Mongolia	2,390	0	45	1,350	0	35	1,040	0	60
Nepal	15,098	20	43	14,538	21	45	560	0	1
Oman	X	X	X	X	X	X	X	X	X
Pakistan	19,364	28	59	18,759	28	59	600	25	74
Philippines	34,996	5	16	27,889	22	51	7,100	−32	−39
Qatar	X	X	X	X	X	X	X	X	X
Saudi Arabia	X	X	X	X	X	X	X	X	X
Singapore	X	X	X	X	X	X	X	X	X
Sri Lanka	8,344	17	35	7,648	16	35	692	36	36
Syrian Arab Rep	40	−6	6	11	129	174	30	−22	−12
Thailand	39,913	14	40	35,720	20	49	4,185	−20	−7
Turkey	20,514	−50	−35	14,125	−59	−49	6,389	−6	61
United Arab Emirates	X	X	X	X	X	X	X	X	X
Viet Nam	23,886	22	46	20,705	20	43	3,188	36	70
Yemen	X	X	X	X	X	X	X	X	X
Yemen, Dem	270	22	44	270	22	44	X	X	X
EUROPE	**338,064**	**5**	**7**	**54,519**	**5**	**−30**	**283,545**	**5**	**19**
Albania	2,330	0	38	1,608	0	40	722	0	33
Austria	13,750	14	20	1,413	41	−1	12,337	12	24
Belgium	3,021	10	7	538	148	131	2,483	−1	−4
Bulgaria	4,818	3	−10	1,732	68	35	3,086	−16	−24
Czechoslovakia	18,976	15	34	1,465	−18	−32	17,511	19	45
Denmark	3,302	103	49	367	365	61	2,935	90	48
Finland	38,980	12	−5	3,233	−48	−65	35,746	25	12
France	38,252	0	2	10,420	−3	−27	27,832	1	19
German Dem Rep	10,588	29	56	695	48	−6	9,893	28	64
Germany, Fed Rep	28,648	−8	1	3,933	30	−9	24,714	−13	3
Greece	2,668	−1	−7	1,872	−6	−24	796	12	91
Hungary	6,330	14	41	2,761	12	17	3,569	15	69
Iceland	X	X	X	X	X	X	X	X	X
Ireland	1,127	229	252	46	475	−5	1,081	223	298
Italy	8,784	34	−28	4,384	38	−2	4,399	30	−43
Luxembourg	X	X	X	X	X	X	X	X	X
Malta	X	X	X	X	X	X	X	X	X
Netherlands	913	−4	10	96	213	357	817	−11	1
Norway	9,892	5	22	799	55	−15	9,093	2	27
Poland	23,590	8	34	2,889	62	56	20,701	3	32
Portugal	8,524	13	42	500	−6	−70	8,024	15	85
Romania	23,373	9	0	4,565	−15	−41	18,808	18	21
Spain	14,131	18	6	1,746	−31	−79	12,386	31	151
Sweden	52,428	−10	2	4,424	75	21	48,004	−14	1
Switzerland	4,415	12	8	897	16	−25	3,518	11	22
United Kingdom	3,993	14	22	140	−30	−66	3,853	17	35
Yugoslavia	15,232	9	−13	3,996	3	−47	11,236	11	13
USSR	**355,700**	**−9**	**−6**	**81,300**	**−2**	**−15**	**274,400**	**−10**	**−3**
OCEANIA	**34,517**	**17**	**40**	**8,382**	**26**	**36**	**26,483**	**15**	**44**
Australia	17,162	23	33	2,472	83	65	14,690	17	28
Fiji	202	22	81	23	156	60	180	15	85
New Zealand	9,547	5	38	50	−80	−90	9,497	8	48
Papua New Guinea	6,910	17	61	5,533	16	41	1,724	52	365
Solomon Islands	512	20	119	210	12	39	302	26	265

Source: U.N. Food and Agriculture Organization.
0 = zero or less than half of 1 percent; X = not available.
For additional information, see Sources and Technical Notes.

Table 20.3 Trade in Forest Products, 1966–84

	Average Annual Trade (thousand cubic meters)											
	Roundwood						Sawnwood					
	Imports			Exports			Imports			Exports		
	1966-68	1974-76	1982-84	1966-68	1974-76	1982-84	1966-68	1974-76	1982-84	1966-68	1974-76	1982-84
WORLD	68,223	108,304	106,308	68,845	109,223	103,290	49,877	59,940	77,571	51,056	60,974	81,333
AFRICA	544	560	901	6,354	6,278	5,293	1,552	2,328	4,272	909	1,010	761
Algeria	27	63	237	0	0	0	175	454	1,084	0	0	0
Angola	0	0	0	129	42	0	2	0	0	23	12	0
Cameroon	0	0	0	310	573	627	0	0	0	35	114	118
Central African Rep	0	0	0	14	114	85	0	0	0	9	41	37
Congo	0	0	0	543	183	213	0	0	10	6	19	27
Cote d'Ivoire	1	0	0	2,205	2,909	2,242	0	0	0	184	265	347
Egypt	60	78	264	0	0	0	339	475	1,711	0	0	0
Equatorial Guinea	0	0	0	436	18	71	0	0	0	11	1	3
Gabon	0	0	0	1,224	1,218	1,276	0	0	0	25	5	7
Ghana	0	0	0	517	406	63	0	0	0	203	158	47
Kenya	0	0	0	160	83	10	11	4	0	23	15	3
Liberia	1	0	0	29	331	212	2	0	11	0	11	12
Libya	59	40	74	0	0	0	126	324	200	0	0	0
Morocco	145	222	144	0	0	0	143	271	425	0	0	0
Mozambique	4	0	0	2	6	3	11	2	0	151	158	3
Nigeria	0	4	0	402	128	10	0	0	0	62	14	2
Somalia	0	10	0	159	0	0	0	10	1	0	0	0
South Africa	96	56	34	21	30	119	372	434	326	16	13	33
Sudan	1	0	0	0	0	0	67	39	80	0	0	0
Swaziland	0	5	72	79	190	271	0	2	0	28	89	76
Tunisia	21	49	28	41	0	0	83	158	284	0	0	0
Uganda	100	2	0	0	0	0	9	0	0	7	2	0
Zaire	0	0	0	66	37	75	0	1	0	34	25	23
Zambia	5	4	9	0	0	0	59	35	6	17	0	0
NORTH & CENTRAL AMERICA	6,257	6,014	6,432	16,408	22,717	24,798	14,322	19,531	29,736	19,012	24,203	38,634
Barbados	4	4	1	0	0	0	27	39	40	0	0	0
Canada	1,972	3,294	3,378	5,419	2,879	4,775	704	1,490	1,266	15,834	19,337	33,213
Cuba	0	5	0	0	0	0	311	567	451	0	0	0
Dominican Rep	0	0	41	1	0	0	38	278	86	0	0	0
El Salvador	1	1	0	0	0	0	70	39	5	3	0	0
Honduras	0	0	0	18	17	9	1	0	0	451	477	295
Jamaica	11	14	1	0	2	0	83	115	77	0	0	0
Mexico	32	15	29	9	14	12	77	163	282	18	11	21
Nicaragua	3	3	0	6	4	0	0	0	0	40	94	8
Trinidad and Tobago	2	1	9	0	0	0	42	26	201	2	1	0
United States	4,223	2,656	2,955	10,588	19,662	19,988	12,850	16,687	27,178	2,640	4,221	5,077
SOUTH AMERICA	309	151	152	462	150	1,031	902	719	848	1,539	1,167	1,719
Argentina	231	11	11	4	0	3	755	422	289	1	0	1
Brazil	0	81	30	85	58	33	1	113	317	1,260	550	544
Chile	3	6	0	0	8	941	0	0	0	73	250	753
Colombia	0	0	0	57	13	0	1	0	1	69	32	2
Paraguay	0	0	0	246	2	0	1	0	0	36	150	317
Peru	8	11	1	0	0	0	84	37	23	4	7	7
Uruguay	37	15	0	0	0	0	48	25	23	1	0	0
Venezuela	1	13	109	1	0	0	8	121	194	0	0	0
ASIA	33,705	63,384	60,375	18,697	36,137	24,977	3,299	6,425	9,965	2,069	4,880	7,232
Bahrain	4	18	79	0	0	0	15	44	48	2	0	0
Burma	0	0	0	75	70	108	0	0	0	106	92	103
China	1,380	4,730	9,456	56	64	77	0	24	422	10	161	67
Cyprus	4	3	6	0	0	0	36	18	58	0	3	1
India	32	10	33	19	50	22	14	2	17	1	10	0
Indonesia	0	36	0	799	17,529	3,221	1	1	0	8	443	1,747
Iran	35	123	118	11	0	0	87	173	285	0	0	0
Iraq	94	35	6	0	0	0	51	293	357	0	0	0
Israel	118	145	150	0	0	0	228	414	294	0	0	0
Japan	28,077	50,377	41,994	34	19	39	1,911	3,174	4,762	253	56	35
Jordan	17	1	3	0	0	0	53	48	82	0	0	0
Kampuchea, Dem	0	0	0	82	6	6	0	0	0	8	0	0
Korea, Rep	2,009	5,465	6,042	0	0	0	20	111	12	1	228	151
Kuwait	80	84	40	19	17	17	116	145	104	1	27	57
Lebanon	72	42	31	6	0	0	130	204	67	0	2	5
Malaysia	99	282	386	9,408	13,737	18,962	24	122	84	926	2,407	3,377
Mongolia	0	0	0	0	94	65	0	0	0	0	67	83
Nepal	0	0	0	174	168	126	0	0	0	0	5	0
Pakistan	28	35	23	0	0	0	207	38	140	0	0	0
Philippines	0	1	3	7,643	4,014	1,453	0	0	0	123	344	620
Saudi Arabia	4	70	238	0	0	0	47	341	1,304	0	0	0
Singapore	1,540	1,304	614	41	44	172	177	808	1,039	538	886	852
Sri Lanka	2	0	0	88	1	184	7	1	6	0	0	0
Syrian Arab Rep	25	28	76	6	3	9	102	142	131	1	6	0
Thailand	5	12	243	226	265	413	27	197	372	48	80	2
Turkey	59	46	2	11	14	73	0	2	11	8	27	61
Viet Nam	16	22	41	0	0	0	3	19	30	0	0	0
Yemen, Dem	0	1	5	0	1	1	43	17	29	9	0	0

Table 20.3

	Average Annual Trade (thousand cubic meters)											
	Roundwood						Sawnwood					
	Imports			Exports			Imports			Exports		
	1966-68	1974-76	1982-84	1966-68	1974-76	1982-84	1966-68	1974-76	1982-84	1966-68	1974-76	1982-84
EUROPE	**26,691**	**37,854**	**38,213**	**12,696**	**20,282**	**22,265**	**28,545**	**29,457**	**31,326**	**19,174**	**21,167**	**25,162**
Austria	1,003	2,893	3,385	435	735	727	53	231	760	2,903	3,329	3,982
Belgium	1,226	2,854	3,609	407	422	996	1,032	1,295	1,316	84	142	300
Bulgaria	310	381	359	68	41	4	126	212	163	67	44	20
Czechoslovakia	76	94	78	1,315	2,462	2,317	167	190	134	712	801	1,149
Denmark	182	221	178	274	437	1,306	1,063	1,265	1,285	105	92	222
Finland	2,895	5,421	6,551	754	635	975	14	21	26	3,744	3,677	4,784
France	2,422	3,027	2,145	2,138	3,040	3,634	1,710	2,211	2,297	715	896	793
German Dem Rep	1,006	901	827	9	434	192	1,407	1,629	1,355	91	53	13
Germany, Fed Rep	3,707	3,180	3,312	995	4,121	3,061	3,331	3,214	4,573	433	1,082	946
Greece	170	280	190	0	1	0	496	364	364	0	6	7
Hungary	1,822	1,800	1,202	280	839	990	987	1,104	739	194	275	110
Iceland	4	8	7	0	0	0	53	57	68	0	0	0
Ireland	30	40	30	0	28	433	345	408	347	3	8	73
Italy	4,405	5,983	5,178	27	14	12	3,641	4,183	4,927	22	55	84
Netherlands	1,163	1,099	808	334	716	621	2,707	2,932	2,789	28	111	251
Norway	2,917	2,223	1,583	252	310	707	297	289	520	75	368	422
Poland	211	153	175	447	1,139	1,449	205	241	181	791	650	529
Portugal	120	342	368	80	185	357	32	23	23	379	489	991
Romania	4	201	130	991	460	204	0	0	62	2,274	1,308	1,174
Spain	448	1,228	970	62	135	646	806	1,244	958	27	85	271
Sweden	596	2,773	4,669	2,803	2,287	1,838	175	195	141	5,655	6,470	8,012
Switzerland	545	806	819	408	834	691	367	278	566	72	134	99
United Kingdom	1,130	571	417	15	52	515	9,450	7,626	7,524	4	48	55
Yugoslavia	300	1,376	1,225	603	956	591	60	228	181	798	1,043	877
USSR	**42**	**264**	**225**	**13,057**	**18,639**	**16,287**	**284**	**325**	**312**	**8,034**	**8,214**	**7,299**
OCEANIA	**133**	**78**	**10**	**1,145**	**5,021**	**8,639**	**906**	**1,156**	**1,112**	**206**	**334**	**525**
Australia	116	65	2	27	2,895	5,896	787	1,068	1,012	60	65	45
New Zealand	17	12	4	925	1,337	1,174	62	41	28	128	215	440
Papua New Guinea	0	0	0	107	568	1,281	2	0	0	13	43	21
Solomon Islands	0	0	0	79	220	283	0	0	0	0	1	8

Source: U.N. Food and Agriculture Organization.
0 = zero or less than one-half the unit of measure; X = not available.
For additional information, see Sources and Technical Notes.

Table 20.4 Extent of Desertification, Early 1980s

	Total Productive Drylands		Productive Dryland Types							
			Rangelands		Rainfed Croplands		Irrigated Lands			
	Area (million hectares)	Percent Desertified	Area (million hectares)	Percent Desertified	Area (million hectares)	Percent Desertified	Area (million hectares)	Percent Desertified		
Total	**3,257**	**61**	**2,556**	**62**	**570**	**60**	**131**	**30**		
Sudano-Sahelian Africa	473	88	380	90	90	80	3	30		
Southern Africa	304	80	250	80	52	80	2	30		
Mediterranean Africa	101	83	80	85	20	75	1	40		
Western Asia	142	82	116	85	18	85	8	40		
Southern Asia	359	70	150	85	150	70	59	35		
USSR in Asia	298	55	250	60	40	30	8	25		
China and Mongolia	315	69	300	70	5	60	10	30		
Australia	491	23	450	22	39	30	2	19		
Mediterranean Europe	76	39	30	30	40	32	6	25		
South America and Mexico	293	71	250	72	31	77	12	33		
North America	405	40	300	42	85	39	20	20		

Source: U.N. Environment Programme.
For additional information, see Sources and Technical Notes.

Sources and Technical Notes

Table 20.1 Forest Resources, 1980s

Sources: J.P. Lanly, Forest Resources Division, United Nations Food and Agriculture Organization (FAO), 1986 (personal communication); FAO, *Forest Resources 1980* (FAO, Rome, 1985); FAO and United Nations Environment Programme (UNEP), *Tropical Forest Resources Assessment Project* (FAO, Rome, 1981); FAO and United Nations Economic Commission for Europe (ECE), *The Forest Resources of the ECE Region* (ECE, Geneva, 1985). Reforestation data for China: State Statistical Bureau, *China: A Statistics Survey in 1985* (New World Press, Beijing, 1985); Reforestation data for Jordan: Library of Congress, Science and Technology Division, *Draft Environmental Report on Jordan* (Library of Congress,

Washington, D.C., August 1979); Reforestation data for Yugoslavia: Socijalisticka Federativna Republika Jugoslavija Savenzi Zavod Za Statistiku, *Statisticki Godisnjak Jugoslavija 1983, 1984, 1985* (Savenzi Zavod Za Statistiku, Belgrade, 1984, 1985, 1986).

The forests and open woodland referred to in Table 20.1 are natural stands of woody vegetation in which trees predominate. In this definition, "natural" means all stands except

Forests and Rangelands

plantations and includes stands that have been degraded to some degree by catastrophic fire, logging, or agriculture. Trees are distinguished from shrubs on the basis of height: a mature tree has a single well-defined stem and is taller than seven meters, and a mature shrub is usually less than seven meters tall.

In this table, deforestation refers to the clearing of closed forest lands and its subsequent use for permanent agriculture or settlements. Other alterations not included here, such as selective logging and slash-and-burn agriculture, can substantially affect forests, forest soil, wildlife and its habitat, and the global carbon cycle. Tropical deforestation is analyzed using a broader definition in Norman Myers, *The Primary Source* (Norton, New York, 1984).

Reforestation refers to the establishment of plantations for industrial and nonindustrial uses. Plantations are formed in two ways: by *afforestation*, forest stands established artificially on land that was previously unforested, and by *reafforestation*, forest stands established artificially on land that was forested within the past 50 years (or within living memory) in which the previous crop has been replaced by a new and essentially different crop. Reforestation does not include regeneration of old crops (through either natural regeneration or forest management), although some countries may have reported regeneration as reforestation. Reforestation data for China, Jordan, and Yugoslavia are official national estimates, and they include afforestation and reafforestation. For all countries, large amounts of tree planting are undertaken for nonindustrial uses, such as village wood lots; reforestation data often exclude this component.

The FAO/UNEP assessment surveyed the moist tropical forests of 76 countries. Data for the study were collected from research institutes; correspondence with the forestry services of most of the countries; visits to national forestry, land use, and survey institutions in some of the major forestry countries and to FAO regional offices; photographic surveys of all or part of five countries; satellite imagery of all or part of 19 countries; and side-looking airborne radar surveys of four additional countries. Three countries (Burma, India, and Peru) prepared their own national reports. In many cases, FAO adjusted data to fit common definitions and to correspond to a base year of 1980.

The FAO/UNEP statistics were selected because of their international coverage, relative timeliness, and extensive documentation. Even so, their quality varies considerably among the countries. Deforestation estimates are considered reliable by FAO for 33 of the 56 countries for which data collection procedures were documented.

The FAO/ECE survey covered all types of forests in the 32 member countries of the ECE. Data for this study were drawn from four types of sources: official data supplied in response to questionnaires, estimates by experts in some countries, recent ECE and FAO publications, country reports, and official articles and estimates by the professional staff conducting the study. Most data refer to the period around 1980, but no attempt was made to adjust the data to a common baseline year.

For an evaluation and detailed comparison of forest statistics, see Alan Grainger, "Quantifying Changes in Forest Cover in the Humid Tropics: Overcoming Current Limitations," *Journal of World Forest Resource Management*, Vol. 1 (1984), pp. 3–23; and J.M. Melillo, *et al.*, "A Comparison of Two Recent Estimates of Disturbance in Tropical Forests," *Environmental Conservation*, Vol. 12, No. 1 (1985).

Table 20.2 Wood Production, 1966–84

Sources: United Nations Food and Agriculture Organization (FAO), *Yearbook of Forest Products 1984* (FAO, Rome, 1986); and P.A. Wardle, Forestry Department, FAO, 1986 (personal communication).

Total roundwood refers to all wood in the rough, whether destined for industrial uses or for use as fuelwood.

Fuelwood includes all rough wood used for cooking, heating, and power production. Wood intended for charcoal production, pit kilns, and portable ovens is included.

Industrial roundwood refers to all round-wood products other than fuelwood and charcoal: sawlogs, veneer logs, sleepers, pitprops, pulpwood, and other industrial products.

FAO compiles forest products data from responses to annual questionnaires sent to national governments. Data from other sources, such as national statistical yearbooks, are also used, and in some cases FAO prepares its own estimates. FAO continuously revises its data using new information; the latest figures are subject to revision.

Statistics on the production of fuelwood and charcoal are lacking for many countries. FAO uses population data and country-specific per capita consumption figures to estimate fuelwood and charcoal production for these countries. Consumption of nonconiferous fuelwood ranges from 0.0016 cubic meters per capita per year in Jordan to 0.9783 cubic meters per capita per year in Benin. Consumption was also estimated for coniferous fuelwood. For both coniferous and nonconiferous fuelwood, the per capita consumption estimates were multiplied by the number of people in the country to determine national totals.

Table 20.3 Trade in Forest Products, 1966–84

Source: P.A. Wardle, Forestry Department, United Nations Food and Agriculture Organization (FAO) 1986 (personal communication).

Trade in roundwood includes sawlogs and veneer logs, fuelwood, pulpwood, other industrial roundwood, and the roundwood equivalent of trade in charcoal, wood residues, and chips and particles.

Trade in sawnwood includes sawnwood and sleepers. This category comprises wood that has been sawn, planed, or shaped into products such as planks, beams, boards, rafters, and railroad ties. With few exceptions, sawnwood is thicker than five millimeters.

Countries shown comprise 99 percent of all roundwood trade. Regional and world totals include countries not shown in the table.

All trade data refer to both coniferous and nonconiferous wood.

Imports are usually on a cost, insurance, freight basis. Exports are usually on a free-on-board basis.

FAO compiles wood trade data from responses to annual questionnaires sent to national governments. Additional data are drawn from national statistical yearbooks, trade yearbooks, and trading partner sources. FAO continuously revises its data using new information; the latest figures are subject to revision.

For further details, refer to FAO, *Yearbook of Forest Products 1984* (FAO, Rome, 1986).

Table 20.4 Extent of Desertification, Early 1980s

Source: Mabbutt, J.A., "A New Global Assessment of the Status and Trends of Desertification," *Environmental Conservation*, Vol. 11, No. 2, p. 106 (1984).

Desertification, the diminution or destruction of the biological productivity of the land, can lead ultimately to desert-like conditions. For this table, the definition was applied only to the world's drylands: hyperarid, arid, semiarid, and subhumid zones of low and variable rainfall. These regions are inherently vulnerable to water stress and droughts, and they are particularly vulnerable to deterioration resulting from unsustainable human use of the land.

Desertification is generally associated with a sequence of interactive processes: impoverishment of and reduction in vegetative cover; exposure of the soil surface to accelerated wind and water erosion; reduction of the soil's organic matter and nutrient content; and deterioration of the structure, moisture-holding capacity, and fertility of the soil.

The principal indicators used to assess desertification include deterioration of rangeland, deterioration of rainfed croplands, waterlogging and salinization of irrigated lands, deforestation and destruction of woody vegetation, decline in availability and the quality of surface and groundwater, and encroachment and growth of sand sheets and dunes.

Moderate desertification generally implies a loss of productivity of less than 25 percent, severe desertification causes a loss of productivity of 25–50 percent, and very severe desertification causes a loss of productivity of over 50 percent. The "percent desertified" used in this table is the fraction of the productive land type that is moderately to very severely desertified.

Data for this table were compiled from many sources, and they involve extrapolation from partial data. More than 100 countries affected by desertification received questionnaires from the United Nations Environment Programme (UNEP) requesting information on land use patterns, the status and trends of desertification, and actions taken to combat desertification. Twenty-five countries submitted extensive reports updating earlier studies conducted for the United Nations Conference on Desertification (UNCOD, 1977). (For additional information on the UNCOD, refer to Chapter 5, "Forests and Rangelands.") Regional assessments were prepared by U.N. regional commissions (including the U.N. Sudano-Sahelian office). Other published and unpublished works by the United Nations Educational, Scientific and Cultural Organization, the World Meteorological Organization, the United Nations Food and Agriculture Organization, UNEP, and others were used. Refer to these sources for further details on data and methods.

21. Wildlife and Habitat

Wildlife resources in many countries are under pressure as habitats are degraded by human encroachment. This chapter presents data on national and international efforts to protect natural ecosystems and on the number of vertebrate species threatened with extinction.

Three international networks of protected areas—Biosphere Reserves, Natural World Heritage Sites, and Wetlands of International Importance—include natural sites judged to be of worldwide importance. (See Table 21.1.) Biosphere Reserves are terrestrial and coastal environments that have been internationally recognized for conservation and research on the interactions between humans and the environment. A major goal of the Biosphere Reserve program (managed by the United Nations Educational, Scientific and Cultural Organization [UNESCO]) is to establish a network of representative samples of the world's biogeographical provinces. Each province is a geographic area characterized by distinctive groups of flora and fauna. As of October 1986, 261 Biosphere Reserves had been established in 70 countries, covering about half the provinces.

World Heritage Sites are natural or cultural sites of "outstanding universal value" identified by individual countries and recognized by the members of UNESCO. Sixty-nine "natural sites" in 32 countries have been established. The 42 countries party to the Convention on Wetlands of International Importance Especially as Waterfowl Habitat (Ramsar, Iran, 1971) have designated wetland sites that are of global importance. These sites, as well as other wetlands, are essential habitat for a variety of plants and animals. (See Chapter 18, "Land Use and Cover," Table 18.2.)

Countries choose sites for inclusion in international protection systems from those sites already protected by national law. Therefore, the sites protected in national and international systems cannot be added together to arrive at a global total of protected areas; many sites would be double-counted. The number and area of nationally protected sites are not the same in Tables 21.1 and 21.2 because more recent, unpublished data were used in Table 21.1.

Table 21.2 presents data on nationally protected sites classified by biogeographical realm and province. By organizing the world's protected sites in a biogeographical framework, resource managers are able to identify which provinces are adequately or inadequately represented in the protected area system. Most of the world's 193 biogeographical provinces are protected to some extent;

however, in 1985, 15 had no protected sites, and 36 others had less than 100,000 hectares protected.

The total area of each province has not been measured, so the fraction that is protected cannot be determined. Because the provinces vary greatly in size, the total area of the protected sites does not indicate how well a province is protected.

Provinces are useful units for identifying gaps in protected area coverage globally, but finer distinctions are required to ensure adequate protection of ecosystems and species at the national level. Because many biogeographical provinces encompass a wide range of biotic communities, a protected site within a given province may not adequately protect the diversity of species found there.

Assessing the *quality* of protection is difficult. Sites officially designated as "protected" by national authorities may not be well protected or managed in fact. Management goals and enforcement practices vary widely within and among countries, and many protected sites are being encroached upon by settlements and polluted by industry.

Species may be threatened with extinction throughout their international range ("globally threatened") or within the borders of a country ("nationally threatened"). Table 21.3 refers to nationally threatened species; Table 21.4 refers to globally threatened species. Although species that are threatened in one country may be abundant in another, many countries try to ensure the continued survival (within their national boundaries) of all endemic species. Some threatened species are endemic to a single country; they are listed as both globally and nationally threatened.

In general, data on the number and status of mammal and bird species are better than those for lower vertebrates; information on invertebrate and plant species is limited, and data for these groups are not included in Tables 21.3 and 21.4.

Data on threats to wildlife and habitat are essential for evaluating the long-term viability of species and natural areas. However, information is lacking on the extent, rate, and impact of habitat destruction, and data on the impacts of pesticides and other chemicals are similarly limited. The economic value of wildlife to indigenous people, necessary for understanding the complex interactions between people and their land, is largely unquantified. Some information is available on the economic value of wildlife in commercial enterprises (trade, tourism, ranching, cropping, etc.). (See Chapter 6, "Wildlife and Habitat.")

Table 21.1 National and International Protection of Natural Areas, 1986

| | National Protection Systems | | International Protection Systems | | | | |
| | | | Biosphere Reserves | | Natural World Heritage Sites | Wetlands of International Importance | |
	Number of Sites	Area (hectares)	Number of Sites	Area (hectares)	Number of Sites	Number of Sites	Area (hectares)
WORLD	**3,514**	**423,774,398**	**261**	**138,917,074**	**69**	**353**	**20,059,723**
AFRICA	**443**	**88,662,296**	**39**	**19,857,799**	**19**	**18**	**1,311,298**
Algeria	5	226,500	1	7,200,000	1	2	8,400
Angola	5	1,517,700	0	0	—	—	—
Benin	2	843,500	1	880,000	0	—	—
Botswana	8	11,644,000	0	0	—	—	—
Burkina Faso	6	682,900	1	16,300	—	—	—
Burundi	0	0	0	0	0	—	—
Cameroon	15	2,228,200	3	850,000	0	—	—
Cape Verde	0	0	0	0	—	—	—
Central African Rep	7	3,904,000	2	1,640,200	0	—	—
Chad	1	114,000	0	0	—	—	—
Comoros	0	0	0	0	—	—	—
Congo	10	1,353,100	1	110,000	—	—	—
Cote d'Ivoire	10	1,865,000	2	1,480,000	3	—	—
Djibouti	0	0	0	0	—	—	—
Egypt	1	17,094	1	1,000	0	—	—
Equatorial Guinea	0	0	0	0	—	—	—
Ethiopia	10	3,027,500	0	0	1	—	—
Gabon	5	1,673,000	1	15,000	—	—	—
Gambia	0	0	0	0	—	—	—
Ghana	8	1,175,075	1	7,770	0	—	—
Guinea	1	13,000	2	133,300	1	—	—
Guinea-Bissau	0	0	0	0	—	—	—
Kenya	28	3,105,307	4	851,359	—	—	—
Lesotho	1	6,805	0	0	—	—	—
Liberia	1	130,700	0	0	—	—	—
Libya	2	130,000	0	0	0	—	—
Madagascar	14	674,662	0	0	0	—	—
Malawi	9	1,081,485	0	0	1	—	—
Mali	6	876,100	1	771,000	0	—	—
Mauritania	2	1,483,000	0	0	0	1	1,173,000
Mauritius	3	4,033	1	3,594	—	—	—
Morocco	2	41,000	0	0	0	4	10,580
Mozambique	6	1,815,000	0	0	0	—	—
Niger	3	372,000	0	0	0	—	—
Nigeria	3	868,082	1	460	0	—	—
Rwanda	2	262,000	1	15,065	—	—	—
Senegal	9	2,176,700	3	1,093,756	2	4	96,750
Sierra Leone	1	98,000	0	0	—	—	—
Somalia	1	334,000	0	0	—	—	—
South Africa	149	5,689,179	0	0	—	6	9,968[a]
Sudan	3	1,915,670	2	1,900,970	0	—	—
Swaziland	4	40,045	0	0	—	—	—
Tanzania, United Rep	15	10,601,775	2	2,337,900	3	—	—
Togo	7	472,550	0	0	—	—	—
Tunisia	3	33,033	4	32,425	1	1	12,600
Uganda	18	1,332,029	1	220,000	—	—	—
Zaire	9	8,827,000	3	297,700	4	—	—
Zambia	19	6,664,400	0	0	0	—	—
Zimbabwe	17	2,757,709	0	0	1	—	—
NORTH & CENTRAL AMERICA	**423**	**161,860,486**	**57**	**85,638,399**	**18**	**22**	**10,778,405**
Barbados	0	0	0	0	—	—	—
Canada	78	22,949,135	4	382,738	5	17	10,380,014
Costa Rica	21	412,469	1	500,000	1	—	—
Cuba	4	24,305	1	10,000	0	—	—
Dominican Rep	5	219,800	0	0	0	—	—
El Salvador	0	0	0	0	—	—	—
Guatemala	2	59,600	0	0	1	—	—
Haiti	2	5,000	0	0	0	—	—
Honduras	4	422,571	1	500,000	1	—	—
Jamaica	0	0	0	0	0	—	—
Mexico	29	938,448	5	1,145,877	0	1	47,480
Nicaragua	2	17,300	0	0	0	—	—
Panama	6	660,902	1	597,000	1	—	—
Trinidad and Tobago	8	16,523	0	0	—	—	—
United States	251	64,946,135	43	12,502,784	10	4	350,911
SOUTH AMERICA	**267**	**50,059,743**	**22**	**11,031,277**	**7**	**3**	**216,877**
Argentina	29	2,594,351	4	2,005,180	2	—	—
Bolivia	12	4,707,690	3	435,000	0	—	—
Brazil	50	11,894,302	0	0	1	—	—
Chile	64	12,737,360	7	2,603,469	0	1	4,877
Colombia	30	3,958,750	3	2,514,375	0	—	—
Ecuador	12	2,627,365	1	766,514	2	—	—
Guyana	1	11,655	0	0	0	—	—
Paraguay	9	1,120,538	0	0	—	—	—
Peru	11	2,407,642	3	2,506,739	2	—	—
Suriname	9	582,400	0	0	—	1	12,000
Uruguay	6	28,778	1	200,000	—	1	200,000
Venezuela	34	7,388,912	0	0	—	—	—

Table 21.1

	National Protection Systems		International Protection Systems					
			Biosphere Reserves		Natural World Heritage Sites	Wetlands of International Importance		
	Number of Sites	Area (hectares)	Number of Sites	Area (hectares)	Number of Sites	Number of Sites	Area (hectares)
ASIA	**790**	**52,413,945**	**31**	**4,640,171**	**6**	**32**	**1,450,883**
Afghanistan	0	0	0	0	0	—	—
Bahrain	0	0	0	0	—	—	—
Bangladesh	3	32,386	0	0	0	—	—
Bhutan	11	950,000	0	0	—	—	—
Burma	0	0	0	0	—	—	—
China	63	2,306,237	4	467,178	0	—	—
Cyprus	0	0	0	0	0	—	—
India	239	11,149,261	0	0	3	2	119,400
Indonesia	140	13,755,239	6	1,319,440	—	—	—
Iran	24	3,055,696	9	2,609,731	0	18	1,297,550
Iraq	0	0	0	0	0	—	—
Israel	5	33,996	0	0	—	—	—
Japan	50	2,195,600	4	116,000	—	2	5,571
Jordan	2	34,300	0	0	0	1	7,372
Kampuchea, Dem	1	10,717	0	0	—	—	—
Korea, Dem People's Rep	0	0	0	0	—	—	—
Korea, Rep	14	475,788	1	37,430	—	—	—
Kuwait	0	0	0	0	—	—	—
Lao People's Dem Rep	0	0	0	0	—	—	—
Lebanon	0	0	0	0	0	—	—
Malaysia	34	1,558,882	0	0	—	—	—
Mongolia	4	4,672,580	0	0	—	—	—
Nepal	10	974,470	0	0	2	—	—
Oman	1	20,000	0	0	0	—	—
Pakistan	52	6,537,311	1	31,355	0	9	20,990
Philippines	26	390,932	1	23,525	0	—	—
Qatar	0	0	0	0	0	—	—
Saudi Arabia	1	450,000	0	0	0	—	—
Singapore	1	2,434	0	0	—	—	—
Sri Lanka	37	642,665	2	9,412	0	—	—
Syrian Arab Rep	0	0	0	0	0	—	—
Thailand	45	2,720,533	3	26,100	—	—	—
Turkey	15	286,850	0	0	1	—	—
United Arab Emirates	0	0	0	0	—	—	—
Viet Nam	12	158,068	0	0	—	—	—
Yemen	0	0	0	0	0	—	—
Yemen, Dem	0	0	0	0	0	—	—
EUROPE	**704**	**17,239,198**	**81**	**3,763,790**	**11**	**237**	**2,113,180**
Albania	4	10,000	0	0	—	—	—
Austria	27	297,007	4	27,600	—	5	102,369
Belgium	4	11,720	0	0	—	6	7,635
Bulgaria	12	56,037	17	27,602	2	4	2,097
Czechoslovakia	28	1,157,022	4	176,909	—	—	—
Denmark	23	125,709	0	0	0	26	593,372
Finland	33	803,400	0	0	—	11	101,343
France	37	1,654,878	4	344,527	1	—	—
German Dem Rep	13	20,881	2	18,884	—	8	49,600
Germany, Fed Rep	45	531,213	1	13,100	0	20	314,315
Greece	14	63,105	2	8,840	0	11	78,600
Hungary	36	420,610	5	128,883	0	8	29,450
Iceland	21	789,420	0	0	—	1	20,000
Ireland	3	20,404	2	8,808	—	5	9,829
Italy	34	516,704	3	3,798	0	40	51,476
Luxembourg	4	114,350	0	0	0	—	—
Malta	0	0	0	0	0	—	—
Netherlands	50	164,314	1	260,000	—	13	263,185
Norway	61	4,716,628	1	1,555,000	0	14	17,545
Poland	15	113,015	4	25,576	1	5	7,090
Portugal	12	381,075	1	395	0	2	30,563
Romania	9	98,255	3	41,213	—	—	—
Spain	56	1,700,659	10	614,977	1	3	52,392
Sweden	67	1,463,146	1	96,500	0	20	271,075
Switzerland	19	120,989	1	16,870	0	2	1,816
United Kingdom	57	1,552,567	13	44,308	2	31	91,334
Yugoslavia	20	336,090	2	350,000	4	2	18,094
USSR	**141**	**15,111,283**	**19**	**9,242,965**	**—**	**12**	**2,880,100**
OCEANIA	**739**	**38,232,488**	**12**	**4,742,673**	**8**	**29**	**1,308,980**
Australia	581	35,413,712	12	4,742,673	6	27	1,294,173
Fiji	2	5,342	0	0	—	—	—
New Zealand	147	2,787,392	0	0	2	2	14,807
Papua New Guinea	2	3,143	0	0	—	—	—
Solomon Islands	0	0	0	0	—	—	—

Sources: International Union for Conservation of Nature and Natural Resources; and United Nations Educational, Scientific and Cultural Organization.
0 = zero; — = country not a full party to the convention.
For additional information, see Sources and Technical Notes.
Note: a. Area for two of the six sites.

Table 21.2 Protected Areas Classified by Biogeographical Realm

Vegetation Type/Province	Protected Areas	
	Number of Sites	Area Protected (hectares)
WORLD	**3,382**	**415,907,820**
NEARCTIC REALM	**329**	**158,212,645**
Temperate Rainforests		
Sitkan	12	3,869,827
Oregonian	6	380,344
Temperate Needleleaf Forests		
Yukon Taiga	12	21,010,636
Canadian Taiga	41	9,311,043
Temperate Broadleaf Forests		
Eastern Forest	39	1,155,364
Austroriparian	43	734,852
Evergreen Sclerophyllous Forests		
Californian	6	52,010
Warm Deserts/Semi-deserts		
Sonoran	11	3,464,499
Chihuahuan	10	493,332
Tamaulipan	1	5,117
Cold-winter Deserts		
Great Basin	15	657,128
Tundra Communities		
Aleutian Islands	7	7,025,370
Alaskan Tundra	9	25,292,471
Canadian Tundra	2	4,557,110
Arctic Archipelago	0	0
Greenland Tundra	0	0
Arctic Desert and Icecap	2	71,050,000
Grasslands	25	387,751
Mixed Mountain Systems		
Rocky Mountains	46	6,783,793
Sierra-Cascade	16	1,251,492
Madrean-Cordilleran	19	285,793
Lake Systems		
Great Lakes	7	444,713
PALEARCTIC REALM	**1,027**	**52,878,456**
Temperate Rainforests		
Chinese Subtropical Forest	10	312,509
Japanese Evergreen Forest	38	1,430,485
Temperate Needleleaf Forests		
West Eurasian Taiga	106	5,061,090
East Siberian Taiga	16	3,402,600
Temperate Broadleaf Forests		
Icelandian	22	791,431
Subarctic Birchwoods	14	258,590
Kamchatkan	1	964,000
British Islands	34	1,463,117
Atlantic	96	1,063,740
Boreonemoral	55	743,047
Middle European Forest	97	1,232,282
Pannonian	22	245,056
West Anatolian	1	11,338
Manchu-Japanese Mixed Forest	22	1,480,074
Oriental Deciduous Forest	36	1,378,671
Evergreen Sclerophyllous Forests		
Iberian Highlands	42	1,835,557
Mediterranean Sclerophyll	80	1,538,599
Warm Deserts/Semi-deserts		
Sahara	2	117,094
Arabian Desert	5	499,440
Cold-winter Deserts		
Anatolian-Iranian Desert	32	5,499,190
Turanian	13	1,170,858
Takla-Makan-Gobi Desert	2	4,507,850
Tibetan	1	266,913
Iranian Desert	9	1,409,356
Tundra Communities		
Arctic Desert	5	3,491,000
Higharctic Tundra	1	795,650
Lowarctic Tundra	2	2,961,254
Temperate Grasslands		
Atlas Steppe	3	51,775
Pontian Steppe	16	581,053
Mongolian-Manchurian Steppe	3	172,580
Mixed Mountain Systems		
Scottish Highlands	20	81,723
Central European Highlands	105	2,037,182
Balkan Highlands	32	390,241
Caucaso-Iranian Highlands	42	2,236,152
Altai Highlands	2	935,093
Pamir-Tian-Shan Highlands	17	616,490
Hindu Kush Highlands	1	14,786
Himalayan Highlands	10	1,708,148
Szechwan Highlands	2	52,000
Mixed Island Systems		
Macaronesian Islands	7	48,095
Ryukyu Islands	2	4,047
Lake Systems		
Lake Ladoga	0	0
Aral Sea	1	18,300
Lake Baikal	0	0

Vegetation Type/Province	Protected Areas	
	Number of Sites	Area Protected (hectares)
AFROTROPICAL REALM	**426**	**88,166,096**
Tropical Humid Forests		
Guinean Rainforest	15	907,720
Congo Rainforest	23	7,754,775
Malagasy Rainforest	6	243,238
Tropical Dry Forests		
West African Woodland/Savanna	53	13,543,787
East African Woodland/Savanna	36	7,873,091
Congo Woodland/Savanna	5	2,990,700
Miombo Woodland/Savanna	33	13,396,995
South African Woodland/Savanna	105	10,437,555
Malagasy Woodland/Savanna	7	388,224
Malagasy Thorn Forest	1	43,200
Evergreen Sclerophyllous Forests		
Cape Sclerophyll	41	1,620,967
Warm Deserts/Semi-deserts		
Western Sahel	7	1,726,000
Eastern Sahel	2	1,719,700
Somalian	18	4,142,182
Namib	7	6,768,070
Kalahari	8	9,282,803
Karroo	15	144,330
Mixed Mountain Systems		
Ethiopian Highlands	5	636,000
Guinean Highlands	2	335,625
Central African Highlands	9	3,622,985
East African Highlands	9	431,108
South African Highlands	13	78,908
Evergreen Sclerophyllous Forests		
Ascension and St. Helena Islands	0	0
Comoros Islands and Aldabra	1	19,000
Mascarene Islands	3	4,033
Lake Systems		
Lake Rudolf	0	0
Lake Ukerewe (Victoria)	1	45,700
Lake Tanganyika	0	0
Lake Malawi (Nyasa)	1	9,400
INDOMALAYAN REALM	**572**	**27,568,406**
Tropical Humid Forests		
Malabar Rainforest	30	1,303,273
Ceylonese Rainforest	1	97,956
Bengalian Rainforest	22	657,352
Burman Rainforest	0	0
Indochinese Rainforest	28	1,780,756
South Chinese Rainforest	21	165,709
Malayan Rainforest	20	1,087,728
Tropical Dry Forests		
Indus-Ganges Monsoon Forest	136	6,835,608
Burma Monsoon Forest	18	515,429
Thailandian Monsoon Forest	20	942,417
Mahanadian	17	1,022,379
Coromandel	3	105,828
Ceylonese Monsoon Forest	36	544,709
Deccan Thorn Forest	8	454,036
Warm Deserts/Semi-deserts		
Thar Desert	35	1,628,854
Mixed Island Systems		
Seychelles and Amirantes Islands	2	2,893
Laccadives Islands	0	0
Maldives and Chagos Islands	0	0
Cocos-Keeling and Christmas Islands	1	1,600
Andaman and Nicobar Islands	8	28,592
Sumatra	29	4,253,807
Java	38	644,930
Lesser Sunda Islands	10	174,155
Sulawesi (Celebes)	22	1,093,265
Borneo	39	3,791,061
Philippines	26	390,932
Taiwan	2	45,137
OCEANIAN REALM	**54**	**4,127,602**
Mixed Island Systems		
Papuan	24	3,747,672
Micronesian	5	13,258
Hawaiian	4	214,502
Southeastern Polynesian	8	53,977
Central Polynesian	4	44,055
New Caledonian	7	48,796
East Melanesian	2	5,342
AUSTRALIAN REALM	**469**	**29,411,357**
Tropical Humid Forests		
Queensland Coastal	53	7,776,347
Temperate Rainforests		
Tasmanian	26	904,976
Tropical Dry Forests		
Northern Coastal	10	934,272

and Province, 1985

Table 21.2

Vegetation Type/Province	Protected Areas Number of Sites	Protected Areas Area Protected (hectares)
AUSTRALIAN REALM (continued)		
Evergreen Sclerophyllous Forests		
Western Sclerophyll	138	2,444,584
Southern Sclerophyll	56	1,413,727
Eastern Sclerophyll	95	2,741,356
Brigalow	12	319,156
Warm Deserts/Semi-deserts		
Western Mulga	10	2,144,280
Central Desert	13	3,657,703
Southern Mulga/Saltbush	10	4,363,400
Tropical Grasslands/Savannas		
Northern Savanna	9	1,458,655
Northern Grasslands	3	582,738
Temperate Grasslands		
Eastern Grasslands and Savannas	34	670,163
ANTARCTIC REALM	**157**	**3,078,315**
Temperate Rainforests		
Neozealandia	145	2,783,281
Tundra Communities		
Maudlandia	6	34,959
Marielandia	1	160,000
Insulantarctica	5	100,075
NEOTROPICAL REALM	**348**	**52,464,943**
Tropical Humid Forests		
Campechean	4	63,918
Panamanian	6	660,902
Colombian Coastal	6	1,019,000
Guyanan	21	2,155,078
Amazonian	14	12,733,681
Madeiran	2	448,150
Serro Do Mar	8	196,468
Temperate Rainforests		
Brazilian Rainforest	16	447,233
Brazilian Planalto	2	15,839
Valdivian Forest	13	4,018,459
Chilean Nothofagus	7	4,367,307
Tropical Dry Forests		
Everglades	9	774,279
Sinaloan	5	462,994
Guerreran	5	66,873

Vegetation Type/Province	Protected Areas Number of Sites	Protected Areas Area Protected (hectares)
NEOTROPICAL REALM (continued)		
Yucatecan	2	106,970
Central American	23	825,207
Venezuelan Dry Forest	26	1,125,794
Venezuelan Deciduous Forest	11	546,930
Equadorian Dry Forest	3	181,300
Caatinga	3	236,100
Gran Chaco	6	1,175,000
Temperate Broadleaf Forests		
Chilean Araucaria Forest	1	5,415
Evergreen Sclerophyllous Forests		
Chilean Sclerophyll	5	38,795
Warm Deserts/Semi-deserts		
Pacific Desert	0	0
Monte	7	1,446,751
Cold-winter Deserts		
Patagonian	4	36,700
Tropical Grasslands/Savannas		
Llanos	3	1,207,000
Campos Limpos	3	3,192,000
Babacu	1	155,000
Campos Cerrados	11	2,457,403
Temperate Grasslands		
Argentinian Pampas	0	0
Uruguayan Pampas	9	70,516
Mixed Mountain Systems		
Northern Andean	9	913,288
Colombian Montane	8	1,397,050
Yungas	9	1,108,268
Puna	13	1,168,439
Southern Andean	47	6,450,237
Mixed Island Systems		
Bahamas-Bermudean	4	122,540
Cuban	4	24,305
Greater Antillean	9	225,230
Lesser Antillean	6	87,875
Revilla Gigedo Island	0	0
Cocos Island	1	3,200
Galapagos Islands	1	691,200
Fernando De Noronja Island	1	36,249
South Trinidade Island	0	0
Lake Systems		
Lake Titicaca	0	0

Source: International Union for Conservation of Nature and Natural Resources. 0 = zero. For additional information see Sources and Technical Notes.

Table 21.3 Nationally Threatened Vertebrate Species, Early 1980s

	Mammals Number of Species Known	Mammals Threatened Number	Mammals Threatened Percent	Birds Number of Species Known	Birds Threatened Number	Birds Threatened Percent	Reptiles Number of Species Known	Reptiles Threatened Number	Reptiles Threatened Percent	Amphibians Number of Species Known	Amphibians Threatened Number	Amphibians Threatened Percent	Fishes Number of Species Known	Fishes Threatened Number	Fishes Threatened Percent	Data Source
NORTH AMERICA																
Canada	94	6	6	434	10	2	32	2	6	54	2	4	800	15	2	OECD
United States	466	35	8	1,090	69	6	368	25	7	222	8	4	2,640	44	2	OECD
ASIA																
Japan	186	4	2	632	35	6	85	3	4	58	1	2	3,144	4	0	OECD
Turkey	31	11	36	217	36	17	X	X	X	X	X	X	X	X	X	OECD
EUROPE																
Austria	83	38	46	201	121	60	X	X	X	X	X	X	92	54	59	OECD
Denmark	49	14	29	190	41	22	5	0	0	14	3	21	166	17	10	OECD
Finland	62	21	34	232	15	7	5	1	20	6	0	0	58	4	7	OECD
France	101	58	57	266	155	58	49	19	39	34	18	53	73	20	27	SOE
Germany, Fed Rep	94	44	47	455	98	22	12	9	75	19	11	58	173	40	23	OECD
Hungary	X	14	X	X	83	X	X	4	X	X	1	X	X	2	X	SOE
Ireland	X	3	X	X	18	X	X	X	X	X	1	X	X	X	X	SOE
Italy	97	13	13	419	60	14	46	24	52	28	13	46	503	70	14	OECD
Netherlands	60	29	48	257	85	33	7	6	86	15	10	67	49	11	22	OECD
Norway	71	10	14	280	28	10	5	1	20	5	1	20	X	X	X	OECD
Portugal	79	X	X	337	X	X	24	X	X	17	X	X	X	X	X	OECD
Spain	100	53	53	389	142	37	49	20	41	23	18	78	137	12	9	OECD
Sweden	63	11	18	250	34	14	6	0	0	11	5	46	X	X	X	OECD
Switzerland	86	X	X	190	74	39	15	X	X	20	X	X	60	X	X	OECD
United Kingdom	51	26	51	200	51	26	6	2	33	6	2	33	37	18	49	SOE
OCEANIA																
Australia	320	40	13	700	36	5	550	8	1	150	6	4	3,200	X	X	SOE
New Zealand	68	14	21	282	16	6	37	7	19	6	X	X	777	3	0	OECD

Sources: Organisation for Economic Co-operation and Development; and national sources. 0 = zero or less than half of 1 percent; X = not available. OECD = Organisation for Economic Co-operation and Development. SOE = national state of the environment reports. For additional information, see Sources and Technical Notes.

Table 21.4 Globally Threatened Vertebrate Species, Early 1980s

	Mammals		Birds		Reptiles		Amphibians		Fishes	
	Number of Species Known	Number Threatened	Number of Species Known	Number Threatened	Number of Species Known	Number Threatened	Number of Species Known	Number Threatened	Number of Species Known	Number Threatened
AFRICA										
Algeria	97	11	X	X	X	X	X	X	X	X
Angola	275	12	X	X	X	X	X	X	X	X
Benin	187	7	X	X	X	X	X	X	X	X
Botswana	154	7	X	X	X	X	X	X	X	X
Burkina Faso	147	6	X	X	X	X	X	X	X	X
Burundi	103	6	X	X	X	X	X	X	X	X
Cameroon	297	16	X	X	X	X	X	X	X	X
Cape Verde	9	3	X	X	X	X	X	X	X	X
Central African Rep	208	7	X	X	X	X	X	X	X	X
Chad	131	11	X	X	X	X	X	X	X	X
Congo	198	11	X	X	X	X	X	X	X	X
Cote d'Ivoire	226	12	X	X	X	X	X	X	X	X
Djibouti	22	6	X	X	X	X	X	X	X	X
Egypt	105	10	X	X	X	X	X	X	X	X
Equatorial Guinea	182	12	X	X	X	X	X	X	X	X
Ethiopia	256	16	X	X	X	X	X	X	X	X
Gabon	190	9	X	X	X	X	X	X	X	X
Gambia	108	4	X	X	X	X	X	X	X	X
Ghana	222	9	X	X	X	X	X	X	X	X
Guinea	188	10	X	X	X	X	X	X	X	X
Guinea-Bissau	109	6	X	X	X	X	X	X	X	X
Kenya	308	9	X	X	X	X	X	X	X	X
Lesotho	33	2	X	X	X	X	X	X	X	X
Liberia	193	11	X	X	X	X	X	X	X	X
Libya	76	9	X	X	X	X	X	X	X	X
Malawi	192	5	X	X	X	X	X	X	X	X
Mali	136	10	X	X	X	X	X	X	X	X
Mauritania	61	10	X	X	X	X	X	X	X	X
Morocco	108	8	X	X	X	X	X	X	X	X
Mozambique	183	6	X	X	X	X	X	X	X	X
Namibia	161	10	X	X	X	X	X	X	X	X
Niger	131	9	X	X	X	X	X	X	X	X
Nigeria	274	18	X	X	X	X	X	X	X	X
Rwanda	147	7	X	X	X	X	X	X	X	X
Sao Tome	7	0	X	X	X	X	X	X	X	X
Senegal	166	10	X	X	X	X	X	X	X	X
Sierra Leone	178	10	X	X	X	X	X	X	X	X
Somalia	173	14	X	X	X	X	X	X	X	X
South Africa	279	16	X	X	X	X	X	X	X	X
Sudan	266	16	X	X	X	X	X	X	X	X
Swaziland	46	3	X	X	X	X	X	X	X	X
Tanzania, United Rep	310	12	X	X	X	X	X	X	X	X
Togo	196	6	X	X	X	X	X	X	X	X
Tunisia	77	8	X	X	X	X	X	X	X	X
Uganda	311	10	X	X	X	X	X	X	X	X
Western Sahara	15	7	X	X	X	X	X	X	X	X
Zaire	409	17	X	X	X	X	X	X	X	X
Zambia	228	6	X	X	X	X	X	X	X	X
Zimbabwe	194	7	X	X	X	X	X	X	X	X
AMERICAS										
Argentina	255	42	927	122	204	18	124	0	X	X
Bahamas	17	3	218	19	39	12	2	0	X	X
Belize	121	18	504	69	107	12	26	0	X	X
Bolivia	267	51	1,177	141	180	19	95	0	X	X
Brazil	394	77	1,567	198	467	38	485	0	X	X
Canada	163	8	X	X	X	X	X	X	X	X
Chile	90	18	393	41	82	4	38	0	X	X
Colombia	358	60	1,665	181	383	36	367	1	X	X
Costa Rica	203	27	796	94	218	18	151	2	X	X
Cuba	39	9	286	38	100	17	39	0	X	X
Ecuador	280	50	1,447	155	345	29	349	0	X	X
El Salvador	129	15	432	64	93	10	38	0	X	X
French Guiana	142	28	628	86	136	24	89	0	X	X
Greenland (Denmark)	26	7	X	X	X	X	X	X	X	X
Guatemala	174	21	666	94	204	18	98	0	X	X
Guyana	198	27	728	98	137	19	105	0	X	X
Hispaniola	23	4	211	26	134	11	53	0	X	X
Honduras	179	23	672	87	161	13	55	0	X	X
Jamaica	29	3	223	23	38	12	20	0	X	X
Lesser Antilles	37	4	193	29	94	14	15	0	X	X
Mexico	439	32	961	123	704	34	272	0	X	X
Netherlands Antilles	9	2	171	18	22	4	2	0	X	X
Nicaragua	177	24	610	81	162	17	59	0	x	X
Panama	217	30	840	98	212	19	155	1	X	X
Paraguay	157	33	630	101	110	11	69	0	X	X

World Resources 1987

Table 21.4

	Mammals		Birds		Reptiles		Amphibians		Fishes	
	Number of Species Known	Number Threatened	Number of Species Known	Number Threatened	Number of Species Known	Number Threatened	Number of Species Known	Number Threatened	Number of Species Known	Number Threatened
AMERICAS (continued)										
Peru	359	61	1,642	159	297	25	233	0	X	X
Puerto Rico	17	2	220	29	46	9	25	1	X	X
Suriname	200	32	670	91	131	19	99	0	X	X
Tobago	29	3	157	15	39	10	8	0	X	X
Trinidad	85	6	347	52	76	15	14	0	X	X
United States	367	25	X	X	X	X	X	X	X	X
Uruguay	77	22	367	50	66	11	37	0	X	X
Venezuela	305	37	1,295	150	246	26	182	0	X	X
AUSTRALIA	299	46	X	X	X	X	X	X	X	X

Sources: The Nature Conservancy International; and International Union for Conservation of Nature and Natural Resources.
0 = zero; X = not available.
For additional information, see Sources and Technical Notes.

Sources and Technical Notes

Table 21.1 National and International Protection of Natural Areas, 1986

Sources: National Protection Systems: International Union for Conservation of Nature and Natural Resources (IUCN), *1985 United Nations List of National Parks and Protected Areas* (IUCN, Gland, Switzerland, 1985); and unpublished IUCN data (IUCN Conservation Monitoring Centre [CMC], Cambridge, United Kingdom, December 1985). Biosphere Reserves: Man and the Biosphere Programme (MAB) of the United Nations Educational, Scientific and Cultural Organization (UNESCO), unpublished data (UNESCO MAB, Paris, October 1986); Natural World Heritage Sites: World Heritage Secretariat of UNESCO, unpublished data (UNESCO, Paris, October 1986); Wetlands of International Importance: IUCN CMC, unpublished data (IUCN CMC, Cambridge, United Kingdom, October 1986).

The protected areas under "National Protection Systems" in Table 21.1 are aggregated from sites classified in five (of the ten) IUCN management categories. Two other categories, Biosphere Reserves and World Heritage Sites—natural areas—are drawn from sites included under "National Protection Systems." Data for the remaining three categories of the IUCN framework are less complete and have therefore been omitted. Resource Reserves are relatively isolated, uninhabited areas that have been little studied. Anthropological Reserves are natural areas in which humans are an integral component, and in which management is oriented toward the maintenance of habitat for traditional societies. Multiple Use Management Areas are large areas in which the principal goal is to manage renewable resources such as timber and game and to provide recreation potential on a sustained basis.

The categories that are aggregated for this table are:

■ *Scientific Reserves and Strict Nature Reserves.* These areas possess outstanding and representative ecosystems. The sites are generally closed to public access. Their size is determined by the area required to ensure the integrity of the site. In many of the sites, nat-

ural perturbations (e.g., insect epidemics, forest fires) are allowed to occur.
■ *National Parks and Provincial Parks.* These sites are relatively large areas of national or international significance that are not materially altered by humans. Access is controlled, but visitors are encouraged to use the areas for recreation and study.
■ *Natural Monuments and Natural Landmarks.* These areas contain unique geological formations, special animals or plants, or unusual habitat. Areas vary in size. Access is usually restricted.
■ *Managed Nature Reserves and Wildlife Sanctuaries.* These sites are protected for specific purposes such as conservation of a nationally significant plant or animal species. Some areas may require management. For example, a particular grassland or heath community may be best protected and perpetuated by livestock grazing. The size of the areas varies. Public access is restricted to scientific and educational purposes.
■ *Protected Landscapes and Seascapes.* Areas so designated may be entirely natural, with no human artifacts, or they may include cultural landscapes, such as scenically attractive agricultural areas. Protected landscapes may be coastlines, lake shores, hilly or mountainous terrain along scenic highways, etc. Areas vary in size, and public access depends on the use of the area.

The figures in Table 21.1 do not include many locally or provincially protected sites, privately owned areas, or sites where hunting and other consumptive uses of wildlife are permitted. Each area, unless an island, is larger than 1,000 hectares.

Biosphere Reserves are an international network of protected areas approved by the International Coordinating Council of UNESCO's Man and the Biosphere Programme. Each area must contain an ecosystem typical of a biogeographical province in terms of diversity and naturalness, and it must be large enough to be an effective conservation unit. (For a definition of biogeographical province, see the technical note for Table 21.2.) Each Biosphere Reserve must include a defined, minimally disturbed core

area for conservation and research, and it must be surrounded by one or more buffer zones. Within the buffer zones, traditional uses of the land may be permitted, as are experimental research on the functioning of ecosystems and rehabilitation of modified or degraded ecosystems.

World Heritage Sites are structures or natural areas of "outstanding universal value." (Only "natural sites" are included in the table.) Sites are nominated by any of the countries party to the World Heritage Convention and are reviewed for the Convention Committee by IUCN. To be accepted, a natural site must contain an example of a major stage of the earth's evolutionary history; a significant ongoing geological process; a unique or superlative natural phenomenon, formation, or feature; or a habitat for endangered or rare species of plants and animals required for survival of the species.

Wetlands of International Importance are wetlands so designated by any of the 42 countries (as of December 1986) that have signed the Convention on Wetlands of International Importance Especially as Waterfowl Habitat (Ramsar, Iran, 1971). IUCN collects wetlands data with the assistance of the International Waterfowl Research Bureau, the International Council for Bird Preservation, and the United Nations Environment Programme.

Many sites are listed under multiple headings: Biosphere Reserves, World Heritage Sites, Wetlands of International Importance, and Protected Areas. Because these categories overlap, the total number of protected sites is less than the sum of the totals for all the categories. Computerized data bases for all four of the protection systems are maintained by the IUCN Conservation Monitoring Centre at Cambridge, United Kingdom.

Continental and world totals include information for countries not included in the table because they have a population of less than 240,000. The Bahamas, for example, have four protected areas totalling 122,540 hectares. Seven protected areas have been established in Antarctica under the Antarctic Treaty System; they are included in the world total under "National Protection Systems." For all categories, China includes Taiwan, Greenland is included in the North American total, and the Ukraine and Byelorussia are included in the USSR figures. The United States and Canada share a World Heritage Site (Kluane-Wrangell/St. Elias National Park), as do Guinea and Cote d'Ivoire (Mt. Nimba Strict Nature Reserve). These sites are listed under each country, but are counted only once in continental and world totals. Under Wetlands of International Importance, the Netherlands includes the Netherlands Antilles. For additional data on the status of wetlands, refer to Chapter 18, "Land Use and Cover," Table 18.2.

Table 21.2 Protected Areas Classified by Biogeographical Realm and Province, 1985

Source: International Union for Conservation of Nature and Natural Resources (IUCN), *1985 United Nations List of National Parks and Protected Areas* (IUCN, Gland, Switzerland, 1985).

For a definition of "protected area," refer to the technical note for Table 21.1.

Each protected site is categorized in the Udvardy system of biogeography. This system classifies the world's landmass according to the dominant floristic, faunistic, and geographical characteristics of an area.

Realms are continent- or subcontinent-size areas with unifying features of geography, flora, and fauna. Realms are further divided into *provinces*, geographic areas characterized by distinctive groups of plant and animal species. For further details, refer to M. Udvardy, *A Classification of the Biogeographical Provinces of the World* (IUCN, Morges, Switzerland, 1975).

The classification system used in Table 21.2 is being revised; rather than the 193 biogeographical provinces shown, the new classification will have about 205.

Global data for Tables 21.1 and 21.2 do not agree because Table 21.1 includes more recent, unpublished data.

Categorizing protected areas by biogeographical province is difficult. Information on species is incomplete, and biogeographic divisions depend upon which groups of plants and animals form the basis of the classification. As a result, transition zones are often used to account for regions where species from two or more biogeographical provinces are found. Similarly, protected areas may have biotic communities representative of more than one biogeographical province.

Table 21.3 Nationally Threatened Vertebrate Species, Early 1980s

Sources: Organisation for Economic Co-operation and Development (OECD), *OECD Environmental Data Compendium 1985* (OECD, Paris, 1985). Data for Ireland, Hungary,

France, United Kingdom, and Australia: national state of the environment reports (1985, 1986, 1981, 1983, and 1982, respectively).

Nationally threatened species are vulnerable to or threatened by extinction within a nation's boundaries. The species may have stable populations in other countries. Data on species that are threatened throughout their ranges ("globally threatened") are presented in Table 21.4.

This table combines data from several sources that use various methods; thus the comparability of the data is limited. OECD compiles its information by means of a questionnaire, and information submitted by several countries was incomplete or varied from standard definitions. Data drawn from national sources use various definitions of "threatened." Listings for countries responding to the OECD questionnaire include only endangered and vulnerable species. For definitions of threatened and endangered, refer to the technical note for Table 21.4.

Table 21.4 Globally Threatened Vertebrate Species, Early 1980s

Sources: Latin America: The Nature Conservancy International, unpublished data (The Nature Conservancy International, Washington, D.C., August 1986); Africa, North America, and Australia: International Union for Conservation of Nature and Natural Resources (IUCN), *The IUCN Mammal Red Data Book, Part I* (IUCN, Gland, Switzerland, 1982), and IUCN Conservation Monitoring Centre (CMC), unpublished data (IUCN CMC, Cambridge, United Kingdom, 1985).

Globally threatened species are threatened by or vulnerable to extinction throughout their range (see definitions below). Species may also be threatened in only a part of their range; data on vertebrate species that are threatened within individual countries are presented in Table 21.3.

The Nature Conservancy International compiles globally threatened species data from IUCN *Red Data Books*, the threatened species lists associated with the Convention on International Trade in Endangered Species of Wild Fauna and Flora (Washington, D.C., 1973), and the list of globally threatened species associated with the U.S. Endangered Species Act. The Nature Conservancy International is also coordinating development of additional data on globally threatened species in Latin America; national institutions will undertake thorough surveys of the endemic biota, identifying species likely to be globally threatened. The Nature Conservancy International will circulate these surveys to other countries, allowing assessment of the degree to which species are globally threatened. Results of this work are expected by 1989.

IUCN has established a standard framework for classification of threatened and endangered species:

■ *Endangered.* "Taxa in danger of extinction and whose survival is unlikely if the causal factors continue operating." Included are taxa whose numbers have been reduced to a critical level or whose habitats have been so drastically reduced that they are deemed to be in immediate danger of extinction. Taxa that may already be extinct but that have been seen in the wild in the past 50 years are also included.

■ *Vulnerable.* "Taxa believed likely to move into the Endangered category in the near future if the causal factors continue operating." Included are taxa of which most or all the populations are decreasing because of overexploitation, extensive destruction of habitat, or other environmental disturbance; taxa with populations that have been seriously depleted and whose ultimate security has not yet been assured; and taxa with populations that are still abundant but are under threat from severe adverse factors throughout their range.

■ *Rare.* "Taxa with world populations that are not at present Endangered or Vulnerable, but are at risk." These taxa are usually localized within restricted geographical areas or habitats or are thinly scattered over a more extensive range.

■ *Indeterminate.* "Taxa known to be Endangered, Vulnerable, or Rare but where there is not enough information to say which of the three categories is appropriate."

■ *Out of Danger.* "Taxa formerly included in one of the above categories, but which are now considered relatively secure because effective conservation measures have been taken or the previous threat to their survival has been removed."

■ *Insufficiently Known.* "Taxa that are suspected but not definitely known to belong to any of the above categories."

In practice, the Endangered and Vulnerable categories may include taxa whose populations are beginning to recover as a result of remedial action, but whose recovery is insufficient to justify their transfer to another category.

The number of threatened species listed for most countries in Table 21.4 includes species that are Endangered, Vulnerable, Rare, Indeterminate, and Insufficiently Known.

The total number of species includes species that were introduced to a country, but the number of threatened species excludes introduced species.

The data on mammals exclude cetaceans (whales and porpoises). See Chapter 24, "Oceans and Coasts," Table 24.2, for data on marine mammals.

Although the list of threatened species is based on the judgment of many experts working in the field and has taken years to compile, it is under continual revision as new species are discovered and as more become threatened.

22. Energy and Minerals

This section provides data on the availability, production, and consumption of energy and minerals.

Table 22.1 presents information on the production and consumption of commercially traded fuels. World commercial energy production increased 33 percent between 1970 and 1984, peaking in 1979 at 46 percent above 1970. Between 1970 and 1984, production of natural gas grew faster than that of any other fuel type, increasing 52 percent worldwide.

Total consumption of commercial energy increased 38 percent from 1970 to 1984. (The apparent difference between production and consumption growth over this period is probably due to statistical anomalies and revisions, with inventory drawdowns playing a minor role.) Many developed countries have reduced their energy consumption relative to Gross National Product by using energy more efficiently and by shifting to less energy-intensive industries. Of the 24 member countries of the Organisation for Economic Co-operation and Development (which consumed 51 percent of the world's commercial energy in 1984), 15 used less energy per unit of GNP in 1984 than in 1970.

Serious gaps still exist in energy data despite the large and growing statistical effort by governments, international organizations, and major petroleum companies. Data on energy consumption by sector (commercial, residential, industrial, and transportation) are virtually nonexistent for developing countries. Fuelwood data are unreliable and are not included in this chapter. (For fuelwood production estimates, refer to Chapter 20, "Forests and Rangelands," Table 20.2.)

Electricity production has increased dramatically over the past 20 years. (See Table 22.2.) Although nuclear electricity production increased by a factor of 15 since 1970, fossil-fuel fired generation still accounts for two thirds of global electricity output. Many countries are increasing hydroelectric and geothermal production to meet their electricity needs. For example, Togo, Zambia, the Dominican Republic, and Argentina all increased their combined hydroelectric and geothermal production by over 500 percent between 1970 and 1984. For additional information on dams, reservoirs and hydroelectric capacity, refer to Table 23.2 in Chapter 23, "Freshwater."

Table 22.3 summarizes the world's reserves and resources of commercial energy as assessed in 1983. The United States, China, and the USSR have 65 percent of the proved reserves (quantities known to exist in specific locations and

qualities, although not necessarily recoverable at current prices) of bituminous (hard) coal. The proved recoverable reserves (technically and economically recoverable) of crude oil held by Saudi Arabia, Kuwait, Iran, and Mexico make up about 55 percent of the world total; the USSR and Iran hold over 50 percent of the world's proved recoverable reserves of natural gas. At 1984 consumption rates, global reserves of petroleum would last 31 years, natural gas 52 years, and bituminous coal 175 years.

Table 22.4 shows the historical and projected status of nuclear power. Nuclear power provides a third or more of the electricity used by six industrialized countries, and several developing countries plan to add nuclear power to their energy economies. The world's nuclear capacity would double if all reactors planned and under construction were operative. However, experience indicates that many of these reactors will not be completed. In the United States, for example, 111 of the 139 power plants ordered between 1971 and 1977 were indefinitely delayed or canceled. Since the nuclear accident at Chernobyl, debate about the future of nuclear power has intensified in many countries.

Table 22.5 provides data on production and consumption of eight metals over the last 20 years. These metals were selected on the basis of importance to national economies and international trade. Consumption of metals is dominated by the major industrialized countries; the USSR, Japan, and the United States are the three largest consumers of the metals listed, with Japan's consumption increasing the most rapidly.

Scrap recovery is often an economically attractive source of raw materials, and it is also promoted to reduce pollution and litter and to conserve resources. Many countries have stepped up scrap recovery efforts over the past two decades. (See Table 22.6.)

Incentives to recover a material vary across countries. For example, national policy may favor material recovery through the imposition of pollution and litter laws or taxes. Scrap supply, demand, and prices are also linked to the supply of and demand for new products and to the price and availability of nonscrap raw materials. The importance of these links varies with the material; copper scrap recovery, for example, is sensitive to the demand for copper products. On the other hand, the price of glass scrap (cullet) is favorable compared with that of noncullet glass, but the supply of cullet is usually limited because cullet markets were established only in the late 1970s.

Table 22.1 Production and Consumption of Commercial Energy,

	Production								Consumption					
	Total[a]		Solid		Liquid		Gaseous		Total		Per Capita		Per Constant (1975) $US of GNP	
	1984 (peta-joules)	Change over 1970 (percent)	1984 (peta-joules)	Change over 1970 (percent)	1984 (peta-joules)	Change over 1970 (percent)	1984 (peta-joules)	Change over 1970 (percent)	1984 (peta-joules)	Change over 1970 (percent)	1984 (giga-joules)	Change over 1970 (percent)	1984 (kilo-joules)	Change over 1970 (percent)
WORLD	274,267	33	82,741	31	121,866	21	58,294	52	259,542	38	55	6		
AFRICA	15,556	9	3,245	107	10,640	−15	1,489	1,834	6,332	112	12	41		
Algeria	2,930	38	0	0	1,982	−4	947	1,380	441	198	21	95	17,528	32
Angola	448	105	X	X	439	103	5	150	30	15	4	−25	X	X
Benin	X	X	X	X	X	X	X	X	5	25	1	−14	6,387	−25
Botswana	X	X	X	X	X	X	X	X	X	X	X	X	X	X
Burkina Faso	X	X	X	X	X	X	X	X	6	200	1	125	7,647	120
Burundi	0	X	0	X	X	X	X	X	2	100	0	51	3,564	41
Cameroon	284	7,000	X	X	276	X	X	X	129	892	13	600	27,148	351
Cape Verde	X	X	X	X	X	X	X	X	2	NM	6	NM	19,305	X
Central African Rep	0	0	X	X	X	X	X	X	3	0	1	−26	7,574	−15
Chad	X	X	X	X	X	X	X	X	3	50	1	12	3,426	−18
Comoros	X	X	X	X	X	X	X	X	1	NM	2	NM	10,965	X
Congo	257	25,600	X	X	256	25,500	0	0	5	0	3	−29	3,617	−64
Cote d'Ivoire	62	6,100	X	X	58	X	X	X	57	78	6	5	13,225	14
Djibouti	X	X	X	X	X	X	X	X	3	200	8	34	X	X
Egypt	1,930	168	X	X	1,784	155	108	3,500	857	237	19	142	35,983	56
Equatorial Guinea	0	0	X	X	X	X	X	X	1	0	3	−24	X	X
Ethiopia	2	100	X	X	X	X	X	X	21	11	0	−34	6,301	−24
Gabon	365	57	X	X	356	54	8	700	37	185	33	139	19,080	45
Gambia	X	X	X	X	X	X	X	X	2	100	3	49	14,837	22
Ghana	10	0	X	X	4	X	X	X	29	−31	2	−55	10,419	−31
Guinea	0	X	X	X	X	X	X	X	12	9	2	−28	8,214	−29
Guinea-Bissau	X	X	X	X	X	X	X	X	1	0	1	−40	8,019	21
Kenya	6	500	X	X	X	X	X	X	55	62	3	−8	12,273	−29
Lesotho	X	X	X	X	X	X	X	X	X	X	X	X	X	X
Liberia	1	0	X	X	X	X	X	X	22	16	10	−26	32,396	−9
Libya	2,493	−63	X	X	2,313	−66	180	NM	384	885	111	463	27,254	933
Madagascar	1	NM	X	X	X	X	X	X	15	15	2	−20	9,363	23
Malawi	2	NM	X	X	X	X	X	X	8	33	1	−10	9,861	−31
Mali	0	0	X	X	X	X	X	X	7	133	1	69	8,160	46
Mauritania	X	X	X	X	X	X	X	X	9	50	5	2	15,734	15
Mauritius	0	0	X	X	X	X	X	X	8	0	8	−18	8,823	−47
Morocco	29	38	24	85	1	−50	3	50	199	137	9	69	15,038	26
Mozambique	17	55	11	10	X	X	X	X	38	15	3	−31	X	X
Niger	2	X	2	X	X	X	X	X	10	233	2	133	12,373	198
Nigeria	3,103	34	1	−50	2,874	24	220	5,400	622	678	7	383	18,925	448
Rwanda	1	NM	X	X	X	X	0	0	6	500	1	280	7,206	215
Senegal	X	X	X	X	X	X	X	X	31	107	5	32	14,786	62
Sierra Leone	X	X	X	X	X	X	X	X	7	−30	2	−44	10,180	−43
Somalia	X	X	X	X	X	X	X	X	16	433	4	228	19,338	282
South Africa	3,140	121	3,123	120	X	X	X	X	2,769	66	88	20	63,014	10
Sudan	2	NM	X	X	X	X	X	X	48	−21	2	−48	8,047	−52
Swaziland	X	X	X	X	X	X	X	X	X	X	X	X	X	X
Tanzania, United Rep	2	100	0	0	X	X	X	X	27	23	1	−24	9,209	−14
Togo	0	NA	0	0	X	X	X	X	6	50	2	6	9,014	14
Tunisia	252	42	X	X	234	32	18	NM	138	221	20	137	19,923	33
Uganda	2	−33	X	X	X	X	X	X	11	−45	1	−64	X	X
Zaire	83	493	4	33	64	X	X	X	59	37	2	2	16,493	20
Zambia	49	172	12	−20	X	X	X	X	64	36	10	−11	27,096	16
Zimbabwe	80	−34	67	−35	X	X	X	X	112	−13	13	−46	25,700	−47
NORTH & CENTRAL AMERICA	77,614	11	21,141	37	31,499	16	21,243	−17	78,791	7	199	−13		
Barbados	4	NM	X	X	4	NM	1	X	9	50	36	42	19,186	9
Canada	9,099	51	1,396	289	3,510	18	2,969	41	7,247	31	288	11	36,054	−18
Costa Rica	11	267	X	X	X	X	X	X	34	79	13	22	14,756	11
Cuba	33	371	X	X	33	371	0	X	428	71	43	47	X	X
Dominican Rep	2	NM	X	X	X	X	X	X	88	120	14	55	19,804	13
El Salvador	6	200	X	X	X	X	X	X	27	35	5	−10	16,609	13
Guatemala	12	1,100	X	X	10	X	X	X	46	53	6	6	14,758	34
Haiti	1	X	X	X	X	X	X	X	10	100	2	43	11,014	35
Honduras	3	200	X	X	X	X	X	X	28	56	7	−3	18,168	−1
Jamaica	1	NM	X	X	X	X	X	X	80	21	35	−2	46,797	78
Mexico	7,746	391	163	163	6,513	545	977	117	3,871	149	50	65	32,150	31
Nicaragua	2	100	X	X	X	X	X	X	26	37	8	−11	17,780	8
Panama	5	400	X	X	X	X	X	X	46	31	22	−6	18,026	−27
Trinidad and Tobago	489	28	X	X	374	21	115	58	172	30	148	15	54,260	−10
United States	60,200	−2	19,589	30	21,056	−8	17,181	−25	66,149	2	280	−12	32,405	−32
SOUTH AMERICA	10,668	−7	375	103	7,714	−25	1,655	131	7,433	78	28	29		
Argentina	1,675	53	13	−13	1,096	27	478	129	1,515	36	50	9	44,204	36
Bolivia	142	173	X	X	49	2	88	8,700	61	110	10	47	27,750	73
Brazil	1,838	235	152	167	1,009	193	81	2,600	2,551	109	19	51	15,578	−5
Chile	205	15	35	−13	99	32	37	−23	320	1	27	−20	35,759	−11
Colombia	808	26	173	162	375	−24	187	240	706	90	25	41	39,756	3
Ecuador	570	5,082	X	X	560	6,122	4	300	180	267	20	140	31,674	60
Guyana	0	X	X	X	X	X	X	X	17	−23	18	−41	42,173	−29
Paraguay	3	200	X	X	X	X	X	X	24	140	7	54	7,986	−15
Peru	466	148	2	−60	390	153	43	169	360	53	19	5	23,341	21
Suriname	5	25	X	X	1	NM	X	X	18	−28	49	−28	35,013	−45
Uruguay	13	225	X	X	X	X	X	X	55	−25	18	−29	15,517	−30
Venezuela	4,944	−43	1	0	4,134	−50	737	93	1,619	125	96	46	54,987	59

1970–84

Table 22.1

	Commercially Traded Fuels												
	Production								Consumption				
	Total[a]		Solid		Liquid		Gaseous		Total		Per Capita		Per Constant (1975) $US of GNP
	1984 (peta-joules)	Change over 1970 (percent)	1984 (peta-joules)	Change over 1970 (percent)	1984 (peta-joules)	Change over 1970 (percent)	1984 (peta-joules)	Change over 1970 (percent)	1984 (peta-joules)	Change over 1970 (percent)	1984 (giga-joules)	Change over 1970 (percent)	1984 (kilo-joules)	Change over 1970 (percent)
ASIA	**64,345**	**37**	**22,781**	**97**	**35,681**	**6**	**4,147**	**266**	**54,415**	**106**	**20**	**55**		
Afghanistan	114	13	5	0	0	0	106	12	29	61	2	24	X	X
Bahrain	243	37	X	X	100	−39	144	929	161	847	388	402	X	X
Bangladesh	97	X	X	X	3	X	91	X	154	X	2	X	7,316	X
Bhutan	0	X	X	X	X	X	X	X	0	X	0	X	X	X
Burma	107	182	1	NM	69	103	33	1,550	88	87	2	40	14,506	−4
China	21,912	146	16,231	119	4,884	274	484	332	20,047	137	19	87	69,143	−3
Cyprus	X	X	X	X	X	X	X	X	37	68	56	56	25,285	−26
India	5,123	158	3,592	128	1,194	312	125	558	5,185	132	7	71	41,868	37
Indonesia	3,900	108	32	540	2,920	61	940	1,900	1,248	207	8	126	24,617	25
Iran	5,055	−42	25	56	4,680	−43	327	−28	1,704	114	39	40	X	X
Iraq	2,515	−24	X	X	2,502	−23	11	−65	238	43	15	−13	X	X
Israel	2	−99	X	X	0	−100	2	−60	288	55	69	10	18,066	−11
Japan	1,271	−15	434	−59	18	−47	92	−11	13,308	36	111	18	17,705	−28
Jordan	X	X	X	X	X	X	X	X	99	450	29	274	43,939	108
Kampuchea, Dem	0	0	X	X	X	X	X	X	1	−92	0	−92	X	X
Korea, Dem People's Rep	1,404	80	1,307	77	X	X	X	X	1,545	85	78	29	X	X
Korea, Rep	449	61	397	44	X	X	X	X	1,800	194	44	131	45,082	2
Kuwait	2,833	−57	X	X	2,619	−60	215	169	336	217	195	37	16,955	61
Lao People's Dem Rep	3	NM	0	0	X	X	X	X	3	−63	1	−72	X	X
Lebanon	2	−33	X	X	X	X	X	X	66	35	25	26	X	X
Malaysia	1,128	2,464	X	X	923	2,395	198	6,500	390	119	26	57	22,186	−21
Mongolia	57	171	57	171	X	X	X	X	88	175	47	85	X	X
Nepal	1	NM	X	X	X	X	X	X	8	60	0	14	3,808	9
Oman	1,320	87	X	X	1,094	55	226	X	467	15,467	391	8,434	153,090	6,636
Pakistan	422	159	37	0	28	40	310	223	624	93	6	30	31,531	−6
Philippines	95	1,088	23	2,200	27	NM	X	X	489	66	9	17	22,644	−11
Qatar	1,004	29	X	X	839	13	165	323	188	337	637	65	110,148	380
Saudi Arabia	10,324	27	X	X	10,274	27	50	NM	1,155	1,381	104	667	20,605	358
Singapore	X	X	X	X	X	X	X	X	496	544	196	429	42,535	100
Sri Lanka	8	167	X	X	X	X	X	X	57	27	4	−1	12,407	−33
Syrian Arab Rep	418	131	X	X	405	124	3	NM	269	290	27	141	26,683	16
Thailand	179	1,527	26	550	49	NM	90	NM	613	213	12	125	24,525	36
Turkey	517	48	380	101	89	−41	0	X	1,237	151	26	84	24,547	28
United Arab Emirates	2,752	70	X	X	2,603	62	149	1,556	282	1,663	223	210	15,598	X
Viet Nam	182	102	176	100	X	X	X	X	210	−43	4	−59	X	X
Yemen	X	X	X	X	X	X	X	X	37	1,750	6	1,243	20,852	468
Yemen, Dem	X	X	X	X	X	X	X	X	52	373	25	241	80,210	X
EUROPE	**39,047**	**46**	**17,744**	**−8**	**9,185**	**462**	**8,689**	**104**	**60,984**	**21**	**124**	**13**		
Albania	211	171	26	189	160	154	17	325	112	195	39	117	X	X
Austria	245	−25	38	−30	51	−57	51	−34	880	23	117	22	18,460	−20
Belgium	272	−19	169	−49	X	X	1	−50	1,430	−10	145	−12	19,560	−35
Bulgaria	557	18	477	10	13	−7	4	−76	1,486	58	166	50	X	X
Czechoslovakia	1,974	6	1,908	5	4	−56	24	−35	2,831	25	183	16	X	X
Denmark	108	10,700	0	−100	99	NM	9	X	681	−13	133	−16	15,403	−33
Finland	156	346	44	4,300	X	X	X	X	712	30	146	23	20,244	−16
France	1,829	3	578	−50	117	−7	247	−9	6,263	10	114	1	15,126	−26
German Dem Rep	2,838	20	2,638	13	47	1,075	105	425	3,710	21	223	24	X	X
Germany, Fed Rep	4,463	−13	3,415	−19	173	−46	570	24	9,982	9	163	8	19,330	−20
Greece	251	318	181	262	56	X	4	X	650	128	66	103	24,222	43
Hungary	666	10	276	−31	121	38	255	124	1,198	40	112	36	87,639	−34
Iceland	14	180	X	X	X	X	X	X	36	44	150	22	23,758	−10
Ireland	142	178	52	6	X	X	88	X	338	52	96	27	32,543	0
Italy	822	9	12	−48	101	58	521	5	5,165	24	90	16	22,079	−9
Luxembourg	0	−100	X	X	X	X	X	X	119	−30	328	−34	33,698	−60
Malta	X	X	X	X	X	X	X	X	17	89	45	62	19,717	−34
Netherlands	2,861	116	0	−100	578	605	2,270	104	2,480	41	172	28	24,888	6
Norway	3,054	1,295	13	0	1,493	NM	1,166	NM	797	54	193	44	20,970	−9
Poland	5,082	33	4,893	35	10	−47	167	−10	4,903	44	133	27	X	X
Portugal	34	17	5	−38	X	X	X	X	383	105	38	74	21,122	35
Romania	2,763	45	621	92	512	−13	1,590	62	3,059	71	134	52	X	X
Spain	783	89	552	83	99	1,550	0	−100	2,474	70	65	50	21,021	15
Sweden	430	185	0	−100	1	NM	X	X	1,142	−16	137	−19	14,377	−33
Switzerland	170	48	X	X	X	X	X	X	693	17	108	14	10,803	−1
United Kingdom	8,302	96	1,221	−67	5,379	76,743	1,493	243	7,759	−2	138	−3	29,339	−23
Yugoslavia	1,020	62	624	51	173	41	107	174	1,676	99	73	77	40,616	11
USSR	**62,469**	**75**	**14,601**	**9**	**26,156**	**74**	**20,469**	**207**	**48,308**	**65**	**176**	**45**	**X**	**X**
OCEANIA	**4,569**	**146**	**2,845**	**110**	**991**	**172**	**603**	**905**	**3,278**	**58**	**135**	**25**		
Australia	4,277	145	2,786	115	954	163	489	773	2,787	57	180	27	23,609	6
Fiji	1	X	X	X	X	X	X	X	8	14	12	−12	9,270	−35
New Zealand	287	166	59	4	37	1,750	114	2,750	370	61	113	38	24,240	15
Papua New Guinea	1	NM	X	X	X	X	X	X	30	173	9	93	21,118	108
Solomon Islands	X	X	X	X	X	X	X	X	2	100	8	26	15,911	X

Source: U.N. Statistical Office; U.N. Population Division; and The World Bank.
Note: a. Includes primary electricity production, shown in Table 22.2.
0 = zero or less than half the unit of measure; X = not available; NM = not meaningful.
For additional information, see Sources and Technical Notes.

Table 22.2 Production of Electricity, 1960–84

	Total			Fossil-Fuel Fired			Hydroelectric and Geothermal			Nuclear	
	1984 (giga-watt-hours)	Change over (percent) 1970	1960	1984 (giga-watt-hours)	Change over (percent) 1970	1960	1984 (giga-watt-hours)	Change over (percent) 1970	1960	1984 (giga-watt-hours)	Change over 1970 (percent)
WORLD	9,267,420	87	303	6,114,340	65	279	1,978,118	69	190	1,174,962	1,392
AFRICA	224,149	156	522	173,797	178	480	46,427	86	669	3,925	NM
Algeria	11,450	479	764	11,200	701	1,046	250	−57	−28	0	0
Angola	1,790	178	1,152	455	267	1,322	1,335	157	1,103	0	0
Benin	5	−85	−50	5	−85	−50	X	X	X	0	0
Botswana	X	X	X	X	X	X	X	X	X	0	0
Burkina Faso	115	326	1,338	115	326	1,338	X	X	X	0	0
Burundi	2	100	X	2	100	X	0	0	0	0	0
Cameroon	2,230	92	146	110	817	1,000	2,120	84	136	0	0
Cape Verde	25	257	2,400	25	257	2,400	X	X	X	0	0
Central African Rep	68	45	750	3	0	NM	65	48	713	0	0
Chad	65	55	713	65	55	713	X	X	X	0	0
Comoros	10	400	X	10	400	X	0	0	0	0	0
Congo	237	212	717	2	−94	−80	235	434	1,137	0	0
Cote d'Ivoire	1,918	271	2,763	878	242	10,875	1,040	300	1,663	0	0
Djibouti	148	244	1,544	148	244	1,544	X	X	X	0	0
Egypt	22,870	201	767	12,360	328	420	10,510	123	3,942	0	0
Equatorial Guinea	15	−6	150	13	−7	160	2	0	100	0	0
Ethiopia	760	46	645	190	−27	245	570	120	1,113	0	0
Gabon	535	452	2,575	275	184	1,275	260	X	X	0	0
Gambia	42	223	740	42	223	740	X	X	X	0	0
Ghana	1,830	−37	389	40	5	−89	1,790	−38	X	0	0
Guinea	499	29	X	419	15	X	80	233	X	0	0
Guinea-Bissau	14	40	367	14	40	367	X	X	X	0	0
Kenya	2,253	286	915	529	114	605	1,724	413	1,073	0	0
Lesotho	X	X	X	X	X	X	X	X	X	0	0
Liberia	897	79	797	555	113	561	342	41	2,038	0	0
Libya	7,270	1,607	6,824	7,270	1,607	6,824	X	X	X	0	0
Madagascar	452	84	322	204	58	343	248	112	307	0	0
Malawi	511	252	X	27	93	X	484	269	X	0	0
Mali	153	168	920	33	14	120	120	329	X	0	0
Mauritania	102	40	X	102	40	X	X	X	X	0	0
Mauritius	455	107	203	390	131	222	65	27	124	0	0
Morocco	6,617	242	554	6,241	960	7,605	376	−72	−60	0	0
Mozambique	1,945	185	761	410	0	225	1,535	462	1,435	0	0
Niger	245	528	2,963	245	528	2,963	X	X	X	0	0
Nigeria	8,835	470	1,495	6,735	3,541	1,367	2,100	54	2,111	0	0
Rwanda	135	67	X	X	−100	X	135	69	X	0	0
Senegal	684	107	439	684	107	439	X	X	X	0	0
Sierra Leone	280	42	583	280	42	583	0	0	0	0	0
Somalia	75	168	650	75	168	650	X	X	X	0	0
South Africa	122,383	140	402	117,758	132	384	700	474	5,285	3,925	NM
Sudan	1,032	163	998	520	78	453	512	412	X	0	0
Swaziland	X	X	X	X	X	X	X	X	X	0	0
Tanzania, United Rep	870	82	X	255	47	X	615	102	X	0	0
Togo	234	244	4,580	149	126	2,880	85	4,150	X	0	0
Tunisia	3,590	352	1,036	3,560	373	1,223	30	−27	−36	0	0
Uganda	655	−16	56	8	−33	X	647	−16	54	0	0
Zaire	4,558	41	86	133	71	329	4,425	40	82	0	0
Zambia	10,080	962	X	35	−87	X	10,045	1,360	X	0	0
Zimbabwe	4,538	−29	X	1,080	−7	X	3,458	−34	X	0	0
NORTH & CENTRAL AMERICA	3,048,728	61	211	2,015,973	39	181	652,420	53	149	380,335	1,567
Barbados	360	147	847	360	147	847	X	X	X	0	0
Canada	437,990	114	283	98,645	110	1,061	286,644	83	171	52,701	5,339
Costa Rica	3,067	198	600	92	5	104	2,975	216	657	0	0
Cuba	12,292	151	312	12,222	155	313	70	−23	250	0	0
Dominican Rep	4,009	300	1,045	3,495	281	1,097	514	505	786	0	0
El Salvador	1,684	151	574	120	−39	757	1,564	230	563	0	0
Guatemala	1,625	114	478	1,024	138	561	601	83	377	0	0
Haiti	375	218	317	115	−3	28	260	X	X	0	0
Honduras	1,060	237	1,065	186	56	148	874	346	5,363	0	0
Jamaica	2,400	56	372	2,250	58	489	150	23	19	0	0
Mexico	87,083	203	705	61,700	350	994	25,383	69	391	0	0
Nicaragua	973	55	420	466	52	156	507	58	10,040	0	0
Panama	2,360	X	X	869	X	X	1,491	X	X	0	0
Trinidad and Tobago	2,725	127	480	2,725	127	480	X	X	X	0	0
United States	2,472,304	51	193	1,813,482	33	161	331,183	32	121	327,634	230
SOUTH AMERICA	330,643	208	544	74,584	68	218	251,418	298	801	4,641	NM
Argentina	44,914	107	329	20,399	1	114	19,874	1,178	2,044	4,641	NM
Bolivia	1,695	115	280	500	242	421	1,195	86	241	0	0
Brazil	175,710	287	668	10,296	84	130	165,414	315	800	0	0
Chile	13,490	79	194	4,165	28	158	9,325	117	213	0	0
Colombia	27,800	221	641	7,600	199	553	20,200	230	681	0	0
Ecuador	4,400	364	1,037	2,650	387	1,150	1,750	332	900	0	0
Guyana	390	21	324	385	19	318	5	X	X	0	0
Paraguay	1,095	402	1,041	209	227	118	886	475	X	0	0
Peru	11,769	113	343	3,065	79	231	8,704	128	403	0	0
Suriname	1,250	−5	1,482	350	9	343	900	−10	X	0	0
Uruguay	3,637	65	192	137	−86	−76	3,500	182	418	0	0
Venezuela	44,330	249	853	24,665	187	441	19,665	379	20,600	0	0

Table 22.2

	Total			Fossil-Fuel Fired			Hydroelectric and Geothermal			Nuclear	
	1984 (giga-watt-hours)	Change over (percent)		1984 (giga-watt-hours)	Change over (percent)		1984 (giga-watt-hours)	Change over (percent)		1984 (giga-watt-hours)	Change over 1970 (percent)
		1970	1960		1970	1960		1970	1960		
ASIA	**1,664,058**	**155**	**630**	**1,182,390**	**143**	**752**	**315,334**	**99**	**254**	**166,334**	**2,277**
Afghanistan	1,045	164	778	280	1,547	4,567	765	102	577	0	0
Bahrain	2,056	391	879	2,056	391	879	X	X	X	0	0
Bangladesh	4,292	X	X	3,395	X	X	897	X	X	0	0
Bhutan	30	650	X	21	950	X	9	350	X	0	0
Burma	1,726	188	300	872	330	221	854	115	434	0	0
China	376,990	225	535	290,210	204	458	86,780	323	1,073	0	0
Cyprus	1,250	105	430	1,250	105	430	X	X	X	0	0
India	165,440	170	722	106,860	219	770	54,745	117	598	3,835	59
Indonesia	21,330	827	1,424	19,105	1,711	3,138	2,225	79	175	0	0
Iran	37,168	450	X	30,834	506	X	6,334	280	X	0	0
Iraq	18,460	571	2,067	17,850	549	1,995	610	X	X	0	0
Israel	14,909	117	545	14,909	117	545	X	X	X	0	0
Japan	647,380	80	461	445,790	62	682	74,803	-7	28	126,787	33
Jordan	2,304	1,052	X	2,304	1,052	X	X	X	X	0	0
Kampuchea, Dem	70	-47	17	40	-63	-33	30	15	X	0	0
Korea, Dem People's Rep	45,000	173	392	18,000	260	2,045	27,000	135	225	0	0
Korea, Rep	58,163	506	3,208	43,972	425	3,633	2,399	96	314	11,792	NM
Kuwait	14,196	433	3,737	14,196	433	3,737	X	X	X	0	0
Lao People's Dem Rep	990	2,052	7,515	40	-13	208	950	X	X	0	0
Lebanon	1,355	10	222	770	118	147	585	-33	437	00	0
Malaysia	13,700	287	X	11,880	407	X	1,820	51	X	0	0
Mongolia	2,206	303	1,981	2,206	303	1,981	X	X	X	0	0
Nepal	350	361	3,082	35	59	775	315	483	4,400	0	0
Oman	1,675	1,495	X	1,675	1,495	X	X	X	X	0	0
Pakistan	21,873	151	892	8,723	50	472	12,826	340	1,786	324	NM
Philippines	20,800	140	662	8,116	24	459	12,684	505	891	0	0
Qatar	3,425	1,115	5,337	3,425	1,115	5,337	X	X	X	0	0
Saudi Arabia	31,150	2,839	X	31,150	2,839	X	X	X	X	0	0
Singapore	9,401	326	1,327	9,401	326	1,327	X	X	X	0	0
Sri Lanka	2,261	177	649	170	83	467	2,091	189	669	0	0
Syrian Arab Rep	6,757	614	1,736	3,880	335	1,048	2,877	5,131	9,490	0	0
Thailand	22,029	385	3,609	17,948	551	2,922	4,081	128	X	0	0
Turkey	30,630	255	988	17,185	208	848	13,445	342	1,242	0	0
United Arab Emirates	6,636	4,640	X	6,636	4,640	X	X	X	X	0	0
Viet Nam	5,800	174	X	4,000	166	X	1,800	193	X	0	0
Yemen	295	1,539	X	295	1,539	X	X	X	X	0	0
Yemen, Dem	280	46	94	280	46	94	X	X	X	0	0
EUROPE	**2,362,999**	**68**	**246**	**1,411,617**	**40**	**218**	**473,655**	**35**	**101**	**477,727**	**956**
Albania	3,020	220	1,457	620	30	749	2,400	413	1,883	0	0
Austria	41,827	39	162	12,913	47	216	28,914	36	143	0	0
Belgium	53,699	76	254	25,595	-15	71	361	47	110	27,743	48,572
Bulgaria	44,601	129	858	27,100	56	878	3,501	63	86	14,000	NM
Czechoslovakia	78,388	74	221	67,880	64	209	3,269	-11	31	7,239	NM
Denmark	22,361	12	332	22,296	11	333	41	71	64	0	0
Finland	43,311	104	402	12,284	4	266	13,245	42	151	17,782	NM
France	306,800	109	325	60,700	-28	92	64,300	12	59	181,800	3,083
German Dem Rep	110,093	63	173	96,605	47	143	1,748	40	183	11,740	2,430
Germany, Fed Rep	376,600	55	217	292,000	33	175	17,400	-2	34	67,200	1,014
Greece	24,820	153	990	21,958	206	1,114	2,862	9	510	0	0
Hungary	26,293	81	245	22,293	54	196	234	166	149	3,766	NM
Iceland	3,853	162	599	9	-78	-64	3,844	169	631	0	0
Ireland	11,236	84	397	10,548	96	693	688	-3	-26	0	0
Italy	179,546	53	219	127,508	82	1,488	45,151	3	-6	6,887	117
Luxembourg	517	-76	-66	425	-66	-72	92	-90	338	0	0
Malta	700	146	945	700	146	945	X	X	X	0	0
Netherlands	62,780	54	280	59,000	46	257	X	X	X	3,780	927
Norway	106,072	84	241	327	-5	59	105,745	85	242	0	0
Poland	134,792	109	360	131,440	110	359	3,352	78	409	0	0
Portugal	19,033	154	483	11,000	573	6,818	8,033	37	159	0	0
Romania	72,530	107	848	61,450	90	747	11,080	300	2,691	0	0
Spain	115,500	104	521	78,850	186	2,537	27,650	-1	77	9,000	874
Sweden	123,503	104	256	4,432	-77	21	68,076	64	119	50,995	90,963
Switzerland	48,141	45	152	884	-37	259	29,861	2	59	17,396	610
United Kingdom	280,491	13	105	222,507	2	69	4,005	-29	28	53,979	108
Yugoslavia	72,253	178	709	40,080	255	1,261	27,753	88	364	4,420	NM
USSR	**1,493,000**	**102**	**411**	**1,148,200**	**87**	**376**	**202,800**	**63**	**298**	**142,000**	**3,742**
OCEANIA	**143,843**	**106**	**365**	**107,779**	**125**	**425**	**36,064**	**64**	**247**	**0**	**0**
Australia	112,947	110	387	99,436	122	419	13,511	47	235	0	0
Fiji	387	145	604	100	-37	82	287	X	X	0	0
New Zealand	26,519	93	288	5,104	307	444	21,415	72	263	0	0
Papua New Guinea	1,495	683	2,523	1,085	1,804	7,650	410	206	853	0	0
Solomon Islands	28	211	2,700	28	211	2,700	X	X	X	0	0

Source: U.N. Statistical Office.
0 = zero or less than half of the unit of measure; X = not available; NM = not meaningful.
For additional information, see Sources and Technical Notes.

Table 22.3 Reserves and Resources of Commercial Energy[a]

| | Bituminous Coal (million metric tons) | | | | Lignite and Sub-bituminous Coal (million metric tons) | | | | Crude Oil (million metric tons) | Natural Gas (billion cubic meters) | Uranium (metric tons) | |
	Year of Data	Proved Reserves in Place	Proved Recoverable Reserves	Estimated Additional Resources	Year of Data	Proved Reserves in Place	Proved Recoverable Reserves	Estimated Additional Resources	Proved Recoverable Reserves (1981)	Proved Recoverable Reserves (1983)	Reasonably Assured Resources (1983)	Estimated Additional Resources (1983)
WORLD[b]	1981	920,000	515,000	X	1981	600,000	431,000	X	84,000	81,000	1,455,800	896,800
AFRICA												
Algeria	1981	X	43	X	X	X	X	X	833	3,150	26,000	0
Angola	X	X	X	X	X	X	X	X	198	0	X	X
Benin	X	X	X	X	X	X	X	X	X	X	X	X
Botswana	1977	7,000	3,500	100,000	X	X	X	X	X	X	X	0
Burkina Faso	X	X	X	X	X	X	X	X	X	X	X	X
Burundi	X	X	X	X	X	X	X	X	X	X	X	X
Cameroon	X	X	X	X	X	X	X	X	66	150	X	X
Cape Verde	X	X	X	X	X	X	X	X	X	X	X	X
Central African Rep	X	X	X	X	1979	4	4	X	X	X	18,000	0
Chad	X	X	X	X	X	X	X	X	X	X	X	X
Comoros	X	X	X	X	X	X	X	X	X	X	X	X
Congo	X	X	X	X	X	X	X	X	177	64	X	X
Cote d'Ivoire	X	X	X	X	X	X	X	X	43	X	X	X
Djibouti	X	X	X	X	X	X	X	X	X	X	X	X
Egypt	1965	25	13	X	X	X	X	X	400	85	X	X
Equatorial Guinea	X	X	X	X	X	X	X	X	X	X	X	X
Ethiopia	X	X	X	X	X	X	X	X	X	X	X	X
Gabon	X	X	X	X	X	X	X	X	66	68	19,400	0
Gambia	X	X	X	X	X	X	X	X	X	X	X	X
Ghana	X	X	X	X	X	X	X	X	X	X	X	X
Guinea	X	X	X	X	X	X	X	X	X	X	X	X
Guinea-Bissau	X	X	X	X	X	X	X	X	X	X	X	X
Kenya	X	X	X	X	X	X	X	X	X	X	X	X
Lesotho	X	X	X	X	X	X	X	X	X	X	X	X
Liberia	X	X	X	X	X	X	X	X	X	X	X	X
Libya	X	X	X	X	X	X	X	X	3,083	690	X	X
Madagascar	1977	1,000	X	X	1977	75	X	X	X	X	X	X
Malawi	1977	25	12	X	X	X	X	X	X	X	X	X
Mali	X	X	X	X	1979	X	X	3	X	X	X	X
Mauritania	X	X	X	X	X	X	X	X	X	X	X	X
Mauritius	X	X	X	X	X	X	X	X	X	X	X	X
Morocco	1981	134	45	X	1981	44	X	X	40	X	X	X
Mozambique	1976	240	240	155	X	X	X	X	X	X	X	X
Niger	1979	5	X	X	X	X	X	X	X	X	160,000	53,000
Nigeria	1979	X	X	21	1979	338	169	1,000	2,251	1,200	X	X
Rwanda	X	X	X	X	X	X	X	X	X	X	X	X
Senegal	X	X	X	X	X	X	X	X	X	X	X	X
Sierra Leone	X	X	X	X	X	X	X	X	X	X	X	X
Somalia	X	X	X	X	X	X	X	X	X	X	191,000	99,000
South Africa	1981	112,000	51,850	17,100	X	X	X	X	X	X	X	X
Sudan	X	X	X	X	X	X	X	X	27	3	X	X
Swaziland	1961	2,020	1,820	3,000	X	X	X	X	X	X	X	X
Tanzania, United Rep	1979	304	200	1,500	X	X	X	X	X	1	X	X
Togo	X	X	X	X	X	X	X	X	X	X	X	X
Tunisia	X	X	X	X	X	X	X	X	231	135	X	X
Uganda	X	X	X	X	X	X	X	X	X	X	X	X
Zaire	1978	600	600	X	X	X	X	X	20	2	1,800	1,700
Zambia	1979	32	24	98	X	X	X	X	X	X	X	X
Zimbabwe	1977	1,535	734	5,820	1979	965	X	X	X	X	X	X
NORTH & CENTRAL AMERICA												
Barbados	X	X	X	X	X	X	X	X	X	X	X	X
Canada	1981	X	1,607	25,687	1981	X	4,299	32,035	901	2,563	176,000	181,000
Costa Rica	X	X	X	X	X	X	X	X	X	X	X	X
Cuba	X	X	X	X	X	X	X	X	X	X	X	X
Dominican Rep	X	X	X	X	X	X	X	X	X	X	X	X
El Salvador	X	X	X	X	X	X	X	X	X	X	X	X
Guatemala	X	X	X	X	X	X	X	X	8	X	X	X
Haiti	X	X	X	X	1979	13	X	27	X	X	X	X
Honduras	X	X	X	X	1979	21	X	X	X	X	X	X
Jamaica	X	X	X	X	X	X	X	X	X	X	X	X
Mexico	1981	1,623	1,295	1,960	1981	620	496	400	6,907	2,134	2,900	3,500
Nicaragua	X	X	X	X	X	X	X	X	X	X	X	X
Panama	X	X	X	X	X	X	X	X	X	X	X	X
Trinidad and Tobago	X	X	X	X	X	X	X	X	82	320	X	X
United States	1979	223,725	125,353	472,103	1979	205,113	131,750	669,321	3,967	5,712	131,300	30,400
SOUTH AMERICA												
Argentina	X	X	X	X	1981	195	130	7,735	790	620	18,800	7,000
Bolivia	X	X	X	X	X	X	X	X	X	X	X	X
Brazil	X	X	X	X	1981	23,000	13,000	X	371	81	163,300	92,400
Chile	X	X	27	291	1978	X	1,150	X	X	X	X	0
Colombia	1979	2,025	1,010	7,200	1979	48	25	790	71	140	X	X
Ecuador	X	X	X	X	1981	X	18	6	228	3,238	X	X
Guyana	X	X	X	X	X	X	X	X	X	X	X	X
Paraguay	X	X	X	X	X	X	X	X	X	X	X	X
Peru	1981	28	X	856	X	X	X	X	116	34	X	X
Suriname	X	X	X	X	X	X	X	X	X	X	X	X
Uruguay	X	X	X	X	X	X	X	X	X	X	X	X
Venezuela	1981	X	275	1,000	1981	X	34	14,058	932	1,318	X	X

	Bituminous Coal (million metric tons)				Lignite and Sub-bituminous Coal (million metric tons)				Crude Oil (million metric tons)	Natural Gas (billion cubic meters)	Uranium (metric tons)	
	Year of Data	Proved Reserves in Place	Proved Recoverable Reserves	Estimated Additional Resources	Year of Data	Proved Reserves in Place	Proved Recoverable Reserves	Estimated Additional Resources	Proved Recoverable Reserves (1981)	Proved Recoverable Reserves (1983)	Reasonably Assured Resources (1983)	Estimated Additional Resources (1983)
ASIA												
Afghanistan	1965	112	66	400	X	X	X	X	X	75	X	X
Bahrain	X	X	X	X	X	X	X	X	29	280	X	X
Bangladesh	1981	1,054	X	X	X	X	X	X	X	192	X	X
Bhutan	X	X	X	X	X	X	X	X	X	X	X	X
Burma	1975	5	2	120	1975	X	X	80	4	250	X	X
China	X	200,000	99,000	1,326,000	X	X	X	40,500	2,714	700	X	X
Cyprus	X	X	X	X	X	X	X	X	X	X	X	X
India	1981	26,331	X	85,547	1981	1,581	1,581	1,943	471	420	32,000	900
Indonesia	1981	102	X	477	1981	591	X	15,445	6,738	900	X	X
Iran	1972	385	193	X	X	X	X	X	7,776	11,000	X	X
Iraq	X	X	X	X	X	X	X	X	4,052	780	X	X
Israel	X	X	X	X	X	X	X	X	3	4	X	X
Japan	1981	8,479	997	X	1981	175	18	X	6	15	7,700	X
Jordan	X	X	X	X	X	X	X	X	X	X	X	X
Kampuchea, Dem	X	X	X	X	X	X	X	X	X	X	X	X
Korea, Dem People's Rep	1978	2,000	300	2,700	1978	300	300	2,200	X	X	X	X
Korea, Rep	1981	366	192	X	X	X	X	X	X	X	X	X
Kuwait	X	X	X	X	X	X	X	X	8,797	1,000	X	X
Lao People's Dem Rep	X	X	X	X	X	X	X	X	X	X	X	X
Lebanon	X	X	X	X	X	X	X	X	X	X	X	X
Malaysia	1981	X	X	88	1981	X	X	380	301	1,370	X	X
Mongolia	X	12,000	X	X	X	12,000	X	X	X	X	X	X
Nepal	X	X	X	X	X	X	X	X	X	X	X	X
Oman	X	X	X	X	X	X	X	X	351	57	X	X
Pakistan	X	X	X	X	1979	145	102	310	13	450	X	X
Philippines	X	X	X	X	1979	170	82	X	3	X	X	X
Qatar	X	X	X	X	X	X	X	X	469	1,800	X	X
Saudi Arabia	X	X	X	X	X	X	X	X	22,456	2,700	X	X
Singapore	X	X	X	X	X	X	X	X	X	X	X	X
Sri Lanka	X	X	X	X	X	X	X	X	X	X	X	X
Syrian Arab Rep	X	X	X	X	X	X	X	X	200	42	X	X
Thailand	X	X	X	X	1981	15	471	1,418	X	112	X	X
Turkey	1978	285	186	924	1978	3,924	1,728	280	38	15	2,500	X
United Arab Emirates	X	X	X	X	X	X	X	X	4,390	750	X	X
Viet Nam	1965	300	150	700	1965	12	X	X	X	X	X	X
Yemen	X	X	X	X	X	X	X	X	X	X	X	X
Yemen, Dem	X	X	X	X	X	X	X	X	X	X	X	X
EUROPE												
Albania	X	X	X	X	X	15	X	X	20	8	X	X
Austria	X	X	X	X	1981	136	60	85	17	9	0	700
Belgium	1981	1,085	627	15,000	X	X	X	X	X	X	X	X
Bulgaria	1979	36	30	1,200	1979	4,418	3,700	700	2	7	X	X
Czechoslovakia	X	5,750	2,700	5,500	X	7,220	2,860	1,620	3	10	X	X
Denmark	X	X	X	X	X	X	X	680	52	65	X	0
Finland	X	X	X	X	1979	X	X	X	X	X	X	0
France	1981	1,050	398	X	1981	100	64	8	20	82	56,200	26,600
German Dem Rep	X	X	X	X	1981	X	X	0	X	X	X	X
Germany, Fed Rep	1981	44,000	29,919	186,300	1979	55,000	35,150	X	43	179	850	1,300
Greece	X	X	X	X	1976	3,600	1,550	1,150	10	110	X	X
Hungary	1966	450	225	350	1966	4,400	4,000	4,200	16	120	X	X
Iceland	X	X	X	X	X	X	X	X	X	X	X	X
Ireland	1981	7	5	39	1981	12	9	33	X	35	X	X
Italy	X	X	X	X	1981	20	78	302	72	190	2,850	X
Luxembourg	X	X	X	X	X	X	X	X	X	X	X	X
Malta	X	X	X	X	X	X	X	X	X	X	X	X
Netherlands	1981	1,406	497	X	X	X	X	X	18	X	X	X
Norway	X	X	X	X	1981	35	30	100	641	471	X	X
Poland	1978	60,000	27,000	84,000	1978	16,000	12,000	24,000	4	130	X	X
Portugal	1981	28	20	39	1981	44	37	7	X	X	6,700	1,000
Romania	X	X	X	X	X	X	X	X	X	X	X	X
Spain	1981	1,085	868	1,801	1981	917	823	918	18	14	15,650	5,000
Sweden	X	X	X	X	1981	4	1	20	X	X	X	300
Switzerland	X	X	X	X	X	X	X	X	X	X	X	X
United Kingdom	1981	X	4,600	185,400	X	X	X	X	1,000	664	X	X
Yugoslavia	1971	80	70	22	1978	17,760	16,500	3,775	41	40	X	X
USSR	**1981**	**136,000**	**108,800**	**1,710,000**	**1981**	**152,000**	**131,500**	**2,407,900**	**X**	**30,700**	**X**	**X**
OCEANIA												
Australia	1981	48,540	27,442	507,000	1981	42,286	38,260	187,400	216	644	314,000	369,000
Fiji	X	X	X	X	X	X	X	X	X	X	X	X
New Zealand	1981	40	37	450	1981	2,167	291	10,728	0	190	X	X
Papua New Guinea	X	X	X	X	X	X	X	X	X	X	X	X
Solomon Islands	X	X	X	X	X	X	X	X	X	X	X	X

Source: U.N. Statistical Office.
Notes:
a. Hydroelectric potential is shown in Table 23.2.
b. Global data include estimates for countries where data are unavailable.
0 = zero; X = not available.
For additional information, see Sources and Technical Notes.

Table 22.4 Nuclear Power and Waste Generation, 1970–85

	Number of Reactors					Net Capacity (Megawatts of Electricity)[a]					Spent Fuel Inventories (cumulative metric tons of heavy metal)[b]			
	Operable				Planned or under Construction as of	Installed				Planned or under Construction as of				
	1970	1975	1980	1985	31 Dec 1985	1970	1975	1980	1985	31 Dec 1985	1970	1975	1980	1985
WORLD TOTAL	66	151	234	372	262	15,471	68,379	132,782	254,178	253,119				
MARKET ECONOMIES	54	128	197	307	160	13,963	62,141	117,573	218,577	157,037	6,219	17,078	36,711	59,600
North America	14	57	77	112	43	6,433	38,553	56,326	89,536	44,919	145	2,494	9,818	19,000
Canada	1	5	9	17	6	22	2,078	5,150	10,007	4,936	96	989	3,314	6,600
Mexico	0	0	0	0	2	0	0	0	0	1,308	0	0	0	0
United States	13	52	68	95	35	6,411	36,475	51,176	79,529	38,675	49	1,505	6,504	12,400
Asia	6	16	31	50	55	1,658	7,019	17,712	32,660	45,869	X	X	X	X
China	0	0	0	0	9	0	0	0	0	5,688	0	0	0	0
India	2	3	4	6	4	400	602	804	1,244	880	X	X	X	X
Japan	4	12	23	33	31	1,258	6,292	15,011	23,669	29,745	X	X	X	X
Korea, Rep	0	0	1	4	7	0	0	564	2,698	6,436	X	X	X	X
Pakistan	0	1	1	1	1	0	125	125	125	600	X	X	X	X
Philippines	0	0	0	0	1	0	0	0	0	620	0	0	0	0
Taiwan	0	0	2	6	2	0	0	1,208	4,924	1,900	X	X	X	X
Europe	34	54	86	140	55	5,872	16,224	42,164	92,966	58,797	6,060	14,220	25,095	35,600
Austria	0	0	0	0	1	0	0	0	0	692	0	0	0	0
Belgium	0	1	3	7	0	0	393	1,656	5,460	0	X	X	X	X
Finland	0	0	4	4	0	0	0	2,266	2,266	0	X	X	X	X
France	3	6	17	43	21	1,190	2,478	12,468	37,813	26,470	X	X	X	X
Germany, Fed Rep	1	4	10	17	11	328	2,744	8,523	16,381	12,304	X	X	X	X
Italy	2	2	3	3	5	397	397	1,270	1,270	3,908	X	X	X	X
Netherlands	1	2	2	2	0	52	497	497	497	0	X	X	X	X
Spain	1	3	3	8	10	153	1,073	1,073	5,667	9,658	X	X	X	X
Sweden	0	5	8	12	0	0	3,130	5,515	9,440	0	X	X	X	X
Switzerland	1	3	4	5	2	350	1,020	1,940	2,882	2,065	X	X	X	X
United Kingdom	25	28	32	38	5	3,402	4,492	6,956	10,670	3,700	X	X	X	X
Yugoslavia	0	0	0	1	0	0	0	0	620	0	X	X	X	X
Other	0	1	3	5	7	0	345	1,371	3,415	7,452	X	X	X	X
Argentina	0	1	2	2	1	0	345	945	945	692	X	X	X	X
Brazil	0	0	1	1	4	0	0	626	626	4,960	X	X	X	X
Egypt	0	0	0	0	2	0	0	0	0	1,800	0	0	0	0
South Africa	0	0	0	2	0	0	0	0	1,844	0	X	X	X	X
NONMARKET ECONOMIES	12	23	37	65	102	1,508	6,238	15,209	35,601	96,082	X	X	X	X
Bulgaria	0	2	3	4	6	0	810	1,215	1,620	5,746	X	X	X	X
Cuba	0	0	0	0	2	0	0	0	0	816	0	0	0	0
Czechoslovakia	0	1	3	6	11	0	104	864	2,094	6,402	X	X	X	X
German Dem Rep	1	3	5	5	10	70	886	1,702	1,702	4,080	X	X	X	X
Hungary	0	0	0	2	6	0	0	0	816	2,448	X	X	X	X
Poland	0	0	0	0	6	0	0	0	0	3,660	0	0	0	0
Romania	0	0	0	0	6	0	0	0	0	3,924	0	0	0	0
USSR	11	17	26	48	55	1,438	4,438	11,428	29,369	69,006	X	X	X	X

Source: U.S. Department of Energy.
Notes: a. Nuclear electricity generation data are shown in Table 22.2. b. "Market Economies" aggregate includes data for "Asia" and "Other." Data for "Nonmarket Economies" are unavailable. 0 = zero; X = not available. For additional information, see Sources and Technical Notes.

Table 22.5 Producers and Consumers of Selected Metals, 1965–85

	Annual Production (thousand metric tons)						Annual Consumption (thousand metric tons)				
	1965	1970	1975	1980	1985		1965	1970	1975	1980	1985
ALUMINUM											
United States	2,499	3,607	3,519	4,654	3,500	United States	2,852	3,488	3,265	4,454	4,400
USSR	840	1,100	1,530	1,760	2,200	Japan	286	930	1,171	1,639	1,816
Canada	753	972	887	1,068	1,282	USSR	1,000	1,281	1,580	1,850	1,750
Australia	88	206	214	303	851	Germany, Fed Rep	387	670	704	1,042	1,158
Germany, Fed Rep	234	309	678	731	745	China	95	180	300	550	700
Norway	279	522	595	653	724	France	249	413	399	601	586
Brazil	33	62	121	260	540	Italy	128	279	270	458	470
China	100	130	200	360	410	Brazil	52	84	209	296	367
Venezuela	0	25	45	321	396	United Kingdom	364	404	393	409	350
Spain	52	120	210	386	370	Belgium	117	175	178	233	285
Ten Countries Total	4,878	7,052	7,999	10,497	11,018	**Ten Countries Total**	5,529	7,904	8,469	11,532	11,882
World Total	6,318	9,653	12,145	15,383	15,289	**World Total**	6,699	9,928	11,299	15,285	16,038
COPPER											
Chile	606	711	828	1,068	1,356	United States	1,819	1,854	1,397	1,868	1,906
United States	1,226	1,560	1,282	1,181	1,106	Japan	428	821	827	1,158	1,231
Canada	461	610	734	716	724	USSR	408	841	1,035	990	935
USSR	323	451	580	590	600	Germany, Fed Rep	536	698	635	748	754
Zaire	289	387	495	540	560	China	120	200	315	386	446
Zambia	696	684	677	596	483	France	287	331	365	433	398
Poland	15	72	230	346	431	Italy	192	274	299	388	362
Peru	180	220	193	367	397	United Kingdom	650	554	451	409	347
Mexico	55	61	79	175	290	Belgium	99	145	177	304	310
Australia	92	158	219	244	258	Canada	204	229	196	209	223
Ten Countries Total	3,943	4,914	5,317	5,822	6,205	**Ten Countries Total**	4,742	5,946	5,696	6,893	6,912
World Total	4,690	6,262	7,000	7,394	8,114	**World Total**	5,750	7,172	7,260	9,086	9,281

Table 22.5 Producers and Consumers of Selected Metals, 1965–85
(continued)

	Annual Production (thousand metric tons)						Annual Consumption (thousand metric tons)				
	1965	1970	1975	1980	1985		1965	1970	1975	1980	1985
LEAD											
Australia	368	457	408	397	491	United States	754	894	820	1,094	1,142
USSR	350	440	480	420	440	USSR	385	486	620	800	660
United States	273	519	564	550	424	Japan	147	211	189	393	395
Canada	275	353	349	297	278	Germany, Fed Rep	271	309	225	333	345
Peru	154	157	184	189	210	United Kingdom	312	262	238	296	274
Mexico	167	177	179	147	200	Italy	94	168	146	275	230
China	100	100	100	160	160	China	100	160	185	210	220
Yugoslavia	106	127	127	121	110	France	145	193	174	213	208
Morocco	77	73	64	115	101	Yugoslavia	43	45	83	128	139
Bulgaria	100	96	114	116	96	Bulgaria	X	77	95	110	115
Ten Countries Total	**1,970**	**2,497**	**2,568**	**2,512**	**2,510**	**Ten Countries Total**	**2,250**	**2,803**	**2,775**	**3,851**	**3,728**
World Total	**2,753**	**3,471**	**3,581**	**3,577**	**3,392**	**World Total**	**3,179**	**3,914**	**4,759**	**5,392**	**5,308**
NICKEL											
USSR	85	110	152	154	180	USSR	110	130	115	132	161
Canada	242	277	242	185	152	United States	156	141	133	142	147
Australia	0	30	76	74	85	Japan	27	98	90	122	136
New Caledonia	31	105	133	87	73	Germany, Fed Rep	31	41	43	68	76
Indonesia	4	16	15	53	49	France	21	36	32	38	32
Cuba	X	35	37	37	32	Italy	9	20	17	27	29
Dominican Rep	0	X	27	16	26	United Kingdom	37	35	21	23	25
South Africa	3	12	21	26	25	China	X	X	18	18	21
Philippines	0	0	9	48	19	Sweden	13	23	22	20	17
Botswana	0	X	6	15	18	India	X	X	3	12	14
Ten Countries Total	**365**	**585**	**717**	**696**	**658**	**Ten Countries Total**	**404**	**524**	**494**	**602**	**658**
World Total	**426**	**628**	**808**	**759**	**777**	**World Total**	**428**	**567**	**570**	**715**	**792**
TIN											
Malaysia	64	73	64	61	37	United States	63	57	56	56	52
USSR	23	27	30	36	23	USSR	29	17	23	25	37
Indonesia	15	19	25	33	22	Japan	18	29	28	31	32
Brazil	2	4	5	7	22	Germany, Fed Rep	13	15	13	16	16
Thailand	19	21	16	34	20	China	15	13	14	13	11
Bolivia	23	29	24	22	18	United Kingdom	21	19	14	10	9
China	25	20	22	15	15	France	10	11	10	10	7
Australia	4	9	10	12	7	Italy	6	7	8	6	5
United Kingdom	1	2	3	3	5	Brazil	2	3	3	5	5
Peru	0	0	0	1	4	Netherlands	4	6	4	5	5
Ten Countries Total	**178**	**204**	**200**	**223**	**173**	**Ten Countries Total**	**180**	**175**	**174**	**177**	**178**
World Total	**205**	**217**	**219**	**236**	**191**	**World Total**	**223**	**225**	**216**	**224**	**232**
ZINC											
Canada	826	1,239	1,229	1,059	1,175	United States	1,221	1,074	839	810	941
USSR	470	610	690	785	810	USSR	401	510	900	1,030	810
Australia	355	487	501	495	734	Japan	322	623	547	752	780
Peru	254	299	385	488	589	Germany, Fed Rep	334	396	297	406	409
Mexico	225	266	289	236	280	China	100	150	220	200	350
United States	554	485	426	317	252	France	186	220	223	330	247
Japan	221	280	254	238	252	Italy	116	178	150	236	218
Spain	39	98	84	183	228	United Kingdom	282	278	207	181	195
Sweden	79	93	111	167	207	Belgium	123	128	103	155	169
Ireland	1	97	67	229	192	Canada	85	110	150	133	157
Ten Countries Total	**3,025**	**3,954**	**4,036**	**4,197**	**4,719**	**Ten Countries Total**	**3,170**	**3,667**	**3,636**	**4,233**	**4,276**
World Total	**4,235**	**5,615**	**6,111**	**6,213**	**6,656**	**World Total**	**4,054**	**5,042**	**5,036**	**6,181**	**6,323**
IRON ORE											
USSR	153,432	195,492	232,803	244,713	248,000	USSR	128,895	159,392	189,177	218,417	201,078[a]
Brazil	20,754	40,200	89,894	114,732	120,000	Japan	62,286	106,708	140,584	140,899	130,451
Australia	6,803	51,189	97,651	95,534	100,000	China	38,500	44,000	66,400	80,900	94,000
China	39,000	40,400	65,000	68,000	80,000	United States	125,132	133,676	115,952	100,461	73,674[a]
United States	88,842	91,201	80,132	70,730	49,533	Germany, Fed Rep	44,392	54,141	48,216	53,353	50,256
India	23,830	31,366	41,405	41,936	44,546	Brazil	5,429	10,476	11,395	19,984	26,424
Canada	36,250	47,459	46,868	48,754	39,889	France	37,735	40,717	34,452	34,483	25,033
South Africa	5,816	7,728	12,298	26,312	24,393	Italy	8,606	12,438	17,916	20,695	20,529
Sweden	29,354	31,509	30,867	27,184	20,454	Czechoslovakia	10,856	15,780	17,720	18,894	17,919
Venezuela	17,510	22,100	24,772	16,102	15,480	Poland	11,664	13,918	14,097	20,985	17,218
Ten Countries Total	**421,592**	**558,643**	**721,691**	**753,999**	**742,295**	**Ten Countries Total**	**473,495**	**591,246**	**655,909**	**709,071**	**656,582**
World Total	**620,982**	**769,163**	**902,018**	**895,867**	**858,817**	**World Total**	**620,982**	**769,163**	**902,018**	**895,867**	**858,817**
CRUDE STEEL											
USSR	91,000	115,886	141,325	147,941	155,000	USSR	91,000	115,873	141,325	147,931	159,945[a]
Japan	41,161	93,322	102,313	111,395	105,281	United States	125,723	124,514	113,945	111,525	103,779[a]
United States	118,985	119,305	105,816	101,455	80,067	Japan	31,548	75,835	73,469	82,784	76,638
China	15,000	18,000	25,000	37,120	46,700	China	X	X	X	37,217	54,351[a]
Germany, Fed Rep	36,821	45,041	40,415	43,838	40,500	Germany, Fed Rep	32,851	41,983	32,959	27,690	31,920
Italy	12,681	17,277	21,836	26,501	23,744	Italy	12,296	20,539	18,618	26,808	22,402[a]
Brazil	3,024	5,390	8,308	15,339	20,456	Brazil[b]	3,013	5,178	8,280	11,740	9,249[a]
France	19,604	23,773	21,530	23,176	18,832	France	16,935	24,175	20,297	16,457	15,945
Poland	9,088	11,795	15,007	19,485	16,100	Poland	8,659	11,739	17,328	15,000	15,352
United Kingdom	27,440	28,316	20,198	11,278	15,722	United Kingdom	24,076	26,416	20,729	14,962	14,667
Ten Countries Total	**374,804**	**478,105**	**501,747**	**537,527**	**522,402**	**Ten Countries Total**	**346,101**	**446,252**	**446,950**	**492,114**	**504,248**
World Total	**459,300**	**594,418**	**643,798**	**713,788**	**714,970**	**World Total**	**459,300**	**594,418**	**643,798**	**713,788**	**714,970**

Sources: U.S. Bureau of Mines; and World Bureau of Metal Statistics (London).
Notes: a. 1984. b. Rolled steel only. 0 = zero or less than half of the unit of measure; X = not available. For additional information, see Sources and Technical Notes.

Table 22.6 Recovery of Selected Materials, 1964–85

	Recovery Ratio											
	Aluminum			Copper			Iron and Steel			Lead		
	1964-66	1974-76	1983-85	1964-66	1974-76	1983-85	1971-73	1977-79	1982-84	1964-66	1974-76	1983-85
AFRICA												
Algeria	X	X	X	X	X	X	X	X	X	X	X	28
Egypt	X	X	X	X	X	X	X	X	X	X	X	X
Ethiopia	X	X	X	X	X	X	X	X	X	X	X	X
Morocco	X	X	X	X	X	X	X	X	X	X	X	56
Mozambique	X	X	X	X	X	X	X	X	X	X	X	X
Nigeria	X	X	X	X	X	X	X	X	X	X	X	X
South Africa	X	8	25	X	37	8^c	X	X	X	X	27	66
Sudan	X	X	X	X	X	X	X	X	X	X	X	X
Tunisia	X	X	X	X	X	X	X	X	X	X	X	3
NORTH & CENTRAL AMERICA												
Canada	12	12	15	8	13	15	15	18	24	56	85	66
El Salvador	X	56^d	41^d	X	X	X	X	X	X	X	X	X
Guatemala	X	X	X	X	X	X	X	X	X	X	X	X
Mexico	X	10	16	X	8^e	20	X	X	X	X	X	35
Panama	7^d	15^d	20^d	X	X	X	X	X	X	X	X	X
United States	21	23	28	23	21	23^f	31	32	37	49	47	48
SOUTH AMERICA												
Argentina	X	19	16	X	X	X	X	X	X	X	X	54
Brazil	6	10	16	X	19	14	X	X	X	X	46	57
Chile	X	X	X	X	X	X	X	X	X	X	X	X
Colombia	X	X	X	X	X	X	X	X	X	X	X	X
Peru	X	X	X	X	X	X	X	X	X	X	X	19
Uruguay	X	X	X	X	X	X	X	X	X	X	X	X
Venezuela	X	4	43	X	X	X	X	X	X	X	X	71
ASIA												
Bahrain	X	X	85	X	X	X	X	X	X	X	X	X
China	X	X	X	X	X	X	X	X	X	X	X	X
Hong Kong	X	X	X	X	X	X	X	X	X	X	X	X
India	X	X	X	X	X	X	X	X	X	X	X	12
Indonesia	X	78^d	X	X	X	X	X	X	X	X	X	X
Iran	13^d	20	2	X	X	X	X	X	X	X	X	X
Israel	X	4^d	X	X	X	X	X	X	X	X	X	X
Japan	27	15	31	26	17	17	25	25	26	41	29	33
Jordan	X	X	X	X	X	X	X	X	X	X	X	X
Korea, Rep	X	6^d	6^d	X	40	24	X	X	X	X	X	20
Malaysia	X	X	X	X	X	X	X	X	X	X	X	X
Pakistan	X	X	X	X	X	X	X	X	X	X	X	X
Philippines	X	X	X	X	X	X	X	X	X	X	X	X
Sri Lanka	X	X	X	X	X	X	X	X	X	X	X	X
Taiwan	9	13	8	X	3^c	7	X	X	X	X	X	78
Thailand	X	X	X	X	X	X	X	X	X	X	X	30
Turkey	X	X	X	X	X	X	18	15	32	X	X	25
EUROPE												
Austria	X	9	21	X	86^e	225	23	36	26	7	6	22
Belgium	9^d	3^d	1^d	11^{c,g}	42^g	25^h	15	22	25	13	8	41
Czechoslovakia	X	X	X	X	X	X	36	44	45	X	X	X
Denmark	X	28^d	40^d	7^{c,i}	21^i	21^i	X	X	X	X	X	76
Finland	X	14^d	32^d	X	X	X	33	28	26	X	X	23
France	19	22	26	8^c	9	11	13	13	13	31	6	42
German Dem Rep	X	X	X	X	X	X	58	57	68	X	X	X
Germany, Fed Rep	32	29	35	33	27	31	33	31	29	15	33	25
Greece	X	X	X	X	36	12^c	X	X	X	X	X	3
Hungary	X	X	X	X	X	X	24	24	29	X	X	X
Ireland	X	X	X	X	X	X	X	X	X	X	X	95
Italy	34	38	39	12^c	17	23	43	47	46	28	34	44
Netherlands	3^d	26	37	X	X	X	22	16	15	21	35	72
Norway	12	7	2	X	X	X	21	20	24	X	4	2
Poland	X	X	X	X	X	X	26	29	27	X	X	X
Portugal	X	10^d	5^d	X	X	9^c	19	32	49	16	X	22
Romania	X	X	X	X	X	X	16	X	X	X	X	X
Spain	X	23	1	5^c	26	36	28	38	45	X	X	38
Sweden	13^d	21	18	X	X	X	42	36	36	X	X	85
Switzerland	24^d	21	21	8^c	15^c	91^c	X	X	X	X	X	20
United Kingdom	36	29	23	23	23	26	47	53	38	40	23	65
Yugoslavia	X	X	19	X	21	42	24	28	23	X	X	32
USSR	X	X	X	X	X	X	11	16	X	X	X	X
OCEANIA												
Australia	14^d	16	16	26^e	34	43	X	X	X	X	71	40
New Zealand	X	6	12	X	X	X	X	X	X	X	X	50

World Resources 1987

Table 22.6

	Tin			Zinc			Paper			Glass
Recovery Ratio	1964-66	1974-76	1982-84	1964-66	1974-76	1982-84	1964-66	1974-76	1982-84	1983-85
AFRICA										
Algeria	X	X	X	X	X	X	X	X	X	X
Egypt	X	X	X	X	X	X	X	30	29a	X
Ethiopia	X	X	X	X	X	X	X	31	15b	X
Morocco	X	X	X	X	X	X	X	5	3b	X
Mozambique	X	X		X	X		X	0	23b	X
Nigeria	X	X	X	X	X	X	X	0	2b	X
South Africa	X	X	X	X	X	X	X	29	23b	X
Sudan	X	X	X	X	X	X	X	5	3b	X
Tunisia	X	X	X	X	X	X	X	30	10b	X
NORTH & CENTRAL AMERICA										
Canada	X	5	6	3	3	X	13	18	20	X
El Salvador	X	X	X	X	X	X	X	X	X	X
Guatemala	X	X	X	X	X	X	X	33	66b	X
Mexico	X	X	X	X	21	23	X	42	39	X
Panama	X	X	X	X	X	X	X	X	X	X
United States	47g	38g	35g	26	30	38	19	25	31a	10
SOUTH AMERICA										
Argentina	X	X	X	X	X	7	X	49	41a	X
Brazil	X	5	5	X	9	10	X	26	37a	X
Chile	X	X	X	X	X	X	X	22	38a	X
Colombia	X	X	X	X	X	X	X	24	30b	X
Peru	X	X	X	X	X	X	X	23	17b	X
Uruguay	X	X	X	X	X	X	X	22	76a	X
Venezuela	X	X	X	X	X	X	X	27	21b	X
ASIA										
Bahrain	X	X	X	X	X	X	X	X	X	X
China	X	X	X	X	X	X	X	5	7b	X
Hong Kong	X	X	X	X	X	X	X	34	29b	X
India	X	X	X	X	X	X	X	6	16b	X
Indonesia	X	X	X	X	X	X	X	1	1b	X
Iran	X	X	X	X	X	X	X	19	24b	X
Israel	X	X	X	X	X	X	0	16	10b	X
Japan	22	16	21	19	30	34	41	43	48b	X
Jordan	X	X	X	X	X	X	X	0	19a,b	X
Korea, Rep	X	X	X	X	X	X	X	31	32	X
Malaysia	X	X	X	X	X	X	X	13	20a	X
Pakistan	X	X	X	X	X	X	X	19	17b	X
Philippines	X	X	X	X	X	X	X	24	14a	X
Sri Lanka	X	X	X	X	X	X	X	X	14	X
Taiwan	X	X	X	X	X	X	X	X	X	X
Thailand	X	X	X	X	X	X	X	82	26	X
Turkey	X	X	X	X	X	X	X	27	X	X
EUROPE										
Austria	X	23	X	7	1	1	26	24	46a	30
Belgium	44	36	67	X	5	9	27	38	35b	37
Czechoslovakia	X	X	X	X	X	X	X	31	56a	X
Denmark	X	26	100	X	X	X	16	31	29	16
Finland	X	X	X	X	X	X	20	30	44a	X
France	56	4	3	18	11	6	27	43	39a	25
German Dem Rep	X	X	X	X	X	X	X	X	X	X
Germany, Fed Rep	77g	52g	27g	13	37	28	27	56	42a	33
Greece	X	X	X	X	X	X	0	13	4b	X
Hungary	X	X	X	X	X	X	X	31	26	X
Ireland	X	X	X	X	X	X	X	X	X	7
Italy	22	58	64	6	7	3	18	30	30b	24
Netherlands	X	25	5	X	X	X	34	47	54	51
Norway	27	93	25	X	X	56	20	22	21	X
Poland	X	X	X	X	X	X	X	31	32b	X
Portugal	X	44	60	X	X	X	0	8	44	11
Romania	X	X	X	X	X	X	X	30	28b	X
Spain	X	46g	23g	X	10	10	28	32	44	13
Sweden	X	X	X	2	3	X	22	29	49a	X
Switzerland	X	X	X	X	X	X	32	41	89a	44
United Kingdom	68g	72g	84g	30	31	30	29	30	35a	10
Yugoslavia	X	X	X	X	X	8	X	31	34	X
USSR	X	X	X	X	X	X	X	X	X	X
OCEANIA										
Australia	3	11	2	X	45	77	0	26	40	X
New Zealand	X	X	X	X	X	X	0	11	9b	X

Source: World Resources Institute and International Institute for Environment and Development.
Notes: a. Waste paper collected as percentage of consumption of recyclable paper and paperboard; b. 1982-83; c. Recovery includes only direct old scrap used by manufacturers; d. Consumption is apparent aluminum consumption; e. Recovery includes only old scrap used in the production of refined copper; f. 1984-86; g. Production of secondary refined tin included; h. Includes Luxembourg and the Netherlands; i. Includes Finland, Norway, and Sweden.
0 = zero or less than half of 1 percent; X = not available.
For additional information, see Sources and Technical Notes.

Energy and Minerals

Sources and Technical Notes

Table 22.1 Production and Consumption of Commercial Energy, 1970-84

Sources: Energy: U.N. Statistical Office, *Energy Statistics Yearbook 1982* and *1984* (United Nations, New York, 1984 and 1986). Population: U.N. Population Division, *World Population Prospects: Estimates and Projections as Assessed in 1984* (United Nations, New York, 1986). Gross National Product: unpublished data (The World Bank, Washington, D.C., November 1986).

Energy data are compiled by the U.N. Statistical Office primarily from responses to questionnaires sent to national governments, supplemented by official national statistical publications. Additional data and analysis are provided by the Organisation for Economic Co-operation and Development, the Organization of Petroleum Exporting Countries, the International Labour Organization, the United Nations Food and Agriculture Organization, the International Atomic Energy Agency, the International Sugar Organization, and the U.S. Department of Energy. When official data are not available, the U.N. Statistical Office prepares estimates based on the professional and commercial literature.

Total production of commercially traded fuels includes the production of solid, liquid, and gaseous fuels and the production of primary electricity (shown in Table 22.2). Solid fuels include bituminous coal, lignite, peat, and oil shale burned directly. Liquid fuels include crude petroleum and natural gas liquids. Gaseous fuel is natural gas.

Fuelwood, bagasse, charcoal, and all forms of solar energy are excluded from production figures, even when traded commercially.

Consumption is defined as domestic production plus net imports, minus net stock increases, minus aircraft and marine bunkers. Total consumption includes energy from solids, liquids, gases, and primary electricity.

All the production data and the total consumption data are in petajoules, or 1 quadrillion joules. One petajoule equals 0.000948 Quads (quadrillion British Thermal Units) and is the equivalent of 163,400 "U.N. standard" barrels of oil or 34,140 "U.N. standard" metric tons of coal. The heat content of various fuels has been converted to coal-equivalent and then petajoule-equivalent values using country- and year-specific conversion factors. For example, a metric ton of bituminous coal produced in Argentina has an energy value of 0.843 metric tons of standard coal equivalent (7 million kilocalories). A metric ton of bituminous coal produced in Turkey has an energy value of 0.929 metric tons of standard coal equivalent. The original national production data for bituminous coal were multiplied by these conversion factors, and the resulting figures in tons of standard coal equivalent were multiplied by 29.3076×10^{-6} to yield petajoule equivalents. Similarly, other fuels were converted to coal equivalent and petajoule-equivalent terms.

A gigajoule is 1 billion joules. A kilojoule is 1,000 joules.

South Africa refers to the South Africa Customs Union: South Africa, Botswana, Lesotho, Swaziland, and Namibia.

Table 22.2 Production of Electricity, 1960-84

Source: U.N. Statistical Office, *Energy Statistics Yearbook 1982* and *1984* (United Nations, New York, 1984 and 1986).

Electricity production data generally refer to gross production. Data for the Dominican Republic, Finland, France, (including Monaco), Iceland, Mexico, Switzerland, the United States, Zambia, and Zimbabwe refer to net production. Gross production is the amount of electricity produced by a generating station before consumption by station auxiliaries and transformer losses within the station are deducted. Net production is the amount of electricity remaining after these deductions. Typically, net production is 5-10 percent less than gross production. Energy production from pumped storage is not included in gross or net electricity generation.

A gigawatt-hour of electricity is 1 billion watt-hours. A gigawatt-hour is the equivalent of 3.4 billion Btus or 83,000 joules.

Electricity production includes both public and self-producer power plants. Public power plants produce electricity for many users. They may be operated by private, cooperative, or governmental organizations. Self-producer power plants are operated by organizations or companies to produce electricity for internal applications, such as factory operations.

The fossil-fuel fired generation figure for Denmark refers to 1983.

Table 22.3 Reserves and Resources of Commercial Energy

Source: U.N. Statistical Office, *Energy Statistics Yearbook 1984* (United Nations, New York, 1986).

Resource data for coal, lignite, crude oil, and natural gas are from World Energy Conference, *1983 Survey of Energy Resources* (World Energy Conference, London, 1983). More recent data will be available in 1987 from the World Energy Conference held in October 1986.

Data for uranium resources are taken from the Nuclear Energy Agency of the Organisation for Economic Co-operation and Development (OECD), and the International Atomic Energy Agency, *Uranium Resources, Production and Demand* (OECD, Paris, 1983).

The total resources of mineral fuels have been assessed with varying degrees of confidence. Fuel resources are grouped according to the degree of confidence in their identification and the economic and technical feasibility of extracting them.

Proved Reserves in Place represent the fraction of total resources that is known to exist in specific locations and in specific qualities.

Proved Recoverable Reserves are the fraction of proved reserves in place that can be extracted with existing technology under present and expected economic conditions.

Estimated Additional Resources include all resources, other than proved reserves, that are of foreseeable economic interest. The estimates reflect a reasonable level of confidence and are based on knowledge of geological conditions that are favorable to occurrence of the resources.

Reasonably Assured Resources of uranium refers to known uranium deposits of a size and quality that could be recovered within specified production cost ranges using currently proven mining and processing technology.

Estimated Additional Resources of uranium are those resources that are expected to occur on the basis of studies of existing deposits and potential deposit areas.

In the lignite and sub-bituminous coal aggregate, lignite accounts for 57 percent of the global proved reserves in place and 61 percent of the global proved recoverable reserves.

Bituminous coal includes anthracite. Because the questionnaire sent to countries did not request a description of bituminous coal, it is not possible to calculate the amount of anthracite included in the figures. Anthracite is probably only a small fraction of the total.

Crude Oil includes natural gas liquids, reservoir gas recovered in liquid form in surface separators or plant facilities.

Data on hydroelectric resources are shown in Table 23.2. Available data for other renewable energy resources—wind, solar, waves, tides, biomass, and geothermal—will be presented in future editions of the *World Resources Report*.

Table 22.4 Nuclear Power and Waste Generation, 1970-85

Sources: Reactor and capacity data: U.S. Department of Energy (DOE), Energy Information Administration (EIA), *Commercial Nuclear Power: Prospects for the United States and the World* (U.S. DOE/EIA, Washington, D.C., 1986). Spent fuel data: U.S. DOE/EIA, unpublished data (U.S. DOE/EIA, Washington, D.C., 1986).

Operable Reactors refers to power reactors that produce electricity for the commercial electrical grid, although not necessarily at full power. Reactors in extended shutdown are included. Retired reactors are excluded. All data are as of December 31 of the year indicated.

The Number of Reactors Planned or Under Construction refers to those plants for which planning or construction was underway as of December 31, 1985.

Installed Capacity is on a net basis. The electricity requirements of generating plants, usually about 5-10 percent of gross generation, have been deducted.

Capacity Planned or under Construction refers to the total additional capacity that is possible if all the reactors planned or under construction were completed.

A megawatt of electricity is 1 million watts of electric power.

Spent Fuel Inventories are expressed as cumulative totals to the years given and are net of reprocessing. "Heavy metal" refers to the actinide elements (uranium, plutonium, etc.) contained in the spent fuel. For additional information on spent fuel inventories, refer to U.S. DOE/EIA, *World Nuclear Fuel Cycle Requirements* (U.S. DOE/EIA, Washington, D.C., 1986).

Table 22.5 Producers and Consumers of Selected Metals, 1965–85

Sources: Production data for 1965, 1970, 1975, and 1980: U.S. Bureau of Mines (U.S. BOM), *Minerals Yearbook 1966, 1976,* and *1981* (U.S. Government Printing Office, Washington, D.C., 1967, 1977, and 1983). Production data for 1985: unpublished data (U.S. BOM, Washington, D.C., December 1986). Consumption data for aluminum, copper, lead, nickel, tin, and zinc: World Bureau of Metal Statistics, *World Metal Statistics* (World Bureau of Metal Statistics, London, April 1970, December 1974, February 1979, June 1985, and October 1986). Consumption data for iron and steel: United Nations Economic Commission for Europe (ECE), *Annual Bulletin of Steel Statistics for Europe* (ECE, New York, 1966, 1972, 1977, 1981, and 1986); and unpublished data (U.S. BOM, Washington, D.C., December 1986). USSR production and consumption data for copper: Vasili V. Strishkov, *The Copper Industry of the USSR: Problems, Issues, and Outlook* (U.S. BOM, Washington, D.C., 1984).

The countries listed represent the top ten producers and the top ten consumers of each material in 1985.

The U.S. Bureau of Mines prepares mineral production statistics based on material from government mineral and statistical agencies, the United Nations, and U.S. and foreign technical and trade literature. This material is continually updated.

Production refers to the first solid state of mined ore after melting.

Zinc is given in zinc content of mined ore.

Iron Ore refers to iron ore, iron ore concentrates, and iron ore agglomerates (sinter and pellets).

Crude Steel refers to the first solid state after melting, in the form of steel ingots, continuously cast primary forms, and steel castings. The U.N. definition of crude steel is the equivalent of the term "raw steel" as used by the United States.

The World Bureau of Metal Statistics publishes consumption data for the metals presented, excluding iron and steel. Data on the metals included were supplied by metal companies, government agencies, trade groups, and statistical bureaus. Obviously incorrect data have been revised, but most data were compiled and reported without adjustment or retrospective revisions.

Metal consumption refers to the domestic use of primary refined metals. These metals include metals refined from either primary (raw) or secondary (recovered) materials. Metal used in a product that is then exported is considered consumed by the exporting country rather than by the importing country.

Consumption of iron ore was calculated by adding net imports to the quantities of iron ore and concentrates reported as delivered to consuming industries. Consumption of crude steel was calculated by adding net imports to the quantities of crude steel reported as delivered to consuming industries.

Global consumption figures for iron ore and crude steel are not consistent with the definitions applied to other metals in Table 22.5. Because world consumption of iron ore and crude steel is roughly equal to world production, world production data were used for the world consumption totals. Worldwide stock inventories are assumed to be negligible.

Refer to the sources for additional details.

Table 22.6 Recovery of Selected Materials, 1964–85

Sources: Aluminum: The Aluminum Association, *Aluminum Statistical Review 1970, 1980, 1984,* and *1985* (The Aluminum Association, Washington, D.C., 1971, 1981, 1985, and 1986). Copper, lead, tin, and zinc: Metallgesellschaft Aktiengesellschaft, *Metallstatistik 1960–1970, 1968–1978,* and *1974–1984* (Metallgesellschaft Aktiengesellschaft, Frankfurt, 1971, 1979, and 1985); and World Bureau of Metal Statistics, *World Metal Statistics* (World Bureau of Metal Statistics, London, 1986). Glass (except the United States): Glass Manufacturers Federation, *Glass Gazette,* Nos. 1–11 (excluding Nos. 2 and 5) (Federation Europeenne du Verre d'Emballage, Brussels, 1980–86). Glass data for the United States: U.S. Department of Commerce, Bureau of the Census, *Current Industrial Reports: Glass Containers: Summary for 1985* (Department of Commerce, Washington, D.C., 1986). Iron and steel: United Nations Economic Commission for Europe (ECE), *Annual Bulletin of Steel Statistics for Europe* (ECE, New York, 1976, 1980, and 1984). Paper: United Nations Food and Agricultural Organization (FAO), *Waste Paper Data* (FAO, Rome, 1984); and FAO, *Yearbook of Forest Products 1975* and *1984* (FAO, Rome, 1977 and 1986).

Materials industries recover scrap from two major sources. Worn-out end products (old automobiles, beverage cans, newspapers, bottles, etc.) are the source of obsolete or old scrap. Scrap is also generated at various stages of materials production. Industrial scrap that never leaves the production facility is usually referred to as "home" or "runaround" scrap; industrial scrap that is bought by dealers and sold to other facilities is "new industrial" scrap.

Definitions of scrap and scrap recovery differ across materials, countries, and time. For example, aluminum scrap recovery reported by the Aluminum Association comprises *recovery* of new industrial and old scrap, evaluated on a recovered metal basis. The Aluminum Association gathers data from industry sources and adjusts these data to reflect unreported scrap recovery. Copper scrap data, however, are for *production* of refined copper from new industrial and old scrap. This method gives a more accurate picture of current scrap recovery in relation to the metal production industry than do aluminum recovery figures. Because the aluminum scrap data are for recovered metal, they do not account for scrap trade and inventory changes; nor do they indicate the destination of the scrap. Some aluminum scrap is consumed by mills rather than by smelters, thereby overstating the ratio of aluminum recovery to new metal production.

The recovery ratio for each material was calculated as follows:

■ *Aluminum.* The numerator of the ratio is recovery of new industrial and obsolete scrap. The denominator is aluminum consumption, defined as production of primary aluminum, plus net imports of ingot and mill products, plus the numerator, minus stock changes. This ratio has several flaws. As noted above, scrap is traded internationally, reducing the comparability of the numerator and denominator. In addition, aluminum recovered in a given year might not be consumed until a later year.

■ *Copper.* The numerator of the ratio is production of refined copper from obsolete and new industrial scrap. The denominator is production of refined copper from all sources (comprising the numerator and refined copper production from new ore). The brass and bronze industries are also major consumers of copper scrap. In the United States, brass mills consumed 75 percent of all new industrial copper scrap, and bronze and brass production consumed 30 percent of all obsolete copper scrap.

■ *Glass.* The numerator is recovered glass (cullet) reported in metric tons. The denominator is total national glass consumption. However, glass recovery ratios may not reflect international trade. The Federal Republic of Germany, for example, imported 89,000 metric tons of cullet in 1984, a figure that is included in the numerator. But because the source of these imports was not reported, it cannot be determined whether the exporting country or countries deducted 89,000 metric tons from its numerator.

■ *Iron and Steel.* The numerator is the sum of blast furnace and steelworks' consumption of scrap. The denominator is the sum of the blast furnace consumption of iron ore and concentrates and agglomerated products and the steelwork output of steel produced from pig iron and from iron ore. These data are net of trade.

■ *Lead.* The numerator is the sum of scrap consumed in remelted lead and lead alloys and the direct use of scrap by industries. Not all countries include both components. The denominator is consumption of refined lead.

■ *Paper.* The numerator is waste paper collected for reuse. The denominator is apparent domestic consumption of paper and paperboard, adjusted for net trade. When the data were available, the denominator was replaced with the apparent domestic consumption of recyclable paper and paperboard. Part of all paper and paperboard cannot be recycled; in Switzerland, for example, about 50 percent of the paper and paperboard consumed cannot be recycled. Substituting consumption of recyclable paper and paperboard in the denominator gives a better indication of a country's efforts to recycle paper products.

■ *Tin.* The numerator is the direct use of scrap by manufacturers plus the production of refined tin from scrap. The second component is included only in the numerators for the United States, the Federal Republic of Germany, Spain, and the United Kingdom. The production of refined tin from scrap is about 20 percent of the numerator for the United States, 30 percent for the Federal Republic of Germany, 65 percent for Spain, and 60 percent for the United Kingdom. The denominator for all countries is refined tin consumption.

■ *Zinc.* The numerator is the sum of scrap used in primary zinc smelters, and for remelted zinc and zinc alloys, zinc scrap used in copper and other alloys, and scrap used directly in chemicals, paints, etc. Only the United States, Japan, and the United Kingdom include all four components in their numerators. All the countries reporting scrap recovery include scrap for remelted zinc and zinc alloys. The denominator is refined zinc consumption.

It is difficult to determine what materials countries include in their scrap figures. Further, there is substantial trade in scrap, especially in Europe, that is not accurately reported. This makes cross-country and cross-material comparisons imprecise.

Refer to the sources for additional information on data limitations.

23. Freshwater

The availability and quality of freshwater are the most important resource concerns in many regions of the world.

Freshwater availability can be defined several ways. In Table 23.1, it refers to a country's annual average surface and groundwater runoff generated by endogenous precipitation and excludes the inflow of international rivers. Upstream and downstream countries usually have rights to international river water, so that only a fraction of the flow of an international river can be claimed by any one country along a river's reach. If all countries sharing an international river counted the river's entire inflow as adding to their availability, a false impression of abundance would be created. (For further details on international water-sharing agreements, refer to Chapter 12, "Policies and Institutions.") However, if river basins were the accounting unit, such double counting would be eliminated.

Dams have been built for thousands of years, and they have served purposes as diverse as recreation, navigation, flood control, irrigation, and power production (mechanical and electric). (See Table 23.2.) Flood control benefits are not quantified in Table 23.2; nor are the benefits of increased agricultural output resulting from dam-controlled irrigation water. (See Chapter 19, "Food and Agriculture," Table 19.3.) Hydroelectric capacity has more than tripled over the past 25 years. In 1984, hydroelectricity represented 21 percent of the world's electricity—without direct emission of pollutants or production of long-lived nuclear wastes. (See Chapter 22, "Energy and Minerals," Table 22.2.)

Dams may also have negative impacts, which are often difficult to quantify. Large numbers of people are displaced when fertile river valleys are flooded by reservoirs. Reservoir impoundments in tropical rainforests may contribute to the extinction of rare species of plants and animals. Reservoirs, and attendant irrigation works, can serve as breeding grounds for water-related diseases such as malaria and schistosomiasis.

Other impacts of dams, such as the alteration of river chemistry, can be beneficial or detrimental. River chemistry may be modified by enhanced evaporation from reservoir surfaces (concentrating dissolved minerals) and by reduced water flow below the dam, causing less dilution of natural and anthropogenic inputs to the river. Dams also capture riverborne sediment, so that less alluvial soil is deposited in the river valley and delta. These and other modifications alter the hydrology and biota of the river.

Freshwater is monitored for several reasons, each with its own criteria for determining water quality. (See Table 23.3.) For example, freshwater used for human consumption is evaluated according to health and aesthetic criteria, but water used for irrigation does not require the same degree of purity. Water quality, therefore, must be assessed in relation to specific uses. Standards have not been included in this table because most pertain to specific uses, and the uses of water vary among sites. Drinking water standards for three water quality indicators used in Table 23.3 are presented in the Technical Note for that table.

Water quality also depends on the type of water body and its location. Groundwater is usually the purest source of water; lakes and rivers are affected by sewage, industrial effluents, agricultural runoff, and atmospheric deposition to a much greater degree. (Rivers, however, can flush out pollutants more rapidly than groundwater can.) The vegetation, soils, and geology of a water basin may also affect the chemical and biological characteristics of water. For example, the Huanghe (Yellow River) in China flows through regions of highly erodible soils. As a result, its sediment load is hundreds of times greater than that of other rivers of similar size.

To account for these basin-specific variations, water quality is best assessed by monitoring over time and by comparing data with established standards for specific uses, rather than by comparing data for several basins. Unfortunately, global coordination of freshwater quality monitoring (under the Global Environmental Monitoring System [GEMS]) began only in 1979; it will be several years before trend data emerge from this program. Many of the world's largest rivers, such as the Amazon, Congo, Orinoco, Yenisei, Lena, Mekong, Ob, and Amur, are not yet monitored within the GEMS framework.

The cost of supplying water is rarely recovered in fees charged to the user. (See Table 23.4.) This practice is often justified on the grounds that water supplied for a specific purpose creates benefits for people other than the immediate user. Governments subsidize water costs, judging that the wider benefits to the country outweigh the direct costs to the treasury. However, the balance between societal and user cost recovery must be carefully maintained. Consumers have little reason to economize if water fees are too low. Further, many water pricing decisions are made on political rather than economic grounds, often conferring great benefits on those least in need of assistance. These distortions often have tremendous costs to national development budgets.

Table 23.1 Freshwater Availability and Use, 1959–85

	Availability		Water Flows from Other Countries (cubic kilometers per year)	Withdrawal			Sectoral Use (percent)		
	Total (cubic kilometers per year)	Per Capita 1987 (thousand cubic meters per year)		Year Of Data	Total (cubic kilometers per year)	Per Capita (thousand cubic meters per year)	Public Use[a]	Industry (self-supplied)	Agriculture (irrigation)
WORLD									
AFRICA									
Algeria	16.90	0.73	0.27	1980	3.38	0.18	21	4	75
Angola	X	X	X	X	X	X	X	X	X
Benin	26.00	6.04	X	X	X	X	X	X	X
Botswana	1.00	0.84	17.00	1980	0.09	0.10	8	17	75
Burkina Faso	X	X	X	X	X	X	X	X	X
Burundi	X	X	X	X	X	X	X	X	X
Cameroon	208.00	19.93	X	X	X	X	X	X	X
Cape Verde	0.20	0.59	0.00	1972	0.04	0.15	8	0	92
Central African Rep	X	X	X	X	X	X	X	X	X
Chad	X	X	X	X	X	X	X	X	X
Comoros	X	X	X	X	X	X	X	X	X
Congo	X	X	X	X	X	X	X	X	X
Cote d'Ivoire	74.00	7.03	X	X	X	X	X	X	X
Djibouti	0.30	0.77	0.00	1973	0.01	0.03	X	X	X
Egypt	1.00	0.02	56.50	1976	45.00	1.18	2	2	96
Equatorial Guinea	X	X	X	X	X	X	X	X	X
Ethiopia	110.00	2.39	X	X	X	X	X	X	X
Gabon	X	X	X	X	X	X	X	X	X
Gambia	3.00	4.48	19.00	1982	0.02	0.03	X	X	X
Ghana	53.00	3.65	X	1970	0.30	0.03	44	3	54
Guinea	X	X	X	X	X	X	X	X	X
Guinea-Bissau	X	X	X	X	X	X	X	X	X
Kenya	14.80	0.66	X	X	X	X	X	X	X
Lesotho	X	X	X	X	X	X	X	X	X
Liberia	X	X	X	X	X	X	X	X	X
Libya	0.60	0.15	0.00	1978	1.47	0.54	17[b]	0	83
Madagascar	40.00	3.77	X	1984	16.30	1.68	1	0	99
Malawi	X	X	X	X	X	X	X	X	X
Mali	X	X	X	X	X	X	X	X	X
Mauritania	0.40	0.20	7.00	1978	0.73	0.47	2	0	98
Mauritius	2.20	2.02	X	1974	0.36	0.41	X	X	X
Morocco	30.00	1.30	0.00	1983	10.50	0.50	4	3	93
Mozambique	X	X	X	X	X	X	X	X	X
Niger	X	X	X	X	X	X	X	X	X
Nigeria	X	X	X	X	X	X	X	X	X
Rwanda	X	X	X	X	X	X	X	X	X
Senegal	X	X	X	X	X	X	X	X	X
Sierra Leone	X	X	X	X	X	X	X	X	X
Somalia	11.50	2.37	0.00	X	X	X	X	X	X
South Africa	50.00	1.47	X	1970	9.20	0.40	17	0	83
Sudan	30.00	1.31	100.00	1977	18.60	1.09	1	0	99
Swaziland	X	X	X	X	X	X	X	X	X
Tanzania, United Rep	X	X	X	1970	0.48	0.04	38	0	63
Togo	11.50	3.66	X	X	0.05	0.02	90	0	10
Tunisia	3.50	0.47	X	1977	1.32	0.22	19	5	77
Uganda	X	X	X	1970	0.20	0.02	43	0	57
Zaire	X	X	X	X	X	X	X	X	X
Zambia	X	X	X	1970	0.36	0.09	72	0	28
Zimbabwe	X	X	X	X	X	X	X	X	X
NORTH & CENTRAL AMERICA									
Barbados	0.05	0.21	X	1962	0.03	0.12	45	35	20
Canada	2,901.00	111.74	X	1980	36.15	1.50	18	70	11
Costa Rica	95.00	34.76	X	1970	1.35	0.78	0	8	92
Cuba	34.50	3.38	X	1975	8.10	0.87	14	4	83
Dominican Rep	20.00	3.06	X	X	X	X	X	X	X
El Salvador	18.95	3.21	X	1975	1.00	0.24	17	0	83
Guatemala	116.00	13.75	X	1970	0.73	0.14	0	18	82
Haiti	11.00	1.59	X	X	X	X	X	X	X
Honduras	102.00	21.90	X	1970	1.34	0.51	0	4	96
Jamaica	8.30	3.45	X	1975	0.32	0.16	3	6	91
Mexico	357.40	4.31	X	1975	54.20	0.90	5	7	88
Nicaragua	175.00	49.97	X	1975	0.89	0.37	18	45	37
Panama	144.00	63.32	X	1975	1.30	0.74	12	11	77
Trinidad and Tobago	X	X	X	1975	0.15	0.15	0	50	50
United States	2,478.00	10.23	X	1975	472.00	2.19	10	49	41
SOUTH AMERICA									
Argentina	694.00	22.03	X	1976	27.60	1.06	9	18	73
Bolivia	X	X	X	1959	X	X	1	1	97
Brazil	5,190.00	36.69	X	X	X	X	X	X	X
Chile	X	X	X	1975	16.80	1.63	5	4	92
Colombia	1,070.00	35.73	X	1960	X	X	14	0	86
Ecuador	314.00	31.64	X	X	X	X	X	X	X
Guyana	X	X	X	1971	5.40	7.62	1	0	99
Paraguay	X	X	X	X	X	X	X	X	X
Peru	40.00	1.93	X	1975	X	X	7	0	93
Suriname	X	X	X	X	X	X	X	X	X
Uruguay	X	X	X	1965	0.65	0.24	15	8	77
Venezuela	856.00	46.86	X	1970	4.10	0.39	37	4	59

World Resources 1987

Table 23.1

	Availability		Water Flows from Other Countries (cubic kilometers per year)	Year Of Data	Withdrawal		Sectoral Use (percent)		
	Total (cubic kilometers per year)	Per Capita 1987 (thousand cubic meters per year)			Total (cubic kilometers per year)	Per Capita (thousand cubic meters per year)	Public Use[a]	Industry (self-supplied)	Agriculture (irrigation)
ASIA									
Afghanistan	50.00	2.76	X	X	X	X	X	X	X
Bahrain	0.00	0.00	0.05	1975	0.20	0.74	10	6	84
Bangladesh	1,357.00	12.72	X	X	X	X	X	X	X
Bhutan	X	X	X	X	X	X	X	X	X
Burma	1,082.00	28.03	X	X	X	X	X	X	X
China	2,800.00	2.58	0.00	1980	460.00	0.46	6	7	87
Cyprus	1.00	1.46	X	1972	0.44	0.72	7	2	91
India	1,850.00	2.35	X	1975	380.00	0.61	3	4	93
Indonesia	2,530.00	14.67	X	1978	X	X	95	5	0
Iran	117.50	2.49	X	1975	45.40	1.36	3	0	97
Iraq	34.00	2.00	66.00	1970	42.80	4.57	2	3	95
Israel	1.65	0.38	X	1975	1.72	0.50	17	6	77
Japan	547.00	4.48	0.00	1980	107.80	0.92	17	33	50
Jordan	0.70	0.18	0.40	1975	0.45	0.17	3[b]	0	97
Kampuchea, Dem	88.10	11.46	X	X	X	X	X	X	X
Korea, Dem People's Rep	X	X	X	X	X	X	X	X	X
Korea, Rep	63.00	1.48	X	1976	10.70	0.30	11	13	75
Kuwait	0.00	0.00	0.00	1974	0.01	0.01	35	4	61
Lao People's Dem Rep	270.00	62.47	X	X	X	X	X	X	X
Lebanon	4.80	1.74	0.00	1975	0.75	0.27	13[b]	0	87
Malaysia	456.00	28.04	X	1975	9.42	0.77	X	X	X
Mongolia	24.60	12.21	X	X	X	X	X	X	X
Nepal	170.00	9.85	X	X	X	X	X	X	X
Oman	2.00	1.50	0.00	1975	0.43	0.56	2	0	98
Pakistan	298.00	2.83	X	1975	153.40	2.05	X	X	X
Philippines	323.00	5.66	X	1975	29.50	0.69	X	X	X
Qatar	0.02	0.06	0.00	1975	0.04	0.23	33	0	67
Saudi Arabia	2.20	0.18	0.00	1975	2.33	0.32	36	6	58
Singapore	0.60	0.23	X	1975	0.19	0.08	X	X	X
Sri Lanka	43.20	2.58	X	1970	6.30	0.50	0	2	98
Syrian Arab Rep	7.60	0.67	X	1976	7.00	0.94	6	0	94
Thailand	110.00	2.07	X	1975	X	X	1	0	99
Turkey	166.00	3.23	6.90	1980	28.90	0.65	12	10	78
United Arab Emirates	0.30	0.21	0.00	1980	0.42	0.43	9	0	91
Viet Nam	X	X	X	X	X	X	X	X	X
Yemen	1.00	0.14	0.00	X	X	X	X	X	X
Yemen, Dem	1.50	0.66	0.00	1975	1.93	1.17	1	0	99
EUROPE									
Albania	10.00	3.14	X	1967	0.20	0.11	1	99	0
Austria	56.30	7.50	34.00	1980	3.13	0.42	20	77	3
Belgium	8.40	0.85	4.10	1980	9.03	0.92	11	88	2
Bulgaria	18.00	1.97	187.00	1980	14.18	1.60	14	15	71
Czechoslovakia	28.00	1.79	62.60	1980	5.80	0.38	24	72	5
Denmark	11.00	2.15	2.00	1977	1.40	0.28	35	32	32
Finland	110.00	22.33	3.00	1980	3.70	0.77	12	86	1
France	170.00	3.09	15.00	1981	37.20	0.69	16	71	13
German Dem Rep	17.00	1.01	17.00	1980	9.13	0.55	14	71	14
Germany, Fed Rep	79.00	1.30	82.00	1981	41.40	0.67	12	87	0
Greece	49.40	4.96	13.50	1980	6.94	0.72	11	2	87
Hungary	6.00	0.56	109.00	1980	5.38	0.50	9	58	33
Iceland	170.00	685.48	0.00	X	X	X	X	X	X
Ireland	50.00	13.51	0.00	1972	0.40	0.14	11	83	6
Italy	185.00	3.22	2.00	1980	56.20	0.98	14	27	58
Luxembourg	1.00	2.75	4.00	1976	0.06	0.17	47	50	3
Malta	0.03	0.06	0.00	1978	0.02	0.07	99	0	0
Netherlands	10.00	0.68	80.00	1980	14.20	1.00	5	64	32
Norway	405.00	97.40	8.00	1980	2.00	0.49	21	74	5
Poland	49.40	1.31	6.80	1980	16.80	0.47	17	62	21
Portugal	34.00	3.29	31.60	1980	10.50	1.06	15	37	48
Romania	37.00	1.59	171.00	1980	25.40	1.14	8	34	58
Spain	109.80	2.82	0.10	1984	24.70	0.64	15[b]	0	85
Sweden	176.00	21.10	4.00	1980	3.98	0.48	24	75	2
Switzerland	42.50	6.66	7.50	1985	3.20	0.50	37	57	6
United Kingdom	120.00	2.14	0.00	1980	28.35	0.51	21	79	1
Yugoslavia	129.00	5.50	115.00	1980	8.77	0.39	17	75	8
USSR	4,384.00	15.44	300.00	1980	353.00	1.33	6	31	64
OCEANIA									
Australia	343.00	21.30	X	1975	17.80	1.31	16	6	77
Fiji	X	X	X	X	X	X	X	X	X
New Zealand	397.00	117.53	X	1980	1.20	0.38	52	11	14
Papua New Guinea	X	X	X	X	X	X	X	X	X
Solomon Islands	X	X	X	X	X	X	X	X	X

Source: Bureau of Geological and Mining Research, National Geological Survey, France.
Notes:
a. Domestic, commercial, public services, and industry supplied by public facilities.
b. Public and industrial sectors combined.
0 = zero or less than half the unit of measure; X = not available.
For additional information, see Sources and Technical Notes.

Table 23.2 Large Dams[a]

	Number of Dams over 15 Meters High Completed			Reservoir Surface Area[b] (million square meters)			Hydroelectric Capacity (megawatts)[c]			
	Before 1961	Between 1961 and 1980	After 1981 or under Construction	Before 1961	Between 1961 and 1980	Since 1981 and Planned for Units under Construction	Technical Potential 1983	Installed		
								1960	1970	1984
WORLD[d]	**7,408**	**5,556**	**1,316**	**130,784**	**177,639**	**32,753**		**149,571**	**290,652**	**541,976**
AFRICA	**251**	**404**	**96**	**7,316**	**16,990**	**3,271**	**307,986**	**1,979**	**7,508**	**15,939**
Algeria	15	6	15	66	71	92	287	186	286	285
Angola	3	7	4	X	297	20	23,000	28	211	400
Benin	0	1	0	0	X	0	500	X	X	X
Botswana	0	3	0	0	X	0	1	X	X	X
Burkina Faso	0	1	1	0	X	220	200	X	X	X
Burundi	X	X	X	X	X	X	800	X	X	2
Cameroon	1	6	1	X	X	X	23,000	152	152	498
Cape Verde	X	X	X	X	X	X	X	X	X	X
Central African Rep	0	0	0	0	0	0	2,000	4	12	20
Chad	0	0	0	0	0	0	30	X	X	X
Comoros	X	X	X	X	X	X	10	X	X	1
Congo	1	1	0	X	X	0	11,000	X	15	120
Cote d'Ivoire	1	18	2	180	2,693	X	3,000	20	50	885
Djibouti	X	X	X	X	X	X	X	X	X	X
Egypt	4	1	0	700	68	0	3,210	350	2,448	2,535
Equatorial Guinea	X	X	X	X	X	X	2,000	1	1	1
Ethiopia	3	4	0	X	X	0	12,000	64	91	222
Gabon	0	1	0	0	X	0	18,000	X	0	100
Gambia	X	X	X	X	X	X	X	X	X	X
Ghana	0	4	1	0	8,534	35	2,000	X	588	952
Guinea	0	2	0	0	28	0	5,000	X	25	50
Guinea-Bissau	X	X	X	X	X	X	60	X	X	X
Kenya	2	5	2	2	136	0	6,000	26	75	354
Lesotho	0	2	1	0	0	0	450	X	X	X
Liberia	0	1	0	0	X	0	2,000	3	38	69
Libya	0	8	3	0	33	4	X	X	X	X
Madagascar	8	2	0	56	1	0	7,800	24	35	45
Malawi	2	1	0	X	X	0	900	X	26	126
Mali	0	0	2	0	0	907	2,000	X	5	20
Mauritania	X	X	X	X	X	X	50	X	X	X
Mauritius	2	3	1	X	X	X	65	11	16	54
Morocco	13	14	4	80	409	19	2,453	290	378	609
Mozambique	2	4	3	121	2,731	149	15,000	47	116	1,523
Niger	0	0	0	0	0	0	235	X	X	X
Nigeria	2	34	11	X	363	796	12,400	20	320	1,900
Rwanda	X	X	X	X	X	X	600	X	22	43
Senegal	0	0	2	0	0	707	500	X	X	X
Sierra Leone	0	1	0	0	X	0	1,300	X	2	X
Somalia	X	X	X	X	X	X	50	X	X	X
South Africa	148	184	24	818	1,331	265	X	11	37	572
Sudan	2	2	0	X	X	0	2,700	X	30	148
Swaziland	0	5	1	0	26	1	600	X	X	X
Tanzania, United Rep	0	2	0	0	X	0	9,500	X	49	259
Togo	0	1	0	0	X	0	270	X	2	10
Tunisia	6	15	9	25	43	53	65	26	29	64
Uganda	1	0	0	X	0	0	1,200	126	156	156
Zaire	4	4	1	X	X	X	120,000	590	809	1,661
Zambia	2	2	0	X	2	0	12,000	0	756	1,538
Zimbabwe	21	66	8	5,268	224	2	3,800	X	705	633
NORTH & CENTRAL AMERICA	**2,258**	**993**	**64**	**16,836**	**11,091**	**1,287**		**53,569**	**88,114**	**146,194**
Barbados	X	X	X	X	X	X	X	X	X	X
Canada	322	174	2	X	X	X	141,409[e]	18,643	28,298	54,949
Costa Rica	1	3	1	X	3	83	9,071	78	182	631
Cuba	2	45	0	X	X	0	X	10	44	45
Dominican Rep	0	8	4	0	X	0	1,900	8	16	165
El Salvador	2	2	0	X	X	0	1,377	56	109	233
Guatemala	1	1	1	X	0	13	5,426	37	102	488
Haiti	1	0	0	0	0	0	152	X	X	50
Honduras	0	7	1	0	420	110	2,800	4	30	130
Jamaica	2	0	0	X	0	0	100	22	21	25
Mexico	183	282	33	2,867	2,233	477	25,250	1,357	3,331	6,621
Nicaragua	0	2	0	X	X	0	4,106	9	57	103
Panama	2	3	0	X	X	0	3,031	X	X	551
Trinidad and Tobago	2	1	1	X	X	X	X	X	X	X
United States[f]	1,746	465	22	13,970	8,435	604	X	33,180	55,752	82,102
SOUTH AMERICA	**415**	**368**	**132**	**4,719**	**34,510**	**8,247**		**6,096**	**14,654**	**55,639**
Argentina	36	46	12	182	2,083	169	46,000	340	609	5,384
Bolivia	2	2	1	X	X	X	18,000	90	172	304
Brazil	259	210	63	2,834	30,966	6,095	213,140	3,642	8,828	35,524
Chile	41	23	11	133	140	111	18,772	595	1,067	1,780
Colombia	10	21	11	X	14	148	94,358	505	1,535	4,300
Ecuador	1	3	7	X	X	X	22,733	40	106	742
Guyana	0	0	0	0	0	0	8,000	X	X	X
Paraguay	0	2	1	0	432	1,350	10,965	0	90	190
Peru	44	17	6	393	93	30	60,000	515	923	1,917
Suriname	0	1	0	0	X	0	2,334	0	180	189
Uruguay	3	1	1	1,177	783	320	2,248	236	236	881
Venezuela	19	42	19	X	X	25	29,227[e]	133	908	4,426

World Resources 1987

	Number of Dams over 15 Meters High Completed			Reservoir Surface Area[b] (million square meters)			Hydroelectric Capacity (megawatts)[c]			
							Technical	Installed		
	Before 1961	Between 1961 and 1980	After 1981 or under Construction	Before 1961	Between 1961 and 1980	Since 1981 and Planned for Units under Construction	Potential 1983	1960	1970	1984
ASIA	**2,235**	**2,027**	**584**	**3,819**	**11,909**	**10,011**		**16,512**	**42,755**	**100,171**
Afghanistan	2	0	0	X	0	0	25,000	38	190	272
Bahrain	X	X	X	X	X	X	X	X	X	X
Bangladesh	0	1	0	0	777	0	800	X	X	130
Bhutan	X	X	X	X	X	X	X	X	1	3
Burma	1	0	0	X	0	0	30,000	84	103	169
China[f]	337	875	130	X	X	X	378,532	X	8,180	28,000
Cyprus	5	27	13	0	5	5	X	X	X	X
India[f]	232	143	120	3,183	4,741	5,089	100,000	1,846	6,386	15,103
Indonesia	15	14	7	33	813	624	32,000	169	312	602
Iran	1	17	7	3	916	174	X	2	517	1,804
Iraq	1	4	3	X	X	418	X	X	X	100
Israel	X	X	X	X	X	X	X	X	X	X
Japan[f]	1,313	389	169	X	96	197	81,918[e]	12,678	19,994	33,919
Jordan	0	4	1	0	2	1	22	X	X	X
Kampuchea, Dem	0	1	1	0	X	195	10,000	0	10	10
Korea, Dem People's Rep	X	X	X	X	X	X	X	X	2,500	4,500
Korea, Rep	257	368	6	84	280	X	2,000	143	329	1,202
Kuwait	X	X	X	X	X	X	X	X	X	X
Lao People's Dem Rep	0	1	0	0	370	0	28,000	0	2	200
Lebanon	2	3	0	X	X	0	X	65	246	246
Malaysia	2	10	9	X	151	507	25,800	X	293	693
Mongolia	X	X	X	X	X	X	X	X	X	X
Nepal	0	0	1	0	0	2	18,250	3	26	128
Oman	X	X	X	X	X	X	X	X	X	X
Pakistan	4	30	4	X	609	10	19,600	X	X	2,548
Philippines	4	3	5	24	108	32	10,048	305	549	1,810
Qatar	X	X	X	X	X	X	X	X	X	X
Saudi Arabia	2	16	20	X	X	X	X	X	X	X
Singapore	0	2	1	0	7	2	X	X	X	X
Sri Lanka	44	23	8	X	X	122	2,500	55	195	542
Syrian Arab Rep	1	11	0	X	X	0	1,282	11	15	823
Thailand	0	29	22	0	2,046	864	20,148	0	452	1,714
Turkey	13	55	57	492	979	1,770	32,000	412	724	3,877
United Arab Emirates	X	X	X	X	X	X	X	X	X	X
Viet Nam	0	1	0	0	10	0	18,000	X	164	300
Yemen	X	X	X	X	X	X	X	X	X	X
Yemen, Dem	X	X	X	X	X	X	X	X	X	X
EUROPE	**1,993**	**1,523**	**365**	**11,892**	**8,932**	**1,990**		**53,879**	**99,365**	**153,608**
Albania	1	76	17	X	X	X	X	X	X	500
Austria	56	47	12	103	132	25	8,562[e]	2,946	5,467	9,923
Belgium	4	10	0	4	9	0	X	54	62	1,326
Bulgaria	31	76	1	16	34	1	3,015[e]	460	816	1,895
Czechoslovakia	71	65	14	161	200	112	X	929	1,447	2,840
Denmark	2	4	0	1	1	0	5[e]	9	8	12
Finland	25	25	0	5,875	1,239	0	3,196[e]	1,559	1,964	2,497
France	247	162	41	291	353	80	7,352[e]	10,231	14,996	21,400
German Dem Rep	3	11	1	X	X	X	X	326	653	1,851
Germany, Fed Rep	90	93	30	107	59	44	2,397[e]	3,349	4,700	6,560
Greece	4	7	9	31	916	26	X	174	1,038	1,714
Hungary	1	3	0	X	X	0	X	19	20	46
Iceland	3	6	5	7	96	50	3,995[e]	109	247	803
Ireland	13	2	0	X	X	0	X	219	240	514
Italy	322	87	38	198	118	366	38,916[e]	12,612	13,335	17,343
Luxembourg	1	2	0	4	1	0	X	15	932	1,332
Malta	X	X	X	X	X	X	X	X	X	X
Netherlands	4	5	1	147	980	350	X	X	X	X
Norway	83	134	10	187	117	80	63,470[e]	6,443	12,783	23,063
Poland	12	12	5	65	123	76	X	261	740	1,976
Portugal	35	29	16	159	166	69	6,000	1,085	1,536	3,014
Romania	8	92	57	1	1,105	291	12,300	210	1,200	4,032
Spain	355	316	68	1,030	1,232	260	17,696[e]	4,600	10,883	13,180
Sweden	68	64	3	2,824	1,593	52	22,374[e]	X	10,862	15,450
Switzerland	67	57	5	70	29	0	X	5,640	9,620	11,480
United Kingdom	445	80	11	382	147	27	1,062[e]	1,171	2,153	4,189
Yugoslavia	43	58	21	230	283	80	17,000	1,450	3,645	6,650
USSR	**40**	**39**	**12**	**84,051**	**90,082**	**6,654**	**125,000[e]**	**14,781**	**31,368**	**59,300**
OCEANIA	**216**	**202**	**63**	**2,150**	**4,124**	**1,294**		**2,755**	**6,888**	**11,125**
Australia	175	171	52	1,808	3,139	643	6,107[e]	1,423	3,806	6,563
Fiji	0	0	2	0	0	9	400	X	X	80
New Zealand	40	29	9	342	986	642	5,708[e]	1,254	2,971	4,295
Papua New Guinea	0	2	0	X	X	0	29,000	9	42	100
Solomon Islands	X	X	X	X	X	X	X	X	X	X

Sources: International Commission on Large Dams; The World Bank; and U.N. Statistical Office.
Notes:
a. More than 20,000 dams between 15 and 30 meters high in China, India, Japan, and the United States are excluded from these statistics. Data for the USSR exclude about 3,000 dams. b. Reservoirs created by dams over 15 meters high. c. Hydroelectric capacity data refer to all dams in the country. Hydroelectric generation data are shown in Table 22.2. d. Global totals are the sum of country data. Many countries fail to report most or all data for several categories. e. Theoretical potential. f. Only dams over 30 meters high are included.
0 = zero or less than half of 1 percent; X = not available.
For additional information, see Sources and Technical Notes.

Table 23.3 River Water Quality, 1979–86

Country	River	Site	Nitrates and Nitrites (mg of nitrogen/liter)			Biochemical Oxygen Demand (mg of oxygen/liter)		
			Number of Samples			Number of Samples		
			Below Detection Limit	Above Detection Limit	Mean[c]	Below Detection Limit	Above Detection Limit	Mean[c]
AFRICA								
Egypt	Nile	Aswan	0	24	0.00	0	24	2
		Assiut	0	24	0.00	0	24	3
		Center of Cairo	12	24	0.03	0	36	3
		Edfina	0	24	1.18	0	24	7
		El Kanater	12	24	0.03	0	36	3
		Farskur	0	24	1.90	0	24	10
		Shobak	12	24	0.03	0	36	3
Sudan	Blue Nile	Khartoum	0	58	0.39	0	57	3
Tunisia	De Zaghouan	35° 35', 7° 37'	0	3	0.10	0	7	4
NORTH & CENTRAL AMERICA								
Canada	Great Bear	Fort Franklin	0	23	0.15			
	Mackenzie	at Arctic Red River	0	35	0.08			
	Nelson	above Weir River	2	19	0.06			
	Roseau	Gardenton	33	38	0.07			
	Saskatchewan	above Carrot River	7	56	0.12	0	3	3
	Slave	Fitzgerald	2	28	0.06			
	St. Lawrence	below Lachine Rapids	1	20	0.20			
Guatemala	Pixcaya	14° 40', 90° 51'	0	13	1.10	0	13	16
Mexico	Bravo	25° 53', 97° 30'	0	1	0.13	0	51	3
	Colorado	32° 42', 114° 43'	0	6	0.37	0	65	6
	Lerma	20° 34', 101° 12'	0	25	2.02	0	46	73
	Panuco	23° 3', 98° 18'	0	10	1.83	0	60	1
Panama[d]	Aguas Claras	9° 14', 78° 41'	1	59	0.06	44	1	2
	San Felix	9° 19', 82° 50'	1	63	0.04	41	5	2
United States	Apalachicola	Chattahoochee, Florida	0	54	0.29			
	Arkansas	Little Rock	0	32	0.26			
	Colorado	below Hoover Dam	0	33	0.38			
	Columbia	Warren Dale, Oregon	1	30	0.20			
	Delaware	Trenton, New Jersey	0	31	0.98	0	39	2
	Dismal	Thed Ford, Nebraska	0	19	0.49			
	Hudson	Green Island, New York	0	30	0.62			
	Mississippi	Vicksburg	0	31	1.39			
	Missouri	Hermann, Missouri	0	33	0.93			
	Niagara	Lake Ontario	0	20	0.24			
	Ohio	Grand Chain, Illinois	0	36	1.05			
	Potomac	Chain Bridge	0	49	1.15			
	Rio Grande	Brownsville, Texas	2	31	0.13	0	43	3
	Sacramento	Freepoint, California	1	29	0.16			
	St. Clair	Lake Huron Outlet	0	27	0.29			
	St. Lawrence	Cornwall, Ontario	0	32	0.20			
	St. Marys	Lake Superior Outlet	0	33	0.28			
	Susquehanna	Harrisburg, Pennsylvania	0	84	0.89			
	Talkeetna	Talkeetna, Alaska	0	21	0.41			
	Tennessee	Paducah, Kentucky	0	30	0.29			
	Yukon	Pilot Station, Alaska	0	14	0.13			
SOUTH AMERICA								
Argentina	Paraguay	Puerto Berme	3	24	0.14	6	19	1
	Parana	Puerto Libertad	0	38	0.23	8	28	1
		Corrientes	4	119	0.27	24	93	1
		Rosario	2	35	3.22	2	24	2
	Plata	Buenos Aires	70	65	0.14	13	124	1
	Uruguay	Concepcion del Uruguay	0	7	0.48	0	3	1
Brazil[d]	Guandu	Tornada D'Agua				0	32	1
	Jacui	29° 56', 51° 40'				0	26	3
	Paraiba do Sul	Aparecida				0	39	2
		Barra Mansa				0	54	1
	Sao Francisco	Petrolandia				3	9	3
	Velhas	Honorio Bicalho				0	9	2
Chile	Maipo	El Manzano	0	103	0.22	0	76	1
	Mapocho	Los Almendros	0	103	0.70	0	71	1
Colombia	Cauca	Juanchito	0	31	0.09	0	31	2
Ecuador	Daule	75° 59', 1° 43'	0	24	0.60	0	17	1
Peru[d]	Rimac	Lima	0	34	2.83			
Uruguay[d]	Plata	Colonia	0	15	0.25	0	15	1
	Uruguay	Bella Union	0	16	0.26	0	16	1
		Salto	0	19	0.42	0	19	1
OCEANIA								
Australia	Mitta Mitta	Hinnomunjie	1	17	0.02			
	Murray	Mannum	9	251	0.15			
Fiji	Watmanu	18° 1', 178° 26'	0	118	0.05	0	114	1
New Zealand[d]	Waikato	Taupo Gates	4	51	0.00	8	48	0
	Waimakariri	43° 28', 172° 19'	3	58	0.09	5	56	1

World Resources 1987

Country	River	Site	Fecal Coliform (number/100 milliliters)			Cadmium (mg / liter)[a]			Mercury (μg/liter)[b]		
			Below Detection Limit	Above Detection Limit	Mean[c]	Below Detection Limit	Above Detection Limit	Mean[c]	Below Detection Limit	Above Detection Limit	Mean[c]
AFRICA											
Egypt	Nile	Aswan									
		Assiut									
		Center of Cairo									
		Edfina									
		El Kanater									
		Farskur									
		Shobak									
Sudan	Blue Nile	Khartoum									
Tunisia	De Zaghouan	35° 35′, 7° 37′	0	12	208						
NORTH & CENTRAL AMERICA											
Canada	Great Bear	Fort Franklin							9	4	0.030
	Mackenzie	at Arctic Red River							4	9	0.032
	Nelson	above Weir River				4	0	0.001	4	4	0.023
	Roseau	Gardenton	22	49	19	11	1	0.001	34	33	0.030
	Saskatchewan	above Carrot River	28	31	5	12	0	0.001	49	11	0.024
	Slave	Fitzgerald				2	0	0.001	4	9	0.026
	St. Lawrence	below Lachine Rapids				16	0	0.001	4	5	0.013
Guatemala	Pixcaya	14° 40′, 90° 51′	0	12	8,717						
Mexico	Bravo	25° 53′, 97° 30′	0	1	230						
	Colorado	32° 42′, 114° 43′	0	47	520						
	Lerma	20° 34′, 101° 12′	0	44	300,000						
	Panuco	23° 3′, 98° 18′	6	67	851	3	0	0.050	3	1	0.126
Panama[d]	Aguas Claras	9° 14′, 78° 41′	0	42	433						
	San Felix	9° 19′, 82° 50′	0	45	1,004						
United States	Apalachicola	Chattahoochee, Florida	6	32	49	3	11	0.001	7	7	0.221
	Arkansas	Little Rock	0	43	841	3	13	0.001	5	11	0.075
	Colorado	below Hoover Dam	24	18	2	8	8	0.001	3	13	0.163
	Columbia	Warren Dale, Oregon	4	35	5	6	8	0.002	4	8	0.167
	Delaware	Trenton, New Jersey	0	39	342	2	13	0.001	9	6	0.200
	Dismal	Thed Ford, Nebraska	0	24	122	2	4	0.001	1	5	0.217
	Hudson	Green Island, New York	0	38	1,104	1	13	0.003	9	5	0.193
	Mississippi	Vicksburg	0	32	512	0	12	0.002	6	7	0.269
	Missouri	Hermann, Missouri	0	44	2,041	1	13	0.069	2	12	0.493
	Niagara	Lake Ontario	0	30	348	2	12	0.009	11	3	0.200
	Ohio	Grand Chain, Illinois	0	36	157	5	19	0.015	11	8	0.237
	Potomac	Chain Bridge	2	41	557	4	36	0.001	14	27	0.193
	Rio Grande	Brownsville, Texas	0	43	3,767	5	9	0.001	2	12	0.236
	Sacramento	Freepoint, California	1	32	122	4	9	0.002	3	9	1.375
	St. Clair	Lake Huron Outlet	14	25	22	2	13	0.001	7	9	0.981
	St. Lawrence	Cornwall, Ontario	2	45	8	3	11	0.001	10	4	0.193
	St. Marys	Lake Superior Outlet	22	20	1	5	8	0.001	7	7	0.236
	Susquehanna	Harrisburg, Pennsylvania	2	36	145	12	36	0.001	33	12	0.138
	Talkeetna	Talkeetna, Alaska	5	14	10	1	5	0.001	1	4	0.100
	Tennessee	Paducah, Kentucky	0	43	29	1	19	0.013	9	6	0.213
	Yukon	Pilot Station, Alaska	7	9	2	2	10	0.002	1	11	0.117
SOUTH AMERICA											
Argentina	Paraguay	Puerto Berme	0	26	643						
	Parana	Puerto Libertad	0	32	1,700						
		Corrientes	0	117	336						
		Rosario	0	8	5,213						
	Plata	Buenos Aires	0	136	2,568						
	Uruguay	Concepcion del Uruguay									
Brazil[d]	Guandu	Tomada D'Agua	0	32	6,584	32	5	0.003	27	10	0.525
	Jacui	29° 56′, 51° 40′	0	18	391	24	0	0.003	19	3	0.000
	Paraiba do Sul	Aparecida	0	39	15,080	0	39	0.001	39	0	0.000
		Barra Mansa	0	44	25,462	48	9	0.003	46	10	0.109
	Sao Francisco	Petrolandia	3	7	2,198	6	0	0.003	3	3	0.339
	Velhas	Honorio Bicalho	0	4	14,083						
Chile	Maipo	El Manzano	0	71	1,143						
	Mapocho	Los Almendros	0	71	24						
Colombia	Cauca	Juanchito	0	13	560,000	0	6	0.000	0	6	0.050
Ecuador	Daule	75° 59′, 1° 43′	0	27	7,200						
Peru[d]	Rimac	Lima	0	11	1,391	9	20	0.232			
Uruguay[d]	Plata	Colonia	0	15	963	0	9	0.000	0	13	0.004
	Uruguay	Bella Union	0	16	355	0	9	0.000	0	14	0.000
		Salto	0	19	73	0	10	0.000	0	14	0.000
OCEANIA											
Australia	Mitta Mitta	Hinnomunjie							4	2	0.123
	Murray	Mannum	0	127	135	18	0	0.001			
Fiji	Watmanu	18° 1′, 178° 26′	0	68	1,848						
New Zealand[d]	Waikato	Taupo Gates	1	51	1	6	0	0.001	6	0	0.100
	Waimakariri	43° 28′, 172° 19′	0	61	186	6	0	0.001	6	0	0.100

(continued on next page)

Table 23.3 River Water Quality, 1979–86 (continued)

Country	River	Site	Nitrates and Nitrites (mg of nitrogen/liter) Below Detection Limit	Above Detection Limit	Mean[c]	Biochemical Oxygen Demand (mg of oxygen/liter) Below Detection Limit	Above Detection Limit	Mean[c]
ASIA								
Bangladesh	Brahmaputra	Bahadurabad Ferryghat	0	7	0.88	0	26	3
	Lower Ganges	Hardinge Bridge	0	10	0.56	0	13	3
	Meghna	90° 59', 24° 02'	0	14	0.84	0	34	3
China[d]	Chang Jiang	Wuhan	0	120	0.23	0	119	1
	Huanghe	Luo Kou Bridge	0	119	1.94	0	118	2
	Zhujiang	Xijiang River Bridge	0	119	0.60	0	119	1
India	Bhima	Takali	0	85	0.22	0	84	6
	Cauveri	Krishnaraja Sagar Dam	0	76	0.03	0	80	1
	Chaliyar	Koolimadu	0	61	0.86	0	60	1
	Godavari	Polavaram	0	65	0.55	0	61	2
	Kallada	Panamthottam Kad	0	14	1.93	0	14	4
	Krishna	Vijayawada	0	70	0.75	0	67	3
	Mahi	Sevalia	0	62	8.96	0	57	2
	Narmada	Garudeshwar	0	60	0.56	0	59	3
	Periyar	Kaladi	0	62	0.96	0	62	1
	Sabarmati	Dhario Dam	0	65	0.34	0	65	2
	Subarnarekha	Mango Bridge	0	1	9.00	0	13	6
	Tapti	Kathore	0	14	0.15	0	14	4
	Wainganga	Ashti	0	80	0.35	0	78	6
Indonesia	Barito	South Kalimantan	1	21	0.26	0	22	5
Iran	Karun	Ahwaz City	0	23	6.22	0	23	3
Japan	Kiso	Shimo-Ochiai	0	72	0.25	0	72	1
Korea, Rep	Han	37° 32', 127° 17'	0	11	0.95	0	52	1
Malaysia	Kelantan	Jambatan Guillemard	0	12	0.22	0	24	2
	Kinta	Tanjong Rambutan Dam				0	55	0
Pakistan[d]	Indus	Kotri	0	147	1.86	0	150	6
Philippines[d]	Cagayan	Cagaya De Oro				0	76	1
Thailand[d]	Chao Phrya	Nakhon Sawan	0	26	0.27	7	46	1
Turkey	Cark Suyu	Beskopruler	0	48	0.39	0	51	1
EUROPE								
Belgium	Escuat	Belharies	0	39	4.44	0	42	7
	Espierre	Leers/Nord	1	27	3.18	0	33	201
	Lys	Warneton	0	29	4.00	0	38	6
	Meuse	Lanaye/Ternaaien	0	75	2.54	0	77	5
	Sambre	Erquelinnes	0	39	2.72	0	40	9
	Scheldt	Doel	0	35	3.93	0	36	6
	Sure	Martelange	0	33	3.44	0	36	4
	Zelzate	Ghent/Terneuzen	0	52	2.49	0	52	6
Denmark	Gudena	Tvilum Bro				3	19	4
	Odense	Broby				0	6	3
	Okjerna	Ahlergard				0	21	7
	Susa	Naby				0	9	1
France[e]	Garonne	Couthures				0	24	2
	Loire	Nantes				0	23	5
	Rhone	St. Vallier				0	24	3
	Saone	Auxonne				0	24	2
	Seine	Paris				0	24	4
Germany, Fed Rep	Danube	Jochenstein	0	14	10.56	0	14	3
	Elbe	Geesthacht	0	13	13.35	0	14	6
	Ems	Herbrum	0	14	24.17	0	14	5
	Moselle	Koblenz/Moselle	0	13	19.06	0	13	3
	Niers	Goch	0	14	22.46	0	14	5
	Rhine	Kleve/Bimmen	0	13	15.74	0	13	4
	Weser	Intschede	0	14	22.42	0	14	5
Hungary[d]	Danube	Budapest	0	84	2.49	0	82	5
Ireland	Barro	Graiguenamanagh Bridge	0	21	12.90	0	21	2
	Blackwater	Killavullen	0	10	7.95	0	10	3
	Boyne	Slane Bridge	0	14	8.14	0	14	2
	Clare	Corofin Bridge	0	17	5.49	0	19	2
Italy	Adige	Trento				0	9	3
Luxembourg	Sure	Wasserbillig				0	25	4
Netherlands[e]	Maas	Belgian Frontier	0	265	2.76	0	259	3
	Rhine	Lex	0	193	3.99	0	189	3
Norway[d]	Glama	Haslemoen	0	27	0.21			
	Otra	Beieholen	0	27	0.19			
Portugal[d]	Tejo	Santarem	1	52	0.86	0	58	2
Spain[d]	Guadiana	Puente Palmas	0	29	1.42	0	43	3
	Mino	Mayor Oroza	0	35	0.52	0	41	1
	Sorbe	Muriel Guoga	0	4	110.10	0	26	1
	Tejo	Puente Barca	0	30	0.26	0	42	29
United Kingdom	Avon	Keynsham	0	51	6.97	0	2	2
	Carron	A-890 Bridge				0	23	1
	Thames	Teddington Weir	0	212	7.10	0	1	3
	Trent	Nottingham	0	97	7.97			

World Resources 1987

Country	River	Site	Fecal Coliform (number/100 milliliters) Number of Samples Below Detection Limit	Above Detection Limit	Mean[c]	Cadmium (mg/liter)[a] Number of Samples Below Detection Limit	Above Detection Limit	Mean[c]	Mercury (μg/liter)[b] Number Samples Below Detection Limit	Above Detection Limit	Mean[c]
ASIA											
Bangladesh	Brahmaputra	Bahadurabad Ferryghat	0	20	2,606						
	Lower Ganges	Hardinge Bridge	0	8	1,963						
	Meghna	90° 59', 24° 02'	0	38	3,193						
China[d]	Chang Jiang	Wuhan	0	120	667	120	0	0.000	120	0	0.215
	Huanghe	Luo Kou Bridge	1	118	4,974	76	43	0.000	117	2	0.251
	Zhujiang	Xijiang River Bridge	0	119	865	9	61	0.000	118	1	0.100
India	Bhima	Takali	0	8	175						
	Cauveri	Krishnaraja Sagar Dam	0	77	439						
	Chaliyar	Koolimadu	0	59	438						
	Godavari	Polavaram	0	48	7						
	Kallada	Panamthottam Kad	0	13	578						
	Krishna	Vijayawada	0	46	57						
	Mahi	Sevalia	7	49	550,000						
	Narmada	Garudeshwar	4	43	260,000						
	Periyar	Kaladi	0	61	767						
	Sabarmati	Dhario Dam	0	62	1,147						
	Subarnarekha	Mango Bridge	0	11	21,455						
	Tapti	Kathore	0	7	37,000						
	Wainganga	Ashti	0	8	3,699						
Indonesia	Barito	South Kalimantan	0	18	220,000	21	0	0.003	17	2	0.001
Iran	Karun	Ahwaz City	0	20	903						
Japan	Kiso	Shimo-Ochiai	0	72	2,700	63	3	0.001	25	0	0.500
Korea, Rep	Han	37° 32', 127° 17'	12	36	60	48	4	0.002	47	4	0.480
Malaysia	Kelantan	Jambatan Guillemard									
	Kinta	Tanjong Rambutan Dam	0	25	204						
Pakistan[d]	Indus	Kotri	0	155	120	0	8	0.000	0	8	0.000
Philippines[d]	Cagayan	Cagaya De Oro	0	62	7,628				0	19	0.146
Thailand[d]	Chao Phrya	Nakhon Sawan	3	49	2,211	0	20	0.001	0	25	0.380
Turkey	Cark Suyu	Beskopruler	0	4	186						
EUROPE											
Belgium	Escuat	Belharies	1	30	118	0	36	0.002	6	29	0.356
	Espierre	Leers/Nord	0	22	43,387	0	29	0.114	2	26	0.778
	Lys	Warneton	0	27	9,510	0	30	0.004	2	28	0.233
	Meuse	Lanaye/Ternaaien	0	69	188	6	64	0.001	1	62	0.492
	Sambre	Erquelinnes	0	33	316	5	27	0.001	1	27	0.076
	Scheldt	Doel	0	25	119	0	31	0.004	0	34	0.391
	Sure	Martelange	0	29	210	1	27	0.000	2	21	0.114
	Zelzate	Ghent/Terneuzen	0	22	22	1	34	0.000	1	31	1.225
Denmark	Gudena	Tvilum Bro	0	18	1,918	20	0	0.005	16	5	0.395
	Odense	Broby	0	6	7,755	2	0	0.002	2	0	1.100
	Okjerna	Ahlergard	0	22	929	11	12	0.015	9	15	8.769
	Susa	Naby	0	7	272	8	1	0.023	9	0	0.178
France[e]	Garonne	Couthures	0	24	6,123	14	10	0.001	20	4	0.085
	Loire	Nantes	0	24	752	0	8	0.000	0	8	0.250
	Rhone	St. Vallier	0	24	6,094	22	2	0.010	5	7	0.258
	Saone	Auxonne	0	24	16,000	0	8	0.005	0	3	0.000
	Seine	Paris	1	22	32,000	19	5	0.001	13	11	0.326
Germany, Fed Rep	Danube	Jochenstein				3	11	0.000	0	14	0.344
	Elbe	Geesthacht				0	11	0.353	6	5	0.127
	Ems	Herbrum				9	5	0.386	8	6	0.134
	Moselle	Koblenz/Moselle				10	3	0.001	0	13	0.192
	Niers	Goch				4	2	0.001	2	4	0.100
	Rhine	Kleve/Bimmen				0	12	0.002	0	13	0.454
	Weser	Intschede				12	1	0.292	9	5	0.070
Hungary[d]	Danube	Budapest	0	84	4,480	8	51	0.000	27	36	0.305
Ireland	Barro	Graiguenamanagh Bridge	0	5	582	6	0	0.002	9	0	0.040
	Blackwater	Killavullen	0	5	2,664	4	0	0.002	7	0	0.049
	Boyne	Slane Bridge	0	6	1,878	9	0	0.002	9	0	0.013
	Clare	Corofin Bridge	0	5	4,332	9	0	0.002	9	0	0.013
Italy	Adige	Trento				0	9	0.000	0	9	0.000
Luxembourg	Sure	Wasserbillig	0	22	2,324	21	3	0.004	7	0	0.200
Netherlands[e]	Maas	Belgian Frontier	0	65	17,275	0	129	0.002	0	123	0.179
	Rhine	Lex	0	70	3,035	0	57	0.001	0	111	0.111
Norway[d]	Glama	Haslemoen	0	35	99	25	0	0.001			
	Otra	Beieholen	0	38	3	26	0	0.001			
Portugal[d]	Tejo	Santarem	0	36	12,000	22	0	0.037	12	6	0.406
Spain[d]	Guadiana	Puente Palmas	0	32	402	18	12	0.000			
	Mino	Mayor Oroza	0	32	12,723	21	2	0.000			
	Sorbe	Muriel Guoga	0	2	31	2	5	0.000			
	Tejo	Puente Barca				2	26	0.001			
United Kingdom	Avon	Keynsham				15	24	0.000			
	Carron	A-890 Bridge				14	20	0.002	29	4	0.123
	Thames	Teddington Weir				102	6	0.001	187	1	0.498
	Trent	Nottingham				25	65	0.002	27	12	0.114

Source: Global Environmental Monitoring System.
Notes:
a. Total cadmium (soluble and particulate) except where indicated.
b. Total mercury (soluble and particulate) except where indicated.
c. Samples outside detection limits were assigned the detection limit value for calculating the mean.
d. Cadmium and mercury data are for soluble forms only.
e. Cadmium data are for soluble form only.
0 = zero or below the limit of detection; X = too few values to calculate statistic; blank = not available; mg = milligrams; μg = micrograms.
For additional information, see Sources and Technical Notes.

Table 23.4 Production Costs and Tariffs for Drinking Water, Early 1980s

	Facility Construction Costs ($US/capita)			Urban Systems		
		Urban				
	Rural	House Connection	Stand-pipe	Operation Cost ($US/m³)	Tariff ($US/m³)	Progressive Tariff
WORLD						
AFRICA						
Angola	25	90	X	X	0.10	no
Benin	51	21ᵃ	X	X	X	X
Botswana	X	35ᵃ	X	X	X	yes
Burkina Faso	25	100	40	0.23	0.40	yes
Burundi	17	160	100	0.39	0.22	no
Cape Verde	26	36	13	1.84	0.16	X
Congo	200	143	80	0.50	0.29	no
Djibouti	X	390	150	0.40	0.55	yes
Gambia	X	X	X	X	X	yes
Ghana	50	100	80	0.30	0.20	yes
Guinea	21	27	2	0.40	0.50	no
Guinea-Bissau	100	160ᵃ	X	0.50	0.50	no
Kenya	15-70	150-300	50-150	X	X	yes
Lesotho	100	400	200	1.00	0.33	X
Liberia	15	92	X	X	0.44	yes
Libya	X	1,000	X	0.80	0.07	yes
Madagascar	38	97	43	X	X	no
Malawi	10	75	45	0.50	0.28	yes
Mali	38	70	14	0.20	0.14	yes
Malta	28	28	X	0.51	0.30	yes
Mauritania	X	X	X	0.62	0.68	yes
Mauritius	X	X	X	0.25	0.20	X
Morocco	115	200	77	X	X	X
Niger	47	144	X	X	X	yes
Nigeria	34	81	43	1.18	0.67	yes
Rwanda	15	120	40	0.65	0.22	no
Senegal	10	13	2	0.40	0.22	yes
Sierra Leone	60	250	200	0.80	0.20	no
Somalia	160	130	90	0.50	0.75	yes
Sudan	17	60	40	0.05	0.05	yes
Tanzania, United Rep	56	80	56	0.45	0.24	no
Togo	19	126ᵃ	X	0.66	0.31	yes
Tunisia	200	250	X	X	0.31	yes
Uganda	40	200ᵃ	X	X	X	yes
Zaire	8	40	X	X	X	yes
Zambia	45-90	127	82	0.34	0.22	yes
NORTH & CENTRAL AMERICA						
Bahamas	X	290	215	1.15	2.50	yes
Barbados	150	170	50	0.28	0.68	yes
Belize	125	25	X	X	X	X
Cayman Islands	X	1,200	X	X	4.40	yes
Costa Rica	55	80	X	0.17	1.50	yes
Dominican Rep	58	94	X	0.05	1.70	yes
El Salvador	100	X	X	X	X	X
Guatemala	48	147	30	0.08	0.03	yes
Haiti	25	120	40	0.15	0.28	yes
Honduras	50	257	X	0.19	0.24	no
Mexico	157	143	X	0.09	0.06	yes
Nicaragua	57	116	24	0.29	0.44	yes
Panama	60	110	X	0.07	0.29	yes
Trinidad & Tobago	410	350	300	1.00	X	yes
SOUTH AMERICA						
Argentina	170	180	50	0.07	0.10	yes
Bolivia	88	119	96	X	X	yes
Brazil	45	75	25	0.10	0.13	yes
Chile	128	170	X	0.11	0.14	yes
Colombia	69	108	30	0.04	0.05	yes
Ecuador	157	230	85	X	0.20	yes
Guyana	120	120	100	0.08	0.03	yes
Paraguay	130	125	X	0.24	0.19	yes
Peru	52	52	5	0.06	0.08	yes
Suriname	75	180	500	0.60	0.80	yes
Uruguay	122	122	45	X	0.16	yes
Venezuela	104	X	X	X	X	X
ASIA						
Bangladesh	3	40	6	0.12	0.06	no
Brunei	X	240	X	0.44	0.11	no
Burma	5-35	65-70	30-35	X	0.20	yes
Cyprus	X	X	X	0.32	0.28	X
Hong Kong	X	X	X	X	0.24	yes
India	7-70	25-70ᵃ	X	0.16	0.10	yes
Indonesia	10-15	60	X	0.10	0.10	yes
Jordan	X	X	X	0.11	0.35	yes
Korea, Rep	29	X	X	X	X	X
Lao PDR	5-50	300-500	0.3-10	0.35	0.38	X
Macao	50	20	X	0.18	0.28	no
Malaysia	35-210	200	X	0.18	0.25	yes
Maldives	12	X	111	1.00	X	no
Nepal	2-30	70ᵃ	X	0.16	0.08	yes
Pakistan	19	38ᵃ	X	X	X	yes
Philippines	37	28	X	0.29	0.12	yes
Qatar	X	X	X	1.74	0.60	no
Saudi Arabia	X	420	X	1.10	0.10	no
Singapore	NA	19	X	0.18	0.25	yes
Sri Lanka	12	150	80	0.19	0.20	yes
Syrian Arab Rep	100	250	X	0.25	0.13	yes
Thailand	4-66	61	X	0.26	0.15	yes
Turkey	93	100	X	0.20	0.25	yes
UAE	85	100	30	1.32	0.90	no
Viet Nam	X	X	X	X	X	no
Yemen	125	300	250	1.10	1.40	yes
Yemen, Dem	240	300	260	0.26	0.30	yes
OCEANIA						
American Samoa	X	1,000	X	0.40	0.80	no
Cook Islands	72	96	X	0.30	0.00	no
Fiji	61	188	233	0.35	0.18	yes
Guam	100	205	X	0.52	X	no
Kiribati	5	X	X	X	X	X
New Caledonia	X	340	X	0.10	0.18	yes
Niue	650ᵇ	680ᵇ	650ᵇ	X	X	no
Pac Isl Trust Terr	120	450	X	0.18	0.07	yes
Papua New Guinea	15	150	50	0.60	0.40	yes
Solomon Islands	40	130	X	0.30	0.25	yes
Tokelau	32	X	X	X	X	X
Tonga	48	63	X	0.80	0.85	no
Vanuatu	50	X	X	0.19	0.31	no
Western Samoa	200	300	150	0.75	0.30	yes

Source: World Health Organization.
Notes:
a. Combined figure for house connections and standpipes.
b. Per house or standpost.
X = not available; NA = not applicable; m³ = cubic meter.
For additional information, see Sources and Technical Notes.

Sources and Technical Notes

Table 23.1 Freshwater Availability and Use, 1959-85

Sources: Water availability and use: J. Forkasiewicz and J. Margat, *Tableau Mondial de Donnees Nationales D'economie de l'Eau, Resources et Utilisation* (Departement Hydrogeologie, Orleans, France, 1980); and J. Margat, Deputy Director, Department Hydrogeologie, Orleans, France, September and December 1986 (personal communications). Population: U.N. Population Division, *World Population Prospects: Estimates and Projections as Assessed in 1984* (United Nations, New York, 1986).

Margat compiles water availability and use data from published documents, including national, U.N. and professional literature. Definitions and data collection methods vary across sources. Data for small countries and countries in arid and semiarid zones are considered less reliable than those for larger and wetter countries. For details on specific country data, refer to the sources.

Freshwater availability refers to the average annual flow of rivers and aquifers generated from endogenous precipitation. These annual averages disguise large seasonal, interannual and long-term variations in water availability. When data for water flows from other countries are not shown, the total availability figure may include these flows.

Other measures of freshwater availability may be more useful, depending on the application. For example, river and aquifer inflows from other countries are usually excluded from availability data in this table. However, countries often have treaty rights to a portion of an international river's flow; because of the definition, the actual availability of freshwater is understated. (See Chapter 12, "Policies and Institutions.") In many countries, the release of water from glaciers and large lakes also contributes to freshwater availability.

Water is *withdrawn* when it is taken from a surface or underground source and conveyed to the place of use. Water is *consumed* when it is no longer available for use because it has been removed from available supplies by evaporation or transpiration, by use in agriculture or manufacturing, or for human consumption.

Water that is withdrawn but not consumed (e.g., irrigation runoff, cooling water from thermoelectric plants) is returned to the water basin. It can be withdrawn again provided the quality has not been degraded.

Per capita *availability* data were created using 1987 population estimates. Per capita *withdrawal* figures were calculated using the total withdrawal estimate for the "year of data" as the numerator and national population data for that year as the denominator. If no "year of data" figures were available, the 1975 population was used to calculate per capita withdrawal statistics.

Water use is classified in three categories: public use (homes, commercial establishments, public services [e.g., hospitals], and publicly supplied industry), agriculture (principally irrigation), and self-supplied industry. In this table, industrial use includes water withdrawn to cool thermoelectric plants. Because not all countries collect data using these categories, the sectoral data are not strictly comparable.

Water use does not include instream uses of water such as hydroelectric power generation, navigation, habitat for fish and other aquatic life, and recreation.

For additional information on water resources, see M.I. L'vovich, *World Water Resources and Their Future* (Mysl' P.H., Moscow, 1974), English translation edited by Raymond L. Nace (American Geophysical Union, Washington, D.C., 1979).

Table 23.2 Large Dams

Sources: Dams: International Commission on Large Dams (ICOLD), *World Register of Dams 1984* (ICOLD, Paris, 1985). Hydroelectric capacity: The World Bank, *A Survey of the Future Role of Hydroelectric Power in 100 Developing Countries* (The World Bank, Washington, D.C., 1984); and U.N. Statistical Office (UNSO), *Energy Statistics Yearbook 1984* (UNSO, New York, 1986).

ICOLD obtains data from national committees of its 74 member countries. Information on dams in nonmember countries (about 1 percent of all reported large dams) was collected by committee members.

Dams measuring at least 15 meters, from the lowest portion of the general foundation area to the crest, are included in the register.

Because of the number of large dams in the United States, China, India, and Japan, only dams over 30 meters high are included in the register. The total number of dams over 15 meters, completed or under construction as of December 31, 1982, was 5,352 in the United States, 18,707 in China, 1,205 in India, and 2,226 in Japan. There are also 1,000 dams over 30 meters in China that are not included in the table; they are included in the total given above. The dams listed for the USSR include only hydroelectric dams controlled by the Ministry of Energy and Electrification. An additional 2,000-3,000 large dams built by the Ministry of Agriculture and local authorities are not included in the table. About 45 additional large dams in the German Democratic Republic (GDR) are not included in the table. The GDR became an ICOLD member in late 1984 and its list was incomplete when the register was published.

Data for reservoir area are also incomplete; the areas of Canadian reservoirs, for example, are not listed in the *World Register of Dams 1984*. Continental and global totals are the sums of listed country data. Refer to the source for additional details.

Theoretical potential represents the energy that would be produced if all runoff ran through turbines to sea level with 100 percent mechanical efficiency. Data are from World Energy Conference, *1983 Survey of Energy Resources* (World Energy Conference, London, 1983). More recent data will be available in 1987 from the World Energy Conference held in October 1986.

Technical potential is limited to the total potential of all sites where it is physically possible to construct dams, with no consideration of economic return or of adverse impacts of site development. The World Bank obtained data on technical hydroelectric potential from information available in published reports and from World Bank files.

Table 23.3 River Water Quality, 1979-86

Source: Global Environmental Monitoring System, unpublished data (Canada Centre for Inland Waters, Burlington, Ontario, December 1986).

The Global Environmental Monitoring System's Water Network (GEMS/Water) is coordinated by the United Nations Environment Programme, the World Health Organization (WHO), the United Nations Educational, Scientific and Cultural Organization, and the World Meteorological Organization. Monitoring stations are operated by national authorities; GEMS/Water establishes network operating protocols and station-siting guidelines, conducts interlaboratory comparison exercises, provides training to national personnel, and operates a central data base at the Canada Centre for Inland Waters (CCIW) in Burlington, Ontario. Monitoring data have been submitted to CCIW since January 1, 1979; data available at CCIW on November 28, 1986, were screened for use in this table (see below).

As of December 1986, 263 stations (on 194 rivers in 52 countries) had reported data to CCIW. To select stations for inclusion in this table, a three-step process was used. In 1983, GEMS/Water rated 204 stations for representativeness in order to evaluate the global coverage of important river basins. A station was considered representative if it sampled pristine water (5 points), was located on an important river (in terms of basin area [0-2], river discharge [0-2], and whether the river is international [2] and discharges into the ocean [1]), monitored rivers important to a country's water supply (0-2), and was located downstream from major water uses (0-2). All stations rated 5 and above and an additional 59 stations that were not evaluated at the time were screened for data comprehensiveness. Developing country monitoring stations were considered comprehensive if they had data for at least two of the five indicators used in the table; developed country stations were included if they had data for at least three of the indicators. Many rivers had several stations that met the criteria for representativeness and comprehensiveness. For most of these rivers, only the monitoring station furthest downstream was included in the table.

The five variables used in the table were chosen to reflect three major types of water contamination: agricultural runoff, sewage, and industrial waste (see below). These variables had the most comprehensive data for the three types of water contamination. For example, of the monitoring stations evaluated by GEMS/Water in 1983, 81 percent monitored nitrates/nitrites and 33 percent monitored mercury. However, only 60 percent monitored phosphates, 20 percent monitored one or more variants and residues of DDT (alternative agricultural runoff indicators), and 8 percent monitored PCBs (an industrial waste indicator).

■ *Agricultural runoff.* The presence of nitrates/nitrites in water usually indicates agricultural runoff (fertilizer and livestock runoff) and industrial and domestic wastes. High concentrations in drinking water may be a health hazard, especially for infants. Excess nitrogen may also enhance eutrophication of natural waters.

■ *Sewage.* Biochemical oxygen demand (BOD) is a measure of the oxygen consumed by microorganisms in oxidizing organic matter over a period of time; it may indicate sewage pollution of water. The GEMS/Water protocol for BOD analysis specifies an incubation period of five days. Fecal coliform bacteria are a group of organisms found in the alimentary tracts and excreta of humans and warmblooded animals. Although not normally disease agents in humans, fecal coliform bacteria usually indicate the presence of sewage and possibly of other microorganisms, such as *Salmonella*, that are hazardous to human health. WHO recommends that 98 percent of a series of 100 milliliter drinking water samples be free from fecal coliform bacteria.

■ *Industrial wastes.* Cadmium enters surface water as an effluent of mining and smelting operations. It is also present in the wastes of electroplating, pigment, textile, and chemical industries. Cadmium is toxic to humans, affecting the kidneys and reproductive organs, and to fish and invertebrates. WHO recommends that drinking water contain less than 0.005 milligrams of cadmium per liter. Mercury is an indicator of industrial activity, emitted in the wastes of chloroalkali plants and a variety of chemical industries (electronics, explosives, pesticides, photography, etc.). Mercury is toxic, causing neurological damage in high doses. WHO recommends that drinking water contain less than 0.001 milligrams (1 microgram) of total mercury per liter.

Data submitted to CCIW include measurements of constituents and a count of the number of samples for which measurements could not be made because of limitations in the sensitivity of analytical techniques. Analytical techniques usually have a lower and upper limit of sensitivity. When detection was not possible, in almost all cases it was because the constituent was present at a concentration too low to be measured. In only a few instances was the constituent present in a concentration too *high* to be measured.

Means shown in the table are arithmetic means. For the purpose of determining the mean, measurements reported as below the detection limit were set equal to the lower

detection limit. The few measurements reported as above the detection limit were set equal to the upper detection limit.

For additional details on site representativeness, data comprehensiveness, and descriptive statistics, refer to WHO, *GEMS/Water Data Evaluation Report 1983* (WHO, Geneva, 1983), and M. Maybeck, "The GEMS/Water Program (1978-1983)," *Water Quality Bulletin*, Vol. 10, No. 4 (1985), pp. 167.

Typically, samples collected at monitoring stations are taken to laboratories for chemical analyses. (Other parameters, such as temperature, pH, dissolved oxygen, etc., are measured on site.) Ideally, sampling frequencies depend on the site, the group of variables being monitored, and cyclic impacts on river quality (such as daily or annual industrial effluent cycles, seasonal agricultural runoff cycles, and seasonal precipitation cycles). In fact, few stations are monitored with ideal frequency. Station siting guidelines, sampling frequency recommendations, and laboratory analysis procedures for several dozen constituents are described in WHO, *GEMS/Water Operational Guide* (WHO, Geneva, 1978).

GEMS/Water has undertaken a program of quality control to improve comparability of data across monitoring stations and analytical laboratories. In 1982, sample concentrates of known values (quality control samples) were distributed for the first time to subnational, national, and regional analytical laboratories for analyses. Laboratories were requested to prepare and analyze the samples and compare their results with the correct values, which were supplied with the samples. Laboratories were also requested to submit the results of their quality control exercise and general comments, confidentially, to the WHO/GEMS central analytical quality control laboratory to aid evaluation of the quality control program. Of 248 samples distributed, results were returned by 32 laboratories (13 percent). Many of them commented on equipment, personnel, and training limitations and lack of reagents. Distribution of quality control samples to WHO/GEMS laboratories continued through 1986.

In 1983, a second type of prepared sample (performance evaluation samples) was mailed to 290 laboratories without documentation of correct values. Seventy replies were received. Overall, about 70 percent of the analyses of these unknown samples were in the acceptable range (within 20 percent of the correct value), although the percentage of acceptable results varied among the constituents. For example, 60 percent of the analyses of trace metals (a category that includes cadmium and mercury) were considered acceptable, as were 70 percent of the nutrient analyses (including nitrates/nitrites) and 56 percent of the "demand" analyses (e.g., BOD). For further details, refer to J.A. Winter, "Quality Assur-

ance to Support the GEMS/Water Program," *Water Quality Bulletin*, Vol. 10, No. 4 (1985), pp. 181.

Table 23.4 Production Costs and Tariffs for Drinking Water, Early 1980s

Source: World Health Organization (WHO), *The International Drinking Water Supply and Sanitation Decade: Review of National Progress (as of December 1983)* (WHO, Geneva, 1986) and *The International Drinking Water Supply and Sanitation Decade: Review of National Baseline Data, 31 December 1980* (WHO, Geneva, 1984), and unpublished data (WHO, Geneva, 1985).

WHO sent two questionnaires to developing country correspondents on the status and progress of the International Drinking Water Supply and Sanitation Decade (IDWSSD). The questionnaires requested information on: the physical, economic, and health status of the country; national plans for the IDWSSD; drinking water and sanitation service levels; institutional structures; manpower and training; investments and external contributions; and unit costs and cost projections. (Service levels for drinking water and sanitation are shown in Table 17.2 in Chapter 17, "Human Settlements.") The first survey asked for information as of December 31, 1980, and the second survey asked for information as of December 31, 1983. A third survey, currently underway, requests information for December 31, 1985. Data from the 1983 questionnaire were used when available; data from the 1980 questionnaire were used in their absence.

The data in this table summarize responses to one set of questions. Country correspondents were asked for the average national cost, expressed in U.S. dollars, of urban and rural water facility construction, the operation cost of urban water facilities, and the urban water tariff. They were also asked if a progressive tariff was in force in urban areas. A few countries reported a range of figures in response to some questions, but most questions were answered by a single figure. It is likely that these figures are the average or median of a wide range of values.

Data have not been adjusted for inflation, nor is there an indication in the source of the exchange rate used by country correspondents in calculating U.S. dollar figures from national currency.

A progressive tariff charges an increasing marginal unit price for water. For example, the first 1,000 cubic meters cost $0.05 per cubic meter, the next 1,000 cubic meters cost $0.07 per cubic meter, etc. Countries listed as having a progressive tariff have one in force in some or all of their urban areas.

24. Oceans and Coasts

Oceans cover more than two thirds of the earth's surface, and they contain huge stores of food, minerals and other resources. This chapter provides information on the abundance and exploitation of marine resources as well as on the legal framework that has been created to manage these resources.

Table 24.1 reports on the length of coastlines, national claims to coastal waters, and marine fish catch by country. Three types of claims are covered: territorial seas, Exclusive Economic Zones (EEZs), and continental shelves. Territorial seas are claimed by a country as sovereign territory; EEZs and continental shelves are jurisdictional claims to living and nonliving marine resources. Seventy-one countries have established EEZs since 1974, bringing about 95 percent of the world's marine resources under national authority.

National fish catches have changed sharply in the past decade because of several factors: establishment of EEZs, fluctuations in species populations, and improvements in fishing methods and technology. With the establishment of 200-mile EEZs, several small Pacific island nations gained control over part of the large tuna fishery in the South Pacific. Some developed countries, such as the United States and Canada, also benefit from establishment of the EEZs. But countries whose fishing fleets operate in foreign waters (e.g., the Federal Republic of Germany and Norway) have seen their fishing grounds come under the control of other countries, and their fish catches have declined.

Data on *populations* of marine mammals are very limited. (See Table 24.2.) Estimating species populations requires censuses of animals in particular regions and information on species' breeding habits, survival rates, and migratory patterns. These data have not been gathered for most marine mammal species.

Catch data for marine mammals, necessary for analyzing the impact of harvests on stocks, are limited in several respects. Although global whaling data have been collected for almost 70 years, the data shown in Table 24.2 do not describe the impact of pre-1920 exploitation of these species. Right whales, commercially hunted since the 16th Century, were near extinction by the early 1900s. Historical catch data for several other commercially exploited marine mammal species, such as southern fur seals, have been reported only for the past few years.

Available catch data vary in quality. Whaling has been internationally regulated for 50 years, and catch data are considered reliable. However, catch data for small cetaceans are often incomplete because not all countries report, and those that do report may monitor only selected regions. Seal harvests have been sporadically recorded over the years, and the quality of current data varies according to region and species. Moreover, catch data for seals and sea lions do not include mortality caused by fishing gear and other plastic debris.

The potential and actual marine fish catches in the world's oceans (a subset of the total fish catch presented in Table 24.1) are shown in Table 24.3. Although the global marine fish catch has risen slightly in the past 15 years, harvests for several regions have changed dramatically. For example, the Pacific Southeast fishery, the source of 23 percent of the world's marine fish catch in 1970, provided only 6 percent in 1973, rising to 13 percent by 1984. This drop reflects the collapse of the Peruvian anchovy fishery in the early 1970s as a result of the abnormally warm El Niño current.

Two fisheries, the Pacific Northwest and the Mediterranean and Black Seas, reached and perhaps exceeded their "estimated maximum sustainable yield" in the past five years. This term—a measure of the biological productivity of a fishery—refers to the maximum catch that can be sustained under average environmental conditions. Experts believe that exploitation of the remaining fisheries potential cannot be achieved by increased fishing effort alone. Realization of the fisheries potential requires improved fisheries management, including protection of depressed stocks such as the North Atlantic herring and the Peruvian anchovy.

Time-series data on one marine pollutant, petroleum from tanker spills, are provided in Table 24.4. The amount of oil spilled into the oceans in the early 1980s was substantially less than that spilled in the late 1970s. But the oil spilled from tanker accidents is only a small fraction of the estimated 3 million metric tons introduced to the world's oceans annually. Other major sources include: river flows, coastal and offshore drilling rigs, tanker flushing, municipal wastes, the atmosphere, and natural seeps.

Several other types of marine pollution can damage renewable coastal resources—sediments, heavy metals, organochlorine compounds, sewage, and other industrial, agricultural, and municipal effluents. However, documented effects of particular marine pollutants are scattered, and almost no data are available on the impacts of pollutants on marine life in the open seas. Refer to Chapter 9, "Oceans and Coasts," for further details.

Table 24.1 Coastal Areas and Resources, 1974-86

	Length of Marine Coastline (kilometers)	Maritime Zones (nautical miles unless otherwise indicated)			Average Annual Marine Catch[a]	
		Territorial Sea	Exclusive Economic Zone	Continental Shelf	1982-84 (thousand metric tons)	Percentage Change Over 1974-76
WORLD					**69,634**	**16**
AFRICA					**2,675**	**-13**
Algeria	1,183	12	X	X	70	93
Angola	1,600	20	X	X	90	-57
Benin	121	200	X	X	4	-41
Cameroon	402	50	X	X	36	-5
Cape Verde	965	12	200	X	11	248
Comoros	340	12	200	X	4	11
Congo	169	200	X	X	19	17
Cote d'Ivoire	515	12	200	200	74	9
Djibouti	314	12	200	X	0	40
Egypt	2,450	12	X	200m/EXP	26	-8
Equatorial Guinea	296	12	200	X	3	-34
Ethiopia	1,094	12	X	X	0	-86
Gabon	885	12	200	X	50	849
Gambia	80	12	X	X	8	-18
Ghana	539	12	200	200m	200	1
Guinea	346	12	200	X	17	62
Guinea-Bissau	274	12	200	X	3	35
Kenya	536	12	200	200m/EXP	6	61
Liberia	579	200	X	X	10	73
Libya	1,770	12	X	X	8	79
Madagascar	4,828	12	200[c]	200m	12	-29
Mauritania	754	70	200	200/CM	45	102
Mauritius	177	12	200	200/CM	10	37
Morocco	1,835	12	200	X	427	61
Mozambique	2,470	12	200	X	37	50
Namibia	1,489	6	X	X	235	-68
Nigeria	853	30	200	200m/EXP	270	13
Reunion	201	12	200	X	3	8
Senegal	531	12	200	200/CM	219	-35
Seychelles	491	12	200	200/CM	4	2
Sierra Leone	402	200	X	200m/EXP	36	-42
Somalia	3,025	200	X	X	15	85
South Africa	2,881	12	X	200m/EXP	607	2
Sudan	853	12	X	200m/EXP	3	315
Tanzania, United Rep	1,424	50	X	X	29	-31
Togo	56	30	200	X	14	43
Tunisia	1,143	12	X	X	68	51
Zaire	37	12	X	X	1	-92
NORTH & CENTRAL AMERICA					**7,115**	**52**
Antigua and Barbuda	153	12	200	X	2	32
Bahamas	3,542	3	X	200m/EXP	5	75
Barbados	97	12	200	X	6	36
Belize	386	3	X	X	1	-9
Bermuda	103	3	X	X	1	-73
Canada	58,808[b]	12	X	200m/EXP	1,272	30
Cayman Islands	160	3	X	X	1	NM
Costa Rica	1,290	12	200	200m/EXP	10	-23
Cuba	3,735	12	200	X	183	11
Dominica	148	12	200	X	1	1
Dominican Rep	1,288	6	200	200/CM	11	89
El Salvador	307	200	X	X	10	37
Greenland	44,087	3	X	X	97	102
Grenada	121	12	200	X	1	-41
Guadelupe	306	12	200	X	9	29
Guatemala	400	12	200	200m/EXP	3	-15
Haiti	1,771	12	200	200m/EXP	4	8
Honduras	820	12	200	200m/EXP	7	77
Jamaica	1,022	12	X	200m/EXP	8	-16
Martinique	290	12	200	X	5	46
Mexico	9,330	12	200	200m/EXP	1,086	148
Nicaragua	910	200	X	X	4	-54
Panama	2,490	200	X	X	141	9
Trinidad and Tobago	362	12	X	200m/EXP	4	-2
United States	19,924	3	200	200m/EXP	4,240	50
SOUTH AMERICA					**8,806**	**39**
Argentina	4,989	200	X	200m/EXP	389	62
Brazil	7,491	200	X	X	679	24
Chile	6,435	12	200	200/350	4,051	257
Colombia	2,414	12	200	200m/EXP	20	-19
Ecuador	2,237	200	X	200m	610	162
French Guiana	378	12	200	X	2	105
Guyana	459	12	X	200/CM	28	29
Peru	2,414	200	X	200	2,676	-33
Suriname	386	12	200	X	3	-42
Uruguay	660	200	X	200m/EXP	132	428
Venezuela	2,800	12	200	200m/EXP	216	55

World Resources 1987

Table 24.1

	Length of Marine Coastline (kilometers)	Maritime Zones (nautical miles unless otherwise indicated)			Average Annual Marine Catch[a]	
		Territorial Sea	Exclusive Economic Zone	Continental Shelf	1982–84 (thousand metric tons)	Percentage Change Over 1974–76
ASIA					**28,391**	**22**
Bahrain	161	3	X	X	5	133
Bangladesh	580	12	200	CM	152	61
Burma	3,060	12	200	200/CM	454	32
China	14,500	12	X	X	3,471	9
Cyprus	648	12	X	200m/EXP	2	81
Hong Kong	733	3	X	X	183	26
India	7,000	12	200	200/CM	1,575	9
Indonesia	54,716	12	200	X	1,612	61
Iran	3,180	12	X	X	37	−39
Iraq	58	12	X	X	6	−32
Israel	273	6	X	200m/EXP	10	0
Japan	13,685	12	X	X	11,156	14
Jordan	26	3	X	X	0	−73
Kampuchea, Dem	443	12	200	200m/EXP	5	−50
Korea, Dem People's Rep	2,495	12	200	X	1,508	51
Korea, Rep	2,413	12	X	X	2,339	24
Kuwait	499	12	X	X	4	−7
Lebanon	225	12	X	X	1	−46
Macau	40	6	X	X	7	−32
Malaysia	4,675	12	200	200m/EXP	684	36
Maldives	644	12	X	X	39	19
Oman	2,092	12	200	X	99	−48
Pakistan	1,046	12	200	200/CM	290	71
Philippines	22,540	X	200	EXP	1,305	12
Qatar	563	3	X	X	3	18
Saudi Arabia	2,510	12	X	X	26	13
Singapore	193	3	X	X	21	23
Sri Lanka	1,340	12	200	200/CM	170	51
Syrian Arab Rep	193	35	X	X	1	−3
Thailand	3,219	12	200	200m/EXP	2,062	45
Turkey	7,200	6/12	X	X	503	329
United Arab Emirates	1,448	3/12	X	X	72	8
Viet Nam	3,444[b]	12	200	200/CM	497	24
Yemen	523	12	X	X	15	2
Yemen, Dem	1,383	12	200	200/CM	76	63
EUROPE					**12,002**	**−5**
Albania	418	15	X	200m/EXP	4	0
Belgium	64	3	X	X	48	3
Bulgaria	354	12	X	200m/EXP	102	−27
Denmark	3,379	3	X	200m/EXP	1,856	2
Faeroe Islands	764	3	X	X	193	−34
Finland	1,126[b]	4	X	200m/EXP	121	35
France	3,427	12	200	200m/EXP	753	−4
German Dem Rep	901	12	X	200m/EXP	214	−34
Germany, Fed Rep	1,488	3	X	200m/EXP	293	−36
Greece	13,676	6	X	200m/EXP	92	2
Iceland	4,988	12	200	200/CM	1,054	8
Ireland	1,448	3	X	X	208	129
Italy	4,996	12	X	200m/EXP	442	11
Malta	140	12	X	200m/EXP	1	−26
Netherlands	451	12	X	200m/EXP	487	54
Norway	3,419[b]	4	200	200m/EXP	2,597	−8
Poland	491	12	X	200m/EXP	657	−9
Portugal	860[b]	12	200	200m/EXP	262	−32
Romania	225	12	200	200m/EXP	181	114
Spain	4,964	12	200	200m/EXP	1,272	−14
Sweden	3,218	12	X	200m/EXP	260	27
United Kingdom	12,429	3	X	200m/EXP	859	−16
Yugoslavia	1,521[b]	12	X	200m/EXP	47	46
USSR	**46,670**	**12**	**200**	**200m/EXP**	**9,275**	**4**
OCEANIA					**417**	**49**
Australia	25,760	3	X	200m/EXP	166	42
Cook Islands	120	12	200	200/CM	1	−17
French Polynesia	2,525	12	200	X	2	−9
Fiji	1,129	12	200	200m/EXP	26	430
Kiribati	1,143	12	200	X	23	43
New Caledonia	2,254	12	200	X	3	202
New Zealand	15,134	12	200	200/CM	144	114
Niue	64	12	200	X	0	NM
Papua New Guinea	5,152	12	X	200m/EXP	3	−93
Solomon Islands	5,313	12	200	X	43	107
Tonga	419	12	200	200m/EXP	2	126
Tuvalu	24	12	200	X	1	NM
Vanuatu	2,528	12	200	200/CM	3	4

Sources: U.S. Department of State; U.N. Law of the Sea Secretariat; and U.N. Food and Agriculture Organization.
Notes:
a. Marine catch includes marine fishes, molluscs, crustaceans, and miscellaneous aquatic animals.
b. Coastline figures exclude islands.
c. Continental shelf limit for Madagascar is 200 nautical miles or 100 n.m. from the 2,500-meter isobath.
0 = zero or less than half of 1 percent; X = no claim made or information not available; NM = not meaningful; m = meters of water (depth);
f = fathom (1.83 meters); CM = edge of continental margin; EXP = limits of exploitable resources.
For additional information, see Sources and Technical Notes.

World Resources 1987

Table 24.2 Marine Mammals, 1920–85

Species (stocks)	Original Abundance (pre-commercial exploitation)	Current	Percentage of Initial Stock Remaining	Data Source	1920–29	1930–39	1940–49	1950–59	1960–69	1970–79	1980–85[a]	Data Source
THREATENED SPECIES												
Great Whales												
Gray whale	X	X	X	NMFS	230	291	438	763[b]	1,650[b]	1,730[b]	650[b]	NMFS
Northeast Pacific	15,000–20,000	13,450–19,210	recovered									
Northwest Pacific	X	near extinction	X									
Blue whale	X	X	X	NMFS	69,130	170,746	46,198	35,948	7,434	23	0	IWS
North Atlantic	1,100–1,500	100	6–9									
North Pacific	4,900	1,400–1,900	29–39									
North Indian Ocean	X	X	X									
Antarctic	150,000–210,000	1,000–8,000	<1–5									
Subantarctic Indian Ocean	10,000	5,000	50									
Fin whale	X	X	X	NMFS	78,140	139,384	111,215	286,212	174,995	22,752	2,015	IWS
North Norway	several thousand	X	X									
West Norway/Faeroe Isl.	>2,700	X	10									
Spain, Portugal, British Isles	>5,000	X	X									
Denmark Strait	X	1,791–11,584	X									
Northwest Atlantic	X	3,590–6,300	X									
North Pacific	42,000–45,000	14,620–18,630	32–44									
Antarctic	400,000	85,200	21									
Sei whale	X	X	X	NMFS	13,628	6,382	8,747	31,689	154,968	55,151	506	IWS
North Atlantic	X	4,957	X									
North Pacific	45,000	22,000–37,000	49–82									
Southern Hemisphere	63,100–64,400	9,800–11,760	15–19									
Humpback whale	X	X	X	NMFS	16,219	27,359	9,334	37,688	12,445	182[b]	78[b]	IWS
Northeast Atlantic	X	X	X									
Northwest Atlantic	>4,400	5,257–6,289	recovered?									
North Indian Ocean	X	X	X									
North Pacific	15,000	1,200	8									
Southern Hemisphere	100,000	2,500–3,000	2–3									
Bowhead whale	X	X	X	NMFS	181[b]	125[b]	99[b]	99[b]	135[b]	236[b]	71[b]	NMFS
East Greenland-Spitsbergen	25,000	near extinction	<1									
Davis Strait	11,000	X	<5									
Hudson Bay	680	X	X									
Western Arctic	18,000	4,417	25									
Sea of Okhotsk	X	X	5–10?									
Right whale	100,000–300,000	3,100–3,200	1–3	NMFS	X	X	X	X	X	X	X	
North Atlantic	X	X	X									
North Pacific	X	X near extinction										
Southern Hemisphere	X	3,000	X									
Sperm whale	1,377,000	982,300	71	NMFS	11,645	27,118	53,800	157,608	249,470	181,023	5,424	IWS
North Atlantic	166,000	99,500	60									
Northeast Pacific	311,000	274,000	88									
Northwest Pacific	309,400	198,100	64									
Southern Hemisphere	590,600	410,700	70									
Small Whales												
Northern bottlenose whale	X	X	X		X	X	X	X	3,464	813	0	IWS
Shepherd's beaked whale	X	X	X		X	X	X	X	X	X	X	
Pygmy killer whale	X	X	X		X	X	X	X	X	X	X	
Dolphins and Porpoises[c]												
La Plata River dolphin	X	X	X		X	X	X	X	X	X	262	IWC
Ganges River dolphin	X	4,000–5,000	X	FAO	X	X	X	X	X	X	X	
Indus River dolphin	X	450–600	X	FAO	X	X	X	X	X	X	X	
Yangtze River dolphin	X	X	X		X	X	X	X	X	X	X	
Amazon River dolphin	X	X	X		X	X	X	X	X	X	7	IWC
Cochito	X	X	X		X	X	X	X	X	X	X	
Sirenians and Otters												
Dugong	X	X	X		X	X	X	X	X	X	925[d]	MMC
Amazonian Manatee	X	>10,000	X	FAO	X	X	X	X	X	X	X	
West African Manatee	X	X	X		X	X	X	X	X	X	X	
West Indian Manatee	X	X	X		X	X	X	X	X	X	X	
Florida	X	>1,000	X	FAO	X	X	X	X	X	X	X	
Sea Otter	X	112,000–132,000	X	FAO	X	X	X	X	X	X	X	
Southern Sea Otter	X	X	X		X	X	X	X	X	X	X	
Seals and Sea Lions												
Caribbean monk seal	X	near extinction	X	FAO	X	X	X	X	X	X	X	
Hawaiian monk seal	X	500–1,500	X	NMFS	X	X	X	X	X	X	X	
Mediterranean monk seal	X	500–800	X	FAO	X	X	X	X	X	X	X	
South American fur seal	X	320,000	X	FAO	X	X	X	X	X	X	18,910	FAO
Cape/Australian fur seal	X	870,000	X	NMFS	X	X	X	X	X	X	273,290	FAO
Africa	1,164,000	850,000	73		X	X	X	X	X	X	X	
Australia	X	20,000	X		X	X	X	X	X	X	X	
New Zealand fur seal	X	X	X	FAO	X	X	X	X	X	X	X	
New Zealand	X	38,000	X		X	X	X	X	X	X	X	
Australia	X	few thousand	X		X	X	X	X	X	X	X	
Antarctic fur seal	X	363,000	X	FAO	X	X	X	X	X	X	X	
Subantarctic fur seal	X	23,400–120,000	X	FAO	X	X	X	X	X	X	X	
Galapagos fur seal	X	1,000–5,000	X	FAO	X	X	X	X	X	X	X	
Juan Fernandez fur seal	several million	705–750	X	NMFS	X	X	X	X	X	X	X	
Guadelupe fur seal	200,000	1,600	1	NMFS	X	X	X	X	X	X	X	
Northern elephant seal	X	45,000	X	FAO	X	X	X	X	X	X	X	
Southern elephant seal	X	600,000	X	FAO	X	X	X	X	X	X	X	

World Resources 1987

Species (stocks)	Original Abundance (pre-commercial exploitation)	Population Current	Percentage of Initial Stock Remaining	Data Source	1920–29	1930–39	1940–49	1950–59	1960–69	1970–79	1980–85[a]	Data Source
NONTHREATENED SPECIES												
Small Whales												
Minke whale	X	X	X		X	31	15	26,126	35,841	90,094	59,753	IWS
Southern Hemisphere	X	580,000	X	FAO								
Barents Sea	X	60,000–90,000	X									
Korean Stock	X	14,000	X									
Pygmy Right whale	X	X	X		X	X	X	X	X	X	X	
Bryde's whale	X	X	X		X	X	X	X	X	9,281[e]	895	IWS
Killer whale	X	X	X		X	X	31	1,133	2,082	1,067	1,195	IWC
Antarctica	X	160,000	X	FAO								
False killer whale	X	X	X		X	X	X	X	X	X	756	IWC
Long-finned pilot whale	X	X	X		X	X	X	X	36,205	10,885	13,666	IWC
Short-finned pilot whale	X	X	X		X	X	X	X	X	X	2,965	IWC
White whale	X	62,000–88,000	X	FAO	X	X	X	3,971	10,001	16,605	9,227	IWS
Narwhal	X	X	X		X	X	X	X	1,511[f]	4,874	4,623	IWS
Canadian Eastern Arctic	X	29,000	X	IWC								
and Inglefield Bay	X	X	X									
Pygmy Sperm whale	X	X	X		X	X	X	X	X	X	X	
Dwarf Sperm whale	X	X	X		X	X	X	X	X	X	X	
Baird's beaked whale	X	X	X		X	6	26	1,223	1,502	548	244	IWS
Northwest Pacific	X	4,220	X	IWC								
Arnoux's beaked whale	X	X	X		X	X	X	X	X	X	X	
Longman's beaked whale	X	X	X		X	X	X	X	X	X	X	
Blainville's beaked whale	X	X	X		X	X	X	X	X	X	X	
Gervais's beaked whale	X	X	X		X	X	X	X	X	X	X	
Strap-toothed whale	X	X	X		X	X	X	X	X	X	X	
Hector's beaked whale	X	X	X		X	X	X	X	X	X	X	
Gray's beaked whale	X	X	X		X	X	X	X	X	X	X	
Stejneger's beaked whale	X	X	X		X	X	X	X	X	X	X	
Andrew's beaked whale	X	X	X		X	X	X	X	X	X	X	
True's beaked whale	X	X	X		X	X	X	X	X	X	X	
Ginko-toothed beaked whale	X	X	X		X	X	X	X	X	X	X	
Hubb's beaked whale	X	X	X		X	X	X	X	X	X	X	
Cuvier's beaked whale	X	X	X		X	X	X	X	X	X	X	
Indo-Pacific beaked whale	X	X	X		X	X	X	X	X	X	X	
Skew's beaked whale	X	X	X		X	X	X	X	X	X	X	
Wonderful beaked whale	X	X	X		X	X	X	X	X	X	X	
Gulf Stream beaked whale	X	X	X		X	X	X	X	X	X	X	
Arch beaked whale	X	X	X		X	X	X	X	X	X	X	
Japanese beaked whale	X	X	X		X	X	X	X	X	X	X	
Scamperdown beaked whale	X	X	X		X	X	X	X	X	X	X	
Bering Sea beaked whale	X	X	X		X	X	X	X	X	X	X	
Southern bottlenose whale	X	X	X		X	X	X	X	X	X	X	
Melon-headed whale	X	X	X		X	X	X	X	X	X	140	IWC
Dolphins and Porpoises[c]												
Rough-toothed dolphin	X	X	X		X	X	X	X	X	X	X	
Tucuxi	X	X	X		X	X	X	X	X	X	7	IWC
Indo-Pacific humpbacked dolphin	X	X	X		X	X	X	X	X	X	10	IWC
Atlantic humpbacked dolphin	X	X	X		X	X	X	X	X	X	X	
Irrawaddy dolphin	X	X	X		X	X	X	X	X	X	X	
White-beaked dolphin	X	X	X		X	X	X	X	X	X	X	
Atlantic white-sided dolphin	X	X	X		X	X	X	X	X	X	23	IWC
Northwest Atlantic	X	24,000	X	NMFS								
Pacific white-sided dolphin	X	X	X		X	X	X	X	X	X	5,293	IWC
Northwest Pacific	X	30,000–50,000	X	NMFS								
Dusky dolphin	X	X	X		X	X	X	X	X	X	17	IWC
Hourglass dolphin	X	X	X		X	X	X	X	X	X	X	
Peale's dolphin	X	X	X		X	X	X	X	X	X	1	IWC
Fraser's dolphin	X	X	X		X	X	X	X	X	X	2	IWC
Southeast Pacific	X	7,800	X	NMFS								
Risso's dolphin	X	X	X		X	X	X	X	X	X	1,171	IWC
Northwest Atlantic	X	10,000	X	NMFS								
Bottlenose dolphin	X	X	X		X	X	X	X	X	X	3,889	IWC
Northwest Atlantic	X	14,000–23,000	X	NMFS								
Spinner dolphin	X	X	X		X	X	X	X	X	X	58,018	IWC
Eastern Pacific	X	900,000	X	NMFS								
Striped dolphin	X	X	X		X	X	X	X	X	X	20,654	IWC
Eastern Pacific	X	2,300,000	X	NMFS								
Spotted dolphin	X	X	X		X	X	X	X	X	X	119,087	IWC
Eastern Pacific	X	2,200,000	X	NMFS								
Clymene dolphin	X	X	X		X	X	X	X	X	X	X	
Common dolphin	X	X	X	NMFS	X	X	X	X	X	X	29,098	IWC
Northwest Pacific	X	900,000	X									
Northwest Atlantic	X	31,000	X									
Southern right whale dolphin	X	X	X		X	X	X	X	X	X	X	
Northern right whale dolphin	X	X	X		X	X	X	X	X	X	48	IWC
Heaviside's dolphin	X	X	X		X	X	X	X	X	X	X	
Black dolphin	X	X	X		X	X	X	X	X	X	1,400	IWC
Hector's dolphin	X	X	X		X	X	X	X	X	X	4	IWC
Commerson's dolphin	X	X	X		X	X	X	X	X	X	X	
Dall's porpoise	X	920,000	X	NMFS	X	X	X	X	X	X	82,937	IWC
Harbour porpoise	X	X	X		X	X	X	X	X	X	12,892	IWC
Burmeister's porpoise	X	X	X		X	X	X	X	X	X	X	
Spectacled porpoise	X	X	X		X	X	X	X	X	X	X	
Finless porpoise	X	X	X		X	X	X	X	X	X	38	IWC

Table 24.2 Marine Mammals, 1920–85 (continued)

Species (stocks)	Population Original Abundance (pre-commercial exploitation)	Current	Percentage of Initial Stock Remaining	Data Source	Total Reported World Catch (number of animals) 1920–29	1930–39	1940–49	1950–59	1960–69	1970–79	1980–85[a]	Data Source
NONTHREATENED SPECIES												
Seals and Sea Lions												
Steller sea lion	X	230,000	X	FAO	X	X	X	X	X	X	8,403	FAO
California sea lion	X	177,000	X	NMFS	X	X	X	X	X	X	X	X
South American sea lion	X	273,000	X	NMFS	X	X	X	X	X	X	X	X
Australian sea lion	X	3,000-5,000	X	FAO	X	X	X	X	X	X	X	X
Hooker's sea lion	X	4,000	X	FAO	X	X	X	X	X	X	X	X
Northern fur seal	X	1,155,000	X	NMFS	252,724[g]	533,137[g]	669,328[g]	724,074[g]	597,396[g]	289,662[g]	162,741[g]	Busch
Walrus	X	160,000	X	FAO	X	X	X	X	X	X	X	X
Harbor seal	X	400,000	X	FAO	X	X	X	X	X	X	993	FAO
Largha seal	X	335,000-450,000	X	NMFS	X	X	X	X	X	X	X	X
Ringed seal	X	6,000,000-7,000,000	X	FAO	X	X	X	X	X	X	366,869	FAO
Baikal seal	X	50,000-60,000	X	FAO	X	X	X	X	X	X	X	X
Caspian seal	X	500,000-600,000	X	FAO	X	X	X	X	X	X	X	X
Harp seal	X	1,650,000-3,250,000	X	NMFS	1,441,549[h]	1,511,852[h]	732,418[h]	2,481,884[h]	3,396,666[h]	1,797,781[h]	622,000[h,i]	Busch
Ribbon seal	X	200,000-250,000	X	FAO	X	X	X	X	X	X	X	X
Bearded seal	X	500,000	X	FAO	X	X	X	X	X	X	4,323	FAO
Hooded seal	X	500,000-600,000	X	FAO	X	X	X	X	X	X	102,711	FAO
Grey seal	X	130,000	X	FAO	X	X	X	X	X	X	4,598	FAO
Crabeater seal	X	15,000,000	X	FAO	X	X	X	X	X	X	X	X
Ross seal	X	220,000	X	FAO	X	X	X	X	X	X	X	X
Leopard seal	X	500,000	X	FAO	X	X	X	X	X	X	X	X
Weddell seal	X	750,000	X	FAO	X	X	X	X	X	X	X	X
Walrus	X	160,000	X	FAO	X	X	X	X	X	X	X	X
Atlantic	X	20,000	X									
Pacific	X	140,000	X									

Sources: NMFS = U.S. National Marine Fisheries Service; IWS = Bureau of International Whaling Statistics; FAO = U.N. Food and Agriculture Organization; IWC = International Whaling Commission; MMC = U.S. Marine Mammal Commission; Busch = *The War against the Seals* (1985).

Notes:
a. 1980-85 for great whales, small cetaceans, and Northern fur seals; 1980-84 for other species.
b. Catches by aboriginal whaling.
c. Catch data for dolphins and porpoises include reported incidental catch; figures shown are incomplete for several species.
d. Refers to incidental take within the United States between 1977 and 1985.
e. 1973-79.
f. 1965-69.
g. Northern fur seal catch data are for the Pribilof Islands only; 1980-84 data supplied by FAO.
h. Data for 1920-54 are for Newfoundland only; data for 1955-84 are for Canada and Norway.
i. Data for 1971-84 are rounded off to the nearest thousand; they exclude native catches.
0 = zero; X = not available.
For additional information, see Sources and Technical Notes.

Table 24.3 Marine Fish Catch, 1970–84

Ocean/Region	Estimated Sustainable Yield[a] (thousand metric tons per year)	Average Annual Marine Fish Catch[b] (thousand metric tons) 1970–71	1972–73	1974–75	1976–77	1978–79	1980–81	1982–83	1984
WORLD	**62,250–90,950**	**54,158**	**50,923**	**53,793**	**56,238**	**55,106**	**56,417**	**58,037**	**62,690**
Atlantic Ocean	25,500-33,400	20,414	21,634	22,043	22,584	21,096	20,590	20,017	19,484
Northwest	3,400-4,300	3,599	3,695	3,128	2,381	1,920	1,907	1,924	1,849
Northeast	10,100-12,300	9,794	10,106	11,136	12,179	10,997	10,902	10,030	10,321
Western Central	3,200-5,100	1,083	1,023	1,112	1,020	1,370	1,294	1,585	1,636
Eastern Central	2,900-3,700	2,688	3,045	3,280	3,472	2,749	3,100	2,874	2,363
Southwest	2,600-3,900	820	753	763	842	1,196	1,135	1,289	1,184
Southeast	2,500-3,100	2,430	3,012	2,623	2,690	2,864	2,252	2,316	2,131
Pacific Ocean	31,000-45,100	30,423	25,542	27,812	29,065	29,544	31,145	33,060	37,744
Northwest	13,500-16,500	11,158	14,040	15,430	16,200	15,229	15,852	17,267	19,983
Northeast	2,600-3,200	2,070	1,958	1,970	1,644	1,416	1,585	1,791	2,192
Western Central	5,800-7,800	3,559	4,192	4,413	4,671	4,604	4,664	4,993	5,254
Eastern Central	2,200-3,000	749	959	1,045	1,507	1,970	2,387	1,759	1,939
Southwest	1,200-2,000	162	241	246	356	273	288	307	313
Southeast	3,700-10,300	12,724	4,152	4,708	4,687	6,054	6,369	6,943	8,063
Mediterranean & Black Seas	1,090-1,410	883	913	1,082	1,454	1,194	1,451	1,528	1,658
Indian Ocean	4,700-7,100	2,438	2,770	2,791	3,023	3,033	3,113	3,271	3,671
West	2,700-4,200	1,677	1,561	1,809	1,889	1,789	1,772	1,844	2,168
East	1,500-2,200	761	1,209	982	1,133	1,245	1,341	1,426	1,503
Antarctic Ocean	X	X	64	65	113	239	118	161	133

Source: U.N. Food and Agriculture Organization.

Notes:
a. Estimated sustainable yield data for oceanic pelagic species (about 3–5 percent of total potential) are unavailable for regions and are excluded from regional "estimated sustainable yields." These species are included in yield estimates for oceans.
b. Fish catch excludes crustaceans, molluscs, marine mammals, and marine plants.
X = not available.
For additional information, see Sources and Technical Notes.

World Resources 1987

Table 24.4 Accidental Oil Spills, 1973–86

Year	Number of Tankers Afloat	Accidental Oil Spills	Accidental Spills per Thousand Tankers	Volume of Oil Lost (metric tons)
1973	3,750	36	9.6	84,458
1974	3,928	48	12.2	67,115
1975	4,140	45	10.9	188,042
1976	4,237	29	6.8	204,235
1977	4,229	49	11.6	213,080
1978	4,137	35	8.5	260,488
1979	3,945	65	16.5	723,533
1980	3,898	32	8.2	135,635
1981	3,937	33	8.4	45,285
1982	3,950	9	2.3	1,716
1983	3,582	17	4.7	387,773
1984	3,424	15	4.4	24,184
1985	3,285	9	2.7	79,830
1986[a]	3,139	12	3.8	5,694

Source: Tanker Advisory Center.
Note: a. 1986 data were estimated by annualizing trends of the first six months of the year.
For additional information, see Sources and Technical Notes.

Sources and Technical Notes

Table 24.1 Coastal Areas and Resources, 1974–86

Sources: Length of marine coastline: U.S. Central Intelligence Agency, *The World Factbook 1986* (U.S. Government Printing Office, Washington, D.C., 1986). Sovereign and jurisdictional claims to maritime zones: Office of the Special Representative of the Secretary General for the Law of the Sea, *Law of the Sea Bulletin*, No. 2 (March 1985); and unpublished data (United Nations, New York, November 1986). Fish catch: United Nations Food and Agriculture Organization (FAO), *Yearbook of Fishery Statistics 1978, 1982* and *1984* (FAO, Rome, 1980, 1984, and 1986).

The Office of the Special Representative of the U.N. Secretary General for the Law of the Sea compiles information concerning coastal claims from: the U.N. Legislative Series, official gazettes, communications to the Secretary General, legal journals, and other publications. National claims to maritime zones fall into five categories: territorial sea, contiguous zone, exclusive economic zone, fishery zone, and continental shelf. Territorial sea, exclusive economic zone, and continental shelf claims are shown in Table 24.1. (Only those countries with marine coastlines are included in the table.)

Relevant legislation, decrees, and treaty commitments for 137 of the 141 coastal countries are excerpted in the *Law of the Sea Bulletin*. As coastal countries seek to secure their claims to maritime resources under the Law of the Sea Convention (not yet in force), the list is revised accordingly.

Territorial sea commonly refers to an adjacent zone of water, seabed and subsoil, and airspace over which a nation claims sovereignty. The nation's right to enforce its laws and regulations is qualified only by the right of innocent passage of foreign ships. Nations may also claim certain jurisdictional rights in a contiguous zone beyond the territorial sea out to 24 nautical miles; these rights usually pertain to customs, taxation, immigration, and sanitation.

Turkey claims six nautical miles of territorial sea in the Aegean and 12 nautical miles in the Mediterranean and Black Seas. Sharja, one of the United Arab Emirates (UAE), claims a territorial sea limit of 12 nautical miles; the limit for the other members of the UAE is three miles.

An Exclusive Economic Zone (EEZ) may be established by a nation out to 200 nautical miles to claim all the resources within the zone, including fish and all other living resources, minerals, energy from wind, waves, and tides, etc. Nations may also claim rights to regulate scientific exploration, protect the marine environment, and establish marine terminals and artificial islands.

Continental shelf claims include the exclusive right to explore for and exploit all mineral ores, energy resources, and benthic plants and animals found on or beneath the shelf. Claims are based on the distance from the shoreline (e.g., 200 nautical miles) and on the outer limit of the continental margin as defined in the 1982 Convention. Limits usually refer to the farthest distance. For Chile, a 350 mile continental shelf limit applies to Sala y Gomez and Easter Island; 200 miles is the limit for the rest of the country.

International fishery data are continually revised. The latest *Yearbook of Fishery Statistics* (1984) contains FAO's most accurate and up-to-date figures.

Data are provided to the FAO Fisheries Department by national fishery offices and regional commissions. Some countries' data are only provisional for the latest year; for other countries, no data are available. If no new data are submitted, FAO uses the previous year's figures or makes estimates based on other information.

Years refer to calendar years except for Antarctic fisheries data, which are for split years (July 1–June 30). Data for Antarctic fisheries are given for the calendar year in which the split year ends.

Catch data shown in Table 24.1 refer to marine fish killed, caught, trapped, collected, bred, or cultivated for commercial, industrial, and subsistence use. Crustaceans, molluscs, and miscellaneous aquatic animals are included in "fish catch" in Table 24.1, but not in Table 24.3. Quantities taken in recreational activities are excluded. Figures are the national totals averaged over a two-year period; they include fish caught by a country's fleet anywhere in the world.

Tables 24.1 and 24.3 present data on nominal catch, which is defined as gross removal (total live weight of fish caught or killed during fishing operations) minus pre-catch losses (total live weight of fish that are not caught but that die in fishing operations), minus discarded catch both live and dead (undersized, unsalable, or otherwise undesirable whole fish discarded at the time of capture or shortly afterwards), minus utilization and losses prior to landing (consumption by crew, use for bait, spoilage, handling losses), minus unrecorded, rejected, or dumped landings (unrecorded dumping at sea, black market landings, unrecorded quantities landed for home consumption, etc.), minus losses from dressing, handling, and processing (dumped viscera, heads, and other parts, loss of fluids), plus gains prior to landing (gain of fluid content, addition of liquids or solids during shipboard processing).

Table 24.2 Marine Mammals, 1920–85

Sources: Population estimates: U.S. National Marine Fisheries Service (NMFS), *Marine Fisheries Review*, Vol. 46, No. 4 (NMFS, Seattle, Washington, 1984); United Nations Food and Agriculture Organization (FAO), *World Review of Interactions between Marine Mammals and Fisheries* (FAO, Rome, 1984); FAO, *Mammals in the Seas*, Vols I–IV (FAO, Rome, 1978, 1979, 1981, and 1982); International Whaling Commission (IWC), *Report of the International Whaling Commission*, Vols. 30–36 (IWC, Cambridge, United Kingdom, 1980–86); and U.S. National Oceanic and Atmospheric Administration, *Annual Report 1984/84: Marine Mammal Protection Act of 1972* (U.S. Department of Commerce, Washington, D.C., 1985). Catch data: Bureau of International Whaling Statistics, *International Whaling Statistics 1964, 1966, 1974,* and *1984* (Bureau of International Whaling Statistics, Oslo, Norway, 1964, 1966, 1974, and 1984); William E.

Schevill, *The Whale Problem: A Status Report* (Harvard University Press, Cambridge, Massachusetts, 1974); FAO, *Yearbook of Fishery Statistics 1983* and *1984* (FAO, Rome, 1985 and 1986); Edward Mitchell, *Porpoise, Dolphin, and Small Whale Fisheries of the World* (International Union for Conservation of Nature and Natural Resources (IUCN), Morges, Switzerland, 1975); Marine Mammal Commission (MMC), *Annual Report of the Marine Mammal Commission* (MMC, Washington, D.C., 1986); Robert L. Brownell, *et al., Preliminary Report on World Catches of Marine Mammals 1966–75* (MMC, Washington, D.C., 1978); Briton Cooper Busch, *The War Against the Seals* (McGill-Queens University Press, Montreal, 1985); NMFS, *Marine Fisheries Review*, Vol. 46, No. 4 (NMFS, Seattle, Washington, 1984); and IWC, *Report of the International Whaling Commission*, Vols. 30–36 (IWC, Cambridge, United Kingdom, 1980–86).

Marine mammal population estimates were compiled by NMFS and FAO after extensive literature reviews. Estimates were derived from mathematical models based on aerial, shipboard, and land-based censuses of animals and on information on their range and population density in a given area as well as on their breeding and migratory habits. The regions listed for some species refer to geographically isolated breeding stocks of the species. Not all stocks for each species are listed. Some disagreement exists among scientists as to stock designations and boundaries. Population estimates for most species of small cetaceans (whales and porpoises) and sirenians (manatees and dugongs) have not been made.

NMFS "original abundance" of species estimates refer to population size before commercial exploitation. Whaling records and historical population estimates, together with assumed natural increase and survival rates, are used to derive a range of estimates of original abundance. These estimates are then run through computer models using varying levels of aboriginal hunting and carrying capacity to estimate the original abundance most compatible with modern census data. The data vary in quality; estimates of original abundance are considered less reliable for humpback and sperm whales than for other great whales.

The populations of several species of small cetaceans, pinnipeds, and sirenians have declined because of incidental take by fisheries, hunting, or other human activity. For most of these species, original abundance has not been estimated.

Catch data on large cetaceans have been collected by the Bureau for International Whaling Statistics since 1929. Pre-1929 data were obtained by the Bureau from international records kept by the Norwegian Whalers' Association. Global whale catch data for 1910–20 are being compiled by the Bureau; earlier data are not available. Since 1929, whale catch data have been collected through questionnaires sent out with each whaling expedition and from official national records. Years refer to calendar years except for Antarctic whaling, which are for split years (July 1–June 30). Catch data for Antarctic whaling grounds are included in the calendar year in which the split year ends.

Figures shown for harvests of whales and seals are those reported to the Bureau, FAO, and the IWC. Catch data include only whales and seals taken; they exclude animals struck and lost or caught by fishing operations and gear. Data for dolphins and porpoises include reported direct and incidental take. Catch data for these species are often incomplete; many countries either do not report, or they report only for certain regions. For small cetaceans, countries often report a range of estimates; figures shown are the mean.

The threatened species list was compiled from the U.S. Endangered Species List, the appendices to the Convention on International Trade in Endangered Species, and the species classified as "endangered," "rare," or "vulnerable" by IUCN. (For a description of these categories, see the Technical Note to Table 21.4, in Chapter 21, "Wildlife and Habitat.")

Table 24.3 Marine Fish Catch, 1970–84

Sources: Marine fish catch: United Nations Food and Agriculture Organization (FAO), *Yearbook of Fishery Statistics 1976, 1978, 1982* and *1984* (FAO, Rome, 1977, 1979, 1984, and 1986). Estimated fishery potential: M.A. Robinson, *Trends and Prospects in World Fisheries* (FAO, Fisheries Department, Rome,

1984).

FAO divides the world's oceans into 18 distinct marine fisheries. Data for three of these areas, the Atlantic Antarctic, the Pacific Antarctic, and the Indian Ocean Antarctic, have been aggregated into an Antarctic total.

Marine fish catch excludes freshwater and diadromous fishes caught in marine areas, crustaceans, molluscs, marine mammals, and marine plants. Global data are therefore not comparable to those in Table 24.1, which include these categories of marine organisms. Refer to the Technical Note for Table 24.1 for the definition of nominal fish catch and additional information on FAO's fishery data base.

Data on estimated sustainable yield are estimates made by FAO of the biologically realizable potential of marine fisheries. These estimates refer to the maximum harvest that can be sustained by a fishery without depleting the resource, given average environmental conditions. An assumed level of incidental take (catching one species while fishing for another) is subtracted from estimates of potential. The figures also exclude the potential harvest from culturing marine fish. Estimates of oceanic pelagic species (about 3–5 percent of the total marine potential) are unavailable at the regional level and are therefore excluded. They are included in estimates of oceanic potential.

Table 24.4 Accidental Oil Spills, 1973–86

Source: Unpublished data (Tanker Advisory Center, New York, October 1986).

The Tanker Advisory Center compiles oil spill accident data from lists of insurance claims and other known accidents maintained by Lloyd's of London and Liverpool Underwriters. Data for the number of tankers afloat are taken from *Tanker Register*, maintained by H. Clarkson and Co., London.

For 1973–82, data refer to tankers of at least 6,000 metric tons deadweight and for 1983–86, to tankers of at least 10,000 metric tons deadweight. Vessels carrying liquefied gas are not included.

Spills refer to oil lost during accidents. Oil lost during cleaning and ballasting operations is not included.

25. Atmosphere and Climate

The tables and figures in this chapter illustrate the extent to which human activities are changing the chemical composition of the atmosphere.

Atmospheric ozone shields the earth against solar radiation in the ultraviolet-B wavelength range. Exposure to this radiation can cause skin cancer in some individuals and may damage the human immune system. It may also have deleterious impacts on crops and marine organisms. The ozone concentration is highest in the stratosphere (upper atmosphere), where it is constantly created and destroyed in a complex series of chemical reactions. Increasing stratospheric concentrations of several "environmentally important trace gases" may disturb this equilibrium, causing a depletion of the ozone layer. (See Tables 25.1 and 25.2 and Figures 25.1 and 25.2.) These increased concentrations are the result of both human activities and natural processes. Nitrous oxide, for example, is naturally emitted by soils, but, with the use of chemical fertilizers, emissions have recently increased.

Many atmospheric gases have "greenhouse" properties: they are transparent to incoming solar radiation and absorb and reemit the longer-wavelength radiation emitted from the earth's surface. By trapping heat in this manner, greenhouse gases cause the lower part of the earth's atmosphere (the troposphere) to warm. However, increasing concentrations of these gases may alter atmospheric heating rates, resulting in global warming and other climatic disturbances.

Until recently, stratospheric ozone depletion and climate modification were treated as separate issues. However, many gases participate in both phenomena, and the phenomena themselves interact. For example, methane, the second most important greenhouse gas, reduces ozone depletion in the troposphere and lower stratosphere (where ozone itself is a greenhouse gas) and enhances the formation of carbon dioxide and water vapor in the stratosphere, increasing the greenhouse effect. CFCs deplete the stratospheric ozone layer and also have a greenhouse impact. Because ozone plays an important part in the atmospheric radiation and temperature regimes, any vertical redistribution of ozone (caused by stratospheric depletion and tropospheric enhancement) would have climate impacts even if the "total column" concentration did not change.

On balance, the net effects of these environmentally important trace gases on ozone depletion and global warming are unlikely to be environmentally benign. Additionally, any effects are likely to vary with altitude and latitude.

The ozone monitoring record is brief and of variable quality. To date, there has been no significant global depletion of ozone, although substantial regional trends (e.g., the Antarctic ozone "hole") have been documented. Although long-term data show a noticeable trend toward increasing global temperature over the past century, this change has not been proven to be statistically significant.

The acidity of precipitation in North America and Europe is illustrated in Figures 25.3 and 25.4. These maps are useful for showing the *distribution* of acid deposition in industrialized regions, but only recently have monitoring efforts been expanded enough to allow charting of acidity *trends*. The United States, for example, did not develop a national acid deposition monitoring program until 1978. With an initial 22 monitoring stations, this national network (which is supplemented by several networks operated by subnational and private organizations) grew rapidly, reaching 195 monitoring stations by the end of 1985. European monitoring efforts began in the 1950s, but monitoring methods and operations were revised in the mid-1970s, reducing confidence in long-term trend data. Neither North American nor European data reflect dry deposition of acidifying compounds, a potentially important factor in acidification of the environment.

The impact of acid deposition depends on the quantity, timing, and acidity of precipitation; the chemical balance of soils, vegetation, and natural waters; the susceptibility of vegetation, animals, and structures to a more acidified environment; and the incidence of other stresses. Acid deposition has been linked to impoverishment of aquatic ecosystems, and it may be a factor in the forest death affecting Europe and North America. (See Chapter 10, "Atmosphere and Climate.")

Indoor air pollution can be more dangerous to human health than is outdoor air pollution. Pollutant concentrations are often higher indoors, where many people spend most of their time. (See Table 25.3.) Biomass fuel combustion (the primary heating and cooking method for half the world's households) emits several pollutants known to have short- and long-term effects on human health. These pollutants may contribute to respiratory illnesses, the leading cause of death in developing countries.

Table 25.1 Atmospheric Concentrations of Environmentally Important Trace Gases, 1959–86

	(parts per million)	(parts per trillion)				(parts per billion)	
	CO_2	CCl_4	CH_3CCl_3	CCl_3F (CFC-11)	CCl_2F_2 (CFC-12)	N_2O	CH_4
1959	316.1	X	X	X	X	X	X
1960	317.0	X	X	X	X	X	X
1961	317.7	X	X	X	X	X	X
1962	318.6	X	X	X	X	X	X
1963	319.1	X	X	X	X	X	X
1964	319.6	X	X	X	X	X	X
1965	320.4	X	X	X	X	X	X
1966	321.1	X	X	X	X	X	X
1967	321.8	X	X	X	X	X	X
1968	322.8	X	X	X	X	X	X
1969	324.2	X	X	X	X	X	X
1970	325.5	X	X	X	X	X	X
1971	326.5	X	X	X	X	X	X
1972	327.7	X	X	X	X	X	X
1973	329.8	X	X	X	X	X	X
1974	330.4	X	X	X	X	X	X
1975	331.0	104	70	120	200	291.4	1,525
1976	332.1	106	78	133	217	293.3	1,555
1977	333.6	115	86	148	239	294.6	1,573
1978	335.2	123	94	159	266	296.4	1,596
1979	336.6	116	112	167	283	296.3	1,619
1980	338.4	121	126	179	307	297.6	1,639
1981	339.5	122	127	185	315	298.5	1,656
1982	340.7	121	133	193	330	301.0	1,671
1983	342.7	126	144	205	350	300.9	1,663
1984	344.3	130	150	213	366	300.4	1,689
1985	345.6	130	158	223	384	301.5	1,711
1986	346.7[a]	X	X	X	X	X	X

Sources: Scripps Institution of Oceanography; and *Science.*
Note: a. Estimated from January–October monitoring data.
X = not available.
For additional information, see Sources and Technical Notes.

Figure 25.1 Trends in Atmospheric Concentrations of Environmentally Important Trace Gases, 1975–85

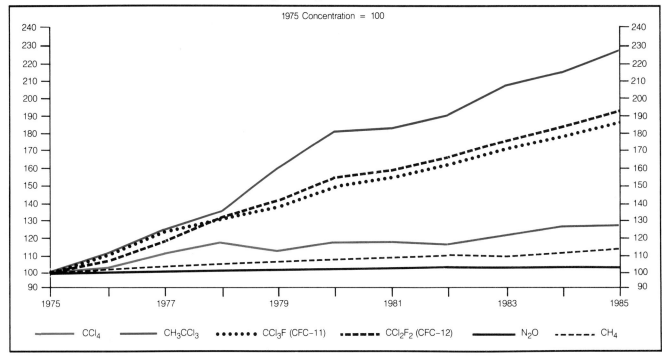

Source: Table 25.1.
For additional information, see Sources and Technical Notes.

World Resources 1987

Table 25.2 Annual Emissions of Environmentally Important Trace Gases, 1925–85

| Year | Chlorofluorocarbons (thousand metric tons) | | Carbon Dioxide (million metric tons of carbon) | | Year | Chlorofluorocarbons (thousand metric tons) | | Carbon Dioxide (million metric tons of carbon) | |
	CCl₃F (CFC-11)	CCl₂F₂ (CFC-12)	Biotic Sources	Fossil Fuel Combustion and Industrial Processes		CCl₃F (CFC-11)	CCl₂F₂ (CFC-12)	Biotic Sources	Fossil Fuel Combustion and Industrial Processes
1925	0.0	0.0	886	X	1956	28.7	56.1	1,655	2,185
1926	0.0	0.0	942	X	1957	32.2	63.8	1,662	2,278
1927	0.0	0.0	997	X	1958	30.2	66.9	1,675	2,339
1928	0.0	0.0	1,045	X	1959	30.9	74.8	1,682	2,470
1929	0.0	0.0	1,059	X	1960	40.5	89.1	1,689	2,586
1930	0.0	0.0	1,073	X	1961	52.1	99.7	1,696	2,602
1931	0.0	0.1	1,087	X	1962	65.4	114.5	1,703	2,709
1932	0.0	0.1	1,101	X	1963	80.0	133.9	1,703	2,855
1933	0.0	0.1	1,115	X	1964	95.0	155.5	1,710	3,016
1934	0.0	0.2	1,135	X	1965	108.3	175.4	1,772	3,154
1935	0.0	0.3	1,149	X	1966	121.3	195.0	1,821	3,313
1936	0.0	0.5	1,163	X	1967	137.6	219.9	1,869	3,420
1937	0.0	0.8	1,184	X	1968	156.8	246.5	1,918	3,595
1938	0.1	1.2	1,191	X	1969	181.9	274.3	1,925	3,808
1939	0.1	1.7	1,205	X	1970	206.6	299.9	1,883	4,116
1940	0.1	2.3	1,218	X	1971	226.9	321.8	1,869	4,267
1941	0.1	3.0	1,225	X	1972	255.8	349.9	1,855	4,435
1942	0.1	3.7	1,239	X	1973	292.4	387.3	1,835	4,678
1943	0.2	4.5	1,253	X	1974	321.4	418.6	1,835	4,684
1944	0.2	6.1	1,267	X	1975	310.9	404.1	1,835	4,660
1945	0.3	8.0	1,288	X	1976	316.7	390.4	1,835	4,924
1946	0.6	13.9	1,302	X	1977	303.9	371.2	1,828	5,065
1947	1.3	21.3	1,315	X	1978	283.6	341.3	1,821	5,108
1948	2.3	24.8	1,336	X	1979	263.7	337.5	1,814	5,345
1949	3.8	26.6	1,350	X	1980	250.8	332.5	1,807	5,255
1950	5.5	29.5	1,454	1,639	1981	248.2	340.7	X	5,115
1951	7.6	32.4	1,516	1,776	1982	239.5	337.4	X	5,079
1952	11.0	33.7	1,565	1,803	1983	252.8	343.3	X	5,068
1953	15.0	37.9	1,620	1,848	1984	271.1	359.4	X	5,252
1954	18.6	42.9	1,634	1,872	1985	280.8	368.4	X	5,400[a]
1955	23.0	48.2	1,641	2,050					

Sources: Chemical Manufacturers Association; *Ecological Monographs*; and University of New Orleans.
Note: a. preliminary.
0 = zero or less than half the unit of measure; X = not available.
For additional information, see Sources and Technical Notes.

Figure 25.2 Annual Emissions of Environmentally Important Trace Gases, 1925–85

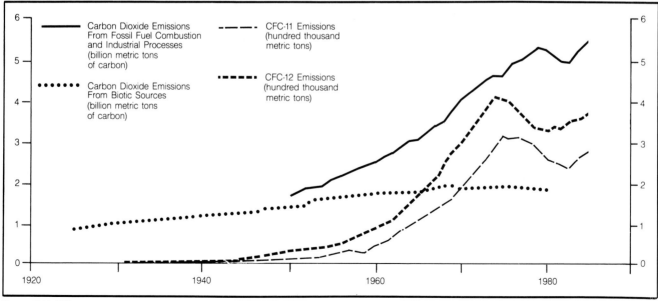

Source: Table 25.2.
For additional information, see Sources and Technical Notes.

Figure 25.3 Acidity of North American Precipitation, 1984
(pH units)

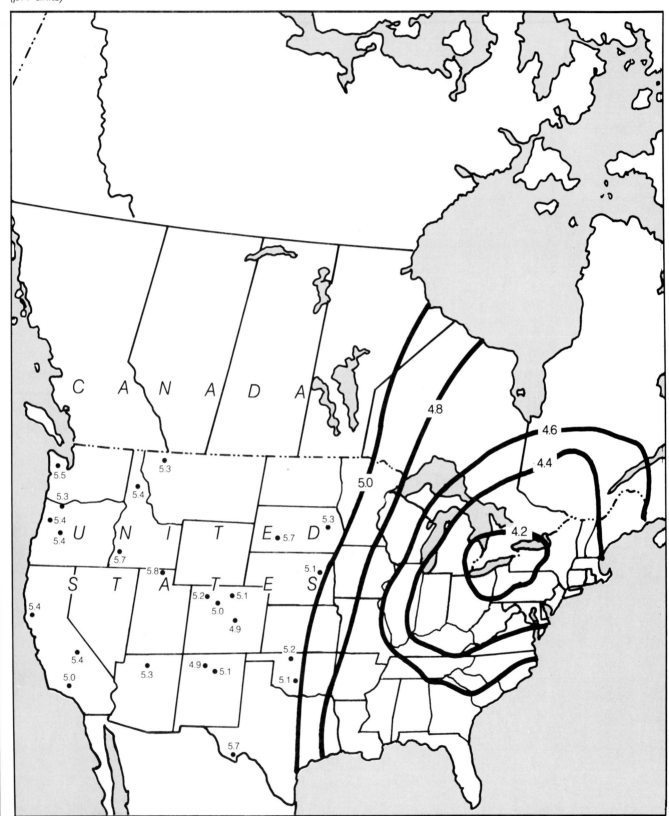

Source: Pacific Northwest Laboratory.
For additional information, see Sources and Technical Notes.

World Resources 1987

Figure 25.4 Acidity of European Precipitation, 1978–82

(pH units)

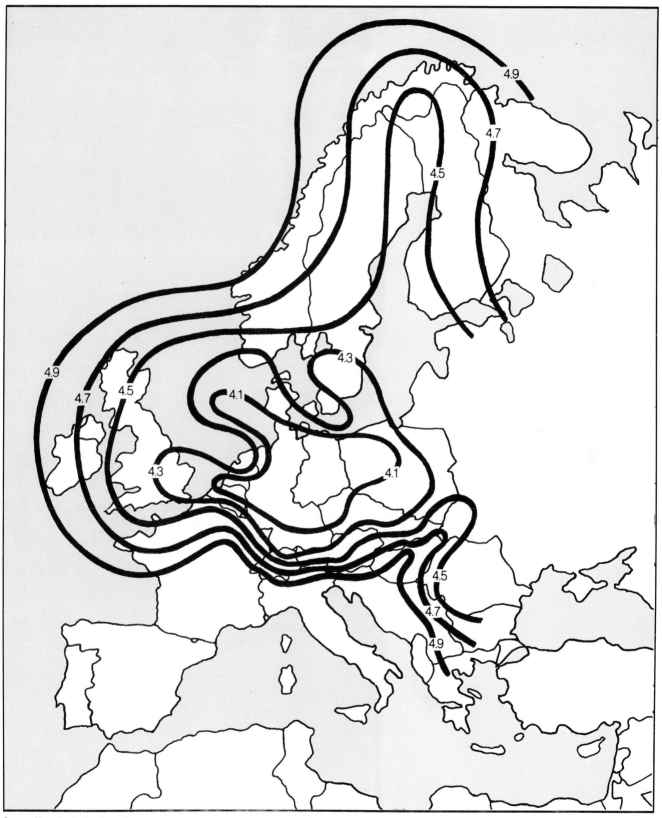

Source: Norwegian Institute for Air Research.
For additional information, see Sources and Technical Notes.

Table 25.3 Indoor Air Pollution in Developing Countries, 1968–86

	Number of Measurements	Duration	Total Suspended Particulates (mg/m³)	Benzo (alpha) Pyrene (ng/m³)	Carbon Monoxide (mg/m³)	Other (mg/m³ or as noted)
AREA MONITORING						
Nigeria						
Lagos	98	X	X	X	X	Nitrogen dioxide: 17 Sulfur dioxide: 100 Benzene: 86 ppm
Papua New Guinea						
Western highlands	6	All night	0.36	X	13	Formaldehyde: 0.84
Eastern highlands	3	All night	0.84	X	36	Formaldehyde: 1.5
Eastern highlands	6	All night	1.30	X	X	
Kenya						
Highlands	5	X	4.00	145	X	Benzo(a)anthracene: 224 ng/m³ Phenols: 1.0 μg/m³ Acetic acid: 4.6 μg/m³
Sea level	3	X	0.80	12	X	Benzo(a)anthracene: 20 ng/m³
Guatemala	180	X				
Poorly ventilated dwelling			X	X	30-58	
Well-ventilated dwelling			X	X	17-36	
India						
Urban households using:						
Wood	22	30 minutes	15.80	1,300	X	Nitrogen dioxide: 0.31; sulfur dioxide: 0.16
Cattle dung	32	30 minutes	18.30	8,200	X	Nitrogen dioxide: 0.14; sulfur dioxide: 0.24
Dung and wood	22	30 minutes	18.40	9,300	X	Nitrogen dioxide: 0.32; sulfur dioxide: 0.25
Wood charcoal	10	30 minutes	5.50	X	X	Nitrogen dioxide: 0.075; sulfur dioxide: 0.83
Coal	14	30 minutes	24.90	4,200	X	Nitrogen dioxide: 0.17; sulfur dioxide: 1.7
Nepal						
Cooking simulation	44	15 minutes	X	X	460-690	
Four villages	18	60-120 minutes	8.80	X	24-28	
Two villages	53	60-120 minutes	X	X	80-340	Nitrogen dioxide: 0.06; formaldehyde: 0.23[a]
China						
Rural households using:						
Wood	X	X	2.60	590	X	Sulfur dioxide: 0.05
Coal	X	X	7.20	3,400	X	Sulfur dioxide: 0.25
Smokeless coal	X	X	1.80	160	X	Sulfur dioxide: 0.48
PERSONAL MONITORING DURING COOKING						
India						
Four villages	65	45 minutes	6.80	3,900	X	
Four villages	68	45 minutes	3.70	X	X	
Two villages	190	50 minutes	3.60	X	X	
Nepal						
Two villages	49	60-120 minutes	2.00	X	X	

Source: Biofuels and Development Program, East-West Center. **Note:** a. Seven-day means. For additional information, see Sources and Technical Notes.
X = not available; mg/m³ = milligrams per cubic meter; ng/m³ = nanograms per cubic meter; μg/m³ = micrograms per cubic meter; ppm = parts per million.

Sources and Technical Notes

Table 25.1 Atmospheric Concentrations of Environmentally Important Trace Gases, 1959–86

Sources: Carbon dioxide: C.D. Keeling (unpublished data, Scripps Institution of Oceanography, La Jolla, California, December 1986). Other gases: R.A. Rasmussen and M.A.K. Khalil, "Atmospheric Trace Gases: Trends and Distributions over the Last Decade," *Science*, Vol. 232, pp. 1623–1624.

The trace gases listed in this table are environmentally important because they affect atmospheric ozone and/or contribute to the greenhouse effect. For further details concerning these processes, refer to the chapter introduction.

■ Carbon dioxide, which now accounts for about 50 percent of the greenhouse effect, is emitted to the atmosphere by natural and anthropogenic processes: volcanic eruptions, fossil and biomass fuel combustion, gas flaring, cement production, forest clearing, soil disturbance, etc. For further details on carbon dioxide emissions, refer to the Technical Note for Table 25.2.

Atmospheric carbon dioxide concentrations are monitored at many sites worldwide; the data presented here are from Mauna Loa, Hawaii (19.53°N, 155.58°W). Trends at Mauna Loa reflect global trends, although carbon dioxide concentrations differ significantly among monitoring sites at any given time.

Some annual mean figures were derived from interpolated data. For details on this procedure, see R.B. Bacastow, *et al.*, "Seasonal Amplitude Increase in Carbon Dioxide Concentration at Mauna Loa, Hawaii, 1959–1982," *Journal of Geophysical Research*, Vol. 90, p. 529ff (1985).

Annual means disguise large daily and seasonal variations in carbon dioxide concentrations. For example, at Barrow, Alaska, the concentrations of carbon dioxide can fluctuate by 15–20 parts per million (ppm) between April and August and by several ppm in a single day. The seasonal variation is caused by photosynthetic plants using carbon during the summer and releasing it in the winter.

Data are revised for several years to correct for drift in instrument calibration, hardware changes, and perturbations to "background" conditions. The sum of these revisions is usually minor. The most recent data may be obtained from the Carbon Dioxide Information Center, Oak Ridge National Laboratory, Oak Ridge, Tennessee, United States.

Details concerning data collection, revisions, and analysis are contained in C.D. Keeling, *et al.*, "Measurement of the Concentration of Carbon Dioxide at Mauna Loa Observatory, Hawaii," in *Carbon Dioxide Review: 1982*, W.C. Clark, ed. (Oxford University Press, New York, 1982).

■ Other Gases:

Carbon tetrachloride (CCl_4) is an intermediate in the production of CFC-11 and CFC-12. (Refer to the Technical Note for Table 25.2.) A small amount is used in other chemical and pharmaceutical applications and for grain fumigation. Compared with other gases, CCl_4 makes a small contribution to the greenhouse effect and to stratospheric ozone depletion.

Methyl chloroform (CH_3CCl_3) is used primarily as an industrial degreasing agent and as a solvent for paints and adhesives. Its contribution to the greenhouse effect and to stratospheric ozone depletion is also small.

CFC-11 (CCl_3F) and CFC-12 (CCl_2F_2), discussed in the Technical Note for Table 25.2, are potent depletors of stratospheric ozone. Together they may contribute one-fourth the greenhouse impact of carbon dioxide.

Nitrous oxide (N_2O) is emitted both by aerobic decomposition of organic matter in oceans and soils by bacteria and by combustion of fossil fuels and biomass (fuelwood and cleared forests). N_2O is an important depleter of stratospheric ozone; it may contribute one-twelfth the greenhouse impact of carbon dioxide.

Methane (CH_4) is emitted in a variety of natural anoxic processes, including enteric fermentation in ruminants and anaerobic decomposition in wetlands, bogs, tundra, and lakes. Emission sources associated with human activities include livestock management, anaerobic decomposition in rice paddies, and combustion of fossil fuels and biomass (fuelwood and cleared forests). Methane acts to increase ozone in the troposphere and lower stratosphere; its greenhouse impact is one-third that of carbon dioxide.

The data shown here are from monitoring at Cape Meares, Oregon (45°N, 124°W). Although gas concentrations at any given time vary among monitoring sites, these data reflect global trends.

Every January, multiple samples of air are collected and are analyzed using a gas chromatograph equipped with electron capture detectors. All measurements are referenced to primary calibration standards maintained since January 1976. These standards were recently reanalyzed, and the data presented here reflect the revisions. For additional details concerning monitoring methods and data manipulation and analysis, refer to R.A. Rasmussen and M.A.K. Khalil, "Behavior of Trace Gases in the Troposphere," *Science of the Total Environment*, Vol. 48 (1986) pp. 169–186.

Table 25.2 Annual Emissions of Environmentally Important Trace Gases, 1925–85

Sources: Chlorofluorocarbons: Chemical Manufacturers Association (CMA), "Production, Sales, and Calculated Release of CFC-11 and CFC-12 through 1985" (CMA, Washington, D.C., 1986). Biotic emissions of carbon dioxide: R.A. Houghton, *et al.*, "Changes in the Carbon Content of Terrestrial Biota and Soils between 1860 and 1980: A Net Release of CO_2 to the Atmosphere," *Ecological Monographs*, Vol. 53, No. 3, pp. 235–262; and unpublished data supporting this study (R.A. Houghton, November 1986). Carbon dioxide emissions from fossil fuel combustion and industrial processes: R.M. Rotty (unpublished data, University of New Orleans, November 1986).

This table presents emissions data for two environmentally important trace gases. (Refer to the chapter introduction for further details of these terms.)

■ Chlorofluorocarbons: The Chemical Manufacturers Association contracts with Grant Thornton and Company, Certified Public Accountants, to collect chlorofluorocarbon (CFC) production and sales data from companies based in countries that are members of the Organisation for Economic Co-operation and Development (OECD) and in Argentina, South Africa, India, Brazil, Venezuela, and Mexico. The data are examined for reporting errors (double-counting of CFC production by subsidiary and parent companies and of company-to-company sales) and inventory

changes. Grant Thornton and Company has compiled or modeled annual production data for CFC-11 and CFC-12 from 1931 to the present.

Emissions of CFCs are estimated based on use-specific release factors. For example, all CFCs used in solvents and aerosols are assumed to be released within six months of production; those used in hermetically sealed refrigeration equipment are assumed to have an early release peak because of product defects and filling losses, with the remainder released over a 12-year period. For details on the modeling of CFC releases, refer to P.H. Gamlen, *et al.*, "The Production and Release to the Atmosphere of CCl_3F and CCl_2F_2 (Chlorofluorocarbons CFC 11 and CFC 12)," *Atmospheric Environment*, Vol. 20, No. 6 (1986) pp. 1077–1085.

CFC production and release data are not available for India (one company has reported data since 1983), Eastern Europe, China, and the USSR. The USSR is thought to be the largest producer of the group, with an estimated *production* of about 68,000 metric tons of CFC-11 and 33,000 metric tons of CFC-12 in 1986. These levels of production are equal to about 21 percent and 9 percent, respectively, of reported 1985 world production of CFC-11 and CFC-12. Emission data are not available. India (except one company since 1983), Eastern Europe, China, and the USSR are not included in the table.

■ Carbon dioxide: Carbon emissions are caused by natural and human factors. Volcanoes emit carbon dioxide, and long-term changes in global vegetation can contribute to, or withdraw from, the atmospheric carbon reservoir. Combustion of fossil fuels adds carbon to the atmosphere, as do gas flaring and cement production. In addition, carbon is released by the burning or decomposition of the biomass when forestland is cleared. For additional information, refer to Chapter 11, "Global Systems and Cycles."

Fossil fuel combustion and industrial processes: Fossil fuel combustion releases carbon dioxide at rates that depend on the amount of each fuel type used (solid, liquid, and gas), the amount of fuel that is burned (a fraction is used for nonenergy purposes), and the carbon content of the fuel that is burned. The U.N. Statistical Office (UNSO) energy data base is the source for fuel production and disposition data. (For further details of the UNSO data base, refer to the Technical Note for Table 22.1 in Chapter 22, "Energy and Minerals.") Because the energy content of a fuel is directly proportional to its carbon content, fuel production data (when converted to energy units) can be used to estimate the amount of carbon dioxide released in combustion.

Fuel production data may require adjustments for carbon budget studies. For example, traditional carbon analyses of coal correlate carbon content with gross heating value. (The gross heating value is the amount of heat that could be extracted from fuel combustion if the water vapor in the flue gases were condensed, releasing its latent heat of vaporization.) Recently, however, UNSO has reported global coal production on a net heating value basis; these data require an adjustment for estimating the carbon con-

tent of global coal production.

It was assumed that approximately 1 percent of the coal used by industry and power plants was not burned (coal dust and char), and an additional few percent was converted to nonoxidizing uses (tar, benzene, etc.). Other oxidative reactions of coal (waste bank fires, coal bank fires, methane releases from coal mines, and carbon dioxide emissions from sulfur dioxide scrubbers) are assumed to be of negligible importance in carbon budget modeling. Overall, the margin of error in the calculation of carbon emissions using fuel production data was estimated at 6–10 percent.

Carbon emissions from gas flaring and cement production are also included in fossil fuel combustion and industrial processes. These two sources emit about 3 percent of the carbon emitted by fossil fuel combustion. For annual data on gas flaring, cement production, and fossil fuel (disaggregated into solid, liquid, and gaseous fuels) emissions of carbon dioxide, refer to *World Resources 1986*, Table 11.1, p. 318.

Biotic emissions: The model used to produce this data series attempts to account for both the emission and uptake of carbon dioxide by the biota and soils. Carbon dioxide is released from vegetation and soils during three processes: clearing land for agriculture (emissions from soils and decomposing natural vegetation), cutting forests for fuelwood and industrial wood, and converting forests to pasture land. Carbon dioxide is removed from the atmosphere by forest growth on abandoned cropland and pasture and by afforestation.

The 11 types of land cover considered in this model have different stocks of carbon in vegetation and soils, amounts and rates of carbon emissions when disturbed, and extent and rates of recovery. Undisturbed vegetation was assumed to be in carbon equilibrium with the atmosphere.

The extent of and changes in each land type were determined from historical data or from models. For further details, refer to the sources or to the Technical Note for Table 18.3 in Chapter 18, "Land Use and Cover."

All fuelwood and industrial wood were assumed to have come from closed forests; it was assumed that no wood was taken from shrublands and grasslands. Fuelwood was assumed to be oxidized in one year, paper and paper products in ten years, and lumber and related products in 100 years. Soils disturbed by logging also suffer a net loss of carbon.

For developed regions (Europe, European USSR, and North America), historical wood harvest data were taken from the literature. For developing regions, pre-1950 fuelwood data were computed using per capita consumption factors. For these regions, industrial wood production was assumed to be one-fifth the volume of fuelwood production. For 1950–80, data on wood harvest in developing countries were taken from the four FAO World Forest Inventories and the *FAO Yearbook of Forest Products*. (For details concerning sources, terms, and computation factors, refer to the Technical Notes for Tables 20.1 and 20.2 in Chapter 20, "Forests and Rangelands.")

Forests were assumed to have been converted to pasture in Latin America only. Afforestation was assumed to have taken place only in China, the USSR, and Europe.

Based on recent research (to be published in R.A. Houghton, *et al.*, "The Flux of Carbon from Terrestrial Ecosystems to the Atmosphere in 1980 due to Changes in Land Use: Geographic Distribution of the Global Flux," *Tellus*, Vol. 39B, Nos. 1 and 2 [February 1987]), the 1980 carbon emission estimate contained in the Houghton, *et al.*, *Ecological Monographs* article has been revised. The *Ecological Monographs* data and model produce a global biotic carbon emission estimate of 2.6 billion metric tons for 1980. However, the authors have since adjusted their estimates of soil carbon loss, improved the vegetational disaggregation, and refined the land use model (to incorporate shifting cultivation). The resultant 1980 biotic carbon emission was estimated at 1.8 billion metric tons. These modifications to the model have not yet been applied to the entire time series; results of the earlier model were multiplied by 1.8/2.6 to produce the numbers shown in the table. Refer to the source documents for further details.

Figure 25.3 Acidity of North American Precipitation, 1984

Source: A.L. Slavich and A.R. Olsen, Pacific Northwest Laboratory, *Acid Precipitation in North America: 1984 Annual and Seasonal Summaries from the ADS Data Base* (U.S. Environmental Protection Agency, Research Triangle Park, North Carolina, 1987, in press).

The pH scale is used to measure acidity or alkalinity. Neutral solutions have a pH of 7, acid solutions have a pH less than 7, and alkaline solutions have a pH greater than 7. Each unit change in pH represents a tenfold change in acidity. For example, rainfall with pH 4 is ten times as acidic as rainfall with pH 5 and 100 times as acidic as rainfall with pH 6. A 0.2 pH decline represents a 58 percent increase in acidity. The pH values in this figure are precipitation-weighted annual means.

Typically, rainfall is regularly collected at monitoring sites using techniques established by the monitoring network operating protocol. Depending on the network operating protocol, samples are collected daily, weekly, or monthly. All the networks represented on this map use "wet only" rather than "bulk" sampling. Wet only samplers are exposed to the atmosphere only during precipitation; bulk samplers are exposed to the atmosphere at all times and are influenced by both wet and dry deposition. Precipitation samples are then chemically analyzed; they may also be checked for validity. For example, a laboratory may reject samples with a positive-negative ion balance that deviates from a given equilibrium number.

This map incorporates data collected at 154 monitoring sites in six North American precipitation monitoring networks: National Atmospheric Deposition Program/National Trends Network, Multi-State Atmospheric Power Projection Pollution Study Precipitation Chemistry Network, Wisconsin Deposition Monitoring Network, Canadian Air and Precipitation Monitoring Network, Acidic Precipitation in Ontario Study (both the cumulative and daily networks), and Utility Acid Precipitation Study Program. Station den-

sity east of the 5.0 isopleth precludes depiction of individual monitoring stations.

The Acid Deposition System (ADS) is a joint data base for nine Canadian and U.S. networks monitoring precipitation chemistry. To join ADS, a network must establish monitoring protocols, screen data, and undertake quality control and quality assurance programs. Analytical laboratories in ADS member networks also participate in interlaboratory comparison studies. Results of these studies indicate that analyses performed by different laboratories are generally comparable.

For this map, ADS eliminated data that did not meet several selection criteria. The first set of criteria relates to the validity of samples. For example, if a sample has insufficient precipitation for a complete analysis of an ion species, the sample is invalid for that species.

A second set of criteria relates to completeness of the data. One important data completeness criterion is the fraction of precipitation events at a site for which there were valid chemical measurements. (See above.) Data completeness is determined separately for each ion species; some sites that had good ratings when evaluated for sulfur monitoring, for example, may have been excluded from this map because of an insufficient number of pH measurements.

A third set of criteria addresses site representativeness. Sites that are far from industrial pollution sources, towns, transportation facilities, and other potentially contaminating influences were considered regionally representative. Sites with good data completeness and site representativeness ratings were included in this map.

For details of data and site selection criteria and for data on other monitored ion species, refer to the source.

Figure 25.4 Acidity of European Precipitation, 1978–82

Source: Co-operative Programme for Monitoring and Evaluation of the Long-Range Transmission of Air Pollutants in Europe (EMEP), *Summary Report from the Chemical Co-ordinating Centre for the Second Phase of EMEP* (Norwegian Institute for Air Research, Lillestrom, 1984).

EMEP is a cooperative air monitoring program undertaken by 23 European countries. National monitoring networks submit air and precipitation chemistry data for selected sites to the central data base supported by EMEP. National analytical laboratories also participate in interlaboratory comparison programs (including analysis of blind samples) to ensure comparability of the many analytical methods used. Comparability is generally satisfactory, although there are a few national laboratories whose analyses of blind samples deviate from correct values more than 10 percent.

All monitoring sites reporting to EMEP collect samples daily. Either wet only or bulk samplers are used at EMEP monitoring sites. For definitions of these terms, refer to the Technical Note for Figure 25.3. Monitoring stations reporting data to EMEP are regionally representative (i.e., far from local pollution sources).

This map incorporates data from 50 of EMEP's 82 monitoring stations; stations were

included if they had least 24 months of measurements over the 60-month period (January 1978–December 1982). Data are precipitation-weighted arithmetic means. Refer to the Technical Note for Figure 25.3 for a definition of pH.

Table 25.3 Indoor Air Pollution in Developing Countries, 1968–86

Source: Kirk R. Smith, East-West Center, *Biofuels, Air Pollution, and Health: A Global Review* (Plenum Publishing Company, New York, 1987, in press).

Indoor air pollution can be caused by vaporization of adhesive solvents from wood paneling and carpets, radon gas emissions from soils, indoor fuel combustion emission, and other factors. This table presents data on indoor air pollution from biomass fuel combustion, the primary heating and cooking method of half the world's households. For information on other forms of indoor air pollution, refer to Chapter 10, "Atmosphere and Climate."

Biomass and fossil fuel combustion releases a number of potentially harmful compounds: particulates, polycyclic organic matter such as benzo(a)pyrene, carbon monoxide, and other chemicals.

Emissions of any specific pollutant vary with the type, size, shape, and amount of fuel used; the rate of fuel combustion; and the method of combustion. The mixture of pollutants emitted by fuel is also determined by these factors.

Indoor concentrations and human exposure to pollutants depend on ventilation and the time an individual spends in a polluted environment. In cold climates, individuals are more likely to spend long periods indoors. Cultural factors are also important; for example, women, who traditionally perform most cooking chores in many regions of the world, spend long periods near cooking fires. Exposure of women (and of their infants and other children if they are kept nearby) is therefore likely to be higher than the exposure of men.

The impacts of pollutant exposure on health depend on the pollutant, individual physiology, acclimation (the irritant effects of a single exposure to some pollutants can decline with repeated or continuous exposure), and other factors. For example, a pregnant woman is at higher risk of carbon monoxide poisoning than is a woman who is not pregnant, and an unborn child may be affected as well. Combinations of pollutants may have different health effects than those of single pollutants.

Health effects may be acute, subacute, or chronic. Acute effects include, for example, smoke inhalation and acute carbon monoxide poisoning. Subacute effects result from irritation or inflammation of the respiratory tract by pollutants such as aldehydes, phenols, and toluene. Chronic effects include a variety of pulmonary and cardiopulmonary conditions, cancers, and other diseases. As yet, however, there are insufficient epidemiological and toxicological data to permit quantitative assessment of the health impacts of indoor pollutants. Extrapolation from occupational and other high exposure studies indicates that health effects may be substantial.

26. Policies and Institutions

This chapter includes data on international treaties for environmental protection, sources of information on the environment, flows of development assistance to developing countries, and public attitudes toward environmental issues.

Table 26.1 lists the countries that have ratified major environmental treaties. It does not include treaties not yet in force in 1986 (such as the Vienna Convention for the Protection of the Ozone Layer) or most regional treaties concerning the environment (such as the Convention on the Conservation of European Wildlife and Natural Habitats, signed by 17 European countries). A country's ratification of these treaties indicates its recognition of the importance of particular forms of environmental protection. However, because most conventions lack enforcement mechanisms, a country's ratification of a treaty does not ensure compliance with its provisions.

Major sources of country-level environmental and natural resource information are shown in Table 26.2. Nearly all governments publish statistical yearbooks, which usually include data on agriculture, fishing, forestry, water use, population, and other natural resources. Several countries publish state of the environment reports and compendia of environmental statistics that provide more detailed environmental information. For many countries, environmental profiles published by nongovernmental organizations are the only sources of natural resource or environmental information available. The U.S. government sponsors two series of environmental profiles of developing countries receiving U.S. assistance.

Country-level environmental information may also be found in other sources, such as the sectoral profiles of forestry, energy, etc., published by multilateral and bilateral development organizations and by government agencies charged with managing these resources. These sources are not shown in Table 26.2.

Official Development Assistance (ODA) comprises grants and concessional loans made to developing countries. (See Table 26.3.) ODA-financed projects can make important contributions to improved health care, access to drinking water and sanitation, and increased agricultural production. (The environmental costs of some ODA-financed projects have begun to receive attention in both donor and recipient countries.) ODA data, taken together with estimates of Gross National Product (GNP) and long-term debt, also indicate a country's reliance on foreign financial inputs. Several countries have increasingly relied on ODA in the past decade: Guinea-Bissau's ODA as a percentage of GNP rose from 0.2 percent in 1971 to 40.8 percent in 1982; Mauritania's rose from 7 to 25 percent over the same period.

Member countries of the Organisation for Economic Co-operation and Development (OECD) Development Assistance Committee are the primary source of ODA, but their share of contributions has declined in the past 30 years, from over 99 percent of all ODA in the mid-1950s to 77 percent in 1983-84. Members of the Organization of Petroleum Exporting Countries now contribute 14 percent, and members of the Council for Mutual Economic Assistance contribute 8 percent. Developing countries provide 1 percent of ODA flows to other developing countries.

Data from public opinion surveys on environmental issues indicate levels of awareness and concern about these issues. Although public sentiment does not always produce political changes or commitments, it can be influential in shaping national policies. In the past decade, most developed countries have strengthened or adopted new environmental laws, largely in response to public concerns.

Environmental protection has received strong and continuing support in many developed countries. (See Table 26.4.) Between 1982 and 1986, 55–90 percent of the people surveyed in 12 European countries described themselves as concerned about national or global environmental issues. In 1986, only 6–38 percent of the people in 11 European countries felt that their governments were handling environmental issues efficiently.

The phrasing of questions and the answers offered for multiple choice questions can have an important impact on the responses received. For example, when asked to choose between economic growth and environmental protection, 61 percent of U.S. respondents favored environmental protection. However, when offered a third option, "we can achieve goals of environmental protection and economic growth at the same time," 61 percent chose that answer.

Other surveys of environmental opinion have been conducted in developed countries, but they could not be included in Table 26.4 because the questions are not comparable. Data on public opinion toward the environment and natural resources for developing countries are limited; they are not shown in Table 26.4.

Table 26.1 Participation in Global Conventions Protecting the

	Wetlands (Ramsar) 1971	World Heritage (Paris) 1972	Endangered Species (Washington) 1973	Migratory Species (Bonn) 1979	Ocean Dumping (London, Mexico City, Moscow, Washington) 1972	Pollution from Ships (London) 1978	Law of the Sea (Montego Bay) 1982	Nuclear Test Ban (Moscow) 1963	Biological and Toxin Weapons (London, Moscow, Washington) 1972	Regional Seas (UNEP)
WORLD										
AFRICA										
Algeria	X	X	X							M,ML
Angola										
Benin		X	X	X				X	X	
Botswana			X					X		
Burkina Faso										
Burundi		X								
Cameroon		X	X	X	X					WCA
Cape Verde					X			X	X	
Central African Rep		X	X					X		
Chad								X		
Comoros										
Congo			X						X	
Cote d'Ivoire		X					X	X		WCA
Djibouti										
Egypt	X	X	X	X		X	X	X		M,ML,MSP
Equatorial Guinea										
Ethiopia		X							X	
Gabon					X	X		X		
Gambia			X					X	X	WCA
Ghana		X	X				X	X	X	
Guinea		X	X				X			WCA
Guinea-Bissau							X	X	X	
Kenya		X			X	X		X	X	
Lesotho								X	X	
Liberia		X				X		X		
Libya		X			X			X	X	M
Madagascar		X	X					X		
Malawi		X	X					X		
Mali	X	X		X			X			
Mauritania	X	X						X		
Mauritius			X					X	X	
Morocco	X	X	X		X			X		M
Mozambique		X	X							
Niger		X	X	X				X	X	
Nigeria		X	X		X	X		X	X	WCA
Rwanda			X					X	X	
Senegal	X	X	X				X	X	X	WCA
Sierra Leone								X	X	
Somalia			X	X						
South Africa	X		X		X	X		X	X	
Sudan		X	X				X	X		R
Swaziland								X		
Tanzania, United Rep		X	X				X	X		
Togo			X				X	X	X	WCA
Tunisia	X	X	X			X	X	X	X	M,ML,MSP
Uganda								X		
Zaire		X	X		X			X	X	
Zambia		X	X					X		
Zimbabwe		X	X				X			
NORTH & CENTRAL AMERICA										
Barbados									X	
Canada	X	X	X		X			X	X	
Costa Rica		X	X					X	X	
Cuba		X			X		X			
Dominican Rep					X			X	X	
El Salvador								X		
Guatemala		X	X		X			X	X	
Haiti		X			X					
Honduras		X	X		X			X	X	
Jamaica		X					X			
Mexico		X			X		X	X	X	C
Nicaragua		X	X					X	X	
Panama		X	X		X	X		X	X	
Trinidad and Tobago			X				X	X		
United States	X	X	X		X	X		X		C
SOUTH AMERICA										
Argentina		X	X		X				X	
Bolivia		X	X					X	X	
Brazil		X	X		X			X	X	
Chile	X	X	X	X	X			X	X	SEP
Colombia		X	X			X		X	X	SEP
Ecuador		X	X					X	X	SEP
Guyana		X	X							
Paraguay			X				X		X	
Peru		X	X			X		X	X	
Suriname	X		X	X	X			X		
Uruguay	X		X			X		X	X	
Venezuela			X					X	X	

Environment, 1986

Table 26.1

	Wetlands (Ramsar) 1971	World Heritage (Paris) 1972	Endangered Species (Washington) 1973	Migratory Species (Bonn) 1979	Ocean Dumping (London, Mexico City, Moscow, Washington) 1972	Pollution from Ships (London) 1978	Law of the Sea (Montego Bay) 1982	Nuclear Test Ban (Moscow) 1963	Biological and Toxin Weapons (London, Moscow, Washington) 1972	Regional Seas (UNEP)
ASIA										
Afghanistan		X	X		X			X	X	
Bahrain							X			P
Bangladesh		X	X					X	X	
Bhutan								X		
Burma								X		
China			X		X	X		X	X	
Cyprus	X	X	X					X	X	M
India	X	X	X	X		X		X	X	
Indonesia			X				X	X		
Iran	X	X	X					X	X	P
Iraq		X					X	X		P
Israel			X	X		X		X		M
Japan	X		X		X			X	X	
Jordan	X	X	X		X			X	X	
Kampuchea, Dem									X	
Korea, Dem People's Rep					X					
Korea, Rep					X					
Kuwait							X	X	X	P
Lao People's Dem Rep								X	X	
Lebanon		X				X		X	X	M
Malaysia			X					X		
Mongolia								X	X	
Nepal		X	X					X		
Oman		X			X	X				P
Pakistan	X	X	X						X	
Philippines			X		X		X	X	X	
Qatar		X							X	P
Saudi Arabia		X							X	P,R
Singapore								X	X	
Sri Lanka		X	X					X		
Syrian Arab Rep		X						X		M
Thailand			X					X	X	
Turkey		X						X	X	M,ML
United Arab Emirates			X		X					P
Viet Nam									X	
Yemen		X								R
Yemen, Dem		X						X	X	
EUROPE										
Albania										
Austria	X		X					X	X	
Belgium	X				X	X		X	X	
Bulgaria	X	X				X		X	X	
Czechoslovakia						X		X	X	
Denmark	X	X	X	X	X	X		X	X	
Finland	X	X	X		X	X		X	X	
France		X	X		X	X			X	M,ML
German Dem Rep	X		X		X	X		X	X	
Germany, Fed Rep	X	X	X	X	X	X		X	X	
Greece	X	X			X	X		X	X	M
Hungary	X		X	X	X	X		X	X	
Iceland	X				X	X	X	X	X	
Ireland	X			X	X			X	X	
Italy	X	X	X	X	X	X		X	X	M,ML,MSP
Luxembourg		X	X	X				X	X	
Malta		X					X	X	X	M,MSP
Netherlands	X		X	X	X	X		X	X	C
Norway	X	X	X	X	X	X		X	X	
Poland	X	X			X			X	X	
Portugal	X	X	X	X	X				X	
Romania									X	
Spain	X	X	X	X	X	X		X	X	M,ML
Sweden	X	X	X	X	X	X		X	X	
Switzerland	X	X	X		X			X	X	
United Kingdom	X	X	X	X	X	X	X	X	X	
Yugoslavia	X	X			X	X		X	X	M
USSR	X		X		X	X		X	X	
OCEANIA										
Australia	X	X	X		X			X	X	
Fiji							X	X	X	
New Zealand	X	X			X			X	X	
Papua New Guinea			X		X				X	
Solomon Islands					X				X	

Sources: U. N. Environment Programme; and U.S. Department of State.
X = ratified member; other symbols refer to specific Regional Sea conventions described in the Sources and Technical Notes.
For additional information, see Sources and Technical Notes.

Table 26.2 National and Regional Sources of Environmental

	National Conservation Strategy	U.S. AID Phase I Draft Environmental Profile	U.S. AID Phase II Environmental Profile	State of the Environment Report	U.S. Foreign Disaster Assistance Country Profile	Country Statistical Yearbook	Environmental Statistical Report	Regional Report on Resources and the Environment	INFOTERRA Participant
WORLD									
AFRICA									
Algeria						P			I
Angola						P			I
Benin									
Botswana	U					P			I
Burkina Faso		P80	P	U(G)	P82	P			I
Burundi		P81				P		P84(NGO)	I
Cameroon		P81				P			I
Cape Verde		P80			P84	P			I
Central African Rep						P			
Chad					P82	P			I
Comoros					P84				
Congo						P			I
Cote d'Ivoire	D					P			I
Djibouti					P81	P			I
Egypt		P80				P			I
Equatorial Guinea						P			
Ethiopia					P81	P			I
Gabon						P			I
Gambia		P			P82	P			I
Ghana		P80			P85	P			
Guinea	D	P83							I
Guinea-Bissau	D								
Kenya					P81	P		P84(NGO)	I
Lesotho		P82				P			I
Liberia		P80				P			I
Libya						P			
Madagascar	P84				P84	P			I
Malawi		P82				P			I
Mali		P80			P83*	P			I
Mauritania		P79	P		P84	P			I
Mauritius					P84	P			I
Morocco		P81				P			I
Mozambique					P*	P			
Niger		P80			P85	P			I
Nigeria						P			I
Rwanda		P81				P		P84(NGO)	I
Senegal	U	P80			P82	P			I
Sierra Leone	D					P			I
Somalia		P79			P81	P			I
South Africa	P80					P			
Sudan		P		U(G)	P81	P			I
Swaziland		P80				P			
Tanzania, United Rep					P81	P		P84(NGO)	I
Togo	D					P			I
Tunisia	D	P80				P			
Uganda	U	P82			P81	P		P84(NGO)	I
Zaire	D	P	P		P82	P			I
Zambia	P85	P82			P81	P			I
Zimbabwe	P	P82				P			I
NORTH & CENTRAL AMERICA									
Barbados		P	D		P82	P		P82(NGO)	I
Canada	D			P(G)86	P82*	P	P86	P79,85(IGO)	I
Costa Rica	D	P	P		P82*	P		P82(NGO);U85(NGO)	I
Cuba						P		P82(NGO)	
Dominican Rep			P		P84	P		P82(NGO)	
El Salvador		P82	P		P84	P		P82(NGO);U85(NGO)	I
Guatemala		P81	P		P82	P		P82(NGO);U85(NGO)	I
Haiti		P79	U		P84	P		P82(NGO)	
Honduras		P81	P		P81	P		P82(NGO);U85(NGO)	I
Jamaica		P	U		P83*	P		P82(NGO)	I
Mexico	D					P		P82(NGO)	I
Nicaragua		P81			P81	P		P82(NGO);U85(NGO)	I
Panama		P	P			P	P85	P82(NGO);U85(NGO)	I
Trinidad and Tobago					P82	P		P82(NGO)	
United States				a		P	P79	P79,85(IGO)	I
SOUTH AMERICA									
Argentina	D					P		P82(NGO)	I
Bolivia		P80	P		P84	P		P82(NGO)	I
Brazil	D					P		P82(NGO)	I
Chile				P(NGO)85	P80*	P		P82(NGO)	I
Colombia						P		P82(NGO)	
Ecuador		P79	P		P83	P		P82(NGO)	I
Guyana		P			P82	P		P82(NGO)	I
Paraguay			P			P		P82(NGO)	I
Peru		P79	D		P83	P		P82(NGO)	I
Suriname						P			
Uruguay						P		P82(NGO)	
Venezuela	D					P		P82(NGO)	I

Information, 1986   Table 26.2

	National Conservation Strategy	U.S. AID Phase I Draft Environmental Profile	U.S. AID Phase II Environmental Profile	State of the Environment Report	U.S. Foreign Disaster Assistance Country Profile	Country Statistical Yearbook	Environmental Statistical Report	Regional Report on Resources and the Environment	INFOTERRA Participant
ASIA									
Afghanistan						P		P84(IGO)	
Bahrain						P			
Bangladesh	D	P80			P83	P		P84(IGO)	I
Bhutan						P		P84(IGO)	
Burma		P82			P80	P		P84(IGO)	
China	D			U(IGO)83		P		P84(IGO)	I
Cyprus		D				P			
India	D	P80		P(NGO)85	P83	P		P84(IGO)	I
Indonesia	D	P			P83	P	P83	P84(IGO)	I
Iran						P		P84(IGO)	
Iraq						P			I
Israel				P(G)79		P			I
Japan				P(G)70-85		P	P80	P79,85(IGO);P84(IGO)	I
Jordan	D	P79				P			
Kampuchea, Dem						P		P84(IGO)	
Korea, Dem People's Rep								P84(IGO)	
Korea, Rep						P		P84(IGO)	I
Kuwait						P			I
Lao People's Dem Rep						P		P84(IGO)	
Lebanon						P			I
Malaysia	D			P(NGO)84		P		P84(IGO)	I
Mongolia						P		P84(IGO)	
Nepal	U	P79			P83	P		P84(IGO)	I
Oman	D	P81				P			I
Pakistan	D	P81			P83	P	P84	P84(IGO)	I
Philippines	U	P80	D	P(G)83	P82	P	P79	P84(IGO)	I
Qatar						P			
Saudi Arabia				U(G)84		P			
Singapore				P(G)80		P		P84(IGO)	
Sri Lanka	U	P78	U		P83	P		P84(IGO)	I
Syrian Arab Rep		P81				P		P84(IGO)	I
Thailand	D	P79				P		P84(IGO)	I
Turkey		P81		P(NGO)85	P82	P		P79,85(IGO)	I
United Arab Emirates						P			I
Viet Nam	P85					P		P84(IGO)	I
Yemen		P82				P			I
Yemen, Dem						P			
EUROPE									
Albania						P			
Austria				P(G)		P	P82	P79,85(IGO)	I
Belgium				P(G)79		P		P79,85(IGO)	I
Bulgaria						P			
Czechoslovakia	D					P			I
Denmark				P(G)		P		P79,85(IGO)	I
Finland				P(G)85		P	P80	P79,85(IGO)	I
France	D			P(G)78-85		P	P83	P79,85(IGO)	I
German Dem Rep						P			
Germany, Fed Rep				P(NGO)		P	P84	P79,85(IGO)	I
Greece	D					P		P79,85(IGO)	I
Hungary				P(G)86		P	P81		I
Iceland						P			
Ireland				P(G)85		P		P79,85(IGO)	I
Italy	U			P(G)		P	P84	P79,85(IGO)	I
Luxembourg				P(G)84		P		P79,85(IGO)	
Malta						P			I
Netherlands	D			P(G)85		P	P80	P79,85(IGO)	I
Norway	D					P	P83	P79,85(IGO)	I
Poland				P(G)85		P	P79		I
Portugal						P		P79,85(IGO)	I
Romania						P			
Spain	D			P(G)		P		P79,85(IGO)	I
Sweden				P(G)83		P	P84	P79,85(IGO)	I
Switzerland						P		P79,85(IGO)	I
United Kingdom	P83					P	P80	P79,85(IGO)	I
Yugoslavia				P(G)80		P	P85	P79,85(IGO)	I
USSR						P			I
OCEANIA									
Australia	P83			P(G)85		P	P83	P79,85(IGO);P84(IGO)	I
Fiji	D				P80*	P		P84(IGO)	I
New Zealand	P85					P		P79,85(IGO);P84(IGO)	I
Papua New Guinea					P85	P		P84(IGO)	I
Solomon Islands						P		P84(IGO)	

Source: World Resources Institute and International Institute for Environment and Development.
P = published; U = unpublished; D = under discussion; * = publication being updated; IGO = prepared by an intergovernmental organization; NGO = prepared by a non-governmental organization; G = prepared by a governmental organization; I = participant in the UNEP INFOTERRA program; a = P(G)70-84;P(NGO)82,84,87.
For additional information, see Sources and Technical Notes.

Table 26.3 Official Development Assistance, 1964–84

	Average Annual Official Development Assistance (ODA) (million $US)			ODA as a Percentage of Gross National Product		
	1964–66	1974–76	1982–84	1964–66	1974–76	1982–84
WORLD						
AFRICA						
Algeria	X	120	57	X	1	0
Angola	X	15	76	X	X	X
Benin	X	49	82	X	10	8
Botswana	X	45	103	X	17	13
Burkina Faso	X	90	195	X	14	18
Burundi	X	43	136	X	11	14
Cameroon	X	107	177	X	4	2
Cape Verde	X	X	59	X	X	46
Central African Rep	X	44	99	X	12	15
Chad	X	69	92	X	15	24
Comoros	X	25	40	X	44	38
Congo	X	56	100	X	8	5
Cote d'Ivoire	X	95	141	X	3	2
Djibouti	X	31	75	X	X	69
Egypt	X	1746	1537	X	15	5
Equatorial Guinea	X	X	13	X	X	X
Ethiopia	X	132	302	X	5	7
Gabon	X	41	67	X	2	2
Gambia	X	10	49	X	8	24
Ghana	X	75	156	X	3	4
Guinea	X	19	94	X	2	5
Guinea-Bissau	X	X	63	X	X	41
Kenya	X	136	439	X	4	8
Lesotho	X	27	97	X	10	13
Liberia	X	21	120	X	4	12
Libya	X	−164	−60	X	−1.30	−0.20
Madagascar	X	70	197	X	4	8
Malawi	X	56	132	X	9	12
Mali	X	117	248	X	20	25
Mauritania	X	110	178	X	25	25
Mauritius	X	24	41	X	4	4
Morocco	X	200	485	X	2	4
Mozambique	X	31	226	X	X	X
Niger	X	136	199	X	21	15
Nigeria	X	34	−9	X	0	−0.01
Rwanda	X	72	155	X	13	10
Senegal	X	133	313	X	8	13
Sierra Leone	X	14	70	X	2	5
Somalia	X	113	384	X	17	25
South Africa	X	X	X	X	X	X
Sudan	X	268	771	X	6	10
Swaziland	X	17	27	X	6	5
Tanzania, United Rep	X	242	621	X	9	11
Togo	X	41	100	X	7	14
Tunisia	X	192	201	X	5	2
Uganda	X	31	144	X	1	3
Zaire	X	193	326	X	3	5
Zambia	X	69	254	X	3	8
Zimbabwe	X	X	241	X	X	4
NORTH & CENTRAL AMERICA						
Barbados	X	6	14	X	1	1
Canada	−122	−821	−1417	−0.34	−0.49	−0.46
Costa Rica	X	26	183	X	1	7
Cuba	X	24	14	X	X	X
Dominican Rep	X	28	146	X	1	2
El Salvador	X	34	260	X	2	7
Guatemala	X	44	68	X	1	1
Haiti	X	48	132	X	6	8
Honduras	X	41	213	X	4	8
Jamaica	X	26	177	X	1	7
Mexico	X	59	118	X	0	0
Nicaragua	X	43	118	X	3	5
Panama	X	33	53	X	2	1
Trinidad and Tobago	X	5	5	X	0	0
United States	−3815	−4065	−8331	−0.55	−0.26	−0.25
SOUTH AMERICA						
Argentina	X	30	42	X	X	0
Bolivia	X	63	164	X	4	6
Brazil	X	148	157	X	0	0
Chile	X	54	1	X	1	0
Colombia	X	90	90	X	1	0
Ecuador	X	64	84	X	1	1
Guyana	X	18	31	X	4	7
Paraguay	X	38	62	X	3	2
Peru	X	77	265	X	1	1
Suriname	X	68	37	X	15	4
Uruguay	X	12	4	X	0	0
Venezuela	X	−57	−107	X	−0.20	−0.18

Table 26.3

	Average Annual Official Development Assistance (ODA) (million $US)			ODA as a Percentage of Gross National Product		
	1964–66	1974–76	1982–84	1964–66	1974–76	1982–84
ASIA						
Afghanistan	X	71	10	X	3	X
Bahrain	X	63	143	X	X	4
Bangladesh	X	691	1206	X	7	9
Bhutan	X	X	14	X	X	8
Burma	X	66	299	X	2	5
China	X	X	664	X	0	0
Cyprus	X	36	23	X	5	1
India	X	1629	1605	X	2	1
Indonesia	X	675	777	X	2	1
Iran	X	−603	81	X	−1.10	0
Iraq	X	−240	17	X	−1.80	X
Israel	X	409	1153	X	3	6
Japan	−215	−1126	−3701	−0.23	−0.22	−0.32
Jordan	X	385	755	X	37	20
Kampuchea, Dem	X	130	33	X	66	X
Korea, Dem People's Rep	X	X	X	X	X	X
Korea, Rep	X	240	14	X	1	0
Kuwait	X	−771	−1059	X	−5.86	−3.95
Lao People's Dem Rep	X	42	34	X	X	28
Lebanon	X	58	129	X	X	X
Malaysia	X	77	213	X	1	1
Mongolia	X	X	X	X	X	X
Nepal	X	43	200	X	3	8
Oman	X	129	92	X	8	1
Pakistan	X	955	739	X	8	2
Philippines	X	175	387	X	1	1
Qatar	X	−221	−53	X	−8.82	−0.94
Saudi Arabia	X	−2543	−3583	X	−7.23	−2.89
Singapore	X	15	25	X	0	0
Sri Lanka	X	140	452	X	5	9
Syrian Arab Rep	X	561	927	X	8	6
Thailand	X	110	432	X	1	1
Turkey	X	90	418	X	0	1
United Arab Emirates	X	−857	−263	X	−9.28	−0.96
Viet Nam	X	414	117	X	X	X
Yemen	X	186	352	X	19	9
Yemen, Dem	X	88	111	X	25	11
EUROPE						
Albania	X	X	X	X	X	X
Austria	−10	−63	−191	−0.11	−0.17	−0.29
Belgium	−83	−330	−471	−0.49	−0.53	−0.55
Bulgaria	X	X	X	X	X	X
Czechoslovakia	X	X	X	X	X	X
Denmark	−15	−196	−420	−0.15	−0.53	−0.78
Finland	−3	−46	−159	−0.03	−0.17	−0.32
France	−775	−1951	−3879	−0.78	−0.61	−0.71
German Dem Rep	X	X	X	X	X	X
Germany, Fed Rep	−445	−1572	−3037	−0.39	−0.38	−0.46
Greece	X	3	−12	X	0	−0.03
Hungary	X	X	X	X	X	X
Iceland	X	X	X	X	X	X
Ireland	X	X	X	X	X	X
Italy	−62	−208	−926	−0.10	−0.11	−0.27
Luxembourg	X	X	X	X	X	X
Malta	X	28	29	X	6	2
Netherlands	−71	−591	−1312	−0.36	−0.69	−0.95
Norway	−12	−178	−562	−0.17	−0.65	−1.04
Poland	X	X	X	X	X	X
Portugal	−36	X	−64	−0.96	X	−0.29
Romania	X	X	X	X	X	X
Spain	X	X	X	X	X	X
Sweden	−43	−525	−827	−0.20	−0.76	−0.85
Switzerland	−11	−95	−286	−0.08	−0.17	−0.28
United Kingdom	−484	−859	−1610	−0.48	−0.40	−0.33
Yugoslavia	X	X	1	X	X	X
USSR	−700	−1312	−3227	X	X	X
OCEANIA						
Australia	−117	−454	−804	−0.54	−0.55	−0.50
Fiji	0	19	33	X	3	3
New Zealand	−9	−53	−60	−0.17	−0.39	−0.26
Papua New Guinea	X	270	322	X	20	14
Solomon Islands	X	18	X	X	X	X

Sources: Organisation for Economic Co-operation and Development; and The World Bank.
Note: Flows to recipients are shown as positive numbers; flows from donors are shown as negative numbers.
0 = zero or less than half of 1 percent for recipient countries and less than five one-thousandths of 1 percent for donor countries; X = not available.
For additional information, see Sources and Technical Notes.

Table 26.4 Public Opinion on Environmental Issues, 1979-86

	Belgium	Denmark	France	Germany, Fed Rep	Greece	Ireland	Italy	Japan	Netherlands	Portugal	Spain	United Kingdom	United States
	1982 1986	1982 1986	1982 1986	1982 1986	1982 1986	1982 1986	1982 1986	1982	1982 1986	1986	1986	1982 1985 1986	1984
1. Where you live now, do you have reason to complain about:	Yes/No	Yes/No	Yes/No	Yes/No	Yes/No	Yes/No	Yes/No	Yes/No[a]	Yes/No	Yes/No	Yes/No	Yes/No	Yes/No
Drinking water purity	16/81 15/81	3/96 7/90	15/84 19/81	25/72 22/77	15/83 20/78	13/86 11/88	27/71 33/66	X	6/92 8/91	26/72	27/71	9/90 11/88 12/87	22/77
Noise	27/71 26/71	13/87 10/89	21/79 17/83	33/65 25/74	24/76 27/72	14/86 9/90	27/73 31/68	22/78	19/80 14/86	28/70	27/71	21/78 17/83 16/84	19/80
Air pollution	27/71 26/70	12/87 12/86	19/80 19/80	35/61 28/71	26/74 31/69	13/86 15/83	25/73 35/63	18/82	17/82 16/83	28/69	29/68	18/81 16/83 15/84	24/74
Lack of access to open space	21/76 16/80	4/96 4/94	17/82 10/89	19/78 14/85	30/66 29/61	11/89 7/91	29/70 28/71	X	8/92 11/88	20/76	30/67	12/87 11/88 12/87	15/83
Loss of good farmland	23/71 22/70	4/79 5/81	26/64 22/72	17/71 19/72	25/65 23/61	10/84 10/83	31/63 33/62	X	17/68 18/71	24/69	24/60	17/74 23/70 18/77	26/69
Deterioration of the landscape	25/70 27/68	8/82 9/82	30/70 25/74	23/72 29/66	36/58 33/58	15/84 20/77	36/61 45/53	14/86	27/69 31/65	27/67	36/59	21/75 31/66 31/65	33/65
(C = concerned; NC = not concerned.)	1982 1986	1982 1986	1982 1986	1982 1986	1982 1986	1982 1986	1982 1986	1982	1982 1986	1986	1986	1982 1985 1986	1984 1985
2. Considering your country as a whole, are you worried or concerned about:	C/NC	C/NC	C/NC	C/NC	C/NC	C/NC	C/NC	C/NC[a]	C/NC	C/NC	C/NC	C/NC	C/NC
Pollution of rivers and lakes	57/38 59/38	65/33 77/21	72/27 76/23	82/14 84/15	60/32 65/31	68/31 71/28	78/20 91/8	34/66	82/17 85/14	75/20	86/11	64/34 76/21 76/23	84/14 94/5
Damage caused to sea life by spillage from oil tankers	59/36 56/39	74/25 79/18	81/18 79/19	78/15 81/17	73/21 73/24	69/30 70/29	78/19 91/8	X	85/14 84/14	73/20	83/13	81/18 86/12 84/14	X 81/16
Air pollution	60/35 61/36	60/37 72/26	65/32 72/26	77/19 82/17	74/23 69/27	58/41 62/37	78/19 89/9	43/57	77/21 85/15	70/24	82/14	54/43 65/32 65/33	X 78/20
Disposal of industrial chemical waste	62/31 59/38	69/27 79/17	75/21 72/24	81/14 77/20	74/16 63/30	70/28 71/27	74/22 89/8	X	85/12 86/11	73/19	80/15	77/20 85/12 80/19	86/11 93/5
Disposal of nuclear waste	65/28 X	68/33 X	72/22 X	72/21 X	54/22 X	66/29 X	67/24 X	X	83/14 X	X	X	77/19 86/10 X	86/11 79/18
Pollution from other countries (acid rain, transboundary river flows, etc.)	54/38 X	66/28 X	71/25 X	78/17 X	54/27 X	61/31 X	64/29 X	X	89/10 X	X	X	69/25 75/20 X	X
(C = concerned; NC = not concerned.)	1982 1986	1982 1986	1982 1986	1982 1986	1982 1986	1982 1986	1982 1986	1982	1982 1986	1986	1986	1982 1986	
3. More generally, are you worried or concerned by:	C/NC	C/NC	C/NC	C/NC	C/NC	C/NC	C/NC	C/NC[a]	C/NC	C/NC	C/NC	C/NC	C/NC
Extinction of plant and animal species	59/36 60/35	68/29 73/24	68/31 76/23	75/19 83/16	58/32 57/36	56/42 55/42	70/28 85/14	12/88	75/23 81/18	73/19	86/10	73/26 79/20	X
The depletion of the world's forest resources	63/32 X	72/23 X	68/29 X	67/28 X	59/28 X	55/43 X	79/19 X	28/72	64/29 X	X	X	73/25 X	X
The loss of natural resources in the world	X 56/39	X 71/25	X 64/33	X 70/28	X 57/30	X 60/37	X 80/16	X	X 67/31	69/20	83/12	X 77/21	X
Possible changes in the earth's climate due to carbon dioxide	51/41 53/42	64/28 72/24	54/40 65/33	69/24 73/24	53/32 59/28	57/39 64/33	71/24 79/16	18/82	52/36 61/33	71/16	76/17	58/37 70/26	X
4. Here are two opinions which are sometimes heard in discussion of the environment and economic growth. Which of them is closer to your point of view?	1982	1982	1982	1982	1982	1982	1982	1982	1982			1982	1982 1984
Priority should be given to protecting the environment, even if this means restricting economic growth	50	75	58	64	56	29	67	28	56	X	X	50	16 61
Priority should be given to economic growth, even if the environment suffers a little as a result	30	14	30	21	26	58	20	11	34	X	X	36	23 28
Environmental protection and economic growth are both possible	X	X	X	X	X	X	X	41	X	X	X	X	61 X
Other responses/Don't know	20	11	12	15	18	13	13	20	10	X	X	14	0 11

Table 26.4

	Belgium	Denmark	France	Germany, Fed Rep	Greece	Ireland	Italy	Japan	Nether-lands	Portugal	Spain	United Kingdom	United States
5. Sometimes, environmental protection measures oblige industries to spend more money and hence increase their prices. In your opinion, which is more important?	1982	1982	1982	1982	1982	1982	1982		1982			1982	1982
To protect the environment	50	74	63	54	67	34	66	X	72	X	X	57	62
To keep prices under control	30	9	19	12	17	53	18	X	13	X	X	28	32
Not sure/Don't know	20	17	18	34	16	13	16	X	15	X	X	15	6
6. Do you agree with the following statement: "Stronger measures need to be taken to protect the environment against pollution."	1979 1983	1979 1983	1979 1983	1979 1983	1983	1979 1983	1979 1983		1979 1983			1979 1983	
	Yes/No	Yes/No	Yes/No	Yes/No	Yes/No	Yes/No	Yes/No	Yes/No	Yes/No	Yes/No	Yes/No	Yes/No	Yes/No
	89/3 86/7	90/5 88/5	94/2 93/4	88/9 91/5	97/0	96/1 88/4	97/1 96/2	X X	95/3 94/4	X X	X X	94/2 65/25	X X
7. Here is a list of problems that people in our country are more or less interested in. Could you please tell me whether you personally consider it a very important problem, an important problem, of little importance, or not important at all?	1983	1983	1983	1983	1983 (4 = very important, 1 = not important at all) (Mean scores by country)	1983	1983		1983			1983	
Fighting unemployment	3.68	3.83	3.77	3.77	3.79	3.86	3.82	X	3.74	X	X	3.76	X
Fighting against terrorism	3.41	3.78	3.58	3.36	3.50	3.56	3.72	X	3.42	X	X	3.66	X
Protecting nature and fighting pollution	3.38	3.79	3.45	3.63	3.68	3.25	3.56	X	3.46	X	X	3.41	X
Ensuring energy supplies are maintained	3.39	3.73	3.36	3.40	3.41	3.47	3.35	X	3.24	X	X	3.53	X
Defend our interests against the superpowers such as the United States and the Soviet Union	3.14	3.33	3.37	3.21	3.53	2.86	3.28	X	2.99	X	X	3.37	X
Try to reduce the number both of very rich people and very poor people	3.34	3.03	3.24	3.11	3.44	3.31	3.33	X	3.18	X	X	2.95	X
Reduce the differences between regions of our country by helping the less developed regions or those most in need	3.03	2.90	3.06	2.97	3.30	3.05	3.13	X	2.80	X	X	3.05	X
Helping poor countries in Africa, South America, Asia, etc.	2.78	3.11	2.89	2.89	2.84	2.68	2.87	X	2.90	X	X	2.73	X
Strengthen our military defense against possible enemies	2.66	2.65	2.81	2.60	3.39	2.67	2.44	X	2.49	X	X	3.15	X
8. Looking forward over the next ten years or so, how do you think things will develop in our world?	1983	1983	1983	1983	1983	1983	1983		1983			1983	
	Yes/No[a]	Yes/No[a]	Yes/No[a]	Yes/No[a]	Yes/No[a]	Yes/No[a]	Yes/No[a]	Yes/No	Yes/No	Yes/No	Yes/No	Yes/No[a]	Yes/No
Progress in science and technology will have allowed us to improve the situation of the poorest countries	50/50	51/49	65/35	53/47	66/34	68/32	61/39	X	52/48	X	X	72/28	X
The world's resources will be used more thoughtfully in the interest of future generations	41/59	59/41	51/49	53/47	56/44	65/35	53/47	X	57/43	X	X	63/38	X
There will be more mutual confidence and trust between the developed countries and the other countries than there is at present	38/62	31/69	42/58	42/58	36/62	49/51	50/50	X	37/63	X	X	41/59	X
Famine will have lessened throughout the world	25/75	19/81	34/66	25/75	44/56	48/52	36/64	X	19/81	X	X	27/73	X
The differences in standards of living between the industrial countries and the poorer countries will have become smaller	28/72	18/82	28/72	28/72	40/60	45/55	27/73	X	23/77	X	X	34/66	X
International tensions will have lessened	26/74	13/87	25/75	25/75	32/68	34/66	24/76	X	17/83	X	X	23/77	X

(continued on next page)

Table 26.4 Public Opinion on Environmental Issues, 1979–86 (con't)

	Belgium	Denmark	France	Germany, Fed Rep	Greece	Ireland	Italy	Japan	Nether-lands	Portugal	Spain	United Kingdom	United States
9. Here are some kinds of fears which are sometimes expressed about the future (say the next 10 or 15 years) of the world we live in. Which of the following really concern or worry you?	1982	1982	1982	1982	1982	1982	1982		1982			1982	
Rise in crime and terrorism	61	60	72	57	72	89	83	X	68	X	X	77	X
Increase in unemployment as a consequence of the automation of jobs	76	68	65	75	60	73	60	X	64	X	X	61	X
Despoiling of natural life and the countryside by pollution of all kinds	50	65	48	77	69	48	55	X	65	X	X	39	X
More and more artificial things are coming into the life we lead (traffic, housing, food, etc.)	43	23	29	62	48	35	52	X	27	X	X	19	X
Rise in tensions between different groups in society resulting in serious and lasting disorders	47	32	29	46	20	49	32	X	40	X	X	46	X
Critical deterioration in international relations	32	44	24	51	53	25	32	X	25	X	X	28	X
The risk that the use of new medical or pharmaceutical discoveries may severely alter the human personality	26	28	24	40	30	32	30	X	26	X	X	20	X
Prolonged breakdown in supplies of oil and natural gas	27	22	16	40	29	21	19	X	13	X	X	18	X
Invasion of your country by low-priced products from the Far East	23	13	27	19	12	23	14	X	11	X	X	27	X
Your country's loss of influence in Europe	12	17	8	23	16	9	9	X	6	X	X	16	X
A reduction in the influence of Western Europe in the world	14	11	6	19	10	6	7	X	9	X	X	8	X
10. Which of the ideas or causes in the following list are sufficiently worthwhile for you to do something about, even if this might involve some risk or giving up some other things?	1982	1982	1982	1982	1982	1982	1982		1982			1982	
Peace	65	61	77	57	85	45	76	X	68	X	X	58	X
Human rights	43	48	53	38	59	41	40	X	54	X	X	44	X
The struggle against poverty	37	34	56	29	54	38	43	X	34	X	X	37	X
Freedom of the individual	34	29	55	31	60	26	34	X	34	X	X	42	X
Protection of the environment (wildlife, nature, etc.)	33	33	37	39	48	20	26	X	40	X	X	36	X
(Our country's) defense	13	18	28	17	44	11	23	X	9	X	X	28	X
Your religious faith	10	8	12	13	41	35	21	X	15	X	X	15	X
Sexual equality	14	22	16	17	34	9	12	X	19	X	X	14	X
Unification of Europe	14	7	14	13	21	4	9	X	9	X	X	5	X
Revolution	3	3	3	3	7	1	3	X	3	X	X	2	X
None of these things	11	14	3	14	5	15	3	X	6	X	X	6	X
11. Do you know if in your country the responsible authorities are concerned with the protection of the environment? If yes: Do you think the authorities are doing an effective job or not?	1986	1986	1986	1986	1986	1986	1986		1986	1986	1986	1986	
They are concerned about it and it's effective	14	38	23	30	23	9	6	X	29	12	15	15	X
They are concerned about it but it's not effective	56	44	49	51	42	48	54	X	55	36	32	42	X
They are not concerned about it	16	5	7	13	10	28	18	X	4	28	29	23	X

Sources: Commission of the European Communities; Gallup Poll; Harris Survey; Opinion Research Corporation; NBC News/Associated Press; and national sources.
Note: All figures are percentages except those for question No. 7.
a. "NC" or "No" includes people answering "Don't know."
0 = zero or less than one half of one percent; X = not available or question not asked.
For additional information, see Sources and Technical Notes.

Sources and Technical Notes

Table 26.1 Participation in Global Conventions Protecting the Environment, 1986

Sources: United Nations Environment Programme (UNEP), "Environmental Law in the United Nations Environment Programme" (UNEP, Nairobi, 1985); unpublished data (U.S. Department of State, Washington, D.C., November 1986).

UNEP's Environmental Law Unit maintains a *Register of International Treaties and Other Agreements in the Field of the Environment*, which summarizes the content and current membership status of more than 100 multilateral conventions and protocols. In order to promote the wider acceptance and use of existing international legal instruments by governments, the *Register* is updated periodically and sent to member countries for review. The complete titles of the conventions and treaties summarized in Table 26.1 are:

1. Convention on Wetlands of International Importance Especially as Waterfowl Habitat (Ramsar, 1971);
2. Convention Concerning the Protection of the World Cultural and Natural Heritage (Paris, 1972);
3. Convention on International Trade in Endangered Species of Wild Fauna and Flora (Washington, D.C., 1973);
4. Convention on the Conservation of Migratory Species of Wild Animals (Bonn, 1979);
5. Convention on the Prevention of Marine Pollution by Dumping of Wastes and Other Matter (London, Mexico City, Moscow, Washington, D.C., 1972);
6. Protocol of 1978 Relating to the International Convention for the Prevention of Pollution from Ships, 1973 (London, 1978);
7. United Nations Convention on the Law of the Sea (Montego Bay, 1982);
8. Treaty Banning Nuclear Weapon Tests in the Atmosphere, in Outer Space, and under Water (Moscow, 1963);
9. Convention on the Prohibition of the Development, Production, and Stockpiling of Bacteriological (Biological) and Toxin Weapons, and on their Destruction (London, Moscow, Washington, D.C., 1972);

Some of the symbols used to indicate ratification of a Regional Sea convention denote ratification of several related conventions and protocols. The full titles of Regional Seas conventions and the abbreviations used in the table are listed below.

M = Convention for the Protection of the Mediterranean Sea against Pollution (1976). Protocol for the Prevention of Pollution of the Mediterranean Sea by Dumping from Ships and Aircraft (1976). Protocol Concerning Cooperation in Combating Pollution of the Mediterranean Sea by Oil and Other Harmful Substances in Cases of Emergency (1976).

ML = Protocol for the Protection of the Mediterranean Sea against Pollution from Land-Based Sources (1980).

MSP = Protocol Concerning Mediterranean Specially Protected Areas (1982).

WCA = Convention for Co-operation in the Protection and Development of the Marine and Coastal Environment of the West and Central African Region (1981). Protocol Concerning Co-operation in Combating Pollution in Cases of Emergency (1981).

R = Regional Convention for the Conservation of the Red Sea and Gulf of Aden (1982). Protocol Concerning Regional Co-operation in Combating Pollution by Oil and Other Harmful Substances in Cases of Emergency (1982).

SEP = Convention for the Protection of the Marine Environment and Coastal Area of the Southeast Pacific (1981). Agreement on Regional Co-operation in Combating Pollution of the Southeast Pacific by Oil and Other Harmful Substances in Cases of Emergency (1981). Supplementary Protocol to the Agreement on Regional Co-operation in Combating Pollution of the Southeast Pacific by Oil and Other Harmful Substances in Cases of Emergency (1983). Protocol for the Protection of the Southeast Pacific against Pollution from Land-Based Sources (1983).

C = Convention for the Protection and Development of the Marine Environment of the Wider Caribbean Region (1983). Protocol Concerning Cooperation in Combating Oil Spills in the Wider Caribbean Region (1983).

P = Protocol Concerning Regional Co-operation in Combating Pollution by Oil and Other Harmful Substances in Cases of Emergency (1979). Kuwait Regional Convention for Co-operation on the Protection of the Marine Environment from Pollution (1979).

Information on the number of Natural World Heritage Sites and Wetlands of International Importance is contained in Chapter 21, "Wildlife and Habitat," Table 21.1. See Chapter 18, "Land Use and Cover," Table 18.2, for additional information on other internationally important wetlands. For information on treaty terms, refer to the sources.

Table 26.2 National and Regional Sources of Environmental Information, 1986

Sources: National Conservation Strategies: International Union for Conservation of Nature and Natural Resources (IUCN), *National Conservation Strategies: A Report to Development Assistance Agencies on Progress and Priorities in Planning for Sustainable Development* (IUCN, Gland, Switzerland, 1983); and IUCN, *World Conservation Strategy in Action*, Bulletin Supplement No. 4 (IUCN, Gland, Switzerland, 1985).

U.S. Agency for International Development (AID) Phase I Draft Environmental Profiles list: Office of Arid Land Studies, University of Arizona, January 1985.

U.S. AID Phase II Environmental Profiles list: International Institute for Environment and Development (IIED), Washington, D.C., July 1986.

State of the Environment Reports: various sources.

Foreign Disaster Assistance Reports list: U.S. AID Office of Foreign Disaster Assistance, October 1986.

Statistical Yearbooks: U.N. Statistical Office, *Directory of Environment Statistics* (United Nations, New York, 1983), and other sources.

Environmental Statistics Reports list: U.N. Statistical Office, New York, November 1985, and other sources.

Regional Reports on Natural Resources and the Environment: Organisation for Economic Co-operation and Development (OECD), *State of the Environment* (OECD, Paris, 1979, 1985); U.N. Economic and Social Commission for Asia and the Pacific, *State of the Environment in Asia and the Pacific* (United Nations, Bangkok, 1984); Program for International Development, *Renewable Resource Trends in East Africa* (Clark University, Worcester, Massachusetts, 1984); U.S. AID, Bureau for Africa, *Natural Resources and Environmental Concerns in Sub-Saharan Africa* (U.S. AID, Washington, D.C., 1986); M.J. Dourojeanni, *Renewable Natural Resources of Latin America and the Caribbean, Situation and Trends* (World Wildlife Fund, Washington, D.C., 1982); IIED, *Natural Resources and Economic Development in Central America* (IIED, Washington, D.C., 1987).

INFOTERRA Participants list: United Nations Environment Programme (UNEP), Nairobi, December 1986.

AID Phase I profiles are compilations of information based on a search of published literature. Phase II profiles are based on more extensive field studies, often written in collaboration with government institutions or local nongovernmental organizations. Phase II profiles are comparable to state of the environment reports in scope and detail.

INFOTERRA, the International Referral System for Sources of Environmental Information, is a network of national focal points—information centers—established by UNEP for the exchange of environmental information. At present, INFOTERRA focal points are located in 127 countries, including 103 developing countries. The system handles about 750 inquiries per month, mostly relating to pollution control technology, chemicals, atmosphere and climate, environmental monitoring, and management and planning.

National Conservation Strategy reports refer to documents that have been prepared in support of the National Conservation Strategy program. Some are endorsed by the national governments; others are not. Countries with a "D" notation ("under discussion") have adopted or endorsed a National Conservation Strategy plan of action or have some other involvement with the program. They may or may not produce a published document. For more detailed information on the status of National Conservation Strategies, see past issues of the *IUCN Bulletin Supplement*.

Policies and Institutions

Table 26.3 Official Development Assistance, 1964–84

Source: Official Development Assistance: Organisation for Economic Co-operation and Development (OECD), *Geographical Distribution of Financial Flows to Developing Countries 1971/1977* and *1981/1984* (OECD, Paris 1978, 1986); OECD, *Twenty Five Years of Development Assistance* (OECD, Paris, 1985); unpublished data (OECD, Paris, 1986). Gross National Product: unpublished data (The World Bank, Washington, D.C., October 1986).

Net Official Development Assistance (ODA) is the net amount of disbursed grants and concessional loans given or received by a country. Grants include gifts, in money, goods, or services, for which no repayment is required. A concessional loan has a grant element of 25 percent or more. The grant element is the amount by which the face value of the loan exceeds its present market value because of below-market interest rates, favorable maturity schedules, and repayment grace periods. Nonconcessional loans are not a component of ODA.

ODA contributions are shown as negative numbers; receipts are shown as positive numbers. For a definition of Gross National Product, see Chapter 15, "Basic Economic Indicators," technical note for Table 15.1.

Sources of ODA include the development assistance agencies of members of the Organisation for Economic Co-operation and Development (OECD) Development Assistance Committee, of members of the Council for Mutual Economic Assistance (CMEA), and of members of the Organization of Petroleum Exporting Countries (OPEC). Grants and concessional loans to and from multilateral development agencies are also included in contributions and receipts.

OECD gathers ODA data through questionnaires and reports from countries and multilateral agencies. Only limited data are available on ODA flows among developing countries.

Data for OPEC countries, many of which both contribute to and receive ODA, were determined by subtracting ODA contributions from ODA receipts for each country. Figures for the USSR are total donations made by all members of CMEA; USSR donations comprise 85–90 percent of the CMEA total.

Table 26.4 Public Opinion on Environmental Issues, 1979–86

Sources: Commission of the European Communities (CEC), *The Europeans and their Environment* (CEC, Brussels, 1982); CEC, *Eurobarometer*, Nos. 16, 17, and 19 (CEC, Brussels, 1981, 1982, 1983); Survey Research Consultants International (SRCI), *Index to International Public Opinion, 1983–84* and *1984–85* (Greenwood Press, Westport, Connecticut, 1985 and 1986). United Kingdom: SRCI, *World Opinion Update* (SRCI, Williamstown, Massachusetts, July 1985). Japan: Environment Agency, *Public Opinion Poll on Environmental Pollution, 1982* (Environment Agency, Tokyo, 1982); United States: The Gallup Poll, "Environmental Protection Preferred Even at Risk of Curbing Economy" (The Gallup Poll, December 16, 1984); The Harris Survey, "Environmental Pollution Causes Deep Concern" (The Harris Survey, April 1, 1985); Opinion Research Corporation, November 20–22, 1981, and NBC News/Associated Press, October 25–26, 1981, cited in Robert C. Mitchell, *Recent Public Opinion about the Environment in the United States* (Resources for the Future, Washington, D.C., 1984).

CEC conducts biennial *Eurobarometer* surveys in member countries of the European Community (EC) on a range of subjects, including attitudes toward the environment. Data for the United States and Japan were taken from national and private surveys similar to the CEC surveys. Questions for these countries were often phrased differently from those asked in the CEC surveys, and sometimes different options were provided for multiple choice questions. Data should be considered more comparable among EC countries than among non-EC countries.

Two questions shown in the table (2 and 3) have been rephrased to allow presentation in a common format. Question 2 originally read: "Concerning your country as a whole, how worried or concerned are you about . . ." Question 3 originally read: "More generally, how worried or concerned are you by . . ." In questions 1–3, the percentage of people answering "yes" or "concerned" is the sum of those people describing themselves as having reason to complain or being concerned "a great deal" or "a fair amount" about an issue. The percentage of people answering "no" or "not concerned" is the sum of those who said they were "not very much" or "not at all" concerned. A portion of the sample surveyed gave other responses, such as "don't know." Except where indicated, these answers are not reflected in the data shown.

Questions in non-EC countries sometimes differed from the EC questions shown in the table. The original questions are:

United States: 1. "Where you live now, do you have reason to complain a great deal, a fair amount, not very much, or not at all about the following? If you have no reason to complain, please don't hesitate to say so." 2. (1984) "Now, concerning this country as a whole, I would like to find out how worried or concerned you are about a number of problems I am going to mention—a great deal, a fair amount, not very much, or not at all." (1985) "I'm going to read you some different kinds of environmental problems. For each, would you please tell me if it is currently a very serious problem, a somewhat serious problem, only a small problem, or not a problem at all in this country." 4. (1982) "I am going to read you three statements about environmental protection and business and new job growth. Please listen carefully and tell me which statement you agree with the most. a) We must accept a slower rate of business and new job growth in order to protect our environment; b) we can achieve our current national goals of environmental protection and business and new job growth at the same time; c) we must relax environmental standards in order to achieve business and new job growth." (The 1984 question is identical to the EC phrasing.) 5. "Sometimes laws that are designed to protect the environment cause industries to spend more money and raise their prices. Which do you think is more important: protecting the environment or keeping prices down?"

Japan: 1. Respondents were asked what major environmental problems would have to be solved in order to provide for a good living environment. They were allowed to choose two items from a list of 11. 2. "Considering the living environment not only in the area where you live but throughout the country, what problem(s) would you especially like to see the government tackle?" 3. "What do you think are the most serious environmental problems facing the world as a whole?" Respondents were allowed to choose up to two items from a list of seven. 4. "Which of the following three views on environmental protection and economic growth best reflects your own thinking? a) A certain amount of economic growth may have to be sacrificed in order to protect the environment; b) environmental protection and economic growth are both possible; c) economic growth should be given priority even if the environment suffers somewhat."

About 1,000 people over age 14 responded to the CEC surveys in each country. In the United Kingdom, the sample size was 1,300, including 300 people in Northern Ireland. The U.S. surveys conducted by the Gallup and Harris organizations polled 1,600 and 1,250 people, respectively, through personal interviews. The Opinion Research Corporation surveyed 1,004 people. Three thousand people over age 20 were personally surveyed in Japan. Sampling errors for the surveys range from 1 to 5 percent.

World Map

World Map

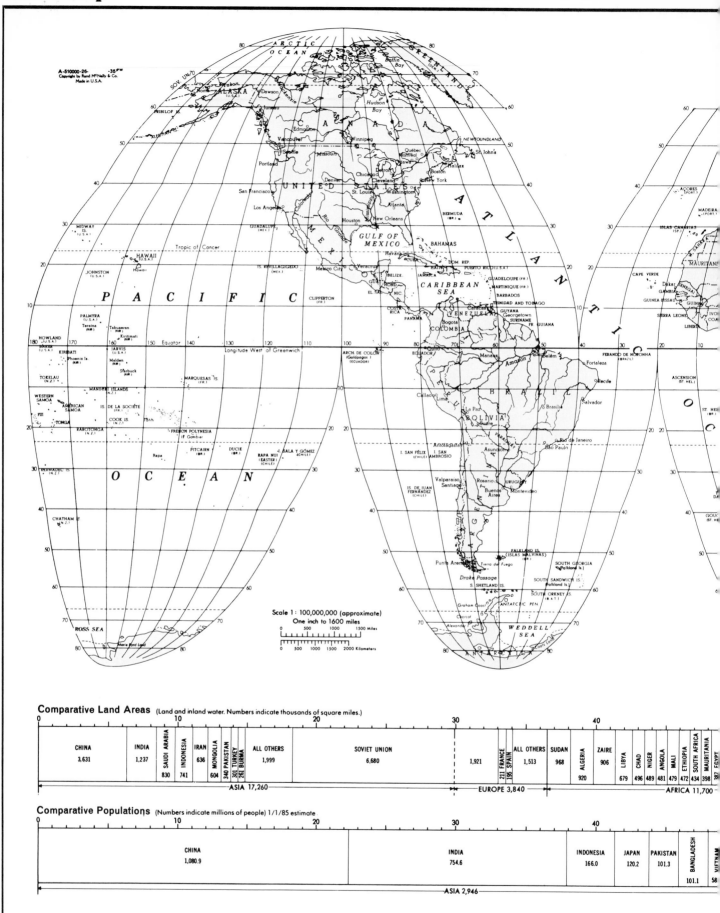

Comparative Land Areas (Land and inland water. Numbers indicate thousands of square miles.)

0				10							20			30					40										

| CHINA 3,631 | INDIA 1,237 | SAUDI ARABIA 830 | INDONESIA 741 | IRAN 636 | MONGOLIA 604 | PAKISTAN 340 | TURKEY 301 | BURMA 261 | ALL OTHERS 1,999 | SOVIET UNION 6,680 | 1,921 | FRANCE 211 | SPAIN 195 | ALL OTHERS 1,513 | SUDAN 968 | ALGERIA 920 | ZAIRE 906 | LIBYA 679 | CHAD 496 | NIGER 489 | ANGOLA 481 | MALI 479 | ETHIOPIA 472 | SOUTH AFRICA 434 | MAURITANIA 398 | EGYPT 387 |

ASIA 17,260 ◄►◄ EUROPE 3,840 ►◄ AFRICA 11,700

Comparative Populations (Numbers indicate millions of people) 1/1/85 estimate

0	10	20	30	40				

| CHINA 1,080.9 | INDIA 754.6 | INDONESIA 166.0 | JAPAN 120.2 | PAKISTAN 101.3 | BANGLADESH 101.1 | VIETNAM 58 |

ASIA 2,946

World Resources 1987

354

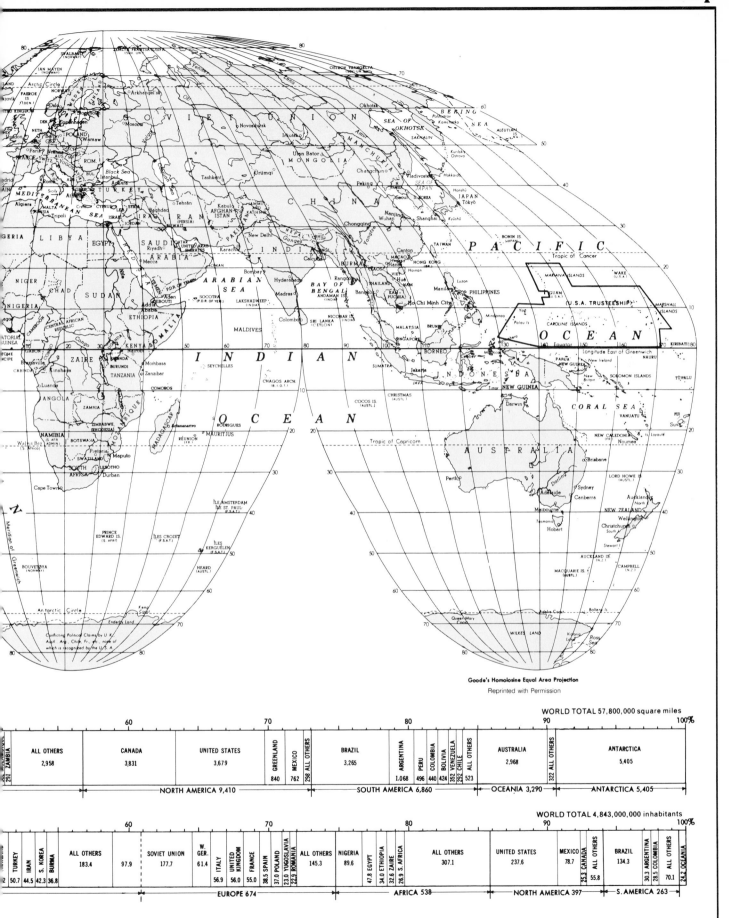

Goode's Homolosine Equal Area Projection
Reprinted with Permission

WORLD TOTAL 57,800,000 square miles

									60		70				80								90		100%

| ZAMBIA 291 | ALL OTHERS 2,958 | CANADA 3,831 | UNITED STATES 3,679 | GREENLAND 840 | MEXICO 762 | ALL OTHERS 298 | BRAZIL 3,265 | ARGENTINA 1,068 | PERU 496 | COLOMBIA 440 | BOLIVIA 424 | VENEZUELA 352 | CHILE 292 | ALL OTHERS 523 | AUSTRALIA 2,968 | ALL OTHERS 322 | ANTARCTICA 5,405 |

NORTH AMERICA 9,410 — SOUTH AMERICA 6,860 — OCEANIA 3,290 — ANTARCTICA 5,405

WORLD TOTAL 4,843,000,000 inhabitants

						60				70								80				90							100%

| TURKEY 50.7 | IRAN 44.5 | S. KOREA 42.3 | BURMA 36.8 | ALL OTHERS 183.4 | 97.9 | SOVIET UNION 177.7 | W. GER. 61.4 | ITALY 56.9 | UNITED KINGDOM 56.0 | FRANCE 55.0 | SPAIN 38.5 | POLAND 37.0 | YUGOSLAVIA 23.0 | ROMANIA 22.9 | ALL OTHERS 145.3 | NIGERIA 89.6 | EGYPT 47.8 | ETHIOPIA 32.6 | ZAIRE 32.0 | S. AFRICA 26.9 | ALL OTHERS 307.1 | UNITED STATES 237.6 | MEXICO 78.7 | CANADA 25.3 | ALL OTHERS 55.8 | BRAZIL 134.3 | ARGENTINA 30.3 | COLOMBIA 28.5 | ALL OTHERS 70.1 | OCEANIA 24.2 |

EUROPE 674 — AFRICA 538 — NORTH AMERICA 397 — S. AMERICA 263

World Resources 1987

Index

A

Acid deposition, 192–93, 333
  forest degradation from, 173
  trends in, 144, 151–53
Acquired Immune Deficiency Syndrome (AIDS), 18
Action Plan for the Protection of the Mediterranean (MAP), 189–92
Advanced Very High Resolution Radiometers (AVHRR), 175, 176
Advisory Group on Greenhouse Gases (AGGG), 159
Africa
  agricultural policy in, 224, 225–26
  agricultural production in, 39, 43, 44–47, 50–53, 222, 223, 228–30, 232
  agriculture in, 222–29, 233–36
  agroforestry in, 3, 51, 63, 64, 230–32
  AIDS in, 18
  artisanal fisheries in, 136
  crop breeding programs in, 226–27
  deforestation in, 3, 58, 63, 222, 229
  droughts in, 52–53, 120, 222, 223, 230
  environmental crisis in, 222–24
  erosion in, 3, 230–31
  external debt of, 47, 52, 222
  food deficits in, 1, 2–3, 116–17
  forest management in, 59, 60, 229–32
  fuelwood shortage in, 230, 232
  green revolution for, 226–27, *235*

habitat loss in, 80
health in, 16, 18, 19, 21
indoor air pollution in, 151
interannual variability of rainfall in, *224*
irrigation use in, 116–17, 224, 228–29
marine pollution in seas of, 126
poaching in, 78, 80, 81, 85
population growth in, 2–3, 6, 8, 9, 12, 222, 223, 236
protected areas in, 78, 85
rangeland in, 65, 66, 67, 70, 72, 73
reforesting, 229–32
soil and climate constraints in, 40–41, *223*
soil conservation in, 227–28
soil fertility in 222–23, 227, 229
sport hunting in, 81, 85
successful development in, 233–36
sustainable wildlife harvests in, 80
water availability in, 111, 112, 113–14, 119, 120
water quality in, 4, 119
wetlands in, 88–89, 132
wildlife-based tourism in, 80–81
wildlife management in, 84–85
see also Middle East; North Africa; sub-Saharan Africa; individual countries
African, Caribbean, and Pacific (ACP) Group, 42
African Convention on the Conservation of Nature and Natural Resources, 84
Agency for International Development, U.S. (AID)
  agroforestry assistance by, 63
  forest rehabilitation by, 229–30
  Integrated Planning Technology, 73

wetlands and, 89
Agreement for the Complete Utilization of the Nile Waters, 184–85, 197
Agricultural Development Agency (Jamaica), 108
Agricultural Finance Corporation (Zimbabwe), 225
Agriculture
  biotechnology use in, 52
  carbon cycle's effect from, 167
  cereal production in, *40*
  crop breeding programs for, 226–27
  ecologically sustainable, 39, 43, 46–50
  economics of, 3, 66
  effect of air pollution on, 153–55
  effect on wetlands of, 88–89
  commodity price trends (1960–85), *43*
  commodity production trends (1960–84), *43*
  groundwater depletion by, 49
  land distribution for (1960–80), *278–79*
  multistory, 231
  nonfood production of, 40, *41*
  price trends in, 41–47
  productivity of (1964–85), *276–77*
  salinization and productivity of, 116, 174
  in sub-Saharan Africa, 222–29
  subsidies for, 39, 43, 46, 47–50
  trends in output of, 2–3, 39–47, *275*
  urbanization and, 25, 27, 32–34
  water use by, 112, *275*
  see also Food
Agroforestry, 50, 63–65
  funding of, 63

Numbers in italics refer to pages with tables or figures.

Index

systems and practices of, *64*
use in Africa, 3, 51, 63, 64, 230–32
see also Agriculture; Food; Forests
Air quality standards, 149, 151, 156
Alaska, 81–82
Aldehydes, indoor concentrations of, 149–51
Algeria, 104
Alley cropping, 3, 51, 64, 231–32
Alliance for Responsible CFC Policy, 2, 195
Amboseli National Park (Kenya), 81
Angola, hunting ban in, 81
Antarctic, 134
 ozone hole over, 1, 2, 144, 158, *158,* 159,
 195–96, 333
Antarctic Treaty, 194–95, 197
Appalachian Mountains, 155, 156
Aquaculture, 125, 135
Aquifers. *See* Drinking Water; Freshwater;
 Groundwater
Arctic Ocean, 126
Argentina
 balanced development in, 33
 food-price policies in, 34
 rangelands in, 66, 67
 renewable energy use in, 102
 Total Fertility Rate of, 11
Arizona, 82
Army Corps of Engineers, U.S., 88–89
Arrhenius, Erik, 204
Asbestos, indoor concentrations of, 151
Asia
 artisanal fisheries in, 136
 forest management in, 59, 60, 63
 groundwater in, 119, 120
 health in, 16, 17, 19, 20, 21
 hybridization use in, 51
 indoor air pollution in, 151
 rangelands in, 66, 71
 reforestation in, 58
 renewable energy use in, 100
 sport hunting in, 81
 water quality in, 4, 119
 water use in, 116
 wetlands in, 86, 132
 women's roles in, 7, *14*
 see also South Asia; Southeast Asia; Southwest Asia; individual countries
"Asian Mediterranean," 129
Aswan High Dam, 185
Atlantic Ocean
 carbon in, 166
 pollution of, 128, 129, 131
Austin Power and Light Company (Texas), 102
Australia
 agroforestry in, 65
 game cropping in, 82
 health problems in, 17
 oil prices in, 94
 rangeland conditions in, 67–70, 73
 sustainable wildlife harvests in, 80
 Total Fertility Rate of, 11
 urbanization in, 26
 water availability in, 112
 water use in, 113
 wetlands in, 132, 134
Austria
 forest degradation in, 155
 hazardous waste cleanup in, 208–9
 hazardous waste contamination in, 201
Austrian Mineral Oil Administration, 208

B

Baltic Sea
 drainage basins and subregions of, 138, *139*
 eutrophication of, 127
 pollution of, 5, 127, 128, 129, 138–39
 "regional seas" profile of, 137–38
 vital statistics of, 138–39
Bangkok (Thailand), 34
Bangladesh
 agricultural production in, 51
 disaster aversion in, 177
 mortality rates in, 17
 population growth in, 10, 11
 resource agreement with India by, 186–87,
 197
 water availability in, 112
Barcelona Convention for the Protection of the
 Mediterranean Sea against Pollution (1976),
 189, 192
Basel (Switzerland), 1, 4, 181, 187–89, 197
Batstone, Roger, 214
Bay of Bengal, 186, 187
Beijing (China), air pollution in, 153
Belgium
 eutrophication in, 50
 ocean waste disposal by, 130, 131
 water availability in, 112
Benson, Delwin E., 83
Bern Convention, 84
Bethlehem Steel Corporation, 133
Bharat Heavy Electricals (India), 122
Binger, Albert, 107
Biogeochemistry, 163–78
Biological oxygen demand (BOD), 4–5, 117
 of the Mediterranean Sea, 126
 at mouth of selected rivers, *117*
Biomass energy, 104–5, 107–8, *104*
Biomass Users Network (BUN), 105, 107–8
Biosphere Reserve program, 291
Biotechnology
 agricultural use of, 52
 for hazardous waste disposal, 214
Birth rates (1965–90), *250–51*
Black Sea, 325
Bolivia, 11
Bombay (India), homelessness in, 36
Borneo, 132
Botswana
 rangeland management in, 73
 revenue from wildlife and national parks in
 (1972–78), 81, *82*
 wetlands in, 88–89
 wildlife consumption in, 66
Boundary Waters Treaty (1909), 183, 196
Brahmaputra River, 186, 187, 196
 wetlands of, 134
Brazil
 acid deposition in, 153
 agricultural subsidies in, 46
 deforestation in, 275
 marine pollution in seas of, 129
 population of, 9
 rangeland in, 66, 67
 renewable energy use in, 100, 102, 104–5,
 107
 rural-urban migration in, 33, 34
 tree improvement in, 62
 urban bias in, 34
 water availability in, 112
 wetlands in, 134
Brezhnev, Leonid, 192
Bruck, Robert L., 155, 156

Brunei, forest diversity in, 61
BT Kemi, 201, 209
Bureau of Census, U.S., 259
Bureau of Land Management, U.S. (BLM),
 rangeland restoration by, 58, 72–73
Bureau of Reclamation, U.S., 123
Burkina Energy Institute, 232–33
Burkina Faso
 agricultural production in, 45, 51
 fuel-efficient stoves in, 232, 233
 water conservation in, 229, 233
Burma
 agricultural production in, 43
 taungya use in, 63
Burundi, 43

C

Calcutta (India), 186
 education in, 32
 population growth in, 28
California
 independent power production in, 95, 101
 land subsidence in, 120
 salinization in, 174
 sport hunting in, 82
California Energy Commission, 101
Caloosahatchee River (Florida), 88
Campbell, Thomas C., 123
Canada
 air pollution agreement by, 192–93
 air pollution in, 144, 146, 147, 155
 CFC ban in, 156, 195
 forest degradation in, 155
 forest management in, 62, 65
 freshwater availability in, 112, 113, 114
 ocean waste disposal by, 130–31
 rangeland condition in, 67
 resource agreement with U.S. by, 182–84,
 196, 197
 sport hunting in, 81
 wildlife value in, 80
Carbon
 atmospheric, 165, 166–67
 fluxes, 165–66, *165*
 in the oceans, 165, 166–67
 reservoirs of, *164,* 165
Carbon cycle, 163, 164–68, *166,* 173
 average residence time for an atom in, *165*
 changes in, 166–67
 interactions with other cycles by, 167–68
Caribbean Basin
 birth rates in, 7, 11
 forest management in, 59
 groundwater extraction in, *120*
 marine pollution in seas of, 126
 population growth in, 9, 11
 renewable energy use in, 101
 water quality in, 119
Caribbean Sea, 126, 129
Central America, 58, 59
Central America and Mexico Coniferous
 Resources Cooperative (CAMCORE), 62
Central Arid Zone Research Institute (CAZRI),
 63
Central Rangelands Development Project
 (Somalia), 58, 72
Centre for Environmental Studies (Netherlands),
 140
Centro Internacional de Agricultura Tropical
 (Colombia), 52

Chang, Williamson B.C., 123
Chemical cycles, 163–68, 173
Chemical Manufacturers Association (CMA), 157
Chemical Waste Act (Netherlands), 206
Cheminova Chemical Company, 208
Chernobyl, nuclear accident at, 1, 5, 93–94, 96, 100, 102–3, 181, 197, 299
Chesapeake Bay, 5
  cleanup of, 133
Chesapeake Bay Commission, 133
Chesapeake Bay Foundation, 133
Chile
  Total Fertility Rate of, 11
  water availability in, 112
China, 4
  agricultural production in, 40, 43, 51
  air pollution in, 153, *153*
  energy conservation in, 106–7
  forest management in, 62, 64
  hazardous waste shipments to, 217
  marine pollution in, 126
  medical care in, 21
  rainwater pH in selected cities (1981–83), *153*
  rangeland in, 65–66, 71
  renewable energy use in, 100, 101, 104
  Total Fertility Rate in, 10–11
  urban area redefinition in, 35–36
  water availability in, 112
  wetlands in, 86
Chinoin (Hungary), 209
Chlorofluorocarbons (CFCs), ozone depletion and, 2, 5, 6, 144, 156–58, 159, 195–96, 333
Cities
  disparities in living conditions between rural areas and, 29–32, *30, 31, 32*
  world's 85 largest (1985), *264*
  see also Urbanization
Clean Air Act (U.S.), 144, 203
Clean Water Act (U.S.), 133, 203
Climate change, 158–59, 333
  carbon cycle and, 167
Coal
  air pollution from use of, 153, 159
  production of, 99, *100*
  reserves, *98*, 99, 299
Cocoa Marketing Board (Ghana), 35
Cogeneration, 98, 99
Colombia
  agricultural production in, 45, 47, 51
  renewable energy use in, 100
  Total Fertility Rate of, 11
Colorado, 121, 164
  sport hunting in, 82
Colorado River, 164
  salinity of, 121
Committee on Climatic Change and the Ocean (CCCO), 169
Commodity
  price index of 33 nonfuel, *243*
  world indexes and prices (1960–86), *244–45*
Commodity Credit Corporation (CCC), 48
Common Agricultural Policy (CAP), 47, 49–50
Commonwealth Forestry Institute (CFI), 62
Company for Disposal of Special Wastes (GSB), 211
Comprehensive Environmental Response, Compensation, and Liability Act (CERCLA) (U.S.). *See* Superfund
Conference on Security and Cooperation in Europe (1975), 192
Congo, silviculture in, 61
Congressional Budget Office, U.S., 213
Conservation Foundation (Washington, D.C.), 205

Consultative Group on Desertification Control (DESCON), 72
Consultative Group on International Agricultural Research (CGIAR), 51
Contraception. *See* Family planning
Convention for the Protection of the Rhine against Chemical Pollution (1976), 188
Convention on the Conservation of European Wildlife and Natural Habitats. *See* Bern Convention
Convention on International Trade in Endangered Species of Wild Flora and Fauna (CITES), 80, 84
Convention on Long Range Transboundary Air Pollution, 192–93, 196
Cool Water Coal Gasification Program (U.S.), 107
Corfu Channel case, 181
Costa Rica
  agroforestry in, 63
  infant mortality in, 17, *17*
Côte d'Ivoire, deforestation in, 3
Council for Mutual Economic Assistance, 341
Council of Europe, 5
  accidental pollution and, 189
Crab Orchard National Wildlife Refuge (Illinois), 91
Cyprus, 12
Czechoslovakia, forest degradation in, 155, 159–60

D

Dams, large, *316–17*
Danish Environmental Board, 208
Danish International Development Agency (DANIDA), 62
Danube River, 118
Dar es Salaam (Tanzania)
  population growth in, 28
  water quality in, 119
Data collection
  on air pollution, 144–45, 146, 147
  on biogeochemistry, 175–77
  on carbon cycle, 167
  on fisheries, 135–36
  on forest resources, 58
  health-related, 16–17, 202, 204–5, 217
  on indoor air pollution, 148
  on marine pollution, 126, 129
  on national and regional sources of environmental information (1986), *344–45*
  on oceanic physics, 169
  on ozone concentrations, 2
  on rangeland resources, 65, 67
  Regional Seas Program and, 191–92
  on rural-urban disparities, 29–30
  on urbanization, 36
  on water pollution, 4
  on water use, 118, 119, 120
  on wetlands, 86–87, 140
Debt, external
  African, 52, 222
  export crops and, 47
  indicators of (1970–85), *242–43*
  in Third World, 239
Deep Seabed Hard Mineral Resources Act (1980), 194
Deforestation, 5, 57, 58, 63, 186, 267, 283
  carbon cycle and, 164, 167
  fuelwood shortages and, 232
  in Africa, 3, 222, 229
  of rangeland, 71–72, 73–74

Delaware River (U.S.), 117
Democratic Republic of Yemen, 70
Demographics
  indicators of, *11*
  see also Population
Denmark
  air pollution agreement by, 193
  air pollution in, 152
  hazardous waste cleanup in, 208
  hazardous waste management in, 210, 211–12
  ocean waste disposal by, 130, 131
  ozone research in, 154
  renewable energy use in, 101
Department of Agriculture, U.S. (USDA), 73, 275
Department of Commerce, U.S., 114
Department of the Environment (Thailand), 259
Department of the Interior, U.S., 90
Desalination, 121–22
  world capacity for, *121*
Desertification, 174, 283
  in Africa, 3, 222
  areas at risk of, *71*
  extent of (early 1980s), *289*
  of rangeland, 70, 71–72
Desertification Hazards Assessment, 177
d'Estaing, Giscard, 13
Developed countries
  agricultural production in, 39, 40
  forest management in, 59, 61, 62, 64–65
  hazardous waste contamination in, 3, 4
  health in, 16, 17–18, 20, 21
  oil consumption in, 93, 94, 96, 98
  oil production in, 96, 98–99
  population growth in, 7, 8, 9–16
  rural populations in, 25, 27
  water use in, 112–13, 113, 114, 116
  see also Organisation for Economic Co-operation and Development; individual countries
Developing countries. *See* Third World
Development
  agricultural, 4, 6, 32–34
  waste generation and, 4–5
  wildlife habitat lost to, 77, 84–85, 88–89, 90, 291
Dredge spoils, dumping of, at sea, 130–31, *131*
Dregne, Harold E., 72
Drinking water
  production costs and tariffs for (early 1980s), *323*
  see also Freshwater; Groundwater
Ducks Unlimited, 89
Dupont de Nemours, Company, E.I., 159, 195
  CFC production by, 2
  hazardous waste generation by, 215

E

Eastern Europe
  agricultural production in, 40
  air pollution in, 192–93
  energy use in, 96, 100, 104, 105
  hazardous waste contamination in, 209
  hazardous waste shipments to, 216
  rural populations in, 27
  water quality in, 3, 5, 118–19
  water use in, 113
  see also Europe
Economic Commission for Europe (ECE)
  accidental pollution and, 189
  hazardous waste control by, 5
  resource sharing agreements and, 192–93, 197

Index

Economics
  of African economic development, 52
  of agricultural support policies, 47–50
  of agriculture, 3, 66, 228
  of agroforestry, 63
  of air pollution, 152–53, 159
  basic indicators of, 239
  of combating desertification, 72, *72*
  of El Niño effects, 172
  of energy use and development, 93, 94, *94,
    95*, 98, 100, 101, 102–4, 105, 106–7
  of fishery trade, 136–37
  of forests, 60–61, 230
  of hazardous waste cleanup, 3, 91, 203,
    205–9, 215
  of hazardous waste management, 211, 215,
    216
  of health provision, 21–22
  of immigration, 15–16
  of livestock use, 66
  of oil pollution, 129
  of ozone damage, 154–55
  of poaching, 81, 85
  of pollution prevention, 215
  of population demographics, 14–15
  of rangeland restoration, 73
  of salinity control, 116, 121–22, 174
  of soil conservation, 228
  of soil erosion, 48
  of urbanization, 25, 28
  of water markets, 122–23
  of wetlands, 87, 89–90, 134
  of wildlife, 78–83
  of Zimbabwe's agricultural transformation,
    225–26
Ecuador, 28
Education, availability of, 32, *32*
Egypt
  food-price policies in, 34
  resource agreement with Sudan by, 184–86,
    196
  Total Fertility Rate of, 12
  water availability in, 113
Electricity
  housing with access to, 31, *31*
  market competition, 94, 95, 100
  production of, 299, *302–3*
  see also Energy; Renewable energy
El Niño, 169, *170*, 325
  causes of, 171–72
  effect of, on primary marine productivity
    (1982–83), *172*
  fisheries and, 135, *172*
  sea surface temperatures and fish catch
    during (1982–83), *172*
Endangered Species Act of 1973, 86
Energy
  conservation, 93, 94, 106–7, 299
  consumption, 94–105, 299, *300–1*
  consumption by region and fuels, *96*
  consumption patterns (regional), *94*
  consumption shares by country groups, *97*
  production, 94–105, 299, *300–1*
  production, by region and fuels, *97*
  reserves and resources of, *304–5*
  sources, 97–105
  see also Electricity; Renewable energy
England. *See* United Kingdom
Environment Canada, 184
Environmental Protection Agency, U.S., (EPA)
  air pollutants and, 143, 144, 145
  air quality standards, 156
  CFC use data by, 157
  chemical classification by, 205
  Chesapeake Bay study by, 133

  drinking water standards of, 121
  hazardous waste list of, 202, 203
  hazardous waste program of, 259
  hazardous waste site estimate by, 207
  National Crop Loss Assessment Network
    (NCLAN), 153–55
  radon and, 143, 149
  water quality report by, 117–118
Erosion, soil, 3, 48–49, 50, 222–23, 230–31, 275
  in selected countries (1970–86), *281*
Estuarine ecosystems. *See* Wetlands
Ethiopia
  medical care in, 20
  Nile River flow from, 185, 186
  renewable energy use in, 104
  soil erosion in, 3
Europe
  acid deposition in, 144, 151–53, 192–93
  acidity of precipitation in (1978–82), *337*
  agricultural subsidies in, 39, 50
  air pollution in, 143, 144–51, 152, 154
  Chernobyl's effect on, 102–3
  equal access to courts in, 188
  forest degradation in, 155
  forest management in, 59, 62, 64–65
  groundwater contamination in, 50
  groundwater in, 119, 120
  hazardous waste disposal in, 212–14
  hazardous waste generation in, 201
  hazardous waste management in, *212–13*
  hazardous waste monitoring in, 210
  hazardous waste storage in, 202, 205–6,
    207–10
  health problems in, 17
  marine pollution in seas of, 127
  pollution prevention in, 215–16
  pollution standards in, 128
  population growth in, 8, 13, 15–16
  radioactive fallout over, 93
  rangeland in, 66, 70, 73
  reforestation in, 58
  soil contamination in, 174
  sport hunting in, 81, 83–84
  transboundary air pollution agreement by,
    192–93, 196
  transboundary waste shipments in, 216–17
  water pollution in, 1, 3–4, 5
  wetlands in, 86, 132, 133
  wildlife management in, 83–84
  wildlife products imports by, 80
  see also Eastern Europe; Organisation for
    Economic Co-operation and
    Development; individual countries
European Air Chemistry Network (Sweden),
  152
European Community (EC)
  accidental pollution and, 189
  agricultural policy of, 47–50
  agricultural production in, 39, 50
  air pollution cleanup costs in, 152–53
  cereal surplus of, *48*
  CFC reduction by, 159, 195–96
  hazardous waste regulation by, 205, 216
  pesticide contamination in, 50
  sport hunting in, 81
  water pollution directives of, 188
European Economic Committee, 5
European Monitoring and Evaluation Program
  (EMEP), 152, 193
Eutrophication, 88, 118, 127
Exclusive Economic Zones (EEZs), 125, 140,
  325
Exxon Corporation, 98

F

Fal Estuary (U.K.), 128
Family planning
  government policies for, 7, 10, *10*, 11, 12, 13,
    22–23
  unmet need for (1980), *256*
Farakka Barrage, 186, 187
Farm Act of 1985 (U.S.), 49
Federal Energy Regulatory Commission, U.S.,
  95
Federal Office of Forestry (Switzerland), 155
Federal Republic of Germany
  agroforestry in, 65
  air pollution agreement by, 192–93
  forest degradation in, 155
  forestry aid by, 73
  hazardous waste cleanup in, 3, 207–8
  hazardous waste management in, 210, 211
  ocean waste disposal by, 130, 131
  pollution in, 1, 3, 4, 5, 50, 148, 152, 155
  resource agreement by, 187–89
  seabed mining by, 194, 197
Federal Waste Disposal Act (West Germany),
  206
Fertility
  consequences of declining, 14–16
  levels, 9–16
  rates (1965–90), *250–51*
  regional patterns of, 10–16
  women's roles effect on, 7, *10*, 14, *14*
Finland
  health problems in, 17
  water use in, 114
  wildlife value in, 80
Fish
  consumption of, 137, *136*
  trade in, 136–37
Fish and Wildlife Conservation Act, 86
Fish and Wildlife Service, U.S., 79, 85, 89
Fisheries
  annual catches of (1950–84), *135*
  artisanal, 135–36, *136*
  coral reef, 136, *137*
  El Niño and, 171–72, *172*
  harvest from marine, 135–36, 325, *330*
Florida Everglades, restoration of, 77, 88–89,
  89, 90
Food
  production (1964–85), *276–77*
  wildlife as, 81–83
  see also Agriculture
Food and Agriculture Organization, U.N. (FAO),
  267, 275, 283
  African agricultural report by, 236
  Desertification Hazards Assessment, 177
  food supply forecasts by, 40, 41
  forest data of, 58
  forest management and, 73, 229
  game cropping projection by, 82
  marine pollution and, 128
  pesticide use by, 53
  rangeland data by, 65
  sustainable fish harvest estimate by, 135
  World Soils Map and, 173
Food and Drug Administration, U.S. (FDA), 127,
  128
Forest Service, U.S., 73
Forests
  distribution of world (1985), *59*
  economic value of, 60–61
  extent of world, 58–59

genetic improvement of, 61–62
management, 59–61, *60*, 229–32, 283
pollution's effect on, 155–56, 159
resources of, 58–59, *284–85*
trade in products of (1966–84), *288–89*
tree growth in boreal, *157*
trends in commercial, 61–62
yields from, *61*, *286–87*
Fossil fuels. *See* Coal; Natural Gas; Oil
France, 1
    agroforestry in, 65
    air pollution agreement by, 193
    birth rates in, 13
    forest degradation in, 155
    forestry aid by, 73
    hazardous waste cleanup in, 208
    hazardous waste legislation in, 206
    nuclear power use in, 94, 99
    ocean waste disposal by, 130, 131
    renewable energy use in, 100
    resource agreement by, 187–89
    water availability in, 112
    wetland conversion in, 49, 50
Freshwater
    effect of, on health, 22
    housing with access to piped, *31*
    monitoring, 313
    quality of river (1979–86), *318–21*
    supply of, 111–12, *112, 113*, 313, *314–15*
    use of, 112–17, *114, 115, 314–15*
Freshwater Foundation (Minnesota), 122
Fuelwood, 104, 283, 299
    energy production from, 96
    deforestation from use of, 71
    shortages, 66, 230, 232

Gabon, 61
Ganges-Brahmaputra River Basin, resource
    agreement for, 186–87, *186*, 196
Ganges River, 134, 186, 187, 196
Geiser, Kenneth, 216
General Electric, 100
Geographical Information System (GIS), 175,
    176, 177
Geothermal energy, 105, 299
    capacity of, worldwide, *105*
German Democratic Republic, forest degrada-
    tion in, 155
Ghana
    food-price policies in, 35
    medical care in, 21
    silviculture in, 61
    Total Fertility Rate of, 12
    water use in, 113
    wildlife consumption in, 66
Global change science. *See* Biogeochemistry
Global Environmental Monitoring Systems
    (GEMS), 143, *146*, 313
Global Habitability Program, 178
Global Strategy for Health for All by the Year
    2000 (WHO), 21–22, 23
GLORIA, 164
Gold, Thomas, 98
Government Accounting Office, U.S., 207
Great Lakes
    resource agreement for, Basin, 182–84, *183*,
        196
    toxics contamination in, 122
Great Lakes Charter, 122
Great Lakes Water Quality Agreements (1972,
    1978), 183, 184

Great Manmade River (Libya), 122
Great Swamp National Wildlife Refuge (New
    Jersey), 90
Greece, 114
Greenhouse effect
    carbon cycle and, 164, 166
    coal use and, 106
    natural, 168
Greenpeace, 214
Green revolution, 39, 50
    for Africa, 226–27, *235*
    carbon cycle and, 167
    impact of, 33
Gross Domestic Product (GDP), 106
    ratio of energy consumption to, 94, *94*
Gross National Product (GNP), 239, *240–41*
Groundwater
    availability, 119–21, 313
    contamination, 3, 50, 120–21, 202, 203, 205
    depletion of, 49, 116
    quality of, 119–21, 313
    withdrawal of, 120, *120*
    see also Drinking water; Freshwater
Guayaquil (Ecuador), 28
Guesselbodi National Forest (Niger), 229–30

Haiti
    Total Fertility Rate of, 11
    water availability in, 112
Hamza, Ahmed, 211
Hawaii, 123
Hazardous waste
    abandoned, dumps, 205–7
    contamination from, 3–4, 121
    economics of cleanup of, 3
    generation estimates, 202
    health effects of, *205, 206*
    incineration, 209, 213–15
    managing, 208–17
    monitoring, 209–10
    multimedia pollution from, 202–3
    source reduction, 215–16
    substances that require priority consideration,
        203
    surface impoundment of, 206, 208, 209,
        212–13
    toxicity standards, 202
    transboundary shipment of, 216–17
    see also Toxic organic compounds
Health
    air pollution's effect on, 145, 149, 150, 151
    economics of, provision, 21–22
    hazard assessment of categories of sub-
        stances, *204*
    indicators of (1964–90), *252–53*
    malaria and cholera incidence and (1979–84),
        254–55
    risks from hazardous waste, 4, 203–5
    socioeconomic indicators related to, *16*
    status of, 16–23
    water quality and, 119
Heavy metals
    emissions of, 144–45
    forest damage by, 156
    health hazards from, 203, 205
    as marine pollutant, 128
    in Superfund cleanup sites, 207
Helsinki Convention on the Protection of the
    Marine Environment of the Baltic Sea,
    138–40
Holcomb Research Institute, 87

Honduras
    pesticide use in, 46
    Total Fertility Rate of, 11
Hong Kong, 11
Hopcraft, David, 83
Hopcraft Ranch (Kenya), 83
Housing conditions, 30–32, *31*
Huanghe (Yellow River), 134, 174, 313
Huang p'u River (China) pollution of, 4, 119
Human Settlements, trends in, 26–29
Hungary
    geothermal use in, 105
    hazardous waste contamination in, 201
    water quality in, 3, 118
Hybridization, plant, 51
Hydranautics (U.S.), 122
Hydrological cycle
    destabilizing, 119
    freshwater supply and, 112
    groundwater and, 120
Hydropower, 299
    environmental and social problems with,
        100–1
    potential of, *101*
    use of, 95, 100–1, *101*, 313

Iceland, geothermal use in, 105
Idaho Power Company, 123
Idaho Snake River Water Bank, 123
Immigration, 15–16
Imperial Dam (Arizona), 121
Incineration of hazardous wastes, 209, 213–15
India
    agricultural production in, 40, 46, 47
    fertilizer use in, 66
    medical care in, 20, 21
    pollution in, 4, 126
    renewable energy use in, 100, 101, 104
    resource agreement with Bangladesh by,
        186–87, 196
    silviculture in, 61
    sustainable wildlife harvests in, 80
    Total Fertility Rate of, 11
    urbanization in, 28
    water availability in, 112, 113
    water use in, 115
Indo-Bangladesh Joint Rivers Commissions
    (JRC), 186
Indonesia
    agroforestry in, 63
    coastal wetlands in, 132–34
    forest value to, 60
    pesticide use in, 46
    population growth in, 9, 11
    water availability in, 112
Industrial Waste Research Center (Egypt), 211
Industrial world. *See* Developed countries
Industry
    hazardous waste source reduction by, 215–16
    pollution from, 4, 144, 145, 146–47, 201
    salinization from, 188
    water use by, 112–15, *114, 115*
INFORM (New York), 215
Institut du Sahel (Senegal), 51
Institut National d'Etudes Demographiques
    (INED), 13
Institute for Local Self-Reliance (Washington,
    D.C.), 215
Institute for Shaping the Natural Environment
    (Poland), 118

Index

Institute of Environmental Medicine (New York), 204
Integrated Global Ocean Station System, 129
Integrated Planning Technology, 73
International Agency for Research on Cancer, 145
International Agreement for the Protection of the Rhine against Pollution (1963), 187–89
International Aquaculture Foundation, 135
International Board for Plant Genetic Resources (IBPGR), 52
International Center for Arid Land Studies (Texas Tech University), 72
International Centre of Insect Physiology and Ecology (Kenya), 221
International Cogeneration Society, 99
International Commission for Scientific Exploration of the Mediterranean Sea, 189
International Conference on Acidification and Its Policy Implications (1986), 193
International Conference on Primary Health Care (Soviet Union), 21
International Council for Research in Agroforestry (ICRAF), 63
International Council of Scientific Unions (ICSU), 178
International Geosphere-Biosphere Programme of, 6
International Crops Research Institute for Semi-Arid Tropics (ICRISAT), 51, 226, 227
International Drinking Water Supply and Sanitation Decade (WHO), 22, 30
International Energy Agency, 107
International Flavors and Fragrances, 215
International Food Policy Research Institute (Washington, D.C.), 116
International Geosphere-Biosphere Programme, (IGBP), 6, 177, 178
International Institute for Environment and Development (IIED), 74, 368
International Institute for Tropical Agriculture (IITA), 51, 63, 64, 227
alley cropping and, 231
International Joint Commission (IJC), 183–84, 196, 197
International Laboratory for Research into Animal Diseases (Kenya), 52
International Livestock Centre for Africa, 232
International Maritime Organization, 193
International Monetary Fund (IMF)
agricultural price trends and, 42
energy use statistics of, 96
International Oceanographic Commission, 129
International Potato Center (Peru), 51
International Red Cross, 190
International Register of Potentially Dangerous Toxic Chemicals (IRPTC), 217
International Seabed Authority (ISA), 193
International Statistical Institute of the Netherlands, 9
International Union for Conservation of Nature and Natural Resources (IUCN)
forest conservation and, 60, 74
forest survey by, 60
threatened protected areas list of, 78, *79*
water pollution and, 119
wetlands conservation program of, 140
wetlands identification by, 86–87
International Year of Shelter for the Homeless (U.N.), 36
Iowa, 89
Iran
rangeland conditions in, 70
Regional Seas Program and, 191

water availability in, 112
Iraq
rangeland conditions in, 70
Regional Seas Program and, 191
Ireland, ocean waste disposal by, 130, 131
Irrawaddy River (Burma), 134
Irrigation, 275
in Africa, 224, 228–29
economics of, 228
growth in (1950–85), *116*
salinization and (1974–84), *280*
water used for, 112, *280*
Israel
resource sharing by, 190
Total Fertility Rate of, 12
water availability in, 112
water use in, 115
Italy
forest degradation in, 155
geothermal use in, 105
marine pollution in, 128
water availability in, 112
Ivory Coast. *See* Côte d'Ivoire

J

Japan
CFC regulation in, 195
contamination in, 128, 146, 147, 174
health problems in, 17
nuclear power use in, 94
renewable energy use in, 104, 105, 106
rural population in, 25, 27
Total Fertility Rate of, 11
urbanization in, 28
water availability in, 112
water use in, 113, 114
Java
agroforestry in, 63
coastal wetlands in, 132
Jayal, N.D., 119
Johnston Atoll (Hawaii), 90
Johnston, Eric, 190
Johnston Plan, 190
Jonglei Canal (Sudan), 88–89, 185
Jordan
rangeland conditions in, 70
resource sharing by, 190
Jordan River Basin, resource sharing of, 190

K

Kalimantan, 132
Kang, B.T., 231
Kano Agriculture Development Project (Nigeria), 228
Kentucky, forest degradation in, 155
Kenya, 4
agricultural production in, 45
agroforestry in, 63
family planning in, 22–23, *22*
hunting ban in, 81, 83
improved charcoal stoves in, 232, 233
land tenure laws in, 228
national soil program in, 228, 233
protected areas in, 78, 85
Total Fertility Rate of, 12, 22
urbanization in, 28
wildlife-based tourism in, 80, 81
Kenya Contraceptive Prevalence Study (KCPS), 22–23, *22*

Kenya Family Planning Programme, 23
Kenya Fertility Survey, 22, *22*
Kenya Renewable Energy Development Project, 232
Kesterson Refuge (California), 90, 91
Kigali (Rwanda), 18
Kinyanjui, Max, 232
Kiribati, 140
Kohl, Helmut, 103
Kommunekemi (Denmark), 208, 211
Krakow (Poland), 5, 118
Kruger National Park (South Africa), 82
Kuwait, 191
desalination in, 122
rangeland conditions in, 70
Kuwait Program, 191

L

LD50, of toxic organic compounds, 127
Lagos (Nigeria)
population growth in, 28
urban subsidies in, 34
Lake Balaton, 118–19
Lake Okeechobee (Florida), 88–89
Land area and use, *268–69, 272*
Landfills, hazardous waste disposal in, 202–3, 206, 208, 209, 212–13
Landsat, 175, 176, 267
La Plata River, 119
Latin America
agricultural development in, 33
agroforestry in, 63
deforestation in, 58
external debt of, 47
groundwater extraction in, *120*
health in, 16, 17, 18, *19*, 20, 21
pollution in, 20, 121, 151
population growth in, 8–9, 11
rural populations in, 27
sport hunting in, 81
waste water treatment in, 119
water quality in, 119
wildlife harvests in, 80
see also individual countries
Legislation, international environmental, 181–82
Lesotho, 113
Libya
Total Fertility Rate of, 12
water availability in, 113, 122
Lima (Peru), 28
urban bias in, 34
Livestock
economics of, use, 66
production, 65–71, *67*, 74, 88
London Dumping Convention (1972), 130, 132
Long Range Transboundary Air Pollution Convention, 182, 192–93, 217
Los Alamos National Laboratory (U.S.), 105
Loucks, Orie L., 87
Love Canal (New York), 201, 204
Lusaka (Zambia), AIDS in, 18
Lutheran World Relief, 228

M

McMillan, Thomas, 122
Majjia Valley (Niger), 230–31
Malaysia, 4
coastal wetlands in, 132
forest diversity, 61, 62

pesticide use in, 46
Malawi
 agricultural production in, 45
 anti-poaching programs in, 84, *84*
Mali
 agricultural production in, 44–45, 51
 water supply in, 112
Mali River (India), pollution of, 4
Malta, freshwater availability in, 112
Maltby, Edward, 134
Manila (Philippines), infant mortality in, 30
Mantaro River (Peru), 119
Mariculture, 135
Marine Pollution Monitoring Pilot Project (MAPMOPP), 129
Masai Mara Game Reserve (Kenya), 78, 85
Mauritius, 43, 51
Mediterranean Sea, 325
 pollution of, 5, 126, 128, 129
 resource agreement for, 189–92, *191*, 196
Mekong Delta, 134
Metals, producers and consumers of (1965–85), *306–7*
Mexico, 20, 28, 120
 agricultural production in, 46
 oil price effect on, 93, 97
 oil reserves in, 98
 rangeland conditions in, 67
 renewable energy use in, 101, 102, 105
 Total Fertility Rate of, 11
 urban bias in, 35
 water availability in, 112
 water use in, 113
Mexico City, 10
 land subsidence in, 120
 pollution in, 20
 population growth in, 28
 urban subsidies in, 35
Mexico City International Population Conference, 10
Middle East
 desalination in, 121–22
 oil resources in, 97–98
 pastoralism in, 66
 rangeland conditions in, *68–69*
 soil degradation in, 70, 174
 water availability in, 112
 see also North Africa; West Asia; individual countries
Midway Island, 128
Migratory Bird Treaty Act of 1916, 87
Miller, George, 123
Minamata Bay (Japan), 128, 201, 203
Mines Dominiales des Potasses d'Alsace (MDPA), 188
Mining
 groundwater, 120
 international seabed, 193–94
 salinization from, 188
 water pollution from, 4, 119, 128
 wetlands degradation by, 88
Minnesota Mining & Manufacturing Corporation (3M), 215, 216
Mission Technologies Propres de la Direction de la Prevention des Pollutions du Ministere de l'Environnement (France), 215
Modeling
 atmospheric, 169
 climate change, 158–59
 economic value of wildlife, 81
 ocean, 169
 ozone depletion, 144, 158
 rangeland management, 73

Modular High Temperature Gas-Cooled Reactor (MHTGR), 103
Molina, Mario, 156
Moltke, Emmerik, 208
Mombassa (Kenya), 28, 30
 water pollution in, 119
Montevideo (Uruguay), 33
Morley, David, 21
Morocco, Total Fertility Rate of, 12
Mortality
 infant, rates (IMRs), 16–17, *17*
 rates (1960–90), 29–30, *29, 250–51*
 from vaccine-preventable disease, *20*
Mount Kilimanjaro, 64, 81, 231
Mount Mitchell (North Carolina), forest damage on, 155, 156, *156*
Mouvement d'Action Rurale (MAR) conference, 90
Mozambique, hunting ban in, 81
Multispectral Scanner System (MSS), 175, 176
Municipal effluents. *See* Sewage; Waste water treatment
Munro, Bob, 204, 208

N

Naam movement, 229
Nairobi (Kenya), 81
 AIDS in, 18
 infant mortality in, 30
 population growth in, 28
Namibia, game cropping in, 82, *82*
Napada River (India), pollution of, 4
Narbara River (India), 174
National Academy of Sciences (U.S.)
 biodiversity conference by, 78
 plastics pollution and, 128
 toxic chemical study by, 204
National Air and Space Administration (NASA)
 Antarctic ozone depletion and, 158
 Earth System Science program, 178
 Global Habitability program, 178
National Audubon Society, 86
National Crop Loss Assessment Network (NCLAN), 153–55
National Marine Fisheries Services (U.S.), 134
 wildlife management by, 85–86
National Meteorological Service (Argentina), 2, 195
National Oceanic and Atmospheric Administration (NOAA)
 meteorological satellites of, 175, 176
 ozone depletion and, 159
National Park Service (U.S.), 88–89
National Priorities List (EPA), 205, 207
National Research Council (U.S.)
 Great Lakes Water Quality Agreement review by, 184
 indoor air pollution and, 149, 151
 international program of research by, 178
National Resources Inventory (U.S.), 48
National Science Foundation (U.S.)
 Global Geosciences program, 178
 ozone depletion and, 159
National Toxicology Program (U.S.), 204
National Wilderness Preservation System (U.S.), 86
National Wildlife Refuges (U.S.), 90–91
Natural gas
 consumption, 95, 96, 97, *97*, 98
 production, 96, *97*, 98–99
 reserves of, 98–99
Nedlog Technology Group, 217

Nepal
 agricultural production in, 47
 deforestation in, 186
 renewable energy use in, 104
 soil erosion in, 174
 storage dams for, 187
 water availability in, 112
Netherlands
 air pollution in, 152
 forestry aid by, 73
 groundwater contamination in, 50
 hazardous waste cleanup in, 3
 hazardous waste contamination in, 201, 207
 hazardous waste storage in, 206
 ocean waste disposal by, 130, 131
 renewable energy use in, 101
 resource agreement by, 187–89
 water use in, 114
New Delhi (India), infant mortality in, 30
New Guinea, sustainable wildlife harvests in, 80
New Hampshire, 152
New Jersey, 205
New York City, pollution in, harbor, 127, 128
New Zealand
 game cropping and ranching in, 82, 83
 ocean waste disposal by, 130, 131
 oil prices in, 94
 Total Fertility Rate of, 11
 water use in, 113
Niagara River, 122
Nicaragua, agricultural production in, 47
Niger
 agricultural production in, 3, 45, 51
 forest management in, 3, 229–31
Nigeria, 4
 acid deposition in, 153
 agriculture in, 47, 51, 227–28
 agroforestry in, 63, 231
 deforestation in, 3
 oil price effect on, 93, 97
 urban bias in, 34
 wetlands in, 134
Nile River, 88–89, 164
 resource agreement for, 184–86, *185*, 196
Nile Water Agreement, 184
Nitrogen cycle, 167–68, 173
Nongovernmental organizations (NGOs)
 in African development, 228–33
 CFC reductions and, 159
 forest conservation programs by, 73–74
 Great Lakes resource agreement and, 184
 resource agreements and, 189, 196
Nordic Convention on the Protection of the Environment (1974), 188
North Africa
 Total Fertility Rate in, 12
 see also Middle East; West Asia; individual countries
North America
 acid deposition in, 151–53, *336*
 agricultural subsidies in, 39
 declining fertility in, 12–16
 forest degradation in, 58, 155
 forest management in, 59, 60, 62, 65
 groundwater in, 119, 120, 121
 hazardous waste disposal in, 212–14
 hazardous waste generation in, 201, 202
 hazardous waste storage in, 202, 205–6, 208–9, 212–14
 health problems in, 17
 marine pollution in, 127, 128
 pollution standards in, 128
 rangelands in, 66, 67
 rural populations in, 27
 salinization in, 174

Index

transboundary air pollution agreement by, 192–93, 196
transboundary waste shipments in, 216–17
urbanization in, 27–29
water availability in, 112, 113
wetlands in, 86, 87, 132
North Carolina
    pollution prevention program in, 215
    wetlands conversion in, 49
North Carolina, University of, 215
North Sea
    hazardous waste incineration in, 214
    pollution of, 127, 129, 131, 208
Norway, air pollution and, 152, 192–93
Nuclear power, 299
    Chernobyl's effect on, programs, 1, 5, 94–95, *95*, 96, *96*, 100, 102–3, 299
    protests over use of, 103
    reactor construction starts and connections, 99–100, *101*
    use of, 94–95, *96*, 99-100, *306*
    waste generation (1970–85), *306*
Nutrients
    inputs of, in Africa, 227
    soil storage of, 173, 174

O

Occidental Chemical, 214
Oceania
    population growth in, 8, 11
    rangelands in, 65, 66
    reforestation in, 58
    wetlands in, 86
Oceans
    carbon in, 165, 166–67
    chemical cycles and, 165, 166–67, 168
    coastal areas and resources (1974–86), *326–27*
    condition of, 125–32
    fundamental characteristics of, 168
    global agreements covering, 193–94
    hazardous waste incineration in, 131, 214
    interaction with the atmosphere by, 168–73
    marine mammals in (1920–85), *328–30*
    role of tropical, 169–73
    waste dumping in, 130–32
Office of Foreign Disaster Assistance (U.S.), 177
Office of Technology Assessment (OTA), 203, 207, 214
Official Development Assistance (ODA), 341, *346–47*
Ogallala Aquifer, 49, 120
Oil
    consumption, 93, 94, 96
    marine pollution from, 125, 126, 128–30, *129, 331*
    prices, 93, 94, *95*, 98, 107
    production, 93, 94, 96, 98, *99*
    reserves of, 97–98, *98*, 299
Okavango Swamps (Botswana), 88
Oland Island, 129
Oman
    rangeland conditions in, 70
    water availability in, 112
Ordinance on Environmentally Hazardous Waste (Sweden), 206
Oregon, rangeland restoration in, 72–73
Organisation for Economic Co-operation and Development (OECD)
    accidental pollution and, 189
    acid deposition research by, 192

air pollution in, 143, 144–51, *145*, 152, 154, 216
agricultural land conversion in, 174
agricultural policy of, 47
CFC use in, 156–57, 159
chemical classification by, 205
energy conservation in, 299
hazardous waste control by, 5
hazardous waste definition of, 202
hazardous waste disposal in, 4, 207–8, 212–14
hazardous waste monitoring in, 209–10
hazardous waste regulation by, 206, 216
marine pollution in, 127, 132
monitoring coastal ecosystems of, 126
Official Development Assistance by, 341
oil pollution estimate by, 128
renewable energy use in, 100, 101, 104, 105, 106
waste generation in, 201, *265*
waste water treatment in, 117, *118*
water pollution in, 4–5, 117, 216
water use by, 113, 114
see also individual countries
Organization of African Unity
    Priority Programme for Economic Recovery, 52
    wildlife management and, 84
Organization of Petroleum Exporting Countries (OPEC)
    Official Development Assistance by, 341
    oil production by, 93, 94, 97
Oslo Convention, 131
Overcash, Michael R., 216
Oxfam, 229, 233
Ozone
    depletion of, 1–2, 144, 156–58, *157, 158*, 159, 195–96, 333
    effect of, on crops, 154, *157*
    global agreements on, protection, 195–96
    trace gases and, concentrations, 157–58, *158*, 159, 333
    use of depleting substances (1985), *157*

P

Pacific Ocean
    circulation in the tropical, 169–71
    Exclusive Economic Zones in, 140, 325
    pollution of, 128
Pakistan
    agricultural production in, 43
    agroforestry in, 63
    food-price policies in, 34
    mortality rates in, 17
    Total Fertility Rate of, 11
    water availability in, 112
Papua New Guinea
    agroforestry in, 63–64
    coastal wetlands in, 132
Paraguay
    rangeland conditions in, 67
    water availability in, 114
Pasig River (Philippines), 4, 119
Pastureland. *See* Rangeland
Peru
    fishery collapse in, 135, 172, 325
    renewable energy use in, 100, 102
    urban bias in, 34
    urbanization in, 28
Pesticides, as hazardous wastes, 202, 203–5
Philippines, 4
    deforestation in, 267
    medical care in, 20–21

renewable energy use in, 100, 104, 105, 107
Total Fertility Rate of, 11
Phosphorus cycle, 167–68, 173
Photovoltaics. *See* Solar power
Plan of Action to Combat Desertification (PACD), 72
Plastics, as marine pollutants, 128
Poland
    forest degradation in, 155
    hazardous waste contamination in, 209–10
    water availability in, 112
Policy
    affecting urbanization, 26, 28, 33, 34–35
    for African sustainability, 234–36
    agricultural, 224, 225–26, 234–36
    agricultural support, 34–35, 39, 41, 43–46, 47–50
    biogeochemistry, 176–77
    family planning, 7, 10, *10*, 11, 12, 13, 22–23
    hazardous waste disposal, 212–16, 217–18
    immigration, 16
    public opinion's effect on, 5
    recycling, 299
    resource agreement, 181–97
    response to climate change, 159
Polish Ecological Club, 209
Pollution
    air, 143, 144–51, 150, 153–55, 333, *338*
    control's effect on water use, 114–15
    effect of, on agriculture, 153–55
    environmental effects of oil, 129–30
    groundwater, 120–21
    human activities causing, 1–5
    indoor, 143, 148–51, 333, *338*
    marine, 126–32, 325
    oil, in major shipping lanes, 129, *130*
    trends in, 143, 144–47, 333
    water, 4–5, 117-19, 120–21, 126–32, 325
Population
    aging of, 14–15, *250–51*
    doubling times at current rates of growth, *12*
    estimated size and growth of (1955–2000), *248–49*
    fertility and, 9–16
    global, statistics, *8*
    growth, 2, 3, 6, *8, 9*, 27
    immigration and, 15–16
    proportion of, living in urban areas, 25, 26–27
    trends in, 7–9, 27
    urban and rural, *27, 260–61*
    with access to drinking water and sanitation, 30, *30*
    see also demographics; fertility; mortality
Port-au-Prince, Haiti, 30
Portugal, 114
Priority Programme for Economic Recovery, 52
Process Inherent Ultimately Safe Reactor (PIUS), 103
Protected areas
    classified by biogeographical realm and province (1985), *294–95*
    condition of, 78–79
    global networks of, *78*, 291
    national and international (1986), *292–93*
Public opinion
    effect on policy of, 5
    on environmental issues (1979–86), 341, *348–50*
Public Utilities Regulatory Policies Act (PURPA), 99
Pudlis, Gene, 209

Q

Quito (Ecuador), 28

R

Radioactive waste, disposal of at sea, 131–32, *132*
Radon, indoor concentrations of, 143, 148–49
Rahman, Mujibur, 186
Ramsar Convention, 140, 291
Rand Corporation, 157
Rangeland
  conditions of, 67–71, *68–69*
  degradation of, 67
  deforestation of, 71–72, 73–74
  desertification of, 3, 70, 71–72
  distribution of world (1955–83), *65*
  extent of world, 65–66
  integrated management of, 73
  restoration of, 72–73
  systems for using, 66
Red Sea, pollution of, 126, 129
Recycling, of selected materials (1964–85), *308–9*
Regional Seas Program, 191–92
Remote sensing, 163–64, 175–76, 267, 283
  characteristics of U.S. satellites, *175*
Renewable energy, 93, 95, 99, 100–6, 299
Research
  acid deposition, 153, 192
  African sustainability, 235–36
  agricultural, 50–52, *50*, 226–27
  AIDS, 18
  air pollution, 154, 155–56
  alley cropping, 232
  Antarctic, 193
  biogeochemistry, 177–78
  forest improvement, 61–62
  hazardous waste disposal, 207
  indoor air pollution, 148–49, 151
  pollution prevention, 215
  renewable energy, 101, 103–4, 105, 106, 107–8
Resource agreements
  global, 193–96, *342–43*
  involving two-four countries, 182–89
  regional, 189–93
Resource Conservation and Recovery Act (RCRA)
  amendments to, 215
  exemptions from, 213
  hazardous waste definition in, 201, 202, 203
  hazardous waste monitoring under, 209–10
Revier, 83, 84
Rhine River
  resource agreement for, 187–89, *187*
  toxic chemical spill in, 1, 4, 5, 181, 187–89, 197
  water quality of, 117
Rhine Salt Convention, 188
Rio de Janeiro (Brazil)
  pollution in, 20
  urban subsidies in, 34
Rio Tinto Estuary (Spain), 128
Rockefeller Foundation, 74
Rockefeller, Godfrey, 133
Rowland, F.S., 156, 158
Royal Society of Canada, 184
Rwanda, agroforestry in, 46, 51, 64

S

Sandoz, toxic spill by, 1, 4, 181, 187–89, 197
Sanitation
  effect of, on health, 22
  housing with access to, *31*
  in the Third World, 113–14, *262–63*
Sanman Gorge Dam (China), 101
Sao Paulo (Brazil)
  pollution in, 20
  urban subsidies in, 34
Saouma, Edouard, 53
Saudia Arabia
  rangeland conditions in, 70
  water availability in, 112
Scandinavia. *See* Europe; Western Europe; individual countries
Schecter, Roger, 215
Schistosomiasis, 313
Seine River (France), water quality of, 5, 117
Senegal
  agricultural production in, 45
  Total Fertility Rate of, 12
Senegal River, 134
Serengeti National Park (Tanzania), 78
Sève, Juan, 230
Sewage, as source of marine pollution, 126–27, 131, *131*
Sewage treatment. *See* Waste water treatment
Shanghai (China), 4
Sitalakhya River (Bangladesh), 119
Silviculture, 61
Smets, Henri, 189
Smithsonian Institution, biodiversity conference by, 78
Smoking, indoor air pollution from, 151
Society for Promotion of Area Resource Centres (SPARC), 36
Soil, 174, 275
  characteristics of, 173–74
  conservation, 227–28
  erosion of, 3, 48–49, 50, *281*
  fertility in Africa, 223, 227, 229
  functions of, 173
Solar power, 102–4
  shipments of units, 103, *104*
Solomon Islands, Total Fertility Rate of, 11
Solomon, Susan, 159
Somalia, rangeland restoration in, 58, 72
South Africa, Republic of, 82, 83
  acid deposition in, 153
South America
  coastal wetlands in, 132
  El Niño and, 171
  forest management in, 59
  rangelands in, 66, 67
  water pollution in, 4
  water use in, 116
  see also individual countries
South Asia
  birth rates in, 7, 11
  population growth in, 8, 9, *10*, 11
  see also Asia; individual countries
South Korea. *See* Republic of Korea
South Pacific Forum's Fisheries Agency, 140
Southeast Asia
  birth rates in, 7, 11
  pesticide use in, 46
  population growth in, 8, 9, 11
  see also Asia; individual countries
Southwest Asia
  birth rates in, 7
  see also Asia; Middle East; North Africa; individual countries

Soviet Union, 99
  agricultural production in, 40
  CFC regulation in, 195
  Chernobyl accident in, 1, 5, 93–94, 96, 100, 102–3, 181, 197, 299
  energy production in, 94, 96, 98, 100
  forest management in, 59, 62
  game cropping in, 82
  groundwater withdrawals in, 120
  population of, 9
  rangelands in, 66, 71
  renewable energy use in, 100
  sport hunting in, 81
  water quality in, 118
  water use in, 112, 116
  wetlands in, 86
  wildlife value in, 80
Spain, renewable energy use in, 101
Spot Image satellites, 176, 267
Sri Lanka
  agricultural subsidies in, 46
  Total Fertility Rate of, 11
Stanford University, 103
Stockholm Conference on the Human Environment, 125, 181–82, 189, 192, 196
Sub-Saharan Africa
  agricultural production in, 2–3, *42*
  cereal consumption, production, and imports in, *42*
  food-price policies in, 35
  labor shortage in, 224, 226
  locust plague in, 53
  population growth in, 222, 223
  seasonal migration in, 32
  substainable development in, 221–36
  Total Fertility Rates in, 12
  water supply in, 112, 228–29
  see also Africa; individual countries
Subsidies
  agricultural, 34–35, 43, 46, 47–50, 225, 236
  water use, 313
Sudan
  agricultural production in, 43
  resource agreement with Egypt by, 184–86, 196
  wetlands in, 88–89
Sudan Agricultural Research Corporation, 51
Sudd Swamp (Sudan), 88–89, 185
Sulfur cycle, 167–68
Sumatra, 132
Superfund
  cleanup sites, 3, 4, 121, 203, 206–7, *209*
  funding for, 206–7
  National Priorities List, 205, 207
Suriname, silviculture in, 61
Sweden, 190
  air pollution agreement by, 192–93
  air pollution in, 144, 145, 152, 155
  CFC ban in, 156, 195
  forest degradation in, 155
  hazardous waste contamination in, 201, 209
  infant mortality rates in, 16
  medical care in, 20
  natural gas exploration in, 99
  radon pollution in, 148, 149
  rangeland conditions in, 70
  renewable energy use in, 100, 101, 106
  resource agreement by, 187–89
  water availability in, 112
  water use in, 114–15
Swedish International Development Agency (SIDA), 228
Systems Planning for the Use of Rangeland (SPUR), 73

Index

T

Tanzania
  agricultural production in, 46–47
  agroforestry in, 63, 64
  hunting ban in, 81
  protected areas in, 78
  renewable energy use in, 104
  urbanization in, 26
Technology
  agricultural production, 3, 39, 50–52
  biogeochemistry, advances in, 175–77
  clean-coal, 107
  desalination, 121–22
  energy efficient, 93, 94, 98, 101, 103–4,
    105–7, 114–17, 299
  forestry, 61–62
  hazardous waste disposal, 207, 212–17,
    212–13
  rangeland restoration, 73
  resource sharing, 196–97
Tennessee, 204
Texas
  irrigation technique in, 116
  sport hunting in, 81
Thailand
  agricultural production in, 43, 46
  agroforestry in, 63
  coastal wetlands in, 132
  Total Fertility Rate of, 11
  urban bias in, 34
Thematic Mapper, 176
Third Lome Convention, 42
Third United Nations Conference on the Law of
  the Sea (UNCLOS III), 193–94
Third World
  acid deposition in, 151, 152, 153
  agricultural innovations in, 50–52, 63–64
  agricultural production in, 39, 40, 43–47, *46*,
    50–52, 63–64, 275
  agricultural research spending in, *50*
  air pollution in, 144, 146, 151, 153, *153*
  coastal wetlands in, 132, 134
  desalination use in, 121, 122
  development in, 93, 107
  disease classification in, *19*
  drinking water in, *262–63*
  educational service access in, 32
  electricity access in, 31, *31*
  energy use in, 96–97, 98, 100, 101, 102, 104,
    105, 106–7
  external debt of, 47, 52, 239
  family planning policies effect on birth rates
    in, *10*
  fisheries in, 135–36, 137
  food consumption trends in, 42
  food deficits in, 116–17
  food production (per capita) in, *41*
  forest management in, 59, 60–61, 62
  freshwater and sanitation access in, 22, 30
  fuelwood use in, 283
  groundwater pollution in, 121
  hazardous waste contamination in, 3, 207,
    210
  hazardous waste generation in, 201, 206
  hazardous waste management in, 211
  health in, 16–17, 18–22
  indoor air pollution in, 151, *338*
  marine pollution, 126, 127
  medical personnel loss in, 21
  natural gas production in, 98
  nuclear power use in, 100
  Official Development Assistance by, *341*
  oil price effect on, 93, 97
  oil production in, 93, 96, 97–98
  protected areas in, 78, 81
  population growth in, 7, 8, 9–12
  rural populations in, 25, 27
  rural-urban disparities in, 29–30
  sanitation in, 113–14, *262–63*
  urban bias in, 34–35
  urbanization in, 25–33
  waste water treatment in, 119
  water use in, 113–14, 114
  water quality in, 119
  renewable energy use in, 299
Thirty Percent Protocol, 192–93
Thomas, Lee M., 122, 133
Thresher, Philip, 81
Tolba, Mostafa, 72
Tibet, 186
Togo, 44
Tokyo, land subsidence in, 120
  Total Fertility Rates (TFR), 9–16
Toxic organic compounds
  emissions of, 145
  pollution by, 1, 4–5, 127–28, 181, 187–89, 197
  sources and environmental presence (1985),
    148–49
  wildlife contamination from, 90–91
Toxic Substances Control Agreement, 122, 184
Trace gases, 144, 157–58
  annual emissions of environmentally
    important (1925–85), *335*
  atmospheric concentrations of environmen-
    tally important (1950–86), *334*
  trends in atmospheric concentrations of
    environmentally important (1975–85), *334*
TRAFFIC (USA), 79
Tropical Forestry Action Plan (U.N.), 6, 73–74
Tropical Agriculture Research and Training
  Center (CATIE), 63
Tropical Forest Advisory Committee, 73
Tropical Ocean and Global Atmosphere Study,
  173
Trypanosomiasis, zones affected by, 223–24,
  224
Tunisia, 112
  Total Fertility Rate of, 12
Turkey
  Total Fertility Rate of, 12
  water use in, 112, 114

U

Uganda, hunting ban in, 81
United Kingdom
  air pollution in, 152, 192–93
  animal-rights movement in, 84
  forest degradation in, 155
  forest diversity in, 61
  hazardous waste cleanup in, 208
  hazardous waste legislation in, 206
  hazardous waste storage in, 206
  medical care in, 20–21
  ocean waste disposal by, 130, 131
  renewable energy use in, 101, 105
  seabed mining by, 194, 197
  water availability in, 112
  water use in, 114
  wetland conversion in, 50
United Nations
  population projections by, 25, 27–28, 36
  Special Session on Africa, 6, 52–53
United Nations Conference on Desertification
  (UNCOD), 58, 72
United Nations Conference on the Peaceful
  Uses of Outer Space
  (UNISPACE), 178
United Nations Convention on the Law of the
  Sea (1982), 140
United Nations Development Programme
  (UNDP)
  fisheries and, 135
  forest management and, 73
  Nile Basin and, 185–86
  wetlands and, 89
United Nations Economic Commission for
  Europe (ECE), 217
  energy efficiency and, 106
  groundwater withdrawals, by countries, 120
United Nations Educational, Scientific and Cul-
  tural Organization (UNESCO), 120
  Biosphere Reserve program, 291
  World Soils Map and, 173
United Nations Environment Programme
  (UNEP)
  accidental pollution and, 189
  CITES and, 84
  desertification estimate by, 71, 72
  Desertification Hazards Assessment, 177
  GEMs and, 143
  groundwater survey by, 120
  hazardous waste control by, 5
  hazardous waste management and, 217
  ocean pollution and, 125, 126, 127, 128
  regional seas concept of, 137, 138
  Regional Seas Programs of, 189, 191–92
  regional seas strategy, 119
  resource sharing agreements and, 189, 191,
    193, 195, 196, 197
United Nations Fund for Population Activities
  (UNFPA), 247
United Nations International Atomic Energy
  Agency (IAEA), 102, 103
United Nations International Drinking Water
  Supply and Sanitation Decade
  Third World domestic water availability and,
    111, 114
*United Nations List of National Parks and Pro-
  tected Areas (1985)*, 80–81
United Nations Medium Variant Projection, 9
United Nations Population Division, 259
United Nations Programme for Action for
  African Economic Recovery and Develop-
  ment: 1986–1990, 52
United Nations Truce Commission, 190
United Nations World Water Conference, 111
United Nations World Meteorological Organization, 129
United States
  aging population in, 14–15
  agricultural policy of, 47–50
  agricultural productivity in, 39, 40
  AIDS in, 18
  air pollution agreement by, 192–93
  air pollution in, 2, 143, 144–51, 153
  CFC ban in, 156, 195
  coastal wetlands in, 132
  costs of ozone damage in, 154–55
  cropland salinization in, 116
  crop surplus and program costs in, *48*
  desalination in, 121–22
  fish harvest of, 137
  forest degradation in, 155
  forest management in, 59, 60, 62, 65
  groundwater mining in, 120
  groundwater pollution in, 121
  hazardous waste contamination in, 3, 4, 201,
    203, 204–5
  hazardous waste disposal in, 4, 121

hazardous waste generation in, 201, 202
hazardous waste monitoring in, 209–10
hazardous waste storage in, 206, 208–9, 212–14
health problems in, 17
independent power production in, 94, 95
industrial water use in, 114, *114*
infant mortality rates in, 16
irrigation use in, 116
meat consumption trends in, 74
medical care in, 20–21
national emissions estimates in (1940–84), *147*
nuclear power use in, 94, 100, 299
ocean waste disposal by, 130–31
oil prices in, 93
oil reserves in, 98
ozone research in, 154
pesticide use in, 46, 49
pollution prevention in, 215–16
population of, 9, *15*
radon pollution in, 143, 148, 149
rangelands in, 66, 67, 72–73
renewable energy use in, 100, 101, 102–3, 104, 105, 106
resource agreement with Canada by, 182–84, 196, 197
seabed mining by, 194, 197
soil degradation in, 48–49, 174
sport hunting in, 81–82, 85
urbanization in, 28
water availability in, 112
water pollution in, 4, 5, 117–18
wetlands harvest in, 87
wildlife-based expenditures in, *80*
wildlife-based recreation in, 80, 85
wildlife management in, 85–86
wildlife product imports by, 80
women's roles in, 14, *14*
USS Chemicals, 215
United Tourist Organization, 189
Upton, Arthur, 204
Urbanization
agriculture's effect on, 25, 27, 32–34
dynamics of, 32–35
economics of, 25–28
trends in, 27–29
see also Cities
Uruguay
rangeland condition in, 67
Total Fertility Rate of, 11
urbanization in, 33

Vac, Hungary, hazardous waste contamination in, 3, 201, 209
Vanuatu, 140
Venezuela, oil price effect on, 93, 97
Vienna Convention for the Protection of the Ozone Layer, 2, 144, 159, 195–96
Viennese Working Group of Concerned Scientists, 208
Vietnam, coastal wetlands in, 132
Vistula program, 118
Vistula River (Poland), 5, 118
Volatile organic compounds, aquifer contamination by, 121
Volga River (Soviet Union), 5, 118

Volgograd (Soviet Union), 5
Voytek, Peter, 204
Vranitzky, Franz, 103

Wadden Sea, 130, 134
Waldsterben, 155, 192
Wash, The (U.K.), 134
Washington (state), conservation reserve in, 49
Waste water treatment
in eastern Europe, 118–19
hazardous wastes and, 202, 209
in OECD countries, 4–5, 117, 118
in Third World, 119
in the United States, 117
Water markets, 122–23
Water quality standards, 121, 313
Water Services of America, 122
Weddell Sea (Antarctica), carbon in, 166
West Africa, forest management in, 60
West Asia
declining fertility in, 12–16
hazardous waste cleanup in, 207–9
population growth in, 8, 12
rangeland conditions in, *68–69*, 70
rural populations in, 25, 27
urbanization in, 27–29
see also Middle East; North Africa; individual countries
West Germany. *See* Federal Republic of Germany
Westinghouse Corporation, 100
Wetlands, 267
agriculture's effect on, 88–89
coastal, 132–34, 140
conversion, 49
economics of, restoration, 89–90
estimated area of world, by climate zone, *86*
freshwater, 86–90
internationally important (1980s), *270–71*
loss of, 87–90, 134
productivity of selected, *132*
size and location of, 86–87, *87*
value of, 87
Wetlands Convention, 90
Wetlands of International Importance, 90
Weyerhaeuser Corporation, 62
Wildlife
cropping of, 82–83
economic value of, 78–83
as food source, 66, 81–83
funding, management, 86
game ranching, 83
internationally threatened, 79–80 *296–97*
nationally threatened, 84, 86, *295*
nonconsumptive uses of, 80–81, 84, 85
regional trends in, management, 83–86
sustainable harvests of, 79–80
trade in, 79–80, 82, *83*
trends in, condition of, 78–79
Wildlife reserves. *See* Protected areas
Wilson, E.O., 78
Wind power, use of, 101–2
Women
roles of, in Africa, 224
roles of, in Asia, 7, *14*

roles of, in U.S., 14, *14*
roles of, and fertility rates, 7, *10*
World Bank
African projects of, 88, 224–25, 228
agricultural subsidization costs and, 47
country categorization (by GNP), 27
energy use estimates by, 96, 98, 99, 100
forest management and, 73
groundwater access and, 120
Livestock III project, 88
population estimate by, 9, 11
wildlands policy, 90
World Census of Agriculture, 275
World Climate Research Program, 173
World Energy Conference, 100
World Fertility Survey, 9
World Health Organization (WHO), 259
AIDS statistics by, 18
Chernobyl and, 103
drinking water guidelines by, 4
GEMs and, 143
hazardous waste definition by, 201
indoor pollution and, 151
malnutrition estimates by, 18
marine pollution and, 128
mental disorder estimate by, 17
mortality trends and, 16–17, *16, 17*
Report on the World Health Situation by, 16
vaccine-preventable diseases and, 20
water availability data by, 114
World Meteorological Organization (WMO), 192
climate change and, 159
El Niño and, 171
World Ocean Circulation Experiment, 169
World Population Conference in Bucharest (1974), 10
World Resources Institute (WRI), 369
CFC reductions and, 159
Tropical Forestry Action Plan and, 73
World Soils Map, 173
World Wildlife Fund (WWF)
illegal trade in wildlife products estimate by, 80
TRAFFIC (USA), 79
wetlands conservation program of, 140
Wright, Peter, 229

Yarmuk River, 190
Yemen Arab Republic, rangeland conditions in, 70
Yodo River (Japan), 117
Yugoslavia
forest degradation in, 155
renewable energy use in, 104
Yuma Desalting Plant (Arizona), 121

Zaire
hunting ban in, 81
renewable energy use in, 100
Zimbabwe
agricultural transformation in, 225–26, 233
sport hunting in, 81

IIED

International Institute for Environment and Development

North America
1717 Massachusetts Avenue, N.W.
Washington, D.C. 20036 U.S.A.

Latin America
c/o CEUR Av. Corrientes 2835,
Cuerpo A 7o Piso
(1193) Buenos Aires, Argentina

Europe
3 Endsleigh Street
London, WC1H ODD, England

IIED's Board of Directors:
Robert O. Anderson, *Chairman*
H. Abdlatif Y. Al-Hamad, *Vice Chairman*
Henrik Beer
Huey Johnson
James W. MacNeill
Robert S. McNamara
Waldemar Nielsen
Sir Arthur Norman
Saburo Okita
Michael S. Perry
Sir Shridath Ramphal
Jack Raymond
Azad Shivdasani
Emil Salim
Maurice F. Strong
Louis von Planta
Brian W. Walker

Officers:
Brian W. Walker, *President*
Richard Sandbrook, *Vice President, Policy*
David Runnalls, *Vice President and Director,*
North American Office
Jorge E. Hardoy, *Director of Buenos Aires Office*

The International Institute for Environment and Development (IIED) is a global organization, established in 1971, to further the wise use of natural resources as necessary to economic growth that serves basic human needs. Inspired by its first president, the renowned British economist and humanitarian Barbara Ward, IIED has made sustainable development its guiding principle.

IIED's programs include policy research, information and field activities. The Institute draws its staff from around the world and operates from offices in London, Washington, and Buenos Aires. The work of the Institute reaches from forests and fisheries to the overcrowded living conditions in Third World cities, from the Antarctic to the tropics, finding the means for renewable energy and sustainable agriculture.

All IIED's activities ultimately concern development; the process involves working alongside the people of the developing world in partnership with them. IIED's research is rigorous, scientific and pioneering. Its origins and applications in the field come from direct interaction with nongovernmental organizations as well as public policy makers in the developing countries. The objective of the IIED process is to enable its partners to become self-reliant and to improve their livelihoods on a sustainable basis.

IIED's Earthscan information service publishes books and articles that reflect the concerns of the developing world. It provides nongovernmental organizations in the Third World with an information network linked to their specific programs and offers them technical assistance.

IIED is funded by private and corporate foundations, international organizations, governments and concerned individuals.

The World Resources Institute (WRI) is a policy research center created in late 1982 to help governments, international organizations, the private sector, and others address a fundamental question: How can societies meet basic human needs and nurture economic growth without undermining the natural resources and environmental integrity on which life, economic vitality, and international security depend?

The Institute's current program areas include tropical forests, biological diversity, sustainable agriculture, global energy futures, climate change, pollution and health, economic incentives for sustainable development, and resource and environmental information. Within these broad areas, two dominant concerns influence WRI's choice of projects and other activities:

The destructive effects of poor resource management on economic development and the alleviation of poverty in developing countries; and

The new generation of globally important environmental and resource problems that threaten the economic and environmental interests of the United States and other industrial countries and that have not been addressed with authority in their laws.

Independent and nonpartisan, the World Resources Institute approaches the development and analysis of resource policy options objectively, with a strong grounding in the sciences. Its research is aimed at providing accurate information about global resources and population, identifying emerging issues and developing politically and economically workable proposals. WRI's work is carried out by an interdisciplinary staff of scientists and policy experts augmented by a network of formal advisors, collaborators, and affiliated institutions in 30 countries.

WRI is funded by private foundations, United Nations and governmental agencies, corporations, and concerned individuals.

World Resources Institute

1735 New York Avenue, N.W.
Washington, D.C. 20006 U.S.A.

WRI's Board of Directors:

Matthew Nimetz, *Chairman*
John E. Cantlon, *Vice Chairman*
John H. Adams
Robert O. Blake
John E. Bryson
Richard M. Clarke
Marc J. Dourojeanni
Alice F. Emerson
John Firor
Curtis A. Hessler
Martin Holdgate
James A. Joseph
Sir Ian MacGregor
Alan R. McFarland
Robert S. McNamara
George P. Mitchell
Paulo Nogueira-Neto
Ruth Patrick
James Gustave Speth
M.S. Swaminathan
Mostafa K. Tolba
Russell E. Train
Arthur C. Upton
Melissa Wells
George M. Woodwell

Officers:

James Gustave Speth, *President*
Jessica T. Mathews, *Vice President and Research Director*
Andrew Maguire, *Vice President for Policy Affairs*
Wallace Bowman, *Secretary-Treasurer*